OXFORD HANDBOOK OF
GOVERNANCE

OXFORD HANDBOOK OF

GOVERNANCE

Edited by

DAVID LEVI-FAUR

*The Hebrew University of Jerusalem
and the Free University of Berlin*

OXFORD
UNIVERSITY PRESS

OXFORD
UNIVERSITY PRESS

Great Clarendon Street, Oxford OX2 6DP

Oxford University Press is a department of the University of Oxford.
It furthers the University's objective of excellence in research, scholarship,
and education by publishing worldwide in

Oxford New York

Auckland Cape Town Dar es Salaam Hong Kong Karachi
Kuala Lumpur Madrid Melbourne Mexico City Nairobi
New Delhi Shanghai Taipei Toronto

With offices in

Argentina Austria Brazil Chile Czech Republic France Greece
Guatemala Hungary Italy Japan Poland Portugal Singapore
South Korea Switzerland Thailand Turkey Ukraine Vietnam

Oxford is a registered trade mark of Oxford University Press
in the UK and in certain other countries

Published in the United States
by Oxford University Press Inc., New York

British Library Cataloguing in Publication Data
Data available

Library of Congress Cataloging in Publication Data
Data available

Typeset by SPI Publisher Services, Pondicherry, India
Printed in Great Britain
on acid-free paper by
CPI Group (UK), Croydon CR0 4YY

ISBN 978–0–19–956053–0

3 5 7 9 10 8 6 4 2

FOREWORD

....

As this volume was written, the Arab world was in turmoil. Tunisia experienced regime change, then Egypt, now half a dozen other states are in turmoil. The changes on offer in these uprisings are disparate. In Palestine, the change is a fragile agreement to create a unity government between Hamas and the Palestine Liberation Organization. Yet what Palestine has in common with Syria, Libya, Yemen, Bahrain and the other uprisings is that the new demand was from the crowd on the streets, reluctantly acceded to by the Hamas and PLO leaders. We have seen this before, with the Carnation Revolution in Portugal (1974), People Power democratic revolutions in the big countries of South-East Asia (the Philippines (1986), Indonesia (1998)), in 1989 with crowds creating the Velvet Revolution in Czechoslovakia, initially led from the streets and shipyards of Poland, then sweeping most of the communist world and almost prevailing in China, followed by successor democratic uprisings in Serbia (2000) with students as usual playing a vanguard role, the Rose Revolution in Georgia (2003), Ukraine's Orange Revolution (2004), Kyrgzstan's Tulip Revolution (2005). And we see it throughout history as George Rudé's (1964) *The Crowd in History* showed with case studies of transformation of the great powers of the 18ᵗʰ and 19ᵗʰ centuries, such as the French Revolution.

As in France, England and Boston, in Egypt, Libya and Yemen there is a struggle among very different political forces on the street to steer the crowd. Networks identified with the idea of Al Qaeda are part of the mix, as are organizers with liberal ideologies, socialists, religious sects, tribal powerbrokers and much more. Are such actors engaged in governance of the crowd and therefore of their country? At the time of writing, government forces have been driven from the eastern ports of Libya, while Colonel Gaddafi's regime continues to control the west. The spirit of this volume might be to say that the Gaddafi family remains the key node in the governance of his tribe and of western Libya, while a variety of rebel leaders are key nodes of the networks governing the east. NATO governs the skies above east and west, enforcing a UN no-fly zone. Yet the governance of the ground is shaped by NATO as well in the sense of Christopher Hood's (1983) typology applied to metagovernance (Jacob Torfing, Chapter 7)—Nodality (occcupying a strategic conjuncture of a governance network); Authority (legitimacy in the eyes of network actors); Treasure (access to key resources); Organization (organizational capability to monitor and manage networks).

A conventional analysis could be that while networked governance might have more Nodal and Organizational capability than government by the state, the state has more Authority (particularly Max Weber's legitimacy to monopolise force) and Treasure under its sway. Moreover, it is the A and T of NATO that is the real deal of statist politics (the stuff of political science). Libya in 2011 hardly fits this account. It is doubtful that Gaddafi enjoys the greater legitimate Authority; it remains to be seen whether the rebels might be able to mobilise the greater Treasure of NATO (the regional intergovernmental organization) in the long haul.

The main point here is that a political science that clings to a preoccupation with government, marginalizing the study of governance, restricts its relevance beyond the politics of settled western democracies, risking irrelevance in understanding moments of political transition. One virtue of the governance perspective is well captured in the pages of this volume. In the study of political transformation, this is that governance nurtures the study of non-government networks enrolling 'bits of state' (Filer 1992) to their projects. Nonviolence networks make much of this. They argue that the crowd is more likely to prevail in history with democratic change when it maintains the discipline of a willingness to absorb the bullets of the regime without returning fire. As the crowd absorbs more and more bullets, the turning point in a struggle has prospects of being more profound, as we saw with the 1991 Santa Cruz massacre of at least 200 in East Timor. This is because with more bullets it becomes more transparent that the state does not secure consent through legitimate authority. It could be said that this Gandhian insight holds from the carnation revolution in Portugal, which made famous the symbol of putting flowers into the barrels of rifles, through to Tunisia and Egypt's Jasmine and Lotus Revolutions. On this analysis, the mistake of the Libyan rebels was to grab through force those regions of the country where they could prevail militarily. As soon as alternative governance networks start shooting at the government, defenders of the state, particularly military professionals, close ranks. Prospects of breaking off bits of government subside. The bit that matters most in this context is the military. That does not necessarily mean the military leadership. Nonviolence training often construes the military leadership as corrupted, enriched by the regime. Hence the crowd might appeal to middle-ranking officers and their troops on the street. One informant in my research said that in the Philippines People Power movement relatives of commanders of particular tanks were assigned to stand in front of those tanks and appeal for support.

There is now an evidence base for nonviolence as a preferred strategy of revolutions that prevail by enrolling bits of state to reform projects. Chenoweth and Stephan's (2011; Stephan and Chenoweth 2008: 8) study of 323 violent and nonviolent resistance campaigns from 1900 to 2006 found that 'major nonviolent campaigns have achieved success 53 percent of the time, compared with 26 percent for violent resistance campaigns', while Abrahms (2006) found terrorism enjoyed an even lower success rate, achieving its policy objectives in only 7 per cent of its long-run campaigns (see also Cronin 2009). Among the reasons advanced for this result are:

First, a campaign's commitment to nonviolent methods enhances its domestic and international legitimacy and encourages more broad-based participation in the resistance, which translates into increased pressure being brought to bear on the target. Recognition of the challenge group's grievances can translate into greater internal and external support for that group and alienation of the target regime, undermining the regime's main sources of political, economic, and even military power. Second, whereas governments easily justify violent counterattacks against armed insurgents, regime violence against nonviolent movements is more likely to backfire against the regime (Stephan and Chenoweth 2008: 8-9).

So, as contributors to this volume such as Jeremy Richardson (Chapter 22) argue, the new governance is not so new, having been understood by practitioners of reform networks enrolling bits of state since at least the French Revolution. E-democracy is certainly a new technology of the crowd in history (Eran Fisher, Chapter 40) that can help a mob to become a smart mob, but it is still a networked swarming strategy for political change prodded by the NATO of nodes like Wikileaks. While states remain the greatest focus of power on our planet, and while many networks can be enhanced by a little dose of bureaucracy (Laurance Lynn, Chapter 4), while they operate in the shadow of hierarchy, this volume richly reveals how state authority is often manifest as bits of state networked to assert power against the claims of other bits of the same state. Robert Putnam's (1988) study of the Bonn G-7 summit revealed an outcome that was not the preference of the majority faction of any G-7 state. It was a result that a set of minority factions of those states, such as environment ministries under pressure from green NGOs, could secure by networking their weaknesses to mobilise state strength. Normatively, a shift from the study of government to governance helps create space for intellectual work in the service of struggles against domination, as opposed to the service of states, or at least research pitched at the non-government, non-business audience. When weak movements from below prevail against the strong in the world system, it is usually when they have a strategy for dividing bits of corporate and state power against one another (Braithwaite and Drahos 2000). At these moments, as illustrated by the flower revolutions, the will of the crowd can be to institutionalize its governance of the government by elections that allow the people to replace regimes on a regular basis without spilt blood.

Another big historical conjuncture at which this volume appears (as discussed by Graham Wilson, Chapter 26, and other chapters) is the aftermath of the Global Financial Crisis. This was a context for regulatory scholars questioning whether even the most powerful government was in command of its economic destiny, or whether it was 'Masters of the Universe' who wield the power of finance capital. Ratings agencies, regulators, and large fractions of the disciplines of accounting and economics seemed to be more servants of Wall Street than servants of the state or its people. Central bankers seemed more independent of the executive government (Ellen Meade, Chapter 28) than of finance capital. Police-prosecutors-courts were quiescent, continuing to go about their business of punishing crimes on Main Street, preserving impunity on Wall Street. Contemplating the shift to governance is as relevant to responding to the limits of the judicial as to the executive and legislative branches of government. As Cynthia Estland points out (Chapter 38), under the 'old governance' of labour rights, threats of strikes and union safety inspectors were more important to protecting workers from occupational health and safety crimes than state enforcement, as evidenced by the strong negative association between the unionization of coal mines and harm to miners' bodies

(Braithwaite 1985). Wikileaks exposure is more relevant to regulating torture than state enforcement. For some crimes of big business, such as those of the pharmaceutical and defence contracting industries, privatization of enforcement through whistleblowers using the False Claims Act in the US to win a reward has been more important than the old public enforcement during the past decade. The gradual growth of restorative justice in western democracies involves a different kind of privatization and hybridity with state justice. So does the Taliban moving in to rural areas of Afghanistan in the 1990s where law and order had collapsed, offering their services, as David Kilcullen has put it, as an 'armed rule of law movement'.

So the governance turn is as relevant to rethinking the intersections of the judicial branch as it is to other branches of government. The New Public Management urged legislative, executive and judicial branches of government to be engaged with markets as a mechanism to solve problems of public provision—by making health providers compete, putting a price on carbon, governing by contract private prisons (Erik Hans Klijn, Chapter 14). 'New governance' encouraged the state to be networked (Rod Rhodes, chapter 3 and many other chapters), responsive to complexity (Volker Schneider, Chapter 9), collaborative (Chris Ansell, Chapter 35; Yannis Papadopoulos, Chapter 36), cybernetic (Guy Peters, Chapter 8), participatory (Frank Fischer, Chapter 32; Yael Yishai, Chapter 37), risk-analytic (Elizabeth Fisher, Chapter 29; Susana Borrás, Chapter 30), learning (Fabrizio Gilardi and Claudio Radaelli, Chapter 11), multi-level (Part VIII), globally attuned (Part IX), experimentalist (Charles Sabel and Jonathan Zeitlin, Chapter 12), institutionally flexible (Jon Pierre, Chapter 13), innovative (Eva Sorensen, Chapter 14), adaptive-transformative (Laurence Lynn, Chapter 4) by harnessing the managerial and technical genius of disparate partners. Because the state was encouraged to consider meta-governance strategies to harness both governance through markets and contracts of the NPM and governance through networks of 'new governance' (or the 'conduct of conduct', Brent Steele, Chapter 50), many of us saw governance as entering an age of regulation. Under regulation of private-public hybridity of networked governance and governance by contract and markets, both markets and regulation (broadly conceived) became stronger. So David Levi-Faur and Jacint Jordana in a series of empirical studies coined the term regulatory capitalism to capture the idea of a world with expanding rules and expansive markets. Even at the definitional core of states as inheritors of a monopoly of force, we moved to a world where private police greatly outnumbered public police and where core functions of warmaking and peacekeeping were contracted out and regulated by national and supra-national authorities (like NATO, the UN, the Red Cross, Amnesty, the International Criminal Court).

No one has done more than David Levi-Faur to build bridges between regulatory scholarship and political science. The rich conversation he has assembled in this volume is the latest contribution of this kind. It stands beside his leadership of the European Consortium for Political Research Standing Group on Regulatory Governance (that has become a pre-eminent global interdisciplinary network in this field) and his founding of the journal *Regulation & Governance*. David really believes in political science, so he was brave or foolish to invite this Foreword from someone who often wonders 'Was political science a bad idea?' 'Would it not be better if the social sciences were less organized around types of institutions, more around ideas?' I do despair during my fieldwork in countries recovering from civil war when political scientists, economists and anthropologists talk past one another. Political scientists sometimes see statebuilding as what matters and wonder how economists think they can get business investing without getting state institutions working first. Some economists, though by no means all, see capitalism as having taken off in a pre-Westphalian world, conceiving democratic institutions as things that follow the growth of capitalism. Anthropologists can see both as arriving from another planet. They sometimes see the development of markets as not very realistic and less important than developing the subsistence and gift economies that decide whether villagers will flourish or starve. And they can view the state as almost irrelevant to the daily lives of villagers, while the quality of village governance has a huge impact and traditional justice does nearly all the work the judicial branch of governance does in the west. It seemed a pathology of the disciplinary structure of the social sciences that anthropologists saw the lived folkways, the social construction of custom in local communities as what matter, economists saw markets as what matter and political scientists the state as what matters.

After reading this volume, littered with so many theoretical and empirical insights, I become encouraged for the future of a social science that conquers this pathology. Many anthropologists today do wonderful work on innovations that might simultaneously strengthen subsistence economies and market economies (high-tech fishing boats that trawl outside the range of traditional canoes, but encourage traditional fishing by buying and refrigerating every surplus fish caught from villagers' canoes). Likewise anthropologists advance splendid diagnoses of how village and state governance can be joined up in ways that can improve lives. Economists and political scientists are more open to learning from each other today, methodologically and institutionally, on the synergies between state and market institutions. So for this outside critic, the governance turn in political science on display in this volume renders the discipline more relevant to making the connections that constitute a social science that matters to human lives (Peer Zumbansen, Chapter 6). This means a social science that identifies why we spew more carbon into the environment (Thomas Bernauer and Lena Maria Schaffer, Chapter 31), why a war occurred, why poverty persists, why women are oppressed, why a Global Financial Crisis occurs, as opposed to the narrow frames of why state or market failure happen.

John Braithwaite

Canberra,
May 2011

REFERENCES

Abrahms, M. 2006. 'Why terrorism does not work,' *International Security*, 31: 42–78

Braithwaite, J. 1985. *To Punish or Persuade: Enforcement of coal mine safety*, Albany: State University of New York Press.

Braithwaite, J. & P. Drahos 2000. *Global Business Regulation*, Cambridge: Cambridge University Press.

Chenoweth, E. & M. J. Stephan 2011. *Why civil resistance works: the strategic logic of nonviolent conflict*, New York: Columbia University Press.

Cronin, A. K. 2009. *How Terrorism Ends: Understanding the decline and demise of terrorist campaigns*, Princeton: Princeton University Press.

Filer, C. 1992. 'The escalation of disintegration and the reinvention of authority', in M. Spriggs and D. Denoon (eds.), *The Bougainville Crisis: 1991 update*, Bathurst: Crawford House Press.

Hood, C. 1983. *The Tools of Government*. Chatham: Chatham House.

Putnam, Robert D. 1988. "Diplomacy and Domestic Politics: The Logic of Two-Level Games." *International Organization* 42: 425–460.

Rudé, G. F. E. 1964. The Crowd in History: A study of popular disturbances in France and England, 1730–1848, London: Lawrence and Wishart.

Stephan, M. J & E. Chenoweth 2008. 'Why civilian resistance works: the strategic logic of nonviolent conflict', *International Security* 33(1): 7–44.

PREFACE

The invitation to edit the *Oxford Handbook of Governance* came from Dominic Byatt of Oxford University Press. After some hesitation, I accepted it in the hope of consolidating and extending the work I had undertaken, with my colleagues, within the framework of the ECPR Standing Group on Regulatory Governance and the *Regulation & Governance* journal. It proved a challenging task because of the scope of the subject but also because I undertook it on top of other commitments, not least the editing of the *Handbook on the Politics of Regulation* (Edward Elgar). Nevertheless, it became a very rewarding project for me and I hope also for the readers of and the contributors to this handbook.

My own interest in governance emerged from my research on interest intermediation, policy networks, and the European Union. This interest was first nurtured by my mentor Yael Yishai, at the University of Haifa, and subsequently developed through my cooperation with Frans van Waarden and David Vogel and my years at Nuffield College Oxford with Jeremy Richardson. It was while I was working at Oxford on the edited collection *The Politics of Regulation: Institutions and Regulatory Reforms for the Age of Governance* (Edward Elgar, co-edited with Jacint Jordana) that I started to note the proximity of the issues covered by the then separate literatures of regulation and governance. Still it took some time before I started to appreciate more seriously the interaction of the two shifts—the shift from government to governance and the shift from Weberian bureaucracy to regulocracy—and consequently emergence of a new regulatory state. Softer and more transnational than the traditional regulatory state, the new regulatory state controls by competition rather than by capping prices, and is European and étatist rather than American and neoliberal. These themes were made still clearer to me while I was working at RegNet at the Australian National University, with John Braithwaite, Peter Drahos, Peter Garbosky, Christine Parker, and Clifford Shearing.

I started working on this handbook in 2008, shortly after moving from the University of Haifa to the Hebrew University of Jerusalem, and was then actively engaged with it for almost three years. It was completed on research leave at the Research College (Kolleg-Forschergruppe) "The Transformative Power of Europe" at the Freie Universität Berlin to whose directors, Tanja Börzel and Thomas Risse, I owe much. I would like to take this opportunity to thank my colleagues and friends at the Hebrew University of Jerusalem who warmly facilitated my integration into the Department of Political Science and the Federmann School of Public Policy. I am also grateful to my hosts in Berlin: Tanja Börzel and Thomas Risse at the Freie Universität, who also supported the production of this book with their grant from the German Research Foundation (Deutsche Forschungsgemeinschaft), and whose generosity and good advice were critical for the success of this handbook. In working on this volume I have drawn on occasional advice regarding both structure and content from very many good and generous colleagues. It is a pleasure to acknowledge the support of Tanja Börzel, Jørgen Grønnegård Christensen, Itzhak Galnoor, Peter Haas, Jacint Jordana, Arie Kacowicz, Orly Lobel, Guy Peters, Jon Pierre, Thomas Risse, Eva Sorensen, David Vogel, and Frans van Waarden. Finally, I want to note my gratitude to the contributors to this volume for their cooperation and their dedication to the project and to the field of governance. Their work both in this handbook and elsewhere extends the scope of research in this field and strengthens the foundations of our understanding of both government and governance. I hope that what we present here justifies optimism as regards the promise of the field and its future.

The Oxford Handbook of Governance is made up of nine sections. The first comprises six chapters that offer a broad overview of the governance literature. The second provides theoretical approaches aimed at situating the study of governance within a broad conceptual context and at extending its core agenda. The chapters in the third section analyze governance as a reform of the state. The fourth section covers actors of governance, their strategies, and their styles. The fifth examines economic governance, its challenges, forms, and causes. The sixth deals with the governance of risk and of science and technology. The seventh moves on to issues of democratic governance, which demonstrate that governance implies a change in our understanding of democracy. The eighth and the ninth sections cover the transnational arena, dealing first with the European Union—one of the exciting laboratories of governance research—while the second addresses issues in global governance. In all, the fifty-two chapters of this handbook fulfill a dual role of representing past achievements and offering directions and insights that may, I hope, allow us to understand the world around us better and to realize the ambitions of the scholarly community concerned with governance.

David Levi-Faur

Berlin, May 2011

Table of Contents

PART I: INTRODUCTION

PART II: THEORETICAL LENSES

PART III: GOVERNANCE AND THE REFORM OF THE STATE

PART IV: ACTORS, STRATEGIES, AND GOVERNANCE STYLES

PART V: ECONOMIC GOVERNANCE

PART VI: GOVERNANCE OF RISKS

PART VII: DEMOCRATIC GOVERNANCE

PART VIII: EUROPEAN GOVERNANCE

Notes on Contributors

Chris Ansell is an Associate Professor of Political Science at the University of California, Berkeley.

Ian Bache is Professor of Politics at the University of Sheffield, UK.

Tim Bartley is an Associate Professor of Sociology at Indiana University.

Christopher Todd Beer is a PhD Candidate in Sociology at Indiana University.

Thomas Bernauer is Professor of International Relations at the Center for Comparative and International Studies (CIS), ETH Zurich.

Susana Borrás is Professor of Innovation and Governance and Head of the Department for Business and Politics at the Copenhagen Business School, Denmark.

Tanja A. Börzel is Professor of Political Science and holds the Chair of European Integration at Freie Universität Berlin. She co-directs the Research College "The Transformative Power of Europe," together with Thomas Risse.

Arwin van Buuren is Associate Professor of Public Administration at the Erasmus University Rotterdam.

Tom Christensen is Professor at the Department of Political Science, University of Oslo, Norway.

William D. Coleman is Professor in Political Science at the Balsillie School of International Affairs and the University of Waterloo in Waterloo, Canada. His research focuses on differing ways of conceptualizing globalization and on global policy making addressing social issues.

Marie-Laure Djelic is Professor in the Management Department at ESSEC Business School, Paris.

William H. Dutton is Professor of Internet Studies at the Oxford Internet Institute at the University of Oxford, where a Fellow of Balliol College and an Emeritus Professor at the University of Southern California.

Jurian Edelenbos is professor of Public Administration at the Erasmus University Rotterdam.

Cynthia L. Estlund is the Catherine A. Rein Professor at the New York University School of Law.

Frank Fischer is Professor of Politics and Global Affairs at Rutgers University in the USA and Senior Faculty Fellow at the University of Kassel in Germany.

Elizabeth Fisher is Reader in Environmental Law at Corpus Christi College and the Faculty of Law, University of Oxford.

Eran Fisher is a Postdoctoral Research Fellow at the Kreitman School for Advanced Graduate Studies and the Department of Communication Studies, Ben Gurion University, Israel.

Matthew Flinders is Professor of Parliamentary Government & Governance at the University of Sheffield, United Kingdom.

Fabrizio Gilardi is Associate Professor of Public Policy, Department of Political Science and Center for Comparative and International Studies, University of Zurich, Switzerland.

Niamh Hardiman is Senior Lecturer in the School of Politics and International Relations at University College Dublin.

Adrienne Héritier holds a joint chair of political science at the Department of Political and Social Science and the Robert Schuman Center for Advanced Studies at the European University Institute in Florence.

Alexandria J. Innes is a Visiting Assistant Professor in the Department of Political Science at Northern Illinois University. Her research interests are in critical and post-colonial theory, security, and migration, and her work has appeared in *International Relations*.

Arie M. Kacowicz is Associate Professor of International Relations at the Hebrew University of Jerusalem. He has recently completed a book manuscript, "Globalization and the Distribution of Wealth: The Latin American Experience, 1982–2008."

Erik Hans Klijn is professor of Public Administration at the Department of Public Administration, Faculty of Social Science, Erasmus University Rotterdam in The Netherlands.

Per Lægreid is Professor at the Department of Administration and Organization Theory, University of Bergen, Norway.

David Levi-Faur is Associate Professor at the Department of Political Science and the Federmann School of Public Policy and Government at the Hebrew University and a Senior Fellow at the Kolleg-Forschergruppe "The Transformative Power of Europe" at the Free University of Berlin.

Orly Lobel is Herzog Endowed Scholar and Professor of Law at the University of San Diego.

Laurence E. Lynn Jr is the Sid Richardson Research Professor at the University of Texas at Austin and the Sydney Stein, Jr, Professor of Public Management Emeritus at the University of Chicago.

Felicity Matthews is Lecturer in Public Policy at the University of York, United Kingdom.

Ellen E. Meade is an Associate Professor in the Department of Economics at the American University.

Catherine Moury is Advanced Research Fellow at CIES-IUL, and Assistant Professor at Lisbon University Institute.

Abraham L. Newman is an Associate Professor in the Edmund A. Walsh School of Foreign Service at Georgetown University.

Yannis Papadopoulos is Professor of Public Policy at the Institut d'Études Politiques et Internationales of the University of Lausanne (Switzerland).

B. Guy Peters is Maurice Falk Professor of American Government at the University of Pittsburgh and Professor of Comparative Governance at Zeppelin University (Germany).

Susan Phillips is Professor and Director, School of Public Policy and Administration, Carleton University, Ottawa, Canada, and Visiting Fellow, Lucy Cavendish College, University of Cambridge and Centre for Charitable Giving and Philanthropy, Cass Business School, City University London.

Jon Pierre is a Research Professor in the Department of Political Science at the University of Goteburg and "Professor 2" at the University of Nordland (Norway).

Dieter Plehwe is a senior fellow at the Social Science Research Center Berlin, Project Group Modes of Economic Governance.

Colin Provost is Lecturer in Public Policy at the School of Public Policy/Department of Political Science, and is Director of Environmental Governance at the Enviromnment Institute at University College London.

Claudio M. Radaelli is Anniversary Chair in Politics and Director of the Centre for European Governance, University of Exeter, UK.

R. A. W. Rhodes is Professor of Government, University of Southampton, UK; and Professor of Governance and Public Policy, Griffith University, Australia.

Jeremy Richardson is an Emeritus Fellow at Nuffield College Oxford, UK and Professor in the National Centre for Research on Europe, University of Canterbury, New Zealand.

Thomas Risse is Professor of International Politics at the Freie Universität Berlin, Germany, and the coordinator of the Collaborative Research Center "Governance in Areas of Limited Statehood."

Wade T. Roberts is an Associate Professor of Sociology at Colorado College.

Amit Ron is an Assistant Professor of Political Science in the New College of Interdisciplinary Arts and Sciences at Arizona State University.

Bo Rothstein holds the August Röhss Chair in Political Science at University of Gothenburg and is co-founder and head of The Quality of Government Institute.

Charles F. Sabel is Maurice T. Moore Professor of Law at Columbia University.

Kerstin Sahlin is Professor in Management at Uppsala University.

Lena Maria Schaffer is a Post doctoral Researcher at the Center for Comparative and International Studies, ETH Zurich.

Frank Schimmelfennig is Professor of European Politics at the Center for Comparative and International Studies, ETH Zurich.

Volker Schneider is Professor of Political Science at the University of Konstanz, Germany. He holds the Chair on Empirical Theory of the State.

Eva Sørensen is Professor in Public Administration and Democracy at Roskilde University.

Brent J. Steele is an Associate Professor of Political Science and International Relations at the University of Kansas.

Diane Stone is a Professor in the Departments of Political Science and International Relations, University of Western Australia; Politics and International Studies, University of Warwick; and Public Policy, Central European University.

Jacob Torfing is Professor of Politics and Institutions at Department of Society and Globalization, Roskilde University and director of Centre for Democratic Network Governance.

Yael Yishai is a Professor of Political Science at the University of Haifa.

Frans van Waarden is Professor of Policy and Organization at Utrecht University and fellow of University College Utrecht.

Graham Wilson is Professor and Chair, Department of Political Science, Boston University. He previously held the same position at the University of Wisconsin-Madison and prior to that had been a member of the Department of Government, University of Essex.

Amos Zehavi, PhD, is a lecturer with a joint appointment in the Departments of Political Science and Public Policy at Tel Aviv University.

Jonathan Zeitlin is Professor of Public Policy and Governance at the University of Amsterdam.

Peer Zumbansen is Professor of Law. Canada Research Chair in Transnational Economic Governance and Legal Theory, Osgoode Hall Law School, York University, Toronto.

Michael Zürn is Director at the Social Science Research Center Berlin (WZB) and Professor at the Freie Universität Berlin. He is also a member of the Berlin-Brandenburg Academy of Science.

LIST OF TABLES

List of Figures

PART I

INTRODUCTION

CHAPTER 1

···

FROM "BIG GOVERNMENT" TO "BIG GOVERNANCE"?

···

DAVID LEVI-FAUR*

GOVERNANCE is said to be many things, including a buzzword, a fad, a framing device, a bridging concept, an umbrella concept, a descriptive concept, a slippery concept, an empty signifier, a weasel word, a fetish, a field, an approach, a theory and a perspective. In this handbook, governance is an interdisciplinary research agenda on order and disorder, efficiency and legitimacy all in the context of the hybridization of modes of control that allow the production of fragmented and multidimensional order *within* the state, *by* the state, *without* the state, and *beyond* the state. The plurality of the modes of control reflect and reshape new ways of making politics, new understanding of institutions of the state and beyond the state and allow us to explore new ways for the control of risks, empowering citizens and promoting new and experimentalist forms of democratic decision-making. As the *Oxford Handbook of Governance* intends to demonstrate, governance is increasingly becoming a broad concept that is central to the study of political, economic, spatial, and social order in general and to the understanding of the dynamics of change of capitalist democracies in particular.

While the origins, meanings, significance, and implications of the concept of governance are often disputed, governance has become an important concept and indeed probably one of the most important manifestations of the rise of neo-institutionalism in the social sciences (March and Olsen 1984). Paradoxically, it is almost as popular to lament the multiple, and sometimes ambiguous, meanings of governance, as it is to employ the term in creative ways. The literature on governance contains narratives and analysis of democratic controls and challenges beyond the traditional institutional literature. In the spirit of Karl Deutsch's classic *The Nerves of Government*, it reflects an understanding that "it might be profitable to look upon government somewhat less as a problem of power and somewhat more as a problem of steering" (1963: xxvii). Institutional technocrats (that is, people who preach the advantages of governance as the technology of control rather than an instrument of power) are often happy to endorse Deutsch's recommendation. Sometimes they are successful in convincing even highly suspicious governments to adopt the approach, at least on the surface (Burns 2010).[1] Yet, putting the political use of the concept aside for the moment, the scholarly value of the approach as a bridging concept is promising (Keersbergen and Waarden 2004: 143). Building on the various manifestations of neo-institutionalism in the social sciences, the governance approach to politics, institutions and policy offers an exciting and fruitful integrative theme for the ever more fragmented and decentered social sciences, with their disciplinary division of labor that is increasingly being called into question (Braithwaite 2005; Hall 2007).

Why, and to what extent, governance can play out its scholarly, intellectual, and normative missions is an issue that will be discussed here and throughout the Handbook's chapters. Let me start, however, by noting that it was not always the case. Governance, while not novel in the sense that it does not entirely reflect new practices and institutions, was for a long time marginal to the scholarly discourse of the social sciences (Pierre and Peters 2000: 1; Keersbergen and Waarden 2004: 143). It is still in the process of being translated (and in this process transformed) into different languages. In most languages, I suspect, it is awaiting official translation. In Hebrew, for example, the term does not yet have an agreed translation. The Chinese academic community had by 2000 agreed that governance should be translated as *zhili* (Burns 2010).[2] While still being adapted to new cultural and institutional contexts, governance is no longer marginal, either in the policy arenas or in scholarly discourse, as will be elaborated in this chapter, for good reasons. Consequently, it became a research agenda that unites scholars across the social sciences, many of whom recognize the growing gaps between the formal constitutional order and the way order is produced and reproduced in everyday life.

The notion of governance, which was rarely used and nearly incomprehensible before the 1980s, appears now in countless book and article titles, in the names of academic journals, educational and research institutions, and academic networks (Offe 2009: 554). It is the subject of handbooks and a recognized focus of teaching programs, research, and institutional and public policy reform (Lynn, Chapter 4, this volume). One could go on, and expose more evidence on the growth of the scholarly interest in governance across major fields and note its relative absence from others. Yet the most important issue that this chapter takes upon itself—especially given the countless useful contributions that already exist in the field—is to contextualize the study of governance in a more general framework of understanding of the processes of institutionalization and of a shift toward poly-centered polities, politics, and policy-making. The chapter identifies four major ways of thinking about governance as complementary to or an alternative to states and governments. It then asserts the theoretical potential of one of these approaches in particular, that is to say, the one which emphasizes the parallel growth of state-centered and society-centered governance. This approach is grounded in arguments about the rise of the regulatory state and of the global diffusion of regulatory capitalism and brings the literatures of governance and regulation together.

THE SCHOLARLY ORIGINS AND GROWTH
OF GOVERNANCE

The concept of governance probably stems from the Greek *kybernan* meaning to pilot, steer or direct, which was translated into Latin as *gubernare*. Our modern concepts of "government" and "governance" are indirectly related to this basic idea (Schneider and Hyner 2006: 155).[3] In the 1950s and the 1960s, the topic of governance was marginal to the production of knowledge in the social sciences and humanities (as reflected in the ISI Web of Knowledge databases). The small number of papers that were classified under this topic concentrated mainly on higher education and urban governance most probably demonstrating that hierarchical modes of control do not capture much of the politics of either universities or local government.

While the notion of governance was always there, it played a limited role in shaping the discourse of the social sciences. The influence of the papers that were classified under this topic, until the end of the mid-1970s, is low when assessed by their impact.[4] The situation changed radically with the publication of Oliver Williamson's *Transaction Costs Economics: Governance of Contractual Relations* (1979) and with the growing interest in law and economics in corporate governance. Williamson's paper had a strong impact. It not only accounted for about 83 percent of the citations of papers on the topic of governance in the period 1975–1980 but it is also one of most cited papers in the literature so far. The period 1981–1985 is characterized by the dominance of issues of corporate governance both generally and within the narrower population of highly cited papers. Urban and higher education governance issues are still there, but with low volume and with low number of citations. The ten highly cited papers that were published between 1981 and 1985 received 74 percent of the citations and eight of these ten dealt with corporate governance in one form or another. The following five years (1986–1990) suggested a further spread of the concept. Yet it is only in the 1990s that governance became a buzz-concept. In the 1980s only 349 papers were classified as dealing with the topic and these papers were cited altogether 3,609 times; in the 1990s, the number of papers and the number of citations both grew more than ten times (3,773 papers and 70,157 citations). Many more papers were influential in this period. Thus, the share of the ten most cited ones in the total number of citations dropped to 25 percent in the first half of the 1990s and to 14 percent for the second half.

The first decade of the second millennium saw further acceleration in the interest of the scholarly community in governance. The number of papers on the topic grew to 18,648 and they drew 104,928 citations. The share of the most cited papers in the overall pie of citation declined even further, to less than 5 percent. The gradual flattening of the influence of a small number of papers may suggest a healthy development in the field. An analysis of 9,366 papers on the topic of governance that were published between 2006 and 2009 reveals that they came from economic journals

(1,312), management (1,121), political science (1,086), business (1,061), environmental studies (993) public administration (911), planning and development (788), geography (758), business and finance (733), international relations (642), law (578), urban studies (436), sociology (383), and over fifty other fields. By comparison, the 158 papers that were published in the years 1981–1985 were published mainly in law journals (44 papers) followed by political science (22), economics (13) and public administration (10).

One way to better understand the growing interest in governance and the popularity of the concept is to look at the tipping points, that is, in influential publications that set the tone for further expansion of the concept. It is tempting to focus in this regard on papers and manuscripts in the field of political science, my own discipline. Nonetheless, if the social sciences at large are considered as a reference point, Williamson's 1979 paper is probably the best representative. The paper examines the preoccupation of the new institutional economics with the origins, incidence, and ramifications of the notion of "transaction costs" and *only* indirectly with the concept of "governance." To explain how actors try to minimize transaction costs he links the characteristics of investment and the frequency of transactions and distinguishes four types of governance: market, unilateral, bilateral, and trilateral. The three non-market governance structures (or institutional frameworks as he defines them) require some form of hierarchical governance (for him the internalization of production in "firms"). Yet his typology of various forms of governance was not adopted widely in the rest of the social sciences. The term governance was more popular than any particular method and definition that were applied by any scholar or scholarly approach. What was also probably taken most from Williamson was his distinction between market and hierarchies (see also Williamson 1975). While Dhal and Lindblom (1953) had for long used the distinction to disaggregate government and to explore other sources of authority, with Williamson the distinction became entrenched in the scholarly imagination. It is vis-à-vis these two modes of governance—markets and hierarchies—that the notion of network attracted more and more attention. Woody Powell's "Neither markets nor hierarchy: Network forms of organization" (1990) and Rod Rhodes's "Policy networks: A British perspective" (1990) served most probably as the earliest and most influential papers in setting the agenda and pointing out the direction of research. The notion of a network, as a governance structure and an institutional arrangement, as well as the recognition of the importance of informal spheres of authority, was quick to spread out. This was not least because political scientists had studied governance beyond government for a long time without calling it so: for example, growing interests in corporatist and alternative modes of interest intermediation (Schmitter 1974; van Waarden 1992), in private interest government (Heclo and Wildavsky 1974; Streeck and Schmitter 1985), issue networks (Heclo 1978), and policy styles (Richardson 1982, and Chapter 22, this volume). All laid the foundation for the study of governance as a research agenda that looked beyond the constitutional arrangements and formal aspects of the polity, politics and policy.

GOVERNANCE AS A SIGNIFIER OF CHANGE:
THE SCIENCE OF SHIFTOLOGY

One reason that made governance such an important concept in the social sciences is that it carries images and meanings of change. This happens of course in a period of turbulence and therefore it is not surprising that scholars started to devote more and more attention to the study of change. Within this process also they became more open to new ways, new concepts, and new issues for research. This "newness," and its relation to "change," is reflected in the following quotation from Rhodes:

> *Governance* signifies a change in the meaning of government, referring to *new* processes of governing; or *changed* conditions of ordered rule; or *new* methods by which society is governed. (Rhodes Chapter 3, this volume: 33, italics in the original; also Rhodes 1996: 652)

The rise of governance coincided with the widespread consensus that ours is (again) an era of change, of shifts, and even of transformation and paradigm change. In the governance literature this was best captured in the observation of "shifts" in governance and controversies about their directions and implications. These shifts suggest that authority is institutionalized, or at least can be institutionalized in different spheres, and by implication these arenas can compete, bargain, or coordinate among themselves or ignore each other. The shifts are conceptualized in three different directions: upward (to the regional, transnational, intergovernmental, and global), downward (to the local, regional, and the metropolitan), and horizontally (to private and civil spheres of authority). Some of the most dominant ways to think about shifts in governance include a shift from politics to markets, from community to markets, from politicians to experts, from political, economic, and social hierarchies to decentered markets, partnerships and networks; from bureaucracy to regulocracy, from service provision to regulation; from the positive state to the regulatory state; from Big Government to small government; from the national to the regional; from the national to the global; from hard power to soft power, and from public authority to private authority.

It is important to note that scholars of different aspects of the political order may have different shifts in mind when thinking about them. Scholars of international relations (or global governance) most often think about governance as denoting a shift from "anarchy" to "regulation" at the global level and have in mind more order and stronger institutions. Scholars of domestic politics by contrast often mean a "softer order" that replaces stagnating bureaucracies and centralized state controls with softer and collaborative forms of policy-making. Both, however, focus on the omnipresence of change. The multiplicity of shifts that can legitimately and usefully capture the notion of the rise of governance invites clarifications and opens a great window of opportunity for both ambiguity-bashers and the rise of "shiftology" as the study of change. For example, it is useful to consider and to define more precisely to what extent the shift away from government is also a shift away from the state and from public and private hierarchies. The choice of words here is significant: government, state, and hierarchies are different signifiers. We can imagine, for example, a shift away from government that is not a shift away from the state, because the state itself is more than government and while governments may shrink, other parts of the state (e.g. courts) may expand. We can also imagine a shift away from hierarchy toward governance that does not signify a shift away from government, because government adapts or reorganizes itself in horizontal or decentered forms. A useful way to think about these shifts is provided by Lynn (2010), who conceptualizes them as schematic trajectories of adaptation and transformations. The departure point is a particular division of tasks and responsibilities in the role of civil society, business, and government in supplying or exerting governance. The movements are not only from different departure points but also in different directions and towards different degrees of division of tasks and responsibilities (see Lynn 2010, fig. 1).

Governance as structure, process, mechanism, and strategy

Governance, much like government, has at least four meanings in the literature: a structure, a process, a mechanism and a strategy (cf. Börzel 2010a; Risse Chapter 49, this volume; Pierre and Peters 2000; Héritierand Rhodes 2011, Jessop 2011, Kjær 2004; Bartolini 2011). While the distinction between these four meanings is often not clearly elaborated, it might be useful to clarify them for analytical and theoretical purposes. As a structure, governance signifies the architecture of formal and informal institutions; as a process it signifies the dynamics and steering functions involved in lengthy never-ending processes of policy-making; as a mechanism it signifies institutional procedures of decision-making, of compliance and of control (or instruments); finally, as a strategy it signifies the actors' efforts to govern and manipulate the design of institutions and mechanisms in order to shape choice and preferences.

Most governance literature focuses on governance as structure, probably as a reflection of the dominance of institutionalism in the social sciences. Structures are understood and conceptualized sometimes as "systems of rules" (Rosenau 1995: 13), "regimes of laws, rules, judicial decisions, and administrative practices" (Lynn, Heinrich, and Hill 2001: 7), "institutionalized modes of social coordination" (Risse Chapter 49, this volume), a "set of multi-level, non-hierarchical and regulatory institutions" (Hix 1998: 39) and "the comparatively stable institutional, socio-economic and ideational parameters as well as the historically entrenched actor constellations" (Zürn, Wälti, and Enderlien 2010: 3). The diverse range of ways in which governance structures are conceptualized is therefore broad enough to allow several approaches to the study of alternative institutions of government such as networks, markets, and private standards.

The conceptualization of governance as a process aims to capture more dynamic interactive aspects than that of governance as structure. Thus, we can think about governance not as a stable or enduring set of institutions but as an ongoing process of steering, or enhancing the institutional capacity to steer and coordinate (Pierre and Peters 2000: 14; Kooiman 2003). The processes are evident in definitions that stress that governance is a "norm generating process" (Humrich and Zangl 2010: 343) as well as from the conceptualization of governance as "practices of governing" (Bevir 2011: 1) and the "exercise of authority, public" (Heinrich 2011: 256).

Governance is also about the institutionalization and naturalization of procedures of decision-making. We can also benefit from a distinction between five major mechanisms of decision-making via monetized exchange, non-monetized exchange, command, persuasion, and solidarity. Monetized exchanges are usually market exchanges and are characterized by minimal or moderate transaction costs. Non-material exchanges involve resources that are hard or impossible to monetize or otherwise assign value to. In both cases of exchange—the monetized and the non-monetized—decision-making involves deciding whether to exchange or not, as well as where, when and how. Command is a decision-making mechanism that involves rule-making with the expectation of compliance from the subject being commanded. It is an authoritative and hierarchical mechanism of decision-making which often is associated with the state but of course is not confined to it. Persuasion in decision-making involves the elaboration of values, preference, and interest as well as the rationalization and framing of options for action and the exchange of ideas and information in a deliberative manner. Finally, solidarity is a mechanism that rests on loyalty rather than voice, love rather than interest, faith rather than critical thinking, and group identity rather than individualism.

Governance as strategy, or "governancing," is the design, creation, and adaptation of governance systems. If governing is the act of government and the design of a hierarchy of governmental institutions, then governancing is about the decentralization of power and the creation of decentralized, informal, and collaborative systems of governance. Governancing therefore refers to governance-in-action (Barkay 2009) and to the institutional designs by actors that go beyond the formal institutions of government. For example, I consider the set of strategies of the European Parliament, to extend its control of the system of comitology, as an example of governancing (Héritier and Moury, Chapter 45, this volume). Another example of governance as strategy is the active design of soft architectures of governance such as networks (Levi-Faur 2011), soft mechanisms of decision-making such as the Open Method of Coordination and hyper innovation and experimentalism as an art of governance (Sable and Zeitlin, Chapter 12, this volume).

It is also useful to define what governance is not. First, governance is not a unified, homogeneous, and hierarchical approach to the study of politics, economics, and society. Indeed, the very notion of homogeneity stands in contrast to the basic underlying belief of a large group of governance scholars who tend to see themselves as (neo)pluralists and pragmatists. Second, governance, so far, is not a theory of causal relations. There is no need to explain governance structures, processes, mechanism, or strategies with new theories. Still governance and governancing can force and revitalize some explanatory strategies at the expense of others. Indeed, this is what Rhodes's (Chapter 3, this volume) third wave of governance studies is all about. Third, governance is not government. It may be considered as more than government or an alternative to government, but it is not synonymous with it.

GOVERNANCE AND THE SEARCH
FOR THEORY OF THE STATE

It is useful to distinguish between four perspectives on the state in the age of governance. I will present the first three in this section and cover a fourth in the next section. The first perspective on the state in governance theory is that of "governance as the hollowing out of the state" (Jessop 1994; Peters 1994; Rhodes 1994). This conceptualizes the shift from government to governance whereby power and authority drift away upwards toward transitional markets and political institutions and downward toward local or regional government, domestic business communities and non-governmental organizations. There are different and interesting variations within this perspective. Yet one of the clearest and to some extent most provocative views was taken by Rod Rhodes, who used the phrase "the hollowing out of the state" to suggest, with some qualifications, that the British state, and by extension other states, is being eroded or eaten away (Rhodes 1997: 100). "The state", he argued, "becomes a collection of inter-organizational networks made up of governmental and societal actors with no sovereign actor able to steer or regulate" (Rhodes 1997: 57). Similarly, Sørensen and Torfing suggested that:

> Although the state still plays a key role in local, national and transnational policy processes, it is nevertheless to an increasing extent "de-governmentalized" since it no longer monopolizes the governing of the general well-being of the population in the way that it used to do. The idea of a sovereign state that governs society top-down through laws, rules and detailed regulations has lost its grip and is being replaced by new ideas about a decentered governance based on interdependence, negotiation and trust. (2005: 195–196)

In the same vein, Klijn and Koppenjan (2000: 135) wrote that an "apparently broad consensus has developed around the idea that government is actually not the cockpit from which society is governed and that policy making processes rather are generally an interplay among various actors." It is hard however to identify a positive theory of the state in the writings of the proponents of the "hollowing out of the state" approach and instead the emphasis is on state failure and a criticism of "reified concepts of the state as a monolithic entity, interest, or actor" (Bevir 2011: 2). This is quite understandable since most efforts were focused on theory and empirical research on policy networks. Still, there is a more important and illuminating point here; this perspective is strongly connected with pluralists and neo-pluralist theories of the state, which tend to see the state as a broker or even a weathervane. The autonomy of the state is constrained and it reflects the preferences of most of the strongest groups in society. While normative, empirical and constructivist pluralists seem to set the tone in this interpretation of the state, this view is often shared by neo-Marxists (Jessop 1994). In short, this governance approach is a society-centered analysis and despite Rhodes's (1997: 29–32, 2007: 7–8) effort to draw lines between his perspective on governance and pluralism, they belong to the same intellectual and scholarly family. Thus, Rhodes's (2007) "Understanding governance: Ten years on" continues to assert the thesis of the hollowing out of the state, to ignore the notion of the regulatory state, and to equate states and governance with core executive:

> The "hollowing out of the state" means simply that the growth of governance reduced the ability of the core executive to act effectively, making it less reliant on a command operating code and more reliant on diplomacy. (Rhodes 2007: 6)

The second perspective may best be described as that of "degovernancing." Like the concepts of deregulation and debureaucratization, it is about the intended and unintended outcomes of limiting the ability to govern via centralized administrative and political mechanisms. Degovernancing is about the hollowing out of the state but also the hollowing out of alternative spheres of authority such as business-to-business regulation, civil regulation, and transnational regulation. Good governance in this approach is "no governance" or "minimal governance" and the preferred mode of control is that of the market. If the first perspective is about the hollowing out of the state, then this perspective is about the hollowing out of politics altogether. It is often associated with the effort to devise market forms of governance as alternatives to political forms. While it is hard to find scholars who explicitly and consistently favor market mechanisms over all other forms of control, including civil and business-to-business regulation, yet there are enough preferences for "*lite*" modes of regulation in issues such as climate change and carbon markets and enough opposition to hierarchical and statist modes of governance for this perspective to be considered here, along with the other three.

The third perspective, "state-centered governance," combines a recognition of the shift and transformation in the organization of the state, the limitations of its policy capacities and the importance of private actors in the policy process and in global governance more generally, with the suggestion that the state is still the most important and central actor in politics and policy. Thus Pierre and Peters suggest that

> although governance relates to changing relationships between state and society and a growing reliance on less coercive policy instruments, the state is still the centre of considerable political power. Furthermore, emerging forms of governance departing from a model of democratic government where the state was the undisputed locus of power and control, hence we cannot think of any better 'benchmark' than the image of the state as portrayed in liberal-democratic theory. For these reasons mainly we look at governance as processes in which the state plays a leading role, making priorities and defining objectives. (Pierre and Peters 2000: 12)

Claus Offe nicely identified two important aspects of this version of governance that together point to the resilience of the state:

> one finds the notion that *governance* can increase the intervention capacity of the state by bringing non-state actors into the making and implementation of public policy, thus making the latter more efficient and less fallible....The catchphrase of this doctrine is that the state should limit itself to *steering* and leave the *rowing* to other actors. One could also speak of auxiliary forces within civil society who, through appropriate means and according to their specific competences and resources, are being recruited for cooperation in the fulfillment of public tasks, become subject to regulatory oversight and economic incentives, and are thus licensed to privately exercise (previously exclusively) public functions. The core intuition is that of a *state-organized unburdening of the state*....Underlying this shift in emphasis is the vision of a "leaner" and at the same time more "capable" state" (Offe 2009: 555)

My own work on the EU regulatory regimes suggested that, in order to understand the institutional gaps between the EU electricity and telecoms regimes, one needs to develop "a state centered multi-level governance" approach (Levi-Faur 1999: 201). This was later reasserted in the portrayal of the leaner and meaner state (Jordana and Levi-Faur 2004). The work of Héritier emphasized the critical importance of the "shadow of hierarchy" (i.e. the state) in the effective and legitimate application of new modes of governance (Héritier and Lehmkuhl 2008; Börzel 2010b). Börzel (2010a) emphasizes the paradox that the lower the effectiveness of government, the greater the need for governance, whose effectiveness (and legitimacy) depends, however, on the presence of government. Schout, Jordan, and Twena (2010) similarly observed that new (and old) instruments in EU governance are highly reliant on administrative capacities. Risse (Chapter 49, this volume) extended the state-centered governance perspective to areas of "limited statehood." Börzel and Risse discussed the possibility of governance without the state (Börzel and Risse 2010). Bell and Hindmoor (2009) claim to go somewhat beyond Pierre and Peters (2000) to develop what they call a "state-centered relational approach," arguing that states have enhanced their capacity to govern by strengthening their own institutional and legal capacities at the same time as developing closer relations with non-state actors. They reject the notion that there has been any general loss of governing capacity and emphasize that governments rely upon hierarchical authority to implement their policies because even when governments *choose* to govern in alternative ways, the state remains the pivotal player in establishing and operating governance strategies and partnerships (Bell and Hindmoor 2009; 2–3; Matthews, Chapter 20, this volume).

"State-centered (multi-level) governance" denotes the high autonomy of the state when the state is not dependent directly or instrumentally on society or capitalists and can shape its preferences both in the context of privatization and liberalization and in the context of globalization and the creation of transnational and intergovernmental institutions in the regional and global arenas (Hooghe and Marks 2001; Bache, Chapter 44, this volume). Taken to the extreme, this view would suggest that polities worldwide are and should be structured around states; governance is either a marginal or temporary solution to state failures. Scholars need to bring the state back in order to tune their theories of politics and policy to the realties out there. Much of the literature of governance, probably most, would be easily classified as belonging to this perspective.

From Big Government to Big Governance

A fourth perspective on the state in the literature of governance is emerging. This is best referred to as Big Governance, and may help to take the literature in this field forward in a significant manner while at the same time providing a better understanding of the role of the state in the age of governance. This perspective explores the relations between governments and governance from the perspective of regulation and with regard to the consolidation of what might best be called regulatory capitalism (Braithwaite 2000, 2008; Braithwaite et al. 2007; Jordana and Levi-Faur 2004; Levi-Faur 2005; Lobel, Chapter 5, this volume; Döhler 2011; Lehmkuhl 2008). It suggests that both governance and regulation are major signifiers of the structure of polities, the processes of politics and of policy outcomes. The approach draws on the governance literature in order to denote the decentralization and diversification of politics and policy beyond the state and draws on the regulation literature in order to denote the expansion of regulatory governance and especially the notion of the regulatory state. By bringing the regulation and governance perspectives together an important aspect of the current capitalist order is becoming clearer: the growth and indeed explosion in the demand and supply of rules and regulation via hybrid modes of governance.

Big Government, that is, a powerful if leaner government that controls, distributes, and redistributes large amounts of the national domestic product, is still with us but it is becoming even bigger, mainly via regulation. If the expanding part of the Big Government program for most of the twentieth century was taxing and spending, in the last three decades the expanding part of the Big Government program is regulation. Still, this is not only about Big Government via regulation and thus not only about the return of the state via regulatory means and in the form of the regulatory state. It is also about the growth and expansion of alternative modes of governance via increasing reliance on regulation. Growth of regulatory functions of public institutions, alongside the growth in the regulatory functions of the other four modes of governance, denotes a shift from Big Government to Big (regulatory) Governance.

The Big Governance perspective, like the state-centered governance perspective, suggests that the shift to governance is potentially about leaner and in many respects more capable states. But unlike the state-centered governance perspective, it suggests that both governance and government can expand. This impression of co-expansion rests largely on observing the co-expansion of civil, business and public forms of regulation and the diversification in the instruments of regulation towards standards, best practices, ranking and shaming. A growing demand for governance is mostly being supplied via regulation. The suppliers of regulation are not only public actors but also civil and business actors who collaborate and compete with each other. Unlike state-centered governance, this co-expansion perspective has a positive theory of controls—the theory of the regulatory state and more generally also with reference to growth in the role, capacities and demand for civil and business regulation—the theory of regulatory capitalism (Levi-Faur 2005). In short, we are in the heyday of Big Governance and the major question of governancing, that is, the strategy of governance designs and control, is to determine not which pure mode of governance is more effective or more legitimate but which hybrids are. We need to conceptualize a world order where governance is increasingly a hybrid of different systems of regulatory control; where statist regulation co-evolves with civil regulation; national regulation expands with international and global regulation; private regulation co-evolves and expands with public regulation; business regulation co-evolves with social regulation; voluntary regulations expand with coercive ones; and the market itself is used or mobilized as a regulatory mechanism.

To understand Big Governance better we will probably need to bring back some of the issues that were dealt with by the now neglected and unfashionable theories of "political development" and bureaucratic and political "modernization." The Big Governance approach draws on the regulatory innovations, experimental governance and learning literatures in order to examine governance development as a feature not only of the economically underdeveloped and politically authoritarian countries but mainly with regards to the developed and democratic countries. The expansion of the demand and supply of legitimate and effective governance is at the same time the problématique and the moral compass of this approach.

Conclusions

To grasp the added value of the agenda of governance better in today's social science discourse, we need to consider the bad reputation of governments and hierarchies; the frustration of reformers and revolutionaries; the statelessness of Anglo-American political theory; the rise of neoliberalism; the transformation of the so-called Weberian hierarchical model of bureaucracy, the end of the Westphalian order; the efforts to reform, update and extend democratic theory via participation and deliberation; the transnationalization of civil politics; the emergence of new transnational risks; the rise of the European Union as a new, surprising, and intriguing transnational order. At the same time we need to consider experimental designs in democracy and governance more generally and the innovative tools that allow the creation of alternative modes of regulation in the private and public sphere and as hybrids of at least five pure modes of governance. Much of this development rests on the steering functions and their promotion via information-gathering, rule-making, monitoring, and enforcement. Rowing via tax collection, distribution, redistribution, and service provision by the government is still here and will most probably stay with us. Yet in order to meet the challenges of complex society, transnationalization, and new democratic expectations, governments and other spheres of authority will need to develop their steering capacities and do it in horizontal rather than hierarchical ways. The following chapters in this handbook shed light on the challenges we face and how governance and governancing can help to meet them.

Notes

* It is a pleasure to acknowledge with thanks the comments I received on this chapter from good and generous colleagues: Ian Bache, Susana Borrás, Tanja Börzel, Cindy Estlund, Frank Fischer, Matthew Flinders, Jacint Jordana, Arie Kacowicz, Johan Olsen, Felicity Matthews, Susan Phillips, Rod Rhodes, Volker Schneider, Diane Stone, Frans van Waarden, Graham Wilson, Amos Zehavi and Michael Zürn. These colleagues offered a large number of highly useful comments and suggestions. I could respond to only some of their comments and suggestions in this chapter. I intend to come back to those comments and insights in my future work on regulation and governance.

1. Burns (2010) offers a fascinating story of the "selling" of the notion of governance to suspicious government officials of China. The ideas about governance which were interpreted as associated with a strong civil society and the rule of law were of course adapted (and marginalized) to keep the Chinese power structure and state ideology intact. Officials use it differently from scholars. It can be interpreted as a supplementary rather than collaborative relationship pattern in Chinese official language context, but scholars lay stress on its partnership collaboration between state and society.

2. In traditional Chinese, *zhili* is a word including two Chinese characters. "*Zhi*" means to rule, govern or put something under control, "*Li*" means management, regulation or put something in order. Therefore, it has a combinative meaning of rule and administration. Generally *zhili* means government should manage and handle social affairs in a comprehensive manner taking into account political, economic, educational, and cultural considerations. It differs significantly from the traditional command-and-control mode of government. In some political contexts, *zhili* also means a government's comprehensive control mode which builds on the socialist legacy, for example, *Shehui Zhi'an Zonghe Zhili* (Social Security Comprehensive Administration). In other words, the notion of governance was diffused but then transformed and adapted to the local political context. I am grateful to Liu Peng for clarifying this.

3. In fourteenth-century France *gouvernance* signified royal officers and in the England of the Elizabethan age people talked about the governance of the family (Pierre and Peters 2000: 1–2; Bell and Hindmoor 2009: 1).

4. All citations and impact data refer to the ISI's Humanities and Social Sciences databases and were updated to March 2011.

References

Barkay, T. 2009. Regulation and voluntarism: A case study of governance in the making. *Regulation and Governance* 3: 360–375.

Bartolini, S. 2011. New modes of governance: An introduction. In *New Modes of Governance in Europe: Governing in the Shadow of Hierarchy*, ed. A. Héritier and M. Rhodes. Houndmills: Palgrave Macmillan, 1–18.

Bell, S. and Hindmoor, A. 2009. *Rethinking Governance: The Centrality of the State in Modern Society*. Port Melbourne, Vic.: Cambridge University Press.

Bevir, M. 2011. Governance as theory, practice, and dilemma. In *The Sage Handbook of Governance*, ed. M. Bevir. Thousand Oaks, CA: Sage, 1–16.

Börzel, T.A. 2010a. *Governance without Government: False Promises or Flawed Premises?* SFB Governance Working Paper Series, Berlin: Freie Universität Berlin: SFB 700.

Börzel, T.A. 2010b. European governance: Negotiation and competition in the shadow of hierarchy. *Journal of Common Market Studies* 48: 191–219.

Börzel, T.A. and Risse T. 2010. Governance without a state: Can it work? *Regulation and Governance* 4: 1–22.

Braithwaite, J. 2000. The new regulatory state and the transformation of criminology. *British Journal of Criminology* 40: 222–238.

Braithwaite, J. 2005. For public social science. *British Journal of Sociology* 56: 345–353.

Braithwaite, J. 2008. *Regulatory Capitalism: How it works, Ideas for Making it Work*. Cheltenham: Edward Elgar.

Braithwaite, J., Coglianese, C., and Levi-Faur, D. 2007. Can regulation and governance make a difference? *Regulation and Governance* 1: 1–7.

Burns, John P. 2010. Western models and administrative reform in China: Pragmatism and the search for modernity. In *Comparative Administrative Change and Reform: Lessons Learned*, ed. Jon Pierre and Patricia W. Ingraham. Montreal: McGill-Queen's University Press, 182–206.

Dhal, R. H. and Lindbloom, E. C. 1953. *Politics Economics and Welfare*. New York: Harper & Brothers.

Deutsch K. W. 1963. *The Nerves of Government: Models of Political Communication*. New York: Free Press .

Döhler, M. 2011. Regulation. In *The Sage Handbook of Governance*, ed. M. Bevir. Los Angeles and London: Sage, 518–534.

Hall, P. A. 2007. The dilemmas of contemporary social science. *Boundary* 2, 34: 121–141.

Heclo, H. 1978. Issue networks and the executive establishment. In *The New American Political System*, ed. A. King. Washington, DC: American Enterprise Institute, 87–124.

Heclo, H. and Wildavsky A. 1974. *The Private Government of Public Money*. London: Macmillan.

Heinrich, C. J. 2011. Public management. In *The Sage Handbook of Governance*, ed. M. Bevir. Thousand Oaks, CA: Sage, 252–269.

Héritier, A. and Eckert. S. 2008. New modes of governance in the shadow of hierarchy: Self-regulation by industry in Europe. *Journal of Public Policy* 28: 113–138.

Héritier, A. and Lehmkuhl, D. (eds.) 2008. The shadow of hierarchy and new modes of governance. *Special Issue Journal of Public Policy* 28.

Héritier, A. and Rhodes, M. (eds.) 2011. *New Modes of Governance in Europe: Governing in the Shadow of Hierarchy*. Houndmills: Palgrave Macmillan.

Hix, S. 1998. The study of the European Union II: The 'new governance' agenda and its revival. *Journal of European Public Policy* 5: 38–65.

Hooghe, L and Marks, G. 2001. *Multi-level Governance and European Integration*. London: Rowman & Littlefield.

Humrich C. and Zangl, B. 2010. Global governance through legislation. In *Handbook of Multilevel Governance*, ed. Henerik Enderlein, Sonja Wälti, and Michael Zürn. Cheltenham: Edward Elgar, 343–357.

Jessop, B. 1994. Post-fordism and the state. *In Post-Fordism: A Reader*, ed. A. Amin. Oxford: Blackwell, 251–279.

Jessop B. 2011. Metagovernance. In *The Sage Handbook of Governance*, ed. M. Bevir. Thousand Oaks, CA: Sage, 106–123.

Jordana, J. and Levi-Faur, D. (eds.) 2004. *The Politics of Regulation: Institutions and Regulatory Reforms for the Governance Age*. Cheltenham: Edward Elgar.

Kjær, A. M. 2004. *Governance*. Cambridge: Polity.

Keersbergen, Van K. and Van Waarden, F. 2004. Governance as a bridge between disciplines: Cross-disciplinary inspiration regarding shifts in governance and problems of governability, accountability and legitimacy. *European Journal of Political Research* 43: 143–171.

Klijn, E. H. and Koppenjan J. F. M. 2000. Public management and policy networks: Foundations of a network approach to governance. *Public Management* 2: 135–158.

Kooiman, J. 2003. *Governing as Governance*. London: Sage.

Lehmkuhl, D. 2008. Control modes in the age of transnational governance. *Law and Policy* 30: 336–363.

Levi-Faur, D. 1999. The governance of competition: The interplay of technology, economics, and politics in European Union electricity and telecom regimes. *Journal of Public Policy* 19: 175–207.

Levi-Faur, D. 2005. The global diffusion of regulatory capitalism. *Annals of the American Academy of Political and Social Science* 598: 12–32.

Levi-Faur, D. 2011. Regulatory networks and regulatory agencification, *Journal of European Public Policy* 18: 808–827.

Lynn, L. E. Jr. 2010. The persistence of hierarchy. In *The Sage Handbook of Governance*, ed. M. Bevir. Thousand Oaks, CA: Sage, 218–236.

Lynn, L. E., Jr., Heinrich, C. J., and Hill, C. J. 2001. *Improving Governance: A New Logic for Empirical Research*. Washington, DC: Georgetown University Press.

March, G. J. and Olsen, P. J. 1984. The new institutionalism: organizational factors in political life. *American Political Science Review* 78: 734–749.

Marin, B. and Mayntz, R. (eds.) 1991. *Policy Network: Empirical Evidence and Theoretical Considerations*. Frankfurt am Main: Campus Verlag.

Mayntz, R. 2003. New challenges to governance theory. In *Governance as Social and Political Communication*, ed. H. P. Bang. Manchester: Manchester University Press, 27–39.

Offe, C. 2009. Governance: An "empty signifier"? *Constellations* 16: 550–562.

Peters, B. G. 1994. Managing the hollow state. *International Journal of Public Administration* 17: 739–756.

Pierre, J. and Peters, B. G. 2000. *Governance, Politics and the State*. Basingstoke: Macmillan.

Powell, W. W. 1990. Neither markets nor hierarchy: Network forms of organization. *Research in Organizational Behavior* 12: 295–336.

Rhodes, R. A. W. 1990. Policy networks: A British perspective. *Journal of Theoretical Politics* 2: 292–316.

Rhodes, R. A. W. 1994. The hollowing out of the state: The changing nature of the public service in Britain. *Political Quarterly* 65: 138–151.

Rhodes, R.A.W 1996. The new governance: governing without government. *Political Studies* 44: 652–667.

Rhodes, R. A. W. 1997. *Understanding Governance*. Buckingham and Philadelphia: Open University Press.

Rhodes, R. A. W. 2007. Understanding governance: Ten years on. *Organization Studies* 28: 1243–1264.

Richardson, J. (ed.) 1982. *Policy Styles in Western Europe*. London: Allen and Unwin

Rosenau J. N. 1995. Governance in the twenty-first century. *Global Governance* 1: 13–43.

Rosenau, J. N. 2007. Governing the ungovernable: The challenge of a global disaggregation of authority. *Regulation and Governance* 1: 88–97.

Scharpf, F. W. 1997. *Games Real Actors Play: Actor-centred Institutionalism in Policy Research*. Boulder, CO: Westview Press.

Schmitter C. P. 1974. Still the century of corporatism? *The Review of Politics* 36: 85–131.

Schneider, V., and Hyner, D. 2006. Security in cyberspace: Governance by transnational policy networks. In *New Modes of Governance in the Global System: Exploring Publicness, Delegation and Inclusiveness*, ed. M. Koenig-Archibugi and M. Zürn. New York: Palgrave, 154–176.

Schout, A., Jordan, A. J., and Twena, M. 2010. From the 'old' to the 'new' governance in the European Union: why is there such a diagnostic deficit?, *West European Politics* 33: 154–170.

Sørsensen, E. and Torfing, J. 2005. Democratic anchorage of governance networks, *Scandinavian Political Studies* 28: 195–218.

Streeck W. and Schmitter C. P. 1985. Community, market, state – and associations? The prospective contribution of interest governance to social order. *European Sociological Review* 1: 119–138.

van Waarden, F. 1992. Dimensions and types of policy networks. *European Journal of Political Research* 21: 29–52.

Williamson E. O. 1975. *Markets and Hierarchies: Analysis and Antitrust Implications*. New York: The Free Press.

Williamson E. O. 1979. Transaction cost economics: The governance of contractual relations. *Journal of Law and Economics* 22: 233–261.

Zürn, M., Wälti, S., and Enderlein, H. 2010. Introduction. In *Handbook of Multilevel Governance*, ed. Henerik Enderlein, Sonja Wälti, and Michael Zürn. Cheltenham: Edward Elgar, 1–13.

....

CHAPTER 2

GOVERNANCE AS POLITICAL THEORY

....

B. GUY PETERS

THE concept of governance has become very fashionable over the past several decades, and indeed has become one of the most commonly used terms in political science, to the point of becoming a "fetish." Further, the term has become used widely by policy-makers and by international organizations, especially those responsible for improving the lives of people around the world experiencing poverty and oppression. The concept of governance also has been used in relation to the management of organizations in the private sector, while interest in corporate governance has become all the more pervasive after major debacles in firms such as Enron and Lehmann Brothers.

The ambiguity of the concept of governance has been one of the reasons for its popularity; it can be shaped to conform to the intellectual preferences of the individual author and therefore to some extent obfuscates meaning at the same time that it perhaps enhances understanding. The concept is, in Sartori's (1971) terms, often weak on intension and therefore very strong on extension. The addition of various adjectives to delineate the meaning may help with the understanding of governance (Collier and Levitsky 2004), but even with those qualifications there are numerous opportunities for stretching the meaning of the concept beyond all utility, so that it threatens to become relatively meaningless.

The purpose of this chapter is not, however, to engage in an extensive exegesis of the concept of governance but, rather, to make a substantially stronger claim about this concept. This claim is that, if conceptualized adequately, then governance can be the foundation of a significant political theory that can be important for developing contemporary political science. In particular, an emphasis on governance enables the discipline of political science to recapture some of its roots by focusing more explicitly on how the public sector, in conjunction with private sector actors, transnational actors, or alone, is capable of providing direction and control for society and the economy. The same questions may arise for transnational governance. The focus on individual level

behavior in much of contemporary political science has tended to obscure the fundamental task of governing, and it is important to place the behavior of individuals into the
broader context of governing.

Therefore, this chapter will develop the concept of governance as a broad political
theory, and demonstrate how the approach could be used to address a range of contemporary concerns, both in academic circles and in the real world of governing. This argument will not attempt to persuade the reader that governance theory and analysis are as
yet capable of providing an encompassing paradigm for political science or public
administration. I will, however, argue that there are opportunities for developing a more
encompassing approach that may have some features of a paradigm and that such an
effort may be important for the discipline. Further, a focus on governance may help to
bring together a range of other approaches and hence can integrate much of contemporary political science. The treatment will be balanced and will therefore include some of
the important questions that continue to arise about governance and its utility for the
discipline.

THE NATURE OF GOVERNANCE

The root of the word governance, and indeed government, relates to steering a boat.
A steering metaphor is indeed a useful way in which to approach the idea of governance
in contemporary societies. Societies require collective choices about a range of issues
that cannot be addressed adequately by individual action, and some means must be
found to make and to implement those decisions. The need for these collective decisions
has become all the more obvious when the world as a whole, as well as individual societies, are faced with challenges such as climate change, resource depletion. and arms control that cannot be addressed by individual actions, and indeed are often cases in which
individual self-interest is likely to result in collective harm (Hardin 1977; Ostrom 1990).
Governance also implies some conception of accountability, so that the actors involved
in setting goals and then in attempting to reach them, whether through public or private
action, must be held accountable for their actions to society (Van Keersbergen and Van
Waarden 2004).

Even for social and economic problems without the complexity and difficulty of common pool resources, there is still a need for collective action, whether to provide for pensions for the elderly, build roads, or cope with common health problems. The
consequences of the absence of a capacity for collective action can be seen in "failed
states" (Niemann 2007; Risse, Chapter 49, this volume), even if there are private actors
capable of managing some economic or even social functions. While these forms of governance may be able to impose some policies on a population, and can be seen as developing collective goals, the goals were selected by some largely unaccountable actors.[1]
Even when usually effective political systems are not capable of providing that collective
action, as with Katrina in the United States, the consequences are often devastating.

Effective governance, except in very rare circumstances, may therefore be better provided with the involvement of state actors, and hence governance is an essentially political concept, and one that requires thinking about the forms of public action. The tendency of some contemporary theories of governance to read the state out of that central position thus appears misguided. Just as more traditional versions of governance that excluded non-state actors ignored a good deal of importance in governing, so too would any conception—academic or practical—that excluded the state from a central role.

There are a variety of ways in which collective problems associated in governance can be addressed. Scholars have advanced some rather important arguments suggesting that autonomous action through voluntary agreements can solve these problems (Ostrom 2005; Lam 1998). This style of solving collective action problems is important but may depend upon special conditions, and perhaps on factors such as leadership. Given the difficulties of imposing collective governance through negotiations in networks or other collections of social actions, the public sector has been the principal source of governance. Governments are the principal source of law in most societies and have, in the Weberian conception of the state, a monopoly on the legitimate use of force in society.

In addition to the monopoly of legitimate force, governments also have *ex ante* rules for making decisions. At the most basic level these are constitutions (Sartori 1997), although there are also rules and procedures within public institutions that enable them to make decisions in the face of conflicts.[2] Although many of the social mechanisms that have been central in thinking about governance may be able to involve a range of actors, these mechanisms may encounter difficulties in reaching decisions, and especially in reaching high quality decisions (but see Klijn and Koppenjann 2004).

Lacking *ex ante* decision rules, networks and analogous structures must bargain to consensus through some means or another. This style of decision-making may appear democratic but it is also slow and tends to result in poor decisions. As Scharpf (1988) argued concerning systems in which all actors have *de facto* vetoes, outcomes tend to be by the lowest common denominator, so that highly innovative and potentially controversial decisions are unlikely to emerge. This "joint decision trap" can be overcome in part by recognizing the iterative nature of decisions and by the capacity of actors involved to build package deals that enable them to overcome marked differences in preferences.

GOVERNANCE AS A FUNCTIONALIST ARGUMENT

In the Parsonian framework for society, the polity was assigned the task of "goal attainment," developing mechanisms for making and implementing collective policy choices to achieve important goals. Thus, in this sweeping conception of the organization of society the public sector is responsible for providing effective guidance to the other institutions such as the economy (adaptation) and even socialization (integration). In such a conception of how societies cope with their environment the public sector is assigned this crucial function. This is a rather simplistic characterization of the place of the state in society, but does identify the crucial role of states in making policy and in steering society.

At a lower level of generalization we can consider the functions that must be performed in the process of governing. The structural-functional approach, for example, argued that the basic decision-making functions were rule-making, rule application, and rule adjudication.[3] Political systems may differ in how they perform those functions, but for the political system to function they all had to be performed. These functions are themselves, however, rather general, and posed severe problems of operationalization for anyone attempting to employ them empirically for comparison.

Governance can be argued to have a relatively similar set of functional requirements, albeit expressed with somewhat greater detail and specificity. We would argue, for example, that successful governance requires the fulfillment of at least the four following activities:

1. Goal Selection. Governing is steering and steering requires some knowledge about the destination toward which one is steering. This function can be performed by state actors alone but also may involve social actors. We do need to remember, however, that goals are not simple, and exist at a variety of levels ranging from broad goals such as "social justice" down to operational goals of departments and programs. Therefore, effective governance requires the integration of goals across all levels of the systems.

2. Goal Reconciliation and Coordination. The multiple actors within government all have their own goals, and effective governance therefore requires establishing some priorities and coordinating the actions taken according to those priorities.

3. Implementation. The decisions made in the first two stages of the process above must then be put into effect, requiring some form of implementation. This stage of the process is more likely to can be performed by state actors along but also may involve social actors.

4. Feedback and Accountability. Finally, individuals and institutions involved in governance need to learn from their actions. This is important both for improving the quality of the decisions being made and also for democratic accountability. Therefore, some well-developed method of feedback must be built into the governance arrangements.

These functions are basic to the process of governance, and can be elaborated further by considering the processes involved, such as decision-making, resource mobilization, implementation, and adjudication.[4] The functions themselves may be excessively broadly conceived, but the process elements involved can be detailed to a much greater extent and can also be related to many processes discussed in other areas of political science. Further, the need to focus on processes will force the discipline to think more about the element of political activity that has often been ignored.

THE CONTRIBUTIONS OF GOVERNANCE
TO POLITICAL THEORY

The functionalist basis of much of governance theory has been questioned, especially in relation to earlier approaches such as structural functionalism (but see Lane 1994; Smith 2003). Despite that rather fundamental problem raised by the critics governance theory can still make a significant contribution to contemporary political theory. Like the earlier efforts to construct general functionalist perspectives on political life, governance approaches do have wide applicability. The problem may be, however, that, like those approaches, there is insufficient specificity to make meaningful comparisons.

I am arguing, however, that there is sufficient detail and sufficient attention to different varieties of governance to warrant greater optimism about this approach to political phenomena. The several versions of governance theory that have been developed make the approach appear incoherent and excessively open. On the other hand, these varieties of theory all address a fundamental and common problem and the several answers provided may enrich the study of governance. The problem is that many approaches to social theory tend to focus on a single explanation or actor, rather than on how the possible explanations can be brought together in a more comprehensive and conjectural way.

For governance theory to make the contribution that appears possible, the style of thinking about the issues may need to change from "or" to "and" and from and to "and + and." Much contemporary theory has stressed the role of social actors as opposed to the role of the state in governing. While that emphasis has been useful to dispel the idea that governing is entirely a function of the formal public sector,[5] it has gone perhaps too far in denying the role of state. What is needed has been an integration of the various approaches and finding a more complete understanding of governance.

A basis for general comparison

For the development of empirical political theory perhaps the most important attribute of governance approaches is that they can be applied in a wide range of settings. As argued above, all societies have to find some means of governing themselves and providing some collective direction, and governance asks questions about how this is done. We have identified a number of dimensions that can be used for comparison and which can be used to specify more exactly how governance functions in different settings, and the consequences of choices made about governance structures and processes.

Governance approaches are also useful beyond the usual pale of studies of government, or state–society interactions, and can be a means of approaching issues such as failed states (Risse and Lehmkuhl 2010). While conventional state institutions and processes are not effective in these settings we have to inquire about what can replace those institutions. In the more effective governance systems many governance functions may be delegated, the informal institutions made responsible for policymaking and implementation function in a "shadow of hierarchy" (Scharpf 1997) with the formal institutions always having the capacity of recapturing their formal control. In the weak or failed states.

Even when there are effective formal institutions in a society, these may be augmented or perhaps contested by informal institutions. There is a tendency to think of formal and informal institutions for governance as alternatives, but these structures may assist one another in providing governance. Helmke and Levistsky (2004), for example, point to the variety of different ways in which the formal and the informal may interact in governing: some informal instruments can supplement the formal actions of governing organizations, while others may contradict those actions.

The same basic governance logic can be applied when attempting to understand "global governance." As the range of governance activities at the transnational level continues to increase there is a need for a framework to interpret those activities and link them to a more generic understanding of governing. International relations theory is largely inadequate for this undertaking, although regime theory does provide some capacity for understanding how particular policy areas are governed. The governance framework, on the other hand, does give substantial leverage for understanding how, at the international level, these relatively unstructured relationships that lack many formal enforcement instruments are capable of steering in the international system.

The logic of governance models can therefore be applied to a range of settings and levels of government. Further, the development of models of multi-level governance is an attempt to link those various levels and to provide ways of understanding intergovernmental politics. The multi-level governance literature does not seem entirely novel to scholars accustomed to the study of federal political systems, but it does help to emphasize the extent to which even formally unitary systems have some of the same patterns of interaction among levels as do formally federal states.

Linking a variety of fields

A second contribution that governance theory can perform in political science is integrating a number of issues and fields within comparative politics to attempt to create a more coherent whole in this sub-discipline. To some extent the variety of dimensions within political science are all concerned with governing, whether they are focusing attention on a single area of the world, a single institution or process, or a particular theoretical approach. Governance can help to bring these together into a more coherent whole.

One of the most important areas of integration is bringing comparative political economy and comparative public policy more closely in touch with scholars who work in political institutions (see Pontussen 1995). Although often interpreted rather differently, these areas are concerned with the activities of the public sector, and the interaction of the political and economic systems. By broadening the range of actors involved in these approaches and by examining a broader range of consequences of public sector action, the governance approach can enrich these sub-disciplines. At the same time, the greater analytic rigor of these approaches can also enrich the study of governance.

American politics is perhaps the odd one out so far. The dominance of rational choice, and to a lesser extent now more behavioral approaches, in American political science has tended to leave little room for interest in governance, especially among the very large community of people who work on American politics per se. That lack of concern with governance may be contrasted with the "governance turn" in studies of the Europe Union (EU) and the desire to understand more fully how the EU is capable of steering this complex political system (Koehler-Koch and Rittberger 2006; Trondal 2007).

The potential integrative function of governance can actually extend beyond the field of comparative politics. There has been something of a "governance turn" in some aspects of international relations: for example, the increased emphasis on "global governance" in international relations (Brodansky 1999) has brought many of the same issues dealt with at the national level into the international arena. Likewise, regime theory in international relations (Wettestad 2001) tends to be asking governance questions, even if the questions are not phrased explicitly as such.

In addition to the increased involvement of international relations with issues of governance, there has been some increased concern in legal research with governing and governance, rather than just with questions of "black letter law." This involvement of legal studies with governance is reflected in part in the need to bring "soft law" (Mörth 2004) into legal studies and also in concerns with reflexive law, or "new law" (Karkkainen 2004). Perhaps especially in continental systems with a strong legalistic foundation for government, the need to integrate law and governance is crucial for its wider applicability.

The contributions of a range of other disciplines to governance could also be discussed here (see Peters et al. 2011, ch. 2) could also be discussed here. Economics has been concerned with some aspects of economic governance, especially corporate governance. Sociology as a discipline has also been concerned with the consequences of governance for society. Development studies has a definite need to consider governance and the means of creating more effective patterns of governance in transitional societies. Thus, the concept of governance has a range of applicability that goes well beyond political science.

Integrating other approaches

As well as integrating a range of fields within comparative politics, governance has the potential to integrate, or at least to utilize, other approaches to political science and to some extent aspects the other social sciences (Van Keersbergen and Van Waarden 2004). I have made the argument above that governance asks very fundamental questions about what the public sector does, and how it does it. That orientation in turn raises important question about how the process of governance functions, who is involved, and what the consequences of different patterns of action are for society.

Governance is perhaps more useful in identifying problems and issues than it is in supplying definitive explanations for those issues. Therefore, governance requires the involvement of a range of other explanations for some aspects of decision-making if we are to understand the internal dynamics of the processes. That said, the same is true for almost any approach in political science, especially one that focuses on structural elements. Further, any approach that claims to explain everything may in fact explain nothing because the purported explanation may not be falsifiable (see Frohlich and Oppenheimer 2006).

Linking normative and empirical questions

Finally, the governance approach to some extent integrates empirical and normative questions into political science. The notion of governance to some extent has a normative content itself, given that a fundamental assumption is that governance is important for the quality of life of citizens, and also for the success of states in their national and international roles. Achieving the United Nations' Millennium goals, for example, may be dependent in large part on the capacity of governments to govern effectively and to provide the range of public services required to produce these services. The actual provision may be conducted in conjunction with non-state actors such as networks, but states will be crucial in organizing the provision of those services.

The normative element of governance becomes most apparent when the term "good governance" is used, as it is increasingly in both academic and practitioner discourse. Perhaps most notably the World Bank has placed a great deal of emphasis on "good governance" as part of its program for development in its donee countries. The World Bank has a rather clear conception of what constitutes "good governance," largely focused on the control of corruption. The assumption is that if government is capable of performing its tasks without significant levels of corruption then it is likely to be able to perform those tasks more efficiently and also it will create trust within the population (see Wagenaar and von Maravich 2010).

While that is a viable and important conception of good governance, it is not the only one and it may be far from the most general conception available. One can also conceptualize good governance as the existence of a state, operating alone or along with its partners, that provides a wide range of services to the public (see Bay 1967). The logic is that the state should use its capacity to tax, spend, and regulate in order to improve the lives of citizens, a version of governance that clearly describes the welfare states of Europe. This conception may indeed be valuable for understanding governance in the advanced industrial democracies, and to some extent also in other areas of the world that have various forms of the Welfare State—especially Latin America.

We must also note that these conceptions of good governance are potentially contradictory, so that emphasizing one may make another more difficult to attain. This is most apparent in the contrast between transparency and effective government. Although public decisions should at some time be made public, the process of building the coalitions and reaching agreement may be best done behind closed doors (see Peters et al. 2011: ch. x; Breton, 2007). For example, some of the success of consociational governance in the Netherlands has been due to decisions being made in secret, enabling leaders to take unpopular positions and reach difficult compromises. Even in network governance the representatives of social groups involved in making decisions will find it difficult to accept positions opposite to those favored by most of their members, if the process is extremely open to the public.

Like most normative questions in political science, there is no definitive answer to what constitutes good governance. The answer to that question depends substantially upon the perspective of the individual who is answering the question. I argue here that, although other perspectives have some validity, for the purposes of political science as a discipline, and to a great extent also from the perspective of citizens, a conception of good governance that depends upon the capacity to achieve stated policy goals is the most appropriate. If that definition can be fulfilled then the targets expressed in other approaches, especially those of the active state, can be achieved more readily.

Remaining questions about governance

I have been making a positive case about governance as a political theory, but there are still a number of significant questions about the utility of the approach as a general approach to politics. The discipline continues to search, perhaps misguidedly, for a paradigm, and governance can be presented as one alternative.[6] As already argued, unlike many contemporary approaches to politics governance begins with structures and processes rather than the individuals within them. Further, governance focuses attention on general patterns of attempted steering in societies but there may still be more specific question about that steering and the capacity of the processes being studied to shape outcomes in the economy and society.

Links among levels of governance action

The first question that must be raised about governance is the linkage between the macro level as contained in most governance studies and micro-level behavior. This question arises within institutional theory (see Peters 2003) and indeed in almost any approach to social life that concentrates on structural explanations. This question is in many ways just another way of addressing the familiar structure versus agency dichotomy that is central to many discussions of social theory (Hay 1996). In the case of governance theory the question is more specifically about whether we can explain the behavior of organizations and networks of organizations through individual behavior.

To some extent this question in relation to governance implies identifying the micro-foundations of governance decisions (see Mayntz 2004). And this question implies also that there are multiple micro-foundations, given the multiple ways in which governance has been defined and used in political science. Given the conventional wisdom in contemporary political science the dominant micro-foundation would be rational choice, guided by the assumption that individuals would make governance decisions that would maximize their own self-interest. As in rational choice versions of institutionalism (see Peters 2005), the structures associated with governance constitute an ecology within which individuals may pursue their own self-interest.

Again, the variations in governance theory provide both a challenge and an opportunity for understanding the micro-foundations of governance. One the one hand, more state-centric approaches to governance involve power, and especially authority as the fundamental resources utilized to gain compliance by the actors involved. On the other hand, the more interactive approaches to governance (see Peters et al. 2011) imply resource exchange among the actors involved (Rhodes, 1992) and the importance of trust and social capital in governing (Rothstein and Toerell 2008).

Perhaps most fundamentally, versions of governance theory tend to raise questions about structure and agency in governing. The state-centric approach tends to rely heavily on structural explanations, with the institutions of the state being responsible for governing and their characteristics being crucial for defining outcomes (see Hooghe and Marks 2003; Duit and Galaz 2008). To some extent even the network models tend to rely heavily on structural explanations, assuming that the nature of the networks also can determine the patterns of interactions (Klijn and Koppenjan 2004).

These largely structural definitions do tend to provide relatively little place for agency in processes of governance. Although the structures are important for shaping decisions and for channeling the activity of individuals and political groups, it is important to remember that the actual decisions made are made by individuals, whether as single actors or through interactions. The integration of various other approaches to political science mentioned above is a means of bringing agency into governance. While that contributes to the explanatory process it does to some extent require moving outside the approach per se in order to have a complete explanation of the phenomenon being investigated. The virtue of involving these multiple approaches may, however, be the capacity to bring together several otherwise competitive approaches to provide a more integrated conception of behavior in governing.

Developing governance theory therefore requires developing means of bringing together individual level behavior with structures and institutions. This problem is also relevant for institutionalism and to some extent any structural approach to politics and government. Unlike many approaches to institutionalism, however, governance approaches do not have any explicit mechanisms for integrating individuals and structures (see Peters 2005). That said, some approaches to political science closely allied with governance, notably public administration, do have strong elements of individual behavioral explanations that can to some extent be carried over into governance.

Measuring governance

A second important question about the utility of governance as a general approach to political science is the ability to provide adequate measures of the phenomenon. Contemporary social science is based on adequate measurement as well as adequate conceptualizatiom, and therefore to advance the case of governance as a general approach to political science requires developing some valid and reliable measures of the concept. Further, these measures need to "travel" (Sartori 1971) well and be viable in a range of circumstances if this concept is to be usable in comparative research.

In political science it appears that the phenomena that are most important for the actual performance of political systems are the most difficult to measure, and vice versa. While voting behavior is interesting and can entertain citizens on election night television its connection to the actual choices made by governments is increasingly remote (see Rose 1974). There are so many steps occurring between elections and policy decisions that elections can hardly be said to shape those policies. That said, however, voting data is readily available and exists at the interval level of measurement so that it can be used readily in all the standard statistical methods. Governance, on the other hand, has few obvious measures, and even fewer, if any, that are at the interval level (see Besancon 2006).

Measuring governance will require investing a great deal of effort and also will require consideration of just what level of measurement may be required to advance the study of this crucial phenomenon. The danger is that many people in the discipline will assume that only if governance can be measured in the same ways as some other familiar political phenomena, and only if the same statistical modeling can be applied to these data, can the approach be considered adequate. This assumption of the dominance of quantitative methodologies (see Seawright 2010) may well be misplaced, and methods such as process-tracing (Bennett and George 2005) may tell us as much or more about how government decisions are made.

Creating good governance

Finally, the normative question of how to ensure good governance remains a central concern in considering governance (see Rothstein, Chapter 10, this volume). As noted, this term is subject to multiple definitions. The minimalist definition already mentioned is that good governance is the capacity to get things done and to have services delivered. In addition, we would want to add that good governance is democratic, or at least open. This remains important for understanding the impact of governance on society. Governance has a pronounced normative element, as well as the empirical element, which must be considered when analyzing governance decisions. Several of the strands of thinking in governance that have attempted to augment or supplant traditional representative democracy have used enhanced democratization as one of the justifications for that change.

In whatever version good governance may be considered, the normative dimension must still be a part of the consideration. This is true for any important issue in political theory and is certainly true for governance. A fundamental issue for any society is how it can govern itself effectively, and in an open manner. It is perhaps especially important to examine carefully assumptions that the quality and democracy of governance can be enhanced by reducing the role of the state in governing. Such an approach may have a rather narrow conception of the public at its heart and therefore democratic governance may be sacrificed in the name of democracy.

Notes

1. Those actors may be economic actors, as when multinational firms control large swathes of territory and are able to impose their own will on the indigenous populations. This style of governing not only existed historically, e.g. the role of the British East India Company in governing India, but it is now present in some enclaves of African and Asian countries. The actors involved in these processes may also be social actors, for example in patrimonial regimes.
2. Not always, of course, do these rules guarantee decisions. In some cases the rules, e.g. requirements for special majorities, are in place to prevent decisions unless there is an overwhelming sentiment in favor of that decision.
3. There were also other functions such as interest articulation and interest aggregation that occurred more on the input side of the political system rather than within government itself.
4. Although often ignored in discussions of governance, the legal processes within the public sector may be important for performing some of these important tasks. This is especially the case as governing becomes increasingly judicialized in many areas of the world, including countries such as the United Kingdom that have long been opposed to the courts adopting a governing role.
5. In fairness, relatively few scholars had adopted such as simple idea, especially given the important of corporatism as a political theory; nevertheless, questioning the role of the state has been useful.
6. Governance may be a candidate for some parts of the world, but appears not be a viable alternative in the United States because of the dominance of rational choice and a relatively weak tradition of concern with the "state." Likewise, the reality of governance models involving social actors in a central role seems to be less viable in many other areas of the world (see Kjaer forthcoming).

References

Bay, C. 1967. *The Structure of Freedom*. Stanford, CA: Stanford University Press.
Bennett, C. and George, A. 2005. *Case Studies and Theory Development in the Social Sciences* Cambridge, MA: MIT Press.
Besancon, M. 2006. *Good Governance Rankings: The Art of Measurement* Boston: World Peace Foundation.

Breton, A. 2007. *The Economics of Transparency in Politics*. Aldershot: Ashgate.

Brodansky, D. 1999. The legitimacy of international governance: A coming challenge for international environmental law. *American Journal of International Law* 93: 596–624.

Duit, A. and Galaz, V. 2008. Governance and complexity: Emerging issues for governance theory. *Governance* 21: 311–335.

Frohlich, N. and Oppenheimer, J. 2006. Skating on thin ice: Cracks in the public choice foundation. *Journal of Theoretical Politics* 18: 235–266.

Hardin, G. 1977. *Managing the Commons*. San Francisco: W. W. Freeman.

Hay, C. 1996. Structure and agency. In *Theory and Methods in Political Science*, ed. D. Marsh and G. Stoker. Basingstoke: Macmillan, 83–103.

Helmke, G. and Levitsky, S. 2004. Informal institutions and comparative politics. *Perspectives on Politics* 2: 725–740.

Hooghe, L. and Marks, G. 2003. Unraveling the central state, but how?: Types of multi-level governance. *American Political Science Review* 97: 233–243.

Karkkainen, B. C. 2004. New governance in legal thought and the world. *Minnesota Law Review* 89: 471–504.

Kjaer, A. M. (forthcoming). *Politics and Society*.

Klijn, E.-H. and Koppennjan, J. 2004. *Managing Uncertainties in Networks: A Network Approach to Problem Solving*. London: Routledge.

Koehler-Koch, B. and Rittberger, B. 2006. The governance turn in EU studies. *Journal of Common Market Studies* 44: 27–49.

Lam, W. F. 1998 *Governing Irrigation Systems in Nepal: Institutions, Infrastructure and Collective Action*. San Francisco: ICS Press.

Lane, H. 1994. Structural functionalism reconsidered: A proposed research agenda. *Comparative Politics* 26: 461–477.

Mayntz, R. 2004. Mechanisms in the analysis if social macro-phenomena. *Philosophy of Social Sciences* 34: 237–254.

Mörth, U. 2004. *Soft Law in the European Union*. Cheltenham: Edward Elgar.

Niemann, M. 2007. War making and state making in Central Africa. *Africa Today* 53: 21–39.

Ostrom, E. 1990. *Governing the Commons: The Evolution on Institutions of Collective Action*. Cambridge: Cambridge University Press.

Ostrom, E. 2005. *Understanding Institutional Diversity*. Princeton, NJ: Princeton University Press.

Peters, B. G. 2003. *The Future of Governing: Four Emerging Models*, 2nd ed. Lawrence: University Press of Kansas.

Peters, B. G. 2005. *Institutional Theory in Political Science: The New Institutionalism*, 2nd ed. London: Continuum.

Peters, B. G., Pierre, J., Sørenson, E., and Torfing, J. 2011. *Interactive Governance: Advancing the Paradigm*. Oxford: Oxford University Press.

Pontussen, J. 1995. From comparative public policy to political economy: putting political institutions in their place and taking institutions seriously. *Comparative Political Studies* 28: 117–147.

Rhodes, R. A. W. 1992. *Beyond Westminster and Whitehall: The Sub-central Governments of Britain*. London: Routledge.

Risse, T. and Lehmkuhl, U. 2010. *Governance in Areas of Limited Statehood*. New York: Basic Books.

Rose, R. 1974. *The Problem of Party Government*. London: Macmillan.

Rothstein, B. and Toerell, J. 2008. What is the quality of governance: A theory of impartial government institutions. *Governance* 21: 165–190.

Sartori, G. 1971. Concept misformation in comparative politics. *American Political Science Review* 64: 1033–1053.

Sartori, G. 1997. *Comparative Constitutional Engineering: An Inquiry into Structures, Incentives and Outcomes*. New York: New York University Press.

Scharpf, F. W. 1988. The joint decision trap: Lessons from German federalism and European integration. *Public Administration* 66: 239–278.

Scharpf, F. W. 1997. *Games Real Actors Play: Actor-Centred Institutionalism in Policy Research*. Boulder, CO: Westview.

Seawright, J. 2010. Regression-based inference: A case study of failed causal assessment. In *Rethinking Social Inquiry*, ed. H. E. Brady and D. Collier. Lanham, MD: Rowman and Littlefield, 123–135.

Smith, B. C. 2003. *Understanding Third World Politics: Theories of Political Change and Development*. Bloomington: Indiana University Press.

Trondal, J. 2007. The public administration turn in integration research. *Journal of European Public Policy* 14: 960–972.

Van Keersbergen, K and Van Waarden, F. 2004. Governance as a bridge between disciplines: Cross-disciplinary inspiration regarding shifts in governance and problems of governability, accountability and legitimacy. *European Journal of Political Research* 43: 143–171.

Wagenaar, H. and Von Maravich, P. 2010. *The Good Cause*. Leverkeusen: Barbara Budrich Verlag.

Wettestad, J. 2001. Designing effective environmental regimes: The conditional keys, *Global Governance* 7: 317–341.

CHAPTER 3

WAVES OF GOVERNANCE

R. A. W. RHODES

GOVERNANCE signifies a change in the meaning of government, referring to *new* processes of governing; or *changed* conditions of ordered rule; or *new* methods by which society is governed (adapted from Finer 1970: 3–4). Of course, nothing in the social sciences is ever that simple. Kjær (2004) provides a useful conspectus. She distinguishes between governance in public administration and public policy, governance in international relations, European Union governance, governance in comparative politics, and good governance as extolled by the World Bank (see also Pierre 2000). So, like Humpty-Dumpty, I have to assert that "when I use a word it means what I choose it to mean—neither more nor less" (Carroll 1965: 269) and wearing my public administration and public policy spectacles, I use governance to refer to the changing boundaries between public, private, and voluntary sectors, and to the changing role of the state. I use the term to explore how the informal authority of networks supplements and supplants the formal authority of government, and to explore the limits to the state and seek to develop a more diverse view of state authority and its exercise. I explore the paradox of strong states confounded by implementation gaps and unintended consequences.

This chapter focuses on the claim there has been a change in the pattern and exercise of state authority from government to governance—from a hierarchic or bureaucratic state to governance in and by networks. I identify three waves in the governance literature: network governance, metagovernance, and interpretive governance. I summarize and illustrate each wave with a brief example drawn from British government. The core theme throughout is the need to put the people back into governance by focusing on the ways in which governance is constructed differently by many actors working against the background of diverse traditions. I conclude that network governance and metagovernance face an intellectual crisis and that there is a growing need for "alternative ways of conceptualizing the institutions, actors and processes of change in government" (Marinetto 2003: 605). I argue that interpretive governance is that new way. [1]

THE FIRST WAVE OF GOVERNANCE:
NETWORK GOVERNANCE

The literature on network governance studies the institutional legacy of neoliberal reforms of the state. Network governance is associated with the changing nature of the state following the public sector reforms of the 1980s. The reforms are said to have precipitated a shift from a hierarchic bureaucracy toward a greater use of markets, quasi-markets, and networks, especially in the delivery of public services. The effects of the reforms were intensified by global changes, including an increase in transnational economic activity and the rise of regional institutions such as the European Union. The resulting complexity and fragmentation are such that the state increasingly depends on other organizations to secure its intentions and deliver its policies. Network governance evokes a world in which state power is dispersed among a vast array of spatially and functionally distinct networks composed of all kinds of public, voluntary, and private organizations with which the center now interacts. Social scientists typically appeal to inexorable, impersonal forces, to logics of modernization, such as the functional differentiation of the modern state or public sector marketization, to explain the shift from hierarchy to governance by markets and especially networks. They offer a modernist-empiricist account of network governance.[2]

The network governance literature has been reviewed and classified so many times before that I offer only the briefest recap. There are several strands.[3] I discuss the "Anglo-governance school" in the United Kingdom below as my main example of network governance. In addition, there is the work of Renate Mayntz, Fritz Schapf, and their colleagues at the Max Planck Institute on *steuerungtheorie*. They were among the first to treat networks, not as interest group intermediation, but as a mode of governance.[4] Others focused on more effective ways of steering networks; for example, Erik-Hans Klijn and Joop Koppenjan pioneered network management.[5] Such ideas caught on rapidly and mutated to embrace working in partnerships and collaborative management.[6] Attention turned from describing the growth of networks to the normative implications of that growth and the question of how to find ways of participating in networks that preserve legitimacy and accountability. The search was on for new forms of democratic governance.[7] Finally, America caught up with Europe and brought its characteristic modernist-empiricist skill set to bear on networks and governance. If European scholars favored case studies, their American colleagues combined "large N" studies of networks with a tool view that sought to make the study of networks relevant to public managers. Frederickson (1999) proclaimed that network and governance theory "repositions" public administration at the forefront of political science in facing the challenges of the fragmenting disarticulated state.[8]

In brief, network governance has four faces. First, it provides a modernist-empiricist description of public sector change whether it is the increased fragmentation caused by the reforms of the 1980s or the search for better coordination of the 1990s. Second, it offers an interpretation or explanation of government change. It argues that hierarchic models of responsible government are no longer accurate. It tells a different story of the shift from hierarchic government to governance through networks. It explains the shift as a consequence of functional differentiation and modernization. Third, it offers policy advice to public managers on how best to steer networks and work collaboratively. Finally, it offers prescriptions on democratic governance, on how networks and governance could increase participation. For many, this network governance literature is becoming "the new orthodoxy" (Marsh 2008: 738).

Network governance: an example[9]

In Britain, the first wave of governance narratives is referred to as the "Anglo-governance school" (Marinetto 2003). Challenging the conventional wisdom of the hierarchic Westminster model, it starts with the notion of policy networks or sets of organizations clustered around a major government function or department. These groups commonly include the professions, trade unions, and big business. So, central departments need the cooperation of such groups to deliver services. They need their cooperation because British government rarely delivers services itself; it uses other bodies to do so. Also, there are too many groups to consult, so government must aggregate interests; it needs the legitimated spokespeople for that policy area. The groups in turn need the money and legislative authority that only government can provide. So, for many policy areas, actors are interdependent and decisions are a product of their game-like interactions, rooted in trust and regulated by rules of the game negotiated and agreed by the participants. Such networks have significant degree of autonomy from the state—they are self-organizing—although the state can indirectly and imperfectly steer them (Rhodes 1997a: 53). In sum, for the Anglo-governance school, governance refers to governing with and through networks.

Policy networks are a long-standing feature of British government; they are its silos or velvet drainpipes. They form a private government of public services, scathingly referred to by the New Right as producer groups capturing government in their own interests. The Conservative government of Margaret Thatcher sought to reduce their power by using markets to deliver public services, bypassing existing networks and curtailing the "privileges" of professions, commonly by subjecting them to rigorous financial and management controls. But these corporate management and marketization reforms had unintended consequences. They fragmented the systems for delivering public services, creating pressures for organizations to cooperate with one another to deliver services. In other words, marketization multiplied the networks it aimed to replace. Commonly, packages of organizations now deliver welfare state services.

The Anglo-governance school conceives of networks as a distinctive coordinating mechanism notably different from markets and hierarchies and not a hybrid of them. They associate networks with characteristics such as interdependence and trust. In their view, trust is essential because it is the basis of network coordination in the same way that commands and price competition are the key mechanisms for bureaucracies and markets respectively (see also Frances et al. 1991: 15). Shared values and norms are the glue that holds the complex set of relationships in a network together. Trust and reciprocity are essential for cooperative behavior and, therefore, the existence of the network (see for example Kramer and Tyler 1996). With the spread of networks there has been a recurrent tension between contracts, on the one hand, with their stress on competition to get the best price and networks on the other, with their stress on cooperative behavior.

According to the Anglo-governance school, the core executive's capacity to steer is reduced or hollowed out from above by international interdependencies such as membership of the EU, from below by marketization and networks, and sideways by agencies. Internally, the British core executive was already characterized by baronies, policy networks, and intermittent and selective coordination. It has been further hollowed out internally by the unintended consequences of marketization, which fragmented service delivery, multiplied networks, and diversified the membership of those networks. Multiplying networks mean that core executive coordination is modest in practice. It is largely negative, based on persistent compartmentalization, mutual avoidance, and friction reduction between powerful bureau and ministries. In this view, coordination is rarely strategic. Almost all attempts to create proactive strategic capacity for long-term planning have failed (Wright and Hayward 2000). The Anglo-governance school explains New Labour's reforms as an attempt to promote coordination and strategic oversight to combat both Whitehall's departmentalism and the unintended consequences of managerialism.

In sum, the Anglo-governance school tells us a story of fragmentation confounding centralization and coordination as a segmented executive seeks to improve horizontal coordination among departments and agencies and vertical coordination between departments and their networks of organizations. The government was hollowed out, swapping direct for indirect controls. Central departments were no longer either necessarily or invariably the fulcrum of a network although the government can still set the limits to network actions: after all, it still funds the services.

THE SECOND-WAVE: META-GOVERNANCE

Critics of the first wave characteristically focus on the argument the state has been hollowed out. For example, Pierre and Peters (2000, 78, 104–105 and 111) argue the shift to network governance could "increase public control over society" because governments "rethink the mix of policy instruments." As a result, "coercive or regulatory instruments become less important and . . . 'softer' instruments gain importance". In short, the state has not been hollowed out but reasserted its capacity to govern by regulating the mix of governing structures such as markets and networks and deploying indirect instruments of control.[10]

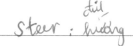

Metagovernance refers to the role of the state in securing coordination in governance and its use of negotiation, diplomacy, and more informal modes of steering. As with network governance, metagovernance comes in several varieties (Sørensen and Torfing 2007: 170–180). They share a concern, however, with the varied ways in which the state now *steers* organizations, governments and networks rather than directly providing services through state bureaucracies, or *rowing*. These other organizations undertake much of the work of governing; they implement policies, they provide public services, and at times they even regulate themselves. The state governs the organizations that govern civil society; "the governance of government and governance" (Jessop 2000: 23). Moreover, the other organizations characteristically have a degree of autonomy from the state; they are often voluntary or private sector groups or they are governmental agencies or tiers of government separate from the core executive. So, the state cannot govern them solely by the instruments that work in bureaucracies.[11]

Nonetheless, there are several ways in which the state can steer the other actors involved in governance (see for example Jessop 2000: 23–24, and 2003). First, the state can set *the rules of the game* for other actors and then leave them to do what they will within those rules; they work "in the shadow of hierarchy." So, it can redesign markets, reregulate policy sectors, or introduce constitutional change, Second, the state can try to steer other actors using *storytelling*. It can organize dialogues, foster meanings, beliefs, and identities among the relevant actors, and influence what actors think and do. Third, the state can steer by the way in which it distributes *resources* such as money and authority. It can play a boundary-spanning role, alter the balance between actors in a network; act as a court of appeal when conflict arises; rebalance the mix of governing structures; and step in when network governance fails. Of course, the state need not adopt a single uniform approach to metagovernance. It can use different approaches in different settings at different times.

Metagovernance—an example

Metagovernance is an apt description of the changing roles of the British central agencies, namely, Treasury, the Prime Minister's Number 10 units, and the Cabinet Office. Between 1997 and 2007, when New Labour was in power and Tony Blair was prime minister, all these agencies sought to increase their capacity for metagovernance over the rest of Whitehall. They did so in three ways. First, the Blair government introduced "joined-up" government (see Cabinet Office 2000; Ling 2002). It sought policy instruments that integrated both horizontally across central government departments and vertically between central and local government and the voluntary sector. Second, the Treasury used the financial levers of public service agreements (PSAs) to spread its tentacles into the departments as never before. These PSAs set targets for key areas in the departments and future funding hinged on meeting the targets. As former Cabinet Secretary Andrew Turnbull (2007) explained, the result was that the Treasury became a policy department. Finally, as Fawcett (2009: ch. 4) argues, the reforms at Number 10 "increased the Prime Minister's capacity to achieve effective metagovernance over the rest of Whitehall." For example, Number 10's Delivery Unit organized "stock takes" at which Ministers reported to the prime minister on the progress made in achieving agreed targets. Fawcett also quotes a senior Number 10 official arguing you have to "strategically manage the landscape" by "rethinking how government can keep control of those things they need to control." Officials forswear line management and speak the language of metagovernance; they strategically manage the landscape with indirect controls.

That is not to say such steering was successful. Civil servants are aware there are limits to such hands-off strategies. One permanent secretary observed that the shift to hands-off controls needed a major cultural change and he opined that no one had attempted cultural change on this scale before. His remarks were not streaked with much optimism. Another official commented, "the relatively subtle changes which have taken place in the reform agenda between 1999 and now don't seem worthy of close analysis from our end of the telescope" (Bovaird and Russell 2007: 319). Or, more bluntly: "they see another piece of paper from the centre and say stuff that." (Rhodes 2011: ch. 8).

Common ground

For all the different emphases, the first two waves of governance share common features. First, proponents of metagovernance take for granted the characteristics of network governance. They agree networks are characterized by trust and diplomacy. They accept that states are becoming increasingly fragmented into networks based on several different stakeholders; and the dividing line between the state and civil society is becoming more blurred because the relevant stakeholders are private or voluntary sector organizations. So, Jessop (2000: 24) concedes "the state is no longer the sovereign authority... [it is] less hierarchical, less centralized, less *dirigiste*." There is a shared modernist-empiricist description of the characteristics of network governance (see also Sørensen and Torfing 2007).

Second, the analysis of metagovernance not only recognizes non-state actors by granting them the power to self-regulate but also distinguishes them from the state, so creating the space for the state to exert macro-control over their self-regulation. The state governs the other actors involved in governance. In other words, metagovernance heralds the return of the state by reinventing its governing role; it is "bringing the state back in (yet again)" (Jessop 2007: 54). This return to the state opens opportunities for policy advice on the practice of metagovernance. The two waves share a common concern with providing advice on network governance. Both assume the role of the state is to manage, directly and indirectly, the networks of service delivery. For example, Part III of Sørensen and Torfing (2007: chs. 10–12) on "metagovernance" is devoted to such topics as governing the performance of networks, institutional design and network management, and the possibilities for public authorities to shape network outputs. They are not alone. Although it is not "rocket science," nonetheless the literature on network steering has proliferated over the past decade. This work treats government departments, local authorities, markets and networks as fixed structures that governments can manipulate using the right tools. It seeks to improve the ability of the state to manage the mix of hierarchies, markets and networks and of state managers to steer these structures.

Third, both narratives rely on a reified notion of structure. The proponents of first-wave governance are self-confessed modernist-empiricists with a reified notion of structure rooted in an explicit social science theory of functional differentiation. The proponents of metagovernance also continue to claim the state is a material object, a structure, or a social form. They draw on critical realist epistemology and such notions as "emergence" and "mechanisms" ostensibly to guard against the charge of reification (see for example Jessop 2007). For example, McAnulla (2006) argues that structures are emergent or temporal mechanisms rather than reifications, but never explains how these structures differ from practices, or how they determine individual actions without passing through intentional consciousness. He provides no clear account of why agents can't change emergent structures. The structure emerges from actions, so presumably if all the relevant people change their actions, they will stop producing that structure, so changing it. The emergent structures are better understood as practices (Bevir and Rhodes 2010). They consist simply of what a bundle of people do and the unintended consequences of these actions. Of course, structure can be used as a metaphor for the way in which practices coalesces into patterns. But the metaphors have a bewitching effect and people treat them as real, reified entities. In short, critical realism and the analysis of metagovernance all too often rely on the reifications of modernist-empiricism and first-wave governance.

THE THIRD WAVE: INTERPRETING
THE CHANGING STATE

An interpretive account of governance represents a shift of topos from institutions to *meanings* in action. It explains shifting patterns of governance by focusing on the actors' own interpretations of their *beliefs and practices*. The everyday practices arise from agents whose beliefs and actions are informed by *traditions* and expressed in stories. It explores the diverse ways in which situated agents are changing the boundaries of state and civil society by constantly remaking practices as their beliefs change in response to *dilemmas*. It reveals the *contingency* and contestability of narratives. It highlights a more diverse view of state authority and its exercise.[12]

An account of the changing state explores the institutions of the state as the contingent meanings that inform the actions of the individuals involved in all kinds of practices of rule. First-wave narratives of the changing state focus on issues such as the objective characteristics of policy networks and the oligopoly of the political market place. They stress power-dependence, the relationship between networks and policy outcomes, and the strategies by which the centre might steer networks. The second wave of narratives focuses on the mix of governing structures such as markets and networks and on the various instruments of control such as changing the rules of the game, story-telling, and changing the distribution of resources. In contrast, an interpretive approach focuses on the social construction of patterns of rule through the ability of individuals to create meanings in action. An interpretive approach highlights the importance of beliefs, practices, traditions, and dilemmas for the study of the changing state.[13]

Any existing pattern of rule will have some failings. Different people will have different views about these failings since the failings are not simply given by experience but rather constructed from interpretations of experience infused with traditions. When people's perceptions of the failings of governance conflict with their existing beliefs, the resulting dilemmas lead them to reconsider beliefs and traditions. Because people confront these dilemmas against the background of diverse traditions, there arises a political contest over what constitutes the nature of the failings and what should be done about them. This contest leads to a reform of governance. The reformed pattern of rule poses new dilemmas, leading to a further contest over meanings and policy agendas. All these contests are governed by laws and norms that prescribe how they should be conducted. Sometimes the relevant laws and norms have changed because of simultaneous contests over their content and relevance. Yet while we can distinguish analytically between a pattern of rule and a contest over its reform, we rarely can do so temporally. Rather, the activity of governing continues during most contests, and most contests occur partially in local practices of governing. What we have, therefore, is a complex and continuous process of interpretation, conflict, and activity that produces ever-changing patterns of rule.

This interpretive approach prompts us to adopt narrative explanations. We cannot explain network and metagovernance adequately by using allegedly objective social processes or locations. Rather, we explain governance by using narratives that relate actions to the beliefs and desires that produce them. Explanation depends on the conditional connections between beliefs, desires, and actions. Narratives point to conditional connections between people, ideas, and events to explain actions and practices. So, to explain the different and changing patterns of rule, we need to understand the beliefs and practices of the actors against the background of particular traditions and in response to specific dilemmas. In short, we have to adopt an actor-centered or bottom-up approach to explaining any pattern of rule.

Interpretive governance: an example

What does this interpretive approach tell us about governance? Bevir and Rhodes (2010) discuss some of the distinctive research topics that spring from an interpretive approach under the heading of the "3Rs" of rule, rationalities, and resistance. Interpretive theory suggests that under *rule*, political scientists should ask whether different sections of the elite draw on different traditions to construct different narratives about the world, their place within it, and their interests and values. An interpretive approach draws attention to the varied *rationalities* that inform policies across different policy arenas. Britain, like much of the developed world, has witnessed the rise of neoliberal managerial rationalities and the technology of performance measurement and targets. I give a brief, interpretive account of such managerial rationalities in the British civil service below.[14] Finally, politics and policies do not arise exclusively from the strategies and interactions of elites. Other actors can *resist*, transform, and thwart the agendas of elites. An interpretive approach draws attention to the diverse traditions and narratives that inform actors at lower levels of the hierarchy, and citizens. For example, we know the role of street-level bureaucrats in delivering services is crucial; in effect, they use local knowledge and local reasoning to decide what policy will be for clients (see; Maynard-Moody and Musheno 2003).

The best way of showing what is distinctive about interpretive research is to give an example. Lack of space makes a detailed case study or "thick description" impractical (see Rhodes 2011). However, I can give a flavor of the approach with a short illustration of the ways in which neoliberal managerial rationalities were understood and embedded in a British government department.

I attended a two-day event that set out to build commitment to the department's business plan and to "drill" (sometimes "drive") reform down the hierarchy. It was targeted at the fifty heads of the management units (HMUs). The event was divided between presentations by senior management followed by small group discussions and report backs. For senior management one of the objectives was to "celebrate" the "realistic overall story" of the department's business plan. I attended the general sessions and moved among the groups with other members of the department who attended as "roving reporters." Here I have one simple aim; to show that managerialism is as widely spoken as it is contested.

Top management took the event seriously. It was not a jamboree. Senior management had several planning meetings before the event and a lengthy debriefing session afterwards. It was seen as integral to change management in the department. There was also a coherent message and it centered on three key words, performance, delivery, and leadership. The documentation was built around this message. Every participant was given a conference notebook, or "journal," and a ring binder with all the PowerPoint slides and handouts. Much care and attention had been given to their design. The journal also contained the outline timetable and, for each group breakout session, it had the questions to be addressed with space for individual and group answers. So, participants were asked to record their "stories" about positive improvements in performance over the past six to nine months. Then, the group moved on to delivery. Again the groups were "tasked" to "build the story" and "add to the story." It continued in this vein for the "ownership of operational objectives"; "bringing the leadership model to life"; and managing poor performance. It is a lexicon of managerialism.

A minister of state was sent to show that the political masters supported the management reforms. He attacked "silos," stressesd delivery, leadership, evidence-based policy, and better performance measurement. So, he was on message. The permanent secretary had doubts about one of the department's director-generals (DGs), but he did not need to worry. That DG told me, "I'm uncomfortable with some of what we are doing but I'm comfortable with what I said this morning." So, all the key speakers gave perorations for change along the right lines. They did not address the issue of how to make it happen, and that was what concerned the HMUs.

If the speakers were on message, the groups were not. They challenged specific objectives. Senior managers were urbane in answering these challenges. Afterwards a DG snapped: "they are challenging set objectives, they can't do that." At the reporting session, the roving reporter commented the group "made a constructive and interesting start." The group howled with laughter. If the group had but one characteristic, it was argumentativeness. The group discussions turned to "how can I change?" The abrupt answers included, "say 'no' more often"; and "the minimum." They talked about finding "real resources" to support change. There was a querulous tone to many of the group meetings. They wanted senior management to "walk it not spout it."

Through the day, the permanent secretary became increasingly impatient with the discussions. He lectured the facilitator for the reporting sessions about getting the groups back on message. He stood at the back and paced. When he sat still, he tapped one foot on the ground continuously. His body language expressed frustration and impatience. When I talked to him he was almost vehement when he said "we have to know how to drill it down"; and "by the end of the year we have to know the story." He thought the groups were too focused on process and there was a lack of action points.

On the second day, the facilitator provided a summary of the HMUs' views, and we split into groups again. I began to spot slogans in the presentations and the discussions; "partnership, not turf war"; "the vision thing—it's so powerful." The groups were more puzzled than querulous on the second day. They asked straightforward but hard questions; "what do you want to drill down?" At the summary session, the facilitator said emotional intelligence would be a key topic for the second day. The group I attended had nothing to say on the subject. They commented, "what you are talking about does not affect me." Their problems were more prosaic. They were not convinced they were leaders and, if they were leaders, they didn't think they had been given permission to lead. They saw internal communication as the biggest problem and wanted top management to talk with the lower levels more often; "staff might value you more if you represented them." On performance measurement, they wanted specific suggestions about what they should do, starting with "clear measurable objectives."

I noted the DGs were networking with one another, not with the HMUs. They skipped group sessions to discuss performance measurement. There was a tough–tender divide over "making space" (that is, redundancies). There was a clear but unstated assumption that too many middle-level managers—that is HMUs—were no good and they needed to get rid of them. The DGs were concerned the reforms had not been drilled down anywhere near far enough. They feared they had not "engaged" with the HMUs. Some HMUs agreed—they had voted with their feet and left early. Those who stayed now confronted the question of "what am I going to do to push this forward?" Everyone faced a colleague and told him or her which two things would be left behind and which two things would be embraced. There was much hilarity but many sensible answers. So, one HMU said he would stop thinking why things can't be done. Another would support his team and say thank you.

At the debriefing session the following day, the DGs and the permanent secretary agreed some basic questions needed to be answered such as "what is the story?" and "have we got the right people?" There were some clichés about the importance of praise and the need to be ruthless about failure. Somewhat to my bemusement there was talk of "getting to grips with emotional intelligence." I think they meant they needed better communication with the HMUs. Whatever it meant, they were going to "stop pussyfooting" and make "painful decisions." Goethe was paraphrased: "boldness has a genius and madness to it." They agreed they have taken an important step forward; "we are on the road."

The event exemplified managerialism. The everyday language was what you would expect. The keywords were delivery, performance, leadership, with a touch of emotional intelligence. Even the gap between senior and middle-level management was predictable. The most relevant point is that the HMUs talked the language of managerialism in criticizing the reforms. They did not reject performance measurement. Rather, they asked for clear, relevant, operational objectives. They wanted better managerialism. Targets and appraisal were part of everyday vocabulary but the practice of measurement lagged some way behind. This view was shared by others in the departments. One management board member observed about the department's business plan: "you don't have the metrics in place to measure progress"; "detailed action plans are missing"; "get some measures and learn as you go along"; and "there is too much waffle, too much wooliness, it needs to be crisp, more precise."

A senior minister, David Blunkett (2006: 441), happily conceded civil servants "talk the language" but, to his obvious irritation, "they don't do anything." That statement is inaccurate. There are business plans and missions statement galore. The British civil service has managerialism, but not as the textbooks know it and the reformers want it. We find this out by observing people at work and listening to what they say; by recovering their beliefs and practices and telling their stories. The contradictions of managerialism are revealed by the different stories told by senior management and by HMUs.

CONCLUSIONS

In sum, network governance was the modernist-empiricist story of the changing state that described the shift from hierarchy to markets to networks. This first-wave narrative reduces the diversity of governance to a social logic of modernization, institutional norms, or a set of classifications or correlations across networks. The second wave of metagovernance reinvents the state's capacity to control. It too relies on modernist-empiricist assumptions. It argues for a top-down narrative of state regulation and control. But there is no necessary logical or structural process determining the form of network governance or the role of the "central state" in the metagovernance of governance. The intrinsic rationality of markets, the path dependency of institutions, and the state's new toolkit for managing both the mix of governing structures and networks do not explain patterns of governance and how they change.

In the third wave, the narrative about the changing state shows how governance arises from the bottom up as conflicting beliefs, competing traditions, and varied dilemmas cause diverse practices. It replaces aggregate concepts such as state, institution, power, and governance with narratives that explain actions by relating them to the beliefs and practices of individual actors. Governance arises out of the diverse actions and practices inspired by varied beliefs and traditions. It is the contingent product of diverse actions and political struggles informed by the beliefs of agents rooted in traditions.

An interpretive approach encourages telling stories about how governance is variously constructed and reconstructed. It has much in common with anthropology, which also seeks to reconstruct the meanings of social actors by recovering other people's stories from practices, actions, texts, interviews, and speeches to write "thick descriptions." I agree with Fenno (1990: 128) that "not enough political scientists are presently engaged in observation." I agree with Agar (1996: 27) that "no understanding of a world is valid without representation of those members' voices." And I agree with Geertz (1973: 9), that the challenge is to write "our own constructions of other people's constructions of what they and their compatriots are up to." In short, an interpretive approach seeks to put the people back into governance.

NOTES

1. Inevitably in an overview chapter, I revisit ground covered in earlier work. This chapter is a personal position statement drawn from Rhodes 1997a, and 2007; Bevir and Rhodes 2010; Rhodes 2011.
2. Modernist-empiricism treats institutions such as legislatures, constitutions and policy networks as discrete, atomized objects to be compared, measured and classified. It adopts comparisons across time and space as a means of uncovering regularities and probabilistic explanations to be tested against neutral evidence (see Bevir 2006).
3. For reviews of these several approaches see: Börzel 1998, 2011; Klijn 1997, 2008; Rhodes 1990, 2006. These strands are best seen as emphases or foci, not schools of thought, as there is much interweaving of ideas and methods.
4. See for example, Marin and Mayntz 1991; Mayntz 1993, 2003; Scharpf 1997.
5. There is an extensive European literature on managing networks including, for example: Kickert et al. 1997; Koppenjan and Klijn 2004; Perri et al. 2002; Rhodes 1997b; Stoker 2004.
6. On collaborative governance see: Ansell and Gash 2007; Bingham and O'Leary 2008; Huxham and Vangen 2005; Sullivan and Skelcher 2002, the special issue of *Public Administration Review* 66 (2006), and this volume, Chapter 23.

7. On democratic governance see: see: Bang and Sørensen 1999; Bevir 2007; Klijn and Skelcher 2007; Sørensen and Torfing 2005; and Part VII of this volume.

8. For a survey of American "large N" studies and more citations see Meier and O'Toole 2005. On how to manage networks see, for example: Agranoff 2007; Goldsmith and Eggers 2004; Goldsmith and Kettl 2009; O'Toole 1997.

9. The Anglo-governance school's proponents include: Rhodes 1997a, 2000; Richards and Smith 2002; Smith 1999; Stoker 2000,2004.

10. See also for example: Holliday 2000; Kjær 2004; Marsh, Richards, and Smith 2003; Taylor 1997.

11. On metagovernance see: Bell and Hindmoor 2009; Jessop 2000, 2003; Kooiman 2003; Sørensen and Torfing 2007. There are marked affinities between the ideas of metagovernance and metaregulation, or "the process of regulating regulatory regimes" (Scott 2006: 664). For a brief review of this topic see: Coglianese and Mendelson 2010.

12. On the debate about interpretive theory see Bevir and Rhodes 2003, 2006, 2010; and the symposia debating this work in *British Journal of Politics and International Relation* 6 (2004): 129–164; and *Political Studies Review* 6 (2008): 143–177. See also: McAnulla 2006; and Hay 2011.

13. See Bevir and Rhodes 2003, 2006, 2010. Although they arrive at this point by a different route, post-structuralism in the guises of governmentality and discourse analysis also stress the constructed nature of the state and governance. See, for example: Dean 2007: ch. 2; Finlayson and Martin 2006; Miller and Rose 2008: ch. 3.

14. For other examples and critical commentary see: Dean 2007; Du Gay 2000; McKinlay and Starkey 1998; Miller and Rose 2008: ch. 2.

References

Agar, M. 1996. *The Professional Stranger*. 2nd edition. San Diego, CA: Academic Press.

Agranoff, R. 2007. *Managing Within Networks: Adding Value to Public Organizations*. Washington, DC: Georgetown University Press.

Ansell, C. and Gash, A. 2007. Collaborative governance in theory and practice. *Journal of Public Administration Theory and Practice* 18: 543–571.

Bang, H. P. and Sørensen, E. 1999. The everyday maker: A new challenge to democratic governance. *Administrative Theory and Praxis* 21: 325–341.

Bell, S. and Hindmoor, A. 2009. *Rethinking Governance: The Centrality of the State in Modern Society*. Port Melbourne, Vic.: Cambridge University Press.

Bevir, M. 2006. Political studies as narrative and science, 1880–2000. *Political Studies* 54: 583–606.

Bevir, M. (ed.) 2007. *Public Governance*. 4 vols. London: Sage.

Bevir, M. and Rhodes, R. A. W. 2003. *Interpreting British Governance*. London: Routledge.

Bevir, M. and Rhodes, R. A. W. 2006. *Governance Stories*. London: Routledge.

Bevir, M. and Rhodes, R. A. W. 2010. *The State as Cultural Practice*. Oxford: Oxford University Press.

Bingham, L. B. and O'Leary, R. 2008. *Big Ideas in Collaborative Management*. New York: M. E. Sharpe.

Blunkett, D. 2006. *The Blunket Tapes: My Life in the Bear Pit*. London: Bloomsbury.

Börzel, T. J. 1998. Organizing Babylon: On the different conceptions of policy networks. *Public Administration* 76: 253–273.

Börzel, T. J. 2011. Networks: Reified metaphor or governance panacea? *Public Administration* 89: 49–63.

Bovaird, T. and Russell, K. 2007. Civil service reform in the UK, 1999–2005: Revolutionary failure of evolutionary success? *Public Administration* 85: 301–328.

Cabinet Office, 2000. *Wiring It Up.* London: Performance and Innovation Unit, Cabinet Office.

Carroll, L. 1965 *The Annotated Alice.* With an Introduction and Notes by Martin Gardner. Harmondsworth: Penguin.

Coglianese, C. and Mendelson, E. 2010. Meta-regulation and self-regulation. In R. Baldwin, M. Cave, and M. Lodge (eds.), *The Oxford Handbook of Regulation.* Oxford: Oxford University Press, 146–168.

Dean, M. 2007. *Governing Societies.* Berkshire: Open University Press.

Du G. P. 2000. *In Praise of Bureaucracy.* London: Sage.

Fawcett, P. 2009. Government, Governance and Metagovernance in the British Core Executive. PhD thesis. University of Birmingham, UK.

Fenno, R. E. 1990. *Watching Politicians: Essays on Participant Observation.* Berkeley, CA: Institute of Governmental Studies, University of California.

Finer, S. E. 1970. *Comparative Government.* London: Allen Lane, The Penguin Press.

Finlayson, A. and Martin, J. 2006. Post-structuralism. In C. Hay, M. Lister, and D. Marsh (eds.), *The State: Theory and Issues.* Basingstoke: Palgrave Macmillan, 155–171.

Frances, J., Levacic, R., Mitchell, J., and Thompson, G. J. 1991. Introduction. In G. Thompson, J. Frances, R. Levacic, and J. Mitchell (eds.), *Markets Hierarchies and Networks: The Co-ordination of Social Life.* London: Sage, 1–19.

Frederickson, H. G. 1999. The repositioning of American public administration. *PS: Political Science and Politics* 32: 701–711.

Geertz, C. 1973. *The Interpretation of Cultures.* New York: Basic Books.

Goldsmith, S. and Eggers, W. D. 2004. *Governing by Networks.* Washington, DC: Brookings Institution Press.

Goldsmith, S. and Kettl, D. F. 2009. *Unlocking the Power of Networks: Keys to High-Performance Government.* Washington, DC: Brookings Institution.

Hay, C. 2011. Interpreting interpretivism, interpreting interpretations: "the new hermeneutics of public administration". *Public Administration* 89: 167–182.

Holliday, I. 2000. Is the British state hollowing out? *Political Quarterly* 71: 167–176.

Huxham, C. and Vangen, C. 2005. *Managing to Collaborate: The Theory and Practice of Collaborative Advantage.* London: Routledge.

Jessop, B. 2000. Governance failure. In G. Stoker (ed.), *The New Politics of British Local Governance.* Basingstoke: Palgrave Macmillan, 11–32.

Jessop, B. 2003. Governance and metagovernance: On reflexivity, requisite variety, and requisite irony. In H. P. Bang (ed.), *Governance as Social and Political Communication.* Manchester: Manchester University Press, 101–116.

Jessop, B. 2007. *State Power.* Cambridge: Polity.

Kickert, W. J. M., Klijn, E-H., and Koppenjan, J. F. M. (eds.) 1997. *Managing Complex Networks: Strategies for the Public Sector.* London: Sage.

Kjær, A. M. 2004. *Governance.* Cambridge: Polity.

Klijn, E-H. 1997. Policy networks: An overview. In W. J. M. Kickert, E-H Klijn, and J. F. M. Koppenjan (eds.), *Managing Complex Networks: Strategies for the Public Sector.* London: Sage, 14–61.

Klijn, E-H. 2008. Governance and governance networks in Europe: an assessment of 10 years of research on the theme. *Public Management Review* 10: 505–525.

Klijn, E-H. and Skelcher, C. 2007. Democracy and governance networks: Compatible or not? *Public Administration* 85: 587–608.

Kooiman, J. 2003. *Governing as Governance*. London: Sage.

Koppernjan, J. F. M. and Klein, E-H. 2004. *Managing Uncertainties in Networks: A Network Approach to Problem Solving and Decision Making*. London: Routledge.

Kramer, R. M. and Tyler, T. (eds.) 1996. *Trust in Organizations: Frontiers of Theory and Research*. London: Sage.

Ling, T. 2002. Delivering joined-up government in the UK: Dimensions, issues and problems. *Public Administration* 80: 615–642.

Marin, B. and Mayntz, R. (eds.) 1991. *Policy Network: Empirical Evidence and Theoretical Considerations*. Frankfurt am Main: Campus Verlag.

Marinetto, M. 2003. Governing beyond the centre: A critique of the Anglo-Governance School. *Political Studies* 51: 592–608.

Marsh, D. 2008. What is at stake? A response to Bevir and Rhodes. *British Journal of Politics and International Relations* 10: 735–739.

Marsh, D., Richards, D., and Smith, M. J. 2003. Unequal plurality: Towards an asymmetric power model of British politics. *Government and Opposition* 38: 306–332.

Maynard-Moody, S. and Musheno, M. 2003. *Cops, Teachers, Counselors: Stories from the Front Lines of Public Service*. Ann Arbor, MI: The University of Michigan Press.

Mayntz, R. 1993. Governing failure and the problem of governability: Some comments on a theoretical paradigm.In J. Kooiman (ed.), *Modern Governance*. London: Sage, 9–20.

Mayntz, R. 2003. New challenges to governance theory. In H. P. Bang (ed.), *Governance as Social and Political Communication*. Manchester: Manchester University Press, 27–39.

McAnulla, S. 2006. Challenging the new interpretivist approach: Towards a critical realist alternative. *British Politics* 1: 113–138.

McKinlay, A. and Starkey, K. P. (eds.) 1998. *Foucault, Management and Organization Theory: From Panopticon to Technologies of Self*. London: Sage.

Miller, P. and Rose, N. 2008. *Governing the Present: Administering Economic, Social and Personal Life*. Cambridge: Polity.

Meier, K. J. and O'Toole, L. J. 2005. Managerial networking: issues of measurement and research design. *Administration and Society* 37: 523–541.

O'Toole, L. 1997. Treating networks seriously: Practical and research based agendas in public administration. *Public Administration Review* 57: 45–52.

Perri 6, Leat, D., Seltzer, K. and Stoker, G. 2002. *Towards Holistic Governance. The New Reform Agenda*. Houndmills, Basingstoke: Palgrave Macmillan.

Pierre, J. (ed.) (2000). *Debating Governance*. Oxford: Oxford University Press.

Pierre, J. and Peters, B. G. 2000. *Governance, Politics and the State*. Houndmills, Basingstoke: Palgrave Macmillan.

Rhodes, R. A. W. 1990. Policy networks: A British perspective. *Journal of Theoretical Politics* 2: 292–316.

Rhodes, R. A. W. 1997a. *Understanding Governance*. Buckingham and Philadelphia: Open University Press.

Rhodes, R. A. W. 1997b. It's the mix that matters: From marketization to diplomacy. *Australian Journal of Public Administration* 56: 40–53.

Rhodes, R. A. W. (ed.) 2000. *Transforming British Governance*, 2 vols. London: Macmillan.

Rhodes, R. A. W. 2006. Policy network analysis. In M. Moran, M. Rein, and R. E. Goodin (eds.), *The Oxford Handbook of Public Policy*. Oxford: Oxford University Press, 423–445.

Rhodes, R. A. W. 2007. *Understanding Governance*: ten years on. *Organization Studies* 28: 1243–1264.

Rhodes, R. A. W. 2011. *Everyday Life in British Government*. Oxford: Oxford University Press.

Richards, D. and Smith, M.J. 2002. *Governance and Public Policy in the UK*. Oxford: Oxford University Press.

Scharpf, F. W. 1997. *Games Real Actors Play: Actor-centred Institutionalism in Policy Research*. Boulder, CO: Westview Press.

Scott, C. 2006. Privatization and regulatory regimes. In M. Moran, M. Rein and R. E. Goodin (eds.), *The Oxford Handbook of Public Policy* Oxford: Oxford University Press, 651–668.

Smith, M. J. 1999. *The Core Executive in Britain*. London: Macmillan.

Sørensen, E. and Torfing, J. 2005. Democratic anchorage of governance networks. *Scandinavian Political Studies* 28: 195–218.

Sørensen, E. and Torfing, J. 2007. Theoretical approaches to metagovernance. In E. Sorsensen and J. Torfing (eds.), *Theories of Democratic Network Governance*. Houndmills, Basingstoke: Palgrave Macmillan, 169–182.

Stoker, G. 2004. *Transforming Local Governance*. Houndmills, Basingstoke: Palgrave Macmillan.

Stoker, G. (ed.) 2000. *The New Politics of British Local Governance*. London: Macmillan.

Sullivan, H. and Skelcher, C. 2002. *Working Across Boundaries: Collaboration in Public Services*. Basingstoke: Palgrave Macmillan.

Taylor, A. 1997. "Arm's Length but Hands On". Mapping the New Governance. The Department of National Heritage and cultural policies in Britain. *Public Administration* 75: 441–466.

Turnbull, Andrew 2007. Permanent Secretary, HM Treasury, "Stalinist Brown," An interview by Nicholas Timmins, *Financial Times*, 20 March.

Wright, V. and Hayward, J. 2000. Governing from the centre: Policy co-ordination in six European core executives. In R. A. W. Rhodes (ed.), *Transforming British Government*, Vol. 2: *Changing Roles and Relationships*. London: Macmillan, 27–46

CHAPTER 4

··

THE MANY FACES OF GOVERNANCE: ADAPTATION? TRANSFORMATION? BOTH? NEITHER?

··

LAURENCE E. LYNN, JR

THE term "governance" has long been used as a generic descriptive term. To paraphrase the *Oxford English Dictionary*, governance is the action or manner of governing, that is, of directing, guiding, or regulating individuals, organizations, nations, or multinational associations—public, private, or both—in conduct or actions. In scholarly usage, governance has been defined simply as "the general exercise of authority" (Michalski, Miller, and Stevens 2001: 9), where authority refers to institutions, public or private or both, for maintaining control and enforcing accountability. Common usage also views "governance" as a synonym for "government": providing direction to society by the state (Krahman 2003; Stoker 1998; World Bank 1989). Recent academic redefinitions of the term "governance" notwithstanding, these usages will remain standard.

In the early 1990s, new meanings of the term "governance" began to enter scholarly discourse (Boyer 1990; Kooiman 1993). These meanings reflect reactions by scholars to the emergence of new types and forms (or tools) of ordered rule and collective action that were said to be transforming the governing of advanced and many developing societies (Rhodes 1996; Stoker 1998). In its new clothes, "governance" is often depicted as taking place beyond the retreating reach of government control: expanding the role of civil society in directing and regulating the uses of public resources and increasing reliance on deliberative, as opposed to representative, forms of democracy.

As with other fashionable ideas in public administration, definitions of governance have proliferated to the point where the construct has become analytically intractable (Offe 2009). This chapter attempts to clarify the conceptual farrago that is "new governance" and to consider empirical claims that a "new governance" is displacing the role of the state across a broad array of policies and societies.

The next section discusses the main conceptualizations of "new governance." This discussion is followed by a consideration of evidence that puts the empirical claims of transformation to the test. Next, the concept of "governance" is viewed as an analytic framework that enables us to compare redefinitions of the term. The chapter concludes by challenging transformist narratives and offering ideas concerning the kinds of empirical research that will move the discussion of governance onto firmer conceptual and empirical foundations.

What is "new governance"?

Believing traditional concepts of governance to be unduly narrow if not obsolete (Hajer and Wagenaar 2003; Sørenson 2006; Osborne 2010), scholars began disassociating the term "governance" from government in favor of forms of governing, often viewed as "ideal types" (see Risse, this volume) that are decentered into civil society and feature plurality, interdependence, and trust.

Two divergent emphases can be discerned in these efforts to redefine governance. One views government and the for-profit sector as integral, although not necessarily dominant, participants in "new governance": governance *with* government. The other views "new governance" as the provision of societal direction primarily by nongovernmental actors: governance becoming centered in civil society. The former emphasizes adaptation, the latter transformation.

Governance with government

"Clearly, we are moving beyond governments to governance," asserted American political scientist William Boyer (Boyer 1990, 51). Boyer defined governance as the "action of government *plus* its interaction with its nongovernmental partners in the process of governing—in their collective relationship with the economy and public policy."

In a more recent conceptualization, governments, says Erik-Hans Klijn (2008, 506), "have become more dependent on societal actors to achieve their goals because of the increasing complexity of the challenges they face.... It is only through collaborative action that societal policy problems can be resolved."

Klijn elaborates this statement, based on his review of European governance literature:

> [T]here is little that distinguishes governance from governance networks....Governance...tends to emphasize the horizontal relationships between governmental organizations and other organizations....[G]overnance is the process that takes place within governance networks...[comprising] web[s] of relationships between government, business and civil society actors .. which are not necessarily equitable (2008: 507, 510, 511).

The widely held European view, Klijn suggests, one also popular in the US, is that governance means, specifically, networks.

Klijn also says what "governance" is not: it is not traditional bureaucratic government, not "New Public Management," not "good government," and not processes operating outside the range of government influence.

Echoing Klijn, Chris Skelcher (2010, 1164) says that "There has been widespread interest across Europe in the engagement of citizens, civil society organizations, and business with government in the formulation and delivery of public policy...A range of democratic innovations has emerged, including citizens' juries, deliberative forums, multisector partnerships, and coproduction," which is a significant change. Direct participative engagement reinforces the role of the citizen as the principal, in relationship to political decision makers and public bureaucracies. Citizens become part of "government" through these mechanisms, which confer authority on their inputs to the policy process.

Governance without government

Of a growing vein of governance literature, Peters and Pierre (1998, 223) say that "governance without government" is becoming the dominant pattern of management for advanced industrial democracies, a view widely associated with Rhodes (1996, 1997). In this bold reconceptualization of governance, emphasis is placed on "the changing boundary between state and civil society" (Bevir, Rhodes, and Weller 2003, 13). "Governance" refers to a particular model of governing that *coexists with* government but functions largely or wholly beyond its influence, that is, with "a significant degree of autonomy from the state" (Rhodes 1997, 53).

Powerful stakeholders and ordinary citizens are, in this view, demanding larger roles in the exercise of public authority. In general, say Maarten Hajer and Hendrik Wagenaar (2003, 2), "The language of 'governance' seems to help practitioners and theorists alike to unlearn embedded intellectual reflexes and break out of tacit patterns of thinking. This stimulates them to rethink governing." Going further, Stoker asserts that "The essence of governance is its focus on governing mechanisms which do not rest on recourse to the authority and sanctions of government" (Stoker : 1998 : 18; see also Rudiger, Wurzel, and Zito 2005).

GOVERNANCE AS ANALYTIC FRAMEWORK

Claims that "new governance" represents a new reality have dominated the governance discourse. Overlooked are references to "governance" as an organizing framework or a perspective for understanding the changing processes of governing (Krahman 2003; Pierre and Peters 2000; Hajer and Wagenaar 2003; Stoker 1998). An attempt to view governance as an analytic framework is depicted in Figure 4.1, which reflects an adaptive view of governance.

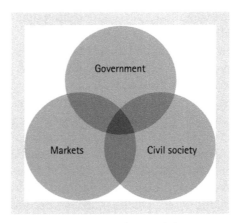

FIGURE 4.1 Types of societal direction.

Societal steering is viewed as having three primary wellsprings: government; the firms of the proprietary private sector; and the organizations of civil society, prominently including non-governmental organizations (NGOs). Governments may provide societal direction by raising revenue through taxes and debt to finance and deliver public goods and services directly to citizens. Charitable NGOs/non-profit organizations (NPOs) do this by providing services to various clienteles financed by gifts and grants from individual donors and foundations. Drawing on loans and investments from individuals and financial institutions, the proprietary for-profit sector provides goods and services directly to customers.

These three sources of societal direction may take place in virtual independence from one another; as such, the three sectors may be said to coexist. In most societies, independence of the sectors is the exception, not the rule. Governments contract with NGOs or with for-profit firms for the delivery of services. Both NGOs and the for-profit sector are generally subject to various forms of regulation by different levels and agencies of government. Non-profit organizations create taxable for-profit subsidiaries to raise revenue and receive grants from corporate donors. To an apparently increasing extent, organizations from all three sectors may form networks or partnerships to serve a collective interest. These types of interaction are depicted in the shaded areas of Figure 4.1.

This analytic framework can be elaborated by identifying specific forms that these different types of interactions take: contracts, subsidies, self-organizing networks, independent regulatory authorities, new organizational formats, participatory budgeting, and the like.

The seven *types* and the extensive array of *forms* of societal direction—each sector acting independently, each sector interacting with each of the other two, and interactions among all three sectors—constitute an analytic framework by which we can understand the "new governance" literature and, at least in principle, consider the extent to which a society uses these types and forms of steering, how societies differ from each other in patterns of steering, how societies change over time, and whether the boundaries between the sectors are being redrawn; Figure 4.2 depicts civil-society-centered governance.

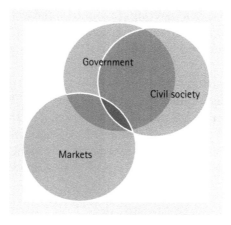

FIGURE 4.2 Governance centered in civil society.

This framework is also useful for comparing different definitions of governance. Traditional, state-centric governance includes all directive activity within the government sphere, both direct government and all types and forms of government interaction with the other two sectors. In contrast, Klijn's definition of governance interpreted only one *form* of governance—networks —as it takes place within the sphere of civil society, that is, including, but not limited to, civil society interactions with government and with the for-profit sector. The civil-society-centered definitions exclude all types of its interactions *except* its interactions with government.

Of all definers of "governance" or "new governance," one might ask: Which spheres, types, and forms of governance, and which particular policy domains, are included in your concept? From an analytic perspective comprising all types and forms of directive activity, definitions that exclude some types or forms are arbitrary. It's one thing to focus attention on *new* or *changed* forms of governance, quite another thing to exclude specific types and forms from a concept, governance, that is inherently comprehensive.

VARIETIES OF EVIDENCE

The growing interest in "new governance" has stimulated a growing body of systematic, empirical research, including diverse types of evidence reflecting the different meanings of governance and the specific interests of investigators. The findings discussed in this section have been selected to show that meta-narratives of convergent transformation toward a "new governance" paradigm should yield to a more complex and nuanced view of how the types and forms of societal governance are in fact evolving.

A substantial literature is associated with the growing popularity of aggregate indicators that rank or assess countries according to a wide variety of measures (Bandura 2008). The most comprehensive project is the World Bank's Worldwide Governance

Indicators (WGI) database now covering 212 countries and territories from 1998 to 2009 and measuring various dimensions of governance defined as "the exercise of authority through formal and informal traditions and institutions for the common good" (Kaufmann 2003).

Although associated mainly with the "governance as good government" perspective, the potential value of these indicators is arguably broader. In a summary analysis of trends in governance during the period 1998 to 2008, for example, Kaufmann, Kraay, and Mastruzzi (2009, 23) conclude that "there is little evidence of significant (or quanti- tatively important) changes in world averages of governance over the past decade." Research based on aggregate indicators is controversial, however, and will not be dis- cussed further.

Assessments of institutional change and reform

Investigations into the consequences of efforts at institutional reform illuminate issues associated with "new governance."

The Organisation for Economic Co-operation and Development (OECD), for exam- ple, conducts comparative analyses of governance in member countries that draw broad conclusions concerning institutional change. OECD reports have identified a transfor- mation in governance, but in the opposite direction from that suggested by "new gov- ernance" narratives: toward what is called "the regulatory state" (cf. Levi-Faur 2005). One such analysis concluded, for example, that

> [a]cross the OECD area, the liberalisation of domestic markets and international trade, coupled with the introduction of regulatory management tools, *has led to a profound reformulation of the state's role in the economy*. Scholars have labeled this trend the 'rise of the regulatory state'.... A vital factor behind this change has been the creation of a host of new institutions – oversight bodies, regulatory agencies, administrative courts and ombudsman commissions – to manage newly liberalized markets. These specialised agencies have developed a host of tools to develop evidenced-based policies and to enforce economic regulations" (OECD 2009, emphasis added).

Another OECD study concluded that countries are relying increasingly on "agencies, authorities, and other autonomous bodies" (OECD 2002). The report concludes that "[i]n public law, awarding the status of legal person *does not usually affect the political responsibility or accountability of the minister* for the activities of such a body" (10, emphasis added). However, these autonomous organizations "should be subsidiary bodies that *belong to government ministerial departments* but benefit from some mana- gerial flexibility" (10, emphasis added).

Research on managerialist reforms such as New Public Management (NPM) reveals similar contradictions between claims of transformation and the extent of actual change. For example, a study of the New Steering Model (NSM), an NPM-style reform in German local government, reported mixed results (Kuhlmann, Bogumil, and Grohs 2008, 860).

The authors conclude that "[a] comprehensive 'paradigm shift' from the Weberian bureaucracy to a managerial NSM administration has not occurred. Many local authorities tend to implement new structures and instruments only formally, without using them in a 'managerial' way. Rather, they seek to make these instruments fit into the traditional bureaucracy. Public administrations in Continental Europe still have no solution for how to make managerialism match with their prevailing legalist 'rule of law' culture."

Of particular interest in reform-oriented research is the analysis of governance reforms in anglophone and European states by Mark Bevir, Rhodes, and Patrick Weller (2003). They ask: "What is the plot of our story?" Their complex plot includes the following: "[T]he beliefs and practices of elite actors [engaged in reform] originate in the traditions they have inherited. They construct issues or dilemmas out of experiences infused with these traditions" (202). Continuing this path-dependent theme, the authors say that "Governance is constructed differently and continuously reconstructed so there can be no one set of tools" (203).

Evidence from theory-based empirical research

Researchers have investigated a wide array of propositions, conjectures, and hypotheses related to the evolution of governing institutions. Following are examples of such studies, which cast a nuanced light on some familiar "new governance" narratives.

Networks, the theme of many "new governance" narratives, are a common subject of empirical research. Mark Considine and Jenny Lewis (2003, 132), for example, "sought to turn the vague reform rhetoric of various countries at the leading edge of change [Australia, Britain, the Netherlands, and New Zealand] into testable propositions about the way real officials should work in the new systems." A sample of over one thousand individuals engaged in governance in the four countries was surveyed concerning "two sequential propositions: (1) the strength of commitment to the traditional bureaucratic or procedural model of governance; and (2) the strength of ... new models of governance" (133). The authors conclude that "enterprise governance"—that is, NPM-style governance—and network governance "now operate as norms in practice, *in addition to* the older form of bureaucratic or procedural organization, in reform-minded countries" (138, emphasis added). A little bureaucracy, moreover, may improve network performance. A series of studies of mental health networks by Brinton Milward and Keith Provan (2000) found that those networks that develop long-term relationships that mimic the stability of bureaucracy actually perform better than those that remain more fluid. In a related vein, Kenneth Meier and Gregory Hill summarize the findings of research conducted by Laurence O'Toole and Meier (2003), as follows: "[S]tability of personnel and management, both traits more associated with bureaucracy than networks, were strongly and positively correlated with higher performance on a wide variety of organizational outputs and outcomes" (2005: 62) Networks may, in Meier and Hill's view (2005: 62), "be more effective to the degree they take on bureaucratic traits." Angela Eikenberry (2007, 194) says that many scholars "show that networks can exacerbate rather than alleviate inequality in the political process." Similarly Rouban (1999, 2) notes, based on several investigations, that "networks are not necessarily democratic and more often create communities than they do citizens... [D]ecentralization procedures have not always led to more local democracy" but may strengthen local elites. Finally, research suggests that collaboration among network participants may obscure both formal and informal governance arrangements or understandings that reflect or create power differentials and hierarchy and that can either strengthen or weaken the collaboration (Bell and Hindmoor 2009).

Studies of direct democracy and citizen participation, another theme of "new governance" narratives, reveal numerous contradictions between their claimed salutary effects and both the reality of local elite domination of deliberative processes and citizen bias (Lynn 2002). One study of how well community service organizations meet community needs concluded: "From a broader policy standpoint, our findings question the ability of community service organizations to identify and respond to community needs" (Markham, Johnson, and Bonjean 1999, 176). A survey of research on neighborhood-representing organizations found "a low level of both participatory and representative democracy" in such organizations (Cnaan 1991, 629). Finally, winners and losers in political contests express different levels of satisfaction with democratic institutions, winners preferring majoritarian government, losers preferring consensual processes (Anderson and Guillory 1997).

In summary, findings concerning citizen involvement in governance are widely varying and highly qualified by context. Findings range from benefits such as "social learning," better agency–public relations, and better alignment of agency and citizen interests to costs such as increased divisiveness, the displacement of reason by passion and persistence, and heightened distrust of and respect for public officials. Empirical research does not support a presumption that the pursuit of self-interest will yield to shared understandings and the accommodation of differences. Indeed, the opposite may be the result.

Two studies of environmental policy-making present findings that qualify the "governance beyond government" narrative. In one, Rudiger, Wurzel, and Zito (2005) investigate the adoption of what they call New Environmental Policy Instruments by eight European countries and the European Union. They ask: Has governance, as they define it, eclipsed government? Their analytic framework postulates four types of interactions between new governance instruments and traditional government: coexistence, fusion, competition, and replacement. They found that "regulation is still the most widely used instrument of environmental policy" (489); no wholesale switch to new policy instruments, from government to governance, has occurred. Rather, new policy instruments are used for new tasks and coexist with traditional regulation.

In a study of Swedish forestry and transport policies, Erik Hysing (2009) asks: "Is *from government to governance* a credible story line for understanding these cases?" The research "is based on a review of existing research on forest and transport governing, as well as new empirical findings from policy documents (evaluations, government bills, programs, strategies, etc.) and qualitative interviews" (648). The author concludes that "The role of the state has changed during the period under study, but not in a unidirectional way.... The general impression... is that governing within both policy areas is characterized by continuity rather than dramatic changes.... While the state seems to be losing ground when studying one dimension, it retains or even increases its role when studying other dimensions" (665, 667).

Evidence from multi-level governance research

The study of multi-level governance illuminates many themes in the "new governance" narrative. Ian Bache (this volume) says: "[multi-level governance] directs attention to increasingly complex relations between actors from public, private and voluntary sectors organized at different territorial levels and raises important questions about the efficiency and accountability of contemporary decision-making in the public sphere. As such, multi-level governance has made a significant contribution to our understanding of contemporary politics."

Carolyn Hill and Laurence Lynn (2005), for example, used a multi-level "logic of governance" to evaluate over 800 published studies that explore multi-level interactions. They found that "the vast majority of studies adopt a top-down perspective on governance.... Influence is modeled as flowing downward from legislation and management toward treatments and consequences" (179). They conclude that "conjectures by hundreds of investigators in specialized domains [are] that the interesting questions of administration and management concern the effects of hierarchical interactions more than of horizontality" (189).

In a study that replicated the Hill and Lynn research but with published studies using non-US data, Melissa Forbes and Lynn (2005) concluded that "[e]vidence based on international data suggests, as do American studies, that [multiple] levels of governance influence one another, that is, that the organization of governance impacts what, how, and for whom public services are provided" (568). These findings have been further replicated in studies by Forbes, Hill, and Lynn (2006) and by Robichau and Lynn (2009). Robichau and Lynn, following an analysis of 300 recently published research studies, concluded that "the presumption is warranted that implementation is generally hierarchical; influences flow downward through a chain of delegation to the retail level of service delivery" (24).

In one multi-level study, for example, Peter May and Søren Winter (2009) seek to explain the extent to which "street-level bureaucrats emphasize actions that reflect higher level policy goals" (3) in reformed Danish employment programs. The authors found that "higher level political [attention by relevant municipal politicians to employment issues] and managerial [supervision, communicating specific goals] influence the policy emphases of frontline workers" (16).

The evolution of the European Union (EU) into a supranational governing entity provides a narrative of institutional transformation among member countries with elements both of transformation and adaptation, hierarchy and cooperation. Rudiger, Wurzel, and Zito (2005, 490), for example, conclude that "the EU is now *the* dominant driver of national environmental policy through issuing regulations that are incorporated into national law." Hysing concludes that "[t]he responsibility for standardization and regulation of environmental impact originating from transport has largely been *delegated to the EU level*" (666, emphasis added).

Qualifying the theme of hierarchy in the EU, Hadii Mamudu and Donley Studlar (2009: 77) examine the emergence of a complex, multi-level governance institution to control tobacco use within the Union involving shared sovereignty, which refers to "how states willingly cede part of their sovereignty to intergovernmental organizations or supranational bodies to deal with issues that cannot be handled singlehandedly." However, when the scope of sovereignty covers specific issue areas, state authority is disaggregated into a combination of state officials, non-governmental organizations, judges, commissions, and interest groups. In tobacco control, for example, non-state entities have become prominent within this system of multi-level governance. Thus multi-level governance in the EU has provided new opportunities for interest groups, especially those frustrated at the state level, to bring their arguments to a new level, one with fewer established insider–outsider power relationships.

* * * * * * *

An appropriate conclusion of the above cited empirical research might have been provided by Jan Kooiman (2003, 13), a progenitor of the governance-as-networks perspective, who conceded that "the state is still very much alive. Although new modes of government [such as subsidiary bodies], with the state as a participant, are on the agenda." He continues: "the state is perfectly capable of giving [managerial flexibility] with one hand and taking [ministerial-level regulation] with the other." Indeed, a significant literature supports the argument that, while the types and forms of governance have evolved, the reach of the state is undiminished and that a "new regulatory state" may be emerging (Levi-Faur 2005; Pierre and Peters 2005; Bell and Hindmoor 2009; Lynn 2010).

TRAJECTORIES OF CHANGE

Many investigators, challenging narratives of transformation and convergence, argue that institutional evolution across nations will take many different trajectories (Dunleavy and Hood 1994; Peters 1996; Pollitt and Bouckaert 2004). The kinds of evidence and arguments just summarized bear out such expectations. As Johan Olsen argues (2006, 13), the notion infusing transformist narratives, that transformation is inevitable and that it will converge on a new paradigm, "is not supported by empirical observations." In general, as the research by Bevir, Rhodes, and Weller, cited above, suggests, the evolution of governance in any country is "path dependent," that is, it is governed in fundamental ways by beliefs, choices, and traditions unique to that country. There is "no universal process of globalization driving public sector reform" (2003, 203).

A schematic depiction of some possible trajectories/pathways/faces of governance evolution is shown in Figure 4.3, which considers the governance spheres of government and civil society and depicts a space encompassing four governance domains:

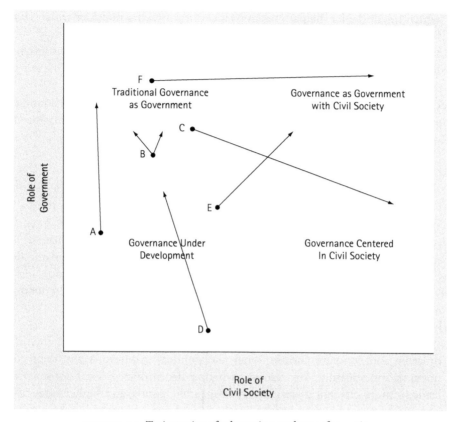

FIGURE 4.3 Trajectories of adaptation and transformation.

governance under development, traditional "governance as government," governance as "government with civil society," and "governance centered in civil society." Possible trajectories of change include:

A which might depict the evolution of Eastern European nations from Soviet governance toward proto-traditional "neo-Weberian states" (Pollitt and Bouckaert 2004), a necessary stage on the way to more balanced governance;

B which might depict the type of adaptation that has been occurring in many developed democracies, for example, new regulation in response to the global financial crises that began in 2008: "the rise of the regulatory state" might be depicted by the left arrow, the general trend toward regulated devolution and third-party government in America the right arrow;

C which might depict the narrative of transformation put forward by those perceiving or advocating "governance without government" (Rhodes 1996, 1997);

D which might depict a typical development path taken by countries emerging from tribal or other forms of local rule toward a functioning central government;

 E which might depict the path taken by a country nearing maturity which chooses to move more directly toward government–civil society integration; and

 F trajectory which might depict the emergence of the complex institutions governing tobacco use in the European Union.

Trajectories other than those in Figure 4.3 might be plotted for individual countries or for similarly disposed countries grouped on the basis of theoretical or empirical premises (cf. Rodriquez, Spink, and Ward 2008).

GOVERNANCE: A RESEARCH AGENDA

Is the evidence sufficient to warrant claims that governance is being transformed? What do we know about how governance is evolving in societies of the developed and developing worlds? The preceding discussion suggests that the answers are "no," and "not nearly enough." As Andrews (2010, 29) argues, "researchers should focus on better understanding what structures governments actually do adopt and why" (29).

What should we study? We might:

- describe and compare constitutional and political institutions and their consequences, investigating, for example, whether decentralized fiscal administration leads to more efficient governance, better public goods, and higher rates of economic growth or whether political institutions shape a country's economic policy;
- compare deliberate government reform initiatives and improvement strategies, investigating, for example, the political and policy consequences of managerialist reforms or whether major reform initiatives have changed the norms of practice among civil servants; or
- compare forms of "new governance" such as networks, hybrid organizations, partnerships, and participatory decision-making, investigating, for example, how the adoption of civil society-oriented administrative technologies has modified the relationships between the authority of governments, communities, and citizens.

As the evidence surveyed in this chapter attests, research of each type is ongoing, but the body of findings is thin. More of each type of investigation will more clearly reveal the different "faces" of governance and yield a richer array of insights into the nature, extent, and direction of institutional evolution in and across both the developed and developing worlds.

Even more synoptic studies of governance are needed (Heinrich, Lynn, and Milward 2010). How, for example, might changes in the boundary between the state and civil society be investigated empirically? Accompanying an authentic transformation might be, for example,

- significant reductions in the proportion of societal resources flowing through governments and thus subject to government authorization, appropriation, and administrative processes;
- evidence of a pattern of devolution and deregulation of administration, such as a reduction in the number of pages of applicable regulations or instances of language changes that reassign policy and regulatory authority to non-governmental or hybrid entities;
- evidence of changes in agency enforcement strategies such as increased reliance on non-coercive, voluntary, and negotiated enforcement across significant swaths of public responsibility;
- testimony from stakeholders, such as public program administrators and their private sector agents and other civil society institutions, that government has become less intrusive, that front-line professionals are feeling more empowered and less burdened by red tape, and that local priorities have increasing weight in service delivery;
- increased interest group and citizen involvement and influence at all levels of policy-making and bargaining over program features;
- redirection of political advocacy from higher to lower levels of government and from targeted political action to broader forms of social mobilization;
- greater coverage (of individuals and households) by alternative, non-traditional service delivery arrangements, evidence, that is, that more aspects of wellbeing for more people are in non-governmental hands; and
- reduced co-optation of the charitable nonprofit sector by government as public resources and guidance are replaced by civil society resources and direction—civil society institutions themselves, for example, foundations, fundraising associations, and large NGOs—might be transferring authority over priorities and methods of implementation to community and grass-roots control.

Little effort has been made to assemble these kinds of evidence. One reason is the ideological basis of reform promotions (Lynn 2010). As Olsen notes (2006, 8), "there has been little felt need to examine assumptions about the extent and consequences of administrative reform because so many reforms have been driven by strong ideological convictions or even a doctrinaire faith in what is the ideal organization and role of public administration in the economy and society." Also, those with ideological commitments to new patterns of governance may be more interested in demonstrating how they can work. Eikenberry, for example, says "[s]tudies on network governance have focused primarily on how to build and manage effective networks in order to improve service delivery and increase the production of public goods, not on the effects of network governance on democracy or social justice/equity issues" (Eikenberry 2007, 193; cf. O'Toole and Meier 2004).

"Governance" has become a recognized focus of teaching, research, and public policy. There is a concomitant need, then, for a research enterprise that will provide it with adequate conceptual and empirical foundations.

REFERENCES

Anderson, C. J. and Guillory, C. A. 1997. Political initiatives and satisfaction with democracy: A cross-national analysis of consensus and majoritarian systems. *American Political Science Review* 91: 66–81.

Andrews, M. 2010. Good government means different things in different countries. *Governance: An International Journal of Policy, Administration, and Institutions* 23: 7–35.

Bandura, R. 2008. A survey of composite indices measuring country performance: 2008 update. UNDP/ODS Working Paper. New York: United Nations Development Programme (UNDP), Office of Development Studies.

Bell, S. and Hindmoor, A. 2009. *Rethinking Governance: The Centrality of the State in Modern Society*. Cambridge: Cambridge University Press.

Bevir, M., Rhodes, R. A. W., and Weller, P. 2003. Comparative governance: Prospects and lessons. *Public Administration* 81: 191–210.

Boyer, William W. 1990. Political science and the 21st century: From government to governance. *PS: Political Science and Politics* 23: 50–54.

Cnaan, R A. 1991. Neighborhood-representing organizations: How democratic are they? *Social Service Review* 73: 614–634.

Considine, M. and Lewis, J. M. 2003. Bureaucracy, network, or enterprise? Comparing models of governance in Australia, Britain, the Netherlands, and New Zealand. *Public Administration Review* 60: 131–140.

Dunleavy, P. and Hood, C. 1994. From old public administration to New Public Management. *Public Money and Management* 14: 9–16.

Eikenberry, A. M. 2007. Symposium—Theorizing governance beyond the state. *Administrative Theory & Praxis* 29: 193–197.

Forbes, M. and. Lynn, L. E., Jr 2005. How does public management affect government performance? Findings from international research. *Journal of Public Administration Research and Theory* 15: 59–84.

Forbes, M. K, Hill, C. J., and Lynn, L. E., Jr 2006. Public management and government performance: An international review. In G. Boyne, K. Meier, L. O'Toole, Jr, and R. Walker (eds.) *Public Services Performance: Perspectives on Measurement and Management*. Cambridge: Cambridge University Press, 254–274.

Hajer, M. and Wagenaar, H. (eds.) 2003. *Deliberative Policy Analysis: Understanding Governance in the Network Society*. Cambridge: Cambridge University Press.

Heinrich, C. J., Lynn, L. E., Jr, and Milward, H. B. 2010. A state of agents? Sharpening the debate and evidence over the extent and impact of the transformation of governance. *Journal of Public Administration Research and Theory* 20: 13–19.

Hill, C. J. and Lynn, L. E., Jr 2005. Is hierarchical governance in decline? Evidence from empirical research. *Journal of Public Administration Research and Theory* 15: 173–195.

Hysing, E. 2009. From government to governance? A comparison of environmental governing in Swedish forestry and transport. *Governance: An International Journal of Policy, Administration, and Institutions* 22: 647–672.

Kaufmann, D. 2003. *Rethinking Governance: Empirical Lessons Challenge Orthodoxy*. Washington: World Bank Institute.

Kaufmann, D., Kraay, A. and Mastruzzi, M. 2009. *Governance Matters VIII: Aggregate and Individual Governance Indicators, 1996–2008*. World Bank Policy Research Working Paper No. 4978. Available at SSRN: http://ssrn.com/abstract=1424591 (accessed 19 September 2011).

Klijn, E.-H. 2008. Governance and governance networks in Europe: An assessment of ten years of research on the theme. *Public Management Review* 10: 505–525.

Kooiman, J. 1993. *Governing as Governance*. London: Sage Publications.

Kooiman, J. 2003. *Governing as Governance*. London: Sage Publications.

Krahman, E. 2003. National, regional, and global governance: One phenomenon or many? *Global Governance* 9: 323–346.

Kuhlmann, S., Bogumil, J., and Grohs, S. 2008. Evaluating administrative modernization in German local governance: Success or failure of the 'New Steering Model'? *Public Administration Review* 68: 851–863.

Levi-Faur, D. 2005. The global diffusion of regulatory capitalism. *Annals of the American Academy of Political and Social Science* 598: 12–32.

Lynn, L. E. Jr 2002. Democracy's 'Unforgivable Sin'. *Administration & Society* 34: 447–454.

———. 2010. The persistence of hierarchy. In M. Bevir (ed.) *The Sage Handbook of Governance*. Thousand Oaks, CA: Sage Publications, 218–236.

Mamudu, H. M. and Studlar, D. T. 2009. Multilevel governance and shared sovereignty: European Union, Member States, and the FCTC. *Governance: An International Journal of Policy, Administration, and Institutions* 22: 73–97.

Markham, W. T., Johnson, M. A., and Bonjean, C. M. 1999. Nonprofit decision making and resource allocation: The importance of membership preferences, continuity needs, and interorganizational ties. *Nonprofit and Voluntary Sector Quarterly* 28: 152–184.

May, P. J. and Winter, S. C. 2009. Politicians, managers, and street-level bureaucrats: Influences on policy implementation. *Journal of Public Administration Research and Theory* 19: 453–476.

Meier, K. J. and Hill, G. C. 2005. Bureaucracy in the twenty-first century. In E. Ferlie, L. E. Lynn, Jr, and C. Pollitt (eds.) *The Oxford Handbook of Public Management*. New York and Oxford: Oxford University Press, 51–71.

Michalski, W., Miller, R., and Stevens, B. 2001. Governance in the 21st century: Power in the global knowledge economy and society. In *Governance in the 21st Century*. Paris: OECD, 7–26.

Milward, H. B. and Provan, K. G. 2000. Governing the hollow state. *Journal of Public Administration Research and Theory* 2: 359–379.

Offe, C. 2009. Governance: An 'Empty Signifier'? *Constellations* 16: 550–562.

OECD. 2002. *Distributed Public Governance: Agencies, Authorities and Other Government Bodies*. Paris: OECD.

OECD. 2009. *Reviews of Regulatory Reform: China, Defining the Boundary between the Market and the State*. Paris: OECD.

Olsen, J. P. 2006. Maybe it is time to rediscover bureaucracy. *Journal of Public Administration Research and Theory* 16: 1–24.

Osborne, S. P. 2010. The (new) public governance: A suitable case for treatment? In S. P. Osborne (ed.) *The New Public Governance: Emerging Perspectives on the Theory and Practice of Public Governance*. London: Routledge, 1–15.

O'Toole, L. J., Jr. and Meier, K. J. 2003. *Plus ça change*: Public management, personnel stability, and organizational performance. *Journal of Public Administration Research and Theory* 13: 43–64.

Peters, B. Guy. 1996. *Governing: Four Emerging Models*. Lawrence: University Press of Kansas.

Peters, B. Guy and Pierre, J. 1998. Governance without government? Rethinking public administration. *Journal of Public Administration Research and Theory* 8: 223–243.

Pierre, J. and Peters, B. G. 2000. *Governance, Politics, and the State*. New York: St Martin's Press.

———. 2005. Governance: A garbage can perspective. In J. Pierre and G. B. Peters (eds.) *Governing Complex Societies: Trajectories and Scenarios*. Basingstoke, UK: Palgrave Macmillan, 49–63.

Pollitt, C. and Bouckaert, G. 2004. *Public Management Reform: A Comparative Analysis*, Second Edition. New York and Oxford: Oxford: Oxford University Press.

Rhodes, R. A. W. 1996. The new governance: Governing without government. *Political Studies* 44: 652–667.

Rhodes, R. A. W. 1997. *Understanding Governance*. Buckingham and Philadelphia: Open University Press.

Robichau, R. W. and Lynn, L. E., Jr 2009. Public policy implementation: Still the missing link. *Policy Studies Journal* 37: 21–36.

Rodriquez, V. E., Spink, P. K., and Ward, P. M. 2008. The changing institutional capacity of subnational government: Toward effective governance. In R. H. Wilson, P. M. Ward, P. K. Spink, and V. E. Rodriquez (eds.) *Governance in the Americas: Decentralization, Democracy, and Subnational Government in Brazil, Mexico, and the USA*. Notre Dame, IN: University of Notre Dame Press, 88–144.

Rouban, L. 1999. Introduction: Citizens and the new governance. In L. Rouban (ed.) *Citizens and the New Governance: Beyond the New Public Management*. Amsterdam: IOS Press, 1–5.

Rudiger, J., Wurzel, A. K. W., and Zito, A. 2005. The rise of 'new' policy instruments in comparative perspective: Has governance eclipsed government? *Political Studies* 53: 477–496.

Skelcher, C. 2010. Fishing in muddy waters: Principals, agents, and democratic governance in Europe. *Journal of Public Administration Research and Theory* 20: i161–175.

Sørenson, E. 2006. Metagovernance: The changing role of politicians in processes of democratic governance. *American Review of Public Administration* 36: 98–114.

Stoker, G. 1998. Governance as theory: Five propositions. *International Social Science Journal* 155: 17–28.

World Bank. 1989. *From Crisis to Sustainable Development: Africa's Long-Term Perspective*. Washington, DC: World Bank.

CHAPTER 5

···

NEW GOVERNANCE
AS REGULATORY
GOVERNANCE

···

ORLY LOBEL*

In recent years, new governance has emerged as a school of thought that focuses on the significance of institutional design and culture for effective and legitimate regulation. The development of new governance theory marks a paradigm shift from the old regulation by command and control to a regulatory governance model, signifying a collective intellectual and programmatic project for a new legal regime. New governance offers a vision of law and policy that draws on the comparative strengths of both private and public stakeholders and highlights the multiple ways in which the various actors in a society contribute to the acts of ordering social fields. New governance scholars begin with an analysis of both market and governance failures to challenge the conventional wisdom that regulation must involve top-down command-and-control rules. Instead they attempt to offer a third-way vision between unregulated markets and top-down government controls. This chapter analyzes the field of new governance from a regulatory perspective and examines the ways in which governments can effectively regulate markets, looking at how regulatory governance has been expanded to offer effective regulation of private actors. Regulatory governance includes a broad range of government-enforced rules and procedures: collaborative private–public rule-making efforts, increased attention to internal processes and organizational dynamics, and the promotion of government-supported self-regulation. A central challenge that new governance takes on is how to promote legitimate, effective, and active participation in the work of regulation by the private regulated parties themselves without devolving into deregulation. From a regulatory perspective, new governance theory systemically maps the range of possibilities in the interaction between regulation and regulated actors (Levi-Faur 2005; Lobel 2004).

Beyond theoretical inquiry, a wide variety of legal fields have increasingly been applying new governance perspective to a diverse set of policy issues. Regulatory agencies are experimenting with a range of collaborative public–private approaches to regulation, enforcement, and compliance. Under the lens of new governance, the regulatory process consists of a wide range of tools, each with its comparative advantages and costs. This chapter introduces the regulatory perspective of the new governance approach from both its theoretical and its practical lenses. First, Section 2 introduces the regulatory governance approach by discussing its central principles and offering examples of its adoption in health and safety laws and anti-discrimination laws. Section 3 discusses the reasons for a shift to regulatory governance and explains new governance's departure from traditional command-and-control regulation. It describes how the alternative perspective of new governance focuses on the ways that government and the private sector can successfully operate together in legal and regulatory processes. The chapter then presents additional examples of the benefits of the new governance approach in environmental law, financial regulation, and organizational sentencing guidelines. Section 4 proceeds to argue that the corollary of a move to self-regulation initiatives is the ability of individuals to speak out when they face internal corporate misconduct. To support a self-regulation structure and to encourage internal reporting, the chapter stresses the importance of whistleblower protections. The chapter concludes with some of the limitations and risks of regulatory governance, as well as directions for further research.

1. RENEWING THE DEAL: REGULATORY NEW GOVERNANCE IN ACTION

Disparate areas of public policy reveal commonalities and require distinct combinations of policy approaches. In *The Renew Deal: The Fall of Regulation and the Rise of Governance*, I describe the new governance model of regulation as consisting of eight clusters of approaches (Lobel 2004):

(1) increased participation of non-state actors;
(2) public–private collaboration;
(3) diversity and competition within the market;
(4) decentralization;
(5) integration of policy domains;
(6) non-coerciveness ("soft law");
(7) adaptability and constant learning;
(8) coordination.

These eight dimensions represent the organizing principles operating together within the governance model. First, the new governance model involves increased participation of non-state actors because it challenges the conventional assumptions that the regulatory policymaking powers of administrative agencies are based on their superior knowledge, information, and expertise. Increased participation of private actors in the regulatory sphere permeates the many levels and stages of legal process—legislation, promulgation of rules, implementation of policies, and enforcement—and enhances citizens' ability to participate in political in civil life. The next three approaches, private–public collaboration, diversity, and decentralization, follow from such participation. Multiparty involvement is advocated as a way to create internal norms, cultivate a culture of learning and manage new market realities by combining "hard law" with more flexible, "softer" requirements. As such, regulatory governance enables us to view the different sectors— state, market, and civil society—as part of one comprehensive, interlocking system. In a system of private–public collaboration, individuals are norm-generating subjects involved in the process of developing and changing the norms of behavior, in contrast to the traditional model, under which private actors are the objects of regulation. Chris Ansell (Chapter 35, this volume) discusses this type of collaborative governance. Next, diversity and competition refer to the notion that a sustainable legal regime must encompass a multitude of values, account for conflict and compromise, acknowledge the diversity and changing interests of many participants, and recognize the legitimacy of private economic interests while appealing to public values. Similarly, decentralization indicates a movement downward and outward, transferring responsibilities to state and localities and to the private sector to promote the governance values listed above.

The fifth dimension of new governance, the integration of policy domains, recognizes that doctrinal divides and boundaries between legal fields are often defined through negotiation and revision. In a traditional regulatory model, laws are fragmented into distinct subfields, such as health and safety, financial regulation, environmental regulation, and social policies. The principles of private participation, collaboration, decentralization, and diversity all potentially lead to revealing the ways in which dispersed issues, such as financial misconduct and environmental regulation, are nonetheless connected at the level of those who are most influenced by them, for example, as shall be further elaborated in Section 4, through adequate reporting requirements, stakeholder involvement and whistleblower protections. Next, the concept of noncoerciveness refers to new governance's aim to create a fluid and flexible policy environment that fosters "softer" processes, which will create an environment more conducive to participation and dialogue. The new governance model also requires adaptability and constant learning, recognizing the inevitability and fertility of change while treating ambiguity as an opportunity rather than a burden to overcome. Finally, legal coordination aims to provide meaning to all other dimensions of new governance by facilitating the communication of local knowledge and the structured interactions of separate groups. A well-orchestrated government can promote and standardize innovations that began locally and privately.

From the perspective of new governance scholars, the question of what works and what fails in regulatory approaches must be constantly examined and re-examined. The answers are fundamentally empirical and can change over time and across different industries. De Búrca and Scott describe new governance as, first and foremost, relying on an empirical observation: "the first line of inquiry is a practical and empirical one, entailing an examination of the actual operation of new regulatory forms" (2006). Increasingly, we have empirical evidence indicating that in most contexts institutional culture and design have a significant impact on the likelihood that individuals will engage in unlaw-ful action.[1] For example, in the discrimination context, policy-makers increasingly rec-ognize that "[e]mployers' organizational choices can both facilitate and constrain the development of discriminatory work cultures" (Green 2005). In other words, the nature of the organization and its procedures is fundamental to goals of equal protection laws.

As a result of these understandings about the internal processes and institutional norms of regulated parties, the Equal Employment Opportunity Commission (EEOC) and some state civil rights agencies have recently guided workplaces to prevent discrim-ination through training programs, guidelines, internal reporting channels, and self-monitoring. (Suk 2006; Sturm 2001). Similarly, the Occupational Safety and Health Administration (OSHA) offers programs requiring private companies to identify, inves-tigate, and monitor their own safety risks and near-miss accidents in return for certifica-tion as "star" members of the OSHA collaborative and assistance from the agencies' officials (Lobel 2005). Occupational health and safety regulation provides a leading example of regulatory failures and demonstrates the need to diversify regulatory and compliance approaches. I have argued that the expansion of governance-based approaches to worker safety can allow agencies to augment targeted enforcement (Lobel 2007). For OSHA to be effective, it must rely on both cooperative compliance and coer-cive enforcement. It is important to emphasize, however, that a dynamic and interde-pendent blend of governance and regulatory approaches to occupational safety is a departure from OSHA's initial design as a regulatory agency. Although OSHA has been experimenting with governance approaches for some time now, these approaches depart from the paradigmatic perception of the agency. The shift to workplace safety govern-ance is the shift to a broader spectrum of public interventions, including both sanc-tioned and semi-voluntary reforms. Notably, much of the experimentation with regulatory governance has been occurring in the context of the workplace and employ-ment-related regulations. This focus on organizations and worker protection is not sur-prising, as the context of the workplace lends itself to the involvement of regulated actors—the firm/employer—as well as the immediate beneficiaries of regulation—the workers. The beneficiaries of regulation are the chief stakeholders and their involvement in enforcement and monitoring, as well as initial standard setting and rule-revision is a key component of the regulatory governance principle of private participation.

2. REGULATORY GOVERNANCE: BETWEEN MARKETS AND COMMAND-AND-CONTROL REGULATION

Traditional command-and-control regulation has long been the subject of scholarly cri-tique on account of its inefficiencies and frequent failures. At the same time, widespread inadequacies of market self-ordering are also well documented. Given the continuing need for government intervention along with the limits of traditional command-and-control regulation and the growing pressures to liberalize markets, regulators around the world are developing innovative third-way approaches to regulation, collectively referred to as the new governance model. New governance can also be understood as a scholarly effort to bring together two distinct academic literatures: empirical studies of regulation and normative thinking about the role of the state. Both in practice and in theory, policy-makers and scholars are focusing their attention on new governance as a set of legal strategies outside the traditional command-and-control toolbox that has the potential to increase the effectiveness and legitimacy of social regulation.

New governance approaches to regulation provide a method of regulating private market actors, such as firms and organizations, which allows regulatory decision-making to become a collective endeavor (Simon 2006). The related approach of regulatory governance, which has appeared as a term in Organisation for Economic Co-operation and Development (OECD) documents since the 1990s, refers to policies aimed to improve the act of regulation (Döhler 2011). Marian Döhler notes the relation of the term "regulatory governance" to "meta-regulation," which refers to the process of regulating a process of regulation itself. (2011, 524 n. 4). Rod Rhodes similarly describes the concept of "metagovernance," under which the state governs organizations that "undertake much of the work of governing…and at times they even regulate themselves" (Chapter 3, this volume, p. 37). Rather than viewing industry as a passive object of regulation from above, regulatory governance aims to harness the knowledge and energy of private actors in the act of regulation. This includes drawing on industry best practices, private standard-making, and non-governmental monitoring. This concept of regulatory governance provides a perspective from which new governance can be understood and applied. These approaches of new governance and regulatory governance do not, however, entail a complete shift from command-and-control regulation to self-regulation. As noted previously, the central challenge of regulatory governance is to maintain an effective role for law and regulation amidst the shifts to more private efforts of governance. Government continues to retain a significant coordination role. John Braithwaite and Peter Drahos have recently described this new approach as the "rise of a 'new regulatory state,' where states do not so much run things as regulate them or monitor self-regulation" (Braithwaite and Drahos 2000: 28; Braithwaite 2000). Jason Solomon describes new governance approaches as "less hierarchical, more transparent, and more democratic than traditional top-down forms of regulation" (2008: 820).

In the scholarly realm, new governance attempts to tie together recent developments in the political economy with advances in legal and democratic theory. David Levi-Faur has characterized "the new regulatory order" as "social, political, and economic," explaining that "[s]tate, markets, and society are not distinct entities" (2005: 14). Emphasizing the interplay between economic and political theory, Levi-Faur explains the theory of "regulatory capitalism," which integrates new regulatory approaches with political economic theories (ibid.). Significantly, new governance theory attempts to renew and intervene in otherwise stalemated debates. Recognizing the shortcomings of the two dominant orthodoxies of regulation and de-regulation, governance as an operative project powerfully promotes an alternative vision that engages innovative public management techniques across legal fields. Douglas NeJaime notes that "new governance strategies spring from a discontent with the results produced by traditional techniques" (2009: 343). In their willingness to synthesize an emerging social vision, scholars and policy-makers move beyond entrenched and failed government structures while resisting simplistic attacks on the role of government intervention.[2]

These approaches share the understanding that overreliance on command-and-control regulation may be ineffective (de Búrca and Scott 2006). Over the past five decades, top-down rules and adversarial enforcement—the hallmark of command-and-control—have often failed to achieve their intended goals of increasing compliance and, at times, have been counterproductive in regulating private industry. In particular, as technology and production methods change rapidly, addressing all the risks of production and work through universal standards is virtually impossible (Braithwaite 1985; Kagan and Scholz 1984; Bardach and Kagan 1982). Often, regulatory rules are too complex, markedly vague, needlessly detailed, or simply unsuited to fit the realities of the new economy (McGarity and Shapiro 1993). Moreover, the nature of production, commerce, work, and other risks has changed in various ways (Lobel 2003). Rapid technological changes as well as unpredictable strains of heightened competition require flexibility and constant adaptation. In the context of regulating work relations, for example, adopting more contingent, flexible, lean, and outsourced employment is a major trend of today's labor market, which has presented new realities in employment relationships. Increased diversity in production and workforces, the move to higher technology production in some sectors, a shift from goods to services, and a decrease in the percentage of workers employed in stable full-time jobs all further exacerbate the challenges for national regulation. The heterogeneity of the workforce and the workplace has made it more difficult for a centralized government agency to promulgate rules that will fit all firms (Osterman et al. 2001).

Among the recent regulatory approaches designed to enhance industry cooperation and self-regulation are the provision of more information and a focus on institutional design and internal compliance processes. Regulation is understood as interdisciplinary problem-solving (Simon 2006). Government agencies encourage transparency, participatory dialogue between industry actors, and inclusive decision-making processes (Lobel 2004). Cooperation instead of adversarialism has become the motto of administrative agencies in the past decade:

> Under the traditional regulatory model, industry and private individuals are the object of regulation. Their agency is limited to choosing whether to comply with the regulations to which they are subjected. Information flows selectively to the top while decisions flow down, following rigid parameters, and leaving decision making to a small, detached group of number-crunching experts. Consequently, the [C&C] regulatory model promotes adversarial relations, mutual distrust, and conflict....In a cooperative regime, the role of government changes from regulator and controller to facilitator, and law becomes a shared problem-solving process rather than an ordering activity. (Lobel 2004)

Instead of focusing on substantive prohibitions and adversarial enforcement, new governance approaches attempt to involve private parties in the legal process. Thus, in place of extensive elaboration of prohibitive standards and high rates of inspection, government facilitates self-regulation and programs of collaborative, semi-voluntary compliance. New governance views adversarial relations as having the potential to reduce firms' willingness to share information and to collaborate with the agency in mutually beneficial problem-solving. Centralized command systems—whether by government agencies or within the hierarchy of private firms—entail social costs. In particular, centralized systems of control can indicate mistrust. Indeed, empirical evidence suggests that the structure of an organization has a significant impact on the likelihood that individuals will engage in unlawful behavior (Arlen and Kraakman 1997; Greenwood 2004; Prendergast 1999; Vaugh 1982). New governance theory therefore encourages government agencies to foster a culture of compliance within regulated industries. Under the new governance model, the agency, when feasible, asks the regulated private companies to identify problems and risks and to continuously reflect on possible solutions—effectively, to self-regulate. In turn, the agency offers consultation and assistance. Agencies also offer practical and reputational rewards through safe havens, variance accommodation, and public certification of responsible practices.[3] To allow continuous improvement through corporation self-monitoring, agencies frequently phrase their regulations as norms rather than rigid rules. In fact, these regulations are often deliberately ambiguous. Instead of regulating the details of behavior, agencies increasingly use broad policy goals such as "risk management" and allow the regulated industries to implement and interpret these mandates (Bamberger 2006). For example, regulators might require actors to give reasons or set their own reflexive processes, self-monitoring, self-checks, reason-giving requirements, and preventative measures such as training, data collection, and continuing education.

New governance initiatives also build on the insight that law has a norm-generating expressive value in addition to its direct control over individuals and corporations. The law offers principled reasons and justifications for action beyond its direct tangible prohibitions and results (Sunstein 1996). In other words, the regulatory regime creates a relational contract between government and industry that in turn supports the generation of private norms (McMaster and Sawkins 1996).

3. Soft Law, Reflexive Law and Regulatory Governance Around the World

Regulatory governance thinking has emerged as a transatlantic exchange and diffusion of ideas. In Europe, Gunther Teubner explicitly links his writing to the idea of democratic experimentalism and the related ideas of a "directly deliberative polyarchy."[4] Similarly, the concept of reflexive law notably informs directly and indirectly those identified with the experimentalist literature (Baxter 1998). For example, Michael Dorf, co-author of *A Constitution of Democratic Experimentalism* (1998), has recently described political scientist Jean Cohen's account of reflexive law (2002), which builds on, and partly modifies, Teubner's theory as "quite similar to what Charles Sabel and I have called 'democratic experimentalism.'" (Dorf 2003: 386). Dorf calls for "an amended account of reflexive law in which data drawn from experience at the relatively local level are continually refined and transmitted to the relatively central standard-setter, which uses the data continually to update the standards all must meet. This amended account is accordingly both top-down and bottom-up" (ibid.: 384). The common theme is the shift to debates about policy through design and the pluralization of forms of public action. The focus is on institutional architecture and the relationships among private and public actors, rather than on the substantive prescription of state legislation, rules, and judicial decisions. Questions about the balance between central coordination, monitoring, and bottom-up reflexivity are at the core of the debates about new governance, and there is still much on the agenda to be deliberated and learned through research and action.

In Europe and in the international arena, new governance has at times been used interchangeably with "soft law." European Union scholar Claire Kilpatrick emphasizes that "soft law is shorthand for 'different from law (in its classical conception),' not 'less than law'" (2005). Moreover, governance processes are often sustained against the background of existing regulatory rules. Even more fundamentally, the very idea of "flexibility" depends on the relative perspective of those affecting and affected by the policy (Lobel 2003). In fact, rather than characterizing the shift to governance as a shift from formal law to informal norms, it is often more accurate to understand new governance initiatives as the formalization of informal practices.

In part, the literature describes new governance as a response to increased globalization. The impact of globalization on national regulation remains heterogeneous. At times, national regulators must adjust to allow greater flexibility and more efficient competitive market production (Agell 1999). At the same time, regulators of less-developed regimes must adjust their standards to incrementally present minimum conditions that fit the norms of the international community. Murphy suggests three possible trajectories: convergence to the lowest common denominator (race to the bottom), persistence of national specificity of regulation, or no race (2002). By and large, the empirical evidence shows that globalization and market integration lead to neither a race to the bottom nor a race to the top. Rather, the impact on national regulation will vary considerably, causing regulatory regimes to remain heterogeneous despite some harmonization (Anderson, Haldrup, and Sørenson 2000). Still, many have argued that in general, the nation-state is significantly less capable in today's economy to govern and regulate markets (Beck 1992). In particular, developing countries have limited abilities to regulate labor conditions, or perhaps they simply have limited economic interest to doing so. Labor standards in developing nations are generally lower than in developed countries, and even minimal international standards are regularly not observed. Thus, it may be that a race to the bottom is most concerning for rapidly industrializing countries (Porter

1999). Globalization has also meant that many large corporations from developed countries operate at a transnational or multinational level, whether through ownership of a foreign subsidiary or by subcontracting core functions of the firm, primarily those of production. These developments further require regulators to better coordinate the levels of regulations from the local to the transnational and focus on the most effective ways of addressing social and economic challenges. Charles Sabel and Jonathan Zeitlin discuss the concept of "experimental governance" later in this book (Chapter 12), which they describe as a transformation of governance occurring at multiple levels beyond the nation-state, partially in response to these types of challenges presented by the conditions of globalization.

4. REGULATORY GOVERNANCE AND SOCIAL ENFORCEMENT

In the aftermath of Enron and other recent corporate scandals, Securities and Exchange Commission Chairman William Donaldson declared that "the most important thing that a Board of Directors should do is determine the elements that must be embedded in the company's moral DNA, as one might call it."[5] As regulators increasingly rely on concepts of corporations' organizational DNA to promote reflexive regulation and self-monitoring, effective law enforcement becomes dependent on an individual's ability and motivation to report illegal conduct. Individual internal dissent is necessary to complement requirements of systematic self-monitoring. The move to new models of governance denotes augmented reliance on the ability of the individual actor to speak within the organization, and at times to report outside the agency to a government regulator when an individual witnesses organizational corruption. This increased reliance on social enforcement—the private action of detecting and reporting illegality—has created a need for legal mechanisms to protect and incentivize whistleblowing. In a series of experimental and theoretical articles, I have argued that if the notion of new governance is to be taken seriously as an effort to diversify the ways workplaces improve work standards, then the balance between exit, voice, and loyalty, to use Hirschman's classic terms, must also be altered (1970).

Reliance on internal grievance procedures has become particularly central to legal rights. Again turning to the context of antidiscrimination law, we can see development in the law's approach to internal prevention, monitoring, and enforcement. In 1998, in two holdings, *Faragher v. City of Boca Raton* and *Burlington Industries v. Ellerth*, the United States Supreme Court held that an employer may assert a two-pronged affirmative defense to claims of sexual harassment, showing

"(a) that the employer exercised reasonable care to prevent and promptly correct any sexually harassing behavior, and
   (b) that the ... employee unreasonably failed to take advantage of any preventative or corrective opportunities by the employer or to avoid harm otherwise."[6]

The Court reasoned that this affirmative defense against a Title VII claim was appropriate because the statute's "primary objective [is] not to provide redress but to avoid harm." A year later, in *Kolstad v. American Dental Association*, the Supreme Court introduced an affirmative defense against Title VII claims for punitive damages when the organization had promulgated antidiscrimination policies and provided antidiscrimination education.[7] The Court again explained that Title VII's primary objective is to prevent rather than remedy harm and, therefore, employers should be encouraged to adopt formal antidiscrimination policies, implement training programs, and inform their employees about antidiscrimination laws.

The principle of "avoidable harm," as developed in these recent discrimination cases, provides insight into how courts encourage employers to systematically implement internal reporting systems. The current legal regime, under which an employer can avoid liability by demonstrating that the employee could have avoided the harm through reasonable effort, stems from tort law, which generally holds that "a victim has a duty 'to use such means as are reasonable to avoid or minimize the damages' that result from violations of the statute."[8] Under these tort principles, courts liberally interpret the reasonableness of the victim's course of action to avoid harm (McCormick 1935). However, the application of the avoidable harm doctrine also indicates the limits of the defense. In *Ellerth*, the plaintiff successfully demonstrated that, although she knew about the employer's antiharassment policy procedures, her conscious decision not to use them was reasonable because a complaint would likely have been futile. *Ellerth* demonstrates that, under some circumstances, internal inaction can be unreasonable. Similarly, in *Sharp v. City of Houston*, the Fifth Circuit held that an employee's failure to report harassment by her supervisor did not absolve the employer of liability because of a prevailing workplace "code of silence."[9] The employer in that case had an unwritten practice that anyone complaining of a fellow worker's misconduct "would suffer such a pattern of social ostracism and professional disapprobation that he or she likely would sacrifice a career."[10]

The "reasonable inaction" principle draws on the fact that, at times, internal reporting is ineffective and entails great costs. At the same time, the EEOC guidelines warn that that an employee could reasonably believe that the employer's internal reporting system was ineffective if "he or she was aware of instances in which co-workers' complaints failed to stop harassment."[11] Similarly, reasonable non-reporting may occur when an employer fails to inform employees about its antiharassment policy and grievance procedures.[12]

New governance approaches to regulation have also appeared in the Federal Organizational Sentencing Guidelines (OSGs), which mitigate a corporation's liability when the corporation can show it has an adequate internal process for reporting wrongdoing (Webb and Molo 1993). The OSGs reduce penalties when a corporation indicates that it has implemented an "effective program to prevent and detect violations of law."[13] At minimum, an effective program includes (1) established standards and procedures that are reasonably capable of reducing the prospect of criminal conduct; (2) oversight by high-level personnel; (3) effective communication of the compliance program to all its employees, including training and the dissemination of published materials; and (4) active monitoring and auditing activities through the institution of a reporting system "whereby employees and other agents [can] report criminal conduct by others within the organization without fear of retribution."[14] Further, the OSGs require the corporation to adequately enforce its compliance procedures, using disciplinary measures and all reasonable steps to correct, prevent, and detect future violations.

The OSGs also recognize that the precise features of the compliance program will vary across different corporations. For example, the larger the organization, the more formal the compliance program must be. The guidelines also describe industry practices as a factor in determining the reasonableness of any particular program. With respect to fines, the OSGs allow up to a 95 percent penalty reduction if the corporation has an adequate compliance program in place. Conversely, the absence of a compliance program can multiply fines up to 400 percent. State courts have also created incentives for corporations to implement monitoring, compliance, and reporting systems. Like the recent developments in implementing principles of new governance to discrimination law, in enacting the OSG framework, the legislature signals that internal problem solving is vital to prevention and that the legal system is willing to reduce liability and penalties in the interest of private structural compliance efforts.

Because new governance relies on the idea of "enforced self-regulation," increased attention must be given to the ability of individuals to speak out against corporate illegality. Like the discrimination and OSG developments, organizations must, more generally under new governance approaches, institute effective procedures for internal dissent.

Ayres and Braithwaite illustrate the regulatory pyramid under a new governance approach where self-regulation constitutes the base of the pyramid and escalated forms of control, command regulation, and punishment constitute the top (1992). Their pyramid structure reflects a regulatory perspective of new governance because it focuses first on private actors' participation in regulation. While self-regulation is the first stage of any organizational problem solving, at the second stage, the regulatory agency negotiates particularized regulations with individual firms, with the threat of a third stage of less tailored and more coercive rules if the firm fails to self-enforce and cooperate with the agency. Similarly, in the context of reporting wrongdoing, a sequenced reporting system will allow organizations to first require their members to report illegal behavior within the internal reporting channels of the company. Only if internal problem solving fails will individuals be allowed to turn to public channels for whistleblowing (Lobel 2008).

New governance thus requires more protection and encouragement of individuals within the organization to point to problems and to engage in active dissent. The legal mechanisms that protect whistleblowers aim to promote responsible practices and counter incentives of concealing misfeasance. The need to react swiftly and flexibly to ever-changing socio-political conditions has led to increased reliance on individual reporting. As a result, developing concepts of accountability emphasize external and vertical controls that are triggered by actors internal to the institution. Whistleblowing protections have expanded in practice over the past few decades. Most notably, following the financial debacles of the new century, the Sarbanes-Oxley Act of 2002 (SOX) significantly strengthened the protections offered to whistleblowers in the context of publicly traded corporations in the United States. Commentators hailed the whistle-blower provision in SOX "the gold standard of whistleblower protection" (Estlund 2005: 376). The tension of promoting internal compliance as a matter of corporate culture, while at the same time ensuring the ability of individuals to speak out against their organization's non-compliance is at the root of the regulatory puzzle. This tension has also led to much uncertainty and diversity in the ways regulators approach whistleblowing laws. A myriad of common law and statutory protections encourage employees to stand up against illegality within their organizations. The subjects of wrongdoing that employees are encouraged by law to report range from public safety and physical health to financial accountability. In the United States, in response to recent corporate scandals where "insiders" revealed illegalities, as at as Enron and WorldCom, both federal and state legislatures have been strengthening whistleblower protections in a variety of statutory protections (Lobel 2008; Kohn, Kohn, and Colapinto 2004). Other countries including England, Australia, New Zealand, and the European Union have similarly been rethinking whistleblower protection laws to ensure detection and deterrence of corporate crime (Schmidt 2005).

Recent experimental studies find that the likelihood and the manner of reporting will vary depending on the type of illegality and is strongly correlated to perceptions of legitimacy, job security, and voice within the workplace (Feldman and Lobel 2008, 2010). The recent research concludes that policy-makers should not treat all misconducts equally when designing enforcement systems. I have argued elsewhere that the corollary to skepticism about government's ability to remedy organizational illegalities or failures is the belief in the ability of individuals within the organization to find ways to solve problems as they arise (Lobel 2008). If government relies more heavily on individuals to prevent improper behavior, then the need for legal protections for whistleblowing increases. Looking at potential conflicts between the value of organizational loyalty and citizenship loyalty, I suggested a companion pyramid to the Ayres and Braithwaite responsive regulation pyramid, which has become central to the new governance literature (Lobel 2008; Ayres and Braithwaite 1992). According to the reporting pyramid (see Figure 5.1), reporting illegality should ideally begin within the organization, and escalate all the way to the biggest guns of external enforcers if and when internal reporting internally becomes ineffective. Thus, the reporting pyramid begins with internal confrontation through the chain-of-command channels, proceeding to internal formal grievance and monitoring systems that promote self-regulation. Only when internal grievance or monitoring systems are absent or suspect of being themselves irresponsive, should the individual be encouraged to turn to regulatory agencies and, in rare cases, the media.

Most regulatory systems have built-in mechanisms designed to promote legal compliance, but great variation exists among these mechanisms. The variation

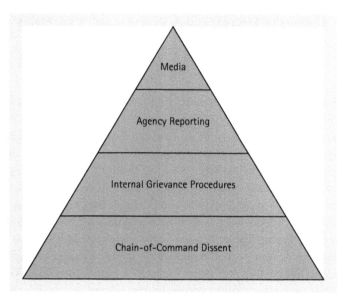

FIGURE 5.1 The reporting pyramid.
Source: Lobel 2008.

among these regulatory mechanisms and incentives is immense. A recent empirical study designed to study the interplay between internal and external enforcement motivation suggests that when non-compliance is likely to trigger strong internal ethical motivation, offering monetary rewards may be unnecessary or, worse yet, counterproductive (Feldman and Lobel 2010). In such circumstances, where legal violation is generally perceived as morally offensive, creating a duty to report may be sufficient. Invariably, reporting illegal behavior in complex organizations requires the resolution of deep tensions. Good governance requires loyalty, organizational accountability, and internal problem solving. At the same time, whistleblowing requires an individual to supersede immediate authorities, even in contexts of sensitive information.

The idea that we need to increase individual voice within the organization is consistent with the move away from traditional command and control. John Stuart Mill spoke of the leader who has "sought for objections and difficulties, instead of avoiding them" (1921: 12). Studies confirm that people generally prefer to confront illegal behavior from within their organization, rather than reporting externally, if they believe such action will be effective. Moreover, when they view the non-compliance as highly unethical, aligning their moral and legal obligations, the choice of regulatory design is less significant. It is when non-compliance becomes more ambiguous or trivial that social enforcement becomes increasingly dependent on optimal external incentives.

5. Conclusion and directions for future research

Law and regulation are mainly problem-solving ventures. Both public and private ordering are imperfect and prone to various biases and systemic failures. The field of new governance explores empirically and calls normatively for improved regulatory design and a shift from command-and-control regulation to more collaborative public–private standard setting. The new governance school of thought represents a synthesis of the emerging theories and entails a plurality of rationales and expression. There is still much to be studied in the realm of legal process and policy design. How do traditionally separate stages of the legal process—legislation, rule-making, implementation, enforcement, adjudication—that have traditionally been kept separate under different governmental branches, departments, and procedures become more dynamic and interdependent? What are the conditions that are most likely to trigger shifts to governance-based approaches? What are contemporary success stories of governance-in-action?

Critical thinkers have long explored the ways that the pluralization of legal and social concepts can expand our imaginative spectrum. Rather than a monolithic concept, "regulation" as a theoretical concept and operational project benefits from the innovative work of governance scholars. No particular collective action process can promise results that follow a priori logic. However, given the current climate of strong disillusionment about the potential of law to effect social change, a shift in the default assumptions about the range of public solutions is a positive development. The departure from a certain set of conventional antagonistic moves in the debates about public policy and the new intellectual energy surrounding the new governance paradigm broadens the range of responses available to lawyers and policy-makers concerned with just and equitable social arrangements.

New governance approaches aim to bring together insights from interdisciplinary research on regulation and the changing demands of a new global economy. Increasingly, legislators, administrators, and courts draw on research from a range of fields to make regulation more effective and sustainable. In a recent article on the role of behavioral economics in the study of regulation, my collaborator and I commented that "[t]he bridge between new governance scholarship and behavioral economics points to future directions for interdisciplinary research. In order to continue applying behavioral insights to create smart and lean policy, more integrated research is required" (Amir and Lobel 2008: 2135). Connecting the insights of experimental psychology and behavioral economics to concrete policy challenges allows regulators to design more effective mechanisms. Alongside behavioral economics, which studies individual behavior, judgment, and decision-making, the fields of organizational behavior and the sociology of institutions provide lessons for regulators about the impact of internal processes on compliance.

As emphasized throughout the chapter, cooperative programs should not be confounded with "deregulation" or "libertarian" non-coerciveness. Regulatory governance calls for a sophisticated analysis and a deep understanding of the comparative advantages between and the dynamic interaction between private and public action in solving social problems. It challenges traditional debates that posit top-down legal rules versus market-based approaches. Most importantly, it illuminates the multiple stages and possibilities within the legal process including standard setting, implementation, compliance, and enforcement and the ways that government can diversify its interaction with regulated parties to bring about more effective and legitimate governance.

NOTES

* The author wishes to thank David Levi-Faur and Cindy Estlund for their valuable insights and Jessica Hartling for her excellent research assistance.
1. Arlen and Kraakman (1997) show how imposing different levels of liability upon firms can influence company culture and employee behavior. Feldman and Lobel (2008) demonstrate the impact of institutional processes on individual decisions about whether to blow the whistle on illegality. Prendergast (1999) illustrates that agents' behavior changes with incentives.
2. On the two oppositional orthodoxies, see, for example, Philippe Nonet and Philip Selznick, who described "the model of rules" as the "ethos of modern bureaucracy" (1978: 64). Herman Schwartz, like many others, describes an "anti-government ethos" that emphasizes privatization and deregulation (1995).
3. An argument that adversarial regulatory frameworks cannot fully utilize these long-term incentives as a means of increasing compliance is found in Lobel 2005. For a description of how market-based incentives may lead some industries to provide agencies with information that they normally would not reveal, see Freeman and Farber 2005.
4. Cohen and Sabel 1997.
5. W. Donaldson, Remarks Before the Economic Club of New York, May 8, 2003.
6. *Faragher v. City of Boca Raton*, 524 U.S. 775, 807 (1998); *accord Burlington Indus., Inc. v. Ellerth*, 524 U.S. 742, 765 (1998).
7. Kolstad v. Am. Dental Ass'n, 527 U.S. 526, 545–546 (1999).
8. *Faragher*, 524 U.S. at 806.
9. 164 F.3d 923, 935 (5th Cir. 1999).
10. *Id.* at 931.
11. U.S. Equal Employment & Opportunity Comm'n, Enforcement Guidance: Vicarious Employer Liability for Unlawful Harassment by Supervisors (1999), *available at* http://www.eeoc.gov/policy/docs/harassment.html (accessed May 14, 2010).
12. *Harrison v. Eddy Potash, Inc.*, 248 F.3d 1014, 1027–8 (10th Cir. 2001); *Boyd v. Snow*, 335 F. Supp. 2d 28, 36 (D.D.C. 2004); *Booker v. Budget Rent-A-Car Sys.*, 17 F. Supp. 2d 735, 747–8 (M.D. Tenn. 1998).
13. *U.S. Sentencing Guideline Manual* § 8A1.2 cmt. n.3(k) (2001).
14. *Id.* § 8A1.2 cmt. n.3(k)(5).

REFERENCES

Agell, T. 1999. On the benefits from rigid labor markets: norms, market failures and social insurance. *The Economic Journal* 109: 143–164.

Amir, O. and Lobel, O. 2008. Stumble, predict, nudge: how behavioral economics informs law and policy. *Columbia Law Review* 108: 2098–2139.

Anderson, T. M., Niels, H., and Sorenson, J. R. 2000. Labor market implications of EU product market integration. *Economic Policy*, 15(30): 107–133.

Arlen, J. and Kraakman, R. 1997. Controlling corporate misconduct: an analysis of corporate liability regimes. *New York University Law Review* 72: 687, 692–693.

Ayres, I. and Braithwaite, J. 1992. *Responsive Regulation: Transcending the Deregulation Debate.* Oxford and New York: Oxford University Press.

Bamberger, K. A. 2006. Regulation as delegation: private firms, decision-making, and accountability in the administrative state. *Duke Law Journal* 56: 377, 380.

Bardach, E. and Kagan, R. A. 1982. *Going by the Book: The Problem of Regulatory Unreasonableness.* Philadelphia: Temple University Press.

Baxter, H. 1998. Autopoiesis and the "relative autonomy" of law. *Cardozo Law Review* 19: 1987.

Beck, U. 1992. *Risk Society.* London: Sage.

Braithwaite, J. 2000. The new regulatory state and the transformation of criminology. *British Journal of Criminology* 40: 222–228.

———. 1985. *To Punish or Persuade: Enforcement of Coal Mine Safety.* Albany: State University of New York Press.

——— and Drahos, P. 2000. *Global Business Regulation.* Cambridge: Cambridge University Press.

——— 2002. *Regulating Intimacy: A New Legal Paradigm.* Princeton: Princeton University Press.

Cohen, J. and Sabel, C. F. 1997. Directly-deliberative polyarchy. *European Law Journal* 3: 313–340. First published online 16 December 2002, doi 10.111/1468-0386.0034.

de Búrca, G., and Scott, J. (eds.) 2006. *Law and New Governance in the EU and the US.* Oxford: Hart.

Döhler, M. 2011. Regulation. In *The Sage Handbook of Governance*, ed. M. Bevir. Los Angeles and London: Sage, 524 n. 4.

Dorf, M. 2003. The domain of reflexive law. *Columbia Law Review*, 103: 384, 386.

———. 2003. Legal indeterminacy and institutional design. *New York University Law Review* 78: 875, 960.

——— and Sabel, C. F. 1998. A constitution of democratic experimentalism. *Columbia Law Review* 98: 267, 322.

Estlund, C. 2005. Rebuilding the law of the workplace in the era of self-regulation. *Columbia Law Review* 105: 319, 376.

Feldman, Y. and Lobel, O. 2008. Behavioral versus institutional antecedents of decentralized enforcement in organizations: An experimental approach. *Regulation & Governance* 2: 165, 171–181.

——— and ———. 2010. The incentives matrix: the comparative effectiveness of rewards, liabilities, duties and protections for reporting illegality. *Texas Law Review* 87: 1151.

Freeman, J. and Farber, D. A. 2005. Modular environmental regulation. *Duke Law Journal* 54: 795.

Green, T. K. 2005. Work and discrimination. *California Law Review*, 93: 623–50.

Greenwood, D. J. H. 2004. Enronitis: why good corporations go bad. *Columbia Business Law Review* 2004: 773.

Hirschman, A. O. 1970. *Exit, Voice, and Loyalty.* Cambridge, MA: Harvard University Press.

Kagan, R. A., and Scholz, J. T. 1984. The criminology of the corporation and regulatory enforcement strategies. In *Enforcing Regulation*, ed. K. Hawkins and J. M. Thomas. Boston: Kluwer-Nijhoff.

Kilpatrick, C. 2005. New EU employment governance and constitutionalism. In *Law and New Governance in the EU and the US*, ed. de Burca and Scott. Oxford: Hart Publishing, 121–151.

Kohn, S., Kohn, M., and Colapinto, D. 2004. *Whistleblower Law: A Guide to Corporate Legal Protections and Procedures*. Westport, CT: Praeger.

Levi-Faur, D. 2005. The global diffusion of regulatory capitalism. *Annals of the American Academy of Political and Social Science* 598: 12–32.

Lobel, O. 2004. The renew deal: The fall of regulation and the rise in governance in contemporary legal thought. *Minnesota Law Review* 89: 342–470.

——— . 2003. The slipperiness of stability: the private employment agency and flexible work arrangements. *Texas Wesleyan Law Review* 10: 109.

——— . 2003. Orchestrated experimentalism in the regulation of work. *Michigan Law Review* 101: 2146–62.

——— . 2005. Interlocking regulatory and industrial relations: the governance of workplace safety. *Administrative Law Review* 57: 1071, 1090–1092.

——— . 2007a. The paradox of extra legal activism. *Harvard Law Review* 120: 937–88.

——— . 2007b. Rethinking traditional alignments: privatization and participatory citizens. In *Progressive Lawyering, Globalization and Markets: Rethinking Ideology and Strategy*, ed. C. Dalton. Buffalo, NY: William S. Hein & Co., 209–232.

——— . 2008. Citizenship, organizational citizenship and the laws of overlapping obligations. *California Law Review* 97: 433–499.

McCormick, C. T. 1935. *Handbook on the Law of Damages*. St Paul: West Publishing Co.

McGarity, T. O., and Shapiro, S. A. 1993. *Workers at Risk: The Failed Promise of the Occupational Safety and Health Administration*. Westport, CT: Praeger.

McMaster, R., and Sawkins, J. W. 1996. The contract state, trust distortion, and efficiency. *Review of Social Economy* 54: 145, 149–156.

Mill, J. S. 1921. *On Liberty*. London and New York: Longmans, Green, and Co.

Murphy, D. 2002. The business dynamics of global regulatory competition. In *Dynamics of Regulatory Change: How Globalization Affects National Regulatory Policies*, ed. D. Vogel and R. Kagan. Berkeley: University of California Press, 84–117.

NeJaime, D. 2009. When new governance fails. *Ohio State Law Journal* 70: 323, 342.

Nonet, P. and Selznick, P. 1978. *Law and Society in Transition: Toward Responsive Law*. New York and London: HarperTorch Books.

Osterman, P., Kochan, T., Locke, R., and Piore, M. 2001. *Working in America: A Blueprint for the New Labor Market*. Cambridge and London: The MIT Press.

Porter, G. 1999. Trade competition and pollution standards: "race to the bottom" or "stuck at the bottom"? *Journal of Environmental Development* 8: 133–151.

Prendergast, C. 1999. The provision of incentives in firms. *Journal of Economic Literature* 37: 7.

Schmidt, M. 2005. Whistle-blowing regulation and accounting standards enforcement in Germany and Europe: an economic perspective. *International Review of Law and Economics* 25: 143–168.

Schwartz, H. 1995. Do economic and social rights belong in a constitution? *American University Journal of International Law and Policy* 10: 1233, 1235.

Simon, W. 2006. Toyota jurisprudence: legal theory and rolling rule regimes. In *Law and New Governance in the EU and the US*, ed. G. de Búrca and J. Scott. Oxford: Hart, 37–64.

Solomon, J. M. 2008. Law and governance in the 21st century regulatory state. *Texas Law Review* 86: 819, 820.

Sturm, S. 2001. Second generation employment discrimination: a structural approach. *Columbia Law Review* 101: 448, 555.

Suk, J. C. 2006. Antidiscrimination law in the administrative state. *University of Illinois Law Review*: 405, 450–451.

Sunstein, C. R. 1996. On the expressive function of law. *University of Pennsylvania Law Review* 144: 2021–2022.

Vaughn, D. 1982. Toward understanding unlawful organizational behavior. *Michigan Law Review* 80: 1377.

Webb, D. K. and Molo, S. F. 1993. Some practical considerations in developing effective compliance programs: a framework for meeting the requirements of the sentencing guidelines. *Washington University Law Quarterly* 71: 375, 378, 390.

CHAPTER 6

GOVERNANCE: AN INTERDISCIPLINARY PERSPECTIVE

PEER ZUMBANSEN*

1. INTRODUCTION

GOVERNANCE, often conceived as an opposite to "government," occupies an ambivalent place in past and present discourses on political (or legal or economic) order and society. Its ambiguity is largely owed to the relative openness of the concept on the one hand and the resulting challenges of neatly demarcating it from other concepts on the other. Governance appears in such a variety of contexts, uses, and functions that it might almost appear of little use as a key notion in contemporary and ongoing social research. But, inspired by the challenge of the similarly intriguing and provocative term "globalization" and its reception in scientific discourse particularly over the last two decades, this chapter seeks to respond to this challenge by addressing the non-finite substantial content and formal/institutional fluidity of the concept of governance through a series of investigations from the standpoint of different disciplinary frameworks. What connects these investigations is an overarching element, which is inherent to each discipline's respective treatment and use of the concept, namely that governance depicts more an empty, still-to-be-defined space for conceptual clarification than a clearly identifiable political construct, institutional framework, or historical period.

As a consequence, all engagement with the concept—as reflected in each of the disciplines touched upon in the following pages—must appear transitional and contentious in nature. Governance points to a reorientation of the language used by a discipline to address architectures of order, hierarchies of norms and values, organizational principles as well as distinct competences and authorities from an uncertain and evolving vantage point. Crucially, governance exposes the tedious relationship between form and substance, which is the paradoxical, mutually irreducible relation between organizational architecture and normative justification and legitimacy. This exposure is perceived differently in each discipline and at different times. While, for example, "governance discourses" in disciplines such as political philosophy or law appear to be closely associated with questions of choice, hierarchy, polarity, conflict or dispute, in other disciplines—say, economics—governance captures above all the experimental and tentative character dimensions of ordering (Williamson 2005). Both these contestable and experimental dimensions of the concept underscore its importance in our present imagination. Governance breaks down boundaries between otherwise distinct discourses, disciplines and theories of order and calls the hitherto employed reference frameworks into question. In cutting across disciplinary boundaries and by reaching deep into the learned semantics of conceptualizations of order, governance signals a fundamental transformation in the communication about the determinants of ordering, including its political, legal, economic, religious nature. The significance of the term lies in its horizontal and vertical irritation of disciplinary discourse as it forces us, on the one hand, to think about the connections between "different" analytical and conceptual frameworks and, on the other, to take seriously the exhaustion of individual disciplines' vocabulary and established patterns of construction. The key to understanding governance then lies in accepting its interdisciplinary and transformative natures.

2. GOVERNANCE: FORM AND SUBSTANCE

The emergence of "globalization studies" in the last two decades of the twentieth century draws attention to the translation challenges facing social studies that had for the longest time been developing their analytical and conceptual toolkit in the context of particular, historically evolved political orders. Despite ubiquitous historical and present evidence of pre-state political order and non-state-based legal regulation such as standardization and private governance, the mindset of the majority of many Western social sciences—with the exception of, say, anthropology—seemed to be shaped by the Westphalian Order since 1648. This context is, at least in part, responsible for the fact that many social sciences today promptly contrast and differentiate the term governance from constructs of (state-based) government. Newly emerging conceptualizations of non-state-based, private or hybrid forms of political and legal order count among the significant traits of the fast proliferating study of globalization (Drahos and Braithwaite 2001; Cutler 2003). In a surprising, almost matter-of-fact way, the national, global or transnational spatial confines of this theorizing has begun to overlap and fuse. Governance, now, is associated with and explained by reference to globalization processes. As a result, *global governance* has become the definitive theoretical-conceptual challenge for scholars still scrutinizing the shift "from government to governance" against the background of a radical transformation of the Weberian rational state, the ensuing post-interventionist paradigm and the relativization of territorial and institutional frameworks.

This raises the question whether governance is merely a bridging concept between state- and non-state-based theories of political-legal order or whether it has further normative dimensions. The introductory sections of the chapter have argued that governance consists of these two sides simultaneously. In the attempt to address the "politics" of international financial institutions such as the World Bank, the World Trade Organization or the International Monetary Fund, but also of transnational, hybrid and networked governance processes, references to governance overwhelmingly serve the purpose of highlighting the troubling, unresolved questions of legitimacy from the viewpoint of political philosophy (Ruggie 1982), democratic theory (Habermas 2008; Held 2004) and, certainly, law (Kingsbury, Krisch, and Stewart 2005; Harlow 2006). The term has frequently been used to highlight the stark discrepancies between established traditions of political institutional frameworks on nation-state level and the fragmentary elements of world government on the global scale. Mirroring this national-global interface are the continuing methodological efforts to invigorate the legal imagination around "global constitutionalism" and "global administrative law" (Walker 2010; Ladeur, 2011; Somek 2011). Meanwhile, the dramatic expansion of global markets for goods, services and capital, spurred by governmental competition in a the "race to the bottom," makes the absence of "domesticating" forms of democratic deliberation and control painfully felt. With the overarching political goal of "good (global) governance," the distributional effects of the new rules that govern globalized markets remain largely unscrutinized (Rittich 2005; Picciotto 2008).

To be sure, governance had become a key notion in contemporary social studies and economics well before the interest in the study of "globalization" as such. The transformation of the Western welfare state in the latter half of the twentieth century is marked by a significant transformation of the role of the state in the establishment and provision of formerly "public" services. In this context, governance has emerged as "theory, practice and dilemma" (Bevir 2010), capturing a multidimensional challenge to conceptual but also very practical approaches to societal order. "Governance is about the constantly shifting and contingent nature of practical political activity." (Bevir 2010: 11). Hardly any term can capture this ambiguous overlap of procedural analysis and substantive assessment of the changing grounds of legitimacy better than the notion of "accountability." This very notion has become front and center of a diversified inquiry into evolving forms and institutions of regulation, not least due to its ambiguous nature. In the context of a pluralized and transnational regulatory landscape, where normative and institutional hierarchies have been displaced by heterarchic, fragmented, and competing spheres of deliberation and rule-production (Calliess and Zumbansen 2010), accountability emerges as the audacious answer to questions of both formal and substantive coherence. In other words, where the grounds of legitimacy have become either questionable or contested, accountability promises the re-establishment of a quasi-legitimating foundation of order, without having to answer to any distinct question of substantive grounding.

Attempts to re-embed this governance-through-accountability approach in the nation-state must remain temporary and contingent at best. Competing impressions of a "retreat" (Strange 1996) or "return" of the state (Jessop 2007) as well as of the "dena-tionalization" of regulatory processes over the past decades (Sassen 2003) have opened important vistas on the impressive role still played by the state in regulation and admin-istration (Harlow 2009). Legal theoretical and sociological depictions of the emergence of "responsive" and "reflexive" modes of law in a regulatory context marked by privatiza-tion, deregulation and contractualization (Teubner 1983; Willke 1999) are importantly complemented by political science studies: the here detected "waves of governance" reveal a significant, continuing—if altered (in form and structure)—regulatory presence of the state. In the "network governance model" of dispersed public power, the state depends on and interacts with a "vast array of spatially and functionally distinct net-works composed of all kinds of public, voluntary, and private organisations" (Rhodes Chapter 3, this volume: 34; Ladeur 2010). The ensuing wave of "metagovernance" is marked by a moderating, informally and indirectly acting state, which has been central to the operation of neoliberal market governance in the latter part of the twentieth cen-tury (Aman Jr. 2007), before giving way to the present wave of "decentred governance," marked by a refocusing on the individual actors in a radically de-hierarchized and trans-nationalized regulatory landscape. The present wave is marked by the contingency and contestability of narratives through which form and substance of governance are described (Rhodes Chapter 3, this volume: 39), and by increasingly interdependent and intertwined processes of transnational norm-production (Black and Rouch 2008; Zumbansen 2010).

In order to appreciate this decisive conceptual and political shift, it is important to reflect on the constitutional order which preceded it. Over the course of the twentieth century, scholars were scrutinizing Max Weber's earlier insights into the facilitative and functional significance of legal rules for an increasingly complex society (Weber 1978: ii, 882 ff), and the rule of law became a central notion in Western democratic and legal the-ory. The "form" of the Rule of Law became associated with rules and procedures pertain-ing to the exercise of democratic participation, political decision-making and control of government (Grimm 1991). Meanwhile, its evolving, shifting and never stable "substance" became expressed, for example, through the formulation of programmatic goals ("social welfare"—"social equality"—"solidarity," etc.) or the adjudication of civil liberties, first as "negative" rights as a protection against state "intervention" into individual (or, collec-tive) rights positions, and then, as "positive rights," as claims *against* the state to provide services, subsidies or institutional guarantees for the exercise of societal freedom (Böckenförde 1991; Grimm 1996). The relationship between form and substance has rightly been characterized as one of interdependence, inseparability and paradox: con-stitutional theory has as such always been confronted with the impossibility to isolate "form" from an underlying "substantive" concept and with the need not to fold substance into form and thereby render it empty. In other words, the formal part of the Rule of Law guarantees the substantive openness of the political order, but in order to do so, the "value" of this political openness, which is often times equated with democratic govern-ance, appears as prerequisite (Waldron 2010). To be sure, while the association of the rule of law with "democratic" governance alone does not spell out the entire content of the associated political order (Kelsen 2006; Brunkhorst 2010: 196–197), it represents a commitment to a general concept of democratic rule, unavoidably resting, as it were, on substantive elements of equal participation, representation, and majority rule (Kingsbury 2009: 35).

It comes as no surprise that this recurring ambivalence of the rule of law as caught between form and substance has not only prompted an early anti-formalist and realist critique (Pound 1939; Kennedy 1976), but an even more radical engagement with the relationship among people ("citizens"), institutions ("state," "market[s]") and "things" (Latour 1993). Political ecologists have thus been questioning the merits of tying govern-ance problems to ideas of democracy or to the state. Dissatisfied by what they describe as an "absurdly unrealistic epistomology," such scholars wish to turn away from a focus on "people" and instead towards "issues," or "things" (Latour 2005: 19, 21). Following from this critique, is the rejection of "facts" as objectively observable or merely representative of different and competing viewpoints and interests (Latour 2010: ch. 1). With the carpet pulled away from underneath the self-assured assertions of what should be *done* about a particular set of "facts," the task for governance (including law) becomes one of captur-ing the various, constituting expectations that constitute "facts" as a governance problem (Vismann 2000a: 286; Pottage 1998: 342).

With law, sociology, and political science seemingly enamoured with the rapid growth of complex regulatory instruments "between state and market" since the 1980s, signifi-cant theoretical and eventually very influential governance thinking was done by econo-mists. Interested in a historically minded analysis of economic development (North 1990; North 2005), New Institutional Economics (NIE) focused on the nature of institu-tions constituting modern societies. Building on the idea and theory of "path depend-ency" (David 2011), NIE over time developed a fine-tuned analytical apparatus to study the dynamics between "formal" and "informal" institutions. While formal institutions are associated with existing political frameworks (state, law), informal institutions are made up of societal rules, customs, routines and "social norms" (Williamson 2005).

Remarkably, against the backdrop of state transformation and globalization, NIE has assumed the status of a fully fledged social theory with tremendous theoretical impulses for other fields of social study. Areas such as law and political science have readily adopted NIE's emphasis on "efficient" modes of social regulation while taking more seri-ously non-state, "informal" regulatory sites and instruments. Yet NIE's place within the very influential expansion of "law and economics" into other social studies remains ambivalent, particularly in light of post-financial crisis reassertions of the "role of the state" in market regulation. The awarding of the 2009 Nobel Prize to two outstanding NIE scholars—the economist Oliver Williamson and the political scientist Eleanor Ostrom—should be seen as an important invitation to look beyond a categorical dis-tinction between formal and informal institutions and to inquire deeper into the dynamic relations between both. It is here, where the study of "economic governance" prompts a more vigorous dialogue with (economic) sociologists and legal scholars. While the former have been reopening the debate around Polanyian concepts of disembedded markets (Williams and Zumbansen 2011), the latter are called upon to complement NIE's depictions of formal/informal institutions with longstanding legal theoretical and legal sociological work into non-legal regulation and "legal pluralism," that is the coexistence of state-originating and other society-based norms (Ehrlich 1962; Moore 1973; Berman 2009; Zumbansen 2010).

Insights are outstanding as well from an increasingly intensified engagement of governance scholars with historians, anthropologists, and geographers. In the development of globalization studies the field of history has experienced a significant surge in recent years as a consequence of mostly younger scholars challenging the state-based frameworks of political history in particular. By positing the need to pay closer attention to both the "crossed" (Werner and Zimmermann 2006) and the "transnational" dimensions of historical evolution (Conrad and Osterhammel 2004), these scholars aim at a reorientation or at least an opening of historical research for a perspective, that seeks to take into view the parallels and complementary processes occurring at particular times in various states. They thereby enrich and complement "national" histories with a highly dynamic perspective on the global dimension of historical development.

The contribution of anthropological research to governance studies as well has been significant. Harkening back to groundbreaking work on regulatory patterns in indigenous societies (Mead, Malinowski, Geertz), present-day anthropologists have taken their discipline into the contested spheres of, say, local rights generation (Merry 2006) or transnational commercial activity (Riles 2005). In addition, legal anthropologists have turned to the intricate functional qualities of social "materialities," "facts," and "media" (Vismann 2000b). In search of the code and the driving forces of societal activity, these scholars have been advancing our understanding of the form and challenges of local human rights adversary activity but also of the fine arteries of real/intellectual property or cross-border contract drafting and dispute resolution. Human rights law meets legal pluralism (Wilson 2006), commercial law meets sociology and anthropology (Dezalay and Garth 1996; Garth 2006), legal theory meets literary criticism (Chakrabarty 2007).

Concluding this cursory glance at different disciplinary engagements with the term governance, the field of geography—itself at the intersection of various fields—occupies a crucial place. Critical economic and social geographers long pointed to the complex undercurrents of existing mappings of territories and landscapes, highlighting the laden assumptions and associations accompanying such respective geographical demarcations (Harvey 2005). Two sites of engagement are of particular importance in this regard. One is concerned with the notion of *space* in a globalizing world. Geographers, combining sociology and social theory, have painted richly structured pictures of "global spaces" constituted by sets of human or organizational activity (Knorr-Cetina and Preda 2005) and particular constellations of, for example, power or violence (Foucault and Miskowiec 1986). The prevalence of space over place in these studies is owed to the belief that the former alone can adequately capture the non-territorial and at the same time epistemological dimension of an area that is determined by a particular set of people, activities or ideas (Sassen 2006). A key focus of attention in this regard has been the city. Urban studies scholars, comprised of geographers, sociologists, anthropologists, legal scholars, and cultural theorists (Sassen 1991; Bakan and Blomley 1992; Blomley 2001; Ford 1999; Blank 2006; Valverde 2009), have relentlessly been pushing the borders of their discipline to make sense of an altogether unruly entity. The city, as part of an often hierarchically structured political and administrative framework, has long been the focus of social critique (Benjamin 2002), political sociology (Weber 1921), and democratic theory (Young 1990; Frug 1980) as well as of a critical strand in border-crossing legal, sociological, and geographic inquiry (Bakan and Blomley 1992). On another level, economic geography has been mapping and investigating the connections between "spatial resource allocation" and economic development (Krugman 1998; David 1999), hereby complementing parallel endeavors undertaken by political economists and sociologists who carve out the particular constellations between institutional structure and economic development (Hall and Soskice 2001; Hancké 2009).

3. Blinded by Light? Learning from Inter-disciplinarity

From this interdisciplinary vanguard, the term governance illustrates the contested grounds of engaging with competing models and theorizations of order. More generally, governance points to the tension between state and non-state based conceptualizations of political and social order. This observation alone does not render the concept any tighter, but it allows to fruitfully trace and to exploit the term's openness and its apparent availability not only in different disciplinary discourses, but also within two allegedly distinct frameworks of political, legal and sociological theorizing—"national" and "global." By prioritizing an acceptance of the concept's ambivalence and dynamic character in the context of continuing attempts to define a particular meaning in which references to governance occur, governance becomes a highly adaptable concept for the complex study of evolving regulatory structures today. Governance, then, emerges less as a term, which depicts a territorially or historically identifiable form of political order, but as an expression of uneasiness in the face of the plurality of interpretations, mappings and definitions of its ongoing transformation, thereby constructing a space to further negotiate such pluralities.

As the term governance cuts across different disciplines in illustrating the wide-ranging variations of its use and historical and theoretical embeddedness, the question of purpose of this interdisciplinary foray moves into the foreground. It becomes obvious that the concept shares essential elements with ideas such as justice, sovereignty, or order. Like these, governance expresses a problematic ambivalence, which results from the concept's two core dimensions. On the one hand, the concept can function to merely identify, describe, and capture an existing form and content of order. In that sense, one speaks of the governance system found in organizations such as business corporations or the church or that which marks a particular area of social activity. On the other hand, however, the concept has a fluid dimension, which can be programmatic in nature or bear critical and investigative character.

This tension can be expressed by the juxtaposition of two distinct intra-disciplinary approaches to and uses of the concept. In law, particularly in legal sociology and in areas of public and private law, references to governance point to the transformational character of existing institutional frameworks of order. For public lawyers, governance gives expression to the fundamental shifts in the organization and implementing of public service delivery as well as rule-making (Aman Jr 2007; Vincent-Jones 2006). Governance, in this context, carries the burden of being the construction site for an encompassing reconsideration of the particularly "public" nature of legislation, administration and adjudication. Meanwhile, in private law, governance appears to be an attractive concept to illustrate the larger, systematic dimensions of societal conduct. Governance studies in the contexts, for example, of contract and corporate law are thus concerned with the critical analysis of the otherwise unquestioned assumptions that lead to the classification of an activity as either private or public (Deakin, Lane and Wilkinson 1997; Friedmann 1957).

In other words, the association of an activity as well as of its regulation with either the public or the private sphere appears as a core trait of many references to governance. At a minimum, they indicate the overarching direction of the regulatory thrust of an existing governance form. As an ample illustration, *corporate governance* is a field that held center stage in company law research and policy-making since the early 1990s and is concerned with the interests of all those invested in the business enterprise. Yet, according to the dominant perception, corporate governance is presented as a focus field for company law, which belongs to private law because its regulatory aspiration extends only to the *private* interests channelled through the corporation (Kraakman et al. 2004). The underlying governance mechanism is categorized as a contract or, a *nexus of contracts* tying together the different interests in the corporation (Williamson 1985: ch. 12). The contestation of this dominating thesis occurs largely internally to the theoretical construction of the concept of the business corporation. Positing that the entering and modifying of contractual relations occurs on the basis of assigned rights, critics of the dominating corporate governance model reject the idea of business regulation as a "private" affair (Bratton 1989).

The tension between these two approaches to capturing the nature of corporate governance is powerfully illustrated from an interdisciplinary perspective: from the point of view of NIE, corporate governance is above all a mechanism of private ordering, which is predominantly construed through informal institutions, including the arrangements among the different contractual partners in the corporation. These private arrangements are seen to be embedded in an ideally "non-interventionist" framework of formal rules, including corporate law and securities regulation. NIE's depiction of the coexistence of informal and formal institutions governing the corporation is echoed by the dominant interpretation of US American corporate law as "enabling." According to this view, corporate law is part of an otherwise unfettered realm of "private," commercial self-regulation. At the core of the models forthcoming from NIE as well as from corporate law is the distinct demarcation of the rule-making processes *in* and *around* the corporation from its regulatory environment. While the majority of arrangements created to govern the corporation are allegedly private in nature and distinct from "external" legal intervention, law is associated only with the institutional and regulatory framework, in which the (private) ordering occurs. As a consequence of this model, the process and the substance of the internal organization of the corporation is represented as the result of private, mostly individual choices. These stand in stark contrast to the political pressure exerted on the corporation "from outside," through the state, the "public" or societal interests, altogether demarcated from the shareholder or investor group as so-called "stakeholders."

This example must serve as a stand-in for what must necessarily be a more extensive illustration of how the concept of governance operates to demarcate different levels or spheres of societal activity. From the political scientist's perspective, corporate governance highlights the complex relations between differently conceived levels of action and control. From the vantage point of economic theory, the firm can be perceived as a crucial nodal point of societal innovation and learning (O'Sullivan 2000). This demarcation has significant consequences for the way in which governance is understood in this particular context. The political-sociological demarcation of a private, allegedly informal, more or less non-legal, self-regulatory, and non-political sphere from a public, "interventionist" legal framework underscores the way in which governance can serve as a quasi-neutral observation of boundaries. Meanwhile, organization-theoretical and, particularly, evolutionary depictions of the firm focus on the dynamics of knowledge transfer, selection, variation and retention within and beyond the unit of the corporation (Zumbansen 2011: 142 ff).

From this example, we can easily infer the existence of other comparable instances, in which references to governance obscure more than they serve to lay bare or clarify. Unsurprisingly, references to governance in different areas are regularly met by contesting allusions to the undisclosed political (and other) assumptions of the use of the concept or by an outcry of protest in view of the matter-of-fact employment of the concept to depict changes in political control, democratic accountability with insufficient capacity to challenge these processes from a critical perspective. The use of the concept and the contestation of that use occur without a necessary interdisciplinary element. The relative ambiguity and the already mentioned conceptual openness and lack of definitional clarity of the term subject governance to a host of critiques, which are internal to a given discipline. Meanwhile, it is this set of characteristics which recurs in different disciplinary uses of the concept and underscores its cross-cutting nature. It is this dimension of governance that renders it crucial within contemporary social theory. Rather than merely being an idea which we find in different disciplinary discourses, governance bridges a series of investigations and inquiries across different disciplinary boundaries. Governance, in other words, is essentially interdisciplinary in that it unfolds its ambivalent role—being potentially both affirmative *and* critical—only through the interplay of different disciplinary approaches to a particular regulatory area.

4. GOVERNANCE AS INTERDISCIPLINARY
AND TRANSFORMATIVE CONCEPT

It follows from an interdisciplinary observation that there cannot be a meaningful use or critique of governance, if it is confined to the analytical and theoretical framework of a single discipline. Instead, the meaning of governance must operate within a contestation of boundaries between disciplines. As illustrated in the example of corporate governance, the tension between the legal and the economic modeling of the corporation is fully captured only through the use of the concept. In the very moment that the distinct assumptions, which inform a particular field's approach to governance (and its respective contestations), are placed side by side, the concept emerges as the crucial bridging element that inseparably ties these different approaches together to unfold into a necessarily pluralistic and interdisciplinary understanding. By unraveling the way in which governance is being theorized within different disciplines, the concept underlines the impossibility of merely sticking to the governance concept of one discipline over the other. Rather, any reference to governance now prompts the inclusion of competing disciplinary interpretations of the regulatory challenge from different disciplinary backgrounds into what might have started out as an analysis of the regulatory challenges arising from a particular field (for a particular discipline).

This cross-cutting dimension of governance reflects the natures of the regulatory landscapes which it is meant to address. As seen from the cursory overview of different emerging disciplinary usages of the concept, with which this chapter began, governance has been arising in response to perceived, dramatic changes in the analytical and conceptual toolkit with which a discipline has been theorizing the idea of "order." As was further seen, such changes have been associated with the transformation of state-based regulation within the nation-state as well as with the transformation of state-based sovereignty and rule-making in areas that by their very nature cut across different national boundaries. Oft-cited examples include environmental and security concerns, but also questions of political or social justice (Beck 2009; Held 1995). What connects these allegedly distinct, "global" regulatory challenges (environment, security, international human rights) to those that mostly remain associated with the nation-state (welfare state reform, corporate law reform, tort law reform) is the way in which such areas are in fact different instantiations of encompassing regulatory arenas.

NOTE

*   This chapter was written during my fellowship at the Hanse Institute of Advanced Study, Summer 2010 and in its concluding phase benefited from the vibrant intellectual atmosphere at Massey College in Toronto. I am grateful for comments from Alexandra Kemmerer, David Levi-Faur, Maria Panezi, Alain Pottage, Fenner Stewart, and the participants of the Summer School on 'Kulturtechniken des Rechts', at the Bauhaus University in Weimar, 23–7 August 2010. This chapter is dedicated to Cornelia Vismann.

References

Aman Jr, A. 2007. Law, markets and democracy: A role for law in the neo-liberal state. *New York Law School Review* 51: 801–815.

Bakan, J. C. and Blomley, N. K. 1992. Spacing out: Towards a critical geography of law. *Osgoode Hall Law Journal* 30: 661–690.

Beck, U. 2009. *World at Risk* [orig. German *"Weltrisikogesellschaft"* (Frankfurt: Suhrkamp); Ciaran Cronin, transl.]. Cambridge and Malden, MA: Polity.

Benjamin, W. 2002. *The Arcades Project*. Trans. H. Eiland and K. McLaughlin. Cambridge, MA: Belknap Press of Harvard University Press.

Berman, P. S. 2009. The new legal pluralism. *Annual Review of Law and Social Sciences*: 225–242.

Bevir, M. 2010. Governance as theory, practice and dilemma. In M. Bevir (ed.), *The Sage Handbook of Governance*. Thousand Oaks, CA: Sage, 1–16.

Black, J. and Rouch, D. 2008. The development of global markets as rule-makers: Engagement and legitimacy. *Law and Financial Markets Review*: 218–233.

Blank, Y. 2006. Localism in the global legal order. *Harvard International Law Journal* 47: 263–281.

Blomley, N. 2001. Landscapes of property. In N. Blomley, D. Delaney, and R. T. Ford (eds.), *The Legal Geographies Reader: Law, Power, and Space*. London: Blackwell, 118–128.

Böckenförde, E.-W. 1991. The rise of the state as a process of secularisation. In E.-W. Böckenförde (ed.), *State, Society and Liberty: Studies in Political Theory and Constitutional Law*. Trans. J.A. Underwood. New York and Oxford: Berg, 26–46.

Bratton, W. W. 1989. The "nexus of contracts" corporation: A critical appraisal. *Cornell Law Review* 74: 407–465.

Brunkhorst, H. 2010. Constitutionalism and democracy in the world society. In P. Dobner and M. Loughlin (eds.), *The Twilight of Constitutionalism?* Cambridge: Cambridge University Press, 179–198.

Calliess, G.-P. and Zumbansen, P. 2010. *Rough Consensus and Running Code: A Theory of Transnational Private Law*. Oxford: Hart.

Chakrabarty, D. 2007. *Provincializing Europe: Postcolonial Thought and Historical Difference*. 2nd edition. Princeton, NJ: Princeton University Press.

Conrad, S. and Osterhammel, J. (eds.) 2004. *Das Kaiserreich transnational. Deutschland in der Welt 1871–1914*.

Cutler, A. C. 2003. *Private Power and Global Authority: Transnational Merchant Law in the Global Economy*. Cambridge: Cambridge University Press.

David, P. A., 1999. Krugman's economic geography of development: NEGs, POGs, and naked models in space. *International Regional Science Review* 22: 162–172.

David, P. A. 2011. Path dependence – A foundational concept for historical social science. In P. Zumbansen and G.-P. Calliess (eds.), *Law, Economics and Evolutionary Theory*. Aldershot: Edward Elgar, 88–108.

Deakin, S., Lane, C., and Wilkinson, F. 1997. Contract law, trust relations, and incentives for co-operation: A comparative study. In S. Deakin and J. Michie (eds.), *Contracts, Co-operation, and Competition. Studies in Economics, Management and Law*. Oxford and New York: Oxford University Press, 105–139.

Dezalay, Y. and Garth, B. 1996. *Dealing in Virtue: International Commercial Arbitration and the Construction of a Transnational Legal Order*. Chicago, IL: Chicago University Press.

Drahos, P. and Braithwaite, J. 2001. The globalisation of regulation. *Journal of Political Philosophy* 9: 103–128.

Ehrlich, E. 1962. *Fundamental Principles of the Sociology of Law (orig. published in German as Grundlegung der Soziologie des Rechts, 1913)*. New York: Russell and Russell.

Ford, R. 1999. Law's territory (A history of jurisdiction). *Michigan Law Review* 97: 843.

Foucault, M. and Miskowiec, J. 1986. Of other spaces. *Diacritics* 16: 22–27.

Friedmann, W. G. 1957. Corporate power, government by private groups, and the law. *Columbia Law Review* 57: 155–186.

Frug, G. 1980. The city as a legal concept. *Harvard Law Review* 93: 1057–1154.

Garth, B. 2006. Introduction: Taking new legal realism to transnational issues and institutions. *Law and Soc. Inquiry* 31: 939–945.

Grimm, D. 1991. Der Wandel der Staatsaufgaben und die Krise des Rechtsstaats. In D. Grimm (ed.), *Wachsende Staatsaufgaben – Sinkende Steuerungsfähigkeit des Rechts*. Baden-Baden: Nomos, 291–306.

Grimm, D. 1996. Der Wandel der Staatsaufgaben und die Zukunft der Verfassung. In D. Grimm (ed.) *Staatsaufgaben*. Frankfurt: Suhrkamp, 613–646.

Habermas, J. 2008. A political constitution for the pluralist world society? In J. Habermas (ed.), *Between Naturalism and Religion. Philosophical Essays*. London: Polity, 312–352.

Hall, P. A. and Soskice, D. (eds.) 2001. *Varieties of Capitalism: The Institutional Foundations of Comparative Advantage*. Oxford: Oxford University Press.

Hancké, B. (ed.) 2009. *Debating Varieties of Capitalism: A Reader*. Oxford: Oxford University Press.

Harlow, C. 2006. Global administrative law: The quest for principles and values. *European Journal of International Law* 17: 187–214.

Harlow, C. 2009. The "hidden paw" of the state and the publicisation of private law. In D. Dyzenhaus, M. Hunt, and G. Huscroft (eds.), *A Simple Common Lawyer. Essays in Honour of Michael Taggart*. Oxford, and Portland, OR: Hart Publishing, 75–97.

Harvey, D. 2005. The sociological and geographical imaginations. *International Journal of Politics, Culture and Society* 18: 211–256.

Held, D. 1995. *Democracy and the Global Order*. Cambridge: Polity Press.

Held, D. 2004. Democratic accountability and political effectiveness from a cosmopolitan perspective. *Government and Opposition* 39: 364–391.

Jessop, B. 2007. *State Power*. Cambridge: Polity Press.

Kelsen, H. 2006. *Verteidigung der Demokratie. Abhandlungen zur Demokratietheorie (ed. by Matthias Jestaedt and Oliver Lepsius)*. Tübingen: Mohr Siebeck.

Kennedy, D. 1976. Form and substance in private law adjudication. *Harvard Law Review* 89: 1685–1778.

Kingsbury, B. 2009. The concept of "Law" in global administrative law. *Eur. J. Int'l L.* 20: 23–57.

Kingsbury, B., Krisch, N., and Stewart, R. 2005. The emergence of global administrative law. *Law and Contemporary Problems* 68: 15–61.

Knorr-Cetina, K. and Preda, A. (eds.) 2005. *The Sociology of Financial Markets*. Oxford: Oxford University Press.

Kraakman, R., Davies, P. L., Hansmann, H., Hertig, G., Hopt, K. J., Kanda, H., and Rock, E. B. 2009. *The Anatomy of Corporate Law: A Comparative and Functional Approach*. Oxford and New York: Oxford University Press.

Krugman, P. 1998. What's new about the new economic geography? *Oxford Review of Economics and Politics* 14: 7–17.

Ladeur, K.-H. 2010. Staat und Gesellschaft. Von der liberalen zur postmodernen Gesellschaft. In O. Depenheuer and C. Grabenwerter (eds.), *Verfassungstheorie*. Tübingen: Mohr Siebeck, 599–633.

Ladeur, K.-H. 2011. The evolution of general administrative law and the emergence of postmodern administrative law. *Osgoode Hall Law School CLPE Research Paper Series* 6: SSRN.

Latour, B. 1993. *We Have Never Been Modern*. Trans. Catherine Porter. Cambridge, MA: Harvard University Press.

Latour, B. 2005. From Realpolitik to Dingpolitik, or how to make things public. In B. Latour and P. Weibel (eds.), *Making Things Public: Atmospheres of Democracy*. Cambridge, MA: ZKM Art and Media Centre; Karlsruhe: MIT Press, 14–41.

Latour, B. 2010. *On the Modern Cult of the Factish Gods*. Durham, NC: Duke University Press.

Merry, S. E. 2006. New legal realism and the ethnography of transnational law. *Law and Social Inquiry* 31: 975–995.

Moore, S. F. 1973. Law and social change: The semi-autonomous field as an appropriate subject of study. *Law and Society Review* 7: 719–746.

North, D. C. 1990. *Institutions, Institutional Change and Economic Performance*. Cambridge: Cambridge University Press.

North, D. C. 2005. *Understanding the Process of Economic Change*. Princeton,NJ, and Oxford, UK: Princeton University Press.

O'Sullivan, M. 2000. The innovative enterprise and corporate governance. *Cambridge Journal of Economics* 24: 393–416.

Picciotto, S. 2008. Constitutionalizing multilevel governance? *International Journal of Constitutional Law* 6: 457–479.

Pottage, A. 1998. Instituting property. *Oxford Journal of Legal Studies* 18: 331–344.

Pound, R. 1939. Public law and Private law. *Cornell Law Quarterly* 24: 469–482.

Riles, A. 2005. A new agenda for the cultural study of law: Taking on the technicalities. *Buffalo Law Review* 53: 973.

Rittich, K. 2005. Functionalism and formalism: Their latest incarnations in contemporary development and governance debates. *University of Toronto Law Journal* 55: 853–868.

Ruggie, J. G. 1982. International regimes, transactions, and change: Embedded liberalism in the postwar economic order. *International Organization* 36: 379–415.

Sassen, S. 1991. *The Global City*. Princeton, NJ: Princeton University Press.

Sassen, S. 2003. Globalization or denationalization? *Review of International Political Economy* 10: 1–22.

Sassen, S. 2006. *Territory – Authority – Rights. From Medieval to Global Assemblages*. Princeton, NJ, and Oxford, UK: Princeton University Press.

Somek, A. 2011. Die Verfassung im Zeitalter ihrer transnationalen Reproduzierbarkeit. Gedanken zum Begriff der Konstitutionalisierung. In C. Franzius, F. C. Mayer and J. Neyer (eds.), *Strukturfragen der Europäischen Union*. Baden-Baden: Nomos, 135–149.

Strange, S. 1996. *The Retreat of the State*. Cambridge: Cambridge University Press.

Teubner, G. 1983. Substantive and reflexive elements in modern law. *Law and Society Review* 17: 239–285.

Valverde, M. 2009. Jurisdiction and scale: Legal "technicalities" as resources for theory. *Social and Legal Studies* 18: 139–157.

Vincent-Jones, P. 2006. *The New Public Contracting. Regulation, Responsiveness, Relationality*. Oxford and New York: Oxford University Press.

Vismann, C. 2000a. *Akten. Medientechnik und Recht*. Frankfurt: Fischer.

Vismann, C. 2000b. Jurisprudence: A transfer science. *Law and Critique* 10: 279–286.

Waldron, J. 2010. Constitutionalism: A skeptical view. *New York University Public Law and Legal Theory Research Paper No. 10–87*. Available at http://ssrn.com/abstract=1722771 (accessed 19 September 2011).

Walker, N. 2010. Out of place and out of time: Law's fading coordinates. *Edinburgh Law Review* 14: 13–46. Available at http://ssrn.com/abstract=1367591 (accessed 19 September 2011).

Weber, M. 1921. *The City.* Glencoe: Free Press.

Weber, M. 1978. *Economy and Society*, ed. Guenther Roth and Claus Wittich. Trans. Ephraim Fishoff et al. 2 vols. Berkeley, Los Angeles, London: University of California Press.

Werner, M. and Zimmermann, B., 2006. Beyond comparison: *Histoire croisée* and the challenge of reflexivity. *History and Theory* 45: 30–50.

Williams, C. and Zumbansen, P. 2011. Introduction: corporate governance after the 'end of history': investigating the new 'great transformation'. In C. Williams and P. Zumbansen (eds.), *The Embedded Firm: Corporate Governance, Labor and Finance Capitalism.* Cambridge: Cambridge University Press, 1–12.

Williamson, O. 1985. *The Economic Institutions of Capitalism.* New York and London: Free Press and Macmillan.

Williamson, O. E., 2005. The economics of governance. *American Economic Review* 95: 1–18.

Willke, H. 1999. The contingency and necessity of the state. In D. Baecker (ed.), *Problems of Form.* Stanford: Stanford University Press, 142–154.

Wilson, R. A. 2006. Tyrannosaurus Lex: the anthropology of human rights and transnational law. In M. Goodale and S. E. Merry (eds.), *The Practice of Human Rights: Tracking Law Between the Global and the Local.* Cambridge: Cambridge University Press, 342–369.

Young, I. M. 1990. *Justice and the Politics of Difference.* Princeton, NJ: Princeton University Press.

Zumbansen, P. 2010. Transnational legal pluralism. *Transnational Legal Theory* 1: 141–189. Available at http://ssrn.com/abstract=1542907 (accessed 19 September 2011).

Zumbansen, P. 2011. The New Embeddedness of the Corporation: Corporate Social Responsibility in the Knowledge Society. In C. A. Williams and P. Zumbansen (eds.), *The Embedded Firm: Corporate Governance, Labour and Financial Capitalism.* Cambridge: Cambridge University Press, 119–148.

PART II

THEORETICAL
LENSES

CHAPTER 7

....

GOVERNANCE NETWORKS

....

JACOB TORFING

THIS chapter focuses on the role and character of governance networks, which are defined as networks of interdependent actors that contribute to the production of public governance. Governance networks proliferate at all levels (Marcussen and Torfing 2007) and they play a crucial role in societal regulation. Hence, in the era of regulatory capitalism (Levi-Faur 2005) societal regulation tends to be a result of sustained interaction between key actors from the state, economy, and civil society.

Governance networks both supplement and supplant the traditional modes of governance in terms of hierarchy and markets. Hierarchical forms of government based on unicentric control and command were the backbone of the modern welfare states that developed in most Western countries in the aftermath of World War II. However, the Trilateral Commission's report from 1975 problematized the role of public bureaucracies due to mounting problems in terms of "government overload" and the "ungovernability of society" (Crozier, Huntington, and Watanuki 1975). This bleak diagnosis spurred neoliberal attempts to enhance the role of multicentric markets in public governance. However, the last decades have shown that competitive markets are difficult to create, have a number of unintended effects, and often fail to provide legitimate, innovative, and proactive solutions to collective problems. The recognition of the limits of both hierarchies and markets has paved the way for the surge of pluricentric forms of network governance.

Governance networks are also prone to failure, but—like hierarchies and markets—they have particular strengths and merits that explain the recent surge of governance networks. Consequently, public governance is produced and delivered through shifting combinations of hierarchies, markets, and networks. As such, today, public problem-solving begins with the fundamental question of how hierarchies, markets, and networks should be combined in order to provide an appropriate solution to the problems or challenges at hand.

Over the years, the study of governance networks has become a truly interdisciplinary endeavor (Kersbergen and Waarden 2004). Nevertheless, the research on governance networks is firmly rooted in political theory, public policy studies, implementation stud-ies, and public organization theory. Hence, many political theorists have abandoned the fruitless dispute between state-centric and society-centric theories in favor of the analy-sis of decentered networks of public and private actors (Jessop 2002). Policy analysts have problematized the basic assertions of pluralism and corporatism and have begun to analyze the interaction between the state, economy, and civil society in terms of more or less institutionalized policy networks (Rhodes 1997). Implementation theorists have transgressed the rigid distinction between top-down and bottom-up implementation studies by conducting a backward mapping of the actors involved in the production and implementation of particular policy outcomes (Winter 2006). Finally, organization the-orists have not only discovered that organizations have an external environment, but also realized that this environment consists of other organizations that together form an interorganizational network (Powell and DiMaggio 1983).

The aim of this chapter is to discuss the recent contribution of political science and public policy research toward understanding the role, functioning, and impact of gov-ernance networks, and to explore how such networks can be governed in order to improve their performance. The plan is as follows. Section 1 defines the concept of gov-ernance networks, discusses its empirical manifestations, and flags a few caveats. Section 2 presents competing explanations of the recent surge of governance networks and pro-vides a brief overview of different theories of network governance. Taking seriously the idea that governance networks are prone to failure, Section 3 discusses the meta-govern-ance of governance networks. Finally, the concluding section lists some new and intrigu-ing questions for further research.

1. Defining governance networks

Globalization, the fragmentation of social and political life, the growing number of wicked problems, and the new ideas of how to govern through "regulated self-regulation" make it clear that public agencies cannot govern alone. Indeed, no actor has the knowl-edge, capacity, and authority to regulate society and the economy single-handedly (Kooiman 1993). This assertion has led numerous scholars in North America, Europe, and around the globe to assert that we are witnessing a "transition from government to governance."

The assertion of a transition from government to governance has an important sign-aling value as it urges us to focus on political processes rather than institutional struc-tures when analyzing public policy-making and societal regulation. However, the assertion of a shift from government to governance carries the danger of invoking a far too simplistic image of a unified past and future. As such, it is implicitly assumed that in the past government was omnipotent and that now it has lost its pivotal role. It also car-ries the danger of portraying the relationship between government and governance as a zero-sum game, according to which governance can only expand at the expense of government. For these reasons we should stop talking about a shift from government to governance and instead see governance as a new analytical perspective aiming to comprehend a new and emerging reality where, to an increasing extent, unilateral action on the part of government gives way to multilateral action involving a plethora of public and private actors.

In its most generic form *governance* can be defined as the attempt to steer society and the economy through collective actions and forms of regulation that link values and objectives to outputs and outcomes. Governance can be produced by hierarchies and markets, but it may also be produced by networks of relevant and affected actors. As such governance networks can be seen as a particular mode of governance.

Drawing on the burgeoning research literature, we can define *governance networks* as a horizontal articulation of interdependent, but operationally autonomous, actors from the public and/or private sector who interact with one another through ongoing negotiations that take place within a regulative, normative, cognitive, and imaginary framework; facilitate self-regulation in the shadow of hierarchy; and contribute to the production of public regulation in the broad sense of the term (Sørensen and Torfing 2007). Let us briefly unfold each of these constitutive features of governance networks in turn.

The driving force in the formation of governance networks is the social and political actors' recognition of their *mutual dependence*. Actors with divergent interests will interact if they realize that they need to exchange and/or pool their resources in order to govern. The interdependent actors might cooperate by sharing information, knowledge, and ideas; coordinate their actions in order to enhance efficiency; or collaborate in order to find joint solutions to problems and challenges that are deemed relevant and important. No matter how they interact, the network actors will tend to retain their *operative autonomy* since, because their participation is voluntary and they are free to leave the network, they cannot be forced to think or act in a certain way. The network actors may have different resources and different structural positions in the network that create asymmetrical power relations. Nevertheless, the relations between the actors are horizontal in the sense that no one actor has the power and authority to resolve, single-handedly, the disputes that emerge in the network.

The network actors interact through *negotiations* that might take the form of either interest-based bargaining or deliberation aimed at a common understanding of problems, challenges, and solutions. In hierarchical forms of government, agents are subordinated to their principals, who can govern them through orders and commands. In markets, buyers and sellers are independent and compete with each other in order to buy and sell goods and services at the right price. In governance networks, public and private actors interact through negotiations that involve conflicts, power, and compromise formation.

The network actors come to the networked negotiations with different rule and resource bases and, in the beginning, there is no common constitution that can regulate the negotiations and facilitate decision-making and compromise formation. However, through time, governance networks will tend to become more and more *institutionalized* as regular patterns of interaction are sedimented into norms, rules, cognitive codes, and joint perceptions, and a particular distribution and deployment of resources becomes accepted as legitimate. There can be varying degrees of institutionalization and some networks might aspire to constitute themselves as formal institutions or even as organizations with a unified leadership and command structure. But there will also be processes of *deinstitutionalization* as the network actors contest and renegotiate rules, norms, and perceptions (Olsen 2009).

The attraction and purpose of creating governance networks is most often that the interdependent actors will interact through more or less institutionalized negotiations in order to produce some kind of *self-regulation*. As such, it is assumed that governance networks have a certain capacity for taking authoritative decisions, whether this is a result of delegation or a result of long-lasting battles through which a network has acquired legitimacy, status, and recognition. However, the self-regulatory capacity of networks is always limited and constrained by public authorities that may aim to frame and influence the institutionalized negotiations in networks and often threaten to take over if governance networks fail to deliver. As Fritz Scharpf puts it, governance networks always operate in the shadow of hierarchy (Scharpf 1994) (see also the discussion of meta-governance below).

Finally, the idea is that the institutionalized negotiations between interdependent actors contribute to the production of *public regulation* in the broad sense of common values, standards, scenarios, plans, regulation, and concrete decisions. There might be competing agendas in governance networks and the actors might aim to pursue their own interests, but networks that do not somehow contribute to public governance do not qualify as governance networks.

Governance networks, as defined above, are proliferating, but they are unevenly spread across different scales and levels. While governance networks are frequently formed in relation to national reforms and the formulation and amendment of specific sector policies, the role and impact of governance networks seem to have become even stronger at the local and regional levels where public policies are reformulated and implemented in a networked collaboration between public and private actors. The European Union (EU) is basically a "networked polity" (Kohler-Koch and Eising 1999), in which hard and soft regulation is produced in and through multi-level governance networks. Finally, the current proliferation of governance networks at the global level, where there is no overarching political authority, is remarkable, although it is a more recent phenomenon and intergovernmental negotiations still prevail in most areas.

Governance networks may have different tasks in terms of knowledge-sharing, coordination of action, or joint problem-solving. They may also take different forms as they can either be initiated from above or self-grown from below, intraorganizational or interorganizational, loosely connected or tightly structured, or short-lived or relatively permanent. Last but not least, governance networks are often labeled differently as they are frequently referred to as think tanks, strategic alliances, public boards and committees, commissions, collaborative arenas, planning cells, and so on. The different tasks, forms, and labels of governance networks attest to the broad relevance of the concept for describing the contemporary forms of interactive governance that seem to proliferate in the era of regulatory capitalism.

Having defined governance networks and discussed their spread and variability, it is necessary to flag a few caveats in order to avoid some common misunderstandings. The first caveat is that the surge of governance networks is not, as some scholars have suggested, resulting in a "hollowing out of the state" (Rhodes 1997, 2007; Jessop 2002). The growth of governance networks is not mitigating the role and impact of the state. The state may have lost its privileged position in public policy-making, but many of the former state powers remain in place and new capacities are developed as central and local state agencies take on the task of initiating, managing, and directing governance networks at different levels. As such, state power is not reduced, but transformed and exercised in new and subtle ways (Pierre and Peters 2000). It could even be argued that the proliferation of governance networks strengthens the regulatory capacity of the state by enhancing its reach, mobilizing private resources, and creating joint ownership of new policies.

The second caveat is that governance networks, despite the recent proliferation and the scholarly attention, are not a new phenomenon. In many countries and policy areas there are long-standing traditions for the involvement of the social partners and other relevant actors in the formulation and implementation of policy. Indeed, interaction between public and private actors is a key feature of modern government and a constitutive trait of liberal democracy. What *is* new, however, is that political scientists and central decision-makers increasingly view governance networks as both an efficient and legitimate way of governing of complex and multilayered societies. This is evidenced by the increasing reliance on governance networks within and across all levels of government (Marcussen and Torfing 2007).

The final caveat is that governance networks are no panacea. When it comes to the exercise of public authority such as tax collection and taking children into care, there are good reasons for placing such tasks in the hands of public bureaucracies that can be held accountable for their action and inaction. Likewise, when it comes to the production and delivery of fairly standardized public goods and services such as public roads and meals for the elderly, private markets will often give us the best value for public money. By contrast, governance networks have their ultimate strength in relation to growing number of "wicked problems" where the nature of the policy problem is uncertain, specialized knowledge is needed, and there are many relevant stakeholders and a high risk of conflict (Klijn and Koppenjan 2004).

2. THEORIES OF GOVERNANCE NETWORKS

In the North American context, the surge of governance networks and their growing impact on public policy-making was observed by Hugh Heclo (1978), who found that policy decisions are frequently moved from macro-level policy systems involving the presidency, congressional leaders, the Supreme Court, mass media, and the general public to policy sub-systems in which issue-specific actors from the public and private sectors interact on the basis of interdependency. Later these empirical findings found theoretical support in the work of Elinor Ostrom (1990), who demonstrated how common-pool resources can be regulated through the development of durable cooperative institutions based on interdependency and negotiation rather than hierarchical command and market competition. In Germany, researchers at the Max Planck Institute in Cologne (Marin and Mayntz 1991; Mayntz 1993a, 1993b) and at the Center for Interdisciplinary Research in Bielefeld (Héritier, Knill, and Mingers 1996) explored the systemic limitations of both hierarchies and markets, which prompt the development of new modes of governance based on negotiated interaction. At the same time, British scholars aimed to replace the much celebrated notion of corporatism with a broader notion of policy networks, which includes both relatively tight and exclusive policy communities and relatively loose and inclusive issue networks (Marsh and Rhodes 1992; Rhodes 1997; Marsh 1998). Their Dutch colleagues focused on growing societal and political complexity and uncertainty, and saw the formation of governance networks as a preferred way of tackling these problems (Kickert, Klijn, and Koppenjan 1997; Klijn and Koppenjan 2004). The recent studies of multi-level governance sought to comprehend the vertical and horizontal interaction in federalist and quasi-federalist systems (Bache and Flinders 2004; Scharpf 2001). Last but not least, international relations theorists problematized the realist paradigm that emphasizes the privileged role of nation-states in international politics and explored the advocacy coalitions, epistemic communities, international regimes, and transnational networks that bring together a host of governmental and non-governmental actors (Haas 1992; Sabatier and Jenkins-Smith 1993; Djelic and Sahlin-Andersson 2006).

The researchers who discovered the surge of networks have been preoccupied with describing the constitutive traits of governance networks, demonstrating their advantages vis-à-vis hierarchy and markets, and mapping their empirical functioning and impact in different policy fields and at different levels. The attempt to explain the proliferation of networks has been less outspoken, but to the extent explanations of the surge of governance networks are offered, they tend to fall within three broad categories.

First of all, there are a large number of system-theoretical explanations that claim that governance networks provide a functional response to the growing differentiation, complexity, and multilayered character of modern societies (Mayntz 1993a, 1993b; Kooiman 1993, 2003). New societal developments call for the development of complex networks that can match the complexity of goals and actors. Since the reference to the effects of particular social and political phenomena cannot explain their initial emergence, there are serious flaws in the functionalist explanations of governance networks.

Second, there are a number of explanations that aim to solve this flaw by insisting that the surge of governance networks is a political and strategic response of elected politicians who are concerned with the lack of input and output legitimacy of public policy (Scharpf 1999), public administrators who are operating within a public sector that has been fragmented by New Public Management (NPM) reforms (Rhodes 1997), and private citizens and organized stakeholders who want to play a more active role in public policy-making (Warren 2009). However, these actor-driven explanations run the risk of exaggerating the intentionality behind the rise of governance networks and of forgetting that actors, to a large extent, are responding to collective and institutionalized ideas that define how public administration should be organized.

Finally, there are a few more discursive explanations that tend to view governance networks as a part of new "governmentality" which recognizes the limits of both the traditional forms of hierarchical government and the neoliberal marketization reforms. The new governmentality recommends that society and the economy be governed through new forms of "regulated self-regulation" that combine "technologies of agency"—aiming to construct free, empowered, and responsible agencies—with "technologies of performance"—aiming to shape the free actions of the constructed subjectivities through the production of standards, performance indicators, storylines, and rationalities that seek to ensure conformity to overall policy objectives (Dean 1999).

The three explanations are not mutually exclusive. Societal transformations tend to problematize traditional forms of governance and encourage social and political actors to search for new ways of governing, while positive experiences with more interactive forms of network governance are gradually sedimented into a new collective and institutionalized way of thinking about how to govern and be governed that further accelerates the surge of governance networks.

The attempt to explain the surge of governance networks points to the need for a theoretical framework that can guide the study of the formation, function, and impact of governance networks. There is no commonly accepted theory of governance networks, but it is possible to identify four different theoretical approaches that tend to subscribe to different strands within the new institutionalism (Peters 1999). Let us briefly consider the different approaches in turn, beginning with "interdependence theory" and "governability theory," which are the two main approaches in the study of governance networks. Both theories tend to view social action as driven by institutionally conditioned calculations, but they differ in their view on the prospect for overcoming conflicts and facilitating a smooth coordination among public and private stakeholders.

Interdependence theory is firmly anchored in historical institutionalism (Kickert, Klijn, and Koppenjan 1997; Rhodes 1997; Jessop 1998). It defines governance networks as an interorganizational medium for interest mediation between interdependent, but conflicting actors, each of whom has a rule and resource base of their own. The formation of governance networks enables the social and political actors to find common solutions to joint problems and to counteract the institutional fragmentation caused by NPM reforms. Governance networks are formed through incremental bottom-up processes, but are often recruited as vehicles of public policy-making by public authorities at higher levels (Rhodes 1997). The network actors pursue different interests through internal power struggles, but they are held together by their mutual interdependence and the development of common norms and perceptions, which facilitate negotiation and compromise and tend to modify and transform the interests and objectives of the public and private actors.

Governability theory combines rational-choice institutionalism with a systems-theo-retical view of societal development (Mayntz 1993a, 1993b; Scharpf 1994, 1999; Kooiman 1993, 2003). It defines governance networks as a means for horizontal coordination between autonomous actors who interact in and through different negotiation games. Governance networks are viewed as game-like structures that facilitate negotiated inter-action between actors from different systems and organizations. The actors are held together by the anticipated gains from the exchange and pooling of resources and the development of mutual trust. A proactive creation of incentive structures helps to over-come collective action problems and mitigate conflicts. The result of the self-interested and relatively trust-based interaction is either negative coordination, where the actors aim to steer free of conflicts by making agreements based on the least common denomi-nator, or positive coordination, based on joint problem definitions and common solutions.

"Institutional theories of normative integration" and "governmentality theory" also provide valuable insights into the intricacies of network governance. These theories do not focus explicitly on governance networks, but they conceive governance as a decen-tered process that involves a plethora of public and private actors who are caught up in different kinds of networks. While differing in their emphasis on the role of power and conflict in societal governance, both theories have an interpretative perspective on social action.

Institutional theories of normative integration perceive governance networks as institu-tionalized fields of interaction that bring together relevant and affected actors who become normatively integrated by the emerging rules, norms, and values that together define a logic of appropriate action (March and Olsen 1995; Powell and DiMaggio 1991). Governance networks are regarded as a particular way of organizing and structuring organizational fields (Powell and DiMaggio 1991). They are formed through a bottom-up process whereby actors contact other actors and extend and deepen those contacts that are positively evaluated (March and Olsen 1995). The proliferation of governance networks may also be further accelerated by isomorphic pressures (Powell and DiMaggio 1983). Network actors interact on the basis of a shared logic of appropriate action that shapes their identity and capacities. Conflicts might occur, but they are civilized through the con-struction of solidarity and the formation of democratic identities (March and Olsen 1995).

Governmentality theory (Foucault 1991; Rose and Miller 1992; Dean 1999) implicitly defines governance networks as an attempt by an increasingly reflexive, facilitating, and regulatory state to mobilize and shape the free actions of actors who are interacting in networked arenas. Citizens, non-governmental organizations (NGOs), interest organi-zations, and private enterprises are encouraged to regulate society and themselves within an institutional framework of norms, standards, and calculative practices that ensures conformity with the overall policy objectives. Governance networks are constructed and framed by particular governmental technologies and narratives that aim to recruit social actors as vehicles of the exercise of power. However, if the social actors resist and oppose the normalizing power strategies to which they are subjected, the result is the prolifera-tion of conflicts.

The four theoretical approaches differ in their perception of the nature of social action and in their view of the role of power and conflicts in interactive governance. However, the four approaches all tend to emphasize the role of institutions for stabilizing, structuring, and framing network governance.

The institutional focus enables us to understand the dynamic processes of institutionalization and deinstitutionalization and the trade-off between flexibility and stability. Johan P. Olsen (2009: 199) defines institutionalization as a process that implies increasing clarity, agreement, and formalization of the content, explanation, and justification of behavioral rules, and the allocation, access to, and control over material and immaterial resources. Consequently, deinstitutionalization implies that existing rules and resource distributions are becoming more unclear, contested, and uncertain. Institutionalization helps to stabilize the precarious governance networks so that we can harvest the flexibility gains associated with the relatively informal forms of interactive governance (Milward and Provan 2006: 12). Now, if the degree of institutionalization becomes too high, it will tend to create rigidities and reduce the flexibility gains. Hence, public authorities and other actors capable of governing governance networks should aim to balance the processes of institutionalization and the processes of deinstitutionalization.

3. GOVERNANCE NETWORK FAILURE AND THE ROLE OF META-GOVERNANCE

Governance networks are praised in the research literature for their ability to ensure a well-informed decision-making process, generate innovative solutions, mobilize private resources, handle conflicts, and create joint ownership of bold ideas (Sørensen and Torfing 2007). Nevertheless, there is also a clear risk of governance failure as networks are not formed spontaneously and may lead to stalemate, poor and biased decisions, or directionless consensus. The risk of governance network failure can be reduced by the exercise of meta-governance, defined as "the governance of governance," or, in the case of governance networks, "the regulation of self-regulation" (Jessop 2002). Governance networks should not be left to drift and possibly fail, since reflexive and strategic meta-governance can help to facilitate, manage, and give direction to networked policy processes without reverting to traditional forms of hierarchical command and control (Kickert, Klijn, and Koppenjan 1997; Jessop 2002; Agranoff 2003; Kooiman 2003).

Any actor fulfilling Christopher Hood's so-called NATO-criteria can exercise meta-governance (Hood 1986). Hence, would-be meta-governors must occupy a central position in relation to the governance network in question (Nodality); must be considered as an legitimate actor in the eyes of the network actors (Authority); must have access to and command key resources (Treasure); and must have an organizational capability to monitor and manage networks (Organization). Government agencies at different levels often have what it takes to become a meta-governor, but private actors and networks at a higher level can also assume the role of meta-governors. Sometimes there will even be tough competition between different would-be meta-governors, while at other times meta-governors, either at the same or at multiple levels, complement each other in facilitating, managing, and giving direction to governance networks. A special problem emerges in relation to governance networks at the global level where, in the absence of anything close to a world government, the task of meta-governing governance networks is often exercised by a mixture of hegemonic nation-states and international organizations such as the United Nations and the World Bank.

Since meta-governance is often exercised by public authorities, the concept of meta-governance helps us to understand the role of the state in relation to governance networks. As mentioned above, the state is not "hollowed out" (Rhodes 2007), but plays a key role in shaping and managing interactive arenas of network governance through a combination of institutional design, political and discursive framing, process management and direct participation. The privileged role of the state in the meta-governance of governance networks contributes to ensuring "the primacy of politics" and provides "democratic anchorage" of networked governance.

The crucial challenge to all meta-governors is to avoid the Scylla of over-steering and the Charybdis of understeering. Meeting this challenge requires maintaining a delicate balance between hands-off and hands-on meta-governance (Sørensen and Torfing 2009). Hand-off meta-governance, through institutional design and political framing of networked policy processes, can help to prevent over-steering, which tends to create opposition amongst, or pacify, the network actors. Likewise, hands-on meta-governance, through process management and active participation, can help to resolve internal conflicts and prevent biased decisions that, other things being equal, tend to reduce the role and influence of governance networks.

4. THE FUTURE RESEARCH AGENDA

Governance networks no longer represent something new and exotic; rather, they are an intrinsic part of modern governance and regulation that we must learn to live with and make the best of. This predicament triggers a number of new and yet unanswered questions that define the ever-expanding research agenda of governance network research.

The first question concerns the role of governance networks in *facilitating and enhancing democratic participation*. Sometimes governance networks are captured by experts, political elites, and public agencies, but they may also facilitate civic engagement of interested groups of citizens (Hirst 1994, 2000). In fact, some scholars perceive network governance as a form of participatory governance that aims to connect state and civil society (Grote and Gbikpi 2002). Focusing on the participatory aspect of networks raises a series of questions concerning which actors are participating in different networks at different levels (Marcussen and Torfing 2007), the role of institutional design in stimulating participation (Smith 2005), and the empowerment effects arising from participating in governance networks (Sørensen and Torfing 2003).

The second question concerns *the role of discourse and storylines* in unifying policy networks and shaping the interaction between the participants. Maarten Hajer (1993, 1995) has opened an interesting line of research that explores how policy actors with diverging interests are brought together in a relatively stable discourse coalition which is held together by a storyline that, in a short and condensed way, defines key problems and solutions. Governance networks are stabilized by policy discourses that shape the way in which problems and challenges are understood and defined, and, over time, the hegemonic discourse will become sedimented into concepts and institutional practices that are taken for granted by the network actors. Storylines and discourses are not only unifying, structuring, and stabilizing governance networks, but also play a crucial role in including and excluding actors, issues, and options (Torfing 2007). The crucial role of discourse in relation to governance networks calls for studies on how discourse and storylines are formed in a battle where situated actors who advance particular arguments aim to get acceptance of these arguments from other actors.

The third question concerns the deployment of *soft rules* in public governance. Soft rules refer to attempts to regulate the behavior of public, social, and economic actors by means of legally non-binding recommendations, guidelines, norms, standards, and accords (Borrás and Conzelmann 2007). Governance networks will often rely on soft rules rather than hard laws because they are based on negotiation and compromise and because they lack the means to enforce black letter laws. An important question is whether soft rules are less effective in governing behavior than hard laws. Of course, hard laws are legally binding and can be backed by severe sanctions, but shaping the logic of appropriate action through the production and dissemination of new vocabularies, standards, and benchmarks might prove to be very effective in regulating behavior in the long term.

The fourth question on the research agenda is the question of how to *evaluate and assess the performance and impact* of governance networks. The assessment of governance networks may invoke an entire range of normative criteria in terms of equity, democracy, goal-attainment, productivity, stability, conflict resolution, learning capacity, and so on. (Provan and Kenis 2008). In recent debates there has been a particular focus on the evaluation of the effectiveness and democratic performance of governance networks (Sørensen and Torfing 2009). Governance networks may contribute to a more effective governance of our complex, fragmented, and multilayered societies, but it is not evident how effectiveness should be measured and what measurement methods should be applied (Jessop 2002; Klijn and Koppenjan 2004). Governance networks may also contribute to a democratization of society (Sørensen and Torfing 2005a; Benz and Papadopoulos 2006; Klijn and Skelcher 2007) and they may also be evaluated in terms of their democratic anchorage (Sørensen and Torfing 2005b). Other assessment criteria such as equity and policy innovation might also be invoked, and the question is whether there is a trade-off between the performance and impact of governance networks on different normative criteria.

The final question concerns the *role of politics and power* in network governance (Kahler 2009). Neither practitioners nor researchers should fool themselves into believing that network governance involves an unpolitical exchange of resources through a rational, consensus-seeking deliberation among policy experts and relevant stakeholders who are merely aiming to make technical adjustments to public policy and secure a harmonious coordination of policy implementation (Moulaert and Cabaret 2006). Network governance involves complex power games and those who fail to understand this will not be able to manoeuvre successfully in the world of interactive governance. In order to grasp the intrinsic link between governance and power we must not only analyze "power *in* governance," but also analyze "power *of* governance," "power *over* governance," and "power *as* governance." We need to explore all the different ways that network governance and power are related if we are to fully understand the essentially political character of interactive governance.

REFERENCES

Agranoff, R. 2003. *Leveraging Networks: A Guide for Public Managers Working across Organisations*. Arlington: IBM Endowment for the Business of Government.

Bache, I. and Flinders, M. (eds.) 2004. *Multi-Level Governance*. Oxford: Oxford University Press.

Benz, A. and Papadopoulos, Y. 2006. *Governance and Democracy*. London: Routledge.

Borrás, S. and Conzelmann, T. 2007. Democracy, legitimacy and soft modes of governance in the EU: The empirical turn. *European Integration* 29: 531–548.

Crozier, M., Huntington, S. P. and Watanuki, J. 1975. *The Crisis of Democracy*. New York: New York University Press.

Dean, M. 1999. *Governmentality: Power and Rule in Modern Society*. London: Sage.

Djelic, M.-L. and Sahlin-Andersson, K. (eds.) 2006. *Transnational Governance: Institutional Dynamics of Regulation*. Cambridge: Cambridge University Press.

Foucault, M. 1991. Governmentality. In G. Burchell, C. Gordon, and P. Miller (eds.), *The Foucault Effect*. Hertfordshire: Harvester Wheatsheaf, 87–104.

Grote, J. R. and Gbikpi, B. (eds.) 2002. *Participatory Governance*. Opladen: Leske and Budrich.

Haas, P. M. 1992. Epistemic communities and international policy coordination. *International Organization* 46: 1–35.

Hajer, M. 1993. Discourse coalitions and the institutionalization of practice: The case of acid rain in Britain. In F. Fisher and J. Forester (eds.), *The Argumentative Turn in Policy Analysis and Planning*. Durham: Duke University Press, 43–76.

Hajer, M. 1995. *The Politics of Environmental Discourse: Ecological Modernization and the Policy Process*. Oxford: Clarendon Press.

Heclo, H. 1978. Issue networks and the executive establishment. In A. King (ed.), *The New American Political System*. Washington, DC: American Enterprise Institute, 87–124.

Héritier, A., Knill, C. and Mingers, S. 1996. *Ringing the Changes in Europe*. Berlin: Walter de Gruyter.

Hirst, P. 1994. *Associative Democracy*. Cambridge: Polity.

Hirst, P. 2000. Governance and democracy. In J. Pierre (ed.), *Debating Governance*. Oxford: Oxford University Press, 13–35.

Hood, C. 1986. *The Tools of Government*. Chatham: Chatham House.

Jessop, B. 1998. The rise of governance and the risks of failure: The case of economic development. *International Social Science Journal* 50: 29–45.

Jessop, B. 2002. *The Future of the Capitalist State*. Cambridge: Polity.

Kahler, M. (ed.) 2009. *Network Politics: Agency, Power and Governance*. Ithaca, NY: Cornell University Press.

Kersbergen, K. V. and Waarden, F. V. 2004. "Governance" as a bridge between disciplines: Cross-disciplinary inspiration regarding shifts in governance and problems of governability, accountability and legitimacy. *European Journal of Political Research* 43: 143–171.

Kickert, W. J. M., Klijn, E.-H. and Koppenjan, J. F. M. (eds.) 1997. *Managing Complex Networks*. London: Sage.

Klijn, E.-H. and Koppenjan, J. F. M. 2004. *Managing Uncertainties in Networks*. London: Routledge.

Klijn, E.-H. and Skelcher, C. 2007. Democracy and governance networks: Compatible or not? *Public Administration* 85: 587–608.

Kohler-Koch, B. and Eising, R. (eds.) 1999. *The Transformation of Governance in the European Union*. London: Routledge.

Kooiman, J. (ed.) 1993. *Modern Governance*. London: Sage.

Kooiman, J. 2003. *Governing as Governance*. London: Sage.

Levi-Faur, D. 2005. The global diffusion of regulatory capitalism. *The Annals of the American Academy* 598: 12–32.

March, J. G. and Olsen, J. P. 1995. *Democratic Governance*. New York: Free Press.

Marcussen, M. and Torfing J. (eds.) 2007. *Democratic Network Governance in Europe*. Basingstoke: Palgrave Macmillan.

Marin, B. and Mayntz, R. (eds.) 1991. *Policy Networks*. Frankfurt-am-Main: Campus Verlag.

Marsh, D. (ed.) 1998. *Comparing Policy Networks*. Buckingham: Open University Press.

Marsh, D. and Rhodes, R. A. W. (eds.) 1992. *Policy Networks in British Government*. Oxford: Oxford University Press.

Mayntz, R. 1993a. Modernization and the logic of interorganizational networks. In J. Child, M. Crozier, and R. Mayntz (eds.), *Societal Change between Markets and Organization*. Aldershot: Avebury, 3–18.

Mayntz, R. 1993b. Governing failure and the problem of governability: Some comments on a theoretical paradigm. In J. Kooiman (ed.), *Modern Governance*. London: Sage, 9–20.

Milward, H. B. and Provan, K. G. 2006. *A Manager's Guide to Choosing and Using Networks*. Arlington: IBM Endowment for the Business of Government.

Moulaert, F. and Cabaret, K. 2006. Planning, networks and power relations: Is democratic planning under capitalism possible? *Planning Theory* 5: 51–70.

Olsen, J. P. 2009. EU governance: Where do we go from here? In B. Kohler-Koch and F. Larat (eds.), *European Multi-level Governance*. Cheltenham: Edward Elgar, 191–209.

Ostrom, E. 1990. *Governing the Commons*. Cambridge: Cambridge University Press.

Peters, B. G. 1999. *Institutional Theory in Political Science*. London: Continuum.

Pierre, J. and Peters, B. G. 2000. *Governance, Politics and the State*. Basingstoke: Macmillan.

Powell, W. W. and DiMaggio, J. 1983. The iron cage revisited: Institutional isomorphism and collective rationality in organisational fields. *American Sociological Review* 48: 147–160.

Powell, W. W. and DiMaggio, J. 1991. *The New Institutionalism in Organizational Analysis.* Chicago: University of Chicago Press.

Provan, K. G. and Kenis, P. N. 2008. Modes of network governance: Structure, management, and effectiveness. *Journal of Public Administration Research and Theory* 18: 229–252.

Rhodes, R. A. W. 1997. *Understanding Governance.* Buckingham: Open University Press.

Rhodes, R. A. W. 2007. Understanding governance: Ten years on. *Organization Studies* 28: 1243–1264.

Rose, N. and Miller, P. 1992. Political power beyond the state: Problematics of government. *British Journal of Sociology* 43: 172–205.

Sabatier, P. A. and Jenkins-Smith, H. C. 1993. *Policy Change and Learning: An Advocacy Coalition Approach.* Boulder, CO: Westview Press.

Scharpf, F. W. 1994. Games real actors could play: Positive and negative coordination in embedded negotiations. *Journal of Theoretical Politics* 6: 27–53.

Scharpf, F. W. 1999. *Governing in Europe: Effective and Democratic?* Oxford: Oxford University Press.

Scharpf, F. W. 2001. Notes toward a theory of multi-level governing in Europe. *Scandinavian Political Studies* 24: 1–26.

Smith, G. 2005. *Beyond the Ballot Box: 57 Democratic Innovations from Around the World.* Report prepared for the Power Inquiry.

Sørensen, E. and Torfing, J. 2003. Network politics, political capital and democracy. *International Journal of Public Administration* 26: 606–634.

Sørensen, E. and Torfing, J. 2005a. Network governance and post-liberal democracy, *Administrative Theory and Praxis* 27: 197–237.

Sørensen, E. and Torfing, J. 2005b. The democratic anchorage of governance networks. *Scandinavian Political Studies* 28: 195–218.

Sørensen, E. and Torfing, J. (eds.) 2007. *Theories of Democratic Network Governance.* Basingstoke: Palgrave Macmillan.

Sørensen, E. and Torfing, J. 2009. Making governance networks effective and democratic through metagovernance. *Public Administration* 87: 234–258.

Torfing, J. 2007. Discursive governance networks in Danish activation policies. In M. Marcussen and J. Torfing (eds.), *Democratic Network Governance in Europe.* Basingstoke: Palgrave Macmillan, 111–129.

Warren, M. E. 2009. Governance-driven democratization. *Critical Policy Analysis* 3: 3–13.

Winter, S. 2006. Implementation. In B. G. Peters and J. Pierre (eds.), *Handbook of Public Policy.* London: Sage, 151–166.

....

CHAPTER 8

INFORMATION AND GOVERNING: CYBERNETIC MODELS OF GOVERNANCE

....

B. GUY PETERS*

GIVEN all the difficulties commonly encountered in governing and steering society, a number of scholars have considered the possibility of constructing and nurturing modes of governance that depend heavily on information collection and processing, in other words, a cybernetic format for governance (Deutsch 1963; Dunsire 1986). Although the cybernetic form of governing, as advanced by Deutsch (1963), Dunsire (1986) and Schick (1998) is the most extreme, all forms of governance do depend crucially on information. The difference among these forms of governance is the extent to which information drives decisions or is only part of a decision process that also involves a number of more deliberative and politicized elements. That is, in some versions of governance the reactions to information tend to be preprogrammed,[1] while in others the responses are indeterminate and involve greater judgment by the actors involved. While generally the analysis of governance involves substantial concern about the goals of governing, in this cybernetic conception goals are largely exogenous to the steering process. This approach is more concerned with how the system maintains itself and reacts to external changes in the pursuit of those exogenous goals. In this view governance is very much about information processing and steering on the basis of the information.

This chapter discusses the role and forms that information and information processing can play in governance. These models of governing all raise important questions about governing, and all face numerous barriers to successful implementation, and these issues will be discussed.

INFORMATION AND GOVERNANCE

Although the use of information is central to any attempt to govern effectively, at least six approaches to governing have attempted to deal with information processing more explicitly, to theorize the role of information in governance, and, in some cases, to enhance the capacity of the public sector to use information effectively. These approaches consider not only characteristics of the public sector in this process, but also the nature of the information available and how the quality and timeliness of that information can be enhanced.

Cybernetic governance

Karl Deutsch's *The Nerves of Government* was the first significant statement of the logic of cybernetic governance. Deutsch was interested generally in the capacity of political systems to utilize communications and information for guidance and control, and used the model from engineering to provide an analytic understanding of the state. In Deutsch's conception of governance (although he did not use the term) the principle elements involved were the information-processing center of government—Dror's "central mind of government" (1986)—and the power of governments to act in response to information.

In terms of contemporary thinking about governance this model depended heavily on a central government, but the idea of connections to society were also central to the argument. In this model the "will" of that center of government to steer and to make policies defined the acts of governing. The will manifested through the center of government is assumed to produce not only the capacity to steer and control in relationship to feedback but also to generate some striving toward the autonomy of the decision-making units within government.[2] Therefore, this conception of governance is to some extent the antithesis of much of the contemporary governance literature that emphasizes close connections, or even dominance, by civil society.

Deutsch was writing his work on cybernetics and the state at the time in which systems theory (Easton 1965), with its homeostatic assumptions, were common in the study of comparative politics and. political theory. Therefore, the basic logic of social systems striving to maintain their equilibrium when confronted with environmental changes was rather common in political science discussions at the time. Deutsch's notion of cybernetics utilized in steering the state was, however, less conservative and was directed toward choosing policies that would adapt to changing conditions and move the polity forward toward a better policy regimen rather than simply maintaining itself. Both systems theory and cybernetic ideas, however, relied heavily on the concept of feedback as a means of signaling to decision-makers that there is a need for some adjustment.

Another major attempt to understand the potential of a cybernetic model for under-standing the public sector was undertaken in the so-called Bielefeld Project, launched in Germany during the 1980s (see Kaufman 1986). This research project was concerned with general questions of guidance, control, and steering in the public sector, including the role of evaluation in providing feedback to government to assist in that steering. Although there was a general concern with control in government in this project, there was also some explicit concern with the possibilities of cybernetic steering (Dunsire 1986). The information that was generated in society would be used to guide policy in a rather smooth and seemingly apolitical manner.

There also have been attempts to apply the basic logic of cybernetic decision-making to the international environment, and to foreign policy decision-making by individual states.[3] John Steinbruner (1974), for example, examined the possibilities of cybernetic foreign policy for the United States, and to some extent more generally. Steinbruner extends the basic logic cybernetic decision-making to consider issues of uncertainty and value trade-offs that are particularly relevant in international politics.

Cybernetic analyses of government have not been at the center of political science, and find less favor in the contemporary world than they did in the time at which systems theory played a more central role. Despite that, this approach to governance does point to the crucial role that information plays in steering policy-making, and also the general importance of the political system being closely connected and responsive to its environment.

The social indicators movement

Although not expressed in terms of guidance and control, the social indicators move-ment was another attempt to utilize social intelligence to improve governance. At about the time that Deutsch was developing his cybernetic model a number of scholars and practitioners were attempting to develop a set of indicators that could be used to guide public policy, especially social policy (Bauer 1966; Zapf 2000). The indicators at the heart of this research were intended to assess the state of society, or the quality of life, and therefore also the final outcomes for society of public interventions.

Although not as concerned with long-term outcomes for society, nor with monitor-ing the state of society per se, the wide-scale use of performance indicators was a part of the New Public Management (NPM) movement (see Bianchi 2010). The logic of per-formance management and performance indicators is to provide relatively short-term measures of how well public sector programs have reached certain targets. These are not attempts to measure the "quality of life" in a comprehensive manner but rather more limited attempts to assess the activities of individual programs and organizations. If the social indicators movement were able to provide comprehensive, valid, and reliable measures of the quality of life there would be significant questions about whether they would be useful for steering society in any conventional political system. These meas-ures tend to cut across the well-established divisions in the public sector, and hence it is difficult for any one minister or organization to drive the pursuit for these broad improvements in the living standards within societies. Further, the linkages between specific policy changes and these broader goals may be difficult to understand and even more difficult to manage.[4]

Evidence-based policy-making

While cybernetic forms of governing have largely remained at a theoretical level, there has been an increased practical interest in "evidence-based policy-making." This concept involves a more extensive use of information for making policy than many other formats for policy-making (see Sanderson 2002), and also attempts to institutionalize learning from the environment. This style of policy-making has been associated with New Labour in the United Kingdom but has also been a more general phenomenon. The basic idea is the rather simple notion that governments can learn from their own experiences, or the experiences of other countries, when designing policy interventions. This perspective relies on feedback just as the cybernetic conceptions does, but it tends to be directed more at changing rather than maintaining particular policy regimes.

Evidence-based policy-making can also be related to general processes of learning about policy in the public sector (see Sabatier and Jenkins-Smith 1988; Howlett 2009). The learning model assumes that policy interventions can be conceptualized as experiments of a sort, with governments having the capacity to learn from those experiments. Unlike cybernetic models, however, these models assume continuing change and that the purpose of using information is not to maintain the status quo but rather to alter it and to improve the policy performance of the governance arrangements in question. This, in turn, requires not only the availability of the requisite information but also a political system that is open to change (see below).

Also, several scholars working in Israel have attempted to understand how to improve decision-making in government and to take information more directly into account when making those decisions. Yehezkel Dror was concerned with the difficulties in making good decisions under conditions of risk and uncertainty (1986). Likewise, Itzhak Galnoor (1982) has attempted to link some ideas of the cybernetic model of governance to decision-making within Israel. These scholars have all been concerned with the capacity of government to respond effectively in an environment that is both complex and potentially hostile, and what information can do to facilitate those processes.

Institutional cybernetics

Volker Schneider (2004) developed the idea of "institutional cybernetics" to describe the shift in political theory away from the conflict-oriented explanations of public choices toward a more integrationist perspective on steering the state. However, rather than the functionalist explanations and the lack of agency in most systems approaches (see also below) this institutional perspective examines the role of specific institutions in the governance process and attempts to understand how the processes of governance actually do produce the requisite steering for the social and economic systems. In particular, institutions use their norms, routines, and links with society to "actuate" steering mechanisms, thus making the cybernetic conception of decision-making more actor-centered than it has been in some earlier versions.

Finally, some of the thinking about institutionalism, and especially the persistence of institutions, has adopted some of the thinking associated with systems models and cybernetics. Paul Pierson, for example, argued (2000) that the path dependency in historical institutionalism was sustained at least in part by positive feedback to elites that reinforced their patterns of behavior. That said, the same logic could apply to negative feedback and deinstitutionalization (Oliver 1992). To be successful all institutions must be to some extent connected with their environments and react to changes in those environments, whether or not that connection has the close connections implied by this model.

Learning and governance

The cybernetic conception of governance can also be considered to be one aspect of learning for governance (see Chapter 11, this volume). Both of these approaches to governance assume that information available in the environment will help public sector organizations to make better policies. Further, both approaches assume that these organizations can be made more or less open to that information, and thus that organizational (institutional) design is important for building more receptive organizations.

Although these approaches have a good deal in common they also have some important differences. Perhaps most importantly, the learning model tends to focus on the capacity of organizations to adapt their internal structures and policy ideas in response to information gained from the environment. This cybernetic model, however, assumes somewhat more immediate reactions to the environment than the more complex and difficult process of learning. That said, however, the cybernetic approach must remain open to learning from successive responses and to developing more efficient means of responding to, or perhaps the means of anticipating, changes in its environment.

Information and implementation

The approaches to using information in governance already discussed have been concerned primarily with using information as a detector (see Hood 1976). Information can also be an effector (in Christopher Hood's term) and can be used to implement public policy. Hood discusses information as "nodality," meaning that governments are major information nodes that collect vast amounts of data to guide policy-making and also can use information to attempt to alter the behavior of citizens.[5]

Providing governance through information is the least expensive option for the public sector. If governments can gain compliance simply by advising the public that some actions are illegal, or other actions are desirable, then there is less need for more expensive options such as policemen or hospitals. And sometimes information is the only instrument available to governments, as when they attempt to enforce environmental regulations in wilderness areas (Bemelmans-Videc, Rist, and Vedung 1998). Governing through information also permits citizens to make some of their own choices and can make government appear less intrusive. Also, in modern societies with seemingly constant connection to information sources the capacity to get information out to the people has been enhanced.

To be capable of relying on information for governance a political system must have substantial legitimacy and trust. If citizens do not trust their governments they are certainly not likely to comply with the suggestions made through public service announcements or other information campaigns. The capacity to govern through information also involves the existence of common symbols that can be manipulated in order to produce the desired reactions. Therefore, in countries with markedly different internal subcultures, the capacity to govern simply through information will be restricted.

Complexity and the limits of control and information-based governance

These cybernetic models of governing stand in marked contrast to the alternative conceptions of governing that are emerging in response to the apparently increased complexity in the social environment, and to some extent in the processes within the public sector itself (see Dobuzinskis 1992). The cybernetic models tend to assume rather linear conceptions of control, and indeed assume a clear capacity to control. That closure in decision-making, and assumptions of linear relationships between changes in the environment and responses is difficult to maintain in real governance situations. The logic of models operating within most cybernetic models, or indeed within many system-based models of governance, is that of a closed system rather than one with more dynamic relations with its environment.

As the world of governing has become more complex, alternative notions have also been developed. For example, scholars such as Duit and Galaz (2008) have sought to apply complexity theory to the study of public administration. Even the punctuated equilibrium models that have been central to historical institutionalism and to the study of political agendas demonstrate the importance of more or less random events, as well as phenomena such as tipping points, in upsetting the rather neat closed systems assumed in other decision-making models such as in cybernetic models (see van Bueren and Gerrits 2008). These various attempts to use complexity theories and associated approaches do not by any means deny the utility of information in making public policy (see Klijn 2008). That said, however, they do approach the use of information differently than scholars who are operating with the more closed, cybernetic conception.

Basic concepts in the cybernetics of governing

The basic logic of cybernetic steering in governing is that the governance system responds to changes in the environment and makes calibrated responses to those changes. If the responses are too great or too small they are adjusted quickly in subsequent rounds of decision-making. The assumption then is that through successive iterations an appropriate governance response can be found so that the policies of the public sector will produce effective outcomes in the economy and society.[6]

Normatively the virtues of the cybernetic state are assumed to be the production of the best possible patterns of governance in a complex society. As will be noted below, politics and the complex processes and structures associated with governance make reaching high-quality public decisions difficult. Fritz Scharpf (1988), for example, has demonstrated that federal systems and systems such as the European Union (EU) that have a number of veto players tend to have difficulty in reaching decisions that extend beyond the lowest common denominator.

Perhaps the most basic concept in cybernetic models of decision-making is feedback. When there is an action, whether it is from a physical operator such as a furnace, or a government, feedback informs the actor of the consequences of that action. Then the system will respond to the information in order to adjust the operations of the system to meet the new conditions. In a physical system that response is automatic, while in governance systems there must still be some form of decision about the changed state, even if that decision has been programmed in advance.

Several concepts help us to understand the responses of cybernetic decision-making systems to their environment. "Lag" in the process appears to be the most commonly encountered concept in the real world of governing. Although the environment of the governance system may change, and even if the actors in the public sector may identify that change, there may still be some delay in the response to the social transformation. These delays in responding may be a function of political inadequacies within the governance systems, lack of faith in the indicators used to detect the change, or conflicting information from other sources.

Although in general lag is dysfunctional in steering systems, it may be more acceptable in governance because of the ambiguity of many indicators and the difficulties in determining the need for action. Further, as the responses in question may be extreme—for example, going to war—then some reflection before responding may be desirable in many cases in the public sector. That said, however, the failure to respond may also produce negative outcomes. Thus, unlike simple systems such as thermostats, governance requires exercising substantial judgment about the quality of the information and the strength of the connection between it and the actions.

Lead is the antithesis of lag. In the best of all worlds of governance, the public sector and its social partners would be able to anticipate some changing needs in society and respond before the potential problems manifest themselves. Demography offers a simple example of this type of anticipation. Most contemporary societies know with reasonable accuracy the number of babies being born each year, and also know that in five or six years those babies will be entering elementary school. The public sector can therefore plan for those incoming students and adjust the number of school places to match that demand.

Most public policies are not as simple as planning for school places,[7] so that anticipation of future demands for policy interventions is not nearly so easy. This capacity to anticipate successfully is even more constrained because of the increasing complexity of many policy areas, with small changes in some aspects potentially producing major changes in others, for example, in the environment or energy. Further, globalization makes containing the effects, or the causes, of any policy to a particular geographical area more difficult, so that anticipation is all the more difficult.

The concept of *gain* is a measure of the extent to which the system responds to any signal, or to particular types of signals. For the signals coming to a thermostat from a change in temperature in the environment, the response is linear, with a one degree change producing an equal response from the furnace or the air conditioner to compensate for that external change. Other signals, for example, a fire alarm, may produce a significantly nonlinear response. Conversely, some signals may produce a minimal response and require more than one repetition in order to generate any significant response. For example, one occurrence of a potentially pandemic disease may not generate much reaction while each subsequent occurrence may produce more and more response.

The task in considering a cybernetic model of governing therefore is to attempt to develop some appropriate level of response to the signals coming into the system. Too little response (low gain) may produce inadequate responses, while too much gain may produce excessive responses when not appropriate. For example, if national security systems have very high gain they run the risk of starting a war because of an airplane off course, or an earthquake that appears to be a nuclear explosion. That said, however, if there is a real problem in the security environment then an inadequate response could be equally devastating.

All of these mechanisms of cybernetic control are intended to produce an *equilibrium* outcome in the policy-making process. The idea of reaching and maintaining an equilibrium is evident in several areas of the social sciences, notably in the neoclassical model of the market in economics. Similarly the logic of checks and balances in constitutional models of governing represents a means of producing equilibrium outcomes (see Dunsire 1990). Systems theory is also premised on finding some sort of equilibrium, and the basic logic of cybernetic thinking for governance is to generate a viable equilibrium.

WHAT IS REQUIRED TO MAKE GOVERNANCE MORE CYBERNETIC?

While creating a cybernetic political system has been an aspiration, and an ideal, for some analysts and indeed for some people actually involved in providing governance, it has some more realistic elements. In particular, citizens and analysts can ask how governments can be moved toward being more closely connected with their environments, and more responsive to any changes in that environment. Even if the ideal cannot be attained, a more responsive political system is likely to produce a better quality of life for citizens, and to also assist policy-makers in understanding how to adjust their policies to changing social dynamics. The conditions for enhancing greater responsiveness are both technical and political, and achieving significantly higher levels of responsiveness may also raise normative questions about the popular control of governance and about technocracy. This section will discuss some of the conditions necessary to make governance more responsive, and also discuss some potential failings of governance systems.

Technical barriers

The cybernetic conception of governing, and indeed any approach to governance that emphasizes the responsiveness of the public sector to changing social and economic conditions, depends upon information processing, just as physical mechanisms for cybernetic controls involve receiving and processing adequate information from the environment and then making the appropriate decisions based on that information. A cybernetic conceptualization of governance in the public sector involves much of the same logic as making decisions, although actually implementing such a system is substantially more difficult. Therefore, we need to understand the technical issues that may constitute barriers to effective cybernetic performance of governance systems.

As noted previously, the development of effective social indicators has been a subject of research for some decades, but remains a question for policy-makers. Despite those decades of research, the reliability and validity of social indicators is still somewhat suspect, especially if we hope to make decisions quickly. Some of the initial development of social indicators was directed at building comprehensive assessments but this ambition has been transformed toward short-term performance indicators measuring the success and failure of particular organizations.

Somewhat paradoxically, the development of performance indicators in the public sector has tended to go in the opposite direction of that which might be required for effective cybernetic forms of governing. Much of the development of performance indicators has been directed toward finding indicators that reflect short-term success or failure so that political actors can hold the administrators accountable for their actions (Bouckaert and Halligan 2007). There is relatively little evidence that these short-term indicators can be effective in longer-term adjustments to changes in policy, and indeed the short-term indications may be totally unrelated, or negatively related, to longer-term steering needs.

The above having been said, however, the short-term nature of many performance indicators does in some ways match the logic of cybernetic governing more closely. The short-term indicators permit more rapid responses by the public sector. Even if the information is not as comprehensive as the social indicators literature might desire, the shorter-term information does permit the state to make continuous adjustments to the environment. However, rather than being directed at maintaining the status quo, these indicators are directed more at altering policies and at evaluating the performance of individual programs.

As well as the time frame represented in an indicator and the technical validity and reliability of the indicator, there may be other political problems that prevent the indicator from playing the role that might be assumed in a cybernetic conception of governing. Although analysts and their advocates may understand the "true" meaning of an indicator, almost any data entering the political arena is subject to interpretation and a constructivist interpretation. For example, during the debates over extending benefits in the US Congress during the summer of 2010, the unemployment rate—a very standard economic indicator—was construed in rather different ways. The Democratic majority argued that the persistently high rate of unemployment represented economic problems and a need to extend the benefits. The Republican majority, on the other hand, argued that this indicator reflected that the social benefit system was too generous and if benefits were cut people would find jobs.

Some economic policies already in place approximate this more or less automatic style of making policy. For example, the "automatic fiscal stabilizers" such as unemployment benefits and tax receipts tend to operate to counteract recessionary or inflationary pressures with little or no decision-making by the government of the day (Baunsgaard and Symansky 2009). If the negative situation in the economy persists then the increases in unemployment and welfare benefits, and declines in tax revenues, will create a budget deficit that should stimulate the economy. Likewise, if the economy is inflationary, reduced deficits of a surplus should slow the economy.

Political barriers to cybernetic and information-based governing

Although there are important technical barriers to implementing a more information-driven, cybernetic style of governance, the political constraints may be more important. The complexities of the political system and the ideological and partisan conflicts that exist within almost any system make rapid and smooth adjustment to the environment difficult at best. At the extreme, some political systems may not be open to information, replying upon their own ideology or their assumptions about their own capacity to make good judgments. For example, with regard to the neoliberal governments of the 1980s, the argument was made that they were largely uninterested in information and argument (Savoie 1994). Ideology is a crucial barrier to effective responsiveness in governance, but there are also other political factors affecting this capacity.

One of the major political barriers to cybernetic patterns of governance is simply that in most contemporary political systems the public sector is massive and difficult to steer. There is a huge inertia in any governing system that information, even information about better ways of performing public tasks, may not be able to overcome. The path-dependency argument in institutional theory (Thelen 1999) makes a strong argument about the persistence of programs, as well as about rather limited forms of change that are likely to occur within most contemporary systems of governance.

In addition to just being large, the public sector is also extremely disjointed and internally competitive, making effective responses to external signals more difficult. Specialization has been built into the public sector for a good reason, but this separation of functions makes effective response to the multifaceted environment more difficult (Bouckaert, Peters, and Verhoest 2010). For example, if there is a decline in an important health indicator then not only health departments in the public sector but other actors—sanitation, agriculture, regulatory organizations of several types to name but a few—would be implicated. Thus, for the system as a whole to respond effectively it must coordinate a number of actors and actions, and coordination is not always the strongest suit of the public sector.

The capacity to coordinate, and to process, information in the public sector is seriously compromised because in an information-based decision-making system, such as contemporary government, information constitutes power. The hoarding of information and the limiting of effective responses within a governance system were very evident in the lead-up to September 11 in the United States, with various intelligence agencies all having some parts of the picture about the planned attack but none willing to share that information with the others. So long as an organization held information that others did not then they had a resource they could use to enhance their own position in bureaucratic politics. Therefore, an attack that might have been prevented was able to proceed.[8]

As well as the problems of coordination and of sharing information in the public sector, there are also internal communications problems within many public organizations. The classic problem of uncertainty absorption as a part of organizational communication can serve to reduce the effectiveness of any information received from the outside, and thus reduce the creation of effective responses. At each stage of the transfer of information through the hierarchical levels of an organization the actors involved will tend to code information to meet their own preconceptions, or to enhance their own position within the organization.

Finally, and perhaps most basically, politics is itself a fundamental barrier to immediate and effective government responses to information coming from the environment. The cybernetic model of governance tends to assume that there will be a rather neat linear response to environmental changes, that the indicators are unambiguous, and that decisions within the system can be made readily. These conditions may be attained more readily in political systems with fewer veto points than in more complex systems (Tsebelis 2000). In addition to the formal structural constraints in political systems there may be political conditions, for example, a coalition government, that can also limit the capacity of governments to make decisions, and especially to do so in a more or less linear fashion.

QUESTIONS ABOUT THE CYBERNETIC MODEL

There are a number of possible normative benefits from adopting a more cybernetic conception of governance. As noted in the introduction to this chapter, the capacity to make and implement high-quality decisions that respond to the changing needs of society is a very positive goal for governance, and may indeed reflect the underlying conception of steering that is at the heart of the theoretical notion of governance (see Chapter 2, this volume). Both cybernetics and governance are derived from the same root word in Greek, and the two concepts are intimately connected. Steering involves a continuing adjustment to changes in the environment and, in effect, results in governance for the society.

Theoretically, one of the major problems in the cybernetic model is the absence of agency. That is to say, decisions emerge because of the desire to produce high-quality, adaptive decisions that will solve social problems. It is not clear, however, who is making these decisions and why they are so enlightened. As noted above, the political system, and perhaps especially political as opposed to administrative actors, may well have priorities that mean that they do not necessarily make technically correct decisions, especially if in the short term those decisions may harm powerful interests in the society.[9] Decisions have to be made by someone in a governance system, so unless one adopts a highly technocratic style of governing then being able to reach many of the decisions that are needed will be difficult.

The tendency of cybernetic approaches, along with many systems models of government, does, in a somewhat paradoxical manner, emphasize the need to consider decision-making in governance. The work of scholars such as Dror, mentioned above, has been focused around the need to build the decision-making capacities of the public sector in the face of risk, uncertainty, and poor information. The automatic responses assumed in cybernetic models are in marked contrast with the difficulties involved in many actual decision-making settings. Both approaches, however, do emphasize the importance of information in governance, as well as some of the difficulties in obtaining valid and reliable information.

Following from the above, one of the inherent difficulties in the use of cybernetic models of decision is that they assume a stable, indeed an ultra-stable, environment (Ashby 1952). The signals coming from the environment tend to concern relatively minor deviations from the preferred state, which will be addressed by the response to that feedback. However, in the rapidly changing and unstable environment that characterizes contemporary society it is difficult to identify such stability. As already noted, complexity models of governance may better show this rapidly changing environment, albeit in so doing they tend inherently to deny the capacity for effective steering and control.

Any model of governing with more or less cybernetic elements embedded in it must also have a stable normative environment. That is, the goals that the system is seeking to track must be stable and widely agreed if the guidance is to be effective. Without that goal stability and consistency steering becomes difficult. Again, the complexity of goals in contemporary governance makes the normative stances more difficult (Tarschys 2006).

Although there are some normative benefits that may be derived from the cybernetic conception of governance, there may also be some normative questions about the cybernetic model that can be added to the empirical questions discussed above. The most central of these concerns is the "primacy of politics," and the need for democratic controls over public governance. While politics can be presented as a barrier to high-quality decision-making, and is often discussed in this light by individuals with a more technocratic conception of governance, the basis logic of any democratic system is that elected political leaders are ultimately responsible for the decisions made in the public sector. While some decisions are made more or less automatically, for example, the automatic fiscal stabilizers, most governance choices must, in democratic terms, be made through political means.

As well as the democratic questions concerning the role of political leaders in making decisions, there are additional democratic concerns about the increased involvement of a range of social actors in governance processes. The various conceptions of interactive governance, or network governance (Sørensen and Torfing 2007), linking social actors to the state, makes the process of reaching decisions all the more difficult. This model of governing contrasts markedly with the rather technocratic conceptions inherent in the cybernetic model. This conception of governance then poses both empirical and normative challenges to cybernetic models of governing.

A related normative concern in any cybernetic model derives from the equilibrium that resides at the heart of many such models. Although some versions of governance, driven by information and concerned with guidance and control in the public sector, have been concerned with more dynamic adjustments in governance, the basic logic of systems seeking to stabilize their functioning has been largely dismissed. Therefore, their relationship with society is rather conservative and may also be rather self-serving, as the state and its institutions are maintained as a first priority. While that conservatism may be functional for maintaining a political system in the face of threats of revolution or entropy, it is less viable from a policy-making perspective, with the danger that a policy-making system fails to respond to changing external conditions and changing political demands.

Conclusions

All governance depends, to some extent, on using information. Governance involves receiving and then acting upon information about the conditions of the environment within which the governing system functions. This process also involves continuously assessing the impacts of interventions into that environment. The question therefore becomes not whether governance utilizes information but rather how that information is used and the extent to which information is processed and politicized prior to being acted upon. Further, the question becomes how effectively political systems can process information and use it for reaching appropriate conclusions about policy interventions.

The cybernetic conception of government action that motivated this chapter posits a rather extreme version of the relationship between information and governance. There is an almost one-to-one correspondence between the signals being received and the actions of the governance system. As already noted, that close connection may be difficult to attain in real-world systems, and may be undesirable even if it were attainable. Still, it presents an interesting intellectual model of governance that can be used to explain the real world of governance and the ability of political systems to process and use information.

Looking at the questions of guidance and control in governance processes forces us to consider more carefully how decisions are made. As already noted there is some tendency in the governance literature to ignore agency and to focus very heavily on functionalist forms of explanation. While the functionalist logic does help to identify the basic issues in governing, there is still a need for decision-makers to act, or to construct systems for responding. The need of the "central mind of government" to govern means that someone must consider the environment, react to information, make decisions, and then continue to consider the consequences of each round of governing.

NOTES

*   I would like to express my appreciation to Professor Jon Pierre for reading and commenting on an earlier version of this chapter.
1. In cybernetic language some decisions are, in essence, servomechanisms that respond automatically to particular types of information.
2. Deutsch's arguments were focused on the state in the international environment but some of the same logic can be applied to individual organizations within the public sector. See Carpenter (2001).
3. As noted, Deutsch's argument, directed toward the state in an international environment, has had much greater influence in international relations than in comparative politics or in policy studies. Its concentration on information and communications has fed into the interest in constructivist models of international relations.
4. Perhaps the best extant example of attempting to make these linkages has been the connection between broad strategic goals and more operational goals in performance management systems as that pioneered by New Zealand.
5. Note that the root of the word "statistics" is from state, implying that governments were responsible for the first systematic collection of information about their territories and their populations.
6. To some extent this logic is similar to that of incrementalism in which successive limited comparisons of policy choices produce (it is expected) better policies.

7. Even this planning may not be so simple given rapid migration in some societies, with a large number of prospective students moving in or out of the school district.
8. There is no guarantee that sharing information would have prevented the attack, but it certainly would have increased the probability of some prevention or mitigation.
9. One need only look at the politics of environmental and energy policies to understand this dynamic.

REFERENCES

Ashby, W. R. 1952. *A Design for a Brain*. New York: John Wiley.

Bauer, R. A. 1966. *Social Indicators*. Cambridge, MA: MIT Press.

Baunsgaard, T. and Symansky, S. A. 2009. *Automatic Fiscal Stabilizers*. Washington, DC: IMF Staff Note, 28 September.

Bemelmans-Videc, M.-L., Rist, R. C., and Vedung, E. 1998. *Carrots, Sticks and Sermons: Policy Instruments and their Evaluation*. New Brunswick, NJ: Transaction.

Bianchi, C. 2010. Improving performance and fostering accountability in the public sector through systems dynamic modelling. *Systems Research and Behavioral Science* 27: 361–384.

Boukaert, G. and Halligan, J. A. 2007. *Performance Management*. London: Routledge.

Bouckaert, G., Peters, B. G., and. Verhoest, K. 2010. *The Coordination of Public Sector. Organizations: Shifting Patterns of Public Management*. Basingstoke: Palgrave.

Carpenter, D. P. 2001. *The Forging of Bureaucratic Autonomy: Reputations, Networks and Policy Innovations in Executive Agencies, 1862–1928*. Princeton, NJ: Princeton University Press.

Deutsch, K. W. 1963. *The Nerves of Government: Models of Political Communication and Control*. New York: Free Press.

Dobuzinskis, L. 1992. Modernist and post-modernist metaphors of the policy process: Control and stability vs chaos and reflexive understanding. *Policy Sciences* 25: 35–80.

Dror, Y. 1986. *Governing Under Adversity*. New Brunswick, NJ: Transaction.

Duit, A. and Galaz, V. 2008. Governance and complexity–emerging issues for governance theory. *Governance* 21: 311–325.

Dunsire, A. 1986. A cybernetic view of guidance, control and evaluation in the public sector. In F. X. Kaufman, G. Majone, and V. Ostrom (eds.), *Guidance, Control and Evaluation in the Public Sector*. Berlin: DeGruyter, 213–244.

Dunsire, A. 1990. Holistic governance. *Public Policy and Administration* 5: 4–19.

Easton, D. 1965. *A Systems Analysis of Political Life*. New York: John Wiley.

Galnoor, I. 1982. *Steering the Polity: Communications and Politics in Israel*. London: Sage.

Hood, C. 1976. *The Tools of Government*. Chatham, NJ: Chatham House.

Howlett, M. 2009. Governance modes, policy regimes and operational plans: A multi-level nested model of policy instrument choice and policy design. *Policy Sciences* 42: 73–89.

Kaufman, F. X. 1986. Introduction: History of the project and background to the problem. In F. X. Kaufman, G. Majone and V. Ostrom (eds.), *Guidance, Control and Evaluation in the Public Sector*. Berlin: DeGruyter, 3–14.

Klijn, E-H. 2008. Complexity theory and public administration: What's new? *Public Management Review* 10: 299–317.

Oliver, C. 1992. The antecedents of deinstitutionalization. *Organization Studies* 13: 563–588.

Pierson, P. 2000. Increasing returns, path dependence, and the study of politics. *American Political Science Review* 94: 251–267.

Sabatier, P. A. and Jenkins-Smith, H. 1988. An advocacy-coalition framework of policy change and the role of policy-oriented learning therein. *Policy Sciences* 21: 129–146.

Sanderson, I. 2002. Evaluation, policy learning and evidence-based policy making. *Public Administration* 80: 1–22.

Savoie, D. J. 1994. *Reagen, Thatcher, Mulroney: In Search of the New Bureaucracy.* Pittsburgh, PA: University of Pittsburgh Press.

Scharpf, F. W. 1988. The joint decision-trap: Lessons from German federalism and European integration. *Public Administration* 66: 239–278.

Schick, A. 1998. The cybernetic state. *Society* 35: 5–16.

Schneider, V. 2004. State theory, governance and the logic of regulation and administrative control. In A. Wantjen and A. Wonka (eds.), *Governance in Europe: The Role of Interest Groups.* Baden-Baden: Nomos.

Sørensen, E. and Torfing, J. 2007. *Theories of Democratic Network Governance.* Basingstoke: Palgrave.

Steinbruner, J. D. 1974. *The Cybernetic Theory of Decision: New Dimensions of Political Analysis.* Princeton, NJ: Princeton University Press.

Tarschys, D. 2006. Goal congestion: Multi-purpose governance in the European Union. In E. O. Eriksen, J. E. Fossum, and A. J. Menendez (eds.), *The Chartering of Europe.* Baden-Baden: Nomos, 178–199.

Thelen, K. 1999. Historical institutionalism and comparative politics. *Annual Review of Political Science* 2: 369–404.

Tsebelis. G. 2000. *Veto-Players: How Political Institutions Work.* Princeton, NJ: Princeton University Press.

Van Bueren, A. and Gerrits, L. 2008. Decisions as dynamic equilibriums in erratic policy processes: Positive and negative feedback as drivers of non-linear policy dynamics. *Public Management Review* 10: 381–399.

Zapf, W. 2000. Social reporting in the 1970s and in the 1990s. *Social Indicators Research* 51: 1–15.

···

CHAPTER 9

GOVERNANCE AND COMPLEXITY

···

VOLKER SCHNEIDER*

1. INTRODUCTION

···

DURING the last two decades, the concept of governance has become remarkably popular. Spreading across a growing number of sub-disciplines in the social sciences, it has also influenced political practice at the national, European, and international levels. The secret of its success clearly lies in the term's polyvalence. "Governance" can be used in diverse scientific discourses, creating a kind of network effect: the more the term is used, the more attractive it becomes within further theoretical contexts. A side effect of this proliferation is its growing fuzziness: the list of competing definitions is getting longer and longer (Kooiman 2003; Van Kersbergen and van Waarden 2004). In his skeptical reflection about the concept's potential, Offe (2009) even called the term an "empty signifier," a purely "verbal frame for largely exchangeable contents" (561). Governance thus seems to get into a similar problem zone as the notion "system" in the last century, which became largely devaluated as an analytical category.

A similar situation exists in the debate on complexity theory. Complexity and some related concepts, such as emergence and self-organization, have become a common point of reference in a growing number of academic circles. In contrast to governance, however, complexity theory is not restricted to social science, but is also used in the natural sciences and engineering. Similarly, dozens of definitions of complexity have emerged in this wide-ranging spectrum (see Section 3). Despite this conceptual diversity, there is a clear research focus that ultimately aims at explaining the emergence of order and self-organization within nature and society.

The aim of this chapter is to explore the way that complexity theories can support governance theory to sharpen its analytical focus and to clarify its analytical potential; namely, to understand the functioning and the generation of order and self-organization in modern societies. At a very general level, these are core questions of both governance and complexity theory, but governance is distinctively applied to society and its various sub-systems. This chapter aims at comparing and contrasting both theories in the way self-organization is explained. It will be argued that complexity theory offers a broader and deeper understanding of emergent mechanisms and modes of operation. Governance analysis can learn a great deal from complexity theory (Schneider and Bauer 2009).

The following section starts with an outline of the major variants of governance theory, their common core, and their relatedness to complexity theory. The subsequent section deals with major orientations of complexity theory as initially developed in science and technology. While the various approaches differ in some respects, they also share some important elements. These include the explicit modeling of heterogeneous agents, systems of interaction, and the role of learning and adaptation, as well as the recognition of the multilayered and multi-relational nature of social systems. The chapter will conclude with a summary of the major features of complexity theory and their implications for governance theory.

2. Governance and the problem of complexity

Governance is itself a complex concept. Different theories and approaches use the term quite differently, and the term shows up in different concepts with distinctive meanings. However, this is not unusual in political science, where concepts are not as precise as, for example, in mathematics.

The broadest meaning of governance is the production of social order, collective goods or problem-solving through purposeful political and social intervention, either by authoritative decisions (hierarchical governance) or by the establishment of self-governing arrangements. The difference between government and governance is that the latter is not restricted to governmental institutions alone, but is extended to several dimensions (Mayntz 2003). A major extension of its meaning implies that the whole variety of mechanisms is emphasized, ranging from hierarchical decision-making to horizontal forms of coordination and other informal institutions. However, similar to the debate on regulation, we can differentiate between broad and narrow perspectives (Jordana and Levi-Faur 2004). This distinction can be applied to at least four dimensions:

- Composition: A narrow perspective relates governance only to a set of private actors (governing without government), whereas a broad view relates it to the full spectrum of actors—including governmental actors, actors with a mixed public–private status and actors who are also purely private in an overall actor population.

- Structure: A narrow view relates governance only to horizontal and polycentric relational structures, whereas the broad version includes all possible relational configurations. These can be demarcated between the most centralized "star network" (nodes are only connected to one central node) and the fully connected "all-channel network" (every node is connected to all other nodes).
- Mechanism: Narrow views merely confine governance to new forms of coordination, such as networks and bargaining systems, whereas the broad perspective embraces all social mechanisms by which coordination and order can be facilitated. The broad view thus includes top-down steering as well as distributed bottom-up control by market decisions.
- Level: A narrow view restricts governance only to a specific level of social activity, such as rule-making, whereas the broad perspective includes all types of actions within the policy-making circuit. For instance, Williamson distinguishes between governance as a middle-range rule-setting, on the one hand, and day-to-day policy-making, long-term rule-setting at the constitutional level, and rule evolution at the cultural level on the other (Williamson 2000).

The most useful and consistent view seems to be the broadest perspective—in which governance is conceived as the process of governing—which includes all four dimensions as a kind of extended view on institutionally shaped policy-making. The major advantage of this concept is to provide for a general frame to cover the broad array of institutional arrangements by which the coordination, regulation, and control of social systems and sub-systems are enabled and facilitated.

In order to evaluate the core of this conceptual innovation, it is useful to take a quick look at the evolution of this concept in four major traditional sub-disciplines of contemporary political science: comparative politics, policy analysis, political economy (public choice), and international relations. In all four domains, the crucial innovations were the micro- and meso-foundation of social and political processes, and the synthesis between holistic integration and individualistic conflict theories. Whereas conflict theory emphasizes the fact that societies are held together despite diverging social interests, integrationist theorists stress cohesion by norms and institutions. Micro-foundation then suggests going beyond the simple black-box models of social dynamics, according to which public policies and collective problem-solving emerge from top-down programmed system behavior. The aim is to reconstruct in detail how multiple actors with diverse interests and different institutional contexts successfully coordinate and cooperate in the production of public goods and problem-solving.

Comparative politics: This area of political science deals with the comparison of political systems to understand the effect of different institutions and actor constellations in the emergence of stability and systemic performance. In this field, governance theory first emerged within interest group research. During the 1960s and 1970s, the dominant perspective was a structural–functionalist version of system theory (Almond and Powell 1966), in which the various actors of the political system (government, parties, interest groups, etc.) had to fulfill structurally predetermined functions, and the role of interest groups was restricted to the articulation and aggregation of interests. This perspective was challenged by new approaches emphasizing that interest associations also had important governing functions, sometimes substituting public policies in their respective sectors (Schmitter 1981). By analyzing institutional structures of associations, these studies contributed to a more differentiated picture about the variety of actors and relations that are involved in modern politics (Streeck and Schmitter 1985). Within the debate of "democratic governance," this perspective was generalized toward all institutional arrangements involved in the governing of modern democracies (March and Olsen 1995); see also Part VII of this book.

Public policy analysis: This sub-discipline is concerned with the content and process of public policy-making, a perspective that emerged in the 1950s. Also, this approach was first dominated by system theory, in which public policies were treated as the top-down execution of functional imperatives. Shaped by the technological optimism of its time, this created a veritable euphoria of planning and social reform. However, in the early 1970s Scharpf (1972) emphasized the complexity of actor constellations as "planning barriers." Due to the failure of many policies, research increasingly focused on specific actor constellations supporting or hampering the successful implementation of policy programs (Mayntz 1983). As implementation problems often could have been avoided by the incorporation of private actors into the policy formulation, the traditional state-centric view was enlarged to an inclusive policy network perspective (Kenis and Schneider 1991; Scharpf 1997).

Political economy: This sub-discipline is strongly influenced by economic theories, creating an individualist counterpart to holistic system theory (Buchanan 1966; Olson 1971; see, for an overview, Holzinger 2009). In addition, this paradigm was firmly based on conflict theory where actors are essentially self-interested and competitive. Seen from an individualistic perspective, the paradigm aimed at avoiding categories such as "the common will" to explain the activities of governments and other organized collectivities. Collective action and the provision of collective goods were solely explained in a bottom-up fashion by the rational interaction of selfish actors. As many of these approaches pointed to social dilemmas in the provision of collective goods, "new institutionalists" began to combine rational action models with a variety of institutional arrangements, shaping individual action in such a way that desired collective outcomes were facilitated (North 1990; Ostrom 1990; Scharpf 1997).

International relations: This sub-domain essentially deals with conflict and cooperation in the international system. The evolution of "global governance theory" in this field was a reaction to the state-centric and realist model of global politics, assuming first that states interact as organized wholes (the billiard ball model), and second that competition and power politics are the dominant interaction in the international system. Building on findings of the "transnational school" of international relations, global governance emphasized the importance of domestic societal and non-governmental actors in global politics (Rosenau and Czempiel 1992; Ronit and Schneider 2000). In a relational perspective, global governance thus went beyond the realist model of interaction, and also accentuated cooperation, information exchange, and mutual learning in global politics (see Chapter 51, this volume).

Beyond these traditional sub-disciplines, the governance approach diffused into a growing number of research areas. In European studies, emerging from international relations, governance and related concepts (networks, multi-level governance) were increasingly used to describe the European Union (EU) as a hybrid political entity (Chapters 43 and 44, this volume). In the area of regulation studies, which combined policy analysis and political economy, regulatory policy-making by independent "non-majoritarian" political institutions was conceptualized as a specific mode of governance (Jordana and Levi-Faur 2004; Majone 1997). Finally, innovation studies use the governance approach to understand the diverse operation of national innovation systems (Kuhlmann 2001).

Although governance theory evolves differently in these various fields of inquiry, there are at least three commonalities:

- The avoidance of holistic (and functionalist) macro explanations in which large "organized wholes" (states, systems, sub-systems, etc.) are the principal actors whose actions are primarily determined by their functions and structural positions;
- The insertion of a variety of new institutional arrangements which enable the coordination, cooperation, and integration, as well as the creation of social order;
- A synthesis between purely conflict-oriented and purely integration-oriented perspectives, implying an increasing variety of political relations and structural configurations.

Therefore, governance theory contributed to a more differentiated picture of contemporary politics and society than previous approaches did. From this perspective, governance theory can be seen as a reflection of growing societal complexity. Schmidt, for instance, refers to Scharpf's perspective as a "complexity theory of democracy" (Schmidt 1997). The proximity of governance and complexity is also stressed by other authors (Pierre and Peters 2005; Kooiman 2003). However, as it will be shown in the next section, because of the broader perspective and deeper foundation of complexity theory, its analytical dimensions and process patterns are spelled out in a much greater precision.

3. COMPLEXITY THEORY AND THE EMERGENCE OF ORDER

Complexity theory emerged in natural sciences, engineering, and mathematics. Its core question is to explain the spontaneous emergence of order by self-organizing processes at multiple levels in nature and society. In this respect, it can be conceived as a sort of modernized version of evolution theory in which computer simulation and artificial intelligence are used to reconstruct—at the most abstract level—the evolution of matter, life, and consciousness. When applied to the social sciences, the variety of adaptive processes is used to explain the emergence of "social orders," such as organizational patterns and institutional structures in political and economic systems. In a long-term perspective, it intends to produce a "unified theory" of complex systems, which may be applied to all kinds of phenomena—regulatory networks in cells, food webs in the ecology, information flows in economies and polities (Holland 1995, 1998; Mitchell 2009).

As various overviews of this field have shown, its roots go back to cybernetics, general systems theory, and information theory at the beginning of the twentieth century (Mitchell 2009; Waldrop 1992). During the last few decades, it was strongly shaped by evolutionary biology (Kauffman 1993), computational theory in the computer sciences (Holland 1995), and the new "network science" as a recent offset of physics (Barabási 2003; Strogatz 2003). In the meantime, this type of theorizing also penetrated a range of sub-disciplines within the social sciences, above all economics (Beinhocker 2006) and sociology (Sawyer 2005). Because of the multiplicity of scientific fields involved in this debate, complexity theory encountered similar or even greater problems of conceptual fuzziness than governance theory. A review in the 1990s reported more than thirty ways to define complexity (Horgan 1995), and a recent guide to complexity theory emphasized nine different definitions (Mitchell 2009). Table 9.1 presents ten important definitions; some of them can be conceived of as "facets of complexity."

Table 9.1 Facets of complexity

	Facets and Definitions	Explanations
1	Compositional	The number and diversity of components that a system contains
2	Relational	The interrelatedness among the components in a system; this is not only a function of the number of the relations (density) but also of frequency (intensity) and diversity (multiplexity)
3	Ecological	The connectedness and nestedness of a system to its external environments and internal (sub-systems) environments
4	Hierarchical	The differentiation and "modularization" of a system across its different hierarchical levels
5	Functional	The number and diversity of functions a system fulfills
6	Mechanismic	The number and diversity of mechanisms operating in a system
7	Statistical	The minimum amount of information on the past behavior of a system necessary to predict its future development
8	Algorithmic	The degree of regularity (described by algorithms) displayed by a system versus its randomness
9	Thermodynamic	The amount of thermodynamic resources necessary to reassemble a system from scratch
10	Fractal	The "fuzziness" and degree of detail a system displays at smaller and smaller scales

Source: Bunge (1996), Horgan (1995), and Mitchell (2009).

Many of these definitions point to common properties: systems in this perspective are not fashioned by few structuring principles but consist of many heterogeneous components, each following local rules of behavior. Interaction, observation, communication, and bargaining then lead to the diffusion of rules and interaction patterns. Complexity scientists can demonstrate by computer simulations that collective order may emerge purely from local interaction at the micro level, without any need of central control. This bottom-up explanation of social phenomena is the most important feature of this approach. A fascinating example of "order from below" is swarm behavior: in swarms of birds and fish, organizational patterns emerge without any leadership or "collective brain." Individuals locally adapt their behavior to the behavior of their neighbors, and the overall program emerges from local interaction (Fisher 2009; Macy and Willer 2002).

In this complexity perspective, systems are inherently dynamic and adaptive. Components (agents) modify their behavior to improve it (in terms of success, fitness, survival, etc.) through learning or evolutionary mechanisms such as variation and selection. This generates new behavioral patterns in the sense that an organized whole is more than the sum of its parts. At the aggregate level, this can be seen as emergent complexity, in order to cope with more and more complex and diverse environments.

The diversity of components and the complexity of interaction impacts on the development processes of these systems. The contingency of constellations and process dynamics lead nonlinear behavior, implying critical mass and threshold effects where small events can lead to significant changes. Small stimuli can amplify and cascade through the entire system.

Although there are multiple perspectives on complexity science—for example, represented in different overviews (Capra 1996; Lewin 2000; Waldrop 1992; Mitchell 2009; Beinhocker 2006)—six key concepts should be emphasized: agents, networks, rules, adaptation, nonlinear dynamics, and emergence.

Agents

Basic assumptions include the fact that agents are partly autonomous, interdependent, diverse, and capable of rule-oriented behavior. Agents represent individuals, organizations, governments, and even societies (Holland 1995). With respect to diversity or heterogeneity, agents can vary in different respects: 1) agents may differ in power, status, and the control of different resources; 2) agents can perceive their environment according to specific "internal models" or belief systems; 3) agents may apply a range of action principles and decision-making criteria and may be more or less constrained by differential access to information and computing power. In contrast to rational choice theory, which emphasizes average behavior, heterogeneity of action is a key feature in complex systems models (Epstein and Axtell 1996; Miller and Page 2007).

Concerning autonomy, an important condition is that there is no central or higher instance which has full control on agent's individual behavior, and also that there are no rules controlling action in a deterministic way. Agents are not robots. Although they are conditioned by macro rules (e.g. social norms and institutions), rules can be partly ignored, interpreted differently, or even changed by subsequent interaction.

Networks

Another core idea is that multiple agents engage in local interaction based on a network of multiple relations. Interaction often goes along with or is preceded by other relationships, such as acquaintance or regular information exchange. Most of the systems are thus multi-relational in the sense that connectivity is not only based on one type of link (e.g. resource exchange, information, etc.) but that actors are enmeshed in multiple webs. This fact is usually expressed by the concept of multiplexity. This view is inspired by ecological thinking and its famous "web of life" metaphor (Capra 1996). In this respect an important relation is the "food chain" in which animals are interlinked by predatory competition. However, ecology cannot be reduced to agonism alone. Ecological research has shown that cooperation, symbiosis, mutualism, and other complex relations between different creatures are widespread. The actual mapping of complex networks in real ecosystems is an important part of biology and ecological science.

The special contribution of the new "network science" in this context was to find network patterns that can be generalized across nature and society (Barabási 2003; Strogatz 2003; Watts 2004). This became feasible with fast-growing computing power during the last decades. Major discoveries were the "small-world" and "scale-free" properties of large networks. Whereas the first denotes a network structure involving many local clusters that are interlinked by few "hubs" (nodes with many links), the second indicates "invariance under rescaling" (Mitchell 2009): many networks display similar power distributions (many nodes with few links, few nodes with many links) regardless of the scale in which they are presented. An important implication of this type of networks is resilience to the disruption of relations and dropout of nodes.

Rules

Agents use prescriptive devices for their action. Rule-guided behavior may react to changes in the environment or to the actions of other agents. A simple rule is an IF-THEN stimulus—a response sequence where a specific situational triggers a particular course of action. Agents may also use interaction rules that specify decision criteria to choose among actions or strategies, for example, to cooperate or defect in a dilemma situation. As Holland shows, rules can also relate to the perception of a situation ("internal model"), and multiple rules can be combined in a complex way to form "schemata" that spread among agents (Holland 1995). His path-breaking idea was to apply general evolutionary mechanisms (crossover, recombination, mutation, etc.) in the reproduction and selective spread of rule combinations. For instance, in a population-based simulation of the prisoner's dilemma, Holland could demonstrate that under certain conditions (e.g. agents informing about their past behavior), an evolutionary stable strategy of mutual cooperation can emerge. This perspective, in which rule combinations are treated as a kind of agents' DNA is also known as the "genetic algorithm" approach (Mitchell 2009), in which the logic of natural evolution is applied to the generative processes of rule systems (Epstein and Axtell 1996; Holland 1995).

Adaptation

In this generative view, agents' properties and action rules lead to dynamic patterns created by iterative and mutual adaptation. Both complexes of rules and properties of agents change and adapt endogenously over time. A key idea is that agents look for improved "fitness" and adjust their actions on the basis of trial and error, feedback, imitation, and learning. It is important to note that fitness does not necessarily equate with generally improved performance; it can just mean appropriateness to certain contexts. Adaptation processes operate at the individual and at the population level. In order to illustrate this iterative and sequential process, complexity scientists use the metaphor of a "fitness landscape" (Kauffman 1993), in which adaptation is compared to hill-climbing in a mountainous region. Elevations in the landscape represent better adaptation, and a peak in the overall scenery indicates supreme "fitness." Multiple peaks imply that there are several combinations with similar degrees of fitness, and a single peak (like the Japanese Fujiyama or the African Kilimanjaro) indicates that there is only one distinct rule combination that is best adapted to its environment. The various schemata are represented by points in a three-dimensional space. Elevations in the landscape express the vertical dimension in the topography, whereas the two horizontal dimensions indicate the proximity (similarity) of the various structural combinations to each other. Similar combinations imply adjacent locations in the topography, whereas dissimilar combinations are located further away from each other.

As Kauffman shows, evolutionary adaptation is shaped by a landscape's topography: variation in a rugged landscape is more risky than in a smooth one, since changes are subjected to stronger forces of selection. In a rugged area, a small variation can drastically reduce the chances of survival. Successful evolution by gradually increasing fitness means a sequence of hill-climbing, leading from small hills to ever higher summits (Kauffman 1993). The metaphor of fitness landscapes is not just an analogy, but integrates some of the most recent conceptual developments: 1) topographies with multiple peaks imply that there is not only one successful strategy of adaptation but often a whole series of local optima; 2) specific topographies may imply a "dead end" when a specific hill-climbing sequence leads to a local optimum where further development is "locked-in"; this phenomenon is called "path dependency"; 3) depending upon the shape of the landscape, variation can also lead to stagnating or even declining fitness, a phenomenon which is dealt with in the "punctuated equilibrium" concept (Gould and Eldredge 1993). The fitness landscape concept also integrates coevolution, which takes place when adaptive change in one population alters the fitness of other populations. This phenomenon is also summarized by the "red queen effect," which stresses a kind of evolutionary "arms race" between species and populations (Kauffman 1995b).

Nonlinearity

An important property of complex adaptive systems is nonlinearity. Structural configurations are nonlinear when the components are interdependent and when changes in one component affect many others. Change in one part may trigger chain reactions within the entire system (Jervis 1998). A dramatic example is the extinction of "keystone species" leading to the disappearance of many other species. A related effect is the "butterfly effect," stressing the fact that small events—such as the wing beat of a butterfly—can produce large effects in the long run. Nonlinearity also exists in processes due to quality changes after passing a critical threshold (size, mass, number, etc.). The concepts of "tipping points," "phase transitions," or "critical mass" relate to such developments. Discontinuities can be triggered by endogenous as well as exogenous events, and a theory explaining developmental jumps by big external events is "punctuated equilibrium" theory (Gould and Eldredge 1993).

A major implication of this kind of pattern is unpredictability. Nonlinearity makes a system's behavior hard to predict, at least in the long run. In the worst case, the system will become chaotic; in a less dramatic situation it just alternates between multiple equilibriums.

Emergence

From a macrostructural perspective, the most important implication of complex systems' thinking is "emergence," that is, the fact that the individual interaction level produces social effects at the macro level, which are not reducible to the aggregate alone. A key idea in this respect is "self-assembly of order" or self-organization as a kind of "order for free" (Kauffman 1995a; Ramage and Shipp 2009). Interaction at the micro level, where agents follow their local rules, will generate collective patterns over time (e.g. coordination, division of labor, etc.).

During the past ten years, some of these concepts have been applied to social sciences. For instance, the concept of "fitness landscapes" was used in organizational sociology and innovation studies (McKelvey 1999; Frenken 2006). In political science, agent-based models were used to explain the emergence and consolidation of nation-states in the international system (Cederman 1997). Their application to the evolution of governance structures in the technology development (Schneider 2001) or to public policy in general is still rare but is growing (Geyer and Rihani 2010; Klijn 2008).

4. IMPLICATIONS OF COMPLEXITY THINKING
FOR GOVERNANCE THEORY

Complexity approaches apply a diversified perspective on political configurations. Complex systems include multiple levels, numerous and heterogeneous components, and multiple relations:

- Complex systems are "systems of systems," in which micro-level processes are nested in meso and macro levels, and macrostructures "emerge" from micro and meso dynamics.
- Multiple and heterogeneous components as distinctive features relate to a variety of actors and "rule works." Actors are heterogeneous with respect to their resources and action orientations. Rules and rule regimes are complex combinations that cannot be reduced to singular principles.
- Multiplex networks imply that various actors are not only tied in by one type of relation but also by other social bonds and relationships.

According to this perspective, social processes are not reducible to few basic principles or "logics" that shape the action and the evolution of overall systems. For instance, in a complexity perspective it makes no sense to reduce the EU or a nation-state to "network governance" or the "network society." In contrast, political systems of all kind are complex combinations of orders in which a multiplicity of factors and conditions has to be taken into account. Social processes are differentiated and nested based on multiple mechanisms, processes, and social forces. In this perspective, order cannot be explained solely by a single governance structure or by development logic. For instance, while hierarchical rules play an important role in political organizations, there are also spontaneous orders merely arising due to adaptive interaction at the micro level. Systems become adaptive and move into ordered processes when agents operate independently in response to individual needs, to environmental pressures, and to the actions of others.

Such a diversified perspective can enhance governance theory in various respects. It contributes not only to a more fine-grained and dynamic perspective, which takes nonlinearity into account. In addition, it enables the integration of multiple levels, relations, and heterogeneous agents into one single picture. In such a view, complex governance systems are composed of many governing agents (organizations or individuals) whose diverse incentives, motives, calculations, and so on at the micro level are important factors in the explanation of regulation and feedback processes at the different levels of the social fabric. At the same time, however, these agents are embedded into political, economic, and cultural rule systems, which distribute rights, resources, and incentives in a complex way. This structure may also extend to actors and conditions in the environment which constrain and influence the actions of internal agents. An important task in this perspective is to explain adaptive capacity and performance of differently structured governance systems (Pierre and Peters 2005).

The analysis of such plural and multilayered order-generating mechanisms must not necessarily be formalized in mathematical models. Qualitative explanatory sketches can, too, improve the understanding of complex systems. However, in order to fully exploit the potential of this type of analysis, quantitative methods and computer simulation are very powerful. For instance, to describe such "hybrid" and "multijuristical" institutional configurations, which are stressed by Bevir (2011) in a precise way, political analysis has to advance its methods to formalize complex combinations. Beyond a certain number of actors, rules, and relations, a qualitative analysis of constellations and interactions will quickly reach its limits. In this respect, complexity theory and agent-based modeling offer a promising perspective from which to advance the analytical power of governance theories.

Governance theory should limit its domain of application to micro- and meso-structures of society. Applications at the level of macrostructures run the risk of oversimplification. When it is argued that modern societies are in a transition from hierarchical to network governance, there is a grain of truth in this statement in the sense that the role of hierarchy has decreased in modern society. However, it would be absurd to assume that modern societies are only governed by networks. Concrete societies are coordinated by a combination of multiple mechanisms, which we perhaps do not fully understand at the moment. If governance theory is used to reintroduce a single all-explaining mechanism, it becomes a similar obscure approach to that of systems theory in the 1960s and 1970s. In order to avoid the danger of speaking of governance in a similar manner, a more detailed analysis of complex interaction processes, rule systems, regulatory mechanisms, and generative processes is indispensible. In this respect, governance analysis can learn a lot from complexity theory.

NOTE

* I am grateful for linguistic assistance to Leonie Fremgen, and for critical and helpful comments to David Levi-Faur, Achim Lang, Thomas Malang, and Holger Pressel.

REFERENCES

Almond, G. A. and Powell, G. B. 1966. *Comparative Politics. A Developmental Approach.* Boston, MA: Little Brown.

Barabási, A.-L. 2003. *Linked: How Everything is Connected to Everything Else.* New York: Plume.

Beinhocker, E. D. 2006. *The Origin of Wealth: Evolution, Complexity, and the Radical Remaking of Economics.* Boston, MA: Harvard Business School Press.

Bevir, M. 2011. Governance as theory, practice, and dilemma. In M. Bevir (ed.), *The Sage Handbook of Governance.* Los Angeles: Sage, 1–15.

Buchanan, J. M. 1966. An individualistic theory of political process. In D. Easten, (ed.), *Varieties of Political Theory.* Englewood Cliffs, NJ: Prentice-Hall, 25–37.

Bunge, M. 1996. *Finding Philosophy in Social Science*. New Haven: Yale University Press.

Capra, F. 1996. *The Web of Life*. New York: Anchor Books.

Cederman, L. E. 1997. *Emergent Actors in World Politics: How States and Nations Develop and Dissolve*. Princeton, NJ: Princeton University Press.

Epstein, J. M. and Axtell, R. L. 1996. *Growing Artificial Societies: Social Science from the Bottom Up*. Cambridge, MA: MIT Press.

Fisher, L. 2009. *The Perfect Swarm: The Science of Complexity in Everyday Life*. New York: Basic Books.

Frenken, K. 2006. *Innovation, Evolution and Complexity Theory*. Cheltenham: Edward Elgar.

Geyer, R. and Rihani, S. 2010. *Complexity and Public Policy: A New Approach to 21st Century Politics, Policy and Society*. London: Routledge.

Gould, S. J. and Eldredge, N. 1993. Punctuated equilibrium comes of age. *Nature* 366: 223–227.

Holland, J. H. 1995. *Hidden Order: How Adaptation Builds Complexity*. Reading, MA: Addison Wesley.

Holland, J. H. 1998. *Emergence: From Chaos to Order*. New York: Oxford University Press.

Holzinger, K. 2009. Vom ungeliebten Störenfried zum akzeptierten Paradigma? Zum Stand der (Neuen) Politischen Ökonomie in Deutschland. *Politische Vierteljahresschrift* 50: 539–576.

Horgan, J. 1995. From complexity to perplexity. *Scientific American* 272: 104–109.

Jervis, R. 1998. *System Effects: Complexity in Political and Social Life*. Princeton, NJ: Princeton University Press.

Jordana, J. and Levi-Faur, D. (eds.) 2004. *The Politics of Regulation: Institutions and Regulatory Reforms for the Age of Governance*. Cheltenham: Edward Elgar.

Kauffman, S. A. 1993. *The Origins of Order: Self-Organization and Selection in Evolution*. New York: Oxford University Press.

Kauffman, S. A. 1995a. *At Home in the Universe: The Search for Laws of Self-Organization and Complexity*. New York: Oxford University Press.

Kauffman, S. A. 1995b. Technology and evolution: Escaping the red queen effect. *McKinsey Quarterly* 1: 118–129.

Kenis, P. and Schneider, V. 1991. Policy networks and policy analysis: Scrutinizing a new analytical toolbox. In B. Marin and R. Mayntz (eds.), *Policy Networks: Empirical Evidence and Theoretical Considerations*. Frankfurt-am-Main: Campus Verlag, 25–59.

Klijn, E. 2008. Complexity theory and public administration: What's new? *Public Management Review* 10(3): 299–317.

Kooiman, J. 2003. *Governing as Governance*. London: Sage.

Kuhlmann, S. 2001. Future governance of innovation policy in Europe: Three scenarios. *Research Policy* 30: 953–976.

Lewin, R. 2000. *Complexity: Life at the Edge of Chaos*. Chicago: University of Chicago Press.

Macy, M. W. and Willer, R. 2002. From factors to actors: Computational sociology and agent-based modeling. *Annual Review of Sociology* 28: 143–166.

Majone, G. 1997. From the positive to the regulatory state: Causes and consequences of changes in the mode of governance. *Journal of Public Policy* 17: 139–167.

March, J. G. and Olsen, J. P. 1995. *Democratic Governance*. New York: Free Press.

Mayntz, R. 1983. The conditions of effective public policy: a new challenge for policy analysis. *Policy and Politics* 11: 123–143.

Mayntz, R. 2003. New challenges to governance theory. In H. P. Bang (ed.), *Governance as Social and Political Communication*. Manchester: Manchester University Press, 27–40.

McKelvey, B. 1999. Self-organization, complexity catastrophe, and microstate models at the edge of chaos. In J. A. C. Baum and B. McKelvey (eds.), *Variations in Organization Science: In Honor of Donald T. Campbell*. Thousand Oaks, CA: Sage, 279–307.

Miller, J. H. and Page, S. E. 2007. *Complex Adaptive Systems: An Introduction to Computational Models of Social Life*. Princeton, NJ: Princeton University Press.

Mitchell, M. 2009. *Complexity: A Guided Tour*. New York: Oxford University Press.

North, D. 1990. A transaction cost theory of politics. *Journal of Theoretical Politics* 2: 355.

Offe, C. 2009. Governance: An "empty signifier"? *Constellations* 16: 550–562.

Olson, M. 1971. *The Logic of Collective Action: Public Goods and the Theory of Groups*. Cambridge, MA: Harvard University Press.

Ostrom, E. 1990. *Governing the Commons: The Evolution of Institutions for Collective Action*. Cambridge: Cambridge University Press.

Pierre, J. and Peters, G. 2005. *Governing Complex Societies: Trajectories and Scenarios*. Basingstoke: Palgrave MacMillan.

Ramage, M. and Shipp, K. 2009. *Systems Thinkers*. London: Open University Press.

Ronit, K. and Schneider, V. (eds.) 2000. *Private Organizations in Global Politics*. London: Routledge.

Rosenau, J. and Czempiel, E. 1992. *Governance without Government: Order and Change in World Politics*. Cambridge: Cambridge University Press.

Sawyer, R. K. 2005. *Social Emergence: Societies as Complex Systems*. Cambridge: Cambridge University Press.

Scharpf, F. W. 1972. Komplexität als Schranke der politischen Planung *Politische Vierteljahresschrift* 13: 168–192.

Scharpf, F. W. 1997. *Games Real Actors Play: Actor-Centered Institutionalism in Policy Research*. Boulder, CO: Westview Press.

Schmidt, M. 1997. *Demokratietheorien*. Wiesbaden: VS-Verlag.

Schmitter, P. 1981. Interest intermediation and regime governability in contemporary Western Europe and North America. In S. Berger (ed.), *Organizing Interests in Western Europe*. Cambridge: Cambridge University Press, 285–330.

Schneider, V. 2001. *Die Transformation der Telekommunikation: Vom Staatsmonopol zum globalen Markt (1800–2000)*. Frankfurt-am-Main: Campus Verlag.

Schneider, V. and Bauer, J. 2009. Von der Governance-zur Komplexitätstheorie: Rekonstruktion gesellschaftlicher Ordnungsbildung. In I. Schulz-Schaeffer and J. Weyer (eds.), *Management Komplexer Systeme*. München: Oldenbourg, 31–53.

Streeck, W. and Schmitter, P. 1985. Community, market, state—and associations? The prospective contribution of interest governance to social order. *European Sociological Review* 1: 119–138.

Strogatz, S. H. 2003. *Sync: The Emerging Science of Spontaneous Order*. New York: Hyperion.

Van Kersbergen, K. and van Waarden, F. 2004. "Governance" as a bridge between disciplines: Cross-disciplinary inspiration regarding shifts in governance and problems of governability, accountability and legitimacy. *European Journal of Political Research* 43: 143–171.

Waldrop, M. M. 1992. *Complexity: The Emerging Science at the Edge of Order and Chaos*. New York: Simon and Schuster.

Watts, D. 2004. *Six Degrees: The Science of a Connected Age*. New York: Norton.

Williamson, O. 2000. The new institutional economics: Taking stock, looking ahead. *Journal of Economic Literature* 38: 595–613.

CHAPTER 10

··

GOOD GOVERNANCE

··

BO ROTHSTEIN[*]

1. WHY GOOD GOVERNANCE?

GOOD *governance* is a relatively new concept that has made a strong impact in some of the highest policy circles since the mid-1990s. The concept has received most attention in circles dealing with developing countries and the so-called transition countries (Smith 2007; Peters, this volume, Chapter 2). It is now used by many national development agencies and international organizations such as the World Bank and the United Nations. An example is the International Monetary Fund, which in 1996 declared that "promoting good governance in all its aspects, including by ensuring the rule of law, improving the efficiency and accountability of the public sector, and tackling corruption, are essential elements of a framework within which economies can prosper" (IMF 2005). However, the recent economic and financial crises have shown that issues about "bad governance" cannot be seen only as a problem for developing and transition countries but also for the highly developed parts of the world (Rothstein 2011).

In this chapter, I will argue that good governance is a concern if a society is in possession of the political, legal, and administrative institutions that make it possible to enact and implement policies that can broadly be understood as "public goods." Such goods can in practice be many things, from systems for sanitation, pensions and other social insurances, defence, and preservation of scarce natural resources, to the respect for the rule of law and protection of property rights. The well-known problem of public goods is that because of the possibility to "free ride," they will not be supplied by standard market operations. Instead, some forms of binding and enforceable regulations are needed. This implies that good governance is closely related to concepts like *state capacity* (Besley and Persson 2011), *quality of government* (Rothstein 2011), and the possibility of establishing sustainable systems for governing various types of "common-pool resources"

(Ostrom 1990). It should also be noted that good governance in many cases does not only refer to certain qualities of government institutions but also to governments' interaction with the various sections of the private sector. Good governance can be produced by the government alone but in many cases there is a need for collaboration with business and/or voluntary organizations (Pierre and Peters 2005).

The intellectual background: the institutional turn in the social sciences

One of the major sources for the rise of the good governance agenda has been the "institutional turn" in the social sciences. Around 1990, three major works were published that have had a profound impact for the analysis of institutions, namely Douglass C. North's *Institutions, Institutional Change and Economic Performance* (1990), James B. March and Johan P. Olsen's *Rediscovering Institutions*, and Elinor Ostrom's *Governing the Commons*. Although coming from different intellectual traditions, they had one aim in common, namely to challenge the then dominating societal view in studies of social and economic outcomes. Instead of variables like economic power or the structure of class divisions, these scholars argued that political institutions, broadly understood as informal as well as formal rules and regulations, were central in explaining social outcomes. In short, instead of focusing on how economic and sociological variables determined politics, the institutional approach turned the causal logic around by arguing that the character of a society's political institutions to a large extent determined its economic and social development.

In addition to the general analyses of the importance of institutions, the good governance agenda has also been inspired by research on the possibility for governments (and international organizations) to produce and implement "optimal" or "good" regulations for various sectors of the economy (Jordana and Levi-Faur 2004). The challenge here is usually understood as producing regulations that serve "the common good" in spite of the power from various special interest groups that try to bend the rules (Croley 2007).

The policy background: from the Washington Consensus to good governance

In development policy circles, the good governance agenda has to a large extent replaced what was known as *the Washington Consensus*. This approach stated that economic growth could be created by massive deregulation of markets, tightening of public spending, guarantees for property rights, and large-scale privatizations (Serra and Stiglitz 2008). The reason why this strategy did not work, according to many observers, was that poor countries lacked the necessary type of institutions that were "taken for granted" in neoclassical economics. Among those, Rodrik (2007: 97) lists "a regulatory apparatus curbing the worst forms of fraud, anti-competitive behavior, and moral hazard, a moderately cohesive society exhibiting trust and social cooperation, social and political institutions that mitigate risk and manage social conflicts, the rule of law and clean government." In former communist countries, so-called shock-therapy capitalism ran into a number of problems, not least because its proponents did not pay adequate attention to the need for institutions that would hinder fraudulent, anti-competitive, and other similar types of destructive behavior (Kornai, Rothstein, and Rose-Ackerman 2004).

Empirical research: good governance and human wellbeing

Another reason for the rise of the good governance agenda is that a number of studies have shown it to have a positive impact on a large set of outcomes related to human wellbeing. The background is the development of a number of widely used measures and indexes that can be said to measure various aspects of "good governance," such as government effectiveness, levels of corruption, and the quality of legal systems. Central in this discussion has been the link between the quality of government institutions that implement policies (control of corruption, the rule of law) and economic growth (Holmberg, Rothstein, and Nasiritousi 2008). There is also some evidence showing that "good governance" leads to lower economic inequality (Chong and Calderon 2000; Chong and Gradstein 2004). In addition, Helliwell and Huang (2008), Frey and Stutzer (2000), Pacek and Radcliff (2008), and Ott (2010) have observed positive links between measures of good governance and subjective wellbeing (a measure of an individual's evaluation of their quality of life in total).

There is also a large body of literature that testifies to the negative consequences of "bad governance," chiefly in the form of corruption and a lack of property rights, for areas such as population health and people's access to safe water (Sjöstedt 2008; Holmberg and Rothstein 2011; Transparency International 2006; Swaroop and Rajkumar 2002). In addition, Rothstein and Stolle (2008) show that high trust in legal institutions has a positive impact on interpersonal trust. Råby and Teorell (2010) show that measures of good governance are stronger in predicting the absence of violent interstate conflicts than measures for democracy, and Lapuente and Rothstein (2010) make the same argument for civil wars. Maybe most surprising are Gilley's findings about political legitimacy. From a study based on survey data from seventy-two countries he concludes that "general governance (a composite of the rule of law, control of corruption and government effectiveness) has a large, even overarching importance in global citizen evaluations of states." He further states that these governance variables have a stronger impact on political legitimacy than variables measuring democratic rights and welfare gains (Gilley 2006: 57; cf. Gilley 2009; Levi and Sacks 2009). In sum, while it has been very difficult to find any positive correlations between measures of the degree of democracy and measures of human wellbeing in cross-country studies, the opposite is true for measures of good governance that relate to the output side of the political system (Råby and Teorell 2010). Thus, policy organizations that have put good governance on their agenda are supported by quite a large number of empirical studies.

2. DIFFERENT CONCEPTIONS OF GOOD GOVERNANCE

As could be expected, an extensive debate exists about how good governance should be defined. Should it be about procedures only (like most definitions of representative democracy) or should it also contain substantial policies? Should the concept be universally applicable all over the globe (like the UN Declaration of Human Rights) or should it be relativized to different cultures? Should the concept be equated with efficiency or should it be understood as something that explains efficiency? Should good governance include how well those who govern represent those who are governed, or should it be about the capacity to steer society? One of the most frequently used definitions of good governance has been launched by the World Bank Research Institute and reads as follows:

> The traditions and institutions by which authority in a country is exercised. This includes (1) the process by which governments are selected, monitored and replaced, (2) the capacity of the government to effectively formulate and implement sound policies, and (3) the respect of citizens and the state for the institutions that govern economic and social interactions among them. (Kaufmann, Kraay, and Zoido-Lobatón 1999: 1)

This definition forms the basis of the World Bank's widely used Worldwide Governance Indicators that has measures for "voice and accountability," "political instability and violence," "government effectiveness," "regulatory quality," "rule of law," and "control of corruption." This is a very broad definition and it has been criticized for including both policy content ("sound policies") and procedures ("rule of law"). It has also been criticized for containing both the institutions for access to political power as well as those that exercise and implement laws and policies. The "sound policies" problem raises the question whether international (mostly economic) experts can be expected to be in possession of reliable answers to the question of what are "sound policies" (Rothstein and Teorell 2008). For example, should pensions or health care or education be privately or publicly funded (or a mix of these)? To what extent and how should financial institutions be regulated? Second, such a definition of good governance that is not restricted to procedures but includes the substance of policies raises what is known as the "Platonian-Leninist" problem. If those with superior knowledge decide policies, the democratic process will be emptied of most substantial issues. The argument against the "Platonian-Leninist" alternative to democracy has been put forward by one of the leading democratic theorists, Robert Dahl, in the following way: "its extraordinary demands on the knowledge and virtue of the guardians are all but impossible to satisfy in practice" (Dahl 1989: 65).

Is small also good?

Another idea that has been put forward is that good governance equals small government. A case in point is Alesina and Angeletos who conclude that "a large government increases corruption and rent-seeking" (2005: 1241). Similarly, Nobel laureate Gary Becker has argued that "to root out corruption, boot out big government" (1998: 210). For Becker, as well as for many other economists, "the source of corruption is the same everywhere; large governments with the power to dispense many goodies to different groups" (ibid.: 203). Therefore, smaller government is "the only surefire way to reduce corruption" (ibid.: 203). However, if we take a look into the empirics, the relationship between government size and corruption runs in the opposite direction. Thus, the comparatively least corrupt countries—to a significant extent situated in the northern parts of Europe—have generally much larger governments than the most corrupt ones. If we take all countries for which data is available, the correlation between total tax revenues as a share of GDP and institutional quality is 0.34. As North, Wallis, and Weingast (2009) show, rich countries have much larger governments than poor countries. They explain this by arguing that not only are infrastructure and the rule of law to be understood as public goods and thus to be financed by the state, but to a large extent education, research, and social insurance programs that mitigate risks are also to be considered thus. This is not an argument for saying that high public expenditure reduces corruption and is a causal factor behind good governance, but, as stated by La Porta and colleagues (1999: 42), the data shows that "identifying big government with bad government can be highly misleading."

Good governance as absence of corruption

One way out of the definitional problem would be to simply define good governance as the absence of corruption. This turns out to be problematic for several reasons. First, corruption is in itself difficult to define. The standard definition is that corruption is "the abuse of public power for private gain." The problem with this definition is that it is relativistic since what counts as "abuse" (or "misuse") would vary in different parts of the world (Kurer 2005: 229). Needless to say, this would dramatically increase problems of operationalization and measurement but it would also carry all the difficulties connected to relativistic definitions that we know from discussions about human rights and democracy. Without a universally accepted normative standard about what forms of behavior are acceptable and appropriate, there is no way to know (and measure) what should count as "abuse" when we compare various systems of governance in order to see if they would qualify for the epithet "good" or not.

The second reason why good governance cannot be equated with the absence of corruption is that there may exist many problems within governing societies that are not confined to what is usually understood as corruption. A high degree of corruption is certainly an antithesis to good governance, but so are many other practices that are usually not seen as corruption, such as clientelism, lack of respect for the rule of law and property rights, nepotism, cronyism, patronage, systemic discrimination, and cases where administrative agencies are "captured" by the interest groups that they set out to regulate and control (Rothstein and Teorell 2008).

Good governance as the rule of law

Perhaps as central as corruption, establishing the rule of law is usually key in any discussion on good governance and is placed high on the agenda for reforming developing and transitional countries (Carothers 1998). Still, although unequivocally embraced as a virtue of any system of good governance, the concept is rarely defined. One reason for this may of course be that the concept is inherently ambiguous and legal scholars argue over its exact meaning (Rose 2004). To begin with, they dispute whether or not the rule of law should be given a purely procedural interpretation bearing no implications for the actual substance of promulgated laws. Those that defend a procedural notion claim that the rule of law must be distinguished from the rule of "good" law. Critics argue that this would allow morally detested regimes, such as Nazi Germany, to be classified as abiding by the rule of law. Against the procedural view, these critics seek to inscribe into the rule of law various substantive moral values of liberal democracy (cf. Bratton and Chang 2006: 1077–1078). Yet, even among proceduralists, who adhere to a narrower conception, ambiguities remain. Usually more attention is paid to the internal qualities of the laws themselves—such as the need for the law to be clear, understandable, general, internally consistent, prospective, stable, and so on—rather than to define the core principles that a political system must abide by in order to be in accordance with the rule of law.

Searching for these core principles, one may instead turn to conceptions developed within political science. Weingast (1997: 245) defines the rule of law as "a set of stable political rules and rights applied impartially to all citizens." Similarly, O'Donnell (2004: 33) states a minimal definition of the rule of law as "that whatever law exists is written down and publicly promulgated by an appropriate authority before the events meant to be regulated by it, and is fairly applied by relevant state institutions including the judiciary." He then specifies his normative term:

> By "fairly applied" I mean that the administrative application or judicial adjudication of legal rules is consistent across equivalent cases; is made without taking into consideration the class, status, or relative amounts of power held by the parties in such cases; and applies procedures that are preestablished, knowable, and allow a fair chance for the views and interests at stake in each case to be properly voiced.

The rule of law thus embodies the principle "equality before the law." It entails "a crucial principle of fairness—that like cases be treated alike" (ibid.: 33–34). However, one problem is that good governance also applies to spheres of state action other than those directly governed by law. When public policy is to be enacted in so-called "human processing" areas, such as, for example, education, health care, welfare benefits, and active labor-market programs, widely discretionary powers usually need to be transferred to lower-level government officials and professional corps responsible for implementing policy. The reason is that they have to adapt actions to the specific circumstances in each case and it has turned out to be administratively impossible to enact precise "rule of law type" laws and regulations that can guide this. In many areas, governance is carried out by professional corps that are for the most part guided by professional standards issued by their organizations, which are not connected to "rule of law" principles. For example, nurses in elderly care homes would probably not think of what they are doing as guided by "the rule of law." This is not a novel insight: Aristotle himself observed that written laws cannot be applied precisely in every situation, since the legislators, "being unable to define for all cases . . . are obliged to make universal statements, which are not applicable to all but only to most cases" (quoted in Brand 1988: 46). The conclusion is that while the "rule of law" principles in most approaches serve as a central ingredient in good governance, they do not cover the full spectrum of the concept.

Good governance and democracy

Establishing representative democracy has often been championed as an effective antidote to everything from corruption to poverty. This because of its link to accountability, which helps to reduce the discretionary powers of public officials (Deininger and Mpuga 2005: 171). This would indicate that democracy and good governance could possibly conceptually overlap, thus raising the question of why we need a concept like good governance since we could just talk about "good democracy." The problem is that, empirically, there is no straightforward relationship between establishing electoral representative democracy and many features of good governance. On the contrary, democracy seems to be curvilinearly related to the level of corruption (Montinola and Jackman 2002; Sung 2004). Empirical research indicates that corruption is worst in countries that have newly democratized, for example, in Peru under its former president, Fujimori (McMillan and Zoido 2004), and in Jamaica since the mid-1970s (Collier 2006).

This issue—that the introduction of representative electoral democracy does not necessarily lead to good governance or increases in the quality of government institutions responsible for implementing laws and policies—has been raised by Larry Diamond. He argues that although there is reason to celebrate the fact that more countries than ever before are democratic, he warns that in many countries, democracy is "haunted by the specter of bad governance," which he defines as "governance that is drenched in corruption, patronage, favoritism, and abuse of power" (Diamond 2007: 119). He also argues that the idea that the pathologies of "bad governance" can be cured with more "democracy assistance" is not convincing because such assistance does not reach the deeper levels of the political culture in societies that are dominated by clientelism or endemic corruption. When, as is often the case, corrupt practices are "deeply embedded in the norms and expectations" of how political and economic exchanges are perceived, improvement will require nothing less than a "revolutionary change in institutions" (Diamond 2007: 120). It is noteworthy that Diamond, one of the most prominent scholars in democratization research and democracy promotion, makes a clear distinction between democracy and good governance and points out that only introducing the former while neglecting the latter will not result in increased human wellbeing. One should also keep in mind that the two states that have made the greatest progress in curbing corruption over the last few decades—Singapore and Hong Kong—have not been and are still *not* democracies (Uslaner 2008). From this, and from the empirical research (referred to above) showing that measures of good governance have much a greater impact on human wellbeing (and perceptions of political legitimacy) than measures of democracy, we may conclude that good governance is different from, and should not conceptually be equated with, democracy.

Good governance as government efficiency

It would certainly be strange to argue that a government that is very inefficient or ineffective could produce *good governance*. Would it then be possible to define good governance in terms of government efficiency or effectiveness? There are two reasons why this is problematic. First, the notion of "good" usually implies other things than just economic efficiency. It is easy to think of things that a government can carry out in an efficient way that normatively would be just the opposite of "good." Second, defining good governance in terms of administrative and regulative efficiency would border on establishing a tautology. One should bear in mind that the good governance agenda largely came about in studies trying to understand why many developing countries were unable to increase growth. Defining good governance in terms of efficiency would be to say that efficiency causes efficiency. Not much would be gained by saying that societies with efficient governance systems produce efficiency. If not a tautology, one could say that such a definition would make the distance between independent and dependent variables minimal. Instead, what we need to know is if societies that are socially and economically efficient, that is, are able to solve the problem of producing the amount and type of public goods they need, have institutions that are qualitatively different in their operative principles than the opposite type of societies.

3. Conclusion: toward a definition of good governance

As seen above, neither the absence of corruption, nor representative democracy, nor the size of government, nor the rule of law, nor administrative effectiveness captures what should be counted as *good governance*. Searching for a definition, it is notable that the conceptual discussion has largely been detached from normative political theories about social justice and the state. It should be obvious that when terms like "good" are placed in political concepts, it is impossible to refrain from entering the normative issues that are raised in political philosophy. One can say that modern political philosophy has been engaged with the issue of "what the state ought to do" but refrained from taking an interest in what the state "can do." There are good reasons for why it is meaningless (or dangerous) to discuss the one without the other (Rothstein 1998). The good governance agenda is a clear case where normative/philosophical theory and positive/empirical approaches should merge. This issue is certainly not confined to internal academic civilities. Without a foundation for ethical standards, the risk is that when approaches like the good governance agenda translates into policies, it may end up in mindless utilitarianism where basic human rights of (often poor) people are sacrificed in the name of some overall utility (Talbott 2005). The first requirement for a definition of good governance is thus that it is based in a normative theory that gives some orientation for what should be regarded as "good" in this context. Second, any definition of good governance must take into account that this approach has clearly shifted the interest away from the "input" side of the political system to the "output" side of the political system.

A third requirement would be universalism, since the good governance approach is *de facto* applied on a global scale. This demand raises the issue of how to deal with the huge variation in institutional configurations that exists between countries which, in most evaluations of good governance, are ranked at the top. As with their institutions for representative democracy, the Swiss, Finnish, British, and German systems of governance are very different in their specific institutional configurations but these countries are all still counted as having "good governance." Obviously, a definition of good governance (or representative democracy) cannot relate to a specific set of institutional arrangements. Instead, we have to look for some basic norm that characterizes the system as whole. For representative democracy, that is, the access to power, Robert Dahl has suggested such a norm, namely "political equality." The issue is what could be the equivalent for good governance given that issues are more related to the implementation side of the political system. Based on the type of rights-based liberal political theory launched by philosophers such as Brian Barry and John Rawls, a suggestion for such a "basic norm" has been put forward by Rothstein and Teorell, namely *impartiality* in the exercise of public power, which they define in the following way: "When implementing laws and policies, government officials shall not take anything about the citizen or case into consideration that is not beforehand stipulated in the policy or the law" (Rothstein and Teorell 2008: 170; Rothstein 2011). Such a definition of *good governance* would make it clear what the norm is—that is, what is being "abused" when corruption, clientelism, favoritism, patronage, nepotism, or undue support to special interest groups occurs when a society is governed in a manner that should be considered as "good." Establishing institutions that are governed by impartiality would then in itself be understood as a "public goods problem," which also seems to be the case given the number of people in the world that have to endure the opposite type of systems of governance.

NOTE

* I would like to thank Rasmus Broms for excellent research assistance and my colleagues at The Quality of Government Institute at University of Gothenburg for all kinds of intellectual support.

REFERENCES

Alesina, A. and Angeletos, G.-M. 2005. Corruption, inequality, and fairness. *Journal of Monetary Economics* 52: 1227–1244.

Becker, G. S. 1998. *The Economics of Life: From Baseball to Affirmative Action to Immigration, How Real-World Issues Affect our Everyday Life*. New York: McGraw-Hill.

Besley, T. and Persson, T. 2011. *Pillars of Prosperity: State Capacity and Economic Development*. Princeton, NJ: Princeton University Press.

Brand, D. 1988. *Corporatism and the Rule of Law*. Ithaca, NY: Cornell University Press.

Bratton, M. and Chang. E. C. 2006. State building in Sub-Saharan Africa: Forwards, backwards, or together. *Comparative Political Studies* 39: 1059–1083.

Carothers, T. 1998. The rule of law revival. *Foreign Affairs* 77: 95–106.

Chong, A. and Calderón, C. A. 2000. Institutional quality and poverty measures in a cross-section of countries. *Economics of Governance* 1: 123–135.

Chong, A. and Gradstein, M. 2004. *Inequality and Institutions*. Research Department Working Paper No. 506. New York: Inter-American Development Bank.

Collier, M. W. 2006. *Political Corruption in the Caribbean Basin*. London: Routledge.

Croley, S. P. 2007. *Regulation and Public Interests: The Possibility of Good Regulatory Government*. Princeton, NJ: Princeton University Press.

Dahl, R. A. 1989. *Democracy and Its Critics*. New Haven, CT: Yale University Press.

Deininger, K. and Mpuga, P. 2005. Does greater accountability improve the quality of public service delivery? Evidence from Uganda. *World Development* 33: 171–191.

Diamond, L. J. 2007. A quarter-century of promoting democracy. *Journal of Democracy* 18:118–120.

Frey, B. S. and Stutzer, A. 2000. Happiness, economy and institutions. *The Economic Journal* 110: 918–938.

Gilley, B. 2006. The determinants of state legitimacy: Results for 72 countries. *International Political Science Review* 27: 47–71.

Gilley, B. 2009. *The Right to Rule: How States Win and Lose Legitimacy.* New York: Columbia University Press.

Helliwell, J. F. and Huang, H. 2008. How's your government? International evidence linking good government and well-being. *British Journal of Political Science* 38: 595–619.

Holmberg, S. and Rothstein, B. 2011. Dying of corruption. *Health Economics, Policy and Law* (forthcoming).

Holmberg, S., Rothstein, B. and Nasiritousi, N. 2008. *Quality of Government: What You Get.* Working Paper No. 21. Gothenburg: Quality of Government Institute.

IMF (International Monetary Fund). 2005. *The IMF's Approach to Promoting Good Governance and Combating Corruption: A Guide*; available at www.imf.org/external/np/gov/guide/eng/index.htm.

Jordana, J. and Levi-Faur, D. 2004. *The Politics of Regulation: Institutions and Regulatory Reforms for the Age of Governance.* Northampton, MA: Edward Elgar.

Kaufmann, D., Kraay, A. and Zoido-Lobatón, P. 1999. *Governance Matters.* Policy Research Working Paper No. 2196. Washington, DC: World Bank Institute.

Kornai, J., Rothstein, B. and Rose-Ackerman, S. (eds.) 2004. *Creating Social Trust in Post-Socialist Transition.* New York: Palgrave Macmillan.

Kurer, O. 2005. Corruption: An alternative approach to its definition and measurement. *Political Studies* 53: 222–239.

La Porta, R., Lopez-de-Silanes, F., Shleifer, A. and Vishny, R. 1999. The quality of government. *Journal of Law, Economics and Organization* 15: 222–279.

Lapuente, V. and Rothstein, B. 2010. *Civil War Spain versus Swedish Harmony: The Quality of Government Factor.* Paper presented at the Annual Meeting of the American Political Science Association. Washington, DC, 31 August–3 September.

Levi, M and Sacks, A. 2009. Legitimating beliefs: Sources and indicators. *Regulation and Governance* 3: 311–333.

McMillan, J. and Zoido, P. 2004. How to subvert democracy: Montesinos in Peru. *Journal of Economic Perspectives* 18: 69–92.

March, J. B. and Olsen, J. P. 1989. *Rediscovering Institutions: The Organizational Basis of Politics.* New York: Basic Books.

Montinola, G. R. and Jackman, R. W. 2002. Sources of corruption: A cross-country study. *British Journal of Political Science* 32: 147–170.

North, D. C. 1990. *Institutions, Institutional Change and Economic Performance.* Cambridge, MA: Cambridge University Press.

North, D. C., Wallis, J. J. and Weingast, B. R. 2009. *Violence and Social Orders: A Conceptual Framework for Interpreting Recorded Human History.* Cambridge, MA: Cambridge University Press.

O'Donnell, G. 2004. Why the rule of law matters. *Journal of Democracy* 15: 32–46.

Ostrom, E. 1990. *Governing the Commons: The Evolution of Institutions for Collective Action.* New York: Cambridge University Press.

Ott, J. C. 2010. Good governance and happiness in nations: Technical quality precedes democracy and quality beats size. *Journal of Happiness Studies* 11: 353–368.

Pacek, A. C. and Radcliff, B. 2008. Welfare policy and subjective well-being across nations: An individual-level assessment. *Social Indicators Research* 89: 179–191.

Pierre, J. and Peters, B. G. 2005. *Governing Complex Societies: Trajectories and Scenarios.* Basingstoke: Palgrave Macmillan.

Råby, N. and Teorell, J. 2010. *A Quality of Government Peace? Bringing the State Back into the Study of Inter-State Armed Conflict*. Working Paper No. 20. Gothenburg: Quality of Government Institute.

Rodrik, D. 2007. *One Economics, Many Recipes: Globalization, Institutions and Economic Growth*. Princeton, NJ: Princeton University Press.

Rose, J. 2004. The rule of law in the Western world: An overview. *Journal of Social Philosophy* 35: 457–470.

Rothstein, B. 1998. *Just Institutions Matter: The Moral and Political Logic of the Universal Welfare State*. Cambridge: Cambridge University Press.

Rothstein, B. 2011. *The Quality of Government: Corruption, Social Trust and Inequality in a Comparative Perspective*. Chicago: University of Chicago.

Rothstein, B. and Stolle, D. 2008. The state and social capital: An institutional theory of generalized trust. *Comparative Politics* 40: 441–459.

Rothstein, B. and Teorell, J. 2008. What is quality of government: A theory of impartial political institutions. *Governance* 21: 165–190.

Serra, N. and. Stiglitz, J. E. (eds.) 2008. *The Washington Consensus Reconsidered: Towards a New Global Governance*. Oxford: Oxford University Press.

Sjöstedt, M. 2008. *Thirsting for Credible Commitments: How Secure Land Tenure Affects Access to Drinking Water in Sub-Saharan Africa*. Gothenburg: Department of Political Science, University of Gothenburg.

Smith, B. C. 2007. *Good Governance and Development*. New York: Palgrave Macmillan.

Sung, H.-E. 2004. Democracy and political corruption: A cross-national comparison. *Crime, Law and Social Change* 41: 179–194.

Swaroop, V. and Rajkumar, A. S. 2002. *Public Spending and Outcomes: Does Governance Matter?* World Bank Policy Research Working Paper No. 2840 (May). Washington, DC: World Bank.

Talbott, W. J. 2005. *Which Rights Should Be Universal?* New York: Oxford University Press.

Transparency International. 2006. *Global Corruption Report 2006*. London: Pluto Press.

Uslaner, E. M. 2008. *Corruption, Inequality, and the Rule of Law: The Bulging Pocket Makes the Easy Life*. Cambridge: Cambridge University Press.

Weingast, B. R. 1997. The political foundations of democracy and the rule of law. *American Political Science Review* 91: 245–263.

CHAPTER 11

....

GOVERNANCE AND LEARNING

....

FABRIZIO GILARDI &
CLAUDIO M. RADAELLI

THE governance turn in political science (Peters, Chapter 2, this volume; Bevir 2010) refers, implicitly or explicitly, to the mechanism of learning. Horizontal arrangements and multi-level settings operate using a logic that is different from the traditional hierarchic logic used by government. One theme in the governance turn is that the relatively decentralized network-based interaction of constellations of public and private actors, given certain institutional properties, triggers socialization, problem-solving, reflexivity, and deliberation—and possibly even collective learning processes (Checkel 1998; Scott 2010; Sanderson 2002, 2009). Governance by epistemic communities and knowledge-based actors (Stone, Garnett, and Denham 1998, Schrefler 2010) is also intimately connected to learning (Boswell 2008), specifically in relation to how rationality, science, and experts' advice bring about change in public policy, and what type of instruments, organizational settings, or institutional devices enable learning to operate.

Turning to learning, recent reviews (Freeman 2006; Grin and Loeber 2007; Dobbin, Simmons, and Garrett 2007) contain only a handful of empirical studies on learning, thus making it difficult to assess what we have collectively and cumulatively learned about this topic. This perhaps explains the frustration expressed by authors such as James and Lodge (2003) and Volden, Ting, and Carpenter (2008) about the overall theoretical leverage of research in this field (although James and Lodge's sharpest criticisms are confined to the subfield of policy transfer). In the meantime, international relations scholars have connected with learning through very different strands of research, including socialization, critical realism, and diffusion. But this has not led to greater conceptual clarification; rather it has opened up a Pandora's box of endless discussions on ontology and epistemology.

In this chapter we discuss learning in the context of governance, and the two-way relationship between them. The next section puts forward four types of learning, namely reflexive social learning, instrumental learning, political learning, and symbolic learning. Then we discuss a series of theoretical problems that emerge when learning is used in the context of governance, and especially the difficulty of moving from the micro to the meso or macro level. The following section considers the challenges that researchers face when studying learning empirically, both qualitatively and quantitatively. Finally, we discuss the relationship between governance and learning, and conclude with the normative implications (Rothstein, Chapter 10, this volume). Perhaps paradoxically, whilst the governance turn was initially concerned with reflexivity and the withering away of government, the theoretical and empirical analysis of learning has brought back hierarchy and the role of governments in political learning. More recently, the field of learning has yet again crossed paths with governance theorists who have rediscovered the role of power and hierarchy, even within network-based governance (Héritier and Rhodes 2011). The challenge for future research is to specify the conditions for different usages of modes of governance (such as deliberation and reflexivity, but also coercion, pressure, and legitimacy) and different types of learning, from learning how to improve on public policy to more political and less benevolent types of learning.

Four types of learning

The literature has drawn attention to four ideal types of learning, namely reflexive social learning, instrumental learning, political learning, and symbolic learning (Grin and Loeber 2007; May 1992; Sanderson 2002).

Reflexive social learning involves society-wide paradigmatic changes affecting not only public policy, but also fundamental social interaction and institutional behavior. By far the most cited article on paradigmatic change is Hall's study on economic policy-making (1993; 488 citations in June 2010, source: Social science citation index). Reflexive learning about governance (Sanderson 2002) results from advanced, sophisticated, participatory usages of governance tools, but also requires dense socialization or other triggers of communicative rationality. Sanderson draws on complexity theory to show how this type of learning emerges, although it is not easy to distinguish between the positive and normative aspects of his research program (Sanderson 2009). Sabel and Zeitlin (2010: ch. 1), instead, draw on theories of experimental constitutionalism and social networks to associate reflexivity with modes of governance that are not based on hierarchy. Their analysis dovetails with the literature on the so-called new modes of governance (Héritier and Rhodes 2011). Although most of these modes are not "new" (e.g. soft law and self-regulation), recent research has drawn attention to the open method of coordination in the European Union—which has similarities with policy benchmarking in international organizations. The open method is a type of international coordination of public policy based on the diffusion of information among social and policy networks at different levels of governance. Its instruments are benchmarking, peer review, common indicators, and iterative appraisal of plans and achievements of the member states. The capacity to learn from local, diffuse innovation and problem-solving is key to the logic of the open method. These are the ambitions and the logic. However, when we move from "how things should work" to "how they actually work" we find a body of empirical research arguing that the open method has generated much more learning from the top than learning from society as a whole and from the local level of innovation (Radaelli 2008). More fundamentally, the case of open coordination in the European Union shows a more general characteristic of the relationship between modes of governance and learning. In fact, the same mode of governance (in our case the open method) can be used for different objectives: one is reflexive social learning, but evidence shows other objectives, such as creating a pressure to converge, and increasing the effectiveness of hard law by accompanying it with softer modes of regulation (Borrás and Radaelli 2010).

Reflexivity is also found in legal systems, as shown by the theory of responsive regulation and more recent advances in legal scholarship on norms (Lenoble and De Schutter 2010). In turn, the explanation of how norms emerge and how they are interpreted, shared, and contested has made its way onto the research agenda in international relations (Wiener 2008). In policy theory, Campbell (1998) has introduced the distinction among programs, paradigms, frames, and public sentiments. Since reflexivity is also about how "ideas" have an effect on policy, Campbell's typology is useful in order to distinguish between different types of ideas. One problem for reflexive scholars, however, is to explain why an organization or a political system would engage with social learning. A possible answer to this question is a legitimacy crisis that induces a profound reassessment of core beliefs: as sociologists have emphasized, conformity with socially valued practices is an important strategy through which actors can protect themselves from criticism (DiMaggio and Powell 1991). Another is socialization: even if it does not lead to a full internalization, standards of accepted behavior may emerge out of the repeated interaction of policy-makers in intergovernmental organizations and other networks.

The second type is *instrumental learning* (Radaelli 2009; Gilardi 2010). It is variably informed by (more or less bounded) rational policy-making, evidence-based policy agendas, and less normative theories of the bureaucracy, and it can be characterized as an updating process based either on Bayesian rationality or cognitive shortcuts. From the Bayesian perspective, estimates of a given quantity of interest are reached via a combination of prior beliefs and evidence, which produce so-called posterior beliefs. Because prior beliefs are revised in the light of new information, this process is also called "Bayesian updating." To illustrate, imagine that policy-makers want to stop an oil spill in the Gulf of Mexico and are considering whether to adopt a specific technique that might work but might also worsen the problem. Based on prior experience, expert advice, and degree of risk aversion, some are quite optimistic about the operation's chances of success, while others are more skeptical, but in the end a series of trials are allowed. After these trials, policy-makers update their beliefs on the effectiveness of the technique and need to decide whether a large-scale operation can be attempted. All policy-makers are exposed to the same evidence, but their posterior beliefs will vary depending on their prior beliefs. Thus, stronger evidence is needed for a skeptical policy-maker to change their mind than for someone who was already relatively confident that the technique could work. Specifically, in Bayesian inference "strong" evidence means that there are many data points (many trials, in this example) and that the variability of results is low. If there are only a few examples and/or if these point to different conclusions, then prior beliefs play an important role and will be updated only marginally.

An alternative, and equally powerful, take on instrumental learning comes from cognitive psychology, especially the influential work of Kahneman and Tversky (2000) and its application to political science by Weyland (2007). Similar to the Bayesian approach, actors want to improve their assessment of some state of the world. Contrary to Bayesian inference, however, actors update their beliefs not in accordance with statistical laws but following "cognitive shortcuts" such as availability and representativeness. First, availability means that not all information carries the same weight. Particularly vivid examples or "success stories" are more influential than equally relevant but less striking cases. Continuing the oil spill example, a major catastrophe, even if it were an isolated accident, can negate many low-key successes by shaping policy-makers' minds regarding the effectiveness of certain types of drilling. By contrast, in Bayesian updating a single outlier will be properly discounted. Second, representativeness refers to the tendency to draw disproportionate conclusions from a limited empirical basis. Short-term trends or a handful of successful examples are interpreted as conclusive evidence, while in Bayesian updating sample size is a critical parameter. Thus, if initial attempts to contain the oil leak seem to work, policy-makers tend to focus on this restricted basis and be more optimistic than they should be if they updated their beliefs following statistical laws.

At the international level, instrumental learning is concerned with drawing lessons from the experience of others. The rationale for this type of learning is straightforward. Policy-makers learn, by trial and error, from their own experiences. They use their policies as experiments. They make trials, observe the mistakes, and improve. However, by borrowing from others policy-makers do not have to wait for their own errors and crises to show the way ahead. This explains why there is an intense international activity concerned with "lesson-drawing." Richard Rose is the political scientist who has developed this field (Rose 1991). Others prefer the notion of policy transfer (Dolowitz and Marsh 1996). In lesson-drawing, policy-makers dissatisfied with the status quo scan the practices in effect in other units (such as countries, regions, or cities) and assess to what extent they could successfully implement them in their jurisdiction. Alternative ways of drawing a lesson exist: from copying a policy almost exactly to just taking inspiration from it, with different degrees of adjustment in between. Lesson-drawing has been criticized by some scholars as being too broad and almost indistinguishable from any type of rational decision-making (e.g. James and Lodge 2003). Thus, it may be useful to define the concept more narrowly.

Policy change is often the product of elected politicians' authority to change legislation and policy, and bureaucratic learning with knowledge about solutions and their feasibility. To make sense of this distinction, it is useful to go back to a classic article by May (1992), who distinguished between instrumental and *political learning*, which is our third ideal type of learning. Broadly speaking, the latter refers to the strategies that help policy-makers control a policy domain. If it is difficult to monitor and attribute responsibility for performance, organizations tend to become "political" rather than seek policy improvement (Brunsson 1989). Qualifying May's original insights, political learning can lead to the following usages of knowledge (Boswell 2008): "strategic" (i.e. to increase the control of elected policy-makers on non-elected regulators, or to increase the popularity of the incumbent in election years), "substantiating" (i.e. to support a prefabricated position, for example for or against asylum seekers and migrants; see Boswell 2008), and "symbolic" (i.e. using governance tools to send signals to the business community or for blame-shifting purposes). Politically competitive environments will ensure that organizations learn how to use governance innovation to exercise control, implement broad political trajectories such as deregulation, increase popularity in the polls, and shift power. Thus, Gilardi (2010) showed that governments are more likely to implement unemployment benefits cuts if other governments did not suffer major electoral losses after doing so.

Further, an organization under pressure to become or remain a respectable member of international environments will engage in *symbolic learning*, which is our fourth ideal type of learning. Organizational theory has long shown that in symbolic usages of learning what matters is legitimacy, not policy performance (DiMaggio and Powell 1991). The distinction between types of learning is important not only analytically but also when it comes to assessing the consequences of learning from a normative perspective, as we discuss below. Different types also suggest variation in micro-foundations and implications for the use of knowledge, as shown in Table 11.1 below.

THEORETICAL PROBLEMS

When scholars set out to examine learning in the context of governance, they typically conceptualize learning as a process of updating beliefs. One difference in the literature is between policy studies and the field of "modes" of governance.

In comparative public policy, this updating refers to the classic components of public policy, such as problem definition, the results achieved at home or abroad, goals, and knowledge—either knowledge about institutional/policy performance or about the volitions and beliefs of the actors involved in strategic interaction. In studies of institutional architectures of governance dealing with more abstract notions such as hierarchy, the shadow of the law, facilitated coordination, and voluntarism, updating is essentially about forms of compliance, emulation, and herding, or, on the other hand, dense communication and reflexivity. Public policy and modes of governance are often combined in studies on how the political economy of specific regimes affects certain policy areas, as is shown by the literature on the European Employment Strategies of the European Union (e.g. Heidenreich and Bischoff 2008). In both cases (i.e. policy and modes), updating is grounded in social interaction within the constellation of actors involved either in the policy-making or in the modes of governance.

Table 11.1 Types of learning, mechanisms, micro-foundations, use of knowledge, and goals of learning

Type of learning	Mechanism: updating beliefs on the basis of …	Micro-foundations	Use of knowledge	Goals of learning
Reflexive social learning	Change of preferences of actors	Legitimacy crisis; identity transformation; socialization	Reflexive, broad social usage	Learning how to learn
Instrumental	Evidence about policy: what seems to work at home or elsewhere	Organizations under pressure to deliver →organizations focus on analysis in order to improve on policy performance →organizations seek to draw lessons from abroad	Fully or bounded rational updating of beliefs	Improving policy effectiveness
Political	Evidence and conjectures about the strategies pursued by other actors	Organizations that compete for control of an organizational field in an environment where it is difficult to measure and attribute responsibility for performance	– Strategic – Substantiating – Symbolic	Gaining political advantages, such as winning elections
Symbolic	What seems to provide legitimacy	Dense, institutional international environments wherein organizations seek legitimacy	Symbolic	Gaining legitimacy

One problem with this approach is that it takes a concept of updating that is rooted in individual behavior and transposes it to the macro level of policy or forms of governance. However, political scientists working on governance tend to work on macro–macro or meso–meso relations. They observe meso phenomena such as policy change, and explain it in terms of institutional variables. Or they are concerned with the emergence of complex macro architectures—such as network governance in industrial districts (Piore and Sabel 1984) or the open method of coordination in the European Union (EU)—and (for their explanations) look at other macro variables such the limitations of hierarchy, and slow institutional adjustment to the environment.

One way or the other, this way of using learning does not stand up to rigorous scrutiny. Following Coleman (1990), a macro–macro (or meso–meso) explanation consists of three steps: (a) the micro-foundations of the macro-level independent variable; (b) the micro–micro mechanisms that characterize interaction in the constellation of individual actors; and (c) the micro-to-macro relations of aggregation, that is, the mechanisms that transform individual phenomena and social interaction into macro (or meso) outcomes of the dependent variable. Although Coleman's bathtub has been criticized, it remains a rigorous standard for explanation. However, one would struggle to find research projects on learning that truly match this standard.

Arguably, this is the root of the frustration of political scientists when they reflect on the state of play in the field of learning (James and Lodge 2003; Grin and Loeber 2007). On micro-foundations, we have to consider individuals or organizations, depending on the unit of analysis. At the individual level, there has been an explosion of projects in the area of cognitive psychology, looking at bounded rationality, heuristics, and the interplay between emotions and calculation. An early study of heuristics and their implications for learning, public policy, and governance is that by Schneider and Ingram (1988), which also ties in nicely with the discussion on lesson-drawing.

The study of micro-foundations has even reached an inner level of analysis, with projects on models of the mind and neuro-politics. This is as far as we can go in exploring the origin of learning and biases in learning processes. The key question remains "Why would an organization or an individual want to learn?" Organizational theory provides different answers (Brunsson 1989) depending on whether the actors are appraised on the basis of their performance or not. Many organizations in the public sector are "political" in Brunsson's sense, that is, they are not judged on their performance because they are not responsible for implementation or there are problems in measuring final policy outcomes as a result of what the organization did or did not do.

With relation to micro–micro interaction, scholars of diffusion have pointed out at pathways in the epidemiology of governance innovations. But we can also go back to Moscovici and other pioneers of social psychology and their insights on how—assuming dense social interaction—individuals respond to the opinion of the majority and the minority in their groups. This strand could usefully tie in with studies on the role of information as symbol, signal, and cognitive device (Levitt and March 1988; March 1981). Finally, the micro–micro exploration of learning has been improved by our understanding of how a constellation of actors gets locked into mechanisms of increasing returns and therefore deviates from its optimal path. One striking observation, however, is that we still do not know much about how communities of social actors—especially policy-makers—learn, as shown by Richard Freeman's comprehensive review of learning in public policy (Freeman 2006). Methods such as participant observation may assist in this direction—a formidable example is Sharon Gilad's study of the ombudsman (Gilad 2009).

Aggregation—the third element of Coleman's explanation—remains a problem. All too often political scientists use the insights of social psychology or the economics of innovations to jump to conclusions about institutions and governance. It is true that individuals think and interact. It is more problematic to show that institutions, like the National Health Service or the World Bank, have learned. On the one hand, there are those who assign *sui generis* cognitive capabilities to institutions, following social anthropologist Mary Douglas (1986). On the other, governance scholars still find it difficult to prove institutional and organizational learning empirically.

THE EMPIRICAL ANALYSIS OF LEARNING

As we have argued above, learning has been over-conceptualized and under-researched empirically. One reason is that the analysis of governance informed by learning is riddled with problems and trade-offs in research design. To begin with, if the null hypothesis of not-learning is not specified, pretty much everything can become "learning" and the measurement of the dependent variable is biased (Radaelli 2009). Second, the time-dimension matters and can bias empirical findings. If one examines learning over a fairly narrow time frame, one may not see the learning buds that are about to blossom. Yet if one takes the long view, it is almost impossible *not* to find instances of learning. Organizations, political systems, pressure groups, and policy officers *must* learn, at least if they are to survive in a dynamic environment. Third, when measurement is carried out via qualitative interviewing—which is still a classic tool in comparative policy studies—the officers in charge of policy tend to overestimate the role of learning as opposed to coercion and classic notions of power politics. For an officer, it is easier to justify organizational behavior in terms of learning from experience or best practice, rather than disclosing features of power politics and conflict. There is also a more subtle syndrome. When organizations experience a crisis, such as mad cow disease or the transfusion scandals in Europe, they use the "we have learned" mantra as a way to re-establish their control and legitimacy in policy fields. Learning (and ironically the crisis too) is therefore used to protect an organization from criticism: "we have learned—hence we are fine now, and the case is closed" is a typical response, as argued by Thomas Alam (2007) in his dissertation on the mad cow disease crisis. If interviewers do not search for the larger picture and "determine" the existence of learning on the basis of their interviews, they may draw grossly biased inferences about governance and power relations.

On the qualitative side, we have recent examples of studies that define their micro-foundations and elaborate on their expectations about evidence for one type of learning or another (Boswell 2008 on migration; Radaelli 2009 on regulatory reform). Schrefler (2010) illustrates the logic behind different types of learning using a knowledge utilization framework. Qualitative studies on hormone growth producers by Dunlop (2010) and Dunlop and James (2007) connect the debate on epistemic communities mentioned above to principal–agent analysis, thus showing empirically how to hybridize models of ideational politics, often linked to reflexive governance, to the rational choice template of delegation models. In her attempt to document empirically the explanatory power of discursive institutionalism, Vivien Schmidt (2008) has provided a template for the empirical analysis of ideational politics in institutional settings. Empirically, learning is a manifestation of the transformative power of discourse. In his book on the diffusion of health and pension reforms, Weyland (2007) has shown how to test alternative causal mechanisms. The advocacy coalition framework has produced both qualitative and quantitative projects (Weible, Sabatier, and McQueen 2009). Peter Hall's concept of third-order, paradigmatic change has been looked at from different angles of historical neo-institutionalism (Beland 2005). Oliver and Pemberton have re-examined economic policy in Britain. They found that policy learning does not necessarily lead to policy change, due to the capacity of institutions to channel forces of change. A paradigm may fail without being necessarily replaced wholesale (Oliver and Pemberton 2004).

On the quantitative side, scholars have generally proceeded from a narrow definition of learning based on belief updating. The first step is the identification of a relevant and measurable policy outcome that can be used to define "success." Then, the main hypothesis is that the adoption or level of the policy in a given country is influenced by that of other countries, with more "successful" countries being more influential. This approach can be implemented relatively straightforwardly in a standard regression framework, with the computation of so-called "spatial lags," or weighted averages of policies elsewhere, in which weights correspond to different degrees of success. Alternatively, information on success can be used in a dyadic framework adapted from the international relations literature. For instance, Volden (2006) studied state children's health insurance policies in the US and found that states were more likely to imitate the programs of other states that had managed to increase the number of insured children, which was one of the main objectives of the policy. Another strategy is to measure the correlation of policies and outcomes and include it as an explanatory variable in the regression. For example, Gilardi, Füglister, and Luyet (2009) showed that specific hospital-financing instruments were more likely to be adopted when they were associated with a slower increase of health-care expenditure abroad. In her study of economic policies, Meseguer (2009) operationalized learning by directly following the Bayesian updating model and showed that, as expected theoretically, both average results abroad and their variability influence the willingness of governments to adopt the same policies. These approaches have contributed to closing the gap between theory and evidence and do not suffer from the looseness of the qualitative approaches discussed above, which is no little achievement; nevertheless they are not always practicable. The identification and measurement of relevant outcomes is often difficult because most policies have multi-dimensional goals, which can be loosely defined, thus complicating the analysis considerably. While this complexity is interesting in itself (Gilardi 2010), practically it makes quantitative analyses of learning feasible only in specific cases. Moreover, quantitative analysis in general has its share of problems, such as a number of simplifying assumptions (i.e. additivity and linearity) that can be at odds both with the theory and the nature of the phenomenon under study, and a limited capacity to identify causal relations (as opposed to correlations) in observational (i.e. not experimental) settings.

CONCLUSIONS AND NORMATIVE IMPLICATIONS

In conclusion, if the governance turn has influenced and rekindled the discussion on learning, there is also evidence that theoretical and empirical research on learning has potentially useful lessons for those working on governance and governments. As shown by the "new" modes of governance (Borrás and Radaelli 2010), whilst governance theorists design modes based on a logic of reflexivity and open, decentralized social learning, learning scholars point out that the same mode can be used both reflexively and in more coercive or hierarchical ways (Héritier and Rhodes 2011). This observation can be taken to a more abstract level: whilst the thrust of the reaction to "government" was an emphasis on private–public relationships and learning in dense networks of interaction, learning studies distinguish between different goals of learning. There are constellations of actors and institutions conducive to genuine improvement and reflexivity, albeit that policy improvement and "better policy" mean different things to different actors (Radaelli 2005). But the literature on learning has also found constellations of actors and institutions leading to more political goals, such as "learning how to gain popularity and win elections." This way, learning scholars have also reminded governance theorists that governments and elected politicians still matter in public policy. Organizational scholars of learning have drawn attention to legitimate symbolic goals of learning and mechanisms of hope that constrain the potential of different types of governance. In the future, the cross-fertilization between governance and learning will continue, as evidenced by recent studies on "new" governance that stress the role of hierarchy (Héritier and Rhodes 2011) and the tradition of actor-centered institutionalism (Scharpf 1997). The emerging research agenda is about setting the conditions for different usages of governance (deliberative but also coercive) in the context of instrumental, political, and symbolic learning.

This leads us to a final observation on the normative implications. Ultimately, this question is crucial for normative assessments of governance structures. Knowing if and under what conditions learning can occur, and to what extent, has sweeping implications for the desirability of alternative forms of governance along a centralized–decentralized (or coordinated–uncoordinated, hierarchical–horizontal) continuum. The literature still has to make significant progress on this issue. A first problem is that learning tends to be unambiguously considered a positive phenomenon. However, we should ask what political actors learn. As Hall (1993: 293), emphasized, "[j]ust as a child can learn bad habits, governments, too, may learn the 'wrong' lessons from a given experience." More than that, political actors may even actively learn how to pursue the "wrong" goal more effectively; terrorists are a case in point (Horowitz 2010).

More realistically, politicians may learn about the policies that help them get re-elected rather than solve problems, as we discussed above. Elected policy-makers are not primarily interested in truth, reflexivity, and "what works." They primarily seek power, bureau expansion, popularity, reputation, and other goals. Knowledge can be used to gain legitimacy for ill-planned policy reforms or to justify prefabricated opinions. For this reason, learning may not be beneficial to politics and public policy-making. Some authors have noted that learning that leads to genuine policy solutions may still occur, but it is unintended. Under these circumstances, policy-makers seek power and other goals, but their interaction produces learning as an unintended effect.

Multi-level governance settings can be equally ambiguous. Majone (2000, 2002) argued that regulatory networks help improve the accountability of independent regulators through peer pressure and reputational incentives that keep them under control. In other words, networks lead to a learning process in which regulators conform to emerging professional norms. While it is possible that this will result in practices that are seen as desirable from the point of view of democratic principles, it is also possible that networks will merely reinforce the autonomy of regulators and their insulation from democratic processes, leading to an increased democratic accountability problem. More generally, networks can fulfill a socialization function and promote the development of shared meaning and values and common definitions of problems and solutions (Börzel and Heard-Lauréote 2009: 142). Again, however, the outcome may or may not be desirable from a normative standpoint. As sociologists have shown, institutional isomorphism is disconnected from the objective characteristics of practices, so that policies can spread regardless of their actual consequences, and even despite their ineffectiveness.

In other words, the literature should overcome the presumption that learning, to the extent that it actually occurs, invariably leads to normatively desirable results. Of course, what is desirable and what is not are fundamentally contested and vary across political actors and over time. Acknowledging the normative ambiguity of learning does not lead to a dilution of the concept but, through new research perspectives, to a sharpening of it. It may even make learning more palatable to researchers who find the original concept too technocratic.

ACKNOWLEDGMENTS

Claudio M. Radaelli wishes to acknowledge his grant, awarded by the European Research Council on Analysis of Learning in Regulatory Governance, ALREG (http://centres. exeter.ac.uk/ceg/research/ALREG/index.php). Fabrizio Gilardi acknowledges the support of the Swiss National Science Foundation (NCCR Democracy).

REFERENCES

Alam, T. 2007. *Quand la vache folle retouve son champ : Une comparaison trasnationale de la remise en ordre d'un secteur d'action publique.* PhD dissertation, CERAPS, Lille.

Beland, D. 2005. Ideas and social policy: An institutionalist perspective. *Social Policy & Administration* 39(1): 1–18.

Bevir, M. (ed.) 2010. *The Sage Handbook of Governance.* London: Sage.

Borrás, S. and Radaelli, C. M. 2010. *Recalibrating the Open Method of Coordination: Towards Diverse and More Effective Usages.* Stockholm: Swedish Institute for European Policy Studies, Sieps WP 2010, 7.

Börzel, T. A. and Heard-Lauréote, K. 2009. Networks in EU multi-level governance: concepts and contributions. *Journal of Public Policy* 29: 135–151.

Boswell, C. 2008. The political functions of expert knowledge: Knowledge and legitimation in European Union immigration policy. *Journal of European Public Policy* 15: 471–488.

Brunsson, N. 1989. *The Organization of Hypocrisy: Talk, Decisions and Actions in Organizations.* Chichester and New York: John Wiley and Sons.

Campbell, J. L. 1998. Institutional analysis and the role of ideas in political economy. *Theory and Society* 27: 377–409.

Checkel, J. 1998. The constructivist turn in international relations theory. *World Politics* 50: 324–348.

Coleman, J. S. 1990. *Foundations of Social Theory.* Cambridge, MA: The Belknap Press of Harvard University Press.

DiMaggio, P. J. and Powell, W. W. 1991. The iron cage revisited: Institutional isomorphism and collective rationality in organizational fields. In P. J. DiMaggio and W. W. Powell (eds.), *The New Institutionalism in Organizational Analysis.* Chicago and London: University of Chicago Press, 63–82.

Dobbin, F., Simmons, B. and Garrett, G. 2007. The global diffusion of public policies: Social construction, coercion, competition, or learning? *Annual Review of Sociology* 33: 449–472.

Dolowitz, D. and Marsh, D. 1996. Who learns from whom: A review of the policy transfer literature. *Political Studies* 44: 343–357.

Douglas, M. 1986. *How Institutions Think.* London: Routledge and Kegan Paul.

Dunlop, C. 2010. Epistemic communities and two goals of delegation: Hormone growth promoters in the European Union. *Science and Public Policy* 37: 205–217.

Dunlop, C. and James, O. 2007. Principal–agent modelling and learning: The European Commission, experts and agricultural hormone growth promoters. *Public Policy and Administration* 22: 403–422.

Freeman, R. 2006. Learning in public policy. In M. Moran, M. Rein, and R. E. Goodin (eds.), *Oxford Handbook of Public Policy.* Oxford: Oxford University Press, 367–388.

Gilad, S. (2009). Juggling conflicting demands: The case of the UK financial ombudsman service. *Journal of Public Administration Research and Theory* 19: 661–680.

Gilardi, F. 2010. Who learns from what in policy diffusion processes? *American Journal of Political Science* 54: 650–666.

Gilardi, F., Füglister, K. and Luyet, S. 2009. Learning from others: The diffusion of hospital financing reforms in OECD countries. *Comparative Political Studies* 42(4): 549–573.

Grin, J. and Loeber, A. 2007. Theories of policy learning: Agency, structure, and change. In F. Fischer, G. J. Miller, and M. S. Sidney (eds.), *Handbook of Public Policy Analysis: Theory, Politics, and Methods.* Boca Raton, FL: CRC Press, 201–219.

Hall, P. A. 1993. Policy paradigms, social learning, and the state. The case of economic policy-making in Britain. *Comparative Politics* 25: 275–296.

Heidenreich, M. and Bischoff, G. 2008. The open method of co-ordination: A way to the Europeanization of social and employment policies? *Journal of Common Market Studies* 46: 497–532.

Héritier, A. and Rhodes, M. (eds.) 2011. *New Modes of Governance in Europe: Governing in the Shadow of Hierarchy*. Basingstoke: Palgrave Macmillan.

Horowitz, M. C. 2010. Nonstate actors and the diffusion of innovations: The case of suicide terrorism. *International Organization* 64: 33–64.

James, O. and Lodge, M. 2003. The limitations of "policy transfer" and "lesson drawing" for public policy research. *Political Studies Review* 1: 179–193.

Kahneman, D. and Tversky, A. (eds.) 2000. *Choices, Values, and Frames*. Cambridge: Cambridge University Press.

Lenoble, J. and De Schutter, O. (eds.) 2010. *Reflexive Governance: Redefining the Public Interest in a Pluralistic World*. Oxford: Hart.

Levitt, B. and March, J. G. (1988). Organizational learning. *Annual Review of Sociology* 14: 319–340.

Majone, G. 2000. The credibility crisis of community regulation. *Journal of Common Market Studies* 38: 273–302.

Majone, G. 2002. The European Commission: The limits of centralization and the perils of parliamentarization. *Governance* 15: 375–392.

March, J. G. 1981. Footnotes to organizational change. *Administrative Science Quarterly* 26: 563–577.

May, P. J. 1992. Policy learning and failure. *Journal of Public Policy* 12: 331–354.

Meseguer, C. 2009. *Learning, Policy Making, and Market Reforms*. Cambridge: Cambridge University Press.

Oliver, M. J. and Pemberton, H. 2004. Learning and change in 20th-century British economic policy. *Governance* 17: 415–441.

Piore, M. J. and Sabel, C. F. 1984. *The Second Industrial Divide: Possibilities for Prosperity*. New York: Basic Books.

Radaelli, C. M. 2005. Diffusion without convergence: How political context shapes the adoption of regulatory impact assessment. *Journal of European Public Policy* 12: 924–943.

Radaelli, C. M. 2008. Europeanization, policy learning, and new modes of governance. *Journal of Comparative Policy Analysis* 10: 239–254.

Radaelli, C. M. 2009. Measuring policy learning: Regulatory impact assessment in Europe. *Journal of European Public Policy* 16: 1145–1164.

Rose, R. 1991. What is lesson-drawing? *Journal of Public Policy* 11: 3–30.

Sabel, C. and Zeitlin, J. (eds.) 2010. *Experimentalist Governance in the European Union: Towards a New Architecture*. Oxford: Oxford University Press.

Sanderson, I. 2002. Evaluation, policy learning and evidence-based policy making. *Public Administration* 80: 1–22.

Sanderson, I. 2009. Intelligent policy making for a complex world: Pragmatism, evidence and learning. *Political Studies* 57: 699–719.

Scharpf, F. 1997. *Games Real Actors Can Play: Actor-Centered Institutionalism in Policy Research*. Boulder, CO: Westview Press.

Schneider, A. and Ingram, H. 1988. Systematically pinching ideas: A comparative approach to policy design. *Journal of Public Policy* 8: 61–80.

Schmidt, V. A. 2008. Discursive institutionalism: The explanatory power of ideas and discourse. *Annual Review of Political Science* 11: 303–326.

Schrefler, L. 2010. The usage of scientific knowledge by independent regulatory agencies. *Governance* 23: 309–330.

Scott, C. 2010. Reflexive governance, regulation, and meta-regulation: Control or learning? In J. Lenoble and O. de Schutter (eds.), *Reflexive Governance: Redefining the Public Interest in a Pluralistic World*. Oxford: Hart, 43–66

Stone, D., Garnett, M., and Denham, A. (eds.) 1998. *Think Tanks across the World: A Comparative Perspective*. Manchester: Manchester University Press.

Volden, C. 2006. States as policy laboratories: Emulating success in the Children's health insurance program. *American Journal of Political Science* 50: 294–312.

Volden, C., Ting, M. M, and Carpenter, D. P. 2008. A formal model of learning and policy diffusion. *American Political Science Review* 102: 319–332.

Weible, C. M., Sabatier, P. A., and McQueen, K. 2009. Themes and variations: Taking stock of the advocacy coalitions framework. *Policy Studies Journal* 37: 121–140.

Weyland, K. 2007. *Bounded Rationality and Policy Diffusion: Social Sector Reform in Latin America*. Princeton: Princeton University Press.

Wiener, A. 2008. *The Invisible Constitution of Politics: Contested Norms and International Encounters*. Cambridge: Cambridge University Press.

....

CHAPTER 12

EXPERIMENTALIST GOVERNANCE

....

CHARLES F. SABEL & JONATHAN ZEITLIN

FAR-REACHING transformations in the nature of contemporary governance are under-way, within and beyond the nation-state. They can be observed across multiple levels and locations, from the reform of local public services such as education and child welfare to the regulation of global trade in food and forest products. At the heart of these transformations is the emergence of what may be called "experimentalist governance," based on framework rule-making and revision through a recursive review of implementation experience in different local contexts. Robust examples can be found in many jurisdictions, including the United States and the European Union (EU). In this chapter we analyze the properties of these experimentalist governance processes.

Most generally, put in terms applicable to the public regulation of private firms as well as the provision of education and other services by public institutions, experimentalist governance is a recursive process of provisional goal-setting and revision based on learning from the comparison of alternative approaches to advancing them in different contexts. (We use "recursive" here in the sense familiar from mathematics and computer science, whereby the output from one application of a procedure or sequence of operations becomes the input for the next, so that iteration of the same process produces changing results.) Experimentalist governance in its most developed form involves a multi-level architecture, whose four elements are linked in an iterative cycle. First, broad framework goals and metrics for gauging their achievement are provisionally established by some combination of "central" and "local" units, in consultation with the relevant civil society stakeholders. Examples of such framework goals, to which we will refer in this chapter, include "good water quality," "safe food," an "adequate education," and "sustainable forests." Second, local units are given broad discretion to pursue these goals in their own way. In regulatory systems, the "local" units will typically be private actors such as firms or the territorial authorities (state regulators in the US, or member state authorities in the EU) to whom they immediately respond. In service-providing organizations, the "local" units will typically be front-line workers, such as teachers, police, or social welfare workers, or the district or regional entities supervising them.

But, third, as a condition of this autonomy, these units must report regularly on their performance and participate in a peer review in which their results are compared with those of others employing different means to the same ends. Where they are not making good progress against the agreed indicators, the local units are expected to show that they are taking appropriate corrective measures, informed by the experience of their peers. Fourth and finally, the goals, metrics, and decision-making procedures themselves are periodically revised by a widening circle of actors in response to the problems and possibilities revealed by the review process, and the cycle repeats (Sabel and Zeitlin 2008, 2010b; Sabel and Simon forthcoming).

Governance processes organized according to these principles may be considered experimentalist in the philosophical sense of American pragmatists like John Dewey (1927) because they systematically provoke doubt about their own assumptions and practices, treat all solutions as incomplete and corrigible, and produce an ongoing, reciprocal readjustment of ends and means through comparison of different approaches to advancing common general aims (Sabel 1994, 2005). These governance processes may also be considered a form of "directly deliberative polyarchy" (DDP). They are *deliberative* because they use argument to disentrench settled practices and open for reconsideration the definitions of group, institutional, and even national interest associated with them. They are *directly deliberative* because they use the concrete experience of actors' different reactions to current problems to generate novel possibilities for consideration rather than buffering decision-makers from mundane experience, the better to elicit their principled, disinterested response to abstractly posed problems. And these governance processes are *polyarchic* because, in the absence of a central, final decider, their constituent units must learn from, discipline, and set goals for one another (Cohen and Sabel 1997, 2003; Gerstenberg and Sabel 2002; Sabel and Zeitlin 2008, 2010a).

Experimentalist governance architectures of this type have become pervasively institutionalized in the EU across a broad array of policy domains. These stretch from the regulation of energy, financial services, and competition through food and drug safety, data privacy, and environmental protection to justice and internal security, anti-discrimination, and fundamental rights. They take a variety of organizational forms, including networked agencies, councils of national regulators, open methods of coordination, and operational cooperation among front-line officials, often in combination with one another (Sabel and Zeitlin (2008, 2010a, 2010b). Governance architectures with similar properties are also widespread in the US, both in the reform of public services like education and child welfare, and in the regulation of public health and safety risks, such as nuclear power, food processing, and environmental pollution (Sabel and Simon forthcoming).

Experimentalist governance in action

The experimentalist architecture in regulation is well illustrated by the EU Water Framework Directive (WFD) and its Common Implementation Strategy (CIS). This legislation was adopted in 2000 after years of intense negotiation and replaces seven detailed prescriptive directives from the 1970s with a single broad, overarching regulatory framework (Scott and Holder 2006; von Homeyer 2010; Sabel and Zeitlin 2008: 309–310, 315). The directive aims to improve the quality and sustainability of water resources across the EU through integrated management of river basins, while requiring member states to achieve "good status of water quality" by 2015. The concept of "good water status" is explicitly open-ended, with the methods, tools, metrics, and values for its assessment to be developed through the implementation process. The WFD also requires member states to "encourage the active involvement of all interested parties" in its implementation, particularly in the "production, review, and updating of . . . river basin management plans" (Barreira and Kallis 2003: 102).

Central to the implementation process is an institution not formally envisaged in the directive itself: the Common Implementation Strategy (CIS). Conceived by national water directors and agreed by the European Commission, the CIS is designed to help member states implement the WFD and avoid regulatory conflicts arising from incompatible approaches. Its primary outputs are non-binding technical guidance documents, such as indicators and values for measuring water quality and defining "good" water status. These are supposed to be "developed in a pragmatic way based on existing practices in member states," embodying best available knowledge, and are conceived as "living documents" subject to ongoing review and updating. But member states are also obliged to submit regular reports on the implementation of the directive, including both river basin management plans and programs for monitoring the water status. The Commission in turn produces its own regular implementation reports, including reviews of EU water status, surveys of member state plans, and proposals for future improvement, all of which draw on scoreboards and benchmarks developed through the CIS (Scott and Holder 2006: 229–231; von Homeyer 2010: 141–144).

It is not only the outputs of the CIS but also its organizational arrangements that are "regarded as provisional and subject to revision in the light of experience." CIS activities more generally feed both directly and indirectly into revisions of the WFD. Thus, legislative proposals for new "daughter" directives are developed "in a spirit of open consultation" through multi-stakeholder expert advisory fora, with representatives from non-governmental organizations (NGOs), industry associations, and outside experts, as well as from national authorities and the Commission. CIS guidance documents may also be given legally binding status by the Commission, subject to approval by member state representatives under "comitology" procedures for scrutinizing use of its delegated regulatory powers (Scott and Holder 2006: 231–233, 237; von Homeyer 2010: 144–147).

In both the EU and the US, experimentalist regulation of private economic activity typically seeks to work through public oversight of firms' own experimentalist governance processes or to induce their development where they do not already exist. This approach responds to the widely acknowledged failures of "command-and-control" regulation in a turbulent, fast-moving world. In such a world, fixed rules written by a hierarchical authority become obsolete too fast to be effectively enforced on the ground, and the resulting gap between rules and practice is bridged by an unaccountable proliferation of discretionary waivers and exceptions. The alternative approach is to build on and monitor firms' own error detection and correction mechanisms by requiring them to develop systematic, verifiable plans for identifying and mitigating possible hazards in their operations in the light of available knowledge about safety failures in similar settings (Sabel 2005; Sabel and Simon forthcoming).

A well-documented example is the worldwide diffusion of Hazard Analysis of Critical Control Points (HACCP) systems for ensuring food safety. These systems replaced historic command-and-control methods based on periodic "poke-and-sniff" inspections of finished products for compliance with minimum health standards. HACCP, by contrast, is a process-based approach, whereby firms are required to analyze their entire production chain for potential hazards, identify critical points where contamination may arise, develop a testable plan for controlling and reducing such hazards, monitor its implementation, verify the results, and take remedial action to correct any performance shortfall. Public authorities review the adequacy of these plans and verification procedures. They may then require their revision to meet rising health and safety standards established by the best performers, although the precise regulatory arrangements vary widely. Increasingly, too, such regulation extends beyond individual firms to require full traceability of products throughout the supply chain (Zeitlin 2011: 7–10; Sabel 2005: 138; Sabel and Simon forthcoming; Henson and Humphrey 2009). In air-traffic safety systems, or the regulation of nuclear power generation, this form of hazard analysis is augmented by rigorous event-notification systems, which require local actors to notify the system regulator of "out-of-control" sequences—near misses, or accidents that only accidentally did not result in catastrophes. The system regulator then reviews the event, collaborates with the local actor to determine its root cause, alerts all other actors in the system to the results of the investigation and potential threats to their own operations, and periodically reviews responses to these alerts (Sabel and Simon forthcoming).

Analogous developments are evident in the provision of public services or the provision of local public goods in domains such as child protection, health care, both "special" and general education, job training, mental health services, disability capacitation (Noonan, Sabel, and Simon 2009), and economic development and community policing (Simon 2001; Fung 2004). The impetus to change is the realization that services must be customized to the needs of individuals or small groups to be effective (Sabel et al. forthcoming). The new institutions accordingly emphasize highly individuated planning, pervasive performance measurement, and efforts to aggregate and disseminate information about effective practices.

The cornerstone of these new programs is the redefinition of the conventional relation between the center and the front-line. The center's role is no longer merely to monitor front-line compliance with promulgated standards. It is responsible for providing the infrastructure and services that support frontline efforts. Thus, the role of the principal in the experimentalist school is not just to verify that the teacher's class is studiously at work, but also to organize the specialized services and framework conditions—remedial reading, testing to diagnose learning difficulties, coaching in team building—on which the teacher's team must rely when formulating and implementing individual learning plans. In child welfare, caseworkers rely on a center that trains and otherwise qualifies foster parents, facilitates contracting with outside specialists, and marshals resources that respond to the unexpected needs of particular families or sudden community-wide problems.

The solitary "street-level bureaucrat," whose tacit discretion under the radar of their superiors in the broad interstices of poorly enforced rules has haunted the organizational literature and limited the ambitions of policy-makers since the 1970s, does not figure in these emerging experimentalist regimes. Experimentalist design departs from the organizational features that gave rise to the street-level bureaucrat in three important ways.

First, the ambiguity and complexity of front-line issues, and hence the need for a flexible response, are openly acknowledged. The social professions increasingly see individual problems as functions of multiple and diverse causes that call for interdisciplinary diagnosis and intervention. In the most highly regarded child protective service programs, the caseworker's chief responsibility is to form and periodically convene a team that typically includes key family members, a health professional, lawyers for the child and the state, a therapist, and perhaps a teacher (Noonan, Sabel, and Simon 2009). In schools, analogous interdisciplinary teams—the classroom teacher, the reading specialist, the behavioral therapist—formulate plans for students with learning difficulties. Group decision-making promotes accountability in two ways. Team members act under the scrutiny of a shifting array of peers, which creates informal pressures to avoid error and excel. Furthermore, collaborative decision requires articulation, and the diversity of the team members' backgrounds ensures that matters likely taken for granted in a more homogeneous setting are explained and subjected to examination.

The second feature of experimentalist service provision that distinguishes it from street-level and other bureaucracies is a distinctive form of monitoring. Like event-notification practices in experimentalist risk regulation, social services monitoring engages in an intensive scrutiny of individual cases to reveal systemic problems. But where event notification is triggered by unexpected disruptions, core monitoring in experimentalist service provision is part of the organizational routine. A particularly well-developed example is the Quality Service Review (QSR) used in child welfare programs in Utah and several other states. The QSR begins with selection of a stratified random sample of cases. A two-person team, composed of an agency official and an outside reviewer, examines the case over two days, beginning with a file review and proceeding to interviews with the child, family members, non-family caregivers, professional team members, and others with pertinent information.

The reviewers then score the case numerically in terms of one set of indicators concerning the wellbeing of the child and his or her family and a second concerning the capacity to build teams, make assessments, formulate and update plans, and execute the plans. The initial scoring is refined in meetings among the reviewers, and then between review teams and the caseworkers and supervisors whose decisions they have reviewed. The final report presents the aggregate scoring and identifies recurring problems with illustrations of these from specific cases.

The QSR is both a process of norm elaboration and compliance enforcement. Agency goals like child safety and family stability ("permanence") are indeterminate in the abstract. The QSR helps establish paradigmatic instances of their meaning and the processes for achieving them. Participation by officials from the child welfare department's central administration promotes consistency across regions. Similarly, QSR data measures performance and helps diagnose systemic problems. The scores can be compared over time, giving rough but serviceable indications of where to focus remedial effort (Noonan, Sabel, and Simon 2009; Sabel and Simon forthcoming).

Third, rules have a different relation to accountability in experimentalist administration than in conventional governance. Workers often have discretion to depart from rules where they believe it would be counterproductive to follow them. This discretion, however, is limited by the requirement that they do so transparently in a manner that triggers review and, if their judgment is sustained, prompt rewriting of the rule to reflect the new understanding. These regimes challenge the premise of the street-level bureaucracy literature that the only escape from the rigidity of mechanical rule following is low-visibility, ad hoc front-line discretion. Instead of the familiar combination of rules and furtive discretion they rely on what might be called "dynamic" accountability, in which actions are justified or compliant if they can be plausibly explained as efforts to advance the organizational purpose, and are well informed by reflection on the best efforts of actors currently responding to like situations.

As these examples suggest, the proliferation of experimentalist governance processes across different sectoral and institutional settings can be understood as a widespread response to a secular rise in environmental volatility and complexity over the past few decades. Some of this can be linked directly to globalization, such as the problems of managing transborder common-pool resources like water or of ensuring the safety of imported food and other products as they move through transnational supply chains. In other cases, the transnational connection is only part of the story, as with the accelerating pace of technological innovation, which has undermined the effectiveness of "command-and-control" regulation in many industries, or the diversification of household and family structures, employment patterns, and populations, which have reduced the effectiveness of standardized public services in fields like education and child welfare. But whatever the precise combination of transnational and domestic factors, the resulting increase in *strategic uncertainty* has overwhelmed the capacities of conventional hierarchical management and principal–agent governance in many settings. The foundation of principal–agent governance is the monitoring of subordinate agents' con-formity to fixed rules and detailed instructions, incentivized through positive and nega-tive sanctions—rewards and punishments, in ordinary language. In a world where "principals" are uncertain of what precisely their goals should be and how best to achieve them, they must be prepared to learn from the problem-solving activities of their "agents." Hence "principals" can no longer hold "agents" reliably accountable by com-paring their performance against predetermined rules, since the more successful the lat-ter are in developing new solutions, the more the rules themselves will change (Sabel 2004, 2005; Sabel and Zeitlin 2008, 2010a).

Experimentalism correspondingly diverges not only from conventional hierarchical governance, but also from other contemporary reform movements focused on reinforc-ing principal–agent relations, whether from the top down, as in the New Public Management (NPM), or from the bottom up, as in devolved or "interactive" govern-ance. Experimentalism is based neither on a sharp separation between policy concep-tion and administrative execution, as in conventional hierarchical governance and NPM, nor on their fusion in the hands of local communities or citizens' councils as in interactive governance (Sabel 2004). Instead, it is based on the reciprocal redefinition of ends and means through an iterated, multi-level cycle of provisional goal-setting and revision, thereby giving structure to apparently fluid practices of "network governance."

Very generally, experimentalist "dynamic accountability," which anticipates the trans-formation of rules in use, offers a potentially effective response not only to contempo-rary challenges of strategic uncertainty, but also to long-standing legitimacy deficits of principal–agent governance within the nation-state itself. For it is an open secret of the modern administrative state that neither legislatures nor the courts have ever fully suc-ceeded in controlling the discretionary exercise of delegated bureaucratic authority in complex technical fields such as regulation and service provision. By obliging adminis-trative authorities to justify their choice of rules publicly, in light of comparable choices by similarly placed peers, the dynamic accountability of experimentalist governance allows old and new political actors of all kinds to contest official proposals on the basis of much richer information about feasible alternatives than has been traditionally availa-ble. In this way, experimentalist governance processes, though not intrinsically demo-cratic in themselves, have a potentially democratizing destabilization effect on domestic politics, especially in transnational settings such as the EU. But whether the potential participants make use of the possibilities thus created, and what effects this may have on public decision-making if they do, remain empirical as much as theoretical questions (Sabel and Zeitlin 2008, 2010a; Sabel and Simon 2004, forthcoming).

Experimentalist governance can be understood as a machine for learning from diver-sity. It is thus especially well-suited to heterogeneous but highly interdependent settings like the EU. There, local units face similar problems and can learn much from each other's efforts to solve them, even though particular solutions will rarely be generalizable in any straightforward way. In this sense, experimentalism transforms diversity from an obsta-cle to integration into an asset for its advancement. If strategic uncertainty is one condi-tion for experimentalist governance, then another is a polyarchic or multi-polar distribution of power, where no single actor has the capacity to impose their own pre-ferred solution without taking into account the views of others. Because the EU has had to face problems of rising strategic uncertainty under conditions of deep internal diver-sity and firm polyarchic constraints, it appears to have found its way more quickly and consistently than other polities to experimentalist solutions (Sabel and Zeitlin 2008, 2010a).

Experimentalist governance in the EU is not confined to policy fields where the Union has weak competences and produces mainly non-binding guidelines, action plans, scoreboards, and recommendations. Recent research has shown that the experimental-ist architecture of framework rule-making and revision outlined earlier is also well developed in domains where the EU has extensive legislative powers. Examples include energy, telecommunications, financial services, competition, data privacy, drug author-ization, food safety, environmental protection, and anti-discrimination rights. In many such cases, the EU's experimentalist decision-making architecture regularly results in the elaboration of revisable standards mandated by law and the enunciation of new prin-ciples, which may eventually be given binding force, as in the WFD and CIS. In others, the ensuing changes may influence only the behavior of national administrations, with no immediate impact on the legal framework of the EU itself (Sabel and Zeitlin 2008, 2010a, 2010b).

Either way, however, dynamic accountability in EU experimentalist governance does not operate through moral suasion or "naming and shaming" alone. Participation in its processes and respect for its outcomes are underpinned by an ensemble of devices that may be called destabilization regimes: mechanisms for unblocking impasses in framework rule-making and revision by rendering the current situation untenable while suggesting—or causing the parties to suggest—plausible and supe-rior alternatives. Some of these mechanisms operate directly, like the requirement to provide public justification for disagreements over scientific risk assessments in EU food safety, or the right to challenge the handling of individual cases by national authorities in the new European Competition Network, which extends horizontally to other members of the network as well as vertically to the Commission (Vos 2010; Dąbrowska 2010; Svetiev 2010; Sabel and Zeitlin 2010a: 13–14). Other destabilization mechanisms, like the penalty default, work indirectly. Rather than obliging the parties to deliberate, the central authority creates stiff disincentives for any refusal to do so by imposing rules sufficiently unpalatable to all parties that each is motivated to contrib-ute to an information-sharing regime that allows fair and effective regulation of their interdependence. In a world where standard rule-making produces such unpredicta-ble consequences as to be unworkable, the easiest way to generate penalty defaults is (to threaten) to engage in traditional rule-making (Sabel and Zeitlin 2008: 305–309; Sabel and Simon forthcoming; Karkkainen 2006). A well-documented example can be found in EU energy policy. There the Commission has periodically threatened to invoke its delegated regulatory and competition law powers to spur member states and private actors to cooperate in framework rule-making (Eberlein 2010; Sabel and Zeitlin 2010a: 14–16.)

Yet even where such destabilization regimes draw on official authority to induce participants to explore novel possibilities and respect the outcome of informed deliberation, they cannot be assimilated into the conventional idea of bargaining in the "shadow of hierarchy." In that view the parties compare two knowns: the value of the payoff of the officially imposed solution to each party, and the value of the jointly bargained outcome. They prefer their bargain because it makes both better off than the official solution. But, by bargaining under conditions of strategic uncertainty, the parties compare two unknowns. The hierarchical authorities are no longer credibly able to directly take over the regulatory functions. They can in effect promise only to make things unworkable: the penalty default is a warning, *in terrorem*, of an incalculable harm. Nor can the regulated parties precisely calculate the payoff they may eventually achieve through mutual engagement: they would not face strategic uncertainty if the outcome of their joint problem-solving was *ex ante* knowable. All that is clear is that the parties will have greater control of their fate, and hence greater chances of finding solutions that are workable for both, by engaging with each other than by choosing the penalty default. In sum, the experimentalist architecture of EU governance is not "soft law" in the sense of monitory guidance that can be flouted without consequence, but neither is it the traditional "hard law" of a form derivable from principal–agent rule-making.

EXTENDING EXPERIMENTALISM TRANSNATIONALLY

Experimentalism appears particularly well-suited to transnational domains, where there is no overarching sovereign with the authority to set common goals even in theory, and where the diversity of local conditions and practices makes the adoption and enforcement of uniform fixed rules even less feasible than in domestic settings. Yet the very polyarchy and diversity that make experimentalist governance attractive under such conditions can also make getting a transnational regime off the ground difficult. Thus, too many participants with sharply different perspectives may make it hard to reach an initial agreement on common framework goals. Conversely, a single powerful player may be able to veto other proposed solutions even if he cannot impose his own.

One possible way forward, though by no means the only one, is for a large jurisdiction like the EU (or the US) to take the lead in extending experimentalism beyond its own borders, for example, by unilaterally regulating transnational supply chains as a condition of market access. An obvious danger, however, is that such unilateral extension will produce resentment and resistance by regulatory addressees in other countries, unless they are given a voice in shaping the standards they are expected to meet. Such one-sided extension may also denature experimentalism itself by cutting out the feedback loop between local learning from rule application to rule revision. Hence some further destabilization mechanism may be required to unblock this impasse, such as by opening up such unilateral regulatory initiatives to joint governance by affected parties in other countries.

Here the disciplines of the world trading system may prove unexpectedly helpful. World Trade Organization (WTO) rules permit member states to restrict imports in order to protect public health and the environment. But they also require states wishing to restrict imports on these grounds to ensure that their proposed measures are non-discriminatory and proportional to the intended goals, to take account of relevant international standards, and to consult with their trading partners to minimize the impact on affected third parties (Weinstein and Charnovitz 2001; Parker 2001; Scott 2007). These disciplines, when they permit such extensions at all, can thus provide a potential mechanism for transforming unilateral regulatory initiatives by developed countries like the EU into a joint governance system with stakeholders from the developing world, if not a fully multilateral experimentalist regime. This role for the WTO points toward the operation of a more general mechanism, whereby the rules of existing multilateral institutions, though not experimentalist themselves, can nonetheless push unilateral extensions of experimentalism in a more reciprocal direction.

By way of illustration, consider the EU's recent initiative on Forest Law Enforcement Governance and Trade (FLEGT). This innovative initiative is aimed at combating illegal logging, an endemic problem in many developing countries, which depresses prices for legally harvested wood and undercuts the adoption of sustainable forestry worldwide. FLEGT responded to the failure of previous attempts by northern governments to tackle the problem of global forest deterioration by negotiating a binding international convention and imposing unilateral trade restrictions. It also responded to the limited take-up of private forest certification schemes in developing countries (Cashore et al. 2007). FLEGT seeks to control exports of illegally logged wood by negotiating Voluntary Partnership Agreements (VPAs) with developing countries to create "legality assurance" licensing systems. These licensing systems are based on jointly defined standards, regular monitoring and performance review, and third-party verification. Local civil society stakeholders participate both in the definition of "legally harvested wood" and in monitoring its certification, each of which are explicitly conceived as revisable in light of the other. The EU provides development assistance to build up the regulatory capacity of both public and private actors. Agreements with these experimentalist features have been signed with Ghana, Cameroon, Congo-Brazzaville, the Central African Republic, Liberia, and Indonesia, while negotiations are currently underway with a number of other Asian and African countries (Overdevest 2009; Brack 2010; Lawson and MacFaul 2010; van der Wilk 2010).

To reinforce FLEGT's effectiveness and extend its geographical scope, the EU has enacted legislation requiring all businesses placing wood products on the European market to demonstrate "due diligence" in ensuring that they have not been illegally harvested, with full traceability throughout the supply chain. Such due diligence can be demonstrated in three possible ways: (1) possession of an export license under a FLEGT VPA; (2) establishment of a private risk management system, with full traceability, risk assessment, and risk mitigation procedures; or (3) participation in a recognized monitoring scheme, based on independent verification of compliance with local forestry legislation. The European Commission, in cooperation with national authorities, is responsible for determining that recognized monitoring bodies are maintaining effective systems of due diligence against illegal logging, including procedures for the remediation of violations (Official Journal of the European Union 2010).

The EU's approach to combating illegal logging appears likely to be accepted as legitimate not only by the WTO but also by developing countries themselves, because it offers them an opportunity to participate in a jointly governed system of legality assurance, while imposing reciprocal obligations on European importers. These EU initiatives are likely to interact productively with parallel efforts to control illegal logging by other developed countries, including the US, which lack some of their experimentalist features, while at the same time reinforcing private forest certification schemes and placing them under public scrutiny. They can likewise be expected to have a major impact on China, now the world's largest trader in wood products, which has signed bilateral coordination agreements with both the EU and the US to reduce illegal logging and promote sustainable forestry in developing countries (Brack 2009, 2010; Lawson and MacFaul 2010; van der Wilk 2010).

FLEGT is just one example of how the extension of experimentalist regulation along global supply chains, disciplined by the rules of the world trading system, may stimulate the construction of a jointly governed transnational regime involving a multiplicity of public and private actors from developed and developing countries. But other pathways are also possible, and comparison among them is likely to prove fruitful (Zeitlin 2011).

Experimentalism and Structural Barriers to Reform

So far experimentalism has been presented largely as a response to strategic uncertainty: the situation where the parties face urgent problems, but know that their preferred problem-solving strategies fail and therefore are willing to engage in a joint, deliberative (potentially preference-changing) investigation of possible solutions. But there are, of course, many situations where at least one party with the power to block reform has doubts about the workability of current arrangements, but defends them nonetheless because of the advantages the present system confers on it, but not others, or (when direct benefits are less salient) because potential alternatives threaten cascading disruptions of ways of life long taken for granted. In these cases there are structural obstacles to reform: deep-seated features of institutions—hiring policies in firms, admissions policies in schools, sentencing practices in courts—or widespread beliefs—about the kinds of people who are "reliable" or "dangerous"—that perpetuate inequalities and the domination of some parties over others. The concern is that, because these obstructions are so deep-seated, they are likely to resist, and ultimately to thwart, most efforts at reform. The failure in the waning decades of the last century to improve schools—and especially to improve, through effective schooling, the educational outcomes predicted by a student's social and economic background—was taken as a near conclusive demonstration of this futility. Experimentalist reforms, however, are proving most promising in some of the domains, such as education, child welfare, and antidiscrimination, where structural obstacles seem most daunting. By way of conclusion, therefore, we briefly contrast conventional and experimentalist responses to the problem of deeply rooted barriers to change.

In the conventional view the best response is to attack the barriers head-on, at the outset. If disparities in power, as evidenced in differential access to authoritative decision-makers, will eventually check change, then power-sharing, in the form of some guarantee of equalized access, is the first objective and precondition for reform. Community organizers in the US have honed this strategy to an art, using collaborative "power mapping" of the decision-making processes in schools or policing to develop the skills of movement leaders, and using skillful leadership to wrest some measure of control from those identified as having it (Oakes, Rogers, and Lipton 2006). However, the general strategy is familiar from the history of the labor movement and the many social movements that subsequently arose. At its limit, expressed in some variants of Marxism, revolution in the sense of a thoroughgoing change in distribution of the political and economic control rights is the precondition of any fundamental change.

Experimentalism shares with many other "postmodern" or "post-sovereigntist" views the assumption that decision-making powers and structural obstacles to reform are not localized at this or that hierarchical apex. Rather, power relations and other such obstructions are diffused throughout society, and therefore present in every locale. Experimentalism belongs to the "optimistic" side of the postmodern family of views, in holding that the absence of a controlling hierarchy of authority, explicit or not, suggests not the omnipresence of controlling disciplines, but instead that local changes can have local effects, and that these effects can percolate horizontally and even upwards (Kjaer 2010: ch. 5). Hence the emphasis in experimentalist reforms is on creating space for local innovation—delegating authority for decision-making, under conditions of dynamic accountability, to local units and front-line workers—rather than on formal power-sharing at the institutional apex.

But the contrast between experimentalism and conventional views of reform in relation to power disparities and other structural impediments is less stark than this juxtaposition alone suggests. Experimentalist reforms plainly recognize that many actors will resist creating spaces for local innovation precisely because of an attachment to things as they are. Hence the recourse to penalty defaults and other destabilizing devices imposed by courts (as in the case of the reform of schools and child welfare institutions in the US), by legislatures (as in the case of US statutes requiring school systems to adopt experimentalist reform programs), or by administrative authorities (as in the EU examples discussed above). The assumption is that given strategic uncertainty and thus the growth of a background recognition of the need for renewal, the parties will prefer joint exploration, even if this leads to a change in preferences and the deep-seated behaviors that go with them, to impotent submission to external forces that no one—including the authorities in whose name they are exercised—truly controls. The assumption, in other words, is that structural impediments can best—and perhaps only—be identified and surmounted in the course of a reform process that generates concrete solutions, not in anticipation of it.

There is some important evidence that reforms of this type work even in the presence of what are conventionally regarded as deeply rooted structural obstacles to change. School systems in US cities such as New York, which adopted experimentalist reforms either by explicit political decision or in response to penalty defaults, are significantly improving the learning outcomes of the least well-off students (Kemple 2011). In Finland the national school system, using a variant of experimentalist reform, has achieved over-all results that rank at the top of international league tables, while all but eliminating the effect of the parents' social and economic background on the pupil's performance (Sabel et al. forthcoming). But it is still too soon to know whether these successes will be further generalized. And even if they are, questions remain about the inclusiveness of reform. Experimentalist reforms of child welfare often involve the children concerned—for example, as members or even leaders of the teams elaborating plans for their future. But the role of parents in school reforms, or of citizens in experimentalist regulatory systems, is less clear. There are related questions about the legislative oversight of experi-mentalist governance arrangements.

Nonetheless, these open questions and more notwithstanding, it is fair to say that experimentalism has created the plausible hope of reform in areas of social life where well-founded concerns about social impediments to change long seemed to allow none.

REFERENCES

Barreira, A. and Kallis, G. 2003. The EU water framework directive and public participation in transboundary river basin management. In J. G. Timmerman and S. Langass (eds.), *Environmental Information in European Transboundary Water Management*, eds.. London: IWA Publishing, 92–103.

Brack, D. 2009. Combating illegal logging: Interaction with WTO rules. *Energy, Enviroment and Resource Governance Illegal Logging Briefing Paper 2009/01*. London: Chatham House.

Brack, D. 2010. Controlling illegal logging: Consumer country measures. *Energy, Enviroment and Resource Governance Illegal Logging Briefing Paper 2010/01*. London: Chatham House.

Cashore, B., Auld, G., Bernstein, S., and McDermott, C. 2007. Can non-state governance "ratchet up" global environmental standards? Lessons from the forest sector. *Review of European Community and International Environmental Law* 16: 158–172.

Cohen, J. and Sabel, C. F. 1997. Directly-deliberative polyarchy. *European Law Journal* 3: 313–340.

Cohen, J. and Sabel, C. F. 2003. Sovereignty and solidarity: EU and US. In J. Zeitlin and D. M. Trubek (eds.), *Governing Work and Welfare in a New Economy: European and American Experiments*. Oxford: Oxford University Press, 345–375.

Dąbrowska, P. 2010. EU governance of GMOs: Political struggles and experimentalist solutions? In C. F. Sabel and J. Zeitlin (eds.), *Experimentalist Governance in the European Union: Towards a New Architecture*. Oxford: Oxford University Press, 174–214.

Dewey, J. 1927. *The Public and Its Problems*. New York: Henry Holt.

Eberlein, B. 2010. Experimentalist governance in the European energy sector. In C. F. Sabel and J. Zeitlin (eds.), *Experimentalist Governance in the European Union: Towards a New Architecture*. Oxford: Oxford University Press, 61–79.

Fung, A. 2004. *Empowered Participation: Reinventing Urban Democracy*. Princeton, NJ: Princeton University Press.

Gerstenberg, O. and Sabel, C. F. 2002. Directly deliberative polyarchy: An institutional ideal for Europe? In C. Joerges and R. Dehousse (eds.), *Good Governance in Europe's Integrated Market*. Oxford: Oxford University Press, 289–341.

Henson, S. and Humphrey, J. 2009. *The Impacts of Private Food Safety Standards on the Food Chain and on Public Standard-Setting Processes*. Paper prepared for FAO/WHO. Rome: Codex Alimentarius Commission.

Karkkainen, B. C. 2006. Information-forcing regulation: Penalty defaults, destabilization rights, and new environmental governance. In G. de Búrca and J. Scott (eds.), *Law and New Governance in the EU and the US*. Oxford: Hart, 293–322.

Kemple, J. J. 2011. Children first and student outcomes: 2003–2010. In J. A. O'Day, C. S. Bitter, and L.M. Gomez (eds), *Education Reform in New York City: Ambitious Change in the Nation's Most Complex School System*. Cambridge, MA: Harvard Education Press, 255–291.

Kjaer, P. F. 2010. *Between Governing and Governance: On the Origin, Function, and Form of Europe's Post-National Constitution*. Oxford: Hart.

Lawson, S. and MacFaul, L. 2010. *Illegal Logging and Related Trade: Indicators of the Global Response*. London, Chatham House.

Noonan, K., Sabel, C. F., and Simon, W. H. 2009. Legal accountability in the service-based welfare state. *Law and Social Inquiry* 34: 523–568.

Oakes, J., Rogers, J., and Lipton, M. 2006. *Learning Power: Organizing for Education and Justice*. New York: Teacher's College Press.

Official Journal of the European Union. 2010. Regulation (EU) No. 995/2010 of the European Parliament and of the Council of October 20, 2010 laying down the obligations of operations who place timber and timber products on the market. *Official Journal* L 295/23–34.

Overdevest, C. 2009. Exporting experimentalism and the case of FLEGT. Unpublished memo prepared for the project on Extending experimentalist governance: From the EU to the world? University of Wisconsin-Madison, March 6–7.

Parker, R. W. 2001.The case for environmental trade sanctions. *Widener Law Symposium Journal* 7: 21–28.

Sabel, C. F. 1994. Learning by monitoring: The institutions of economic development. In N. Smelser and R. Swedberg (eds.), *Handbook of Economic Sociology*. Princeton, NJ: Princeton University Press, and New York: Russell Sage Foundation, 137–165.

Sabel, C. F. 2004. Beyond principal–agent governance experimentalist organizations, learning and accountability. In E. Engelen and M. Sie Dhian Ho (eds.), *De Staat van de Democratie. Democratie voorbij de Staat*. Amsterdam: Amsterdam University Press, 173–195.

Sabel, C. F. 2005. A real time revolution in routines. In C. Heckscher and P. S. Adler (eds.), *The Firm as a Collaborative Community*. Oxford: Oxford University Press, 106–156.

Sabel, C. F. and Simon, W. H. 2004. Destabilization rights: How public law litigation succeeds. *Harvard Law Review* 117: 1015–1101.

Sabel, C. F. and Simon, W. H. (forthcoming). Minimalism and experimentalism in American public law. *Georgetown Law Review.*

Sabel, C. F. and Zeitlin, J. 2008. Learning from difference: The new architecture of experimentalist governance in the European Union. *European Law Journal* 14: 271–327.

Sabel, C. F. and Zeitlin, J. 2010a. Learning from difference: The new architecture of experimentalist governance in the European Union. In C. F. Sabel and J. Zeitlin (eds.), *Experimentalist Governance in the European Union: Towards a New Architecture.* Oxford: Oxford University Press, 1–28.

Sabel, C. F. and Zeitlin, J. (eds.) 2010b. *Experimentalist Governance in the European Union: Towards a New Architecture.* Oxford, Oxford University Press.

Sabel, C. F., Saxenian, A., Miettinen, R., Kristensen, P. H., and Hautamäki, J. (forthcoming). *Individualized Service Provision as the Key to the New Welfare State: Lessons from Special Education in Finland.* Helsinki: SITRA.

Scott, J. 2007. *The WTO Agreement on Sanitary and Phytosanitary Measures: A Commentary.* Oxford: Oxford University Press.

Scott, J. and Holder, J. 2006. Law and new environmental governance in the European Union. In G. de Búrca and J. Scott (eds.), *Law and New Governance in the EU and the US.* Oxford: Hart, 211–242.

Simon, W. H. 2001. *The Community Economic Development Movement: Law, Business, and the New Social Policy.* Stanford: Stanford University Press.

Svetiev, Y. 2010. Networked competition governance in the EU: Centralization, decentralization, or experimentalist architecture? In C. F. Sabel and J. Zeitlin (eds.), *Experimentalist Governance in the European Union: Towards a New Architecture.* Oxford: Oxford University Press, 79–120.

van der Wilk, N. 2010. China and the EU's normative approach to Africa: Competitor or collaborator? A case study of forest law enforcement, governance and trade (FLEGT). Unpublished MA thesis, University of Amsterdam.

von Homeyer, I. 2010. Emerging experimentalism in EU environmental governance. In C. F. Sabel and J. Zeitlin (eds.), *Experimentalist Governance in the European Union: Towards a New Architecture.* Oxford: Oxford University Press, 121–150.

Vos, Ellen. 2010. Responding to catastrophe: Towards a new architecture for EU food safety regulation? In C. F. Sabel and J. Zeitlin (eds.), *Experimentalist Governance in the European Union: Towards a New Architecture.* Oxford: Oxford University Press, 151–176.

Weinstein, M. M. and Charnovitz, S. 2001. The greening of the WTO. *Foreign Affairs* 80: 147–156.

Zeitlin, J. 2011. Presidential address: Pragmatic transnationalism: Governing across borders in the global economy. *Socio-Economic Review* 9: 1–20.

PART III

GOVERNANCE AND THE REFORM OF THE STATE

....

CHAPTER 13

GOVERNANCE AND INSTITUTIONAL FLEXIBILITY

....

JON PIERRE*

GOVERNANCE reform and public management reform has been high on the agenda in the advanced democracies for the past decades. Both types of reform could be seen as strategies to adapt the public sector to meet new challenges, and in both types of reform the purported rigidity of government institutions and decision-making processes have been an important target. Governance reform and management reform are both predicated on some degree of institutional flexibility in public sector organizations. In order to engage civil society, non-government organizations (NGOs), and private sector actors, political and administrative institutions need to partially redefine their roles and modus operandi.

This reform process creates tensions between institutions' new and traditional roles. Thus, the key issue addressed in this chapter is the tension between the traditional role of public institutions, geared to uphold values of equal treatment and the rule of law on the one hand, and the more recent role, emphasizing contextualization and flexibility on the other. How have governments sought to reconcile the tension between institutional stability and flexibility? This chapter argues that institutions have responded to this challenge in a variety of ways such as deregulation, the introduction of "soft steering" instruments, and institutional innovation (Sørensen, Chapter 15, this volume; Zehavi, Chapter 17, this volume). Also, flexibility has been achieved not so much through intraorganizational reform but by increased reliance on collaborative forms of governance, where the main role of government institutions is to ensure fairly traditional political and administrative authority. While there are a number of different response strategies available to governments, the fundamental problem of instilling flexibility into traditional government structures remains. In both new modes of governance and public management there is an emphasis on process over institutions, interaction over command, performance over procedure, and outcomes over deliberation and input. Adapting traditional government structures to a new role and introducing a new modus operandi has triggered many of the expected institutional obstacles to change.

This chapter thus looks at some specific aspects of the institutional dimension of governance—the capacity of institutions to change. Administrative reform in the Western democracies has included some very real institutional and organizational reform both with regard to institutional structure and the management of that structure (Christensen and Lægreid, Chapter 18, this volume). It is common in the institutional literature to view change as an organizational response to exogenous forces. In the present analysis, however, change has been driven by endogenous forces; government institutions were given a partially new role to play by their political masters. Kathleen Thelen's (2004) distinction between functionalist and "path dependence" models of institutional change is somewhat helpful since it seems to separate institutional change driven by endogenous factors from exogenously driven change. The institutional changes in the public sector that were part of the administrative reform had clear functionalist features; they represented a distinct break with "path dependence" and were in many respects a means to another and more far-reaching end of bringing managerialism into the public bureaucracy.

The magnitude of the challenges triggered by this reform varied considerably among different national contexts. Some countries adopted public management reform swiftly and extensively while others were more tentative, restricted, and slow in the adoption of New Public Management (NPM) (Peters 2001; Pollitt and Bouckaert 2004). Similarly, some governments already had long experience with consultation with social partners, whereas such exchanges were more novel in other contexts. Also, the "new governance" argument probably overstates the centrality of the state in society some decades ago (Olsen 2007); the capability of government has always, albeit to a larger or smaller extent, been constrained by factors related to the economy or to social complexity or simply to opposition among strategic social partners.

More specifically, then, this chapter focuses on the tensions between the stability of public organizations on the one hand and the adoption of a more flexible and contextualized modus operandi of those organizations on the other. How did government agencies adopt a flexible modus operandi in order to engage a complex society demanding flexible solutions? What challenges and organizational obstacles are encountered in adapting such an organizational strategy, and what traditional values embedded in public administration are jeopardized by flexible administration? The key argument of the chapter is that although administrative reform has included profound institutional change, particularly at the executive side of government, "flexible government" and a new government role in governance has not been attained by making government itself flexible but rather by making governance and management more flexible and contextually defined. The role of government in that governance remains, to a large extent, to ensure due process and legalism.

The remainder of the chapter is organized as follows. The next section will briefly discuss the main tenets of administrative reform in the advanced democracies. The chapter then turns to review different types of institutional response and adaptation to the new role outlined in administrative reform, emphasizing a more flexible modus operandi. After that, we assess the consequences of increased institutional flexibility for state–society interactions. A summarizing section closes the chapter.

GOVERNANCE REFORM AND PUBLIC MANAGEMENT REFORM

The governance "turn" in the 1990s identified a partially new role for public bureaucracies. Government and its bureaucracy was to serve as a political and administrative "hub," defining collective objectives, allocating resources, and overseeing the quality of services delivered by other actors. This new role had significant intraorganizational consequences for the public administration. Previous strategies of command and control were replaced by more interactive processes of information, negotiation, and bargaining between the public administration and significant players in its external environment, including the targets of public policy.

The organizational challenges dictated by governance reform were, however, a quiet breeze compared to the reform pressures catalyzed by the NPM (Hood 1991). NPM insisted that public service delivery, and management in the public sector more broadly, should be conceived of as "generic" tasks. Therefore, the public sector should be reformed so that it could emulate private sector practices, focusing on improved services, cost-efficiency, and "customer" satisfaction. Thus, one of the differences between governance reform and management reform was that while the former acknowledged the unique and critical role of the state as the carrier of collective interests in the process of governing, the latter largely denied any specificity of the public sector in service production and therefore aimed to adopt private sector management models and roles to solve problems of inefficiency and lack of responsiveness to the recipients of services.

In terms of their institutions' ramifications, governance and management reform shared several common features (Klijn, Chapter 14, this volume). Both assumed some degree of institutional flexibility in public sector organizations. In order to engage civil society, NGOs, and private sector actors, political and administrative institutions needed to partially redefine their roles and modus operandi; a type of reform that easily creates tensions between conventional and emergent roles. Against this backdrop, we need to know how governments have sought to reconcile the tension between institutional stability and flexibility. While there are a number of different response strategies available to governments, the fundamental problem of instilling flexibility into traditional government structures remains. In both new modes of governance and public management there is an emphasis on process over institutions, interaction over command, performance over procedure, and outcomes over deliberation and input. Adapting traditional government structures to a new role and a new modus operandi has triggered many of the expected institutional obstacles to change.

The magnitude of the challenges triggered by this reform varied considerably among different national contexts. Some countries adopted public management reform swiftly and extensively while others were more tentative, restricted, and slow in the adoption of NPM (Peters 2001). Similarly, in the "neo-corporatist" group of countries, government already had long experience with consultation and collaboration with social partners whereas such exchanges were more novel in other contexts (Katzenstein 1984). Thus, the "new governance" argument probably overstates the centrality of the state in society some decades ago (Olsen 2007); the capability of government has always been constrained by factors related to the economy or to social complexity or simply to opposition among strategic social partners.

The remainder of the chapter is organized as follows. The next section will briefly discuss the main tenets of administrative reform in the advanced democracies. The chapter then turns to review different types of institutional response and adaptation to the new role outlined in administrative reform, emphasizing a more flexible modus operandi. After that, we assess the consequences of increased institutional flexibility for state–society interactions. A summarizing section closes the chapter.

ADMINISTRATIVE REFORM: OBJECTIVES AND DESIGN

One of the diagnoses preceding the public management reform process in the 1980s and 1990s was that government lacked flexibility (Peters 2001). At about the same time, the governance "turn" defined a partially new role for public bureaucracies.

We need to distinguish between governance reform and public management reform as two subcategories of administrative reform. The former type of reform aims at redefining the structures, processes, and roles of the public sector in order to enhance the capacity of the bureaucracy to contribute to democratic governance. The latter type of reform has the objectives of increasing efficiency, cutting costs, and helping the public sector deliver higher-quality service. The need for greater institutional flexibility is obvious in both types of reform. As a result, governments have sought to develop new and more flexible models both in the field of management and in governance (Sørensen, Chapter 15, this volume).

Governance reform and NPM reform overlapped to some extent as they both emerged in the late 1980s and 1990s. Both types of reform are still underway, although management reform appears to have lost some momentum over the last few years (Pierre and Ingraham 2010). The main normative beliefs, ideas, and objectives sustaining governance reform relate to the capacity and desirability of state control in a complex society. The system of government that had evolved over centuries was no longer believed to be geared to govern the increasingly complex and multilayered society (Kooiman 1993, 2003). Another more normative idea was that politics and government as we know them had run their course, with growing skepticism toward politicians, tax fatigue, and growing support for neoliberalism following in their wake (see Pierre and Peters 2000).

Based on these overarching beliefs and normative images of state, society, and governance, management reform and governance reform aimed at increasing the points of contacts between state and society and partially redefining the role of the state in governing and service delivery (Hood 1991; Osborne and Gaebler 1992). In a complex society, the chief task of government should be to coordinate its actions with those of a wide variety of societal actors. Civil society, voluntary associations, and the market should all become involved in the pursuit of collective projects and service delivery. The role of government was to define the long-term policy goals and to ensure that governing was conducted through the democratic process: "governance is the business of government," as Osborne and Gaebler (1992) put it. The key criteria guiding the role of the public sector were its performance in service delivery and its capacity to coordinate political and social action toward collective objectives.

Adapting the organizational framework to the new state role advocated by NPM required massive government restructuring. Also, the new forms of state–society interaction required an empowerment of the lower levels of the public service and a contextualization of the role of government in governance. The "trajectory" (Pollitt and Bouckaert 2004) of public management reform has been closely documented and the present space does not allow a more detailed account of various specific components of that reform (see Cheung 1997; Light 1997; Pollitt and Bouckaert 2004; Pierre and Ingraham 2010; Savoie 1994). Suffice it to say that several reform components addressed organizational issues in the public sector. One organizational target of reform is related to leadership and control. Public organizations serve political masters whose directives are communicated in a fairly strict top-down process, from the senior public servant level down to the staff that deliver services. However, NPM reform sought to reduce politicians' operative responsibilities and to bring managerialist thinking into the stale public bureaucracy.

A second type of organizational reform refers to changes in resource allocation and the strategic use of the budget as an instrument for organizational steering (see Caiden 1998). A leitmotif in administrative reform has been to focus on performance and to supplement input-based control with output-based measurement and management. Performance management has a profound impact on organizational steering, control, and coordination since it accords operations a leading role in the organization and basically sees all other elements of the organization as subordinate to the operative segments of the organization. Again, these changes accorded the lower levels more autonomy in relation to the senior levels of the bureaucracy.

Finally, a third important intraorganizational consequence of the recent management reform has been an increasing openness vis-à-vis societal actors. As already mentioned, the new role envisaged for the state in governance reform and public management reform was a coordinating role. Public bureaucracies obviously had extensive contacts with clients before reform but much of those interactions were through the public service, and were conducted through a regulated process. The new governance role of the institutions meant that they had to devise structures and processes that helped create new points of contact with society. Those contacts could take place at the peak organizational level but the more day-to-day contextualized exchange processes were more likely to take place at the lower levels of the organization.

Let us now see how the public bureaucracy responded to these challenges.

The institutional dimension of reform

Across the Western world, management reform has been embedded in a larger neoliberal project aiming at redefining the role of the state in society (Suleiman 2003). This rolling back of the state generated opportunities, or what Pierce (1993) refers to as "governance gaps," for non-state actors to engage in different forms of collective problem-solving. This could be done either in networks or as social partners in public service delivery.

Deregulation. One type of institutional adaptation in administrative reform was quite simply to abolish regulatory control over strategic policy sectors or markets in the spirit of the neoliberal regime. In this perspective, rearranging institutions to take a lower profile is relatively easy. With less public control and regulation follows less public accountability, and the bureaucracy no longer needs to concern itself with the degree to which a previously regulated sector continues to cater to collective interests (but see Bozeman 2007; Horwitz 1986). Deregulation became hugely popular in the United States and the UK during the 1980s. Privatization, too, was important, albeit more so in Europe than in the US, simply because state ownership was more extensive in the European countries than in America. This initial deregulation was not the end of the story, however. The 1990s and 2000s have witnessed cycles of deregulation and reregulation in many countries and specific sectors, partly to ensure safety, security, and quality considerations or because the market could not deliver on any other criteria.

Obviously, deregulation and privatization are not strategies of increasing institutional flexibility. They are, rather, strategies for the public institutions to exit their regulatory role. That role had come under attack from Reagan and Thatcher, with other political leaders of similar neoliberal ideology following suit (Savoie 1994). To the public bureaucracy, deregulation could be said to have provided an alibi for not having to embark on a complex process of organizational change and adaptation.

Creating networks. Another, far more common and challenging type of adaptation of the bureaucracy to new management and governance roles has been to alter the modus operandi of institutions in order to engage social partners. Government departments and agencies opened up to societal actors and requested policy advice and input. Through such networks, government institutions can help ensure societal consent on policies. For instance, a survey among civil servants in the Swedish Central Government Office shows that a significant proportion of central government bureaucrats believe that steering through networks is an efficient governing strategy and, similarly, a significant number of those civil servants are already engaged in such networks. Informal steering mechanisms such as bargaining and information are seen as suitable in contexts where the policy sector is densely organized, for example, in the environmental policy sector, or where social complexity makes the use of obtrusive instruments less efficient.

In the case of networks, any meaningful involvement for public servants is predicated on their ability to commit the institution they represent to particular policy arrangements (see Eva Sørensen's chapter). The reciprocity of networks suggests that in the context of policy implementation they are two-way streets: they convey policy-makers' ideas and goals to the targets of the policies at the same time as they provide societal actors with access into the policy process. Other elements of management and governance reform provided front-line staff with such autonomy, thus enabling public sector institutions to create networks or to engage in existing networks.

An additional aspect of networks is related to the growing importance of transnational networks. This applies not least to the countries in the European Union where transnational networks and other forms of cross-border communication are strongly encouraged. However, today we can see any number of transnational networks emerge, frequently addressing issues that transcend nation-state borders, such as climate change (Betsill and Bulkeley 2004; van der Heiden 2010).

Soft law steering and partnerships. Another type of interaction and unobtrusive policy instrument that evolved during this governance reform was the institutionalization of bilateral contacts between public organizations and key players in their external environments. Here, public–private partnerships offer a good example. During the 1980s and early 1990s, such partnerships emerged primarily at the urban level in many countries where political or administrative institutions at the local level created institutionalized forms of cooperation with the local business community (see Pierre 1998). Later, public–private partnerships became popular instruments for a wide variety of purposes, such as economic development, service delivery, and even privatization, and now can be found in all levels of institutions, from the European Union to the local level (see Ball, Heafey, and King 2001; Mörth 2008).

"Soft law" steering is another important type of "new governance" policy instrument (see Zehavi, Chapter 17, this volume). Since performance management links budget allocation to what the public service unit has actually achieved in terms of quantity and quality, service producers translate these criteria into objectives for service delivery (see Mörth 2004). Performance evaluation, for instance in the context of certification "Best Practice" or other standards related to performance, thus become powerful steering instruments without the exercise of obtrusive policy instruments.

Steering with "soft," unobtrusive policy instruments and forging partnerships with external actors required increased autonomy at the lower-level operative elements of public institutions. In order to accomplish a shift toward more managerial public institutions, operative control therefore had to be divorced from the political echelon of the organization. Politicians were to define the long-term goals of the public administration and then give managers considerable autonomy in the management of the organization. Empowering the lower levels of public organizations, however, distorts the relationship between politics and administration and confuses the hierarchy in the administrative sphere, which is an important precondition for accountability. Most importantly perhaps, it is a model of performance-based administrative reform that "introduces an important bottom-up influence to counter traditional top-down control. It demands that administrators perform a new role and build a very different capacity to fill it. And it requires elected legislators and executives alike to change the way they think and act toward bureaucratic control" (Kettl 1997: 456). The benefits in steering capacity generated from networks and other informal arrangements with societal actors must thus be weighed against the costs embedded in the intraorganizational challenge of handling the new bottom-up channel of influence that these arrangements entail.

Thus, depoliticization and managerialism changed the pattern of command and control within the public organizations. It is a reform concept that helps citizens, or customers, interact with a more flexible bureaucracy. While it is a reform that helps provide more flexibility at the lower organizational levels it has significant intraorganizational consequences. Furthermore, as we will discuss later in this chapter, both flexibility and stability in the institutional system of government have their pros and cons, something that further complicates an understanding of the relationship between the governance role of government and the degree of flexibility of its institutions.

Budgetary reform. The national budget is one of the most important instruments of steering and coordination in government and the public sector. During the 1980s and perhaps even more so the 1990s, many governments in Europe, Asia, and North America reformed the budgetary process and also to some extent the role of the budget in the public sector. This reform had several drivers, the most important being austerity and structural imbalances in the national budgets. Management reform was predicated on de-emphasizing input and, instead, linking budgets to performance.

To help facilitate these changes, budget cycles changed from single to multiple years; budget allocations became more aggregated, giving more budgetary control for agencies; and performance measures were brought into the budget allocation process (Osborne and Gaebler 1992; Caiden 1998). In terms of cutback management, the previously standard model of across-the-board cutbacks was replaced with more strategic models like "Planning, Programming, and Budgeting" (PPB), targeting specific programs for cutbacks. These changes reflect different views of the capacity of government organizations to change and adapt; the former system assumes that organizations had very limited adaptive capacity, whereas the latter, more strategic, approach implies a greater capacity to change.[1]

Agencification. Yet another institutional strategy in management reform has been to create new institutional structures to provide public services rather than trying to change the function of existing organizations. This strategy has been a key component of management reform in a large number of countries and represents the most distinct case of government restructuring in the context of administrative and management reform (Aucoin 1998). The policy–operations divorce was seemingly definite and institutionalized with the creation of executive agencies. This split allowed government departments to focus on their policy role while agencies could pursue managerial efficiency. Also, this reform allowed operative units in the public sector to develop their own interfaces and exchanges with society (Campbell and Wilson 1995; Pollitt and Talbot 2003).

Creating these new agencies helped the political leadership of the public sector escape the arduous task of trying to change the modus operandi of existing institutions. The strategy echoes Daniel Tarschys's observation some time ago in a Royal Commission report in Sweden that it seemed easier for government to create a new agency than it was to change the course of an already existing agency (SOU 1983: 39). In some ways, agencification squared the circle of accommodating coterminous continuity and change in the public sector; it significantly reduced the pressure for change in government departments; and it created new organizations, with no organizational luggage to take into consideration, which were geared to support a managerial "turn" in the public sector.

Agencification began with the Next Steps reform in the UK in the 1980s and was quickly transmitted around the world. The Anglo-American countries—Australia, New Zealand, Canada, and the United States—in particular adopted the agency model of public sector organization (Pollitt et al. 2001). Its impact on the modus operandi of public administration cannot be exaggerated. Agencification was integral to performance management, and redefined to a significant extent the relationship between the public sector and its environment by facilitating competitive tendering and management by contract. Thus, devising separate institutional structures for the operative segment of public service delivery was the gateway to a wide range of market-based administrative reform concepts.

If the creation of executive agencies was thus critical to the many different forms of market-based reform that we have witnessed over the past couple of decades, it was also a major source for many of the coordination problems that have emerged in the wake of that reform. In addition, decentralization, which was implemented in a number of countries during the 1980s and was consistent with management reform objectives of empowering line managers and front-line service staff, exacerbated problems of coherence and coordination in government. The "joined-up government" and "whole of government" strategies in the UK reflect the coordination problems of which the executive agencies were part (Christensen and Lægreid 2007, Chapter 18, this volume).

That having been said, the problems of integrating new ideas of performance management into internal markets with the traditional structures and modus operandi of the public administration would prove more complex than perhaps anticipated (Radin 2006). Again, this is not to argue that management reform has no place in the public sector but it does seem to suggest that much of the reform implemented thus far has underestimated the significance of preexisting institutional arrangements and procedures (see Allison 1986).

Equally important, more recent management reform recognizes, to a larger extent than previous reform efforts, the role of the public administration in democratic governance and the need for such reform to cater to a wider set of objectives (Halligan 2007, 2010). The public bureaucracy has an essential role in governance and, in order to be efficient and sustainable, any alteration in its role, structure, or procedures needs to be assessed against the criterion of how it impacts on those aspects of the public adminis-tration (Peters 2008; Suleiman 2003).

Status quo ante. Finally, a fourth response to the organizational challenges inherent in administrative and governance reform has, interestingly, been to conduct business *status quo ante.* There are some core values related to public service embedded in adminis-trative institutions. Altering or dismissing those values may enhance institutional efficiency and capabilities in the short run, but state–society relationships will also be negatively affected. Based on an extensive review of public management research, Hill and Lynn (2005) show that traditional forms of top-down hierarchical governance still seem to characterize much of the governance role of public institutions. To some degree, this strategy illustrates the reality of government in the midst of administrative reform. Despite the pressure, and need, for change, government remains tied to a set of constitu-tional mandates that significantly reduce the scope for reform.

Status quo ante might appear to be a strategy of sticking one's head in the sand hoping that the problems of governance and organizational inflexibility will somehow go away. However, while management reform has distinct institutional consequences, govern-ance reform has played out differently. An intriguing question is to what extent the par-ticipation of government institutions in "new governance" arrangements entails an impetus to radically transform its structure or procedures, or if the role of government in governance is to deliver traditional forms of government functions. The fundamental logic of interactive forms of governance is not so much about isomorphism but rather a matter of facilitating concerted action among different types of actors and interests, where each partner contributes with their particular competence or resources or author-ity. In this perspective, government's main contribution to governance is formal author-ity, legality, consent, and legitimacy—in other words, good old-fashioned government. This way, government could meet the challenge presented by new modes of governance by delivering "government" more interactively than before without necessarily chang-ing the nature of that "government."

All of these responses to the challenge of adapting the public bureaucracy to a new role in governance can be easily detected in the advanced democracies (see Pollitt and Bouckaert 2004). They should be seen as different facets of a larger undertaking aiming at modernizing the public sector and, indirectly, reassessing the role of the state in soci-ety. Deregulation, relying on less obtrusive policy instruments, reforming the budget, and restructuring government by creating executive structures with considerable auton-omy in relationship to the political leadership are examples of the organizational changes and adaptation that administrative reform has entailed (Aucoin 1998).

To sum up the discussion thus far, public management reform's focus on creating a more flexible public service driven by bottom-up processes related to performance and customer preferences manifested itself first and foremost in an institutional split between policy and operations, or what Aucoin (2006) and others refer to as "autonomi-zation." The objectives of public management reform were beyond what could have been accommodated within the existing institutional system. While this institutional reform was conducive to increased efficiency and a more demand-driven public service, the main governance consequence of this development has been a growing problem in coordinating the public sector.

Institutional flexibility as a problem and a solution

Institutional rigidity has been a perennial criticism against the public sector. However, flexible government as an objective of administrative reform is far more complex and multidimensional than a first glance at the issue might suggest (Peters 2001). On the one hand, flexibility is a prerequisite for accommodating changes in the environment of the organization and adapting public services to changing demand patterns. Also, given the tremendous changes in society over the past century or so it is certainly noteworthy that the basic structures of government look quite similar to those of the late nineteenth century.

On the other hand, flexibility sits at odds with entrenched public sector values like due process, procedural fairness, equal treatment, and, indeed, public law. These values are contingent on institutional stability. Moreover, the clients of the public administration appreciate some degree of consistency in the bureaucracy's organizational structure as it reduces transaction costs and uncertainty. The challenge to the architects of reform, then, has been to combine the positive aspects of institutional stability with the positive aspects of increased institutional flexibility. Earlier in this chapter we looked at a couple of different organizational strategies that aimed to respond to this challenge. We will now briefly look somewhat closer at institutional stability and flexibility in the context of governance and legitimacy.

A basic strand in organization theory is the interactive relationship between organizations and their environments; organizations need to have the capacity to adapt to their environment in order to maintain their core functions and roles. In the public sector such adaptation is complicated by organizational multifunctionality, which may suggest different adaptive strategies for different functions (cf. Christensen et al. 2007). More importantly, perhaps, the functions of the institutions of governments are characterized by a high degree of institutionalization; we need only think of democratic input and control, legislation, taxes and budget allocation, and regulation to see the need for institutional and procedural stability.

Thus, in the midst of demanding more flexible government, the architects of reform need to consider the virtues related to institutional consistency as well. Increased flexibility in government helps increase the long-term efficiency of the government system and helps adapt the public sector to changes in its environment and to changes in public policy. At the same time, however, state–society relationships benefit from consistency and a high degree of institutionalization so that citizens/clients/customers recognize the public administration and are familiar with its setup and modus operandi (Peters 2001).

CONCLUSIONS

One of the objectives of administrative reform in the advanced Western democracies has been to increase the institutional flexibility in the public service. Enhancing that flexibility has been an end in itself and a means to adapt the bureaucratic "hardware," that is, organizational structure, to a new organizational "software," that is, management reform. A key strategic objective in this respect has been the institutional separation of the policy and operative functions of government. This split was essential to the introduction of market-based models of service delivery that such flexibility brought into the public sector. Agencification and decentralization also empowered line managers and front-line staff in the public service and paved the way for public management reform focusing on the performance in service delivery. Thus, there has been a logical chain of reform, from structural change in the public sector to the introduction of a new management philosophy.

At the same time, the role of government in the "new governance" arrangements emphasize not so much a flexible approach to collective problem-solving as a formal–legal component to governance. Most public administration clients probably want flexibility in terms of the services they deliver but they might not want that flexibility at the expense of other and more traditional values that we accord the public sector. Thus, what appears to a be a conflict of goals for government in "new governance" and public management reform can to some degree be accommodated by recognizing the significance of the traditional roles of administration in the new or emergent public sector.

Administrative reform, particularly the more extreme forms of market-based reform, has had a profound impact on governance. Critical observers argue that market-based reform has been detrimental to the role of the public administration in democratic governance (Peters 2008; Suleiman 2003; Ventriss 2000). Others tend to argue that increased institutional flexibility in the public sector has helped make the bureaucracy better equipped to deliver cheap service of good quality and be responsive to the needs of the clients. Governments in a large number of countries are now trying to find the balance between the governance role and the service role of the public administration and how those roles are best accommodated. Administrative reform is no longer a one-off event but more a continuous process.

NOTES

* I appreciate David Levi-Faur's and B. Guy Peters's comments on a previous draft of this chapter. The research for this chapter was conducted while the author was a Visiting Research Fellow to the University of Melbourne. The support from the Swedish Science Council and the Wenner-Gren Foundations is gratefully acknowledged.
1. I owe this insight to B. Guy Peters.

REFERENCES

Allison, G. T. 1986. Public and private management: Are they fundamentally alike in all unimportant respects? In F. W. Lane (ed.), *Current Issues in Public Administration*. New York: St Martin's Press, 184–200.

Aucoin, P. 1998. Restructuring government for the management and delivery of public services. In B. G. Peters and D. J. Savoie (eds.), *Taking Stock: Assessing Public Sector Reform*. Montreal and Kingston: McGill-Queens University Press, 310–347.

Aucoin, P. 2006. Accountability and coordination with independent foundations. In T. Christensen and P. Lægreid (eds.), *Autonomy and Regulation: Coping with Agencies in the Modern State*. Cheltenham: Edward Elgar, 110–136.

Ball, R., Heafey, M. and King, D. 2001. Private finance initiative: A good deal for the public purse or a drain on future generations? *Policy and Politics* 29: 95–108.

Betsill, M. M. and Bulkeley, H. 2004. Transnational networks and global environmental governance: The cities for climate program. *International Studies Quarterly* 48: 471–493.

Bozeman, B. 2007. *Public Values and Public Interest: Counterbalancing Economic Individualism*. Washington, DC: Georgetown University Press.

Caiden, N. 1998. A new generation of budget reform. In B. G. Peters and D. J. Savoie (eds.), *Taking Stock: Assessing Public Sector Reform*. Montreal and Kingston: McGill-Queens University Press, 252–264.

Campbell, C. and Wilson, G. K. 1995. *The End of Whitehall: Death of a Paradigm?* Oxford: Blackwell.

Cheung, A. B. L. 1997. Understanding public-sector reforms: Global trends and diverse agendas. *International Review of Administrative Sciences* 63: 435–457.

Christensen, T. and Lægreid, P. 2007. The whole-of-government approach to public sector reform. *Public Administration Review* 67: 1059–1066.

Christensen, T., Lægreid, P., Roness, P. G. and Rövik, K. A. 2007. *Organization Theory and the Public Sector*. London: Routledge.

Halligan, J. 2007. Reintegrating government in third generation reforms in Australia and New Zealand. *Public Policy and Administration* 22: 217–238.

Halligan, J. 2010. Reforming management and management systems: Impacts and issues. In J. Pierre and P. Ingraham (eds.), *Comparative Administrative Change And Reform: Lessons Learned: A Festschrift To Honor B. Guy Peters*. Kingston and Montreal: McGill-Queen's University Press, 139–158.

Hill, C. J. and Lynn, Jr., L. E. 2005. Is hierarchical governance in decline? Evidence from empirical research. *Journal of Public Administration Research and Theory* 15: 173–195.

Hood, C. 1991. A public management for all seasons? *Public Administration* 69: 3–19.

Horwitz, R. B. 1986. Understanding deregulation. *Theory and Society* 15: 139–174.

Katzenstein, P. J. 1984. *Corporatism and Change*. Ithaca Cornell University Press.

Kettl, D. F. 1997. The global revolution in public management: Driving themes, missing links. *Journal of Policy Analysis and Management* 16: 446–462.

Kooiman, J. (ed.) 1993. *Modern Governance: New Government-Society Interactions*. London: Sage.

Kooiman, J. 2003. *Governing as Governance*. London: Sage.

Light, P. 1997. *The Tides of Reform: Making Government Work, 1945–1995*. New Haven, CT: Yale University Press.

Mörth, U. 2008. *European Public–Private Collaboration: A Choice between Efficiency and Democratic Accountability?* Cheltenham: Edward Elgar.

Mörth, U. (ed.) 2004. *Soft Law in Governance and Regulation: An Interdisciplinary Analysis.* Cheltenham: Edward Elgar.

Olsen, J. P. 2007. *Europe in Search of Political Order.* Oxford: Oxford University Press.

Osborne, D. and Gaebler, T. 1992. *Reinventing Government.* Reading, MA: Addison-Wesley.

Peters, B. G. 2001. *The Future of Governing: Four Emerging Models*, 2nd ed. Lawrence, KA: University of Kansas Press.

Peters, B. G. 2008. *The Politics of Bureaucracy*, 6th. ed. London: Routledge.

Peters, B. G. and Pierre, J. 1998. Governance without government: Rethinking public administration. *Journal of Public Administration Research and Theory* 8: 223–242.

Pierce, N. R. 1993. *Citistates.* Washington, DC: Seven Locks Press.

Pierre, J. (ed.) 1998. *Partnerships in Urban Governance: European and American Experience.* Basingstoke: Palgrave Macmillan.

Pierre, J. and Peters, B. G. 2000. *Governance, Politics and the State.* Basingstoke: Palgrave Macmillan.

Pierre, J. and Ingraham, P. (eds.) 2010. *Comparative Administrative Change and Reform: Lessons Learned.* Montreal and Kingston: McGill-Queen's University Press.

Pollitt, C. and Talbot, C. (eds.) 2003. *Unbundled Government: A Critical Analysis of the Global Trend to Agencies, Quangos and Contractualisation.* London: Routledge.

Pollitt, C. and Bouckaert, G. 2004. *Public Management Reform: A Comparative Analysis.* Oxford: Oxford University Press.

Pollitt, C., Bathgate, K., Caulfield, J., Smullen, A. and Talbot, C. 2001. Agency fever? Analysis of an international policy fashion. *Journal of Comparative Policy Analysis: Research and Practice* 3: 271–290.

Radin, B. A. 2006. *Challenging the Performance Movement: Accountability, Complexity, and Democratic Values.* Washington, DC: Georgetown University Press.

Savoie, D. J. 1994. *Thatcher, Reagan, Mulroney: In Search of a New Bureaucracy.* Pittsburgh: Pittsburgh University Press.

SOU. 1983. Politisk styrning: administrativ självständighet (Political control: Administrative autonomy). Report from a Royal Commission, 39.

Suleiman, E. 2003. *Dismantling Democratic States.* Princeton: Princeton University Press.

Thelen, K. 2004. *How Institutions Evolve: The Political Economy of Skills in Germany, Britain, the United States, and Japan.* Cambridge: Cambridge University Press.

Van der Heiden, N. 2010. *Urban Foreign Policy and Domestic Dilemmas.* Colchester: ECPR Press.

Ventriss, C. 2000. New public management: An examination of its influence on contemporary public affairs and its impact on shaping the intellectual agenda of the field. *Administrative Theory and Praxis* 22: 500–518.

....

CHAPTER 14

NEW PUBLIC MANAGEMENT AND GOVERNANCE: A COMPARISON

....

ERIK HANS KLIJN

1. INTRODUCTION

....

GOVERNMENTS worldwide appear to be experimenting with new forms of horizontal governance, such as public–private partnerships (Osborne 2000; Hodge and Greve 2005), collaboration (Ansell, Chapter 35, this volume), stakeholder involvement (McLaverty 2002; Edelenbos and Klijn 2006), and other forms of citizen involvement (Lownes, Pratchett, and Stoker 2001) that are encompassed under the label governance. Many reasons have been offered to explain this phenomenon, with the most common one being that the role of governments is changing in modern network society (Castells 2000). Governments in recent years have become more dependent on societal actors to achieve their goals because of the increasing complexity of the challenges they face. Many of these involve conflicting values, and addressing them requires governments that are multifaceted and increasingly horizontal (Kickert, Klijn, and Koppenjan 1997; Sørensen and Torfing 2007). The growing demand for integrated service provision also stimulates horizontal networks through, for instance, cooperation between various organizations.

Thus the *governance perspective* tells us that various actors have to be included in the policy-making and implementation process. Private actors, social alignments, and citizens are in themselves important resources, with the power to obstruct policy interventions. Although governance emphasizes horizontal coordination to solve policy problems and bind resources for collective action that is not the only direction of movement. Depending on the nature of the resource dependencies between the actors, governance can still show vertical or asymmetrical travel.

At the same time we see a different development in modern government, that is, a continuation of the New Public Management (NPM), which originated in the eighties. Here governments are trying to provide service delivery and public policy through a wide range of private and non-profit actors. Using techniques of rational management and through a separation of policy formation and policy implementation, governments try to enhance the efficiency and effectiveness of service delivery and policy implementation. We see trends of agentification (Pollitt et al. 2000) and privatization accompany this attempt.

Actually one could also regard both NPM and governance as answers to the growing complexity of society and the difficulties of the classical welfare state to cope with that complexity. Growing specialization in modern society causes increasing interdependencies (Castells 2000) while the growing individualizing has resulted in citizens who have a more critical attitude to their governments but also in societies where several traditional forms of ties (family, religion, neighborhood) seem to have lost at least some of their strength.[1] This creates a need for tailor-made government arrangements that take citizens' wishes into account. These arrangements must, on the one hand, satisfy demands for more integrated service delivery, with citizens participating, and yet, on the other hand, must deal with the growing complexity of decision-making resulting from interdependence and more "assertive" citizens and other interest groups. Both NPM and governance recognize this growing complexity but have different attitudes toward coping with it.

DIFFERENCES BETWEEN NPM AND GOVERNANCE: WHAT TO COMPARE?

Both trends, the continuation of NPM since the eighties and the emergence of governance in the late nineties, are clearly visible in the real-life world of public administration. It is far from simple to separate them, since policy documents, politicians, and managers draw freely from arguments that come from the two different perspectives. While essentially quite distinct they are often confused, yet both major paradigms reinforce each other. The NPM leads to a proliferation of separate bodies, comprised of actors focusing on their specialized task. But that proliferation itself creates a network, or as some would say a "hollow state" (Milward and Provan 2000), that tries to secure policy and service delivery through other agencies. Those have to be coordinated in turn, especially if we want integrated service provision or policy-making. And then we find ourselves in a governance network where actors need each other's resources. The difficulties of coordinating networks calls for clearer guidelines and performance indicators to create order in the chaos.

But before we start a comparison it is essential that we are clear about what is being compared. That is not the practice of everyday life, since we already mentioned that

practitioners freely "shop" between ideas from NPM and governance. We are comparing the basic ideas from both perspectives as they originate in the literature. We also use
a slightly restricted definition of governance, as modes of horizontal steering that are
effected by networks of actors. There are wider definitions of governance (see
Introduction; Pierre Chapter 13, this volume; Christensen and Lægreid, Chapter 18, this
volume) that sometimes even include NPM. Here, however, I apply a narrow definition
to allow us to distinguish between governance and NPM.

In this chapter we will begin by exploring NPM, as it was the first to arrive in the field
of public administration in the eighties. This is done in Section 2. After that we deal with
the phenomenon of governance in Section 3. In both cases we start by examining what is
understood by the two paradigms and then look at the conditions that make the perspective work. Section 4 contains a brief comparison where we focus on a few themes.
We end with some conclusions and observations.

2. THE NEW PUBLIC MANAGEMENT: STRIVING FOR INTERNAL EFFICIENCY

New public management as a practice and as a set of ideas in public administration
emerged in the late seventies and eighties. It was strongest in the Anglo-American countries like the UK, New Zealand and Australia, and the US. The NPM solution consists of
a number of elements. The central notion is that when policy-making is separated from
execution, uncertainties are made more manageable—and this includes the separation
of responsibilities.

The new public management as inspiration: market-like mechanisms

It is difficult to provide a definitive image of NPM. Pollitt and colleagues conclude in
their book *New Public Management in Europe*: "NPM is chameleon: it changes its
appearance to blend in with the local context" (Pollitt, van Thiel, and Homburg 2007:
199). But in general one can say that NPM can be characterized by a number of features
that are connected to each other but do not all necessarily have to be present at the same
time (see Hood 1991; Kickert 1997; Kettl 2000; Lane 2000; Pollitt, van Thiel, and
Homburg 2007). The main features focus on:

1. improving the effectiveness and efficiency of government performance;
2. ideas and techniques that originate from the private sector;
3. the use of privatization and contracting out of governmental services, or parts of
   governmental bodies, to improve effectiveness and efficiency;

4. the creation or use of markets or semi-market mechanisms, or at least on increasing competition in service provision and realizing public policy;
5. the use of performance indicators or other mechanisms to specify the desired output of the privatized or autonomized part of the government or the service that has been contracted out. This also means a shift from *ex ante* to *ex post* control.

Through instruments such as contracting-out and privatization, not only do we acquire a different relationship between the public and private sectors, but we also disentangle the complex responsibilities that were created during the evolution of the welfare state. The reform agenda of NPM in itself needs a lot of work to succeed. Strict regulation is required to create the conditions for separation, and to create possibilities for monitoring and control. Not surprisingly, various authors emphasize the emergence of a regulatory state and regulatory capitalism (Levi-Faur 2005), or stress the enormous growth of auditing and control (Power 1999). Others have stressed that the "post NPM reforms" advocate a more holistic approach and put more emphasis on the horizontal dimension of the reforms. Christensen and Lægreid (Chapter 18, this volume) mention developments such as creating coordinative structures inside the central structures (task forces, interministerial collaborative units, etc.) of the central state in order to cut across traditional boundaries and move away from the fragmentation that is a feature of the early NPM reforms.

Lean, effective, and clearly separated responsibilities

The aim of most NPM reforms was to transform governments into leaner but more effective steering organizations or, according to two of the proponents of these government reforms, to do "more with less" (Osborne and Gaebler 1992). Governments should be steering, that is, setting goals and trying to achieve them, instead of rowing, that is, doing all of the service provision themselves.

> Governments that focus on steering activily shape their communities, and nations. They make more policy decisions. They put more social and economic institutions in motion. Some even do more regulating. Rather than hiring more public employees, they make sure other institutions are delivering services and meeting the community's need. (Osborne and Gaebler 1992: 32)

Osborne and Gaebler's plea for an entrepreneurial government essentially comes down to a plea for a clear specification of desired products or services and the outputs that have to be achieved. This information should come from political officeholders and provide more control over bureaucracy or other implementing units. But it also implies a separation of responsibilities between decision-making and delivery and between political actors and providers. With these ideas, new substance is given to the doctrine of the primacy of politics because politically responsible actors need to focus only on formulating objectives and starting points.

Of course, some authors have observed that the promises of the NPM seem to harbor some contradictions. Pollitt and Bouckaert (2000) identified ten of what they called "incompatible statements." These include elements like: the tension between gaining political control over bureaucracies versus free managers; making savings versus improving performance; motivating staff versus weakening tenure; and improving quality versus cutting costs. Another important observation that has been made is that the image of the NPM's innovations and practices has been strongly dominated by the Anglo-American literature, while the NPM reforms in Europe have been less strong and have certainly been colored by the national institutional contexts of these countries (see Kickert 1997; Pollitt, van Thiel, and Homburg 2007). Other authors have questioned the emphasis on consumer sovereignty because it might weaken the position of elected political officeholders and it is not always easy to accommodate to the characteristics of the goods (Aberbach and Christensen 2005).

Conditions that make the NPM ideas work

In the NPM view, governments operate as skillful buyers who decide what they want, specify outputs, and then decide which organization—public but autonomous, non-profit or private—can best deliver the service. Furthermore, the process can be tested with well-defined output performance indicators. But to make this idea work, apart from some institutional changes in regulation that, for instance, allow agencies to be relatively independent, and so on, two very important conditions have to be met: goal specification and monitoring possibilities.

Product specification is essential because you have to know precisely what you are contracting out. It is also important because it makes it possible to evaluate the performance of the contractor. Some authors have argued that this makes the NPM approach most suitable for relatively simple problems, like garbage collection, or the building of roads and schools (although these are already more difficult), and less successful with more complex problems where defining the problem and choosing performance indicators is harder (Klijn 2002; see also Van de Walle 2009 regarding the problems of performance indicators).

Because the quality of output depends on the effort that the contractor puts into the production process, monitoring is important. After all, the contractor might have an incentive to exert less effort (Deakin and Michie 1997; Williamson 1996). Thus, monitoring is used to protect against the potential for self-serving behavior.

Opportunism becomes more important as actors become more dependent on each other due to specific investments (Williamson 1996). Safeguards in the contract are often used to protect oneself against the opportunistic behavior of other actors. But monitoring and including safeguards in the contracts assume that interactions *can be* monitored and that behavior to at least some extent can be foreseen.

3. GOVERNANCE AS AN EMERGING
STEERING CONCEPTION

New public management may be difficult to define; the problems are, however, probably even greater in the case of governance. Many definitions and conceptualizations have been used in the wide variety of literature on governance.

Governance?

We will not discuss all of these since that has already been done in the introduction of this book. In his widely cited article, Rhodes (1997) provided six interpretations of the word "governance". His overview covered corporate governance, new public management, good governance as a socio-cybernetic system, governance as a self-organizing network, and other aspects. We can discuss whether it is fruitful to enlarge the definition in such a way because there seems to be no limit to what governance can mean. Even more classical forms of government could be included, for a more elaborate discussion (Klijn 2008), but for this chapter we need a narrower definition of governance for comparison with NPM. Following the ideas of Rhodes (1997, Chapter 3, this volume) we shall focus on the meaning of governance as networks. At best, we can make a faint distinction by saying that governance relates to the interaction process and its guidance, whether it is called network management (Agranoff and McGuire 2001; Mandell 2001) or meta-governance (as in Sørensen and Torfing 2007; Torfing, Chapter 7, this volume). Meanwhile networks relate to the empirical phenomenon of policy issues or public services that are solved within networks of actors. Thus, governance networks will be used here as an indication of *more or less stable patterns of social relationships (interactions, cognitions, and rules) between mutually dependent (public, semi-public, and/or private) actors, that arise and build up around complex policy issues or policy programs* (Koppenjan and Klijn 2004: 69–70). Governance then refers to the interaction processes that take place within those networks.

Its most important characteristics emphasize:

1. a strong focus on the interorganizational dimension of policy-making and service delivery and the interdependencies of organizations in achieving policy aims and service delivery;
2. horizontal types of steering (network management, meta-governance, etc.) that are supposed to be better able to acquire cooperation from societal actors (Rhodes 1997; Agranoff and McGuire 2001; Mandell 2001; Torfing, Chapter 7, this volume). These horizontal types of steering supposedly ensure that actors will use their power of veto less frequently (*enhance support*);

3. using the knowledge from societal actors in order to improve the quality of policy and public services and to make better use of information dispersed by various actors (*enhancing quality and innovative capacity*);

4. the early involvement of societal actors, stakeholders, and citizens' groups so that the legitimacy of decisions is enhanced (*enhancing democratic legitimacy*) (Sørensen and Torfing 2007).

Thus, through more horizontal forms of steering and organizing (like partnerships, interactive decision-making, etc.) we also acquire, just as with the NPM perspective, different relations between societal and (semi) private actors and governmental actors. Where in NPM this is a strongly contractual relationship, in governance it is a more interdependent horizontal relationship. This does not mean that governance networks are completely horizontal. In governance networks there are also vertical elements because actors have different resources and these cause inequalities in the relations through asymmetrical resource dependencies, while formal contacts between various layers of governmental levels, for instance, create some vertical relationships. But even in these there is often mutual dependency.

Thus policy and service delivery are achieved in networks of actors who may be public-only intergovernmental networks or multi-level governance or mixtures of public and private actors. Managerial effort in the sense of facilitating, mostly called network management (Agranoff and McGuire 2001; Meier and O'Toole 2001, 2007), or meta-governance (Torfing, Chapter 7, this volume) is then crucial to make these governance processes work.

Governance: solving wicked problems in an interdependent network of actors

Governance is mostly used or "advertised" in situations involving wicked problems (Rittel and Webber 1973). These stem from policy issues that involve many actors, where the actors often disagree about the nature of the problem and the desired solution. In addition, the actors are usually hampered by insufficient or controversial knowledge. It is no easy task to come up with a solution for complex policy problems since they almost always involve tricky conflicts between values. What values should we prioritize in environmental decision-making: transport values, livability values, economic values, or environmental values? In cases of integrated service delivery too, governance has to solve difficult coordination and value problems.

This means that in most governance processes it is not possible to specify the definitions and goals at the start (see Hanf and Scharpf 1978; Kaufmann, Majone, and Ostrom 1986; Rhodes 1997). Actually, various actors are involved with different problem definitions, value judgments, and desired solutions (Fischer 2003; Koppenjan and Klijn 2004).

Actors may lack the capacity for problem-resolving, have vested interests, or not have the necessary resources, and so on. A central requirement is that the actors involved are in some way connected to each other (interdependency). Solving policy problems or delivering public services has to be achieved by cooperation.

In governance literature, public managers and political officeholders are pictured as skillful network managers who are able to bind actors together, search for solutions that satisfy various values, and sustain winning coalitions for difficult decision-making processes (see Agranoff and McGuire 2001; Mandell 2001; Meir and O'Toole 2001; Koppenjan and Klijn 2004). The basic characteristics of governance create slightly more difficulties with the model of representative democracy when compared with NPM. If other stakeholders are engaged in the formation of policy the question is raised of how this can be combined with the responsibility of elected officeholders, as we will see in the section that compares the two perspectives.

Conditions for success: stakeholder involvement and horizontal coordination

Many conditions are mentioned in the literature on governance, like the sense of urgency, strong interdependencies, embeddedness of the actors, and available process rules that guide interactions, but the most important are the involvement of stakeholders and active network management (see Scharpf 1978; Gage and Mandell 1990; Meir and O'Toole 2001.). Governance works from the assumption that policy problems and service delivery are formed and implemented in networks of interdependent actors (public organizations and involved stakeholders). Participation of these actors in the decision-making process is essential, as is the employment of their resources to solve a problem. But since actors perceive different problems and have different interests it is important to develop policy solutions that satisfy various stakeholders' problems, perceptions, and interests. After all, why would the involved actors give their support and resources to move the process onward? Thus, flexibility in developing content and activities to facilitate such forward movement is important in governance processes.

That means horizontal coordination, or as it is mostly called network management, is crucial (Gage and Mandell 1990; Agranoff and McGuire 2001; Meir and O'Toole 2001) to explore new content, activate and bind actors, organize platforms for interaction, or develop temporary rules for interactions (Mandell 2001; Koppenjan and Klijn 2004). Actually, recent research on network management does show that these activities are crucial for achieving outcomes (see Meir and O'Toole 2001, 2007; or Huang and Provan 2007 for US data; Klijn, Steijn, and Edelenbos 2010 for European data on this). Thus, contrary to NPM, it is not the precise problem definition and the monitoring that are crucial but the willingness of the actors involved to participate in the governance process and their ability to manage that process.

4. New public management versus governance: a comparison

The two major perspectives in public administration portray "ideal types" but the descriptions do make it clear that the perspectives differ considerably in focus, key ideas, management strategies, and the role of politics.

While governance tends to emphasize the horizontal relationships between governmental and other organizations, NPM can be considered an opposing paradigm to governance in many ways since it emphasizes central steering and political control, whereas governance tends to emphasize the limits of central control. The title of the classical Hanf and Scharpf book from 1978 about networks was after all: *Interorganizational Policy Making: Limits to Coordination and Central Control* (Hanf and Scharpf 1978)! Table 14.1 summarizes some of the main differences.

Table 14.1 Two dominant perspectives in public administration

	New Public Management	Governance
Focus	Organizational and institutional changes and adaptations within the public sector (intraorganizational focus)	Changes and adaptations in the relations between governments and other actors (interorganizational focus)
Objectives	Improving effectiveness and efficiency of public service delivery and public organizations	Improving interorganizational coordination and quality of decision-making
Core ideas/ management techniques	Using business instruments (modern management techniques, market mechanisms, performance indicators, consumer boards) to improve service delivery	Using network management: activating actors, organizing research and information-gathering (joint fact-finding), exploring content, arranging interactions, process rules, etc.
Politics	Elected officials set goals, and implementation is achieved by independent agencies or market mechanisms on the basis of clear performance indicators	Goals are developed during interaction and decision-making processes; elected officeholders are part of the process or are meta-governors
Complexity	Modern society is complex but we need clear goals and flexible implementation for that. Keep away from complex interactions with society. If necessary use consumer boards or market incentives to govern implementing units	Modern society is complex and requires interdependence; citizens do not take the decisions of public actors at face value. Taking part in complexity by interacting with actors in society is unavoidable and/or necessary to reach satisfactory outcomes

Thus, where NPM is mainly intraorganizational, trying to improve the internal operation of governments, governance is mainly interorganizationally oriented, trying to improve coordination of governments with the other actors who are necessary to deliver services or implement policies. One could also say that NPM is more occupied with efficiency and improving existing services and policies, while governance is more concerned with delivering new solutions for complex problems by improving coordination between the various actors.

The role of elected officials: central steering or meta-governor?

An important difference is how the two approaches view the role of elected politicians. Certainly, in the beginning, NPM presented itself as technical. Goals were set by elected politicians and the NPM role was to implement their wishes. One could also say that NPM was more focused on output legitimacy (Scharpf 1997) in the sense that it wanted to achieve outputs that met the political goals. NPM, certainly in its early appearance, (re)introduced the separation between politics and administration. Politics set the goals while implementers, whoever they are, do the job. Of course, one of the problems is that politicians do not always formulate clear goals or when they do, they tend to change them if circumstances change (Schedler 2003); a natural reaction if one wishes to survive in the political landscape. But, after a while, changing goals is not very compatible with organizing service provision and policy implementation by contracts and performance indicators. It is not particularly easy to break the contract open to include new performance indicators. The representation of the NPM method as purely technical is not entirely correct. As has been said, the idea is to put the consumer at the center, and this might conflict with the prominent role of politicians.

In governance the position of elected officials and politicians is less clear, or one could say more problematic. If governance allows other stakeholders to enter the decision-making process and the formulation of goals then the consequence is that the elected officials have to share their authority, at least some respects, with other actors. This is actually an explicit aim with some of the governance experiments like interactive decision-making (Edelenbos and Klijn 2006) and various forms of citizens' and stakeholders' involvement (Lowndes, Pratchett, and Stoker 2001). Whether it is done with the idea that these actors are necessary for achieving policy aims because they veto power or whether this provides democratic legitimacy in both cases, the role of elected politicians tends to change from sole initiator of political decisions to joint authority or to a meta-governor who sets basic constraints and rules in which interactions can take place. Thus the governance perspective also tends to look at the input legitimacy, especially since the discussion recently has shifted with relation to which rules and organizational principles are required to enhance the democratic legitimacy of its processes (Sørensen and Torfing 2007).

Managing complexity: jumping in or staying out?

If we look at both dominant views on management and the way they view complexity in society, we see that it is treated differently. New public management tries to ignore or reduce complexity by abstaining from detailed governance and instead focusing on governing by output criteria and by organizing the playing field through market mechanism, privatization, etc. In NPM the manager tries to keep as far as possible from the complex interaction system itself. The system is treated as a black box, which reacts to its emerging characteristics by changing the output criteria or by organizing the service provision differently by choosing other providers.

Governance tries to address complexity by stepping into the complex system and designing mechanisms and strategies that are specifically targeted at the situation and characteristics of the process. It acknowledges that the processes are very dynamic and that systems show emergent properties, which can be addressed by being part of the interactive system through influencing the strategies and choices of the agents and coordinating the interactions of agents.

5. CONCLUSIONS

We have argued in this chapter that governance and NPM originated from two different sets of concerns and theoretically are quite different. Still, in the last decade both perspectives have incorporated each other's ideas. The governance literature has embraced, for example, ideas of performance indicators and NPM literature has adopted more horizontal steering mechanisms.

Thus, both in real life and in scientific literature ideas about the two aspects overlap. A good example is the discussion on public–private partnerships (PPP). These can be described as a "*more or less sustainable cooperation between public and private actors in which joint products and/or services are developed and in which risks, costs and profits are shared*" (Klijn 2010). Policy-makers and researchers assume that a more intensive cooperation between public and private parties will add value by producing better and more efficient policy outcomes (Ghobadian et al. 2004; Hodge and Greve 2005). Private parties are involved earlier in the decision-making process and are said to contribute more intensively than is the case in more traditional client–supplier or principal–agent relationships.

But in the policy discussions and the scientific literature we find that the basic assumptions incorporated in the idea and effectiveness of PPPs come from both NPM and governance (see Klijn 2010). From the NPM literature, the PPP idea takes the assumption that separate bodies should be organized at some distance from political life (arm's length, see Pollitt et al. 2004). Performance indicators are often mentioned in discussions of PPP. On the other hand, many scientific and policy documents on PPP stress that public and private partners can together add value by exchanging information and by forming real partnerships. These are ideas that clearly come from the governance literature and demonstrate the influence each has on the other. Maybe both perspectives reflect the way order and complexity in public administration need each other. NPM offers the possibility of order and control but has difficulty coping with the real-life complexity of governing, while governance may help with that but cannot satisfy our longing for forms of control and our search for mechanisms to evaluate, in a clear-cut way, the performance of governments.

This means that the two major perspectives will probably continue to coexist and flourish because they depend on each other. The NPM perspective will be attractive because it provides an answer as to how to govern complex society from one political center. In a world dominated by the media, where the political process is personalized, it fits our desire for clear, strong leaders. In that sense the governance perspective will have more difficulty surviving as a "brand." On the other hand, there remains the question of whether governance is better able to cope with the day-to-day complexity of administrative life. There is still room for the development of the two perspectives.

NOTE

1. See SCP (2009) for figures about citizens' attitudes derived from the Euro barometer. For social capital see Putnam (1995).

REFERENCES

Aberbach, J. D. and Christensen T. 2005. Citizens and consumers: An NPM dilemma. *Public Management Review* 7: 225–245.

Agranoff, R. and McGuire, M. 2001. Big questions in public network management research. *Journal of Public Administration Research and Theory* 11: 295–326.

Castells, M. 2000. *The Rise of the Network Society: Economy, Society and Culture.* Cambridge: Blackwell.

Deakin, S. and Michie, J. (eds.) 1997. *Contracts, Co-operation, and Competition: Studies in Economics, Management and Law.* Oxford: Oxford University Press.

Edelenbos, J. and Klijn, E. H. 2006. Managing stakeholder involvement in decision making: A comparative analysis of six interactive processes in The Netherlands. *Journal of Public Administration Research and Theory* 16(3): 417–446.

Fischer, F. 2003. *Reframing Public Policy: Discursive Politics and Deliberative Practices.* Oxford: Oxford University Press.

Fischer F. and Forester, J. 1993. *The Argumentative Turn in Policy Analysis and Planning.* London: Duke University Press.

Gage, R.W. and Mandell, M.P. (eds.) 1990. *Strategies for Managing Intergovernmental Policies and Networks.* New York: Praeger.

Ghobadian, A., Gallear, D., O'Regan, N. and Viney, H. (eds.) 2004. *Public Private Partnerships: Policy and Experience.* Houndmills, Basingstoke: Palgrave Macmillan.

Hanf, K. and Scharpf, F. W. 1978. *Interorganizational Policy Making: Limits to Coordination and Central Control.* London: Sage.

Hodge, G. and Greve, C. (eds.) 2005. *The Challenge of Public Private Partnerships.* Cheltenham: Edward Elgar.

Hood, C. C. 1991. A public management for all seasons. *Public Administration* 69(1): 3–19.

Huang, K. and Provan, K. G. 2007. Structural embeddedness and organizational social outcomes in a centrally governed mental health service network. *Public Management Review* 9: 169–189.

Kaufmann, F. X., Majone, G. and Ostrom, V. (eds.) 1986. *Guidance, Control and Evaluation in the Public Sector: The Bielefeld Interdisciplinary Project.* Berlin: Walter de Gruyter.

Kettl, D. F. 2000. *The Global Public Management Revolution: A Report on the Transformation of Governance.* Washington, DC: Brookings Institution Press.

Kickert, W. J. M. (ed.) 1997. *Public Management and Administrative Reform in Western Europe.* Cheltenham: Edward Elgar.

Kickert, W. J. M., Klijn E. H. and Koppenjan, J. F. M. (eds.) 1997. *Managing Complex Networks: Strategies for the Public Sector.* London: Sage.

Klijn, E. H. 2002. Governing networks in the hollow state: Contracting out, process management or a combination of the two. *Public Management Review* 4: 149–165.

Klijn, E. H. 2008. Governance and governance networks in Europe: An assessment of 10 years of research on the theme. *Public Management Review* 10: 505–525.

Klijn, E. H. 2010. Public private partnerships: Deciphering meaning, message and phenomenon. In G. Hodge, C. Greve, and A. Boardman, *International Handbook on Public–Private Partnerships.* Cheltenham: Edgar Elgar, 68–80.

Klijn, E. H., Steijn, B., and Edelenbos, J. 2010. The impact of network management strategies on the outcomes in governance networks. *Public Administration* 88(4): 1063–1082.

Koppenjan, J. F. M. and Klijn, E. H. 2004. *Managing Uncertainties in Networks: A Network Approach to Problem Solving and Decision Making.* London: Routledge.

Lane, J. E. 2000. *New Public Management.* London: Routledge.

Levi-Faur, D. 2005. The global diffusion of regulatory capitalism. *Annals of the American Academy* 598: 12–32.

Levi-Faur, D. 2012. *The Oxford Handbook of Governance.* Oxford: Oxford University Press.

Lowndes, V., Pratchett, L. and Stoker, G. 2001. Trends in public participation: Part 1: Local government perspectives. *Public Administration* 79: 205–222.

McLaverty, P. (ed.) 2002. *Public Participation and Innovations in Community Governance.* Aldershot: Ashgate.

Mandell, M. P. (ed.) 2001. *Getting Results through Collaboration: Networks and Network Structures for Public Policy and Management.* Westport: Quorum Books.

Meier, K. and O'Toole, L. J. 2001. Managerial strategies and behaviour in networks: A model with evidence from U.S. public education. *Journal of Public Administration and Theory* 11(3): 271–293.

Meier, K. and O'Toole, L. J. 2007. Modeling public management: Empirical analysis of the management-performance nexus. *Public Administration Review* 9: 503–527.

Milward, H. B. and Provan, K. G. 2000. Governing the hollow state. *Journal of Public Administration Research and Theory* 10: 359–379.

Osborne, D. and Gaebler, T. 1992. *Reinventing Government: How the Entrepreneurial Spirit is Transforming the Public Sector.* Reading, MA: Addison-Wesley.

Osborne, S. P. (ed.) 2000. *Public-Private Partnerships: Theory and Practice in International Perspective*. London: Routledge.

Ostrom, E. 1986. A method for institutional analysis. In F. X. Kaufmann, G. Majone, and V. Ostrom (eds.), *Guidance, Control and Evaluation in the Public Sector: The Bielefeld Interdisciplinary Project*. Berlin: Walter de Gruyter, 459–479.

Pierre, J. (ed.) 2000. *Debating Governance: Authority, Steering and Democracy*. Oxford: Oxford University Press.

Pollitt, C. and Bouckaert, G. 2000. *Public Management Reform: A Comparative Analysis*. Oxford: Oxford University Press.

Pollitt, C., Talbot, C., Caulfield, J. and Smullen, A. 2004. *Agencies: How Governments Do Things Through Semi-Autonomous Organizations*. Basingstoke: Palgrave Macmillan.

Pollitt, C., van Thiel, S. and Homburg, V. 2007. *New Public Management in Europe*. Basingstoke: Palgrave Macmillan.

Power, M. 1999. *The Audit Society: Rituals of Verification*. Oxford: Oxford University Press.

Putnam, R. D. 1995. Tuning in, tuning out: The strange disappearance of social capital in America. *Political Science and Politics* 12: 664–683.

Rein, M. and Schön, D. A. 1992. Reframing policy discourse. In F. Fischer and J. Forester (eds.), *The Argumentative Turn in Policy Analysis and Planning*. Durham, NC: Duke University Press, 145–166.

Rhodes, R. A. W. 1997. *Understanding Governance*. Buckingham: Open University Press.

Rittel, H. J. W. and Webber, M. M. 1973. Dilemmas in a general theory of planning. *Policy Sciences* 4: 155–169.

Rogers, D. L. and Whetten, D. A. (eds.) 1982. *Interorganizational Coordination: Theory, Research, and Implementation*. Ames, IA: Iowa State University Press.

Scharpf, F. W. 1978. Interorganizational policy studies: Issues, concepts and perspectives. In K. I. Hanf and F. W. Scharpf (eds.), *Interorganizational Policy Making: Limits to Coordination and Central Control*. London: Sage, 345–370.

Scharpf, F. W. 1997. *Games Real Actors Play: Actor-Centered Institutionalism in Policy Research*. Boulder, CO: Westview Press.

Schedler, K. 2003. And politics? Public management developments in the light of two rationalities. *Public Management Review* 5: 533–550.

Social Cultureel Planbureau (Social and Cultural Planning Bureau). 2009. *Crisis in aantocht?* (Crisis at hand?). The Hague: SCP 2009/13.

Sørensen, E. and Torfing, J. (eds.) 2007. *Theories of Democratic Network Governance*. Cheltenham: Edward Elgar.

Van de Walle, S. 2009. International sector comparison of public sector: How to move along. *Public Management Review* 7: 39–56.

Williamson, O. E. 1996. *The Mechanisms of Governance*. Oxford: Oxford University Press.

···

CHAPTER 15

GOVERNANCE AND INNOVATION IN THE PUBLIC SECTOR

···

EVA SØRENSEN

TODAY, the pressure on public sectors to be innovative is as large as ever. The aim of this chapter is to show that public administration research offers two relatively distinct strategies for promoting the innovation capacity of the public sector, and to argue that these strategies, which are often seen as alternatives, should rather be seen as complementary. Both strategies take their departure in the assumption that the public sector's innovation capacity has been seriously hampered by the strict regulatory regimes imposed by bureaucratic forms of government that neither provide space for nor encourage entrepreneurial behavior. In addition, the two strategies share the view that public sector innovation is enhanced by institutional conditions that spur ongoing interaction between relatively autonomous public and private actors. The main difference between them is that they propose different institutional designs for structuring and driving this interaction. The New Public Management (NPM) strategy calls for an institutionalization of *competition*-based forms of interaction that motivate individual as well as collective actors to develop, implement, and disseminate new policies and services. In contrast, the governance strategy builds on the assumption that public sector innovation is best achieved through the institutionalization of *collaboration* among interdependent stakeholders. The chapter sets out to show that both of these strategies offer important insights about how to strengthen the innovation capacity of the public sector, and that much can be achieved by recognizing the innovative drivers and barriers of competition as well as of collaboration.

The chapter is structured as follows. First, I analyze how and why innovation in the public sector has risen to the top of the agenda in debates about how to govern advanced liberal democracies. Next, I point out how recent strands of public administration theory establish a positive correlation between interactive forms of governance and public

sector innovation and show how this correlation finds support in new economic innovation theories. Then follows an outline and critical assessment of the NPM and governance strategies for enhancing the public sector innovation proposed by public
administration researchers. Finally, I show how a combination of the two strategies
appears to be the most promising path to take in advancing the innovative capacities of
the public sector.

INNOVATION IN THE PUBLIC SECTOR: AN EMERGING AGENDA

Up until the 1980s there was limited interest in public sector innovation. Innovation was
something that took place in the private sector, and the role of the public sector was to
provide the best possible conditions for private sector innovation, for example, the protection of private ownership of new innovations and the provision of well-educated and
skillful innovators (Edquist and Hommen 1999). As a result of the governability crisis of
the late 1970s (Mayntz 1991) public sector innovation entered the policy agendas all over
the Western world in the shape of a massive call for public sector reforms. The manifest
outcome has been a persistent stream of reforms of the regulatory framework in which
public governance is exercised (Levi-Faur 2011). These reforms waged war against the
inflexibility and inefficiency of traditional rule-based, compartmentalized, and top-
down structured forms of bureaucratic government, which leave little room for agency,
problem-driven creativity, and decentered entrepreneurship (Hood 1991; Osborne and
Gaebler 1993).

Although the call for a more innovative public sector is not new, the global financial
crisis in 2008 has brought public innovation to the top of the policy agenda in many
welfare states. Hence, the crisis has left them with a huge gap between the demand for
public services and the resources available to meet these demands. While the first
wave of public sector reforms in the 1980s and 1990s aimed to make the public sector
work harder, recent reforms aim, in addition, to make the public sector work smarter
in innovative ways that would make it possible to do more with less (Armstrong and
Ford 2000). Hence, *public sector innovation understood as the development, implementation, and dissemination of new policies and services* is seen as exceeding the available
resources.

Given these expectations and high hopes it is no wonder that public authorities all
over the world are embracing the new public innovation agenda. The result is a mush-
rooming of all sorts of government-initiated programmes and funding schemes that
encourage public sector innovation, and research in public sector innovation. The task
placed on the shoulders of those involved in these programmes is to find ways for the
public sector to work smarter. As we shall see, public administration theory has something to offer in this respect.

THE INTERACTIVE TURN IN PUBLIC
ADMINISTRATION THEORY

Public administration theory is increasingly occupied by the question of how to increase the ability of public organizations to change. Early twentieth-century public administration theory was primarily interested in identifying modes of governance and organizational principles that could create stable and legitimate rule, predictable decisions, efficient implementation procedures, and top-down control. Max Weber's ideal-typical model of bureaucracy delivers on all counts due to its legal–rational foundation, rule-governed practices, horizontal division of labor, and hierarchical decision-making structure (Weber 1976). Whereas Weber perceived stability as a positive contribution to public governance, Anthony Downs (1967) conceived the high degree of stability in public bureaucracies as a problem, because it prevents a dynamic adaptation of the public sector to societal changes and conditions. He argued that public bureaucracies tend to become more and more ossified as they grow bigger and use more and more energy and resources on internal coordination and external boundary wars. This reduces their ability to change as a response to changes in the environment.

Efforts to make the public sector more dynamic have brought interaction between public and private actors to the center of attention as a driver of public governance (Hood 1991; Kooiman 1993; Osborne and Gaebler 1993; Rhodes 1997; Mitchell and Shortell 2000; Feiock 2002; Agranoff and McGuire 2003; Kettle 2003; Pollitt and Bouckaert 2004; Greve 2008). Hence, interactive forms of governance such as quasi-markets, partnerships, and networks are increasingly seen as a means to enhance governance efficiency and effectiveness through a dismantling of the traditional bureaucratic, compartmentalized, and supply-side driven forms of regulation and coordination. The strength of interactive forms of governance is that they can be applied in flexible ways and that they empower and encourage decentered actors to perform well, as measured not only in terms of top-down imposed standards but also with reference to bottom-up demand-side criteria.

The mobilization of the self-governing capacity of decentered actors is particularly important for dealing efficiently and effectively with what has been known as wicked problems, that is, governance tasks where there is uncertainty about the cause of the problem, ambiguities related to its definition, disagreements concerning how to address it, and/or difficulties in evaluating governance outcomes (Rittel and Webber 1973; Rhodes 2000; Klijn and Koppenjan 2004). Among the wicked problems that currently range high on the governance agenda are finance, health issues, migration, security, and climate change. Interactive forms of governance provide a way to involve relevant actors in reaching a better understanding of the nature of these problems, in spurring and exploiting their commitment to finding and implementing viable solutions, and in evaluating the quality of governance outcomes.

While the main focus of attention among recent public administration researchers has been on how interactive forms of governance can enhance the efficiency and effectiveness of public governance, some have pointed to the positive impact that interactive forms of governance might also have on public innovation (Osborne and Gaebler 1993; O'Toole 1997; Newman, Raine, and Skelcher 2001; Borins 1998; Hess and Adams 2007; Nambisan 2008; Eggers and Singh 2009; Moore and Hartley 2008). The thrust of the argument made by these researchers is that institutional arrangements that push for decentered agency and self-governance provide spaces in which a plurality of competent actors are able to use their knowledge, creativity, entrepreneurship, and resources to find new and better ways of getting things done.

However, the construction of self-governing spaces for individual as well as for collective actors is not perceived as sufficient to promote innovation. As pointed out by many, self-governing spaces can sometimes be both inefficient and ineffective, and can hamper innovation (Scharpf 1994; Greve 2008; Kenis and Provan 2009). A realization of the potential benefits of interactive forms of governance calls for a particular type of innovation management that is exercised through the construction of institutional designs that reward entrepreneurial behavior (Hartley 2005). The concept of meta-governance offers itself as a conceptual frame for categorizing this kind of innovation management, which aims to enhance the innovation capacity of self-governing actors though a strategic framing of different patterns of interaction (Jessop 1998; Gray and Lowery 2000; Sørensen 2007; Meuleman 2008). The increasing interest among public administration researchers in mapping the potential role that interactive forms of governance and meta-governance might have for enhancing public innovation finds resonance in the huge and well-established body of innovation theory that focuses on private sector innovation.

INTERACTION AS A DRIVER OF PRIVATE SECTOR INNOVATION

The assumption is that interaction between decentered and institutionally motivated actors with relevant competencies and capacities finds support in state-of-the-art economic innovation theory. The theoretical development within this strand of theory can be described as a gradual development from a single-actor and supply-side driven innovation model to a systemic multi-actor perspective. This new theoretical framework views private sector innovation as a result of complex chains of interactions within and between firms, with numerous feedback loops that take into account the new and emerging demands of the customers (Godin 2006; Edquist and Hommen 1999), the day-to-day experiences of the employees (Coyne, Clifford, and Dye 2007), and skillful interventions of innovation managers that shape spaces and processes in which innovation are to take place (den Hertog and de Jong 2007; Westland 2008). As such, there are

many parallels between the interactive approach to public innovation and recent theories of private sector innovation: *Innovation is seen as driven by institutionally structured
interactions between multiple actors with different resources, competencies, and perspectives, and the task of innovation managers is to design institutional conditions that promote and give direction to this interaction.*

Since economic innovation theory is a well-established research field with a long history, efforts to understand and promote public innovation can gain important insights
from these theories about how different institutional designs can contribute to enhancing public innovation. In the early stages of theory development, economic innovation
theory viewed competition as the main driver of innovation: Market-based competition
motivates individual entrepreneurs, as well as firms, to develop new products and production processes. However, over time, collaboration within firms, between firms,
between firms and their consumers, and between firms and public authorities has been
brought into focus as an important driver of private sector innovation (Braczyk, Cooke,
and Heidenreich 1998).

The fact that both competition and collaboration can trigger innovation raises a series
of interesting questions for meta-governors about when to motivate self-governing
actors to compete and when to push them to collaborate. This debate is currently intense
among economic innovation researchers (Jorde and Teece 1992; Teece 1992; Raco 1999).
As we shall see, public administration theorists are engaged in similar considerations:
Some theories lay the ground for a competition-driven innovation strategy while others
speak in favor of collaboration as a main driver of innovation. The relationship between
the first and the second group of researchers is rather polarized, to the effect that few
recognize that both might actually have something to contribute within enhancing public sector innovation. Hence, it is possible to identify two competing strategies for promoting public sector innovation. The NPM strategy that views competition as the main
driving force for enhancing public innovation, and the governance strategy that argues
for the potential benefits of collaborative forms of governance for promoting public
innovation.

THE NPM STRATEGY

The NPM strategy's critique of traditional bureaucratic ways of governing is inspired by
the Public Choice theory (Niskanen 1987), which views public institutions as an incentive structure framing battles for power and resources among self-interested individuals
with pre-given preferences. Accordingly, the exercise of public management is understood in terms of a principal–agent relationship that makes traditional forms of rule and
command obsolete (Moe 1984). Since the principals (politicians and high-ranking public managers) do not have sufficient knowledge and resources to control the agents (the
public employees), they must govern them through a skillful modeling of the incentives
structures that motivate the agents to act in ways desired by the principal.

Informed by this theoretical perspective, the NPM strategy advocates for the institu-tionalization of market-based incentives structures and management forms that moti-vate utility, maximizing employees and agencies to constantly engage themselves in developing new and innovative production processes and services. Competition between providers of public services, increased consumer choice, performance-based budgeting and salaries, and so on are some of the means to promote public sector inno-vation (Hood 1991). As evidenced by the big wave of NPM reforms that saw the light of the day in the late 1980s and 1990s, the impact of the NPM strategy has been considera-ble (Pollitt and Bouckaert 2004).

There is little doubt that the many NPM reforms have increased the public sectors' ability to adapt to contextual changes and its capacity to develop and pursue new ideas and practices. The public sector is not quite as ossified as it once was. This is among other things due to the disaggregation of large bureaucracies into many partly self-governing agencies, the increased space for the exercise of strategic management, the performance-based budget and career systems, and the introduction of consumer choice.

However, at the same time, NPM has unwittingly produced new barriers to change and innovation in the public sector. First, the one-sided focus on competition as a driver of innovation disregards and even diminishes the prospects for enhancing innovation though knowledge-sharing. Individuals as well as institutions that are placed in a com-petitive relationship with each other have little incentive to share their ideas, knowledge, and experiences. On the contrary, it will be in their interest to hold their cards close to their chest. This is problematic as it is widely recognized that knowledge-sharing is an important driver of innovation (Tsai 2001; Spencer 2003). Second, the NPM strategy builds on the assumption that the goals that the governance process aims to reach do not need to be innovated—or that self-governing, decentered actors have nothing to offer in this respect. Principals are seen as innovation heroes who are fully capable of formulating and innovating the goals by themselves, and the innovative capacities of self-governing, decentered actors is merely regarded as relevant in relation to the implementation proc-ess. As such, the NPM strategy might in fact hamper the innovation of the goals that give the overall direction to public governance processes. Third, innovation can be hampered by too many and too detailed top-down-initiated performance measurement exercises. The problem is that such measurements encourage the self-governing actors to do what is measured rather than to experiment and search for new context-dependent and flexible ways of understanding and solving governance tasks (Ridgway 1956).

THE GOVERNANCE STRATEGY

The governance strategy that emerged in the wake of the many NPM reforms was inspired by the new governance theories, which were consolidated as a strong new research field in the 1990s (Kenis and Schneider 1991; Rhodes and Marsh 1992; Kooiman 1993; O'Toole 1997; Scharpf 1994; Jessop 1998). These theories view collaborative forms of interaction as an important driver of innovation because they bring together interdependent actors with different kinds of relevant knowledge in a jointly negotiated effort to perform concrete governance tasks. The differences in knowledge, views, and interests between the participants is seen as a means to destabilize sedimented world views, problematize routinized practices, and reevaluate the functionality and relevance of traditional role perceptions and patterns of interaction. As such, collaboration fertilizes the ground for the development of new perspectives, ideas, and practices. The governance strategy underlines the fact that bringing together actors with different knowledge, interests, and perspectives does not necessarily lead to collaboration. The willingness of the involved actors to collaborate and use the differences between them constructively rather than as sources of conflict and contestations presupposes that the relationship between them is founded on the presence of interdependency: they collaborate and innovate because each of the actors cannot do what they want to do on their own.

Seen from this theoretical perspective, public innovation can be enhanced through the construction of self-governing arenas in which public and private actors are motivated to collaborate in formulating and implementing new creative policies and services through the construction of strong interdependencies between them. Much of the debate among governance theorists about how this can be done has evolved around the question of how to meta-govern governance networks (Hartley 2005; Nambisan 2005; Goldsmith and Eggers 2004; Sørensen and Torfing 2007). Meta-governance of governance networks, defined as interactive arenas in which interdependent but operationally autonomous actors formulate and pursue negotiated goals, can be exercised hands-off through the framing of autonomous spaces in which self-governance can take place, the design of decision-making and implementation arenas composed of different groups of stakeholders, and the evaluation procedures and incentives structures that reward collaborative arenas that succeed in defining and pursuing shared goals. However, meta-governance can also be exercised hands-on through direct dialogue and interaction between the meta-governors and decentered self-governing collaborative arenas, where the meta-governor takes on the role of facilitator and/or participant in governance networks (Sørensen 2007).

The governance strategy avoids the three innovation barriers caused by the NPM strategy. First, collaborative forms of governance promote knowledge-sharing between interdependent actors. Second, policy goals are not placed outside the innovation process. The close and ongoing dialogue between a meta-governor and the decentered self-governing actors establishes feedback loops between goal-innovation and implementation innovations. Finally, the governance strategy subscribes to bottom-up forms of self-evaluation rather than to top-down performance assessments, to the effect that post-bureaucratic-standard following that blocks innovation endeavors can be avoided.

The governance strategy, however, contains its own innovation barriers. First, negotiated decision-making tends to favor solutions that are close to the status quo and thus block more radical innovation alternatives. Second, entrepreneurs are often bad at making compromises. They are passionate and visionary and unwilling to follow the complex rules and norms that govern negotiated decision-making. Consequently, they might end up either being excluded or exclude themselves from the collaboration process. Finally, interactive network arenas that exist outside the "ordinary" rule and command hierarchy might prove to be innovative, but the consequence of the secluded position of these arenas might be that it is difficult to get the innovation accepted by and disseminated to the larger system. The interactive governance arenas become isolated innovation islands with limited impact (Burt 1992).

ADVANCING THE GOVERNANCE APPROACH
TO PUBLIC INNOVATION

The NPM strategy has taken a big step forward in advancing a viable strategy for enhancing public innovation, and the governance strategy has come even further. However, the overly critical stance that many governance theorists take toward NPM means that the important insights that the NPM strategy brings to the fore have not been sufficiently recognized and incorporated in the governance strategy. By bringing important insights from the NPM strategy and the governance strategy together we achieve a better understanding of the drivers and barriers of public innovation, and thus develop an innovation strategy for the public sector that does not produce new innovation barriers, be they those imposed by the NPM strategy or those brought about by the governance strategy.

Efforts to develop a joint innovation strategy should recognize: 1) that competition and collaboration are equally important and interrelated innovation drivers; and 2) that public innovation is equally dependent on top-down and bottom-up forms of management. With regard to the first point, neither the NPM strategy nor the governance strategy has fully recognized the close ties and linkages between competition and collaboration.

The NPM strategy has overlooked the fact that while competition is essential for motivating actors to take the risks and trouble related to innovative endeavors and to invest in uncertain outcomes, it does not necessarily provide actors with the resources they need to be able to carry out the actual innovation. Likewise, competitive games do not necessarily install processes that accommodate innovation. Innovation does not only thrive on motivation. It also calls for destabilizations of sedimented patterns of thought and behavior, resource-pooling, and knowledge-exchange. Collaboration produces this innovation fuel. Just as economic innovation theories increasingly recognize the importance of collaboration as a supplement to competition, traces of the same recognition can be found in the NPM strategy when it advocates for the formation of public–private partnerships and the formulation of relational contracts that set up rules and procedures for an ongoing dialogue between public and private contract parties (Greve 2008; Milward and Provan 2000; Bertelli and Smith 2009; Ferlie et al. 1996; Ferlie, Musselin, and Andresani 2008; Norton and Blanco 2009). These institutionalized forms of collaboration are not only regarded as necessary for coordinating governance initiatives taken by meta-governors and service-providing public and private agencies but also as a way of sharing the burdens and risks of developing new policies and services.

The governance strategy, on its side, has not taken fully into account that collaborative governance arenas, in order to be innovative, must be subject to competition from other collaborative arenas. If not they will often be content with avoiding conflicts, sticking to the status quo, and reaching for the lowest common denominator. Competition provides the external pressures needed for the collaboration partners to overcome the troubles and conflicts that are often associated with making more radical and path-breaking negotiated decisions. For collaboration to result in innovations the participants must share a feeling that if they are unable to reach convincing outcomes others will and all will be lost. To put it differently, competition produces that feeling of shared destiny and "we-identity" that drives collaborative innovation processes. As was the case with the NPM strategy, the governance strategy has indirectly realized this connection between collaboration and competition. This connection is expressed in the claim that interdependency is a core driver of collaborative forms of governance. When it comes to the heart of the matter, this interdependency is founded in a group's competitive relationship to other external actors (Anghel et al. 2004; Franke and Piller 2003). Without the presence of external contestants, the need to collaborate is diminished and so is the participants' willingness to pay the price that it takes to develop and implement new innovative ideas.

Summing up the argument made above, it can be said that competition and cooperation should be seen as interrelated innovation drivers. This has already indirectly been recognized by the NPM and governance strategies. However, an advancement of a strategy for public innovation calls for a more direct and outspoken reflection on and exploitation of this connection between competition and collaboration.

In advancing our understanding of public innovation, it should also be recognized that the objective is not to choose between top-down and bottom-up forms of governance. An enhancement of public innovation calls for both. As pointed out in both strategies, innovation relies on the presence of autonomous spaces in which decentered entrepreneurs can develop and pursue innovative ideas. However, in order to be effective this bottom-up interaction is in need of skillful top-down meta-governance that frames the interaction in ways that motivate the involved actors to innovate through the strategic institutional design of incentive structures that balance competitive and collaborative patterns of action. This firm meta-governance helps to activate the knowledge, ideas, commitment, and energies of street-level bureaucrats, users of public services, employees, and private stakeholders in formulating, implementing, and disseminating new, innovative ideas. Proactive top-down meta-governance is crucial because it nurtures and gives direction to these interactions.

The strength of the NPM strategy is that it insists that public authorities send clear signals to self-governing actors about what is expected of them, in the shape of the overall goal they are expected to achieve. Furthermore, it points to the necessity of sketching out the conditions of the autonomy available to self-governing actors. Thereby the NPM strategy triggers the interesting question of how to strike the right balance between over-regulation and under-regulation in the exercise of meta-governance. Over-regulation of self-governing actors diminishes their motivation for engaging in governance processes because they lose the feeling of ownership that comes with influence. Under-regulation means a lack of pressure on self-governing actors to engage in radical innovations, and/or the production of innovations that target goals different from those set by central public authorities.

The governance strategy, on its side, makes it clear that meta-governance and decentered self-governance should not be institutionalized as separate processes. Fruitful public innovation calls for institutional conditions that install continuous two-way communication and feedback loops between meta-governors and self-governing actors. This is necessary to avoid decoupling between policy innovation and implementation of innovations.

Conclusion

Although public innovation has been on the research agenda of those studying public administration and public governance for some time now, questions about how innovative the public sector is, what the main barriers and drivers of public innovation are, and what can be done to enhance public innovation have not gained a prominent position on the research agenda until recently. The aim of this chapter has been to show that it is possible to identify two strategies for enhancing public sector innovation, and to argue that much can be gained from merging the insights from these two strategies rather than choosing one over the other.

Although a lot of energy has been put into stipulating the differences between the NPM strategy and the governance strategy, the similarities between them are striking. Both criticize traditional bureaucratic forms of governance for being inflexible, for favoring stability over change and flexibility, and for celebrating rule-following over entrepreneurship. In addition, both view interaction between public and private actors as an important driver of public innovation, and view a balance between top-down meta-governance and decentered self-governance to be decisive for enhancing public innovation.

There are admittedly also important differences between the two strategies: one celebrates competition and directional top-down management while the other speaks in favor of collaboration and two-way dialogue between meta-governors and self-governing actors. A closer scrutiny of the strategies shows, however, that both of them do in fact indirectly recognize that both competition and collaboration are crucial for innovation, although they weigh the importance of the two drivers of innovation radically differently.

An important difference between the two strategies is that the NPM strategy offers an understanding of meta-governance, which is more in line with traditional top-down understanding of public rule, while the governance strategy proposes an interactive understanding of the relationship between meta-governance and self-governance. By doing so, each strategy gives its particular contribution to understanding how self-governing actors can be meta-governed in ways that promote public innovation.

In conclusion, NPM strategy and the governance strategy provide a good starting point for future endeavors to advance our theoretical understanding and develop strategies for enhancing public innovation. It is important, however, to direct the focus of attention toward creating a better understanding of the interconnectedness between competition and collaboration, and between meta-governance and self-governance, and to use this better understanding to illuminate how to design public governance processes in a way that promotes innovation.

REFERENCES

Agranoff, R. and McGuire, M. 2003. *Collaborative Public Management: New Strategies for Local Governments*. Washington DC: Georgetown University Press.

Anghel, M., Toroczkai, S., Bassler, K. E. and Korniss, G. 2004. Competition-driven network dynamics: Emergence of a scale-free leadership structure and collective efficiency. *Physical Review Letters* 92: 0587011–0587014.

Armstrong, J. and Ford, R. 2000. "Public sector innovations and public interest issues." *The Innovation Journal* 6(1); available at http://www.innovation.cc/discussion-papers/ps-innova tion-public-interest.html.

Bertelli, A. M. and Smith, C. R. 2009. Relational contracting and network management. *Journal of Public Administration, Research and Theory* 29(suppl. 1): i21–40.

Borins, S. 1998. *Innovating with Integrity*. Washington, DC: Georgetown University Press.

Braczyk, H.-J., Cooke, P. and Heidenreich, M. 1998. *Regional Innovation Systems*. London: UCL Press.

Burt, R. S. 1992. *Structural Holes*. Cambridge, MA: Harvard University Press.

Coyne, K. P., Clifford, P. G. and Dye, R. 2007. Break through thinking from inside the box. *Harvard Business Review* 85: 70–78.

den Hertog, P. and de Jong, G. 2007. Randstad's business model of innovation: Results from an exploratory study in the temporary staffing industry. *Innovation: Management, Policy and Practice* 9: 351–364.

Downs, A. 1967. *Inside Bureaucracy*. Boston: Little Brown.

Edquist, C. and Hommen, L. 1999. Systems of innovation: Theory and policy for the demand side. *Technology in Society* 21: 63–79.

Eggers, W. D. and Singh, S. K. 2009. *The Public Innovator's Playbook: Nurturing Bold Ideas in Government*. Deloitte Research; available at http://www.deloitte.com/innovatorsplaybook.

Feiock, R. C. 2002. A quasi-market framework for local economic development competition. *Journal of Urban Affairs* 24: 123–142.

Ferlie, E., Musselin, C. and Andresani, G. 2008. The steering of higher education systems: A public management perspective. *Higher Education* 56: 325–348.

Ferlie, E., Ashburner, L., Fitzgerald, L. and Pettigrew, A. 1996. *The New Public Management in Action*. Oxford: Oxford University Press.

Franke, N. and Piller, F. T. 2003. Key research issues in user interaction with user toolkits in a mass customisation system. *International Journal of Technology Management* 26: 578–599.

Godin, R. 2006. Talking politics: Perils and promise. *European Journal of Political Research* 45: 235–261.

Goldsmith, S. and Eggers, W. D. 2004. *Governing by Networks: The New Shape of the Public Sector*. Washington DC: Brookings Institutional Press.

Gray, V. and Lowery, D. 2000. Where do policy ideas come from? A study of Minnesota legislators and staffers. *Journal of Public Administration Research and Theory* 10: 573–598.

Greve, C. 2008. *Contracting for Public Services*. London: Routledge.

Hartley, J. 2005. Innovation in governance and public service: Past and present. *Public Money and Management* 25: 27–34.

Hess, M. and Adams, D. W. 2007. Innovation in public management: The role and function of community knowledge. *The Innovation Journal* 12: 1–20.

Hood, C. 1991. A public management for all seasons? *Public Administration* 69: 3–19.

Jessop, B. 1998. The rise of governance and the risk of failure: The case of economic development. *International Social Science Journal* 50: 29–45.

Jorde, T. M. and Teece, D. J. 1992. *Antitrust, Innovation, and Competitiveness*. Oxford: Oxford University Press.

Kenis, P. and Schneider, V. 1991. Policy networks and policy analysis: Scrutinizing a new analytical toolbox. In B. Marin and R. Mayntz (eds.), *Policy Networks: Empirical Evidence and Theoretical Considerations*. Frankfurt: Campus Verlag, 25–59.

Kenis, P. and Provan, K. G. 2009. Towards an exogenous theory of public network performance. *Public Administration* 87: 440–456.

Kettle, D. 2003. *The Transformation of Governance: Public Administration for Twenty-First Century America*. Baltimore: Johns Hopkins University Press.

Klijn, E. H. and Koppenjan, J. F. M. 2004. *Managing Uncertainties in Networks: A Network Approach to Problem Solving and Decision Making*. London: Routledge.

Kooiman, J. (ed.) 1993. *Modern Governance: New Government-Society Interactions*. London: Sage.

Levi-Faur, D. 2011. Jerusalem papers in regulation and governance. In D. Levi-Faur (ed.), *Handbook on the Politics of Regulation*. Cheltenham: Edward Elgar.

Mayntz, R. 1991. Modernization and the logic of interorganizational networks. *MPIFG Discussion Paper* 91. Cologne: Max-Planck Institut für Gesellschaftsforschung.

Meuleman, L. 2008. *Public Management and the Metagovernance of Hierarchies, Networks and Markets*. Berlin: Springer.

Milward, H. B. and Provan, K. G. 2000. Governing the hollow state. *Journal of Public Administration Research and Theory* 10: 359–379.

Mitchell, S. M. and Shortell, S. M. 2000. The governance and management of effective community health partnerships: A typology for research, policy, and practice. *The Milbank Quarterly* 78: 241–289.

Moe, T. M. 1984. The new economics of organization. *American Journal of Political Science* 28: 739–777.

Moore, M. and J. Hartley 2008, Innovations in governance. *Public Management Review* 10: 3–20.

Nambisan, S. 2005. Preparing tomorrow's technologists for global networks of innovation. *Communications of the ACM* 48: 29–31.

Nambisan, S. 2008. *Transforming Government through Collaborative Innovation*. Washington, DC: Harvard Kennedy School of Government.

Newman, J. E., Raine, J. W. and Skelcher, C. 2001. Transforming local government: Innovation and modernization. *Public Money and Management* 21: 61–8.

Niskanen, W. A. 1987. Bureaucracy. In Charles K. Rowley (ed.), *Democracy and Public Choice*. Oxford: Blackwell, 130–140.

Norton, S. D. and Blanco, L. 2009. Public–private partnerships: A comparative study of new public management and stakeholder participation in the United Kingdom and Spain. *International Journal of Public Policy* 4: 214–231.

Osborne, D. and Gaebler, T. 1993. *Reinventing Government: How the Entrepreneurial Spirit is Transforming the Public Sector*. Reading: Addison-Wesley.

O'Toole, L. J. 1997. Implementing public innovations in network settings. *Administration and Society* 29: 115–138.

Pollitt, C. and Bouckaert, G. 2004. *Public Management Reform: A Comparative Analysis*. Oxford: Oxford University Press.

Raco, M. 1999. Competition, collaboration and the new industrial districts: Examining the institutional turn in local economic development. *Urban Studies* 36: 951–968.

Rhodes, R. A. W. 1997. *Understanding Governance: Policy Networks, Governance, Reflexivity and Accountability*. Buckingham: Open University Press.

Rhodes, R. A. W. 2000. Governance and public administration. In J. Pierre (ed.), Debating Governance: Authority, Steering, and Democracy. Oxford: Oxford University Press, 54–90.

Rhodes, R. A. W. and Marsh, D. 1992. New directions in the study of policy networks. *European Journal of Political Research* 21: 181–205.

Ridgway, V. F. 1956. Dysfunctional consequences of performance measurements. *Administrative Science Quarterly* 1: 240–247.

Rittel, H. W. J. and Webber, M. M. 1973. Dilemmas in a general theory of planning. *Policy Sciences* 4: 155–169.

Scharpf, F. W. 1994. Games real actors could play: Positive and negative coordination in embedded negotiations. *Journal of Theoretical Politics* 6: 27–53.

Spencer, W. J. 2003. Firms' knowledge-sharing strategies in the global innovation system: Empirical evidence from the flat panel display industry. *Management Journal* 24: 217–233.

Sørensen, E. 2007. Public administration as metagovernance. In G. Gjelstrup and E. Søresnen (eds.), *Public Administration in Transition*. Copenhagen: DJØF Publishers, 107–126.

Sørensen, E. and Torfing, J. (eds.) 2007. *Theories of Democratic Network Governance*. Basingstoke: Palgrave Macmillan.

Teece, D. J. 1992. Competition, cooperation, and innovation: Organizational arrangements for regimes of rapid technological process. *Journal of Economic Behaviour and Organization* 18: 1–2.

Tsai, W. 2001. Knowledge transfer in intraorganizational networks. *The Academy of Management Journal* 44: 996–1004.

Weber, M. 1976. *Wirtschaft und Gesellschaft: Grundriß der verstehenden Soziologie*. Tübingen: Mohr.

Westland, J. C. 2008. *Global Innovation Management: A Strategic Approach*. Houndsmill: Palgrave Macmillan.

CHAPTER 16

GOVERNANCE AND STATE STRUCTURES

NIAMH HARDIMAN

THE term "governance" denotes, among other things, "the changing boundaries between public, private, and voluntary sectors" (Chapter 3, this volume). This may include a range of themes including the process of engagement (politics), the substantive issues (policy), and the institutional structures through which state and other actors relate to one another (polity) (Treib, Bähr, and Falkner 2005; also Chapter 1, this volume). This chapter is concerned with the third of these considerations. The analysis of governance as "polity" converges with core preoccupations of comparative political economy. But we take a more selective approach here, and focus specifically on the significance of state structures for explaining cross-national variations in processes of securing coordination and implementing rules within the domestic political context, where the underlying concern is with the provision of collective goods in the form of stable administrative systems and effective government.

During the three decades between about 1980 and the onset of international financial crisis in the late 2000s, state institutions were reconfigured quite extensively in many of the advanced industrial societies. Postwar confidence in managed markets had collapsed with the crisis of "embedded liberalism." A general shift can be traced toward adopting a new paradigm associated with the liberalization of international markets in goods and of capital flows. This did not involve any simple rollback in the size of budgets or the scope of state powers, but rather a reconfiguration of the way states were structured in order to support a new market-conforming approach to public policy (Levy 2006). The withdrawal of the state associated with the privatization of utilities and services was paralleled by the rapid growth in regulatory functions (Levi-Faur and Gilad 2004). States increasingly took on "the logic of discipline," constraining the scope of elected politicians, allocating new ranges of tasks to technocratic control, and curtailing the responsiveness of policy implementation to democratic debate (Roberts 2010). These issues were already contentious prior to the international financial crisis. In view of the damage wrought on domestic economies and the speed with which the contagion spread internationally through interlinked financial systems from 2008 on, it was no longer possible to vest confidence in the belief that markets were self-correcting or that steady growth would continue uninterrupted. The crisis opened up new adaptive challenges to the governance capabilities of states, which imply further changes in the structured linkages between politics and markets, state and society.

Shifts in the design of state structures have been crucial to governance patterns in three ways. First, changing conceptions of the proper role of the state resulted in organizational innovation within the state's administrative structures. "New Public Management" (NPM) was associated with adopting private sector management priorities into the public sector. The associated creation of new agencies and the diversification of the organizational structures of the state changed the governance capabilities of the state itself. Second, states increasingly delegated powers to bodies beyond the direct control or oversight of democratically elected politicians, such as central banks and regulatory agencies. Third, variations in state structures shape the capacity to govern the macro-economy: the politics of fiscal consolidation once again occupies center stage in contemporary political debate. The three sections in this chapter deal with each of these themes in turn.

DEVOLVED GOVERNANCE: NEW PUBLIC MANAGEMENT AND ITS AFTERMATH

The institutional configurations through which domestic public power is exercised take a variety of forms, and the boundaries between politics and administration have been subject to often extensive reorganization in recent decades. There is no single agreed definition of "New Public Management," but it stems from a radical challenge to the capacity of the state to organize and deliver public goods in a manner that is both efficient and effective. The impetus to restructure public administration dates from the 1980s and it is associated with the new market-conforming ideas that gathered pace internationally after the end of the postwar consensus. The most radical break with previous practices originated in Britain under the Conservative government of Margaret Thatcher. New Zealand, Australia, and Canada followed suit. All these countries featured strong executive power, and an ideological affinity with market-led solutions (Pollitt and Bouckhaert 2004).

Prior to the 1980s, it was generally held to be appropriate that the public sector should be animated by values different from those obtaining in the private sector, prioritizing themes such as the common good, public service, and equality of access. The core idea behind NPM was that public sector performance could be measured and optimized, and outputs linked to budget allocations, just as in the private sector. But as state bodies lacked the profit-driven disciplines of private sector organizations, new ways of securing value for money would need to be introduced. The principal mechanisms for doing this involved the organizational reconfiguration of state institutions themselves. "Agencification" thus became a hallmark of NPM (Pollitt and Talbot 2004). Regulatory bodies show a particularly marked expansion in virtually all countries (Hardiman and Scott 2010; Levi-Faur 2005).

NPM aimed to ensure not only that public sector managers would be enabled to manage effectively, but also that they would be required to manage. Agencies had to reach quantifiable targets; they were subject to budget controls and financial disciplines. The assumption was that this would not only make the public sector more cost-effective, it would also bring it more closely into line with end users' needs and preferences and would therefore provide a more direct and market-led way of achieving the democratic responsiveness of public services. Inevitably, this was seen from the outset as creating new tensions between the organizational autonomy taken to be a prerequisite for achieving efficiency, and democratic political responsibility for the quality of government and the equity of outcomes.

No single classification system fully captures national variations in public administration, so it is difficult to track with certainty the degree to which countries adopted key tenets of NPM. Indeed, states may selectively adopt some but not other institutional innovations (Eymeri-Douzans and Pierre 2011). Apart from Britain, New Zealand, and Canada, who led the field, the Netherlands and Denmark were early adopters of some of the features of NPM. Germany was more cautious, France a late adopter, Ireland a notable laggard (Pollitt and Talbot 2004). But even in the more statist and corporatist traditions of public administration, we see changes in the mode of recruitment to the public service and in the delivery of public services that are consistent with the priorities of NPM (Gualmini 2008).

Not all reforms to state structures and service delivery were driven by ideas about market efficiency. For example, the expansion of the role of the private sector in education provision in Sweden was initially motivated by democratic decentralization and parental choice, though it seems to have had somewhat mixed implications for the equality of educational provision and participation (Lindvall and Rothstein 2006).

For some commentators, NPM seemed to betoken the fragmentation of the state, resulting in a more extensive allocative role for the market and the encroachment of non-state governance mechanisms into what had previously been core political prerogatives. Hence the equation of these trends with a shift "from government to governance," involving a "hollowing-out of the state" (Rhodes 1994). With time though, these claims came to appear to have been overstated. At a minimum, governments were required to set the meta-governance framework for devolved and decentralized bodies operating under the "shadow of hierarchy." That is, the state retained or even intensified the capacity to exercise direct executive authority in order to enforce performance standards or to reform accountability mechanisms (Goetz 2008; Rhodes 2006). Devolved and networked governance should therefore be seen as part of a spectrum of more or less institutionalized modes of governance through which states did not necessarily become weaker.

But an enhanced capacity to solve problems and produce collective goods through devolution, regulation, and networked governance entailed other sorts of costs. The vogue for NPM encountered limits of both efficiency and of democratic acceptability. Agency specialization risked fragmenting policy delivery, compounding inefficiencies. Myriad problems emerged when attempting to enforce performance targets and to quantify outputs. Not only was "gaming" with the targets a rational response for many public sector managers, but the argument was made that the quality of performance was itself undermined by the attempt at quantification, especially in areas such as education and health services. Further, securing adequate levels of accountability from privatized service providers, though entirely possible in principle, proved increasingly difficult in practice (Hood et al. 2005).

During the 1990s and 2000s a shift was discernible toward "post-New Public Management" in a quest for improved policy coordination and a "whole-of-government" approach to streamlining public administration (Chapter 18, this volume). The classic Weberian model of public administration came in for positive reappraisal (Olsen 2006; Rothstein and Teorell 2008; Chapter 14, this volume). A marked if selective trend toward "de-agencification" and organizational rationalization became apparent. Yet the trend toward a post-NPM approach does not imply any direct reversal or return to the *status quo ante*. Privatized utilities and public service delivery systems are not easily dismantled and are expensive to renationalize. Segmented adaptation is more likely, with the reassertion of some powers at the center and continuing delegation and decentralization of others (Bouckaert, Peters, and Verhoest 2010). This means that state capacity is not in any simple sense restored to where it was during the postwar decades, but involves new compromises with market actors and networked interests.

Delegated governance and non-majoritarian institutions

Removing political institutions from direct political control is a well-established and often constitutionally mandated principle in some areas. Judiciaries are perhaps an obvious example, although there is much variation in the degree of political involvement in making appointments to senior judicial office and in the politicization of judicial review of executive decisions (Shapiro, Skowronek, and Galvin 2007).

But in recent decades there has been a marked increase in the number and scope of "non-majoritarian" institutions, that is, bodies permitted to exercise powers that are not subject to direction by or immediate accountability to democratically elected politicians. The most prominent examples include independent central banks to create stable monetary and exchange rate policies; regulatory bodies designed to manage prices, set standards, and otherwise compensate for the absence of markets, particularly in the wake of privatization; and competition authorities that are meant to ensure competition when there is concern about the dominant market power some actors might otherwise be able to exercise. We might also include here the increasing trend toward relying on private regulatory conventions as the standard-setting instruments of public policy (Rudder 2008).

The principal rationale for delegating state power to independent institutions is technical competence and specialist expertise. Transaction cost analysis proposes that it may be rational for political actors to constrain their field of action in order to establish credible commitment to policy objectives that are held to be desirable but which are politically contentious in some way. A stable exchange rate may be best supported by a low-inflation regime, but pursuing this objective may require distributing adjustment costs in ways that elected politicians find unpalatable because they believe they will lose electoral support. But binding state policy into a low-inflation regime may secure credibility among investors and improve growth prospects. The creation of new institutions constrains decision-making beyond a single election cycle and therefore normally commits opposition parties to maintaining temporal consistency, which in turn enhances the credibility gains that may be obtained (Majone 2001; North 1990).

The institutional design of regulatory bodies varies cross-nationally, and the choice of institutional design is not easily explicable in terms of political conditions such as partisan contestation over policy (Scott 2003). Policy internationalization, especially the regulatory demands emanating from European integration, may generate convergence in regulatory institutional design; in particular, political executives may share an interest in countering the influence of domestic veto players (Thatcher 2009). The diffusion of institutional design may take place through top-down policy innovation, or may emanate from bottom-up convergence pressures, or may be attributable to sectoral interdependencies (Radaelli 2004; Way 2005).

In general, though, the design of new institutions appears to be strongly conditioned by preexisting administrative traditions: "when making decisions about delegation to non-majoritarian institutions, politicians behave rationally, but select from a menu of choices that has emerged from wider social processes" (Thatcher and Stone Sweet 2002: 15). Thus, for example, regulatory bodies might prioritize "public interest" considerations, as in Britain, or "efficiency" considerations, as in Germany.

There does not seem to be any general trend toward adopting similar institutional solutions to the problems arising from the globalization and liberalization of product and capital markets: these are mediated by existing institutional models. And not all new challenges result in significant institutional reform. In the case of securities trading, changes in technical and economic markets across European countries were met by institutional inertia and resistance from coalitions with vested interests. Economic diffusion was not sufficient to displace these; national institutions were modified rather than transformed to meet the new requirements (Thatcher 2002).

The vogue for regulation grows, as Levi-Faur has argued, "when we cease to trust." But while delegated governance may bypass one set of problems, it also generates new ones. Solving transaction costs is not, or not only, a technical matter, but a social and political decision that may have contentious distributive consequences (Levi-Faur

2005: 19, 22). Institutions are designed in a particular political context and involve building coalitions of support behind them, which may involve the preferment of some interests and the marginalization of others. Delegated governance may itself enable regulatory capture or insider influence by precisely those powerful interests whose behavior they intend to control. Once in place, it becomes more difficult to challenge the inbuilt distributive biases or the prioritization of particular objectives or values over others. But changes in relative power resources may alter payoffs. Institutions may thus be seen to change through "displacement, layering, drift, conversion," depending on the relative power of the policy-makers and of those with vested interests in continuity or change, as well as contextual features of the institutional setting (Mahoney and Thelen 2010).

Institutional design is therefore never politically neutral, and depoliticizing issues and removing them from the purview of democratic deliberation is not a value-free choice. Delegated governance has raised problematic issues in two areas central to democratic discourse: problems of legitimacy and of accountability. Since delegated powers are designed to be beyond the reach of elected politicians, their activities must be justified in terms of the effectiveness or efficiency of their outcomes, or "output legitimacy" (Scharpf 1999). But if performance is the principal means of legitimating institutional design, its acceptability may be more thinly rooted and more contingent upon continuing good economic performance than is the case when there is the possibility of democratic representation and contestation, or "input legitimacy." Performance standards in delegated governance are less likely to be attuned to democratic conceptions such as citizenship entitlements, public interest, and common good, and more likely to be framed in terms drawn from market participation, where citizens become consumers and efficiency may outweigh entitlement. There is a potential clash of values involved, and this was apparent even before the scale of mismanagement and indefensible risk-taking by financial institutions became clear; this has thus undermined the public credibility of arm's length regulatory governance (Helleiner and Pagliari 2011).

The second issue involves an associated concern about accountability. State structures that have delegated powers are not only permitted but required to operate at a remove from the normal fora of debate about what they are doing, how well they are doing it, and what the consequences are. If their legitimacy principally rests upon the technical aspects of their operation and the performance outcomes they achieve, it becomes all the more important to have effective means of holding them to account for their performance (Bovens 2007). There is no optimal way to do this without undermining the procedural advantages of political independence. Weberian legitimating criteria such as transparency of rule implementation and procedural impartiality are often invoked (Hood and Heald 2006). But this pushes the question back recursively one point, because the question still arises as to who has the right to scrutinize the extent of impartiality, and to whom they are to be transparent. Besides, some of the greatest problems of political management are now cross-national in scope—reform of banking regulation, for example. There is no obvious international political forum within which these issues can be decided. The need to establish authority and maintain legitimacy must be negotiated repeatedly within structures as diverse as the G20, the International Monetary Fund (IMF), and the World Trade Organization (WTO) on the one hand, and a whole variety of non-governmental bodies on the other (Koppell 2010). Public policy decisions are increasingly embedded in structures that have overlapping jurisdictions and multiple stakeholders, with even greater scope for inequalities of influence and more problematic issues for democratic accountability.

Economic governance

Fiscal governance is at the heart of government's responsibilities. The global financial crisis brought new issues to the fore concerning the institutional structures through which domestic tax and spending decisions are made and implemented, particularly in the context of the European Monetary Union.

How states raise taxes shapes not just their capacity to secure order, maintain administrative structures, and provide public goods; it also conditions the terms on which they are most likely to commit their spending. Funding state expenditures may require them to run fiscal deficits at times, either as a counter-cyclical measure in a downturn or as a means of increasing growth capacity through increased investments (Barro and Sala-I-Martin 1995). Most countries have learned to do this flexibly, but most have also found they could not long sustain deficits without incurring adverse consequences in the form of increased interest rates (although the USA, with its international reserve currency, is an exceptional case).

The politics of fiscal consolidation became a central political preoccupation during the 1980s and 1990s. Europe's Economic and Monetary Union was intended to require particularly tight fiscal disciplines of its member states. But the international financial crisis after 2008 resulted in many countries incurring sizeable fiscal deficits once again.

The structural and governance conditions underlying successful domestic fiscal stabilization have been much studied. Analysts during the 1990s largely agreed that it was most likely when governments controlled spending rather than increasing their tax take (Alesina, Perotti, and Tavares 1998). Economic constraints may matter, such as the cyclical position of the domestic economy, the stance of monetary policy, the sustainability of the government's fiscal position. But in addition, the fragmentation of political decision-making was argued to have a significant bearing on the capacity to achieve fiscal consolidation. Federal governments were more likely to have difficulties in imposing fiscal disciplines (Coram 2001). Coalition governments were said to be more likely to choose revenue-based adjustments, and these strategies were less likely to be sustainable or growth-friendly (Persson and Tabellini 2003; Poterba and von Hagen 1999). Coalition and single-party governments might best resort to different decision-rules in order to secure their commitment to fiscal discipline. Prebinding "contractual" rules work best for coalitions; "delegation" of discretionary powers to finance ministers works best for the single-party majority governments. Where the appropriate policy rules have been in place, and where governments are committed to these ends, fiscal disciplines have been most successfully maintained (Hallerberg, Strauch, and von Hagen 2007).

The policy implications of these analyses were far-reaching. Arguments often fitted well with an aversion to big-state spending commitments and generous social provision that arguably had ideological as much as technical origins. But these analyses were often cast in terms of problems of common-pool resource management, viewed as discrete time-bound decisions. They tended to overlook the path-dependent political constraints within which governments are obliged to make choices. They also risk underestimating the distributive consequences of fiscal choices and therefore the electoral implications for government of choosing between alternative courses of action (Dellepiane and Hardiman 2010; Dellepiane 2010; Mulas-Granados 2004).

These analyses of the structural conditions underlying stable fiscal governance in domestic politics have been further challenged by the problems that emerged within the Eurozone after 2008. Fiscal disciplines had already proven difficult to sustain during the 2000s—after the introduction of the Euro—because fiscal, monetary, and financial policy interacted in unexpected and uncoordinated ways. A "one-size-fits-all" monetary policy set interest rates too low for the boom conditions that resulted from access to cheap credit in the peripheral economies. The expectation that tight domestic fiscal disciplines would contain economic pressures proved unrealistic. Not only were the sanctioning powers of the European Central Bank (ECB) too weak to be effective, but Germany and France themselves breached the rules with impunity when domestic conditions dictated it (Blavoukos and Pagoulatos 2008; Debrun et al. 2008; Hallerberg and Bridwell 2008; Heipertz and Verdun 2010). Meanwhile regulation of the financial sector continued to be a function of national central banks and not the ECB, and the countries in which the banking system grew fastest were the ones most prone to crisis (Moghadam and Vinals 2010).

After 2008, the consequences of dealing with the dual problems of fiscal imbalances arising from recession and public rescue of the distressed banking system imposed marked asymmetrical burdens on Eurozone member states. In a system that had been designed with a light institutional apparatus, and in which the very possibility of sovereign default was not to be countenanced, the global financial crisis exposed the multiple obstacles to political coordination and effective economic governance at the European level. As it became clear that the peripheral countries (Greece, Ireland, Portugal) were in deep crisis, loan programmes funded jointly by the European Union (EU), the ECB, and the IMF were put into place. But while the symptoms of fiscal imbalance were to be addressed through the imposition of fiscal austerity, the issue of how to resolve the European banking crisis was postponed, compounding the stresses on peripheral countries' sovereign debt.

The design gaps in the EU's "unfinished architecture" were exposed by the crisis: the Eurozone's cross-national monetary and exchange rate regime lacked countervailing fiscal or regulatory instruments, European leaders had conflicting preferences, and the priorities of the independent ECB weighed heavily in shaping outcomes. This impelled some to argue that the only way to save the Euro would be to embrace the logic of federalism and move rapidly toward deeper political integration (Münchau 2011; Schmidt 2010). But problems of political coordination, and electoral resistance to new centralizing European treaties, meant that such an outcome seemed unlikely.

Commitment to managing crises at the level of individual member states had consequences for both domestic and EU-wide fiscal policy institutions. Within the Eurozone, a new and tougher regime was introduced for designing and implementing fiscal rules, and intensifying European oversight of domestic budget planning (Van Rompuy 2010). At national level, a new generation of delegated governance institutions began to emerge in the form of fiscal councils with varying powers of advice, oversight, scrutiny, and amendment of tax and spending policies (Calmfors 2011; Fabrizio and Mody 2006). But the problems associated with the risk of sovereign debt default, and the need to rebuild the fragile European banking system, continued to present new challenges. Economic governance problems had transcended the domestic state level, but had not yet found structured solutions at the transnational level. The EU was left with an uneasy hybrid answer to the "trilemma" of governance in an age of globalization (Rodrik 2011, O'Rourke 2011).

Conclusion

We have noted three areas in which research on state structures has contributed to our understanding of changing patterns of governance: devolved governance in the organization of public administration; the trend toward delegated governance, especially in regulatory policy; and new issues in fiscal governance. In all three areas, we have seen that change has been shaped since the 1980s by a sense not only that politics needs to accommodate market forces, but also that technical considerations require the removal of many areas of decision-making from direct political accountability.

While these shifts in the architecture of states had already been contested in various ways, the international financial crisis at the end of the 2000s threw them into sharp focus. The dominant international discourse for almost three decades had been about the primacy of markets and the need to curtail state power. But within a short time after the onset of crisis, the boundaries between state and market shifted again with measures such as the nationalization of banks and the channeling of massive volumes of public funding into support for the financial sector. The ideological supremacy of the concept of the self-correcting market had been toppled, and it was no longer plausible to assume that technocratic decision-making would produce socially or economically optimal or even acceptable outcomes. Intensive debates about the relative merits of fiscal stimulus to avoid prolonged recession, as opposed to fiscal retrenchment to reduce debt exposure, signaled a shift in the terms of debate not only about the most appropriate way of managing the macro-economy, but also about the distributive balance of power that underpinned the dominance of neoliberal ideas (Palma 2009).

However, there are three reasons why it is not possible to go back to an earlier balance between politics and markets, such that the future design and functioning of states remains unclear. First, the terms on which states might reimpose new domestic political solutions to the crisis of markets are problematic. The neoliberal premises of the "logic of discipline" were thrown into question by economic crisis, and international political coordination prevented the early phase of the global financial crisis from turning into another Great Depression (Eichengreen and O'Rourke 2010).

But many features of the market-liberalizing paradigm remain relatively untouched. The appeal of delegated governance, with the ensuing problems of democratic account-ability and oversight, has not been seriously undermined. Trade openness continues to be valued and, indeed, institutionalized within the rapidly expanded networks of bilateral and multilateral trade agreements. Governments continue to need to prioritize the competitiveness of their domestic economies, particularly within the Eurozone where devaluation is not a possibility. The emphasis of state spending is likely to tilt even further toward promoting productive capacity, including human capital formation through education and skill development. This is a very different agenda from the efforts to contain capitalism through the national institutions of the welfare state and demo-cratic accountability (Streeck 2009, 2011). Further, the basic fiscal contract on which the welfare state was constructed is thrown into question by the ongoing commitment of states to raise revenues in order to rescue the banking system from failure. There is evi-dence that the legitimacy of tax and spending will vary, with the institutional design shaping who pays and who benefits (Kumlin and Rothstein 2005). Where citizens no longer see any real equivalence between tax compliance and collective benefits, the legit-imacy of taxation itself is called into question (Levi 1988).

Second, the transnational dimension of the crisis underscores the limits to solutions grounded in the politics of the nation-state. We can no longer speak of "markets within states," but must recognize the reality of what Streeck calls "states within markets" (Crouch et al. 2007: 540). What is emerging is a complex network of transnational regu-latory frameworks, some intergovernmental, some private. But the overlapping risk management and accountability frameworks these involve bear little resemblance to conventional structures of democratic representation and deliberation (Deeg and O'Sullivan 2009).

Third, the capacity for democratic legitimation and accountability may be badly com-promised in any case, even at the level of the nation-state. Democratic societies still rely on political parties to provide routes to compete for power and for the orderly alterna-tion of power. But the distinction between parties and state structures has been eroded through the weakening capacity of parties to mobilize support through civil society net-works, the growing diversity of electorates due to shifts in economic activity and often also in the ethnic composition of electorates, and the growing tensions in the support for formerly inclusive policies of redistribution between economic or social insiders and outsiders (Kymlicka and Banting 2006; Rueda 2007). Parties' reliance on state funding further removes them from dependence on the mobilization of interests, increasing the risk of disaffection by those left behind by market-driven priorities. While organized interests and social movements may provide an alternative route toward making state structures more responsive, the same solution may well be attractive to radical or extremist groups that are less readily amenable to integration within conventional political processes (Crouch 2004; Mair 2009). It was quite plausible to identify domestic state structures as the core of governance capabilities during the postwar decades, but this became more problematic over the three decades since 1980, and the patterns of governance through domestic and international structures are likely to become ever more complex in the future.

REFERENCES

Alesina, A., Perotti, R. and Tavares, J. 1998. The political economy of fiscal adjustments. *Brookings Papers on Economic Activity* 1: 197–266.

Amable, B., Eichhorst, W., Fligstein, N. and Streeck, W. 2010. On Wolfgang Streeck, re-forming capitalism. *Socioeconomic Review* 8: 559–580.

Barro, R. and Sala-I-Martin, X. 1995. *Economic Growth*. Basingstoke and New York: Macmillan.

Blavoukos, S. and Pagoulatos, G. 2008. The limits of EMU conditionality: Fiscal adjustment in Southern Europe. *Journal of Public Policy* 28: 229–253.

Bouckaert, G., Peters, B. G. and Verhoest, K. (eds.) 2010. *The Coordination of Public Sector Organizations: Shifting Patterns of Public Management*. Basingstoke: Palgrave Macmillan.

Bovens, M. 2007. Analysing and assessing accountability: A conceptual framework. *European Law Journal* 13: 447–468.

Calmfors, L. 2011. The role of independent fiscal policy institutions. *SSRN eLibrary*. Available at http://ssrn.com/paper=1775797 (accessed 19 September 2011).

Coram, A. 2001. Some political aspects of taxation and distribution in federal governments: An application of the theory of the core. *European Journal of Political Research* 39: 417–429.

Crouch, C. 2004. *Post-Democracy*. Oxford: Polity.

Crouch, C., Streeck, W., Whitley, R., and Campbell, J. L. 2007. Institutional change and globalization: colloquium. *Socioeconomic Review* 5: 527–567.

Debrun, X., Moulin, L., Turrini, A., Ayuso-i-Casals, J. and Kumar, M. 2008. Tied to the mast? National fiscal rules in the European Union. *Economic Policy* 23: 297–362.

Deeg, R. and O'Sullivan, M. A. 2009. The political economy of global finance capital. *World Politics* 61: 731–763.

Dellepiane, S. 2010. Review article: The politics of fiscal policy in Europe. *European Political Science* 9: 454–463.

Dellepiane, S. and Hardiman, N. 2010. *Fiscal Politics In Time: Pathways to Budget Consolidation 1980-2000*. Dublin: UCD Dublin European Institute.

Eichengreen, B. and O'Rourke, K. H. 2010. A tale of two depressions: What do the new data tell us? Vox, 8 March 2010. Available at http://www.voxeu.org/index.php?q=node/3421 (accessed 19 September 2011).

Eymeri-Douzans, J.-M. and Pierre, J. (eds.) 2011. *Administrative Reforms and Democratic Governance*. Basingstoke: Routledge.

Fabrizio, S. and Mody, A. 2006. Can budget institutions counteract political indiscipline? *Economic Policy* 21: 689–739.

Goetz, K. H. 2008. Governance as a path to government. *West European Politics* 31: 258–279.

Gualmini, E. 2008. Restructuring Weberian bureaucracy: Comparing managerial reforms in Europe and the United States. *Public Administration* 86: 75–94.

Hallerberg, M. and Bridwell, J. 2008. Fiscal policy co-ordination and discipline: The crisis of the stability and growth pact and domestic fiscal regimes. In K. Dyson (ed), *The Euro at Ten: Europeanization, Power and Convergence*. Oxford: Oxford University Press, 69–86.

Hallerberg, M., Strauch, R. and von Hagen, J. 2007. The design of fiscal rules and forms of governance in European Union countries. *European Journal of Political Economy* 23: 338–359.

Hardiman, N. and Scott, C. 2010. Governance as polity: An institutional approach to the evolution of state functions. *Public Administration* 88: 170–189.

Heipertz, M. and Verdun, A. 2010. *Ruling Europe: The Politics of the Stability and Growth Pact*. Cambridge: Cambridge University Press.

Helleiner, E. and Pagliari, S. 2011. The end of an era in international financial regulation? A postcrisis research agenda. *International Organization* 65: 169–200.

Hood, C. and Heald, D. 2006. *Transparency: The Key to Better Governance?* Oxford: Oxford University Press.

Hood, C., James, O., Peters, B. G. and Scott, C. (eds.) 2005. *Controlling Modern Government: Variety, Commonality and Change*. Cheltenham: Edward Elgar.

Koppell, J. 2010. *World Order: Accountability, Legitimacy, and the Design of Global Governance*. Chicago: University of Chicago Press.

Kumlin, S. and Rothstein, B. 2005. Making and breaking social capital: The impact of welfare-state institutions. *Comparative Political Studies* 38: 339–365.

Kymlicka, W. and Banting, K. 2006. *Multiculturalism and the Welfare State: Recognition and Redistribution in Contemporary Democracies*. Oxford: Oxford University Press.

Levi, M. 1988. *Of Rule and Revenue*. Berkeley, CA: University of California Press.

Levi-Faur, D. 2005. The global diffusion of regulatory capitalism. *The Annals of the American Academy of Political and Social Science* 598: 12–32.

Levi-Faur, D. and Gilad, S. 2004. Review article: The rise of the British regulatory state: Transcending the privatization debate. *Comparative Politics* 37: 105–124.

Levy, J. 2006. Introduction: The state also rises: The roots of contemporary state activism. In J. Levy (ed.), *The State After Statism: New State Activities in the Era of Liberalization*. Harvard, MA: Harvard University Press, 1–28.

Lindvall, J. and Rothstein, B. 2006. Sweden: The fall of the strong state. *Scandinavian Political Studies* 29: 47–63.

Mahoney, J. and Thelen, K. 2010. Introduction: A theory of gradual institutional change. In J. Mahoney and K. Thelen (eds.), *Explaining Institutional Change: Ambiguity, Agency, and Power*. Cambridge: Cambridge University Press, 1–37.

Mair, P. 2009. *Representative Versus Responsible Government*. Cologne: Max Planck Institute for the Study of Societies.

Majone, G. 2001. Non majoritarian institutions and the limits of democratic governance: A political transaction-cost approach. *Journal of Institutional and Theoretical Economics* 157: 57–78.

Moghadam, R. and Vinals, J. 2010. *Cross-Cutting Themes in Economies with Large Banking Systems*. Washington, DC: IMF.

Mulas-Granados, C. 2004. Voting against spending cuts: The electoral costs of fiscal adjustments in Europe. *European Union Politics* 5: 467–493.

Münchau, W. 2011. Original sin: The seeds of the euro crisis are as old as the euro itself. *Foreign Policy* (7 April). Available at http://www.foreignpolicy.com/articles/2011/04/07/original_sin (accessed 19 September 2011).

North, D. 1990. *Institutions, Institutional Change and Economic Performance*. Cambridge: Cambridge University Press.

Olsen, J. P. 2006. Maybe it is time to rediscover bureaucracy. *Journal of Public Administration Research and Theory* 16: 1–24.

O'Rourke, K. H. 2011. A tale of two trilemmas. Paper presented at Institute for New Economic Thinking, Conference on The Challenge of Europe. Bretton Woods, NH, April.

Palma, J. G. 2009. The revenge of the market on the rentiers: Why neo-liberal reports of the end of history turned out to be premature. *Cambridge Journal of Economics* 33: 829–869.

Persson, T. and Tabellini, G. 2003. *The Economic Effects of Constitutions*. Cambridge, MA: MIT Press.

Pollitt, C. and Bouckhaert, G. 2004. *Public Management Reform: A Comparative Analysis*, 2nd ed. Oxford: Oxford University Press.

Pollitt, C. and Talbot, C. (eds.) 2004. *Unbundled Government: A Critical Analysis of the Global Trend to Agencies, Quangos and Contractualisation*. London: Routledge.

Poterba, J. and von Hagen, J. (eds.) 1999. *Fiscal Institutions and Fiscal Performance*. Chicago, IL: University of Chicago Press.

Radaelli, C. 2004. The diffusion of regulatory impact analysis: Best practice or lesson-drawing? *European Journal of Political Research* 43: 723–747.

Rhodes, R. A. W. 1994. The hollowing out of the state: The changing nature of the public service in Britain. *Political Quarterly* 65: 138–151.

Rhodes, R. A. W. 2006. Understanding governance: Ten years on. *Organization Studies* 28: 1–22.

Roberts, A. 2010. *The Logic of Discipline: Global Capitalism and the Architecture of Government*. Oxford: Oxford University Press.

Rodrik, D. 2011. *The Globalization Paradox*. Oxford: Oxford University Press.

Rothstein, B. and Teorell, J. 2008. What is quality of government? A theory of impartial government institutions. *Governance* 21: 165–190.

Rudder, C. E. 2008. Private governance as public policy: A paradigmatic shift. *The Journal of Politics* 70: 899–913.

Rueda, D. 2007. *Social Democracy Inside Out: Partisanship and Labor Market Policy in Industrialized Democracies*. Oxford: Oxford University Press.

Scharpf, F. W. 1999. *Governing in Europe: Effective and Democratic?* Oxford: Oxford University Press.

Schmidt, V. A. 2010. The unfinished architecture of Europe's Economic Union. *Governance* 23: 555–559.

Scott, C. 2003. Organizational variety in regulatory governance: An agenda for a comparative investigation of OECD countries. *Public Organization Review* 3: 301–316.

Shapiro, I., Skowronek, S. and Galvin, D. (eds.) 2007. *Rethinking Political Institutions: The Art of the State*. New York: New York University Press.

Streeck, W. 2009. *Re-Forming Capitalism: Institutional Change in the German Political Economy*. Oxford: Oxford University Press.

Streeck, W. 2011. Taking capitalism seriously: Towards an institutionalist approach to contemporary political economy. *Socio-Economic Review* 9: 137–167.

Thatcher, M. 2002. Analysing regulatory reform in Europe. *Journal of European Public Policy* 9: 859–872.

Thatcher, M. 2009. *Internationalization and the State: Reforming Regulatory Institutions.* Dublin: UCD Geary Institute.

Thatcher, M. and Stone Sweet, A. 2002. Theory and practice of delegation to non-majoritarian institutions. *West European Politics* 25: 1–22.

Treib, O., Bähr, H. and Falkner, G. 2005. Modes of governance: A note towards conceptual clarification. *EUROGOV No. N–05–02.*

Van Rompuy, H. 2010. *Strengthening Economic Governance in the EU: Report of the Task Force to the European Council.* Brussels: European Council.

Way, C. 2005. Political insecurity and the diffusion of financial market regulation. *Annals of the American Academy of Political and Social Science* 598: 125–144.

....

CHAPTER 17

NEW GOVERNANCE AND POLICY INSTRUMENTS: ARE GOVERNMENTS GOING "SOFT"?

....

AMOS ZEHAVI

A constitutive question for governance scholars is *how* common goods are obtained. The answer to this question necessarily involves an investigation of policy instruments. Neither government nor governance is possible without the use of a diverse set of policy instruments. This chapter is dedicated to an investigation of the nexus between policy instruments and governance, with an emphasis on how questions and research that deal with the former should inform the literature that is dedicated to the latter. While this relationship has not been overlooked (see Bressers and O'Toole 1998; Peters and Pierre 2000; Salamon 2002), discussions of governance would benefit from an engagement with policy instrument classifications, theories, and insights. In what follows, I argue that it is time for the governance literature to move beyond debates centered on the question of whether states are moving from hierarchy to networks, and concurrently from the use of "hard" to "soft" policy instruments, because such generalizations are too crude to constitute a useful basis for explorations of governance trends, effectiveness, and political feasibility. Investigations of governance would do well to employ a more nuanced classification of policy instruments than the "hard–soft" dyad and think about governance styles in terms of different policy instrument mixes matched to varying sectoral and national circumstances. In this chapter, I argue that in recent years we have witnessed a proliferation of *all* generic types of policy instruments, not just soft ones, and that when combined these instruments could produce more effective governance than when employed separately. In what comes next, I briefly present the hard versus soft policy instrument debate in the governance literature and then introduce an alternative policy instrument conceptualization—Vedung's trichotomy—which I argue provides a superior foundation for analysis. A brief exposition of one case study—governance of the Australian non-government school sector—illustrates what I believe is a general trend toward increasingly dense policy instrument terrains: terrains in which different types of policy instruments often complement each other and produce effective policy cocktails, although such outcomes are far from a foregone conclusion.

THE HARD VERSUS SOFT INSTRUMENT DEBATE

The move from government to governance centers on a shift from hierarchy to networks (Rhodes 1997; Salamon 2002). Correspondingly, much of governance theory indicates a movement away from "hard" policy instruments toward "soft" ones. Policy instruments are hard or soft with respect to the degree of government intrusiveness and coercion involved in the use of a specific instrument. On one end of this continuum, we find governments that unilaterally lay down laws that apply to non-government actors, actively monitor compliance, and punish transgressions. On the soft end, governments limit their intervention to that of advocates and information providers. On occasion, governments might not even present their favored line of action but simply implore non-government actors to address certain problems.

According to numerous influential commentators, the policy world is in the midst of a pronounced shift from hard to soft policy instruments (Peters 2002; Rhodes 1997; Salamon 2002; Stoker 1998). This development can be explained in several ways. Most notably, this trajectory might reflect the demise of national state capacity. The shift to networks increasingly makes "command-and-control" instruments more difficult to apply because policy implementation is highly dependent on the cooperation of a plethora of non-government actors—cooperation that coercive measures is bound to undermine (Salamon 2002: 15; and also Matthews on the first wave of governance literature, in this volume). Of course, this begs the question of why one should move to networks in the first place. There are a number of advantages in network, as opposed to hierarchy-based, governance. For example, governments are eager to leverage non-government actor resources: community trust, expertise, ground-level information, and, of course, money and manpower. These advantages (and others, see Jordan, Wurzel, and Zito 2003: 12–16) suggest that instead of weakening state capacity, networks extend state reach and enhance its effectiveness. Hence, soft instruments are not necessarily weak or less effective than hard instruments. Against the backdrop of these alleged advantages, several commentators have discerned a clear trend toward greater use of soft instruments (Rhodes 1997; Salamon 2002; Stoker 1998). The general claim they share—some more strongly than others—is that the command-and-control mode of governance is progressively replaced by persuasion and negotiation, that is, instruments that are appropriate for network-based governance.

The hard-to-soft narrative has not gone uncontested. In the 2000s, numerous studies with a strong empirical bent have challenged this theory. Jordan and colleagues, for example, studied environmental policy in nine nations and found that state legislation and penalization—the archetypical hard instrument—are alive and well (2005). In recent years, soft environmental policy instruments—eco-labels for instance—have spread, yet these new instruments do not supplant the older, harder ones. Rather they coexist and complement each other.

Some commentators not only argue that hierarchy is still important, they also claim that hierarchal instruments have actually become *more* common, not less. Richardson, for instance, in an investigation of policy-making in Britain, argued that British policy-making in the past was predicated on negotiation and persuasion of interest groups—certainly a "soft" approach. Thatcher's rise, however, heralded a new era in which government showed greater willingness to assault traditional policy networks that represented distributional arrangements which were at odds with government goals (Richardson 2000; see also Moran 2003). Government choice of *more* hierarchy does not necessarily conflict with the proliferation of non-government-centered arrangements. Bell and Hindmoor, like much of the earlier governance literature, find intensification in the use of soft instruments. However, they argue that there is a concurrent expansion of hierarchy. At first this might appear puzzling, but the combination of the emergence of new technologies (e.g. nanotechnology) and the continued public expectation for government regulation helps explain this result (Bell and Hindmoor 2009).

Even voluntary networks continue to depend on government support. Sager, using a study of alcohol abuse policy in Switzerland, argues that although networks could produce voluntary agreements, they will nonetheless seek government intervention—and potentially coercion—to make agreements stick (2009). As Sager argues, governments add "teeth" to voluntary arrangements. Government intervention could be invaluable for optimal network performance. In what is often called "meta-governance," the debate regarding how government governs is transposed to the network level. Network evolution is not always spontaneous and governments often take a hand, by use of a broad range of policy instruments, in the creation, maintenance, and direction of networks (Bell and Hindmoor 2009). One of the fascinating twists of the governance literature is that the activity and even the very existence of networks could depend on the implicit threat of government action. In order to preempt undesirable government intervention, non-government actors pursue voluntary network agreements that otherwise might not have emerged (Heritier and Eckert 2008). Studies dedicated to this so-called "shadow of hierarchy" stress that the presence in the background of a capable state is often needed as an incentive for what outwardly might appear as independent non-government voluntary action.

In sum, contrary to claims that we are witnessing a decline in the use of hard instruments and an increased emphasis on network-directed soft ones, numerous studies show that not only is hierarchy still a dominant feature in many policy systems, in some instances, the use of hard policy instruments might actually be on the rise. While governments might indulge in network governance more than was the norm in the past, this does not mean that hierarchy diminishes. In fact, network organization often requires an active government role (meta-governance) or a passive one (shadow of hierarchy). Persistent public demands for government intervention, and even coercion, indicate that a simple soft-to-hard trajectory does not capture complex policy instrument reality. For a more accurate description of the policy instrument world in which governments, markets, and networks act, we should move beyond the hard–soft dyad.

Policy instruments beyond hard and soft

The hard–soft distinction offers little analytical leverage when one goes beyond an exploration of historical trends and investigates policy effectiveness and feasibility. This is the case for at least two reasons. First, the fit between the hard and soft categories and actual policy instruments is often quite tenuous. As mentioned before, governments might refrain from taking any active measure to regulate networks and in this respect they are in the realm of soft instrument use (e.g. persuasion). However, the veiled threat of hierarchy lurks behind the scenes as the hard instrument that could come into play, and this prods networks into action (Heritier and Eckert 2008). Conversely, the quintessential "hard" instrument—statutory authority—cannot always be considered as such. Not all laws are "hard". They might lack clear obligations, they could be vague, and their enforcement might be delegated to actors that interpret them in a minimalist way (Slominski 2008). In short, the hard–soft distinction is often overdrawn.

Second, hard and soft do not present a satisfactory description of one very important type of instrument: finance. Governments push non-government actors to act (or avoid action) by structuring financial incentives such as subsidies and taxes. It is not entirely clear where to map finance on the hard–soft instrument dimension because finance does not directly involve coercion. However, financial levies can be onerous—sometimes much more so than "light" legal penalties (Vedung 1998). Policy-makers who ponder what policy instrument to use take into account the degree to which an instrument requires coercion, but coercion-level is certainly not the only criteria used. Effectiveness and cost are at the center of public administration thinking and in the context of these values the treatment of finance as a separate category is justified.

There are numerous classifications of policy instruments and this is not the place to go, in any depth, into the distinctions among them. Some studies opt for elaborate categorization systems that distinguish between numerous institutional arrangements. This approach obviously enjoys the advantage of detail and accuracy. However, this is achieved at the price of generalization (Hood and Margetts 2007). An opposite approach, adopted here, is to seek the bare minimum in terms of categories. Vedung's trichotomy of carrots, sticks, and sermons stands out among such classifications (1998). Carrots relate to incentives (and disincentives)—primarily financial ones. Both monetary rewards for safe drivers and speed bumps, for example, are carrots. Sticks refer to legal injunctions that demand or prohibit certain actions: for instance, speed limit laws. Finally, sermons are associated with different modes of discourse—persuasion, negotiation, propaganda, and so on; A "drive safely" media campaign would fall into this category. The latter two categories roughly correspond to the hard and soft poles, but carrots add the finance dimension that is missing in the standard governance dyad.[1] The trichotomy is at a higher level of abstraction (therefore more parsimonious) than discussions of regulatory instruments. In some cases, a new instrument—say intra-public sector competition—constitutes a specific manifestation of a generic policy instrument (primarily the use of carrots in this case). In other cases, what might be referred to in the regulation literature as instruments—autonomous regulatory agencies for example (Levi-Faur 2005)—should be viewed, from Vedung's theoretical perspective, as institutions, that is, as institutions that employ different policy instruments to achieve their goals.

Where the policy instrument research differs from, and can contribute to, the governance writings is in the careful description of the instrument characteristics that are associated with its effectiveness and feasibility. Moreover, a discussion of generic policy instruments, and their mixes, helps flesh out, and better describe, the evolution of governance modalities across time and space. Studies in the governance literature offer several helpful insights on how policy instruments might complement each other, as in the case of self-regulation under the shadow of hierarchy. Yet more must be said. An important starting point that constitutes a strong suit of the policy instrument literature is an understanding of both specific policy instrument advantages, and weaknesses dependent on policy context. In what follows, carrot, stick, and sermon traits will be briefly discussed in turn.

Carrots can be considered an effective substitute for more coercive sticks—a problematic trait in a network environment characterized by high government–private actor interdependence. Indeed, Rhodes, for one, perceives a growing role for finance in governance although he is somewhat skeptical with respect to the core executive's ability to fully control private actors through this imperfect means (Rhodes 1997). However, carrots suffer from at least two major disadvantages. First, carrots in the form of subsidies tend to be costly relative to the two other generic instruments. In an era of economic austerity, few governments willingly accept high relative costs. Second, finance, definitely when in the form of levies, has a clear punitive side to it. Governments do not make friends by withholding funding, especially when funding previously granted is withdrawn. Although the politics of funding need not take an "all or nothing" form—compromises can be struck—it is difficult to avoid the conclusion that, in many cases, the opposition to any government allocation of carrots would be little different from opposition to the deployment of sticks.

The observation that the use of sticks is rarely a government's preferred option because of the antagonism it is likely to create is not new (see, for example, Doern and Wilson 1974). Governments might be particularly averse to the use of sticks when they face powerful non-government actors, and a common assumption of the governance literature is that both the number and power of non-government actors is on the rise (Bell and Hindmoor 2009; Salamon 2002). Nevertheless, because of their direct effect sticks are often considered effective. They also tend to be less expensive than carrots (or at least the costs are less visible) (Lemaire 1998). However, the distinction often drawn between the effectiveness of sticks (supposedly high) and their political feasibility (low) is problematic. There is no reasonable way of discussing effectiveness without a consideration of the effects a policy would have on target groups—resistance to implementation withstanding. In other words, to the extent that sticks are effective, they are effective despite resistance to their implementation. Effectiveness presupposes feasibility.

In contrast to sticks, there is little question that sermons are politically feasible and inexpensive. The nagging concern with respect to sermons is whether they achieve results. The evidence in favor of sermons as a policy instrument is patchy at best (Vedung and van der Doelen 1998). In fact, the choice of sermons as an exclusive policy instrument could suggest that either the government is uninterested in going beyond symbolic gestures or that it simply has no other viable choices (Baumol and Oates 1979). The policy instrument literature acknowledges the importance of different forms of discourse and information transfer. However, it is questionable whether sermons on their own are likely to sway actors whose interests are incompatible with executive goals. Governments could use sermons in the form of advocacy to prod private actors to enter voluntary agreements among themselves that commit them to desirable policy goals. Without question this approach is politically feasible, but the same cannot be said in any confidence for its effectiveness (Skjærseth 2000).

What this brief summary of the trichotomy's characteristics suggests is that so-called soft instruments that belong primarily to the sermon category have an advantage in terms of legitimacy and feasibility but their effectiveness, especially when employed in the face of opposition, is questionable. Sticks could provoke opposition and entail related implementation problems but their direct effect is said to contribute to effectiveness. Carrots can take a punitive form (e.g. taxes) and then suffer from the same liability as sticks without such direct advantage. Or they can focus on stimulation (e.g. grants), but then high costs should be taken into account as a major weakness.

Given these characteristic advantages and weaknesses it is abundantly clear why policy mixes are prevalent. Some policy instruments might be viewed as effective but politically problematic (e.g. environmental taxes) while others are deemed politically acceptable but relatively ineffective (e.g. environmental awareness campaigns directed at industry and the public). A combination could capture the best of all worlds and offer policy-makers a more diverse toolbox.[2] Indeed, distinct contributions in the governance literature, for instance Torfing's chapter in this volume, have explicitly recognized that public problem-solving would be best served by a *combination* of hierarchy, markets, and networks—which roughly parallel sticks, carrots, and sermons. Nevertheless, it would be unwise to ignore the possibility that an addition of new instruments would make extant instruments less effective, not more so (Osborn and Datta 2006). It is therefore imperative that policy-informing research investigate instrument interactions.

Accordingly, as Howlett and Rayner implore, research should focus on instrument mixes (2006). Indeed, there are already some examples of such work (e.g. Persson 2006). Nevertheless, there is a dearth of studies that evaluate policy mix effectiveness and feasibility. These should consider not just instrument identity, but also the national and sectoral context in which they are employed.

GOVERNANCE STYLES AND POLICY INSTRUMENT VARIATION

Governance scholars have recognized the danger of over-generalization (Marinetto 2003; Rhodes 2007). Focus on governance styles largely coincides with an emphasis on national policy styles in a discussion of policy instruments. Howlett, in a review of policy instrument theories, argued that many of the differences between theories originates from differences across national policy systems (1991). Hence, contrasting theoretical conclusions are often caused not by faulty research but by a focus on different nations and their associated varying policy styles. Thus, for example, the fact that policy-makers in England are reluctant to use coercive policy instruments should be considered an important component of the English policy tradition, but it does not necessarily travel well to other locales. Cross-country comparisons do not only uncover commonalities, they highlight considerable variation across governance systems, variation that is primarily rooted in different institutional structures and traditions.

While the national policy style approach is an important corrective to overstated generalizations, it too concentrates on only one, albeit important, source of variation. First, as presented before, temporal change has received the lion's share of attention in the governance literature and it must not be discounted. For instance, while Howlett's characterization of English policy as persuasion-based jibes with much of what had been written at the time, Richardson claims that by the 1990s it no longer constituted an accurate representation of the English policy style. Thatcher introduced a far more confrontational policy style than was previously the case, a style that involved far more use of "sticks" (2000). Second, as Freeman forcefully argued, there is good reason to believe that variation across policy sectors is greater than across political systems (1985). The main issues addressed by policy-makers in specific policy sectors across countries tend to be quite similar (e.g. population aging in the pension field), and given high, and increasing, levels of policy-learning, it is only to be expected that policy solutions, including what instruments are employed, are replicated across nations (Pollitt and Bouckaert 2000). Indeed, research from recent years has demonstrated striking policy similarities that are sector-specific (Levi-Faur 2005). It would seem that theories of policy instrument choice, legitimacy, and effectiveness must not sacrifice attention to national, sector, and temporal-based variation on the altar of comprehensiveness (Rhodes 2007).

GOVERNANCE AND PRIVATE SCHOOLS:
VARIATION IN POLICY INSTRUMENT MIXES

The policy instrument literature rejects simple narratives that single out one type of policy instrument as most desirable, effective, or dominant. Instrument mixes are, and have always been, the norm. Similarly, most of the recent governance-related writing has come to the realization that a simple "hard to soft" storyline cannot capture the complex reality of present-day governance. Perhaps no meaningful generalizations can be made about governance and policy instruments. This, however, might be going a bit too far. At the very least, it would appear that in most policy sectors there has been an increase in the number and type of actors who are involved in policy implementation, regardless of policy instrument type. I would argue, following Bell and Hindmoor, that the general trend is toward a richer policy mix (Bell and Hindmoor 2009). The fact that the policy instrument mix is becoming more diverse, however, does not imply that it is sermons (or soft) instruments that are being added to the mix. This very much depends on policy sector or political system specifics. In fact, there are sectors in which sticks have only recently been introduced and implemented. The case of the governance of private schools in Australia, as presented below, demonstrates the diversification of the instrument mix, and a brief comparison with other cases highlights cross-national and cross-sectoral variation.

The relationship between private schools and public authorities in Australia has traditionally been quite loose. Up until the mid-1970s, non-government schools were subject to government regulation, at least in principle, and were legally required to register with state governments in order to open their gates. However, private schools were hardly ever inspected beyond the initial state inspection that is a prerequisite for mandatory school registration in most states (Gurr 2007). At least, in terms of academic content, there was little contact—coercive or non-coercive—between government(s) and non-government schools. What was truly peculiar about government–non-government school relations in Australia was that since the mid-1970s, non-government schools received substantial Commonwealth support but such aid was, by and large, unconditional. Non-government schools were left to their own devices, despite financial support, for a period of roughly twenty years (Senate Report 2004).

During the 1990s and 2000s, Australian governments, on both the federal and state levels, gradually became more involved in non-government school governance than was the case in previous decades. It is unnecessary to describe the full scope of change. It would suffice, for the purposes of this chapter, to illustrate how new policy was formulated and implemented by the use of a mix of all three generic policy instruments. By the mid-1990s, the state government of Victoria set out to establish a state curriculum and a standardized testing regime for all state schools. Although standardization was directed primarily at government schools, the government sought non-government school participation as well. Quite differently from the top-down approach for the implementation of the common curriculum and standardized testing in government schools, the government approach to non-government schools was based primarily on dialogue and negotiations (Zehavi 2009). The result was a new accountability system that afforded flexibility and was based on arrangements with the representative bodies of both the Catholic and independent school sectors (which together comprise the non-government school sector). Catholic schools, which represent a majority of non-government schools, voluntarily adopted the new system; a system that greatly increased state oversight. A major reason for collaboration was associated with "the shadow of hierarchy." Catholic leaders feared that, absent a consensual agreement, they might be forced into submission by the state government (Pascoe 2008).

On the national level, the push for a national curriculum, standards and testing, in non-government schools gained steam in the second half of the 2000s. Three elements should be stressed. First, as was true in Victoria, non-government school associations deliberated among themselves and with the government in order to arrive at a voluntary agreement. The Commonwealth government did not impose the new arrangements. In fact, Kevin Rudd's Labor government placed both representatives of the Catholic and independent school sectors on the board of the newly established Australian Curriculum, Assessment and Reporting Authority, which is in charge of devising a national curriculum and national standards for both non-government and public schools. Non-government schools, however, have more flexibility in adapting curriculum content than government schools (*Education Week* 2007). Private actors now have an official seat next to the policy table. Second, government financial aid for non-government schools, which was established over thirty-five years ago, has finally become a carrot in the sense that full participation in the new accountability system is a prerequisite for government support. Non-government schools accept testing and standards, at least in part, because they fear to lose government support (Stewart 2009). Third, although the government made extensive use of sermons in the form of government–private deliberation, and also increased the role of private representatives in the policy-making process, this does not imply that the current system is coercion-free. The accountability system is designed in a mostly consensual manner and allows non-government schools considerable leeway. Nevertheless, the new arrangements are anchored in law (primarily in the Schools Assistance Act 2008). The legal and practical accountability requirements for non-government schools are, in fact, more extensive than ever before.

The picture that emerges of the change in the governance of Australian non-government schools is complex. On the one hand, policy networks have become deeper in the sense that private actors have increased their involvement with government in general, and engaged in the formulation of education standards in particular. On the other hand, there has been no shift away from hard policy instruments. Undoubtedly, sermons are more important than they were in the past and the government does not unilaterally pass laws or fix subsidies. Nevertheless, government aid has transformed into carrots due to an addition of conditionality, which constitutes the "hard" aspect of carrots. Consensual agreements also constituted the basis for statutory instruments. Or, in other words, sermons enabled sticks. This policy instrument mix provides us with lessons about governance in general. Sticks (in the form of the shadow of hierarchy) created the conditions under which fruitful deliberation could take place. Sermons concluded in voluntary agreements, which in turn provided the basis for new laws (sticks) and effective carrots, which taken together lead to near-universal compliance. Sermons appear to create trust, legitimacy, and judicious policy. Carrots and sticks motivate private action and facilitate effective implementation. It is the mix of these three generic instruments that enables effective governance in the non-government school sector.

Of course, policy instrument mixes do not have fixed effects. Temporal, sectoral, and national variations imply that policy instruments do not interact in uniform ways. For example, if we remain in the narrow world of private school governance but explore other Anglo-Saxon countries, we find different types of changes over the last decade or so. The accountability mechanisms applied to independent schools in England have become more elaborate over the last decade, with considerably more emphasis on government curricular requirements and oversight (Department for Education and Employment 1998). As is true of the Australian case, private actors are involved in oversight and there is a fair bit of self-regulation (Ofsted 2008). Nevertheless, unlike Australia, carrots do not play any significant role in the English policy mix. Private schools do not receive public aid, hence funding is not a government control lever. In the United States, on the other hand, the No Child Left Behind legislation has allowed the government to introduce standardized testing in return for (limited) public aid for private schools (Wenning, Herdman, and Smith 2002).

Apart from cross-country variation there are also cross-sector differences. Environmental governance has generally moved, in accordance with much of the new governance literature, from an emphasis on traditional statutory legal instruments to "new" instruments that tend to be more voluntary, market-based, and participatory than the "old" regulatory instruments (Jordan, Wurzel, and Zito 2003). The general move from traditional statutory instruments to the new instruments appears to apply in the Australian case as well (Papadakis and Grant 2003; Ross 2008). Australian environmental governance, unlike private school governance, has a strong statutory tradition. The adoption of carrots and sermons definitely constituted a new development. Nevertheless, even here it would be a mistake to argue that the new instruments supplant, so much as supplement, "sticks" (Ross 2008).

CONCLUSION

The governance literature in terms of its emphasis on how governments promote policy has reached an impasse. Discussions of hierarchies versus networks and hard versus soft policy instruments are gravitating toward the unsurprising conclusion that there is no straightforward movement away from hard instruments and that government capacity has not significantly declined (however, see Matthews in this volume). Furthermore, it is clear that there is considerable variation in governance across fields. The contemporary challenge is to go beyond this. In this chapter, I argued that although recent temporal trends vary across sectors and nations, it is generally the case that there is an increase in the number and type of policy instruments employed in most policy domains. Rarely are policy instruments dropped by the wayside. Addition is more prevalent than subtraction. This inevitably leads to increasingly diverse policy instrument mixes. These mixes, as demonstrated above, could create functional complementariness and therefore afford policy-makers more effective solutions than those possible when using instruments separately.

The movement toward a more densely populated instrument field could be explained in terms of institutionalist theory. Discarding "old" policy instruments is not an easy task because of path dependency: actors that benefit from a specific type of public intervention will fight to preserve it, public administrators will stick to the instruments they know, and so on. One important implication of this is that change will occur through "patches" or institutional layering and, consequentially, changes in governance would be incremental in nature. If we believe that the additions would lead to beneficial instrument complementariness then this is a positive development. However, there is no guarantee that the "new" instruments superimposed on the "old" layer will be a good fit. In some cases, policy outcomes would not improve despite the addition of instruments, in others, the new combination might even undermine overall policy effectiveness (Osborn and Datta 2006).

Clearly, emerging instrument mixes should not be viewed as simply the choice of policy-makers seeking more effective policy. Neither do policy-makers exercise unconstrained choice, nor are they exclusively, or even primarily, motivated by considerations of effectiveness. Still, to better inform policy-making, it would seem that the governance literature must take more interest in policy instruments, how they interact, and to what effect. Given the impact of national and sectoral policy environments such research is bound to be laborious, yet—one hopes—ultimately rewarding.

NOTES

1. Admittedly, the trichotomy does not include the primarily *non-government* instrument of voluntary agreements (see Jordan, Wurzel, and Zito 2003), which cannot be neatly subsumed under these categories.
2. For example, fuel taxes (carrots) effectively reduce emissions but are often subject to political attack due to the price they exact from both producers and consumers. A public relations campaign (sermons) focused on the reduction of fuel consumption could legitimize this measure.

REFERENCES

Baumol, W. J. and Oates, W. E. 1979. *Economics, Environmental Policy, and the Quality of Life.* London: Prentice Hall.
Bell, S. and Hindmoor, A. 2009. *Rethinking Governance: The Centrality of the State in Modern Society.* Cambridge: Cambridge University Press.

Bressers, H. T. A. and O'Toole, L. J. 1998. The selection of policy instruments: A network-based perspective. *Journal of Public Policy* 18: 213–239.

Department for Education and Employment. 1998. Tough independent school inspections will raise standards. 29 July.

Doern, B. and Wilson, V., (eds.) 1974. *Issues in Canadian Public Policy*. Toronto: Macmillan.

Education Week. 2007. Australia grapples with national content standards, 26 March.

Freeman, G. P. 1985. National styles and policy sectors: Explaining structured variation. *Journal of Public Policy* 5: 467–496.

Gurr, D. 2007. Diversity and progress in school accountability systems in Australia. *Educational Research for Policy and Practice* 6: 165–186.

Heritier, A. and Eckert, S. 2008. New modes of governance in the shadow of hierarchy: Self-regulation by industry in Europe. *Journal of Public Policy* 28: 113–138.

Hood, C. C. and Margetts, H. Z. 2007. *The Tools of Government in the Digital Age*. Basingstoke: Palgrave Macmillan.

Howlett, M. 1991. Policy instruments, policy styles, and policy implementation. *Policy Studies Journal* 19: 1–21.

Howlett, M. and Rayner, J. 2006. Understanding the historical turn in the policy sciences: A critique of stochastic, narrative, path dependency and process-sequencing models of policy-making over time. *Policy Sciences* 39: 1–18.

Jordan, A., Wurzel, R. K. W. and Zito, A. 2003. "New" instruments of environmental governance: Patterns and pathways of change. In A. Jordan, R. K. W. Wurzel, and A. R. Zito (eds.), *"New" Instruments of Environmental Governance? National Experiences and Prospects*. London: Frank Cass, 3–24.

Jordan, A., Wurzel, R. K. W. and Zito, A. 2005. The rise of "new" policy instruments in comparative perspective: Has governance eclipsed government? *Political Studies* 53: 477–496.

Lemaire, D. 1998. The stick: Regulation as a tool of government. In M-L Bemelmans-Videc, R. C. List, and E. Vedung (eds.), *Carrots, Sticks and Sermons: Policy Instruments and their Evaluation.* London: Transaction Publishers, 59–76.

Levi-Faur, D. 2005. The global diffusion of regulatory capitalism. *The Annals of the American Academy of Political and Social Science* 598: 12–32.

Marinetto, M. 2003. Governing beyond the centre: A critique of the Anglo-governance school. *Political Studies* 51: 592–608.

Moran, M. 2003. *The British Regulatory State: High Modernism and Hyper-Innovation*. Oxford: Oxford University Press.

Office for Standards in Education, Children's Services and Skills (Ofsted). 2008. "Independent schools." Available at http://ofsted.gov.uk/Ofsted-home/Forms-and-guidance/Browse-all-by/Education-and-skills/Independent-schools.

Osborn, D. and Datta, A. 2006. Institutional and policy cocktails for protecting coastal and marine environments from land-based sources of pollution. *Ocean and Coastal Management* 49: 576–596.

Papadakis, E. and Grant, R. 2003. The politics of "light handed regulation": New environmental policy instruments in Australia. *Environmental Politics* 12: 27–50.

Pascoe, S. 2008. Telephone interview with former director of education for the Catholic Education Commission of Victoria.

Persson, Å. 2006. Characterizing the policy instrument mixes for municipal waste in Sweden and England. *European Environment* 16: 213–231.

Peters, B. G. 2002. The politics of tool choice. In L. M Salamon and O. V. Elliott (eds.), *The Tools of Government: A Guide to the New Governance*. Oxford: Oxford University Press, 552–564.

Peters, B. G. and Pierre, J. 2000. *Governance: Politics and the State*. New York: St Martin's Press.

Pollitt, C. and Bouckaert, G. 2000. *Public Management Reform: A Comparative Analysis*. Oxford: Oxford University Press.

Rhodes, R. A. W. 1997. *Understanding Governance: Policy Networks, Governance, Reflexivity, and Accountability*. Buckingham: Open University Press.

Rhodes, R. A. W. 2007. Understanding governance: Ten years on. *Organization Studies* 28: 1243–1264.

Richardson, J. 2000. Government, interest groups and policy change. *Political Studies* 48: 1006–1025.

Ross, A. 2008. Australia. In A. Jordan and A. Lenschow (eds.), *Innovation in Environmental Policy? Integrating the Environment for Sustainability*. Cheltenham: Edward Elgar, 289–312.

Sager, F. 2009. Governance and coercion. *Political Studies* 57: 537–558.

Salamon, L. M. 2002. The new governance and the tools of public action: An introduction. In L. M Salamon and O. V. Elliott (eds.), *The Tools of Government: A Guide to the New Governance*. Oxford: Oxford University Press, 1–47.

Senate Report. 2004. *Commonwealth Funding for Schools*. Melbourne, Australia.

Skjærseth, J. B. 2000. Environmental voluntary agreements: Conditions for making them work. *Swiss Political Science Review* 6: 57–78.

Slominski, P. 2008. Taking hybridity of hard and soft forms of governance seriously: Concept, choice and interaction of legal instruments in the EU. Paper presented at ECPR, Standing Group on the European Union, Fourth Pan-European Conference on EU Politics. Riga, Latvia, 25–27 September.

Stewart, C. 2009. Montessori hit by reporting scandal. *Weekend Australian*, 6 June.

Stoker, G. 1998. Governance as theory: Five propositions. *International Social Science Journal* 50: 17–28.

Vedung, E. 1998. Policy instruments: Typologies and theories. In M-L Bemelmans-Videc, R. C. List, and E. Vedung (eds.), *Carrots, Sticks and Sermons: Policy Instruments and their Evaluation*. London: Transaction Publishers, 21–58.

Vedung, E. and van der Doelen, F. 1998. The sermon: Information programs in the public policy process: Choice, effects and evaluation. In M-L Bemelmans-Videc, R. C. List, and E. Vedung (eds.), *Carrots, Sticks and Sermons: Policy Instruments and their Evaluation*. London: Transaction Publishers, 103–128.

Wenning, R. J., Herdman, P. A., and Smith, N. 2002. No child left behind: Who is included in new federal accountability requirements? Paper presented at Will No Child Be Left Behind? The Challenges of Making this Law Work. Washington, 13 February.

Zehavi, A. 2009. When the piper gets paid in advance: State funding and accountability in Australian and Israeli private schools. Paper presented at American Political Science Association Annual Conference. Toronto, 3–6 September.

CHAPTER 18

....

GOVERNANCE AND
ADMINISTRATIVE REFORMS

....

TOM CHRISTENSEN & PER LÆGREID

Over the past decade multi-level governance and post-NPM issues have moved to the core of public sector reforms. The concept of working across jurisdictions has become increasingly important in public administration and management theory and practice, reflecting the increased complexity and fragmentation that New Public Management (NPM) reforms have brought (Christensen and Lægreid 2010; Halligan 2010). The need for more coordination has become a focal issue.[1] A commonly held notion is that working across organizational, jurisdictional and political/administrative boundaries will enable more efficient and/or effective policy development and implementation and service delivery.

In post-NPM reform, efforts have focused particularly on the problems that arose as a result of greater vertical and horizontal specialization in NPM (Christensen and Lægreid 2007). On the vertical dimension, using more central resources to coordinate subordinate institutions and levels and using stronger instruments of central control have enabled political executives to regain a degree of political control and pursue consistent policies across levels. On the horizontal dimension, cross-sectoral bodies, programs or projects are increasingly being used to modify the "siloization" of the central public administration brought about by the strong specialization by sector (Pollitt 2003a).

We will argue that reform involves processes of layering or sedimentation (Streeck and Thelen 2005) in the sense that reforms do not normally replace each other, but instead, new reforms are often added to old ones producing hybrid administrative systems. Our view is that when existing political-administrative systems are confronted with new reforms they become partly deinstitutionalized. However, they also retain some traditional elements that continue to coexist with reform elements, producing an ever more complex and layered system as these new elements in turn are adapted and institutionalized. If this view is a valid one, public organizations will consist of elements from different eras and reform waves that become balanced and rebalanced over time.

We will use the term governance to describe changes in the nature and role of the government brought about by public sector reforms over the last two decades whereby the previous focus on hierarchy has given way to a greater emphasis on networks and partnerships (Bevir 2009). Thus governance used in this specific meaning expresses a belief that the organs of government increasingly depend on other organizations—be they local government, supra-government, or private sector organizations—to implement their policies and deliver public services.

Two reform waves have been prominent in recent decades: New Public Management and post-New Public Management (Christensen and Lægreid 2007). Like NPM, post-NPM—often labeled governance reforms (Pollitt and Bouckaert 2011; Klijn, Chapter 14, this volume)—offers a kind of 'shopping basket' of different elements (Pollitt 1995). There are also, however, some rather clear differences between the two reform waves. While NPM had a more internal focus on improving efficiency, post-NPM governance-inspired reforms are mainly interorganizationally oriented. They seek to improve the horizontal coordination of governmental organizations and also to enhance coordination between the government and other actors (Klijn, Chapter 14, this volume; Pollitt and Bouckaert 2011). NPM implied proliferation and unbundling, contractualization, marketization, a private sector management style, explicit performance standards and output/outcome control. In contrast post-NPM implies a mixed pattern of in-house, marketized services and delivery networks, a client-based, holistic management style, boundary-spanning skills, joined-up targets, a procedural focus, impartiality and ethical norms and stronger centralized control (Lodge and Gill 2011). Under NPM politicians had a strategic, goal-setting role, and civil servants were supposed to be autonomous managers held to account through performance arrangements and incentives (Pollitt and Bouckaert 2011). Under post-NPM politicians are guarantors of compromise deals between multiple stakeholders, while civil servants are network managers and partnership leaders.

We will mainly relate governance to post-NPM because it has a flavor of joining-up, collaboration and coordination but there are obviously also governance-related elements in the NPM movement, such as public–private partnerships, networks and user participation. Since networks are often seen as an organizational mode different from markets and hierarchy (Bouckaert, Peters, and Verhoest 2010), we will put a specific emphasis on this when discussing governance-related reforms. Thus governance reforms and NPM reforms partly overlap, especially when it comes to more specific reform tools.

We will focus on three issues in this chapter. First, we will address the concepts of governance, networks and partnership in a reform context. Second, we will examine the typical features of the post-NPM reform wave, especially as they relate to governance. Third, we will discuss to what extent this latest reform movement has replaced previous reforms or whether it has merely supplemented them. Finally, we will draw some conclusions and look at some implications.

Our major argument is that administrative reforms represent a mixed order (Olsen 2010). The old public administration exemplified by hierarchy and Weberian forms of bureaucracy was supplemented during the NPM reform movement by disaggregation, autonomization, agencification, and marketization. This was followed by post-NPM, which entailed patching up the administrative bodies of the state, bringing about stronger integration between the state and the private sector and civil society and increasing central government capacity. Thus, what we have seen is not pendulum swings from government to governance and back again, but rather one reform supplementing another in a complementary process whereby the trade-off between different administrative modes has changed, resulting in increased complexity and hybrid organizational forms.

GOVERNANCE, NETWORKS, PARTNERSHIPS, AND REFORMS

In the post-NPM reforms governance elements and networks are supplementing hierarchy and market as coordination mechanisms. Organizational forms such as partnerships and collegial bodies spanning organizational boundaries are being used more intensively. Networks have been introduced in most Western democracies as a way to increase the capacity of the public sector to deliver services. Governance networks can be seen as part of a transition from a hierarchical state government to a network form consisting of decentralized nodes of authority, but they can also be seen as a supporting tool that powerful governmental actors use to increase their capacity to shape and deliver public policy in a complex world (Klijn and Skelcher 2007: 598). This view challenges the 'governance without government' thesis of Rhodes (1996) which asserts that networks are self-organizing, that the government is only one of many players and that there is a strong horizontal component in the networks (Bache 2000). In contrast, this instrumental conjecture implies that the central government is a powerful actor that creates networks in order to realize its projects and does so in response to a national mandate to be a delivery arm for a national policy initiative that requires inter-organizational cooperation at the local level (Skelcher, Mathur, and Smith 2005).

For complex, unstructured and rapidly changing problems a network approach may be suitable (Kettl 2003). This approach understands coordination as the interaction of interdependent actors from different traditional hierarchical structures and from outside such structures. Such actors pay less heed to formal top-down authority and rely more on negotiations and mutual adjustments and on bringing together organizations to pool resources and knowledge. This network model scores high on adaptability and flexibility, but accountability may be reduced and ambiguous, and steering may be more difficult.

The governance literature is in large part concerned with networks as a phenomenon in which private actors are a central feature (Skelcher , Mathur, and Smith 2005). But there is also a more state-centric approach to governance in which public–public networks are a main component (Peters and Pierre 2003). Here civil servants have networking and boundary-spanning competences allowing them to act as go-betweens and brokers across organizational boundaries both vertically and horizontally. Public–public networks bring civil servants from different policy areas together to trump hierarchy (Hood and Lodge 2006: 92)—in other words, they act as facilitators, negotiators and diplomats rather than exercising only hierarchical authority. Individual, people-oriented skills, and not technical skills, are central to this kind of competence, and may be especially important in tackling 'wicked issues' that transcend traditional sectors and policy areas. The ability to further cooperation is also valued.

Partnerships have become a popular tool in the governance of welfare services (Fimreite and Lægreid 2009). They are designed to enhance collaboration and cooperation across boundaries in public services (Sullivan and Skelcher 2002). Repeated efforts to achieve coordination are a main argument behind using partnership models in the public sector. There are different kinds of partnerships, but a common feature is lack of hierarchy. Mörth and Sahlin-Andersson (2006) classify partnerships along two dimensions—degree of formality and degree of permanence. We will add two further dimensions to these: the degree to which private actors are involved and the degree of voluntariness (Fimreite and Lægreid 2009). Some partnerships can be very informal, time-limited, voluntary and include a strong private component. Others can be highly formalized, mandatory and permanent with a weak private component. In the welfare state administration one-stop shops have become an emerging instrument for joining up and strengthening governance relations, but there is significant diversity between countries regarding the task portfolio, participant structure, level of autonomy, proximity to citizens and instruments used in these arrangements (Askim et al. 2011).

In addition to the partnership model we also have a multi-level governance system in which tasks are carried out at different levels of government, implying increased interdependence of public agencies operating at different territorial levels, often in a complex system of overlapping jurisdictions (Bache and Flinders 2004). Tasks can rarely be treated independently of each other, the different levels have to collaborate, and coordination between levels is an important precondition for coordination between sectors. Multi-level governance does not necessary imply state decline, but rather state transformation and adaptation (Pierre and Peters 2000).

A main concern that arises when partnership is used within the public sector is the problem of accountability. Accountability is a multidimensional concept. In a hierarchical model the concept of accountability is primarily related to upward accountability to political sovereigns (Christensen and Lægreid 2002). The network or partnership models will make a model of strictly hierarchical responsibility from the top down less applicable. Partnerships need some level of independence but at the same time they should be accountable upwards to politicians, horizontally to other agencies and local government and downwards to citizens. They thus have to face the challenges of political as well as administrative and bureaucratic, legal and professional accountability (Pollitt 2003b).

A central accountability issue is thus how the relationship between government and networks impinges on ministerial responsibility (Christensen and Lægreid 2008). It is generally accepted that ministries should be allowed to give some interpretative guidance to partnerships in how to carry out their tasks. Partnerships might also weaken accountability to political bodies at the local level. A joint front-line unit is supposed to balance local accountability to the municipal council with vertical ministerial accountability. Weaker upwards accountability to the parliament and accountability to the local council may, however, be supplemented by stronger downwards accountability to users, clients, and citizens. Partnerships scoring high on formality and permanence are constrained by procedural and substantive rules that define their discretion. Autonomy from direct political control does not automatically mean immunity from public accountability. Thus, responsiveness towards users and clients might become a substitute for accountability in the control of autonomous central agencies.

We will claim that networks as a coordinating mechanism in partnership models supplement rather than replace the traditional welfare state hierarchy (Bouckaert, Peters, and Verhoest 2010). One consequence of this is that accountability relations are challenged.

GOVERNANCE AND POST-NPM REFORMS

The main goal of post-NPM reforms has been to gradually counteract the disintegration or fragmentation brought about under NPM and to restore public sector organizations to a situation of greater integration and coordination (Christensen and Lægreid 2007). This is closely related to the development of governance measures in a modern political-administrative system. First, fragmentation under NPM increased pressure for more horizontal integration and coordination. Second, political executives were reluctant to accept the undermining of political control that resulted from NPM. This has resulted in efforts to strengthen central capacity and control, particularly in sectors seen as politically salient (Gregory 2003; Halligan 2006). There is an increasing striving for coordination and coherence in public policy, and one answer seems to be a return to the centre. While the latter trend is more about restoring the hierarchy, the former is more about governance in the sense of networks and partnerships. Thus we will focus mainly on these horizontal elements of the post-NPM movement.

The post-NPM generation of reforms advocates a more holistic strategy (Bogdanor 2005). The slogans "joined-up-government" and "whole-of-government" provided new labels for the old doctrine of coordination in the study of public administration (Hood 2005). In addition to the issue of coordination, the problem of integration was a main concern behind these reform initiatives (Mulgan 2005). The purpose has been to work across portfolio boundaries and administrative levels to achieve shared goals and an integrated government response to particularly complex issues. Attempts to coordinate government policy-making and service delivery across organizational boundaries are, however, not a new phenomenon (Kavanagh and Richards 2001).

The concept of working across boundaries gained popularity in public administration and in management theory and practice from the late 1990s (Gregory 2003). The new mantra was an increased focus on the notion of stronger coordination, integration and connecting the dots. The notion that working across organizational boundaries will enable more efficient and/or effective policy development and implementation and service delivery runs counter to the NPM claim that greater efficiency can be achieved via more fragmented arrangements.

The horizontal dimension of post-NPM is regarded as even more important than the vertical one. In Australia and New Zealand, for example, new organizational units, such as new cabinet committees, inter-ministerial or inter-agency collaborative units, inter-governmental councils, the lead agency approach, circuit-breaker teams, super networks, task forces, cross-sectoral programs or projects, tsars, etc. have been established with the main purpose of getting government units to work better together (Gregory 2006; Halligan and Adams 2004). In 2003, a new Cabinet Implementation Unit was established in Australia to support whole-of-government activities. Creating coordinative structures inside existing central structures, increasing the strategic leadership role of the Cabinet, and focusing more on following up central decisions are typical hierarchical efforts in Australia. Their aim is to put pressure on the sectoral authorities to collaborate and coordinate better (Halligan 2006). In Norway a new minister of coordination was established in the Prime Minister's Office in 2009. Other examples are merging agencies to form larger bodies, such as the Department of Homeland Security in the USA, the Ministry of Social Development in New Zealand or the new welfare administration in Norway.

The horizontal dimension typically concerns policy areas that cut across traditional boundaries, so-called "wicked issues." How this dimension is handled ranges from mergers to softer collaborative measures. The Canadian government launched what were labeled horizontal management initiatives from the mid-1990s to tackle policy issues such as innovation, poverty, and climate change (Bakvis and Juillet 2004). Other examples of these were seen in Australia in 2002, where attempts were made to bring more coordination to such areas as national security, demographics, science, education, environmental sustainability, energy, rural and regional development, transportation, and work and family life (Halligan and Adams 2004).

Procedural efforts have also been made to enhance post-NPM initiatives. In New Zealand there is a stronger emphasis on effectiveness, broader long-term "ownership" interests and outcomes in contrast to the shorter-term and narrower "purchaser" efficiency and output focus that characterized the NPM reforms (Boston and Eichbaum 2005).

Post-NPM seems generally to be more about working together in a pragmatic and intelligent way than about formalized collaboration. This is especially true in Canada where working horizontally has been an issue of ongoing importance since the mid-1990s (Bakvis and Juillett 2004). The approach to major stakeholders in the environment, including private actors, is more heterogeneous and involves joined-up governance efforts and the use of networks and partnerships.

Collaborative efforts aimed at delivering a seamless service, like Australia's one-stop shops, can be seen as control from above to secure coordinated and efficient service delivery, but also as a real local collaborative effort requiring autonomy from central control (Halligan 2006). A comparative study of service delivery organizations in the UK, New Zealand, Australia, and the Netherlands concludes that procedural bureaucratic models are being superseded by network governance (Considine and Lewis 2003).

The post-NPM reforms are also culturally oriented governance efforts. They focus on cultivating a strong and unified sense of values, teambuilding, the involvement of participating organizations, trust, value-based management, collaboration and improving the training and self-development of public servants (Ling 2002). The argument is that there is a need to re-establish a "common ethic" and a "cohesive culture" in the public sector because of the reported corrosion of loyalty and increasing mistrust brought about by NPM, which was rooted in diverse economic theories (Norman 1995). All agencies should be bound together by a single, distinctive public service ethos, as emphasized in Australia (Shergold 2004). Under the slogan "working together", the Australian government has emphasized the need to build a supportive public sector culture that encourages whole-of-government solutions by formulating value guidelines and codes of conduct.

NPM is also related to governance efforts. Directly influencing public services is the "real thing." In a democracy it is up to citizens to choose which institutional arrangements they prefer, and if they are dissatisfied with the existing system it is their privilege to try other arrangements. But we can also take a more skeptical view of the democratic value of people's status as customers. A managerial concept of democracy might weaken civic responsibility, engagement and political equality and enhance the role of administrators and managers (Christensen and Lægreid 2001). It is a paradox that while one goal of NPM is to open public administration to the public, it may ultimately reduce the level of democratic accountability and lead to erosion of the "publicness" of public service, a development that post-NPM has tried to counteract (Haque 2001; Peters 1999).

GOVERNANCE AS REPLACING OR SUPPLEMENTING PREVIOUS REFORMS

A further central question is whether governance-related post-NPM is transcending NPM. There are rather different views on this. One view is that we are seeing a process of substitution and pendulum swings. Just as NPM was a substitute for the "old public administration", post-NPM will replace NPM, simply because the time is ripe for it. This "zeitgeist" approach focuses on the deinstitutionalization and (re)institutionalization of reforms, rather than combinations of reforms (Røvik 2002). Another possibility is simply that political priorities have changed and that leaders have therefore decided to scrap one set of reforms and embark on another, or that dominant coalitions have been renegotiated and have decided to move beyond NPM. Dunleavy et al. (2006) simply claim that NPM is dead and has been replaced with Digital-Era Governance.

Another take on this is that governance components are transcending the NPM-post-NPM divide, a view that stems partly from the ambiguity of the concept itself. As indicated earlier there are obvious governance elements in the NPM movement related to public–private partnerships, increased market orientation, introduction of quasi-markets and arrangements for increased user participation. To complicate the picture further there are also non-governance components in the post-NPM movement, such as bringing the central government back in and strengthening the hierarchy. In contrast to the proliferation and fragmentation that followed the NPM reforms, the post-NPM reforms have focused more on integration and coordination. The structural arrangements for increasing horizontal coordination and coordination across administrative levels via networks and partnerships are the main governance features of the post-NPM movement (Christensen and Lægreid 2007).

One implication of this understanding is that different reform waves will be combined. In reality reform waves influence the development of public organizations and their activities in a gradual process of change, so that it is difficult to identify the end of one reform wave and the beginning of another. The claim is that NPM is by no means over (Pollitt 2003b), but is being supplemented by other reform initiatives. The next question is then how we may characterize this combination, that is, what kind of dynamics and mechanisms does it involve? Some would say that NPM is the dominant reform wave and that post-NPM has simply modified certain aspects of it. Another possible version is that both reform waves are important and are used in different ways according to policy area or just combined differently in different reforms.

Another take on how reform waves interact is inspired by a combination of structural, cultural and myth perspectives (Christensen et al. 2007) and sees the different reforms as a process of layering or sedimentation (Olsen 2009; Streeck and Thelen 2005). If we look at the historical development of public institutions, we see that at certain points in time elements of their basic structures and cultures are either pushed aside or deinstitutionalized when a new reform wave comes along or else manage to remain viable and influence the further development of the organization, regardless of new reform waves. This layering of various elements from the "old public administration", NPM and post-NPM makes public organizations increasingly complex. Governance elements seem to thrive amid this complexity.

One reason for layering processes may be the simple instrumental fact that executive leaders decide to keep reform elements they support or like when introducing new reforms. Another reason may be that a diversity of reform elements from different waves makes it easier to make flexible political compromises, decrease conflicts and increase legitimacy. A third and more culturally oriented reason could be that path-dependent mechanisms make it difficult to remove all elements from an old reform when a new one emerges. It is never easy to start from scratch, and continuity in norms and values helps a public organization to cope with periods of transition. A fourth and more symbolically oriented reason is related to the labeling of reforms (Meyer 1979). Often reforms are sold as new, modern and efficient, whereas in actual fact there is far more continuity than reform entrepreneurs would have us believe. Continuity that incorporates some new structural and cultural elements—sold as modernization—may be a better option than reforms that turn an organization upside down.

Summing up, we would tend to subscribe to the argument that reform movements are characterized by combination, complexity, layering and hybridization, rather than by dominance, substitution and pendulum swings (Christensen et al. 2007). Our main argument is that public reforms are driven by a number of different forces. Public administration faces increasingly complex environmental and internal conditions, reflected in multifunctional organizational forms, and the administrative reforms in the public sector can be understood as compound reforms that combine different organizational principles based on multiple factors working together in a complex mix (Egeberg and Trondal 2007). Compound administrative reforms are multidimensional and represent "mixed" orders and combinations of competing, inconsistent and contradictory organizational principles and structures that coexist and balance interests and values (Olsen 2007). It is not a question of hierarchy, market or networks but of how the mixtures of these forms of coordination change in different reform movements and how the trade-off between them is altered.

Multidimensional orders are considered to be more resilient to external shocks and therefore preferable to uni-dimensional orders (March and Olsen 1989). Compound reforms thus depart from "either/or" theorizing by assuming that executive governance rests on the mobilization of multiple and complementary sets of institutions, actors, interests, decision-making arenas, values, norms, and cleavages, reflected in what we call a transformative approach to reforms (Christensen and Lægreid 2001). In a pluralistic society, where there are many criteria for success and different causal understandings, we have to go beyond the idea of a single organizational principle to understand how public organizations work and are reformed and look at them as composite organizations (Olsen 2007).

Our argument is that we face a dialectical development in which the old public administration has been combined with NPM and post-NPM features to create new hybrid organizational forms. The central component in the old Weberian bureaucratic model is sustainable and robust, but in the strong modern state it has been supplemented with neo-Weberian components such as performance management and user participation, responsiveness and professional management (Pollitt and Bouckaert 2011) and also with new public governance initiatives (Osborne 2010).

Conclusion

Public administration faces increasingly complex, semi-autonomous and multifunctional organizational forms. The proliferation of these organizational forms in the public sector is one of the reasons why many countries have now launched initiatives to enhance coordination (Christensen and Lægreid 2007). In such initiatives, strengthening the link between individual public sector organizations and the larger objectives of government as well as with other public sector organizations seems crucial. On top of this, governance efforts to collaborate and coordinate with the private sector through partnerships, networks and participation are becoming more important for governmental decisions and policy implementation.

Post-NPM initiatives in different countries vary according to the starting points and national administrative cultures. But a common characteristic is that post-NPM reforms do not represent a break with the past, nor do they fundamentally transform existing organizational modes. Rather it is a question of rebalancing existing administrative systems without changing them in any fundamental way (Gregory 2006). These post-NPM reforms have not replaced the NPM reforms. Countries show complex combinations of organizational autonomy on some issues, increased centralized control and network-like coordination mechanisms alongside remnants of traditional hierarchical control (Bouckaert, Peters, and Verhoest 2010).

In the last decade there has been no dominant model (Pollitt and Bouckaert 2011). NPM has been supplemented by post-NPM, including key concepts such as governance, networks and partnerships. What is more the big models of NPM and post-NPM overlap and are not mutually exclusive when it comes to specific reform tools. Both paradigms incorporate ideas from the other perspective, and both in practice and in the academic literature ideas from both models are combined (Klijn, Chapter 14, this volume).

Summing up, post-NPM reforms imply an increased focus on integration, horizontal coordination in line with a governance approach and enhanced political control (Pollitt 2003b; Lægreid and Verhoest 2010). The emergence of post-NPM reforms can be understood as a combination of external pressure from the technical and institutional environments, learning from NPM reforms and deliberate choices by political executives. An increasing number of scholars are arguing that these post-NPM trends are a reaction to the organizational proliferation and resulting fragmentation induced by NPM doctrines (Pollitt 2003a; Boston and Eichbaum 2005; Gregory 2006; Halligan 2006; Christensen and Lægreid 2007; Bouckaert et al. 2010; Lægreid and Verhoest 2010). This counter-reaction to organizational proliferation entailing increased central control and coordination has been observable in many countries (Bogdanor 2005; Bouckaert, Peters, and Verhoest 2010). External and internal pressures have questioned the effectiveness of a proliferated public sector. These include internationalization and Europeanization, security threats and crisis management needs as well as a call for more integrated service delivery and holistic policies, e-government and regulatory reform initiatives, and the loss of a common civil service culture.

However, it remains unclear what these coordination initiatives imply for public-sector organizations in terms of actual autonomy, control, coordination and performance. One take is that this is a new "one best way" orientation with a lot of symbolic flavor. Another is that such post-NPM initiatives have made a substantial contribution to a better organized public sector. The question is whether post-NPM and governance efforts will continue to be a strong reform movement or whether they will gradually fade away and be supplemented by new reform initiatives.

NOTE

1. Such efforts are typically referred to as joined-up government, whole-of-government, holistic government, collaborative governance, networked government, connected government, cross-cutting policy, horizontal management, partnerships and collaborative public management (Gregory 2003, Ansell, Chapter 35, this volume). Osborne (2006) labels this new reform trend New Public Governance focusing on networks, boundary spanning and relational contracts.

REFERENCES

Askim, J., Fimreite, A. L. Moseley, A., and Holm Pedersen, L. 2011. One stop shops: An emerging instrument for joining up the 21st century welfare state. *Public Administration.* First published online: 30 May 2011, doi 10.1111/j.1467–9299.2011.01933.x

Bache, I. 2000. Government with governance: Network steering in Yorkshire and the Humber. *Public Administration* 78: 575–592.

Bache, I. and Flinders, M. (eds.) 2004. *Multi-level Governance.* Oxford: Oxford University Press.

Bakvis, H. and Juillet, L. 2004. *The Horizontal Challenge: Line Departments, Central Agencies and Leadership.* Ottawa: Canada School of Public Services.

Bevir, M. 2009. *Key Concepts in Governance.* London: Sage.

Bogdanor, V. 2005. Introduction. In V. Bogdanor (ed.), *Joined-Up Government.* British Academy Occasional paper 5. Oxford: Oxford University Press.

Boston, J. and Eichbaum, C. 2005. State Sector Reform and Renewal in New Zealand: Lessons for Governance. Paper presented at the Conference on 'Repositioning of Public Governance—Global Experiences and Challenges', 18–19 November, Taipei.

Bouckaert, G. Peters, B. G., and Verhoest, K. 2010. *The Coordination of Public Sector Organizations: Shifting Patterns of Public Management.* London: Palgrave Macmillan.

Christensen, T. and Lægreid, P. 2001. A transformative perspective on administrative reforms. In T. Christensen and P. Lægreid (eds.), *New Public Management: The Transformation of Ideas and Practice.* Aldershot: Ashgate.

Christensen, T. and Lægreid, P. 2002. New public management: Puzzles of democracy and the influence of citizens. *Journal of Political Philosophy* 10: 267–295.

Christensen, T. and Lægreid, P. 2007. The whole-of-government approach to public sector reform. *Public Administration Review* 67: 1059–1066.

Christensen, T. and Lægreid, P. 2008. The challenge of coordination in central government organizations: The Norwegian case. *Public Organization Review* 8: 97–116.

Christensen, T. and Lægreid, P. 2010. Increased complexity in public sector organizations— The challenge of combining NPM and post-NPM. In P. Lægreid and K.Verhoest (eds.), *Governance of Public Sector Organizations: Proliferation, Autonomy and Performance.* London: Palgrave Macmillan.

Christensen, T., Lægreid, P., Roness, P.G, and Røvik, K.A. 2007. *Organization Theory and the Public Sector.* London: Routledge.

Considine, M. and Lewis, J. 2003. Bureaucracy, network or enterprise? Comparing models of governance in Australia, Britain, the Netherlands and New Zealand. *Public Administration Review* 63: 131–140.

Dunleavy, P., Margetts, H., Bestow, S., and Tinkler, J. 2006. New public management is dead—Long live digital-era governance. *Journal of Public Administration Research and Theory* 16: 467–494.

Egeberg, M. and Trondal, J. 2007. National agencies in the European administrative space: Government driven, commission driven or networked? *Public Administration* 87: 779–790.

Fimreite, A.L. and Lægreid, P. 2009. Reorganizing the welfare state organization: Partnership, networks and accountability. *Public Management Review* 11: 284–297.

Gregory, R. 2003. All the king's horses and all the king's men: Putting New Zealand's public sector back together again. *International Public Management Review* 4 41–58.

Gregory, R. 2006. Theoretical faith and practical works: De-autonomizing and joining-up in the New Zealand state sector. In T. Christensen and P. Lægreid (eds.), *Autonomy and Regulation: Coping with Agencies in the Modern State*. London: Edward Elgar.

Halligan, J. 2006. The reassertion of the centre in a first generation NPM system. In T. Christensen and P. Lægreid (eds.), *Autonomy and Regulation: Coping with Agencies in the Modern State*. London: Edward Elgar.

Halligan, J. 2010. Post NPM responses to disaggregation through coordinating horizontally and integrating governance. In. P. Lægreid and K. Verhoest (eds), *Governance of Public Sector Organizations: Proliferation, Autonomy and Performance*. London: Palgrave Macmillan.

Halligan, J. and Adams, J. 2004. Security, capacity and post-management reforms: public management changes in 2003. *Australian Journal of Public Administration* 63: 85–93.

Haque, M.S. 2001. Recent transition in governance in South Asia: Contexts, dimensions, and implications. *International Journal of Public Administration* 24: 1405–1436.

Hood, C. (2005). The idea of joined-up government: A historical perspective. In V. Bogdanor (ed.), *Joined-Up Government*. Oxford: Oxford University Press for the British Academy.

Hood, C. and Lodge, M. 2006. *The Politics of Public Service Bargain*. Oxford: Oxford University Press.

Kavanagh, D. and Richards, D. 2001. Departmentalism and joined-up government: Back to the future? *Parliamentary Affairs* 54: 1–18.

Kettl, D. F. 2003. Contingent coordination: Practical and theoretical puzzles for homeland security. *American Review for Public Administration* 33: 253–277.

Klijn, E. J. and Skelcher, C. 2007. Democracy and governance networks: Compatible or not? *Public Administration* 85: 587–608.

Ling. T. 2002. Delivering joined-up government in the UK: Dimensions, issues and problems. *Public Administration* 80: 615–642.

Lodge, M. and Gill, D. 2011. Towards a new era of administrative reform? The myth of the post-NPM in New Zealand. *Governance* 24: 141–166.

Lægreid, P. and Verhoest, K. (eds.) 2010. *Governance of Public Sector Organizations: Proliferation, Autonomy and Performance*. London: Palgrave Macmillan.

March, J. G. and Olsen, J. P. 1989. *Rediscovering Institutions: The Organizational Basis of Politics*. New York: The Free Press.

Meyer, M. W. (1979). Organizational structure as signaling. *Pacific Sociological Review* 22: 481–500.

Mulgan, G. 2005. Joined-up government: Past, present, and future. In V. Bogdanor (ed.), *Joined-Up Government*. British Academy Occasional Paper 5. Oxford: Oxford University Press.

Mörth, U. and Sahlin-Andersson, K. (eds.) 2006. *Privat-Offentliga Partnerskap (Public–Private Partnership)*. Stockholm: SNS Förlag.

Norman, R. 1995. New Zealand's reinvented government: Experiences of public managers. *Public Sector* 18: 22–25.

Olsen, J. P. 2007. *Europe in Search for Political Order*. Oxford: Oxford University Press.

Olsen, J. P. 2009. Change and continuity: An institutional approach to institutions of democratic government. *European Political Science Review* 1: 3–32.

Olsen, J. P. 2010. *Governing through Institution Building*. Oxford: Oxford University Press.

Osborne, S. 2006. The new public governance? *Public Management Review* 8: 377–388.

Osborne, S. (ed.) (2010). *The New Public Governance?* London: Routledge.

Peters, B. G. (2011). Responses to NPM: From input democracy to output democracy. In T. Christensen and P. Lægreid (eds.), *The Ashgate Research Companion to New Public Management*. Farnham: Ashgate.

Peters, B. G. and Pierre, J. 2003. Multi-level governance and democracy: A Faustian bargain? In I. Bache and M. Flinders (eds.), *Multi-Level Governance*. Oxford: Oxford University Press.

Pierre, J. and Peters, B. G. (2000). *Governance, Politics and the State*. London: Macmillan.

Pollitt, C. 1995. Justification by works or by faith? Evaluation of new public management. *Evaluation* 1: 133–154.

Pollitt, C. 2003a. Joined-up government: A survey. *Political Studies Review* 1: 34–49.

Pollitt, C. 2003b. *The Essential Public Manager*. Maidenhead: Open University.

Pollitt, C. and Bouckaert 2011. *Public Management Reform: A Comparative Analysis—NPM, Governance and the Neo-Weberian State*. 3rd ed. Oxford: Oxford University Press.

Rhodes, R. A. W. 1996. The new governance: Governing without government. *Political Studies* 44: pp 652–667.

Røvik, K.A. 2002. The secrets of the winners: Management ideas that flow. In K. Sahlin-Andersson and L. Engwall (eds.), *The Expansion of Management Knowledge—Carriers, Flows and Sources*. Stanford. CA: Stanford University Press.

Shergold, P. 2004. Regeneration: New structures, new leaders, new traditions. *Australian Journal of Public Administration* 54: 3–6.

Skelcher, C., Mathur, N., and Smith, M. 2005. The public governance of collaborative spaces: Discourse, design and democracy. *Public Administration* 83: 573–596.

Streeck, W. and Thelen, K. (eds.) 2005. *Beyond Continuity: Institutional Change in Advanced Political Economies*. Oxford: Oxford University Press.

Sullivan, H. and Skelcher, C. 2002. *Working across Boundaries: Collaboration in Public Services*. London: Palgrave.

CHAPTER 19

GOVERNANCE AND PATRONAGE

MATTHEW FLINDERS

As each of the chapters in this section has emphasized from varying perspectives, the transition from government to governance creates new challenges in terms of coordinating and controlling the vast array of actors that are now involved in the regulation and delivery of public services. The central argument of this chapter is that patronage provides a critical tool through which politicians can seek to steer and control the complex networks that the study of governance highlights. Understanding or "rethinking governance" therefore demands that scholars pay far greater attention than they have in the past to the relationship between patronage and interorganizational relationships, due to the manner in which it offers a form of *linkage* at three levels: between politicians and the state, between the state and society, and between society and politicians.

The study of patronage has generally been conducted, as Kopecky, Scherlis, and Spirova (2008) emphasize, through a conceptual lens that sees it as synonymous with corruption. This chapter adopts a more sophisticated approach that dares to suggest that patronage may have evolved to fulfill a more positive and critical role within modern democratic governance. In relation to balancing autonomy and control patronage offers politicians a form of social or organizational glue through which to establish low-cost high-trust relationships. In democratic terms patronage also provides a form of political recruitment through which underrepresented or socially alienated sections of society can be reconnected to the political sphere. The simple argument of this chapter is that too little attention has been given to the manner in which patronage provides a form of risk-reduction mechanism for politicians that is not necessarily corrupt or undemocratic. Moreover, *The Logic of Discipline* (Roberts, 2010), which views all politicians as shortsighted and self-interested and has, as a result, fueled a trend toward reducing the patronage capacity of politicians, risks not only eviscerating the governing capacity of executives but also further narrowing the terrain and jurisdiction of democratic politics.

In order to develop this argument this chapter is divided into three sections. The opening section attempts to rescue the concept from the generally negative normative baggage that has traditionally surrounded it by distinguishing between patronage as a component of democratic governance (labeled *open patronage*) and patronage as a tool of corrupt or premodern governance (referred to as *closed patronage*). The second section then adopts a comparative interdisciplinary approach by briefly exploring the utilization of patronage by politicians in three countries (one authoritarian regime, one hybrid or "party democratic" regime, and one democratic regime). The main aim of this section is to reveal the manner in which patronage forms a critical tool of governance in each of these countries but with quite different intentions. The final section then locates the issue of patronage within a number of much broader themes and particularly within the topic of regulatory governance.

1. A CONCEPT IN NEED OF SALVATION

Patronage is best conceptualized as an incentive system denoting an exchange relationship in which a patron (i.e. an individual, group, country, or institution) exerts control over another agent through the provision of certain goods or services (money, food, protection, jobs, sex, knowledge, etc.). Within this broad ambit this chapter focuses on *party patronage* as a specific form of patronage politics, and defines this as "the power of a party to appoint people to positions in public and semi-public life" (Kopecky and Scherlis 2008: 357). It is therefore concerned with what Daalder (1966) has defined as the "reach" and "permeation" of politicians to allot individuals to powerful positions within the state—the extended area of *sottogoverno* (positions on state enterprises, agencies, boards, and commissions) that form the basis of particularistic exchanges in many countries around the world. This focuses attention back on the theme of linkages in the context of patronage–governance–democracy as different rules, customs, practices, and assumptions concerning the distribution of senior positions within the wider state sector reveal much about the nature of democracy and the operation of the state. In this regard it is useful to reflect on the key insights emanating out of two specific sub-disciplinary streams (that of party politics and development studies).

The literature in the field of party politics has for some time examined the "colonization" of the state and how parties may seek to utilize public appointment powers as an *intra*-party resource through which to command loyalty and create incentives, and as an *extra*-party resource through which to embed partisan players within the broader topography of the state (see, for example, Muller 2006; van Biezen and Kopecky 2007). Party patronage is therefore commonly associated with selective incentives, clientelistic practices, and the use of appointments as rewards for loyalty or payments for previous support. It is also viewed as a mechanism or critical resource through which parties can develop and sustain their organizational structures in the face of diminishing membership levels. The field of development studies has, by contrast, tended to focus predominantly on the interplay between regime types and political behavior. Consequently, the research of many scholars has, each in its own way, shown how various elements of modernization (changes in relation to class, social cleavages, education, and social deference; the integration of previously isolated communities into larger networks; the social provision of collective services; the fulfillment of basic material needs; the emergence of broad ideological affiliations; the emergence of a merit-based public service ethos; the mediating role of the media; etc.) have undermined *traditional* patron–client relationships to the point at which it is possible to suggest that those forms of closed, secretive, and self-perpetuating patronage networks tend to wither in the face of social expectations, which are increasingly intolerant of such practices. The "waning of old corruption," as Harling (1996) describes this process, does not mean that party patronage is not present or important within contemporary socio-political relationships but it does demand a more sophisticated bifurcation.

For this reason Table 19.1 distinguishes between *Closed patronage* (CP) and *Open patronage* (OP). The analysis of the former (CP) is by some way the most dominant

Table 19.1 Dissecting patronage systems

	Closed patronage	Open patronage
Party patronage	Yes	Yes
Ministerial discretion	High/pure	Low/constrained
State structure	'Partitocracy'	Meritocracy
Impact on state	Divisive	Integrative
Directional thrust	Vertical	Horizontal
Logic	Capture support of specific group, individual, constituency	Demonstrate governing competence
Process	Private	Public
Advertised position	No	Yes
Application field	Single interviewee	Competitive interview process
Relevant expertise/experience	No/cronyism	Yes/merit-based
Nature of competition	Closed	Open
Sinecures	Yes	No
Independent regulation	No	Yes
Perceived as democratically legitimate	No	Yes
Power	Focused	Diffused
Benefit	Particularistic/clientelism	Universal/public interest
Politics	Covert	Open
Instrument of…	Favor	Governance
Essence	'Spoils system'	Pubic service bargain
Party appointee	Patron	Partisan
Reach	Extensive	Limited
Capacity for political discretion	Yes/pure discretion	Yes/constrained discretion
Motivation behind appointment	Repayment/loyalty/votes	Delivery/risk-reduction/votes

focus of the wider literature; whereas the aim of this chapter is to emphasize the latter (OP) as a potentially more fertile avenue for research due to the manner in which appointees attempt not to secure the support of specific individuals, groups, or constituencies within a polity (i.e. vertical/agent-focused linkage) but to demonstrate a much broader governing competence and, through this, secure electoral support (i.e. horizontal/generic-societal linkage). OP is therefore distinct from "pork barrel" politics in which government funds are strategically deployed to garner electoral support in specific constituencies and can thus be viewed as a mode of governing rather than a normatively questionable, innately corrupt, and largely hidden aspect of modern governance. The great value of examining OP is that it dovetails and complements a nascent strand of research that rejects the default interpretation of party patronage as a "bad" thing but instead offers a more balanced approach that contextualizes the topic within the challenges of governing an increasingly disaggregated and fluid state. As Kopecky and Scherlis (2008: 356) argue, "patronage reappears on the stage of European politics less in the conventional form of a particularistic exchange between patron and client, and more as a critical organizational and governmental resource employed by political parties."

This is actually not a new argument but the rediscovery of a line of reasoning that first surfaced over half a century ago in Frank Souraf's study of American politics. As the role of the state increased in many countries throughout the twentieth century, Souraf argued, so the role and capacity of political parties and local patrons to act as a dominant form of societal linkage or resource-broker lessened. At the same time a number of factors (growing economic wealth, higher education standards, declining social deference, the elimination of absolute poverty, etc.) fueled public resistance to corrupt and nepotistic practices. In 1960 Sorauf wrote of a "silent revolution in patronage" based upon the imposition of transparent and merit-based appointment processes, "while the traditional political machines, long the major consumers of patronage, are everywhere in hurried retreat... the naked *quid pro quo* no longer seems to many a natural and reasonable ingredient of politics" (Sorauf 1960: 28). Souraf's work was quickly supported by Ari Hoogenboom's *Outlawing the Spoils* (1961) and, by the turn of the century, Fiorina (2002: 22) felt confident enough to write that in nineteenth-century America "it paid—literally to participate in politics and government, with predictable results, positive and negative. But modern politics is much 'cleaner'." This was institutionally reflected in the creation of reflected civil service commissions, to assume responsibility for appointments from ministers in Canada, the United States, and the United Kingdom (in 1908, 1883, and 1855 respectively). The main implication being that persons with liberal democratic values would not tolerate the existence of those secretive, suspicious, and generally corrupt practices associated with CP (Table 19.1, second column).

This line of argument flows into two critical issues. First, in those countries that embraced liberal democratic frameworks (and the emphasis upon transparent and merit-based appointment procedures that form core tenets of modern conceptions of "good governance") patronage has not been eliminated but *recast*; second, to focus on stages of democratic development risks neglecting the continuing role that patronage plays in those countries that are not democracies or that remain hybrid regimes. Patronage arguably remains a more powerful form of political and social resource in those less developed countries, in which the absence of the social protections afforded by modern democratic states allows the continuation of crude "machine politics" (discussed further below). This is a critical point: CP generally feasts on the existence of scarcity, fear, and poverty or what Bruce Berman (1998) powerfully describes as "the politics of the belly." Understanding governance, in general, and the role of patronage as a form of socio-political and politico-administrative linkage (in particular) therefore brings with it the demand that scholars of governance shift their analytical and empirical focus away from those advanced liberal democracies that were most affected by the administrative fashion of New Public Management (NPM) toward a broader approach that is sensitive to the fact that of the 193 countries in the world only eighty-nine are considered "free" democracies. Authoritarian, theocratic, autocratic, or hybrid regimes arguably provide a rich counterpoint from which to understand and conceptualize the role of patronage as a steering mechanism, as a form of linkage, and as tool of regulatory governance with many dimensions. More importantly, they provide valuable empirical reference points through which to map, trace, and understand the transition from CP to OP systems and the demise of the traditional clientelistic patterns of control and coercion.

Having interrogated the concept of patronage at the conceptual level, and attempted to rescue it from the generally negative assumptions and connotations that have to some extent restricted research in this field, it is now necessary to locate these conceptual reference points within an empirical account of modern governance. The value of this shift from theory to practice is that not only does it confirm the bifurcation set out in Table 19.1, but by exploring the nature of "reach" and "permeation" vis-à-vis party patronage, it is possible to understand the manner in which a polity's mega-constitutional orientation (i.e. its core values, principles, and assumptions about the appropriate distribution of power) shapes certain behavioral trends and socio-political expectations. It is to this broader field of comparative politics that this chapter now turns.

2. PATRONAGE, GOVERNANCE, TRANSITION

This chapter is exploring the relationship between governance and patronage. The previous section offered a distinction between "closed" and "open" patronage regimes and dared to suggest that a trend from CP to OP may have occurred due to a range of factors, and, as a result, although the link between patronage and governance had not been broken the link between patronage and corruption possibly has. The aim of this section is to move from theory to empirics by briefly examining the manner in which patronage has been deployed as a tool of governance in three countries, in order to add further weight to this chapter's argument about the dangers of not questioning "self-evident truths" about not only patronage and governance but also the governance *of* patronage. It therefore draws on insights from a range of disciplines (comparative politics, development studies, social anthropology, etc.) in order to deepen our understanding of governance as a form of linkage. Comparative analysis is by its very nature something of an intellectual balancing act between breadth and depth, and achieving an acceptable balance within the restrictions of a book chapter is a challenging endeavor. Nevertheless the cases of Qatar, Thailand, and the United Kingdom provide a range of contrasting dimensions, not least in relation to democratic governance, as they are defined by Freedom House (respectively) as an "authoritarian regime," a "partly free" hybrid regime, and a "free" and developed democracy. At the very least these cases allow the chapter to interrogate empirically those arguments that were made about the role of patronage as a form of linkage and a tool of governance in the previous section. Put slightly differently, each of these cases allows us to stress-test mainstream assumptions about the relationship between patronage and governance on the one hand, and patronage and democracy on the other.

Qatar

To study patronage is to basically study the distribution of power and resources. Qatar, like many of the oil states, is therefore a distinctive case study due to its immense natural resources in the form of oil and gas. Qatar's GDP of around $100 billion a year, with a population of just 1 million, make it one of the wealthiest countries in the world. This wealth has shaped the nature of governance–patronage–democracy linkage by facilitating a "rentier effect" based upon: an absence of taxation; greater spending of patronage, which tends to dampen demands for democratization; and the emergence of politically dependent social groups. Qatar does not, therefore, provide a case of *party* politics but a closely related and highly relevant example of *elite/family* patronage with ramifications for conceptualizing governance relationships.

The fact that Shaykh Hamad's assumption of power in 1995 was predicated on the promise of introducing far-reaching democratic reforms represented a potentially seismic shift in Qatari politics. In 2003, after several significant reforms surrounding elections and participation, Qataris went to the polls and overwhelmingly approved a new constitution, Article 1 of which commits Qatar to being "a democratic" country. Nevertheless, progress toward a functioning democracy appears to have stalled. The parliamentary elections that were promised for 2005 have yet to take place and traditional patterns of rule based upon a reliance on personalized patronage networks continue to remain intact. The existence of large oil revenues lubricates a regime type, as Onley and Sulayman (2006) illustrate, in which goods and services are provided at an artificially low price, and the ruling elite are able to dispense resources in order to sate political demands or potential opposition. "The discovery of oil and the flooding of the coffers of the state with rent income" Kamrava (2009: 417) argues "has only expedited and strengthened the ruling elite—meaning the state's ability to expand and deepen its patronage networks across Qatari society."

Of particular significance has been the rapid creation of a range of well-funded, semi-governmental, semiprivate institutions by the government, including the Qatar Charity and the Qatar Foundation, in order to provide a structural network of patronage positions into which the children of the amir and close friends could be placed in order to consolidate the elite control of society. The state and the ruling elite have therefore become synonymous and indistinguishable in the Qatari context. A rich mixture of hereditary monarchy, family networks, co-option, and clientelism generally ensures a depoliticized society in which demands for democracy are usually eviscerated through the state–society linkage afforded by patronage networks (and oil revenues). Levels of corruption are also reduced by the simple fact that levels of pay and state benefits are generous and, therefore, to corrupt a biblical lesson, "the shepherd has little need to eat his sheep."

The promotion of close and trusted family or tribal members to senior positions within the state and semi-state in order to ensure the survival of the ruling elite is a form of statecraft that is intimately bound-up with the maintenance of CP and has formed part of a regional pattern of governance in the Middle East for many decades (see Herb 1999; Alsharekh 2007). The uprisings across North Africa and the Middle East in 2011 suggest that many of the social pressures that drove Souraf's "silent revolution" may be surfacing across the region. Younger generations are not only better educated and less deferential but are also technologically connected to the expectations of established democracies and are, as a result, more willing to protest against corruption and the suffocation of job opportunities by closed patronage systems. Developments in North Africa and the Middle East and the possibility of democratization processes therefore encourage us to examine whether the demise of authoritarian regimes automatically lead to a shift from CP to OP or simply to cosmetic changes that veil the injection of a different elite (i.e. CP–CP).

Thailand

The previous subsection presented Qatar as a regime in which governance was engineered and maintained through a system of CP. Thailand provides a similar model of bureaucratic colonization using a system of CP but what makes this a particularly interesting case is the manner in which the rhetoric of democratization and "good governance" have been deployed as a veil through which to disrupt and dislocate traditional arenas of bureaucratic power and, in their place, install new arenas of party patronage. The transition from military-authoritarian rule in Thailand to a semi-democratic or hybrid state has therefore not brought with it a transition from CP to OP but has simply seen the use of preexisting patronage networks by a new elite (and, as a result, it remains a fragile democracy).

The modern history of Thailand is indelibly linked to notions of "bureaucratic authoritarianism" in which deference and loyalty trump merit and transparency. The withdrawal of the military from day-to-day politics in the 1990s and the ascendancy of a new business class within a pre-democratic political culture led to the emergence of new forms of corrupt and clientelistic behavior. The turn of the millennium brought with it two major reforms that sought to rebuild public confidence in politics by shifting from a CP to an OP system. First, a new constitution established a raft of new independent regulatory agencies charged with rooting-out corrupt behavior and activities (Constitutional Court, National Committee on Human Rights, State Audit Commission, Election Commission, National Counter Corruption Commission). In order to protect the independence and legitimacy of these new constitutional watchdogs not only were vacancies advertised publicly but the Senate of Thailand was also required to undertake US-style confirmation hearings on all appointees. The second reform focused on widespread bureaucratic reform and the need to "reinvent government" in order to respond to the popular belief that the state had become too slow, cumbersome, inflexible, and corrupt (see Bidya 2006). The election of Thaksin Shinawatra as prime minister in 2001 therefore brought with it a rhetorical commitment to creating a transparent, merit-based, and entrepreneurial approach to the business of government that would deliver a clear shift from CP to OP.

The outcome of both reform processes (the first democratic in focus, the latter administrative) reveals not only a rhetoric–reality gap but also the importance of patronage as a tool of governance (irrespective of whether it is engineered to deliver sectional or public benefits). The process of "Thaksinization" of the state did not deliver a transition from CP to OP but simply a transition in who controlled the patronage networks. The new constitutional regulators were rapidly colonized by Thaksin in a process Mutebi (2008: 306) describes as "symptomatic of the cronyism, manipulation, political interference, and even outright capture by influential governmental figures" that they were designed to prevent. The broader reform of the bureaucracy delivered similar outcomes as components of the dominant "good governance" paradigm, as the research of Martin Painter (2006) has illustrated, like creating agencies, hiving-off functions, and establishing new regulatory agencies that were simply used to *politicize* the state and expand the patronage positions that lay in the hands of Thaksin and his supporters. Thailand therefore provides an interesting case of the repackaging of CP rather than a transition to OP; this forces us to examine a polity where a transition has genuinely occurred—the United Kingdom.

United Kingdom

A power-hoarding political system founded upon party government, the existence of a large and complex sphere of semi-state organizations, the existence of around 20,000 public appointments within the gift of national politicians, and a welter of newspaper articles and think-tank pamphlets bemoaning cronyism, nepotism, and endemic corruption may well combine to convince the casual observer that the United Kingdom exhibits a classic CP system in which the state monopolizes access to jobs and services, and in which elected officials have discretion in the allocation of jobs and services at the disposal of the state (see, for example, Adam Smith Institute 2009; Centre for Policy Studies 2000). The reality is, however, quite different. Since the introduction of an independent regulatory system for public appointments in 1995 the reach and permeation of politicians' appointment powers have been subject to wave after wave of reforms that have each in their own way reduced party patronage and delivered a transition from CP to OP. This transition is based upon three main institutional reforms (for a detailed review see Flinders 2009).

First, the introduction of a vast regulatory system enforces many of the dimensions highlighted in the third column of Table 19.1 (e.g. transparency, merit-based, open interviews, etc.). The role of politicians is constrained to devising the initial job specification at the beginning of the process and then selecting from a limited shortlist of candidates at the end. Very often politicians are presented with just two or even just one candidate and although theoretically they could reject the shortlist, in reality this rarely happens due to a combination of lack of time and knowledge on the part of the appointee plus an awareness that the rejection of a shortlist (irrespective of the actual reasons) will inevitably be defined by the media as evidence of corruption, sleaze, and cronyism.

The second element of this reform process focuses on the creation of a vast raft of independent appointment commissions to either regulate the public appointments system or, in some areas, to actually make senior public appointments without any political involvement at all. The topography of the state in the UK therefore includes the Appointments Commission, Judicial Appointments Commission, Supreme Court Appointments Commission, Public Appointments Commission, and the House of Lords Appointments Commission. The governance of patronage has therefore involved the creation of a vast tier of independent regulatory bodies since the mid-1990s, and since the turn of the millennium these have been complemented by a shift in the balance of power between the executive and legislature that has focused very sharply on patronage powers. The final element of the transition from CP to OP has therefore been the introduction of pre-appointment hearings for a large number of the most senior public appointments, and in some cases the empowerment of the relevant scrutiny committee with a statutory veto over the minister's favored candidate (see Maer 2008). The discretion of government ministers has thus been further constrained by the knowledge that any favored candidate must also be willing and able to survive an appearance before a generally aggressive and partisan scrutiny committee in the House of Commons.

The aim of this section has been to demonstrate the relationship between governance, patronage, and regulation in a range of political systems. The focus on Qatar, Thailand, and the United Kingdom provides just a flavor of this relationship and could profitably have been expanded and deepened to include, for example, the manner in which the Cambodian People's Party has utilized party patronage in order to develop and augment its dominant position (see Un 2005); the evolving nature of traditional patron–client networks in Southern Europe and South America (see, for example, Pappas 2009); or the use of patronage in order to engineer power-sharing relationships within the broader state sector in consociational polities (see van Thiel 2011). What each of these cases reveals is the role of patronage as a critical steering mechanism or linkage between politicians and the increasingly complex and disaggregated govern-ance networks through which they are required to deliver public goods. These cases also pose distinctive questions about the changing nature of regulation vis-à-vis patronage and governance at two distinct levels. First, in relation to the use of patron-age by politicians as a form of regulatory control mechanism over the bureaucracy, based upon the appointment of trusted individuals to strategic posts within the infra-structure of the state. And second, in relation to the growth of independent regulatory bodies to actually police the use and prevent the abuse of patronage powers by politi-cians. The link between patronage and regulation as a facet of modern governance therefore has both *internal* and *external* dimensions that each in their own way fits within broader debates concerning what Vibert labels "the rise of the unelected" (2007), Keane's (2009) sees as "monitory democracy", and Roberts (2010) deconstructs as the "logic of discipline." It is to these broader issues and particularly the theme of regula-tory governance that we now turn.

3. REGULATORY GOVERNANCE AND PATRONAGE

Governance is a concept that spans a number of worlds (e.g. academic, public, political) and it may not be overstating the case to suggest that it has emerged as the über-concept of contemporary times. As a result, state-of-the-art analyses, like Bell and Hindmoor's *Rethinking Governance* (2010), encourage us to approach the topic from a range of view-points (through networks, through associations, through persuasion, etc.) in order to clarify the boundaries and implications of the concept. This chapter has attempted to contribute to this agenda by examining the role of patronage as a vital control or coordi-nation mechanism through which politicians can attempt to retain an element of con-trol over increasingly fragmented state structures. Patronage as a resource, as a form of power, and as a means of reconciling the centrifugal and centripetal pressures of govern-ing can be deployed through a number of processes and for a number of purposes and this chapter has attempted to reveal these through a distinction between *closed patron-age* (CP) and *open patronage* (OP). This distinction was then developed by examining a polity in which CP dominates (Qatar), where a transition from CP to OP was promised but not developed (Thailand), and where a far-reaching shift in the power and capacity of politicians can be identified (United Kingdom). The role of this final section is to deal with the *so what?* question by exploring some of the broader implications of this chap-ter's focus on patronage. The global financial crisis, increasing public expectations, and the need to tackle climate change and resource depletion—to mention just a few major challenges—conspire to emphasize the capacity of politicians to control, coordinate, and regulate an increasingly fluid and interdependent institutional terrain and for this reason this section highlights the relationship between patronage and emergent models of regulatory governance, and focuses on three interrelated issues (multi-level govern-ance, democratic governance, and the logic of discipline).

Marks and Hooghe's (2004) "contrasting visions of governance" forms a central ele-ment of contemporary debates regarding the emergent framework of multi-level gov-ernance (MLG) (see, for example, Piattoni 2010). Type I MLG focuses on a relatively small number of general-purpose governing levels or tiers (and might therefore more accurately conceived of as multi-level govern*ment*); Type II MLG by contrast focuses attention on the vast array of quasi-autonomous bodies, independent commissions, and public–private partnerships that have emerged around Type I structures and are increas-ingly responsible for the regulation and delivery of public policy. The theory of multi-level governance, however, has rarely focused on the nature of the linkages and relationships between Type I and Type II organizations and for this reason arguably remains more of a proto-theory than a fully fledged analytical lens. Focusing on rela-tionships rather than forms emphasizes the role of patronage as the bond or link between Type I and Type II, and the basis of both formal and informal connections.

From this argument it is just a small (analytical) step to Bevir's book *Democratic Governance* (2010a) and his identification of the need for "new governing strategies to span jurisdictions, link people across levels of government and mobilize a variety of stakeholders" (2010b: 2). At the heart of this chapter has been an argument that patron-age is not necessarily undemocratic but can in fact be deployed in order to develop new opportunities for public participation and political recruitment. *Open* patronage pro-vides a method of linking and spanning that has simply not received a great amount of scholarly attention. The residual dilemma, however, rests in reconciling the use of patronage within a democratic structure—a dilemma that has been laid out in Keane's *The Life and Death of Democracy* (2009) and Crouch's *Post-Democracy* (2004). The argu-ment of this chapter is that there is no dilemma as long as closed patronage systems mutate into open systems due to the manner in which the procedures and values of the latter locate both the powers of the appointee and appointed back within the contours of democratic oversight.

Placing patronage powers back within the sphere of public scrutiny brings us neatly to a final focus on regulatory governance and the "logic of discipline." The "logic of disci-pline" encapsulates a lack of trust in elected politicians and brings with it a preference for depoliticized agencies, boards, and commissions on the basis that reducing the power of politicians will curb their self-interested behavior while also solving the "cred-ible commitment" dilemma that Majone's work (2001) on the regulatory state has pro-moted with such vigor. The wholesale acceptance of the "logic of discipline" is clearly represented in relation to the creation of a range of independent appointment commis-sions in the UK as a new element of regulatory governance. This raises two core issues. First, although scholars such as Majone and Keane recommend or welcome the creation of "regulatory states" or "monitory democracies" (different terms for very similar phe-nomena) in which appointed ABCs (i.e. agencies boards and commissions) exert ever greater powers over elected politicians, they say far less about *quis custodiet custodes*; second, the "rise of the unelected" in the form of powerful independent appointment commissions with powerful regulatory or plenipotentiary powers risks further eviscerating the governing capacity of politicians. Governing capacity is a requirement of any political system and this chapter has attempted to highlight the role of patronage as a form of linkage across a variety of dimensions. The "logic of discipline's" emphasis not just on a transition from CP to OP but then to a form of depoliticized patronage in which politicians enjoy few formal powers and very limited discretion (as has occurred in UK and is being considered in a number of Continental European states) risks hollowing-out not just the state, in terms of the central steering capacity of politicians, but also democracy, in terms of narrowing the realm of activity for which elected politicians are responsible. It is for exactly this reason that this chapter has sought to emphasize the relationship between governance and patronage.

References

Adam Smith Institute. 2009. *Hunting of the Quango*. London: ASI.

Alsharekh, A. (ed). 2007. *The Gulf Family: Kinship, Policies and Modernity*. London: Saqi.

Bell, S. and Hindmoor, A. 2010. *Rethinking Governance*. Cambridge: Cambridge University Press.

Berman, B. 1998. Ethnicity, patronage and the African state. *African Affairs* 97: 305–341.

Bevir, M. 2010a. *Democratic Governance*. Princeton: Princeton University Press.

Bevir, M. 2010b. *The Sage Handbook of Governance*. Los Angeles: Sage.

Bidya, B. 2006. Autonomisation of the Thai state. *Public Administration and Development* 26: 27–34.

Centre for Policy Studies. 2000. *Quango Report*. London: CPS.

Crouch, C. 2004. *Post-Democracy*. Cambridge: Polity

Daalder, H. 1966. Parties, elites and political developments in Western Europe. In J. LaPalombra and M. Weiner (eds.), *Political Parties and Political Development.*. Princeton: Princeton University Press, 43–77.

Fiorina, M. 2002. Parties, participation and representation in America. In I. Katznelson and H. Milner (eds.), *The State of the Discipline*. New York: Norton, 511–541.

Flinders, M. 2009. *Delegated Governance and the British State*. Oxford: Oxford University Press.

Harling, P. 1996. *The Waning Of "Old Corruption"*. Oxford: Oxford University Press.

Herb, M. 1999. *All in the Family*. Albany: SUNY Press.

Hoogenboom, A. 1961. *Outlawing the Spoils*. Urbana: University of Illinois Press.

Kamrava, M. 2009. Royal factionalism and political liberalization in Qatar. *Middle East Journal* 63: 401–420.

Keane, J. 2009. *The Life and Death of Democracy*. London: Simon and Schuster.

Kopecky, P. and Scherlis, G. 2008. Party patronage in contemporary Europe. *European Review* 16: 355–371.

Kopecky, P., Scherlis, G. and Spirova, M. 2008. *Conceptualising and Measuring Party Patronage*. Committee on Concepts and Methods, Working Paper, Series No. 25.

Maer, L. 2008. *Parliamentary Involvement in Public Appointments*. London: House of Commons Library.

Majone, G. 2001. Two logics of delegation. *European Union Politics* 2: 103–122.

Marks, G. and Hooghe, L. 2004. Contrasting visions of multi-level governance. In I. Bache and M. Flinders (eds.), *Multi-Level Governance.*. Oxford: Oxford University Press, 15–30.

Muller, W. 2006. Party patronage and party colonization of the state. In R. Katz and W. Crotty (eds.), *Handbook of Party Politics*, London: Sage, 189–194.

Mutebi, A. 2008. Explaining the failure of Thailand's anti-corruption regime. *Development and Change* 39: 147–171.

Onley, J. and Sulayman, K. 2006. Shaikly authority in the pre-oil Gulf. *History and Anthropology* 17: 189–208.

Painter, M. 2006. Thaksinisation or managerialisation? *Journal of Contemporary Asia* 36: 26–47.

Pappas, T. 2009. Patrons against partisans. *Party Politics* 15: 315–334.

Piattoni, S. 2010. *The Theory of Multi-Level Governance*. Oxford: Oxford University Press.

Roberts, A. 2010. *The Logic of Discipline*. Oxford: Oxford University Press.

Sorauf, F. 1960. The silent revolution in patronage. *Public Administration Review* 20: 28–34.

Un, K. 2005. Patronage politics and hybrid democracy. *Asian Perspective* 29: 203–330.

Van Biezen, I and Kopecky, P. 2007. The state and the parties. *Party Politics* 13: 235–254.

Van Thiel, S. 2011. Party patronage in the Netherlands. In P. Mair, P. Kopecky, and M. Spirova (eds.), *Party Government and Party Patronage*. Oxford: Oxford University Press, 00–00.

Vibert, F. 2007. *The Rise of the Unelected*. Cambridge: Cambridge University Press.

CHAPTER 20

....

GOVERNANCE AND STATE CAPACITY

....

FELICITY MATTHEWS[*]

THE concept of state capacity is a perennial issue in political analysis, and a range of competing interpretations exists (see Pierre and Painter 2005 for a detailed analysis). Briefly put, state capacity can be seen as comprising a range of distinct, but interrelated, facets. At the broadest level, state capacity is the capacity to create and maintain order over a sovereign territory, which in turn entails the capacity to enact measures to protect its sovereignty such as raising taxes, declaring war, and administering legal justice. State capacity also hinges upon its democratic authority and legitimacy, wherein the state's right to make authoritative decisions is popularly accepted, and the state is still routinely viewed as the main organ through which problems are solved and society is steered. Finally, in terms of its administrative capacity, state capacity can be defined as the capacity of the state to effectively achieve its chosen policy outcomes, wherein the exercise of power and deployment of resources, such as those detailed above, are key. The issue of state capacity is at the heart of the governance narrative, and this chapter develops an alternative "waves of governance" lens (cf. Chapter 3, this volume) in order to distinguish between two clear waves of opinion regarding state capacity within the field of governance. In terms of understanding state capacity, the first wave argued that the state had been "hollowed out" (e.g. Rhodes 1997) and that its capacity to control the policy process had diminished, as emerging interactions between the state, the market, and civil society had resulted in "governance mechanisms which do not rest on recourse to the sanctions and authority of government" (Stoker 1998: 17). Yet whilst first-wave theories of governance enjoyed a period of ascendency, wherein they were perceived as a "paradigmatic orthodoxy" (Marinetto 2003: 597), a second wave of scholarship emerged that rejected the diminution of state capacity and instead sought to emphasize the continuing resource advantage of states to argue for a countervailing process of "filling in."

However, the dichotomous debate between the "hollowing out" versus "filling in" of the state risks overstating the observable exogenous challenges to state capacity, and in turn neglecting the ways in which states have both consciously and unconsciously sought to fetter their powers, or have missed opportunities to shore up their capacity (for a notable example, see Pierre 2009). This chapter will therefore seek to address this lacuna and also highlight the cognizant and unconscious roles of political actors in shaping state capacity—a third wave of governance. Whilst the "wave" analogy developed in this chapter has a different focus from that set out by Rhodes earlier in this volume, the "third wave" metaphor deployed does complement the notion of a "third wave" developed by Rhodes (Chapter 3) by highlighting the prevailing influence of governing norms and traditions, and the ways in which these have affected the capacity of states to respond to the challenges associated with the governance narrative. The "third wave" approach to understanding state capacity therefore seeks to challenge the implicit assumption within first and second wave accounts that state capacity has been externally drained in order to posit a more refined way of understanding the redistribution of power within modern polities. As the heart of the third wave within this chapter is "the paradox of state capacity," which identifies a simultaneous process wherein states have sought to develop new forms of state capacity whilst at the same time transferring key control levers to a range of semi-independent organizational forms. Viewed from this perspective, the paradox of state capacity develops the analytical leverage of existing scholarship, whilst illuminating the linkage between governance debates and broader socio-political concerns including rising public expectations, antipolitical public sentiment, the impact of the global financial crisis, and the emergence of significant and long-term policy challenges such as climate change.

The chapter is divided into three sections. The first section presents an overview of the first wave literature, which characterizes the state as a hollowed-out and fragmented entity. The second section outlines the challenge presented by the second wave literature, wherein focus upon the active deployment of state resources prompted greater circumspection regarding the capacity of the state. Reflecting upon the first and second waves of governance, the third section develops an alternative way of understanding state capacity: of governance as understood through the paradox of state capacity.

1. THE FIRST WAVE OF GOVERNANCE: THE EROSION OF STATE CAPACITY

The first wave of governance developed in response to the unintended consequences of the New Public Management (NPM) reforms of the 1980s and 1990s, which swept across a range of liberal democracies, as detailed by Klijn and colleagues (Chapter 21, this volume). NPM reforms were driven by the three "E"s—economy, efficiency, effectiveness—to "achieve more bang for each buck" (Osborne and Gaebler 1992). Ambitious reforms were undertaken within many states, intended to reform state–economy relationships by collapsing the public–private distinction. Yet, rather than reducing bureaucracy and overcoming perceived inefficiencies, NPM reforms served to disaggregate the state, which led it to become increasingly dependent upon the internationalized economy and on non-state actors, many of which existed beyond traditional state boundaries. The net effect of these changes highlighted tensions between traditional aspects of state capacity vis-à-vis supranational and international actors, and its monopoly of the policy process and service provision. Whilst governments were still formally responsible for the policy process, they were perceived as increasingly less capable of acting alone, an idea captured in a series of metaphors that highlighted the "hollowing-out" (Rhodes 1997), "unravelling" (Hooghe and Marks 2003), and "unbundling" (Pollitt and Talbot 2004) of the state. In responding to this critique, first wave governance scholars suggested a new role for the state, wherein government was no longer "the cockpit from which society is governed" (Klijn and Koopenjan 2000: 136). In turn, it was suggested that the function of the state should be one of "steering, not rowing" (Osborne and Gaebler 1992: 25), which implied that whilst no longer the central source of economic and political dynamism, the state retained an important, if residual, role in defining goals and making priorities on behalf of the polity.

First wave accounts were predominantly society-centered, suggesting that the ordered hierarchy which had enabled states to control the policy process and achieve their desired outcomes had been usurped by the fluid and dynamic exchanges of power that take place within broader society. Challenging the hegemony of states, first-wave narratives highlighted the "large number of decision-making arenas...differentiated along both functional and territorial lines...interlinked in a non–hierarchical way" that engaged in the governance transactions (Eberlein and Kerwer 2004: 128), which in turn reduced the control capacity of the state and led to "more autonomy and self-governance for social institutions" (Kickert 1993: 204). The notion of self-governance was echoed by a number of scholars. Rhodes, for example, argued that governance is exercised through "self-organizing, inter-organizational networks" (1997: 15). Similarly, Jessop rejected the "rigid polarisation between the anarchy of the market and the hierarchy of imperative co-ordination" in favor of "heterarchy"; a form of "horizontal self-organization among mutually dependent actors" (1999: 15). In turn, as shown by Zehavi (Chapter 17, this volume), the crowding of the policy arena was seen as necessitating the development of new "soft" policy instruments, based upon deliberation, bargaining, and compromise-seeking, which stood in direct contrast with the "hard" top-down, command-and-control instruments traditionally deployed by hierarchical states.

First wave theories therefore perceived the state as a single entity within a multiplicity of actors, which undermined its capacity to control the policy process. Salamon, for example, suggested the emergence of a "third party government", as "government simply lacks the authority and independence to enforce its will on other actors in the way [steering] implies" (2002: 609). Indeed, in the context of political and economic globalization, some argued that the "growing complexity and continuing disaggregation" led to the complete bypass of the nation-state, resulting in a system of "governance without government" (Rosenau 2000: 184). Thus, "where states were once the masters of markets, now it is the markets, which, on many crucial issues, are the masters over the governments of states" (Strange 1996: 4). The challenge to state capacity has been further exacerbated by the commonly experienced emerging disjuncture between declining levels of popular trust in politicians on the one hand, and increasing expectations upon the public sector on the other, which has undermined the capacity of elected officials to provide effective political leadership (Togeby 2003), and, in turn, the democratic legitimacy of the state to intervene in society. Whilst factors feeding into this growing cynicism have been discussed at length elsewhere (notably Torcal and Montero 2006; Hay 2007), Stoker suggested that popular disenchantment may actually be symptomatic of the challenges associated with the governance narrative, "reflect[ing] a sense of frustration because, in an interdependent world, politics has struggled to respond with a new effective practice" (Stoker 2010: 56).

Whilst there was broad agreement regarding the transformation of state capacity, a number of first wave scholars remained circumspect regarding the absolute diminution of the state. Pierre and Peters argued that the marginalization state capacity was "exaggerated at best and misleading at worst," and risked replacing previous state-centric discourses with "an image of governance in which institutions are largely irrelevant." Citing a range of evidence, including the raft of non-governmental organizations engaged in the policy process and the emergence of public–private networks, they suggested that in order to meet the challenge of governance, most states have "deliberately relaxed their organizational cohesion in order to enable different segments of the state to develop their own forms of exchange" (2000: 75–82). The resource advantage afforded to states was also highlighted by Chhotray and Stoker, who suggest that states are often able to "dominate the exchange" within governance transactions (2009: 22), reflecting the importance of "meta-governance" as a form of state capacity, as discussed by Torfing (Chapter 7, this volume). Nonetheless, despite such caveats, the limits to state capacity were still emphasized; for example Pierre and Peters maintained that the state was no longer the preeminent actor whose "centrality can be taken for granted," as the "actual role which the state plays in governance is often the outcome of the tug of war between the role the state *wants to play* and the role which the external environment *allows it to play*" (2000: 26, 82, emphasis mine).

2. THE SECOND WAVE OF GOVERNANCE: THE RESURGENCE OF STATE CAPACITY

Whilst the role of the state in governance transactions was contested at the margins, an implicit assumption of first wave theories of governance was that challenges—such as the crowding of the policy arena and the transfer of key powers away from the state—were externally imposed, which rendered state capacity contingent upon exogenous forces. Yet, numerous scholars rejected the relevance of the first wave of governance, arguing that there is "no reason to assume that the rise of governance necessarily leads to a decline of government" (Anderson 2004: 10). The explanatory power of the first wave of governance as a theory of state capacity was fiercely critiqued by second wave scholars. Goetz, for example, stated that "governance as a concept is neglectful of political power," rendering it "ill-positioned to capture how governments establish new needs for government intervention and build up institutional capacity" (2008: 263). Theories of the regulatory state, for example, argued that rather than diminishing state capacity, the hiving-off of policy functions and the decentering of the state actually led to states developing innovative forms of, often "soft," regulation to extend and consolidate their steering capacity (e.g. Braithwaite 2000; Moran 2003; Scott 2004). Indeed, Bell and Hindmoor asserted that the governance debate was "overblown," arguing that the society-centric focus inherent in many governance narratives fails to recognize the role of structurally advantaged state institutions within governance frameworks, which effectively "rule[s] out the use of state authority" as a subject of analysis (2009: xiii, 70). A similar argument was advanced by Walters, who suggested that the pluralistic epistemology inherent within many governance narratives results in "a certain ambivalence towards politics," which serves to "depolitici[ze] events that we should see more properly as questions of power," and in turn downplays the role of the state in governance transactions (2004: 36). In turn, Smith argued that the state's marginalization in theories of governance was part of a broader pattern of the theoretical neglect of the state that has occurred since the 1980s, as "discussion of the state has been subsumed into discussions of globalization and governance" (2009: 6).

A forceful challenge to the perceived erosion of the state capacity was developed in the British context, as numerous scholars have instead relocated the role and power of the state to suggest its transformation as opposed to its diminution. Reflecting on the creation of a raft of coordinating units and tasks forces in the center of government, Taylor countered the notion of "hollowing-out," as the ability of the government to promote joined-up government and assert itself upon networks suggest that a process of "filling-in" has occurred (2000: 51). The notion of filling-in was echoed by Marinetto, who cites the British government's efforts at boosting the coordination capacities of the Cabinet Office and the Treasury as evidence of "further centralization rather than the haemorrhaging of power and authority" (2003: 600). Similarly, Moran argued that rather than precipitating a hollowing out of the British state, the rise of state intervention through regulation had enabled the state to extend and consolidate its reach into new and existing areas of social and economic life (Moran 2003). Such evidence prompted scholars to highlight the privileged position of government, suggesting that its "centrality and control of resources means that it continues to have dominance over other organizations and networks" (Smith 1999), and that "in dealing with non-core actors it is certainly not lacking in extensive power and resources of its own" (Holliday 2000: 173). Theories of governance were therefore criticized for "ignor[ing] the fact that networks do not always emerge fully formed and complexity may enable the centre to dominate networks by determining their operational parameters and objectives," which in turn "must question the extent to which the state has hollowed out" (Taylor 2000: 51).

Empirical evidence from other geopolitical settings was also deployed to reject the diminution of state capacity. In their study of environmental policy instruments across nine jurisdictions, Jordan, Wurzel, and Zito found that the patterns of instrument use (including regulation, voluntary agreements, and market-based instruments) had remained relatively stable since the 1970s, and in turn that there had been "no wholesale and spatially uniform shift from government to governance" (2005: 490). There was also evidence that many states had responded to the challenges of governance in the post-NPM era, by developing innovative tools to retain their control of policy-making and implementation through improved coordination (6 2004: 103). Canada and the Netherlands, for example, successfully developed outcome-focused targets to drive the policy process; and attempts to affect coordination led to greater inclusiveness in the decision-making process in the Netherlands and Sweden, with central government shaping the overarching framework (Ling 2002). Indeed, it has been suggested that the emergence of complex new policy areas have precipitated "enlargement of state compe-tencies," providing opportunities for states to reassert their political authority and inter-ventionist capacity (Anderson 2004: 10). Climate change, for example, is an issue that requires international cooperation and solutions, but sovereign states remain crucial to policy-making due to the numerous political and institutional tools at their disposal, such as tax instruments and regulation, and because of their democratic capacity to make and impose difficult decisions upon society. Similarly, the global financial crisis of 2008 onwards led to a range of states reasserting themselves upon hitherto seemingly unaccountable economic markets, including the nationalization of failing banks in the United Kingdom (e.g. Northern Rock) and the United States (e.g. Citigroup); increases in public investment to stimulate growth in Australia, Canada, and Mexico; special sup-port for the automobile industry in Germany and the United Kingdom; and programs of tax relief and/or cuts in Spain, Portugal, and Turkey. Thus, during the crisis the state "appears to have ripped up the script and reassert[ed] itself as the only agent capable of preventing economic collapse" (Thompson 2010: 130). It has also been argued that despite falling levels of political satisfaction, the state is still the main conduit between electors and the elected, and there is "little, if any" evidence of a "downgrading of elected politicians and the progressive marginalization of parliaments" (Goetz 2008: 263).

Together, such evidence prompted second wave scholars to criticize the universaliz-ing tendencies of the first wave of governance. In particular, the relevance of first wave theories to those states that did not embrace the NPM revolution with the same enthusi-asm as countries such as the United Kingdom and New Zealand has been challenged. In a comprehensive analysis of the take-up of NPM-inspired reforms across Western Europe, Goetz suggested that the United Kingdom is "atypical in its response to the scepticism and sense of overload in the 1970s and 1980s, and the extent to which the gov-ernment narrative is relevant to state practice in the UK may also be atypical." Placing the UK at one end of the spectrum of reforms, and France at the other (as France under-went a wide-ranging program of left-wing-inspired state expansion in the early 1990s), he argued that "neither case was, however, typical of West European developments more broadly," and that the "driving forces behind the spread of governance" were not uniform (2008: 260–261). In addition to the apparent lack of transferability to other geopolitical settings, first wave theories of governance have also been criticized for being historically parochial. "Governance theory exists in twentieth-century political thought like a fish in water: it would be unlikely to breathe elsewhere" (Marinetto 2003: 597). More specifically, it has been argued that first wave theories are built on false assumptions regarding a zenith of state capacity in the past; a "myth" that Pierre sought to debunk (Chapter 13, this volume). Walters criticized governance for employing a "somewhat exaggerated conception of the power of the post-war welfare state," which in turn served to overstate "the novelty and significance of many of the phenomena of 'steering,' 'regulation,' and indirect control typically grouped under the rubric of 'new' governance" (2004: 38). This was echoed by Bell and Hindmoor, who argued that "those writing about governance risk exaggerating not only the extent to which governments now govern through markets, associations and community engagement, but also governments' past dependence upon hierarchy" (2009: 8).

Reflecting upon such evidence, second wave scholars argued that first wave theories neglected the opportunities that governance provided for state innovation in terms of shoring up its policy-making and implementation capacity, as shown by Sørensen (Chapter 15, this volume). Indeed, "viewed from this perspective, evidence of governance... is not an indication of a shift away from government; rather, it signals a shift towards government, as problems and decision-making authority move from the societal to the state sphere" (Goetz 2008: 263). Bell and Hindmoor argued that endogenous challenges to state capacity were overstated in governance, as states "have an authority, not possessed by any other actors, to choose governance rules," and that "having chosen which governance mechanism to employ, governments can also choose how to structure governance arrangements" (2009: 13). Reflecting on the phenomenon of depoliticization, whereby decision-making capacities have been devolved to non-governmental bodies, Flinders and Buller argued that it is "politicians who make decisions about what functions should be 'depoliticized,'" and it is politicians who "commonly retain significant indirect control mechanisms." In turn, they suggest that the devolution of key competencies away from state auspices is an entirely rational "defensive risk management technique," which "can help to insulate politicians in office from the adverse consequences of policy failure" (2006: 296–297). In a similar vein, Walters highlighted the way in which privatization was "a privileged policy initiative of many governments," arguing that the implicit passivity of concepts such as "complexification" and "interdependence" has meant that the governance narrative "misses" the fact that privatization is "a highly political strategy," instead treating it as a "natural, inevitable response to increasing complexity" (2004: 41). Similarly, in reflecting upon the notion of the regulatory state, Levi-Faur and Gilad argued that the state is "still a major pillar of the new order and leader in the creation and proliferation of nonstate mechanisms of control," and that "the debate on the decline of the state misses the important ways that public interest is re-asserted in the shadow" (2004: 114). Flowing out of this, it has been suggested that regulation can be seen "as a large subset of governance that is about steering the flow of events and behaviour, as opposed to providing and distributing" (Braithwaite, Coglianese, and Levi-Faur 2007: 3).

3. THE THIRD WAVE OF GOVERNANCE: THE RECONSTRUCTION OF STATE CAPACITY

So far, this chapter has shown that the first wave of governance has focused on the exogenous challenges to state capacity at the expense of an appreciation of the inherent resource advantage of the state. Yet, whilst the second wave draws attention to the unique resources at the disposal of states, and the ways in which states have sought their deployment to buttress their capacity, it does not sufficiently account for the unintended consequences of such activity, and the extent to which they have undermined the measures that were instead intended to shore up the capacity of the state. The remainder of this chapter will therefore seek to move beyond the "filling-in" versus "hollowing-out" debate in order to furnish analysis with a more refined appreciation of state capacity, which highlights both the conscious and unconscious roles of political actors in shaping their own context, and in turn the interplay between the range of exogenous challenges and state-led reforms. There is little doubt that governing in the twenty-first century is messy and complex, drawing in a multiple of actors— who exist at overlapping (and sometimes competing) geopolitical jurisdictions—into the policy cycle. This complexity is exacerbated as the state expands into important new policy areas, such as the management of global financial markets and the prevention of environmental degradation, which in turn stimulates popular expectations upon government.[1] And yet, whilst the *volume* and *scale* of these challenges to state capacity may be novel, the *governing implications* are not, and the effective management and coordination of a diversity of competing interests is a perennial and core task of government. Thus in arguing that the state has been hollowed out and its capacity eroded, first wave theories of governance overstate the criticality of this juncture and assume the existence of a unique historic milieu. In turn, the capacity of the state is more nuanced than its construction within theories of governance suggest. An implicit underlying assumption of the first and second waves of governance is that challenges to state capacity have been externally imposed, which renders capacity contingent upon exogenous forces. Even governance narratives that ascribe greater reflexivity to the state capacity, such as the theories of meta-governance discussed by Torfing (Chapter 7, this volume), arguably fail to sufficiently engage with the existence of agent volition and endogenous challenges, instead continuing to privilege the role of external drivers in framing governance transactions. For example, Sørensen and Torfing highlight the "isomorphic pressures to reshape public governance in accordance with the principles specified by the advanced liberal governmentality," which serve to "force politicians to rely on network-based policy processes and adjust to their new role as metagovernors" (Sørensen and Torfing 2009: 245).

The marginalization of the state, and the lack of volition ascribed to actors within its auspices, was partially rectified and rebalanced by second wave scholars, who highlighted the resources available to the state, and the capacity of actors to respond to their surroundings whilst rejecting the notion of a historically critical juncture. However, whilst it is important to recognize the resource advantage of the state, it is also necessary to understand that many of the constraints upon the effective exercise of state capacity are self-created, as political actors have inadvertently constructed proverbial rods for their own backs. Yet the existence of such unintended consequences has been largely under-explored, and it is therefore to the notions of volition and the unintended consequences of the exercise of agency that the remainder of this section will now turn. Many changes to state structures have been consciously instigated by state actors, and predicated upon seemingly rational assumptions. Thus, it is states who ultimately decide to implement programs of hiving-off and privatization; to introduce tools such as depoliticization; to reenter or reshape the political space through programs of regulation; and who have chosen to over-promise (although in some respects the ratchet effect of electoral politics often means that this is a self-fulfilling phenomenon). This rational volition has been recognized by several authors. Reflecting on the deregulation of global financial markets, for example, Thompson argued that those states that "eschewed more regulation did not do so because financial globalization made regulation impossible, but because they wanted to procure political gain from economic growth" (Thompson 2010: 140). The phenomenon of depoliticization has also been perceived as a logical response to the pressures of modern governance, implemented to reduce the risk of political overload (e.g. Birch 1984) and to "insulate politicians in office from the adverse consequences of policy failure" (Flinders and Buller 2006: 296–267). This conception of the state as a rational actor is not new, and in the field of public policy such forms of delegation and hiving-off have been perceived as desirable tactics for politicians who are tied into a short-term electoral cycle—as they serve to discourage politicians from making unpopular decisions—and for enhancing the credibility of policy commitments through the deployment of independent expertise (Majone 2001).

In many cases, therefore, states have actively sought to cede or delegate powers. Yet, whilst many of the changes implemented by the state have been intended to shore up and maximize its capacity to govern, they have resulted in a range of unintended consequences such as the emergence of new, multiple veto points and the creation of rubber levers at the center of government. It is therefore possible to identify a "paradox of state capacity" to reflect this simultaneous—yet counterintuitive—drive by national governments to assume responsibility for a vast range of new and emergent policy problems whilst delegating responsibility for day-to-day delivery to a vast flotilla of semiautonomous organizational units. In turn, it highlights the way in which this seemingly rational process has instead served to exacerbate constraints upon state capacity; to paraphrase Pierre and Peters (2000: 2) the paradox of state capacity argues that governments are the "very root and cause" of governing problems, a phenomenon that has been exacerbated as politicians have increasingly lost the confidence of the public. The impact of this self-inflicted, yet unintended, damage has been striking described by Pierre:

> These parallel processes would at first glance appear to contradict each other. The explanation to the paradox seems to be that there is a concentration in the political executive of those powers and capabilities that are still controlled by the centre. It is also clear that devolution and presidentialization both undercut the position of representative institutions. Institutional reform, either in a structural or a procedural sense, thus seems to take place everywhere except in the traditional institutions of political representation. (2009: 599)

A significant cause of this paradox is the path-determinacy created by prevailing governing norms and traditions, which have shaped the response of state actors to internal and external challenges. Indeed, the fact that Smith's assertion that "the structures of government have changed, and the value system governing those structures need to change with them" (1999: 254) remains relevant over a decade later underlines an unwillingness, or perhaps inability, within states to reassess the appropriateness of traditional governing norms. The failure of states to fundamentally appraise the extent to which their institutional structures are fit for purpose in relation to modern governance has made these challenges without adequate resolution, with the potential for future governance failure. The inherent path-determinism of traditional governing structures and institutions, and the continued predominance of the cultural norms embedded within, has served to blinker state actors and inhibit their ability to constructively engage with the (sometimes unintended) consequences of their actions. This suggests the emergence of an institutional deficit, wherein many of the tools and instruments created emerge as being insufficiently robust and unable to effectively fulfill their intended functions. The criticality of the disjuncture between state structures and governance challenges has been exacerbated as states have sought, or been compelled by growing public expectations, to move into important new policy areas including climate change mitigation and adaptation, and the reregulation of global financial markets. In turn, the disjuncture has been further widened by growing public disenchantment, as governments fail to deliver on the vast range of commitments and pledges that they undertake, which simultaneously undermines the state's authority and legitimacy, whilst encouraging governments to undertake further governing and policy functions in order to recapture their democratic mandate as the main hub of societal steering, thus further exacerbating the risk of failure.

Conclusion

In the context of governance, states need to "learn the appropriate operating code which challenges past hierarchical modes of thinking" (Stoker 1998: 24). However, whilst the context of governing has changed, the continued influence of the traditional, hierarchical models of state power suggests that states have still to fully acknowledge the emergent topography and its impact upon state capacity. And yet the maintenance of traditional assumptions about state power and its ability to control the policy process is exactly what threatens its capacity in the long term. The challenge for states is thus in ensuring the continued responsiveness of its strategic political leadership and institutional apparatus in order to avoid the worst excesses of fragmentation, hollowing out, and, ultimately, governance failure. Success, however, is ultimately predicated upon an active acknowledgement of the complexity and interdependencies across the political arena, and the way in which this interacts with state resources and structures. Herein lies the greatest challenge of all for states: the willingness to undertake a fundamental reappraisal of the normative underpinnings of state capacity, due to their incompatibility with the emergent political landscape. Failure to do so will result in a fundamental disjuncture, thereby diminishing the capacity of the state to exercise its powers and deploy its resources in order to achieve key policy goals.

NOTES

* The author would like to acknowledge the support of the Leverhulme Trust (Grant Reference EFC/2009/0224).
1. Döhler develops a similar argument in relation to regulation to suggest that the increasing "social consciousness of risks" continues to stimulate popular and political demand for increased risk regulation (2010: 530).

REFERENCES

6, P. 2004. Joined-up government in the Western world in comparative perspective: A preliminary literature review and exploration. *Journal of Public Administration Research and Theory* 14: 103–138.

Anderson, H. 2004. Governance and regime politics in copenhagen. Eurz Lecture 16, University of Copenhagen.

Bell, S. and Hindmoor, A. 2009. *Rethinking Governance—The Centrality of the State in Modern Society*. Cambridge: Cambridge University Press.

Birch, A. 1984. Overload, ungovernability and delegitimation: The theories and the British case. *British Journal of Political Science* 14: 135–160.

Braithwaite, J. 2000. The new regulatory state and the transformation of criminology. *British Journal of Criminology* 40: 222–238.

Braithwaite, J., Coglianese, G. and Levi-Faur, D. 2007. Can regulation make a difference? *Regulation and Governance* 1: 1–7.

Chhotray, V. and Stoker, G. 2009. *Governance Theory: A Cross-Disciplinary Approach*. Basingstoke: Palgrave Macmillan.

Döhler, M. 2010. Regulation. In M. Bevir (ed.), *The Sage Handbook of Governance*. London: Sage, 518–534.

Eberlein, B. and Kerwer, D. 2004. New governance in the European Union: A theoretical perspective. *Journal of Common Market Studies* 42: 121–142.

Flinders, M. and Buller, J. 2006. Depoliticisation: Principles, tactics and tools. *British Politics* 1: 293–318.

Goetz, K. H. 2008. Governance as a path to government. *West European Politics* 31: 258–279.

Hay, C. 2007. *Why We Hate Politics*. London: Polity.

Holliday, I. 2000. Is the British state hollowing out? *Political Quarterly* 71: 167–176.

Hooghe, L. and Marks, G. 2003. Unravelling the central state, but how? Types of multi-level governance. *American Political Science Review* 97: 233–243.

Jessop, B. 1999. The dynamics of partnership and governance failure. In G. Stoker (ed.), *The New Politics of Local Governance in Britain*. Oxford: Oxford University Press, 11–32.

Jordan, A., Wurzel, R. and Zito, A. 2005. New environmental policy instruments in the European Union: From government to governance? *Political Studies* 53: 477–496.

Kickert, W. 1993. Complexity, governance and dynamics: Conceptual explorations of public network management. In J. Kooiman (ed.), *Modern Governance*. London: Sage, 191–204.

Klijn, E-H. 2012. The Impact of Governance. In D. Levi-Faur (ed.), *The Oxford Handbook of Governance*. Oxford: Oxford University Press.

Klijn, E-H. and Koopenjan, J. 2000. Public management and policy networks: Foundations of a network approach to governance. *Public Management* 2: 135–158.

Levi-Faur, D. and Gilad, S. 2004. The rise of the British regulatory state. *Comparative Politics* 31: 105–124.

Ling, T. 2002. Delivering joined-up government in the UK: Dimensions, issues and problems. *Public Administration* 80: 615–642.

Majone, G. 2001. Two logics of delegation: Agency and fiduciary relations in EU governance. *European Union Politics* 2: 103–122.

Marinetto, M. 2003. Governing beyond the centre: A critique of the Anglo-governance School. *Political Studies* 51: 592–608.

Moran, M. 2003. *The British Regulatory State: High Modernism and Hyper-Innovation*. Oxford: Oxford University Press.

Osborne, T. and Gaebler, D. 1992. *Reinventing Government*. Reading, MA: Addison-Wesley.

Pierre, J. 2009. Reinventing governance, reinventing democracy? *Policy and Politics* 37: 591–609.

Pierre, J. and Peters, B.G. 2000. *Governance Politics and the State*. Basingstoke: Palgrave Macmillan.

Pierre, J. and Painter, M. 2005. Unpacking policy capacity: Issues and themes. In M. Painter and J. Pierre (eds.), *Challenges to State Policy Capacity*. Basingstoke: Palgrave Macmillan, 1–18.

Pollitt, C. and Talbot, C. (eds.) 2004. *Unbundled Government: A Critical Analysis of the Global Trends to Agencies, Quangos and Contractualisation*. London: Routledge.

Rhodes, R. A. W. 1997. *Understanding Governance*. Buckingham: Open University Press.

Rosenau, J. 2000. Change, complexity and governance in a globalizing space. In J. Pierre (ed.), *Debating Governance: Authority, Steering and Democracy*. Oxford: Oxford University Press, 167–200.

Salamon, L. M. 2002. The tools approach and the new governance: Conclusions and implications. In L. M. Salamon (ed.), *The Tools of Government: A Guide to New Governance*. Oxford: Oxford University Press, 600–620.

Scott, C. 2004. Regulation in the age of governance: The rise of the post-regulatory state. In J. Jordana and D. Levi-Faur (eds.), *The Politics of Regulation in an Age of Governance*. Cheltenham: Edward Elgar, 145–174.

Smith, M. J. 1999. *The Core Executive in Britain*. Basingstoke: Macmillan.

Smith, M. J. 2009. *Power and the State*. Basingstoke: Palgrave Macmillan.

Sørensen, E. and Torfing, J. 2009. Making governance networks effective and democratic through metagovernance. *Public Administration* 87: 234–258.

Stoker, G. 1998. Governance as theory: Five propositions. *International Journal of Social Science* 155: 17–28.

Stoker, G. 2010. The rise of political disenchantment. In C. Hay (ed.), *New Directions in Political Science*. Basingstoke: Palgrave Macmillan, 43–63.

Strange, S. 1996. *The Retreat of the State: The Diffusion of Power in the World Economy*. Cambridge: Cambridge University Press.

Taylor, A. 2000. Hollowing out or filling in? Task forces and the management of cross-cutting issues in the British Government. *British Journal of Politics and International Relations* 2: 46–71.

Thompson, H. 2010. The character of the state. In C. Hay (ed.), *New Directions in Political Science*. Basingstoke: Palgrave Macmillan, 130–147.

Togeby, L. 2003. *Magt og demokrati I Denmark (Power and Identity in Denmark)*. Aarthus: Aarthus Universitetsforlag.

Torcal, M. and J. R. Montero (eds.) 2006. *Political Dissatisfaction in Contemporary Democracies. Social Capital, Institutions and Politics*. London: Routledge.

Walters, W. 2004. Some critical Notes on "Governance." *Studies in Political Economy* 73: 27–45.

CHAPTER 21

THE IMPACT OF GOVERNANCE: A NORMATIVE AND EMPIRICAL DISCUSSION

ERIK HANS KLIJN,
ARWIN VAN BUUREN, &
JURIAN EDELENBOS

1. INTRODUCTION: WHAT IS THE IMPACT OF GOVERNANCE?

Now that governance has spread around the world and is becoming the major perspective on decision-making, policy-making, implementation, and service delivery in political sciences and public administration, the question whether it works seems one of the most important to ask. However, it is not easy to give a straightforward answer.

The first reason is that traditional ways of evaluating outcomes are not very suitable for applying to network governance. Since governance processes take place in networks of diverse actors within fragmented systems (we will call them governance networks in this chapter) it is difficult to evaluate the outcomes by using tools that consider the present goals of a single actor, as is often done in evaluations. But it is also difficult because the ambitions of governance networks are high and highly varied (Rhodes 1997; Kickert, Klijn, and Koppenjan 1997; Osborne 2010).

Why governance networks?

Since the word governance has by now been associated with so many meanings, it is impossible to discuss its impact without first narrowing down what it is. In this chapter we mean by governance more or less horizontal forms of steering, which take place in networks of essentially interdependent actors (public, private, and non-profit). We shall use the word governance for the interaction process and governing attempts that take place in these networks. This conception of governance is close to what Rhodes describes in Chapter 3, this volume.

There are several arguments mentioned in the literature why governance networks should be "the answer" to steering problems in our society (see, for instance, Kooiman 1993; Rhodes 1997; Pierre and Peters 2000; Koppenjan and Klijn 2004). Governance can be seen as a way to organize collective action in a context that can be characterized by mutual dependencies and veto power, uncertainty and ambiguity, and a growing gap between government and society. Governance viewed from the perspective of management can be helpful in overcoming these problems:

1. Because actors have important resources (strengthened by the growth of out-sourcing, etc.), they are indispensible for policy-making and therefore interdependent networks of them emerge (Pierre and Peters 2000; Agranoff and McGuire 2003). Governance approaches are aimed at mobilizing mutually dependent actors, bringing them together and organizing fruitful interaction in order to achieve coordinated action.

2. In decision-making processes information is often incomplete, inconsistent, or conflicting and actors have their own interpretation of this information. Controversies easily result in report wars and information stagflation. Governance approaches are aimed at realizing authoritative knowledge and processes of frame reflection in order to overcome the problems of uncertainty and ambiguity (Van Buuren 2009; Koppenjan and Klijn 2004)

3. A part of the literature on governance networks emphasizes that those processes allow for more direct involvement of stakeholders and thus could contribute to narrowing the growing gap between citizens and politicians (Hirst 2000; Sørensen and Torfing 2007), or are at least an indication of the search for new forms of citizen participation (Lowndes, Pratchet, and Stoker 2001; Young 2000). Whether these new forms of including stakeholders by various processes conflict with the classical representative institutions or not is a debate between scholars (see, for an overview, Klijn and Skelcher 2007).

This chapter: exploring three types of outcomes

These three promises of governance thus point to three possible "impacts." They presume that governance (as a way of organizing collective action) can be successful in:

- mobilizing actors, bringing them together, and organizing effective interaction;
- organizing authoritative and inclusive "content" with which binding decisions can be taken;

- providing additional means for accountability and a voice that can add to the legitimacy of governmental action.

In this chapter we look at these three dimensions of impact that governance could have. We explore the literature on each and try to assess what the empirical findings tell us about it. Before we address these questions we first elaborate on the issue of how we can evaluate outcomes in networks, the fundamental question we raised at first in this section.

2. DEFINING THE IMPACT OF GOVERNANCE: AN ALTERNATIVE PERSPECTIVE

Governance networks pose three problems for the evaluator compared with the traditional ways of evaluating. The first problem is that there are a lot of actors involved and they all have their own perceptions, goals, and strategies. It is not clear which goal the evaluator should take as a starting point, especially if more than one public authority is involved. If one looks at interactions in policy-making and management with multiple actors, it seems logical to evaluate from a multi-actor perspective, too. It is highly unlikely, however, that the different actors will have a collectively formulated goal at the beginning of policy interactions that can serve as a keystone for evaluation.

But there are other problems too. Governance processes are complex and knowledge is spread among actors. This means that a lot of information which could contribute to a satisfactory way of dealing with societal problems (and provide interesting solutions) has to be mobilized and assembled during the interaction. If actors change their perceptions or goals as a result of additional information this can be an indication of learning, and learning is considered a very important interorganizational benefit (Mandell 2001). These learning effects cannot be taken into account if the evaluation is only carried out according to an a priori stated and static goal.

And last, but certainly not least, there is the problem of exclusion. If a policy is being formed and implemented in networks of actors there is a danger of closeness and group-think. It is possible that actors will agree on packages of goals that lay the burden of the costs outside the network onto actors who are not represented or onto the next generation. Evaluation criteria of outcomes in networks should take these aspects into account.

Finding multi-actor evaluation criteria

Some of the network literature comes with suggestions for multi-actor measurement. This means that evaluation has to be carried out by some method of weighting the benefits for various actors (a kind of balance sheet) or by assessing their satisfaction afterward. Thus an outcome of interactions in networks is good if it satisfies a significant number of the actors. This not only takes into account their preferences and goals, but it also measures whether they consider the time and energy spent on achieving those outcomes has been worthwhile (Kickert, Klijn, and Koppenjan 1997).

There is of course a danger that actors will suggest rationalizations to hide their potential dissatisfaction with outcomes. A solution might be to take a wider look at the range of potential outcomes (Koppenjan and Klijn 2004) and to try to relate these to the interests of the various actors. In this way the evaluator could produce a kind of shortlist or balanced scorecard of effects and how they relate to actors' interests, goals, or perceptions. This evaluation step is not without its problems because one has to decide which effects have to be taken into account and how they should be weighted. In that sense evaluation can become an ongoing discussion between evaluator and evaluated. Furthermore, we have to bear in mind the warning of Sabatier and Focht (2005) that stakeholders—due to their good feeling about the process of collaboration—have a greater satisfaction with the outcomes than can be justified by the actual quality of the result. This means that the evaluator has to evaluate critically all possible effects and attribute them to the involved actors.

The notion of weighted interests or satisfying actors meets the need to take learning processes and the shifting of goals into account, as well as the need to evaluate outcomes in a multi-actor setting. It does not, however, provide a solution for the exclusion problem. To address this, evaluation also needs to pay attention to the way the process is conducted. In other words it is important that third parties have access to the decision-making process, that processes have legitimacy, and that they meet criteria of juridical and procedural scrupulousness. These process norms are thus important additional criteria by which to judge outcomes of interaction in network and interorganizational settings. If the decision-making is open to actors who are interested or have a stake in the issue and if the actors involved are satisfied, then this usually creates favorable conditions for ensuring that outcomes are socially good and preferable.

3. GOVERNANCE AND PROCESS: TOWARD SUPPORTING AND BINDING INTERACTIONS

All over the world, local, regional, and national governments are exploring various governance approaches ranging from public–private partnerships to civic engagement and citizen participation. All of these meet the interdependency character of complex decision-making processes: actors need each other's resources to establish outcomes that satisfy them. In this section we discuss in what way these approaches have an impact on two key dimensions: collaboration and trust-building.

Collaboration

Governance is mostly applied to prevent the use of veto power that results from resource dependencies (Koppenjan and Klijn 2004; Edelenbos and Klijn 2006). Complex decision-making processes affect a multitude of different actors, who typically have the means to, at least partially, influence the outcome of their activity (Agranoff and McGuire 2003; O'Toole 1988). By involving these actors at an early stage, it is hoped that the use of veto power will decrease and support for the decisions will increase. This should accelerate decision-making processes, because stakeholders are satisfied and will not wish to cause delay through opposition. Moreover, stakeholder involvement prevents people going to court and averts lengthy legal procedures (Edelenbos 2005). Some scholars stress that through governance the chance of policy errors is reduced: "The fundamental concept behind (...) participation is that the experts in a bureaucracy do not have all the information, or perhaps even the right type of information, for making policy (...). Therefore, isolating important decisions from public involvement will generate policy errors." (Peters 1996: 55) Wicked problems in networks need to involve many actors because they are difficult to tackle and therefore there is a need to draw on the knowledge and other resources of the various actors (Koppenjan and Klijn 2004).

In this way, variety within governance also raises the quality of decisions. "No single actor, public or private, has all knowledge and information required to solve complex dynamic and diversified problems; no actor has sufficient overview to make the application of needed instruments effective" (Kooiman 1993: 4). Through the mobilization and use of a broad array of values, knowledge, and resources, the problem-solving capacity is enlarged. Since, with governance, not only different perspectives on and ideas about problems and solutions are interacting in the process, but also multiple types of knowledge, information, skills, and experience are employed, a better analysis of the problem is possible and better solutions can be created. Collaborative processes stress the need for integral processes that involve different sectors and domains. Collaboration seems inescapably to induce the integration of values, interests, knowledge, and policy domains. Through integral and collaborative decision-making a broader and better assessment can take place of the different perspectives on the problem at hand, and of policy alternatives that may solve it (Young 2000; Huxham and Vangen 2005).

A similar argument can also be found in the literature on new forms of democracy that stresses the importance of openness and accessibility (Dryzek 2000). There is empirical evidence that governance by networks does indeed have an impact on processes. Edelenbos and colleagues (2010), for example, conducted quantitative research on a large enough sample to show that the openness of the governance process for stakeholder participation has a significant impact on the outcome of governance networks. They looked at complex forms in Dutch environmental projects, and considered a number of outcomes in which support and ongoing interaction were important parameters. In the study, substantial outcomes, like innovation, the integrated character of the solution, and so on, were also assessed. The research results showed that collaboration in governance networks had positively significant effects on the perceived process and substantial outcomes of complex decision-making processes (Edelenbos, Steijn, and Klijn 2010).

Generating trust

An important impact involving stakeholders in governance is the generation of trust. Where in other areas, like the New Public Management (NPM), trust is not important since performances are achieved by contracts, performance indicators, penalties, and monitoring, it is important in governance processes.

Trust refers to a positive expectation that other actors refrain from opportunistic behavior even when they have the opportunity to do so (see, e.g. Klijn 2010a). Trusting another actor means that one is willing to assume an open and vulnerable position. It is expected that the other actor will refrain from opportunistic behavior even if the chance arises (Deakin and Wilkinson 1998). Thus, the actors believe that each will take the other's interests into account (Nooteboom 2002), showing that trust is significantly important. It thus reduces strategic uncertainty, reduces the necessity of complex contracts, and enhances the possibility that actors will share information and develop innovative solutions. The literature on trust (see Lane and Bachman 1998; Nooteboom 2002) emphasizes this.

Intensifying interaction in governance networks can generate trust because actors are getting better acquainted. Mutual understanding and a collective history is developed (Lane and Bachman 1998). Then a positive cycle can be generated in which the facilitation of interaction through trust leads to more frequent interaction between actors (both formal and informal), and in return further develops and strengthens trust. Trust is developed and solidified in joint interaction and so can enhance network performance (Huxham and Vangen 2005; Klijn 2010a).

Empirical research shows that the level of trust (that is, high or low trust) has an influence on network performance. Klijn and colleagues (2010a), for example, have shown in their quantitative research on complex environmental projects that a higher level of trust generated in governance networks has a positive impact on process and content outcomes.

4. GOVERNANCE AND CONTENT: TOWARD AUTHORITATIVE INFORMATION AND SHARED MEANINGS

Governance networks involve actors with different ways of knowing in processes of decision-making (van Buuren 2009). This variety of frames and values implies that realizing consensus is a difficult job. However, to attain consensus about ambitions and interests it is equally important to achieve convergence between the level of perceptions, values, and cognitions (van Buuren and Nooteboom 2010). A significant set of strategies within governance networks aims at deliberation, frame reflection, and joint image-building. That means that—when we try to evaluate the impact of governance—we have to look at the effects of governance on learning (Sabatier 1993), reflection (Rein and Schön 1996), and inclusion (Feldman et al. 2006).

Governance networks can be a means of organizing a process of learning or reflection. We can distinguish three levels of joint action within frame reflection:

1. *Fact-finding*: Actors are willing to organize a collaborative process of formulating factual questions, supplying information, conducting researches, and interpreting results;
2. *Problem-defining*: Actors are willing to look at ways of coordinating their ideas to form a shared definition that can be used as a legitimate basis for decision-making;
3. *Image-building*: Actors are willing to adjust their own values and beliefs in the light of a collectively framed problem.

The governance literature is rather exhaustive in dealing with the impact of governance on learning and reflexivity. Most of the studies are highly conceptual and deal with single case studies. And, until now, the impact of governance on processes of frame reflection shows mixed results.

Joint fact-finding

The first level, fact-finding or collaborative analysis, can prevent a battle between actors in the interpretation and analysis of information concerning the problem and solutions, which could seriously hamper the accomplishment of collective agreements. It provides actors with a common basis of information, which can be used to interpret the problem at hand, the consequences of various solutions, and the remaining uncertainties. In particular it can generate a more complete account of the information necessary for a deliberative choice. The literature also promises that including other sources of knowledge, rather than just expertise, can contribute to the quality, the legitimacy, and the creativity of public decisions (Koppenjan and Klijn 2004).

Such cooperation is quite successful as a means to realize consensus about the factual information used within a decision-making process, when a couple of conditions are met. These conditions have to do with an intermediate level of conflict, a prestigious forum, which is dominated by scientific norms, neutral funding, consensus decision rules, and so on (Sabatier and Focht 2005). Busenberg (1999) compares collaborative styles of analyses and adversarial styles and concludes that the latter are much less able to contribute to legitimate decision-making. There seems to be a positive correlation between carefully involving stakeholders in the processes of fact-finding and the consensus about this information and its actual use (van Buuren and Nooteboom 2010).

Joint problem-defining

The second level, problem-defining, goes one step further and results ideally in a commonly shared definition of what the problem is, how urgent it is, and thus which issues have to be tackled. It presupposes a collaborative dialogue in which actors engage in an open and constructive dialogue where they can draft a broadly shared problem definition (Lubell 2000).

There are indicators that governance contributes to joint problem-defining and conflict resolution (Lubell 2005). Organizing participatory processes can have a significant impact upon the mutual understanding between actors, mutual trust, and a sense of reciprocity. Diversity between actors can be a valuable source of creativity (van Buuren and Loorbach 2009).

Joint image-building

The third level is the deepest learning level. It presupposes the mutual adjustment of policy beliefs between actors with their own frames and values. Consensus achieved at this level can form a stable basis for collaborative problem-solving in the long run. According to Sabatier, this level of learning is aimed at the lasting adjustment of the deep core beliefs of actors (Sabatier 1993). On this level they change their own belief system, and not only for the duration of the process.

This most significant level of frame reflection is, however, the most difficult to attain. It requires convergence between the deep-rooted convictions and values of the actors to develop mutual trust and a team spirit. Therefore Sabatier (2003) concludes that learning on this level normally requires external shocks which challenge existing perceptions and values and trigger a process of transformative learning (Fischer 2009).

At least four remarks are necessary to nuance the learning effects of governance practices:

- First of all, frequently a pragmatic attitude dominates. A pragmatic agreement between conflicting interests is often seen as more relevant then realizing a sustainable consensus about values and problem frames. Collaborative processes are focused on problem-solving and therefore it is quite rare that enough energy is devoted to organizing a time-consuming and demanding process of frame reflection and learning;
- Second, a newly established consensus about values and problem frames is often only temporary and not very lasting because of the erratic dynamics and the unpredictable strategic choices of actors within complex governance. The outcomes of learning processes are only temporary equilibriums within an ongoing process (van Buuren and Gerrits 2008);
- Third, the selection of actors within governance oftentimes forms a serious restriction for the reflexive impact of governance practices. The participating

actors are frequently only those who are willing to reflect and to learn. Other actors—with fundamentally different opinions—are often not activated within collaborative processes;

- Finally, the fact that most participants within governance practices are representatives from their home organization means that the reflexive impact of governance practices remains usually limited to these representatives and does not easily spread among the corporate actors within a network.

5. GOVERNANCE AND DEMOCRACY: TOWARD MORE LEGITIMATE GOVERNMENTAL ACTION

Governance is aimed at involving stakeholders as we saw in the third section. But the reasons for that are not only connected to veto power and mobilizing resources which governments do not have themselves. Networks are also supposed to enhance the influence of citizens or even to bridge the gap between politicians and citizens, although there are many critical accounts about the problems of representation in governance (Chapter 36, this volume). Lowndes and colleagues write: "enhancing public participation lies at the heart of the Labour government's modernization agenda for British local government" (Lowndes, Pratchet, and Stoker 2001). Bekkers and colleagues (2007) observed, when they studied policy documents of four European countries, that the strongest rhetoric in the documents is the one that wants to provide citizens with more power over their service delivery and decision-making. So, one of the intended impacts of the trend toward governance certainly is enhancing the influence of citizens and other stakeholders, although we must recognize that this aim is not equally strongly represented in all the literature and practices of the various countries. The US literature for instance tends to emphasize issues of efficiency and coordination. The political decisions on goals are often taken in specific arenas or taken as a given, after which the complex coordination process to implement that decision in a network of actors proceeds. Complexity in that perspective mainly concerns the coordination problem and not the problem of how to deal with the various value judgments different actors have.

The democratic impact of governance can be threefold (see van Buuren, Klijn, and Edelenbos 2011):

- It can add to the *accountability* for decision-making by broadening the range of possibilities for actors to be involved and to take responsibility;
- It can provide additional opportunities for *voice*, whereby citizens are able to influence and add their input to processes of decision-making (see Chapter 37, this volume);
- It can contribute to additional rules and procedures, which improve the quality of *due deliberation*.

Accountability

In a world of mutually dependent actors the notion of accountability is often prob-lematic. One governmental actor may be formally accountable for what is done and have to justify what has happened in processes of decision-making or service delivery, but in practice a complex chain of interactions between a variety of actors constitutes these processes. Governance—seen as an acknowledgement of this complexity—attempts to organize other, more horizontal and informal forms of accountability (in addition to the formal political accountability of officeholders). In this way various stakeholders get the opportunity to become actively involved in processes of decision-making and implementation, and are thereby able to check the legality and legitimacy of officials' actions.

However, many authors recognize tensions between the idea of representative democ-racy with a more vertical accountability structure, and governance processes, which have a more horizontal accountability. This tension is confirmed by empirical research (Klijn and Koppenjan 2000; Edelenbos 2005; Skelcher, Mathur, and Smith 2005). In the literature about governance networks we find four main positions concerning this issue (Klijn and Skelcher 2007):

1. Incompatible position: Classical representational democracy is incompatible with governance processes because these are a threat to the position of democratic institu-tions. The authority and accountability of these institutions is "hollowed out" by the involvement of other stakeholders.

2. Complementary position: Governance processes provide for additional links to society and can perfectly coexist beside classical democratic institutions. Elected offi-cials are provided with more information, political officeholders retain their important place but accountability is shared.

3. Transition position: Governance networks offer greater flexibility and efficiency and will gradually replace representative democracy as the dominant model in the net-work society.

4. Instrumental position: Governance networks provide a means for democratic institutions to increase their control in a situation of societal complexity. By setting performance targets or constraint, elected officeholders secure their dominant position.

Voice

In the literature distinctions are made between the depth of participation (the intensity and influence of stakeholders), the width of participation (how many stakeholders are allowed to participate (see Berry, Portney, and Thomson 1993), and the different levels of participation (Arnstein 1971), all of which lead to conceptualizing the idea of voice.

The literature on participation stresses that involvement of stakeholders enhances the support for policy proposals, because more information becomes available (see Berry, Portney, and Thomson 1993). Stakeholders get a better picture of the arguments used in order to arrive at a certain assessment and decision. When actors are involved earlier and more intensely in the governance process, it is expected that they will be more willing to accept both the process and the decisions reached. However, empirical research shows that involvement only is not enough to ensure support. Stakeholders want to recognize themselves in the decision reached. Their input must be traceable in the results (Edelenbos 2005; Mayer and Edelenbos 2005).

Due deliberation

This source of democratic legitimacy is strongly connected to the argumentation process that takes place and not to its relation with official democratic institutions (accountability) or the degree of stakeholder involvement (voice). The criteria come from deliberate theories of democracy. An essential aspect of most forms of deliberative democracy is that preferences are not fixed, but can change in a debate. Democratic legitimacy, the way in which the interaction and the deliberation between actors are organized, is important. In this sense, they is tied to procedures and rules of the game (Goodin 1996) about fair entry, reciprocity, freedom of coercion, open information access, and transparency, which should result in a good argumentation process (Edelenbos 2005). Explicit and clear rules of the game within governance networks are an important building block for realizing due deliberation. Governance can secure rules and help to guide actions in a situation that is often very complex and chaotic because, in an institutional sense, governance processes are always messy. Many different rules seem to apply because governance involves many actors, decisions, and policy sectors.

Is the promise fulfilled?

An important question is then: Are these ambitions of governance fulfilled to enhance democratic legitimacy in general and the influence of citizens and stakeholders specifically? This question is not so easy to answer since the empirical material is not large. But from the existing research the first impression is that, despite the aims to improve democratic legitimacy by enhancing stakeholder involvement, many governance processes still often have a more technocratic domination. Despite the ambitions to be flexible and involve stakeholders in the formulation of policy it is still the original government goals that seem to dominate the discussions and have an impact on stakeholders. The quality of the discussions are lower than the expectations (see Griggs and Howard 2007; Skelcher, Mather, and Smith 2005). In general the formal accountability rules are met in the sense that representative bodies do have to approve decisions in the end but they do not seem to have a very large influence on the content (see Skelcher, Mather, and Smith

2005; Edelenbos and Klijn 2006), although that may be quite different in the case of city alderman (see Le Galès 2001). In practice we often find a situation where multiple criteria of legitimacy can be found in governance (van Buuren, Klijn, and Edelenbos 2011).

Thus we may conclude that although the intentions for more participation and different forms of democratic legitimacy are there, the practice is only slowly emerging and falls a bit short of the high expectations of the policy documents. A lot of the research stresses that governance practices and representative democracy have to be reconciled by clear process rules, that the participation has to be broad and meaningful enough to make it worthwhile, and that it is important that the impacts of deliberation are visible (Dryzek 2000; Edelenbos 2005).

6. Conclusion and discussion: how governance can make an impact through management actions

We have seen that impacts or results of governance can be looked for in three areas: process, content, and legitimacy. With regard to the first two issues, we saw that governance networks can indeed contribute to the quality of the process and the content of public decision-making, as far as the literature and research on governance can inform us.

At the same time the picture is somewhat mixed. Organizing collaboration and participation can also result in very time-consuming and indecisive processes. Organizing joint content can also result in negotiated nonsense, that is, in content that is agreed by the participating actors, but which is scientifically invalid.

This ambiguity is much stronger when we look at the issue of legitimacy. Here we see serious problems when it comes to synchronizing governance networks with traditional government and representative democracy; traditional ways of organizing legitimacy are difficult to align with new, participative forms of organizing it.

At the same time it is clear that the positive impacts of governance networks cannot be achieved without active and continuing network management or meta-governance. Because networks consist of many actors with different values, and because actual outcomes are achieved by complex interactive processes among autonomous actors operating strategically, meaningful outcomes involve active nurturing, guiding, and managing. These are activities usually indicated by the concept of network management.

It is thus not surprising that many studies find relations between the outcomes of governance processes and active networking or network management activities. Agranoff and McGuire (2003: 123) conclude, in their study of how city officials work with other layers of government and organizations to develop their city economics: "From the perspective of the city government, there is not one cluster of linkages to manage but several clusters—some horizontal some vertical, and some that include both within a context of a single project or program." This statement is very much in keeping with the scarce large N studies on network management and outcomes of governance networks. Huang and Provan (2007) have shown that network involvement, or network embeddedness, is positively related to social outcomes. Meier and O'Toole (2007) have shown that networking by district managers is positively correlated with the performance of the district. Klijn and colleagues (2010b) show that there is a very strong correlation between the perceived outcomes of respondents in environmental projects and the intensity and number of network management activities they report.

Thus, network management activities seem crucial if governance is to have an impact. Although governance networks are to a degree self-regulatory (Rhodes 1997), they sometimes need a push in the right direction by management activities.

References

Agranoff, R. and McGuire, M. 2003. *Collaborative Public Management: New Strategies For Local Governments*. Washington, DC: Georgetown University Press.

Arnstein, S. R. 1971. Eight rungs on the ladder of citizen participation. In S. C. Edgar and B. A. Passett (eds.), *Citizen Participation: Effecting Community Change*. New York: Praeger, 69–91.

Bekkers, V., Dijkstra, G., Edwards, A. and Fenger, M. 2007. *Governance and the Democratic Deficit: Assessing the Democratic Legitimacy of Governance Practices*. Aldershot: Ashgate.

Berry, J. M., Portney, K. E. and Thomson, K. 1993. *The Rebirth of Urban Democracy*. Washington, DC: The Brookings Institute.

Busenberg, G. J. 1999. Collaborative and adversarial analysis in environmental policy. *Policy Sciences* 32: 1–11.

Deakin, S. and Wilkinson, F. 1998. Contract law and the economics of interorganizational trust. In C. Lane and R. Bachman (eds.), *Trust Within and Between Organizations: Conceptual Issues and Empirical Applications*. Oxford: Oxford University Press.

Dryzek, J. S. 2000. *Deliberate Democracy and Beyond: Liberals, Critics, Contestations*. Oxford: Oxford University Press.

Edelenbos, J. 2005. Institutional implications of interactive governance: Insights from Dutch practice. *Governance* 18: 111–134.

Edelenbos, J. and Klijn, E. H. 2006. Managing stakeholder involvement in decision making: A comparative analysis of six interactive processes in the Netherlands. *Journal of Public Administration Research and Theory* 16: 417–446.

Edelenbos, J., Steijn, B. and Klijn, E. H. 2010. Does democratic anchorage matter? *American Review of Public Administration* 40: 46–63.

Feldman, M. S., Khademian, A. M., Ingram, H. and Schneider, A. S. 2006. Ways of knowing and inclusive management practices. *Public Administration Review* 66: 89–99.

Fischer, F. 2009. *Democracy and Expertise: Reorienting Policy Inquiry*. Oxford: Oxford University Press.

Goodin, R. E. (ed.) 1996. *The Theory of Institutional Design*. Cambridge: University of Cambridge.

Griggs, S. and Howard, D. 2007. Airport governance, politics and protest networks. In M. Marcussen and J. Torfing (eds.), *Democratic Network Governance in Europe*. Basingstoke: Palgrave, 66–89.

Hirst, P. 2000. Democracy and governance. In J. Pierre (ed.), *Debating Governance: Authority Steering and Democracy*. Oxford: Oxford University Press, 13–35.

Huang, K. and K. G. Provan. 2007. Structural embeddedness and organizational social outcomes in a centrally governed mental health service network. *Public Management Review* 9: 169–189.

Huxham, C. and Vangen, S. 2005. *Managing to Collaborate: The Theory and Practice of Collaborative Advantage*. London: Routledge.

Kickert, W. J. M., Klijn, E. H. and Koppenjan, J. F. M. (eds.) 1997. *Managing Complex Networks: Strategies for the Public Sector*. London: Sage.

Klijn, E. H. and Koppenjan, J. M. F. 2000. Public management and policy networks: foundations of a network approach to governance. *Public Management* 2: 135–158.

Klijn, E. H. and Skelcher, C. K. 2007. Democracy and governance networks: Compatible or not? Four conjectures and their implications. *Public Administration* 85: 587–608.

Klijn, E. H., Edelenbos, J. and Steijn, B. 2010a. Trust in governance networks: Its impact and outcomes. *Administration and Society* 42: 193–221.

Klijn, E. H., Steijn, A. J., and Edelenbos, J. 2010. The impact of network management on outcomes in governance networks. *Public Administration* 88: 1063–1082.

Klijn, E. H, Steijn, B. and Edelenbos, J. 2010b. The impact of network management strategies on the outcomes in governance networks. *Public Administration* 88: 1063–1082.

Kooiman, J. (ed.) 1993. *Modern Governance: New Government–Society Interactions*. London: Sage.

Koppenjan, J. F. M. and Klijn, E. H. 2004. *Managing Uncertainties in Networks: A Network Approach to Problem Solving and Decision Making*. London: Routledge.

Lane, C. and Bachman, R. (eds.) 1998. *Trust Within and Between Organizations: Conceptual Issues and Empirical Applications*. Oxford: Oxford University Press.

Le Galès, P. 2001. Urban governance and policy networks: On the boundedness of policy networks: A French case. *Public Administration* 79: 167–184.

Lowndes, V., Pratchet, L. and Stoker, G. 2001. Trends in public participation: Part 1 local government perspectives. *Public Administration* 76: 205–222.

Lubell, M. 2000. Cognitive conflict and consensus building in the National Estuary Program. *American Behavioral Scientist* 44: 629–648.

Mandell, M. (ed.) 2001. *Getting Results Through Collaboration: Networks and Network Structures for Public Policy and Management*. Westport: Quorum Books.

Meier, K. and O'Toole, L. J. 2007. Modelling public management: Empirical analysis of the management-performance nexus. *Public Administration Review* 9: 503–527.

Nooteboom, B. 2002. *Trust: Forms, Foundations, Functions, Failures and Figures*. Cheltenham: Edgar Elgar.

Osborne, S. P. 2010. *The New Public Governance: Emerging Perspectives on the Theory and Practice of Public Governance*. London: Routledge.

O'Toole, L. J., Jr 1988. Strategies for intergovernmental management: Implementing programs in interorganizational networks. *Journal of Public Administration* 11: 417–441.

Peters, G. P. 1996. *The Future of Governing, Four Emerging Models*. Kansas: University Press of Kansas.

Pierre, J. and Peters, B. G. 2000. *Governance, Politics and the State*. Basingstoke: Macmillan.

Rein, M. and Schön, D. 1996. Frame-critical policy analysis and frame-reflective policy practice. *Knowledge, Technology & Policy* 9: 85–104.

Rhodes, R. A. W. 1997. *Understanding Governance: Policy Networks, Governance, Reflexivity, and Accountability*. Buckingham: Open University Press.

Sabatier, P. A. 1993. Policy change over a decade or more. In P.A.Sabatier and H. C. Jenkins-Smith. (eds), *Policy Change and Learning*. Boulder, CO: Westview Press, 13–39.

Sabatier, P. A. and Focht, W. (eds.) 2005. *Swimming Upstream: Collaborative Approaches to Watershed Management*. Cambridge: MIT Press.

Skelcher, C., Mathur, N. and M. Smith. 2005. The public governance of collaborative spaces: Discourse, design and democracy. *Public Administration* 83: 573–596.

Sørenson, E. and Torfing, J. (eds.) 2007. *Theories of Democratic Network Governance*. Cheltenham: Edward Elgar.

van Buuren, M. W. 2009. Knowledge for governance, governance of knowledge. Inclusive knowledge management in collaborative governance processes. *International Public Management Journal* 12: 208–235.

van Buuren, M.W. and Gerrits, L. 2008. Decisions as dynamic equilibriums in erratic policy processes. *Public Management Review*,10: 381–399.

van Buuren, M. W. and Loorbach, D. 2009. Policy innovation in isolation: Conditions for policy-renewal by transition arenas and pilot projects. *Public Management Review* 11: 375–392.

van Buuren, M. W. and Nooteboom, S. 2010. The success of SEA in the Dutch planning practice: How formal assessments can contribute to collaborative governance. *Environmental Impact Assessment Review* 30: 127–135.

Young, I.M. 2000. *Inclusion and Democracy*. Oxford: Oxford University Press.

PART IV

ACTORS, STRATEGIES, AND GOVERNANCE STYLES

CHAPTER 22

NEW GOVERNANCE OR OLD GOVERNANCE? A POLICY STYLE PERSPECTIVE

JEREMY RICHARDSON

NATIONAL POLICY STYLES

THE simple concept of national "policy styles" (Richardson 1982) was meant to help identify the defining characteristics of how nations went about making public policy. It was based on the assumption that researchers could identify commonly used national "standard operating procedures" to which governments turned when solving public policy problems. In its original formulation, two main policy styles were identified, namely, *impositional* and *consensual*. Of particular relevance here was the linking of the consensual style to an emphasis on governing via extensive consultations with interest groups and other policy actors via policy communities and policy networks. These two "poles" (impositional and consensual) might be seen as *hierarchical* and *nonhierarchical* styles of governing.

Much has been written about the emergence of a new, nonhierarchical style of governing, namely, *governance* as opposed to *government*. The purpose of this chapter is not to explore the many meanings and definitions of this relatively new term. I am content with the definition formulated by Rod Rhodes, namely that the shift from government to governance is essentially a shift "from a hierarchical state to governance in and by networks" (Chapter 3, this volume). Thus, "new governance" is often presented as a new "style" of governing. A common argument in support of the (alleged) emergence of new governance is that societies have become more complex and that this complexity demands a new style of governing. Thus, Héritier and (Martin) Rhodes argue that "in a highly complex society, with problems extending across borders, central actors are unable to muster the knowledge required to shape effective instruments of intervention. They depend on the expertise and knowledge of private and local actors. *In these conditions, centralized and hierarchical steering is doomed to failure*" (Héritier and Rhodes 2011: x, emphasis added).

A subtext in the literature is the claimed decline in the effectiveness and legitimacy of traditional institutions of government. Thus, Bartolini argues that "governance practices and theory reflect the erosion of the role played by central government institutions (parliaments, executives and bureaucracies) and by central political actors (parties and unions), and the decline of public confidence in them" (Bartolini 2011: 4). The thrust of my argument is that the current focus on styles of "governance" is more a rediscovery of an aspect of governing that has been observed for many decades and an old intellectual fashion, than a new research finding or new theorizing in an attempt to explain how modern government works. Nonhierarchical styles of government are not at all new. Governments of all persuasions have always consulted with and often bargained with a range of private actors in the formulation and implementation of public policy. As Bill McKenzie observed over fifty years ago, "it is often tactically important for the government to unify the experts and interests concerned in a problem, so as to be able to make a bargain that will stick" (Mackenzie 1955: 145). Current new governance theorists, such as Bartolini, appear to be going much further than this, however. Thus, he refers to the growing international mobility options for actors and even to the decline of the nation-state as strengthening new governance trends (Bartolini 2011). Yet the core behavioral trait, namely the drawing into the policy process of a range of (often private) actors, is surely the same. There might be more of it or there might even be less of it (that is an empirical question, to be tested).

Moreover, even if one were to concede that new governance is really new, I have doubts about any suggestion that it is now the dominant style of governing. If one's focus is on current modes of policy-making within nation-states, then it might be argued that there has been a recent shift in the policy style toward a more "impositional" (hence hierarchical) style of governing. Rather than a decline of the state, we might be now witnessing the reemergence of (domestically) strong states. Thus, we should be cautious in arguing a) that "governance" is new, and b) that it is ubiquitous. The phenomenon of what we now term "new" governance may well have been the dominant (though never exclusive) policy style of most Western democracies for quite long periods. However, both exogenous and endogenous forces can at times force a change in national policy styles. As Kingdon argued, the policy process consists of a number of "streams," one of which is the "problem stream" (Kingdon 1995: 90–115). Some problems are so severe that they demand that some existing policy-making modalities be set aside, however well-established they might appear. We need look no further than the financial crisis within Europe (2010–2011) to see that some kinds of problems engender quite radical shifts in policy style from a traditional consensual/bargaining, nonhierarchical style, in which extended network governance is common, to a much more impositional/confrontational style, and, indeed, overtly *dirigiste* and hierarchical style of governing. Domestic policy networks may encounter restricted access to national governments and be confined to bargaining over minor policy adjustments. Under certain circumstances, *government* (even hierarchical government) can become fashionable again at the national level. As Lynn suggests, hierarchy has a degree of persistence, not least because, as he argues, "the problems emergent in the twenty-first century are placing even greater demands on central institutions ... for leadership in arranging coordinated, purposeful action" (Lynn 2010: 16). Governing styles might go through periods of great stability, yet experience shocks that bring about major changes in policy style.

The next section argues that what we now term "new governance" has a long pedigree, both in the real world of policy-making and in the academic literature. I then go on to analyze changes in the British policy style, briefly noting rather similar changes else-where in Europe, followed by a discussion of the EU-level policy style, before making some concluding observations.

NEW GOVERNANCE OR OLD GOVERNANCE?

Writing in the first half of the nineteenth century, the American political theorist and Seventh Vice-President of the US, John C. Calhoun, made the distinction between a numerical majority and a concurrent majority. To Calhoun, government by a numerical majority alone is to "confuse part of the people with the whole of the people, and is in fact no more than the rule of the smaller by the larger part." On the other hand, in a con-current majority the community is regarded as being made up of different and conflict-ing interests, with these interests having an effective veto over the majority. Thus Calhoun argued:

> It is the negative power—the power of preventing or arresting action by govern-ment—be it called by what term it may—veto, interposition, nullification, checks or balance of power—which in fact forms the constitution. They are all but different names for negative power. In all its forms, and under all names, it results from the concurrent majority. (Quoted in Wiltse : 417)

The concurrent majority is necessary, according to Calhoun, because under a system of numerical majority, government could degenerate into absolutism (Wiltse 1951: 417). The notion that governments should develop some kind of ongoing *exchange relationship* with groups subsequently became embedded in the study of American politics. Thus, the father of interest group studies, Arthur Bentley, argued in 1908 that "all phenomena of government are phenomena of groups pressing one another, form-ing one another and pushing out new groups and group representatives (the organs and agencies of government) to mediate the adjustments" (Bentley 1908). In the post-war period, David Truman's classic study of American politics, *The Governmental Process: Political Interests and Public Opinion*, first published in 1951, echoed early works by emphasizing the often close relationship between groups and government in the making of public policy.

Though I think he did not use the term governance, Hugh Heclo, writing in 1978, identified a phenomenon now described as network governance. Thus, he noted that policy
problems often escape the confined and exclusive "worlds" of professionals and are
resolved in a much looser configuration of participants in the policy process. Heclo
argued that the nature of power in Washington had begun to change. Exercising power
was not as much fun as it used to be in the "clubby" days of Washington politics (Heclo
1978: 94). Thus "as proliferating groups have claimed a stake and clamoured for a place in
the policy process, they have helped diffuse the focus of political and administrative
leadership" (Heclo 1978: 94–95).

Indeed, in a passage of special relevance to our current focus on "new governance" he
coined the term "issue network." Thus he wrote,

> Looking for the few who are powerful, we tend to overlook the many whose webs of
> influence provoke and guide the exercise of power. These webs, or what I will call
> "issue networks," are particularly relevant to the highly intricate and confusing wel-
> fare policies…increasingly, it is through networks of people who regard each other
> as knowledgeable, or at least as needing to be answered, that public policy issues
> tend to be refined, evidence debated, and alternative options worked out—though
> rarely in any controlled, well-organized way. (Heclo 1978: 102)

In Continental Europe, something akin to "new governance" was also well recognized.
Stein Rokkan also argued (when discussing Norwegian politics) that we had moved a
very long way from systems of government that can accurately be described as by
numerical majority. Writing as early as 1966, he argued that the Norwegian government
can "rarely, if ever, force through decisions on the basis of its electoral power but has to
temper its policies in complex consultations and bargains with major interest organisations" (Rokkan 1966: 107). Rokkan recognized that hierarchical, top-down government
was not really the norm at that time.

Similar observations can be found in much of the European literature in the 1970s.
Indeed, Heisler and Kvavik (in formulating a systematic characterization of what they
termed the "European polity") saw much of Europe as exhibiting a policy style "…char-
acterized by continuous, regularized access for economically, politically, ethnically and/
or subculturally based groups to the highest levels of the political system—i.e. the decision-making sub-system, as one of the central features of the European polity model"
(Heisler and Kvavik 1974: 48). The term governance was not used, but the thrust of the
analyses was that government was not simply hierarchical but was a process of consultation and bargaining between government and other (often private) policy actors. In
Britain in the late 1970s, academic studies shifted in focus from the study of traditional
institutions toward a different world of power—essentially a "post-parliamentary" polity
(Richardson and Jordan 1979). The policy process was characterized in terms prescient of
the currently popular "network governance": "in describing the tendency for boundaries
between government and groups to become less distinct through a whole range of pragmatic developments, we see policies being made between a myriad of interconnecting,
interpenetrating organizations. It is the relationships involved in committees, the policy

community of departments and groups, the practices of co-option and the consensual style, that perhaps best account for policy outcomes than do examinations of party stances, of manifestos or of parliamentary influence" (Richardson and Jordan 1979: 74). As Judge later commented, the "post-parliamentary thesis" was, for over a decade, a characterization that was largely unchallenged and found reflection in other important commentaries (Judge 1993: 123). In the British case, as Judge comments, "the concern for descriptive accuracy has led a whole generation of British scholars to follow ..." (121). (See particularly Rhodes, Chapter 3, this volume. For an historical overview see Richardson 1999.) Interestingly, the analyses of the policy process by the range of authors cited above is not dissimilar to many current analyses, which emphasize the newness of "new government." For example, Bartolini places considerable emphasis on the phenomenon of "co-production" and sees governance as "... a system of co-production of norms and public goods where the co-producers are different kinds of actors" (Bartolini 2011: 27).

However, it is important to recognize that (as new governance theorists also recognize) most political systems exhibit a mixture of policy styles and that the mix of styles can change over time. Governments can seize power over established institutions such as policy communities and networks. Ironically, just as *Governing under Pressure* was published, the British case was about to see a fairly dramatic shift in policy style.

BRITAIN: DOING LESS BY DOING MORE OR A SHIFT IN POLICY STYLE FROM "GOVERNANCE" TO "GOVERNMENT"

Britain is an important test case of the degree to which "governance" has become the default policy style in modern democracies. In the British case it can be argued that the consensual/governance policy style was a clear feature of postwar politics (Beer 1956, 1965). This is not to say that groups were never challenged by governments. Britain, like other European states, no doubt exhibited a mixture of policy styles, which occasionally included an impositional/hierarchical style of governing. However, confrontation and imposition was not the *preferred* policy style. Network governance was the procedural ambition. It took Margaret Thatcher's succession of Conservative governments to give policy community and policy network politics a severe jolt, as the new policy style unfolded. Her basic objective was "less government" but, paradoxically, she ended up "doing more" via some very interventionist policies (Richardson 1994).

It is true that consultation with interest groups continued under the Thatcherite "revolution." However, to argue that the pattern of consultation was "scarcely touched by supposed Thatcherite antipathy to groups" (Jordan and Maloney 1994: 37) is misleading as it places insufficient emphasis on the extent to which the Conservatives systematically changed the *underlying bases* of consultations. The consultations were often only after the extensive rewriting, by government, of old public policy "franchises." There was consultation, but after the main policy decisions had been taken and on the government's terms. If it was still "network governance" then it was conducted under asymmetric power relationships. It is difficult to see Mrs Thatcher's governments as "nonhierarchical" or "bottom-up." Even the Cabinet was often treated with disdain, let alone the whole raft of private (and semi-public) policy actors hitherto drawn into the UK policy process. (The style of Cabinet government was perhaps best summed up by the joke about a dinner being held for the whole Cabinet. Mrs Thatcher was asked whether she wanted fish or meat, and chose meat. When asked by the waiter "What about the vegetables?" she replied "Oh, they will have the same as me.") Mrs Thatcher (and at least *some* of her ministers—see Dudley and Richardson 1996, for a discussion of *ministerial* styles) had their own strong policy preferences, which often diverged very sharply from those actors within established policy networks. The 1979 election was the start of a period of party and ministerial (though still post-parliamentary) government. Relatively few of the new policy ideas emanated from the plethora of embedded policy communities and policy networks that had grown up in the postwar years. The Thatcher government's preference formation process became detached from the traditional consensual postwar institutions of British policy-making. Policy-making became more "internalised" (Jordan and Richardson 1982: 97–99) in the sense that key decisions were made *within* government rather than emerging from existing policy communities or networks. Governance appeared to give way to hierarchical and even impositional government, hence the invention of the new verb "to handbag" (coined because Mrs Thatcher always carried a large handbag and it was said that she could not look at any existing British institution without hitting it with her handbag). As Peters suggests, governments may challenge existing networks (and create new ones) because existing networks may approximate to the world of the "joint decision trap" described by Scharpf (Peters 1997: 57; Scharpf 1988). Networks can easily produce decisions that are suboptimal for society. In the face of lowest common denominator decisions, "the role of government then becomes providing the leadership to shape the debate and move decisions away from that lowest common denominator realm into a more socially desirable space" (Peters 1997: 57).

In Britain, by the mid-1980s, the balance of power had shifted decidedly in favor of government in terms of setting the agenda and initiating policy change. The policy process could often take on an episodic character—bouts of a hierarchical/impositional style as new policy ideas were introduced by the government, followed by old style consultation via (often reconstructed) policy communities and networks over the fine details.

AND THE REST OF EUROPE FOLLOWS SUIT?

It might be argued that Britain under Mrs Thatcher was unique in Western Europe and that there was no German, French, Italian, or Scandinavian equivalent of the "handbagging" of policy communities and networks by governments. Certainly, it seems that Britain was special in the degree of governmental determination to push through tough reforms against resistance, and in the sheer range of policy sectors that were subject to this desta-bilization process. However, it does seem that the kinds of pressures which helped the British government to tackle the many reform deficits (themselves often testament to the accuracy of the policy community concept as a descriptive tool in the past) eventually spread to the rest of Western Europe. In many Western European states, a gradual shift in policy style also seems apparent, although usually in ways more subtle than Mrs Thatcher's "handbagging" approach. (For examples from Denmark, France, Germany, Italy, Norway, and Sweden see Christiansen and Rommetvedt 1999; Cole and Drake 2000; Hewlett 1998; Lequesne 1993, 1996; Zohlnhöfer 1999; Della Salla 1997; Dente 1995; Radaelli 1998; Micheletti 1995). Thus, in varying degrees, many Western European states have been active in address-ing a range of "reform deficits" (for example, within pension systems), particularly over the past decade or so, and this has entailed a shift to a more hierarchical style of governing. As Héritier and Lehmkhul rightly argue, old forms of government and new forms of govern-ment are very frequently linked. The *shadow of hierarchy* is important not only in prompt-ing the emergence of new modes in order to avoid legislation, but also as a credible threat to secure their effectiveness' (Héritier and Lehmkhul 2011: 72).

There is a return of hierarchy in Europe nowadays in response to the huge debt crisis faced by many countries within the European Union (EU). Waiting for policy ideas and consensus to emerge from existing policy communities, policy networks, and issue net-works is not really an option when the international bailiffs are at a government's door. Actors quite exogenous to the domestic policy-making institutions and processes (such as the European Central Bank, the International Monetary Fund (IMF), credit rating agencies, and, above all, international financial markets) demanded (and got) quite dra-conian policy change in a process that could never be described as "new governance." The reform processes are best described as government with a capital G. The default position "standard operating procedures," which have emphasized widespread actor involvement, consultation, bargaining, and consensus formation have been set aside in the face of a financial crisis of Great Depression proportions. "Normal service" may or may not be resumed when the resource position improves but for the moment the dem-onstration and the riot have often replaced more conventional modes of participation by the affected interest in response to what is a very clear "impositional" policy style. My claim is rather more than the argument advanced by Peters (Chapter 2, this volume) that it is wrong for governance theorists to read the state out of the central position in gov-ernance. It is that the state, at least in moments of crisis, reverts to a strong sense of hier-archy, hence my use of the term "impositional policy style."

EUROPEAN UNION GOVERNANCE STYLES

I now turn to an analysis of policy formulation styles at the EU level where, I shall argue, there are some special institutional and cultural constraints which suggest that govern-ance, rather than government, is (and always was) alive and well. However, my main focus here is on the style of EU-level policy-*making*, not on the types of policy instruments that emerge from this style, or on policy implementation. I make a distinction between *how* policy is made at the EU level and the *form* in which policy outputs are constructed. It is conventional wisdom to claim that the EU is *sui generis*. However, we need to recognize that the EU is now a mature policy-making system. It is also a very *productive* policy-making system. In a sense, there is a policy-making engine at work within the EU that continues to churn out a mass of EU-level public policy that the member states then have to implement. Thus the EU is a "policy-making state," by which I mean the *locus* of public policy-making has shifted to the European level in many policy areas (Richardson 2006, 2012). It is the change in the locus of power that has provoked some profound changes in the behavior of private actors in the policy process, moving much of their lobbying resources to the European level.

From the perspective of interest groups and other private (and public) actors, the changing policy-making balance between nation-states and the EU has obvious implications (for a very useful discussion see Bartolini 2011: 35–36). The practical reality for a huge number of interest groups within the EU is that if they are to influence public policy in their sector they need to act cross-nationally and get themselves to Brussels. Thus, the *logic of influence* simply drives them to the regional (and increasingly global) level if they are to stand a chance of influencing, let alone controlling, their organizational environment. This "pull" is reinforced by the "push" of shifts in domestic policy styles, which, I argue, have become somewhat more hierarchical.

In turn, EU-level policy-makers have developed processes and "standard operating procedures" for dealing with this high level of interest group (and other actor) mobilization. It should occasion no surprise to discover that, from the very outset, they turned to familiar "ways of doing things," namely a characteristically "governance" approach to problem-solving. The central thrust of this section is that at the EU level we can see a system of governance in the sense that it is nonhierarchical, generally non-impositional (but see below regarding the growing importance of judicialization), and is underpinned by a need (and desire) to proceed by consensual agreement.

The phenomenon of European-level pluralist forms of interest group intermediation is not new. Some fairly stable "policy networks" involving European Coal and Steel Community (ECSC) officials and corporatist interests were apparent as early as the mid-1950s, reflecting the founding fathers' own domestic experiences (Mazey 1992). However, the significant expansion of the Community's legislative competence following the adoption of the 1986 Single European Act (SEA), and subsequent treaty reforms has prompted a sharp increase in the volume and intensity of interest group activity at the European level.

It is clear, therefore, that there has been a huge increase in the *supply* of lobbying at the European level as groups have calculated that it is rational to allocate increasing amounts of lobbying resources to this relatively new venue. Moreover, the same rational calculations are true for other actors at the EU level, especially the EU's main institutions, the Commission, the Council, the European Parliament (EP), and the European Court of Justice (ECJ). Based on a rational calculation of self-interest, each of these institutions has, in varying degrees, created incentives for interest groups to mobilize beyond their national borders. Thus, there has also been a demand pull from the policy-makers themselves, leading to a shared *interest* in the creation of an institutionalized EU-level governance system, at the core of which is a strong commitment to consultation with policy networks of various kinds. Rod Rhodes's definition of governance, cited above (namely "governance in and by networks") captures at least one of the key features of the workings of the EU policy formulation processes. To be sure, governance via networks of various kinds is not the *only* policy formulation style to be found in the EU, but it is so widespread that it is close to being the default style, almost regardless of whatever policy instruments (such as hard or soft law instruments) are used in the actual implementation process.

As we have argued above, the founding fathers brought with them to Brussels some familiar institutional baggage. However, some strong institutional constraints mean that the governance style for policy formulation is probably more embedded within the EU than at the level of the nation-state. The chief (and most obvious) institutional constraint is that the EU has no actual government in the conventional sense. Thus hierarchical modes of governing, which are available to nation-states, are not really available at the EU level. The closest institution to a government in the EU is probably the European Commission. First, it has a legal responsibility, under the treaties, for making formal policy proposals to the other EU institutions such as the Council and European Parliament. Second, and more importantly, we know that bureaucracies occupy a special position within the Executive. Whilst the specific origin of public policies is often unclear, and bureaucracies such as the European Commission are usually keen to deny that they are the main source of policy initiatives (reflecting their lack of legitimacy), we know that bureaucracies are almost invariably key players in the policy game. As Mazey argues, the Commission has always been active in helping to *create* an EU-level interest group system. She suggests that this *constituency mobilization* strategy is consistent both with theories of bureaucratic expansion and neo-functionalist models of European integration (Mazey 1995: 606, ; Eberlein2012). More importantly, bureaucracies and interest groups have a mutual self-interest in developing close relations, *even under circumstances of policy disagreement*.

Mutual gains are to be had in the essentially long-running game in which EU institutions and organized interest groups are engaged. The mutuality of the relationship is aptly summarized in a quotation from the Commission's 2002 document, *General Principles and Minimum Standards for Consultation of Interested Parties by the Commission*. Thus, "By fulfilling its duty to consult, the Commission ensures that its proposals are technically viable, practically workable and based on a bottom-up approach. In other words, good consultation serves a dual purpose by helping improve the quality of the policy outcomes and at the same time enhancing the involvement of interested parties and the public at large" (COM 2002: 704). The Commission has a strong belief that consultation of interests represents a "win–win" situation for all parties, that is, that cooperation brings greater mutual gains. In fact relations between the Commission and an increasingly Europeanized interest group system have developed along predictable lines. Indeed, despite the aforementioned reference to the EU as a *sui generis* political system, there is nothing new or unique about the EU's now well-developed interest intermediation system or about the way it has come about. This is in part underpinned by a legal obligation to consult. For example, Protocol No. 7 on the application of the principles of subsidiarity and proportionality, annexed to the Amsterdam Treaty, states that the Commission should consult widely before proposing legislation, and, wherever appropriate, publish consultation documents. More recently, the new Constitutional Treaty also stresses the importance of open, transparent, and regular dialogue between European institutions and representative associations and civil society.

Although the Commission is uniquely small in relation to its tasks, and exhibits marked cultural diversity, it also has very familiar bureaucratic features, such as strong sectorization, serious problems of coordination, and, of special relevance here, a strong *penchant* for developing close relations with organized interests. The latter reflects the Commission's organizational culture, which has arguably been more important than legal obligations in fostering the development of an EU-level interest group system. For their part, interest groups have been keen to exploit the Commission as a new *venue* or opportunity structure to gain influence over public policy-making. The continued development of the EU as a political system, has, as Bouwen suggests, considerably increased the Commission's responsibilities in terms of competences and geographical spread. As he argues, the institutional changes "entail a substantial increase in the workload of the Commission and have thereby increased this supranational institution's dependence on outside resources. This increasing resource dependence has only been strengthening the interaction of the Commission with private interests" (Bouwen 2009: 33).

A major problem for the Commission, as an unelected body, is its lack of legitimacy. For the Commission to try a hierarchical form of government would be the equivalent of writing a suicide note. Thus, even in the field of regulation (where one might expect hierarchy to be more present) Eberlein and Radaelli note that "majority voting and hierarchical direction are in short supply. Consensus based on negotiation constitutes the overriding norm..." (Eberlein and Radaelli 2010). Even the European Parliament, though directly elected, appears to suffer from the same legitimacy deficit. Thus, Lehmann notes that the Commission and the Parliament find themselves competing for legitimacy (Lehmann 2009: 50). In so doing the Parliament itself sucks in lobbyists, to the extent that there is an ongoing debate about how to manage what many see as an oversupply of lobbying, with a reported 70,000 individual contacts per year between members of the European Parliament (MEPs) and interest groups (reported by Lehmann 2009: 51). The discussion above is, of course, entirely focused on policy-making, not policy implementation As Bartolini observes, there is a distinction between coproduction as a process and what is actually produced, in terms of policy instruments (Bartolini 2011: 29). At the policy implementation level, the EU often struggles to reconcile its undoubted policy formulation and policy-making power with its often limited powers over policy implementation. For example, the experimentation with new (often soft) policy instruments and, more importantly, the whole Open Method of Co-ordination (OMC) project, is more a reflection of current power relationships in certain policy areas than a fundamental change in EU policy processes. As Idema and Kelemen argue, EU policy-makers in areas where the EU has no legal basis for issuing binding regulation, have little choice but to rely on OMC. (For examples in the area of gender equality, see Mazey 2012.) Yet Idema and Kelemen also identify a rather different EU policy implementation style, quite different to "governance." They argue that in other policy areas EU policy-makers rely on the "growing judicialisation of regulatory processes" (Idema and Kelemen 2006: 115). Far from the "new governance" of OMC, they see a shift toward a policy (implementation) style "characterized by an emphasis on detailed rules, substantial transparency requirements, adversarial procedures for resolving disputes, costly legal contestation involving many lawyers and frequent judicial intervention in administrative affairs" (Idema and Kelemen: 115). This alternative "face" of the EU policy process is in sharp contrast to the picture of network governance in the policy formulation process that I paint above, and in contrast to much of the new governance literature relating to the EU. It reminds us that in most policy systems one can find multiple policy styles and that changing circumstances can change the balance between competing policy styles. In the conclusion below, I reflect briefly on why such contrasting accounts have emerged.

Conclusion

The analysis by Idema and Kelemen is an important warning to all of us who claim to have identified a dominant style (such as "policy community politics" or "new governance" or, in their case, citing Kagan 2001, "adversarial legalism"). Most policy systems exhibit multiple policy styles because governments have learned that the power situation surrounding any given policy problem is a key variable determining what form of policy-making is possible at a given time. The power situation may vary across sectors (as in the EU) and, certainly, over time (as in the UK). Moreover, the nature of the policy problem might also affect the choice of governing style. Thus, the 2010/2011 crisis in the public finances in Greece, Ireland, and the UK (and probably Italy, Portugal, and Spain) was so grave that top-down, *dirigiste*, hierarchical, impositional govern*ment* was inevitable. It is difficult to imagine a package of expenditure cuts of the proportions that were implemented, as having emerged from any form of "network governance." Power is also related to available resources. It is no accident that network governance became common in the 1950s, 1960s, and 1970s. These were periods of steadily rising prosperity when public resources were gradually expanding. Periods of severe resource contraction produce a different kind of domestic politics with new rules of the game. Just as new governance writers argue that the "new" style is necessary to deal with increased complexity, I argue that crisis in national public finances also demands a change in policy style, back to hierarchical government and the de-emphasis of networks. Thus, we may now have two rather different kinds of politics in Europe. On the one hand, we see domestic politics with rather less network governance, very asymmetric power relations, and possibly a greater emphasis on what we might see as "hard law." This is a policy style somewhat distant from "new governance." On the other, we see a form of European-level governance that is sectorally biased in terms of the choice of hard or soft law policy instruments but which, in terms of the policy formulation and policy-making processes, is *generally* characterized by various forms of network governance, almost irrespective of the forms of policy instruments that emerge.

REFERENCES

Bartolini, S. 2011. New modes of governance: An introduction. In A. Héritier, and M. Rhodes (eds.), *New Modes of Governance in Europe: Governing in the Shadow of Hierarchy.* Houndmills: Palgrave Macmillan, 1–18.

Beer, S. 1956. Pressure groups and parties in Great Britain. *American Political Science Review* 50: 1–23.

Beer, S. 1965. *Modern British Politics.* London: Faber and Faber.

Bentley, A. 1908. *The Process of Government: A Study of Social Pressures.* Chicago: Chicago University Press.

Bouwen, P. 2009. The European Commission. In D. Coen and J. Richardson (eds.), *Lobbying the European Union: Institutions, Actors and Issues.* Oxford: Oxford University Press, 19–38.

Chritiansen, P. and Rommetvedt, H. 1999. From corporatism to lobbyism? Parliaments, executives, and organized interests in Denmark and Norway. *Scandinavian Political Studies* 22: 195–220.

Cole, A. and Drake, H. 2000. The Europeanization of the French polity: Continuity change and adaptation. *Journal of European Public Policy* 7: 26–43.

Commission of the European Communities (COM) 2002. *Communication from the Commission: Towards a Reinforced Culture of Consultation and Dialogue,* 11 December.

Della Salla, V. 1997. Hollowing out and hardening the state: European integration and the Italian economy. *West European Politics* 20: 14–33.

Dente, B. 1995. *Riformare la Pubblica Amministrazione.* Turin: Fondazione Agnelli.

Dudley, G. and Richardson, J. 1996. Promiscuous and celibate ministerial styles: Policy change, policy networks, and British roads policy. *Parliamentary Affairs* 49: 566–585.

Eberlein, B. 2012. Inching towards a common energy policy: Entrepreneurship, incrementalism, and windows of opportunity? In J. Richardson (ed.), *Constructing a Policy-Making State? Policy Dynamics in the European Union.* Oxford: Oxford University Press, 00–00.

Eberlein, B. and Radaelli, C. 2010. Mechanisms of conflict management in EU regulatory policy. *Public Administration* 88: 782–799.

Heclo, H. 1978. Issue networks and the executive establishment. In A. King (ed.), *The New American Political System.* Washington, DC: American Enterprise Institute, 87–124.

Heisler, M. and Kvavik, R. 1974. Patterns of European politics: The "European Polity Model". In M. Heisler (ed.), *Politics in Europe: Structures and Processes in Some Post-Industrial Democracies.* New York: David McKay.

Héritier, A and Lehmkhul, D. 2008. The shadow of hierarchy and new modes of governance *Journal of Public Policy* 28: 1–17.

Héritier, A. and Lehmkhul, D. 2011. Governing in the shadow of hierarchy: New modes of governance in regulation, In A Héritier and M. Rhodes (eds.), *New Modes of Governance in Europe: Governing in the Shadow of Hierarchy.* Basingstoke: Palgrave, 48–73.

Hewlett, N. 1998. *Modern French Politics Analysing Conflict and Consensus since 1945.* Cambridge: Polity.

Idema, T. and Kelemen, D. 2006. New modes of governance, the open method of co-ordination and other fashionable red herring. *Perspectives on European Politics and Society* 7: 108–123.

Jordan, G. and Richardson, J. 1982. The British policy style or the logic of negotiation? In J. Richardson (ed.), *Policy Styles in Western Europe.* London: Allen and Unwin, 80–110.

Jordan, G. and Maloney, W. 1994. Insider groups and public policy: The insider/outsider model revisited. *Journal of Public Policy* 14: 1.

Judge, D. 1993. *The Parliamentary State.* London: Sage.

Kagan, R. 2001. *Adversarial Legalism: The American Way of Law,* Cambridge, MA: Harvard University Press.

Kingdon, J. 1995. *Agendas, Alternatives and Public Policies.* New York: HarperCollins.

Lehmann, W. 2009. The European parliament. In D. Coen and J. Richardson (eds.), *Lobbying the European Union: Institutions, Actors and Issues.* Oxford: Oxford University Press, 39–69.

Lequesne, C. 1993. *Paris-Bruxelles.* Paris: Presses de la FNSP.

Lequesne, C. 1996. French central government and the European political system. In Y. Mény, P. Muller, and J.-L. Quermonne (eds.), *Adjusting to Europe.* London: Routledge, 00–00.

Lynn, L. 2010. The persistence of hierarchy. In M. Bevir (ed.), *The Sage Handbook of Governance.* London: Sage, 218–236.

Mackenzie, W. 1955. Pressure groups and British government. *British Journal of Sociology* 6: 133–148.

Mazey, S. 1992. Conception and evolution of the high authority's administrative services (1952–1958): From supranational principles to multinational policies. In R. Morgan and V. Wright (eds.), *Yearbook of European Administrative History.* Baden Baden: Nomos, 31–48.

Mazey, S. 1995. The development of EU equality policies: Bureaucratic expansion on behalf of women? *Public Administration* 73: 591–609.

Mazey, S. 2012. Policy entrepreneurship, group mobilisation and the creation of a new policy domain: Women's rights and the European Union. In J. Richardson (ed.), *Constructing a Policy-making State? Policy Dynamics in the European Union.* Oxford: Oxford University Press.

Micheletti, M 1995. *Civil Society and State Relations in Sweden.* Aldershot: Avebury.

Peters, G. 1997. Shouldn't row, can't steer: What's a government to do? *Public Policy and Administration* 12: 51–61.

Radaelli, C. 1998. Networks of expertise and policy change in Italy. *South European Society and Politics* 3 (autumn): 1–22.

Richardson, J. (ed.) 1982. *Policy Styles in Western Europe.* London: Allen and Unwin.

Richardson, J. 1994. Doing less by doing more: British government 1979–93. *West European Politics* 17: 178–197.

Richardson, J. 1999. Pressure groups and parties: A "Haze of Common Knowledge" or the empirical advance of the discipline? In J. Harward, B. Barry, and A. Brown (eds.), *The British Study of Politics in the Twentieth Century.* Oxford: Oxford University Press, 181–222.

Richardson, J. 2006. Policy-making in the EU: interests, ideas and garbage cans of primeval soup. In J. Richardson (ed.), *European Union: Power and Policy-Making,* 3–30.

Richardson, J. 2012. Supranational state building in the European Union. In J. Richardson (ed.) *Constructing a Policy-Making State? Policy Dynamics in the European Union.* Oxford: Oxford University Press.

Richardson, J. and Jordan, G. 1979. *Governing under Pressure: The Policy Process in a Post-Parliamentary Democracy*. Oxford: Martin Robertson.

Rokkan, S. 1966. Norway: Numerical democracy and corporate pluralism. In R. Dahl (ed.), *Political Opposition in Western Democracies*. New Haven: Yale University Press, 70–115.

Scharpf, P. W. 1988. The joint-decision trap: Lessons from German federalism and European integration. *Public Administration* 66: 239–278.

Truman, D. 1951. *The Governmental Process: Political Interests and Public Opinion*. New York: Knopf.

Wiltse, J. 1951. *John C. Calhoun, Sectionalist 1840–1850*. New York: Bobs Merrill.

Zohlnhöfer, R. 1985. Economic policy in the 1980s. *West European Politics* 8: 141–160.

CHAPTER 23

....

NGOs: BETWEEN ADVOCACY, SERVICE PROVISION, AND REGULATION

....

CHRISTOPHER TODD BEER, TIM BARTLEY, & WADE T. ROBERTS

SINCE the end of World War II, non-governmental organizations (NGOs) have become key actors at national, international, and transnational levels. Neoliberalism, globalization, and the end of the Cold War fueled the growing prominence of NGOs, such that by the turn of the twenty-first century, NGOs were carrying out most of the tasks of governing complex societies—delivering development assistance, mediating social conflicts, setting standards for business, developing expert knowledge, and reconstructing societies after natural and social disasters. The growth of NGOs has directed international attention to a variety of problems, from human rights abuses to climate change, and helped to diffuse particular scripts for understanding and responding to such problems. By some accounts, the proliferation of NGOs and their incorporation into development and governance projects amount to an associational revolution that "may constitute as significant a social and political development of the latter twentieth century as the rise of the nation state was of the nineteenth century" (Edwards and Hulme 1996: 2).

The rise of NGOs goes hand in hand with a multifaceted shift from government to governance. By many accounts, political authority has undergone a significant transformation—from command and direct provision by governments to "hollow states" that govern through networks and contracts (Milward and Provan 2000; Rhodes, Chapter 3, this volume); from states both "steering" and "rowing" the policy boat to states mostly "steering" while markets and civil society do the "rowing"(Braithwaite 2000; Jordana and Levi-Faur 2004; Osborne and Gaebler 1992); from nation-state-centered regimes to multi-level, multijurisdictional, and multi-stakeholder forms of governance (Sabel and Zeitlin, Chapter 12 and Klijn, Chapter 14, this volume); and "command and control" regulation to soft and responsive forms of regulation (Chapters 5 and 52, this volume); and from planning to experimentalist governance (Sabel and Zeitlin, Chapter 12, this volume). Notably, in each of these transformations and visions of governance, NGOs play pivotal roles. For instance, multi-stakeholder forms of transnational governance assume the existence of NGOs that can effectively voice collective interests. Likewise, the "New Public Management" goal of remaking government on a market model depends heavily not just on markets but on NGOs as service providers, in both affluent and developing countries.

Despite their pivotal role in governance, NGOs tend to be conceptualized more in terms of what they are *not* (i.e. "non-governmental") than in terms of their distinctive activities and patterns of affiliation. Legally, NGOs are formal voluntary organizations with specific privileges and restrictions—that is, tax exemptions but no excessive private gain by insiders—granted by the state. Their authority derives not from democratic representation or military force but from normative forces, rooted in modern conceptions of justice, science, and rational planning. Some analysts distinguish NGOs from the broader category of non-profit organizations by emphasizing NGOs' tendency to articulate humanitarian goals and public interest orientations (Haque 2010). Yet rigid definitional schemes break down under the diversity of organizations commonly dubbed NGOs (including some based more on expertise than humanitarianism) and the range of literatures that make claims about them.

Instead of seeking a universal definition and conceptualization of NGOs, much can be gained by interrogating two features of the world of NGOs. First, NGOs do a variety of things, especially given their linkages to the transformations of governance described above. We highlight three modal NGO activities—advocacy, service provision, and regulation—and discuss strands of scholarship on each. As advocates, NGOs mobilize attention and resources toward a variety of social problems, often by linking local concerns to global audiences. As service providers, NGOs play prominent roles in the delivery of social services and especially of development assistance in failed and weak state contexts. In some settings, NGOs also serve as quasi-regulators of business and government activity, either through their own watchdog and "naming and shaming" activities or by constructing private regulatory bodies. Scholars have shed light on the social conditions facilitating each of these activities, but they have also shown how each is beset by distinctive tensions and contradictions, which limit the ability of NGOs to do all that they are assumed to do by theories of "governance without government."

Second, the population of NGOs includes organizations operating at different levels, often with dramatically different levels of resources and power. A professionalized, transnational NGO is a dramatically different organization to a local NGO, though both may be participating in the same project or field. The multi-level character of NGO fields is crucial to NGOs' role in governance, and the relationship between local, domestic, and transnational NGOs is an important focus of inquiry. Here, scholars have developed

several competing accounts, which view transnational NGOs as either seeding, supporting, or controlling domestic NGOs.

By highlighting what NGOs do and how they interact across levels, this chapter
both provides an overview of some of the voluminous literature on NGOs and raises
some critical questions about the role of NGOs in governance. For instance, as states
devolve service provision to NGOs, questions about NGO accountability, capacity,
and coordination come to the fore, which become even more vexing when operating
across multiple levels. As NGOs become global regulators, and enforcers of "soft law,"
questions arise about how far such regulation can go without the consent of states or
the use of "hard" binding sanctions. Such questions are too often glossed over in discussions of governance.

NGOs as advocates

One core activity of many NGOs is to mobilize attention to social problems and organize pressure on states and international organizations. In this way, they are a "critical
social safety valve" for social problems (Salamon 2003: 13) and a key organizational
infrastructure for broader social movements, both domestic (Andrews and Edwards
2004) and transnational in scope (Bandy and Smith 2005; Keck and Sikkink 1998).
Within most democratic countries, as well as many authoritarian and quasi-authoritar-
ian ones, the NGO has become the standard way of organizing constituencies for indigenous rights, gender equality, environmental protection, and many other causes.
Internationally, NGOs have become prominent actors in intergovernmental arenas, with
growing opportunities for NGOs to be officially recognized in the United Nations (UN),
World Trade Organization (WTO), and World Bank (Finger 1994; Raustiala 1997). At
times, NGO advocacy has proven to be a powerful influence on the agendas of intergovernmental organizations, as evidenced by UN conventions on indigenous rights, the
incorporation of environmental standards into EU governance and some trade agreements, and the formation of intergovernmental agreements, like the Montreal Protocol
on ozone depletion. Yet it should not be assumed that NGO advocacy necessarily
expands global governance. In some cases, international organizations have proven
quite resistant to NGO campaigns, as with attempts to influence WTO policies on intellectual property and embed labor standards in international trade agreements (Evans
and Kay 2008). Scholars have also shown that NGOs are selective in the causes they
champion, depending less on the absolute scale of the problem than on how well it fits
with dominant frames about blame, opportunities for media attention, and the organization of advocacy networks (Bob 2005; Carpenter 2007).

Other parts of the literature demonstrate that NGO advocacy also has a second, more
subtle face. By their very form, NGOs are advocates for particular modes of organization. As stressed by world society theorists, organizing as an NGO—as opposed to, say, a
clan, militia, or religious body—carries powerful assumptions and messages about the

character of modern society. The NGO signifies a world of voluntarism, rationalization, and scientific knowledge (Boli and Thomas 1999; Lechner and Boli 2005). As such, the rise of NGOs helps to make particular organizational logics a taken-for-granted feature of the social world. It is this process that theorists in this tradition view as a primary link between the rise of NGOs and the adoption of policies for the rationalized management of the environment, education, and human rights. Though the evidence for this mechanism is indirect, in a series of studies scholars have found that countries with more ties to international non-governmental organizations (INGOs) are more likely to adopt policies for environmental protection, mass education, and population control, controlling for more functional requisites for these policies (Barrett and Frank 1999; Frank, Hironaka, and Schofer 2000; Meyer, Ramirez, and Soysal 1992; Roberts 2009).

Transnational NGO networks clearly offer new pathways for advocacy. Yet NGO advocacy in the age of governance is beset by a tension between calls for the expansion of rights and protections—that is, for state-building—on one hand, and a trend toward state retrenchment on the other. If the growth of governance beyond the nation-state has empowered NGOs, the neoliberal project of minimizing states' capacities to buffer citizens from the market has made it difficult for NGO advocacy to result in the institutionalization of new rights and protections. One partial resolution of this contradiction involves NGOs themselves taking on greater roles as regulators and service providers, as we describe in the following sections.

NGOs AS SERVICE PROVIDERS

The increasingly pivotal role of NGOs in service provision and development efforts is one of the most striking transformations of the past several decades (Anheier and Salamon 1998). Within affluent countries, and particularly those that aggressively implemented NPM doctrines, the growing importance of non-profit service delivery is linked to visions of moving the state away from "rowing" to "steering" activities. Yet it is in low-income countries and those suffering from state failure that the role of NGOs in service provision has been most striking.

Scholars have identified several interlinked processes behind the proliferation and mainstreaming of NGOs in development service provision. In the 1980s, following decades of disappointing results, international donors sought alternative, non-state pathways for delivering development aid (Fowler 2000; Smillie 1997). State failures, brought about by indebtedness, corruption, and conflict, only added further impetus to the search. The subsequent redirection of funds away from governments to NGOs was instrumental in fuelling the expansion of the NGO sector worldwide. States, too, succumbing to declining capacity, rising social demands, and external pressures, had little choice but to cede traditional state responsibilities to NGOs, accepting them, often reluctantly, as surrogate partners in development and service delivery (Anheier and Salamon 1998; Smillie 1997).

The rapid embrace of NGOs was based in no small part on their idealized qualities and traits. NGOs, it is regularly argued, offer a more efficient and flexible means of reaching constituencies than do bureaucratically constrained state agencies (Dichter 1999). This is thought to be particularly true in the case of impoverished and marginalized communities. NGOs are also thought to utilize a more participatory model of development, strengthening civil society and cultivating social capital in local communities (Fowler 2000). As Kamat (2004) notes, "NGOs have been identified as the preeminent, if not sole, organizational form that can implement the global commitment to 'bottom up' development" (155). In this way, NGOs' contributions are thought to add to the organizational capacity of communities and contribute to good governance, not only by delivering services, but operating as intermediaries that link donors to grassroots organizations and constituencies to governments (Carroll 1992; Renshaw 1994).

Yet the mainstreaming of NGOs brought about corresponding challenges and tensions regarding their role in governance. As the use of NGOs spread, so did cases of corruption and fraud, compromising the reputation and legitimacy of the entire NGO sector and, by extension, the funding sources of legitimate organizations (Edwards and Hulme 1996). As stakeholders sought new ways of organizing NGO activity and establishing accountability, novel forms of governance have emerged within the NGO sector (Brinkerhoff and Brinkerhoff 2002; Milward and Provan 2000). Donors and governments have sought to formalize their collaborations with NGOs by establishing NGO liaison offices, collaborative guidelines, and other forms of regulation (Kamal 1996). The crisis of legitimacy has also led NGO sectors in many countries to take an active role in governing themselves through the development of self-regulatory mechanisms such as national-level guilds, voluntary codes of conduct, organizational self-assessments, and certification programs (Gugerty 2008, 2009; Lloyd 2005). Though questions about the effectiveness and accountability of NGO development efforts persist, the field has clearly become far more structured over time.

Further tension exists between NGOs' service provision, democracy, and the dominant neoliberal market paradigm. Some scholars question whether the turn to NGOs in service provision and international aid cloaks prevailing economic arrangements in a veil of participatory development (Kamat 2004; Kihika 2009; Powell and Seddon 1997). As Kamat (2004) argues, "the agentic role prescribed to NGOs is not an innocent one but one that foretells a reworking of democracy in ways that coalesce with global capitalist interests" (156). Some also question whether the reliance on NGOs undermines statebuilding, particularly in weak or failed state contexts (Batley and Mcloughlin 2010). Though it is precisely in these contexts where the need for NGOs is most acute, the reliance on NGOs to provide core services may undermine efforts to build some resilient state capacity and legitimacy. Some scholars have argued that the way out of this bind involves establishing truly complementary relationships between states and NGOs (Evans 1996). Understanding the conditions for state–NGO complementarity is one portion of the crucial task of understanding whether NGOs will operate merely as "band-aid solutions" at the margins of the neoliberal model or live up to their potential to foster more systematic changes in political–economic orders (Bebbington, Hickey, and Mitlin 2008; Kihika 2009).

NGOs AS REGULATORS

NGOs have become regulators and quasi-regulators in their own right. This trend is closely connected with larger transformations of governance and the rise of regulatory capitalism, including shifts toward soft law, voluntary programs, and transnational governance. Though "regulation" is typically associated with state-imposed controls of industry, scholars of governance have increasingly embraced more extended conceptions of regulation as social control. Doing so reveals a variety of informal social controls, stakeholder pressures, and private standards that carry some degree of regulatory authority both domestically and globally (Abbott and Snidal 2009; Bartley 2007; Vogel 2008). It has become increasingly clear that neoliberalism and globalization have led not to deregulation per se but to changing forms of regulation and a growing density of regulatory standards (Djelic and Sahlin, Chapter 52, this volume; Levi-Faur and Jordana 2005; Schneiberg and Bartley 2008). NGOs have been especially important in designing and enforcing private forms of regulation, in at least two ways.

First, as watchdogs, NGOs have directed attention to questionable practices of companies and governments, seeking to "name and shame" actors into changing course. NGOs like Friends of the Earth, Greenpeace, Oxfam, Global Exchange, and Global Witness have "named and shamed" a variety of major corporations in the oil, timber, mining, garment, and agriculture industries. Such "market campaigns" typically couple protest at corporate headquarters or retail outlets with the use of mass media or the Internet to raise consumer awareness or organize boycotts (O'Rourke 2005; Seidman 2007; Spar and LaMure 2003). In some instances, such campaigns have become an important social control of business. Campaigns focused on animal cruelty, "blood diamonds," deforestation, and global warming have led some retailers and food brands to cut ties with particular suppliers and support efforts to certify best practices (Conroy 2007). Campaigns over sweatshops have succeeded in casting a pall over the brand reputations of targeted firms and limiting at least some of the most egregious forms of labor abuse in global supply chains (Harrison and Scorse 2010; Spar and LaMure 2003). Of course, this strategy was modeled on human rights campaigns that were primarily geared toward holding governments to higher standards (Seidman 2007), and NGOs like Amnesty International and Transparency International continue to direct their scrutiny toward governments.

A second way in which NGOs have become regulators is through their role in developing and maintaining private associations for standard-setting, monitoring, and certification. Voluntary and transnational standards for business have grown at a dizzying rate since the 1990s, generating dense webs of governance (Djelic and Sahlin-Andersson 2006), or what Gereffi and colleagues call an "NGO-industrial complex"

(Gereffi, Garcia-Johnson, and Sasser 2001). This includes standards for sustainable forestry, agriculture, and fisheries (e.g. Forest Stewardship Council, Roundtable on Sustainable Palm Oil, Marine Stewardship Council), as well as responsible investment, fair labor, and responsible mining. Many of these initiatives would not have been possible without NGOs' efforts to forge coalitions with companies, sponsor standard-setting projects, and build markets for certified products(Bartley 2007; Cashore, Auld, and Newsom 2004). In fact, a handful of environmental and development NGOs are largely responsible for carrying the certification model to a variety of different industries (Bartley and Smith 2010).

However, more attention needs to be given to the tensions that arise as NGOs engage in watchdogging and private regulation. NGOs' "naming and shaming" campaigns have their limits. They typically reach only those segments of consumer products industries exporting to affluent countries, and the responses of targeted firms often fail to sufficiently address the root of the problem (Seidman 2007). Additionally, while NGOs have helped to build a variety of private regulatory initiatives, the effects of these programs are not entirely clear. Some scholars have argued that well-designed voluntary programs might be able to both attract sufficient participation from firms and improve performance (Prakash and Potoski 2006), but others have raised doubts about the causal impact of certification and the ability of voluntary programs to overcome the entrenched practices of state and industry actors (Ponte 2008; Seidman 2007). As private regulatory systems have grown and matured, the limitations of voluntary authority and non-binding standards have become clearer. Scholars have increasingly pointed out the importance of state support in allowing private regulation to gain authority, and the limitations of private regulation have in some circumstances led to calls for strengthened governmental and intergovernmental regulation. Here, one sees how the tensions involved in NGOs functioning as regulators might lead to a shift toward more state control.

THE MULTI-LEVEL WORLD OF NGOS

It would be a mistake to talk about NGOs as if this were a monolithic category, since it characterizes a wide array of actors, with vastly different degrees of power and capacity, operating in vastly different political and socioeconomic settings. Yet it is not merely the diversity that needs to be noted, it is the multi-level character of NGO activities and the relationship between transnational and local organizations that deserve careful attention. Advocacy, service provision, and regulation by NGOs all require coordination across levels. Transnational NGOs may rely on domestic or local NGOs to gather information or implement projects, while local and domestic NGOs may rely on transnational groups for resources, expertise, or legitimacy. The increased vertical interactions among states described by theories of multi-level governance (Bache, Chapter 44, this volume) has a parallel in the world of NGOs, with even more radical differentials in power at play in the NGO field. In some circumstances, the power of higher-level, transnational NGOs may subtly undermine the impact of NGO projects at the local level. For instance, scholars of NGOs in development have shown how the dictates of donor support and "upward accountability" may make it difficult for domestic NGOs to remain downwardly accountable to beneficiaries, inwardly accountable to their own mission, and horizontally accountable to partnering NGOs (Edwards and Hulme 1996; Lloyd 2005).

Scholars have made three main types of theoretical claims about the relationship between domestic NGOs on one hand and the international NGOs (INGOs) of "transnational civil society" on the other. By one account, INGOs typically precede and "seed" domestic NGOs. This account is central to world society theory, which attaches widespread consequences to the growth of association at the global level (Meyer et al. 1997). By this account, rather than domestic NGOs emerging primarily from isolated grassroots mobilization, they emerge only after INGOs have "set up shop" in a particular country. Specifically, scholars in this camp have shown that ties to INGOs increase the rate of the founding of domestic environmental NGOs in developing countries, above and beyond variation in domestic environmental conditions, trade openness, education levels, or wealth (Longhofer and Schofer 2010). In this light, the expansion of governance at the transnational level may put NGOs in a more central position in governance at the domestic level, relatively independently of domestic NGOs' actual capacities to carry out their various activities.

A second line of research posits that domestic NGOs have a bit more autonomy and agency in their interactions with the transnational sphere. Keck and Sikkink (1998) argue that transnational advocacy networks are "horizontal ... fluid and open" (8) rather than hierarchical, with reciprocal sharing of information, resources, personnel, and tactics. Here, INGOs are points of leverage for domestic NGOs, rather than prerequisites for them. Under some conditions, domestic NGOs have been able to leverage the support of transnational NGOs to amplify their local activities. In the case of human rights violations in Argentina in the 1970s, it was information gathered by local NGOs and passed on to Amnesty International that led the US Congress to cut off military funding and to pressure the Argentine state (Keck and Sikkink 1998). In addition, scholars have shown how the influence of INGOs can be muted if they rely solely on global norms and arenas without connecting with domestic actors. For instance, Khagram (2004) finds that the success of international campaigns to resist state-supported hydropower dam projects depended on the presence of well-mobilized domestic NGOs and democratic institutions. Tarrow (2005) makes a similar argument about the importance of local organization in explaining the effects of international campaigns for workers' rights in Mexican *maquiladoras*. In these accounts, effective global governance depends crucially on the articulation of NGO activities across the levels.

A third line of research argues that INGOs largely coerce and control domestic NGOs, since the relationship between transnational actors and domestic actors in developing nations is reflective of the core-dominant structure of global geopolitics. By this account, INGOs directly impose their preferred advocacy scripts, service models, or private regulations onto their weaker partners, leaving domestic NGOs in developing countries subservient and disempowered. Domestic NGOs may adopt the language and scripts of transnational actors to increase their chances of funding, making the domestic actor's agenda and their governing activities more responsive to international funding than to the local context (Eccleston 1996; Gariyo 1995; Michael 2004; Tvedt 2002; Vogel 2006). In a study of Madagascar's environmental policy, domestic NGOs and even the national government were heavily influenced by and captive to the policy recommendations and funding made available from a collection of external INGOs (Duffy 2008). In addition, interaction with INGOs may professionalize domestic NGOs to the point where their willingness to use disruptive protest to pressure the state is drastically reduced (Minkoff and Agnone 2010; Staggenborg 1988). Hughes (2007), for instance, argues that INGOs in Cambodia in the human rights and labor sectors steered activists into more professional and individual actions, dampening the chances for mass mobilization, disruptive protest, and deep political engagement.

It is the neoliberal, Eurocentric character of "transnational civil society" that worries many scholars in this camp (Munck 2002; Petras 1997), with INGOs channeling popular resistance into local micro-projects that fail to question ongoing structural inequalities (Petras and Veltmeyer 2001). Others maintain that global scripts are too far removed from the site of their intended impacts to work effectively (Brown, Brown, and Desposato 2002; Hearn 1998), and others worry that local NGOs have had their voices silenced as more powerful elite INGOs have become the *de facto* voice for impoverished individuals and communities (Batliwala 2002). Whatever the precise mechanism, scholars in this third group tend to argue that attempts at "governance without government" are overwhelmed or distorted by the massive inequalities in resources and power across the different levels of NGO fields.

These three perspectives, which see INGOs alternately as seeding, supporting, or controlling domestic NGOs, each draw attention to important aspects of NGO relations and their implications for governance. Rather than adopting one approach in a totalizing way, scholars should investigate the particular conditions under which these processes are most likely to occur and the impact of these on the manner in which NGOs are involved in governance. For instance, in the relatively rare circumstances where domestic NGOs are organizationally robust, they may be able to leverage INGO support, while INGO projects may prove more constraining when domestic NGOs are young, politically tenuous, or disorganized. Scholarship on the multi-actor sphere of governance would be considerably strengthened by taking each of these relational accounts seriously and developing the evidentiary basis for fully specifying their insights.

CONCLUSION

As scholars and practitioners of governance look to NGOs to fill various roles related to advocacy, service provision, or regulation, they should consider both the multi-level character of NGO fields and the tensions that come to the fore as each set of activities unfolds over time. These tensions may even have the ability to shift NGO action from one focus to another, though the contours of this process are only hinted at in existing research. Of course, some large NGOs engage in advocacy, service provision, and regulation simultaneously, and many other NGOs specialize in just one of these activities. Indeed, there may be powerful reasons to specialize, as with service provision NGOs that refrain from vocal advocacy in order to avoid political conflict that could threaten their work. Still, there may be shifts from one focus to another, whether as strategic choices of particular NGOs or as central tendencies of NGO activity at particular historical moments.

We see two general principles that may shift action between advocacy, service provision, and regulation. First, it is clear that a broad shift toward market-oriented, neoliberal policy scripts has tended to privilege NGO service provision and participation in private regulatory partnerships and associations more than NGO advocacy. Studies of private regulation, for instance, have shown how large environmental NGOs shifted away from advocacy targeting states and intergovernmental organizations toward the construction of market-based, voluntary private regulatory bodies (Bartley 2007; Cashore, Auld, and Newsom 2004). Conversely, the tensions of NGO service provision and the limits of private regulation may shift action in the opposite direction, toward advocacy that demands the expansion of state capacity and responsiveness. The reliance on NGOs for development assistance, for instance, may reach a point at which the limits of voluntarism are hard to ignore, signaling a pendulum swing back toward the state as a direct service provider. In the sphere of transnational regulation, enthusiasm for NGO-led systems has gradually evolved into hybrid forms of governance in which states play central roles (Zeitlin 2011). While it is difficult to say precisely how the tensions of NGO activity will play out, future research could productively examine the conditions under which one sees historic shifts between these activities and ways in which particular NGOs decide how to focus their energies.

References

Abbott, K. and Snidal, D. 2009. Strengthening international regulation through transnational new governance: Overcoming the orchestration deficit. *Vanderbilt Journal of Transnational Law* 42: 501–578.

Andrews, K. T. and Edwards, B. 2004. Advocacy organizations in the U.S. political process. *Annual Review of Sociology* 30: 479–506.

Anheier, H. K. and Salamon, L. M. (eds.) 1998. *The Nonprofit Sector in the Developing World*. Manchester: Manchester University Press.

Bandy, J. and Smith, J. 2005. *Coalitions Across Borders: Transnational Protest and the Neoliberal Order*. New York: Rowman and Littlefield.

Barrett, D. and Frank, D. J. 1999. Population control for national deveopment: From world discourse to national policies. In J. Boli and G. M. Thomas (eds.), *Constructing World Culture: International Nongovernmental Organizations Since 1875*. Stanford, CA: Stanford University Press, 198–221.

Bartley, T. 2007. Institutional emergence in an era of globalization: The rise of transnational private regulations of labor and environmental conditions. *American Journal of Sociology* 113: 297–351.

Bartley, T. and Smith, S. 2010. Communities of practice as cause and consequence of transnational governance: The evolution of social and environmental certification. In M. Djelic and S. Quack (eds.), *Transnational Communities: Shaping Global Economic Governance.* Cambridge: Cambridge University Press, 347–374.

Batley, R. and Mcloughlin, C. 2010. Engagement with non-state service providers in fragile states: Reconciling state-building and service delivery. *Development Policy Review* 28: 131–154.

Batliwala, S. 2002. Grassroots movements as transnational actors: Implications for global civil society. *Voluntas: International Journal of Voluntary and Nonprofit Organizations* 13: 393–409.

Bebbington, A., Hickey, S. and Mitlin, D. C. 2008. *Can NGOs Make a Difference? The Challenge of Development Alternatives.* London: Zed Books.

Bob, C. 2005. *The Marketing of Rebellion: Insurgents, Media, and International Activism.* New York: Cambridge University Press.

Boli, J. and Thomas, G. M. (eds.) 1999. *Constructing World Culture: International Nongovernmental Organizations Since 1875.* Stanford, CA: Stanford University Press.

Braithwaite, J. 2000. The new regulatory state and the transformation of criminology. *British Journal of Criminology* 40: 222–238.

Brinkerhoff, J. M. and Brinkerhoff, D. W. 2002. Government-nonprofit relations in comparative perspective: Evolution, themes and new directions. *Public Administration and Development* 22: 3–18.

Brown, D. S., Brown, J. C. and Desposato, S. W. 2002. Left turn on green? The unintended consequences of international funding for sustainable development in Brazil. *Comparative Political Studies* 35: 814–838.

Carpenter, R. C. 2007. Setting the advocacy agenda: Theorizing issue emergence and nonemergence in transnational advocacy networks. *International Studies Quarterly* 51: 99–120.

Carroll, T. F. 1992. *Intermediary NGOs: The Supporting Link in Grassroots Development.* West Hartford, CT: Kumarian Press.

Cashore, B., Auld, G. and Newsom, D. 2004. *Governing Through Markets: Forest Certification and the Emergence of Non-State Authority.* New Haven: Yale University Press.

Conroy, M. E. 2007. *Branded! How the Certification Revolution Is Transforming Global Corporations.* Gabriola Island, BC, Canada: New Society Publishers.

Dichter, T. W. 1999. Globalization and its effects on NGOs: Efflorescence or a blurring of roles and relevance? *Nonprofit and Voluntary Sector Quarterly* 28: 38–58.

Djelic, M. and Sahlin-Andersson, K. (eds.) 2006. *Transnational Governance: Institutional Dynamics of Regulation.* New York: Cambridge University Press.

Duffy, R. 2008. Non-governmental organizations and governance states: The impact of transnational environmental management networks in Madagascar. In B. Doherty and T. Doyle (eds.), *Beyond Borders: Environmental Movements and Transnational Politics.* New York: Routledge, 35–53.

Eccleston, B. 1996. Does north-south collaboration enhance NGO influence on deforestation policies in Malaysia and Indonesia? In D. Potter (ed.), *NGOs and Environmental Policies: Asia and Africa.* Portland, OR: Frank Cass, 66–89.

Edwards, M. and Hulme, D. 1996. *Beyond the Magic Bullet: NGO Performance and Accountability in the Post-Cold War World.* West Hartford, CT: Kumarian Press.

Evans, P. 1996. Government action, social capital and development: Reviewing the evidence on synergy. *World Development* 24: 1119–1132.

Evans, R. and Kay, T. 2008. How environmentalists greened trade policy: Strategic action and the architecture of field overlap. *American Sociological Review* 73: 970–991.

Finger, M. 1994. Environmental NGOs in the UNCED process. In T. Princen and M. Finger (eds.), *Environmental NGOs in World Politics*. London: Routledge, 186–216.

Fowler, A. 2000. *Civil Society, NGDOs and Social Development: Changing the Rules of the Game*. Geneva: United Nations Research Institute for Social Development.

Frank, D. J., Hironaka, A. and Schofer, E. 2000. The nation-state and the natural environment over the twentieth century. *American Sociological Review* 65: 96–116.

Gariyo, Z. 1995. NGOs and development in East Africa: A view from below. In M. Edwards and D. Hulme (eds.), *Beyond the Magic Bullet: Non-governmental Organizations Performance and Accountability*. London: Earthscan, 156–165.

Gereffi, G., Garcia-Johnson, R. and Sasser, E. 2001. The NGO-industrial complex. *Foreign Policy* 125: 56–65.

Gugerty, M. K. 2008. The effectiveness of NGO self-regulation: Theory and evidence from Africa. *Public Administration and Development* 28: 105–118.

Gugerty, M. K. 2009. Signaling virtue: Voluntary accountability programs among nonprofit organizations. *Policy Sciences* 42: 243–273.

Haque, M. S. 2010. Non-governmental organizations. In M. Bevir (ed.), *The Sage Handbook of Governance*. Thousand Oaks, CA: Sage, 330–341.

Harrison, A. and Scorse, J. 2010. Multinationals and anti-sweatshop activism. *American Economic Review* 100: 247–273.

Hearn, J. 1998. The "NGO-isation" of Kenyan society: USAID and the restructuring of health care. *Review of African Political Economy* 25: 89–100.

Hughes, C. 2007. Transnational networks, international organizations and political participation in Cambodia: Human rights, labour rights and common rights. *Democratization* 14(5): 834–852.

Jordana, J. and Levi-Faur, D. 2004. The politics of regulation in the age of governance. In J. Jordana and D. Levi-Faur (eds.), *Politics of Regulation: Institutional and Regulatory Reform in the Age of Governance*. Cheltenham: Edward Elgar, 1–28.

Kamal, A. 1996. Civil society finding its place in the twenty-first century. *Development* 39: 68–69.

Kamat, S. 2004. The privatization of public interest: Theorizing NGO discourse in a neoliberal era. *Review of International Political Economy* 11: 155–176.

Keck, M. E. and K. Sikkink. 1998. *Activists Beyond Borders: Advocacy Networks in International Politics*. Ithaca, NY: Cornell University Press.

Khagram, S. 2004. *Dams and Development: Transnational Struggles for Water and Power*. Ithaca, NY: Cornell University Press.

Kihika, M. 2009. Development or underdevelopment: The case of non-governmental organizations in neoliberal Sub-Saharan Africa. *Journal of Alternative Perspectives in the Social Sciences* 1: 783–795.

Lechner, F. J. and Boli, J. 2005. *World Culture: Origins and Consequences*. Malden, MA: Blackwell.

Levi-Faur, D. and Jordana, J. 2005. Globalizing regulatory capitalism. *The Annals of the American Academy of Political and Social Science* 598: 6–9.

Lloyd, R. 2005. *The Role of NGO Self-Regulation in Increasing Stakeholder Accountability.* London: One World Trust.

Longhofer, W. and Schofer, E. 2010. National and global origins of environmental association. *American Sociological Review* 75: 505–533.

Meyer, J. W., Ramirez, F. O. and Soysal, Y. N. 1992. World expansion of mass education, 1870–1980. *Sociology of Education* 65: 128–149.

Meyer, J. W., Boli, J., Thomas, G. M. and Ramirez, F. O. 1997. World society and the nation-state. *The American Journal of Sociology* 103: 144–181.

Michael, S. 2004. *Undermining Development: The Absence of Power Among Local NGOs in Africa.* Bloomington, IN: Indiana University Press.

Milward, H. B. and Provan, K.G. 2000. Governing the hollow state. *Journal of Public Administration Research and Theory* 10(2): 359–380.

Minkoff, D. C. and Agnone, J. 2010. Consolidating social change: The consequences of foundation funding for developing movement infrastructures. In H. K. Anheier and D. C. Hammack (eds.), *American Foundations Roles and Contributions.* Washington, DC: Brookings Institution, 347–368.

Munck, R. 2002. Global civil society: Myths and prospects. *Voluntas: International Journal of Voluntary and Nonprofit Organizations* 13: 349–361.

O'Rourke, D. 2005. Market movements: Nongovernmental organization strategies to influence global production and consumption. *Journal of Industrial Ecology* 9: 115–128.

Osborne, D. and Gaebler, T. 1992. *Reinventing Government: How the Entrepreneurial Spirit is Transforming the Public Sector.* New York: Addison-Wesley.

Petras, J. 1997. Imperialism and NGOs in Latin America. *Monthly Review* 49: 10–27.

Petras, J. and Veltmeyer, H. 2001. *Globalization Unmasked: Imperialism in the 21st Century.* New York: Zed Books.

Ponte, S. 2008. Greener than thou: The political economy of fish ecolabeling and its local manifestations in South Africa. *World Development* 36: 159–175.

Powell, M. and Seddon, D. 1997. NGOs and the development industry. *Review of African Political Economy* 24: 3–10.

Prakash, A. and Potoski, M. 2006. *The Voluntary Environmentalists: Green Clubs, ISO 140001, and Voluntary Environmental Regulations.* New York: Cambridge University Press.

Raustiala, K. 1997. States, NGOs, and international environmental institutions. *International Studies Quarterly* 41: 719–740.

Renshaw, L. R. 1994. Strengthening civil society: The role of NGOs. *Development and Change* 4(1): 46–49.

Roberts, W. T. 2009. World society, family planning programs and the health of children. *International Journal of Sociology and Social Policy* 29: 414–425.

Salamon, L. M. 2003. *The Resilient Sector: The State of Nonprofit America.* Washington, DC: Brookings Institution Press.

Schneiberg, M. and Bartley, T. 2008. Organizations, regulation, and economic behavior: Regulatory dynamics and forms from the 19th to 21st century. *Annual Review of Law & Social Science* 4: 31–61.

Seidman, G. 2007. *Beyond the Boycott: Labor Rights, Human Rights and Transnational Activism.* New York: Russell Sage Foundation/ASA Rose Series.

Smillie, I. 1997. NGOs and development assistance: A change in mind-set? *Third World Quarterly* 18: 563–578.

Spar, D. L. and LaMure, L. T. 2003. The power of activism: Assessing the impact of NGOs on global business. *California Management Review* 45: 78–101.

Staggenborg, S. 1988. The consequences of professionalization and formalization in the pro-choice movement. *American Sociological Review* 53: 585–605.

Tarrow, S. 2005. *The New Transnational Activism.* New York: Cambridge University Press.

Tvedt, T. 2002. Development NGOs: Actors in a global civil society or in a new international social system? *Voluntas: International Journal of Voluntary and Nonprofit Organizations* 13: 363–375.

Vogel, A. 2006. Who's making global civil society: Philanthropy and US empire in world society. *The British Journal of Sociology* 57: 635–655.

Vogel, D. 2008. Private global business regulation. *Annual Review of Political Science* 11: 261–282.

Zeitlin, J. 2011. Pragmatic transnationalism: Governance across borders in the global economy. *Socio-Economic Review* 9: 187–206.

CHAPTER 24

....

AGENTS OF KNOWLEDGE

....

DIANE STONE

THIS chapter addresses knowledge agents in governance. A limited notion of knowledge will be deployed. The discussion focuses on the codified products produced by socially recognized experts and scientists. That is, "knowledge" will be taken to include: first, research and evaluation studies and other in-house expert products originating from within official or public domains; second, scholarly and scientific knowledge that is used, abused, or adapted for governance activities and deliberations; third, independent policy analysis and advice commissioned or given on the basis of recognized expertise of individuals or organizations.

Knowledge has been long used by governments to inform or legitimize policy. However, knowledge agents have helped propel the shift from government to governance. The understanding of governance in this chapter parallels that given by Rod Rhodes: "the changing boundaries between public, private and voluntary sectors; to the changing role of the state" (Chapter 3, this volume, page oo). The discussion outlines the manner in which knowledge agents are involved in a triple devolution of governance. First, there is a sideways partial delegation of governance responsibilities to non-state or quasi-state knowledge agents who hold some authority on the basis of their epistemic credentials. Second, there is an upwards decentralization of governance into an intersecting array of new global and regional decision-making forums of mixed public–private composition. Finally, knowledge agents have intrinsic governance capacities in their power to define problems, shape the climate of debate, or engage in standard-setting, rule-making, or other regulatory activity.

The discussion progresses through a general categorization of knowledge actors (individuals), knowledge institutions (in their organizational format), and knowledge networks. In the past, with the ontological separation between knowledge and power, or science and politics, firmly ensconced in the public imagination, the scholar traveled out of the ivory tower to deliver advice to the government. Today, the great diversity of knowledge organizations and knowledge networks intersperse and overlap multiple domains of governance.

The first section focuses on individuals. Researchers often consider that there is no political audience for their work despite the important observations they make and policy-relevant explanations they develop. By contrast, policy-makers believe that what researchers contribute does not resonate with the needs of policy because it is irrelevant or too esoteric and theoretical (Court and Maxwell 2006). Research groups may have a huge impact on the media or among non-governmental organizations (NGOs) but little or none on government. This section outlines the role of *individuals* as knowledge actors—individuals such as a "chief scientific officer," policy advisers, and other "experts."

The second section addresses *organizations* and their strategies to promote and propel knowledge (products and actors) into governance. This includes temporary bodies like commissions of inquiry as well as more permanent bodies like philanthropic foundations and independent think tanks, plus private sector advice from NGOs and consultancy firms. The third section introduces knowledge *network* concepts such as epistemic community and discourse coalitions.

For want of a better term these disparate organizations, networks, and associations will be referred to under the umbrella term of "knowledge agents." These agencies contribute to our understanding of the dimensions of policy problems and develop the conceptual tools to help manage issues of governance. They create "codified knowledge"; that is, concrete intellectual and scientific product found in publications, conferences, websites, and declarations of advisory groups. This kind of knowledge is most amenable to governance as it can be packaged for regulation. However, knowledge agencies also produce "tacit knowledge"—shared understandings, on-the-ground knowledge, and common identities taking shape in "interpretative communities" (Yanow 2009). This position resonates with Sabel and Zeitlin's argument in Chapter 12 of this volume concerning experimentalist governance being the provision of "good explanation" for policy choices.

Finally, in the fourth section some of the politics of knowledge are touched upon. Researchers and experts disagree. There is scientific competition. Rarely is there a single body of thinking, data, or literature that is consensually recognized and accepted without demur. To the contrary, there are struggles between different modes of "knowledge" or what are often described as "discourses," "worldviews," and "regimes of truth" (Jacobson 2007) rather than "truth speaking to power."

1. KNOWLEDGE ACTORS

Where once the "knowledge actor" may have been easy to discern, fitting the stereotype of the scientist in the laboratory or the scholar in the academy, today knowledge actors are much more diverse in both their career profile and their organizational affiliations. The increasing complexity of society and economy in the Organisation of Economic Co-operation and Development (OECD) countries generated demand for analysis and expertise to help control and manage the attendant policy problems. More recently, the information technology revolution has facilitated knowledge exchange and dispersion of "free" knowledge and advice via websites and blogs.

The dispersion and at the same time the massive proliferation of knowledge complicates the absorption of information by policy-making communities. There are questions of assurance on the credibility and quality of knowledge(s) from disparate scientific and advocacy groups. A problem of governance, as much at local as at transnational levels, becomes one of "editing" the oversupply of evidence and analysis from research NGOs, universities, and advocacy groups for the most reliable expertise and scientific advice.

On the demand side, knowledge uptake is thwarted by the ignorance of politicians or overstretched bureaucrats. Knowledge creation is a lengthy process, whereas political problems usually require immediate attention. Consequently, politicians often employ information from trusted sources close to the center of power. Alternatively, there can be a tendency for anti-intellectualism in government. Varying from one country or regime to the next, anti-intellectualism can undermine knowledge use when the policy process itself is riddled with a fear of the critical power of ideas. Censorship or the oppression of critical researchers is not uncommon in some authoritarian states.

Problems can also arise from the politicization of research dealing with sensitive social or economic issues. Via selective use, decontextualization, or misquotation, scientific findings are easy to abuse. Decision-makers face incentives to do so to reinforce their policy positions (or prejudices).

These dynamics cast doubt on the policy relevance of scholars and scientists. More often than not, these actors are out of sight of the public and play a "behind-the-scenes" role in governance. Renditions of John Maynard Keynes's famous dictum are often recounted to convey the impact of ideas in governance.

> The ideas of economists and political philosophers...are more powerful than is commonly understood. Indeed the world is ruled by little else. Practical men who believe themselves to be quite exempt from any intellectual influences, are usually the slaves of some defunct economist. Madmen in authority who hear voices in the air are distilling their frenzy from some academic scribbler of a few years back. (Keynes 1936: 383)

Keynes himself was one who traversed both the scholarly and policy worlds. There are many other significant scholar-practitioners in contemporary affairs. For instance, the sociologist and former President of Brazil, F. H. Cardoso, and Nobel laureates such as the political scientist Henry Kissinger and the economist Joseph Stiglitz. However, the vast majority of scientists and scholars have limited engagement with bureaucracy or policy-making. Below, experts, researchers, and scientists using their knowledge (in an attempt) to inform policy are categorized into three different roles based on the type of relationship that they have with policy-makers.

(i) *"In-house" researchers* are usually public servants such as statisticians, or the chief medical officer, or parliamentary researchers. They can also be located away from the center of government in non-department public bodies (better known as quangos) like the scientists in Australia's Commonwealth Scientific and Industrial Research Organisation (CSIRO). Various international organizations also have experts operating as in-house researchers such as the economists employed by the International Monetary Fund (IMF) Institute or the World Bank (Broad 2006). It is not necessarily the case that these researchers have greater influence on policy simply because of their institutional location. Like many other public sector bodies, researchers are bound by budgetary constraints, bureaucratic politics, and the policy preferences of political leaders.

(ii) The *political advisor* appointed by political leaders is likely to conform to the political and ideological interests of those in power. Sometimes these advisors have a scientific or scholarly background prior to their government appointment. For example, people like Geoff Mulgan, who had think tank and university experience prior to joining the No. 10 Policy Unit in the UK; and likewise Christina Romer, chair of the Council of Economic Advisers, an agency within the Executive Office of the US president charged with offering the president objective economic advice. If they are in close proximity to, and are trusted by, political leaders they can have significant impact on the direction of policy even if it only means "screening" or "editing" the kind of evidence that eventually makes its way into policy deliberations.

(iii) Some scholars and scientists adopt the role of "research broker" or *policy entrepreneur* and actively seek to disseminate research. (Less flattering labels are "policy wonk" or "talking head.") These entrepreneurs engage in a variety of strategies to win support for ideas—identifying problems, networking in policy circles, shaping the terms of policy debates, and building coalitions (Court and Maxwell 2006). Usually these individuals have a significant scientific standing or scholarly reputation in their own right, as well as a knack for interpreting and communicating the technical or theoretical work of their colleagues. They tend to have strong personalities or are motivated by a cause that generates publicity or controversy. They aim to synthesize, market, and popularize research knowledge through a variety of means including writing short nontechnical books or commentary for newspapers, by seeking appointment to commissions or delegations and testifying before legislative committees, as well as by mobilizing others from the research community to contribute to policy deliberations with relevant research.

There is considerable scope for interaction and research collaboration between these different kinds of researcher, often within networks (see below). However, the relationships and interactions between these actors can also be very poor. There is competition for funds, political access, media attention, and scientific recognition, and significant disagreements over the causes, consequences, and solutions to particular problems. This is particularly evident in scientifically contested policy arenas concerning HIV/AIDS, climate change, and genetically modified organisms. Lack of scientific consensus can make it difficult for policy-makers to incorporate disparate knowledge into governance processes.

Nevertheless, returning to Keynes's quote earlier in this chapter, the influence of knowledge actors may be of a longer-term character. Paradigmatic change usually occurs over a generation. Rather than influence resting in the scientific work of significant scholars, it rests in the aggregate contributions of the research community as whole, which develops consensual knowledge and the evidence base over time.

2. KNOWLEDGE ORGANIZATIONS

Universities have often been portrayed as engaged in the disinterested pursuit of knowledge rather than involved in governance. In the US, universities have long interacted with both business and government. The relationship has appeared more "at arm's length" in Europe and elsewhere in the world. However, as mass higher education put severe strain on the public fisc in most OECD countries, so too greater political pressures resulted for universities to demonstrate their social and economic relevance (Alferoff and Knights 2009). These institutions are seen as integral to the "knowledge economy" via the production of human capital and technological applications.

Rather than this instrumental view of universities as a human capital production line, they can also be regarded as technologies of governance that regulate, normalize, and discipline. Governance takes many forms where some modalities operate as sovereign, negative, and controlling, while others enable, encourage, and authorize. Foucault's concept of "governmentality" widens our understanding of power dynamics within governance to include social control in disciplinary institutions (hospitals, psychiatric, and educational institutions). Power can manifest itself positively by producing knowledge and certain discourses that are internalized by individuals and guide the behavior of communities. In the case of neoliberal governmentality based on the predominance of market mechanisms and limited powers of state, the knowledge and expert meanings produced allows the construction of autoregulated selves—individuals as well as institutions. Contemporary reconfiguring of the university is part of a neoliberal governmentality where this knowledge institution is remade as an entrepreneurial agent by deepening administrative rationalities and adopting practices from corporate strategies for streamlining work, efficiently allocating resources to maximize profit, and building flexibility in order to respond quickly to market demand. In this way the university and its subjects (faculty, students, support professionals, and government and corporate sponsors) are better integrated into global capitalism (such as via the trade in educational services).

Central importance is also ascribed to knowledge practices of universities continually feeding into and informing political discourses by interrogating sovereignty and conceptualizing new modes of governance above the state (Chapter 52, this volume). Indeed, the academic contributors to this volume (and many other scholars) are indirectly imbricated in governance and the changing boundaries of state, market, and civil society by constantly reworking governance concepts and creating expert narratives and scholarly stories about the state (see Rhodes on interpretive governance in this volume, Chapter 3).

Third sector and market sector

Much has been written on the different types of private organizations that undertake policy research. "Think tanks," for example, are a form of knowledge organization that directly seeks to influence policy (Weidenbaum 2009). Think tanks often claim that their analysis is "independent" and therefore more credible than government or corporate findings. These organizations also claim that this allows more freedom to "think the unthinkable" and question policy orthodoxy. More skeptical observers suggest that many think tanks recycle ideas and pander to donor priorities (Stone 2007).

Historically, philanthropic foundations have played an important role in both advancing knowledge and in its utilization (Roelofs 2003). Notable are the independent foundations such as Ford, Nuffield, Aga Khan, McArthur, and Sasakawa. In health research, the Gates Foundation is significant. The Soros Foundations Network makes no secret of its aim to promote "open society" liberal values through scholarships, research grants, scientific advocacy, and other knowledge creation initiatives.

NGOs are becoming influential knowledge providers and adjudicators. Their expert standing is derived from the professional status and experience of their staff and their capacity to gather data. Oxfam, Greenpeace, and Transparency International undertake research and attempt to use the findings to influence policy-making at national levels as well as in international policy communities. This kind of expertise or research can compensate for a lack of government-sponsored research in some areas or, more frequently, can present alternative perspectives that may criticize government policy. Indeed, sometimes such research units disdain links into government. The aim may be to influence society more broadly (by promoting their research toward pressure groups and the media) rather than to directly influence government thinking and policy.

More select gatherings of experts and policy practitioners such as the World Economic Forum in Davos engineer elite policy dialogue between corporate leaders, public sector officials, and specialist social scientists. The business and government leaders and high-status intellectuals they are able to assemble bestow a patina of power and authority. Scholarly associations and professional bodies also fall into this category of third sector organizations for the advancement of knowledge, which occasionally venture into policy deliberations.

Consultancy firms are increasingly involved with public policy. Many have been instrumental in the international spread and application of ideas concerning the "new public management". In some highly technical or legal policy fields, it makes sense to contract research services. It is a well-established practice for governments or international organizations to do so in areas where they lack expertise or capacity. This does not necessarily entail that the research results will be utilized as other objectives are also pursued, such as engaging with stakeholders, using "evidence" to propel policy change, or deploying "independent" expertise as a façade to generate legitimacy via processes of consultation and external review.

In sum, the boundaries between the public and private became blurred once the policy relationships of both quasi-state bodies and third sector knowledge organizations are highlighted. As Djelic and Sahlin note in Chapter 52, these "soft actors" are institutionally embedded. Co-constitutive governance emerges via contracting out of research or the consultations of official bureaus with non-state knowledge organizations.

Official bureaus

Within the architecture of the state there are many types of knowledge agencies. For instance, Statistics Norway is a central government body for data collection and analysis of the type found in other political systems. Likewise, national (social) science funding regimes have been established to promote merit-based knowledge creation throughout the OECD. Many states maintain scientific laboratories like CSIRO, which is a partner institute to the international Consultative Group of International Agricultural Research (CGIAR). Of a more temporary character, "commissions of inquiry" or "blue ribbon task forces" are convened to investigate what are usually significant problems of public policy (Ashforth 2006).

Traditionally, policy-making has been the preserve of government. Consequently, most "policy knowledge" has been bundled at the nation-state level. Attempts by scientific communities and policy researchers to inform policy are limited by time and funding, so activities have tended to focus on what is perceived as the crucial decision-making level. In the past, this has been at the level of national government. Only when regional or local governments have significant powers (as in a federal system) do they act as a magnet for experts and policy entrepreneurs. However, globalization has facilitated the instantaneous spread of information and allowed for greater "connectivity" and collaboration between knowledge institutions. Globalization has also created new nodes for the interspersion of knowledge, challenging but not displacing the role of the state in governance.

The recent historical trend toward multi-level governance between institutions at the transnational, national, regional, and local levels outlined by Bache in Chapter 44 complicates governance processes and widens the points at which knowledge actors can intervene. Compared to 100 years ago, the problems of government were of a smaller scale and (mis)managed by relatively few state agencies or ministries. Today, with industrialization, urbanization, rapid technological development, population explosion, and resource depletion alongside privatization, liberalization, and financial deregulation, the problems of governance spill beyond the control of any one state. The increased demand for data, models, scientific evidence, and analysis in order to better comprehend the dimensions of these problems borders on exponential. It is paralleled by the sharp rise from the 1990s of "regulocrats," regulatory agencies, and regulatory networks (Levi-Faur 2011).

New sources of advice are emanating through regional arrangements such as the European Union (EU). Global taskforces from the Club di Roma in the 1970s to the Intergovernmental Panel on Climate Change today, by necessity draw in scientific expertise. As international organizations have proliferated and consolidated in the past half century so too has the establishment of in-house research departments. The IMF, the World Trade Organization (WTO) and the OECD are just some of the international organizations that are important financiers and consumers of research and policy analysis. Scientific and professional knowledge is also used extensively in multilateral initiatives such as the Global Water Partnership, which is reliant on various expert communities such as geologists and engineering specialists for scientific input as well as for monitoring and evaluation. Similarly, the "development economics research group" of the World Bank is a stronghold for the economic examination of questions of development; some say to the exclusion of other disciplines (Broad 2006). United Nations agencies such as the United Nations Educational, Scientific and Cultural Organization (UNESCO) have a direct interest in building the knowledge base of society while the World Health Organization (WHO) has been an important sponsor of health research.

Governments, international organizations, and a variety of non-state actors have reacted to cross-border policy issues with multilateral initiatives, public–private partnerships, global funds, and private standard-setting regimes. In a self-reinforcing dynamic, these new governance structures generate further demand for information sharing, research collaboration, and cooperation on other activities that promote the international diffusion of scientific ideas. In short, knowledge networks are on the rise, assisting in the distribution of power and the decentralization of governance upwards to new global and regional policy forums.

3. KNOWLEDGE NETWORKS

Network governance has long been recognized at the national level (see Rhodes, Chapter 3, this volume). Through their collective action, networks become a mode of governance whereby the resources of public and private actors are mobilized toward common policy objectives in domains outside the hierarchical control of governments. This tendency is particularly noticeable in transnational affairs where governance structures and public institutions lack the central coordination hierarchy and sovereign authority that are characteristic of national polities.

Knowledge production in the global system tends to be based on a complex interweaving of network interactions. Sometimes these are loose, ad hoc relationships with like-minded policy institutes, university centers, and government agencies, in a given issue area to exchange information, ideas, and keep abreast of developments. At other times, advisors and their institutes act as policy entrepreneurs within tighter networks such as an epistemic community (see below). Networks are important both in embedding knowledge agents in a relationship with more powerful actors, and in increasing their audience or constituency, thereby potentially amplifying their impact.

There are those multi-actor networks like the Global Water Partnership that incorporate knowledge actors as just one type of resource alongside the financial, political, and economic resources that other players bring to the coalition. But there are some networks that are primarily founded on knowledge. Knowledge networks are characterized by shared scientific interest and understandings. A knowledge network is a system of coordinated research, results dissemination and publication, intellectual exchange, and financing across national boundaries (Parmar 2002).

For example, the Association of SouthEast Asian Nations Institutes of Strategic and International Studies (ASEAN-ISIS) was officially recognized as influential during the 1990s in helping governments conceptualize a common security community (Morrison 2004). Think tanks and university research institutes were venues for informal diplomacy, organizing exclusive meetings, policy dialogues, and elite working groups to facilitate policy innovation. These semi-official, "off-the-record" negotiations over several years served the intangible governance role of crafting discourses of "region" and "Asian identity" that were gradually internalized by policy elites and decision-makers, and regularized into policy.

Knowledge networks take quite different shape and many are impermanent entities (Alferoff and Knights 2009). For example, the scholarly network GR:EEN (Global Re-ordering: Evolution Through European Networks), funded for four years by the European Commission, is different on criteria of legal status, membership, degree of institutionalization, and issue focus compared to more permanent scientific bodies like CGIAR. Moreover, there are alternative positions for conceptualizing the influence of such networks and their sources of power.

"Epistemic communities" are argued to have considerable influence in circumstances of policy uncertainty. Indeed, there is a common theme in the ideational literature that ideas matter more (or at least their impact is more observable) in circumstances of uncertainty where interests are unformed or some kind of crisis (war, environmental catastrophe, election swings) disrupts established policy patterns and provokes paradigmatic revision. Knowledge actors are presented with a "window of opportunity" to redefine the policy context. Epistemic communities assert their independence from government or vested interest on the basis of their shared notions of validity, or on internationally defined criteria for validating knowledge in their area of know-how. They also share casual beliefs that result from their analysis of practices that contribute to problems in their issue area, which then allows them to see the multiple links between policy and outcomes. This concept builds in (social) scientific knowledge as an independent force in policy development. It is a rationalist concept that stresses the external impact of science on governance, and knowledge as "evidence" inputs to decision-making.

The epistemic community concept is built on the assumption that science is value free, hence independent of the uses to which it is applied. Such distinctions demarcate science from nonscience, facts from values. A more fruitful approach is to see the shades of grey and address the quite complex set of relationships between researchers and policy-makers, recognizing the "co-production" of (social) science in policy-making.

The "interpretative communities" (Yanow 2009) and "discourse coalitions" (Arts and Buizer 2009) concepts are founded on constructivist and postmodernist thinking. These perspectives identify symbols, language, and policy narrative as a source of power. They emphasize, first the social interactions of professional groups and, second, the role of discourse. Sometimes drawing upon Foucault, discourse approaches locate expert deliberation at the interface of power and knowledge. Discourses generate "effects of truth"; that is, naturalizing specific ways of thinking and normalizing certain ways of doing things that are broadcast and replicated through social and institutional practices such as network.

In yet another explanatory frame, neo-Gramscian concepts of knowledge networks (Parmar 2002) and others with a post-Marxist sensibility (Broad 2006) do not regard science, policy expertise, or knowledge as delinked and free-floating, but harnessed to social forces, and in particular to the interests of the state and of capital. In these perspectives, knowledge is not value free or neutral but represents a tool of hegemonic power for the ideational sustenance and global spread of capitalism.

As knowledge networks, CGIAR, GR:EEN, and ASEAN-ISIS could be analyzed from any of these analytical standpoints. But they are also a mode of governance. GR:EEN does not simply do research but is a "large-scale integrating project" for the EU and the European project. CGIAR undertakes international agricultural research but is also constituted as a global policy partnership with developing and industrialized country governments, foundations, and international and regional organizations. With official support, ASEAN-ISIS constructed the scholarly concepts and elaborated policy narratives of security cooperation on which governments then proceeded to build new institutions of regional governance. These networks are part of the ecology of governance.

Diffusion of ideas and expertise

Knowledge production and utilization does not take place simply within the confines of a nation-state. Instead knowledge is diffused, ideas are spread, and policies are transferred beyond territorial boundaries and legal jurisdictions. A key role of knowledge and policy networks is not only to produce ideas but to facilitate their spread through regular interaction via international conferences, government delegations, websites, and sustained e-mail communication. Over time, experts and professionals may form common patterns of understanding regarding policy in the manner of epistemic or interpretative communities. In a further step, the network modality itself has also been diffused as a tool of governance to be adopted by governments around the world. For instance, in Canada, "knowledge-based networks" are promoted by the government as its "approach to development" (Gross Stein et al. 2002: viii).

Of concern to a regional government, national polity, or local community is the process of the knowledge transmission. Technical cooperation, overseas training, and the role of international consultants in institutional development can be a "one-way transaction" from aid organizations or developed countries to recipient countries. Simple advocacy of "best practice" does not confront deep-rooted asymmetries of power that exist in numerous developing and transition countries that may confound effective knowledge utilization. Such "lessons" and "best practice" represent codified, formal, and technical knowledge to be found in the reports and websites of government and OECD documentation centers. This codified knowledge can squeeze out tacit and practical knowledge that is generated in local settings and processes. In other words, traditional, "grassroots," and practitioner knowledge rooted in communal understandings or local practices do not easily connect to the technocratic order of contemporary governance.

International standards and modes of verification are often generated under the canons of academic research and intellectual collaboration. This does not allow an even playing field for the many NGOs and community organizations without the expertise or resources to conduct the intellectually coherent and technically proficient studies of the regulocracy. Practitioner insights, grassroots knowledge, and communal voices do not have the same credence or value as "expert" deliberations. The character of knowledge networks—technical, codified, and homogenized language—produces new inequities. Those with elite knowledge skills and meritocratic attributes—graduate degrees, professional experience in international organizations—are better positioned to participate in the devolved policy dialogues around the expert groups of the G20 or the standard-setting bodies of the OECD.

Social epistemology interrogates the scientific status of "experts" and knowledge agencies as simply one kind of narrative that is no more legitimate than the knowledge of indigenous groups, practitioners, or social movements. Postmodernist explanations regard knowledge as not only bound to time and place but to the person or agency that created it. Cultural and historical context determine the character of truth. Rationalist understandings of scientific objectivity are not regarded as "truth" but as contingent and contestable knowledge claims. In other words, social power relations—rather than access to fundamental (scientific) truths—have elevated rationalism over other modes of knowledge in contemporary policy-making (*inter alia*, Alferoff and Knights 2009; Jacobson 2007).

Accordingly, experts exercise some authority because of the scientific status they claim, or are perceived, to hold. They appropriate authority, first, on the basis of their scholarly credentials and institutional location in (quasi-)academic organizations; and, second, on their establishment in organizations that are in some degree independent from both the state and market, thus strengthening such organizations' reputation as knowledge-driven actors.

4. "SPEAKING TRUTH TO POWER"?

While many aspire to inform governance, the more frequent reality is that those in policy-making milieux do not use research or scientific evidence either rationally or comprehensively. Knowledge agents may be ignored or patronized at will by governments.

Furthermore, some bureaucracies lack capacity in the form of in-house policy units or well-trained staff to absorb effectively either global or local knowledge (Court and Maxwell 2006). The irrelevance of research and the absence of knowledge utilization is a good counterfactual, suggesting that material interests or the institutional inertia of bureaucracies determine policy and politics.

There are many variables intervening between knowledge creation and communication on the road to policy design and implementation. Experts are one small and relatively unimportant group compared to the vested interests of transnational corporations, governments, and other political actors seeking to direct the course of policy. Consequently, rather than the agency of individual experts, think tanks, or university institutes, it is their collective weight and the longer-term structural impact of scientific consensus that institutionally embeds certain knowledge as dominant or hegemonic within international organizations, government programs, and other architectures of governance.

The paradigmatic influence of knowledge in governance, as Keynes noted, is more incremental and "atmospheric." Yet, due to the passage of time and other intermediary factors, it is methodologically difficult to demonstrate in positivist terms ideational cause and subsequent governance effect. Indeed, this structural influence is quite different from the more mundane and instrumental policy uses of knowledge agents on the one hand, and the symbolic or ritualistic use of knowledge artifacts for legitimacy in governance on the other.

The utilitarian value of knowledge for governance is seen in the concern for universities to produce graduates with skills that allow nations to better traverse the global political economy or the pragmatic concern for evidence-based policy for the resolution of societal problems. The use of knowledge agents is also to be found in the day-to-day deliberations of government departments and international organizations. Experts provide a range of services for official consumers such as informed judgments and analysis of existing programs. Building data sets or instigating survey research is a means to map, systematize, and order unruly social and economic phenomena. Knowledge agents are also useful as "independent" evaluators monitoring progress in accordance with legislation or international treaties and agreements. In other words, think tanks, university institutes, and scientific researchers develop the theories, methods, and models to interpret such phenomena and the conceptual language that shapes policy discourse. But information technology has also enlarged the amounts and types of empirical evidence and scientific theories available not only to scholars and policy-makers but the general public. The welter of information necessitates knowledge sifters or editors to distinguish between poor and rigorous research, to discern policy-relevant knowledge, or to synthesize, distill, and repackage knowledge into a manageable format for bureaucratic protocols.

Those who demand and fund research usually set the broad parameters of research agendas even if there is a high degree of autonomy in how scientific inquiry is conducted. However, government inquiries or multilateral initiatives that commission research or establish taskforces of experts may be less indicative of the power and influence of knowledge agencies and more symptomatic of circumstances where research and expertise is used to legitimate preestablished policy positions.

By the same token, academic bodies are used routinely by political leaders to announce policy initiatives. For example, most American presidents and a host of distinguished international leaders have delivered presentations at the Council on Foreign Relations in New York as a prestigious platform from which to make policy announcements. Similarly, scientists are appointed to government committees to lend a scholarly veneer as well as to provide advice. Other experts from think tanks, foundations, scientific charities, and professional associations perform similar roles organizing seminars, delivering mid-career training for civil servants, or providing expert commentary on the issues of the day. Because of their professional image, they are viewed as a more benign or cooperative partners when compared to the relatively more critical stance and occasionally disruptive lobbying of some NGOs. Accordingly, knowledge agents have often built stable relationships with official actors in governments and international organizations. They get access to information and entry to official policy communities, while state agencies can legitimize their policy position by arguing that they consulting independent experts or civil society organizations. These are recursive processes of mutual endorsement that again tie knowledge to governance.

Likewise, the media makes use of scientists and scholars because these "talking heads" can provide authoritative "sound bites" and governance stories. Conversely, scientists and scholars are under pressure to demonstrate their economic relevance or social impact. Media exposure, advisory positions, or consultancy contracts are symbolic of the utility of their expertise and training. These modes of brokering knowledge are not neutral. Institutional and individual interests are served through activity that goes beyond the mechanical sharing of information. There is indirect giving of legitimation for both the "expert" as a reputable analyst with scholarly/scientific/epistemic credibility, and legitimation for the commissioning government department or international agency in having sought an "evidence base" or scientific foundation for governance. "Replenishment from the 'lay intelligentsia' is essential for the continuing vitality of official discourse, allowing the authorities to govern according to principles of knowledge generally deemed 'true'" (Ashforth 2006: 3).

REFERENCES

Alferoff, K. and Knights, D. 2009. Making and mending your nets: Managing relevance, participation in academic-practitioner knowledge networks. *British Journal of Management* 20: 125–142.

Arts, B. and Buizer, M. 2009. Forests, discourses, institutions: A discursive-institutional analysis of global forest governance. *Forest Policy and Economics* 11: 340–347.

Ashforth, A. 2006. Reckoning schemes of legitimation: On commissions of inquiry as power/knowledge forms. *Journal of Historical Sociology* 3): 1–22.

Broad, R. 2006. Research, knowledge and the art of "paradigm maintenance": The World Bank's development economics vice-presidency [DEC]. *Review of International Political Economy* 13: 387–419.

Court, J. and Maxwell, S. (eds.) 2006. *Policy Entrepreneurship for Poverty Reduction: Bridging Research and Policy in International Development.* Rugby: Overseas Development Institute and Practical Action Publishing.

Gross Stein, J., Stren, R., Fitzgibbon, J. and MacLean, M. 2002. *Networks of Knowledge: Collaborative Innovation in International Learning.* Toronto: University of Toronto Press.

Jacobson, N. 2007. Social epistemology: Theory for the "Fourth Wave" of knowledge transfer and exchange research. *Science Communication* 29: 116–127.

Keynes, J. M. 1936. *The General Theory of Employment, Interest, and Money.* New York: Harcourt, Brace and World.

Levi-Faur, D. 2011. *The Handbook of the Politics of Regulation.* Cheltenham: Edward Elgar.

Morrison, C. E. 2004. Track 1/Track 2 symbiosis in Asia-Pacific regionalism. *The Pacific Review* 17: 547–565.

Parmar, I. 2002. American foundations and the development of international knowledge networks. *Global Networks* 2: 13–30.

Roelofs, J. 2003. *Foundations and Public Policy: The Mask of Pluralism.* Albany, NY: State University of New York Press.

Stone, D. 2007. Garbage cans, recycling bins or think tanks? Three myths about policy institutes. *Public Administration* 85: 259–278.

Weidenbaum, M. 2009. *The Competition of Ideas: The World of Washington Think Tanks.* New Brunswick: Transaction.

Yanow, D. 2009. Dear author, dear reader: The third hermeneutic in writing and reviewing ethnography. In E. Schatz (ed.), *Political Ethnography: What Immersion Contributes to the Study of Power.* Chicago: The University of Chicago Press, 275–302.

PART V

ECONOMIC GOVERNANCE

CHAPTER 25

THE GOVERNANCE OF MARKETS: ON GENERATING TRUST IN TRANSACTIONS

FRANS VAN WAARDEN

GOVERNANCE is something that goes beyond "government," or, in the words of Héritier and Rhodes (2011), "a mode of production of norms and public goods by co-production of public and private actors and from multi-level polities." Rhodes (Chapter 3, this volume) speaks of a change "from a hierarchic or bureaucratic state to governance in and by networks," which involves "changing boundaries between public, private, and voluntary sectors." It is essential that norms, sanctions, and other incentives to steer the behavioral choice of societal actors—and thus coordinate activities and (re)allocate resources—can come from three types of sources: state, market, and civil society.

States steer social actors to obey rules and to pay, in exchange for the promise of the utility of public goods, backed up by a latent threat of violence, which is constrained by the rule of law. Markets steer social actors through the lure of private utility from immediate exchange, mediated and facilitated by money; the money functions not only as generalized means of exchange, but also as a unit to calculate and compare value, up to the point at which it acquires a virtual value itself. Civil society induces social actors to "obey and pay" through less formal means, such as social contact and contract, social pressure, non-monetized exchange, and social control. Each of these modes of governance has its specific strengths and weaknesses, and in combination— that is, in governance—they can compensate with their assets for the liabilities, limits, and weaknesses of the other modes.

Markets may provide instruments for governance, yet they themselves are also an object of governance. Markets are no spontaneously emerging and persisting social orders, but have specific problems, and require some governance to work well. This chapter charts and compares the three sources or modes of regulating market behavior that together make for the governance of markets.

First, a central problem of markets, which calls for some form of governance of markets, is identified—distrust. Then governance solutions from four different types of sources will be discussed, compared, and assessed: a) markets and commercial businesses; b) informal communities and networks; c) formal private organizations like associations and firm hierarchies; and d) the state, both its judicial branch (producing case law) and the executive/legislative branches, producing statutory law and taking care of bureaucratic enforcement. The chapter ends with the argument that "hybrid" combinations of these sources have often developed, that they are not new as is often claimed in the governance literature, but that what is new is the piling up of different governance modes on top of each other, with the one controlling others.

1. The trust problem of markets

Markets are more than abstract mechanisms to determine prices. They are sub-societies, populated by people of flesh and blood who seek each other to trade. As such, markets have all the characteristics and problems that also torment other places where people meet, seek, need each other, cooperate, and compete: ambitions, needs, interdependence, inequality, power, risk, uncertainties, misunderstandings, distrust, abuse, guile, cheating, conflict.

Such conditions and problems haunt markets in particular because of the information problems involved in transactions. To make rational choices, prospective buyers need to collect, process, compare, and evaluate information before entering into transactions about what they really want, why they may want it, where they can get it, how reliable products and sellers are, how to value them, and so on. That takes time, money, effort, and energy. Hence, transactions involve transaction costs.

Information advantages may provide transaction partners—usually the seller but occasionally also the buyer—with opportunities for profit, by sketching an overly rosy picture of what the seller/buyer offers, or, in the extreme, by the one cheating the other. Frequently, what you see is not what you get. Thus, food adulteration has been a practice from time immemorial. Bread has been diluted with plaster, sand, or bonemeal; wine and milk with ditchwater; and beer given a more hop-like flavor with arsenic (Rougoor, van der Weijden, and Bol 2003: 24). Among others, Nobel Prize-winner Oliver Williamson (1975) identified this as the risk of opportunistic behavior, but long before economists discovered this, society was aware of it, as testified by age-old proverbs. The Dutch warn the buyer not to "be sold turnips for lemons" (*"je knollen voor citroenen laten verkopen"*) the British that "the buyer needs a hundred eyes, the seller but one," and the Bavarians claim that *"Wenn die Narren zu Marckt kommen, lösen die Kremer Geldt"* ("when the fools come to the market, the hawkers cash in").

The risk of getting cheated produces distrust between potential transaction partners. Such distrust is sand in the cogwheels of the economy and society. When distrust strikes, buyers may strike too. This could result in a negative spiral of ever less transactions, as analyzed by Akerlof (1970) in his well-known "lemons" problem. Information asymmetries make prospective consumers wary about engaging in a transaction in which they risk buying a poor-quality product (symbolized by a "lemon," American slang for a bad secondhand car). Lower prices are needed to entice them to do so nevertheless, which increases the pressure on producers to lower product quality so that they can still earn something despite the lower prices, thus confirming the suspicion of the buyers. Conversely, producers of good-quality products refrain from offering their goods on the market, as they cannot get the real value for their product, because prospective buyers reduce their price offer with a premium for the risk they run of ending up with poor-quality goods. Thus bad products and producers drive good ones from the market, resulting in a negative spiral of ever lower prices and lower quality.

In theory, this would eventually destroy the market. Consumers would not be willing to buy anything any more, and sellers would no longer offer anything for sale. No transactions would mean no market. This would be a literal case of "market failure": the market would fail to materialize and to work. The consumers' strike of beef consumption after the BSE scandal or the plummeting shares of corporations who cooked the books—like Enron and Ahold—are cases in point. Following the crisis of confidence caused by the Enron–Andersen scandal, 35 billion dollars of investment capital went up in smoke. Fraud is not only unfair or immoral; it is also dysfunctional. Paradoxically, this type of market failure increases as markets seem to work better. The fiercer the competition, the greater the temptation—or even pressure—to try to take advantage of information asymmetries.

This theoretical logic of the lemons problem depends, however, on the unrealistic assumption that buyers can wait to engage in a transaction. It may hold for buying a car or stocks, but not for procuring the vital necessities of life: food, shelter, clothing, energy, health care. When hungry, one may have to accept whatever food is on offer. The same holds for labor markets: poor workers cannot wait to sell their labor, even if they receive only a starvation wage. Thus, not only do asymmetries in information (1) affect the power relations in potential transactions, but so do (2) asymmetries in the ability to wait, as well as (3) asymmetries in the availability of alternatives.

The last condition is a classic one in economics: monopoly/monopsony or oligopoly/oligopsony positions on markets—that is, less alternatives for one transaction partner—bias bargaining relations and allow the other transaction partner to extract undeserved rents. The first one, information asymmetries, has in the meantime become common knowledge in institutional economics. The middle one, asymmetries in the ability to wait, has not received much attention in mainstream economics. However, it has been stressed in Marxist economics (Mandel 1975).

The rich have all three power advantages: they can increase their alternatives by traveling to where there are more suppliers; they can wait; and they can afford to collect information or recruit expert advice before entering in transactions. Use of power may be abuse of the market, which is again abuse of power. Economists often posit equity and efficiency as opposites, as trade-offs: more equity should mean less efficiency, and vice versa. But greater equity—in transactions—may be a precondition for transactions to happen and hence for efficient allocation.

Under conditions of information asymmetry, distrust, or absence of alternatives, but where buyers are able to wait, transactions may be discouraged or even blocked. Hence, markets are frequently not the natural social orders many economists believe them to be. As Hobbes (1651) and Polanyi (2001 [1944]) argued, markets need to be "governed." They need a Leviathan, a market superintendent, which guarantees social order on the market and reduces the risks of deceit and distrust to at least such a level that people are willing to engage in transactions. In their absence "there is no place for Industry; because the fruit thereof is uncertain: and consequently no Culture of the Earth; no Navigation, nor use of the commodities that may be imported by Sea; no commodious Building; no Instruments of moving, and removing such things as require much force;... and which is worst of all, continuall feare" (Hobbes, 1968 [1651]: 186).

2. MARKET SOLUTIONS: COMMERCIAL INFORMATION PROVIDERS AND CERTIFIERS

Can the market itself provide solutions to its own problems of information asymmetries and distrust? It has been tried, in many different ways and with varying success, depending on the nature of the product, the location of the market, the position of the transaction partners and, more broadly, the temporal, cultural, and societal embeddedness of the specific market.

First of all, the seller may provide information to the prospective buyer in order to convince him or her to buy. He could do so through a) marketing and advertisement; b) labeling his product with information about it, its use, and perhaps even its production process; or c) providing "money-back" guarantees to the buyer.

But how can the buyer be sure that the information given by the producer is true, objective, and complete, and that he will live up to his promise of a money-back guarantee? Again, the market could do the job. The seller has an incentive to care about his reputation, in the interest of future business transactions. In transparent and competitive markets, sellers may compete for the best reputation.

However, satisfying these conditions merely displaces and repeats the information problem: from knowing the product to knowing the seller. The buyer would need to know both the identity and the "quality" of the seller. Is the seller he deals with the same as the one he has reputation-information about? In certain markets, for example for taxis, that may not be easy to establish. Second, the buyer needs information about the reputation of the seller.

He could base such information upon own past experience, but that requires again certain conditions to be present. First of all that he was able to truly ascertain the past performance of the seller. But how to rate the service of a physician or a lawyer? Second, that one is enough of a repeat buyer to sanction the seller by declining to do business with him again.

In cases of limited competition, intransparent markets, or low frequency of transactions between the same actors, third-party involvement may be needed. Such third-party services have again been provided through the market mechanism. Detectives, book and magazine publishers, appraisers, auditors, certifiers, rating agencies, hallmark producers, accreditors, mediators, real estate agents, art experts, brokers, dealers, experts, and product-comparing websites have presented themselves. They provide information about the quality of product and producer, including on issues such as social and environmental responsibility or their agreement with specific belief systems, as with kosher or halal products. Such information has itself become a commodity traded in markets.

Even unions have reached for the instrument of certification to defend workers' interests. Rather than relying on strikes or negotiations with the government over protective regulation, they have introduced quality certificates—for working conditions. Thus, the Dutch union for film and TV crews has developed a certificate for film and TV producers who "treat their crew-members decently" (*De Volkskrant*, 29 January 2010). Rather than using working class power, the unions seek now recourse to consumer power.

Third parties also provide services that aid in negotiating, closing, and enforcing contracts, and in protecting property rights. Such services are provided by lawyers, accountants, notaries, bailiffs, debt collection agencies, and, in some places, the mafia (Gambetta 1993). Some have developed ingenious methods of enforcement. Thus, the Indian company Unique Recovery Service employs eunuchs to aid in debt collection. According to Indian superstition, castrates bring curses and misfortune, and their appearance at a house or wedding party will scare the debtor enough to make him pay back his debt immediately. As a consequence, the outcasts have a socially acceptable profession and make a decent living (*De Volkskrant*, 17 February 2001).

The commercial initiatives of private information providers may help in reducing information asymmetries and distrust in transactions. However, history has exposed their shortcomings.

First, how to trust the information providers and certifiers? The problems caused by information asymmetries and fraud threats, which haunted the original products, concern their quality certificates just as much. Moreover, the certificate producers follow similar strategies in attempting to raise the reputation of their certificates: advertising, labeling, guarantees, brand names, and eventually third-party verification/certification of the certificates and certifiers. This is usually called accreditation of the certifier. But the problem then gets repeated for the accreditor as well. Elsewhere we have called this the "homunculus problem of free markets" (van Waarden and van Dalen 2010), meaning a repetition of the same problem.[1]

The trust problem concerning the private certifier can be exacerbated by several conditions. First, where does the certifier get his income from? In principle, that should be from those who profit from the information, the prospective buyers. However, in the case of a mass-produced product, whose quality certificate is addressed to a mass of anonymous customers, the certifier cannot directly charge those, as he cannot identify them. Only the producer or seller is available to pay the certifier for certifying his products, and he may do so for marketing reasons. That is like "trusting the cat to keep the cream". Indeed, the wisdom of proverbs tells us what to expect in such cases: "He who pays the piper calls the tune." Thus information, ratings and certificates may be(come) biased. Already that suspicion would be sufficient to make the buyer distrust both the product and its certificate, making the latter practically useless and unsaleable, that is, creating a crisis on the market. The recent financial scandals, first the Enron case, which destroyed the reputation of its accountant Andersen, and then the mortgage-backed securities crisis, which seriously hurt the reputation of their rating agencies, Standard and Poor's (S&P), and Moody's, have underlined that once again.

A second problematic condition could be the presence of several competing certifiers, that is, a situation where a market for certifiers has developed, who may differ in degree of seriousness and professionalism, and hence quality. This may provide the customer with choice, but can also create intransparency and confusion. Information hallmarks are standards, and, as with other standards, such as technical and administrative ones, the customer is interested in one reliable and universal standard. What is more, the resulting competition could focus on what is easiest to compare, that is, the price, and price competition tends to exert a downward pressure on quality.

Third, private organizations, which try to build up a hallmark reputation, will have to protect these against copycats, especially dabblers who sell lower-quality information under the same "brand" name. Such free riders can destroy the reputation of an image or brand of a group of producers. For protection against this, sellers may need external support, which could again either come from commercial services, such as the mafia, or from a state-like authority.

3. CIVIL SOCIETY SOLUTIONS 1:
SELF-REGULATION BY INFORMAL COMMUNITIES AND MORE FORMAL NETWORKS

A less biased and usually cheaper solution to the information problems can and has come from noncommercial sources, that is, not from the market, but from civil society. The latter has provided the following bases for trust in transactions: a) personal acquaintances in somewhat durable mutual dependencies or small groups; b) communities bound together by shared norms, values, and identities; c) informal networks; and d) formal non-profit organizations like churches, associations, or foundations.

Transaction partners, who depend on each other for some time and transact frequently—such as a baker and his neighborhood customers or a shipbuilder and his suppliers and workers—get personally acquainted and may develop trust relations. Their interdependence provides them with an interest in continuing their relationship and supporting it by trusting and trustworthy behavior, and with a sanction in case their confidence gets betrayed, namely exiting the relationship—by dismissal, or by a buyers' or workers' strike.

Furthermore, parties in enduring relations will develop mutual expectations, which over time may develop into unwritten rules regarding, for example, the inappropriateness of deception and the need, possibilities, and conditions for trust. Thus, trust in such relations may no longer be founded only on dependency, interest, and sanctions, but also on informal social norms regarding appropriate behavior.

These bilateral social relations tend to be embedded in webs of socioeconomic relations, which eventually form networks, groups, communities, and cultures, bound by common activities, tasks, specialized language, interests, and/or interdependencies, and which subsequently develop norms and values of socioeconomic interaction and shared identities, which enhance these bonds. Such was the case with medieval merchants, who had to fend off threats both from "below"—highwaymen—and from "above"—predatory rulers—up until current communities of, for example, horse traders, construction companies, or financial dealers. Like the medieval merchants, they too try to counter the threats from "below"—dishonest clients or fly-by-night competitors—and the modern-day version of "predatory rulers": governments who "burden" them with taxes and costly regulations.

Transactions make communities, but communities also make transactions. Preexisting communities based on habitat, linguistic, ethnic, and/or religious identities may also embed and facilitate transactions due to trust based on these shared identities and values, which increase the predictability of the behavior of others. The social structure of such communities is the institution that reduces uncertainty and transaction costs. Subsequently, Ouchi (1980), Piore and Sabel (1984), Porter (1990), and Fukuyama (1995) have pointed to the importance of clan and culture for economic transactions. The extensive social capital literature is also relevant here (e.g. Putnam 1993).

Such communities and cultures facilitate transactions through channels of information about social reputations. Gossip is also an important sanction. Most people are quite sensitive to the opinion of their fellow men. Furthermore, the multidimensional character of such community relations provides for other forms of social interdependence, social control, and sanctions like ostracism. Hillmann and Aven (2011) showed how industrial capital was mobilized and allocated during Russian industrialization through networks of entrepreneurs of similar ethnic, kinship, and regional origins.

Most communities sanction theft, deceit, and dishonesty, and these may be fortified by religious norms. The Christian Ten Commandments forbid theft—even the desire of it—(nr. 7) and "giving false testimony" (nr. 8). These have been elaborated in the Catholic and Protestant Catechisms, the Jewish Torah (a.o. 613 mitzvot), and the Qu'ran (Surahs 2: 283 and 5: 38). These and other norms increase the predictability of mutual expectations. Jews will not trade on the Shabbath, Catholics are not allowed to charge interest, and Calvinists are expected to be thrifty and frugal. This has as its effect—if not intention—the mitigation of mutual distrust among the members of the same group. Cultures include also norms relating to whom one trusts: family members and businesses, strangers, or large organizations (Fukuyama 1995).

One strategy to reduce risks in transactions is hence to conclude transactions only or preferably with fellow community members. That might limit the use of this community governance institution to local, small, personal, less differentiated, that is, more "primitive" societies, and might make it outdated in a time of globalization of markets. Indeed, classic examples are the industrial districts of middle-Italy or the Jewish clothing industry in New York. However, the competitive advantage of social, linguistic, and cultural bonds pays off, especially among geographically dispersed communities, such as the diasporas of the Jews in Europe or of the trading Chinese in Asia. The diffusion of world religions may help as well. Another curious local/global "microstructure" is that of the community of traders in financial dealing rooms, as investigated by Knorr Cetina and Bruegger (2000, 2002). They describe in detail how financial traders across the globe communicate and sanction a "misbehaving" dealer instantly by refusing to trade with him for a few minutes or even seconds.

Though such informal community norms, values, and sanctions may be powerful, they often do not suffice. The history of capitalism shows that the pressure of competition can get so high that such mutual expectations are broken and trust disappears. Agencies were needed to back up such norms, to interpret, monitor, and enforce them. Thus, communities have, over time, organized informally in networks or formally in associations and firm hierarchies.

4. Civil society solutions 2:
Self-regulation by formal associations and firm hierarchies

A borderline case between informal and formal cooperation, that is, between communities and associations, are social clubs, with predominantly business people as members, such as the Free Masons, local elite societies, and service clubs such as the Rotary or the Lyons. Such clubs are places where the local elite, including potential business partners, can meet informally, exchange information and opinions, and check mutual expectations. It still is a golden rule for building contractors to belong to such local clubs. They have to "network," for example, with local dignitaries and politicians who may tender out work.

More important are formal and specialized interest associations of economic actors: trade associations, trade unions, and consumer organizations. Many of them have developed into private "self-governments", which enact and try to enforce internal rules binding their members. They set quality standards, engage in product certification, set market-entry conditions, and organize training programs as one of those conditions for market entry. Thus, they try to increase market transparency and force dabblers from the market, in order to raise the collective reputation of the industry. Medieval guilds are the classic example, and they live on today in the German, Austrian, and Swiss *Handwerkskammern*, which still engage in these activities.

Some other present-day examples: the Dutch Insurance Association prescribes members how to list prices, returns, and risks of life insurances in order to facilitate comparison. Dutch associations of building contractors and travel agencies have created guarantee funds, to compensate customers who were cheated by companies that went bankrupt before the home was finished or the holiday started. Cartels mitigate competition, and thus reduce the pressure on market parties to behave opportunistically. Associations of electricity companies have set minimal safety standards for electrical products as well as standards for interconnectivity.

Consumer and workers' associations also help to reduce uncertainty. The first attract members with their service of product quality comparisons. They may also create market regulations, such as a contract with a bankers' association, which regulates liability in electronic payments, thus increasing consumer trust in automatic teller machines (ATMs). Distrust initially limited the popularity of such ATMs. Trade unions conclude collective wage agreements, thus reducing workers' fear of exploitation by employers.

Though risk-reducing, associations can in turn suffer from risks and be risks for others. Competition from unorganized bunglers, not bound by costly associational regulations, may induce members to defect and lower prices and quality, eventually undercutting the value of the associational hallmark, while still free riding on its reputation. Illegal copying of associational certificates threatens such associations' credibility. In turn, associational activities can become risks for others, when they acquire characteristics of cartels.

Another strategy to reduce uncertainty in transactions using "formal organization" is the internalization of transactions into corporate hierarchies through mergers and acquisitions, thus making them susceptible to hierarchic control. Horizontal market relations are thus transformed into vertical hierarchic ones. "Hierarchy" replaces "market" as the allocation and coordination principle (Williamson 1975). This could reduce information asymmetries, and allow for the control of opportunistic behavior. Competing technical standards, which produce uncertainty, can be co-opted and adopted, abolished, or pushed out of the market by the greater market power of the larger firm.

Large hierarchies do not hold power only internally, but also externally. They can use their market power to impose standards upon their suppliers and even customers. Organizations at the end of a product chain, like supermarkets, department stores, or final assembly industries, like car- or shipbuilders, are, especially, in a position to regulate the value chain.

5. THE STATE

Private solutions to the risks and uncertainties of the market have problems. Detectives and other reputation-rating agencies threaten the privacy of economic actors. Accountants—supposed to be independent and neutral—have turned out to be subject to temptations of favoritism. Customs and norms of clans and communities can be quite strict market-entry barriers. Associations suffer from the threat of free riders and have difficulty in enforcing self-regulation. And a proliferation of competing private standards can become self-defeating as they may obfuscate markets rather than increase transparency.

Such problems of certificate inflation, product laundering, and free ridership have produced calls for support from higher or more respected authorities. Eventually that has been the state, in two forms, that of courts, producing case law, and of governments, producing statutory law. States have more power to enforce standards, and a more neutral image as a) their certificates do not need to be directly paid by those certified, but can be funded out of the general tax income; and b) they are accountable to the general public, that is, to the control institutions typical of a democratic constitutional state.

Courts and case law

Many economic transactions, sooner or later, produce conflicts, over the quality of the products supplied, over the payment of product or labor, over the observation of contracts. Such conflicts ultimately come, possibly after an outburst of violence and social unrest, to some arbitrator for settlement. Already, early on, the state has—given its responsibility for social order—provided such arbitrators, that is, the judiciary financed and employed by, but relatively independent from, the other state powers. For the implementation and enforcement of its decisions, the judiciary is supported by the legitimate monopoly of the state over the exercise of force. As judges orient themselves in their decisions to earlier decisions by other judges, these have acquired power of precedence. The accumulated decisions have produced de facto regulation: case law, which regulates economic transactions, and which has substantially contributed to the reduction of uncertainty. Already in this manner the state has become involved in the regulation of economic transactions. Even governments that are otherwise wary of intervention in the economy and advocate a liberal "nightwatch" state, have in this way, willy-nilly, become market regulators, and are becoming more regulatory every day.

The legislative and executive powers, with statute law

Whereas the uncertainty-reducing role of the state via the courts is still a passive one—it reacts to conflicts, which are brought to it from civil society—the state has also come to intervene more actively in economic transactions.

There were various reasons for a special role of the state. First, it has the advantage of its monopolies on the legitimate exercise of force, taxation, and binding regulation. Many forms of uncertainty reduction require such a monopoly. That helped establish needed uniform standards, and could prevent and discourage free ridership. Furthermore, of all actors, the (democratic) state could most legitimately claim to represent a "general interest." That is important for creating trust in uncertainty-reducing regulations.

Market ordering was done first through private and criminal law, which emerged out of local customs and conventions, but was sanctioned and eventually codified by the state. Basic rules of the market game were set as regards the mutual obligations of transaction partners: information provision, contracting, honest trade, liability. Fraud and deception were sanctioned under criminal law, but aggrieved parties could also claim damage compensation under tort law.

Often, a first reaction of the state to deficiencies of private risk and uncertainty-reducing institutions has been to support them. It does so, of course, already with the basic legal infrastructure (property rights, contract law, judicial conflict resolution), without which markets, commercial risk reducers, communities, and associations could not function.

Furthermore, the state tolerated, recognized, sanctioned, or extended self-regulation by private actors. It the process, it set conditions for such self-regulation. State law established the rights and responsibilities of the limited liability company, the insurance company, and the stock market, all risk-reducing innovations that needed state sanctioning to increase trust among investors.

Brands and quality certificates were registered and protected by intellectual property right (IPR) law, reducing the risk of certificate inflation due to illegal copying. A next step was to investigate the value of private certificates and accredit them. Public trust in commercial risk and uncertainty reducers, like insurers and accountants, was increased by the fact that they themselves were held to standards. Collective action problems of associational self-regulation were solved by the statutory extension of cartels and collective wage agreements, or by the recognition of private standards in public law and court decisions. Thus French wine quality regulations are enacted and enforced by private *syndicats* of local wine growers, but are recognized, authorized, and backed by the French state. The Dutch, German, and Austrian states went even further and elevated some private sectoral trade associations to a status under public law not unlike that of municipalities, though not with a territorial but a functional/sectoral jurisdiction, complete with compulsory membership, board elections, and the authority to impose taxes and regulations on the "population" of the economic sector.

States also supplemented or replaced private regulations by public ones. Where the market produced a proliferation of standards, which threatened to make them again intransparent, it set uniform authoritative standards for weights and measures, pricing units, university degrees, or food quality certificates. Public law also corrected inequalities in transactions, by protecting the weaker parties in them, such as children, workers, individual consumers, and smaller businesses. This implied setting minimum standards for goods and transactions in general labor and consumer law, and in legislation for specific goods and sectors, like food, drugs, housing, finances, insurances, or health care. This limited the transaction partners' freedom of contracting. What was originally possible became impossible, what was voluntary became compulsory.

Such public regulations reduce the competitive pressure to cheat and lower quality standards. They generate trust in transactions. Public oversight of the professions or the stock exchange increases their trustworthiness. State supervision and guarantees of banks and insurances induce people to "entrust" their money to private "trusts." Thus the English term "trust" has not only become synonymous for hope, faith, loyalty, duty, and responsibility, but for custody, care, and credit.

The most important general function of the state regarding uncertainty reduction is to provide a stable and predictable legal, political, and social environment for firms, which allows them to calculate risks better. This includes guarantees against arbitrary state interventions and is a central function of the rule of law—the state itself is bound by the law.

6. GOVERNANCE HYBRIDS: A NEW INTERPRETATION OF "RESPONSIVE REGULATION"

The various governance arrangements provided by the market, civil society, and the state can be considered alternative solutions to the trust problems of markets. They differ in that each has its own specific characteristics, structure, problems and solutions, strengths and weaknesses, costs and benefits. But they perform similar functions and hence can be considered *functional alternatives* for each other. Where some have been abolished or have disappeared, other modes may develop to fill the void. They may relate to each other as "communicating vessels" (van Waarden 2002): less of the one may produce more of another. Thus, neoliberalism has turned the hallmark business into a booming market, as prospective transaction partners run more risks in freer markets. Deregulation of telecom and bus services has produced an increase in commercial conflicts in court, with statutory regulations being replaced by case law (Hildebrand 2010).

Being functional alternatives does not mean that all governance modes are equally effective. The various modes have different strengths and weaknesses, assets and limitations. Therefore, in addition to being *alternatives*, market, state, and civil society regulations can and do *complement* each other through cooperation and regulatory joint ventures. The strengths of the one mode may compensate for the weaknesses, problems, and constraints of another. States can correct "failures of markets and civil society", such as difficulties in producing collective goods (including law binding for all, in essence also a collective good), externalization of costs to other parties, ruinous competition, regulatory races-to-the-bottom, bias and particularism, limited enforcement powers of private actors, and so on. Conversely, markets and civil society can compensate for "state failures," such as long principal–agent chains, limited knowledge among the regulators about the world/market to be regulated, lack of legitimacy among the regulatees, and ineffectiveness of command and control, leading to enforcement problems. Where the credibility of private certification becomes questionable, more neutral state accreditation may solve the problem of dwindling trust. And the international reach of many multinational organizations (MNOs) and non-governmental organizations (NGOs) can compensate for the jurisdictional limits of nation-states.

Hence, cooperation is frequently based on dependency relations. The one needs the other, for enforcing one's own power, effectiveness, or legitimacy. Unions need states to raise wage agreements—which set standards for wages and working conditions—to the status of statutory law, and extend the validity to non-organized free-riding entrepreneurs, while state regulations may gain in legitimacy among the regulatees if supported by the latter's interest association. But, as always, dependence can turn into habituation and even "addiction". Nevertheless, such cooperation has stabilized dependency relations between market, state, and civil society. In the meantime, this also holds true for global regulation.

A typical and current example of international public–private regulatory cooperation is the Hazard Analysis and Critical Control Points (HACCP) system for ensuring food safety. This system of process standards requires firms to identify critical points in their production chains that are susceptible to hazards like contamination, and sets procedures for controlling and reducing hazards, monitoring, verifying results, and benchmarking firms' performance with others. The systems, originally developed by the American government, have now become joint products of trade associations, firm hierarchies, scientific and professional organizations, NGOs, national governments, and international organizations. They have acquired a quasi-legal status by being imposed by the US Food and Drug Administration (FDA), the European Union (EU) and its European Food Safety Agency (EFSA), and international organizations as the Codex Alimentarius (UN) and the Sanitary and Phytosanitary (SPS) Agreement of the WTO.

This combination of the regulatory efforts of markets, states, and civil society requires "responsive regulation" of state, market, and civil society actors, albeit in a somewhat different meaning from the familiar one Ayres and Braithwaite (1992) gave it. Rather than being "responsive" to the reactions of regulatees, here it concerns states being responsive to regulatory initiatives of markets and civil society and vice versa, with responses varying from banning or blocking, to support or even adoption. Joint ventures, mergers, and takeovers could even result, though here not of corporations but of economic governance institutions.

The best mix of market, civil society, and state is not so much a matter of design as of discovery, experimentation, and development. For one, the appropriate combination will be contingent upon—that is, responsive to—the nature of the product and market. Given their various strengths and weaknesses, some governance modes may work better in one transaction relation, market, or country than in another. This will depend on what is traded; the extent of the market (local, global); frequencies of transactions; the number, power, and expertise of transaction partners; the risks and uncertainties involved; regulatory histories; and the technical, cultural, political, and legal embeddedness. The latter determine, for example, trade customs and the legitimacy and legality of different modes. And, obviously, illegal markets cannot seek recourse to state regulation to solve trust problems. Therefore, more in general, effective, efficient and legitimate economic governance will have to be custom governance.

Second, the economic governance mix is also contingent upon history. Over time, societies have discovered and developed a great variety of modes of governing markets, in response to problems that presented themselves and their experiences with solutions tried. The development of the balance between markets, state, and civil society is very much like the development of law, as described by US Justice Oliver Wendel Holmes in his 1881 Treatise on the Common Law (2009 [1881]: 1):

> "The life of law has not been logic; it has been experience. The felt necessities of the time, the prevalent moral and political theories, intuitions of public policy, avowed or unconscious, even the prejudices which judges share with their fellowmen, have had a good deal more to do than the syllogism in determining the rules by which men should be governed. The law embodies the story of a nation's development through many centuries, and it cannot be dealt with as if it contained only the axioms and corollaries of a book of mathematics. In order to know what it is, we must know what it has been and what it tends to become. We must alternately consult history and existing theories of legislation."

What holds for the development of law, holds in particular for the development of market governance. Ordering and regulating economic activity has been a process of muddling through, conditioned by path dependency; by the already existing configurations, their performance, and other experiences people have with them; by their influence on societal interests, cultural values, and belief systems; and by the expected costs and benefits of change. Over time markets, civil society organizations, and states have emerged to produce a great variety of private and public goods including all kinds of regulations of markets. The history of state formation is closely linked to the increased importance of markets, and that in turn is linked to the rise of organizations of civil society, such as guilds and charitable organizations.

History continues to unfold. New technologies, products, services, markets, transactions, transaction partners, circumstances, ICT, and globalization create new challenges and opportunities, including for more effective, efficient, appropriate, and legitimate— that is, "better"—governance. The various old modes of economic governance, discussed here, offer ingredients for such "better regulation." Global markets, being beyond the jurisdiction of nation-states, exhibit a renewed importance of private market regulation. Supermarket chains set food standards and the Marine Stewardship Council sets sustainability norms.

7. Conclusion: a new Keynesianism?

It is often claimed in the burgeoning recent "governance literature" that such hybrid governance is a new phenomenon. Nothing could be further from the truth. History and anthropology provide us with rich sources of information about the many different forms of economic governance that societies have generated over time and across space to reduce deceit and distrust in the marketplace and thus facilitate transactions: from the merchant and craft guilds in medieval Europe and the commercial eunuch organizations in India, to the EU. An early extreme case is that of the Dutch East India Company (VOC) (1602–1795). This was a private commercial hierarchy, association, network, market, and state, all in one. While engaging in long-distance trade between Asia and Europe, it coordinated and regulated it, set product quality standards, countered smuggling and dabbling in order to protect its monopoly and reputation, and so on. Furthermore, it had public authority in its trade settlements and its occupied territories across the globe, and was authorized by the Dutch state to regulate, tax, and engage in diplomacy and even in war in the name of that state.

But what is new is the piling up of governance modes on top of each other. There is a long-term secular trend of more controls and longer chains and networks of them. This is facilitated through increased ease of exchange and aggregation of information, necessary for governance. And it is motivated by greater scientific knowledge about possible risks. As we know more about risks and possibilities to avoid those, the pressure to apply such knowledge and to shield people from "unnecessary" risk has risen. Scandals lead to outcries for greater accountability and more oversight of the responsible—yet apparently negligent—regulators. The Enron–Andersen scandal produced the US Sarbanes–Oxley Act (2002), creating a new oversight layer, the Public Company Accounting Oversight Board, over the already existing internal private ones of the accountancy profession and the accountancy firms. The scandal made actors in the control chain also more fearful of liability suits and hence more careful. This made them establish more internal control layers. The recent dioxin scandals in animal feed in Germany have led to new controls over controls, public as well as private ones. Currently there are at least eight levels of control of control of control in the feed-producing industry. First several internal controls in the companies involved, which are checked by controllers of trade associations, those in turn by national governments, and those again by the EU.

The need for controls is, in principle, insatiable. Each higher level of control can raise again distrust and calls for controllers of these controllers. But no matter how many levels of control are being built in, in the end we cannot avoid trusting the last and highest level of oversight. Otherwise, the upward spiral of controls of controls of controls and so on is, in principle, endless.

Thus, in addition to production chains there are control chains that aim to reduce risks and uncertainties in production and transactions. While ever fewer people work in the first ones due to the mechanization of production, more and more jobs are found in the control chains. Economies become like chemical factories, where "controllers" in control rooms do most of the work. Elsewhere (van Waarden 2006) I calculated that around 1 million people or 14 percent of the Dutch working population earn their living by controlling others, who are reducing risks and uncertainties for yet others. Seen from this perspective, distrust is no curse but a blessing. It has become a booming business and a main source of employment. Economists may have long thought that transaction costs are there for the transactions. But perhaps the opposite is also true:

transactions are there for transaction costs: read jobs! Thus we have unexpectedly landed a new Keynesianism. Keynes had an eye for the virtues of waste. He argued that two pyramids were better than one and that it would be even beneficial for the economy to dig holes and immediately fill them up again (1936: 131). He expected such benefits from the state. But in this modern variation of dissipation the private sector participates vehemently. Luckily, its products, virtual organizational pyramids and holes, may be more environmentally friendly.

Note

1. The "homunculus problem" concept stems from alchemy, psychology, and neurosciences. In order to explain how people can become conscious of images, including words, in their head, people used to think that there was a little man in their head, who revealed the images and words for us. Of course, that was no explanation, but a mere repetition of the problem: How did that little freak in our brains become conscious of the images and words in *his* head?

References

Akerlof, G. A. 1970. The market for "Lemons." *Quarterly Journal of Economics* 84: 488–500.

Ayres, I. and Braithwaite, J. 1992. *Responsive Regulation*. Oxford: Oxford University Press.

Fukuyama, F. 1995. *Trust: The Social Virtues and the Creation of Prosperity*. London: Penguin.

Gambetta, D. 1993. *The Sicilian Mafia: The Business of Private Protection*. Cambridge, MA: Harvard University Press.

Héritier, A., and Rhodes, M. (eds.) 2011. *New Modes of Governance in Europe*. Basingstoke: Palgrave Macmillan.

Hildebrand, Y. 2010. Freer Markets, More Court Rulings? PhD dissertation, University of Utrecht.

Hillmann, H. and Aven, B. 2011. Fragmented networks and entrepreneurship in late imperial Russia. *American Journal of Sociology* 117: 484–538.

Hobbes, T. 1968. *Leviathan*. Harmondsworth: Penguin.

Holmes, O. W. 2009. *The Common Law*. New York: Cosimo.

Keynes, J. M. 1936. *The General Theory of Employment, Interest, and Money*. Rpt. 1997, Amherst, NY: Prometheus Books.

Knorr Cetina, K. D. and Bruegger, U. 2000. The market as an object of attachment: Exploring postsocial relations in financial markets. *Canadian Journal of Sociology* 25: 141–168.

Knorr Cetina, K. D. and Bruegger, U. 2002. Global microstructures: The virtual societies of financial markets. *American Journal of Sociology* 107: 905–950.

Mandel, E. 1975. *Late Capitalism*. London: Humanities Press.

Ouchi, W. G. 1980. Markets, bureaucracies, and clans. *Administrative Science Quarterly* 25: 129–141.

Piore, M. J. and Sabel, C. 1984. *The Second Industrial Divide*. New York: Basic Books.

Polanyi, K. 2001. *The Great Transformation*. Boston: Beacon Press.

Porter, M. 1990. *The Competitive Advantage of Nations*. New York: Free Press.

Putnam, R. 1993. *Making Democracy Work*. Princeton: Princeton University Press.

Rougoor, C., van der Weijden, W. and Bol, P. 2003. *Voedselveiligheid tot (w) elke prijs?* The Hague: Ministry of Agriculture.

van Waarden, F. 2002. Market institutions as communicating vessels: Changes between economic coordination principles as a consequence of deregulation policies. In J. R. Hollingsworth, K. Mueller, and E. J. Hollingsworth (eds.), *Advancing Socio-Economics: An Institutionalist Perspective*. New York and Oxford: Rowman and Littlefield, 171–212.

van Waarden, F. 2006. Werk in een wantrouwende wereld. *Beleid en Maatschappij* 33: 232–251.

van Waarden, F. and van Dalen, R. 2010. Het homunculusprobleem van vrije markten: Over het halal-geval van handel in vertrouwen. *Beleid en Maatschappij* 37: 259–278.

Williamson, O. 1975. *Markets and Hierarchies*. New York: Free Press.

· ·

CHAPTER 26

GOVERNANCE AFTER
THE CRISIS

· ·

GRAHAM WILSON

DEBATE continues about the causes of the global financial crisis (GFC) of 2008–2010 (FCIC 2010). Many explanations of the GFC have linked its origins to trends in governance preceding it, including beliefs and practices such as faith in the superiority of markets, central bank independence, binding commitments by policy-makers to rules, independent, "non-majoritarian" regulatory agencies, and increased reliance on regulation or preferably civil regulation. Together these beliefs and practices made up a coherent approach to governance that the GFC was to call into question but that was also to prove surprisingly resilient. We discuss each element in the governance package in turn before turning to examine the impact of the GFC on them.

MARKETS

· ·

Faith in and reliance on markets increased considerably in the three decades before the GFC. With varying enthusiasm, governments moved to expand the impact of market forces by privatizing government-owned industries, contracting out services, and making citizens more dependent on markets, for example, through defined contribution retirement schemes (Hacker 2002, 2006; Hacker and Pierson 2010). New Zealand and the UK were leaders in this movement, privatizing key utilities as well as transportation or manufacturing firms, public housing, and agencies such as those operating ports and airports that had always been government entities, even in the USA (Wilson 1983; Roberts 2010). However, most countries moved in this direction. Even France privatized much of the stock in government-owned enterprises, although retaining an important degree of control through special stock holdings (Schmidt 1999). Privatization in the United States primarily took the form of "contracting out" a wide variety of government activities ranging from prisons to policy-making. An important indicator of faith in markets in the USA was the decline of antitrust activity. If markets in their wisdom created a monopoly situation, then monopoly must be desirable; in any case excess profits would soon result in the movement of new enterprises into the industry (Eisner and Meier 1990). Where real markets could not be achieved through privatization, governments should create internal markets, contracts between core departments and agencies, and use cost–benefit analysis.

The prestige of economics made trends within it unusually important. These included the decline of Keynesianism, with its core idea that markets are not always self-correcting, and the rise of the efficient market hypothesis, with its implication that regulation was undesirable. The spread of microeconomic reasoning to new policy areas was also evident in the "welfare reform" movement that influenced policy in countries as varied as Sweden and the Netherlands, the USA and the UK. Poverty was explained by perverse incentives that welfare had created to stay out of the labor market, more than by social problems. Changes in welfare reflecting this approach in the USA meant that when the GFC resulted in high unemployment, the social "safety net" was less adequate than in any downturn since the 1930s (DeParle 2009; Greenhouse 2008; Hacker 2006).

DEPOLITICIZING GOVERNANCE: REDUCING POLITICAL CONTROL

A second trend was increased acceptance that politics and government pose threats to benign market forces, resulting in a loss of welfare (Roberts 2010). These threats included interest groups intent on receiving "rents" by biasing public policy in their favor, for example through protectionist trade policies and "government failure," which supplanted concerns about market failure, previously a central feature of policy analysis. Government failure resulted from democratically elected politicians interfering in markets in order to achieve re-election, and from bureaucrats motivated by quests for larger budgets, more personnel, and other sources of prestige or power (Buchanan and Tullock 1962; Niskanen 1968; Becker 1983). Democracy itself might be a threat as it enabled voters to interfere with market forces, for example by redistributing income or wealth. Such redistribution would, of course, like all political interference with market forces, be misguided and bound to cause harm; nonetheless, it might happen. Democracy might also lead voters, encouraged by self-interested politicians, to expect government to solve more and more of their problems, resulting in a governance crisis known as "overload" (Crozier, Huntington, and Watanuki 1975; King 1975; Rose 1980). Voters demanded more even while the capacity of governments to deliver declined. The "governance crisis" of the late 1970s combined with the economists' critique of "governmental failure" to suggest that it was desirable to reduce the opportunities for elected politicians to cause harm. Good policy and an end to the governance crisis could both be fostered through "binding commitments."

CENTRAL BANK INDEPENDENCE
AND MONETARISM

Central bank independence exemplified the belief that democratic political control should be limited (Blinder 2002; Roberts 2010). Monetarism made central banks more important. However, central bank independence placed macroeconomic policy, including making obviously political trade-offs (e.g. inflation versus unemployment), in the hands of non-elected experts. Wiser countries (Germany, the United States) had long had independent central banks. Now countries that had subordinated central banks to democratic control followed suit. The European Central Bank (ECB), created to manage the euro, enjoys high autonomy, replacing many national central banks with very little. In 1997, the New Labour government placed the Bank of England on a similarly autonomous footing. Central bank independence was the product of both a shift in fashion in economics (away from Keynesianism and toward monetarism) and of the "overload crisis" concern about the unsuitability of democratic government for making important policy decisions.

A core aspect of Keynesian economic policy had been the belief that governments could choose the trade-off between goals, especially between full employment and inflation. Governments in many countries, even the USA, had attempted to improve this trade-off through incomes policies. Inflation would be contained at low unemployment by holding down wage increases. This generally required the cooperation of unions, which in turn resulted in governments according unions access and influence. This approach failed in the UK in the 1970s, but what became known as neocorporatism worked for several decades in Scandinavia. Monetarists believe there is a naturally occurring level of unemployment that governments cannot change. This meant in turn monetarists had no interest in incomes policies and so the cooperation of unions was unnecessary. Monetarism therefore facilitated moves toward a smaller, stronger state, not only reducing the power of elected politicians through central bank independence but also reducing government dependence on societal interests.

AUTONOMOUS REGULATORY AGENCIES

A third trend was the global diffusion of the autonomous regulatory agencies model (Levi-Faur 2005). Ironically, privatization increased regulation. Few were willing to allow newly privatized utilities such as water, natural gas, or electricity untrammeled power over their customers. The British generated numerous inelegantly named regulatory agencies (Ofwat, Ofgem, etc.) with the power to regulate newly privatized industries. Political control of such agencies was avoided. Elected politicians might focus on the interests of customers/voters to improve their own prospects for re-election rather than the interests of investors in the privatized utilities, as the history of nationalized industries in the UK warned (Foster 1971). Without care, the same fate might befall regulatory agencies. How much autonomy the new regulatory agencies enjoy in practice is unknown but there was one interesting and important development during the GFC. The UK Financial Services Authority (FSA) blocked the acquisition of the failing Lehman Brothers by Barclays even though the British government supported the deal. The FSA saw it as giving Barclays too much exposure to risk. American policy-makers and bankers were disconcerted, one of whom was reported as saying "but I thought they were our ally" (Sorkin 2009).

The trends in the UK supported Majone's contention that the interventionist state was giving way to the regulatory state not only as a consequence of the rise of the European Union (EU), which has considerable regulatory powers and very limited powers to tax and spend, but also of trends at the national level. "Strategic adaptation to [the] new realities has resulted in a reduced role for the positive, interventionist state and a corresponding increase in the role of the regulatory state; rule making is replacing taxing and spending" (Majone 1997). States increasingly relied on regulatory approaches to control not only non-governmental actors but even the state sector itself. Majone here conflates two trends: the growth in regulation that most observers would accept and, more debatably, a claim that this makes the state less interventionist (Levi-Faur and Gilad 2004). There are certainly policy areas such as education in which regulation has taken state activism to unprecedented levels. If state activism continues through regulation it is, however, activism that is primarily carried out by experts ("regulocrats") rather than by elected politicians.

Regulation appeals to governments because it costs them far less than direct government expenditure. Regulation does impose significant costs on those regulated. Successive American Administrations have developed ever more complete forms of assessing proposed regulations. Given the intellectual dominance of economics in this period, it is not surprising that the evaluation of proposed regulations was based primarily on a cost–benefit analysis approach, derived from microeconomic thinking. Cost–benefit analysis was quite old on the eve of the GFC. It had been quite controversial when first deployed some half a century previously. Critics charged that it emphasized costs rather than benefits, perhaps because costs were generally more readily defined than benefits. Critics further claimed that the attempts to measure costs often involved the use of seriously misleading if superficially scientific measures (Self 1970; Wildavsky 1969). The use of cost–benefit analysis nonetheless became the core of Regulatory Impact Assessment (RIA). RIA spread to European countries (notably the UK) and can also be construed as an attempt to limit political discretion. New regulations needed to pass some variant of cost–benefit analysis to proceed, not merely address what elected politicians considered to be a problem (Radaelli 2004, 2010; Peci and Sobrai 2011).

DEREGULATION AND REGULATION-FOR-COMPETITION

Increased regulation by autonomous regulatory agencies coexisted with a drive toward deregulation and regulation-for-competition. Deregulation reflected both the faith in markets and competition and the decline in the faith in democratic control noted above, and was evident on both the left and the right. On the left, the progressive view of regulation as the means by which the public good can be protected from selfish, predatory interests gave way to a view that deregulation was.an instrument of corporate power (Kolko 1965). Whereas the left tended to talk about "capture," conservative economists stigmatized regulation as a quest for "rents," that is, earnings above market rates. Perhaps the widespread skepticism about regulation helps explain why calls for increased regulation of the financial sector at the turn of the century failed to gain traction. Certainly in the financial sector, changes in regulations failed to match the dynamism and innovation of the financial service industries. This reluctance also reflected the efficient markets doctrine and a desire not to disadvantage one's own financial center by regulating it more strictly than rivals'. Joseph Stiglitz has argued that there was an international "race to the bottom" in financial regulation and Iceland won—or more accurately, after the crisis its citizens lost, as they were handed the tab for the errors of their banks. "Iceland may have been the winner of the race but its citizens were the losers" (Stiglitz 2010).

CIVIL REGULATION

Another approach to limiting the role of the state was to replace state action with activity by private sector organizations.

Critiques of "command-and-control" modes of regulation were common in the late twentieth century on the grounds that they specified inefficient and overly costly requirements. Regulators faced an incentive structure that encouraged them to pay little attention to cost and more attention to risks, no matter how remote (Bardach 1982). Regulation seemed to be both a more commonly used policy instrument in the USA than in other countries and yet also more common defective. Relations between regulators and regulated were typically more adversarial than in countries such as Sweden (Lundqvist 1980; Kelman 1981) or the UK (Wilson 1985). Many reasons were advanced for this. American business was instinctively hostile to government authority (Vogel 1978); American society was inherently litigious or the fragmented nature of government in the USA made it inherently more difficult to establish closed, iterative games between the parties; losers always had another governmental venue (Congress, the courts, etc.) to appeal to (Wilson 2002). The belief that "command-and-control" regulation had reached its limits was not limited to the USA, however. Whereas command-and-control regulations had succeeded with low-hanging fruit such as fixed point source pollution, a combination of technical factors, political constraints, and the likelihood of successful resistance made it unlikely that it would achieve any future gains (Kettl 2002).

Civil regulation was a plausible alternative. Civil regulation came in different forms, ranging from pure self-regulation to regulation by organizations and onto regulation by non-governmental organizations (NGOs) (see Chapter 23, this volume; Levi-Faur 2011). At one end of the continuum was extensive dependence on corporations to comply with best practices, a practice that was to prove controversial in both the GFC and the criticisms of oil drilling in the Gulf of Mexico following the catastrophe at BP's Deepwater Horizon well. Self-regulation by associations is perhaps typified by the Eco-Management and Audit Scheme (EMAS) in Europe (particularly Germany). Regulation by association is comparable to traditional regulation except that it is carried out by a private sector organization such as a trade association. The organization would set standards, send in inspectors, and demand compliance if necessary. A rare US example is the American Chemistry Council's Responsible Care scheme, adopted after the Bhopal disaster, which killed thousands and threatened to result in stringent legislation. At the other end of the spectrum were initiatives such as the Sustainable Forestry schemes, which were based on certification by NGOs. Producers who met sustainability standards could use a logo to demonstrate their good behavior, allowing them to charge more and perhaps borrow more cheaply. Other schemes were oriented more toward process than toward outcomes. The ISO 14001 certificate, for example, was obtained when a firm dedicated itself to monitoring its environmental performance, seeking to improve it, and continually revising its goals upward. Thus, a firm could obtain ISO 14001 certification while starting from a below average level of actual performance as long as it complied with the requirements for self-monitoring and improvement. The most dramatic spread of ISO 14001 came when Ford and General Motors imposed it as a requirement on all their suppliers. There was considerable debate about the degree to which self-regulation worked before the crisis. Some doubted whether consumers would adequately reward good business performance. Others raised the *quis custodiet* issue: Who ensured that the organizations certifying compliance had the capacity and motivation to do so adequately? After all, at the end of the day the company being certified paid the bill. The pendulum had already started to swing away from faith in self-regulation before the crisis struck. However, as should be clear from the preceding comments, civil regulation came in different forms, which were therefore more or less subject to the charge that the GFC revealed their limitations.

CONSTRAINING GOVERNMENT
THROUGH TARGETS

Attempts to replace decision-making by politicians on taxation and spending with decision-making by autonomous agencies or boards have never worked. President Obama and Congress did set up the National Commission on Fiscal Responsibility and Reform to explore ways to reduce the government's deficit but it did not reach the level of agreement among its members required to trigger a vote in Congress on its proposals contained in its December 2010 report, *The Moment of Truth*. Divisions within the Commission lessened its impact. However, it is still hard to believe that Congress or the president would have really turned over their authority to it and obediently implemented all its recommendations. In fiscal policy, unlike monetary policy, politicians kept control. If politicians could not be displaced, then at least they could be controlled through specifying limits for annual government deficits and total government borrowing. These targets might actually be enforced (e.g. by the World Bank if the country had a loan from it) or were inculcated in the minds of policy-makers through the work of organizations such as the Organisation for Economic Co-operation and Development (OECD). Countries that did not respect such targets might, at least, be regarded as badly governed, at worst regarded as poor risks financially, and embarrassed in "peer review" proceedings through which members of the OECD and EU evaluate each other's economic performance (Slaughter 2003).

SHORT-TERM RESPONSES IN GOVERNANCE TO THE CRISIS

The immediate aftermath of the crisis witnessed major challenges to these trends in governance.

The most obvious was reduced faith in markets. In countries that had not fully succumbed to adoration of the market, such as France and Germany, the crisis was met with a mixture of anger at being caught up in the consequences of the crisis and considerable *schadenfreude* over the discomfiting of the "Anglo-Saxons" who had promoted market liberalization. One of the most fervent advocates of deregulation and believers in the efficient markets hypothesis, Alan Greenspan, admitted to a Congressional committee that he had been forced to reconsider his beliefs in the light of events. Greenspan noted that he had believed in the "self interest of lending institutions to protect shareholder equity" but under questioning accepted that his ideology had been challenged.

> You had the authority to prevent irresponsible lending practices that led to the subprime mortgage crisis. You were advised to do so by many others," said Representative Henry A. Waxman of California, chairman of the committee. "Do you feel that your ideology pushed you to make decisions that you wish you had not made?"
>
> Mr. Greenspan conceded: "Yes, I've found a flaw. I don't know how significant or permanent it is. But I've been very distressed by that fact." (Andrews 2010)

There was general agreement that more regulation in areas such as trading in financial instruments was required. If some financial institutions were indeed "too big to fail," both the Obama Administration and the British government suggested that a new regulator was needed who would pay attention to the "systemic risks" that such institutions might be generating. In an apparent return to industrial policies of the 1970s, governments in countries with supposedly very different "varieties of capitalism" (Hall and Soskice 2001) rushed to subsidize their automobile industries and take into public ownership a surprising variety of failing concerns. In the United States, for example, in which public ownership of industries had been prohibited by the American liberal tradition (Hartz 1955), the government ended up owning two automobile companies, a massive insurance company, and a variety of banks. Even more remarkably, this major wave of nationalization was carried out by an Administration headed by a conservative Republican, George W. Bush. Similarly, in the UK, the British government took into ownership major banks such as Royal Bank of Scotland. The prime minister during this wave of nationalizations was Gordon Brown who, some fifteen years earlier, had worked with Tony Blair to build a "New Labour" that rejected old nostrums such as government ownership of the means of production, distribution, and exchange.

Central bank independence was also compromised by the crisis. Under the pressure of events, boundaries between government departments (i.e. the Treasury) and central banks (the Federal Reserve (Fed), the Bank of England) disappeared. Governors of central banks played a crucial role but as part of the team coordinating responses to the crisis, not as separate, independent actors. Fed chairman Bernanke and Treasury Secretary Paulson in the United States were the key policy-makers responding to the crisis as a bemused President Bush looked on, struggling to comprehend what had happened. Indeed the activities of the Federal Reserve and other banks were more important than the fiscal stimulus packages adopted by politicians. The Federal Reserve not only made loans to foreign banks (e.g. the British bank, Barclays) as well as American, but bought huge quantities of worthless ("toxic") assets and stimulated the economy through printing money ("quantitative easing"). The value of assets purchased from the banks in the USA by the Fed was approximately ten times the value of the toxic assets purchased by the Treasury Department. As central bankers became visibly part of the rescue team, they also became politically vulnerable figures. Whereas for most of his term as chair of the Federal Reserve, Greenspan had been lionized, his successor Bernanke has been much criticized. The Governor of the Bank of England, Mervyn King, has been subjected to criticism almost amounting to mockery. As *The Economist* reported, "public confidence in central banks has plummeted" even though "the world is relying more than ever on its central banks" (*The Economist*, 2011).

The GFC prompted a renewed enthusiasm for strong government regulation and a swing in opinion away from both self- and collaborative regulation. This swing reflected suspicions that self-regulatory schemes had allowed financial institutions to conceal the truth and evade effective controls but the mood change was evident in other areas too. Critics in the United States charged that cooperative approaches to regulation had compromised both airliner and automobile safety; Federal Aviation Administration (FAA)'s policy of allowing airlines to report faults without penalty and in some cases (Southwest) to keep on flying the planes, posed unacceptable risks, and the NHTSA, it was alleged, had not imposed recalls on Toyota early enough. Toyota's alleged failure to inform the agency of the problems of sudden acceleration called into question the reliability of even the largest corporations as partners with government. Fatalities in a West Virginia coal mine suggested that Massey Energy, its owner, had placed profits above safety and that the Mine Safety and Health Agency had not been sufficiently active in regulating the industry. Most dramatically, the disastrous oil spills following an explosion in one of its Gulf oil wells destroyed BP's reputation as the most environmentally aware and trustworthy of the major oil companies as well as the willingness of the regulatory agency, the Minerals Management Service, to allow corporations to regulate their own safety procedures. Many concluded that the close partnership between the agency and the oil companies had led to inadequate safety standards in the Gulf. It should be noted, however, that all these examples were of what we have termed pure self-regulation as opposed to regulation by association or by NGO. Nonetheless, and however unfairly, these events temporarily made popular demands for a return to government, rather than civil, regulation.

Finally, controls by targeting for government deficits and debts were swept away. Both the UK and USA racked up unprecedented peacetime debt equivalent to over 10 percent of GDP in attempts to ward off another depression. In a further political irony, the right of center parties such as the Republicans in the USA, who had most avidly argued against strict regulation, now denounced the deficits that were products of programs to contain the crisis, such as the stimulus package. Most economists agreed that though these deficits were necessary and appropriate during a recession, they should not be sustained in the medium or long term. Governments and administrations that inherited the crisis (such as Obama's in the United States), could therefore anticipate passing through the painful politics of deficit reduction as they raised taxes and cut spending in order to shrink the deficits.

Long-term consequences

Initially it seemed clear that the GFC would result in more activist governance. It soon became clear that any such shift was unlikely. Most strikingly, no country had adopted a new system of financial regulation in spite of the consensus that regulatory failures had caused the crisis. The closest attempt was the US Dodd–Frank Wall Street Reform and Consumer Protection Act of 2010, a voluminous piece of legislation whose impact is not yet clear, in part because it requires the adoption of 243 regulations to give it effect. By and large, it focuses on monitoring systemic risks arising from the actions of financial institutions more carefully, integrating the work of different regulatory agencies more effectively, and providing for the smoother winding up of failed financial institutions whose demise may have systemic consequences. Perhaps the only fundamental change in financial institutions that it required was that in adopting the "Volker Rule," it sharply limited the degree to which banks could use deposits to trade on their own behalf; they were required to set up a legally separate company to engage in such activities. The legislation also promoted greater transparency by requiring more financial instruments to be traded in exchanges rather than "over the counter." However, the legislation crucially failed to address the most conspicuous issues arising from the GFC, namely the existence of financial institutions that are too big to fail and of the fragmented, weak, and competing regulatory agencies supposedly controlling them. The GFC resulted in further concentration in the US shadow banking industry, leaving behind even fewer firms that were, in consequence, "even too bigger to fail." In the UK, the commission (Vickers) to recommend changes in the financial sector produced an interim report that was greeted with relief by bankers; rejecting calls for a separation of retail and investment banks, the commission merely suggested that there should be clearer separation of the activities within companies and that capital requirements for retail banking be raised above the Basle III levels. As this latter proposal would place British banks at a competitive disadvantage, it seemed unlikely to be enacted. The EU made more aggressive-sounding moves to regulate hedge funds but again the practical effect of the proposals was unclear. Government ownership of banks, insurance companies, and automobile manufacturers resulting from the GFC was regarded as a temporary and unfortunate development that should be reversed as soon as possible, rather than as a means by which governments could pursue economic or social objectives. In short, no coherent alternatives to pre-GFC policy thinking or policy practice emerged.

WHY DID THE CRISIS NOT RESULT IN MORE CHANGE IN GOVERNANCE?

The first reason is that many of the failures in governance related to very complex practices. In a sense, the ability of people to make large amounts of money trading in financial instruments relates to the complexity of the products they handle. The number of people in government who understood the issues involved was very small and the number of people who could analyze the consequences of reforms was even smaller. Similarly, for all the criticism of the Minerals Management Service over BP's Gulf catastrophe, government officials had to admit that only the major oil companies had the technical resources and knowledge to deal with the problems. The complexity of issues also resulted in complex interdependencies and the consequent risk of generating unintended adverse consequences. Restrictions intended to curb risky behavior by banks, for example, could result in restricting the ability of automobile dealerships or even farmers' cooperatives to manage their businesses effectively.

Second, competition between countries inhibited both collective action and reforms by individual states. Governments retained an appreciation, perhaps all the keener, for the contribution the financial sector made to employment and their own revenues. Governments feared that moves to reform particular sectors of the financial industry might harm their own financial sectors disproportionately and they therefore resisted imposing additional controls on their own financial sectors without a guarantee that other countries would follow suit. Although the Dodd–Frank Act in the USA was voluminous, it did almost nothing to change the fundamental causes of the US crisis—fragmented and weak regulatory agencies facing highly concentrated financial institutions. Similarly, after vociferous threats by bankers such as Barclay CEO Jack Diamond to leave London if stringent regulations were introduced, as we have seen, the British commission on banking (Vickers) recommended modest changes that seemed likely to be watered down further as they placed British-owned banks at a competitive disadvantage with foreign banks operating in London.

Third, the political power of business militated against change. As many studies have shown, the US interest group system is dominated by business, which employs far more lobbyists and makes larger campaign contributions than any other interest. The financial industry is partially active and in the ten years preceding the GFC spent $2.7 billion on lobbying and over $1 billion on campaign contributions (FCIC 2010). These contributions went to strategically placed politicians of both parties including, among the Democrats, Senator Charles Schumer of New York. He was both a major recipient of contributions from the financial industry and an avid opponent of increasing regulation of risky financial instruments. Goldman Sachs invested far more heavily in the Obama campaign in 2008 than in the Republican presidential campaign of Senator John McCain. The industry increased further its activism as the GFC produced more government involvement in the industry and industry dependence on government. Baumgartner and colleagues argue that, in general, resources are not crucial in shaping policy in the USA (Baumgartner et al. 2009). However, in this particular case, lobbyists for the financial industry were able to capitalize on the considerable technical knowledge required to understand the issues and the absence of an organized, countervailing interest pressing for stricter regulation. Admittedly, the GFC created to be seen to appear to be acting to prevent a recurrence of the GFC. Passage of Dodd–Frank was secured in part by demonizing Goldman Sachs, a firm that ironically had contributed heavily to the Obama campaign. However, once the sprawling, ambiguous law was passed, the drafting of regulations to give it effect was carried out by experts, unnoticed by the general public but heavily lobbied by the financial industry.

Fourth, no new intellectual movement had arisen from the crisis. This was a contrast with previous events of comparable magnitude. The Depression of the 1930s had famously produced a spurt of interest in socialism in many different forms and National Socialism. The crisis of the 1970s also produced a neoliberal governance package, including the "smaller but stronger" state, privatization, deregulation and tax cutting. Why did the GFC not produce a package of governance ideas? The GFC seemed to provide the left with obvious openings beyond the argument that neoliberal policies had made the crisis possible. The GFC provide a vivid reminder that there is a difference between what was profitable on the one hand, and what was socially desirable on the other. Admittedly, the left still faced the constraints of popular resistance to high tax levels and the competitive pressures arising from globalization that had given rise to "the third way." However, justifications for government bailouts of the banks, such as the argument that some financial institutions were "too big to fail," seemed to suggest the possibility of a "social contract" between these large institutions on the one hand and government or society on the other. Surely financial institutions owed some social obligations in return for government guarantees? If banks or automobile manufacturers have an implicit promise from government that if necessary they will be rescued, then one might ask what they owe society in return when times are good. Bailouts seemed at the least to provide the opportunity for an expansion of corporate social responsibility (CSR) in terms of new commitments to environmental protection, opportunities for the underprivileged, or improved labor practices.

In practice the striking characteristic of long-term responses to the GFC has been the dominance of what in the United States are called conservative and elsewhere are called neoliberal ideas. Debate in the United States has been focused on the attempt to move back not to the governance patterns of the early years of this century but to the governance patterns of the early twentieth century, most notably in the policies of the Tea Party movement, a highly publicized, supposedly grassroots conservative movement that succeeded in having the Republican Party choose many of its nominees as candidates in the 2010 midterm elections. While many of these candidates were defeated in well-publicized races for the Senate, forty out of 130 Republican House candidates backed by the Tea Party were elected. Although the GFC had begun under a Republican Administration and was popularly linked to malfeasance on Wall Street, the Democrats suffered the worst midterm losses numerically since 1938, and the worst as a percentage of seats held since 1922 (Campbell et al. 2011). In the autumn of 2011, the "Occupy" movement ("Occupy Wall Street", imitated in many cities including London, Boston, and Los Angeles) mobilized hundreds of thousands for left-wing protests against the power of finance. The movement attracted the sympathy of millions. Opinion polls suggested over forty percent of Americans supported the values of the movement, though not necessarily its tactics. Those values were not translated into specific policy proposals, however, and as winter came on, participation in the movement declined and the authorities in many cities moved to close the camps that had been the hallmark of the movement. The generalized discontent articulated by the Occupy movement produced no specific demands comparable to the Tea Party's opposition to tax increases and demands for budget cuts.

The large losses by the Socialdemokratische Partei Deutschlands (SPD) in Germany in 2009, the victory of a coalition dominated by the Conservatives in the UK in 2010, and the re-election of a center-right government in Sweden suggested that the swing to the right in the United States was not limited to that country. The 2010 report, *British Social Attitudes*, concluded that the GFC had not brought about any change in the UK public's beliefs about the appropriate role of government in the economy and that British attitudes were more "Thatcherite" (hostile to welfare policies) than when Thatcher herself was prime minister (Curtice and Park 2010).

Why have responses to the GFC taken this rightward turn? In the United States, conservative politicians have been able to invoke the old Jacksonian tradition of opposition to "bigness." As Jackson himself would have argued about the Bank of the United States, which he opposed, "big government" is likely to team up with "big business" against the interests of ordinary citizens. Right-wing populism in the USA has been capable of attacking both Washington DC and Wall Street, while local "Main Street" capitalism has been seen as the depository of all virtues. American right-wing populism has faint echoes in Europe where the decisive influence on European governments was the Greek financial crisis of 2010. Greece not only had a large fiscal deficit but had been lying about its size. Once the truth emerged, Greece was thrown into a financial crisis that threatened not only its sovereign debt but also the future of the Euro. Conservatives in many countries, including those that faced no problems borrowing, argued that unless government deficits were reduced sharply by cutting expenditures, their country would suffer the same crisis as Greece. Such arguments were also made in the USA, for example in Representative Paul Ryan's official Republican response to President Obama's 2011 State of the Union address.

Cutting government programs is harder than denouncing deficits, however. An abundance of opinion poll data shows that even in the USA, the public is far less supportive of specific cuts in government programs than it is of promises of severe action to reduce deficits in the abstract. More generally, the strength of the American right has ruled out apparently plausible policy responses to the fiscal crisis, such as increasing personal taxation, and has limited their scope in Europe. We might characterize the post-US midterm elections, post-Greek crisis situation as, to adapt Roberts's phrase, the reimposition of discipline. Whereas the immediate aftermath of the crash had seen the tearing down of the walls that had constrained government action—fiscal targets, central bank independence, and so on, the aftermath was one in which walls were rebuilt and strengthened. Surprisingly, in spite of the huge costs the GFC imposed on states, it has had led to no long-term change in the balance of power between states and business.

Nor was the GFC likely to result in changes in the "micro" techniques of governance. The great wave of experimentation with New Public Management (NPM) had run out of steam by the beginning of the twenty-first century, even in countries that had been most influenced by it (Lodge and Gill 2011). An era of tight budgets makes NPM's emphasis on flattening hierarchies less appealing. The old bureaucratic order, decaying prior to NPM (Campbell and Wilson 1995), will not return. Rather, executive branches will consist of a mixture of apparently contradictory administrative approaches and constitutional doctrines (King 2007; Hood and Lodge 2006) that cannot be reduced to a single paradigm. Experimentation in regulation is also likely to be limited. Suspicions of civil regulation were increased by the GFC even though the more interesting and complex forms of civil regulation played no part in causing the GFC. Business interests and their political supporters are currently more interested in deregulation than alternatives to regulation. In the longer term, however, if the past is guide to the future, a new administrative doctrine will emerge. Very often a new reform doctrine is promulgated before the previous round has even been implemented (Light 1997). There are political rewards for promoting new doctrines promising greater efficiency, accountability, and responsiveness. As governments struggle to meet continuingly high expectations and, in the aftermath of the GFC, highly constrained resources, there is a market for new administrative doctrines. Currently, however, at both macro and micro levels it is the absence of change in governance after the GFC that is striking.

REFERENCES

Andrews, E. L. 2010. Greenspan concedes flaws in deregulatory approach. *New York Times*, 24 October, Business Section B1.

Bardach, E. 1982. *Going By the Book: The Problem of Regulatory Unreasonableness*. Philadelphia: Temple University Press.

Baumgartner, F., Berry, J., Hojnacki, M. and Leech, B. 2009. *Lobbying and Policy Change: Who Wins, Who Loses and Why*. Chicago: University of Chicago Press.

Becker, G. S. 1983. A theory of competition among pressure groups for political support. *Quarterly Journal of Economics* 98: 371–400.

Blinder, A. 2002. *Quiet Revolution: Central Banking Goes Modern*. New Haven: Yale University Press.

Buchanan J. M. and Tullock, G. 1962. *The Calculus of Consent: Logical Foundations of Constitutional Democracy*. Ann Arbor: University of Michigan Press.

Campbell, C. and Wilson, G. K. 1995. *The End of Whitehall? Death of a Paradigm*. Oxford: Blackwell.

Campbell, J. E. et al. 2011. Postmortems of the 2010 midterm election forecasts. *PS: Political Science and Politics* 44: 1–6.

Crozier, M., Huntington, S. P. and Watanuki, J. 1975. *The Crisis of Democracy: Report on the Governability of Democracies to the Trilateral Commission*. New York: New York University Press.

Curtice, J. and Park, A. 2011. A tale of two crises: Banks, MPs' expenses and public opinion. In A. Park, J. Curtice, E. Clery, and C. Bryosn (eds.), *British Social Attitudes 27th Report*. London: Sage, 00–00.

DeParle, J. 2009. Slumping economy puts test to an aid System tied to jobs. *New York Times*, 1 June.

Economist, The. 2011. Central banks: A more complicated game. 17 February.

Eisner, M. A. and Meier, K. J. 1990. Presidential control versus bureaucratic power: Explaining the Reagan revolution in anti trust. *American Journal of Political Science* 34: 269–287.

FCIC (Financial Crisis Inquiry Commission). 2010. *Financial Crisis Inquiry Report: Final Report of the Commission on the Causes of the Financial and Economic Crisis in the United States*. Washington, DC: GPO.

Foster, C. 1971. *Politics, Finance and the Role of Economics*. London: Allen and Unwin.

Greenhouse, S. 2008. Will the safety net catch the economy's casualties? *New York Times*, 16 November.

Hacker, J. S. 2002. *The Divided Welfare State: The Battle over Public and Private Benefits in the United States*. Cambridge: Cambridge University Press.

Hacker, J. S. 2006. *The Great Risk Shift: The Assault on American Jobs, Families, Health Care and Retirement—And How You Can Fight Back*. New York: Oxford University Press.

Hacker, J. S and Pierson, P. 2010. *Winner Take All Politics: How Washington made the Rich Richer and Turned Its Back on the Middle Class*. New York: Simon and Schuster.

Hall P. and Soskice, D. (eds.) 2001. *Varieties of Capitalism: The Institutional Foundations of Comparative Advantage*. Oxford: Oxford University Press.

Hartz, L. 1955. *The Liberal Tradition in America: An Interpretation of Political Thought In America Since the Revolution*. New York: Harcourt.

Hood, C. and Lodge, M. 2006. *The Politics of Public Sector Bargains: Reward, Competency Loyalty— and Blame*. Oxford: Oxford University Press.

Kelman, S. 1981. *Regulating Sweden, Regulating America: A Comparative Study of Occupational Safety and Health Policy*. Cambridge, MA: MIT Press.

Kettl, D. F. 2002. *Environmental Governance: A Report on the Next Generation of Environmental Policy*. Washington, DC: Brookings Institution.

King, A. S. 1975. Overload: Problems of governing in the 1970s. *Political Studies* 23: 284–296.

King, A. S. 2007. *The British Constitution*. Oxford: Oxford University Press.

Kolko, G. 1965. *Railroads and Regulation 1877–1916*. Princeton: Princeton University Press.

Levi-Faur, D. 2005. The global diffusion of regulatory capitalism. *Annals of the American Academy of Political and Social Science* 598: 12–32.

Levi-Faur, D. 2011. Regulation and regulatory governance. In D. Levi-Faur (ed.), *Handbook of the Politics of Regulation*. Cheltenham: Edward Elgar, 00–00.

Levi-Faur, D. and Gilad, S. 2004. Review: The rise of the British regulatory state: Transcending the privatisation debate. *Comparative Politics* 37: 105–124.

Light, P. C. 1997. *The Tides of Reform: Making Government Work 1945–1995*. New Haven: Yale University Press.

Lodge, M. and Gill, D. 2011. Towards a new era of administrative reform? The myth of post NPM in New Zealand. *Governance* 24: 141–166.

Lundqvist, L. J. 1980. *The Hare and the Tortoise: Clean Air Policies in Sweden and the United States*. Ann Arbor: University of Michigan Press.

Majone, G. 1997. From the positive to the regulatory state. *Journal of Public Policy* 17: 139–167.

Niskanen, W. 1968. The peculiar economics of bureaucracy. *American Economic Review* 58(2): 293–305.

Peci, A. and Sobrai, F. 2011. "Regulatory impact assessment: How political and organizational forces influence its diffusion in a developing country." *Regulation and Governance* 5: 204–220.

Radaelli, C. 2004. The diffusion of regulatory impact analysis: Best practice or lesson drawing? *European Journal of Political Research* 43: 723–747.

Roberts, A. 2010. *The Logic of Discipline: Global Capitalism and the Architecture of Government*. Oxford: Oxford University Press.

Rose, R. 1980. *Challenge to Governance: Studies in Overloaded Politics*. Beverly Hills, CA: Sage.

Schmidt, V. 1999. Privatization in France: The transformation of French capitalism. *Government and Policy* 4: 445–461

Self, P. 1970. Nonsense on stilts: Cost benefit analysis and the Roskill commission. *Political Quarterly* 41: 249–260.

Slaughter, M. 2003. Every day global governance. *Daedalus* 132: 83–90.

Sorkin, A. R. 2009. *Too Big To Fail: The Inside Story of How Washington and Wall Street Fought to Save the Financial System—And Themselves*. New York: Viking.

Stiglitz, G. 2010. Watchdogs need not bark together. *Financial Times*, 10 February.

Vogel, D. J. 1978. Why businessmen distrust their state: The political consciousness of American corporate executives. *British Journal of Political Science* 8: 45–78.

Wildavsky, A. 1969. Rescuing policy analysis from PPBS. *Public Administration Review* 29: 189–202

Wilson, G. K. 1983. Planning: Lessons from the ports. *Public Administration* 61: 265–281.

Wilson, G. K. 1985. *The Politics of Safety and Health*. Oxford: Oxford University Press.

Wilson, G. K. 2002. *Business and Government: A Comparative Introduction*, 3rd ed. Chatham, NJ: Chatham House.

....

CHAPTER 27

MODES OF ECONOMIC GOVERNANCE: THE DYNAMICS OF GOVERNANCE AT THE NATIONAL AND FIRM LEVEL

....

DIETER PLEHWE

RESEARCH on economic governance entails an implicit, if not explicit, acknowledgement of the limits of democratic and political governance. Particular rules that apply within corporations and between economic actors differ from the general rules of society. Modes of economic governance need to be understood better since they constitute an important realm of institutionalized power relations that affect social, economic, and democratic life. Research on modes of economic governance explores the variety of institutions that govern economic relations and informs the search for superior institutional alternatives. This chapter introduces this research, focusing on modes of economic governance at the national level, in the form of varieties of capitalism, and corporate governance at the firm level. The analysis of different modes of governance at the *national level* suggests that economic governance is not uniform across time and space. Institutions governing economic relations developed over time and differ between nations. Analysts consequently developed insights into the ways in which economic action is embedded in cultural and social practices (van Waarden, Chapter 25, this volume). The roots of research on different modes of economic governance can be traced back to the early history of research on comparative capitalism. Classical economic sociology and political economy scholarship by Karl Marx, Max Weber, and Werner Sombart in Germany, and Thorstein Veblen and John R. Commons in the USA established important insights into causes of divergent economic models and developments. More recent research on varieties of capitalism is useful for establishing the existence, endurance, and dynamics of national differences despite the processes of convergence via Europeanization and globalization.

At the *firm level*, neo-institutional economic research has focused on the economic impact of alternative governance regimes (Coase 1937; Williamson 1981). Although corporate governance scholarship shares the concern for noneconomic influences in economic relations, the interpretation of institutions differs markedly from the structural understanding of the historical school. Most economists focus on economic governance arrangements that are potentially subject to change in the short or medium run. The literature of corporate governance is useful in analyzing performance-oriented comparisons of alternative modes of corporate governance and especially in contrasting shareholder and stakeholder-oriented governance structures.

Overall, the discussions at both the national and firm levels of analysis developed under the pressure of the rise of Anglo-Saxon modes of governance and shareholder value perspectives over three decades (Wilson, Chapter 26, this volume). Recently, efforts to better understand the contemporary capitalist dynamics of economic development and their impact on modes of governance have taken over the older debates oscillating around issues of divergence and convergence. The rise of narrow shareholder value perspectives may, in the meantime, be reversed due to the financial and sovereign debt crisis.

1. MODES OF ECONOMIC GOVERNANCE AT THE NATIONAL LEVEL

The crisis of the post-World War II regime of economic growth based on mass production and consumption and the expansion of the welfare state ("Fordism") has presented strong challenges to established modes of economic governance in Europe and elsewhere since the late 1970s. Rising unemployment and declining growth rates, as well as a whole range of economic, social, and ecological problems, suggested a lack of adaptability in many countries. A deep sense of calamity affected welfare state capitalism in the north, socialism in the east, and developmental capitalism in the south. The rise of Thatcherism in the UK and of Reaganism in the USA promised an end to muddling through in the developed world, while the dynamism of a few developing countries like Singapore and South Korea in Southeast Asia demonstrated the superiority of export-oriented market economies. Leading scholars observed a new dynamic of global capitalism and predicted a "borderless world" (Ohmae 1989), which was also presented as converging on the Anglo-Saxon model of arm's-length capitalism. Others presented the Toyota system of "lean production" as a universal model to which all the competitors would have to adapt or face extinction (Womack, Jones, and Roos 1991). Capitalism seemed to be a synonym for sweeping change and adaptation to a universal model.

Against the backdrop of simplistic notions of convergence and universal models, often reflecting the economic and intellectual dominance of the Anglo-Saxon world, a renewed interest developed in studying the prevailing national modes of economic governance. Contrary to globalization pundits, comparative scholarship pointed to the good performance of both the Japanese and German economies vis-à-vis their Anglo-Saxon competitors. Lester Thurow (1992) explained the competitive advantages of the high degree of coordination of economic activities in both countries compared with the UK and the USA.

The new generation of comparative literature on modes of economic governance started with Michel Albert's (1991) juxtaposition of Anglo-Saxon market capitalism, characterized by individualism, flexibility, and a short-term orientation of high returns, and the coordinated capitalism prevalent in Continental Europe and Japan. The latter are consensus-oriented and display longer-term commitments between economic actors. Unsurprisingly, a number of authors took issue with putting all the apples in just two baskets. Many subsequent efforts were dedicated to refining Albert's original distinction. A few examples include Vivien Schmidt (2002), who suggested distinguishing market, managed, and state capitalism and Bruno Amable (2003), who relied on the regulation school theory to separate market-based, social democratic, Continental European, Asian, and Mediterranean variants. Most recently, scholars have pointed to the peculiarities of dependent Eastern European varieties of capitalism emerging from the post-communist transformation (Nölke and Vliegenthart 2009; Bohle and Greskovits 2007).

All these authors share an interest in identifying differences and similarities of important components of economic governance, such as the system of financing corporations, education and training, research and development, industrial relations or business state relations. Countries are sorted into different clusters according to the prevalent set of institutional characteristics (compare Whitley's (1999) most elaborate typologies).

A common thread of the comparative literature is the observation of path-dependent historical development due to the structural influence of institutions. Both particular institutional spheres (e.g. corporate finance) and linkages between institutions (say between institutions important to industrial relations and institutions influencing corporate governance) are held to shape up as significantly different modes of economic governance and peculiar national path dependencies (Vitols 1998; Höpner 2005). Institutional configurations in turn result in differing practices. Cooperative relations coincide with investment in education and training independent of individual companies, like the Austrian or German dual education system. Voluntarism instead produces the company-specific training regimes preferred in the United States, for example. Researchers studying R&D practices have contrasted the Anglo-Saxon focus on radical innovation and new products with the emphasis on incremental innovation in coordinated market economies (Casper 2007), though Taylor (2004) challenges a variety of capitalist theories of technological innovation because of the exceptional and contradictory character of the US system of innovation. Still, the careful comparison of national systems and the particular institutional practices of education and training, industrial relations, and corporate finance yields rich insights into a range of factors influencing specific aspects of national modes of governance, and explains the reasons for different approaches to similar ends.

Contrary to convergence arguments, the theory Varieties of Capitalism (VoC) of economic modes of governance observes lasting, if not increasing, divergence (Hall and Soskice 2001). Historical developments are thought to create and subsequently bolster institutional foundations of comparative advantage. Since particular institutional configurations provide firms in different countries with specific competitive advantages, countries are advised to optimize given configurations rather than make futile attempts to radically alter their national mode of governance. Various perspectives on capitalism convincingly back moderate reform efforts, or muddling through, rather than radical reforms. It is difficult, however, to explain instances of breaking with the past based on the strong version of institutional path dependency (Mahoney 2000).

The tension between historical accounts of path dependencies emphasizing contingency and unintended consequences in the process of institutional development, and functionalist accounts of different types of complex systems, has been noted by O'Sullivan (2005). While interrelations between institutions are convincingly held accountable for fortifying the longevity of national variety, the emphasis on coherent national systems can also make it increasingly difficult to observe, let alone explain, significant changes cutting across national systems and affecting them in similar or different ways and sometimes both (Plehwe 2001). The increasing rigidity of the variety of *national* capitalism literature resulted in an almost complete lack of interest in institutional developments above and below the nation-state (Bohle and Greskovits 2009).

Not least as a result of the perceived dogmatism of the national variety scheme, the dynamics of institutional change and resulting transformations of national systems have been moved higher up the research agenda. A focus on social relations and organizations rather than national configurations distinguishes work in the tradition of the French *effet societal* school, which avoided the fallacies of methodological nationalism in a convincing effort to relate the local and the global in the pursuit of explaining economic modes of governance (Sorge 2005). The treatment of national modes as if they are isolated from each other is increasingly hard to reconcile with the budding dynamic of capitalist transformation across borders after the collapse of the socialist universe of states, which contributed to yet another round of intensified globalization and European integration. The adoption of the single European market program in the late 1980s led to a transfer of political competencies to the supranational level, and was followed by a wave of European legislation. The 1990s furthermore witnessed three more European treatises and the creation of the European Central Bank and currency. The frozen picture presented in works that maintain the idea of a more or less complete reproduction of national modes of governance clearly failed to account adequately for such developments. Theoretical closure at evidence in the varieties of capitalism paradigm alarmed erstwhile supporters of the comparative research agenda like Colin Crouch (2005), who began to object to the isolated and coherent system perspective. Streeck's (2009) call to "bring capitalism back in" suggests a strong desire to consider processes and consequences of capitalist development again, rather than focusing on rock solid institutional architecture. As a result, the erstwhile emphasis on diversity has clearly been modified by new efforts at accounting for changes that are common to different national systems and by a stronger interest in commonalities across systems rather than one-sidedly pointing to differences. The latest contributions on macroeconomic modes of governance can be roughly divided into those focusing on institutional change within national systems (endogenous dynamics) and those focusing on institutional developments beyond the nation-state.

Streeck and Thelen (2005) have developed a new toolkit to study gradual institutional change at the domestic level. Reconsidering institutions as regimes that are subject to conflicts and struggles between rule-makers and takers, the authors aim to develop an actor-centered theory of institutional change. Institutions and rules can be stable or subject to controversy and modification, depending on all kinds of factors. Instead of the notion of a complete and identical reproduction of society due to institutional configurations, the resulting notion of the imperfect reproduction of social relations suggests a continuous process of modification of individual institutions, and consequently also of relations between institutions. The authors identify different types of change for which there are ample examples: first, the displacement of once dominant institutions by the rise of others; second, the layering of institutions as a result of differential growth; third, institutional drift, conversion, and exhaustion (Streeck and Thelen 2005: 31). If previous work had to rely more or less exclusively on exogenous shocks to explain rare moments of significant institutional change, the identification of endogenous processes of gradual change can be regarded a huge step forward in the effort to analyze more subtle, though in the long run no less important, transformations of economic modes of governance. The issue of subnational diversity of economic governance has so far been ignored by most contributions to national literatures. If scholars came across examples that did not fit a national stereotype, such cases were interpreted as anomalies constituting statistical noise. Not only can subnational variety now be considered as an important subject of inquiry in varieties of business systems in their own right (e.g. as industrial districts or regional clusters; compare Grabher 2003) but subnational variety must be considered tremendously important in explaining endogenous institutional change. The shifting fortunes of Belgium's major regions, for example, display both continuities and discontinuities that strongly affect the country's national system (Jessop and Oosterlynck 2008).

Above and across nation-states, scholars have brought a range of supra- and transnational institutions into the discussion of modes of economic governance. Vivien Schmidt (2002) has developed a discursive sociological institutionalism as a better means to account for the narrowing variety of European capitalism affected by neoliberal perspectives of economic governance. Scholars have pointed to a supranational centralization of European regulatory authority and examined the corresponding growth of European legislation (Sandholtz and Stone Sweet 1998). The shift of authority from the national to the supranational level in the European Union (EU) has been marked by a coevolution of European interest groups. Transnational business associations of large corporations operate alongside European federations of national associations to cope better with Europe's new regulatory statehood. With regard to private interest groups, Eising and Kohler-Koch (2005) observe a peculiar mode of European network governance, which differs from both pluralist and corporatist arrangements. Supranational and transnational dimensions of economic modes of governments are found to complement the Europeanization of national systems (Djelic and Quack 2003). Against the backdrop of research on telecom deregulation, Levi-Faur (2006) has argued convincingly for a systematic multi-level approach to the comparative analysis of economic modes of governance at the sector level.

Sigrid Quack (2007, 2011) has pointed to the role and heterogeneity of organizations in order to advance international perspectives in research on economic modes of governance. Rather than being coherent and fully determined, organizations (can) display features of internal division that are crucial with regard to the dynamics of institutional change. Quack also suggests considering organizations as socially embedded yet reflexive actors, which corresponds to the language of imperfect reproduction employed by Streeck and Thelen. Last but not least, Quack directs attention to the dynamics of cross-border interaction, which can lead to the strategic development or unintended evolution of transnational organizations. Different modes of supranational institutionalization include optional, forced, and negotiated diffusion on the one hand, and emerging or negotiated recombination on the other. Quack thereby goes beyond theories of institutional isomorphism, which have distinguished between normative pressures, mimetic processes, and coercion, to explain processes of organizational assimilation (DiMaggio and Powell 1983).

The research program directed at studying the interplay of domestic and nondomestic institutions and their implications for new modes of economic governance is still at an early stage. The literatures on European integration and national varieties of capitalism have developed in parallel, without taking much notice of each other. In addition to what has so far mostly been a horizontal comparison of closed systems mainly focused on differences, the next generation of comparative research will need to provide a better account of vertical dimensions of economic governance, characterizing, for example, open systems and interrelations between supranational and domestic systems in Europe. While the Anglo-Saxon model has certainly not led to wholesale convergence, the market-oriented reform strategies pursued since the 1980s (Wilson, Chapter 26, this volume) did infuse stronger dynamics of transformation within and across the different modes of economic governance. The rise of shareholder value perspectives in corporate governance is a strong case in point.

2. CORPORATE GOVERNANCE: FROM SHAREHOLDER VALUE TO SOCIAL RESPONSIBILITY?

Ownership concerns have been critical in corporate governance research in the United States right from the very beginning. Adolf Berle and Gardiner Means (1967 [1932]) were early in pointing out problems arising from the separation of (dispersed stock) ownership and control in their book *The Modern Corporation and Private Property*. Joseph

Schumpeter (1962 [1942]) later would go further in forecasting the demise of capitalism due to the decline of family-owned corporations in his famous *Capitalism, Socialism and Democracy*. But Berle and Means had already vividly described the dangers of corporate oligarchy coupled with plundering by managers. According to their account, scattered owners had no voice option in the United States and could therefore only exit, that is, sell their shares, in order to express dissent. In a nutshell, the major concern of the "principal agent" (here: owner/manager) theory already laid out at this stage occupies economic neo-institutionalism to this day (Miller 2005).

More technically, the mainstream of corporate governance research is grounded in the original work of Ronald Coase (1937), who was the first to theorize firms (hierarchy) as an alternative to unconstrained market relations reliant on contracts between individuals. His contribution was crucial in alerting the neoclassical mainstream in economics, which had strongly rejected the historical school because of its alleged lack of theory, to reconsider the importance of nonmarket relations in economics. Coase's rational choice explanation of the reality and economic rationality of firms paved the way for comparative research on corporate governance. His work was crucial in establishing the role of organizations as either additionally or as a potential alternative to market relations.

Organizations have been found to reduce the burden and cost of transactions and thus provide agents with options to choose between different modes of coordination or governance. Following Coase, Oliver Williamson (1985) generalized the transaction cost approach, which along with principal–agent and property rights theories constitutes the basis for the larger neo-institutional research programs of law and economics (Klein 1998). Economic neo-institutionalists generally aim to examine alternative and complementary modes of economic governance in principle (e.g. market, network, and hierarchy), which have formed the basis of intense discussions, mainly among economists, to inform competition policy and corporate governance arrangements. More recently, scholars have started to investigate hybrid forms and combinations as well, in recognition of the exercise of authority in the absence of organizational hierarchies in public–private partnerships, for example (Ménard 2004). The comparative approach of the new generation of institutional economists is quite peculiar, however, driven by universal a priori abstractions rather than by insights derived from temporal and societal diversity. Historically, contingent ownership concerns are thereby turned into apparently universal shareholder concerns.

In a two-step procedure, neo-institutional economists first conduct a positive analysis of the reality perceived to point to (in)efficiencies that are considered to be due to institutional incentives (not) conducive to market transactions based on rational choice axioms. The second step constitutes a normative analysis of how to change the institutional configuration in order to achieve greater efficiency by way of a better incentive system (institutional design). This is typically equated with an expansion of market relations or market-friendly governance mechanisms within and between organizations ("external corporate governance"). The procedure adopted is clearly restricted to a problem-solving approach within a given setting, unless the wholesale conversion of planned economies to market economies is concerned. Evidently, normative dimensions of step one, dubbed positive analysis, are rarely acknowledged. Critics therefore point to the effort to depoliticize power relations and corporate decision-making under conditions of globalized capitalism couched in an apparently neutral language of "efficiency" (Soederberg 2010).

The resulting mainstream corporate governance research is focused on the governance relationships at the top of the firm: board, senior managers, and stockholders. This research is designed to tackle the problems of costs associated with managerial agency due to a theoretically deducted difference from "principal" interests (shareholders) in the vertical dimension, and costs associated with dominant shareholders or problems of corporate legitimacy in the horizontal perspective (Roe 2005). Key elements of governance arrangements examined include markets, boards, information distribution and gate-keeping functions, shareholder influence, executive compensation, or professional norms. This list of important elements of governance arrangements readily displays the distance of economic institutionalism from the sociological understanding of institutions that affect agents on a more profound level (Meyer and Rowan 1977; DiMaggio and Powell 1991). Concepts like "governance structures" or "institutional arrangements" developed by Oliver Williamson and Ronald Coase, respectively, are distinct from what is considered an "institutional environment" (Ménard 2005). Consequently, the "law and economics perspective interprets institutions through a backward inference. The diversity of institutional frameworks is analysed through the functions they ultimately serve" (Goyer 2010: 430).

While efforts to compare and contrast corporate governance within and across countries go back a long time, the post-World War II era of managerialism and planning reduced the original controversy. Only the rise of the shareholder value movement in the 1970s strongly revived the comparative debate. Shrinking profit margins due to the structural crisis of capitalism at the time (Fordism) lowered the standing of corporate managers, and new institutional investors increased the options for shareholders to exert influence (pension funds, hedge funds, etc.). The old "Wall Street Rule" with dispersed ownership and shareholder passivism came to an end (Soederberg 2010).

The rise of neoliberalism (Plehwe, Walpen, and Neunhöffer 2006), the law and economics movement, and economic neo-institutionalists in the United States were partly responsible for the redirection of the comparative frame to focus on "shareholder value": "Corporate governance deals with the ways in which suppliers of finance to corporations assure themselves of getting a return on their investment" (Shleifer and Vishny 1997: 737). If the original debate was driven by worries about the abuse of corporate power, the new concern was how to secure financial investors the highest return. Superior financial performance of US corporations and the larger share of profits disbursed to stockowners compared with European or Japanese competitors helped to draw attention to the Anglo-Saxon-style corporate governance. In addition to internal controls (of the board by investors), external control via capital markets (short-time financial flows, hostile takeovers, etc.) is held to discipline managers (Manne 1965). Continuous monitoring efforts by various private and public institutions like rating agencies or the Security Exchange Commission complete the regime. US corporate governance arrangements in particular were turned into the model that reformers tried to promote in many countries that had previously emphasized stability-oriented governance regimes involving bank control (house banks) or strong employee representation on the supervisory board (Hopt et al. 1998). A research program developed originally to assess corporate governance and to direct reforms at the level of individual firms was suddenly turned into a general program of institutional reform (Lazonick and O'Sullivan 2000), promoted by international organizations like the Organisation for Economic Co-operation and Development (OECD) (Taylor 1997).

The corporate accounting scandals of the early 2000s (leading to giant collapses like WorldCom, Enron, Arthur Andersen), which almost all occurred in the USA, presented a challenge to the narrow focus of economic neo-institutionalism and underlined the relevance of alternative modes of corporate governance at the same time. The United States witnessed a range of new legal requirements laid down in the Sarbanes–Oxley Act of 2002. The law stipulated a new regulatory agency, albeit with limited powers (Soederberg 2010: 48f.). But the apparent contradictions and inefficiencies of governance arrangements in the USA, previously celebrated for the high returns to shareholders, had not yet turned the tide of shareholder-oriented reforms elsewhere. "Corporate governance systems throughout the world are converging on a shareholder-centric ideology," wrote a group of authors just before the onset of the global financial crisis (Buchholtz, Brown, and Shabana 2008: 328).

Although shareholder orientation appears to prevail in general, there has been a shift of focus from profitability as the sole criterion of performance to a language of sustainability in corporate governance. A fresh emphasis on responsibility and shareholder pluralism gave rise to a new wave of literature on corporate social responsibility (CSR). Rapidly increasing interest in it was reinforced by the widespread adoption and institutionalization of CSR practices beyond the USA (Kinderman 2009). Corporate governance debates shifted to issues of reconciliation: "Corporate governance is concerned with holding the balance between economic and social goals and between individual and communal goals . . . The aim is to align as nearly as possible the interests of individuals, corporations and society" (Sir Adrian Cadbury quoted in Buchholtz, Brown, and Shabana 2008: 327).

Due to the scope of the global financial crisis, efforts to address sustainability concerns, by and large within a corporate governance model inspired by Anglo-Saxon concerns of shareholder value, have arguably lost much of their previous appeal. Theoretically, the new direction of CSR is driven by sociological inroads into the mainstream of neo-institutional economics: scholars challenge the crude principal–agent dualism, pointing out greater shareholder and management diversity. A rigid conceptualization of conflicts of interests between officials and owners cannot account for the alignment of (parts of) management and (groups of) shareholders characteristic of the reality in many corporations (Shapiro 2005). Stewardship theory challenges the basic assumptions of rational choice conceptualizations of agency, and thereby reintroduces sociological man as a basic unit of management analysis (Mitnick 1992). The role of corporate networks influencing the adoption of management models has been demon-strated by relying on social network analysis (Davis and Greve 1997).

The sociological turn of corporate governance research (Goyer 2010: 430f.) has also led to a renewal of interest in (international) comparisons. Scholars concerned about more responsible *management* emphasize board composition, and promote the inclu-sion of minorities on supervisory boards to lower the dangers of social closure, neglect of important causes, and collusion. Corporate democracy, according to this perspec-tive, requires a better representation of relevant groups at the board level. Unlike Williamson (1985), who argued against workers' representation at the supervisory board level in the name of shareholder interests, Ray (2005) pleads in favor of a regime *between* the German model of codetermination and the American model. It is evident from this formulation that the performance-oriented stewardship theory is still quite restricted by traditional corporate governance concerns. A more comprehensive stakeholder theory would have to make an effort to better account for the different positions of groups like workers and owners in corporations in different countries, beyond the problem-solving and integration concerns dominating managers and scholars in the United States. So far the shift toward responsibility concerns in corpo-rate governance research has remained centered on management. Since many man-agement activities are dedicated to defending key characteristics of the shareholder value orientation, a profound change of institutional arrangements is unlikely to result from managerial responsibility alone. A deeper analysis would require a renewed interest in the role of conflicts and struggles within and beyond individual corpora-tions (Burawoy 1979).

Much of economic corporate governance research is still far away from a more pro-found comparative analysis of politics in production and economic modes. Ultimately, the research program of neo-institutional economics remains both more restricted and specific than the research conducted in economic sociology with regard to internal and external groups, organizations, and institutions (Campbell 2007). This weakness of eco-nomic institutionalism may be considered a strength in reform-oriented debates. Insights to be gained by scholarship steeped in historical and sociological institutional-ism are likely to emphasize path dependency, which fundamentally lowers expectations regarding the feasibility of reform and strategic choice, and certainly lacks the norma-tive enthusiasm and clarity of economic neo-institutionalism.

CONCLUSION: WINDS OF CHANGE?

Although the major developments in research on modes of corporate governance and varieties of capitalism sketched above were well underway before the onset of the global financial crisis in 2008, the redirections from shareholder value to corporate responsi-bility and from national diversity to common challenges of financialization and regula-tory reform have since gained increasing urgency (Meade, Chapter 28, this volume). To be sure, major insights obtained from national research were confirmed by the global crisis because liberal market economies suffered more than coordinated market economies. Since many coordinated market economies display pockets and problems of liberal market economies (bank failures, housing bubbles, lack of oversight of regulatory institutions, etc.), and since a private sector financial crisis has rapidly turned into a fiscal crisis in Europe and the United States, the primary focus on isolated national systems has clearly become inadequate to tackle processes of transformation and programs of regulatory reform (Nölke 2009).

Within the varieties of research on capitalism, the distance from national to other business systems (local, regional, transnational, etc.) is still hard to overlook. So far, European research on integration and varieties research on capitalism are worlds apart from one another. This is highly unfortunate because of recent European developments in economic governance. In the aftermath of the financial crisis the EU has developed components of a supranational mode of economic governance in ways that were unthinkable before.

The next generation of economic governance research is likely to move beyond traditional oppositions of market and state, although an open climate of discussion about traditional theories of market and state failure (like welfare economics and public choice, neo-institutional economics and economic sociology) has yet to emerge. The sociological turn of corporate governance research is promising in this regard. The work of some economic neo-institutionalists (such as Douglas North or Deepak Lal) is also converging with historical sociology despite epistemological differences regarding the explanation of institutions. North concludes that "economics of scope, complementarities, and network externalities of an institutional matrix make institutional change overwhelmingly incremental and path dependent" and hopes that this insight "puts to rest for good any simplistic general nostras such as 'big bang' or 'shock therapy' theories to magically overcome lack of development" (North 2005: 22, 28). Deepak Lal (1998) introduced culture as the key variable in explaining different economic equilibria. Historical economic neo-institutionalists and economic sociologists share many of the key research questions regarding the explanation of institutional change beyond strategic choice. At the same time, economic sociology and economic institutionalism are likely to remain complementary, since economists tend to focus on inefficient institutions, resulting from political interference in market relations. Sociologists challenge universal notions of efficiency arising from the distributional limits of markets and entrepreneurship. There is still some way to go to bridge the divide between economics and society in ways that are adequate to the age of globalized capitalism.

A number of modifications are currently discussed and promoted in many countries and supranational arenas, both with regard to corporate governance arrangements and the institutional configuration of financial markets. Closing regulatory loopholes and increasing the level of responsibility is the order of the day. There is little evidence so far of a strong impact of social responsibility on financial institutions, despite the history of the global financial crisis. If and to what extent reforms at the level of financial institutions will in turn have an impact on corporate governance cannot yet be determined. So far it is safe to say only that the glamour of the Anglo-Saxon mode of governance has lost much of its appeal.

REFERENCES

Albert, M. 1991. *Capitalisme Contre Capitalisme*. Paris: Seuil.

Amable, B. 2003. *The Diversity of Modern Capitalism*. Oxford: Oxford University Press.

Berle, A. and Means, G. 1967. *The Modern Corporation and Private Property*. New York: Harcourt, Brace and World.

Bohle, D. and Greskovits, B. 2007. The state, internationalization, and capitalist diversity in Eastern Europe. *Competition and Change* 11: 89–115.

Bohle, D. and Greskovits, B. 2009. Varieties of capitalism and capitalism tout court. *Archives Européennes des Sociologie* 3: 1–31.

Buchholtz, A. K., Brown, J. A., and Shabana, K. M. 2008. Corporate governance and corporate social responsibility. In A. Crane, A. McWilliams, D. Matten, J. Moon, and D. S. Siegel (eds.), *The Oxford Handbook of Corporate Social Responsibility*. Oxford: Oxford University Press, 327–345.

Burawoy, M. 1979. *Manufacturing Consent: Changes in the Labor Process under Monopoly Capitalism*. Chicago: University of Chicago Press.

Campbell, J. L. 2007. Why would corporations behave in socially responsible ways? An institutional theory of corporate social responsibility. *Academy of Management Review* 32: 946–967.

Casper, S. 2007. *Creating Silicon Valley in Europe: Public Policy towards New Technology Industries*. Oxford: Oxford University Press.

Coase, R. 1937. The nature of the firm. *Economica* 4: 386–405.

Crouch, C. 2005. Models of capitalism. *New Political Economy* 10: 439–456.

Davis, G. F. and Greve, H. R. 1997. Corporate elite networks and governance changes in the 1980s. *American Journal of Sociology* 103: 1–37.

DiMaggio, P. J. and Powell, W. W. 1983. The iron cage revisited: Institutional isomorphism and collective rationality in organizational fields. *American Sociological Review* 48:147–160.

DiMaggio, P. J. and Powell, W. W. 1991. Introduction. In W. W. Powell and P. J. DiMaggio (eds.), *The New Institutionalism in Organizational Analysis*. Chicago: University of Chicago Press, 1–38.

Djelic, M-L. and Quack, S. 2003. *Globalization and Institutions: Redefining the Rules of the Economic Game*. Cheltenham: Edward Elgar.

Eising, R. and Kohler-Koch, B. (eds.) 2005. *Interessenpolitik in Europa*. Baden-Baden: Nomos.

Goyer, M. 2010. Corporate governance. In G. Morgan, J. L. Campbell, C. Crouch, O. K. Pedersen, and R. Whitley (eds.), *The Oxford Handbook of Comparative Institutional Analysis*. Oxford: Oxford University Press, 423–451.

Grabher, G. (ed.) 1993. *The Embedded Firm: On the Socioeconomics of Interfirm Relations*. London and New York: Routledge.

Hall, P. A. and Soskice, D. 2001. *Varieties of Capitalism: The Institutional Foundations of Comparative Advantage*. Oxford: Oxford University Press.

Höpner, M. 2005. What connects industrial relations and corporate governance? Explaining institutional complementarity. *Socio-Economic Review* 3: 331–358.

Hopt, K. J., Kanda, H., Roe, M. J., Wymeersch, E., and Prigge, S. (eds.) 1998. *Comparative Corporate Governance: The State of the Art and Emerging Research*. Oxford: Clarendon Press.

Jessop, B. and Oosterlynck, S. 2008. Cultural political economy: On making the cultural turn without falling into soft economic sociology. *Geoforum* 39: 1155–1169.

Kinderman, D. 2009. *Why do Some Countries get CSR Sooner, and in Greater Quantity, than Others? The Political Economy of Corporate Responsibility and the Rise of Market Liberalism across the OECD: 1977–2007*. WZB Discussion Paper SP III 2009-301. Berlin: Wissenschaftszentrum Berlin für Sozialforschung.

Klein, P. G. 1998. New institutional economics. In B. Bouckeart and G. de Geest (eds.), *Encyplopedia of Law and Economics*. Cheltenham: Edgar Elgar, 456–489.

Lal, D. 1998. *Unintended Consequences: The Impact of Factor Endowments, Culture, and Politics on Long-Run Economic Performance*. Cambridge: MIT Press.

Lazonick, W. and O'Sullivan, M. 2000. Maximizing shareholder value: A new ideology for corporate governance. *Economy and Society* 29: 13–35.

Levi-Faur, D. 2006. Varieties of regulatory capitalism: Getting the most out of the comparative method. *Governance* 19: 367–382.

Mahoney, J. 2000. Path dependence in historical sociology. *Theory and Society* 29: 507–548.

Manne, H. G. 1965. Mergers and the market for corporate control. *The Journal of Political Economy* 73: 110–120.

Ménard, C. 2004. The economics of hybrid organizations. *Journal of Institutional and Theoretical Economics* 160: 345–376.

Ménard, C. 2005. A new institutional approach to organization. In C. Ménard and M. M. Shirley (eds.), *Handbook of New Institutional Economics*. Dordrecht: Springer, 281–318.

Meyer, J. W. and Rowan, B. 1977. Institutionalized organizations: Formal structure as myth and ceremony. *American Journal of Sociology* 83: 340.

Miller, G. J. 2005. Solutions to principal–agent problems in firms. In C. Ménard and M. M. Shirley (eds.), *Handbook of New Institutional Economics*. Dordrecht: Springer, 349–370.

Mitnick, B. M. 1992. The theory of agency and organizational analysis. In N. E. Bowie and R. E. Freeman (eds.), *Ethics and Agency Theory*. Oxford: Oxford University Press, 74–96.

Nölke, A. 2009. Finanzkrise, finanzialisierung und vergleichende kapitalismusforschung. *Zeitschrift für Internationale Beziehungen* 16: 123–139.

Nölke, A. and Vliegenthart, A. 2009. Enlarging the varieties of capitalism. The emergence of dependent market economies in East Central Europe. *World Politics* 61: 670–702.

North, D. C. 2005. Institutions and the performance of economies over time. In C. Ménard and M. M. Shirley (eds.), *Handbook of New Institutional Economics*. Dordrecht: Springer, 21–30.

Ohmae, K. 1989. Managing in a borderless world. *Harvard Business Review*: 152–161.

O'Sullivan, M. 2005. Typologies, ideologies and realities of capitalism. *Socio-Economic Review* 3: 547–558.

Plehwe, D. 2001. National trajectories, international competition, and transnational governance in Europe. In G. Morgan, P. H. Kristensen, and R. Whitley (eds.), *The Multinational Firm: Organizing across Institutional and National Boundaries*. Oxford: Oxford University Press, 281–305.

Plehwe, D., Walpen, B., and Neunhöffer, G. (eds.) 2006. *Neoliberal Hegemony: A Global Critique*. London: Routledge.

Quack, S. 2007. *Grenzüberschreitende Institutionenentwicklung: Akteure und Regelwerke im Wandel*. Habilitationsschrift, Berlin, Freie Universität Berlin.

Quack, S. 2011. Recombining national variety: Internationalisation strategies of American and European law firms. *Journal of Strategy and Management* (forthcoming).

Ray, D. M. 2005. Corporate boards and corporate democracy. *Journal of Corporate Citizenship* 20: 93–105.

Roe, M. J. 2005. The institutions of corporate governance. In C. Ménard and M. M. Shirley (eds.), *Handbook of New Institutional Economics*. Dordrecht: Springer, 371–397.

Sandholtz, W. and Stone Sweet, A. 1998. *European Integration and Supranational Governance*. Oxford: Oxford University Press.

Schmidt, V. A. 2002. *The Futures of European Capitalism*. Oxford: Oxford University Press.

Schumpeter, J. A. 1962. *Capitalism, Socialism, and Democracy*. New York: Harper Torchbooks.

Shapiro, S. P. 2005. Agency theory. *Annual Review of Sociology* 31: 263–284.

Shleifer, A. and Vishny, R. W. 1997. A survey of corporate governance. *Journal of Finance* 52(2): 737–783.

Soederberg, S. 2010. *Corporate Power and Ownership in Contemporary Capitalism: The Politics of Resistance and Domination*. RIPE Series in Global Political Economy. London: Routledge.

Sorge, A. 2005. *The Global and the Local: Understanding the Dialectics of Business Systems*. Oxford: Oxford University Press.

Streeck, W. 2009. *Re-Forming Capitalism: Institutional Change in the German Political Economy*. Oxford and New York: Oxford University Press.

Streeck, W. and Thelen, K. 2005. Introduction: Institutional change in advanced political economies. In W. Streeck and K. Thelen (eds.), *Beyond Continuity*. Oxford: Oxford University Press, 1–39.

Taylor, L. 1997. Editorial: The revival of the liberal creed—the IMF and the World Bank in a globalized economy. *World Development* 25: 145–152.

Taylor, M. Z. 2004. Empirical evidence against varieties of capitalism's theory of technological innovation. *International Organization* 58: 601–631.

Thurow, L. 1992. *Head to Head: The Coming Economic Battle among Japan, Europe and America*. New York: William Morrow and Company.

Vitols, S. 1998. Are German banks different? *Small Business Economics* 10: 79–91.

Whitley, R. 1999. *Divergent Capitalisms: The Social Structuring and Change of Business Systems*. Oxford: Oxford University Press.

Williamson, O. E. 1981 The economics of organization: The transaction cost approach. *American Journal of Sociology* 1981: 548–577.

Williamson, O. E. 1985. *The Economic Institutions of Capitalism*. New York: Free Press.

Womack, J., Jones, D., and Roos, D. 1991. *The Machine that Changed the World*. New York: HarperCollins.

CHAPTER 28

THE GOVERNANCE OF CENTRAL BANKS

ELLEN E. MEADE*

1. INTRODUCTION

THE earliest central banks date from the late seventeenth century: Sweden's Riksbank was established in 1668 and Britain's Bank of England in 1694. In the modern world, the central bank is a creation of government, rather than the private banker to the king; an organization shaped by public law, with delegated formal powers and dominated by technocrats, rather than an organization ruled by public law and dominated by private actors. Policy delegation in a democratic society creates an inevitable trade-off between the desire to have officials be accountable, on the one hand, and the need, on the other hand, to create an environment in which those officials will choose the best policies for society over the long run. Governance addresses this trade-off. In his famous 1873 treatise *Lombard Street*, Walter Bagehot (1915 [1873]: 229) wrote about the need to amend governance, to "adapt its structure most carefully" with the changing role of the central bank. Over the past two decades, central bank governance has changed considerably in many countries. In this chapter, I discuss important elements of governance: independence, accountability, and transparency. Moreover, I distinguish these elements, which are important for the *external* governance of the central bank—the institution's public face, its role and responsibilities in society—from other elements that pertain to the *internal* governance of the central bank's monetary policy committee.

Most central banks exist within a single country and control monetary policy for that country alone. A few, however, are supranational and control monetary policy for more than one country as part of a transnational monetary union. My focus is on the governance of the national or supranational central bank, not on the policy regime that it follows. The policy regime, which these days is usually an objective for inflation or the exchange rate, is typically chosen by the government.

Each section of this chapter addresses one aspect of central bank governance. The next section discusses central bank independence, first reviewing the mainstream or orthodox view on why independence is necessary, how to measure it, and what it means for macroeconomic aggregates, and then discussing alternative perspectives on the orthodox view of independence. Section 3 reviews central bank accountability and transparency, the necessary counterparts to delegated authority. Section 4 discusses internal governance procedures of central banks. Section 5 concludes.

2. CENTRAL BANK INDEPENDENCE

In most countries, the central bank is entrusted with powers and obligations by the government or legislature; that is, power is delegated from the government or legislature to the central bank via statute. This delegation of powers provides the central bank with *independence* to pursue its monetary policy objective. Debelle and Fischer (1995) distinguish between two types of independence: a central bank with *instrument* independence is assigned a goal by the government but is given freedom to use policy instruments to achieve that goal; in contrast, a central bank with *goal* independence is given freedom to establish its goal as well as to use policy instruments to achieve that goal. *De jure* or formal independence refers to the legal statutes of the central bank, whereas *de facto* or informal independence refers to the actual behavior of the central bank—a distinction that is important when assessing the degree of independence. The central bank coexists alongside many independent regulatory agencies in the modern market economy. Levi-Faur (2005: 12) has pointed to a "new order of regulatory capitalism" in which independent regulatory agencies have gained increased power and breadth, and proliferated across borders.

The problem of time inconsistency

According to the orthodox view, central banks require independence in order to credibly commit to low inflation and keep politicians from manipulating monetary policy to gain votes—known as the problem of *time inconsistency*. The implication of this argument is that inflation will be directly related to the magnitude of central bank independence and, in addition, the cost of disinflation will be lower in countries with greater central bank independence because independence signals a commitment to price stability.

The time-inconsistency problem originates with the work of Phillips (1958), who documented a negative relationship between unemployment and wage inflation in the United Kingdom. In the 1960s and 1970s, the Phillips curve came to be thought of as outlining a menu of policy options.[1] Friedman (1968) and Phelps (1967) observed independently that the Phillips trade-off between inflation and unemployment was a fallacy.

There was no trade-off in the long run; rather, there was a fixed long-run productive capacity (and an unemployment rate consistent with it) to which the economy would return, and this fixed capacity was independent of the rate of inflation.

Kydland and Prescott (1977) and Barro and Gordon (1983) formalized an analytical framework in which policy-makers seeking to exploit the Phillips curve trade-off would generate policy that was *time inconsistent*. This policy could succeed in reducing unemployment only if workers' expectations of future inflation were not rational. The incentive for time-inconsistent policy was political: the party in power, desirous of re-election, would favor higher inflation in hopes of reducing unemployment and gaining votes. Several solutions to this time-inconsistency problem emerged: Rogoff (1985) proposed the delegation of monetary policy to a set of conservative central bankers who were not subject to re-election, while Walsh (1995) suggested the provision of appropriate incentives (through employment contracts) and a well-defined objective for those central bankers. Either way, ensuring that the central bank had independence would equip it to resist political pressure and pursue a low inflation policy.

Measuring central bank independence

Several scholars have endeavored to measure formal independence and catalog its value across countries. One widely used measure of independence is owed to Cukierman, Webb, and Neyapti (1992), who evaluated legal statutes of central banks in seventy-two industrial and developing countries. Their *de jure* measure is comprised of many characteristics coded on a range of zero to one and weighted to produce an overall score; a higher score is indicative of greater independence.[2] Their measure captures four broad aspects of legal independence: (1) the insulation of the central bank's management from the political process (greater independence exists when the governor is appointed for a term of more than eight years and cannot be dismissed); (2) the insulation of central bank decision-making from government influence (the highest rating accords to central banks whose governments have no right to participate in or overturn monetary policy decisions); (3) the legal mandate or objective of the central bank (the highest rating is given to institutions with a single mandate for price stability); and (4) the strength of provisions that limit government borrowing from the central bank (because so many episodes of high inflation have had their roots in excessive spending financed by the central bank).

Independence scores based upon this methodology show a clear trend toward greater central bank independence since the 1980s. Table 28.1 provides a frequency distribution of scores based upon legal statutes from the 1980s and from 2003. The average independence score for the 2003 sample is above 0.6, compared with about 0.3 in the 1980s. Of the twenty-eight central banks with scores above 0.8 in the 2003 sample, more than one-half relate to the new central banks in Eastern European countries, while the remainder relate to countries whose central bank laws have been revised to permit greater independence; the countries in Europe's monetary union, for example, all changed their

Table 28.1 Frequency distribution of central bank
independence (x) for two time periods[§]

	1980–1989	2003
$x \leq 0.2$	6	1
$0.2 < x \leq 0.4$	39	13
$0.4 < x \leq 0.6$	24	34
$0.6 < x \leq 0.8$	3	20
$x > 0.8$	0	28
Total number of countries	72	96

[§]The 1980–1989 scores are from Cukierman, Webb, and Neyapti (1992) while
the 2003 scores are from Crowe and Meade (2007) using the same methodology. The latter have a larger country sample mainly because of the addition of
new central banks in independent states that were formerly part of the Soviet
Union.

central bank statutes to conform with the independence requirements of the Maastricht
Treaty. The shifting distribution toward greater formal independence is consistent with
Levi-Faur's (2005) observation about the uptrend in regulatory capitalism.

A potentially significant problem is that a high formal independence score does not
necessarily equate with high actual independence. Cukierman, Webb, and Neyapti (1992)
and Cukierman and Webb (1995) proxy actual or informal independence with a measure
of how frequently the central bank governor resigned or was replaced.[3] Higher turnover
shortens the average term in office of the governor relative to that of the executive, opening
the door to political influence; therefore higher turnover may be negatively correlated with
de facto independence. An alternate approach is proposed in Cukierman (1998), which
suggests using surveys to obtain information from central banks that can be used to gauge
actual independence. Surveys are naturally subject to reporting bias, in that the questions
may be interpreted differently by different individuals and the answers may reflect subjectivity but, as Cukierman notes, the responses provide a check on *de jure* measures.

Effects of independence according to the orthodox view

Alesina and Summers (1993) demonstrated a significant inverse relationship between
central bank independence and inflation for industrial countries over a thirty-year
period, beginning in the mid-1950s. Moreover, because the authors found no connection between independence and growth or unemployment, their work implied that a
reduction in inflation could be achieved without incurring a cost of lost output or jobs.

The Alesina–Summers finding of an inverse relationship between independence and
inflation was reproduced in other work so long as the sample of countries was confined
to the industrial nations; when developing countries were included, the statistical

relationship between independence and inflation was typically much weaker, and when the sample consisted only of developing countries, there was no apparent relationship at all.[4] This puzzle is easily resolved by including the informal independence measure (turnover of the central bank governor) in the regressions: several studies find evidence of a significant, positive relationship between turnover and inflation (see Eijffinger and DeHaan 1996). If governments in developing countries are less likely to observe *de jure* independence than industrial countries, and turnover is an adequate proxy for actual independence (with the two variables having a negative relationship), then these findings can be viewed as consistent with those of Alesina and Summers (1993).

Crowe and Meade (2008) revisit the early empirical work using updated measures of central bank independence based on legal statutes from 2003. Figure 28.1 plots independence against average inflation over the 2002–2006 period. Perhaps not surprisingly, the authors find no evidence of a statistical relationship between the average level of inflation and independence (or turnover) for a sample of fifty-six industrial and developing countries.[5]

What Crowe and Meade (2008) do uncover is a statistically significant effect of the *change* in central bank independence and turnover (negative and positive, respectively) on the *change* in inflation between the late 1980s and the early 2000s, indicating that central banks with larger increases independence had a greater decline in inflation. Quantitatively, the results suggest that an increase in *de jure* independence of about 0.25 is associated with a drop in inflation of more than 5 percentage points when inflation is initially in single digits; the decline in inflation is even greater when its initial value is higher.

A major concern is that independence may not be exogenous to inflation—causality could run either way, for instance, if a country with high inflation grants its central bank more independence so that it can fight inflation. Crowe and Meade repeat their statistical analysis using alternative governance indicators as instruments for independence, and the results remain robust. Overall, their findings are in line with earlier studies in suggesting that independence helps the central bank to deliver a monetary policy that is consistent with low inflation.

Alternatives to the orthodox view

The major objection to the orthodox view of central bank independence centers around the presumed exogeneity of independence. Critics have argued that greater independence does not "cause" lower inflation but is merely correlated with it (Forder 1996). Rather, it is cultural, political, or social processes and norms in a society that produce an environment in which central bank independence is high and inflation is low (or vice versa). Understanding these cultural, political, or social processes and norms is difficult and complex; therefore, there is no magic formula that a country can use to reduce its inflation rate.

Posen (1995, 1998) contends that the financial sector in a country can act as an interest group that opposes inflation; he finds that measures of financial sector opposition to inflation predict both inflation and formal measures of independence. Bernhard (1998)

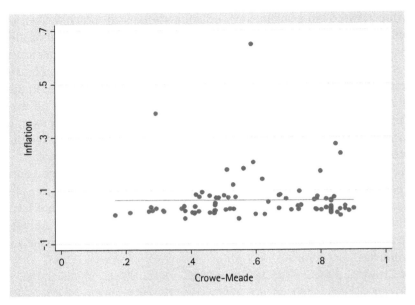

FIGURE 28.1 Inflation and independence for 96 countries, 2003.*

* The Crowe–Meade independence index, reported on the *x*-axis, is constructed using the methodology outlined by Cukierman, Webb, and Neyapti (1992). Inflation, on the *y*-axis, is transformed to mitigate the effects of hyperinflationary outliers, using $\pi/(1+\pi)$ where π is the average annual increase in consumer prices during 2000–2004.

hypothesizes that there is a greater likelihood of conflict over monetary policy and inflation in federalist systems which have legislatures and politicians at several different levels; he argues that politicians in federalist systems will choose to make the central bank independent in order to avoid conflict over monetary policy.

Empirical studies provide some support for these arguments. Scheve (2004) finds that there is significant variation across twenty advanced economies with respect to inflation aversion, using survey data from the mid-1970s to the mid-1990s. Hayo (1998), using survey data for the European Union over the same time period, finds that residents of a country with historically low inflation are more sensitive to an increase in inflation than residents of a country with historically higher inflation.

3. THE DEMOCRATIC DEFICIT: ACCOUNTABILITY AND TRANSPARENCY OF CENTRAL BANKS

As independence involves the delegation of authority to a nonelected body, a democratic void is created, which is filled by requiring the central bank to be *accountable* to the body that granted independence (the government or legislature). Of the types of independence distinguished by Debelle and Fischer (1995), instrument independence involves less delegation than goal independence, because in the former case the government directly sets the central bank's objective. Importantly, most central banks today— even those with a high degree of measured independence such as the European Central Bank (ECB)—have only instrument independence.

Legal accountability requirements typically involve the publication of reports and the testimony of the central bank's governor before the legislature on some regular cycle. For example, the chairman of the Federal Reserve (Fed) is required under the Federal Reserve Act to testify before the Senate Committee on Banking, Housing, and Urban Affairs, and the House Committee on Financial Services, in February and July of each year. The testimony must address "the efforts, activities, objectives, and plans of the Board of Governors and the Federal Open Market Committee (FOMC) with respect to the conduct of monetary policy, as well as economic developments in the United States and the prospects for the future" (Board of Governors of the Federal Reserve System 2005: 5). This testimony is accompanied by the submission of a report. Similarly, the ECB president testifies each quarter before the Committee on Economic and Monetary Affairs of the European Parliament, the appropriate counterpart body to the supranational central bank. This testimony arises from an obligation to report "at least quarterly" in Article 15 of the Statute of the European System of Central Banks and of the ECB, which also sets forth other requirements including the publication of reports, a weekly consolidated financial statement, and an annual report.

Accountability is generally perceived as a responsibility of the institution; in other words, the central bank's policy-makers are collectively accountable for the decisions that they take. In the case of the Bank of England, however, members of its Monetary Policy Committee are also *individually* accountable to parliament. This individual accountability may explain why the Bank's policy-makers feel so free to express their individual views both in voting on policy rates and also in public speaking. In her study of the Bank of England's Monetary Policy Committee, Gerlach-Kristen (2003) finds that dissents are the norm, with dissenting votes cast at about two-thirds of all meetings. This contrasts sharply with dissents for the Federal Reserve's monetary policy body, which have averaged about 8 percent of total votes.[6] Individual accountability may explain why UK policy-makers dissent so much more often than their counterparts in the United States.

Central bank *transparency* relates to the provision of timely and useful information to the public about policy decisions and the factors underlying those decisions. Transparency is clearly necessary for institutional accountability, although the term generally applies to information that is not required by law. Economists emphasize a particular role for transparency: to reduce uncertainty and guide the expectations of private sector investors, thereby promoting efficiency in financial markets. While the accountability role of transparency has its roots in political science and democratic deficits, the uncertainty role is based on the economic theory of the term structure of interest rates. Since most central banks in the modern world target a short-term nominal interest rate (for instance, an overnight interbank rate such as the Federal funds rate), the goal of transparency is to affect longer-term interest rates, which the central bank does not directly control through the provision of information that signals policy-makers' views about the likely direction of policy over the longer term. Operating through this channel, transparency helps to steer longer-term interest rates and direct the public's expectations of inflation. As financial markets have become larger and more influential, transparency has become more critical.

The move toward greater transparency has paralleled the adoption by central banks in many countries of a monetary policy regime known as *inflation targeting*, in which the central bank devotes its policy to the achievement of an announced value of inflation at some specified date in the future. With inflation targeting, the government typically directs the central bank to achieve a specified range or target value for inflation (for background, see Bernanke and Mishkin 1997; Truman 2003). Inflation targets were adopted first in New Zealand in 1991, shortly thereafter in Australia, Canada, Israel, Sweden, and the United Kingdom, and subsequently in a number of emerging market and developing countries.

Since the central bank cannot set the inflation rate directly, adequate transparency is necessary for private sector actors to interpret and judge whether the actions of the central bank are consistent with meeting its inflation target. When the focus of policy was an intermediate target, such as the monetary targets adopted by many countries in the 1970s after the collapse of the Bretton Woods system, it was possible to observe the behavior of that intermediate target directly via high frequency data published by the central bank. But inflation targeting is just that—a target for future inflation, typically in two years time—and it is impossible for the public to judge progress toward that goal without substantial additional information. Modern macroeconomics gives a key role to expectations, and transparency is crucial in steering the private sector's expectations of inflation.

While there is no consensus as to measurement, Geraats (2002) proposes the evaluation of transparency on the basis of five components: the clarity of the central bank's mandate; the timely release of forecasts and other economic information; the provision of ample information about the decision-making procedures of the monetary policy committee, including its votes; the immediate release of policy decisions; and the evaluation by the central bank of its own performance *ex post*. In the Internet age, many central banks provide this sort of information on their websites, and it is difficult to see how this sort of transparency could be achieved without the Internet. Rankings of institutions by their degree of transparency, as in Blinder and colleagues (2001), Eijffinger and Geraats (2006), and Crowe and Meade (2008), give higher marks to inflation-targeting central banks than to central banks with other sorts of monetary regimes.

Many of the studies that examine the implications of transparency for economic outcomes have focused on the predictability of monetary policy and inflation forecasts. Ehrmann and Fratzscher (2007) find that as the Federal Reserve has increased the information it provides about its policy decisions, US monetary policy has become more predictable. Gerlach-Kristen (2004) shows that information about votes cast by policy-makers at the Bank of England can be used to predict future interest rates. Using transparency scores for twenty-eight countries, Crowe and Meade (2008) provide evidence that improved transparency reduces the variation in inflation projections made by private sector forecasters. This is broadly consistent with Crowe (2010), who shows that the introduction of inflation targeting is associated with an improvement in private sector forecasts of inflation. Chortareas, Stasavage, and Sterne (2003) find that greater information dissemination is associated with lower costs of disinflation (reduced sacrifice ratios) in twenty-one OECD countries, while Dincer and Eichengreen (2007) provide evidence that greater transparency reduces the variation in inflation rates.

4. INTERNAL GOVERNANCE OF CENTRAL BANKS

A small literature on the internal behavior of central bank policy committees has emerged over the past decade, concentrating on the decision-making process within the institution—how officials collect and share information, whether they change their views during the course of discussion, and whether the views of specific members (such as the chairman) are dominant.[7] The focus of the work is the individual preferences of policy-makers rather than the collective policy outcome that has been the traditional focus of monetary policy research. Thus, much of the study has concerned the Bank of England, Federal Reserve, or Riksbank, which publish information about committee voting, either in terms of agreements and disagreements with the policy outcome or in terms of the specific policy interest rate preferred by dissenters. Transcripts of Fed policy meetings, published with a five-year lag, provide a source for the study of meeting dynamics and deliberation.

Blinder and Morgan (2005) note that many central banks now make decisions by committee, whereas several decades ago decisions were made by a lone governor. Using an experimental framework, they demonstrate that groups outperform individuals in terms of the quality of their decisions; in addition, groups do not require more information when making those decisions, indicating that committees can be as activist in their policy-making as individual decision-makers. Although there is no firm consensus on what constitutes an optimal size for the monetary policy committee, Sibert (2006) uses evidence amassed in psychology and sociology to suggest that five members may be appropriate—thus, optimal committee size may be smaller than what is observed at the most studied central banks such as the Bank of England, ECB, and Federal Reserve, which have nine, twenty-three, and twelve voting members, respectively.

Internal governance also concerns the role played by different types of members on the monetary policy committee. The Federal Reserve's policy committee is comprised of officials appointed by the President as well as officials representing regions of the United States. This hub-and-spoke system also characterizes the ECB's policy committee, but the regional representatives on the latter are the governors of the national central banks that participate in the monetary union. In the United Kingdom, the membership types are differentiated not by geography but by their work experience:

career central bankers are the "internal" members, while professionals with no prior central bank experience are the "external" members (who are typically part of a broader network of professionals in economics and finance). A number of studies have demonstrated that different types of policy-makers vote differently: Gerlach-Kristen (2003) shows that external members at the Bank of England are more likely to dissent, while Meade and Sheets (2005) find that Federal Reserve policy-makers are more likely to dissent for higher (lower) interest rates if unemployment in their region is low (high) relative to the national average. Chappell, McGregor, and Vermilyea (2005) estimate the policy preferences of Federal Reserve officials—examining the weights that each individual places on price stability versus output stability—and find, not surprisingly, that there are differences. Studying individual policy-makers at the Bank of England, Riboni and Ruge-Murcia (2008) draw a similar conclusion. Collectively, this research points to an important role to be played by "outsiders" in the formulation of monetary policy, whether those outsiders are defined by differences in background (education and career) or geography.

The specifics of the meeting agenda and how those specifics relate to the policy determined at the meeting are also addressed in this literature. In some committees, the chairman dominates by speaking first and framing the agenda, voting first, or both. Gerlach-Kristen and Meade (2010) find a relationship between the order of voting at Federal Reserve policy meetings during Alan Greenspan's tenure and the number of dissents cast, with officials who vote first more likely to cast dissents.[8] Blinder (2004) suggests that the Fed's committee, at least under Greenspan, operated as an "autocratically collegial" body in which dissent was suppressed. By examining the policy preferences voiced by Fed policy-makers during the meeting discussion and comparing those preferences with actual votes, Meade (2005) shows that the magnitude of disagreement voiced during the discussion is about double that of the official tally. This compares with the Bank of England's decision-making body where a high frequency of dissent is not uncommon, and suggests that there is something in the nature of the body itself, or perhaps in the societal or political context in which the central bank operates, that contributes to voting behavior.

Finally, some scholars have employed textual analysis software to analyze the Federal Reserve transcripts, as these transcripts provide the only public source of information about internal central bank discussions. Bailey and Schonhardt-Bailey (2009) catalog and quantify the decision-making process, while Woolley and Gardner (2009) study whether the nature of deliberation has changed since the Fed's decision in 1993 to publish verbatim transcripts of policy meetings. Meade and Stasavage (2008) find that the publication of transcripts has resulted in a possible repression of internal disagreement. Before transcript publication, FOMC meetings had free and flowing discussion with frequent interruption of one official by another; since 1993 there has been a noticeable change, with officials reading pre-prepared statements and little or no interruption. Since transcript publication, officials are less likely to disagree with the policy proposal put forth by the chairman. These results suggest that, although transparency has unquestionable benefits, certain forms of publicity might stifle debate.

5. CONCLUDING REMARKS

Central banks are old and important institutions whose external governance has been much debated, first by Walter Bagehot in the 1800s and much more recently by scholars in economics and political science. Much attention has been paid to institutional independence, the merits or demerits of it, and the democratic deficit created by the delegation of authority for monetary policy. Filling the democratic void is the concern of legal requirements for accountability and information requirements for transparency. Recent research on the internal governance of central banks provides guidance on how to best structure the monetary policy committee.

The financial crisis of 2007–2008 begs the question of whether central bank governance could be amended to prevent future crises of this sort. While it is clear that central bank policies—low interest rates and insufficient regulation—contributed to the onset of the crisis, how to think about the role of governance in generating those policies is less clear (in part because political authorities wholeheartedly supported those policies in the run-up to the crisis). Graham Wilson (Chapter 26, this volume) focuses on institutional independence as the main culprit; while I agree with him, I would not go so far as to say that the crisis has called into question the "desirability" of central bank independence but rather its magnitude. What seems clear is that, because central bankers in the United Kingdom and United States possessed independence, they moved much more quickly and efficiently to respond to the crisis than politicians did or could do, in some cases undertaking measures that were clearly monetary in nature and in other cases acting in a capacity traditionally occupied by the fiscal authority. Unlike the fiscal authority, however, the central bank is not directly accountable to the electorate. So, does this argue for scaling back central banks' mandates because they went too far, or leaving them alone because they responded so quickly to the crisis?

Goodfriend (2011) distinguishes traditional monetary policy, in which the central bank exchanges government securities for bank reserves, from credit policy, in which the central bank exchanges assets other than government securities. Credit policy amounts to providing loans to private sector borrowers and involves picking some borrowers over others, which Goodfriend sees as tantamount to the picking of winners and losers—an activity that politicians should engage in but not their technocrats in the central bank. The worry in this case is not that the government has compelled the central bank to do something political, but rather that the latter has trodden on territory normally occupied by the former.

Even though, as Wilson notes (Chapter 26, this volume), it seemed clear just after the crisis that there would be some rethinking of governance and the emergency powers of the central bank, it seems now that such a rethink is unlikely. If economic performance is eventually restored and unemployment is reduced, politicians will be satisfied and their re-election prospects will be enhanced. Central banks will have trodden broadly but their mandates are unlikely to be curtailed.

Notes

* Acknowledgements: The author thanks David Levi-Faur, David Stasavage, Jacint Jordana, and Arie Krampf for helpful comments on an earlier draft.
1. King (2008) provides a nice discussion of Phillips's original work and the chronological development of the Phillips curve concept.
2. For more details, see also Cukierman (1998: ch. 19) and Crowe and Meade (2007, 2008). Bade and Parkin (1982) and Grilli, Masciandaro, and Tabellini (1991) develop alternative methods for measuring independence.
3. Gilardi and Maggetti (2010) consider many additional factors when measuring the informal independence of regulatory agencies.
4. For a comprehensive review of this literature, see Eijffinger and DeHaan (1996).
5. Turnover for each country is measured as the average number of central bank governors from 1995 through 2004.
6. Meade and Sheets (2005).
7. Many of the issues addressed by this research were initially raised in Alan Blinder's provocative monographs (2002, 2004) in which he reflected upon his experience as vice-chairman of the Federal Reserve.
8. Chappell, McGregor, and Vermilyea (2005) have studied speaking order and its effects on Fed policy during the chairmanship of Arthur Burns.

References

Alesina, A. and Summers, L. H. 1993. Central bank independence and macroeconomic performance: Some comparative evidence. *Journal of Money, Credit, and Banking* 25: 151–162.

Bade, R. and Parkin, M. 1982. *Central Bank Laws and Monetary Policy.* Working Paper, University of Western Ontario.

Bagehot, W. 1915. *Lombard Street: A Description of the Money Market*, 14th ed. London: John Murray.

Bailey, A. and Schonhardt-Bailey, C. 2009. *Deliberation and Monetary Policy: Quantifying the Words of American Central Bankers, 1979–1999.* Political Science and Political Economy Working Paper, London School of Economics.

Barro, R. and Gordon, D. 1983. Rules, discretion, and reputation in a model of monetary policy. *Journal of Monetary Economics* 12: 101–121.

Bernanke, B. S. and Mishkin, F. S. 1997. Inflation targeting: A new framework for monetary policy? *Journal of Economic Perspectives* 11: 97–116.

Bernhard, W. 1998. A political explanation of variations in central bank independence. *The American Political Science Review* 92: 311–327.

Blinder, A. S. 2002. *Central Banking in Theory and Practice.* Cambridge, MA: MIT Press.

Blinder, A. S. 2004. *The Quiet Revolution: Central Banking Goes Modern.* New Haven, CT: Yale University Press.

Blinder, A. S. and Morgan, J. 2005. Are two heads better than one? Monetary policy by committee. *Journal of Money, Credit, and Banking* 37: 789–811.

Blinder, A. S, Goodhart, C., Hildebrand, P., Lipton, D. and Wyplosz, C. 2001. *How Do Central Banks Talk? Geneva Reports on the World Economy 3.* London: Centre for Economic Policy Research.

Board of Governors of the Federal Reserve System, *Purposes and Functions*. 2005. Washington, DC: Board of Governors of the Federal Reserve System.

Chappell, H. W., McGregor, R. R. and Vermilyea, T. A. 2005. *Committee Decisions on Monetary Policy: Evidence from Historical Records of the Federal Open Market Committee*. Cambridge, MA: MIT Press.

Chortareas, G., Stasavage, D. and Sterne, G. 2003. Does monetary policy reduce disinflation costs? *The Manchester School* 72: 521–540.

Crowe, C. 2010. Testing the transparency benefits of inflation targeting: Evidence from private sector forecasts. *Journal of Monetary Economics* 57: 226–232.

Crowe, C. and Meade, E. E. 2007. Evolution of central bank governance around the world. *Journal of Economic Perspectives* 21: 69–90.

Crowe, C. and Meade, E. E. 2008. Central bank independence and transparency: Evolution and effectiveness. *European Journal of Political Economy* 24: 763–777.

Cukierman, A. 1998. *Central Bank Strategy, Credibility, and Independence: Theory and Evidence*. Cambridge, MA: MIT Press.

Cukierman, A. and Webb, S. 1995. Political influence on the central bank: International evidence. *The World Bank Research Observer* 9: 397–423.

Cukierman, A., Webb, S. and Neyapti, B. 1992. Measuring the independence of central banks and its effect on policy outcomes. *World Bank Economic Review* 6: 353–398.

Debelle, G. and Fischer, S. 1995. How independent should central banks be? In J. Fuhrer (ed.), *Goals, Guidelines and Constraints Facing Monetary Policymakers*. Boston: Federal Reserve Bank of Boston Conference Series, 195–221.

Dincer, N. and Eichengreen, B. 2007. *Central Bank Transparency: Where, Why, and with What Effects?* Working Paper 13003, National Bureau of Economic Research.

Ehrmann, M. and Fratzscher, M. 2007. *Social Value of Public Information: Testing the Limits to Transparency*. Working Paper 821, European Central Bank.

Eijffinger, S. C. W. and DeHaan, J. 1996. The political economy of central-bank independence. Special Papers in International Economics, 19. International Finance Section, Department of Economics, Princeton University, Princeton, NJ.

Eijffinger, S. C. W and Geraats, P. 2006. How transparent are central banks? *European Journal of Political Economy* 22: 1–21.

Forder, J. 1996. On the assessment and implementation of "institutional" remedies. *Oxford Economic Papers* 48: 39–51.

Friedman, M. 1968. The role of monetary policy. *American Economic Review* 58: 1–17.

Geraats, P. 2002. Central bank transparency. *Economic Journal* 112: F532–F565.

Gerlach-Kristen, P. 2003. Insiders and outsiders at the Bank of England. *Central Banking* 14: 96–102.

Gerlach-Kristen, P. 2004. Is the MPC's voting record informative about future UK monetary policy? *Scandinavian Journal of Economics* 106: 299–313.

Gerlach-Kristen, P. and Meade, E. E. 2010. *Is There a Limit on FOMC Dissents? Evidence from the Greenspan Era*. Working Paper, American University.

Gilardi, F. and Maggetti, M. 2010. The independence of regulatory authorities. In D. Levi-Faur (ed.), *Handbook of Regulation*. Cheltenham: Edward Elgar,

Goodfriend, M. 2011. Central banking in the credit turmoil: An assessment of Federal Reserve practice. *Journal of Monetary Economics* 58: 1–12.

Grilli, V., Masciandaro, D. and Tabellini, G. 1991. Political and monetary institutions and public financial policies in the industrial countries. *Economic Policy* 13: 341–392.

Hayo, B. 1998. Inflation culture, central bank independence and price stability. *European Journal of Political Economy* 14: 241–263.

King, R. G. 2008. The Phillips curve and US macroeconomic policy: Snapshots, 1958–1996. Federal Reserve Bank of Richmond. *Economic Quarterly* 94: 311–359.

Kydland, F. and E. Prescott. 1977. Rules rather than discretion: The inconsistency of optimal plans. *Journal of Political Economy* 85: 473–490.

Levi-Faur, D. 2005. The global diffusion of regulatory capitalism. *Annals of the American Academy of Political and Social Sciences* 598: 12–33.

Meade, E. E. 2005. The FOMC: Preferences, voting, and consensus. Federal Reserve Bank of St Louis. *Review* 87: 93–101.

Meade, E. E. and Sheets, D. N. 2005. Regional influences on FOMC voting patterns. *Journal of Money, Credit, and Banking* 37: 661–677.

Meade, E. E. and Stasavage, D. 2008. Publicity of debate and the incentive to dissent: Evidence from the US Federal Reserve. *The Economic Journal* 118: 695–717.

Phelps, E. S. 1967. Phillips curves, expectations of inflation and optimal employment over time. *Economica* NS 34: 254–281.

Phillips, A. W. H. 1958. The relation between unemployment and the rate of change of money wage rates in the United Kingdom, 1861–1957. *Economica* NS 25: 283–299.

Posen, A. S. 1995. Declarations are not enough: Financial sector sources of central bank independence. *NBER Macroeconomics Annual* 10: 253–274.

Posen, A. S. 1998. Central bank independence and disinflationary credibility: A missing link? *Oxford Economic Papers* 50: 335–359.

Riboni, A. and Ruge-Murcia, F. J. 2008. Preference heterogeneity in monetary policy committees. *International Journal of Central Banking* 4: 213–233.

Rogoff, K. 1985. The optimal degree of commitment to an intermediate monetary target. *Quarterly Journal of Economics* 100: 1169–1189.

Scheve, K. 2004. Public inflation aversion and the political economy of macroeconomic policymaking. *International Organizations* 58: 1–34.

Sibert, A. 2006. Central banking by committee. *International Finance* 9: 145–168.

Truman, E. M. 2003. *Inflation Targeting in the World Economy*. Washington, DC: Institute for International Economics.

Walsh, C. 1995. Optimal contracts for central bankers. *American Economic Review* 85: 150–167.

Woolley, J. T. and Gardner, J. 2009. *Does Sunshine Reduce the Quality of Deliberation? The Case of the Federal Open Market Committee*. Conference Paper, American Political Science Association.

PART VI

....

GOVERNANCE
OF RISKS

....

CHAPTER 29

....

RISK AND GOVERNANCE

....

ELIZABETH FISHER

IN this chapter the relationship between the concepts of risk and governance is considered. That relationship is by no means straightforward. While both concepts are used to connote new methods of governing (Ewald 2000; Rhodes, Chapter 3, this volume), the phenomena they refer to are quite different. The turn toward governance is often used as shorthand to connote the turn toward markets and multi-level networks of public and private actors (Bevir 2010). In contrast, the turn toward risk, while encompassing many different developments, is generally understood as the promotion of quantification and analysis of knowledge in the process of governing (Fisher 2010).

With that said, risk and governance do overlap in three important ways. First, in certain circumstances risk has been promoted as a governance technique, particularly in the context of New Public Management (NPM). Second, the emphasis in risk discourses upon analysis, while not directly about governance, enables a greater range of public and private actors to be involved in the process of governing. Third, discourses about risk highlight the coproduction of modes of governing and understandings of the problems being governed. Thus, risk is a technique of governance, which enables governance and forces a discourse about the coproduction of governance regimes and the issues they address. These overlaps are important for governance scholars not only because they highlight the fact that the concept of risk is relevant to governance, but also because they require governance scholars to take a harder look at the contentious role that knowledge, and in particular quantitative knowledge, plays in governance regimes.

This chapter is structured as follows. First, I provide an overview of the diverse ways risk is deployed in governing. I highlight four different contexts in which risk is utilized as a concept. These different contexts, as well as the fact that risk is defined differently by different disciplines and is deployed for different reasons, highlight the fact that the role of risk in governing is a multifaceted one. With that said, a common theme across these different contexts is that the deployment of risk promotes the use of and reliance on the analytical and objective assessment of knowledge. Second, I consider the relationship between risk and different forms of governance and examine how risk can be a technique of governance, enable governance, and highlight the coproduction of understandings of governance and the problems that governance addresses. Finally, I consider the most significant implication of these interrelationships, which is that they require governance scholars to think more carefully about the role of knowledge and expertise in governance. In particular, scholars must think about the ability of such knowledge to provide an authoritative basis for decision-making; the interrelationship between knowledge and accountability; and the need to reflect on the role that knowledge plays in coproduction.

Two important points should be made before starting. First, the use of risk has not been limited to the realms of governance. Indeed, it could be argued that it has been primarily utilized in the context of traditional forms of government (Black 2010). For that reason, in the first section, the focus is on risk and *governing*, not risk and *governance*. Second, my conclusions in this chapter are about the need for governance scholars to reflect more critically on aspects of what they study and in particular the role of knowledge. I do not offer a definitive formula for that process of reflection beyond the framework of understanding provided here. For those who want neat answers this will be frustrating, but as will become clear from the analysis, understanding the nature of the interrelationships between risk and governance is an important first step.

1. RISK AND GOVERNING

It has become popular to talk of "risk governance" as if there were discrete reified risks that are subject to particular governance regimes. While the simplicity of this image is appealing, it is also wrong. Risk itself is subject to many different definitions and plays many different roles in the processes of governing. An important starting point is thus to gain some appreciation of the complexity of risk and the many different governing contexts in which it is embedded.

At its simplest, risk is "a situation or event in which something of human value (including humans themselves) has been put at stake and where the outcome is uncertain" (Jaeger et al. 2001: 17). Avoiding such situations or events has been a constant leitmotif in the history of human civilization (Eidinow 2007) and has been a major theme in: how we live our personal lives (Slovic 2000); how economic actors behave (Knight 1964); and how the role of the state is understood (Beck 1992). Risk has thus figured in public and private, and individual and collective, spheres of action. What is new is that in the space of thirty years, the concept has gone from being understood as an obscure technical concept mainly utilized by engineers and public health specialists, to one that is used regularly in the practice and scholarship of governing.

Broadly speaking, four very wide categories of risk discourse in the context of governing can be identified (Fisher 2010). First, risk has become an important concept in public sector management reform (Treasury Board of Canada 2001). In this context risk is part of the NPM discourse and is understood as a threat to the successful operation of public administration; "[e]ffective risk management is then needed to enable the organ-isation to deliver its objectives in the light of those risks" (Audit Commission 2001: 19).

The second way in which risk has become an important feature of governing is that the objects of regulatory activity are redefined in terms of risk. Thus, for example, environmental and public health regulation is now understood to be about regulating environmental and public health risks, and financial regulation is now understood to be about regulating market risk. For regulators, this means that to regulate they must identify a "risk" and then use a range of analytical methodologies to assess and manage that risk (NRC 1994). Understanding the role of regulators in terms of risk usually results in their discretion being more constrained because they must justify their decisions on the basis of a framework for assessment and management. To not act on this basis is under-stood to be unaccountable (Fisher 2000). Risk in this regard is usually understood as a scientific basis for action. Thus, as one former US Environmental Protection Agency (EPA) administrator has noted:

> Risk assessment at [the] EPA must be based only on scientific evidence and scien-tific consensus. Nothing will erode…public confidence faster than the suspicion that policy considerations have been allowed to influence the assessment of risk. (Ruckelshaus 1983: 1027)

Risk is thus closely bound up with the promotion of objective knowledge. This can be seen across all areas but significantly in relation to this second category. The importance of this will be discussed below.

The third area in which risk is being deployed is in relation to enforcement and crimi-nal justice. Thus, risk is now playing a role in decisions that concern how to apply and enforce regulatory schemes (Black and Baldwin 2010). The most obvious example of this is the "risk-based" approaches to enforcement promoted by the Hampton report in the UK, which has resulted in different UK regulators adopting a range of "risk-based" enforcement policies that vary in their detail and in how much they require decision-makers to rely on analytical methodologies (Hampton 2005). More significantly, risk and the assessment of individuals as "risky" are playing an increasingly important role in the criminal justice system and have been related to the re-characterizing of that sys-tem as providing "security" (Zedner 2009). Similar developments can also take place in relation to mental health and social services (DH 2007). All these different techniques are based on the premise that methodologies exist which can accurately assess and man-age an individual's future behavior so as to ensure compliance and enforcement.

Finally, risk is being promoted as an overarching concept that explains and justifies the role and nature of the state at the meta level (Beck 1992). From this perspective, the three different understandings above are largely seen as one development (Strategy Unit of the Cabinet Office 2002). This has resulted in policies that attempt to collate all risks together in risk management strategies (Fisher 2003), as well as discussions about what role the state should play in the private life of individuals and in regulating activities more generally (BRC 2006). On this basis, risk provides a new narrative for explaining, and justifying, the role of the state.

The identification of these four categories above makes it clear that to talk in terms of risk in regard to governing is to refer to a diverse set of phenomena that are promoted for a range of different reasons. It is also the case that there are different disciplinary understandings of risk (Bammer and Smithson 2008). Thus, risk means something different in economics, engineering, criminology, and environmental protection (Fisher 2010: 53–54). Moreover, the institutional contexts in which risk can operate are diverse. The public sector manager's preoccupation with financial risk will be driven by an institutional preoccupation with fiscal responsibility (KPMG 1999). The regulatory scientist concerned with assessing the health risks from a particular chemical will be normally concerned with determining a "safe" level of exposure under the relevant legislative mandate (NRC 1994). Enforcement regimes are usually being designed on the basis that enforcement resources are used wisely (FSA 2006). Probation officers will be attempting to assess the risk of re-offending (NPS 2004).

With that said, what is common across the different ways risk is utilized and defined is that risk is primarily understood as requiring some form of analysis, quantification, and objectivity. Risk thus requires the mobilization of knowledge, in particular scientific knowledge, in decision-making. For that reason, the growing popularity of risk in governing has been the growing popularity of analytical tools such as risk assessment and risk management, and there is a considerable body of guidance concerned with ensuring the rigor and accuracy of decision-making about risk. Understanding governing in terms of risk is therefore largely conceptualizing governing as requiring forms of analysis of information. Nearly every single one of the reforms discussed above requires decision-makers to engage in some form of technical analysis, and provides guidance and frameworks for them to do so.

In this regard, risk is regulating decision-making by "governing behaviour" (Collins 1999: 7), in particular behavior in regard to knowledge. Risk is thus a "regulatory concept" (Fisher 2010) and it is one that provides a basis on which to ensure a decision is "worthy to be recognised" (Habermas 1984: 178). Thus a decision based on a risk assessment or some other form of analytical assessment is understood to be more legitimate than one that is not (Porter 1995).

2. RISK AND GOVERNANCE

The discussion above was in relation to risk and all processes of governing. I now turn to the relationship between risk and governance. As noted in the introduction, that relationship is by no means straightforward. Governance, as is clear from this book, is a notoriously difficult term to pin down, but here it is understood to refer to a less hierarchical form of governing in which public and private actors have a role to play (Bevir 2010). Risk, as we can see from the discussion above, refers to a diverse range of different governing techniques that rely on analysis and objectivity, and many of these techniques have been used within the traditional boundaries of the state, particularly the administrative state. Yet while there is no obvious direct relationship between risk and govern-ance there are three important overlaps.

The first of these is that in some cases, particularly where risk is being used as a con-cept to manage public administration (the first category above), it is a technique to fur-ther governance based on an NPM ideal. This is the first wave of governance as described by Rhodes in Chapter 3 of this book. In this context, risk is a means of encouraging the public sector to do two things. First, it encourages them to model themselves on the pri-vate sector by adopting financial risk management techniques (HM Treasury 2004). The distinction between public and private institutions thus becomes blurred and less hier-archical. Second, risk regulates public and private interactions. Thus for example, the proper "transfer of risks" to the private sector has been a key concern in public–private partnerships (OECD 2008). In both cases, risk is providing a framework by which to judge the legitimacy of behavior within a narrow framework grounded on NPM ideals. The important point is that this role for risk is only one of the categories above.

The second overlap between governance and risk is in relation to what Rhodes would describe as "meta-governance"—the second wave of governance literature (Chapter 3, this volume). The focus in regard to "meta-governance" is on the larger role of the state in coordinating different actors in the process of governing. Using risk in governing contributes to this discourse because the concept of risk acts as an "immutable mobile" in that it allows what is being governed to be "mobilised, gathered, archived, coded, recalculated and displayed" (Latour 1987: 227). The activity of analysis is freed from the confines of a hierarchical state and can be carried out by any actor. This is particularly due to the fact that the legitimacy of a decision is understood to depend on the quality of analysis rather the identity of who carries out the analysis. As that is the case, the use of risk to define regulatory subject matter or in enforcement or criminal justice allows a range of different actors to be involved. The requirement of involvement is not whether actors are public or private, national or international, but whether the quality of analysis can be guaranteed.

This can be seen in a number of different areas of environmental and public health regulation. Thus, for example, Article 5.1 of the World Trade Organization (WTO) Sanitary and Phytosanitary (SPS) Agreement requires decisions to be based on "an assessment... of the risks to human, animal or plant life or health." This has commonly been understood as requiring the identification of risks and the assessment of them. This process of identification and assessment need not be carried out by a national regu-lator. Indeed, it has been made clear in WTO Panel and Appellate Body reports pub-lished as part of the dispute settlement process, that such an assessment need not be carried out by the state who is relying on the results (Appellate Body report 1998: para. 196). Likewise, Article 3.1 encourages states to base their measures on international standards. In other words, as the assessment of risks is understood to be an objective process then it can be carried by anyone. The SPS Agreement thus promotes an under-standing of this form of regulation decoupled from the nation-state. Or to put it another way, the inclusion of the concepts of risk and "risk assessment" encourages governance over government in the WTO context.

Another example can be seen in regard to the new European Union (EU) chemicals law—REACH (Registration, Evaluation and Authorisation of Chemicals)—a governance regime that is concerned with assessing and managing risk, albeit outside the confines of command-and-control regulation. Article 5 of Regulation (EC) No. 1907/2006 of the European Parliament and of the Council of 18 December 2006 posits the "no data, no market" rule that requires that "substances on their own, in mixtures or in articles shall not be manufactured in the Community or placed on the market unless they have been registered in accordance with the relevant provisions of this Title where this is required." Registration requires the provision of a risk assessment, which is carried out by a private actor in accordance with the Regulation. REACH is radical in that rather than regulating public decision-making it primarily regulates the conditions of market operation (Fisher 2008). Private actors carry the burden of information analysis and through the provision of that information to market actors it is hoped historical market failures are addressed. All this is possible, if chemicals control is understood to be about the assessment and management of risk. If it is understood this way, then it need not be carried out in traditional command-and-control terms. What becomes important is that rigorous assessment is carried out and that information is accessible to market actors. A focus on risk and governing thus enables a wider and more open-ended meta-governance technique in the regulating of chemicals.

The third overlap between risk and governance is a more subtle one and is less an overlap than an interrelationship. A focus on risk highlights the fact that governance regimes and the problems that are governing are coproduced (Jasanoff 2006). In this regard, although perhaps more tangentially, risk relates to what Rhodes has described as the third wave of governance discourses—interpretative governance (Chapter 3, this volume). Jasanoff has described the idea of coproduction as

> shorthand for the proposition that the ways in which we know and represent the world (both nature and society) are inseparable from the ways in which we chose to live in it. Knowledge and its material embodiments are at once products of social work and constitutive of forms of social life ... [Scientific knowledge] both embeds, and is embedded in social practices, identities, norms, conventions, discourses, instruments and institutions. (Jasanoff 2006: 2–3)

Any particular example of risk being used in governing is thus not only embedded in specific narratives and disciplines but intimately interrelated with them (Expert Group on Science and Governance 2007: ch. 7). Thus, for example, the language of risk in criminal justice is deployed as part of a narrative in which "[p]rudentialism or the logic of actuarialism, which underpin measures designed to locate, sort and manage diverse risks, become at least as important as reactive penal measures" (Zedner 2007: 265). Likewise, the concept of risk in public–private partnerships is closely bound up with a discourse about value for money in public services (Froud 2003). Moreover, meta-discourses about risk and the state are narratives about how the relationship between the state and the individual should be understood (BRC 2006). A "risk" is thus not a free-floating concept that can be easily moved from context to another.

Moreover, casting a light on the process of coproduction makes clear that narratives about risk are both performative and normative (Expert Group on Science and Governance 2007: ch. 7). These narratives "not only represent the world" but also "tacitly define the horizons of possible and acceptable action" (Expert Group on Science and Governance 2007: 73–75). Thus risk is not just regulating governance behavior but also providing the structure by which to understand what is legitimate. This structure is not just a structure concerning a governance network but also the context in which that network is embedded. If action can only be taken in relation to risks then those risks must be identified before any action can be taken, and everything else largely becomes irrelevant. Therefore, for example, in regard to the WTO SPS Agreement what is important is not whether a sovereign state wishes to take action, but whether risks have been identified and assessed. Indeed, aspects of state sovereignty are pushed to the background and this enables a role for public and private networks in this area of regulation.

Coproduction can also be understood as a process of "framing," which acts as an "interpretative context" that allows things to be made sense of and acted upon. This activity of framing is incredibly powerful.

> Problems that have been framed with particular causal explanations can also, in principle, be controlled by addressing the perceived causes. At the same time, framing is by its nature also an instrument of exclusion. As some parts of an issue come within a problem frame, other parts are left out as irrelevant, incomprehensible, or uncontrollable. (Winickoff et al. 2005: 94)

This framing can occur both explicitly and implicitly. An example of the former can be seen in relation to many risk policies. For example, the Risk and Regulation Advisory Council (RRAC), set up by the UK Labour Government in 2008 described their role as leading an "experimental offensive against the mishandling of risk in society," and in particular addressing

> how distorted perceptions of risks can encourage poor policy-making and unnecessary laws, leading people to feel that Government is interfering too much in their lives. (RRAC 2009: 2)

Likewise, the focus on risk in the context of enforcement is explicitly linked with the ethos that "scarce resources should not be used to inspect or require data from businesses that are low-risk, either because the work they do is inherently safe, or because their systems for managing the regulatory risk are good" (Hampton 2005: 27).

In other cases, the way in which risk frames understandings of problems is more subtle and is tied to how a particular discipline operates. Understanding risk from a particular disciplinary standpoint privileges one understanding of a problem over another. Thus Jasanoff highlights that the technical discourse over risk assessment in the United States understands risk in terms of causation, agency, and uncertainty (Jasanoff 1999). The divergent ways in which risk issues can be framed is most obviously seen in a cross-cultural perspective where the "risks" of a particular activity are understood in fundamentally different ways (Winickoff et al. 2005).

A study of how risk issues are implicitly framed also it makes clear that the "framing" is derived from the two-way relationship between expertise and power (Jasanoff 1999). Wynne puts it rather beautifully when he states that public concerns about public risk decision-making are not primarily about being excluded from decision-making but

> about the presumptive hegemonic imposition of what the salient concerns thus salient knowledge-questions, thus salient knowledges, are recognized to be in the first place, as the public frame of meaning of the issue at stake. (Wynne 2008: 23)

Or to put the matter another way—the concern about risk and governance is about how it privileges one meta-narrative concerning how to make collective decisions about the future over other narratives (Jaeger et al. 2001: 251). To return to the WTO SPS Agreement, we can see the way in which that Agreement, by focusing on risk, does indeed promote a "particular set of knowledge questions" and thus "salient knowledges." It is also the case that there is considerable debate over what those questions and knowledges are, and should be.

3. MOVING FORWARD

These overlaps between risk and governance are of more than just academic interest. In particular, these overlaps make it clear that governance scholars must think more carefully about knowledge and the related concept of expertise. This is because the use of risk is primarily about the deployment of knowledge, particularly knowledge that is perceived as objective. Indeed, what can be seen above is that knowledge can be a technique of governance in itself, is enabling governance, and is part of a process of coproduction of governance regimes and the issues such regimes address.

The importance of scholarly engagement with these issues is all the more important in light of the fact that the deployment of risk in governing has by no means gone unanalyzed. Evaluation, often critical in nature, has been from different perspectives including social theory, philosophy, cultural theory, sociology, political theory, psychology, and science and technologies studies (Bammer and Smithson 2008). While there is much that is important in this literature, there are three particularly pertinent issues for governance scholars to take on board.

First, there has been literature and policy commentary concerned with how successful the use of risk is at providing a sound analytical basis for decision-making. It has therefore been noted that a reliance on risk in governing results in: the complexity of uncertainty being underrated (Wynne 1992); things that cannot be assessed objectively being ignored (Rayner and Cantor 1987); the manipulation of assessment by ideological interests (Michaels 2008); illusionary accountability (Power 1997); and decision-making based on inaccuracies (Shrader-Frechette 1993). These criticisms relate to the use of risk in the four contexts identified in Section 1 and they all highlight the fact that the analytical requirements imposed in relation to risk may not be as authoritative as was hoped. The relevant point for governance scholars is that the efficacy of risk as a governance technique, whether in regard to NPM, or in other areas, must be questioned.

Second, and following on from this, governance scholars must also note the relationship between knowledge, accountability, and legitimacy. Thus, as we saw above, risk was used in governing as a means of regulating behavior as well as setting out the horizons for legitimate action. Risk therefore becomes a major vehicle for accountability and associated ideas. Yet at the same time, the expert discretion necessary for risk decision-making makes such decisions opaque and difficult to hold to account (Fisher 2007: 27). For this reason, a significant focus of much of the literature concerning risk and governing, is whether, and how, it contributes to accountability. It is thus not just whether risk and the analytical requirements that relate to it provide an accurate basis for decision-making but whether they provide a means of ensuring accountability and legitimacy. This is particularly the case when the process of calling someone to account is occurring over a disciplinary divide—for example, a generalist judge must rule on whether a risk assessment is a reliable basis for a decision.

The relevance for governance scholars is that the accountability and legitimacy of those regimes is not a foregone conclusion. Thus there is a vibrant debate about the role of risk in ensuring the legitimacy and accountability of the WTO SPS regime (Howse 2000) as well as in other areas where risk has enabled multi-level and multi-actor governance. An interesting and significant point that emerges out of these discourses that focus on accountability is how much these governance regimes can ever properly be decoupled from ideas of the hierarchical state (Fisher 2006). In holding those in governance regimes to account there is often a reversion to ideas from liberal democratic constitutionalism, such as the separation of powers and ideas of democratic accountability. For example, the legal framework of emissions trading schemes in the EU are subject to judicial review challenges where the legal validity of such schemes are argued in terms of mainstream EU constitutional/administrative law principle (Bogojevic 2010). This may be because accountability mechanisms are still very traditional, but the important thing to note is that while the impositions of knowledge requirements may seemingly enable the involvement of public and private networks, the legitimacy of the networks is often still open to question. Governance scholars thus must look more closely at the interrelationship between governance, accountability, and risk.

The third and final point for governance scholars to take away from the risk and governing literature flows on from this, and that is the importance of reflecting on the process of coproduction and, in particular, the role of knowledge in that process of coproduction. Risk is not a reified single thing, out there, waiting to be regulated by a governance regime. Rather governance regimes and the risks they regulate are coproduced. Financial governance regimes are coproduced with ideas of markets (MacKenzie 2006). Biotechnology governance regimes frame understandings of what a biotechnology risk is (Jasanoff 2005). In doing this, to paraphrase Jasanoff, governance regimes "are made of knowledge" (Jasanoff 2006: 3); they are not just networks of public and private multi-level actors but are networks of the physical and the social (Latour 2007).

Governance regimes are thus constitutive of the world around them and in being so are often shaped by concerns internal to them. Thus, I have shown elsewhere, the ways in which understandings of risk, law, and public administration are coproduced relate to questions internal to legal cultures (Fisher 2007). In the US, the concept of risk in regard to health and safety regulation was interpreted to make sense of a legally odd legislative regime. In the UK, decision-making in regard to the BSE crisis was shaped by the internal dynamics of UK public administration, and these dynamics also shaped understandings of the possible health risks that could arise from that disease. The list could go on, but the important point to appreciate is that governance regimes are, therefore, not just embedded in particular contexts but also shape those contexts. More significantly, the process of coproduction is a malleable and pluralistic one (Jasanoff 2005) and in some governance regimes competing processes of coproduction can be going on (Fisher 2007). Thus, for example, WTO disputes are not just exercises in legalistic nit-picking but disagreements over how the whole regime should be understood (Winickoff et al. 2005). There is therefore much for governance scholars to think about—all in the spirit of Rhodes's "interpretative governance."

4. CONCLUSION

The analysis in this chapter has been very brief, but despite that it provides much for governance scholars to reflect upon. At the very least it has highlighted the fact that the concept of "risk governance" is not a monolithic and reified "thing." Nor is the relationship between risk and governance a straightforward one. Both are different concepts that are referring to a different set of changes in the process of governing. With that said, there are three overlaps. First, in some circumstances, risk is a technique of governance. Second, a focus on risk enables governance by de-shackling ideas of risk assessment and risk management from the hierarchical state. Third, a focus on risk in governing highlights how governance regimes and the issues they govern are coproduced. These three different overlaps can be understood to relate to Rhodes's three different waves of governance discourse (Chapter 3, this volume). These overlaps also highlight the need for governance scholars to think more carefully about the role of knowledge and expertise in governance. This is particularly the case in terms of the efficacy of that role, the relationship between that role and accountability and legitimacy, and the need to reflect on the role of knowledge in coproduction. In conclusion, the relationship between risk and governance is not straightforward. Indeed, it is a relationship that forces governance scholars to take a harder and more subtle look at governance.

REFERENCES

Appellate Body report. 1998. *European Communities: Measures Concerning Meat and Meat Products (Hormones)*. WT/DS26/AB, 16 January.
Audit Commission. 2001. *Worth The Risk?* London: UK Government.

Bammer, G. and Smithson, M. (eds) 2008. *Uncertainty and Risk: MultiDisciplinary Perspectives*. London: Earthscan.

Beck, U. 1992. *Risk Society: Towards A New Modernity*. London: Sage.

Better Regulation Commission (BRC). 2006. *Risk, Responsibility and Regulation: Whose Risk Is It Anyway?* October.

Bevir, M. 2010. Governance as theory, practice and dilemma. In M. Bevir (ed.), *The Sage Handbook of Governance*. Los Angeles: Sage, 1–16.

Black, J. 2010. The role of risk in regulatory processes. In R. Baldwin, M. Cave, and M. Lodge (eds.), *The Oxford Handbook of Regulation*. Oxford: Oxford University Press, 302–348.

Black, J. and Baldwin, R. 2010. Really responsive risk based regulation. *Law And Policy* 32: 181–213.

Bogojevic, S. 2010. Litigating the NAP: Legal challegnes for the emisisons trading scheme of the European Union. *Carbon and Climate Law Review* 4: 219–227.

Collins, H. 1999. *Regulating Contracts*. Oxford: Oxford University Press.

Department of Health (DH). 2007. *Best Practice in Managing Risk*. National Mental Health Risk Management Programme. London: Department of Health, June.

Eidinow, E. 2007. *Oracles, Curses, and Risk Among the Ancient Greeks*. Oxford: Oxford Uinversity Press.

Ewald, F. 2000. Risk in contemporary society. *Connecticut Insurance Law Journal* 6: 365.

Expert Group on Science and Governance. 2007. *Taking European Knowledge Society Seriously*. Brussels: European Commission.

Financial Services Authority (FSA). 2006. *The FSA's Risk-Based Approach*. London: Financial Services Authority.

Fisher, E. 2000. Drowning by numbers: Standard setting in risk regulation and the pursuit of accountable public administration. *Oxford Journal Of Legal Studies* 20: 109–130.

Fisher, E. 2003. The rise of the risk commonwealth and the challenge for administrative law. *Public Law*: 455–478.

Fisher, E. 2006. Unpacking the toolbox: Or why the public/private divide is important in EC environmental law. In M. Freedland and J-B. Auby (eds.), *The Public Law/Private Law Divide: Une Entente Assez Cordiale?* Oxford: Hart, 205–232.

Fisher, E. 2007. *Risk Regulation and Administrative Constitutionalism*. Oxford: Hart.

Fisher, E. 2008. The "Perfect Storm" of REACH: Charting regulatory controversy in the age of information, sustainable development, and globalization. *Journal of Risk Research* 11: 541–563.

Fisher, E. 2010. Risk regulatory concepts and the law. In OECD (ed.), *Risk and Regulatory Policy: Improving the Governance of Risk*. Paris: OECD, 45–92.

Froud, J. 2003. The private finance initative: Risk, uncertainty and the state. *Accounting, Organizations and Society* 28: 567–589.

Habermas, J. 1984. *Communication and the Evolution of Society*. Cambridge: Polity.

Hampton, P. 2005. *Reducing Administrative Burdens: Effective Inspection and Enforcement*. London: HM Treasury.

HM Treasury. 2004. *The Orange Book: Management of Risk—Principles and Concepts*. London: HM Treasury.

Howse, R. 2000. Democracy, science, and free trade: Risk regulation on trial at the WTO. *Michigan Law Review* 98: 2329–2357.

Jaeger, C., Renn, O., Rosa, E. and Webler, T. 2001. *Risk, Uncertainty, and Rational Action*. London: Earthscan.

Jasanoff, S. 1999. The songlines of risk. *Environmental Values* 8: 135–152.

Jasanoff, S. 2005. *Designs on Nature: Science and Democracy in Europe and the United States.* Princeton: Princeton University Press.

Jasanoff, S. 2006. The idiom of co-production. In S. Jasanoff (ed.), *States of Knowledge: The Co-Production of Science and Social Order.* Abingdon: Routledge, 1–12.

Knight, F. 1964. *Risk, Uncertainty, and Profit.* New York: Century Press.

KPMG. 1999. *Annotated Bibliography for the Study On: Best Practices in Risk Management: Private and Public Sectors Internationally.* Ottowa: Treasury Board of Canada.

Latour, B. 1987. *Science in Action.* Cambridge, MA: Harvard University Press.

Latour, B. 2007. *Reassembling the Social: An Introduction to Actor-Network Theory.* Oxford: Oxford University Press.

MacKenzie, D. 2006. *An Engine Not a Camera: How Finanical Models Shape Markets.* Cambridge: MIT Press.

Michaels, D. 2008. *Doubt Is Their Product: How Industry's Assault on Science Threatens Your Health.* New York: Oxford University Press.

National Probation Service (NPS). 2004. *Risk Management Policy and Strategy: A Guide for Probation Areas and NPD.* London: Home Office.

National Research Council (NRC). 1994. *Science and Judgement in Risk Assessment.* Washington, DC: National Academy Press.

Organisation for Economic Co-operation and Development (OECD). 2008. *Public–Private Partnerships: In Pursuit of Risk Sharing and Value For Money.* Paris: OECD.

Porter, T. 1995. *Trust in Numbers: The Pursuit of Objectivity in Science and Public Life.* Princeton: Princeton University Press.

Power, M. 1997. *The Audit Society: Rituals of Verification.* Oxford: Oxford University Press.

Rayner, S. and Cantor, R. 1987. How fair is safe enough? The cultural approach to societal technology choice. *Risk Analysis* 7: 39.

Risk and Regulation Advisory Council (RRAC). 2009. "Response with responsibility: Policy-making for public risk in the 21st century." May; available at http://www.bis.gov.uk/files/file51459.pdf.

Ruckelshaus, W. 1983. Science, risk and public policy. *Science* 221: 1026–1028.

Shrader-Frechette, K. 1993. *Burying Uncertainty: Risk and the Case Against the Geological Disposal of Nuclear Waste.* Berkeley: University Of California Press.

Slovic, P. 2000. *The Perception of Risk.* London: Earthscan.

Strategy Unit of the Cabinet Office. 2002. *Risk: Improving Government's Capability to Handle Risk and Uncertainty, Full Report: A Source Document.* London: HMSO.

Treasury Board of Canada. 2001. *Risk Management Policy.* Ottawa: Government of Canada.

Winickoff, D., Jasanoff, S., Busch, L., Grove White, R. and Wynne, B. 2005. Adjudicating the GM food wars: Science, risk and democracy in world trade law. *Yale Journal of International Law* 30: 81–123.

Wynne, B. 1992. Uncertainty and environmental learning. *Global Environmental Change* 2: 111–127.

Wynne, B. 2008. Elephants in the rooms where publics encounter "science"?: A response to Darrin Durrant, "Accounting for expertise: Wynne and the autonomy of the lay public". *Public Understanding of Science* 17: 21–33.

Zedner, L. 2007. Pre-crime or post-criminology? *Theoretical Criminology* 11: 261–281.

Zedner, L. 2009. *Security.* Abingdon: Routledge.

CHAPTER 30

THREE TENSIONS IN THE GOVERNANCE OF SCIENCE AND TECHNOLOGY

SUSANA BORRÁS

1. INTRODUCTION

SCIENCE and technology are fundamental factors for human and economic development, defining almost every detail of our lives. Pertinent examples of this are the Internet's effect on radically new forms of social communication and business models; nuclear weapons' redefinition of security threats and warfare; and the supply of clean water in households, determining basic sanitary and hygienic conditions. Yet, there are many paradoxes in all this. Science and technology continue to be scarce goods for most of the developing world, whereas in the industrialized world there is a hot debate on whether the "soft" innovations in the service sector will prevail over the "hard" science and technology in the manufacturing sector as the main sources of economic growth. Furthermore, even if there is a widespread understanding that science and technology are behind the improvements in life quality and human progress, not all aspects of science and technology are consistently accepted by society. Fundamental controversies regarding the causes of global warming or the use of embryonic stem cells for therapeutic purposes continue to unravel.

The remarks above serve to underline a series of fundamental premises of this chapter, some of which are not entirely uncontroversial, namely that science and technology shape and are shaped by specific forms of social, political, and economic organization; that science and technology are far from being uniformly institutionalized, developed, exploited, or even accepted by the society; and that the forms in which science and technology are governed are highly diverse according to the way in which a society organizes itself.

Social scientists have analyzed the role of science and technology from different angles, in what seems to be a very rich pool of research endeavors. Scholars in science and technology studies (STS), economics, and political science disciplines have been concerned with the complex micro- and macro-level dimensions of the science—society/economics/politics relations and their mutually shaping interactions. With few happy encounters these research endeavors have run parallel, with an unfortunate disregard for each others' contributions. Yet, during the past few years these three traditions have coincided in embracing the notion and perspective of "governance," in what appears to be a growing but unnamed common ground among them. Economists' interest in issues of governance stems from the evolutionary and institutional economic theory's view that technical change in the economy takes place in compound systems of socioeconomic and political institutional arrangements (OECD 2005; Foray and Lundvall 1996). Likewise, the STS scholarship has recently put forward the notion of "scientific governance" as a way of grasping the changing role of scientific knowledge in different dimensions of social organization (Irwin 2008). Political scientists, for their part, being those who initiated the scholarly attention on "governance," have been looking at multi-level governance (Edler, Kuhlman, and Behrens 2003; Kaiser and Prange 2004), new modes of governance (Lyall and Tait 2005), legitimate governance of socio-technical systems (Borrás 2006a), and various forms of policy instrumentation and coordination (Braun 2008; Smits and Kuhlmann 2004).

This chapter suggests that the governance of science and technology (S&T) is characterized by three sets of persistent tensions, namely the tension between the self-organization of S&T and the politics of purpose; the tension between hierarchy, network, or market forms of organizing interactions; and the tension between the role of citizens and that of scientific experts in the decisions about collective problems and solutions involving science and technology. The main argument of this chapter is that these three tensions have become more intense during the past few decades, and that, as a result, there has been an overall move from government to governance. The shift from government to governance has happened because there has been considerable multiplication and sophistication of the institutional arrangements that mediate and govern these three intensified tensions. Tensions that were once resolved in a rather straightforward and hierarchical way are now subject to many different coexisting and heterogeneous institutional arrangements that define solutions in complex, dynamic, and even overlapping ways.

The next sections set out to examine, one by one, each of the three tensions and the way they fit into the general claim of a gradual shift from "government to governance" (Kooiman 1993; Pierre 2000; Bevir, 2011; Rhodes, Chapter 3, this volume), by looking carefully at the features of their institutional arrangements and the changes in the patterns of (state) authority in the field of science and technology. The concluding section is devoted to looking further into the argument that there is a growing heterogeneity and hybridity of the institutional arrangements (Levi-Faur, Chapter 1, this volume) addressing these increased governance tensions, with a view to succinctly defining some crucial aspects for a renewed interdisciplinary research agenda about the effectiveness and legitimacy of S&T governance.

2. BETWEEN SELF-ORGANIZATION AND
THE POLITICS OF PURPOSE

The organization of science and technology has historically been trapped in a tension between the autonomy of creativity and the politics of purpose: between the scientists' and the technicians' own organizational rules, and the state's interest in using science and technology for purposes of defence, economic growth, public health, and others. This was reflected in the well-known debate in England in the 1940s between Polanyi and Bernal. In his ardent support of scientists' autonomy in the "Republic of Science" Polanyi stated that "Any attempt at guiding scientific research towards a purpose other than its own is an attempt to deflect it from the advancement of science" (Polanyi 1962). In contrast to this, Bernal claimed that science had an essential socioeconomic function, which invariably required the grand mobilization of knowledge in order to achieve explicitly formulated goals in planned economies (Bernal 1967 [1939]). Much of these two contesting views has to do with a centuries-long debate about the organization of science, its nature, and its relation with political life (Turner 2008), as well as about the role of scientific–technical knowledge and governmental intervention in economic development (Freeman 1995).

This tension persists today. On the one hand, since the advent of the welfare state and the Cold War there has been a continuously growing governmental involvement in science and technology. Massive investments in "big science" reflect political ambitions of military superiority and security (Hughes 2003: James 2006). In the 1970s, the political willingness to emulate the "Asian miracle" triggered substantial efforts to increase the levels of R&D expenditure in strategic industries, as well as policies for the knowledge-based economy in the 1990s (Lundvall and Borrás 2005). On the other hand, the substantial upscaling of scientific and technological endeavors has been based on a tacit "social contract for science" that regards the autonomy and self-organization of the scientific community as a premise for its ability to deliver reliable results to these purposeful objectives. In a sense, the massive state involvement in the twentieth century created a space for the development of resilient institutions, norms, and values emanating from the scientific community itself (i.e. peer review, use of specific scientific methods, etc.), and for the unfolding and use of science and technology in the society and economy.

During the past few decades, however, the tension between the politics of purpose and the self-organization of S&T has become more intense, as the "social contract" described above has been under pressure from several interrelated fronts. The first front has to do with the changing societal expectations about the role of science in society. The traditional "social contract of science" is based on an unveiled positive view of science as an "ivory tower," in the expectation that science produces reliable knowledge and communicates it to the society in a one-way fashion. Dissatisfaction with the "ivory tower" of science means the old "social contract" is giving way to a new contract, the shape of which is still not clear. This is also related to the view that alternative sources of knowledge production that are nonacademic, non-disciplinary, and more grounded in social problems have been emerging in relation to the upsurge of non-governmental non-profit social organizations. Green movements, patient associations, and traditional knowledge communities are today collecting, processing, and using sophisticated knowledge, which complements (and sometimes challenges) conventional scientific knowledge (Desai 2007). This is a "mode-2" of knowledge production that departs significantly from the "mode-1" of self-contained scientific academia (Gibbons et al. 1994).

The second front involves the changing nature of governmental involvement in the specific field of science and technology policy. Among the most important elements of this are changes in the forms of funding of research conducted at universities, public research organizations, and firms (Lepori et al. 2007); new forms of management requirements (Rip 1994); and changes in the mechanisms for verifying science's integrity and productivity (Guston 1996). In a sense, the changing nature of governmental involvement in the core organizational dimension of science and technological knowledge production is not only related to the styles and instruments of science policy, but to a large extent to the changing boundaries between governmental action and the self-organized dimensions in the governance of knowledge production.

The third front involves the ownership of scientific–technical knowledge. Merton's ideal feature of science's disinterestedness (as a non-commercial altruistic concern with the benefit to humanity) is largely based on a notion of openly available and free science. However, there has been an increasing tendency toward the privatization and commodification of knowledge (particularly academic knowledge), in a way that is far from being seen as socially, economically, and normatively unproblematic (Callon 1994; Jacob 2009). The scientific community itself has also been concerned with this. The privatization of knowledge might pose problems for the methodological robustness of the scientific endeavor because data cannot be exchanged nor the results of scientific analysis verified. This is behind the scientific community's own mobilization to support the idea of "open science," in what seems to be a return to the Mertonian ideal of self-organized science.

What the three "fronts" above show us with all clarity is that the tension between the self-organization of S&T and the politics of purpose (either governmental or commercial) has been exacerbated during the past years. Most importantly, perhaps, they show us that this has resulted in a multitude of different institutional arrangements. Institutions like peer review, increased power of research councils, and non-commercial mechanisms of knowledge dissemination have been reinforced and coexist with a series of new institutional arrangements like centralized scientific verification instruments, competitive sources of research funding, and commercialization of public research outputs, in what seems to be a "push" toward more purposefulness of S&T with a parallel strengthening of the institutions based on the ideal of S&T self-organization. This means that the governance of S&T is today more heterogeneous and complex than it was a few decades ago, and that the general shift to "governance" has run parallel with a visible governmental action.

3. REGULATING NEW TECHNOLOGIES: MARKETS, NETWORKS, OR HIERARCHICAL COORDINATION

The coordination of new technologies and their use in the society and economy is a major issue in the governance of S&T. Problems of coordination might be particularly important in technologies where there is a high degree of technical interdependency (interoperability) and high levels of positive network externalities (the more members joining, the lower costs for all, but with high costs for individual defectors or "orphan users"). In such cases, striking the balance between the opportunities of the economies of scale that the positive network externalities offer and the risk of technological/economic lock-in (suboptimal technical/economic solutions "trapped" in such arrangements) is particularly convoluted. From the perspective of governance, a tension emerges in terms of different modes of coordination, namely between the market, network, or hierarchical coordination of these technologies.

One field where tensions related to coordination mechanisms are most evident is technical standard-setting. Virtually all products today have to comply with a series of product specifications of a technical character. Yet, when looking at how these are defined and implemented, there is a wide range of forms of coordination mechanisms. Unilaterally defined standards are forms of hierarchical coordination, either because the standard of one producer dominates the market (like Microsoft's operating system "Windows") or because a single government has unilaterally legislated and defined an obligatory technical standard. Simple hierarchical forms of coordination are becoming less common. For example, technical standards concerning safety and consumer protection in Europe are typically defined in a broad legislative mandate that is further negotiated in independent standardization organizations by networks of governmental officials, producers, and consumer representatives. Other more privately driven forms of coordination are to be found in the so-called "sponsored standards," where firms hold proprietary interests and define the standard collectively (like in the DVD case). Yet, the definition of standards is far from being a technical matter: it is a highly political matter, particularly in the international context because standards are associated with trade matters (Mattli and Buthe 2003). In some cases, the shadow of the state in those international standardization processes might be very long (Abbott and Snidal 2009).

Another field where interoperability is most remarkable is information and telecommunication technologies (ICT). Here the tensions related to coordination mechanisms refer to the (de)regulatory frameworks defining the patterns of economic interactions and incentives, as well as the competitiveness and dynamism of this strategic industrial sector. The regulation of the ICT sector since the mid-1980s has been highly linked to privatization and liberalization trends in national contexts, and is therefore part of the effort to create regulation-for-competition in a new and rapidly changing industrial context (Levi-Faur 1999; Jordana and Levi-Faur 2004). There are different models of regulatory frameworks for the ICT sector, and some are perceived to be more effective than others depending on their ability to coordinate interoperability efficiently and dynamically by stimulating ICT standards, their ability to spur innovation and technological development in a decentralized manner, and the way in which information within the regulatory framework is collected and distributed. Yet, the ICT revolution since the second half of the 1980s is not only the story of a generic and disruptive technology. It is also the story of technological advancements that are largely shaped by wide societal dynamics (McDowell, Steinburg, and Tomasello 2008).

The diversity in the mechanisms of governance (market, network, hierarchy) and the tensions between them, as described above, are also observable in other science–technology-intensive areas, for example the life sciences or aerospace, which have different features in terms of interdependency and externalities. Furthermore, when looking at the regulatory aspects of science, technology, and innovation governance, it is most important not to forget crucial crosscutting regulatory issues like intellectual property rights, phytosanitary codes, or environmental standards. Social studies in these fields point at important issues regarding the different bottlenecks and effectiveness of national regulatory frameworks on the patterns, flows, and use of knowledge. Regulatory frameworks of intellectual property rights are of particular importance because they have an all-encompassing effect on the economic regimes of knowledge appropriation, so fundamental to science–industry relations and innovation processes. More specifically, patent regulations have recently been under the critical scrutiny of economists at the national (Jaffe and Lerner 2004), regional (Guellec and van Pottelsberghe de la Potterie 2007), and international levels (Drahos and Braithwaite 2002) regarding the extent to which they strike a balance between the private interests of patent owners and the overall social gains of the patent system. This is ultimately a balance between the public and the private, and between different modes of governance.

Again, what the regulation of new technologies tells us is that the tension between hierarchical, network, and market-based forms of coordination has increased during the past years, and that different arrangements coexist in time and place under a general trend toward "governance."

4. TECHNO-SCIENTIFIC KNOWLEDGE AND DEMOCRACY: EXPERTS OR CITIZENS?

When dealing with the governance of science and technology another fundamental tension deserves our attention, namely the roles of techno-scientific experts and of citizens in contemporary liberal democracies. Recalling previous chapters in this book, governance has to do with the identification and solution of collective problems. Hence, the way in which scientific knowledge interacts with citizens, and the democratic nature of

Table 30.1 Normative theories' views on the democratic dimension of socio–technical knowledge

	Empowering citizens	Empowering experts
Representative democracy	Improving the public understanding of science for an informed public debate.	Ensuring "sound science" in agencies with effective problem-solving capacity
Participatory democracy	Actively participating "science citizens" generating deliberation.	Participation of a wide range of experts producing "socially robust knowledge."

the procedures that define such interaction, are central parameters for the ultimate legitimacy of those collective efforts. Having said that, however, the way of articulating the interaction of citizens–experts and establishing democratic procedures is a highly complex matter: first, because there are different normative theories of democracy with significantly different views on what democracy is; and, second, because empirical analysis tells us about an overwhelming number of coexisting institutional arrangements within and across advanced liberal democratic systems.

A rapid examination of the burgeoning literature on science and democracy shows us that the most dominant propositions can be characterized according to two important parameters, namely their anchorage on normative theories of representative or participatory democracy and their different views regarding the empowerment of citizens or experts. These two dimensions involve the different models of democracy as alternative institutions of voice (Ron, Chapter 33, this volume), and are also based on the recent creation of more elaborate procedures for representation and participation (Chapter 32, this volume). This results in the matrix shown in Table 30.1.

Taking the first row of the table, normative theories of representative democracy tend to address this issue either from the empowerment of citizens or from the empowerment of scientific experts. In the first case, the focus tends to be on empowering the citizens through the provision of careful scientific information and communication. Fostering the public understanding of science (Miller 2001) will allow for an informed public debate on crucial science–technology decisions. Those advocating the empowerment of experts instead see the delegation of decision-making to non-majoritarian independent regulatory agencies run by scientists as being of the utmost importance. The production of "sound academic science" within those agencies and its subsequent problem-solving capacity (even in contexts of uncertainty) will generate output legitimacy in advanced democracies (Majone 2010).

From the point of view of participatory democracy this issue is again regarded differently. Considering those who advocate the empowerment of citizens, the crucial issue is to ensure their constitution as "science citizens" and their engagement in participatory mechanisms that generate deliberation (Hagendijk and Irwin 2006; Liberatore and Funtowicz 2003). Last but not least, those focusing on the empowerment of experts see the rise of knowledge associations and their "expertization" as the crucial issue (Turner 2003). Widening the notion of expertise to include not only conventional academic science but knowledgeable experts from non-governmental organizations (NGOs), patient organizations, and the like will produce the "socially robust knowledge" that advanced liberal democracies need (Nowotny 2003).

The tensions between the role of citizens and that of experts have augmented during the past few decades, as seen in the multiple scientific controversies like the safety of genetically modified organisms, concerns regarding xeno-transplantation, or the food scandals of BSE (mad cow disease) and dioxin levels in food. Seeking to accommodate democracy and scientific–technical knowledge, many countries have introduced a number of new institutional arrangements, often of a participatory nature (Hansen 2010). The design of these institutional arrangements shows considerable diversity, as it can be linked to those different normative principles. For example, normative world views are behind the US's preference for independent regulatory agencies (delegating decisions to scientific experts), in contrast with the European preference for "advisory-only" agencies (Jasanoff 2005). However, no matter how clearly defined state philosophies might appear, the myriad of new institutional arrangements during the past two decades demonstrates an increasing heterogeneity of solutions within each country, not only across countries. This institutional complexity underpins the argument of an overall shift toward more varied forms of governance, beyond the traditional "government" forms.

5. STUDYING THE EFFECTIVENESS AND LEGITIMACY OF S&T GOVERNANCE

The previous sections have illustrated the omnipresence of science and technology in our contemporary societies, and the persistent tensions in the governance of S&T. The main argument of this chapter is that the tensions implicit in the governance of S&T have become more intense during the past few decades. This reflects a process of transformation from government to governance, as the institutional arrangements organizing science and technology and their interactions with the society and economy have multiplied and become more diverse and heterogeneous. Besides, this multiplication and increasing hybridity of the institutional arrangements in the particular field of science and technology supports the notion of a co-expansion of governance and government suggested in the introduction of this handbook (Levi-Faur, Chapter 1, this volume).

The question that naturally arises from this is whether this multiplication and heterogeneity of institutional arrangements is having a positive or negative impact in terms of the effectiveness and legitimacy of S&T governance. The extensive literature in science and technology studies in the fields of economy, sociology, and political science has taken different stances on this matter. However, the strong disciplinary boundaries have generated some remarkable blind spots. In the light of the tensions described above, it is my personal interpretation that two aspects regarding effectiveness and legitimacy deserve further academic attention.

The first aspect for a research agenda has to do with a new analytical perspective on "effectiveness." Economists tend to discuss issues of effectiveness in terms of Pareto optimality, namely a situation in which no individual can be made better off without making another individual worse off. Furthermore, economists have considered effectiveness as being opposed to issues of "market failure" and/or "government failure." These are related to the malfunctioning of markets and governments due to a series of possible problems. Yet, whereas the economists' perspective is an attractive one when considering effectiveness, it is still not sufficient to understand the when, how, and why some institutional arrangements in the governance of S&T are better than others for creating the expected outcomes and avoiding systemic bottlenecks. The problem is that the notion of optimality is based on a single understanding of rationality, and it does not take into account the multiplicity of axioms of social behavior and the corresponding multiplicity of the socioeconomic and political context in which S&T governance is embedded. For that reason, a research agenda that studies the effectiveness of the new and heterogeneous institutional arrangements in the governance of S&T needs to have a broader analytical framework, anchored not only in notions of "bounded rationality" but also in the understanding that institutional arrangements are effective if they are able to shape/be shaped by social behavior in a particular way. In this sense, studies of effectiveness need to take into account the diversity of sociocultural contexts, and the way in which society and the economy shape the organization of science and technology (and vice versa). One possible starting point in that regard could be to anchor research about the effectiveness of S&T governance on the literatures of socio-technical systems (Geels and Schot 2007), of innovation systems (Edquist 1997), and of regulatory systems (Borrás 2006b). These systemic approaches allow the examination of the effectiveness of individual institutional arrangements within the context of their wider institutional frameworks. Yet, even if these systemic approaches are proving very fruitful in avoiding analytical traps of "one size fits all," their empirical endeavors have far too often focused on single case studies with little generalizability. Therefore, if a research agenda looking at the effectiveness of complex institutional arrangements from a systemic approach is to take off, it will require more decidedly cross-country and cross-temporal comparative studies to distil the theoretical consequences of broader empirical research.

A second important aspect in a renewed and more interdisciplinary research agenda would be to reconsider the dominant analytical perspectives on questions about the legitimate governance of S&T. The normative approaches examined in the previous section have provided very rich and suggestive alternative normative solutions for the tension between experts and citizens in the search for a legitimate and democratic governance of S&T. However, this large literature has tended to address these issues more normatively than empirically. Just as above, this literature has plenty of examples of single case studies, typically from the developed world and typically with a micro-level methodological approach. These rich but empirically limited studies in many cases focus heavily on the normative dimension of the case, rather than on its empirical value in terms of generalizability. However exciting, this methodological choice suffers from some important limitations in terms of bringing forward the "lessons" of a multiplicity of situations and contexts where the governance of S&T is (or is not) perceived by the people to be democratically legitimate. This calls for undertaking more decidedly broad empirical efforts in this area, putting emphasis on the use of a wider range of methodologies (quantitative and qualitative), as well as cross-country and cross-temporal comparative studies. Such an empirical turn should be based on the understanding that the democratic legitimacy of S&T governance is based not only on the question of the extent to which reality complies with a theoretically and deductively defined understanding of legitimacy, but also the extent to which it corresponds to the on-the-ground popular support for it. This is so because, at the end of the day, normativity is not only defined by social scientists, but is to a large extent defined by a popular feeling of what is just and democratic (and what is not). Therefore, a new research agenda would need to put more emphasis on empirical studies of popular attitudes, preferences, and behaviors, regarding what is perceived to be a legitimate governance of S&T. In so doing, this new empirical turn in the study of the legitimate governance of S&T will provide useful inputs to the normative approach by pointing at changes in popular trends and behaviors, and by considering the extent to which some of the normative theories' assumptions hold true (Borrás, Koutalakis, and Wendler 2007).

All the remarks above serve to underline the fact that studying the tensions in the governance of S&T, and the institutional arrangements set up to deal with them, needs to be addressed from a multidisciplinary approach. Political science, economics, and sociology offer considerable opportunities for combining insights into what is ultimately an empirical research agenda of one of the most fundamental dimensions that characterize the history of humanity and its organization, namely science and technology.

References

Abbott, K. W. and Snidal, D. 2009. The governance triangle: Regulatory standards institutions and the shadow of the state. In W. Mattli and N. Woods (eds.), *The Politics of Global Regulation*. Princeton: Princeton University Press, 44–88.

Bernal, J. D. 1967 (1939). *The Social Function of Science*. Cambridge, MA: MIT Press.

Bevir, M. 2011. Governance as theory, practice, and dilemma. In M. Bevir (ed.), *The Sage Handbook of Governance*. London: Sage, 3–24.

Borrás, S. 2006a. Legitimate governance of risk at EU level? The case of GMOs. *Technological Forecasting and Social Change* 73: 61–75.

Borrás, S. 2006b. The governance of the European patent system: Effective and legitimate? *Economy and Society* 35: 594–610.

Borrás, S., Koutalakis, C. and Wendler, F. 2007. European agencies and input legitimacy: EFSA, EmEA and EPO in the post-delegation phase. *Journal of European Integration* 29: 583–600.

Braun, D. 2008. Organising the political coordination of knowledge and innovation policies. *Science and Public Policy* 35: 227–239.

Callon, M. 1994. Is science a public good? *Science, Technology and Human Values* 19: 395–424.

Desai, P. N. 2007. Traditional knowledge and intellectual property protection: Past and future. *Science and Public Policy* 34: 185–197.

Drahos, P. and Braithwaite, J. 2002. *Information Feudalism: Who Owns the Knowledge Economy?* London: Earthscan.

Edler, J., Kuhlman, S. and Behrens, M. (eds.) 2003. *Changing Governance of Research and Technology Policy: The European Research Area*. Cheltenham: Edward Elgar.

Edquist, C. (ed.) 1997. *Systems of Innovation: Technologies, Institutions and Organizations*. London: Pinter.

Foray, D. and Lundvall, B. Å. 1996. The knowledge-based economy: From the economics of knowledge to the learning economy. In OECD (ed.), *Employment and Growth in the Knowledge-Based Economy*. Paris: OECD, 27–43.

Freeman, C. 1995. The national innovation systems in historical perspective. *Cambridge Journal of Economics* 19: 27–43.

Geels, F. W. and Schot, J. 2007. Typology of sociotechnical transition pathways. *Research Policy* 36: 399–417.

Gibbons, M., Limoges, C., Nowotny, H., Schartzman, S., Scott, P. and Trow, M. 1994. *The New Production of Knowledge: The Dynamics of Science and Research in Contemporary Societies*. London: Sage.

Guellec, D. and van Pottelsberghe de la Potterie, B. 2007. *The Economics of the European Patent System*. Oxford: Oxford University Press.

Guston, D. H. 1996. Principal–agent theory and the structure of science policy. *Science and Public Policy* 23: 229–240.

Hagendijk, R. and Irwin, A. 2006. Public deliberation and governance: Engaging with science and technology in contemporary Europe. *Minerva* 44: 167–184.

Hansen, J. 2010. *Biotechnology and Public Engagement in Europe*. London: Palgrave Macmillan.

Hughes, J. A. 2003. *The Manhattan Project: Big Science and the Atom Bomb*. New York: Columbia University Press.

Irwin, A. 2008. STS perspectives on scientific governance. In E. Hackett, O. Amsterdamska, M. Lynch, and J. Wajcman (eds.), *The Handbook of Science and Technology Studies*. Boston: MIT Press, 583–607.

Jacob, M. 2009. On commodification and the governance of academic research. *Minerva* 47: 391–405.

Jaffe, A. B. and Lerner, J. 2004. *Innovation and its Discontents: How Our Broken Patent System is Endangering Innovation and Progress, and What to Do About It*. Ithaca: Princeton University Press.

James, A. 2006. *Science and Technology Policies for the Anti-Terrorism Era*. Amsterdam: IOS Press.

Jasanoff, S. 2005. *Designs on Nature: Science and Democracy in Europe and the United States*. Princeton: Princeton University Press.

Jordana, J. and Levi-Faur, D. 2004. The politics of regulation in the age of governance. In J. Jordana and D. Levi-Faur (eds.), *The Politics of Regulation: Institutions and Regulatory Reforms for the Age of Governance*. London: Routledge, 3–28.

Kaiser, R. and Prange, H. 2004. Managing diversity in a system of multi-level governance: The open method of coordination in innovation policy. *Journal of European Public Policy* 11: 249–266.

Kooiman, J. (ed.) 1993. *Modern Governance: New Government–Society Interactions*. London: Sage.

Lepori, B., van den Besselaar, P., Dinges, M., Potĭ, B., Reale, E., Slipersaeter, S., Thèves, J. and van der Meulen, B. 2007. Comparing the evolution of national research policies: What patterns of change? *Science and Public Policy* 34: 372–388.

Levi-Faur, D. 1999. The governance of competition: The interplay of technology, economics, and politics in European Union electricity and telecom regimes. *Journal of Public Policy* 19: 175–207.

Liberatore, A. and Funtowicz, S. 2003. "Democratising" expertise, "expertising" democracy: What does this mean, and why bother? *Science and Public Policy* 30: 146–150.

Lundvall, B.-Å. and Borrás, S. 2005. Science, technology and innovation policy. In J. Fagerberg, D. C. Mowery, and R. R. Nelson (eds.), *The Oxford Handbook of Innovation*. Oxford: Oxford University Press, 599–631.

Lyall, C. and Tait, J. (eds.) 2005. *New Modes of Governance: Developing an Integrated Policy Approach to Science, Technology, Risk and the Environment*. Aldershot: Ashgate.

Majone, G. 2010. Foundations of risk regulation: Science, decision-making, policy learning and institutional reform. *European Journal of Risk Regulation* 1: 5–19.

Mattli, W. and Buthe, T. 2003. Setting international standards: Technological rationality or primacy of power? *World Politics* 56: 1–42.

McDowell, S. D., Steinberg, P. E. and Tomasello, T. K. 2008. *Managing the Infosphere: Governance, Technology, and Cultural Practice in Motion*. Philadelphia: Temple University Press.

Miller, S. 2001. Public understanding of science at the crossroads. *Public Understanding of Science* 10: 115–120.

Nowotny, H. 2003. Democratising expertise and socially robust knowledge. *Science and Public Policy* 30: 151–157.

Organisation for Economic Co-operation and Development (OECD). 2005. *Governance of Innovation Systems:*, Vol. 1: *Synthesis Report*. Paris: OECD.

Pierre, J. 2000. Introduction. In J. Pierre (ed.), *Debating Governance: Authority, Steering, and Democracy*. Oxford: Oxford University Press, 3–21.

Polanyi, M. 1962. The republic of science: Its political and economic theory. *Minerva* 1: 54–74.

Rip, A. 1994. The republic of science in the 1990s. *Higher Education* 28: 3–23.

Smits, R. and Kuhlmann, S. 2004. The rise of systemic instruments in innovation policy. *International Journal of Foresight and Innovation Policy* 1: 4–32.

Turner, S. P. 2003. *Liberal Democracy 3.0: Civil Society in an Age of Experts*. London: Sage.

Turner, S. P. 2008. The social study of science before Kuhn. In E. Hackett, O. Amsterdamska, M. Lynch, and J. Wajcman (eds.), *The Handbook of Science and Technology Studies*. Boston: MIT Press, 33–62.

CHAPTER 31

....

CLIMATE CHANGE GOVERNANCE

....

THOMAS BERNAUER &
LENA MARIA SCHAFFER

1. INTRODUCTION

....

WITHIN less than three decades, climate change has developed from a rather obscure
scientific topic into a key item on the global political agenda. It has also attracted strong
attention in many areas of scientific research, including the social sciences. Social scientists, and notably governance experts focusing on climate change, have addressed a wide
range of important questions, including the following ones, on which we will focus in
this chapter:[1]

- What are the key political challenges in establishing and implementing governance systems to cope with climatic changes?
- Why are some countries in the international system more cooperative than others
  in this respect?
- To what extent can subnational governance efforts in climate policy support
  national and global efforts?

In this chapter, we argue that the nature of the climate change problem, notably the
incentives, the risks, and the uncertainties associated with it, makes governance at the
global level difficult. To this end, we start with a discussion of the problem to be solved
and the international institutions that have thus far been established (Section 2). We
then look at the reasons why global cooperation for climate change mitigation is difficult
to achieve (Section 3). Section 4 shows that, even though cooperation at the global level
is difficult, there is strong variation in countries' national governance efforts. We examine how this variation in effort can be explained. After having moved from the global

(systemic) to the national level of climate change governance, we then move on to explore climate policy-making at the subnational level (Section 5). Local policy-making is, from an analytical viewpoint, particularly interesting in the case of federal political systems.

2. EVOLUTION OF THE GLOBAL GOVERNANCE SYSTEM

Science plays a major role in climate policy. Hence, we start by discussing what the basic goals of the global governance effort are from the viewpoint of many scientists and policy-makers. We then describe the Intergovernmental Panel on Climate Change (IPCC), the principal global institution for knowledge-generation in this policy area. Following this we discuss the UN Framework Convention on Climate Change (FCCC) and the Kyoto Protocol (KP). The latter two are, from a legal viewpoint, the backbone of the existing global governance system.

Goals of the global governance effort

A strong global consensus has emerged over the past few years, that is, that climatic changes must be addressed through the *mitigation* of greenhouse gas (GHG) emissions and—because some major climatic changes are unavoidable even with extremely ambitious mitigation efforts—*adaptation*. The key questions in this respect are:

(1) By how much should GHG emissions be reduced, and in what time frame?
(2) How much would this cost, and how should the burden be distributed among countries and over time?
(3) How much should be invested in adaptation and who should pay for it?

(1) The policy positions of many countries have, over the past few years, converged on the goal of limiting the global average temperature increase to 2°C, relative to the mid-eighteenth-century level. From the perspective of most scientists, a temperature target makes more sense than an emissions or concentrations target, because it is ultimately temperature that affects ecosystems and humanity. The 2°C target emerged from discussions among scientists and policy-makers in Germany in the mid-1990s. The 2°C temperature increase was initially used as a rather arbitrarily chosen parameter to examine climate change impacts, for example, impacts on the Earth's major ice sheets. When many models indicated major damages or uncertainties beyond that level (e.g. with respect to the long-term stability of the Greenland ice sheet), the 2°C developed into a

political target, even though there is no clear-cut scientific reason for this particular choice.

(2) Various studies have tried to estimate by how much global carbon prices (the total cost an emitter of a unit of GHG would have to pay) would have to increase in order to reach specific reduction targets. The IPCC (2007), for instance, notes a figure of $20–80 per ton of CO_2 equivalent by 2030 to stabilize GHG concentrations at 550ppm (roughly a doubling of pre-industrial concentrations, which were 280ppm then and 379ppm in 2005) by 2100. Optimistic studies indicate $5–65 (IPCC 2007).

The IPCC's best estimates of the costs of stabilizing GHG concentrations at 535–590ppm, which would probably meet the 2°C target, are in the order of a 0.1 percent reduction of average annual GDP growth rates. The Stern Review arrives at a similar estimate.

On the more pessimistic side, Nordhaus (2010) estimates that reaching the 2°C target would require a carbon price of $64 in 2010 (at 2005 prices), whereas the global average price today is around $5, and rapid growth of this price is expected over the next few years.

How to share the burden of GHG reductions remains a disputed issue. At the most general level, there is agreement that industrialized countries must shoulder most of the mitigation costs over the coming decades. The Kyoto Protocol (see below) in fact assigns that responsibility to this group of countries in the 2008–2012 period. But there is no consensus on how to deal with very large and rapidly growing developing countries, notably Brazil, China, and India.

(3) As noted by the IPCC (2007): "Much less information is available about the costs and effectiveness of adaptation measures than about mitigation measures." In any event, the costs are likely to be high and can most probably not be met by poor countries, which tend to be most vulnerable to climatic changes. Estimates of adaptation costs range from lower two-digit billion figures to $200 billion and more per year. At the Copenhagen conference in late 2009, industrialized countries promised support in the order of $100 billion per year in the future. But it remains unclear how firm these promises really are, how much each industrialized country would contribute, and how the funding mechanism should be designed.

IPCC

The IPCC is an intergovernmental institution. Its task is to summarize and assess existing scientific knowledge on human-induced climate change and its impacts, as well as options for mitigation and adaptation. It was set up in 1988 by the UN World Meteorological Organization (WMO) and the UN Environment Program (UNEP). Its secretariat is located in Geneva, Switzerland. Its activities are funded by WMO, UNEP, and by direct contributions from governments.

The IPCC does not carry out "in-house" research, nor does it act as a monitoring agency in implementing global climate agreements. It acts primarily as manager of a large network of scientists worldwide. Its activity centers around so-called assessment reports. Such reports have thus far been published in 1990/92, 1995, 2001, and 2007. The next report is scheduled for 2014. The scientists involved, usually several thousand from more than 100 countries, review the relevant scientific literature and, with the help of lead authors and editors, summarize and assess the existing knowledge. This process is organized in three working groups: Working Group I examines geophysical aspects of the climate system and climate change; Working Group II examines vulnerability of socioeconomic and natural systems to climate change consequences and adaptation options; and Working Group III examines options for limiting GHG emissions and mitigating climate change in other ways. The synthesis work and summaries for policy-makers are also exposed to political influence because the IPCC, which is composed of government delegates from all member countries, ultimately decides on their adoption. However, governments have thus far hesitated to modify, for political purposes, the main conclusions drawn from scientific assessments.

FCCC and Kyoto Protocol

The UN Framework Convention on Climate Change (FCCC) was formally adopted at the UN Conference on Environment and Development, UNCED (also known as the Rio, or Earth Summit) in 1992. Its aim is

> [the] stabilization of greenhouse gas concentrations in the atmosphere at a level that would prevent dangerous anthropogenic interference with the climate system. Such a level should be achieved within a time-frame sufficient to allow ecosystems to adapt naturally to climate change, to ensure that food production is not threatened and to enable economic development to proceed in a sustainable manner. (FCCC, Art. 2)

This global treaty does not set forth mandatory emission constraints, overall or for specific countries. Yet it has established the basic legal structure for future agreements and has defined, at a very general level, the goals to be achieved in climate policy. The FCCC entered into force in March 1994 and, as of April 2011, has attracted 194 member countries. Supported by the IPCC Task Force on National Greenhouse Gas Inventories and the FCCC secretariat in Bonn, Germany, FCCC members have established national inventories of GHG emissions and removals. These inventories served to identify the 1990 emission levels that are the benchmarks for emission reduction obligations under the Kyoto Protocol. The so-called Annex I countries (Organisation for Economic Co-operation and Development (OECD) countries and transition economies) are committed to periodically updating these inventories.

Since 1995 the member countries of the FCCC have met each year in Conferences of the Parties (COP). These meetings serve to review the implementation of the agreement and negotiate follow-up agreements. The most important outcome thus far is the Kyoto Protocol (KP). This Protocol was adopted in December 1997 and entered into force in February 2005 (after fifty-five countries representing 55 percent of global CO_2 emissions in 1990 had ratified). The Protocol has (as of April 2011) 192 member countries. The most important non-members are the United States and Afghanistan.

Under the KP, industrialized countries (Annex I countries) have undertaken to reduce six GHGs (carbon dioxide, methane, nitrous oxide, sulfur hexafluoride, hydrofluorocarbons, and perfluorocarbons[2]), of which carbon dioxide and methane are the most important in terms of the size of their greenhouse effect. Thirty-nine of forty potential Annex I countries (except the US) have ratified, and thirty-four countries have committed to emission reductions—five of the KP Annex I members are allowed to maintain or increase their 1990 emission levels (e.g. Russia, Australia, Iceland). The European Union is treated as a "bubble": it received a single target and then allocated emission rights to its member countries. Total reductions are supposed to be in the order of 5.2 percent by 2012, from the 1990 level (each GHG is weighed by its global warming potential). The KP also provides for "flexible mechanisms," such as emissions trading, the clean development mechanism, and joint implementation. The purpose of these economic instruments is to make GHG emissions cuts more cost-efficient, with the assumption that countries are willing to curb their emissions more if doing so is cheaper. Monitoring of compliance relies primarily on annual reports of GHG emissions by Annex I countries and (on a voluntary basis) by other countries.

Most observers of the KP agree that many Annex I countries are currently experiencing difficulties in meeting their emissions targets domestically and are likely to make use of flexible mechanisms in order to be able to meet their legal obligations. Also, the US, which has not ratified the KP but could still seek to implement its Kyoto targets voluntarily, has in fact increased its emissions quite dramatically (its Kyoto target was −7 percent relative to the 1990 level). Moreover, negotiations on a follow-up agreement to the KP, which ends in 2012, have thus far failed, most recently in Copenhagen and Cancun. A recent study (Rogelj et al. 2010) suggests that, even if all unilateral reduction pledges made at Copenhagen and Cancun were implemented, the probability of limiting global warming to 3°C by 2100 would only be 50 percent, while global emissions would increase by 20 percent over 2010 levels. If emissions were cut by 50 percent by 2050 the probability of exceeding 2°C would still be 50 percent.

3. WHY IS GLOBAL GOVERNANCE FOR CLIMATE CHANGE MITIGATION DIFFICULT?

GHG reduction targets set forth in existing governance arrangements are still far from what would be required to limit temperature increases to 2°C. It remains unclear whether those rather non-ambitious targets will be reached by 2012, and even greater uncertainty exists with respect to unilateral pledges for the post-2012 period and the prospects for formal follow-up international agreements.

At the most general level, namely the global political and economic system, climate change mitigation is difficult because it has the character of a global public good. Moreover, there is considerable disagreement over the costs and benefits of GHG mitigation, arising from uncertainties and risks associated with climate change. We discuss these two problems in this section.

Global public goods and the free-rider problem

Climate change mitigation is one of the most typical public goods problems imaginable. Efforts to reduce GHGs correspond by and large to an N-actor prisoner's dilemma, which is similar to the tragedy of the commons (Hardin 1968). The Earth has one indivisible atmosphere that can be used as a sink for GHG emissions worldwide; that is, it is a common-pool resource characterized by open access and rivalry in consumption (Ostrom, Gardner, and Walker 1994). By implication, GHG reductions by any country generate costs and benefits (in terms of avoided damages) for that country, but also benefits for other countries (positive externalities). Since in the climate case positive externalities from emission cuts are quite large in relation to national benefits, international cooperation is necessary, but countries are reluctant to cooperate.

Assuming that countries follow a rationalist, interest-based logic when deciding on their climate policy, they will not implement any major unilateral GHG emission cuts unless other countries credibly commit to a similar policy (e.g. Barrett 2003; Mitchell 2006). The Kyoto Protocol reflects this problem very clearly. It requires ratification by fifty-five countries representing 55 percent of global emissions before entry into force. This clause protects countries from getting "caught up" in legal obligations to reduce emissions if they ratify early but other countries (and major emitters in particular) end up not joining.

In essence, global governance in climate change policy uses mechanisms of reciprocity to prevent free riding on positive externalities. Reciprocity implies that each country exchanges its commitment to reduce emissions against similar commitments by other countries. The international climate change regime described above is quite typical in this regard. It offers an arena for step-by-step cooperation and exchanges of information (monitoring). As is the case with most global governance systems, the climate regime has no centralized enforcement mechanisms but relies on monitoring instruments inside and outside the regime to identify noncomplying countries, and on decentralized enforcement in the form of political and economic pressure imposed by governments and other actors on such countries.

Several cases of successful international cooperation for the provision of global public goods, such as cooperation to protect the stratospheric ozone layer, demonstrate that problems of this type can be solved. Hence, the public goods character of climate change mitigation alone cannot explain why climate policy is progressing much slower than, say, cooperation in the ozone case (Barrett 2003). We need to account for costs and benefits as well. Notably, the costs of climate change mitigation are much higher than the costs of dealing with the stratospheric ozone problem. Further, mitigation costs and benefits remain contested. This circumstance, together with the global public goods character of the climate change issue, makes global cooperation difficult.

The contested economics of climate change mitigation

As noted above, scientific uncertainty with respect to climate change and its consequences, and more specifically concerning the costs of failing to reduce GHG emissions (and, conversely, the benefits of GHG reductions) remains rather high and poses challenges for climate change governance (cf. Borrás, Chapter 30, this volume). The same holds for the costs of reducing GHG emissions. Uncertainty with respect to both benefits and costs combines to create serious difficulties in estimating the net benefits (benefits minus costs) of reducing emissions. The IPCC and the Stern Review arrive at a favorable net benefit assessment because they use rather pessimistic assumptions about climate change-related damages, rather optimistic assumptions about mitigation costs, and a low discount rate.

Net benefit estimates by other social scientists, for example, Nordhaus (2010) and Tol (2009), are more pessimistic. The main reason is that they use higher discount rates, which leads to lower estimates of the present value of (discounted) future climate change-related damages and lower costs of mitigation the more mitigation is postponed. Based on their respective assessments, the IPCC and the Stern Review arrive at very different conclusions compared to Nordhaus, Tol, and some other economists. While the former point to large net benefits of starting early with major GHGs reductions, the latter advocate starting slowly and implementing deep cuts only in the long run. Note, however, that none of these studies denies that human-induced climate change exists and poses very serious problems, and that major emission cuts are necessary. But they disagree on *when* emissions should be cut and by *how much* in order to generate net benefits to present-day decision-makers.

It is easy to see why many policy-makers are more attracted to the Nordhaus-type estimates than the Stern-type estimates. Policies that incur rather high costs in the short term and uncertain, even though potentially high, benefits in the medium to long run are inherently less attractive than policies that generate a "return on investment" within the near future.

Finally, even though collective action at the global level is indispensable for solving the climate change problem, climate change policies are ultimately adopted and implemented at the national level (Meadowcroft 2009). The next section discusses variation in climate policies across countries.

4. NATIONAL CONTRIBUTIONS TO THE GLOBAL PUBLIC GOOD

Most research on climate change governance concentrates on describing and explaining the climate change policies of individual countries or regions. Few studies focus explicitly on explaining observed variation across a large number of countries in national contributions to global climate change mitigation. This section focuses on the main explanations for this variation.

Explaining variation in mitigation efforts

The most prominent explanations of variation in mitigation efforts focus on economic, political, and risk-related factors.

The environmental Kuznets Curve

Among economists the most popular explanation for differences in environmental behavior across countries and over time is the environmental Kuznets Curve (EKC). The latter holds that an inverted U-shaped relationship exists between income and pollution. Grossman and Krueger (1995) are usually credited for the first empirical test of the EKC (cf. Dinda 2004) in their study of the relationship between pollutants (SO$_2$ and smoke) and income per capita, where they identify such a relationship.

Recent research argues, however, that economic growth has somewhat more complex effects on pollution, including GHG emissions. Three types of effects are usually considered: a *scale effect*, a *composition effect*, and a *technology effect*. Since more economic output due to economic growth tends to increase pollution and waste, economic growth is assumed to have a negative *scale effect* on the environment. The *composition effect* is argued to have a positive impact on environmental performance because economies usually develop from (dirtier) manufacturing toward (cleaner) services industries. As long as the composition effect does not simply lead to a relocation of dirty production to poorer and less regulated countries, the composition effect can also reduce global (rather than only local) pollution levels. Economic growth is usually associated with technological innovations that help replace old technologies with newer and cleaner ones (*technology effect*). In addition, growing income is presumably associated with increasing public demand for environmental protection once a country's population has satisfied its basic needs and becomes willing to invest in "postmaterial" goods.

While the basic tenets of the EKC may well be plausible, critics argue that it conveys the message to developing countries that they should "grow first, then clean up" (Dasgupta et al. 2002: 147). This has obvious implications for the discount rate. There is a lively academic (and also policy) debate on the empirical relevance of the EKC in general and CO_2 and other GHG emissions in particular. While many studies identify a statistically significant relationship between income and different local pollutants (notably, SO_2, NOX, CO; cf. Lempert, Scheffran, and Sprinz 2009), global pollutants such as CO_2 tend to either increase monotonically with income or have high turning points (cf. Dinda 2004). Some studies also point to a less favorable N-shaped curve to describe the relationship between income and CO_2 (e.g. Galeotti, Lanza, and Pauli 2006). Moreover, Galeotti, Lanza, and Pauli (2006) find that the inverted U-shaped relation for some pollutants exists for OECD countries, but not for other countries.[3] Arguably the key conclusion from this research (cf. Huang, Lee, and Wu 2008) is that gambling on an automatic reduction of GHG emissions as income grows would be risky and probably a mistake.[4]

Yet another problem with empirical results for the EKC is that they do not take into account regulatory policies. This implies that it remains hard to tell whether observed decreases in GHG emissions are due to income, technology, or composition effects, or whether they are also caused by the effects of regulatory policies or other factors (cf. Bartle 2011; Levi-Faur 2011). Moreover, it remains contested to what extent GHG reductions observed in some countries are due to "bad" composition effects, meaning the relocation of GHG-intensive production to pollution havens. The main long-term problem with "bad" composition effects is that they may allow richer countries to reap the "low-hanging" fruits and could eventually leave poor countries at the bottom of the risk-shifting cascade, where beneficial composition effects must be achieved within the respective country.

Effects of the political system

The political system of a country is likely to have implications for climate change mitigation policy. Several studies show that democracies tend to be better providers of environmental quality (e.g. Bernauer and Koubi 2009). Even though democracy offers greater political access for nongreen interests as well, and the median voter may not always prefer more environmental protection, existing theories expect, on balance, a positive net effect of democracy on environmental protection. The gist of the argument is that, in democracies, freedom of information and political rights enable networks of citizens and other non-state actors to acquire more information on environmental risks and express their demands more easily vis-à-vis policy-makers (Rhodes, Chapter 3, this volume). These networks are crucial in shaping national climate change governance since policy-makers in democracies have greater incentives than autocrats to meet citizen demands because they are more dependent on broad public support, notably in elections (Baettig and Bernauer 2009; Gleditsch and Sverdrup 2002). Note that this argument is relative, not absolute. While the environmental performance of democracies may well be dismal, the performance of non-democracies is likely to be even worse.

Whether democracies outperform non-democracies with respect to climate change policies is ultimately an empirical question. Existing studies on policy outcomes (usually defined as GHG emissions) arrive at mixed results. For instance, Gleditsch and Sverdrup (2002) find that democracy is associated with lower CO_2 emissions. Congleton (1992) finds that democracies emit less methane. Midlarsky (1998) observes that democracies emit more CO_2. Li and Reuveny (2006) find that democracy is associated with less per capita CO_2 emissions.

The relationship between democracy and climate policy *output* appears to be more robust than the relationship between democracy and climate policy *outcomes* (e.g. Neumayer 2002). Von Stein (2008) observes a positive effect of democracy on climate change treaty participation. Baettig and Bernauer (2009) compare climate policy output and outcomes side by side. They find that democracies contribute more to the global public good in terms of policy output, that is, political commitments, but that the effect on policy outcomes is ambiguous. They describe this result in terms of a "word–deeds" gap, which appears to be larger in democracies than in autocracies. Reasons include the fact that mitigation efforts have started only a few years ago, and that, relative to local public goods, such as air pollution, there is a stronger free-rider problem. One major gap in this research area is whether the positive democracy effect is driven more by public demand or the policy supply side (e.g. Ward 2008).

Researchers have recently started to disaggregate democracy and examine the implications of different types of democracy, such as presidential versus parliamentary systems, consensus democracies versus other types, and so on. Ward (2008), for instance, finds that presidential democracies perform worse than parliamentary democracies in environmental terms. Fredriksson and Millimet (2004) observe that governments set stricter environmental policies under proportional than under majoritarian systems. Whether different types of autocracies vary in their climate policy behavior, and if so why, remain to be studied.

Effects of the natural system

The natural (i.e. geophysical climate) system may, on the one hand, influence the emissions behavior of countries. On the other hand, it may also affect their vulnerability to climatic changes and thus their willingness to contribute to the global public good.

Neumayer (2002), for instance, examines natural factors such as climatic conditions, the availability of renewable and fossil fuel resources, and transportation requirements. He finds that these factors have significant effects on cross-country differences in CO_2 emissions, though the income level remains the most important determinant.

Natural system characteristics may also contribute to variation in climate risk exposure, which in turn could affect countries' willingness to commit to climate change mitigation. Sprinz and Vaahtoranta (1994), for example, argue that countries facing greater vulnerability and lower costs of cooperation are more likely to commit to stronger international environmental policies. However, empirical research on climate policy has thus far not been able to identify such a vulnerability effect. For instance, Baettig and Bernauer (2009) do not find any evidence that climate risk exposure has a positive effect on policy output or policy outcomes. Their analysis uses a climate change risk exposure index (Baettig, Wild, and Imboden 2007) and several other indicators for risk exposure. One potential explanation for the absence of a positive vulnerability-cooperation effect is that the available scientific information has not yet spurred sufficient public demand for risk mitigation. Another explanation is that the most vulnerable countries may have greater incentives to invest in climate adaptation, which is a national, "private" good, rather than mitigation, which is a global public good associated with positive externalities; or they may be poor countries that are unable to invest in either adaptation or mitigation.

5. ALTERNATIVE FORMS OF CLIMATE CHANGE GOVERNANCE: LOCAL DYNAMICS IN FEDERAL SYSTEMS

As noted in Section 3, mitigation of climate change through effective global treaties to which all countries adhere has proven very difficult. In this last section we look at other forms of governance that have emerged out of this conundrum. The focus is on subnational climate change governance.[5]

Local climate policy-making is particularly interesting in the case of federal political systems. One noteworthy example is the United States, a typical federal country that is also important because it accounts for around 25 percent of global GHG emissions, but has thus far refused to ratify the Kyoto Protocol. The absence of federal laws and regulations on GHG emissions has led to a plethora of state- and city-level initiatives concerning the governance of climate change over the past few years.

As of April 2011, thirty-two US states have adopted a climate action plan, twenty-one states have adopted GHG emission targets, and twelve states have adaptation plans (Pew Center 2011). Furthermore, the first mandatory cap-and-trade program for CO_2 in the US started in 2009 for the ten member states of the Regional Greenhouse Gas Initiative (RGGI). Similar regional initiatives have been initiated in the Western US states as well as in the Midwest (Pew Center 2011). At the city level, the US Conference of Mayors Climate Protection Agreement (MCPA) is the largest agreement. It involves more than 1000 US cities. It was initiated in February 2005 by the then Seattle mayor, Greg Nickels. Yet another local initiative is the International Council for Local Environmental Initiatives (ICLEI)'s Cities for Climate Protection (CCP) program. The ICLEI is an international initiative that involves around 600 cities worldwide. It started in 1991 and has also helped generate political support for reducing local GHG emission in US cities (Betsill 2001).

Such local and regional activities are interesting from an academic viewpoint, but they also beg the question of whether bottom-up activity can substitute for absent national-level climate policy. Lutsey and Sperling (2007) examine the effects of decentralized climate change policies in US states and cities on GHG emissions, exploring the development of emissions based on current inventories and chosen subnational policies. They argue that "efforts of states and cities are so pervasive at this point that future federal policy will benefit by adopting the most popular and best functioning GHG mitigation programs [...]" (Lutsey and Sperling 2007: 683). Selin and VanDeever are less optimistic about the emission-reducing effects of local climate initiatives. But they also stress the importance of such programs because they allow policy-makers to "[...]

see which of the many available policy options are gaining support in the public and private spheres" (2007: 22) and thereby which are most likely to influence future federal policy development. Tang and colleagues (2010) study forty local climate change action plans in US cities. They find that, although these plans reflect a high level of environmental awareness, they have only limited effects on emissions.

While existing research has not yet been able to demonstrate the effectiveness of local and regional initiatives in terms of reducing GHG emissions, recent research offers interesting insights into the factors that affect the dynamics of such initiatives. With respect to CCP county-level participation patterns, Brody and colleagues (2008) observe that counties with landscape characteristics of high risk, low stress, and high opportunity are more likely to join the CCP campaign. Schaffer (2011) examines county-level participation patterns for the MCPA. She highlights the importance of natural system characteristics, such as whether the county is a coastal county, as well as the political preferences of the inhabitants, in identifying where participation rates in this initiative are highest.

By and large, existing studies suggest that local and regional climate policy initiatives have gained ground in recent years, particularly in federal political systems. There is little evidence that such initiatives can substitute for slow progress in adopting and implementing ambitious mitigation policies at national and international levels. Nonetheless, evidence from the US and other countries indicates that such activities can serve as policy experiments in trying to find efficient mitigation options and changing the "mindset" of business actors and citizens in a climate-friendly direction.

NOTES

1. In a more extensive version of this contribution (Bernauer and Schaffer 2010) we also deal with normative issues. Other important questions regarding climate change governance pertain to issues of regulatory approaches to climate change mitigation (Bartle 2011), transnational governance (Djelic and Sahlin, Chapter 52, this volume), as well as the involvement of civil society in the governance process (Beer, Bartley, and Roberts, Chapter 23, this volume).
2. CO_2, CH_4, N_2O, HFC, PFC, SF6.
3. One explanation is that poorer countries are still on the upward slope of the EKC (Lempert, Scheffran, and Sprinz 2009).
4. Huang, Lee, and Wu (2008: 246) argue that an expansion of the Annex I group under the KP is necessary.
5. As mentioned above, for reasons of space, we cannot discuss other forms of governance in climate policy, such as public–private partnerships and civil society involvement.

REFERENCES

Baettig, M. B. and Bernauer, T. 2009. National institutions and global public goods: Are democracies more cooperative in climate change policy? *International Organization* 63(2): 281–308.

Baettig, M. B., Wild, M. and Imboden, D. 2007. A climate change index: Where climate change may be most prominent in the 21st century. *Geophysical Research Letters* 34: 1–6.

Barrett, S. 2003. *Environment and Statecraft: The Strategy of Environmental Treaty-Making*. Oxford: Oxford University Press.

Bartle, I. 2011. Regulation and climate change mitigation. In D. Levi-Faur (ed.), *Handbook on the Politics of Regulation*. Cheltenham: Edward Elgar, 00–00.

Bernauer, T. and Koubi, V. 2009. Effects of political institutions on air quality. *Ecological Economics* 68: 1355–1365.

Bernauer, T. and Schaffer, L. M. 2010. *Climate Change Governance*. Working Paper No. 60. Zurich: CIS ETH.

Betsill, M. 2001. Mitigating climate change in US cities: Opportunities and obstacles. *Local Environment* 6: 393–406.

Brody, S. D., Zahran, S., Grover, H. and Vedlitz, A. 2008. A spatial analysis of local climate change policy in the United States: Risk, stress, and opportunity. *Landscape and Urban Planning* 87: 33–41.

Congleton, R. D. 1992. Political institutions and pollution control. *The Review of Economics and Statistics* 74: 412–421.

Dasgupta, S., Laplante, B., Wang, H. and Wheeler, D. 2002. Confronting the environmental Kuznets curve. *Journal of Economic Perspectives* 16: 147–168.

Dinda, S. 2004. Environmental Kuznets curve hypothesis: A survey. *Ecological Economics* 49: 431–455.

Fredriksson, P. G. and Millimet, D. L. 2004. Electoral rules and environmental policy. *Economics Letters* 84: 237–244.

Galeotti, M., Lanza, A. and Pauli, F. 2006. Reassessing the environmental Kuznets curve for CO_2 emissions: A robustness exercise. *Ecological Economics* 57: 152–163.

Gleditsch, N. P. and Sverdrup, B. O. 2002. Democracy and the environment. In E. Page and M. R. Redclift (eds.), *Human Security and the Environment: International Comparisons*. Cheltenham: Edward Elgar, 45–70.

Grossman, G. M. and Krueger, A. B. 1995. Economic growth and the environment. *The Quarterly Journal of Economics* 110: 353–377.

Hardin, G. 1968. The tragedy of the commons. *Science* 162: 1243–1248.

Huang, W., Lee, G. and Wu, C. 2008. GHG emissions, GDP growth and the Kyoto Protocol: A revisit of environmental Kuznets curve hypothesis. *Energy Policy* 36: 239–247.

Intergovernmental Panel on Climate Change (IPCC) 2007. *Climate Change 2007: The Physical Science Basis: Summary for Policymakers*. Fourth Assessment Report. Geneva: IPCC.

Lempert, R., Scheffran, J. and Sprinz, D. 2009. Methods for long-term environmental policy challenges. *Global Environmental Politics* 9: 106–133.

Levi-Faur, D. (ed.) 2011. *The Handbook of the Politics of Regulation*. Cheltenham: Edward Elgar.

Li, Q. and Reuveny, R. 2006. Democracy and environmental degradation. *International Studies Quarterly* 50: 935–956.

Lutsey, N. and Sperling, D. 2007. America's bottom-up climate change mitigation policy. *Energy Policy* 36: 673–685.

Meadowcroft, J. 2009. *Climate Change Governance*. World Bank Policy Research Working Paper No. 4941. World Bank Policy Research, 1–42.

Midlarsky, M. I. 1998. Democracy and the environment: An empirical assessment. *Journal of Peace Research* 35: 341–361.

Mitchell, R. B. 2006. Problem structure, institutional design, and the relative effectiveness of international environmental agreements. *Global Environmental Politics* 6: 72–89.

Neumayer, E. 2002. Can natural factors explain any cross-country differences in carbon dioxide emissions? *Energy Policy* 30: 7–12.

Nordhaus, W. 2010. Economic aspects of global warming in a post-Copenhagen environment. *Proceedings of the National Academy of Sciences* 107: 11721–11726.

Ostrom, E., Gardner, R. and Walker, J. 1994. *Rules, Games, and Common-Pool Resources.* Ann Arbor: University of Michigan Press.

Pew Center. 2011. U.S. Climate Policy Maps. Available at http://www.pewclimate.org/what_s_being_done/in_the_states/state_action_maps.cfm.

Rogelj, J., Nabel, J., Chen, C., Hare, W., Markmann, K., Meinshausen, M., Schaeffer, M., Macey, K. and Höhne, N. 2010. Copenhagen accord pledges are paltry. *Nature* 464: 1126–1128.

Schaffer, L. 2011. Voluntary climate change initiatives in the U.S.: Analyzing participation in space and time. Dissertation No. 19475, Zurich: ETH.

Selin, H. and VanDeveer, S. 2007. Political science and prediction: What's next for U.S. climate change policy? *Review of Policy Research* 24: 1–27.

Sprinz, D. and Vaahtoranta, T. 1994. The interest-based explanation of international environmental policy. *International Organization* 48: 77–105.

Stern, N., Peters, S., Bakhshi, V., Bowen, A., Cameron, C., Catovsky, S., Crane, D., Cruickshank, S. and Dietz, S. 2006. Stern Review: The economics of climate change. London: HM Treasury.

Tang, Z., Brody, S., Quinn, C., Chang, L. and Wei, T. 2010. Moving from agenda to action: Evaluating local climate change action plans. *Journal of Environmental Planning and Management* 53: 41–62.

Tol, R. S. J. 2009. The economic effects of climate change. *The Journal of Economic Perspectives* 23: 29–51.

Von Stein, J. 2008. The international law and politics of climate change: Ratification of the United Nations Framework Convention and the Kyoto Protocol. *Journal of Conflict Resolution* 52: 243.

Ward, H. 2008. Liberal democracy and sustainability. *Environmental Politics* 17: 386–409.

PART VII

DEMOCRATIC GOVERNANCE

··

CHAPTER 32

PARTICIPATORY GOVERNANCE: FROM THEORY TO PRACTICE

··

FRANK FISCHER

PARTICIPATORY governance is a variant or subset of governance theory that puts emphasis on democratic engagement, in particular through deliberative practices. In academic circles, the concerns of participatory governance have rapidly become important topics in social and policy sciences. Moreover, during the past several decades participatory governance has made its way into the political practices of a significant spectrum of political organizations, both national and international. Generally advanced as a response to a "democratic deficit" characteristic of contemporary political systems, participatory governance has been embraced by major organizations such as the World Bank, the US Agency for International Development, UN Habitat, and the European Union (EU); all have put money and effort into the development of participatory processes. Many of these initiatives have drawn their inspiration from the progressive projects of political parties in India, Brazil, Spain, Mexico, and the UK. To this list one can add civil society organizations, such as Oxfam, Action Aid, and the International Budget project, actively disseminating information and promoting participatory practices.

Both theory and empirical experience with governance demonstrates that there are numerous patterns of participation and non-participation, from non-democratic elitist top-down forms of interaction to radically democratic models from the bottom up. Governance, as such, tends to refer to a new space for decision-making, but does not, in and of itself, indicate the kinds of politics that take place within these spaces. Participatory governance, grounded in the theory of participatory democracy more generally, offers a theory and practices of public engagement through deliberative processes. It focuses, in this regard, on the deliberative empowerment of citizens and aligns itself in varying degrees to work on deliberative democracy in political theory and deliberative experimentation in policy-related fields of contemporary political and social research, as well as political activism on the part of various public organizations and foundations. Participatory governance thus includes, but moves beyond, the citizen's role as voter or watchdog to include practices of direct deliberative engagement with the pressing issues of the time.

Whereas citizen participation in the governmental process has traditionally focused on measures designed to support and facilitate increased public access to information about governmental activities, efforts to extend the rights of the citizens to be consulted on public issues which affect them, and to see that the broad citizenry will be heard through fair and equitable representative political systems, participatory governance seeks to deepen this participation by examining the assumptions and practices of the traditional view that generally hinders the realization of a genuine participatory democracy (Gaventa 2002). It reflects a growing recognition that citizen participation needs to be based on more elaborate and diverse principles, institutions and methods. Essential are a more equal distribution of political power, a fairer distribution of resources, the decentralization of decision-making processes, the development of a wide and transparent exchange of knowledge and information, the establishment of collaborative partnerships, an emphasis on inter-institutional dialogue, and greater accountability. All these measures seek to create relationships based as much or more on trust and reciprocity than advocacy, strategic behavior, and deceit. Participatory governance involves as well the provision of means to engage individuals and organizations outside government through political networks and institutional arrangements that facilitate supportive collaborative-based discursive relationships among public and private sectors.

Emerging as a result of a multiplication of existing kinds of participatory arrangements in the 1990s, participatory governance has established new spaces and given rise to different types of civil society actors to inhabit them. In both the developed and developing countries, these have involved a number of important shifts in problem-solving and service delivery, including more equitable forms of support for economic and social development. Along the way it has often meant a transition from professionally dominated to more citizen—or citizen-based—activities, frequently taking place within the new civic society organizations.

The following discussion proceeds in six parts. It first takes up the interrelated questions of citizen competence, empowerment, and capacity-building as they relate to participatory governance, and then turns to its impact on service delivery, social equity, and political representation, including the distribution of power. These implications are seen to depend in significant part on participatory designs. The discussion thus presents the prominent theory of "empowered participatory governance," which offers principles for design. These points are further illustrated by pointing to several experiences with participatory governance, in particular the cases participatory budgeting in Brazil and the people's planning project in Kerala, India. Before concluding, the chapter also raises the question of the relation of citizens and experts in participatory governance and the possibility of new forms of collaborative expertise.

Citizen competence, empowerment, and capacity-building

Democratic participation is generally considered a political virtue unto itself. But participatory governance claims to offer even more; it is seen to contribute to the development of communicative skills, citizen empowerment, and community capacity-building. First, with regard to citizen competence and empowerment, the practices of participatory governance are put forth as a specific case of the broader view that participation contributes to human development generally, both intellectual and emotional. Empowerment through participation has, as such, been part of the progressive educational curriculum and numerous citizen-based deliberative projects bear out its influence on personal development (Joss 1995; Dryzek 2008).

Many NGOs engaged with the practices of participatory governance, in particular in the developing world, speak of "people's self-development" and empowerment as primary goals, emphasizing, political rights, social recognition, and economic redistribution in the development of participatory approaches (Rahman 1995). Rather than merely speaking for the poor or marginalized citizens' interests and issues, they have labored to assist people develop their own abilities to negotiate with public policy-makers. Beyond institutionalizing new bodies of client or user groups, they have created new opportunities for dialogue and the kinds of citizen education that it can facilitate, especially communicative skills.

The issue is critical for *participatory* governance as it has little or no meaning if citizens are neither capable nor empowered to participate. Studies show that many people in the middle rungs of society can competently deal with policy discussions (Fishkin 2009; Delli Carpini, Lomax Cook, and Jacobs 2004). Research finds, for example, that lay panelists on citizen juries increase their knowledge of the subject under discussion and often gain a new confidence in their ability to deal with complex policy issues generally (Joss 1995). Many participants tend to describe such participatory experiences as having had a stimulating impact on their personal lives, often leading to further involvement in public affairs.

Much more challenging, however, is the situation for marginalized members of society, those who might benefit from participatory governance the most. But here too there are positive signs. The participatory projects in Porto Alegre and Kerala, taken up below, as well as other experiences in developing and underdeveloped countries, show that citizens with less formal education can also, under the right conditions, participate with surprisingly high levels of competence. In the case of Kerala, most of the members of the local deliberative councils would be described as simple farmers. Nonetheless, they participated impressively in planning projects, the likes of which one very seldom finds in the advanced industrial world.

Participation, it also needs to be noted, is more than a matter of competence. Competent people may not perceive an incentive to participate. Thus, getting them to do so is another important issue. Engagement in the public realm is not without its costs, and most people have little interest in participating unless the costs of engagement are outweighed by the possibility of benefits from it (Osmani 2007). Local people, including competent citizens, may themselves be highly skeptical about the worth of investing their time and energy in participatory activities. In some situations, participation will lack immediate relevance; it may carry more significance for outsiders than it does for those in the relevant communities. Moreover, not everyone within the communities will be able or motivated to participate. Even when there is sufficient interest in participation there may be time barriers. Sometimes decisions have to be taken before deliberative projects can be set up and carried out.

Finally, questions of participation and competence also bear directly on the issue of capacity-building. Capacity-building, as the development of a community's ability to deal collectively with the problems that it confronts, can contribute to a sense of social togetherness. Rather than the relative passive role of the individual associated with traditional conceptions of citizen participation, participatory governance helps to connect and enable competent individuals in local communities build together the kinds of "social capital" needed for joint problem-solving (Putnam 2000). It does this in part by building social trust and the kinds of mutual understanding that it can facilitate.

Basic to the development of building capacity is a devolution of power and resources from central managerial control and toward local democratic institutions and practices, including street-level administrators willing and able to assist community members in taking charge of their own issues. Whereas community members under conventional forms of representative government are more often than not relegated to a vicarious role in politics, under participatory governance they move to a more direct involvement in the political process, as illustrated below by citizen panels but even more importantly participatory budgeting in Brazil.

SERVICE DELIVERY AND EQUITY

For many, the underlying goal of building capacity for action is to increase the efficiency and effectiveness of the provision and management of public services. For others concerned with participatory governance, as Ron has explained, a primary goal of capacity-building "is to provide citizens with the tools that are needed to reflect on the normative principles that underlie the provision of public services."[1] That is, the goal is to provide citizens with opportunities to critically reflect on the norms and values justifying the equity of the outcomes.

A range of experiences shows that community participation can improve the efficiency of programs (in terms of uses of resources) and effective projects (that achieve their intended outcomes) in the provision and delivery of services, in both the developed and developing worlds. In fields such as education, health care, environmental protection, forestry, and irrigation, it is seen to lead to quicker responses to emerging issues and problems, more effective development and design of solutions appropriate to local resources, higher levels of commitment and motivation in program implementation, and greater overall satisfaction with policies and programs (Ojha 2006). Furthermore, an emphasis on efficiency typically leads to improved monitoring processes and verification of results.

While there is no shortage of illustrations to suggest the validity of the claim, there is a methodological issue that can make it difficult to establish such outcomes (Osmani 2007). When local participatory governance is found to contribute to efficiency, firmly establishing the cause–effect relationships can be problematic. It is always possible that a positive association between efficiency and participation may only reflect a process of reverse causation—that is, community members had already chosen to participate in those projects which promised to be efficient. To know if participation has in fact contributed to efficient outcomes, investigators have to discern if such extraneous factors are at work. Although this is theoretically possible, it is a difficult technical requirement. Such information is often unavailable or difficult to come by.

Participation also has the potential to combine efficiency with equity. Research shows that decisions made through the participation of community members rather than by traditional elites or unaccountable administrators offers less powerful groups in the community better chances of influencing the distribution of resources (Heller 2001; Fischer 2000). This view is founded on the presumption that through critical reflection in participatory processes disadvantaged citizens have improved chances of expressing their preferences in ways that can make them count.

But this is not always the case. Empirical investigation tends to be mixed on this issue (Papadopoulus and Warin 2007). Many studies suggest that participatory approaches in local arenas can be of assistance to the poor and disadvantaged members of the community, but other research fails to clearly confirm this. Overall, investigation shows that community participation can lead to more equitable outcomes, but it is particularly difficult to achieve such results in inequitable social contexts. Equitable outcomes more commonly occur in combination with other factors, such as those related to the distribution of power, motivation levels of the participants, and the presence of groups that can facilitate the process. One of the difficulties in assessing the impact of such participation is that there is often no reliable information about the distribution of benefits and costs to households, thus making it difficult to render comparative assessments (Osmani 2007).

Some also argue that by diffusing authority and control over management, decentralized participation can also weaken efficiency (Khwaja 2004). But, depending on the design, this need not be the case. And others argue that it can lead to resource allocations that violate the true preferences of community members, as some may withhold or distort information about their preferences and choices. This problem is perhaps most acute in developing countries, in which community participation is related to external donor-funded projects. All too often in these cases, such participation can intentionally advance preferences that are seen to be more in line with the interests of the donors than local interests. The participants simply try to increase their chances of obtaining available resources by telling the donors what they want to hear (Platteau 2007).

In short, while participation can lead to important payoffs, there are no guarantees. It cannot be said without qualifications that decentralized participation leads to greater efficiency and/or equity. What the experiences suggest is that the conditions of success depends on conscientious effort and design, both of which depend heavily on the ability of the participants to effectively present their views. This depends, in turn, on the degree of political representation and the distribution of power that it reflects.

POLITICAL REPRESENTATION AND THE DISTRIBUTION OF POWER

The theory and practice upon which such efforts rest are based on a number of varied sources, including academic theorizing, political activists, social movements, NGOs, and governmental practitioners. On the theoretical front, many of these projects have been influenced by work on deliberative democracy in political theory, an influential orientation designed to revitalize a stronger conception of democracy and the public interest based on citizen participation through public deliberation (on the forms of democratic governance, see Ron, Chapter 33, this volume). It focuses on promoting "debate and discussion aimed at producing reasonable, well-informed opinion in which participants are willing to revise preferences in light of discussion, new information, and claims made by fellow participants" (Chambers 2003: 309). It is grounded in the idea that "deliberate approaches to collective decisions under conditions of conflict produce better decisions than those resulting from alternative means of conducting politics: Coercion, traditional deference, or markets." Thus, "decisions resulting from deliberation are likely to be more legitimate, more reasonable, more informed, more effective and more politically viable" (Warren 2007: 272).[2]

A critical issue is the relationship of such participation to the larger representative structure of society. Because participatory governance is largely introduced to compensate for the failures of representative government to adequately connect citizens to their elected representatives, the ability to bring these two political models together is important (Wampler 2009). Examples of how this can be done are introduced in the next section presenting the experiences from Porto Algre and Kerala.

Closely related to representation is the question of power, or what Osmani (2007) calls the "power gap." A function of the asymmetrical power relations inherent to modern societies, especially those created by the inequalities of rich and poor, this poses a difficult barrier to meaningful participation. When inequalities are embedded in powerful patriarchies such projects are prone to be captured and manipulated by elites, whether they be political leaders and their patronage networks or those providing development assistance from the outside. Again, we can gain insights into this process in the following discussion of Porto Algre and Kerala.

In many ways, participatory governance is a response to this power problem, as it seeks to give a voice to those without power. But one has to be careful in assessing the degree to which it can generate unmanipulated participation. At the current state of development, participatory governance itself often exists as much or more as a strategy for struggling against political imbalances rather than for counterbalancing them outright.

A manifestation of this struggle is the problem of co-optation, which makes it difficult to judge the significance of participation in successful projects. All too often they are in jeopardy of being co-opted (Malena 2009). Experience shows that success is frequently rewarded by governmental institutionalization, at which point they are often manipulated to serve purposes other than those intended. The World Bank, for example, has deftly co-opted various participatory projects and their methods to generate support for their own agendas. Having discovered of the relevance of local involvement and participation from many of its Third World investment failures, the Bank took an interest in the advantages and institutionalized a participatory program designed to facilitate direct local contact with the communities it seeks to assist (World Bank, 1994). Not only have senior bank staff members been directed to get to know a particular region better through personal participation in programs and projects in its villages or slums, the bank has pioneered a technique called participatory poverty assessment designed "to enable the poor people to express their realities themselves" (Chambers 1997: xvi). It has been adapted from participatory research experiences in more than thirty countries around the world (Norton and Stephens 1995).

Such instrumentalization of participation can be seen as a "political technology" introduced to control processes and projects, hindering the possibilities of popular engagement. Bourdieu (1977) refers to these as "officializing strategies" that domesticate participation, direction attention to less active forms of political engagement. Given the widespread manipulation of participatory techniques, Cooke and Kothari (2001) are led to describe participation as "the new ideology."

As is the case with service delivery and equity, there is nothing simple or straightforward about either political representation and equitable power arrangements in participatory projects. Indeed, there is no shortage of things that can block effective political participation. It is a question that again raises the issue of participatory design and brings us to a discussion of "empowered participatory governance" which has sought to set out principles for design.

EMPOWERED PARTICIPATORY GOVERNANCE

Examining a range of cases designed to promote active political involvement of the citizenry, Fung and Wright (2003) have labored to sort out what works. Acknowledging that complexity makes it difficult for anyone to participate in policy decision-making, they speculate that "the problem may have more to do with the specific design of our institutions than with the task they face." Toward this end, they have examined a range of experiences in the participatory redesign of democratic institutions (including Porto Alegre and Kerala), innovations that elicit the social energy and political influence of citizens—especially those from the lowest strata of society—in pursuit of solutions to problems that plague them.

Even though these reforms vary in their organizational designs, the policy issues to be deliberated, and scope of activities, they all seek to deepen the abilities of ordinary citizens to effectively participate in the shaping of programs and policies relevant to their own lives. From their common features they isolate a set of characteristics that Fung and Wright define as "empowered participatory governance." The principles they draw from these cases are designed to enable the progressive "colonization of the state" and its agencies. Relying on the participatory capabilities of empowered citizens to engage in reason-based action-oriented decision-making, the strategy and its principles are offered as a radical political step toward a more democratic society.

As a product of this work, they isolate three political principles, their design characteristics, and one primary background condition. The background enabling condition states that there should be rough equality of power among the participants. The political principles refer to (1) need of such experiments to address a particular practical problem; (2) a requirement that deliberation rely upon the empowered involvement of ordinary citizens and the relevant; and (3) that each experiment employs reasoned deliberation in the effort to solve the problems under consideration. The institutional design characteristics specify (1) the devolution of decision-making and the powers of implementation power to local action-oriented units; (2) that these local units be connected to one another and to the appropriate levels of state responsible for supervision, resource allocation, innovation, and problem-solving; and (3) that the experimental projects can "colonize and transform" state institutions in ways that lead to the restructuring of the administrative agencies responsible for dealing with these problems.

While this work is an important step forward, a theory of the design of deliberative empowerment still requires greater attention to the cultural politics of deliberative space (Fischer 2006). Beyond formal principles concerned with structural arrangements, we need as well research on the ways the social valorization of a participatory space influences basic discursive processes such as who speaks, how knowledge is constituted, what can be said, and who decides. From this perspective, decentralized design principles are necessary but insufficient requirements for deliberative participation. We need to examine more carefully how political-cultural and pedagogical strategies can facilitate the deliberative empowerment in participatory governance.

Projects and practices: citizens' panels, participatory budgeting, and people's planning

Of particular significance on the practical front have been experimental projects in participatory governance, all designed to bring citizens' reasoned preferences to bear on the policy process (Gastil and Levine 2005). Most of these projects are dedicated to goals closely related to those spelled out by the theory of deliberative democracy, although many do not emerge from it per se. Some scholars, though, have argued that deliberative democratic theory should strive to be a "working theory" for the deliberative experiments of participatory governance (Chambers 2003). There are now some prominent examples of such interaction, in particular on the part of scholars such as Fishkin (2009), Warren and Pearce (2008), and Dryzek (2008). They clearly illustrate constructive "communication between the theorists of deliberative democracy and empirical research on deliberation" (Fischer 2009: 87).

The projects in participatory governance are to be found across the globe, from Europe and the US to the developing and underdeveloped world. In Europe and the US numerous projects have focused on efforts to develop fora through which citizens' views on complex economic and social issues can be brought to bear directly on policy decisions. Some of these have been organized from the bottom, whereas others have emerged from the top down. Such research has ranged from investigations of the traditional citizen survey and public meetings to innovative techniques such as deliberative polling, televoting, focus groups, national issue conventions, and study circles on to more sophisticated citizen juries, scenario workshops, planning cells, consensus conferences, and citizens' assemblies (Gastil and Levine 2005; Fishkin 2009; Joss 1995). These experiences offer important insights as to how to bring citizens into a closer participatory relationship with public decision-makers.

Most important among these efforts have been the citizen jury and the consensus conference. Developed in Northern Europe and the United States before spreading to a range of countries around the world, these two deliberative processes permit a high degree of citizen deliberation on important matters of public policy. They provide citizens with an opportunity to deliberate in considerable detail among themselves before coming to judgment or decision on questions they are charged to answer. During the process, they hear from experts and pose their own questions to them, before deliberating among themselves. But citizens' panels are largely advisory in nature; they supply additional information that can be useful to politicians and the public. Given the limited amount of space available here, the present discussion will focus more specifically on those deliberative arrangements built into the governmental structure itself.

The most progressive projects have developed in the developing world, especially in Brazil and India. These innovations include deliberative processes analogous to citizen juries but have more formally integrated them into the policy processes of established governmental institutions. Of particular importance are the practices of public budgeting in Porto Alegre, Brazil and people's development planning in Kerala, India. These innovations have been influenced by both social movements, NGOs, and left-oriented political parties, both theoretically and practically. Turning first to participatory budgeting in Porto Alegre, by all standards one of the most innovative practices in participatory governance, it has becomes a model widely emulated around the world.

Under public budgeting in Porto Alegre significant parts of local budgets are determined by citizens through deliberative fora (Baiocchi 2003; Wampler 2009). In a city of 1.3 million inhabitants, long governed by a clientelistic pattern of political patronage, a left coalition led by the Workers' Party took office in 1989 and introduced a publicly accountable, bottom-up system of budgetary deliberations geared to the needs of local residences. Involving a multi-level deliberative system, the city of Porto Alegre has been divided into regions with a Regional Plenary Assembly that meets twice a year to decide budgetary issues. City administrators, representatives of community groups, and any other interested citizens attend these assemblies, jointly coordinated by the municipal government and community delegates. With information about the previous year's budget made available by representatives of the municipal government, delegates are elected to work out the region's spending priorities. These are then discussed and ratified at a second plenary assembly. Representatives then put these forward at a city-wide participatory budgeting assembly which meets to formulate the city-wide budget from these regional agendas. After deliberations, the council submits the budget to the mayor, who can either accept the budget or send it back to the council for revisions. The Council then responds by either amending the budget or overriding the mayor's veto through a vote of two-thirds of the council representatives.

The second case, that of Kerala, has involved a full-fledged process of people's resource planning (Issac and Heller 2003; Fischer 2000). Located in the southwestern corner of the country, Kerala has gained attention in the development community for its impressive economic and social distributional activities in the 1980s. In the mid-1990s, a coalition of left parties led by the Communist Marxist/Party of India decided to extend these activities to include a state-wide, bottom-up system of participatory planning, the goal of which was to develop the Kerala Five-Year Plan to be delivered to the central government in New Delhi.

Pursuing a devolutionary program of village-level participatory planning as a strategy to both strengthen its electoral base and improve governmental effectiveness, the government decided that approximately 40 percent of the state's budget would be redirected from the administrative line departments and sent to newly established district planning councils, about 900 in number. Each village, supported by the Science for the People social movement and the Center for Earth Sciences, formulated a specific development plan that spelled out local needs, development assessment reports, specific projects to be advanced, financing requirements, procedures for deciding plan beneficiaries, and a system of monitoring the outcomes. These developments were then accepted or rejected by vote in village assemblies. The final plans were send to the State Planning Board and incorporated into the state's Five-Year Plan, sent to New Dehli for inclusion in the overall development plan of the national government.

As a consequence of these activities, from citizen juries to People's Planning, participation has gained a place across the political spectrum in the 1990s as a central feature of "good governance." Promoting decentralization, good governance practices have added an additional layer of local participatory institutions to an increasingly complex institutional landscape that in some cases has given rise to transfers of both resources and decision-making powers.

Returning to the question of political representation, in the case of the citizen jury and the consensus conference, the outcomes are merely advisory. They offer politicians and decision-makers a different kind of knowledge to consider in their deliberations, a form of understanding often more closely akin to the types of thinking they themselves engage in (as opposed to complex technical reports). But in Kerala and Porto Algre, by contrast, deliberation was integrated into the policy decision process. In Kerala, local discussions were hierarchically channeled up to the State Planning Board for inclusion in the official planning document. In Porto Algre they were linked into the official governmental budget-making process; the outcomes of the deliberations determined an important portion of the budget. Success, in both cases, is seen to depend as much on support from political parties at the top as it does from grass-roots movements from below. The top and the bottom of the power structure must work together (Fischer 2009). Given that the dramatic successes of these two experiences are exceptions to the rule, we need much more investigation into this process.

Participatory expertise: a new type of expert?

Of particular significance in these projects is a breed of NGOs working to represent and serve the needs of marginalized or excluded groups. In many of the newly created participatory spaces activists have assisted excluded peoples—such as the poor, women, AIDS victims, and the disabled—in developing a collective presence that has permitted them to speak for themselves. Through such efforts activists and their citizen groups have in many cases succeeded in influencing the policies of mainstream institutions. In some cases, these activities have given rise to a new breed of public servant—frequently schooled in NGOs—devoted to offering assistance to these groups. As government officials or independent consultants to parallel institutions—they have often played an essential role in the development and spread of participatory approaches to governance (Fischer 2009).

The result of these participatory activities has also given rise to a new kind of professional orientation, one that challenges the standard techno-bureaucratic approaches of the modern state (Fischer 2009). These professionals, along with their respective theoreticians, have sought to reconceptualize the role of the public servant as facilitator of public engagement. Feldman and Khademian (2007), for example, have reconceptualized the role of the public manager as that of creating "communities of participation." In their view, the challenge confronting those working in the public sector is to interactively combine knowledge and perspectives from three separate domains of knowing—the technical, political and local/experiential domains. Bringing about more inclusive practices of governance involves inventing participatory contexts in which the representatives of these forms of knowing can discursively share their perspectives in the common pursuit of problem-solving. Beyond merely identifying and disseminating information from these various ways of understanding and analyzing policy problems, such work involves translating ideas in ways that facilitate mutual understanding and deliberation among the participants and discursively promotes a synthesis of perspectives that helps to stimulate different ways of knowing relevant to the problem at hand.

In many cases participatory expertise involves the development of citizen–expert alliances and the use of practices such as community-based participatory research and participatory action research, as was the case in Kerala (Fischer 2000). These methods involve professional experts in the process of helping lay participants conduct their own research on problems of concern to local residents. While there have been important efforts to facilitate deliberation between citizens and experts, there are a number of problems that still need to be dealt with (Fischer 2009). Perhaps most important, professionals are not trained to facilitate participation and many—maybe most—do not believe there is any point in engaging citizens in such issues. The successful efforts, more often than not, are the result of activities engaged in by professionals involved in progressive social movements of one sort or another (Fischer 2009). In addition, they raise difficult but important epistemological questions related to the nature of such knowledge. Does it just involve a division of labor organized around the traditional separation of empirical and normative issues? Or does it require a new hybrid form of knowledge, involving a fusion of the empirical and the normative and perhaps a special role for local lay knowledge? Included in this question is the need to explore the relationship of reason to emotion. Although everybody in politics knows that emotion and passion are basic to the politics of governance, this topic has yet to receive the attention it deserves in the literature on democratic governance and policy.

Concluding perspective

Many of these participatory activities have offered significant new insights into questions that have long been ignored in traditional political analysis and in democratic theory in particular. Four of these new perspectives stand out especially. The first concerns the need to fill the "institutional void" that the theory of representative government fails to address. The second involves the degree to which citizens are able to participate meaningfully in the complex decision processes that define contemporary policy-oriented politics. The third is the ability to improve service delivery and social equity. And fourth, we have also noted the implications of participatory governance for the nature of professional practices.

Beyond the theoretical realm, however, it should be clear from the foregoing discussion that much of the practical work on governance involves a collection of separate experiments and projects that have common threads but often offer somewhat limited outcomes, projects in Porto Alegre and Kerala being important exceptions. In this regard, it is essential to recognize that the experiences with these efforts have by no means been all positive. It is a story of mixed outcomes, with the experiences ranging across the spectrum from very impressive to disappointing. Indeed, the failures far out-number the successes. The successful cases, moreover, offer few uniformities.

The task of sorting out the positive and negative elements contributing to the success and failure of such participatory projects thus takes on particular importance. Given that there is no shortage of factors that come into play, such an assessment is challeng-ing. What can be said is that, independent of a good deal of the rhetoric associated with discussions about participation, the evidence about new forms of participatory govern-ance illustrates that participation poses difficult issues with no simple solutions. A closer look reveals that while citizens can participate and that participatory governance can improve both democratic decision-making and efficient service delivery, participation has to be carefully organized, facilitated—even cultivated and nurtured.

Given the difficulties involved in designing and managing participatory processes, it comes as no surprise to learn that citizen participation schemes rarely follow smooth pathways. In the absence of serious attention to the quality and viability of citizen par-ticipation, it is usually better to forgo such projects. Participatory governance, despite its promise, is a complicated and uncertain business that needs to be carefully thought out in advance (Fischer 2000). This should be the first priority of those engaged in both the theory and methods of the practice.

NOTES

1. The observation is drawn from Amit Ron's helpful comments on this chapter.
2. While the theory of deliberative democracy has had the most influence on these projects, the theory of agonistic democracy can also support the theory and practices of participa-tory governance.

REFERENCES

Baiocchi, G. 2003. Participation, activism, and politics: The Porto Alegre experiment. In A. Fung and E. O. Wright (eds.) *Deepening Democracy*. New York: Verso, 77–102.

Bourdieu, P. 1977. *Outline of a Theory of Practice*. Cambridge: Cambridge University Press.

Chambers, R. 1997. *Who Reality Counts? Putting the First Last*. London: Intermediate Technology Publications.

Chambers, S. 2003. Deliberative democratic theory. *Annual Review of Political Science* 6: 307–326.

Cooke, B. and Kothari, U. 2001. *Participation: The New Tyranny?* London: Zed Books.

Delli Carpini, M. X., Lomax Cook, F., and Jacobs, L. R. 2004. Public deliberation, discursive participation, and citizen engagement: A review of empirical literature. *Annual Review of Political Science* 7: 315–344.

Dryzek, J. 2009. The Australian citizens' parliament: A world first. *Journal of Public Deliberation* 5: 1–9.

Feldman, M. S. and Khademian, A. M. 2007. The role of the public manager in inclusion: Creating communities of participation. *Governance* 20: 305–324.

Fischer, F. 2000. *Citizens, Experts, and the Environment: The Politics of Local Knowledge.* Durham, NC: Duke University Press.

Fischer, F. 2006. Participatory governance as deliberative empowerment: The cultural politics of discursive space. *The American Review of Public Administration* 36: 19–40.

Fischer, F. 2009. *Democracy and Expertise: Reorienting Policy Inquiry.* Oxford: Oxford University Press.

Fishkin, J. S. 2009. *When the People Speak: Deliberative Democracy and Public Consultation.* Oxford: Oxford University Press; New Haven, CT: Yale University Press.

Fung, A. and Wright, E. O. 2003. *Deeping Democracy: Institutional Innovations in Empowered Participatory Governance.* New York: Verso.

Gastil, J. and Levine, P. (eds.) 2005. *The Deliberative Democracy Handbook: Strategies for Effective Civic Engagement in the 21st Century.* San Francisco: Jossey-Bass.

Gaventa, J. 2002. Towards participatory governance. *Currents* 29: 29–35.

Heinelt, H. 2010. *Governing Modern Societies: Towards Participatory Governance.* London: Routledge.

Isaac, T. H. and Franke, R. 2000. *Local Democracy and Development: People's Campaign for Decentralized Planning in India.* New Dehli: Left World Press.

Isaac, T. H. and Heller, P. 2003. Democracy and development: Decentralized planning in Kerala. In A. Fung and E. O. Wright (eds.) *Deepening Democracy.* New York: Verso, 77–102.

Joss, S. 1995. Evaluating consensus conferences: Necessity or luxury. In S. Joss and J. Durant (eds.) *Public Participation in Science: The Role of Consensus Conferences in Europe.* London: Science Museum, 89–108.

Khwaja, A. I. 2004. Is increasing community participation always a good thing? *Journal of European Economic Association* 2: 2–3.

Malena. C. (ed.) 2009. *From Political Won't to Political Will: Building Support for Participatory Governance.* Sterling, VA: Kumarian Press.

Misar, D. 2005. *Participatory Governance Through NGOs.* Jaipur: Aalekh Publishers.

Ojha, H. 2006. Techno-bureaucratic doxa and challenges for deliberative governance: The case of community forestry policy and practice in Nepal. *Policy and Society* 25: 11–176.

Ojha, H. N., Timsina, N. P., Chhetri, R. B., and Paudal, K. P. 2008. Knowledge systems and deliberative interface in natural resource governance. In H. N. Ojha, N. P. Timsina, R. B. Chhetri, and K. P. Paudal (eds.) *Knowledge Systems and Natural Resources: Management Policy and Institutions in Nepal.* New Delhi: Cambridge University Press, 1–22.

Osmani, S. R. 2007. Participatory governance: An overview of the issues and evidence. In *Participatory Governance and the Millennium Development Goals.* New York: United Nations, 1–48.

Papadopoulus, Y. and Warin, P., 2007. Are innovative, participatory and deliberative procedures in policy making democratic and effective? *European Journal of Political Research* 46: 445–472.

Putnam, R. 2000. *Bowling Alone: The Collapse and Revival of the American Community.* New York: Simon and Schuster.

Rahman, M. D. A. 1995. *People's Self-Development.* London: Zed Books.

Norton, A. and Stephens, T. 1995. *Participation in Poverty Assessment.* Environmental Department Papers Participation Series, Social Policy and Resettlement Division, World Bank, Washington, June.

Platteau, J. 2007. Pitfalls of participatory development. In *Participatory Governance and the Millennium Development Goals.* New York: United Nations, 127–162.

Rowe, G. and Frewer, L. J. 2004. Evaluating public participation exercises: A research agenda. *Science, Technology and Human Values* 29: 512–557.

Wampler, B. 2009. *Participatory Budgeting in Brazil*. University Park: Penn State.

Warren, M. E. 2007. Institutionalizing deliberative democracy. In S. Rosenberg (ed.) *Deliberation, Participation and Democracy: Can the People Govern?* London and New York: Palgrave Macmillan, 272–288.

Warren, M. E. and Pearce, H. (eds.) 2008. *Designing Deliberative Democracy: The British Columbia Citizens Assembly*. Cambridge: Cambridge University Press.

World Bank 1994. *The World Bank and Participation*. Washington, DC: Operations Policy Department.

CHAPTER 33

....

MODES OF DEMOCRATIC
GOVERNANCE

....

AMIT RON*

THE language that we use to describe social processes is simultaneously descriptive and evaluative. When we describe a phenomenon using a specific term—bureaucracy, corruption, the public, and so forth—we also pass judgment about its desirability. In our present context, the term democracy is such a descriptive–evaluative term. In using it to describe a situation we are performing a speech-act commending it (Skinner 1973: 298). In contrast with "democracy," the term "governance" has not yet acquired the same descriptive–evaluative qualities. The contention that motivates this chapter is that we have to be very careful when we affix the notion of democracy to the notion of governance. I am particularly worried that too loose a description of certain practices as "democratic governance" can unintentionally become a speech act endorsing them. I therefore seek to be careful, even pedantic, in what I am choosing to label as democratic governance.

Thus, in seeking to discuss the different forms of democratic governance, this chapter has two goals. The first is to elaborate a working definition of democratic governance. As I explain in the next section, I understand governance to imply decision-making in an environment where there is no single institution with agency—that is, the power to carry out its decisions. Particularly, it is an environment in which government is unwilling or is unable to be the body with the overarching authority to design and watch over the implementation of policies. Accordingly, I define *democratic* governance as attempts to institutionalize spaces for the expression of the voice of the people where these institutions of voice do not have the capacity to guarantee the implementation of their decisions. In short, democratic governance happens where democratic voice is not tied to agency. My definition of democratic governance tries to capture the domain of governance that can properly be called democratic. My discussion of forms of democratic governance refers to the institutional forms of practices of governance that can be described as democratic.

Processes of democratic governance try to create a space for reaching resolutions that can claim to be a legitimate expression of the voice of the people. However, according to the very definition I just proposed, these processes are attempts to speak in the dark, so to speak. Unlike the traditional model of government, where an executive branch carries the decision of a legislative one, in an environment of governance there is no single agency that carries out the resolutions reached by the democratic process. But if no one is guaranteed to be listening, then what is the rationale for creating a space for voice? My second goal in this chapter is to offer a classification of forms of democratic governance according to the answers that they provide to this question. The answer that underlies and motivates each form of democratic governance is based on an assessment of the working of the institutions of voice of democratic government, and an explanation of what factors necessitate the creation of alternative institutions of voice. I will call this account the moral sociology (or moral political sociology) that undergirds the institutionalization of voice. The notion of moral sociology is an adaptation of John Rawls's "moral psychology" (1999: 429ff.), which he introduced to contend that any theory of human psychology embodies a normative conception of the good life. I use the term moral sociology in a similar way to explain how the institutional design of different forms of democratic governance is based simultaneously on a normative ideal of democratic legitimacy and a sociological account of the functioning of existing democratic institutions.

I. WHAT IS DEMOCRATIC GOVERNANCE?

The different forms of democratic governance that I study in this chapter are ideal types of institutions that seek to express the voice of the people. It is useful to begin the discussion with an exploration of the ideal form of democratic government. The form of democratic government is tied to an understanding of the public as sovereign in democracy. This understanding emerges from a merger of a classical account of democracy and a traditional top-down account of policy-making. In this view, the democratic institutions that stand for the voice of the people are in control over the executive power of state. These institutions serve both as the voice of the people and as their agent. This form of decision-making is commonly described as democratic government: "democratic" because decisions are made by representative institutions that stand for the voice of the people; "government" because the decisions of these institutions are carried out by the bureaucracy of the state. I want to distinguish between challenges to the "democratic" element of this ideal type—that representative institutions can claim to speak for the voice of the people—and challenges to the "government" element—that policies are implemented in a top-down manner.

The challenge to the claim of representative institutions of modern democracies to stand for the voice of the people is twofold. The first part is conceptual: the increased complexity of modern society puts pressure on the very idea of a unified "people" with a single "voice" that underlies traditional democratic theory. The model of a small closed community—where the decisions of the governing body affect the members of the community and no one but them—has little resemblance to the global and interconnected nature of today's societies (Held 1995).

The second part is political: despite a system of "one person, one vote," many argue that modern democracies are tilted toward wealth and social power. I will not elaborate here on these familiar claims (for the case of the USA, see Winters and Page 2009).

The second challenge is to the understanding of policy-making and implementation that focuses on a government that governs. Studies in public policy suggest that policy-making should not be viewed as a top-down process. Instead, such studies use the term "governance" to describe situations in which policy decisions and, even more so, policy outcomes, are the product of complex interactions between different groups within and outside government (and that the distinction between what counts as inside and outside government is itself becoming more blurred). The scholarly work on governance originated from a set of processes that took place at an accelerated pace beginning in the early 1980s. These processes shifted organizational and decision-making power away from government into the hands of private and civil society organizations. These organizations mainly interact with government agencies and among themselves through the mechanism of the market and through policy networks (Bevir and Rhodes 2003, 2006; Rhodes, Chapter 3, this volume). In our context, it is important to keep in mind that for the most part the battle cry of these policy reforms was "efficiency" and not "democracy."

The very rationale of decision-making in an environment of governance is different from that of government. The legitimacy of democratic decision-making does not emerge simply from counting votes but from the institutional spaces where the interest of the public can be articulated through exchange of reasons both about the topics of the day and about the fair procedures for resolving conflicts and reaching decisions (see Urbinati 2006). What we count as the voice of the people always depends on the institutions through which it is expressed. Democratic government is based on the discursive logic of deliberations and the procedural logic of elections. When decisions about policies and their implementation are made in collaboration with markets and policy networks, they follow different logics. Markets operate based on procedural rationality that is based on preferences rather than on reasons (Elster 1997). Networks "make decisions and regulate various issues in and through negotiations between interdependent and autonomous actors that might facilitate negative or positive coordination" (Sørensen and Torfing 2005: 198). Thus, the main feature of the decision-making environment of governance, which I describe as the loss of agency, is that there is no single institutional player with the capacity to make decisions or implement them.

Generally speaking, the response of democratic theorists who want to hold on to the notion of democratic legitimacy is to develop a complex understanding of democratic legitimacy that corresponds to the complexity of modern societies. In this complex view, the burden of democratic legitimacy cannot fall on one institutional setting (such as a parliament) that generates one voice on behalf of the people. Rather, it requires a multilayered and diverse set of institutions that would allow democratic voices rather than one voice (Bohman 2007). Furthermore, democratic legitimacy requires engaged citizens who take an active part in the discussions about the rules that shape their own lives, and therefore it requires the blurring of the distinction between government and civil society. The model of complex democratic legitimacy serves as an ideal against which to understand the "deficits" of current democratic institutions.

Now, some scholars use the term democratic governance to describe the ideal of complex democratic government (Hirst 1994; Cohen and Rogers 1992; Elstub 2008; Sørensen and Torfing 2005; and, in a different context, de la Porte and Nanz 2004). I believe that the use of the term democratic governance in this context is misleading. Such an ideal of complex democracy would not be an instance of democratic governance but rather one of democratic government properly understood. Indeed, democratic legitimacy requires the blurring of the fault lines between government and civil society, and the disentanglement of powerful centralized authority: processes that are similar to what happens in systems of governance. However, their modus operandi is different. In a complex system of democratic government, the various institutions of voice interact with each other mainly based on agreed-upon procedures whose reasons are subject to scrutiny and deliberations and not, as in systems of governance, mainly based through bargaining and markets. Again, we need to attend to the speech act of affixing democratic to governance. Initiatives where policy-makers encourage themes like empowered participation, focused deliberation, and attentiveness to those affected by decisions (what Mark Warren 2009: 3, describes as "governance driven democratization") can be designed to perform different functions. They can intend to ensure that government follows the voice of the people, and be designed accordingly, and in that case they should be understood to be part of democratic government. However, they can perform other functions such as ensuring efficient delivery of services, appeasing powerful stakeholders and removing objections, or creating an aura of legitimacy. While these latter practices of governance are not necessarily antidemocratic and can fit within an overall democratic system, there is no reason for them to be dubbed democratic (Papadopoulos, Chapter 36, this volume; Klijn and Skelcher 2007).

Thus, I want to reserve the term *democratic* governance to democratic practices that take place in a public administration environment that is based on the principles of governance. In such an environment, the discursive and procedural logic that governs democratic voice-making does not have priority over the procedural logic of the market and the bargaining logic of the governance network. The voice of the people does not have any preferred status in the system of decision-making. The people have to "play" with other participants in the "game" of governance.

Democratic societies allow organizations that seek to represent the interests of common people or of vulnerable groups to participate in the "game" of governance. They can engage in demonstrations, negotiate with the chamber of local businesses, or rely on the power of their constituencies as consumers (Bevir and Trantmann 2007; Christensen and Lægreid 2011). However, it is not self-evident that groups that claim to stand for the common interest or for vulnerable groups have a valid claim to represent these groups.

Democratic forms of governance are attempts to create space where people can articulate, using democratic procedures, what they take to be their common interest, with the intention of carrying this voice forward by participating in the "governance game" of policy-making and implementation. These institutions of voice seek to participate in the process of governance not in virtue of any political power they possess but in virtue of the legitimacy of the voice that is coming out of the institution.

I want to stress the point that democracy, which I understand as the sovereignty of the voice of the people, requires institutions that allow for the expression of this voice. For this reason, I would caution against understanding all forms of social activism or of citizens' participation as instances of democratic governance (Fischer, Chapter 32, this volume; McLaverty 2011; Bang and Sørensen 1999). To be sure, as I have argued above, social activism and participation are important components of democracy. Given the complexity of modern societies, the burden of democratic legitimacy cannot rest on few representative institutions but must be distributed widely across society. However, social activism and participation are not in themselves democratic. The crucial question is whether the forms of participation or activism can claim to stand for the voice of the people.

2. FOUR FORMS OF DEMOCRATIC GOVERNANCE AND THEIR UNDERLYING MORAL SOCIOLOGY

In the previous section, I defined democratic forms of governance as attempts to participate in policy-making by representing the voice of the people in an environment where there is no guarantee that the voice of the people will prevail. In this section, I want to look in more detail at the reasoning that underlies these attempts and the manner in which they claim to stand for the voice of the people. I do so by examining what I described as the moral sociologies that underlie four different forms of democratic governance.

By introducing the notion of moral sociology, I intend to bring together two important contributions to the theorization of democratic experimentations. First, Archon Fung (2003; also Smith 2009) identifies the relationship between the institutional design of spaces for democracy and their claim for legitimacy. He argues that decisions that might appear as technical or innocuous, such as how participants are selected, how long they meet, or who moderates the discussion, actually have a significant effect on the plausibility of claims for democratic legitimacy of the process.

Second, Robert Goodin and John Dryzek (2006) introduce the notion of a "macro-political uptake" of democratic spaces. They argue that alternative institutions of voice do not operate in a social and political vacuum. To understand the claim of these initiatives to legitimacy, one has to take into account how they are situated vis-à-vis the public sphere at large and other political institutions. Alternative institutions can perform an entire range of functions, such as to have a mandate or have the aspiration to make binding decisions, make recommendations, educate the participants or the public at large, and so on.

I argue that different forms of democratic governance take different aspects of the procedure through which voice is expressed as essential to their claim for legitimacy based on the moral sociology with which they operate. The design of the institution of voice has to be understood in the context of the intended macro-political uptake, which, in turn, depends on the way the institution of voice is understand itself in relation to the broader political and social environment in which it is situated. Thus, the classification of forms of democratic governance that I present below is based on their *claim* to express the voice of the people (Saward 2006). The classification consists of four ideal types of forms of democratic governance. I discuss their view about the legitimacy of the voice that is coming from existing democratic government, their claim for legitimacy, and their understanding of their relationship to government and other powerful players.

Voice as a Supplement: The first form of democratic governance understands the institutionalization of voice as a supplement to the system of government. The moral sociology that underlies this form of democratic governance is the closest to the ideal form of democratic government. In this view, the representative institutions of modern democracy are essentially functioning. Overall, the decisions of the formal representative institutions reflect the voice of the people and that government has the capacity—if it wishes—to see it that these decisions are implemented. Practices of governance supplement an essentially functioning system of government. They are responses to local deficits in democratic legitimacy based on the belief of the capacity of the existing system to rehabilitate itself.

In general, institutions of voice within this form of democratic governance direct their voice toward the agency of the state. Initiatives of this form are likely to be carried out with the support of some officials and even with financial and organizational support from government. The decisions reached by the forum or the summary report of the process are likely to be sent to the government or to other important stakeholders that have the capacity to influence government.

The moral sociology that underlies this form of governance takes the main burden of democratic legitimacy to fall on the representative institutions of democratic government. Since the institutions of governance only supplement existing institutions, the details of the internal working of the institutions are not essential for legitimacy. The main concern of the institutional design is to establish the contention that the recommendations, decisions, or insights that emerge from the alternative institution are not the same as those of any interest group, but that they intend to provide the outcome of a democratic process. It would therefore be essential to provide room for expressing diversity of opinions and procedures to deal, negotiate, or resolve disagreements. The process can claim legitimacy if the "losers" in the process—those whose positions did not carry the day—would still recognize the process as legitimate.

Voice as Corrective: This form of democratic governance seeks to correct for the biases of the voice of the institutions of democratic government, which is understood as failing to represent the diversity of perspectives in society by marginalizing and silencing certain voices. These alternative voices, according to the moral sociology that underlies the institutions of this form, are speaking loud and clear. The problem is that the institutions of democratic government and other powerful players choose not to listen to them. This hearing impairment is not innocuous. The systemic silencing of certain voices in society allows powerful groups to maintain their position of power while claiming democratic legitimacy.

The institutions of democratic governance can perform two functions. First, they can provide a stage for the silenced positions to be expressed (so to make their voice louder). Second, they can provide an alternative site for the formulation of a real dialogue that includes all voices in society. The product of this dialogue can provide policy proposals that will be able to claim wider democratic legitimacy.

To the extent that the sociology underlying this form of governance is accurate, institutions of voice of this form cannot hope to have the same cozy relationship with government and other institutional stakeholders as those who understand their voice as the corrective. Government and other stakeholders do not want to listen. Thus, the purpose of these institutions of voice is to discredit the government's claim for democratic legitimacy and to blow up the democracy-friendly image of other players. For this reason, their impact is highly dependent on their ability to become visible and to be perceived as a legitimate extension of democracy. Once they achieve the required visibility, institutions of this form can hope to be invited to the table to engage in processes of governance on behalf of the people they represent. Their power in the governance process emerges from the alleged legitimacy of the process (and not from any status as an interest group).

Institutions of this form understand themselves as working in a political environment in which there are significant democratic deficits. Therefore, more of the burden of democratic legitimacy falls on their inner working. One key issue for such institutions is the recruitment of participants. If participants are coming only from groups whose voices are marginalized, the voice that is coming out of the institution resembles the voice of an interest group and can lack democratic legitimacy. However, when divisions in society are deep, it may be difficult to get "ordinary" people to meet and discuss with members of marginalized groups. Furthermore, since the discussion is more likely to address the legitimacy of the allocation of power and resources in society (for them, that is the point of having the discussion) the dialogue is likely to become contentious and divisive. There is likely to be more attention given to the procedures for dealing with these divisions and especially to those who demarcate the discussion: which issues are on and which issues are off the table, what phrases can be used, and so on.

Voice as Transformative: Both the forms of democratic governance that see voice as corrective and those that see it as transformative take the voice that is claimed by democratic government as it is practiced in modern democracies to be essentially illegitimate. However, their explanation for the lack of legitimacy is different and it carries different implications for the design of democratic governance. For those who see voice as corrective, power operates by blocking certain views that exist in the public sphere from entering the decision-making arena. For those who see it as transformative, social powers enter into the public sphere itself and shape the very process of opinion formation, particularly through control over the media, advertisement, and the system of education (I follow here the discussion of power in Lukes 2005; see also Ron 2008). Modern democracies do not block free discussion and debate and many times they encourage it. However, these debates take place in an environment in which most participants in these debates are 1) not particularly interested in political issues; 2) have significant gaps in their knowledge about political issues; and 3) understand issues through the narrow frames in which they are discussed in the media.

There are a number of social theories that undergird this moral sociology. Not all of these social theories see the formation of voice as a useful route for rectifying the failure of democratic government (the question is discussed in Young 2001; for elaborations, see Talisse 2005; Fung 2005). Given the topic of this chapter, I refer here only to those who take democratic or deliberative activism to be a viable option for social change (for a theoretical exploration of democracy in radical social movements, see Polletta 2002; Juris 2008). These social theories believe that the creation of spaces for voice is a worthwhile endeavor, even in an unaccommodating political environment, for a mix of three reasons. First, they believe that free and open discussion has the capacity to unsettle deeply held beliefs. Thus, they can make people aware of the inadequacies of the frames with which they discuss social issues and encourage them to develop more adequate ones (see Bohman 2000: 57ff.). Second, there is no legitimate way other than discussion to identify the goals toward which social change should strive. Social activism that is not informed by an active and open discussion with the community it seeks to represent can end up failing to pursue the real interest of the community. Third, carefully planned and executed expressions of voice can ultimately have some political traction even in a hostile political environment.

Typically, these institutions of voice do not try to affect everyday governance in the same way in which the previous two forms do. The transformation they seek to generate is broader and deeper than this or that policy. Therefore, they do not seek to cultivate relationships with official or semiofficial institutions. They see themselves as working with and speaking to the public. However, their position vis-à-vis the public is complex (and even paradoxical). They do not seek to provide a voice for the public as it stands now. Rather, they are seeking to represent the voice of the public as it could be had it had the chance to engage in free deliberation. The institution of voice can be understood as a laboratory for social activists to discuss with the public the viability and desirability of ideas and policies that are outside the boundaries of conventional discourse.

The design of transformative institutions has to face two zones of tension. The first is the choice of participants. These institutions expect participants to undergo some "transformation" as a result of the process. To the extent participants are aware of the nature of the institution of voice and of this expectation prior to participating in the institution, they are already somewhat committed to the goal. This does not mean that the process is not important and that no meaningful transformation can take place. Nevertheless, the *democratic* credentials of this process are questionable. Members of the congregation can undergo significant transformation when listening to an effective preacher, but preaching to the converted is not the same as preaching to nonbelievers. As a consequence, the more the participants are being transformed, the less they stand for other people in their community.

The second zone of tension is the learning process. The process that takes place in the institutions of democratic governance provides legitimate outcome in part because participants get the opportunity to be exposed to information, knowledge, opinions, and expertise that they do not have otherwise. However, transformative institutions understand themselves to operate in an epistemic and discursive environment that is already structured in a way which makes existing power relations appear legitimate and part of the commonsense order of the world (for a discussion of hermeneutic injustice see Fricker 2007; Morgan-Olsen 2010). The entire point of these institutions is to unsettle this perception. Therefore, they do not see themselves as obliged to follow any principles of neutrality and offer an equal chance for all relevant voices to be heard. However, to the extent that the conversation is constrained by the information and expertise that are provided or by implicit or explicit boundaries on the scope of the discussion, then it becomes harder to make the distinction between real democratic transformation and brainwashing.

Voice as Participation: So far, I presented the three moral sociologies in a way that ties together the systemic failure of democratic government and the existence of social power. In particular, for the moral sociologies of those who understand voice as corrective or transformative, there are causal relations (albeit complex ones) between the failure of democracy and the dominance of certain groups in society. However, it is possible to identify a different moral sociology in which the failure of democratic government is not the product of power but rather of historical contingencies, increasing complexity, the education system, and other factors. In this view, democratic government needs to undergo fundamental changes so that it can provide multiple spaces for wider participation and public deliberation; what prevents these changes from occurring are timid conceptions of citizenship and not asymmetries of social power. Democratic governance is needed to demonstrate the possibility and plausibility of wider and more informed public participation. According to this moral sociology, the problem with those who see democratic governance as corrective or transformative is that they have fallen prey to the "blame fallacy," which asserts that whenever "something did not turn out as intended, someone must be to blame" (Dowding 1996: 16). They unnecessarily understand themselves as operating in a hostile environment and cut themselves some unjustifiable slack when they set the procedures for the institutions of voice.

For this moral sociology, even though the failure of democratic government is systemic and not local, there is no reason why democratic governance should not seek to appeal to the agency of government. Institutions of democratic governance of this form see themselves as providing a model and a laboratory for what democratic government should emulate. Institutions of this form will be careful to maintain the integrity (if not the purity) of internal procedures such as random sampling, inclusion of all relevant positions, and neutral moderation. The belief is that good examples of the promise of wider public participation can be replicated, and, in the long run, become part of democratic government.

The main zone of tension for this moral sociology is the question of significant change in the views of the participants. It is not hard for those who understand voice as participation to explain how participants changed their position on questions on which they did not have any strong knowledge or opinion beforehand (such as in the cases of forums that address the legitimacy of technological innovations). However, if we move from topics that are at the periphery of the attention of the public toward its center, it becomes harder to explain why citizens would significantly change their minds. If the epistemic and discursive environment is not structurally biased, then there is no reason to expect citizens to arrive at views that are different from those arrived at by their representatives. But if there is no reason to hold such an expectation, it is not clear why there is a need to resort to governance in the first place.

3. CONCLUSION: GOVERNANCE AND DEMOCRACY

Numerous experiments of very different sorts are taking place these days that integrate citizens and civil society organizations into the process of policy-making and implementation. Some of these take place within government, some outside government, and many are hybrid. I have argued that, to the extent that participants in these initiatives can expect the recommendations or decisions that are made to carry the day in the following stages of implementation, these initiatives should be understood to be part of democratic government and that any conception of democratic government that fits the complexities of modern society must provide plenty of room for such initiatives. To be sure, many times, despite the expectations of participants, some of these initiatives end up not carrying the day. Their recommendations or decisions are ignored or are subverted by other powerful players. This is another indication that democratic government can be democratic only in name.

However, other experiments seek to get citizens involved and to form what they take to be a legitimate expression of the voice of the people, knowing that there is no expectation that their voice will be heard or that the reasons they provide will be engaged with. These experiments are forms of democratic governance. But are they truly democratic? Do they really express the voice of the people? Rather than sketching a normative ideal of democratic governance, I have tried in this chapter to address this question by comparing the different claims that institutions of democratic governance make for their democratic legitimacy, the presuppositions of each form, and the challenges that each form has in claiming democratic legitimacy.

Table 33.1 Four forms of democratic governance and their underlying moral sociology

	Voice as a Supplement	Voice as Corrective	Voice as Transformative	Voice as Participation
Why Democratic Governance?	Democracy is essentially functioning. Problems are local and are related to the fixation tendencies of existing institutions. Alternative voice allows for expertise, innovation, fresh solutions.	Problem of representation. Existing democratic institutions systemically silence certain voices in society. The silencing maintains the power of the groups that are represented. Alternative voice needed to ensure that the authentic voice of the people is heard.	Problem in the process of opinion formation in society. Existing democratic institutions operate within a public sphere that is dominated by forces that suppress real meaningful discussion on social issues. Alternative voice needed for people to be able to recognize their real interests.	Democratic institutions of representation are insufficient without robust public discussion and participation. For historical reasons, modern democratic institutions were developed in a way that closed venues of public participation. These reasons are not related to asymmetries of power. Therefore, to transform democratic institutions there is no need to overcome or transform actual resistance but only to provide good workable models.
Form of cohabitation with government.	Speaking directly to formal authorities.	A display of the illegitimacy of the formal institutions of voice, directed both to formal authorities and to other players in the game of governance.	Typically in opposition to formal institutions. A laboratory for discussion of ideas and policies that lie outside the boundaries of conventional discourse.	The purpose is to provide workable models of democratic policy-making that can be picked up and adopted by other participants in the governance process (government, businesses, civil society).
The internal design of the institutions of voice and the burden of legitimacy.	Overall, weak burden of legitimacy. Avoiding the appearance of being an interest group. Focus on the unique expertise of participants. Focus on innovation, freshness, maverickness.	The main burden falls on the representation of the diversity of voices in society. Can seek to provide a space for all voices in society or only for the voice of the marginalized.	Tension between legitimacy and the appearance of legitimacy. The choice of participants: preaching to the converted vs recruiting ordinary people. The role of the moderator: education vs indoctrination.	Participants have to be a representative sample (of some sort). Emphasis on appearing neutral and impartial. In core issues, difficulty in accounting for significant divergence from the status quo.

NOTE

* I would like to thank David Levi-Faur and Frank Fischer for their helpful comments on an earlier version of this chapter, and Julia Ketchum for editorial assistance.

REFERENCES

Bang, H. and Sørensen, E. 1999. The everyday maker: A new challenge to democratic governance. *Administrative Theory and Praxis* 21: 325–342.
Bevir, M. and Rhodes, R. A. W. 2003. *Interpreting British Governance*. New York: Routledge.
Bevir, M. and Rhodes, R. A. W. 2006. *Governance Stories*. New York: Routledge.
Bevir, M. and Trantmann, F. (eds.) 2007. *Governance, Consumers and Citizens: Agency and Resistance in Contemporary Politics*. Basingstoke: Palgrave Macmillan.
Bohman, J. 2000. *Public Deliberation: Pluralism, Complexity, and Democracy*. Cambridge, MA: MIT Press.
Bohman, J. 2007. *Democracy across Borders: From Dêmos to Dêmoi*. Cambridge, MA: MIT Press.
Christensen T. and Lægried, P. 2011. Democracy and administrative policy: Contrasting elements of new public management (NPM) and post-NPM. *European Political Science Review* 3: 125–146.
Cohen, J. and Rogers, J. 1992. Secondary associations and democratic governance. *Politics and Society* 20: 393–472.
de la Porte, C. and Nanz, P. 2004. The OMC: A deliberative-democratic mode of governance? The cases of employment and pensions. *Journal of European Public Policy* 11: 267.
Dowding, K. 1996. *Power*. Buckingham: Open University Press.
Elster, J. 1997. The market and the forum: Three varieties of political theory. In J. Bohman and W. Rehg (eds.), *Deliberative Democracy: Essays on Reason and Politics*. Cambridge, MA: MIT Press, 3–34.
Elstub, S. 2008. *Towards a Deliberative and Associational Democracy*. Edinburgh: Edinburgh University Press.
Fricker, M. 2007. *Epistemic Injustice: Power and the Ethics of Knowing*. Oxford: Oxford University Press.
Fung, A. 2003. Survey article: Recipes for public spheres: Eight institutional design choices and their consequences. *The Journal of Political Philosophy* 11: 338–367.
Fung, A. 2005. Deliberation before the revolution: Toward an ethics of deliberative democracy in an unjust world. *Political Theory* 3: 397–419.
Goodin, R. E. and Dryzek, J. S. 2006. Deliberative impacts: The macro-political uptake of mini-publics. *Politics Society* 34: 219–244.
Held, D. 1995. *Democracy and the Global Order: From the Modern State to Cosmopolitan Governance*. Stanford, CA: Stanford University Press.
Hirst, P. Q. 1994. *Associative Democracy: New Forms of Economic and Social Governance*. Cambridge: Polity.
Juris, J. S. 2008. Spaces of intentionality: Race, class, and horizontality at the United States Social Forum. *Mobilization: An International Journal* 13: 353–372.
Klijn, E. and Skelcher, C. 2007. Democracy and governance networks: Compatible or not? *Public Administration* 85: 587–608.

Lukes, S. 2005. *Power: A Radical View*, 2nd ed. New York: Palgrave Macmillan.

McLaverty, P. 2011. Participation. In M. Bevir (ed.), *Sage Handbook of Governance*. London: Sage., 402–418.

Morgan-Olsen, B. 2010. Conceptual exclusion and public reason. *Philosophy of the Social Sciences* 40: 213–243.

Polletta, F. 2002. *Freedom Is an Endless Meeting: Democracy in American Social Movements*. Chicago: University of Chicago Press.

Rawls, J. 1999. *Collected Papers*. Cambridge, MA: Harvard University Press.

Ron, A. 2008. Power: A pragmatist, deliberative (and radical) view. *Journal of Political Philosophy* 16: 272–292.

Saward, M. 2006. The representative claim. *Contemporary Political Theory* 5: 297–318.

Skinner, Q. 1973. The empirical theorists of democracy and their critics: A plague on both their houses. *Political Theory* 1: 287–306.

Smith, G. 2009. *Democratic Innovations: Designing Institutions for Citizen Participation*. Cambridge: Cambridge University Press.

Sørensen, E. and Torfing, J. 2005. The democratic anchorage of governance networks. *Scandinavian Political Studies* 28: 195–218.

Talisse, R. B. 2005. Deliberativist responses to activist challenges: A continuation of Young's dialectic. *Philosophy Social Criticism* 31: 423–444.

Urbinati, N. 2006. *Representative Democracy: Principles and Genealogy*. Chicago: University of Chicago Press.

Warren, M. E. 2009. Governance-driven democratization. *Critical Policy Studies* 3: 3–13.

Winters, J. A. and Page, B. I. 2009. Oligarchy in the United States? *Perspectives on Politics* 7: 731–751.

Young, I. M. 2001. Activist challenges to deliberative democracy. *Political Theory* 29: 670–690.

CHAPTER 34

....

THE NEW CITIZENSHIP AND GOVERNANCE: ALTERNATIVE INTERSECTIONS

....

SUSAN D. PHILLIPS[*]

THE idea that the nature of governing has shifted away from "a hierarchic or bureaucratic state to governance in and by networks" (Rhodes, Chapter 3, this volume) is now widely accepted, even to the point where it can animate a volume of this scope and size. In this new "governance" the boundaries between public and private have become blurred, and practice increasingly blends "features of state, market, and community" (Bevir 2011: 16). Our conventional analytical tools, which have been largely state-centric, need to be recast to make sense of this collaborative, pluralistic, hybrid, and multijurisdictional mode of governing. While the involvement of civil society as a partner is core to the theory and practice of these governance arrangements, few of our analytical tools have much to say about civil society.

What governance needs is a concept of citizenship, one that brings civil society into full view and helps us understand the evolving intersections between civil society and governments. "Civil society" refers to the constellation of voluntary associations, non-profits, charities, social movements, social enterprises, and advocacy organizations in a political community—here collectively called "civil society organizations" (CSOs). For analytical purposes, it is helpful to think of this diverse set of organizations as a "sector," often referred to as the "voluntary and community" or "third" sector—whether or not the actors see themselves as a unified "sector"—because it impels us to consider structure as well as agency as factors in the construction of citizenship.

The contemporary concept of citizenship has moved beyond a narrow notion of a legal right to a passport based on nationality to a framework for assessing the reciprocity of relationships among citizens and between citizens and the state as well as the mix of responsibilities between the state, market, and community. In particular, the "new citizenship" emphasizes the important roles that CSOs play as places for the participation of citizens as political actors. At the same time, these organizations are more heavily involved in the delivery of services in increasingly mixed economies. Their multiple roles as comanagers of services, partners in governance, and vehicles for participation often do not sit easily with each other, however.

This chapter explores the intersections of citizenship and governance. It begins by examining the concept of social citizenship and provides a brief assessment of unfolding changes in civil society. It then takes a closer look at the enthusiasm for governance, contending that theory has gotten ahead of reality, in part because the attention paid to collaboration has masked other significant aspects of contemporary government, some of which are closing rather than opening spaces for engagement with civil society. In exploring intersections in the third section, it is evident that citizenship and governance are not necessarily mutually reinforcing in ways that readily open paths for CSOs to be the governing partners the literature wants them to be.

WHAT'S NEW IN CITIZENSHIP?

The traditional, and still dominant, view of citizenship focuses on the conferral by nation-states of certain civil and political rights on individuals who legally qualify as citizens (Isin and Turner 2002; Schuck 2009). This narrow, legalistic view of citizenship is inherently exclusionary, demarcated by both geography (the sovereign state) and individual qualifications (birth or naturalization). Given that it does not serve well in addressing many of the complexities of diverse, modern societies in a globalized environment, a separate strand of *social citizenship* has flourished since the mid-1990s. The value of this "new," albeit now well-established, approach to citizenship is that it enables us to better understand relationships of civil society with the state.

Social citizenship draws its lineage from British sociologist T. H. Marshall who, in the developmental period of the modern welfare state, was concerned with inequality of access to social benefits, even among full legal citizens. For Marshall (1950), social rights (a modicum of security, education, and economic welfare) have to sit alongside political and civil rights, but formal rights alone do not necessarily achieve equality of benefits. Rather, citizenship requires "a bond of a different kind, a direct sense of community membership based on loyalty to a civilization that is a common possession" (Marshall 1950: 8). Not surprisingly, given the historical context, Marshall looked primarily to the welfare state to ensure that people would be full members of a common community and would receive equal treatment in the distribution of social benefits. The model of social citizenship that has evolved out of Marshall is much less state-centered (see Kymlicka and Norman 1994). It embodies "the bundle of rights and obligations that define the identity of members of a political community, thereby regulating access to the benefits and privileges of membership" (Turner 2009: 66). The sense of belonging and membership in a political community is held together and reinforced through active participation and the exercise of responsibilities by citizens.

Citizenship as engagement is expressed not only, or primarily, through the traditional mechanisms of representative democracy such as voting or joining political parties, but through the relationships of citizens with other citizens, which occurs largely through voluntary participation in CSOs. Here, citizens learn and practice the skills of citizenship—public debate, deliberation, compromise, and accountability—and supposedly develop greater trust for one another and for governments (Putnam 2000; cf. Kymlicka and Norman 1994). Indeed, as Walzer (1991: 104) notes, "the civility that makes democratic politics possible can only be learned in the associational networks" of civil society. And, as proponents would suggest, the more diverse forms of CSOs available the better, including social movements and advocacy groups whose primary goal is policy and social change, non-profits and charities, which are mainly involved in the delivery of services, as well as a broad range of other social/cultural organizations (Waters 2003).

The inclusiveness of these vehicles for engagement is a central concern to social citizenship, in both an analytical and a normative sense: Who is the citizen, and can citizens engage with equal ease? Which citizens are treated as full members of the political community and which are treated as "second-class"? If the citizens are women, for instance, the degree and nature of their engagement may be different than men for a variety of reasons, including historical limitations on political rights and access to power, caregiving responsibilities, and socialization (see Jenson 2009; Lister 2007; Phillips 1991 as part of the major contribution of feminist/gender analysis to citizenship).[1] Gender is, of course, not the only basis for inclusion/exclusion. Indeed, Banting (2010) argues that one of the most difficult challenges facing Western democracies is how to reconcile increasing levels of ethno-cultural diversity with a common sense of identity so as to maintain broad public support and social solidarity.

In contrast to the legalistic view of citizenship, the geographies of political community are not necessarily equated with the boundaries of nation-states. As with the sustainability or human rights movements, the frame of reference may be global, with engagement taking place primarily through organizations that are transnational in nature. Alternatively, the political community could be quite local, such as the neighborhood or city, a trend that is currently being reinforced by the Big Society in England and various brands of a "new localism" elsewhere (Brenner 2004). And, like governance, citizenship may be multilayered: citizens may have more than one scale of identity and sphere of participation, and different scales may be interconnected in the ways issues are framed and political strategies constructed (Desforges, Jones, and Wood 2005; Mahon 2006). In addition, as Dutton (Chapter 41, this volume) observes and the 2011 contagion of activism in the Arab world vividly demonstrated, the rise of the "fifth estate," Internet-enabled online social networking, has revolutionized the ability of citizens to engage other citizens, enabling them to take "bottom-up" action that is not place-based and that may both compete with and enhance other institutions of citizenship and democracy by making them more accountable. While the introduction of scale into citizenship has not displaced the primacy of national citizenship, it has added dimensions of pliability and, with it, complexity. It also compels us to look beyond theory to the "spaces and places in which lived citizenship is practised" (Lister 2007: 49) to assess how citizenship is experienced in the light of differing policy frameworks and responsibility mixes and with differential opportunities for civil society to engage in governance.

Although not the sole basis for defining citizenship, the state has by no means become irrelevant to it. Governments use a variety of policy instruments to shape civil society. Through their funding practices governments can stimulate development and build capacity in civil society; they regulate and consult so as to advantage certain types of organizations over others or to constrain advocacy (for example, by regulating which types of organizations are officially recognized as "charities" and able to issue tax receipts, and by putting limits on their political activities); and they may encourage more conservative strategies of collective action over oppositional ones (Goss 2010; Phillips 2006). As with governance, however, the concept of citizenship has evolved with a focus on interdependence—on action through regimes of state and civil society actors. A "citizenship regime" (Jenson and Phillips 1996; Jenson 2009) embodies the mix of responsibilities between state, the market, family, and community, and the institutional arrangements and processes that give access to the state and to various services and that promote the representation and engagement of different sets of actors.

Civil society as part of a citizenship regime

In varying mixes, CSOs play three key roles in citizenship regimes. As *voluntary* organizations, they are vehicles for participation and, more specifically, as private self-governing organizations, they require at least some citizens to take leadership roles (Warren 2001). Second, they represent and advocate for interests, identities, and causes, and push both state and society for change, sometimes working in the new spaces of governance in a collaborative fashion but often mobilizing in opposition to government (Taylor, Howard, and Lever 2010). In this *representative* capacity, the question of who they represent is a central question: How connected are they to members? How diverse are their boards, and do they give voice to marginalized citizens? Third, as part of a mixed economy CSOs deliver services, either on behalf of governments or independent of them, making their staff and volunteers the real "street-level bureaucrats."

Whether civil society in any given political community is an activist and inclusive space, and how it manages the mix of responsibilities is an empirical question, not a normative assumption. There is often both an organizational and sectoral tension in balancing advocacy and service provision, a dynamic in which governments can have a significant influence (Frumkin 2002; Phillips forthcoming). Because most CSOs cannot sustain themselves on membership dues alone, and governments and donors are reluctant to fund advocacy, many advocacy groups get driven into services and projects as a means of survival. More extensive and sophisticated service provision often produces greater professionalization, leading to the classic bureaucracy versus democracy dilemma (Smith and Lipsky 1993). So, too, does more sophisticated advocacy, as the professionalization of research and lobbying often reduces attention to members and collective action (Skocpol 2003). The tension also plays out at a sectoral level as a growing gap between advocacy-oriented organizations, especially those willing to use protest tactics, and those providing services, often in very cooperative, comanagement relationships with governments (Phillips forthcoming). It is also producing increased hybridization as CSOs innovate with more sustainable financing models and flexible organizational forms, producing an increasingly complex mix of social enterprises, for-profit subsidiaries of non-profits, affiliated foundations, joint ventures, and so on (Brandsen, van de Donk, and Putters 2005; Evers and Laville 2004; Skelcher 2005; Smith 2010).

The collective capacity of CSOs to be inclusive largely depends on both the vertical and horizontal structure of the sector: on whether federations and other infrastructure organizations provide cross-scalar integration to connect the local to the national (and perhaps transnational), and whether diverse networks serve as sources of ideas, research, financing, or influence. A complicating ingredient to these networks is that many of the participating CSOs are competitors, increasingly so as government funding became more restrained. However, competitive and fragmented markets for services or representation by CSOs are now being seen by many governments (and by foundations and citizens) as inefficient, thus raising questions of the need for rationalization of CSOs (Smith 2010).

All of this has put pressure on public policy to modernize legal and regulatory frameworks and develop more innovative, flexible financing instruments. Many of these frameworks and instruments are still premised on a traditional model of charity, which is substantially dedicated to "charitable" services and is inherently local in nature, working within the confines of the nation-state. The extent to which governments have responded effectively to these challenges varies greatly (Phillips and Smith 2011).

WHAT'S NEW IN GOVERNANCE?

The case for a transformation in the mode of governing to one that is collaborative, participatory, and networked, operating in a globalized context, is well articulated in many chapters in this volume and does not need to be repeated here. It is easy to get caught up in the enthusiasm for the possibilities of this mode of governing, and it is no wonder there are few dissenting voices. But, there are a few. For example, in assessing state–civil society relationships in Continental Europe, Bode (2011) provides a correction to the anglo-centric notion that the markets created under New Public Management (NPM) in the 1980s and 1990s have gradually given way to collaboration and networks. The more accurate picture in much of Europe is that a creeping marketization has found its way into existing forms of collaboration—corporatism—producing a similar result to most anglo countries but with a different narrative and dynamic. In the US, Hill and

Lynn (2005; see also Lynn 2010; Considine and Lewis 2003) have put governance to one of its few empirical tests. Their research indicates that, although there is a diversity of experimentation, there is little evidence of a uniform transformation to collaborative governance, and hierarchy remains quite firmly entrenched. From the perspective of a small but growing group of neo-Weberian scholars (see Drechsler 2005), the persistence of bureaucracy is not seen as a cause for regret or reform, but as the way forward, subject to some modifications. In effect, just as the concept of citizenship compels us to investigate actual practice, so too should the theory of governance. If we were to examine contemporary governing arrangements across a variety of jurisdictions, a task that is well beyond the scope of this chapter, we would find forces at play that are at least as significant as collaboration and networks for governmental relationships with civil society.

The first of these is the legacy of markets, whether created under NPM or insinuated into corporatism. More than simply being vehicles for creating greater efficiency through competition, they transferred considerable state power, as well as the micropolitics, for the provision of services from governments to CSOs (and private sector firms). Over time, these markets have moved service provision from being stable contractual relationships with relatively few organizations to more fluid and fragmented ones involving many more players (Smith 2010; Dunleavy et al. 2005). An important consequence was the privatization of decision-making about social citizenship—the decisions about who actually gets what kind, level, and quality of services (see McDonald and Marston 2002). The relative invisibility of these tough decisions has enabled many governments to avoid dealing publicly with the full implications of redistribution, leaving challenging issues of allocation and sustainability to CSOs.

The second set of factors pertains to control, which few governments have surrendered to any significant degree. The markets of NPM were, for the most part, highly regulated through various means, and because regulation is a very durable policy instrument, these arrangements have not been easily altered (Levi-Faur 2008). In effect, the market state was also the "regulatory state" (Majone 1997; Jordana and Levi-Faur 2004; Scott 2004; Yeung 2010). Goss (2010) makes a convincing case that the regulations applied to civil society, alongside the resource dependencies of service contracting, have altered the composition of civil society and the distribution of participatory activities of organizations, and this has trickled down to affect the behavior of individuals. One way in which this occurs is through the favorable treatment of charities (which serve others as defined under the law); those that have "political" or advocacy purposes do not qualify, and the advocacy activities of charities are strictly limited. Because charities tend to take a management rather than political stance with their users and "clients," they reinforce clients' roles as passive beneficiaries of services. By placing limits on the right of charities to advocate for policy change, the tax laws deprive these citizens of effective representation, essentially making them second-class citizens. The result, Goss (2010: 132) suggests, has been "to channel civic engagement towards 'safe' charitable behavior, such as giving and service volunteering, and away from risky advocacy activities."

Over the past decade, regulation has morphed into a mixed array of incentive systems, targets, benchmarking, certification, and voluntary codes, among other forms of negotiated soft law (Doern 2007; Levi-Faur 2008; Provost, Chapter 39, this volume). Its reach has extended to both greater regulation *of* private governance (of ensuring the governance systems of private organizations are up to state-determined standards) and greater regulation *by* private governance (through independent third-party certification and other systems of self-regulation). Undoubtedly, the incursion of the state into private governance was driven to a large degree by the spectacular failure of major private firms, from Enron to Lehman's, but it has extended into civil society as well and is forcing CSOs to pay much more attention to and report publicly on their own governance. For example, in justifying the intent of the US Internal Revenue Service (IRS) to become an even more active regulator of tax exempt organizations and, in particular, to ask more questions about their governance and management systems on the annual return that all must file, a senior IRS official noted that governance is a key component of accountability and, while some may think the tax agency should stick to the tax code and "get out of the governance business," the IRS is "in this discussion to stay" (Williams 2010).

Accountability remains a preoccupation for most governments, particularly in a "wikileaks" era of radical transparency and an environment in which politicians' tolerance for risk and the public's tolerance for failure are very low. The accountability imperative has imposed stringent reporting requirements on contracts and other forms of state funding and has forced CSOs to be much more transparent in all aspects of their operations, including fundraising, administrative costs, salaries, and their own governance. Such demands have created administrative burdens for CSOs, particularly smaller ones, often without much real impact on enhancing the quality of outcomes because the focus is on the control and audit of public spending rather than on learning through the meaningful evaluation of results (Smith and Smyth 2010). Many governments have devoted considerable attention in recent years to cutting through the morass of rules on government funding, with fairly limited success. While the interest in accountability has extended to demanding much greater demonstration of outcomes and impact, this too has had limited success due to the inherent difficulties in measuring outcomes in the short-term horizons of most project funding, the strained capacities of CSOs to conduct such evaluation, and little follow-through by governments in making strategic use of evaluation (ACEVO 2010; Shepherd 2010).

The third immutable component of modern governing is security. Although the security state is felt in a variety of ways, perhaps the most consequential for CSOs is the worldwide enactment of anti-terrorism legislation following 9/11. Such legislation is extraordinarily sweeping in its definitions of what kinds of actions could be seen as facilitating terrorism, and draconian in its enforcement mechanisms, potentially with little regard to due process. The real impact may not be in its direct application, as there have been few prosecutions so far, but in the "shadow of the law," that is, in coping with the fear of the law, which may make CSOs particularly reluctant to engage in international partnerships (Carter 2005: 2).

Finally, governance faces pressures for innovation, either because many long-standing programs are not achieving the expected results or because changing contexts have created new problems. One has only to look to the coalition government in the UK to marvel at how many different policy balls—welfare, family benefits, education, pensions, forestry, decentralization—can be thrown into the air at the same time. As a result of austerity measures, many of these reforms need to be accomplished with no new investment, or indeed with fewer resources, and with very little public tolerance for failure. This pressure on governments has been transferred to CSOs as they are increasingly expected to be major sources of social innovation (Mulgan 2006).

ALTERNATIVE INTERSECTIONS: WHEN GOVERNANCE MEETS CITIZENSHIP

What happens when the evolving forms of governing meet the unfolding patterns of citizenship: Is a particular model emerging that will become the new norm? I argue there is no consistent pattern, rather that three distinct models are possible and are taking root in different places and to varying degrees.

When governance that is collaborative and networked meets an active and engaged citizenry, one would expect them to be mutually *reinforcing*, creating a coequal regime. Such mutual reinforcement does not happen by lucky coincidence, however. In any country where there is any significant degree of reciprocity and mutual support between government and civil society, there is a vision on the part of government, supported by sustained political leadership, that values CSOs as constructive forces in promoting active citizenship and democracy, not just as providers of services (Phillips and Smith 2011). Implementation of this vision depends on a supporting social architecture, which includes: adequate capitalization of CSOs and a diversity of financing instruments; recognition of CSOs using a modern "public benefit" test rather than a narrow, outdated view of "charity," thereby acknowledging advocacy as legitimate; a variety of legal forms that enable hybridization; and appropriate measures of accountability, which make it a tool for learning rather than for mere control and which include mechanisms for

Table 34.1 Alternative intersections of civil society and government

	Type of relationships	
Regulatory	Reinforced	Autonomous
government focus on accountability	reciprocal regime	separate regimes
meta-regulation	government vision for civil society	split scales, transnational
civil society fragmented, weak infrastructure and networks	supporting architecture	limited trust in government
	inclusive, engaged civil society with policy capacity	civil society financially independent

horizontal accountability among governing partners. It also implies that CSOs have developed effective research and policy capacities, means of engaging their members and users so as to bring individual citizens into full citizenship, and both diverse horizontal networks and well-developed vertical integration so as to be able to work across scales.

In reality, reinforcing models have been slow to develop. The UK set off on such a path in the late 1990s under New Labour's Third Way, which promoted active citizenship and led to a package of reforms, including the introduction of compacts to guide sector–government relationships, new charity legislation, and new financing tools. This general route has been continued in England, albeit rebranded, under the coalition government's Big Society, which provides a bold vision for empowered citizenship, scaled to a local level with less controlling national government (Cabinet Office 2010). The implementation of the Big Society programs has been undermined, however, by massive cutbacks to the public sector, so its future remains in question (Barnard 2010).

If the control and security aspects of governing remain dominant, however, a different scenario is likely—that of *regulatory* citizenship. Governments still maintain considerable command-and-control-type regulation of civil society, but have also become more extensively involved in meta-governance, in steering civil society by setting the rules of the game, distributing resources, requiring other actors to take responsibility and self-regulate, and by establishing the narratives that shape the nature of problems to be solved and the kinds of policy instruments deemed appropriate for solving them (see Coglianese and Mendelson 2010; Peters 2010; Rhodes, Chapter 3, this volume; Skelcher and Sullivan 2008). Governments have a freer hand in such steering when civil society is fragmented and its infrastructure organizations are weak, so that CSOs do not see their common interests as a sector. There is considerable evidence that governments are increasingly governing good (private) governance. Recent legislation in several countries (the UK, Ireland, and Canada) concerning charitable fundraising provides a good example: civil society is, in the first instance, expected to effectively self-regulate its fundraising practices, but the government reserves the power to step in if this responsibility is not taken seriously or if self-regulation fails (Breen 2009). In addition, the state regulator has identified in considerable detail the types of planning systems and controls—the good governance systems—that it expects CSOs to have in place.

The state-centric analysis of governance generally assumes a civil society willing to collaborate if given the opportunity, and rarely contemplates a situation in which civil society sees itself as relatively autonomous, leading the construction of citizenship rather than reacting to government policy. Yet, a more *autonomous* form of citizenship may arise under several scenarios. One is as a consequence of effective markets. The long-term use of vouchers in education and social services, which allow citizens to pick their service providers, for instance, means that governments have less control over how CSOs deliver services (Smith and Smyth 2010). If civil society is supported by strong philanthropic institutions and innovative social enterprises that provide alternative sources of funding to service contracting, it is afforded a greater degree of independence of government. In repressive regimes or where public trust in government is limited, citizens may look to CSOs rather than governments for representation as well as for services (Heurlin 2010). The autonomy of civil society is perhaps most evident at the transnational level, where a variety of new forms of collective action are emerging, aided by the fifth estate and the difficulties of meta-regulation by nation-states in this arena.

It is likely that aspects of reinforced regimes, regulatory citizenship, and autonomous action will be present in most countries to varying degrees and with different consequences. To date, however, our theorizing has tended to focus on changes in governments *or* in civil society without serious investigation of the intersections. Yet it is precisely in these intersections that the future for both governance and citizenship will be determined.

CONCLUSION

Governing is in an important transition driven by the need to be more innovative, accountable, and sustainable. The outcomes may produce new forms of governance, yet the current focus on networks and collaboration does not tell the whole story. The framework of citizenship, when joined to governance, offers a vehicle for integrating and understanding many of the evolving changes at the nexus of civil society and the state. This chapter urges both better theory and more sophisticated empirical analysis of this nexus.

Analysis of the intersections of citizenship and governance suggest several major challenges that governments and civil society need to address, both separately and collectively.

Undoubtedly, one is the formation of better partnerships that are more than one-off collaborations but that have the potential to be transformative. We live in a world with expectations of radical transparency, which includes transparency in the governance of private organizations such as CSOs. NPM left a legacy of regulation, but also an explosion of different kinds of regulatory instruments, many of which require complementary and interlocking regimes of state and self-regulation. Pressures for social innovation mean that organizations cannot afford to stand still, continuing to do what they do best in a tried and true manner. While there is an appetite for innovation, governments' tolerance for risk, which is necessarily the flip side of innovation, is generally low. One of the areas of considerable innovation is in organizational form, as a mélange of hybrids are being created that blend aspects of public benefit and entrepreneurship, substantially dissolving the traditional boundaries of public, private, and non-profit. Governments need to figure out how to adapt to, (meta-)regulate, and work with these new entities, which do not fit the old categories of charity versus business and service versus advocacy. Finally, civil society must face its own shortcomings of human capital, leadership succession, inadequate capitalization, and limited financing tools, as well as questions about its effectiveness in representing societal diversity and being truly inclusive.

In sum, the key challenge for governance will be to create or modernize the supporting architecture and develop the appropriate meta-governance—the policy, regulatory, and financing frameworks—that can deal with these rapidly changing realities and new intersections of state and civil society.

NOTES

* My appreciation to Leslie Pal, Amit Ron, and David Levi-Faur for helpful comments on an earlier draft of this chapter.
1. Although a recent empirical study of gender differences across eighteen industrialised democracies (Bolzendahl and Coffé 2009) showed no differences in the emphasis that women and men give to political responsibilities, women were found to put greater weight on the social and civil dimensions of citizenship.

REFERENCES

Association of Chief Executives of Voluntary Organizations (ACEVO) 2010. *High Level Report of the ACEVO Task Force on Better Regulation: Public Impact Centred Regulation for Charities*. London: ACEVO.

Banting, K. G. 2010. Is there a progressive's dilemma in Canada? Immigration, multiculturalism and the welfare state. *Canadian Journal of Political Science* 43: 797–820.

Barnard, H. 2010. *Big Society, Cuts and Consequences: A Thinkpiece*. Discussion Paper, Center for Charity Effectiveness. London: Cass Business School, City University.

Bevir, M. 2011. Governance as theory, practice and dilemma. In M. Bevir (ed.), *Sage Handbook of Governance*. Thousand Oaks, CA: Sage, 1–16.

Bode, I. 2010. Creeping marketization and post-corporatist governance: The transformation of state-nonprofit relations in Continental Europe. In S. D. Phillips and S. Rathgeb Smith (eds.), *Governance and Regulation in the Third Sector: International Perspectives*. London: Routledge, 115–141.

Bolzendahl, C. and Coffé, H. 2009. Citizenship beyond politics: The importance of political, civil and social rights and responsibilities among women and men. *The British Journal of Sociology* 60: 763–791.

Brandsen, T., van de Donk, W. and Putters, K. 2005. Griffins or chameleons? Hybridity as a permanent and inevitable characteristic of the third sector. *International Journal of Public Administration* 28: 749–766.

Breen, O. 2009. Regulating charitable solicitation practices: The search for a hybrid solution. *Financial Accountability and Management* 25: 115–143.

Brenner, N. 2004. *New State Spaces: Urban Governance and the Rescaling of Statehood*. Oxford and New York: Oxford University Press.

Cabinet Office. 2010. "Building the big society." London: Cabinet Office; available at http://www.cabinetoffice.gov.uk/media/407789/building-big-society.pdf.

Carter, T. S. 2005. Charities and compliance with anti-terrorism legislation: The shadow of the law. *The Philanthropist* 19: 43–79.

Coglianese, C. and Mendelson, E. 2010. Meta-regulation and self-regulation. In R. Baldwin, M. Cave and M. Lodge (eds.), *Oxford Handbook of Regulation*. Oxford: Oxford University Press, 146–168.

Considine, M. and Lewis, J. M. 2003. Bureaucracy, network, or enterprise? Comparing models of governance in Australia, Britain, the Netherlands, and New Zealand. *Public Administration Review* 63: 131–140.

Desforges, L., Jones, R. and Woods, M. 2005. New geographies of citizenship. *Citizenship Studies* 9: 439–451.

Doern, G. B. 2007. *Red Tape, Red Flags: Regulation for the Innovation Age*. Ottawa, ON: Conference Board of Canada.

Drechsler, W. 2005. "The rise and demise of the new public management." *Post-Autistic Economics Review* 33 (September); available at http://www.paecon.net/PAEReview/issue33/Drechsler33.html.

Dunleavy, P., Margetts, H., Bastow, S., and Tinkler. J. 2005. New public management is dead—Long live digital era governance. *Journal of Public Administration Research and Theory* 16: 467–494.

Evers, A. and Laville, J. L. 2004. Social services by social enterprises: On the possible contributions of hybrid organizations and a civil society. In A. Evers and J-L. Laville (eds.), *The Third Sector in Europe*. Cheltenham and Northampton: Edward Elgar, 237–256.

Frumkin, P. 2002. *On Being Nonprofit*. Cambridge, MA: Harvard University Press.

Goss, K. A. 2010. Civil society and civic engagement: Towards a multi-level theory of policy feedbacks. *Journal of Civil Society* 6: 119–143.

Heurlin, C. 2010. Governing civil society: The political logic of NGO–state relations under dictatorship. *Voluntas* 21: 220–239.

Hill, C. J. and Lynn, L. E., Jr. 2005. Is hierarchical governance in decline? Evidence from empirical research. *Journal of Public Administration Research and Theory* 15: 173–195.

Isin, E. F. and Turner, B. S. 2002. *Handbook of Citizenship Studies*. London: Sage.

Jenson, J. 2009. Lost in translation: The social investment perspective and gender equality. *Social Politics* 16: 446–483.

Jenson, J. and Phillips, S. D. 1996. Regime shift: New citizenship practices in Canada. *International Journal of Canadian Studies* 14: 11–36.

Jordana, J. and Levi-Faur, D. 2004. The politics of regulation in the age of governance. In J. Jordana and D. Levi-Faur (eds.), *The Politics of Regulation: Institutions and Regulatory Reforms for the Age of Governance*. Cheltenham: Edward Elgar, 1–28.

Kymlicka, W. and Norman, W. 1994. Return of the citizen: A survey of recent work on citizenship theory. *Ethics* 104: 352–381.

Levi-Faur, D. 2008. Regulatory capitalism and the reassertion of the public interest. *Policy and Society* 27: 181–191.

Lister, R. 2007. Inclusive citizenship: Realizing the potential. *Citizenship Studies* 11: 49–61.

Lynn, L. E., Jr. 2011. The persistence of hierarchy. In M. Bevir (ed.), *The Sage Handbook of Governance*. Thousand Oaks, CA: Sage, 218–236.

McDonald, C. and Marston, G. 2002. Patterns of governance: The curious case of non-profit community services in Australia. *Social Policy and Administration* 36: 376–391.

Mahon, R. 2006. Introduction: Gender and the politics of scale. *Social Politics* 13(4): 457–461.

Majone, G. 1997. From the positive to the regulatory state: Causes and consequences of changes in the mode of governance. *Journal of Public Policy* 17: 139–167.

Marshall, T. H. 1950. *Citizenship and Social Class*. Cambridge: Cambridge University Press.

Mulgan, G. 2006. The process of social innovation. *Innovations* (spring): 145–162.

Peters, B. G. 2010. Meta-governance and public management. In S. P. Osborne (ed.), *The New Public Governance? Emerging Perspectives on the Theory and Practice of Public Governance*. London: Routledge, 36–51.

Phillips, A. 1991. *Engendering Democracy*. London: Polity.

Phillips, S. D. 2006. The intersection of governance and citizenship: Not quite the Third Way. *Policy Matters* 7: 8–31.

Phillips, S. D. (forthcoming). Restructuring civil society in Canada: Muting the politics of redistribution. In K. Banting and J. Myles (eds.), *Fading of Redistributive Politics: Policy Change and Policy Draft in Canada*. Vancouver: UBC Press.

Phillips, S. D. and Smith, S. Rathgeb 2011. Between governance and regulation: Evolving government–third sector relationships. In S. D. Phillips and S. Rathgeb Smith (eds.), *Governance and Regulation in the Third Sector: International Perspectives*. London: Routledge, 1–36.

Putnam, R. D. 2000. *Bowling Alone: The Collapse and Revival of American Community*. New York: Simon and Schuster.

Schuck, P. H. 2009. "Three models of citizenship." Yale Law School, Public Law Working Paper No. 168. New Haven, CT: Yale University; available at http://papers.ssrn.com/sol3/papers.cfm?abstract_id=1267356.

Scott, C. 2004. Regulation in the age of governance: The rise of the post-regulatory state. In J. Jordana and D. Levi-Faur (eds.), *The Politics of Regulation*. Cheltenham: Edward Elgar, 145–176.

Shepherd, R. P. 2010. In search of a balanced evaluation function: The state of federal program evaluation in Canada. Paper presented to the International Research Society on Public Management (IRSPM). Berne, Switzerland, April.

Skelcher, C. 2005. Public–private partnerships and hybridity. In E. Ferlie, L. E. Lynn, Jr., and C. Pollitt (eds.), *The Oxford Handbook of Public Management*. New York: Oxford University Press, 347–370.

Skelcher, C. and Sullivan, H. 2008. Theory-driven approaches to analysing collaborative performance. *Public Management Review* 10: 751–771.

Skocpol, T. 2003. *Diminished Democracy: From Membership to Management in American Civic Life*. Norman, OK: University of Oklahoma Press.

Smith, S. Rathgeb 2010. Hybridization and nonprofit organizations: The governance challenge. *Policy and Society* 29: 219–229.

Smith, S. Rathgeb and Lipsky, M. 1993. *Nonprofits for Hire: The Welfare State in the Age of Contracting*. Cambridge, MA: Harvard University Press.

Smith, S. Rathgeb and Smyth, J. 2010. The governance of contracting relationships: "Killing the Golden Goose". In S. P. Osborne (ed.), *The New Public Governance? Emerging Perspectives on the Theory and Practice of Public Governance*. London: Routledge, 270–300.

Taylor, M., Howard, J., and Lever, J. 2010. Citizen participation and civic activism in comparative perspective. *Journal of Civil Society* 6: 145–164.

Turner, B. S. 2009. T. H. Marshall, social rights and English national identity. *Citizenship Studies* 13: 65–73.

Walzer, M. 1991. The civil society argument. *Dissent* (spring): 293–304.

Warren, M. E. 2001. *Democracy and Association*. Princeton, NJ: Princeton University Press.

Waters, S. 2003. *Social Movements in France: Towards a New Citizenship*. Basingstoke: Palgrave Macmillan.

Williams, G. 2010. IRS continues its focus on governance matters, official says. *Chronicle of Philanthropy*, 22 April; available at http://philanthropy.com/blogPost/IRS-Continues-Its-Focus-on/23358/.

Yeung, K. 2010. The regulatory state. In R. Baldwin, M. Cave, and M. Lodge (eds.), *Oxford Handbook of Regulation*. Oxford: Oxford University Press, 64–83.

....

CHAPTER 35

COLLABORATIVE GOVERNANCE

....

CHRIS ANSELL

COLLABORATIVE governance is a strategy used in planning, regulation, policy-making, and public management to coordinate, adjudicate, and integrate the goals and interests of multiple stakeholders. In its narrowest sense, collaborative governance is a technique used to resolve conflict and facilitate cooperation among public agencies, interest groups, and citizens. As a technique, it is often used in high-conflict situations, such as those that arise in natural resource disputes or in divisive rule-making. It is also used as a technique to bring citizens and stakeholders together around common projects or agendas, such as community health improvement or educational reform. In a more ambitious sense, however, collaborative governance refers to a strategy for reconstructing democracy along less adversarial and managerial lines. From this perspective, collaborative governance can transform the way that the state interacts with citizens and non-governmental organizations. As a strategy of democratic reconstruction, collaborative governance seeks to restore trust in government and expand democratic consent by deepening participation and deliberation in public affairs.

Definitions of collaborative governance can vary along a number of dimensions, including (1) who collaborates; (2) who sponsors collaboration; (3) what the term collaboration means; and (4) how collaboration is organized. Rather than assume a single authoritative definition of collaborative governance, it is useful to start with a fairly general definition and then to treat these dimensions as "scope conditions." Ansell and Gash define collaborative governance as:

> A governing arrangement where one or more public agencies directly engage non-state stakeholders in a collective decision-making process that is formal, consensus-oriented, and deliberative and that aims to make or implement public policy or manage public programs or assets. (2008: 544)

Consider how the elements of this definition might expand or contract depending on each of the four scope conditions:

(1) *Who collaborates?* The definition suggests that public agencies and non-state actors collaborate. This is fairly inclusive. However, some discussions of collaborative governance focus more narrowly on collaboration between public agencies or use the term to refer to collaboration only among non-state actors. The scope of the concept might also be narrowed by defining the term "non-state stakeholders" to include "citizens" but not organized stakeholders. We may also want to widen the scope of who collaborates. State participation, for example, may be widened beyond public agencies to explicitly include legislatures or courts.

(2) *Who sponsors collaboration?* The definition suggests that public agencies initiate and sponsor collaborative governance. This emphasis is useful if attention is being focused on collaborative governance as a form of policy-making. However, it may be too narrow if the goal is to understand community mobilization, because (non-state) community groups sometimes take the lead in initiating collaborative processes.

(3) *What does collaboration mean?* The definition indicates that collaboration "aims to make or implement public policy or manage public programs or assets." One purpose of this definition is to distinguish collaboration from consultation. Public agencies often consult the public about their views, but this may represent little more than a gauging of public opinion. The definition implies that participants must have a concrete decision-making role. Arguably, however, it may be useful to include a wider range of activities under the term collaboration. "Visioning" exercises, for example, have become common at the local level. These exercises do not strictly decide anything, but they may contribute to decision-making.

(4) *How is collaboration organized?* According to the definition, collaboration is "a collective decision-making process that is formal, consensus-oriented, and deliberative." The description is intended to distinguish collaborative governance from various other patterns of cooperation and interaction that can take place between public agencies and the public. For example, some may wish to argue that public hearings are a form of collaborative governance. But public hearings are typically neither consensus-oriented nor deliberative (in the sense of two-way flows of discussion and debate). Informal cooperation between agencies and specific stakeholders would also be rejected by the definition because this cooperation would be neither collective (including all relevant stakeholders) nor formal (publically designated as a collaborative process). Depending on the context and analytical purpose, these criteria may be too restrictive or not restrictive enough.

The concept of collaborative governance is very similar to several related concepts. Collaborative governance shares with "collaborative management" or "collaborative government" the goal of bringing different groups together to facilitate dialogue and cooperation among them. However, the latter concepts are specifically used to stress the importance of bringing public agencies together to increase the efficiency and effectiveness of public management (McGuire 2006). The British term for collaborative management—"joined-up" government—evokes the goal of bringing different government units together to provide better services for the public. The emphasis is on breaking down bureaucratic silos, and hence, on collaboration *within* government. The term "governance," by contrast, focuses our attention on "the changing boundaries between public, private, and voluntary sectors" (Rhodes, Chapter 3, this volume). Collaborative governance typically emphasizes collaboration *between* and *among* public, private, and voluntary stakeholders. Despite these differences in emphasis, these concepts share a common spirit, are sometimes used interchangeably, and often overlap in practice.

Collaborative governance also overlaps considerably with the concept of "network governance." As Rod Rhodes's review of network governance in this volume suggests, both ideas share an image of politics and public management as pluralistic, differentiated, and fragmented. Both point to the relative weakness of vertical, hierarchical authority as a means of achieving cooperation and coordination, stressing instead the relative importance of deliberation, trust, reciprocity, and interdependence. Again, however, the emphasis is somewhat different. "Collaboration" points to adjudicative and deliberative processes among a set of stakeholders working together in a common forum. "Network" stresses a structural relationship of coordination and concertation among a set of stakeholders, who may not be working together in a common forum. Nevertheless, in practice, the concepts often overlap.

As a technique, collaborative governance promises a range of possible benefits. Stakeholders may discover opportunities for mutual gains, improve their understanding of and trust in other stakeholders, pool knowledge and information, enhance the efficiency and effectiveness of coordination, and improve the legitimacy of decisions. But this technique may also incur a distinct set of costs and be limited in its applicability. It may be time-consuming and resource-intensive, produce "least common denominator" agreements, and be plagued by inequities among stakeholders, raising fears of co-optation. Yet it is difficult to judge collaborative governance in some absolute sense as a "good" or "bad" technique for governing. To appreciate its advantages and disadvantages, it must be judged relative to alternative strategies and in specific contexts.

TYPES OF COLLABORATIVE GOVERNANCE

The term "collaborative governance" is a generic one. Concrete experiments with collaborative governance are often described using sector-specific terms, such as community policing, site-based school management, or community health partnerships. It is not possible to fully canvas these more specific literatures in this chapter. However, to give readers a flavor for the range of variation, we can describe three distinct "species" of collaborative governance: collaborative planning, watershed councils, and regulatory negotiation.

Collaborative planning: The governance of land use and development—sometimes called "spatial" planning—can be conceptualized as a collaborative process between planning agencies and stakeholders (Healey 1998). Collaborative planning is typically contrasted with earlier approaches to comprehensive planning, where plans were drafted by planning experts with little input from the public. When these plans moved into the implementation stage, they frequently raised the public's ire and were often shelved. By contrast, collaborative planning emphasizes the place-based character of spatial planning and argues that planning projects are unlikely to be successful unless stakeholders can first resolve their conflicts. Collaborative planning seeks to involve stakeholders directly in the planning process and aims to produce consensus among stakeholders (Innes and Booher 1999; Innes 2004).

Watershed partnerships: Watersheds transcend political jurisdictions and contain many different stakeholders. However, there is an increasing appreciation of the need to manage interdependent activities within watersheds in an integrated fashion. Collaborative governance has become a favored way of organizing this integrated watershed management (Imperial 2005; Weber, Lovitch, and Gaffney 2005; Leach, Pelkey, and Sabatier 2002; Bentrup 2001). Leach, Pelkey, and Sabatier suggest that the typical form of collaborative watershed management is the stakeholder partnership, which consists of "...representatives from private interest groups, local public agencies, and state or federal agencies, who convene as a group, periodically and indefinitely, to discuss or negotiate public policy within a broadly defined area" (2002: 646). Moore and Koontz (2003) distinguish between three types of watershed partnerships—citizen-based, agency-based, and mixed groups. These partnerships engage in a wide range of activities related to watershed management, including restoration, monitoring, integrated planning, education, and advocacy.

Regulatory negotiation: Regulatory rule-making is often a highly contested process. Traditional mechanisms of notice-and-comment rule-making can require considerable investments of agency effort and time, only to end up embroiled in slow and costly legal battles (Freeman 1997; Harter 1982). The difficulty with what is sometimes called "command-and-control" regulation has led public agencies to experiment with an alternative strategy to rule-making known as regulatory negotiation. "Reg-neg," as it is colloquially known, brings stakeholders together early in rule-making processes in order to search for acceptable agreements. Although agencies typically retain the right (and responsibility) to promulgate the new regulations, they can base their decisions on agreements reached by stakeholders in reg-neg processes (Coglianese 1997).

Each of these three "species" of collaborative governance use collaboration as a technique to address problems that arise with traditional or conventional approaches to governing. Collaborative planning and regulatory negotiation both arose in response to the conflicts, delays, and failures of comprehensive planning and command-and-control regulation. Watershed collaboration arose in response to problems of coordination, which stem from the political and institutional fragmentation of watersheds. A common dynamic that links all three types is that participants have considerable incentives to exercise "voice" over "exit" (Hirschman 1970). Collaborative planning and watershed governance are both place-based forms of governance, which often means that stakeholders cannot easily resort to "exit" strategies. Being co-located also tends to accentuate stakeholder interdependence. Therefore, even in situations of high conflict, place-based stakeholders often have a strong incentive to engage with each other—that is, to exercise "voice." Regulatory negotiation is not place-based, but the underlying dynamic is similar. The regulatory process typically makes exit strategies difficult. While a regulated industry may escape new regulations by taking agencies to court, legal proceedings are themselves often lengthy and costly. Losing stakeholders rarely simply disappear, but instead live to fight another day. Thus, stakeholders in regulatory arenas often have an incentive to work together more collaboratively.

Collaborative governance may appear to be a strategy for depoliticizing conflict and, hence, for reasserting the primacy of rationality over politics. Yet that would be a misleading, or at least limiting, conclusion. For the most part, strategies of collaborative governance start from the assumption that stakeholders and citizens have different interests and values and that these differences are legitimate and, at some level, irreconcilable. Models of collaboration do strive to encourage dialogue and cooperation across differences, because they assume that this can produce more desirable outcomes. But no presumption is made that collaboration will yield the "most" rational solution to a problem or reveal the public interest. Instead, advocates for collaborative governance embrace two weaker assumptions about democratic politics. The first is that interests and values are often quite plastic and that dialogue and face-to-face engagement can help to reveal commonalities and opportunities for mutual gains. The second is that political communities are often better off when they build public policy around these commonalities and mutual gains. This discussion brings us to a consideration of collaborative governance as democratic theory.

COLLABORATIVE GOVERNANCE AS DEMOCRATIC RECONSTRUCTION

In collaborative planning, watershed partnerships, and regulatory negotiation, the technique of collaborative governance has been driven by challenges specific to each sector. However, a number of scholars and practitioners see in collaborative governance a more general strategy for democratic reconstruction. For them, collaborative governance represents a different style of democratic engagement with citizens, one that can rejuvenate trust in government by enhancing public participation and deliberation (Newman et al. 2004; Innes and Booher 1999). Booher provides a good summary of the anticipated benefits of reconstructing democracy along collaborative lines:

...the evidence shows that [collaborative governance] can be an effective strategy to address the challenges for democracy imposed by contemporary society. Collaborative governance practice can resolve seemingly intractable public policy conundrums and produce successful policy outcomes. It can also produce important outcomes in addition to agreement. It can increase the capacity of communities, organizations, and individuals to work together in the future to solve collective problems. It can create innovative changes to practice. Finally it can yield new understandings and information to serve as the basis for better decision making in the future. (2004: 43)

Collaborative governance can be portrayed as an alternative to "adversarial" or "managerial" approaches to democracy. Adversarial democracy is fostered by an emphasis on the competitive aspects of democracy, particularly by majoritarian "winner-take-all" electoral rules and institutions, and by reliance on legal strategies of agency oversight and control, such as those that characterize regulatory strategies in the USA. Neither electoral nor legal adversarialism produce many incentives for opposing stakeholders to search for common ground. Managerialism, by contrast, refers to an emphasis on the primacy of experts and expertise in decision-making, to the attempt to clearly differentiate policy-making from administration, and to the goal of keeping agencies free from political influence and corruption. Each of these factors seeks to depoliticize public agencies and improve their efficiency by insulating them from direct public input. Adversarialism and managerialism are, in fact, two sides of the same coin: the more politicized and adversarial decision-making becomes, the stronger the incentive to buffer some decisions and actions from politics.

Collaborative governance seeks to reconstruct both sides of this relationship. On the adversarial side, collaborative governance creates forums that encourage opposing stakeholders to find areas of consensus or compromise. On the managerial side, the goal is to open up the decision-making process to more direct public input. If it is true that adversarialism and managerialism are two sides of the same coin, then agencies will open themselves to public input only if collaborative forums successfully channel adversarial politics into more cooperative directions.

One view of collaborative governance as democratic reconstruction sees it as an extension of "alternative dispute resolution" or ADR (Wondolleck, Manring, and Crowfoot 1996; Susskind and Cruikshank 1987). Collaborative governance draws heavily on mediation techniques developed by ADR, and the ADR profession has been a natural constituency advocating collaboration. As Freeman and Langbein observe of regulation, "Regulatory negotiation proved more popular in alternative dispute resolution circles than among administrative law scholars" (2002: 71). In several respects, however, ADR is an overly restrictive image of collaborative practice. ADR seeks to "resolve" conflict and therefore focuses on settling disputes and moving negotiations forward ("getting to yes" in Fisher and Ury's (1991) memorable phrasing). Collaborative governance, by contrast, is often thought of as a more inclusive process of deliberation, engaging a set of stakeholders beyond the main disputants. Moreover, the scope of deliberation is often wider under collaborative governance. Rather than simply resolve disputes, collaborative governance often strives to establish a platform for longer-term and more open-ended cooperation. While nothing prevents ADR from having these more ambitious goals, the typical ADR process has limited and short-term objectives. It is important to note that a more inclusive, deliberative, long-term, and open-ended process can impose greater demands on stakeholder commitment (Margerum 2002).

A second image of collaborative governance is as a form of "democratic problem-solving," which reconstructs managerialism by engaging broader publics in the policy-making process (Siriani 2009; Weber, Lovitch, and Gaffney 2005; Lasker and Weiss 2003; Bryson, Cunningham, and Lokkesmoe 2002; Andranovich 1995). This image often stresses the increasingly complex and "wicked" character of public problems and the need to bring government, citizens, and stakeholders together to engage in creative problem-solving. It has led Weber, Lovitch, and Gaffney (2005) to analyze the "horizontal" capacity of community groups to engage in problem-solving. To be effective problem-solvers, they argue, communities need social capital and a sustainable institutional framework that facilitates a multidimensional and integrated consideration of community problems.

A third image portrays collaboration as a "partnership" (Leach, Pelkey, and Sabatier 2002; Huxham et al. 2000). Like the image of democratic problem-solving, the partnership image is used to reform or reconstruct managerialism. Many contemporary governance problems, for example, revolve around the fragmentation of public management. Collaborative "partnerships" are used to facilitate interagency cooperation and "joined-up" government (Huxman and Vangen 2000). The term "partnership," however, may also signify a mechanism for expanding public engagement in policy-making. Partnerships may be formed either between public agencies and non-state stakeholders or among different sets of non-state stakeholders, typically for the purpose of pursuing specific projects like community health care improvement or school reform. As Lasker, Weiss, and Miller observe, partnership enables "different people and organizations to support each other by leveraging, combining, and capitalizing on their complementary strengths and capabilities" (2001: 180).

A fourth image of collaborative governance is put forward under the rubrics of "democratic experimentalism" (Sabel and Zeitlin 2008; Dorf and Sabel 1998) and "empowered participatory governance" (Fung 2004; Fung, Wright, and Abers 2003). Like the images of democratic problem-solving and partnership, the experimentalist and the participatory governance literatures envision a direct and expanded role for citizen deliberation in administration and policy-making. What sets them apart from other discussions, however, is their attention to accountability. Both envision the ways in which a transparent and deliberative process among citizens and stakeholders can offer an alternative to more hierarchical, representative forms of accountability.

To understand whether collaboration governance offers a useful framework for participation, deliberation, and accountability, we turn to an examination of the collaborative process.

Process outcomes: factors contributing to collaborative success

Whether used as a technique for addressing specific issues or seen as a basis for more ambitious democratic reconstruction, much rests on whether collaborative processes can actually succeed. Can opposing stakeholders actually work together in a collaborative fashion? Can they get beyond their differences to deliberate in good faith? Can they commit to the process of collaboration? The answer is a cautious "yes," but expectations must be tempered by the difficulty of achieving collaboration. Collaborative governance has often been a strategy of last resort prompted by the recognition that conflicts have become "intractable" or that public problems are "wicked." Therefore, attempts to collaborate are often fraught with opportunities for failure. Consequently, scholars have been particularly attentive to what they often call "process outcomes"—that is, to whether collaborative processes actually succeed at becoming collaborative. Their work has identified many factors that can either undermine collaborative efforts or lead to their success.

One of the major challenges to successful collaboration is whether the agencies and non-state stakeholders are actually committed to the collaborative process in the first place. Public agencies often participate only grudgingly in collaborative processes, feeling their managerial prerogatives are compromised by the need or requirement to collaborate (Ebrahim 2004). In other situations, agencies are internally divided. Top managers may instruct reluctant field staff to collaborate, or, more commonly, field staff collaboration may be undermined by top managers (Yaffee and Wondolleck 2003; Gray 1989).

Stakeholders also vary in their willingness to collaborate (Murdock, Wiessner, and Sexton 2005). One of the factors influencing receptivity to collaboration is a past history of conflict. On the one hand, a history of conflict can leave a legacy of distrust between stakeholders that can erect a barrier to collaboration. On the other hand, stakeholders may come to recognize the value of collaboration only after conflicts have reached a certain level of intensity. Even when this barrier is crossed, weaker stakeholders may be skeptical about participating in collaborative processes, fearing that they will be co-opted or manipulated (Saarikoski 2000).

These deficiencies can be mitigated to some degree by providing weaker stakeholders with additional skills, resources, and information, though power imbalances may still undermine stakeholder commitment. Stronger stakeholders may feel that they have a better chance of getting their way by going it alone (Gunton and Day 2003). The incentives for participation are often determined by conditions that lie outside the process of collaboration. For example, an industry group may be more likely to collaborate if it fears boycotts or legal proceedings from opposing stakeholders or if it worries that governments will otherwise make decisions unilaterally (Frame, Gunton, and Day 2004; Bentrup 2001). Legislative mandates, financial incentives, and recognition of stakeholder interdependence are other factors that may affect collaborative commitment (Margerum 2002; Schneider et al. 2003).

Even when agencies and stakeholders agree to participate in a collaborative process, they may still be deeply suspicious of one another (Weber, Lovitch, and Gaffney 2005). Therefore, collaborative governance may require an active process of trust-building. This is not an easy task in circumstances where stakeholders have an antagonistic relationship. In a study of resource management cases, Beierle and Konisky (2001) found mixed results, with trust increasing in some cases, but staying the same or declining in others. Murdock, Wiessner, and Sexton (2005) found more favorable results for trust-building in their study of six US Environmental Protection Agency (EPA) pilot projects. They found that face-to-face interaction was a key component of positive trust-building.

Leadership is often understood to be a critical aspect of collaborative governance (Page 2010; Ansell and Gash 2008; Huxham and Vangen 2000). Since collaboration is often voluntary and stakeholders have diverse perspectives and interests, leadership must facilitate the exchange of perspectives and assist stakeholders in exploring their mutual interests and concerns. Page (2010) calls this "integrative" leadership. Collaborative leaders must also be able to establish the integrity of the collaborative process by ensuring that stakeholders abide by the "rules of the game." Finally, leaders must often empower weaker stakeholders to participate more fully and authentically in the collaborative process, preventing stronger stakeholders from "running away" with the process. The skills and requirements for effective collaborative leadership can pull in different directions. Collaborative leaders must often establish strong credibility as "honest brokers," while authoritatively intervening to redress imbalances of power and maintain procedural integrity.

The institutional design of collaborative processes is also important. Siriani (2009) has identified eight very general design principles for collaborative governance. These include the principles that 1) citizens should coproduce public goods; 2) community assets should be mobilized; 3) expert knowledge should be shared; 4) citizens should deliberate together; 5) partnerships should be encouraged to be sustainable; 6) assets and governance networks should be strategically mobilized and deployed; 7) institutional cultures should be transformed to support community empowerment and civic problem-solving; and 8) mutual accountability among collaborative partners should be ensured.

The collaborative governance literature has also been attentive to more specific aspects of institutional design. Murdock, Wiessner, and Sexton (2005), for example, found that collaborative processes were more effective when they had clear objectives and adequate technical support. The composition of stakeholder groups is also very important. Generally, the literature supports greater inclusiveness of stakeholders, while acknowledging that larger groups are harder to work with (Margerum 2002; Gray 1989; Susskind and Cruikshank 1987). Most collaborative processes aim for consensus. Consensus rules have the positive attribute of equalizing power among stakeholders, and proponents argue that they create strong incentives for an exploration of mutual interests. Unfortunately, they also have the negative attribute of giving minority groups a veto power and, consequently, critics argue that they produce "least common denominator" outcomes.

Even when stakeholders are committed to the process, when effective leaders are present, and when the design of the process is sound, collaborative processes can still fall short of expectations. For example, collaborative governance processes are often not fully representative of the affected or interested public. As in many participatory processes, individuals or groups with more education, skills, or resources are more likely to become involved and to sustain involvement (Beierle and Konisky 2001). Collaborative governance is also quite time-intensive, because building trust and consensus is naturally time-consuming (Margerum 2002; Gunton and Day 2003). This can make it harder for citizens or groups with fewer resources to remain involved. Once agreements are reached, however, collaborative governance may speed and facilitate policy implementation.

Evaluating collaborative governance

How should we evaluate the success of collaborative processes? Gunton and Day (2003) point to four criteria for evaluating collaboration: 1) success in reaching agreement; 2) efficiency of the collaborative process relative to alternative processes; 3) satisfaction of stakeholders with the process and the outcome; and 4) achievement of other "social capital" benefits such as improved relationships among stakeholders and enhanced stakeholder skills and knowledge. Below, regulatory negotiation is used to illustrate how these criteria can be used as basis for judging process outcomes.

Achieving agreement: As case study evidence shows, adversarial stakeholders can reach agreement in reg-neg processes (e.g. Weber and Khademian 1997). More systematic evidence is, however, scarce. Coglianese (1997) finds that of sixty-nine negotiated rule-making proceedings in the US between 1983 and 1996, thirty-five rules were issued and nineteen were pending. Thirteen reg-negs were abandoned before they reached a consensus, though abandonment did not result from an inability to achieve consensus. In a survey of participants involved in eight EPA regulatory negotiations and six comparable conventional negotiations, Langbein and Kerwin (2000) offer additional insight into the character of negotiation and agreement. They find that participants in reg-negs perceive greater complexity in the issues associated with regulatory negotiation, but participants also felt that reg-negs settled more issues than conventional rule-making processes.

Efficiency: In a study of thirty-five EPA rules produced by regulatory negotiation, Coglianese (1997) found that reg-neg did not produce regulation more quickly and did not reduce litigation when contrasted with conventional regulation. Harter (2000) challenges Coglianese's methodology and argues that a revised methodology produces a more favorable assessment. Langbein and Kerwin (2000) find support for Coglianese's finding that reg-negs are no less prone to litigation than conventional rules. They also find that participants spend considerably more resources on reg-neg than on conventional rule-making. However, 78 percent of their respondents felt that the benefits of reg-neg outweigh the costs.

Stakeholder satisfaction: Langbein and Kerwin (2000) found that participants were significantly more satisfied with reg-neg than with conventional rule-making, primarily because they believed the final rule was better. In a further analysis of this data, Langbein (2002) created a "responsiveness" (satisfaction) index based on the quality of scientific analysis, the use of technology, the efficiency of the rule, the cost-effectiveness of the rule, the implementation of the rule, the overall process, and the net benefits of the rule (for one's organization). She finds that respondents regarded reg-negs as significantly more responsive than conventional rule-making processes.

Social capital and knowledge benefits: The Langbein and Kerwin study (2000) found that respondents were more likely to report learning something new during reg-neg processes than in conventional rule-making. Forty-five percent of respondents reported learning from "other participants" during regulatory negotiation, while 0 percent reported learning from others during conventional rule-making. They also report that participants in reg-negs appear to have a clearer understanding of issues than participants in conventional rule-making.

To summarize this evidence, we can tentatively conclude that regulatory negotiation helps stakeholders achieve agreements in complex disputes. An important benefit of a collaborative approach to regulation is that it produces higher stakeholder satisfaction and more learning than conventional approaches. The evidence for the efficiency of regulatory negotiation, however, is not decisive. An important limitation of this evidence is that it is almost exclusively drawn from regulatory negotiations sponsored by the US EPA.

Conclusion

The first generation of experimentation with collaborative governance has demonstrated "proof of concept," showing that stakeholders can be brought together to work in a collaborative fashion on problems of mutual concern and interest. Many of these experiments have been localized and driven by the needs of specific communities to overcome policy stalemate or wicked problems. These experiments have proliferated in circumstances where public agencies are embattled or where stakeholders are strongly interdependent and have few options for "exit." Under these conditions, even bitterly opposed stakeholders can, with remedial trust-building and skilled leadership, effectively collaborate.

Now that we know that collaborative governance can be usefully employed in some contexts and for some purposes, our attention must turn to whether it is a more general model for reconstructing democratic relationships. Can it be used to mitigate the worst excesses of adversarial democracy or invigorate civic engagement? Does it overcome collective action problems and thus promote better democratic problem-solving? Can it rebuild citizen trust in government? Proponents of collaborative governance are hopeful. However, these are open questions that should guide future research on collaborative governance.

REFERENCES

Andranovich, G. 1995. Achieving consensus in public decisionmaking: Applying interest based problem-solving to the challenges of intergovernmental collaboration. *Journal of Applied Behavioral Research* 31: 429–445.

Ansell, C. and Gash, A. 2008. Collaborative governance in theory and practice. *Journal of Public Administration Theory and Practice* 18: 543–571.

Beierle, T. and Konisky, D. 2001. What are we gaining from stakeholder involvement? Observations from environmental planning in the Great Lakes. *Environmental and Planning C: Government and Policy* 19: 515–527.

Bentrup, G. 2001. Evaluation of a collaborative model: A case study of analysis of watershed planning in the intermountain west. *Environmental Management* 27: 739–748.

Booher, D. E. 2004. Collaborative governance practices and democracy. *National Civic Review* 93: 32–46.

Bryson, J. M., Cunningham, G. L. and Lokkesmoe, K. J. 2002. What to do when stakeholders matter: The case of problem formulation for the African American Project of Hennepin County, Minnesota. *Public Administration Review* 62: 568–584.

Coglianese, C. 1997. Assessing consensus: The promise and performance of negotiated rule-making. *Duke Law Journal* 46: 1255–1349.

Dorf, M. C. and Sabel, C. 1998. A constitution of democratic experimentalism. *Columbia Law Review* 98: 267–473.

Ebrahim, A. 2004. Institutitonal preconditions to collaboration: Indian forest and irrigation policy in historical perspective. *Administration and Society* 36: 208–242.

Fisher, R. and Ury, W. 1991. *Getting to Yes: Negotiating Agreement Without Giving In.* New York. Penguin.

Frame, T. M., Gunton, T. and Day, J. C. 2004. The role of collaboration in environmental management: An evaluation of land and resource planning in British Columbia. *Journal of Environmental Planning and Management* 47: 59–82.

Freeman, J. 1997. Collaborative governance in the administrative state. *University of California Los Angeles Law Review* 54: 1–98.

Freeman, J. and Langbein, L. I. 2000. Regulatory negotiation and the legitimacy benefit. *New York University Environmental Law Journal* 9: 61–151.

Fung, A. 2004. *Empowered Participation: Reinventing Urban Democracy.* Princeton, NJ: Princeton University Press.

Fung, A., Wright, E. O. and Abers, R. 2003. *Deepening Democracy: Institutional Innovations in Empowered Participatory Governance.* Brooklyn, NY: Verso.

Gray, B. 1989. *Collaborating: Finding Common Ground for MultiParty Problems.* San Francisco: Jossey-Bass.

Gunton, T. I. and Day, J. C. 2003. The theory and practice of collaborative planning in resource and environmental management. *Environments* 31: 5–19.

Harter, P. J. 1982. Negotiating regulations: A cure for the malaise? *Environmental Impact Assessment Review* 3: 75–91.

Harter, P. J. 2000. Assessing the assessors: The actual performance of negotiated rulemaking. *New York University Environmental Law Journal* 9: 32–59.

Healey, P. 1998. Collaborative planning in a stakeholder society. *The Town Planning Review* 69: 1–21.

Hirschman, A. O. 1970. *Exit, Voice, and Loyalty: Responses to Decline in Firms, Organizations, and States.* Cambridge, MA: Harvard University Press.

Huxham, C. and Vangen, S. 2000. Leadership in the shaping and implementation of collaboration agendas: How things happen in a (not quite) joined-up world. *The Academy of Management Journal* 43: 1159–1175.

Huxham, C. Vangen, S., Huxham, C. and Eden, C. 2000. The challenge of collaborative governance. *Public Management Review* 2: 337–358.

Imperial, M. 2005. Using collaboration as a governance strategy: Lessons from six watershed management programs. *Administration and Society* 37: 281–320.

Innes, J. E. 2004. Consensus building: Clarifications for the critics. *Planning Theory* 3(1): 5–20.

Innes, J. E. and Booher, D. E. 1999. Consensus building and complex adaptive systems: A framework for evaluating collaborative planning. *Journal of the American Planning Association* 65: 412–423.

Langbein, L. I. 2002. Responsive bureaus, equity, and regulatory negotiation: An empirical view. *Journal of Policy Analysis and Management* 21: 449–465.

Langbein, L. I. and Kerwin, C. M. 2000. Regulatory negotiation versus conventional rulemaking: Claims, counterclaims, and empirical evidence. *Journal of Public Administration Research and Theory* 10: 599–632.

Lasker, R. D. and Weiss, E. S. 2003. Broadening participation in community problem solving: A multidisciplinary model to support collaborative practice and research. *Journal of Urban Health: Bulletin of the New York Academy of Medicine* 80: 14–57.

Lasker, R. D., Weiss, E. S. and Miller, R. 2001. Partnership synergy: A practical framework for studying and strengthening the collaborative advantage. *The Milbank Quarterly* 79: 179–205.

Leach, W. D., Pelkey, N. W. and Sabatier, P. 2002. Stakeholder partnerships as collaborative policymaking: Evaluation criteria applied to watershed management in California and Washington. *Journal of Policy Analysis and Management* 21: 645–670.

McGuire, M. 2006. Collaborative public management: Assessing what we know and how we know it. *Public Administration Review* 66: 33–43.

Margerum, R. D. 2002. Collaborative planning: Building consensus and building a distinct model for practice. *Journal of Planning Education and Research* 21: 237–253.

Moore, E. A. and Koontz, T. M. 2003. Research note: A typology of collaborative watershed groups: Citizen-based, agency-based, and mixed partnerships. *Society and Natural Resources* 16: 451–460.

Murdock, B. S., Wiessner, C. and Sexton, K. 2005. Stakeholder participation in voluntary environmental agreements: Analysis of 10 Project XL case studies. *Science, Technology and Human Values* 30: 223–250.

Newman, J., Barnes, M., Sullivan, H. and Knops, A. 2004. Public participation and collaborative governance. *Journal of Social Policy* 33: 203–223.

Page, S. 2010. Integrative leadership for collaborative governance: Civic engagement in Seattle. *The Leadership Quarterly* 21: 246–263.

Saarikoski, H. 2000. Environmental impact assessment (EIA) as collaborative learning process. *Environmental Impact Assessment Review* 20: 681–700.

Sabel, C. F. and Zeitlin, J. 2008. Learning from difference: The new architecture of experimentalist governance in the EU. *European Law Journal* 14: 271–327.

Schneider, M., Scholz, J., Lubell, M., Mindruta, D. and Edwardsen, M. 2003. Building consensual institutions: Networks and the national estuary program. *American Journal of Political Science* 47: 143–158.

Siriani, C. 2009. *Investing in Democracy: Engaging Citizens in Collaborative Governance.* Washington, DC: Brookings Institution.

Susskind, L. and Cruikshank, J. 1987. *Breaking the Impasse: Consensual Approaches to Resolving Public Disputes.* New York: Basic Books.

Weber, E. P. and Khademian, A. M. 1997. From agitation to collaboration: Clearing the air through negotiation. *Public Administration Review* 57: 396–410.

Weber, E. P., Lovitch, N. P., and Gaffney, M. 2005. Collaboration, enforcement, and endangered species: A framework for assessing collaborative problem-solving capacity. *Society and Natural Resources* 18: 677–698.

Wondolleck, J. M., Manring, N. J., and Crowfoot, J. E. 1996. Teetering at the top of the ladder: The experience of citizen group participants in alternative dispute resolution processes. *Sociological Perspectives* 39: 249–262.

Yaffee, S. L. and Wondolleck, J. M. 2003. Collaborative ecosystem planning processes in the United States: Evolution and challenges. *Environments* 31: 59–72.

CHAPTER 36

THE DEMOCRATIC QUALITY OF COLLABORATIVE GOVERNANCE

YANNIS PAPADOPOULOS

INTRODUCTION: COLLABORATIVE GOVERNANCE AS A FUNCTIONAL REQUISITE AND A DEMOCRATIC GAIN?

THERE is nowadays a widespread perception that public officials do not enjoy sufficient authority, or do not possess sufficient resources to produce legitimate and efficient policy measures by themselves. The diffusion of mechanisms of collaborative governance is then deemed to enhance the governability of modern societies. These mechanisms can be defined as "ways of governing that are non-hierarchical and involve networks of actors, both public and private, determining policy though negotiation, bargaining and participation" (Weale 2011: 58). Collectively binding political decisions are thus formulated or implemented through decisional circuits where nonpublic actors such as interest groups, non-governmental organizations (NGOs), experts, or even private firms are in fact coproducers of public policy.[1] The state loses de facto "its monopoly on collectively binding decision-making and on the production of public goods" (Grande and Pauly 2005: 15), and becomes an authority "manager" (Zangl and Genschel 2008). In a recent piece Blomgren Bingham (2011: 386–388) offers a thorough picture of the actors and processes associated with collaborative governance:

> Governance suggests steering rather than top-down directing...It requires coordination across multiple organizations and stakeholders from public, private, and non-profit sectors that combine in a network to address a common and shared problem...Collaborative governance includes collaboration with the broadest

definition of partners within and outside government, meaning the general public, national, state, regional, and local government agencies, tribes, non-profit organizations, voluntary associations and other manifestations of civil society, business, and other non-governmental stakeholders...Collaborative governance entails shared, negotiated, and deliberative consultation and decision-making.

Collaborative governance can be seen as a response to functional constraints posed by complex—by that meaning, highly differentiated—societies.[2] In fragmented societies, the task of the political system largely consists of arbitrating conflicts between their numerous organized components, such as economic interests, professional groups, and cultural or lifestyle communities. Renate Mayntz (1997) expressed this role eloquently when she portrayed the state as the only legitimate "specialist of the general" (*Spezialist des Allgemeinen*) in such societies. In Mayntz's words, it is widely expected from the state that it conducts the "management of interdependence" of the various social subsystems (such as the economy or the scientific system). This regulatory function is necessary because the actors of each subsystem operate in a self-referential manner, often ignoring or disregarding the negative externalities they cause (such as environmental or safety risks, health problems, etc.). On the other hand, state authorities frequently lack the organizational or financial resources to regulate effectively. In addition, they may lack adequate expert knowledge because the causes at the origin of public problems are uncertain, intricate, controversial, and changing. They also sometimes lack the necessary authority to implement policies because their target groups can oppose ("voice") or escape ("exit") undesired measures. State authorities are thus dependent on resources or support that are provided by other segments of society, and such a weakness allows the latter to become involved in the coproduction of decisions to which they are formally subject.

Collaborative forms of governance can also be expected—at first glance at least—to have, as an indirect positive effect, an increase in the quality of democracy, by including a broader set of nonpublic actors in the policy-making process and by favoring less hierarchical forms of regulation.[3] Referring to deliberative procedures involving ordinary citizens, for example, a leading specialist of the contribution of associations to democracy speaks about "governance-driven democratization" (Warren 2009). Considine and Afzal (2011: 379) suggest that "networks can also be viewed as the practical manifestation of participatory or deliberative democracy in governance structures, where the direct involvement of citizens and community organizations in networks—with public action becoming grounded in their participation and trust—can potentially enhance public sector legitimacy." However, a detailed and critical scrutiny of the compatibility of collaborative governance with the fundamental principles of legitimization of democratic government is necessary. Assessing the democratic quality of collaborative governance especially requires more careful scrutiny of the following characteristics of this mode of policy-making:

- "Horizontal" forms of governance frequently entail the formation of "policy networks" that take charge of the preparation or the implementation of political decisions.[4] The composition of such networks should be taken into consideration, as they usually involve, along with legislators, executive officials, members of the bureaucracy, and experts, as well as representatives of more or less broad interests and of the affected populations ("stakeholders").[5]

- Value conflicts or conflicts of interests are not excluded from policy networks, but interactions therein are mostly driven by a cooperative logic. Decisions are the outcome of deliberative or at least bargaining processes: through deliberation, network members are expected to learn from one another, to develop mutual empathy, and to attain a consensus favorable to the common good, or at least to be able to reach compromises through an exchange of concessions. Whatever the mechanism, a problem-solving orientation is privileged and confrontation is avoided.

- In collaborative governance, policy networks are more or less uncoupled from the institutions of representative democracy, most notably from the parliamentary arena.[6] In addition, networks may lack formalization, and their operating principles are often weakly codified. They are frequently set up in an ad hoc manner and are not visible in the public space, although lack of visibility is a structural feature of networks and should not be attributed to a deliberate strategy of concealment.

This chapter is structured as follows:

The next section analyses the reasons why collaborative forms of governance are likely to cause problems with respect to the democratic quality of policy-making.

Another section discusses to what extent a loss of democratic quality can be compensated for by an improvement in the problem-solving capacity of government and in the quality of political decisions.

In the concluding section, the need for an empirical assessment not only of collaborative governance performance, but also of its democratic credentials is asserted.

"Horizontal" policy-making: more democratic?

Although the aura of collaborative governance is related to an inclination to value participatory decision-making (Mayntz 2008: 47), one should not forget that the primary goal of collaborative decision-making procedures remains instrumental (Bevir 2010: 118). Additionally, a cornerstone of democratically legitimate government is the principle of authorization. Those producing collectively binding decisions should be authorized *ex ante*—through competitive elections—on behalf of those subject to these decisions to act in their name. The principle of democratic accountability also requires that decision-makers provide *ex post* reasons to justify their decisions, that such reasons

be subject to public debate, and that decision-makers be sanctioned if they fail to convince their audiences. It is precisely the shadow of sanctions—and particularly of
removal from office—that is expected to act as a disciplining device, inducing policy-
makers to be responsive to the preferences of policy-takers.

Obviously this is an idealized narrative of the operation of real existing democracies (Papadopoulos 2003: 486–492), and this is amply demonstrated by numerous
indices of a "crisis of representation," such as increasing distrust for political elites,
cynicism with regard to politics, or support for populist anti-establishment parties.
On the other hand, one should seriously consider the risk that collaborative governance accentuates the elitist tendencies in democratic polities. Regarding authorization
ex ante, in governance networks the policy influence of democratically elected politicians is in competition with the influence of actors who enjoy only sector- or issue-
specific electoral authorization (interest group representatives), only very indirect
delegated authorization (members of the bureaucracy), or who do not enjoy any form
of democratic authorization at all (experts). And as we shall see, whether these actors
operate under the shadow of sanctions *ex post* is an open question. As a matter of fact,
the processes of collaborative governance are not immune to the risk of a number of
democratic "deficits."

1) There is first the problem of a possible lack of inclusiveness of governance
networks. This has to be empirically established case by case; for instance, the earlier literature on policy networks[7] used to distinguish between homogeneous, stable, and closed "policy communities" and more pluralist and fluid "issue networks."
However, well-organized interests are in a better position to articulate claims for
participation, and if we think about Mancur Olson's (1965) paradox of collective
action, such interests are likely to be fairly narrow. Narrow interests can organize
themselves more easily than broad interests because they provide more positive
(gains in case of success) and negative (stigmatization of "free riders") incentives
for collective action. Besides, once they have established themselves as network
participants, the representatives of narrow interests will tend to externalize the
costs of decisions to outsiders (Pierre and Peters 2000: 20), and they will probably
also seek to block access to newcomers, in order to protect their "rents."[8] In a subsequent piece Mancur Olson has called such groups of actors "distributive coalitions" (Olson 1982).

On the other hand, public authorities also have instruments that prevent "rent-seeking" behavior. Elected members of the executive branch and unelected members of the
bureaucracy play a leadership role in the so-called process of "meta-governance": they
are the designers of processes of collaborative governance and are in charge of their
management. They have an interest in co-opting encompassing organizations, and can
steer the behavior of the co-opted interests. When an organization is recognized as an
official negotiation partner by the administration, this usually entails advantages for it.
In return, public authorities can require from network participants that they internal-
ize the state logic and objectives (Offe 1981). Network participants are induced to

behave in a responsible way, so that the risks of free riding and particularistic drift can be reduced.

2) This is, however, a double-edged sword, as it can cause another kind of loss of pluralism, not to the benefit of the most powerful, but through "normalization" (Fung and Wright 2001: 34) and predominance of the state logic. Alternatively, it can weaken social movements by splitting them between those that accept compromise and the more radical actors who refuse it or who are considered as unrealistic. The constraints of deliberation may also lead to such a loss of pluralism. It has been argued, for example, that the norms of deliberation (such as the use of rational arguments or of moderate discourse) favor those actors who are able to comply with them (Sanders 1997). Furthermore, the decline of social pluralism may be accompanied by a decline in intraorganizational pluralism, too. As established by the literature on "neo-corporatism," the cooperative "logic of influence" that animates organizational elites participating in policy-making tends to prevail over the "logic of members" (Schmitter and Streeck 1999). More importantly, representation and accountability relations may be unclear (Papadopoulos 2010): in policy networks, as in society at large, a multitude of representatives "claim to represent a wide variety of goods: human rights and security, health, education, animals, rainforests, community, spirituality, safety, peace, economic development, and so on" (Urbinati and Warren, 2008: 403). The problem is, however, that self-proclaimed representatives often speak in the name of groups who have not authorized them to represent them, and to whom they do not have to justify their options.

These kinds of problems related to representation are by no means new or specific to collaborative governance. Since the work of Edmund Burke and of the American Federalists in the second half of the eighteenth century, it even appears as legitimate that representatives have some latitude to deliberate with each other, and this is not possible if they are tied with too tight a mandate to their constituencies (Benz 2000). Instead of viewing representatives merely as a "microcosm" of the represented, and the representation act as a "transmission belt" for the preferences of the latter, the contemporary conception of representation implies that representatives should be considered as "trustees" enjoying a broad degree of latitude (Pitkin 1972), so that they can devote themselves to the necessary "brainstorming" (Elster 1998) for politically sustainable and technically appropriate decision-making. The problem is that there seems to be a trade-off between deliberation and democracy (Fishkin 1991), the former being more easily achievable in narrow circles and behind closed doors; besides, it is difficult to justify any democratic deficits with the advantages of deliberation, given that a public committed to democratic values does not value the latter as such (Hermet 2001: 16).

3) Moreover, to problems related to representation should be added problems related to a lack of transparency in mechanisms of collaborative governance. The latter often lack codification and thus visibility. The lack of transparency can impede accountability in several respects. For example, the problem of "many hands" (Thompson 1980) arises when external publics are unable to distinguish whom among the numerous network

members to praise or to blame, so network members can claim credit for positive out-comes due in reality to their partners, and also evade accountability by shifting to their partners the blame for failure or misdeeds. Besides, collaborative governance is some-times accompanied by the informalization of regulation itself ("soft law") because those actors affected by regulation who are powerful enough to block policy can use networks to negotiate informal agreements with state actors. This drift from the classic principles of the rule of law is likely to generate criticism, too, for its lack of procedural legitimacy. By overstating the importance of "output" legitimacy relying on decisions commonly perceived to be adequate because they promote an alleged public interest, the literature on governance has probably neglected the importance of "throughput" legitimacy for the acceptance of decisions.

4) Another problem is that networks of collaborative governance may be uncou-pled from the formal institutions of representative democracy.[9] This problem is not specific to collaborative forms of governance either, as for several decades now the rise of technocratic policy-making has been considered to be a cause of the decline of parliamentary dominance. Moreover, there is substantial cross-national variation in the relationship between governance networks and representative institutions, depending on patterns of democracy (majoritarian or consensual) and on the vibrancy of the associational nexus, as shown by a recent comparative study on the United Kingdom, Switzerland, the Netherlands, and Denmark (Skelcher et al. 2011). However, the—admittedly anecdotal—available empirical evidence tends to corrob-orate technocratic dominance in collaborative governance. A comparative study of three policy sectors in seven European democracies concluded that state agents are the most powerful group in policy networks (Kriesi et al. 2006: 354). According to that study, the influence of state agents is stronger than the influence of political par-ties, which are the traditional sources of preference aggregation and policy forma-tion. Another comparative study (Bache and Olsson 2001) showed that elected officials participated in partnership bodies in Sweden but not in the United Kingdom; however, this hardly made any difference because even in Sweden the influence of politicians was negligible.

The problem is not only that elected politicians are not necessarily the key players in processes of collaborative governance. One might expect authorized bodies such as par-liaments to be at least able to oversee the operations of collaborative governance bodies effectively. If this were the case, then parliaments would be able to constrain network members to deliberate under the threat that their decisions could be overruled, thus forcing them to anticipate objections made by MPs. It may make a difference, for instance, whether mechanisms of collaborative governance are established in the proc-ess of law-making (the formulation of principles, norms, and rules of a policy) or in the process of implementation (decisions on how to interpret and implement what is in the law). In the first case, it is more likely that the preferences of elected politicians will be taken into account, because they are the target group that must be convinced. In the sec-ond case, however, it is mainly segments from the administration (often at the local or regional level) that cooperate and deliberate with nonpublic actors, and this happens remotely from the politicians who first made the decisions (as we are taught by implementation research).[10]

In sum, in order to ensure that more horizontal forms of policy-making have sufficient democratic "anchorage points" (Sørensen and Torfing 2009: 244), one should scrutinize whether the following (all necessary) conditions are fulfilled:

- the inclusiveness of collaborative forms, which allows equity and a fair amount of pluralism in participation and in deliberation;
- the publicity of debate, which allows effective accountability, consent, and contestation from outside;
- the direct presence of, or indirect supervision by, elected officials, which prevents formally authorized representative bodies from being "hollowed out" by collaborative governance.[11]

"Horizontal" policy-making: less democratic but more enhancing to collective welfare?

On the other hand, notwithstanding any democratic deficits, collaborative forms of governance can claim alternative sources of legitimacy. It is increasingly argued that collaborative procedures lead to more adequate policy measures, and that they remedy the deficiencies of majority rule in complex societies. To put it in a nutshell, collaborative governance may be friendlier to the "management of interdependence" than decision-making through the official democratic institutions.

If they indeed enable technically more adequate and politically feasible decisions, then collaborative forms of governance may contribute to the production of legitimacy by enhancing both "specific" support to policy programs and "diffuse" support to the power holders. Democracies enjoy popular legitimacy if policy-takers feel that their preferences are endorsed by policy-makers ("input" legitimacy) or if they consider policy processes to be fair enough, so that they can even accept decisions they disagree with ("throughput" legitimacy). But the necessity of "output" legitimacy should be considered too (Scharpf 1999), given that poor policy performances can undermine belief in the competence of governments. Hence it is also useful to ask what kind of governance forms allow the production of decisions widely considered as beneficial to the common good, assuming that the performance of the classic (majoritarian) procedures of representative (or direct) democracy is not necessarily optimal in that respect.

This is particularly true when political decisions apply to contemporary, highly fragmented societies; nevertheless, the issue of democratic procedures being insufficiently complex in themselves to deal with social complexity has often been neglected.[12] For example, social fragmentation is a challenge to representation; even participatory theorists agree that it is illusory to believe that democratic representation can produce a "microcosm" of real society, because not only is society as a whole heterogeneous, but the same applies to the individual constituencies that are recognized as deserving representation (Young 2000: 121). This is not only true for territorial units represented in parliaments, but also for sectoral interests. It suffices to think, for instance, about the increasing heterogeneity of the labor force (between blue-collar workers and service employees, between members of the public and the private, or between the export and the sheltered sectors), which generates considerable strategic dilemmas for trade unions when they claim to articulate its preferences.

Considering these difficulties in ensuring adequate representation in the input process, and thus input legitimacy, it may be argued that legitimacy should rather be achieved through policy outputs of good quality. One needs then not only pragmatic criteria to assess the adequacy of outputs (positive evaluation by target groups), but also normative benchmarks. Reasonable standards seem to be those established by Offe and Preuss (1991), according to whom policy outputs should be *fact-*, *future-*, and *other-regarding*. This means that political decisions should take into account limitations in the availability of resources; should be concerned with durability (not externalize costs to future generations that have no say in present decision-making); and should promote (or at least not undermine) solidarity, especially in fragmented societies where incentives for "free riding" or "rent-seeking" are high. Such criteria are, of course, contestable, and it is not certain that they can serve as a basis for output legitimization. For example, solidaristic policies are sometimes criticized for generating irresponsible behavior on behalf of the groups benefitting from them. There is often controversy about who should profit from public measures, what resources are available, or how high policy costs are and how they are distributed (Offe 2008). This has led, for example Majone (1994), to maintain that redistributive policies can only be legitimized by majority decisions, but this is questionable from a governance perspective. It appears that majoritarian legitimization may not be sufficient to convince those endorsing the costs of a given policy, and that collaborative forms of governance may facilitate finding an agreement for the allocation of costs and benefits.

1) Collaborative forms of governance may have two advantages with respect to the fact- and future-regardingness of decisions: they are expected to enhance evidence-based policy-making, and by (partially) removing decisions from the parliamentary arena where concerns for responsiveness to constituencies' claims prevail, they reduce incentives for "short-termism" or "overpromising" (similarly to other depoliticization strategies, such as the delegation of monetary policy to central bankers and of regulatory tasks to independent agencies). The setting of collaborative governance procedures looks propitious to collective deliberation, which is expected in turn to be conducive to fact- and future-regardingness. Here, deliberative thinking can be defined as "a particular way of thinking: quiet, reflective, open to a wide range of evidence, respectful of different views. It is a rational process of weighing the available data, considering alternative possibilities, arguing about relevance and worthiness, and then choosing about the best policy or person" (Walzer 1999: 58).

The question is, of course, to what extent real deliberation in networks fulfills these conditions. If networks take the form of "policy communities," convergence in beliefs may mean common closure and a reluctance to learn. Hence the problem here may not only be restricted pluralism, but also limited adjustment capability to changing environments due to groupthink. Besides, one should not idealize networks by considering them as settings of disinterested deliberation aiming at the common good. They are also propitious to bargaining among participants: not only can collusion among insiders then lead to the externalization of costs to outsiders, but utility calculations often underestimate long-term and diffuse costs, which are less easily discernible. Empirical research (see, for example, Elgström and Jönsson 2000) shows that for genuine deliberation to take place, some very particular conditions need to be fulfilled, such as remoteness from the moment of decision and a low level of politicization, which is unlikely on important matters.

2) By focusing only on resource constraints and durability, one runs the risk of adopting a technocratic conception of policy-making. Particularly in fragmented societies, the issue of "other-regardingness" of collectively binding decisions is crucial. It is hard to decide whether advanced societies are characterized by a general lack of solidarity. For example, the decline of "social capital" and the individualism that is supposed to accompany it are not so far proven in an empirically robust way.[13] In general, it seems that in order to become part of the circle of the legitimate beneficiaries of social benefits one must increasingly satisfy eligibility conditions, such as nationality, morality, and so on. This also has to do with the fragmentation and openness of societies. Fragmentation reduces feelings of a common belongingness, while openness provides more "exit" options to those reluctant to endorse the costs of solidarity.[14]

Under such conditions, ensuring "other-regardingness" in decision-making is no easy task. However, most works on collaborative governance assume that if it takes place "in the shadow of hierarchy" (Börzel 2008: 123–127) (under the Damoclean sword of scrutiny by formally authorized decision-makers), then the risk of particularistic drift is reduced. It is more or less explicitly believed that the official state institutions serve the common good. These works do not sufficiently consider that politics is largely about "who gets what" (see, however, Mayntz 2008 and Offe 2008), and that this—to some extent at least—influences the behavior of the numerous actors participating in the governance process. Hence, there is no guarantee that officials who are formally authorized through election are immune to rent-seeking behavior.

Actually, the perspective could even be reversed as regards the normative superiority of mechanisms of representative democracy based on electoral competition. As a consequence of social fragmentation, the aggregation of preferences through majority vote is insufficient, because it does not allow for the weighing of preferences. It could be argued that it would be problematic on normative grounds (thus undermining legitimacy) if a majority of weakly affected (and as a result probably also poorly informed) voters made decisions that negatively affected the vital interests of sectoral, regional, or cultural minorities. Majority rule must itself be legitimate, and this is difficult in fragmented societies. Designers of so-called "consociational" political systems are aware of this problem, and have sought to ensure that the political influence of the various groups composing segmented societies be proportional to their social anchorage.[15] In practice this means that the leaderships of these groups search for compromise solutions that overcome the need to resort to the mathematical aggregation of votes.

The risk of a legitimacy deficit of majority decisions is higher when voters behave as self-interested utility maximizers, and this is even more true if we assume that the secrecy of the vote allows them to elect officials (in representative democracy) or to take decisions (in direct democracy) without being called to account for possible negative externalities on their fellow citizens or on minorities who are not entitled to participate. When individuals or social groups do not display sensitivity toward collective interdependence, there is a risk that decision-making under majority rule becomes detrimental to solidarity and redistributive justice (Scharpf 1993: 26). Hence, aggregative usages of democracy that rely on vote counting and on the victory of the most numerous are insufficiently complex to ensure the "management of interdependence" needed to deal with sources of conflict in complex societies. Such management requires deliberation between actors with divergent worldviews and negotiation between competing interests.

On the other hand, there may be indeed a trade-off between deliberation and democracy. The problem is not only that deliberation can only take place in small circles, as stated above—this can be solved if participants are considered representative of the "demos"—but also that publicity may be inimical to deliberation (Chambers 2004). Networks of governance allow the overcoming of policy blockades due to the presence of multiple "veto players" in complex political systems, but this often happens at the expense of transparency (Benz 2003). An important aspect of the uncoupling (Leca 1996) that we observe between the sphere of *politique d'opinion* (electoral politics) and the sphere of *politique des problèmes* (problem-solving policy-making) is that the former is considerably mediatized, so that actors are induced to "go public,"[16] whereas actors in the latter seek subterfuges to mediatization—and thus to public scrutiny—in order to better negotiate with each other (Spörer-Wagner and Marcinkowski 2011).[17] Is democracy then the price we must pay for the "management of interdependence" in complex societies? It is conceivable that elitist networks, where ordinary citizens are absent, better serve the promotion of the common good than democratic procedures through deliberation and concertation, and provided they are widely inclusive. Goodin (1996: 340), for example, argues: "Whatever we say against them, ossified elites and iron triangles at least have the virtue of ensuring ongoing discursive engagement of a sort which may well lead interlocutors to inculcate more expansive public-spirited concerns."

It must nevertheless be admitted that the empirical validation of claims about the virtues and vices of collaborative forms of governance is fragmentary. For example, though it is assumed frequently that collaborative governance has a positive effect on policy efficiency few empirical works address this question (Kenis and Raab 2008). One can mention in addition that concepts such as those of policy "efficiency" or "effectiveness" are controversial. Policy goals are ambiguous, there is seldom agreement on adequate solutions to problems, and even problem definition is controversial. In view of that, it is not certain that the loss of democratic quality that may be caused by collaborative modes of governance is compensated for by advantages in terms of a "management of interdependence."[18]

CONCLUSION: GAINS AND COSTS OF COLLABORATIVE GOVERNANCE

It appears that the gains and costs induced by collaborative forms of governance are very much an empirical matter. It is often assumed that they increase the efficiency of policy-making for a number of reasons presented above; but even if this is true, it presupposes a consensus on the meaning of "efficiency," which is hard to achieve. On the other hand, there is risk of a trade-off as regards the democratic quality of political decisions, but there is no certainty, either, on the magnitude of such a problem. Again, to what extent governance networks are dominated by technocrats or captured by particular interests, to what extent their outcomes become the object of debate and contestation, or to what extent collaborative forms of governance are uncoupled from the formal institutions of representative democracy—all these are empirical questions and there is no answer to them that would not be contingent on local or sectoral conditions.

We have also seen that there may even be normative justifications to collaborative governance that do not only rely on technocratic views about policy efficiency, but rather on the limits of traditional, basically majoritarian, conceptions of democracy. For participatory conceptions of democracy, being a "stakeholder" rather than simply a citizen is a more solid ground for inclusion in decision-making structures than the "one man one vote" aggregative conception of democracy that does not allow for any weighing of preferences. Should designers of decision-making procedures opt for egalitarian criteria of inclusion, or rather for the criterion of affectedness? There is no straightforward answer to such dilemmas. Of course, in the real world, the definition of who is affected by collectively binding decisions does not always result from a transparent application of uncontroversial criteria; co-option may not only have to do with affectedness but may be a function of the blackmailing power of the most powerful, and so on. All this translates into limits for pluralism; yet it may also be argued that these kinds of problems can be corrected by a design ensuring that collaborative forms of governance are representative, accountable, and coupled with democratic institutions. Therefore, it is important that analysts take into account these dimensions too, and do not confine themselves to a "managerial" reading of the gains and costs of collaborative governance.

NOTES

1. See also the chapters by Chris Ansell (Chapter 35, this volume) and R.A.W. Rhodes (Chapter 3, this volume). In cases of "multi-level" governance, public authorities that interact with nonpublic actors represent distinct decisional levels, such as the European, the national, the subnational (regional), and the local levels. The European Union encourages this kind of partnership (see Ian Bache, Chapter 44, this volume).

2. In reality, this is not a simple functional adjustment of the political system to its environment, but the outcome of reflection on behalf of policy-makers, where beliefs on constraints and strategic calculations matter.

3. For empirical analyses of the role of civil society organizations in contemporary governance see Susan D. Phillips, Chapter 34, this volume.

4. According to Börzel and Heard-Lauréote (2009: 137) "networks can be conceived as a particular form of governance, defined as institutionalized modes of coordination through which collectively binding decisions are adopted and implemented...They involve non-hierarchical modes of coordination constituted by mutual resource dependencies and/or informal norms of equality among the actors involved."

5. Considine and Afzal (2011: 379) refer to "the emergence of new types of network governance in which state agencies are found operating key functions through somewhat self-organizing arrangements comprising bureaucrats, private enterprises, not-for-profit agencies, community organizations, and even citizens themselves."

6. Bevir (2010: 3) writes that "representative institutions are at most a small part of a larger policy process in which a range of actors, many of whom are unelected and unaccountable, negotiate, formulate, and implement policies in accord with their particular interests and norms." Outside the democratic nation-state, this problem is even more acute (Benz and Papadopoulos 2006): The European Union is not a fully fledged parliamentary system, and beyond the EU level, the traditional features of a democratic polity are even less discernible.

7. This body of literature did not particularly deal with collaborative forms of governance, and did not assume that some form of policy-making would result in "better" or more legitimate outcomes. Although, in the literature on collaborative governance, the notion of network is generally used as a metaphor, interactions between individual actors and organizations in political decision-making have been identified through "network analysis" techniques in studies concentrating on empirical descriptions of the policy process: See, for instance, Kriesi et al. (2006).

8. Lord (2004: 114) suggests: "Instead of balancing and checking one another, networks or their members may collude to suspend competitiveness between themselves, to reduce prospects of challenge from the constituencies to which they are supposedly accountable and to freeze new entrants out of access to the benefits of engagement with the political system."

9. Weale (2011: 62) suggests, for instance, that "to the extent to which new modes of governance remove important decisions from the sphere of representative control, they appear to lack procedural legitimacy." See also note 6.

10. See, for example, Bache and Chapman (2008) on the implementation of structural funds policy, an exemplar case of "multi-level" governance in South Yorkshire (United Kingdom).

11. Bellamy and Castiglione (2010), and Follesdal (2010) share similar concerns regarding "new modes of governance" (especially the "open method of coordination") in the European Union.
12. For a significant exception, see Zolo (1992).
13. For a critical assessment, see Pharr and Putnam (1999).
14. See the various contributions in Streeck (1998).
15. See the classic book on "pillars" in the Netherlands by Lijphart (1974).
16. Manin (1997) speaks about the advent of an "audience" democracy.
17. This is not to say that network participants do not compete with each other to draw media attention to their claims (Blatter 2007: 278).
18. Bellamy (2010) presents a similar argument regarding the input–output balance in the European Union.

References

Bache, I. and Olsson, J. 2001. Legitimacy through partnership? EU policy diffusion in Britain and Sweden. *Scandinavian Political Studies* 24(3): 215–237.

Bache, I. and Chapman, R. 2008. Democracy through multilevel governance? The implementation of the structural funds in South Yorkshire. *Governance* 21(3): 397–418.

Bellamy, R. 2010. Democracy without democracy? Can the EU's democratic "outputs" be separated from the democratic "inputs" provided by competitive parties and majority rule? *Journal of European Public Policy* 17(1): 2–19.

Bellamy, R. and Castiglione, D. 2010. Democracy by delegation? Who represents whom and how in European governance? *Government and Opposition* 46(1): 101–125.

Benz, A. 2000. Politische Steuerung in lose gekoppelten Mehrebenensystemen. In R. Werle and U. Schimank (eds.), *Gesellschaftliche Komplexität und kollektive Handlungsfähigkeit*. Frankfurt-am-Main: Campus Verlag, 97–124.

Benz, A. 2003. Compounded representation in EU multilevel governance. In B. Kohler-Koch (ed.), *Linking EU and National Governance*. Oxford: Oxford University Press, 82–110.

Benz, A. and Papadopoulos, Y. 2006. Actors, institutions and democratic governance: Comparing across levels. In A. Benz and Y. Papadopoulos (eds.), *Governance and Democracy: Comparing National, European, and International Experiences*. London: Routledge, 273–295.

Bevir, M. 2010. *Democratic Governance*. Princeton, NJ, and Oxford: Princeton University Press.

Blatter, J. 2007. Demokratie und legitimation. In A. Benz, S. Lütz, U. Schimank, and G. Simonis (eds.), *Handbuch Governance: Theoretische Grundlagen und empirische Anwendungen*. Wiesbaden: VS Verlag, 271–284.

Blomgren Bingham, L. 2011. Collaborative governance. In M. Bevir (ed.), *The Sage Handbook of Governance*. London: Sage, 386–401.

Börzel, T. 2008. Der "Schatten der Hierarchie—Ein Governance-Paradox?" *Politische Viertlejahresschrift* Special issue 41: 118–131.

Börzel, T. and Heard-Laréote, K. 2009. Networks in EU multi-level governance: Concepts and contributions. *Journal of Public Policy* 29(2): 135–152.

Chambers, S. 2004. Behind closed doors: Publicity, secrecy, and the quality of deliberation. *The Journal of Political Philosophy* 12(4): 389–410.

Considine, M. and Afzal, K. A. 2011. Legitimacy. In M. Bevir (ed.), *The Sage Handbook of Governance*. London: Sage, 369–385.

Elgström, O. and Jönsson, C. 2000. Negotiation in the European Union: Bargaining or problem-solving? *Journal of European Public Policy* 7(5): 684–704.

Elster, J. 1998. Introduction. In J. Elster (ed.), *Deliberative Democracy*. Cambridge: Cambridge University Press, 1–18.

Fishkin, J. 1991. *Democracy and Deliberation*. New Haven, CT: Yale University Press.

Follesdal, A. 2010. The legitimacy challenges for new modes of governance: Trustworthy responsiveness. *Government and Opposition* 46(1): 81–100.

Fung, A. and Wright, E. O. 2001. Deepening democracy: Innovations in empowered participatory governance. *Politics and Society* 29: 5–41.

Goodin, R. E. 1996. Institutionalizing the public interest: The defence of deadlock, and beyond. *American Political Science Review* 90: 331–343.

Hermet, G. 2001. *Les populismes dans le monde*. Paris: Fayard.

Kenis, P. and Raab, J. 2008. Politik als governanceform: Versuch einer bestandsaufnahme und neuausrichtung der Diskussion. *Politische Vierteljahresschrift* Special issue 41: 132–148.

Kriesi, H., Adam, S., and Jochum, M. 2006. Comparative analysis of policy networks in Western Europe. *Journal of European Public Policy* 13(3): 341–361.

Leca, J. 1996. La "gouvernance" de la France sous la Cinquième République: Une perspective de sociologie comparative. In F. D'Arcy and L. Rouban (eds.), *De la Ve République à l'Europe*. Paris: Presses de Sciences Po, 329–365.

Lijphart, A. 1974. *Democracy in Plural Societies*. New Haven, CT: Yale University Press.

Lord, C. 2004. *A Democratic Audit for the European Union*. Basingstoke: Palgrave Macmillan.

Majone, G. 1994. Décisions publiques et délibération. *Revue Française de Science Politique* 44(4): 579–598.

Manin, B. 1997. *The Principles of Representative Government*. Cambridge: Cambridge University Press.

Mayntz, R. 1997. Politische Steuerung: Aufstieg, Niedergang und Transformation einer Theorie. In R. Mayntz, *Soziale Dynamik und Politische Steuerung: Theoretische und Methodologische Überlegungen*. Frankfurt-am-Main: Campus Verlag, 263–292.

Mayntz, R. 2008. Von der Steuerungstheorie zu global Governance. *Politische Vierteljahresschrift* Special issue 41: 44–60.

Offe, C. 1981. The attribution of public status to interest groups. In S. Berger (ed.), *Organizing Interests in Western Europe*. Cambridge: Cambridge University Press, 123–158.

Offe, C. 2008. Governance: Empty signifier oder sozialwissenschaftlicher Forschungsprogramm? *Politische Vierteljahresschrift* Special issue 41: 61–76.

Offe, C. and Preuss, U. 1991. Democratic institutions and moral resources. In D. Held (ed.), *Political Theory Today*. Cambridge: Polity, 143–171.

Olson, M. 1965. *The Logic of Collective Action*. Cambridge, MA: Harvard University Press.

Olson, M. 1982. *The Rise and Decline of Nations*. New Haven, CT: Yale University Press.

Papadopoulos, Y. 2003. Cooperative forms of governance: Problems of democratic accountability in complex environments. *European Journal of Political Research* 42(4): 473–501.

Papadopoulos, Y. 2010. Accountability and multi-level governance: More accountability, less democracy? *West European Politics* 33(5): 1030–1049.

Pauly, L. W. and Grande, E. 2005. Reconstituting political authority: Sovereignty, effectiveness, and legitimacy in a transnational order. In E. Grande and L. W. Pauly (eds.), *Complex*

Sovereignty: Reconstituting Political Authority in the Twenty-first Century, Toronto: University of Toronto Press, 3–21.

Pharr, S. J. and Putnam, R. D. (eds.) 1999. *Disaffected Democracies: What's Troubling the Trilateral Democracies?* Princeton, NJ: Princeton University Press.

Pierre, J. and Peters, B. G. 2000. *Governance, Politics and the State.* London: Macmillan.

Pitkin, H. 1972. *The Concept of Representation.* Berkeley and Los Angeles: University of California Press.

Sanders, L. 1997. Against deliberation. *Political Theory* 25: 347–376.

Scharpf, F. W. 1993. Versuch über Demokratie im verhandelnden Staat. In R. Czada and M. G. Schmidt (eds.), *Verhandlungsdemokratie, Interessenvermittlung, Regierbarkeit.* Opladen: Westdeutscher Verlag, 25–50.

Scharpf, F. W. 1999. *Governing in Europe: Effective and Democratic?* Oxford: Oxford University Press.

Schmitter, P. C. and Streeck, W. 1999. *The Organization of Business Interests: Studying the Associative Action of Business in Advanced Industrial Societies.* Discussion Paper 99/1. Cologne: Max-Planck-Institut für Gesellschaftsforschung.

Skelcher, C. Klijn, E.-H., Kuebler, D., Sørensen, E. and Sullivan, H 2011. Explaining the democratic anchorage of governance networks: Evidence from four European countries. *Administrative Theory and Praxis* 33: 7–38.

Sørensen, E. and Torfing, J. 2009. Making governance networks effective and democratic through metagovernance. *Public Administration* 87: 234–258.

Spörer-Wagner, D. and Marcinkowski, F. 2011. Politiker in der Oeffentichkeitsfalle? Zur Medialisierung politischer Verhandlungen in nationalen Kontexten. *Politische Viertlejahresschrift* Special issue 44: 416–438.

Streeck, W. (ed.) 1998. *Internationale Wirtschaft, nationale Demokratie: Herausforderungen für die Demokratietheorie.* Frankfurt-am-Main: Campus Verlag.

Thompson, D. F. 1980. Moral responsibility of public officials: The problem of many hands. *American Political Science Review* 74: 905–916.

Urbinati, N. and Warren, M. E. 2008. The concept of representation in contemporary democratic theory. *Annual Review of Political Science* 11: 387–412.

Walzer, M. 1999. Deliberation, and what else? In S. Macedo (ed.), *Deliberative Politics: Essays on Democracy and Disagreement.* Oxford: Oxford University Press, 58–69.

Warren, M. E. 2009. Governance-driven democratization. *Critical Policy Studies* 3: 3–13.

Weale, A. 2011. New modes of governance, political accountability and public reason. *Government and Opposition* 46: 58–80.

Young, I. M. 2000. *Inclusion and Democracy.* Oxford: Oxford University Press.

Zangl, B. and Genschel, P. 2008. Metamorphosen des Staates: Vom Herrschaftsmonopolisten zum Herrschaftsmanager. *Leviathan* 36: 430–454.

Zolo, D. 1992. *Democracy and Complexity: A Realist Approach.* Cambridge: Polity.

CHAPTER 37

....

PARTICIPATORY GOVERNANCE IN PUBLIC HEALTH: CHOICE, BUT NO VOICE

....

YAEL YISHAI

THIS chapter focuses on participatory policy-making in the health domain. Participatory governance denotes democratic engagement of individuals and groups in the policy-making process. It is a configuration in which "the people literally rule themselves, directly and participatorily, day in and day out, in all matters that affect them in their common life" (Barber 1995: 921). Participatory policy-making involves collaboration among public agencies, interest groups, and citizens in the decision-making process (Ansell and Gash 2008), which extends beyond consultation to a meaningful partnership between stake-holders. It involves the provision of means to engage individuals and organizations outside government through political networks and institutional arrangements that facilitate supportive collaborative-based discursive relationships among public and private sectors (Ansell, Chapter 35, this volume). Students of participatory governance have argued that when practiced, "an equal voice is given to all participants, and space is made for new arguments, ones that counter hegemonic discourse, to be heard" (Davies, Wetherell, and Barnett 2006: 60). Participatory governance, however, is not based on "different voices" only but on the institutionalization of public voice in the policy process. Public representatives, in the form of civil society organizations, are not only heard but share the responsibility and accountability of authoritative decision-making.

While participatory governance has become a customary political structure in recent years in both developed and developing countries (Fung and Wright 2003), not all policy domains are equally subject to democratization. The major argument presented in this chapter is that the health domain has largely remained impervious to democratic governance. When power is officially monopolized, backed by vested interests and unwavering legacy, the principles of participatory governance do not apply. The case of health policy-making illustrates these circumstances. Policy forums, dominated by medical experts, serve as a vivid example of "governance without government" (Peters and Pierre 1998), authorized by the state not only to control their area of expertise but also to craft health policy at large. Although some measures of openness and equality have been introduced into the health domain (Blank and Bureau 2007; Allsop and Jones 2008; Kuhlmann and Allsop 2008), collaborative forms of policy-making are sparse. Patients have gained a measure of autonomy by increasing their consumer choice but they have failed to contravene physicians' monopoly of power. Their voice has not matured into political clout. This chapter attempts to examine the contours of this reality, and to understand its origins.

In their capacity as patients those in need of medical attention act in two forms: as consumers and as citizens. The distinction between these two concepts, although often blurred in the literature (Newman and Vidler 2006; Allsop and Jones 2006, 2007), is quite clear. Consumers act as private individuals able to choose among providers of goods and services, wishing to augment their material benefits and satisfy their wants, on condition they can afford them (Allsop and Jones 2007). Citizenship, on the other hand, embodies "decommodification of public life" (Clarke 2007). It is depicted in terms of structured involvement in political affairs. Both choice and voice underscore patient empowerment. When practicing their choice patients may opt for "exit"; when acting as citizens, patients demand a "voice" that will enable them to be heard. In the first instance, patients mimic customers in the marketplace (Thompson 2007); in the second instance, they tend to act within organized voluntary associations, forming a variegated civil society.

The major argument herein presented is that the practices of participatory governance and accommodation, based on partnership and cooperation between providers and consumers, have not materialized in the health policy domain as patients have not had a chance to raise a substantial voice. They do make choices, but their (limited) discretion does not yield the political clout essential for the emergence of participatory governance. Put differently, professional power has withstood worldwide changes in patterns of policy-making. Choice has not been supplemented by voice. The absence of public voice from the health policy arena is detrimental as governance of health extends far beyond matters of professional concern. Whether or not to adopt a new surgery technique is a professional matter that is not subject to amateur considerations. But the allocation of resources among various health branches, the determination of priorities in medical care, and the introduction of equity into the provision of health services are issues to be determined within the framework of the participatory governance that is gaining momentum in many public policy domains. The extent to which medical professionals have joined the participatory trend by adopting accommodative practices of policy-making is the subject of this chapter.

PROFESSIONAL POWER

In many countries medical care is regarded as a public responsibility. Yet there has been a strong tradition of professional autonomy and medical dominance in health care politics. Physicians are perceived to be both servants and officers not only of the welfare state but also of human wellbeing in general (Bertilsson 1990). Doctors are often granted the statutory right not only to self-regulate but also to dominate health govern-ance. This has been achieved in a number of ways. Under state authority medical associ-ations have various authorities, including the registration of those eligible to practice medicine, supervising and licensing education and training, laying down standards and codes of practice, and holding disciplinary measures against those who breech the rules. Likewise, doctors have maintained dominance in clinical decision-making. Consequences for policy-making are self-evident. Physicians are responsible for negoti-ating fees, distributing resources among health care targets, determining the priorities of medical needs, and so on. (Hogg 2007).

There has been wide discussion on how different professions—most noted among them, the medical profession—attained their autonomy, and especially the ways in which professional autonomy was extended to prevent interference and management from outside. A main theme in this work (e.g. Freidson 1970) related to the ways in which the members of the medical profession augmented their power vis-à-vis the state and the patients. The ability to monopolize jurisdictions of work, the core body of knowledge, and the control of access to training, accreditation, and the labor market were accompanied by professional ideology, justifying professional autonomy and spe-cial privileges on the grounds of technical competency and social trusteeship. The medi-cal profession has had an especially persuasive claim to authority even among the sciences. One of the reasons for physicians' predominance in the public arena is their presence at critical transitional moments in human life in ways unmatched by other pro-fessionals. Their expertise provides care and cure. They heal the wounded and alleviate misery and pain. Doctors interact with vulnerable and frail individuals, whose life and health are in their hands.

Ideal-type professional power has significantly deteriorated. More than ever before physicians are employed by large organizations where bureaucratic regulatory authority can conflict with professional codes of behavior. As a result, new ways of collaboration between managers and professionals are emerging. There has been a growing demand for professionals to accommodate to organizational needs. Governance procedures, however, were not swayed by the introduction of managerial considerations into the health domain. Drives for change emerged from different directions.

DRIVES FOR CHANGE

Theoretically, it is inconceivable that the health domain will not be affected by the changes sweeping the administrative–political world. Potent economic, social, and political developments have elicited movement toward new forms of governance in many policy domains. Demographic trends, changing notions of citizenship, and the transformations of welfare states were the major causes. To begin with, economic pres-sures within the health sector have played a major role in introducing change. Although national incomes continue to rise, expenditure on health care has become a source of concern in many countries. Organisation for Economic Co-operation and Development (OECD) health expenditure has grown by more than 4 percent annually over the past ten years (OECD 2009). Increase in spending on health care has been noticeable not only in the national arena but also in private households. Data (although somewhat dated) reveal that in half the OECD countries reviewed, the proportion of privately funded health care increased. The share of out-of-pocket payments was between 10 and 30 percent of the total for most countries. Furthermore, out-of-pocket spending for health care rose as a share of total household consumption during the 1990s. Of the nineteen OECD countries for which this measure is available, all but four experienced such an increase (Huber 2003: 13–15).

The rising costs of modern medical technologies, coupled with public pressures to expand access to health care to peripheral groups, has overloaded health care services and increased expenditure. Many states are struggling to tackle the issues of growing demands for services and the perceived inefficiency of both governments and providers in responding to these demands. The new patterns of morbidity and mortality, with increased incidence of long-term illness, have also burdened health care services. Both state regulation of the health domain and self-regulation of the medical profession have come under pressure not only to increase resources for health but primarily to raise quality and enhance efficiency. As a result, government relations with the medical profession are no longer unilaterally supportive, as the focus of state policy has shifted toward improving the effectiveness of health care and controlling costs. Various reforms have been introduced across Western countries to raise standards and accountability. These goals were to be achieved by introducing some ingredients of participatory governance, based on varying patterns of partnership between state, physicians, and patients. The challenge of finding resources in the face of ever-rising expectations and increasingly costly new treatments have expanded the issue of medical care, brought it to the forefront of the political agenda, and contested traditional forms of policy-making (Davies, Wetherll, and Barnett 2006).

The spirit of change has engulfed patients as well. As suggested by Allsop (2006) there have been significant changes in public attitudes to medical care. Users of medical services have become less accepting and less fatalistic regarding their health care. Tendencies toward "reflexive modernity" (Clarke 2007: 100) had their impact on the health market. The individualization of society has given rise to the commodified consumption of many products and to the rise of self-monitoring individuals (Beck and Beck-Gersheim 2002). This has been accompanied by the erosion of traditional structures on which people depended, such as class, gender divisions, family, and the nation-state. The reconfiguration of state sovereignty implied more individual self-sufficiency and responsibility. One manifestation of this trend has been a declining trust in doctors, fueling an increased awareness of physicians' fallibility and uncertainties in diagnoses. Increasing skepticism toward medicine in particular and science in general was the outcome of this process (Beck 1992). Individualization of society has made people more autonomous and self-directed. It has also produced rampant preoccupation with issues of personal self-realization and health preservation outside conventional medical care.

The participatory revolution in the political arena is the third factor triggering change in governance patterns. A backlash evolved against the principles of representative democracy, whereby "some of the people, chosen by all, govern in all public matters all the time." In most contemporary democracies, "all of the people govern themselves in at least some public matters at least some of the time" (Barber 1984: xiv). The health domain has not remained impervious to these winds blowing in industrial societies. Patients demanded rights to raise their voice and be heard. The outcomes of these drives for change in the health domain were mixed: more (though somewhat inhibited) choice but not more voice.

CHOICE: PATIENTS AS CONSUMERS

The movement from state to market, from hierarchy to contract, and from the public domain to the private sphere has turned patients into consumers. "Choice" has become a keyword in public policy as a whole. The ubiquity of the choice paradigm was attributed to the "personalization agenda," whose goals are to reframe the role of state-led initiatives in terms of empowering individuals "to make informed choices, based on information provided by government" (Malpass et al. 2007: 231). The notion of choice coincides with the emergence of "the consumer," derived from the market economy, as the privileged figure of policy discourse. The underlying assumption is that consumerism has transformed people's expectations so that public services are structured in line with their aspirations and choices. It serves as an impetus for efficiency and responsiveness. The rhetoric of consumer empowerment has been used to justify reform in the health care service and to construct an image of a responsive system (Newman and Vidler 2006).

The introduction of choice into the health arena has raised moral as well as practical problems. Consumerism was viewed as inappropriate to care relationships, especially in health. As noted by Barber (2007: 141), "private choice can be overwhelming." Empirical studies show that regardless of intelligence, people do not always choose well. A "choice overload" has been identified where "more can actually feel like less" (Schwartz 2004) and people can't make up their minds. As the number of options increases choice becomes more onerous. Barber (2007: 141) concludes by asserting that we are "worse off and have less liberty despite having more private choices."

Notwithstanding the problematic aspects of choice, two manifestations are visible in the health domain: gathering information and exercising the right of complaint. Information enables patients to challenge professional authority and gain expertise in their own right. Internet access is rapidly changing the landscape of health care, making patients more educated and therefore presumably less dependent on providers of medical services (Murray et al. 2003). It has been reported that in North America, 80 percent of the general population accessed health information on the internet for themselves, family, or friends (Ahmad et al. 2006). Moreover, the number of patients bringing

Internet-based health information to physicians is on the rise. Patients reported that Internet-based information enhances their understanding and their ability to manage their health condition. Consequently, medical providers are facing new challenges as patients are increasingly acquainted with options for choice (Diaz et al. 2000). Doctors' reaction to patients' growing autonomy tends to be negative. Studies point that many among them feel challenged by "Internet patients." Expressions such as "awkward," "hard time," "headache," "nightmare," "annoying," "irritating," and "frustrating" indicate the magnitude and nature of the burden such information has placed on physicians (Ahmad et al. 2006: 6). Patients who used the Internet for self-diagnosis, if not self-treatment, were regarded as a threat to medical expertise.

The second manifestation of choice is the right to make a complaint. On the face of it this right is limited by the fact that patients have no option to forgo health care or in many cases even to change providers. Yet, increasingly, patients express their autonomy through a complaint, manifesting discontent (Hogg 1999: 32). Patients, in their role as plaintiffs, act as consumers seeking redress in the legal arena. Although in a judicial process an expert's testimony is always required, the very option of suing members of the medical profession and challenging their power accentuates consumerism in the health care domain. Complaints are waged against individual doctors, but they can have a radiating effect on the profession as a whole. Studies (Charles, Wilbert, and Franke 1985) show that sued physicians significantly reported that they were likely to think of retiring early, and to discourage their children from entering medicine. Malpractice litigation, however, is not a weapon targeted only at individual physicians but also an instrument for consumer choice, revealing the growing power of the patient as an independent actor in the health market.

Even though a minority of people who are dissatisfied complain, claims for medical negligence or malpractice have been on the rise (Allsop 2006) in both democratic and non-democratic countries (e.g. Kassim 2007). In the past, deferential attitudes, trust, and a narrow gateway offered by complaints systems have acted as barriers to voicing complaints (Allsop and Jones 2007). The marketization of health care opened wide gates for the expression of grievance. Yet here too the process has stalled due to strong incentive on the part of physicians, backed by tacit consent of the state, to resist expanding and institutionalizing the complaint process. Furthermore, patients are often not aware of their rights and do not have full information regarding access and possible outcomes (Allsop 1994; Bevan and Hood 2006). The heavy financial burden put on the provision of health care by litigation procedures prompted those involved, including the state health authorities, to restrain the process and offer less contentious alternatives.

To conclude, the road to consumerism in the health market is widening but at the same time is strewn with obstacles. Physicians show dissatisfaction with increasing patients' knowledge and resist litigation. They steadfastly adhere to their professional monopoly, acknowledging, however, the rising economic power of the patient. Fierce competition on the patients' pocket spurred the process of marketization centered on consumer power. Choice in the health domain is on the rise.

VOICE: PATIENTS AS CITIZENS

For both ideological and practical reasons the inclusion of patients in health care deci-sion-making is a current policy imperative in many countries around the world (Thompson 2007). Patients raise their voice within the context of "participatory govern-ance." The principles in which participatory governance are couched are (1) a focus on specific, tangible problems where governance structures are geared to concrete con-cerns; (2) the involvement of ordinary, non-professional people affected by these prob-lems; and (3) deliberative solutions to problems. The underlying characteristic of participatory governance is the devolution of decision authority to empowered units. These structures diverge from public attempts to influence policy-making by exerting pressures from the outside (Fung and Wright 2003: 25). They are also not confined to consultation practices. A good example for participatory governance is health councils in Brazil (Smismans 2008). Unlike the consultative bodies that exist in many countries to engage citizens in discussions about health problems, priorities, and policies, Brazil's health councils are empowered by law to approve the budgets, accounts, and spending plans of the executive, on which funding from the federal budget depends. The compo-sition of these bodies follows a mandatory principle of parity between professionals and laypeople (Cornwall 2008: 510).

The Brazilian experience is perhaps unique in the sense patients can have power over decision-making. Most forms of citizen participation center, at best, on "involvement" rather than on the exertion of influence. A study conducted in various countries (Norway, Sweden, Israel, the Netherlands, Denmark, New Zealand, and the United Kingdom, and in the state of Oregon in the United States) revealed the extent to which citizens and their representatives are involved in health policy decision-making bodies (Sabik and Lie 2008). These countries vary in the form of health care but all have insti-tuted, since the 1980s, some form of citizen involvement. In all but one exception (the Netherlands) lay public representatives were legally included in the policy process (see also Ham and Robert 2003; Davies, Wetherell, and Barnett 2006). But even this proce-dure did not craft a tangible and effective patients' voice.

The fact that health groups are occasionally involved in the policy process did not, however, enhance the power of "voice." Generally speaking, the impact of civil associa-tions on health policy-making is quite limited. Data gathered in a study of health groups in the UK revealed that they have developed skills and knowledge in policy advocacy and formed alliances to build support, pool resources, and use each other's knowledge and skills (Baggott, Allsop, and Jones 2004). The government did increase opportunities for participation. However, the majority of commentators assert that the professional iron curtain has not been lifted and that the patients' voice remains weak (Hogg 1999). Doctors perceive patients' groups to have unrealistic expectations and to take an emo-tionally based and populist stance on medical issues, which are detrimental to the col-lective interest (Tallis 2004). One may conclude that granting statutory rights does not guarantee influence. Although many health groups in the UK reported being involved in a number of official advisory committees, they also believed that various barriers inhibited their contribution, among which were poor communication and feedback on policy (Baggott, Allsop, and Jones 2004: 326).

A common explanation for patients' failure to impact the policy process is physicians' ingrained resistant to incorporating "outsiders" (Kuhlmann, Allsop, and Saks 2009) into the process. Public representatives are perceived by physicians as lacking expertise, as being reluctant to raise their voice, and as being partial and subjective. Often membership in policy-making bodies is merely token and patients' sentiments are overlooked. Even when a commitment to meaningful public involvement is made, often no more than one or two public members are included, which reduces the effectiveness of public voice. As noted by Chessie (2009: 721), "*real* citizen engagement is easier to profess than to accomplish." Patients may be becoming more assertive and knowledgeable about health care, but they carry relatively low political leverage. Even though there has been a tendency for more participation there is no guarantee that citizens' views carry additional weight. Access to decision-making does not automatically impact on decisions.

The drives for change noted above, namely, rising costs of health care, individualization of society, and particularly the participatory revolution, did prompt the state to give patients more voice. The need to legitimate difficult and contentious rationing decisions and to act as a counterweight to existing interests, particularly those of doctors, pushed the state toward devolution of power. But this devolution is limited to the margins and is not meaningful in contentious issues. Governments are reportedly reluctant to cede power to patients if this is counter to the thrust of state policies (Kuhlmann, Allsop, and Saks 2009). This does not mean that the status quo was adamantly preserved. New regulatory bodies were created, standards and use of performance indicators were set, inspection, audit and evaluation were proliferated (Newman and Kuhlmann 2007), and consumer involvement in the health policy process has been a widely adopted policy aim. Yet these changes were curbed by the eminent distribution of power within the newly formed governing bodies. Under state auspices physicians continue to control processes of decision-making in the health arena.

IMPEDIMENTS TO PARTICIPATORY GOVERNANCE IN PUBLIC HEALTH

This chapter has focused on governance patterns in the health policy domain sparked by economic, social, and political circumstances: rising costs (including out-of-pocket) of medical care, individualization of society, and the expansion of participatory politics. The underlying question was whether health policy-making incorporated patterns of participatory governance based on some form of power-sharing. The answer, based on this discussion, is equivocal. Patients do have more choice, serving as a leverage for influence. However, consumerism, aided by knowledge and sustained by vocal criticism and litigation, has changed power relations only on the margins. There is little evidence, based on comparative studies, that choice has been converted to voice.

Participatory governance in the health domain is based on a new concept of citizenship, invoked to signify much more than an individual's legal membership in a sovereign state. One of its modern manifestations has been termed "biocitizenship," entailing the process by which individuals contest power relations on matters of health and illness (Hunter 2010). The foregoing discussion elaborates the shortcomings of biocitizenship. More often than not citizens are getting their say, but it is doubtful whether they are getting their way (Quennell 2001). There has been a noticeable "metamorphoses in patienthood" (Landzelius 2006), yet most commentators agree that there has been a democratic deficit. Although laypeople are appointed to various health policy-making bodies, their impact is marginal. As noted by Hogg (1999: 176), "the NHS is run by people who have been selected, not elected," and selection tilts toward doctors, who are the medical specialists.

There are several obstacles that inhibit the influence of patients as citizens. Bureaucratic power is the first impediment. Civil servants in the health domain are often professionals themselves paying due respect to their colleagues (Yishai 1992). By and large, bureaucratic bias against patients and their representative health groups is widely evident. There are some illuminating exceptions to this rule. Patients' influence is augmented when officials wish to introduce change and use health groups to support them in the face of professional opposition. Occasionally, patients are also drawn into partnerships with physicians to impede bureaucratic initiatives. Even under these circumstances patients do not exert influence on the policy process but serve as cogs in the machine.

The second factor is commercial power. Public interests are often marginalized by more powerful economic interests, where lobbies often work against the development of public health policies. Health groups often depend on pharmaceutical companies for their organizational resources. The lack of independence and competition for funding also divides the patients' movement, ultimately weakening its impact and undermining its representation on a national level (Hogg 1999: 137).

Third, participatory governance emerges under few conditions—the most important of which is a balance of power between actors—where strategic domination is absent, and where exit is not attractive. When individuals cannot dominate others to secure their first preferences participatory governance occurs (Fung and Wright 2003: 26). These conditions are absent from the health arena. There is no balance of power between patients and physicians, on whom the former rely in critical moments in their lives. Exit is not an option and dependence is inherent. That patients can be partners with government and professionals is more a myth than a reality as the risks and benefits of joint ventures are not shared.

The final impediment to power-sharing is professional clout. Professionals have developed strong mechanisms to resist and redefine the idea of citizen power. But it is precisely in health issues that citizens' voice is essential. Difficult decisions are taken:

Who should receive dialysis treatment when there are more patients than machines? Who should enjoy the benefits of a sparse and costly medication under budgetary constraints? Members of policy networks, including providers of health services, their clients, and users cannot give an adequate answer. But professional expertise generates an ingrained power structure that so far has been immune to economic, social, and political changes.

Conclusions

Patients have crossed the threshold of consumerism, as they have more choice regarding health care services. They are wooed by service providers but they are not considered equal cohorts. Citizen patients, though armed with knowledge, expertise, and litigation power are not bold and savvy enough to claim their rights. They may enjoy choice-making power and even deliberative power, but their voice remains frail. The scripts of their play are highly edited by institutional and professional powers (Newman and Kuhlmann 2007: 109). As summarized by Cohen and Rogers (2003: 251), the problem of generating new forms of governance is not that "subordinate groups are unable to hold their own in deliberation, but that those with power advantages will not willingly submit themselves to the discipline of reason if that discipline presents large threats to their advantage." This does not imply that health policy is totally impervious to change. In many countries reforms were enacted, affecting both structures and procedures of medical services. But patterns of open and fluid governance typical of many policy domains are hardly applicable to health.

The case of health policy-making teaches us three lessons regarding the theory and practice of participatory governance. First, participatory governance, in terms of power distribution and the introduction of more egalitarian elements to the process, is unlikely to occur under conditions of ingrained inequality. Networks can be established between equals, possessing similar attributes of power, property, or prestige. They are hardly expected to emerge when members of one party in the partnership are sick, weak, and/ or vulnerable. The idea of accommodative governance is thus applicable to the economic or social arenas, where potential associates possess similar, if not equal, assets. This is far less the case regarding the welfare domain, particularly health, where some of those involved tend to be on the frail side of society.

Second, participatory forms of governance are likely to emerge when actors stand to gain from their mutual relationship. This relationship is irrelevant to the health domain where one actor is totally dependent on the other and where so much is at stake for prospective losers. Historically and socially doctors have not only dominated but in fact monopolized the health scene. In case of illness, patients do not have an alternative to modern medicine. Furthermore, one of the major challenges to successful collaboration is whether the agencies and non-state stakeholders are actually committed to the collaborative process in the first place. This is not the case regarding the health arena.

Professionals are not trained to facilitate participation and many, maybe most, do not believe in its utility (Fischer 2009).

Finally, forms of participatory governance are more likely to be present where the state is not only actively involved in the process of policy-making but actually condones democratization. Devolving decision-making power to medical experts has not relieved the state from its responsibility to health care. In fact, many important reforms were adopted in the past two decades under political leadership. The state is also involved in making moral–ideological choices concerning questions of life and death. Yet the fundamental aspects of health policy-making are governed mainly by physicians, either in their capacity as state employees or as independent professional actors. And they, as recurrently noted above, are less than eager to open their ranks to new forms of governance. The state does not endorse change but continues to count on physicians to conduct and manage health care. The power of expertise holds back participatory governance. Physicians prefer the old halo of being a magic healer, performing their civic duties within traditional patterns of hierarchical governance in which they have a dominant voice.

References

Ahmad, F. P., Hudak, L., Bercovitz, K., Hollenberg, E., and Levinson, W. 2006. Are physicians ready for patients with internet-based health information? *Journal of Medical Internet Research* 8: 1–14.

Allsop, J. 1994. Two sides to every story: Complaints' and doctors' perspectives in disputes about medical care in general practice setting. *Law and Policy* 16: 149–184.

Allsop, J. 2006. Regaining trust in medicine: Professional and state strategies. *Current Sociology* 54: 621–636.

Allsop, J. and Jones, K. 2006. The regulation of health care professions: Towards greater partnership between the state's professions and citizens in the UK. *Knowledge, Work and Society* 4: 31–57.

Allsop, J. and Jones, K. 2007. Withering the citizen, managing the consumer: Complaints in healthcare settings. *Social Policy and Society* 7: 233–243.

Allsop, J. and Jones, K. 2008. Protecting patients: International trends in professional governance. In E. Kuhlmann and M. Saks (eds.), *Rethinking Professional Governance: International Directions in Healthcare*. Bristol: Policy Press, 15–28.

Ansell, C. and Gash, A. 2008. Collaborative governance in theory and practice. *Journal of Public Administration Theory and Practice* 18: 543–571.

Baggott, R., Allsop, J., and Jones, K. 2004. Representing the repressed? Health consumer groups and the national policy process. *Policy and Politics* 32: 317–331.

Barber, B. 1984. *Strong Democracy: Participatory Politics for a New Age*. Berkeley, CA: University of California Press.

Barber, B. 1995. Participatory democracy. In S. M. Lipset (ed.), *The Encyclopedia of Democracy*. London: Routledge, 921–924.

Barber, B. 2007. *Consumed: How Markets Corrupt Children, Infantilize Adults and Swallow Citizens Whole*. New York: Norton.

Beck, U. 1992. *Risk Society: Towards a New Modernity*. London: Sage.

Beck, U. and Beck-Gersheim, E. 2002. *Individualization: Institutionalized Individualism and its Social and Political Consequences*. London: Sage.

Bertilsson, M. 1990. The welfare state, the professionals and citizens. In R. Torstendahl and M. Burrage (eds.), *The Formation of Professions: Knowledge, State and Strategy*. London: Sage, 114–133.

Bevan, G. and Hood, C. 2006. What's measured is what matters: Targets and gaming in the English public health care system. *Public Administration* 84: 517–538.

Blank, R. H. and Burau, V. 2007. *Comparative Health Policy*, 2nd ed. Basingstoke: Palgrave Macmillan.

Charles, S. C., Wilbert, J. E. and Franke, K. J. 1985. Sued and nonsued physicians' self reported reactions to malpractice litigation. *American Journal of Psychiatry* 142: 437–440.

Chessie, K. 2009. Health system regionalization in Canada' provincial and territorial health systems: Do citizen governance boards represent, engage, and empower? *International Journal of Health Services* 39: 705–724.

Clarke, J. 2007. Citizens, consumers and the reform of public services. In M. Bevir and F. Trentmann (eds.), *Governance, Consumers and Citizens: Agency and Resistance in Contemporary Politics*. London: Palgrave Macmillan, 97–118.

Cohen, J. and Rogers, J. 2003. Power and reason. In A. Fung and E. O. Wright (eds.), *Deepening Democracy: Institutional Innovations in Empowered Participatory Governance*. London: Verso, 237–257.

Cornwall, A. 2008. Deliberating democracy: Scenes from a Brazilian municipal health council. *Politics and Society* 35: 508–531.

Davies, C., Wetherell, M. and Barnett, E. 2006. *Citizens at the Centre: Deliberative Participation in Healthcare Decisions*. Bristol: Policy Press.

Diaz, J. A., Griffith, R. A., Ng. J. J., Reinert, S. E., Friedmann, P. D., and Moulton, A. W. 2000. Patients' use of the internet for medical information. *Journal of General Internal Medicine* 17: 180–185.

Fischer, F. 2009. *Democracy and Expertise: Reorienting Policy Inquiry*. Oxford: Oxford University Press.

Freidson, E. 1970. *Professional Dominance: The Social Structure of Medical Care*. New York: Atherton.

Fung, A. and Wright, E. O. 2003. *Deepening Democracy: Institutional Innovation in Empowered Participatory Governance*. London: Verso.

Ham, C. and Robert, G. 2003. *Reasonable Rationing: International Experience of Priority Setting in Health Care*. Maidenhead: Open University Press.

Hogg, C. 1999. *Patients, Power and Politics: From Patients to Citizens*. London: Sage.

Hogg, C. 2007. Patient and public involvement: What next for the NHS? *Health Expectations* 10: 129–138.

Huber, M. 2003. Health expenditure trends in OECD countries 1990–2001. *Health Care Financing Review* 25: 1–22.

Hunter, N. D. 2010. Rights talk and patient subjectivity: The role of autonomy, equality and participation norms. *Wake Forest Law Review* 45: 101–125.

Kassim, P. N. 2007. Reducing medical complaints and litigation in Malaysia: Turning patients' voices into opportunities. *Journal of Law and Medicine* 15: 303–311.

Kuhlmann, E. and Allsop, J. 2008. Professional self-regulation in a changing architecture of governance: Comparing health policy in the UK and Germany. *Policy and Politics* 36: 173–189.

Kuhlmann, E., Allsop, J., and Saks, M. 2009. Professional governance and public control: A comparison of healthcare in the United Kingdom and Germany. *Current Sociology* 57: 511–528.

Landzelius, K. 2006. Editorial: Patient organization movement and new metamorphoses in patienthood. *Social Science and Medicine* 62: 529–537.

Malpass, A., Barnett, C. Clarke, N. and Cloke, P. 2007. Problematizing choice: Responsible consumers and citizens. In M. Bevir and F. Trentmann (eds.), *Governance, Consumers and Citizens: Agency and Resistance in Contemporary Politics*. London: Palgrave Macmillan, 231–256.

Murray, E. L., Pollack, L., Donelan, K., Catania, J., and Lee, K. 2003. The impact of health information on the internet on health care and the physician-patient relationship: National U.S. survey among 1.050 U.S. physicians. *Journal of Medical Internet Research* 5: e17: 1727–1734.

Newman, J. and Vidler, E. 2006. Discriminating customers, responsible patients, empowered users: Consumerism and the modernisation of health care. *International Social Policy* 35: 193–209.

Newman J. and Kuhlmann, E. 2007. Consumers enter the political stage? Modernization of health care in Britain and Germany. *European Journal of Social Policy* 17(2): 99–111.

Organisation for Economic Co-operation and Development (OECD) 2009. Health data; available at http://www.oecd.org/health/healthdata (accessd 19 September 2011).

Peters, G. B. and Pierre, J. 1998. Governance without government? Rethinking public administration. *Journal of Public Administration Research and Theory* 8: 223–243.

Quennell, P. 2001. Getting their say, or getting their say? Has participation strengthened the patient "voice" in the National Institute of Clinical Excellence? *Journal of Management in Medicine* 15: 202–219.

Sabik, L. M. and Lie, R. K. 2008. Priority setting in health care: Lessons from the experience of eight countries. *International Journal for Equity in Health* 7: 4–19.

Schwartz, N. 2004. *The Paradox of Choice: Why More is Less*. New York: HarperCollins.

Smismans, S. 2008. New models of governance and the participatory myth. *West European Politics* 31: 874–895.

Tallis, R. 2004. *Hippocratic Oaths: Medicine and its Discontents*. London: Atlantic Books.

Thompson, A. G. H. 2007. The meaning of patient involvement and participation in health care consultations: A taxonomy. *Social Science and Medicine* 64: 1297–1310.

Yishai, Y. 1992. From an iron triangle to an iron duet: Health policy making in Israel. *European Journal of Political Research* 21: 91–108.

....

CHAPTER 38

A RETURN TO
GOVERNANCE IN THE
LAW OF THE WORKPLACE

....

CYNTHIA ESTLUND

ALL the major economies of the world are now largely market-oriented; most goods and services are produced by private economic organizations and networks subject to the pressures and rewards that markets entail. Those private economic actors are not only the primary engines of economic growth and prosperity, but also the locus of harms that societies seek to control: pollution and depletion of natural resources, dangerous products and processes, the defrauding of consumers and investors, and discrimination, to name several. The challenge of controlling those harmful spillover effects without smothering or driving away the engines of economic growth has spawned much of the expansion of the modern regulatory state since the 1930s and 1940s in the USA and elsewhere. That challenge has become more acute with the increasing globalization of production and investment, and with the increasing complexity of the technology and organizational networks through which economic actors produce and distribute goods and services.

In response to these challenges, the techniques and strategies of social regulation have evolved. Developed societies have turned away from primary reliance on direct regulation (especially what is called "command-and-control" regulation) toward governance-based approaches to the regulation of economic actors. That is, they have turned to strategies such as "regulated self-regulation" and "responsive regulation" that seek to advance societal objectives by steering organizations' own internal governance mechanisms in socially desired directions(Braithwaite 2008; Braithwaite and Drahos 2000; Levi-Faur 2005).[1] This dimension of the turn to governance reflects in part the recognition that powerful dynamics and incentives operating *within* regulated organizations and networks can either frustrate or advance societal objectives, and that the key to effective regulation lies in channeling those organizational dynamics, not merely imposing and enforcing commands from without.[2]

Leading theories of regulated self-regulation hold that both the efficacy of these regulatory strategies and their democratic legitimacy require meaningful participation by stakeholders within regulated entities' internal governance processes and in their oversight—in organizations' self-regulation and in its regulation (Ayres and Braithwaite 1992; Parker 2002). But, in practice, stakeholder participation is hardly a universal feature of existing systems of regulated self-regulation. This has contributed to skepticism among many proponents of regulation toward the "New Governance" enterprise, as regulated self-regulation without meaningful stakeholder participation risks devolving into self-deregulation.

One major arena of social regulation within advanced capitalist societies has been the workplace and the conditions under which members of the society are employed, especially within private firms. The regulation of work has some distinctive features as compared to other forms of social regulation. First, when it comes to the regulation of work, we are seeing not a turn to governance so much as a *return* to governance (as well as a shift in its nature), for governance-based approaches to the regulation of wages and working conditions took root across the industrialized world over a century ago in the form of collective bargaining. Moreover, these structures of industrial self-governance were democratic at their inception; unions, as democratically self-governing associations, democratized workplace governance and improved members' wages and working conditions through collective bargaining. These systems, more or less regulated by legislation and administrative agencies, became the centerpieces of national labor relations systems across the industrial democracies in the early to mid-twentieth century. Direct regulation of labor standards played a decidedly secondary role in improving terms and conditions of employment in these schemes.

Collective bargaining has ceded ground in recent years across much of the Western world, especially in the USA (Bercusson and Estlund 2010a). The decline what we may call of "Old Governance" in the workplace has coincided with the rise, first, of more extensive direct regulation of the terms and conditions of employment, and, more recently, of New Governance and meta-regulatory strategies for pursuing those regulatory objectives. This chapter will examine the shift from Old Governance to New Governance in the workplace, and the role that the participatory mechanisms that developed under the former play in the latter. I argue here that the institutions of employee participation that were central to twentieth-century labor relations regimes will also play crucial roles in speeding or slowing, and in any case shaping, the development of New Governance strategies for workplace regulation.

THE RISE AND FALL OF OLD GOVERNANCE

Participatory governance took hold in the workplace long ago because the workers whose wages and working conditions were at stake were (mostly) competent adult participants in the organizations that society sought to regulate. In most regulatory contexts—pollution, unsafe or deceptive consumer products, or financial fraud, for example—society seeks to mitigate harms that emanate from inside economic organizations but that primarily affect those outside the organization. Even when those affected are physically inside the organization, like hospital patients, or in contractual privity with it, like investors and some customers, they are not integral participants in the organizations' daily operations. But workers are just that, and they began demanding a role in workplace governance from the earliest emergence of the factory system. Moreover, those demands had clout behind them, for workers' role in production gave them a source of potential power. Strikes and labor unrest got the attention of employers and policy-makers, bringing the "labor question" to the top of national political agendas and amplifying workers' political demands for legal recognition of their chosen vehicles for participation in workplace governance. Across the Western market economies, national legislation created frameworks for collective bargaining through labor unions, and "industrial self-governance" became a primary mode of workplace regulation (Commons 1921; Stone 1981).

There is, of course, considerable diversity among labor relations systems in the developed economies. In democratic nations with a strong corporatist dimension to their labor relations systems, and in the European Union (EU), the trade unions have an institutionalized political voice and a role in wage-setting that is not strictly dependent on their membership. In those systems, institutions of "social dialogue," in which the major trade union federations are leading actors, exist alongside electoral mechanisms of political representation (EC 2008; Bercusson and Estlund 2007). In those systems, too, unions often play a comparatively limited role within the workplace itself; workers participate in workplace governance through other structures, such as works councils, and sometimes through employee representation on corporate boards, to which I will return.

In the USA, by contrast, unions have no institutionalized role in the political process, though they actively participate in it. In those workplaces where a union represents the workers (by majority rule), the union has a bigger role in daily workplace governance than do most European unions; but in the now overwhelming majority of workplaces where there is no union, there is no other legally recognized form of employee representation. That is because US labor law contains a uniquely broad prohibition on employers' dominating, interfering with, or assisting labor organizations (Lobel 2005). That prohibition, enacted in 1935, has resisted reform largely because US unions have been unwilling to support alternative forms of worker representation that might become rivals and threats to their own shrinking role in workplace governance (Estlund 2002).

In recent decades, collective bargaining has ceded its central role in many capitalist democracies. The reasons are many and complex, and include, at least in the USA, intensified employer resistance to unionization and the law's inadequate response (Estlund 2010b; Kaufman 2007; Weiler 1983). But unions have lost membership and power across the developed world with the greater mobility of people, production, and capital, the rise of globalized and competitive product markets, and the shift from large integrated manufacturing enterprises to flexible and fractured networks and supply chains (Stone 2007; Wachter 2007). New workplace concerns, such as discrimination and work–family conflict, gained political traction, while unions' capacity to address both old and new concerns seemed to erode. For a variety of reasons, direct regulation of wages and working conditions, legislation of workers' rights, and litigation over those rights have mushroomed since the 1960s (Estlund 2010b). Governments have sought to shape the behavior of regulated entities through both *ex ante* prescriptive rules and *ex post* liability rules. The USA, in particular, relies quite heavily on private litigation as a regulatory technique—sometimes quite successfully, as in the context of employment discrimination (Dobbin 2009).

With the rise of labor standards laws and litigation as tools of workplace regulation, some policy-makers and scholars have turned again to the idea of governance—of regulating firms by regulating their own internal governance structures. The return to governance in workplace regulation is both especially urgent and especially difficult in the USA, given the decline of union representation and collective bargaining and the legal and political barriers to nonunion forms of employee representation in workplace governance.

THE RISE OF REGULATED SELF-REGULATION
IN THE WORKPLACE

Modern governance-based approaches to regulation aim to take account of the prodigious internal regulatory capacity by which large firms manage both their response to the proliferating regulatory demands of governments and the increasingly complex networks through which they produce and deliver goods and services (Ayres and Braithwaite 1992; Estlund 2010b; Parker 2002; Lobel 2004, 2005). Corporate compliance systems make up an important part, but still only part, of firms' self-regulatory capacity.[3]

The idea of using law to stimulate and shape firms' self-regulation is, in one sense, nothing new. Governments activate firms' internal self-regulatory capacity, whether or not they pay explicit attention to it, by imposing traditional forms of *ex ante* regulation and *ex post* enterprise liability rules. If the law requires a particular kind of machine guard, firms will deploy rules, resources, and procedures to ensure that the guards are in place (provided that the penalties and probability of detection are large enough). Similarly, if the law makes firms liable for injuries caused by their products, or for racially discriminatory discharges, firms will presumably take organizational precautions against such incidents (subject to the same proviso). So even the most conventional forms of regulation, when applied to complex organizations, trigger and rely on governance mechanisms within those organizations (Estlund 2010b). But traditional regulators treat the regulated organization as a "black box," looking at outputs while ignoring internal organizational dynamics. Organizations are left to figure out for themselves what organizational precautions to take to avoid sanctionable outcomes. Unfortunately, the "black box" approach may induce firms to take precautions that reduce the risk of detection or punishment without reducing bad outcomes (Arlen 1994; Arlen and Kraakman 1997; Khanna 2000). That approach also ignores wide variations in the disposition and capacity of regulated actors to comply with social norms, thus wasting regulatory resources on those that are willing and able to regulate themselves, and devoting inadequate resources to policing those that most need policing (Ayres and Braithwaite 1992).

These are some of the considerations that have led regulators and courts to attend explicitly to firms' internal structures in deciding how rigorously to police firms and how to deal with incidents of non-compliance—whether through harshly deterrent sanctions, milder sanctions, or capacity-building remedial approaches. Braithwaite's influential model of "responsive regulation," for example, would place firms that maintain mechanisms of effective self-regulation on a more cooperative regulatory track. Crucially, firms that fail to effectively self-regulate, whether for lack of capacity or of will, should garner closer scrutiny and harsher sanctions; that helps to drive firms to invest in self-regulation and protects self-regulators from destructive competition, and it is part of what distinguishes regulated self-regulation from deregulation (Ayres and Braithwaite 1992; Braithwaite 1985, 2008). Such regulatory strategies have been taking hold across the developed world and across many arenas of social regulation (Braithwaite and Drahos 2000).

Consider the evolution of antidiscrimination law and practice in the USA (Dobbin 2009; Edelman, Abraham, and Erlanger 1992; Edelman, Erlanger, and Lande, 1993; Edelman 1999). First, the prospect of costly discrimination lawsuits (or loss of federal contracts) led large firms to institute internal equal employment opportunity (EEO) programs. Initially those programs had no direct bearing on their liability, except perhaps by preventing or remedying discrimination and avoiding litigation. But eventually the courts began to take explicit notice of effective internal EEO programs, and to mitigate some elements of liability for firms that maintained them. That gave further momentum to the adoption and spread of internal antidiscrimination procedures, and helped foster the growth of an internal EEO constituency that, in turn, helped to generate corporate support for "diversity" and "inclusion" initiatives that went "beyond compliance." The significant improvement of corporate life for previously excluded groups suggests some of the positive potential that lies in the return to governance in the law of the workplace.

PARTICIPATION IN THE WORKPLACE: PART OF THE NEW GOVERNANCE?

The scholarly proponents of governance-based approaches to regulation emphasize the need to engage stakeholders to monitor self-regulation and to guard against cheating and regulatory capture (Ayres and Braithwaite 1992; Estlund 2010b; Parker 2002, 2007;

Lobel 2009). It is not clear, however, that we should *define* governance-based regulatory strategies as involving stakeholder participation. Not all governance is good governance, and not all governance is participatory; even autocrats engage in governance. Similarly, a regulatory strategy that relies on, engages with, and shapes organizations' internal self-regulatory mechanisms—like the judicial doctrines calibrating employment discrimination liability in part on the basis of internal EEO structures—is a governance-based strategy even if it fails to ensure workers a meaningful role in governance.

So a "return to governance" in the workplace may or may not signify a return to *participatory* governance. Even as workplace regulators allocate scrutiny, rewards, and sanctions based on firms' maintenance of particular compliance structures, they may or may not require worker participation as part of those structures. In the USA thus far, they have not, and that is a problem (Estlund 2010b). Participatory self-governance mechanisms (at work and elsewhere) enable workers to engage cooperatively with fellow citizens to shape decisions that affect them; they also help ensure compliance with publicly mandated labor standards and employee rights. Collective bargaining was once expected to deliver those intrinsic and instrumental benefits, among others, for most workers; but as collective bargaining has waned in power and reach, a crucial question is whether alternative mechanisms for employee participation in workplace governance can fill that vacuum. So let us turn to the question of what forms worker participation in workplace governance might take in a world in which industrial self-governance through collective bargaining must be regarded as merely one possibility. Let us begin by arraying forms of workplace participation in terms of their "democratic-ness," or their resemblance to democratic modes of collective decision-making.

It is worth noting at the outset that, on a yardstick of "democratic-ness," collective bargaining is a decidedly truncated form of worker participation in governance. Workers do elect their own representatives, but those representatives generally have no actual decision-making power in the enterprise. They can only attempt to wrest concessions from management by exerting whatever bargaining power they can muster given extant labor market conditions, workers' position in production, and their solidarity. Other forms of worker participation in governance may be more democratic, including worker-ownership, with the election of management by all workers in the enterprise (Dow 2003). But collective bargaining may be the most democratic form of worker participation that is historically consistent with capitalism and the modern private corporation as we know it in most of the world. Moreover, when US-style collective bargaining takes hold, it does give workers genuine collective influence in workplace governance and dispute resolution through jointly bargained rules and jointly administered grievance-arbitration procedures.

At the other end of the spectrum, the least democratic level of worker participation that is practicable within the modern corporation is far from zero. At a minimum, workers participate within the modern corporation as ordinary employees; employees, with varying degrees of autonomy and authority, make and carry out organizational decisions of all kinds. Moreover, employees whose skills are scarce and highly valued may have considerable individual "voice" within their organizations. These individual, market-inflected forms of employee involvement might not be conceived of as "participation" in governance at all. But much as autocratic governance is still governance, it may be analytically cleaner to define these forms of involvement as "participation"— neither democratic nor effective for most rank-and-file employees, but quite effective for others. This usage suggests, controversially, that there is an irreducible minimum of "participatory governance" by employees in the modern corporation, however hierarchical. But it highlights the fact that employees inevitably play crucial roles within the governance of their organizations because organizations are made up of employees; this sets them apart from other external stakeholders, and may provide a platform for more extensive forms of participation.

So, for example, one organizational innovation that has become ubiquitous in internal compliance systems is the creation of reporting systems through which employees can report violations of internal rules or external laws, anonymously or otherwise, to managers responsible for compliance (Lobel 2009). Those internal reporting systems are supposed to improve compliance with environmental laws, securities laws, and consumer safety laws, among others; they are among the formal requisites of effective self-regulation within some regulatory schemes (USSC 2009: § 882.1). In the case of employment laws, these reporting systems play a larger role, for employees are not only observers and potential monitors but also victims of misconduct with formal recourse to judicial or administrative remedies against the employer. Employee reporting systems in the employment context tend to be more elaborate, often with one or more levels of appeal. These systems may be mere formalities, or they may be formal manifestations of a broader organizational commitment to procedural fairness and to a "culture of compliance" that is a linchpin of effective self-regulation (Tyler, Dienhart, and Thomas 2008). Either way, employee reporting and grievance systems have become obligatory within large and medium-sized corporations (Edelman 1999).

The dual role that employees play within a workplace grievance procedure—as both monitors and victims of non-compliance—captures a paradox in the nature of self-regulation of employment practices, and a challenge for the return to governance in the workplace. On the one hand, self-regulation of employment practices may be strengthened by the convergence of self-interest and insider knowledge that employees bring to the self-regulatory process. On the other hand, employees might be bribed, threatened, or pressured into silence by the organization that employs them; such vulnerability potentially undermines their role both in internal compliance and in external enforcement of workplace laws. In the case of laws protecting consumers, the environment, or investors, the victims of misconduct are outside the firm's control; their private remedies, judicial and administrative, supplement both self-regulation and public enforcement. In employment law, however, both private enforcement litigation and internal complaints emanate from within the regulated organization, from employees who are subject to both economic pressures and subtler pressures of organizational loyalty.[4] The threat of external enforcement through litigation, which helps to keep internal compliance systems honest, is muffled by the same fears and pressures that can undermine employees' willingness to utilize internal reporting systems. The paradoxical mix of strengths and vulnerabilities that employees bring to their role in both internal compliance and external enforcement thus gives a distinctive character to the return to governance in the workplace.

The solution to this paradox is hardly mysterious. Employees need independent collective representation—with a foot both inside and outside the organization—in order to overcome the social and economic pressures and the fears of reprisal that inhibit individual efforts to redress grievances both internally and externally (Estlund 2010b). Collective representation can also solve the collective action problems that plague individual efforts to redress shared grievances. Many workplace violations stem from conditions or policies that inevitably affect many workers at once; the benefits realized by any one complainant are swamped by both the collective benefits to employees and the cost to employers of redressing those grievances. Collective representation is a well-understood solution to the collective action problems that result (Freeman and Medoff 1984). US-style unions rather neatly resolve both the collective action problems and the fear of reprisals that inhibit individual participation in workplace governance and internal compliance mechanisms. Not surprisingly, employee rights and labor standards are more reliably respected in unionized workplaces (Wachtman 1994; Weil 1991).

Thus, the agnosticism of our definitions gives way to a preliminary conclusion: While governance-based strategies for workplace regulation do not necessarily entail *participatory* governance, and employee participation is not necessarily *collective* participation, it is the case that *effective* governance-based regulatory strategies generally do require collective employee participation in workplace governance.

FORMS OF PARTICIPATION IN WORKPLACE GOVERNANCE

Of course that brings us back to the problem that underlies the return to workplace governance: the decline of collective bargaining. Collective bargaining still dominates the law and the politics of employee participation in workplace governance, at least in the USA, where federal labor law bars most alternative forms of employee representation.[5] Unions in the USA tend to regard alternative structures for employee representation more as rivals than as aids in the protection of workers' interests (Dunlop Commission 1994). So they hold fast to the seventy-five-year-old ban on "company unions," and pin their hopes on labor law reforms that would better enable workers to form a union and bargain collectively. But once we recognize that even a tripling of union density in the USA would leave three-fourths of the private sector workforce without collective representation, it becomes clear that alternatives are needed. The crucial challenge facing the return to workplace governance in the USA is whether we will see the rise of institutions of collective representation other than unions and collective bargaining organizations.

In Europe, Australia, and elsewhere, union decline has been both less dramatic and less consequential for workers. That is because unions effectively represent many non-members through corporatist channels, including mechanisms of "social dialogue" and sectoral wage agreements, and because many workers are represented through works councils as well as through unions.[6] Elected works councils are entitled to receive information and to consult (but not usually bargain) with employers on a range of matters affecting employees (Rogers and Streeck 1994). Works councils may work best in conjunction with a union, with the possibility of industrial action to back up employee voice. Indeed, works councils may help fill what might otherwise be a workplace "representation gap" in Europe, for collective bargaining does not generally serve as the sort of vehicle for workplace-level participation and dispute resolution that it does (where it exists) in the USA.

Works councils alone may compare unfavorably to a well-functioning US-style collective bargaining relationship. But such relationships are dwindling. As compared to the nonunion workplace, works councils would represent a big step toward participatory governance, and are seen by some US labor scholars as a potential solution to the "representation gap" (Levine 1998; Weiler 1990; Befort 2004; Hirsch and Hirsch 2007; Kochan 2006). In particular, works councils play a useful part in both firms' self-regulation and in the regulation of self-regulation (Ayres and Braithwaite 1992). Unfortunately, the academy appears to be the primary constituency in the USA for works councils; neither unions nor employers have shown the slightest inclination to go down that road.[7] Employers oppose them, fearing they will open the door to unionization, while most union observers have traditionally viewed them as potential rivals and impediments to unionization, for much the same reasons that they oppose loosening the statutory ban on voluntary, employer-sponsored vehicles of employee representation.[8]

Union objections to forms of employee representation that exist solely inside firms, without the independence that stems from affiliation with a trade union, are not limited to the USA, and are not a simple matter of turf protection. It is no easy matter to devise adequate safeguards against employer capture and manipulation of employee representatives who share the vulnerability and dependence of individual employees (Barenberg 1994). But that is just one facet of the broader challenge of identifying criteria of "effective self-regulation" that are strong enough to ensure efficacy and to guard against "self-deregulation." At least in North America, much of the vocabulary of New Governance—terms like "cooperation," "voluntary compliance," and "self-regulation"—has been badly tarnished by its use by others as a thin cloak for a neoliberal deregulatory agenda (Arthurs 2002; Blackett 2001; Krawiec 2003). For their part, the proponents of New Governance, while keen to distance themselves from that agenda, acknowledge the difficulty of developing reliable indicators of both good faith and capacity on the part of supposedly responsible self-regulators (Parker 2002). How can regulators and the public be confident that the appearance of self-regulation is real rather than a ploy to garner the less vigilant policing and less punitive sanctions that are reserved for those taking the high road?

In the context of workplace regulation and governance, the central challenge is sharpened as it is refracted through the institutional legacy of Old Governance—the labor movement and its long history of collective self-help and collective bargaining on behalf of workers. Even as their membership and power decline, the unions are loathe to give up the symbolic and political primacy of collective bargaining in favor of alternatives that appear to be untested, toothless substitutes for union representation. So New Governance is a very hard sell among the unions in some quarters of the developed world. That is a serious problem. For unions remain the only broad-gauged representatives that working people have within the political process. If they do not participate constructively and vigorously in policy discussions about new approaches to workplace regulation, then those new approaches are likely to evolve without adequate provisions for worker participation—and probably without adequate attention to the need for a strong backdrop of public enforcement. We are more likely to see flawed and undemocratic forms of governance-based regulation than a reinvigoration of stronger and tougher adversarial enforcement.

The freedom of employees to form a union and bargain collectively remains a crucial part of the labor landscape, as well as a core labor right under international law. Even though unions cannot be the only institutions through which workers participate in workplace governance, the option of union representation must be a real one. At a minimum, the "threat" of unionization can help to encourage nonunion employers to maintain decent working conditions and respect for workers' rights, much as the background threat of adversarial public enforcement helps to encourage firms to self-regulate (Doorey 2010). But, especially if unions are conceived as a kind of punishment for firms that misbehave, it is clear that there is a need for other, less "threatening" mechanisms for employee participation within firms seeking to take the "high road" of responsible self-regulation.

Conclusion

Across the advanced economies of the world, the consolidation of "regulatory capitalism" and the rise of New Governance-based strategies of regulation have coincided with the decline of traditional collective bargaining. Those developments have lent some urgency to the project of cultivating mechanisms of worker participation in workplace governance to supplement collective bargaining. Unions—the central institutions of Old Governance in the workplace—inevitably play crucial roles in shaping New Governance institutions for representation of workers. Outside the USA, and especially in Europe, unions have maintained enough political and economic power, both within and beyond the sphere of collective bargaining, to participate confidently in the development of other institutions for participatory workplace governance. In the USA, unions are currently shaping the rise of New Governance-based approaches to regulation mainly by their absence from the discussion, and their insistence on fortifying traditional collective bargaining and adversarial enforcement mechanisms. The result has been a serious lack of public engagement and policy analysis with regard to the nonetheless-emerging forms of governance-based regulatory strategies, and, in particular, a serious neglect of the participatory dimension of those strategies.

Notes

1. I use the term "governance-based approaches to regulation" here to describe a subset of meta-regulatory or reflexive regulatory strategies (both of which describe regulation by one actor of another's regulatory processes (Parker 2002; Levi-Faur, Chapter 1, this volume)). The focus here is on regulation by the state (sometimes with other actors) of the self-regulatory or internal governance processes of private firms.
2. My primary focus here is on how societies pursue their regulatory objectives, not on what those objectives are or how they are chosen. For present purposes I assume (optimistically, perhaps) that societal objectives, including labor rights and standards, are determined through a functioning democratic political process.
3. For large branded firms, both the operational and compliance sides of the self-regulatory enterprise increasingly extend to suppliers. Multinational firms have thus become not only part of the problem of the exploitation of workers and resources in developing countries, but potentially part of the solution (Braithwaite 2008; Fung, O'Rourke, and Sabel 2001, Gereffi, Humphrey, and Sturgeon 2005).
4. Employees rarely sue their current employers (Donohue and Siegelman 1991). The predominance of ex-employee plaintiffs tilts private enforcement toward laws regulating discharge (versus laws regulating ongoing conditions such as harassment or unpaid overtime); and toward retrospective, monetary relief (versus prospective remedies that benefit current and future employees) (Estlund 2007).
5. The National Labor Relations Act prohibits employer assistance or domination of "labor organizations," which include "any organization of any kind ... in which employees participate and which exists for the purpose, in whole or in part, of dealing with employers" on terms and conditions of employment (National Labor Relations Act 2006).
6. Workers are also represented on firms' boards of directors pursuant to "co-determination" schemes pioneered in Germany (EC 2008).
7. Indeed, a modest 1995 proposal for mandatory workplace safety committees, as part of an occupational safety and health reform bill, met both strong employer opposition and union skepticism (Estlund 2010).
8. A proposal to loosen the NLRA's restrictions on employer-sponsored forms of employee representation narrowly passed both Houses of Congress in 1996 but was vetoed by President Clinton (Estlund 2010).

References

Arlen, J. 1994. The potentially perverse effects of corporate criminal liability. *Journal of Legal Studies* 23: 833–867.

Arlen, J. and Kraakman, R. 1997. Controlling corporate misconduct: An analysis of corporate liability. *New York University Law Review* 72: 687–779.

Arthurs, H. W. 2002. Private ordering and workers' rights in the global economy: Corporate codes of conduct as a regime of labour market regulation. In J. Conaghan, R. M. Fischl, and

K. Klare (eds.), *Labour Law in an Era of Globalisation: Transformative Practices and Possibilities.* New York: Oxford University Press, 471–487.

Ayres, I. and Braithwaite, J. 1992. *Responsive Regulation: Transcending the Deregulation Debate.* New York: Oxford University Press.

Barenberg, M. 1994. Democracy and domination in the law of workplace cooperation: From bureaucratic to flexible production. *Columbia Law Review* 94: 753–983.

Befort, S. E. 2004. A new voice for the workplace: A proposal for an American works councils act. *Missouri Law Review* 69: 607–651.

Bercusson, B. and Estlund, C. (eds.) 2007. *Regulating Labour in the Wake of Globalisation.* Oxford: Hart.

Bercusson, B. and Estlund, C. 2007. Regulating labour in the wake of globalisation: New challenges, new institutions. In B. Bercusson and C. Estlund, *Regulating Labour in the Wake of Globalisation.* Oxford: Hart, 1–18.

Blackett, A. 2001. Global governance, legal pluralism and the decentered state: A labor law critique of codes of corporate conduct. *Indiana Journal of Global Legal Studies* 8: 401–447.

Braithwaite, J. 1985. *To Punish or Persuade: Enforcement of Coal Mine Safety.* Albany, NY: State University of New York Press.

Braithwaite, J. 2008. *Regulatory Capitalism: How it Works, Ideas for Making it Work Better.* Cheltenham: Edward Elgar.

Braithwaite, J. and Drahos, P. 2000. *Global Business Regulation.* Cambridge: Cambridge University Press.

Commons, J. 1921. *Industrial Government.* New York: Macmillan.

Dobbin, F. 2009. *Inventing Equal Opportunity.* Princeton, NJ: Princeton University Press.

Donohue, J. and Siegelman, P. 1991. The changing nature of employment discrimination litigation. *Stanford Law Review* 43: 983–1033.

Doorey, D. 2010. Decentring labor law. Unpublished paper presented at CRIMT, Employee Representation in the New World of Work. Quebec City.

Dow, G. K. 2003. *Governing the Firm: Workers' Control in Theory and Practice.* New York: Cambridge University Press.

Dunlop Commission on the Future of Worker–Management Relations. 1994. *Final Report*; available at http://digitalcommons.ilr.cornell.edu/key_workplace/2/ (accessed 19 September 2011).

Edelman, L. B. 1999. The endogeneity of legal regulation: Grievance procedures as rational myth. *American Journal of Sociology* 105: 406–454.

Edelman, L. B., Abraham, S. E. and Erlanger, H. S. 1992. Professional construction of law: The inflated threat of wrongful discharge. *Law and Society Review* 26: 47–83.

Edelman, L. B., Erlanger, H. S. and Lande, J. 1993. Internal dispute resolution: The transformation of civil rights in the workplace. *Law and Society Review* 27: 497–534.

Estlund, C. 2010a. Working together under antidiscrimination law: Paradoxes and possibilities. In M. Gulati and M. Yelnosky (eds.), *NYU Selected Essays on Labor and Employment Law: Behavioral Analyses of Workplace Discrimination* 3. New York: Kluwer Law International, 331–351.

Estlund, C. 2010b. *Regoverning the Workplace: From Self-Regulation to Co-Regulation.* New Haven, CT: Yale University Press.

European Commission (EC) 2008. *Employee Representatives in an Enlarged Europe*, 2 vols. Luxembourg: Office for Official Publications of the European Communities.

Freeman, R. and Medoff, J. 1984. *What Do Unions Do?* New York: Basic Books.

Fung, A., O'Rourke, D. and Sabel, C. 2001. *Can We Put an End to Sweatshops?* Boston, MA: Beacon Press.

Gereffi, G., Humphrey, J. and Sturgeon, T. 2005. The governance of global value chains. *Review of International Political Economy* 12: 78–104.

Hirsch, J. M. and Hirsch, B. T. 2007. The rise and fall of private sector unionism: What next for the NLRA? *Florida State University Law Review* 34: 1133–1180.

Kaufman, B. E. 2007. What do unions do? Evaluation and commentary. In J. T. Bennett and B. E. Kaufman (eds.), *What Do Unions Do? A Twenty-Year Perspective*. New Brunswick, NJ: Transaction, 548–562.

Khanna, V. S. 2000. Corporate liability standards: When should corporations be held criminally liable? *American Criminal Law Review* 37: 1239–1283.

Kochan, T. A. 2006. Updating American labor law: Taking advantage of a window of opportunity. *Comparative Labor Law and Policy Journal* 28: 101–123.

Krawiec, K. D. 2003. Cosmetic compliance and the failure of negotiated governance. *Washington University Law Quarterly* 81: 487–544.

Levi-Faur, D. 2005. The global diffusion of regulatory capitalism. *Annals of American Academy of Political and Social Science* 598 (March): 12–32.

Levine, D. I. 1998. *Working in the Twenty-First Century, Policies for Economic Growth through Training, Opportunity, and Education*. Armonk, NY: M.E. Sharpe.

Lobel, O. 2004. The renew deal: The fall of regulation and the rise of governance in contemporary legal thought. *Minnesota Law Review* 89: 342–470.

Lobel, O. 2005. Interlocking regulatory and industrial relations: The governance of workplace safety. *Administrative Law Review* 57: 1071–1144.

Lobel, O. 2009. Citizenship, organizational citizenship, and the laws of overlapping obligations. *California Law Review* 97: 433–499.

National Labor Relations Act. 2006. 29 U.S.C. §§ 152(5), 158(a)(2).

Parker, C. 2002. *The Open Corporation: Effective Self-Regulation and Democracy*. Cambridge: Cambridge University Press.

Parker, C. 2007. Meta-regulation: Legal accountability for corporate social responsibility? In D. McBarnet, A. Voiculescu, and T. Campbell (eds.), *The New Corporate Accountability: Corporate Social Responsibility and the Law*. Cambridge: Cambridge University Press, 207–237.

Rogers, J. and Streeck, W. 1994. Workplace representation overseas: The works councils story. In R. B. Freeman (ed.), *Working under Different Rules*. New York: Russell Sage Foundation, 97–156.

Stone, K. V. W. 1981. The post-war paradigm in American labor law. *Yale Law Journal* 90: 1509–1580.

Stone, K. V. W. 2007. Flexibilization, globalization, and privatization: Three challenges to labour rights in our time. In B. Bercusson and C. Estlund, *Regulating Labour in the Wake of Globalisation*. Oxford: Hart (eds.) 115–135.

Tyler, T., Dienhart, J. and Thomas, T. 2008. The ethical commitment to compliance: Building value-based cultures. *California Management Review* 50: 31–51.

USSC (United States Sentencing Commission) 2009. *Guidelines Manual*. Washington, DC: Government Printing Office.

Wachter, M. 2007. Labor unions: A corporatist institution in a competitive world. *University of Pennsylvania Law Review* 155: 581–634.

Wachtman, G. R. 1994. Safe and sound: The case for safety and health committees under OSHA and the NLRA. *Cornell Journal of Law and Public Policy* 4: 65–126.

Weil, D. 1991. Enforcing OSHA: The role of labor unions. *Industrial Relations: A Journal of Economy and Society* 30: 20–36.

Weiler, P. 1983. Promises to keep: Securing workers' rights to self-organization under the NLRA. *Harvard Law Review* 96: 1769–1827.

Weiler, P. 1990. *Governing the Workplace*. Cambridge, MA: Harvard University Press.

CHAPTER 39

···

GOVERNANCE AND
VOLUNTARY REGULATION

···

COLIN PROVOST

REGULATION of business through voluntary means (also known as self-regulation) has grown increasingly prominent in the international business community and has attracted considerable attention from scholars of law, economics, and political science. The increasing prevalence of voluntary regulation coincides with the rise of the concept of "governance" in political science and public administration. Broadly speaking, the study of governance involves the analysis of actors and institutions inside government, and also the organized interests, voters, and networks of all of the above. Moreover, it involves the study of how these actors interact with each other to produce policy. Thus, a key assumption of the governance framework is that policy outcomes are shaped by a multitude of actors. Actors within government do not dictate policy outcomes by themselves, rather the policy-making environment is characterized by dynamic relationships between multiple actors that involve negotiation and information exchange. As Rhodes states in Chapter 3 of this volume, "network governance evokes a world in which state power is dispersed among a vast array of spatially and functionally distinct networks composed of all kinds of public, voluntary, and private organizations with which the centre now interacts."

Similarly, in regulatory governance, regulators and firms have a dynamic relationship in which they bargain over the enactment and implementation of regulatory policies. In this relationship, governments have a variety of policy tools at their disposal with which they regulate firm behavior. First, they can impose specifically prescribed behavior, a method that has come to be known as command and control (C&C). Second, they can pursue more cooperative solutions, by allowing firms to propose their own solutions to regulatory problems, perhaps while pushing them to meet particular performance targets. Third, governments can pursue market-oriented solutions, such as taxes, subsidies, and markets for tradable permits. Market solutions have been most frequently advocated by economists as solutions to negative externalities, such as pollution. Finally, governments can allow firms to regulate themselves.

This last method—voluntary regulation—has become a prevalent mode of regulatory governance. In environmental regulation, many firms have implemented their own environmental management systems, which require them to establish specific goals, redesign production processes with the aim of reducing emissions and waste, and allow monitors to measure the firm's progress. Firms may adopt such policies because they are part of trade association voluntary programs or may be members of international standard-setting bodies such as the International Organization for Standardization (ISO), or they may adopt such policies entirely on their own. Firms that provide financial services may also regulate their own behavior in the interest of being transparent to stockholders or creating uniform behavior across their profession, in order to make the business more stable and predictable.

But why do firms volunteer to regulate themselves? After all, if firms are profit-maximizing, why would they not choose to offer minimal compliance or even evasion in the face of government regulations? An equally important question is why would governments agree to such an arrangement of regulatory institutions? How can governments know whether firms will credibly police themselves to ensure they are in compliance with regulations? Firms and politicians have different incentives, as firms are motivated by profit, and politicians are motivated by the desire to be re-elected, but also the desire to make policy as they see fit. These differing sets of motivations may produce suboptimal outcomes as electoral incentives lead politicians to seek C&C-style regulation, which may, in turn, induce firms to evade regulations. The lack of cooperation in such a case represents a collective action problem in which the government must consequently spend more on monitoring and enforcement than it would if firms legitimately regulated themselves. The monitoring and enforcement costs represent transaction costs that both sides may be able to reduce through effective cooperation.

For example, firms might choose to regulate themselves because they believe it will help them to innovate and reduce the cost of production. Governments, on the other hand, know that while C&C techniques might spur firms to pollute less, the costs of monitoring firms and enforcing the regulations can be significant. Thus, analyzing voluntary regulation through the lenses of collective action and transaction costs can inform our understanding of its evolution.

In this chapter, I survey the extant literature and seek to address three broad research questions. First, what regulatory governance arrangements preceded the proliferation of voluntary regulations and why? Second, what are the motivations for government and business to come together and adopt business self-regulation as regulatory policy? Finally, what institutional designs do we see in modern voluntary governance and what effect do these designs have on regulatory policy outcomes? I attempt to answer these questions in five sections. While voluntary regulation can happen in almost any area of regulatory governance, it has been particularly salient in environmental and financial regulation and, thus, I focus most on those areas. First, I discuss the classic collective action problems that plague governments and firms when faced with market failures, and how high transaction costs feed into these problems. Second, to illustrate the problem of transaction costs, I examine environmental regulatory governance in the 1970s and 1980s, particularly in the United States. Third, I spell out the motivations for both governments and firms to adopt voluntary regulatory policies. Fourth, I analyze the institutional design of modern voluntary governance, while describing the features that may increase the likelihood of meaningful compliance. Finally, I present concluding thoughts on what voluntary programs mean for the future of regulatory governance, particularly in the environmental and financial policy domains.

Regulatory governance and collective action

When governments choose policy instruments to regulate business (and businesses choose the policies by which they want to abide), there are potential collective action problems lurking. Numerous scholars have analyzed similar versions of game-theoretical models in which policy outcomes are determined by governments' choice of regulatory policies and firms' corresponding decisions to comply with or evade the regulations (e.g. Ayres and Braithwaite 1992; Potoski and Prakash 2004a; Scholz 1984). When the government prescribes flexible methods of regulation and firms choose to regulate themselves, the optimal outcome has been achieved. In this case, the desired regulatory outcome has been achieved at a minimal cost to the state. However, if firms do not effectively police themselves, then the market failures continue and the government is cheated by the firms' defection. Conversely, if firms want to self-regulate, but the government wants to employ a C&C approach, market failures may be reduced, but at a greater cost to the firm than if the government had prescribed flexible methods. Instead, firms may choose to evade regulations if the government employs a C&C approach, which yields a suboptimal outcome for both, as the government spends resources on regulation that may prevent market failures, yet at a higher cost than we see in the first scenario.

That the optimal outcome is the one in which government and businesses cooperate with each other is not new. Early on in the discussion, Scholz theorized that regulators and firms can maintain cooperation through a tit-for-tat (TFT) strategy (1984). Regulators refrain from applying harsh punishment to firms until they defect from regulatory compliance, at which time regulators must employ punitive measures in order to reduce the payoff to firms evading compliance. According to Scholz, the punishment firms face for evading regulations gives them the incentive to cooperate again with regulators. Ayres and Braithwaite attempt to refine Scholz's research by arguing that regulators have a multitude of regulatory tools, beyond just those that produce cooperation or punishment (1992). They argue that prosecution costs valuable time and resources, and that regulators will prefer to persuade and negotiate, but that these tactics will not be effective with firms unless the threat of prosecution is credible. Thus, if persuasion does not work, regulators can gradually escalate the level of punishment until firms are persuaded to comply.

Echoing these findings, there has recently been an emphasis on the distinction between management-based regulation and C&C-style regulation. Coglianese and Lazer (2003) praise management-based approaches as those in which governments nudge firms toward compliance, while giving them the flexibility to design their own production processes. Conversely, the authors' term for C&C approaches—"technology-based regulation"—is named as such because these methods specify precisely how technology is to be used, without affording firms process flexibility. Tallberg adopts similar terminology, as he argues that the European Commission uses management techniques to attempt to bring member states into compliance with European Union (EU) directives and only applies sanctions (through a referral to the European Court of First Instance or the European Court of Justice) when a member state has been consistently in violation of directives (2002).

Voluntary regulation represents one form of regulatory governance in which governments and firms attempt to cooperate with each other. Before moving to a discussion explicitly about voluntary regulation, I examine environmental regulation in the 1970s and 1980s and how its design often fell short of cooperative goals.

MODES OF ENVIRONMENTAL GOVERNANCE

Politicians are motivated to reduce transaction costs in policy when constructing regulatory policy institutions, but this is certainly not their only motivation. Politicians also want to be re-elected and this motivation may lead them to believe that they must be seen to be doing something to combat market failures. In such a case, they might be more likely to adopt a C&C approach, particularly if consumer, labor, or environmental interests are strong and well-organized. Economists have long pointed out that this is why C&C approaches often win out over market-based approaches. To the average voter, the benefits of command and control are more visible as firms are told to stop polluting in no uncertain terms. On the other hand, the same average voter, who may have no background in economics, might not understand how taxes can reduce pollution (Barthold 1994; Stavins 1998), rather they only see higher costs. Politicians also may be reluctant to establish environmental taxes because they are easily portrayed by environmental interests as "licenses to pollute" (Stavins 1998). Finally, the creation of an environmental tax is built on the assumption that the marginal social cost of pollution can be quantified and measured and that the corresponding tax will match this amount. Measuring the costs of pollution is not a simple task and, even when it is feasible, other political factors, such as the need to balance budgets, may determine the level of tax (Barthold 1994).

To better understand the role of transaction costs and collective action issues in regulation, it is instructive to examine environmental regulatory governance in the United States from the 1970s onwards. When President Nixon signed legislation in 1970 that created the Environmental Protection Agency (EPA), it marked the commencement of an era of dominant, C&C-style environmental regulation. Rising air and water pollution levels in urban areas, as well as concerns about overpopulation and pesticides in food, galvanized environmental interests, and pushed environmental policy toward the top of the federal policy-making agenda. The Clean Air Act of 1970 stipulated that firms had to develop new pollution-abating technology according to strict timetables and if they failed to do so, they were subject to heavy fines and penalties. As Eisner recounts, "The environmental legislation addressing air and water pollution described the substances the EPA was to regulate and provided relatively precise, if overly ambitious, implementation timetables" (1993: 128). Such regulations were often administered uniformly across thousands of firms that had heterogeneous production processes, outputs, and sizes (Bardach and Kagan 1982). Consequently, the EPA reported that, by 1990, the annual costs of controlling pollution had reached $125 billion (USEPA 1990). American environmental regulations resembled suboptimal situations for both businesses and the government, due to the high costs of compliance and the subsequent higher probability of non-compliance.

The lack of business input into regulatory rules prompted many observers to argue that costs could be reduced if all affected interests could come together, offer input, and negotiate solutions upon which all parties could agree.[1]

In 1982, the Administrative Conference of the United States (ACUS) formally recommended that government agencies utilize Alternative Dispute Resolution (ADR) techniques and, soon after, negotiated rule-making was born. Through a cooperative framework, the goal of negotiated rule-making was to achieve higher levels of consensus from all affected parties, with the hope of preventing the delays, litigation, and lack of compliance that had come to characterize the C&C approach. However, negotiated rule-making produced mixed results, as some scholars found that it saved time and improved information sharing (Fiorino 1988), while other scholars found no time savings when compared to conventional rule-making (Coglianese 1997). Additionally, Weber and Khademian found that not all parties involved credibly committed to negotiated rule-making as, in at least one high-profile case, one party in the negotiations sought and received an exemption to the new rules from President George H. W. Bush (1997). Thus, collective action problems between regulators and firms remained a significant problem even after the advent of a more cooperative approach.

The motivation for self-regulation

Voluntary regulation has demonstrated that such collective action problems can be overcome, but in order to understand which institutional arrangements bring cooperation, it is important to understand why governments and businesses seek self-regulatory arrangements. Governments will sometimes accept arrangements in which businesses are responsible for regulating themselves because business self-regulation can reduce transaction costs for politicians and for regulators. In complex policy areas, such as environmental, health, safety, or financial regulation, actors within firms often have a better understanding of their own activities than do regulators, thus creating an information asymmetry between the regulators and the regulated. This asymmetry is exacerbated by the fact that firms vary significantly in terms of size, production process, and output. If firms choose to exploit this information asymmetry, it means that regulators must spend more resources monitoring the firm's behavior.

Recall that electoral incentives may drive governments to choose C&C-style regulatory regimes. If a government chooses a technology-based regulatory approach that specifies how firms ought to produce particular goods (Coglianese and Lazer 2003), the process of monitoring the firm's behavior will be more demanding and more difficult. And, in a large economy, the ratio of regulators to firms is often so lopsided that few firms are properly monitored. For example, between 1996 and 1998, only 1 percent of all large, regulated firms in the United States were monitored for hazardous waste, air, and water pollution (Hale 1998). However, if firms see self-regulation as in their best interest, then regulators need not spend as many resources on monitoring and enforcement as they would if the firm were in frequent violation of regulations. Similarly, politicians need not spend as many resources ensuring that regulators are effectively policing regulated interests.

Business firms have a more extensive set of reasons for why they would potentially want to self-regulate. First, self-regulation offers firms the opportunity to innovate and eliminate resource waste in their production processes. Through the implementation of management systems, firms can analyze what goes into their products to see if there are cheaper methods of production. The implementation of such systems is contrasted with C&C-style governance which, in environmental regulation, focuses on "end of pipe" solutions that are designed to reduce emissions, but only after the production process has nearly reached its conclusion. Analyzing the whole process has the potential to reduce waste and costs in production, and enable the firm to offer its products at a lower price. Moreover, by reducing negative externalities, firms are better able to shield themselves from regulatory enforcement actions. Many firms recognize that long-term compliance with environmental regulations is costly and they strive to reduce the costs of compliance through innovation. Firms with the organizational and resource capacity to innovate and cut costs will be more likely to regulate themselves voluntarily, while firms that have already demonstrated a prior commitment to environmental protection, usually continue to exercise this (Florida, Atlas, and Cline 2001).

Second, the self-regulation of production methods enables firms to differentiate their products from others on the market. Many consumers want to buy products from socially responsible firms that, for example, minimize environmental damage and pay all their employees reasonable wages. Traditionally, consumers have had to engage in extensive search costs in order to determine whether a company was green or whether it treated its employees well, but business membership in a voluntary regulatory body has the potential to transmit a clear signal to consumers about the level of a firm's social responsibility. In this way, membership in a voluntary organization with a strong reputation enables a firm to benefit from the brand name of that organization, thereby signaling to consumers that the business takes its commitment to regulate itself seriously. Prakash and Potoski have characterized the reputation a voluntary organization offers as a "club good" (2007).

Typically, firms must pay to join, as they must bear the costs of certification and of implementing management systems, but the reputation benefit is available to any firm that wants to join the organization. Later, I discuss the conditions under which the signal is likely to be a legitimate one and not one tainted by corporate shirking.

Third, firms may be motivated to self-regulate if there is a legitimate threat of new regulations from the government. Héritier and Eckert find that in the EU, when governing coalitions are able to demonstrate a credible threat to issue new legislation, firms are more likely to organize and implement new, voluntary codes through their trade association (2009). In this case, self-regulation acts as a preemptive strike before the government adopts its own codes.

Fourth, self-regulation may also appeal to firms because of the identity or professional orientation of those performing the inspections. Representatives of firms are inclined to prefer inspector visits from members of their own industry, as opposed to government inspectors, who they fear do not share the same attitudes or beliefs. Rees has found that in occupational health and safety, workers are often less inclined to heed the advice of a government inspector simply because "he's just not one of us" (1988: 147). Similarly, Prakash argues that firm managers are welcoming of ISO inspectors (who are often peers within the industry) because they have a "problem-solving attitude," which stands in stark contrast to the attitudes displayed by government inspectors (2000: 117). Thus, firms may adopt a more positive attitude to regulation in general if they are inspected by people with whom they can identify on a professional basis.

Finally, governments and firms may both seek business self-regulation in the interests of policy harmonization. In some policy areas, most notably financial regulation, there is demand from stockholders and from the firms themselves to hold all firms to the same standards in order to reduce uncertainty when doing business on a global scale. In banking for example, global interdependence of banks means that a bank failure in one country can produce bank failures and unstable economies in other countries. This provides a powerful incentive to regulators and to bankers themselves to establish predictable norms of behavior that will minimize such destabilizing economic events. In accounting, if all firms are held to the same standards of reporting, it creates a more transparent situation by enabling stockholders to compare numbers more easily across firms. Many of the modern standards by which financial service firms abide come from international organizations, such as the Basel Committee (banking supervision) or the International Accounting Standards Board (IASB) (accounting supervision), which are comprised of industry members and technical experts.

THE DESIGN OF SELF-REGULATORY PROGRAMS

Self-regulatory programs have the potential to create effective regulatory governance while minimizing transaction costs for businesses and for governments, but whether such programs are successful depends heavily on the design of such programs and on the institutions employed to carry them out. For example, if firms are bound by a particular agreement to regulate themselves voluntarily, yet there are no mechanisms to prevent cheating or free riding, then the agreement may fall apart, as honest firms do not want to be "suckers" who carry the weight of firms that do not abide by the agreement. Similarly, if firms can claim to be voluntarily reducing emissions, yet are not subject to any type of verification or auditing, then it is easier for them to engage in a type of green marketing that is entirely symbolic and devoid of substance (also known as "greenwashing"). If a government relaxes its own regulations in response to a promise from a firm or set of firms to voluntarily self-regulate, then it too will feel like the sucker if self-regulation is not meaningful. In such a case, the government is likely to reimplement its regulations, knowing that trust has broken down between the regulators and the regulated. Thus, in order for self-regulation to work, firms that want to self-regulate must credibly commit to it and avoid the temptation to merely appear to be self-regulating, and governments must also consider how their own regulations can be compatible with business self-regulation.

Environmental self-regulation

A common method through which firms regulate their own environmental practices is through trade association codes. Well-known examples include the American Forest and Paper Association's (AFPA) Sustainable Forestry Initiative and the American Chemistry Council's (ACC) Responsible Care Initiative. According to Eisner, each association developed its standards in response to public relations disasters, which damaged the industries' reputations (2007). In the case of the AFPA, the controversy over the endangered spotted owl in the forests of the American Pacific Northwest spurred the organization into action, while the Union Carbide chemical leak in Bhopal, India, led the ACC to create the Responsible Care Initiative. Both programs outlined a broad set of principles designed to reduce environmental waste and damage, but differences in the structure of each program have resulted in varying perceptions of each program's success.

As Eisner points out, the Sustainable Forestry Initiative (SFI) has several features that have enhanced its effectiveness (2007). First, it outlines specific performance indicators against which firms are to be measured; these data are, in turn, available to the public. Second, the SFI is a mandatory program for all members of the AFPA, which is an essential feature, as it only takes one well-publicized accident for the entire industry to take a reputation hit (Prakash and Potoski 2007). Thus, if all AFPA members are forced to join the SFI, firms that are committed to it cannot be cheated by members who refuse to join. Finally, third-party auditing is used to verify each firm's performance, and firms whose performance does not measure up to the SFI's standards can be asked to leave the association.

With the Responsible Care Initiative, the ACC also laid out a list of principles and targets, and required that its members join the program, but it did not create a system of independent verification, as the AFPA did in the SFI. Rather, firm auditing was to be done by member-company and community representatives. Moreover, there was no system of sanctions in place for firms that failed to abide by the program's code. Consequently, the available evidence does not suggest that the environmental management performance of the Responsible Care participants was any better than firms outside the ACC (King and Lenox 2000).

While trade association programs cover specific industries, some standard-setting bodies have been able to attract a significant proportion of the international business community as members.[2] Perhaps the most well-known of these is the International Organization for Standardization (ISO), a non-governmental organization (NGO) based in Geneva, which is comprised of private, domestic standard-setting bodies, which in turn, are comprised of industry officials and technical experts (Mattli and Buthe 2003; Prakash and Potoski 2006). The ISO 9000 series deals with quality control standards while the ISO 14000 series deals with environmental management standards (Eisner 2007). ISO 14001, which was launched in 1995, has become the most widely adopted of the ISO standards, as well as perhaps the most studied (Prakash and Potoski 2006). As Prakash and Potoski have indicated, if firms want to join, they must demonstrate seriously that they are willing to improve their environmental standards. This typically involves implementing environmental management systems, training employees in environmental management, establishing procedures to ensure that the firm's new management systems are transparent and then finally undergoing an initial certification audit. Perhaps most importantly, signing up to ISO 14001 involves continual auditing from independent, third parties, who can verify whether each firm is living up to its responsibility under the standard (Prakash 2000).

ISO 14001 meets many of the theoretical criteria necessary to have a successful voluntary regulatory program. First, by imposing significant costs on firms through the certification procedure, ISO ensures that firms are actually committed to maintaining meaningful environmental management systems. Second, by employing a system of third-party auditing and verification, ISO ensures that none of its members shirk its responsibility under the standard. Third, because of its status as a legitimate standard-setting body with an international reputation, ISO is able to attract firms by the thousands, who in turn can abide by similar standards. Prakash argues that such a feature also has the potential to reduce trade barriers, since concerns about harmonizing environmental practices are not as significant when firms apply the same standards (2000). Moreover, as the large membership in ISO indicates that many firms are subject to the same standards, the ISO has a clear advantage over trade association codes, "which may vary widely with respect to their rigor and enforcement" (Eisner 2007: 167).

To date, the evidence regarding the potential effectiveness of ISO 14001 has been mostly positive. US firms that join ISO 14001 are more likely to be in compliance with government regulations (Potoski and Prakash 2005a), and more likely to have lower emission levels (Potoski and Prakash 2005b) than their counterparts that have not joined. Moreover, in contrast to the "race to the bottom" hypothesis, which predicts that international trade can lead to weakened domestic regulations, Prakash and Potoski find that trade linkages can boost ISO 14001 participation, if a given country's export market also contains a high number of ISO participants (2006). Thus, trade can ensure that high levels of ISO participation abroad beget high levels at home. Finally, another way in which ISO participation is part of a self-expanding dynamic is that many firms demand their parts suppliers also be ISO certified (Héritier, Mueller-Debus, and Thauer 2009). Because of these high standards, Héritier and colleagues also find that firms with this requirement are significantly more likely to carry out inspections of the supply firms themselves, rather than simply delegate this to government regulators (2009).

Despite the overall success of ISO 14001, it still suffers from a low participation rate among American firms (Eisner 2007; Potoski and Prakash 2004b). Potoski and Prakash find that countries with strict environmental regulations have higher levels of ISO participation, yet when such regulations are coupled with an adversarial legal system, such as that of the United States, ISO adoption is likely to be lower (2004b). But why is this? Implementing environmental management systems involves a thorough and transparent examination of the production processes in a firm, and sometimes this may uncover processes that are in violation of current regulations. In order to embark on a path of self-regulation, many American firms have asked the EPA for immunity from prosecution for potential violations uncovered, so that they can work toward correcting those failures. However, the EPA believes that such immunity would represent a compromise of regulations, especially if firms used their immunity to then renege on their pledge to self-regulate. "Within regulatory agencies, enforcement and program staffs are often skeptical of changes they fear will allow too much flexibility for regulated entities" (Fiorino 1999: 442). The end result is a collective action problem of paralysis, as regulated and regulator each fear being cheated by the other.

Comparative research has also revealed that European firms are often in a better position than American firms to join international standards, for a variety of reasons. Mattli and Buthe examine private standard-developing organizations (SDOs) in the United States and the EU, and the effects they can have on participating in international standards set by organizations such as ISO (2003). They state that SDOs in the United States operate in a fragmented and competitive arena, in which there is no centralized, standard-setting organization, and that they consequently only share information about new international standards with their dues-paying members. Conversely, SDOs in European countries coordinate their information, rather than compete, and they frequently work under the auspices of centralized standard-setting bodies, such as the German Institute for Standardization or the British Standards Institution. As a result of these institutional arrangements, European SDOs receive information about proposed international standards more rapidly and are therefore in a better position to influence the creation of the standards. Because such information does not travel as rapidly in the fragmented American SDO system, American firms receive such information later and are not well-positioned to shape standards. American firms must then pay the switching costs to adopt the new standards, while European firm standards are already closely aligned. Faced with the high costs of changing practice, many American firms simply opt not to join ISO standards.

Financial service self-regulation

Self-regulation in the financial sector has been driven, to a very large extent, by the sheer complexity of finance policy. Representatives of firms that offer financial services have specialized knowledge of economics and finance, giving them a strong information advantage over government regulators, thus creating the potential for a significant principal–agent problem. Additionally, the overwhelming ratio of financial institutions to financial regulators in government makes it difficult to effectively keep a watchful eye on such institutions. Consequently, at the domestic level, some countries regulate their banking sectors according to levels of risk. Thus, banks are expected to regulate themselves from the inside, but if their behavior appears to pose high levels of risk to the financial sector as a whole, then government regulators are forced to monitor them more closely.

But how are banks to regulate themselves? The interdependent nature of financial institutions in a global economy underscores the need for firms to maintain standards that prevent market failures, whose negative effects can ripple through the world economy. Many of the international standards currently set for financial service firms are established by international organizations, such as the Basel Committee, for banking, or the IASB, for accounting. Further coordination of these standards may be implemented by financial trade associations, or government regulators may rely on firm self-regulation while employing a philosophy of risk regulation.

The design of international institutions that are responsible for the coordination of national regulatory policy has been examined extensively. Keohane has argued that such institutions have been established in order to prevent cheating on multination agreements and to prevent market failures from spilling across borders (1984). Similarly, Braithwaite and Drahos argue that a series of disruptive bank failures in the 1970s led to the creation of the Basel Committee, whose job was to set standards that would generate predictable and stable banking behavior (2000). And Kapstein argues that minimum capital requirements were created for banks because of regulators' knowledge of the dangers posed by banks that did not carry enough capital reserves (1989). However, just as the motivation to reduce transaction costs could not explain the existence of C&C-style environmental regulation in the United States, a number of scholars have argued that a transaction-cost framework is not sufficient to explain fully the institutional design of many international organizations.

The domestic political situation of participating countries has a significant impact on the design of international organizations tasked with the responsibility of coordinating economic policy. Oatley and Nabors argue that politicians in the United States responded to the less-developed-country debt crisis of 1983 by raising capital requirements on American banks, while simultaneously writing these new requirements into international banking agreements, thereby preventing any erosion of American banks' market share (1998). Singer argues that regulators will seek international harmonization only when there has been a negative shock to the confidence or competitiveness of their

banking system (2004). Thus, while establishing international capital reserve requirements for banks is grounded in the collective desire to bring stability and predictability
to global business, it is also driven by domestic politics.

In accounting, the motivation to reduce transaction costs has manifested itself in the
creation of the IASB, a private organization responsible for accounting standard-setting
at an international level. Mattli and Buthe argue that governments respond to investor
demand for harmonized accounting rules by creating a private body, such as the IASB,
whose members come from within the industry and possess a higher collective level of
expertise than government officials do (2005). Because the IASB is a relatively new creation, Mattli and Buthe make the American counterpart, the Financial Accounting
Standards Board (FASB), the subject of their analysis. They argue that a private regulatory body like the FASB has multiple principals, the public overseers—in this case, the
public Securities and Exchange Commission—and private stakeholders, in the form of
accounting companies who must abide by the FASB's standards. Regulatory policy outcomes will, in turn, be shaped by the tightness of the bonds in each of these P/A relationships. For example, the fact that the FASB's funding came from regulated accounting
firms created the perception, particularly in the wake of the Enron and Worldcom scandals in 2001–2002, that accounting firms were able to exercise high levels of influence
over the FASB, at the expense of the public interest (Mattli and Buthe 2005). Thus, in
such a situation, if the private regulator leans too far in favor of regulated interests, then
the government can end up playing the role of the sucker and, consequently, may choose
to redesign the regulatory institutions. This is precisely what happened after the Enron
and Worldcom scandals, as Congress passed the Sarbanes-Oxley Act, which mandated
changes in the way funding was distributed from firms to the FASB (Mattli and Buthe
2005), and created an additional agency, the Public Company Accounting Oversight
Board (PCAOB) to monitor the behavior of accounting firms.

CONCLUSION

In this chapter, I have attempted to spell out the reasons why self-regulation has proliferated in recent years, and analyze some of the institutional features of voluntary governance. Such programs can reduce transaction costs in regulatory policy and foster
cooperation between government and firms, but particular institutions need to be in
place for such programs to arise and then to succeed. For example, making the implementation of an environmental management system sufficiently costly to a firm can
ensure that the firm's commitment to green production is genuine. If industry trade
associations implement self-regulation programs, compulsory program participation
for all association members can prevent free riding from laggard members. Finally, the
presence of independent auditors can ensure that firms maintain their commitments.

Despite this accumulated body of knowledge, self-regulation programs are an evolving phenomenon and there still are a number of salient research questions in this area.

First, as climate change remains an important issue, and agreements on binding emissions reductions remain elusive, the view from the bottom up becomes increasingly important. If there continues to be a proliferation of voluntary participation, from both trade associations as well as increased ISO membership, this may mitigate the effects of the lack of international action.

Second, if we accept that increased ISO membership can reduce polluting emissions, this presents questions about how to deal with the low participation rates in the United States. Potoski and Prakash find that particular US states have created incentives for firms to join ISO 14001 (2004a), but this still leaves unresolved the auditing issue between firms and the EPA. Unless the two sides can reach a compromise in which firms can transparently reveal the flaws in their production processes, participation in ISO 14001 will remain comparatively low. The research of Mattli and Buthe (2003) also provides material for future research in this area. If low ISO participation is also caused by a lack of coordination among domestic standard-setting bodies, this provides an incentive to conduct further state-level research. If the levels of coordination are greater in some American states than others, this would provide further corroboration to Mattli and Buthe's findings and would be potentially instructive for the goal of raising ISO participation.

Finally, the financial crisis of 2007–2009 has not resulted in a consensus about how to prevent such crises from recurring in the future; however, discussions, as of the time of writing, have not included increased voluntary regulation as a viable solution. To be sure, the causes of the crisis are numerous, but the banks' perceived inability to regulate themselves continues to be mentioned prominently. But how did this "inability" manifest itself precisely? Were the standards set by the Basel Accords too imprecise? Was the monitoring and enforcement of their provisions too variable across countries? Already, a burgeoning literature has developed in response to these questions, and the questions will continue to be relevant as long as the reform of banking regulations remains high on national agendas. Moreover, as reforms are passed and implemented, what will be the future of voluntary regulation in the banking sector? We may witness an erosion of self-regulation in this area, as the state tightens its leash. Whatever happens, voluntary regulatory programs will remain salient in regulatory governance and ought to continue to provide a fruitful area for research.

Notes

1. Space limitations prevent a full discussion of environmental regulatory reforms implemented post-1980. For discussion and evaluation of marketable permits for emissions, see, for example, Hahn (1989) and Stavins (1998). See Eisner (2007) for more information about other EPA programs designed to foster cooperation between firms and the EPA, such as Project XL and the 33/50 Program.
2. Some programs count nations and firms as their members. For example, in the Kimberley Process, diamond producers and retailers joined diamond-producing nations to prohibit diamond sales used to finance civil conflict.

References

Ayres, I. and Braithwaite, J. 1992. *Responsive Regulation: Transcending the Deregulation Debate.* Oxford: Oxford University Press.

Bardach, E. and Kagan, R. A. 1982. *Going by the Book: The Problem of Regulatory Unreasonableness.* Philadelphia: Temple University Press.

Barthold, T. A. 1994. Issues in the design of environmental excise taxes. *Journal of Economic Perspectives* 8: 133–151.

Braithwaite, J. and Drahos, P. 2000. *Global Business Regulation.* Cambridge: Cambridge University Press.

Coglianese, C. 1997. Assessing consensus: The promise and performance of negotiated rule-making. *Duke Law Journal* 46: 1255–1350.

Coglianese, C. and Lazer, D. 2003. Management-based regulation: Prescribing private management to achieve public goals. *Law and Society Review* 37: 691–730.

Eisner, M. A. 1993. *Regulatory Politics in Transition.* Baltimore: Johns Hopkins University Press.

Eisner, M. A. 2007. *Governing the Environment: The Transformation of Environmental Regulation.* Boulder, CO: Lynne Rienner Publishers.

Fiorino, D. J. 1988. Regulatory negotiation as a policy process. *Public Administration Review* 48: 764–772.

Fiorino, D. J. 1999. Rethinking environmental regulation: Perspectives on law and governance. *Harvard Environmental Law Review* 23: 441–468.

Florida, R., Atlas, M. and Cline, M. 2001. What makes companies green? Organizational and geographic factors in the adoption of environmental practices. *Economic Geography* 77: 209–224.

Hahn, R. W. 1989. Economic prescriptions for environmental problems: How the patient followed the doctor's orders. *Journal of Economic Perspectives* 3: 95–114.

Hale, R. 1998. *The National Expansion of Star Track.* Boston: Environmental Protection Agency, Region 1.

Héritier, A. and Eckert, S. 2009. Self-regulation by associations: Collective action problems in European environmental regulation. *Business and Politics* 11: 1–22.

Héritier, A., Mueller-Debus, A. K. and Thauer, C. R. 2009. The firm as an inspector: Private ordering and political rules. *Business and Politics* 11: 1–32.

Kapstein, E. B. 1989. Resolving the regulator's dilemma: International coordination of banking regulations. *International Organization* 43: 323–347.

Keohane, R. 1984. *After Hegemony: Cooperation and Discord in the World Political Economy.* Princeton, NJ: Princeton University Press.

King, A. A. and Lenox, M. J. 2000. Industry self-regulation without sanctions: The chemical industry's responsible care program. *Academy of Management Journal* 43: 698–716.

Mattli, W. and Buthe, T. 2003. Setting international standards: Technological rationality or primacy of power. *World Politics* 56: 1–42.

Mattli, W. and Buthe, T. 2005. Accountability in accounting? The politics of private rule-making in the public interest. *Governance* 18: 399–429.

Oatley, T. and Nabors, R. 1998. Redistributive cooperation: Market failure, wealth transfers, and the Basel Accord. *International Organization* 52: 35–54.

Potoski, M. and Prakash, A. 2004a. The regulation dilemma: Cooperation and conflict in environmental governance. *Public Administration Review* 64: 137–148.

Potoski, M. and Prakash, A. 2004b. Regulatory convergence in nongovernmental regimes? Cross-national variation in ISO 14001 adoption. *Journal of Politics* 24: 885–905.

Potoski, M. and Prakash, A. 2005a. Green clubs and voluntary governance: ISO 14001 and firms' regulatory compliance. *American Journal of Political Science* 49: 235–248.

Potoski, M. and Prakash, A. 2005b. Covenants with weak swords: ISO 14001 and facilities' environmental performance. *Journal of Policy Analysis and Management* 24: 745–769.

Prakash, A. 2000. *Greening the Firm: The Politics of Corporate Environmentalism*. Cambridge: Cambridge University Press.

Prakash, A. and Potoski, M. 2006. Racing to the bottom? Trade, environmental governance, and ISO 14001. *American Journal of Political Science* 50: 350–364.

Prakash, A. and Potoski, M. 2007. Collective action through voluntary environmental programs: A club theory perspective. *Policy Studies Journal* 35: 773–792.

Rees, J. 1988. *Reforming the Workplace: A Study of Self-Regulation in Occupational Safety*. Philadelphia: University of Pennsylvania Press.

Scholz, J. T. 1984. Deterrence, cooperation and the ecology of regulatory enforcement. *Law and Society Review* 18: 179–224.

Singer, D. A. 2004. Capital rules: The domestic politics of international regulatory harmonization. *International Organization* 58: 531–565.

Stavins, R. N. 1998. What can we learn from the grand policy experiment? Lessons from SO_2 allowance trading. *Journal of Economic Perspectives* 12: 69–88.

Tallberg, J. 2002. Paths to compliance: Enforcement, management and the European Union. *International Organization* 56: 609–643.

USEPA (US Environmental Protection Agency). 1990. *Environmental Investments: The Costs of a Clean Environment*. Washington, DC: US Environmental Protection Agency.

Weber, E. P. and Khademian, A. M. 1997. From agitation to collaboration: Clearing the air through negotiation. *Public Administration Review* 57: 396–410.

CHAPTER 40

E-GOVERNANCE AND E-DEMOCRACY: QUESTIONING TECHNOLOGY-CENTERED CATEGORIES

ERAN FISHER

E-GOVERNANCE is commonly conceived as the first and necessary step in revitalizing democracy. It promises to make government practices not only more efficient but also more open and interactive, to make information more accessible, and to shift power from government to individuals. E-governance is therefore seen as leading to e-democracy (described here as the evolutionary model) or at the very least as compatible with it (the complementary model). This chapter offers a critique of these prevailing theses by questioning two of their fundamental assumptions: that e-governance and e-democracy are essentially policy decisions made by governments to improve governance practices and revitalize democracy, and that these projects materialize by implementing new information and communication technology. Instead, I propose to take into account both the social and political context within which these projects emerge, and the role of technology discourse in the legitimation of a given political culture and a given constellation of power. Rather than follow policy-defined conceptualizations, I argue that we should identify and criticize the problematic assumptions behind those concepts and offer alternative, more theoretically based, concepts by uncovering the broader social transformations of which these policies are part. In light of this critique, the chapter concludes by offering an alternative model (the contradictory model), according to which e-governance is not necessarily compatible with e-democracy, and a project of e-governance might actually exacerbate the democratic deficit that e-democracy is set to solve.

ELECTRIFYING THE POLITICAL: THE RISE OF E-GOVERNANCE AND E-DEMOCRACY

The development of information and communication technology (ICT) has led to a growing interest in e-governance. E-governance, the management of government and governance practices through the use of ICT, is assumed to make government more accessible to citizens and strengthen communication amongst citizens, civil society and market players, and government agencies. Due to its networked nature, ICT also holds the promise to reinvigorate the democratic process by providing the material infrastructure required to make democracy more direct, or representative democracy more participatory, by engaging citizens in consultation and deliberation (Chadwick 2003; Ron, Chapter 33, this volume). E-governance, with its ability to foster participation may lead to e-democracy (Fischer, Chapter 32, this volume).

The integration of communication networks and the Internet into virtually every sphere of life has rendered ICT an ecology to be reckoned with by all its inhabitants (Poster 1997). The question has shifted from being one of *adoption* (how one might use ICT) to one of *adaptation* (how one is transformed by ICT and reacts to it) (Bryant 2007), and discussions on e-governance and e-democracy emerge in this context. According to Nugent (2001), e-governance entails a few distinct, but interrelated facets: computerization of intra- and intergovernmental agencies' systems, online publication of government documents and information, interactive delivery of services online, and creation of communication channels between government and citizens and amongst citizens (Nugent 2001). Bryant (2007) outlines four aspects of e-governance: government computer systems, Web-based service delivery, transaction handling, and e-democracy. And UNESCO sets out the goals of e-governance as improving the internal organizational processes of governments, providing better information and service delivery, increasing government transparency, reinforcing political credibility and accountability, and promoting democratic practices through public participation and consultation. In accordance, three fields of implementation of e-governance are identified: e-administration, e-services, and e-democracy (Budd and Harris 2009).

Such conceptions of e-governance see technological systems as the enablers of a new type of governance. These new technological tools are presumed to make government not only more efficient but also more democratic. They include first and foremost the Internet, which increasingly serves as the virtual arena within which digital applications are implemented, as well as more specific applications such as online forums, e-mails, websites, and open source initiatives. This represents a prominent outlook, which sees e-governance as contributing to the revitalization of democracy, or even to the creation of a new form of e-democracy. A weaker version of this outlook sees a tight link between e-governance and e-democracy, that is, that the two are compatible (the *complementary* model). A somewhat stronger version sees e-governance as a preliminary step, leading toward e-democracy (the *evolutionary* model). In the follow-ing, I will synthesize key tenets of these models, analyze their problematic assumptions, and offer an alternative model.

While acknowledging the diverse "economic and political reasons underpinning" the integration of ICT into government systems, Gunter (2006) nevertheless argues that they are compatible with one another: ICT makes public service delivery more efficient but may also help in re-engaging "politically alienated electorates in civic processes." According to him, democratization by technological means takes place at two levels: governing practices themselves become more democratic (i.e. open and transparent), and these in turn contribute to a process of democratization of politics in general. E-governance makes government more consumer-oriented, facilitating more individual empowerment, participation, and interactivity. By conflating consumerism and citizen-ship Gunter is able to think of e-governance and e-democracy as complementary. "E-government," he says, "would therefore open up government administrations and render their internal processes more transparent and accountable...Government organisations' web sites are required to be citizen-focused...sites must contain devices designed to make it as easy as possible for users to find the information or services they seek" (Gunter 2006: 366). In other words, the mechanisms of e-governance, produced by pressures to be more consumer-oriented and follow market logic, also lead toward greater democratization.

An even more direct link between e-governance and democracy is suggested by the evolutionary model, according to which e-governance develops through stages that are defined almost exclusively in technological terms. As government websites become more interactive, allowing citizens more active engagement, the level of e-governance is conceived to be more "advanced." The most developed stage of e-governance also becomes a starting point for e-democracy: "At the final stage all departments and gov-ernment organizations in the country are brought together in a unified government portal, which offers a complex of different services for the population. The portal gives citizens an opportunity to take part in online discussions, comment on policy and legis-lation proposals and vote online. Ideally at this stage e-government may be used to fur-ther the means of democracy" (Netchaeva 2002: 468).

Commonly, e-governance and e-democracy are described as comprised of a sequence of three steps. The first two steps are the presence of government agencies on the Web, followed by the ability of citizens and businesses to conduct transactions with govern-ment. The third step—making government interactive—is assumed to be a springboard for e-democracy, that is, for revitalizing civil society and the public sphere (Kampen and Snijkers 2003). In this model, then, e-democracy is seen as an evolution of e-governance, which in turn is founded on ICT. Indeed, two classic works in the literature see e-govern-ance and e-democracy as outcomes of the adoption of technology: Nolan and Gibson (1974) describe a process through which organizations learn to utilize computers, and McFarlan, McKenny, and Pyburn (1982) describe a process by which organizations assimilate technology. In both cases, technology is conceived as an environment to which systems have to adapt (Bryant 2007).

The ultimate stage of e-governance, then, combines efficiency with democracy, allowing cheaper, more efficient channels of transactions between government and citizens/businesses, *and* enhancing democratic participation. Netchaeva (2002: 469) summarizes this position thus: "in the final stage e-government portals perform two main functions: to help the population in their everyday life (online services) and provide citizen participation in the democratic process." However, Netchaeva points out that these are in fact distinct issues: "On the one hand, e-government is an instrument for better governance…On the other hand…IT use in governance may intrinsically change relationships in society, help to achieve real democratic means and even transform people's social and political consciousness" (Netchaeva 2002: 469). What, then, is the nature of the link between e-governance and e-democracy that allows these dominant models to conceptualize them as complementary or even evolutionary? Two interrelated "media" are assumed to make e-governance conducive to e-democracy: information and communication.

Information, communication, and democracy

Underlying these models is an assumption that information is a vital component for better communication, which in turn enhances democracy. Hence, the digitization of information (which makes information more accessible) is assumed to better democracy. The most oft-quoted theorist in this context is Jürgen Habermas. His abstract formulation of the public sphere (1991) seems to come alive and materialize with ICT. Froomkin (2004: 3) emphasizes the role of information in Habermas's theory of democracy, and sees in the digitization of information a vehicle to fulfill the Habermasian promise. According to Froomkin, "an informed and engaged citizenry enriches the political process in at least two ways": stimulating better decisions by the political echelon, and legitimating the process of decision-making by the very act of mass participation.

Habermas suggests that the forces for such democratic revitalization are likely to come from "a reenergized, activist, engaged citizenry, working together to create new small-scale communicative associative institutions that over time merge into larger ones, or at least join forces." Habermas recommends decentralization "in order to allow pluralistic decision making" and to "counteract the 'generation of mass loyalty'" sought and increasingly achieved by political parties and states. The Internet, which facilitates information flows, decentralization, openness, and interactivity, seems to fulfill the abstract demands put forth by Habermas for a vibrant public sphere. The Internet—particularly tools such as social networks and online forums—is seen as a technological response to the democratic deficit which has been infecting Western societies (Froomkin 2004: 4).

Froomkin sees the Internet as a technology for democracy, since it facilitates discourse and enables communicative action. He points to the democratizing effects of technology forms such as hardware, blogs, and wikis. Arguably, the most popular claim about Internet hardware is that its distributive architecture makes it inherently democratic (Benkler 2006). It is precisely this position that brings up the specter of a digital divide since inequality in Internet access and digital literacy hampers inclusion and participation and hence diminishes legitimation (Norris 2001). In the most technologically advanced democratic nations, however, the digital divide is becoming less of a problem (Froomkin 2004). Blogs are another democratizing tool since they allow everyone to express themselves. Moreover, the networked nature of the Internet facilitates conversations because bloggers link to each other. By interlinking diverse voices, blogging—"a medium that is architecturally one-to-many"—is thus rendered "effectively a hybrid, a peer-to-peer conversation with many eavesdroppers." Froomkin predicts that the blogosphere may "evolve into a miniature public sphere of its own." Lastly, Froomkin hails wiki and other collaborative drafting tools as enhancing democracy, arguing that the very act of collaboration requires democratic deliberation (Froomkin 2004: 10).

But it is not simply the ease of communication that encourages Froomkin to conceive of the Internet as a technology for democracy, but also the availability of information. Froomkin (2004) argues that open government initiatives (such as government websites) that improve information flows between government and citizens also improve discourse—hence contributing to democracy—since they allow more access to information, which is a key ingredient for a full-fledged public discourse. The trouble with the digitalization of government, according to Froomkin, is that it is not participatory enough, that not enough has been done "for the direct integration of the popular will into political decision-making processes" (Froomkin 2004: 15). This requires the construction of new tools and structures "that enhance democracy, supplement debate, and encourage citizen involvement in what ultimately will be more like, and feel more like, self-governance" (Froomkin 2004: 16). Practices involved in e-governance, then, which are essentially about the presentation and delivery of information, turn, according to this account, into self-governance or e-democracy, by serving as a basis for better, more *informed* communication, or better discourse.

Noveck (2004: 21) follows suit on the notion that Internet architecture is inherently democratizing. She notes that deliberation involves "a special form of speech structured according to democratic principles and designed to transform private prejudice into considered public opinion and to produce more legitimate solutions," a definition reminiscent of Habermas's notion of communication in the public sphere. According to her, the Internet could enhance democracy not simply because it allows people to express themselves, "but because software can impose that structure that transforms communication into deliberation." The very structure of technology can transform social practices: "Democratic rules of conversation can be 'coded' into the software itself to ensure, for example, that each participant speaks once before anyone else speaks again"; the normative components of an ideal deliberative procedure are inscribed into technological procedures.

Information flows, both between citizens and government and amongst citizens regarding government, are the crux of e-governance, according to Mayer-Schönberger

and Lazer (2007). They identify three distinct meanings to e-governance in the literature. At the very minimum e-governance means that government services become
available online. This "transactional approach" focuses on the ease with which transactions are made between citizens and government; for example, paying bills online. A
second approach sees e-governance as a further rationalization of the bureaucratic
machine, making the public sector more efficient. In this case as well, the Internet is
seen as a tool to "achieve better government," and to improve the internal functioning
of government agencies. A third approach to e-governance points to the potential of
incorporating democratic processes into e-governance. Mayer-Schönberger and Lazer
(2007: 5) approach this multiplicity by offering the notion of *information government* as
a "conceptual lens that offers a complementary perspective to understand the changing
nature of government and its relationship to the citizenry." They focus on information
flows because, at heart, governing concerns acquiring, possessing, storing, and deciding
upon information. Information is a source of power; more so the more a society
becomes informational. In that approach as well, e-governance and e-democracy are
seen as complementary, as interrelated outcomes of improving information flows. If
information as such—"independent of the medium," as Mayer-Schönberger and Lazer
(2007: 6) are careful to point out—is at the heart of governing and democracy, how do
ICTs nevertheless transform governance and democratic practices? According to them,
"[ICTs] allow for much greater malleability of how information might flow." The greater
malleability makes governance more flexible, "moving from pyramidal, silo-based
structures, to more decentralized, networked (in terms of information flows) systems"
(Mayer-Schönberger and Lazer 2007: 7). It also transforms information flows between
government and citizens, making them more intense, two-directional, and hence
democratic.

Chadwick (2003) articulates one of the most developed positions of the complemen-
tary/evolutionary model, upholding the close link between e-governance and e-democracy. The claims made on e-governance and e-democracy, he argues, are "steadily
diverging," as "public administration scholars, public policy analysts, and public management specialists focus on e-government, whereas political communication specialists, social movement scholars, and democratic theorists sharpen their analytical tools
on e-democracy." This divergence plasters over the link between the two processes:
"contemporary digital ICTs facilitate new forms of e-government-enabled public sector policy making that enshrine some of the important norms and practices of
e-democracy." New developments, he argues, create a reality in which "the practices and
norms of e-government and those of e-democracy become intertwined" (Chadwick
2003: 444). Chadwick finds even the most instrumental aspects of e-governance—such
as the marketization and consumerization of government—democratizing, proposing
that "public services exposed to the same kinds of stringent tests as private sector firms
operating within the realm of e-commerce will in the long term become more responsive to the demands of their users or customers..." Chadwick, then, sees in the integration of market mechanisms into the operation of government via ICT, a move toward
democratization: "e-government brings government 'closer to the people' by meeting

the expectations of service users regarding convenience, accessibility, and timeliness" (Chadwick 2003: 445).

But Chadwick indicates that e-governance includes more radical aspirations, which "seek to use ICTs to incorporate citizens' deliberation into the initial stages of policy development or the very process of 'reengineering' public services...this form of e-government would entail a radical overhaul of the modern administrative state as regular electronic consultations involving elected politicians, civil servants, pressure groups, and other affected interests become standard practice in all stages of the policy process" (Chadwick 2003: 445). Here, then, lies a promise that e-governance will transform into e-democracy, the more its procedures become open to citizens' involvement (Chadwick 2003). Chadwick outlines four points of convergence between e-governance and e-democracy. The first is "the integration of e-democratic activities in civil society with policy-making processes." Such activities transform how government operates: "E-government potentially blurs the distinctions between executive and legislative functions by creating opportunities for citizens to have direct political influence on public bureaucracies in ways that have not existed before" (Chadwick 2003: 450). The second point of convergence concerns the role that e-governance and e-democracy play in the internal democratization of the public sector: "Flatter hierarchies of more creative and cooperative officials permanently plugged in to wider informational networks that organically include the online presence of citizen groups and affected interests is thus one way of injecting e-democratic practices into e-government." The third point of convergence concerns what Chadwick calls the "politics of convenience": "In seeking to emulate the private sector by capitalizing on shifts in consumption patterns... e-government reformists forecast the demise of monolithic and cumbersome state provision. In its stead will emerge a newly flexible and dynamic model of the public sector that will give users, in all their post-Fordist diversity, what they want...The effects of these developments...are not the erosion of citizenship values but their metamorphosis into forms more suited to postindustrial politics." The convergence of e-governance and e-democracy transcends the purely consumerist benefits, "as customers not only have a greater choice but come to play a role in the design and delivery of public service themselves" (Chadwick 2003: 451–452).

The fourth and last point of convergence between e-governance and e-democracy is "the context for the design and maintenance of the hardware and software that allows e-government systems to run." For example, the adoption of open source software is "predicated on the argument that cooperative and collaborative sharing of expertise results not only in technically better software but also socially and politically progressive technologies that are more flexible, transparent, and cost-effective to maintain." Chadwick upholds the architecture of ICT as inherently liberating and democratizing; if e-governance adopts these technologies, the argument goes, the democratizing benefits will percolate toward e-democracy as well: "the intrinsically democratic values of open source...would align the public sector with an already existing culture of voluntarism that exists in cyberspace..." (Chadwick 2003: 452).

Questioning e-governance
and e-democracy

Notwithstanding these dominant views, which see e-governance as complementing or even evolving toward e-democracy, I wish to outline an alternative model, which sees e-governance and e-democracy as contradictory trends, by questioning these concepts as analytically and theoretically viable. This questioning revolves on two critical objections: the fact that e-governance and e-democracy are analyzed as government policies, and the technologically centered outlook dominating the analysis. My argument is that rather than accepting and following these policy-defined conceptualizations, we should identify and criticize the problematic assumptions behind them and offer alternative, more theoretically based concepts by uncovering the broader social transformations of which these policies are part.

Two origins of the concepts of e-governance and e-democracy are an important starting point for such discussion. One is the popular discourse on ICT that emerged during the 1980s and 1990s, which heralded the ushering in of a new society, where old practices and institutions are reinvigorated, improved, or completely revolutionized by ICT (Fisher 2010). One of the symbolic emblems of such an approach is the prefix "e-," added to virtually any existing institution to pronounce the transcendence of the pitfalls and limitations of old practices by their "electrification": e-commerce, e-learning, e-publishing, and so forth. E-governance and e-democracy are part of that lineage. Another important source for the emergence of these concepts was governments themselves, which were trying to catch up with the technological revolution, and became the main purveyors and proponents of e-governance and e-democracy (Gunter 2006).

These two historical coordinates of e-governance and e-democracy—as government projects and as technological fixes—should also serve as leverages for some critical reflections, presented here along two arguments: (1) that e-governance and e-democracy are not merely technical and technological issues but are part of a political project that involves a reconfiguration of power relations; and (2) that ICT is not merely a material expression of instrumental rationality but also a discursive category that legitimates this new political constellation. To set the stage for these arguments we first need to consider the relations between politics and technology.

Technology discourse and political legitimation

Uncritically employing the notions of e-governance and e-democracy, one can easily slide toward a "technologistic" view, which gives precedence to technology over other sociological coordinates (Robins and Webster 1999). Such analysis tends to be deterministic and oblivious of the social power structures within which technology is developed and implemented. Such a viewpoint is clearly evident in an analysis that forecasts that "the Internet will revolutionise democratic systems" (Wright 2006: 236). Even more careful and nuanced analyses tend to put the "e" of e-governance at the center, thus inevitably ending up reifying technology. Actually, to account for e-governance one should "forget" technology, and depict the web of social power relations and institutions within which technologies are caught up. An effective route to do that is by shifting attention from technology as a material tool, to technology as discourse. This approach suggests that technology discourse—the common truths, models, and frameworks about technology and about the meaning of living in a technological society—is not simply a reflection of the centrality of technology in the operation of modern societies, but plays a constitutive role in their operation, and enables that centrality. Technology discourse is a projection of social realities through which transformations of political, economic, and social nature are filtered (Heffernan 2000).

With modernity and the harnessing of technology to capitalism and the state, technology discourse has come to play a central role in the legitimation of a techno-political order, that is, a political order legitimated by technology and techniques. In this political context technology becomes an unquestionable "good," a "religion" (Noble 1999), and a "myth" (Robins and Webster 1999: 151; Mosco 2004), which suggests that virtually any social problem is subject to a technical and technological fix. Furthermore, technology functions as an "ideological tool that mystif[ies] mechanisms of power and domination" (Best and Kellner 2000: 376). In this vein, Habermas (1970) points to the substitution of technical and technological discussions with their emphasis on instrumental rationality, for political debate based on communicative action and aimed at arriving at substantive rationality. The role of politics is reduced to finding the technical means to achieve goals that in themselves are understood to lie outside the realm of politics (Habermas 1970).

In the context of contemporary political culture, then, rather than theorizing the transformations entailed by the rise of e-governance solely within a technologistic framework (i.e. as a consequence of the introduction of ICT into government practices), they should be understood as social and political transformations brought about with the aid of—and legitimated by—ICT. Viewed in this light, e-governance could be examined as a new technology discourse, which emerges concurrently with shifts in the nature of governance itself. E-governance emerges at an intersection of momentous transformations: the decline of the welfare state and a crisis in the legitimacy of welfarism as such; the shift from the Keynesian, interventionist state, which regulates and manages large parts of the economy, to the neoliberal state, which deregulates, privatizes, and generally takes a step back from the market; a revenue crisis of the state; the opening up of national, protected economies to a global market; the marketization of social relations, including the privatization of public goods and the rise of consumerism; the rise of postindustrial politics, based on image, persona, and personal connection between voter and politician; and an exacerbation of the democratic deficit characterized by low rates of participation in democratic politics and a deepening legitimation crisis (Budd and Harris 2009).

All these entail new relations between three arenas of action, key to the political scene of Western capitalist democracies: the state, the market, and the public sphere. In this intricate triangle, there has been a growing dominance of the market vis-à-vis the other two arenas: not only did the market gain more power, but the state and the public sphere were partially refashioned in accordance with market principles. The decline of social democracy and the rise of neoliberal democracy in the last few decades have been accompanied by the rise of the practices and discourse of governance. The literature on governance makes this broader political context clear. Bevir (2011) points to the correlation of governance with markets and networks and explains governance as a result of the withdrawal of the state and the rise of market mechanisms and market players (or otherwise non-governmental agencies) in the provision of social services and in processes of policy decision-making. Governance signifies a new way of ruling and ordering, which essentially displaces the old way of governing by governments (Rhodes, Chapter 3, this volume). It signals the transfer of governing practices from government to non-governmental actors such as citizens, groups in civil society, and businesses (Lobel, Chapter 5, this volume).

Rhodes (Chapter 3, this volume) succinctly posits that governance entails "the changing boundaries between public, private and voluntary sectors," that is, "the changing role of the state." ICT plays a central role as a facilitator and enabler of this shift, as it is presumed to allow a more distributed and collaborative form of governance. In this context the discourse on networks that displaces the discourse on states emerges (Rhodes, Chapter 3, this volume; Bevir 2011). And in this context, the Internet emerges as the material manifestation of networks.

The policy and discourse of e-governance and e-democracy have arisen at a historical moment when the scope of the political is shrinking, and when the public sphere is undergoing a process of increased colonization by private interests (Bevir and Rhodes 2006). The Internet and the notions of e-governance and e-democracy are constructed as *deus ex machina*, presumed to amend the democratic deficit and solve the legitimation crisis (Budd and Harris 2009). The decline in state provision of public programs and the corollary shrinkage and failures of the public realm were accompanied by a new ideology that justified this shrinkage, by portraying the public sector as incapable and inefficient: "In a seemingly dynamic and consumer-oriented culture, the delivery of public services is seen to be hidebound by a lack of innovation, creativity, and flexibility. In this view public organizations are bureaucratic, impotent and increasingly sterile" (Budd and Harris 2009: 2). As Lobel (Chapter 5, this volume) argues, one of the central reasons for the shift toward new governance is the ineffectiveness of government regulation in an environment of a more flexible, competitive, globalized market; "the nation state is significantly less capable in today's economy to govern and regulate markets" (Lobel, Chapter 5, this volume, p. 72). In that context, ICT occupied a central place: "the idea of digital means to overcome these incapacities has gained currency to deliver optimal outcomes for public policy and service delivery" (Budd and Harris 2009). The new political culture of neoliberal democracy was legitimated by the technological capabilities of ICT, seen as well adept to respond to the new challenges of neoliberal democracy. Thus, a crisis of governance was accompanied by an emerging space of e-governance.

One of the major transformations epitomized and facilitated by e-governance is the privatization of the public realm. The implementation of e-governance is in fact an exemplar of government–business partnership, and involves outsourcing the very political mechanisms of democratic politics. Due to the complexity of ICT systems, the building and maintenance of e-governance hardware and software are increasingly outsourced, and managed by large, global corporations such as Electronic Data Systems, IBM-Accenture, Cap Gemini-Ernst and Young, and Lockheed Martin, which "monopolize ... the necessary expertise and organizational capacities to service and develop the very large-scaled government systems of big nation states" (Dunleavy et al. 2006: 5). Dunleavy and colleagues (2006) therefore speak of "digital era governance" as more fully dependent on technology and on market players who are able to provide the necessary technological services. This trend will intensify as many government agencies "*become* their websites—where the electronic form of the organization increasingly defines the fundamentals of what it is and does" (Dunleavy et al. 2006: 3).

Concurrent with the decline and critique of the provisionist, interventionist state, and with the rise of a neoliberal ethos championing marketization, a new culture of consumerism, which has affected politics in general and governance in particular, arose. In this new ethos, citizens are increasingly conceptualized as consumers, and the relations between them and government is refashioned as a market-like transaction. In that context, e-governance plays a vital discursive role, since ICT is assumed to facilitate a shift in power from the old, silo-based governance of social democracy to neoliberal democracy, which empowers citizens-*cum*-consumers (Chadwick 2003; Mayer-Schönberger and Lazer 2007).

E-governance versus e-democracy: the contradictory model

These reflections demand that we investigate e-governance not only as a governmental policy but also as a legitimation discourse that employs a technologistic framework to account for what is, in essence, a new constellation of power between states and markets, and a new definition of governing. It should also encourage us to critically rethink the relations between e-governance and e-democracy. As a final exercise, then, it might be fruitful to highlight the contradictory nature of e-governance and e-democracy. The literature on e-governance and e-democracy tends to limit itself to Habermas's discussion of the public sphere, thus highlighting the communicative aspect of his theory. Habermas's more developed theory (Habermas 1985) highlights the contradictory and tenuous relations within the social structure between system and the lifeworld, and between two forms of rationality. Accordingly, we might conceptualize e-governance as the transfer of government activities into online forms with the aim of improving *efficiency*, and e-democracy as the transfer of democratic practices into online forms with the aim of improving *deliberation*. At the heart of these projects is a process of rationalization by technological means, but a very different kind of rationality: e-governance is concerned with further instrumentalization of governmental practices, that is, with further rationalizing systems, while e-democracy is concerned with improving democratic practices, that is, with further rationalizing communication or the lifeworld. These distinctions suggest that e-governance and e-democracy might actually be contradictory, rather than complementary, trends.

In this vein, McCullagh (2003) asserts that e-governance and e-democracy are different issues: one does not emanate from the other, and thus far governments have been concerned much more with the "administrative or business-like role of government" than with "the issue of engaging citizens in the democratic process" (McCullagh 2003: 155). My argument is that this divergence might not be a coincidence, or a failure, but symptomatic: that e-governance and e-democracy might in fact be antithetical, that their underlying rationales as well as their social effects are divergent, and that "electrifying" governance is not the same as electrifying democracy. E-governance and e-democracy are aiming toward, and in effect constructing, two contradictory subjects: the consumers and the citizens. For the customer of government services e-governance should offer as little work as possible. The ideal of e-governance would be the putting together of electronic processes so streamlined that they become virtually transparent. The ideal customer is passive, asked to do the least possible to get errands done. The success of e-governance is measured in terms of instrumental rationality.

The citizen—that which e-democracy promises to reconstruct and reinvigorate through ICT—is a completely different subject. The citizen is asked to be active and engaged. She is required to "work": obtain information about issues of the day, learn about alternative positions, follow political and social events, forge her opinions, express them, and take an active part in discussions and deliberations. As McCullagh asserts, "[c]itizenship requires individual Internet users to play an active role in the democratic process, by engaging in online discussion forums, participating in debates and offering their expertise, so that issues may be explored and addressed in a consensual manner" (McCullagh 2003: 156).

E-governance and e-democracy are also structurally contradictory. E-governance requires a top-down management by the state with an active participation of market players; it is necessarily a governmental project. A project of e-democracy in the spirit of the Habermasian public sphere requires autonomy from the state and the market; it should spring from the bottom up and preserve its critical distance from both state and market (Dahlberg 2001). E-governance, then, is a project of systems (improving instrumental reason); e-democracy is a project of the lifeworld (improving communicative reason).

Hence, the integration of ICT into government activities does not necessarily enhance democracy. According to Johnson (2006), the technological infrastructure of e-democracy in fact makes it unsuitable, and even contradictory, to liberal democracy, "because of the underlying technological culture of e-democracy." Johnson presents us with his version of "soft" technological determinism (see Winner 1978), according to which, the adoption of complex technological systems requires society to adhere to the implicit political and ideological coordinates embedded in it. "Electronic liberal democracy cannot be constructed by simply adapting Internet-based technologies as is because the underlying culture of those technologies, when implemented in specifically political practices, runs counter to the principles of liberal democracy." Johnson refers specifically to the Internet as a commodity and as "an individualized public forum" that "shape[s] the culture of e-democracy in ways that undermine key practices of liberal democracy" (Johnson 2006).

Likewise, Kampen and Snijkers (2003) argue that the main problems of democracy cannot be solved by the Internet. In this realm of truly reforming democracy, they argue, lies "the ultimate e-dream: that ICT can solve the problems that are inherent to modern representative democracies" (Kampen and Snijkers 2003). The dream of e-democracy postulates that "accelerated communication of citizens and politicians through the means of ICT will lead to increased participation of citizens in the making of policy in democratic nations." However, according to Kampen and Snijkers (2003), key problems of representative democracy are not necessarily solvable by ICT, such as the tendency of representatives to act in the interest of preserving their power, or that of "the politically active few to obtain influence disproportionate to their number."

The very framing of the project of revitalizing democracy with the notion of "e-democracy" is problematic: "The mere fact that ICT helps us bridge some practical problems of a direct democracy (e.g. the problem of scale) is no justification to actually install a direct democracy. There still is a large difference between technical possibility and a democratic feasibility" (Kampen and Snijkers 2003). They recommend a complete separation between these projects: "of all possible reasons to use the Internet, e-democracy is the least impressive. The Internet seems to be a source for information and routine transactions and not for political actions." Contrary to the complementary/ evolutionary model, they see no direct link between the availability of online information and democracy (Kampen and Snijkers 2003).

Conclusion

Academic and popular discourse about the intersection of contemporary democratic politics with ICT largely asserts that e-governance—the integration of ICT into governing practices—also enhances democracy and may lead to a form of e-democracy. Such discourse also assumes that e-governance is essentially a government-led initiative, fueled by the need to adapt to the digital revolution and aimed at improving governance practices. Rather than viewing e-governance as a purely technical matter, I suggest an alternative framework according to which e-governance emerges at the nexus of political transformations toward neoliberal democracy. The networked, distributed, emergent, and flexible nature of the Internet serves as both the material infrastructure and the legitimizing metaphor for shifts in the balance of power between states and markets, and the ushering in of a new model of governance. Rather than seeing e-governance simply as a governmental policy aimed at increasing efficiency and improving democracy, it should be seen as a discursive and practical configuration that accompanies the structural transformations toward neoliberal democracy.

Adopting a non-technologistic framework, the chapter also questions the prevailing assumption that the electrification of governance will also lead to e-democracy. Rather, it postulates that e-governance and e-democracy are in fact contradictory trends. The problem with the notions of e-democracy and e-governance is the very conflation of technology and politics, the idea that the problems of democratic institutions are ultimately technical problems ready to be solved by technology. As Netchaeva (2002) puts it, the very term e-democracy is "wrong by definition" because, unlike government, democracy is not an object but an abstract idea. One can literally "electrify" governance by incorporating ICT into its practices in a way that cannot be achieved with democracy. The equation of e-democracy with other "electrification" projects, such as e-governance or e-commerce, then, is wrongheaded and misleading. While governance is a systemic activity, aimed at achieving instrumental goals, democracy is a utopian horizon that combines the components of system (such as parliament and elections) with those of the lifeworld (such as values and norms), and cannot be "electrified" in the same manner.

REFERENCES

Benkler, Y. 2006. *The Wealth of Networks: How Social Production Transforms Markets and Freedom*. New Haven, CT: Yale University Press.

Best, S. and Kellner, D. 2000. Kevin Kelly's complexity theory: The politics and ideology of self-organizing systems. *Democracy and Nature* 6: 375–400.

Bevir, M. 2011. Governance as theory, practice, and dilemma. In M. Bevir (ed.), *The Sage Handbook of Governance*. London: Sage, 00–00.

Bevir, M. and Rhodes, R. 2006. *Governance Stories*. New York: Routledge.

Bryant, A. 2007. Government, e-government, and modernity. In D. Griffin, P. Trevorrow, and E. Halpin (eds.), *Developments in e-Government: A Critical Analysis*. Amsterdam: IOS Press, 3–15.

Budd, L. and Harris, L. 2009. Introduction: Managing governance or governance management. Is it all in a digital day's work? In L. Budd and L. Harris (eds.), *E-Governance: Managing or Governing?* New York: Routledge, 1–25.

Chadwick, A. 2003. Bringing e-democracy back in: Why it matters for future research on e-governance. *Social Science Computer Review* 21: 443–455.

Dahlberg, L. 2001. "Extending the public sphere through cyberspace: The case of Minnesota e-democracy." *First Monday* 6. Available at http://firstmonday.org/htbin/cgiwrap/bin/ojs/index.php/fm/article/view/838/747 (accessed 19 September 2011).

Dunleavy, P., Margetts, H., Bastow, S. and Tinkler, J. 2006. *Digital Era Governance: IT Corporations, the State, and E-Government*. Oxford: Oxford University Press.

Fisher, E. 2010. *Media and New Capitalism in the Digital Age: The Spirit of Networks*. New York: Palgrave Macmillan.

Froomkin, M. 2004. Technologies for democracy. In P. Shane (ed.), *Democracy Online: The Prospects for Political Renewal through the Internet*. New York: Routledge, 3–20.

Gunter, B. 2006. Advances in e-democracy: Overview. *Aslib Proceedings: New Information Perspectives* 58: 361–370.

Habermas, J. 1970. *Toward a Rational Society: Student Protest, Science, and Politics*. Boston: Beacon Press.

Habermas, J. 1985. *The Theory of Communicative Action*, 2 vols. Boston: Beacon Press.

Habermas, J. 1991. *The Structural Transformation of the Public Sphere: An Inquiry into a Category of Bourgeois Society*. Cambridge, MA: MIT Press.

Heffernan, N. 2000. *Capital, Class, and Technology in Contemporary American Culture: Projecting Post-Fordism*. London: Pluto Press.

Johnson, J. A. 2006. The illiberal culture of e-democracy. *Journal of E-Government* 3: 85–112.

Kampen, J. and Snijkers, K. 2003. E-democracy: A critical evaluation of the ultimate e-dream. *Social Science Computer Review* 21: 491–496.

McCullagh, K. 2003. E-democracy: Potential for political revolution? *International Journal of Law and Information Technology* 11: 149–161

McFarlan, F. W., McKenny, J. L. and Pyburn, P. 1982. The information archipelago: Maps and bridges. *Harvard Business Review* 60: 109–119.

Mayer-Schönberger, V. and Lazer, D 2007. From electronic government to information government. In V. Mayer-Schönberger and D. Lazer (eds.), *Governance and Information Technology: From Electronic Government to Information Government*. Cambridge: MIT Press, 1–14.

Mosco, V. 2004. *The Digital Sublime: Myth, Power, and Cyberspace*. Cambridge, MA: MIT Press.

Netchaeva, I. 2002. E-government and e-democracy: A comparison of opportunities in the North and South. *Gazette: The International Journal for Communication Studies* 64: 467–477.

Noble, D. 1999. *The Religion of Technology: The Divinity of Man and the Spirit of Invention*. New York: Penguin.

Nolan, R. and Gibson, C. 1974. Managing the four stages of EDP growth. *Harvard Business Review* 52: 76–78.

Norris, P. 2001. *Digital Divide: Civic Engagement, Information Poverty and the Internet Worldwide*. Cambridge: Cambridge University Press.

Noveck, B. 2004. Unchat: Democratic solution for a wired world. In P. Shane (ed.), *Democracy Online: The Prospects for Political Renewal through the Internet*. New York: Routledge, 21–34.

Nugent, J. 2001. If e-democracy is the answer, what's the question? *National Civic Review* 90: 221–233.

Poster, M. 1997. Cyberdemocracy: The internet and the public sphere. In D. Porter (ed.), *Internet Culture*. New York: Routledge, 201–218.

Robins, K. and Webster, F. 1999. *Times of Technoculture: From the Information Society to the Virtual Life*. London: Routledge.

Winner, L. 1978. *Autonomous Technology: Technics-Out-of-Control as a Theme in Political Thought*. Cambridge, MA: MIT Press.

Wright, S. 2006. Electrifying democracy? 10 years of policy and practice. *Parliamentary Affairs* 59: 236–249.

CHAPTER 41

THE FIFTH ESTATE: A NEW GOVERNANCE CHALLENGE

WILLIAM H. DUTTON*

THE FIFTH ESTATE: A NEW DIMENSION OF GOVERNANCE

SINCE the 1980s, the Internet has been transformed from an exciting innovation to an increasingly significant information and communication technology (ICT) tied to everyday life and work. However, the implications of its use have been perceived primarily through institution-centric lenses in government, business, education, and other fields. For instance, government use of the Internet started with initiatives focused on enhancing existing structures of government through "e-government" and "e-democracy" initiatives around the world that placed public information and services online (Fisher, Chapter 40, this volume). Computer-based communication systems such as the Internet were also seen as the development of new media that would be encompassed by the traditional communication media industries. This is true, but also a new Internet-enabled phenomenon is challenging such institution-centric views.

The blossoming since the turn of the century of Internet-enabled online social networking, e-mail, the Web, blogging, texting, tweeting, and other "Web 2.0" digital channels and services are enabling networked individuals to reconfigure their access to alternative sources of information, people, and other resources. They can then move across, undermine and go beyond the boundaries of existing institutions, thereby opening new ways of increasing the accountability of politicians, press, experts, and other loci of power and influence. This is representative of what might be called a "Fifth Estate" (Dutton 2009) shaping new modes of governance across sectors of increasingly networked societies (Castells 1996; Rhodes, Chapter 3, this volume).

THE FIFTH ESTATE

The concept of a Fifth Estate is defined here to reference the ways in which the Internet is being used by increasing numbers of people to network with other individuals and with information, services, and technical resources in ways that support social accountability across many sectors, including business and industry, government, politics, and the media. Just as the press created a Fourth Estate in the eighteenth century, the Internet is enabling a Fifth Estate in the twenty-first.

The concept of "estates of the realm" originally related to divisions in feudal society between the clergy, nobility, and the commons. Much license has been taken with their characterizations over the centuries. For example, American social scientists identified the three estates with the legislative, executive and judicial branches of government. However, the eighteenth-century philosopher Edmund Burke first identified the press as a fourth estate, arguing (according to Carlyle 1905: 104): ."there were Three Estates in Parliament; but, in the Reporters' Gallery yonder, there sat a Fourth Estate more important far than they all. It is not a figure of speech, or witty saying; it is a literal fact—very momentous to us in these times."

The rise in the twentieth century of press, radio, television, and other mass media consolidated this reality as a central feature of pluralist democratic processes. Growing use of the Internet, Web 2.0, mobile ICTs and other digital online capabilities is creating another new "literal fact": networked individuals reach out across traditional institutional and physical boundaries into what Castells (2001: 235) has called a "space of flows," rather than a "space of places," reflecting contemporary perspectives on governance processes as "hybrid and multijurisdictional with plural stakeholders who come together in networks" (Bevir 2011: 2).

Within this hybrid space of flows, people increasingly go to find information and services. These could be located anywhere in the world and relate to local issues (e.g. taxes, political representatives, schools) and regional, national or international activities. This is significant because it signals that more and more people are likely to go first to a search engine or to a site recommended through their favorite social networking site, rather than to a specific organization's site or to a place, such as to a government office, library, newspaper, university, or other institution (Dutton 2009).

Discovering the Fifth Estate

The central social and political role of the Internet and related ICTs is in reconfiguring access to people, information, services and other resources (Dutton 1999, 2005). How the Internet reconfigures access is shaped by patterns of "digital choices" (Dutton et al. 2007), which can change the communicative power of individuals, groups, and nations. Outcomes of these changes are inherently unpredictable, at micro and macro levels, because they depend on the interaction of numerous strategic and non-strategic choices made by a pluralistic array of actors as they seek to shape access to and from the outside world, in what could be called an "ecology of games," where the term "game" indicates an arena of competition and cooperation structured by a set of rules and assumptions about how to achieve a set of objectives (Dutton 1999: 14–16). This is shown, for instance, in the strategies of government agencies, politicians, lobbying groups, news media, bloggers, and others trying to gain access to citizens over the Internet.

Use of the Internet can reconfigure access in two main ways, by:

1. changing how we do things, such as how we get information, how we communicate with people, obtain services, and access technologies; and
2. altering the outcomes of these activities by changing what we know, whom we know, whom we keep in close touch with, what services we obtain, what technologies we use, and what know-how we require to deploy them.

A frequent response from traditional institutions, such as the fourth estate, to the Internet challenge is to suggest that they will retain their central position because of the trust they have built over the years. However, Internet users say they trust what they can find on the Internet at least as much as they trust broadcast news or the newspapers (e.g. Dutton et al. 2009). Generally, the more experience people have with the Internet, the more they develop a "learned level" of trust in the information they find and the people they meet online. They remain skeptical, with more educated individuals relatively more so, rather than expressing a blind faith in any source of information. However, the most distrustful are those who have never used the Internet, suggesting that the Internet is an "experience technology" (Dutton and Shepherd 2006). As experience online continues to build, more users are likely to develop such a learned level of trust, and rely more on the Internet as a source of information and expertise. These empirical findings support a new perspective on the social role of the Internet.

A NEW PERSPECTIVE ON THE SOCIAL AND POLITICAL ROLE OF THE INTERNET

Expectations of the consequences that would result from the use of ICTs often circle around utopian or dystopian perspectives. The optimists see new uses of ICTs leading to better connections between people in virtual communities of interest, which they believe will enrich everyday life and work. Pessimists expect the use of ICTs will tend to isolate individuals by substituting online and machine working for direct human interaction. This would undermine family and local networks of communication fundamental to the building of "social capital" in geographically based communities. Wellman's (2001) idea of "networked individualism" identifies trends for individuals to mix a variety of real and virtual ties that support their particular needs. The Internet provides more choices of association. This is less polarizing and can reveal the social dynamics that lead to uses of a technology resulting in different outcomes in different contexts. It shows how individuals representing groups, movements, or industries can find opportunities embedded in the design of technologies to promote their interests through mixes of different forms of online and offline associations.

Earlier conceptions

The Fifth Estate provides an alternative conception to a phenomenon that others have sought to capture. For example, many view the Internet as creating a "public sphere" as articulated by Jürgen Habermas (1991). This offers valuable insights, but is too closely tied to a romantic view of the past and therefore not able to capture the rise of an entirely new sphere of influence. The notion of an "information commons" (Kranich 2004) and its many variants is often used by many to characterize aspects of Internet space, especially the open sharing of information free or at low cost. However, the Internet and Web contain much that is trademarked, copyrighted, licensed, or otherwise owned, in addition to its enormous range of free material, such as a Wikipedia, making the concept of a commons problematic.

Social science perspectives that the Internet creates a new "space of flows" are supported across other disciplines. For instance, a key creator of the Web, Tim Berners-Lee, and his Web Science colleagues speak of the Web as an engineered space creating a distributed "information space" (Berners-Lee et al. 2006). They realize this space is being shaped by an increasingly diverse set of actors, including users, and for a wide range of purposes, some of which may not be those originally sought by its designers.

It is within this information space that a Fifth Estate is being formed, but the Fifth Estate is only one component of this space. Institutional networks are also occupying this information space, as discussed below. The interplay within the Fifth Estate and its interactions with other estates of the Internet realm are a key aspect of the pluralistic processes reshaping governance and social accountability in contemporary politics and society.

Politics of the Internet in society

The concept of a Fifth Estate challenges three major perspectives on the political role of the Internet in society:

1. *The Internet as an unimportant political resource—a technical novelty or passing fad.* This view has become less credible as Internet use has continued to grow and diversify around the world, but it continues to arise around particular themes (e.g. regarding the Internet as just a transient novelty that is of little importance to political campaigns and elections), despite growing examples that arguably

contradict this view, such as in the 2011 pro-democracy protests across the Middle East and North Africa.

2. *Deterministic perspectives, such as the idea that the Internet is a technology of freedom v. control.* de Sola Pool (1983), for example, saw computer-based communication networks as inherently democratic by empowering individuals. A contrasting dystopian view contends that institutions will adopt, design, and use the Internet to enhance their control of existing institutional structures and organizational arrangements (e.g. as in George Orwell's *1984* vision of a "surveillance society" where pervasive "Big Brother" networks monitor and control citizens' behavior).

3. *Reinforcement politics.* This conception of reinforcement politics (Danziger et al. 1982) accepts that the Internet can support and reinforce many different forms of networking, each shaped by its context and stakeholders to reinforce or challenge the interests of networked individuals, as in the Fifth Estate, or existing organizations and institutions. For example, Evgeny Morozov (2011) falls into this perspective, arguing that states have used the Internet to reinforce their control of citizens.

The Fifth Estate differs from each of these more traditional perspectives. It takes the Internet as a significant political resource that is changing patterns of governance across multiple sectors, though it does not view this impact as inevitable or an inherent feature of the technology, but, rather, as a pattern of use observed over time that can be undermined by other estates. It differs from reinforcement politics by not seeing any single actor to be in control of the Internet and political use and implications. A pluralistic interplay among an ecology of multiple actors has given rise to the Fifth Estate and its role in governance.

The social shaping of the Fifth Estate

The Internet's broad social roles in government, politics, and other sectors have similarities with those of traditional media. However, the Fifth Estate crucially differs from traditional media in how it helps to open up opportunities for greater social accountability in the governance of important institutions, including the media. This contributes to significantly distinctive features of the Fifth Estate that make it worthy of being considered a new estate of at least equal importance as the fourth—and the first not to be essentially institution-centric.

The underlying dynamics of the Fifth Estate are best understood through a social shaping lens (Dutton 1999). Long-term observations reveal how networks can be designed to operate as either horizontal, peer-to-peer communications or for more hierarchical and centralized structures, depending on the aims of designers and users. Two key distinctive Fifth Estate characteristics emerge from this viewpoint:

1. *Shifts in communicative power.* Networked individuals and institutions are enabled to build and exercise their "communicative power" (Garnham 1999). This derives from the use of ICTs to reconfigure networks in ways that can lead to real-

world power shifts. Instead, it supports access to online resources that incorporate and go beyond more traditional institutions. Individuals can then network with information and people to change their relationships with more institutionalized centres of authority in the other estates, thereby holding them more socially accountable through the interplay between ever-changing networks of networks. For instance, the relationship between media producers, gatekeepers and consumers are changed profoundly when previously passive audiences generate and distribute their own content and when search engines point to numerous sources reflecting different views on a topic.

2. *Networks of accountability*. Capabilities are provided that enable the creation of independent sources of information and collaboration that are not directly dependent on any one institutional source or any single estate. Internet-enabled individuals whose primary social aims in their networking activities are social can often break from existing geographical, organizational, and institutional networks, which themselves are frequently being transformed in Internet space (e.g. by local government officials engaging with individuals on community websites within and beyond their constituencies) to hold other institutions accountable.

This results from the role networks can play in altering the biases of communication systems, such as by changing cost structures, eliminating and introducing gatekeepers, and expanding or contracting the geography of access.

Reconfiguring access can also reconfigure the geography of information and communication networks. It can help to both overcome geographical distances through virtual networks or make geography more important by enabling people to be where they need to be to have face-to-face communication (e.g. Rice et al. 2007). This can blur the boundaries of households, organizations, local communities, nations, and other institutions, while not erasing underlying geographical or institutional boundaries.

The digital choices institutions and individuals make will afford greater or lesser control to citizens, viewers, consumers and other users. Appreciating how the use and diffusion of technologies is socially shaped reveals why the development of any particular platform has not been inevitable, including those supportive of a Fifth Estate. They have evolved through the unpredictable interaction of strategic or unintentional choices by many actors, with many different competing and complementary objectives. For instance, the ability to forge local and global networks is illustrated by the mobilization of political and financial support around the world for causes as varied as climate change, terrorism, struggles against state control, disaster relief, and campaigns against corporate tax avoidance.

Digital choices and divides and the significance of a critical mass

Use of the Internet continues to diffuse across the world, and in the variety of applications it supports, and devices that can be used for access (e.g. see www.worldinternetproject.net). As a result, the Internet has become such a crucial infrastructure of everyday life that disparities in its availability and take up are of substantive social, economic and political significance—placing great emphasis on reducing digital divides which often follow and reinforce socio-economic inequalities in society.

However, social and economic status does not explain all patterns of adoption and use (Rice et al. 2007). The making of "digital choices" about whether or not to use the Internet also comes into play. For example, many people choose not to use the Internet even when they have opportunities to do so. It may be generally understandable that more elderly citizens are significantly less likely to use the Internet than younger generations who have appropriate skills and greater familiarity with the technology. Yet, many older people in homes with access to the technology and other support are still not motivated to go online.

Despite these continuing digital divides, the Internet has achieved the critical mass that enables networked individuals to become a significant force. The existence of a Fifth Estate therefore does not depend on universal access, but on reaching a critical mass of users. This enables the Fifth Estate to play an important political role even in nations such as China or Iran with low proportions of Internet users.

Networked individuals and institutions across Fifth Estate arenas

There are complementary patterns to the use of the Internet in everyday life across various institutional arenas, such as those identified in Table 41. 1.

The Internet is enabling networked individuals in each arena in Table 41. 1 to associate in new ways—creating a Fifth Estate that helps them to reconfigure and enhance their communicative power. Citizens, or civil society, achieves this, in general or specialists in a particular sphere (e.g. medical professionals and patients), by going beyond their institutional sphere to reach alternative sources and contacts over the Internet (Dutton 2007). Of course, institutions rooted in the other estates are also using the Internet to maintain and enhance the communicative power of their organizations and institution, such as through the opening of new online communication channels by print and broadcast media. In addition, institutional networking is supporting strategic shifts in organizational activities, including e-government, e-commerce, and e-learning, but these are distinctly different from the activities of networked individuals.

As a result of these developments, challenges are being made to traditional institution-based forms of authority (e.g. information gathered from the Web being used by a citizen contacting their political representative or a patient visiting a doctor). The Fifth Estate's network of networks is becoming increasingly separate and independent from any single government department, agency, business, or other entity.

The following sections illustrate the more concrete role of the Fifth Estate in the key arenas identified in Table 41.1.

Table 41.1. A categorization of networked institutions and individuals

Arena	Networked individuals of the Fifth Estate	Networked institutions of the other Estates
Governance and democracy	Social networking, net-enabled political and social movements, and protests	E-government, e-democracy
Press and media	Bloggers, online news aggregators, Wikipedia contributors	Online journalism, radio and TV, podcasting
Business and commerce	Peer-to-peer file sharing (e.g. music downloads), collaborative network organizations	Online business-to-business, business-to-consumer (e.g. e-shopping, e-banking)
Work and the organization	Self-selected work collaborations, systems for co-creation and distribution (e.g. open source software)	Flatter networked structures, networking to create flexible work location and times
Education	Informal learning via the Internet, checking facts, teacher assessment	Virtual universities, multimedia classrooms, online courses
Research	Collaboration across disciplinary, institutional and national boundaries	Institutional ICT services, online grant/proposal submissions

Source: Adapted from Dutton (2009): 7.

Government and democracy on the line

Many administrations have made major strides in putting public information and services online, even though they have not generally kept pace with the commercial sector. This means that citizens and businesses can go online to complete tax returns or apply and pay for various public services. Many initiatives around the world have sought to build such e-government services.

E-government initiatives have been paralleled by innovations in e-democracy, efforts to use the Internet to support democratic institutions and processes (Fisher, Chapter 40, this volume). However, in political campaigns, elections and other democratic engagements, many still view the Internet as largely irrelevant, marginal, or likely to undermine democratic institutions. Some critics suggest e-democracy could erode traditional institutions of representative deliberative democracy by offering simplistic "point and click" participation in public policy-making. However, these criticisms are normally aimed at institution-centric views of the Internet.

The Fifth Estate presents new opportunities and threats. It can enable political movements to be orchestrated among opinion leaders and political activists in "Internet time." This can provide a novel means for holding politicians and mainstream institutions to account through ever-changing networks of individuals, who form and re-form continuously depending on the issue generating the particular network (e.g. to form ad hoc "flash mob" meetings at short notice through social networks and mobile communication). An example is the use of texting after the March 2004 Madrid train bombings to organize anti-government rallies that challenged the government's claims and contributed to unseating that administration. Similar examples include the pro-democracy protests across the Middle East and North Africa in early 2011.

Politicians are increasingly seeking to use the Internet to engage with citizens, including finding new sources of funding, as was achieved successfully for the campaign leading to the election of US President Obama in 2008. A key element in open government initiatives in the USA, UK and other nations is to publish more information online in "user friendly" forms, such as linked data, including detailed departmental plans and budgets, as a means for promoting greater transparency, enabling the public to hold politicians to account. In such ways, other estates are supporting the role of the Fifth.

The media and freedom of expression

The Internet has been criticized for eroding the quality of the public's information environment and undermining the integrative role of traditional fourth estate media in society. This includes claims that the Internet is marginalizing high-quality journalistic coverage by proliferating misinformation, trivial non-information and propaganda created by amateurs (Keen 2007) and creating "echo chambers" where personal prejudices are reinforced as Internet users choose to access only a narrow spectrum from the vast array of content at their fingertips (Sunstein 2007).

Such views fail to recognize the two-edged nature of all communication technologies, including the traditional mass media's equivalent weaknesses (e.g. a focus on sensational negative news stories, poor quality reporting and celebrity trivia). More importantly, there is often an unjustified assumption that the Internet will substitute for, rather than complement, traditional media. Many Internet users read online newspapers or news services, although not always the same newspaper as they read offline (Dutton et al. 2009). In these ways, the Internet can be realistically seen as a source of news that in part complements, or even helps to sustain, the Fourth Estate. At the same time, citizen journalists, bloggers, politicians, government agencies, researchers, and other online sources provide a related alternative that is independent and often competing.

The enhanced communicative power of networked individuals has led to many attempts to censor and control the Fifth Estate, even disconnect the Internet, in an equivalent way to tactics used against traditional media. The Internet's opening of doors to an array of user-generated content allows in techniques deployed by governments and others to block, monitor, filter, and otherwise constrain Internet traffic (e.g. Deibert et al. 2008). These are typified by the Chinese government's efforts to control Internet content, by creating the "Great Firewall of China," the Burmese government's closing down of the country's Internet service during political protests in 2007, and efforts by a number of governments to block Internet access and create a "kill-switch" to block the Internet.

At the same time, networked individuals are using the Internet to challenge attempts to control access, such as circumventing censorship. For example, www.herdict.org accepts and publishes reports from Internet users of inaccessible websites around the world and the OpenNet Initiative and Reporters Sans Frontières supports worldwide efforts to sustain and reinforce the Internet's openness.

Business organizations and work

Growing numbers within institutions rooted in the other estates are networking beyond the boundaries of their organizations. This includes geographically distributed individuals networking together to form collaborative network organizations (CNOs) to co-create or coproduce information products and services (Dutton 2008). The online encyclopaedia Wikipedia and open source software products such as the Firefox Web browser are examples of this phenomenon, becoming widely used and trusted despite initial doubts about the merits of their methods of creative coproduction. This is just one way in which the Fifth Estate has a crucial transformative potential at all levels in businesses and other private sector organizations.

There are concerns that CNOs may blur the boundaries and operations of the firm, or undermine the firm's productivity. Instead, individuals generally choose to join CNOs primarily to enhance their own productivity, performance, or esteem. Organizations need to understand how to capture the value of such innovations for the benefit of the enterprise as a whole, and not simply for individual users. Moreover, as consumers become increasingly empowered to hold businesses accountable, such as through Internet orchestrated boycotts, or better informed consumer groups, the role of the Fifth Estate in business and industry will be even more visible.

Education and research

E-learning networks can move beyond the boundaries of the classroom and university (Dutton and Eynon 2009). Many of these follow and reinforce existing institutional structures (e.g. with the teacher as the primary gatekeeper in a multimedia classroom or virtual learning environment). Nevertheless, students are challenging their teachers by bringing in other authorities and views through their networking with one another and with a variety of sources of knowledge, perhaps in classrooms in real time. This can be a positive force, better engaging students in the learning process, or a disruption in teaching, depending on how well preparations have been made to harness online learning networks.

Universities are building campus grids, digital library collections, and institutional repositories to maintain and enhance their productivity and competitiveness. Researchers are also increasingly collaborating through Internet-enabled networking, often across institutional and national boundaries (Dutton and Jeffreys 2010). These researchers are more likely to go to an Internet search engine before they go directly to their library; as likely to use their personal computer to support network-enabled collaboration as meet their colleagues in the next office; and tend to post work on websites, such as disciplinary digital repositories, and blogs rather than in institutional repositories. Indeed, freely available social networking sites offer tools for collaboration that could be as, or more, useful to researchers than systems for collaboration in which universities and governments have invested much money. Academics are engaged in their own Fifth Estate, for instance by online mobilization around both local issues (e.g. university governance) and more international topics (e.g. copyright and open science).

The Fifth Estate's governance challenge: sustaining its vitality

The vitality of the Fifth Estate within the space accorded by the Internet is not inevitable and can be undermined or sustained by the strategies of the other estates of the Internet realm. For example, the modern equivalent of the first estate clergy could be seen as the public intellectuals and critics who undermine the value of the Internet by depicting it as a space over-occupied by an ill-informed, ill-disciplined cult of the amateur. The power base of twenty-first-century "nobility" is reflected in economic elites, for example global

Table 41.2 The Fifth Estate and other institutions: partnerships and threats

Traditional Estate	Modern Parallel	Partnership opportunity	Type of threat to Fifth Estate
1st: Clergy	Public intellectual	Worldwide research networks; science commons; experts' websites and blogs.	Internet as an amateurs' space without expert knowledge and analytical rigour.
2nd: Nobility	Economic elites	Collaborative network organizations; online interactions with customers.	Centralization of information utilities; commercialization of Fifth Estate spaces.
3rd: Commons	Government	Innovations in engagements with citizens (e-democracy; e-government).	Censorship, regulation and other controls that constrain and block Internet access.
4th: Press	Mass media	Use of Fifth Estate spaces to complement traditional media.	Competition for audiences, funding; charging for online access.
Mob	Civil society, including citizens, audiences, consumers, Internet users, and the unorganized	Organized groups and interests, informed, helpful specialist forums (e.g. health care); greater democratic engagement.	Putting the legitimacy of other estates at risk; undermining of trust in the Internet through malicious (e.g. spam, hacking) and accidental uses.

corporations competing to dominate and commercialize Internet spaces. Traditional media are also competing with, co-opting and imitating the Internet's space of flows. Finally, there is the emerging major force of the lay public and civil society, empowered by networked individuals—a modern and dramatic contrast to what Burke might have called "the Mob." There may be mobs in contemporary society, and they can be enabled by the Internet, such as a group of hackers in December 2010 calling themselves Anonymous, who sought to attach institutions that did not support WikiLeaks. Yet mobs can also have a positive role as in some spontaneous protests, orchestrated online.

Table 41. 2 highlights potential threats to the Fifth Estate as well as areas of productive and creative cooperation between estates.

Questions about the governance of the Fifth Estate are likely to become more prominent as the realization grows that the Internet is a social phenomenon with deep societal implications. The greatest threat to the Fifth Estate's enormous potential as an aid to democratic participation and accountability will be from the commons, such as if regulations, online gatekeepers and other controls constrain or block the Internet's original design as an open, end-to-end network allowing a free flow of content.

Summary: a challenge to estates of the Internet realm

Internet use can play a positive role at local and global levels by enabling the emergence of a Fifth Estate—networked individuals who can access sources of information and expertise independent of key geographically and institutionally based organizations. This enhances the relative communicative power of networked individuals, relative to other actors, and enables them to hold other estates more accountable, such as by challenging their authority. Whether this potential is realized in a particular context depends on myriad factors shaping the choices of individual and institutional users. The Internet does not in itself cause people to be more or less strategic, but it can be used to reinforce and extend networks that support individuals and local communities as well as institutional actors.

The role that the Fifth Estate plays by enhancing the communicative power of networked individuals is likely to have profound implications for governance across every sector of society. But the continued vitality of the Fifth Estate depends on preventing excessive regulation or inappropriate regulation of the Internet, while providing safeguards against the main risks to users and the community at large. Regulation of the Internet, including innovations in self-regulation, such as typified by the "peer production of Internet governance" (Johnson et al. 2004) and other self-governing processes where users participate in establishing and monitoring governance rules (e.g. as achieved with Wikipedia and the eBay online auction service) will be key to the future of this new estate of the Internet realm.

NOTE

* The author thanks Malcolm Peltu for his assistance and the volume's editor and reviewers for their comments.

REFERENCES

Berners-Lee, T., Hall, W., Hendler, J. A., O'Hara, K., Shadbolt, N., and Weitzner, D. J. 2006. A framework for Web science. *Foundations and Trends in Web Science* 1: 1–134.

Bevir, M. 2011. Governance as theory, practice, and dilemma. In, M. Bevir (ed.), *The SAGE Handbook of Governance*. London: Sage, 1–16.

Carlyle, T. 1905. *On Heroes: Hero Worship and the Heroic in History*. Repr. of the Sterling Edition of Carlyle's *Complete Works*. Teddington, Middlesex: The Echo Library.

Castells, M. 1996. *The Rise of the Network Society*. Oxford: Blackwell.

Castells, M. 2001. *The Internet Galaxy*. Oxford: Oxford University Press.

Danziger, J. N., Dutton, W. H., Kling, R., and Kraemer, K. L. 1982. *Computers and Politics*. New York: Columbia University Press.

de Sola Pool, I. 1983. *Technologies of Freedom*. Cambridge, MA: Harvard Press.

Deibert, R., Palfrey, J., Rohozinski, R., and Zittrain, J. (eds.) 2008. *Access Controlled*. Cambridge, MA: MIT Press.

Dutton, W. H. 1999. *Society on the Line: Information Politics in the Digital Age*. Oxford and New York: Oxford University Press.

Dutton, W. H. 2005. The Internet and social transformation: Reconfiguring access. In W. H. Dutton, B. Kahin, R. O'Callaghan, and A. W. Wyckoff (eds.), *Transforming Enterprise*. Cambridge, MA: MIT Press, 375–97.

Dutton, W. H. 2007. Through the network (of networks) – the fifth estate. Inaugural lecture, Examination Schools, University of Oxford, 15 October. Available at http://webcast.oii.ox. ac.uk/?view=Webcast&ID=20071015_208 (accessed 19 September 2011).

Dutton, W. H. 2008. The wisdom of collaborative network organizations: Capturing the value of networked individuals. *Prometheus* 26: 211–230.

Dutton, W. H. 2009. The fifth estate emerging through the network of networks. *Prometheus* 27: 1–15.

Dutton, W. H. and Shepherd, A. 2006. Trust in the Internet as an experience technology. *Information, Communication and Society* 9: 433–451.

Dutton, W. H. and Eynon, R. 2009. Networked individuals and institutions: A cross-sector comparative perspective on patterns and strategies in government and research. *The Information Society* 25: 1–11.

Dutton, W. H. and Jeffreys, P. 2010. *World Wide Research: Reshaping the Sciences and Humanities*. Cambridge, MA: MIT Press.

Dutton, W. H., Shepherd, A. and di Gennaro, C. 2007. Digital divides and choices reconfiguring access. National and cross-national patterns of Internet diffusion and use. In B. Anderson, M. Brynin, J. Gershuny, and Y. Raban (eds.), *Information and Communication Technologies in Society. E-Living in a Digital Europe*. London: Routledge, 31–45.

Dutton, W. H., Helsper, E. J., and Gerber, M. M. 2009. *The Internet in Britain*. Oxford: Oxford Internet Institute, University of Oxford.

Garnham, N. 1999. Information politics: The study of communicative power. In W. H. Dutton (ed.), *Society on the Line: Information Politics in the Digital Age*. Oxford and New York: Oxford University Press, 77–78.

Habermas, J. 1991. *The Structural Transformation of the Public Sphere*. Cambridge, MA: MIT Press.

Johnson, D. R., Crawford, S. P., and Palfrey, J. G. 2004. The accountable net: peer production of Internet Governance. *Virginia Journal of Law and Technology* 9. Available at http://ssrn.com/abstract=529022 (accessed 19 September 2011).

Keen, A. 2007. *The Cult of the Amateur: How Today's Internet is Killing Our Culture*. New York: Doubleday.

Kranich, N. 2004. *The Information Commons: A Policy Report*. New York: Democracy Program, Brennan Center for Justice, NYU School of Law. Available at www.fepproject.org/policyreports/InformationCommons.pdf (accessed 19 September 2011).

Morozov, E. 2011. *The Net Delusion: How Not to Liberate the World*. London: Penguin Books.

Rice, R. E., Shepherd, A., Dutton, W. H., and Katz, J. E. 2007. Social interaction and the Internet: A comparative analysis of surveys in the US and Britain. In A. N. Joinson, K. Y. A. McKenna, T. Postmes, and U.-D. Reips (eds.), *Oxford Handbook of Internet Psychology*. Oxford: Oxford University Press.

Sunstein, C. R. 2007. *Republic.com 2.0*. Princeton, NJ: Princeton University Press.

Wellman, B. 2001. Physical place and cyberplace: The rise of personalized networking. *International Journal of Urban and Regional Research* 25: 227–252.

CHAPTER 42

....

THE GOVERNANCE
OF PRIVACY

....

ABRAHAM L. NEWMAN

PERSONAL information—credit card transactions, medical records, retina scans—is constantly collected, organized, and transmitted. Given the possibilities for abuse inherent in the processing of such data, governments have faced the dilemma of how to allow their productive use in society while guarding against potential violations of civil liberties. Far from being a new concern, lawmakers across the advanced industrial democracies first faced this challenge with the spread of the mainframe computer in the 1960s (Hondius 1975; Flaherty 1989). With the emergence of digital data networks and rising demands for surveillance in a globalized economy, the stakes and challenges involved have only grown and often become transnational and multi-jurisdictional (Farrell 2003; Newman 2008a).

The governance of data privacy includes a complex web of regulation, self-regulation, and technology at the national and transnational levels, which interact to manage how personal information may be used and shared in and across modern societies (Bennett and Raab 2006). The backbone of these efforts is formal regulatory rules. While states have tinkered with and adapted these to their national contexts, two broad approaches exist—comprehensive and limited regimes. Comprehensive regimes rely on a general set of Fair Information Practice Principles, which are enforced across the public and private sectors. These principles are monitored and implemented by an independent regulatory agency, which has a set of powers to investigate and sanction regulatory infractions. Limited regimes, by contrast, focus formal rules on the public sector and, with the exception of a few sensitive industries such as health care, rely on self-regulation and technology to manage concerns in the private sector (Newman 2008b; Schwartz and Reidenberg 1996). Within the context of these two legal regimes, industry efforts and technology are used to supplement/supplant public sector governance.

While not the sole determinant of the level of privacy protection in society, such privacy regimes have a significant effect on the level of information sharing and commodification in a society. In the United States, which has a limited regime, there are some 500 million credit reports, more than two for every man, woman, and child. In France, by contrast which has a comprehensive regime, there are no private sector credit reports. While France in this instance might represent an extreme case, it is critical to underscore that the goal of data privacy regulation is not to eliminate data transfers but rather to put a set of rules in place that balance the interests of the individual against those of the organization that hopes to employ the data.

For much of the 1970s and 1980s, data privacy regulation was limited to advanced industrial democracies concentrated in Western Europe and North America (Bennett 1992; Regan 1995). Starting in the 1990s, however, such regulation has spread to over forty nations reaching from Argentina to Albania. While the diffusion of such regulation is still limited primarily to democracies, it can be found in emerging markets and all the world regions. Importantly, the spread of privacy regulation has privileged the comprehensive model, where less than a handful of countries continue to maintain limited regimes. In fact, over the last fifteen years, at least eight nations have shifted from the limited to the comprehensive model of governance. Taken together the diffusion and success of the comprehensive regime marks a significant change in the governance of privacy globally (Bach and Newman 2007). In order to make sense of the rise of privacy regulation and the subsequent diffusion of the comprehensive model, this chapter argues that it is best to examine privacy governance as a sequence of policy decisions in which events at the national level have impacted regional policy which in turn has shaped global debates. In each round, political institutions have played a central role in organizing interests and mediating their influence. Since the 1990s, a network of independent regulatory agencies in Europe—data privacy authorities— has played a central role in promoting the spread of comprehensive rules regionally and globally. This rapid diffusion was far from inevitable but, rather, the result of a series of political fights. Recent challenges to the comprehensive regime stemming from surveillance demands suggest that its stability may once again be called into question.

In terms of central governance challenges, the privacy domain offers examples of several key phenomena. Digital networks and cross-border security operations have elevated privacy to a transnational issue in which citizens and governments face multiple jurisdictional demands. In response, transgovernmental networks of public sector actors have emerged to manage these global governance challenges, harmonizing regulations regionally, and shaping standards internationally. At the same time, private sector self-regulatory initiatives such as the adoption by multinational corporations of codes of conduct and chief privacy officers offer a complementary approach. Both, however, raise important issues of democratic accountability as transnational networks of non-elected regulators and firms play a critical role in international privacy governance.

The chapter proceeds in three sections. The first section lays out the principle underpinnings of data privacy regulations, how regulatory systems differ across countries, and the broader governance tools available. The second section delves into the politics of privacy regulation examining the national, regional, and international fights that have resulted in the rise and diffusion of the comprehensive model. The final section concludes with some thoughts on new challenges and emerging trends in data privacy governance.

GOVERNING PRIVACY

From the 1960s, democratic societies across the globe started debating the appropriate response to the threats posed by the rapidly expanding ability of governments and organizations to collect and process personal information facilitated by computer technology. These debates continue to inspire privacy protection today and form the backbone of regulatory regimes. This section will first describe the common set of privacy principles that underpins most modern privacy regulation before turning to the scope and structure of regulatory institutions. Finally, the section looks at the broader privacy governance toolkit.

The Fair Information Practice Principles

During the early years of the computer, a group of legal scholars in Western Europe and the USA began exploring the implications of the technology for the law. These experts quickly transitioned from studying the effect of computers on the law to larger questions surrounding the relationship between computers and society (Hondius 1975). These discussions produced a set of general norms based on the principle that individuals about whom data is collected (i.e. data subjects) have certain rights that must be balanced against the interests of those who collect and process personal information (i.e. data controllers). These principles may include the right to be notified before the collection of information, the right to consent to the further distribution of information, the right to access data held by a data controller, the right to object to incorrect data, or the right to demand erasure of incorrect or disputed information. The principles are termed the Fair Information Practice Principles (FIPPs). They were first elaborated in the Freedom of Information Act adopted in the United States in 1966 and were latter codified internationally in the Organisation for Economic Co-operation and Development (OECD) *Guidelines on the Protection of Privacy and Transborder Flows of Personal Data* of 1980 and the Council of Europe's *Convention for the Protection of Individuals with Regard to Automatic Processing of Personal Data* which came into force in 1985 (OECD 1980; Bennett 1992). While the exact formulation varies across national legislation and sometimes stresses one of the principles over another, the general formulation of the basic concepts are listed in Table 42.1.

Most evaluations of national and international legislation and private sector self-regulation are based on their consistency with or reflection of the FIPPs.

Table 42.1 The Fair Information Practice Principles

Collection limitation: personal information collection should be limited and lawful

Purpose: the purpose of data collection should be disclosed and data should not be used for other purposes without consent

Openness: individuals should be informed about privacy policies

Accuracy: data should be accurate, complete, and current

Participation: individuals may request information about data held by organizations and challenge incorrect data

Security: stored data must be secure from theft or corruption

Accountability: organization must be held accountable to measures that implement the above principles

---

Institutional variation in regulatory scope and structure

Despite the fact that most modern data privacy regulations reflect the spirit of the FIPP, there is still considerable variation in the scope and structure of national data privacy regimes. Most important is the distinction in scope—comprehensive versus limited regimes (Newman 2008b). In comprehensive regimes, public and private organizations face formal regulation. While the exact rules may vary slightly between public and private sectors with some sectors facing additional rules, data processing in the economy and society is covered by some form of regulation. Additionally, comprehensive regimes include an independent regulatory agency which monitors and implements privacy rules. Generally speaking, data privacy authorities are independent in the sense that they have control over personnel, enjoy long-term leadership tenure, and exercise budget autonomy. As is the case with all such regulatory institutions, some are more independent than others. Nevertheless, there are many examples of data privacy authorities that have opposed policies of their governments and maintained their leadership appointments and faced little political intervention. In addition to independence, data privacy authorities have a range of powers that they may employ in day-to-day enforcement and implementation which include the authority to investigate breaches of regulation, consultative responsibilities concerning, new legislative development, citizen complaint management, and in some cases the ability to impose sanctions. As is the case with independence, the exact powers vary among authorities, although the regional legislation within Europe has harmonized at a high level the powers that these regulators may use.

The limited regime, by contrast, focuses regulatory efforts on the public sector and generally lacks an independent regulatory agency that may monitor and enforce data privacy rules. In terms of regulatory scope, the public sector must comply with some form of FIPP rules. In the private sector, however, only a limited number of sensitive sectors face privacy regulations with the majority of sectors engaging in self-regulation or no regulation at all. These systems lack an independent regulator with oversight at times provided by a government ministry or an ombudsman with limited authority (Schwartz and Reidenberg 1996).

Differences in privacy regimes, while certainly not the only measure of privacy protection in a society, do shape the collection and transmission of information in an economy and a polity. Take two examples. Mailing lists that are aggregated and sold to companies for marketing are significantly more expensive in countries such as Germany where comprehensive rules reign than in the USA (Turner and Buc 2002). Similarly, there are no private sector credit reports in France, while there are some 500 million in the USA. This alters the types of information available to both businesses attempting to segment markets and to governments hoping to rationalize services or monitor citizens.

In addition to the scope of privacy regimes, there is considerable variation in their institutional structure. The primary difference in this regard centers on the level of centralization in oversight and implementation. In some jurisdictions, for example France and Sweden, one centralized data privacy authority is responsible for the domain. For much of their history, these centralized systems relied on licensing and registries of databases to keep abreast of the policies of data controllers (Flaherty 1989; Bennett 1992). Other countries, by contrast, opted for decentralized systems whereby regulatory oversight is shared among a number of government agencies and private sector actors. In Germany, for example, each Land has its own data privacy authority, which is responsible for monitoring privacy regulations in Land administrations as well as private companies that have their company headquarters in the Land. Additionally, private companies are required to appoint in-house data privacy officials, who are legally responsible for upholding data privacy regulations in the firm. In other countries, such as Australia, co-regulation has developed in which industry associations may develop sector codes that, if accepted by the data privacy authority, supplant government rules. If industry does not opt to develop a code, the national regulations apply to the sector. Formal legislation, then, acts as a regulatory backstop for industry-specific regulations. Different regulatory structures are then differentially positioned to oversee certain types of regulatory issues. Centralized systems, for example, may be well situated to manage large ologopolistic firms in the telecommunications or financial services industry. Decentralized regulatory structures have more local monitors that may uncover emerging challenges in data protection.

The structure of regulatory institutions naturally interacts with the scope of the privacy regime. Comprehensive regimes may have more centralized (e.g. France) or more decentralized structures (e.g. Germany). Similarly, limited regimes may be more centralized (e.g. South Korea) or more decentralized (e.g. the USA). The tasks and functions conducted by either a centralized or decentralized regulator, however, are embedded and defined by the regulatory scope of data privacy rules.

While formal rules play a critical role in setting the boundary conditions for privacy governance, there are also a number of other tools that contribute to privacy protection (Bennett and Raab 2006). Technology, for example, plays a critical role in modern privacy protection regimes. At the most basic level, for example, computer programs frequently come with a set of defaults concerning the amount of personal information revealed and exchanged. Individual users may then use technology to limit access to that information and to increase their control over information exchange. Companies have developed a host of privacy enhancing technology (PETs), which offer further protection for individuals or companies concerned about personal privacy. Another set of governance tools center on private sector efforts to manage privacy challenges. Many companies have voluntarily appointed chief privacy officers, who review and monitor company policy vis-à-vis personal data. Some sectors have also looked into self-regulatory codes of conduct or best practices. These technological and self-regulatory efforts, however, are significantly influenced by the legal environment. The threat of government intervention, for example, may bolster such efforts and the lack of government rules may undermine their efficacy (Newman and Bach 2004; Scharpf 1999).

THE POLITICS OF PRIVACY GOVERNANCE

Early national debates

Formal proposals for privacy regulation swept the advanced industrial democracies in the early 1970s. Frequently supported by an odd-couple alliance between the progressive left and the libertarian right, a host of parties, scientific experts, and civil society organizations participated in the lobbying effort. Despite the similar set of legislative proposals and constellation of privacy advocates, the ultimate national rules differed considerably in the regulatory scope and structure. Most important for future international debates, some countries adopted comprehensive rules that covered both the public and private sector and established an independent regulatory agency—data privacy authority—which oversaw the implementation and enforcement of these regulations.

Although initial draft laws often centered on a similar set of privacy principals, grounded in the FIPPS, the reaction by bureaucracies and private sector organizations varied considerably. In some countries, such as France, private sector involvement in the development of such legislation was minimal, although the regulations put in place clear restrictions on how such data could be used. In the USA, by contrast, industry played an active and decisive role in shaping the final rules. The intensity of industry preferences and the success of its involvement were largely shaped by differences in the domestic organization of business and politics.

To understand organizational privacy preferences, it is first critical to examine the broader institutional environment in which such organizations are embedded. Some companies or bureaucracies, for example, have large internal databanks which require little external enhancement from other organizations. One can, then, think of these organizations as enjoying a relatively ologopolistic information position. In such a setting, privacy rules bolster that position by making it more difficult for new firms or government agencies to acquire similar data and defends the organization against claims by others hoping to gain access to their data. In other sectors or countries, however, firms may sit in a fragmented market where data is spread across a number of smaller firms and agencies. In such settings, these organizations rely on data sharing in order to obtain enough data to perform their required function. Privacy rules, thus, impose a considerable cost for such organizations as they restrict the flow of data in the economy and bureaucracy (Newman 2010).

Not only do such rules differentially affect organizational preferences, but these organizations face distinct institutional opportunity structures. In some countries, the legislative process is ripe with possibilities for interest groups to intervene and shape legislation. Veto points such as bicameral legislatures, judicial review, and presidentialism offer a few examples of institutional structures that expand the ability of interest groups to exercise their political voice in the legislative process. Other more unitary governments, by contrast, enjoy considerable autonomy in the legislative process and are better able to push their policy agenda against the preferences of interest group lobbying.

Early national politics on privacy, then, were significantly influenced by the organization of industry and politics. French banks, for example, found much to support in new privacy rules as they enhanced the banks' already dominant oligopolisitic position. Banks in the USA, by contrast, were much more fragmented and thus stood to lose from such rules. Additionally, these banks could use single member districts and presidentialisms to get their preferences heard. As a result of these domestic political battles, several key countries such as France and Germany emerged from the 1970s with comprehensive rules while others including the USA adopted limited regimes (Newman 2008b).

Regional ratcheting up

Starting in the 1980s, the European Union (EU) began a concerted effort to deepen economic cooperation across borders. While a number of European countries had adopted comprehensive rules, several EU member states including Belgium, Greece, Italy, Portugal, and Spain had not. This opened up the possibility for regulatory arbitrage in the face of the deepening integration of the European single market. Data privacy authorities in countries with comprehensive rules, therefore, worried that this effort might threaten their regulatory authority.

Data privacy authorities cooperating with their peers in other countries through transgovernmental networks worked to develop regional rules that would mitigate the asymmetric regulations in Europe. These regulators used their expertise, authority over market access, and network ties to build an agenda for pan-European rules and alter the costs to other political actors of inaction. For example, a set of member states attempted to integrate border control through an agreement known as the Schengen Agreement. The European Commission was very interested in the agreement as it would facilitate the free flow of labor with in the EU. In order to facilitate the agreement, the participants needed to construct a system of information exchange—the Schengen Information System—that would allow for proper implementation and monitoring. Belgium, however, did not yet have comprehensive data privacy rules and thus threatened to undermine the regulations in place in other countries. The data privacy authorities from France, Luxembourg, and Germany (which has all previously adopted comprehensive rules) threatened to block data transfers to the Schengen system without pan-European rules. It was at this point that the Commission and the member states recognized the importance of regional data privacy rules for the broader European effort. Sub-state actors—data privacy authorities—working across borders used their power resources to alter the European debate (Newman 2008a).

The result of this political dance was the 1995 European Data Privacy Directive. The directive requires all member states to adopt rules for the public and private sector and establish an independent data privacy authority (Swire and Litan 1998). Importantly, it required a harmonization of implementation and enforcement authorities of these regulators, significantly boosting the regulatory powers of many existing regulators. The directive also includes an important international requirement contained in Article 25. This article requires that data about European citizens may only be transferred to other countries if those other countries have adequate rules domestically (Long and Quek 2002). In order to assist the European Commission in the development of new rules and to assess the privacy rules of other countries, the directive created the Article 29 Working Party. The Working Party is a novel governance mechanism composed of a network of national regulators with a secretariat in Brussels. It reviews emerging data privacy issues, offers opinions concerning the adequacy of privacy laws in other countries, and follows the implementation and enforcement of privacy laws within the member states (Eberlein and Newman 2008).

Political entrepreneurship by data privacy authorities, then, contributed to the further expansion of comprehensive rules within Europe. The directive also boosted the authority of existing regulators and put them in a position to contribute to the governance of market access into and out of the EU.

The diffusion of European rules

Since the passage of the directive, a host of countries ranging from Argentine to Albania have adopted comprehensive data privacy rules. In total over forty jurisdictions now have comprehensive rules. This includes eight countries (from Canada to the Czech Republic) that had previously relied on limited regimes and have switched their rules. This shift is due in significant part to the international repercussions of the European privacy directive.

On the one hand the passage of the directive shifted the international status quo best practice. Article 25 of the directive limits the transfer of data concerning European citizens to countries that maintain adequate privacy rules. This adequacy clause transformed international debates as it raised the costs in non-European countries that either lacked privacy rules or used a limited regime. While the EU could not force other countries to alter their national rules, the directive changed national privacy debates in many countries. It served as model legislation for advocates of privacy rules and altered the economic calculus of multinational corporations that actively worked in or traded with Europe but were based in other countries. In short, the directive coordinated regulatory authority within Europe so as to leverage the internal market at the international level (Bach and Newman 2007).

At the same time, European data privacy authorities used their expertise in the field to promote policy changes in other jurisdictions and offered the Commission the technical resources to evaluate policy in those countries. In some cases, particularly for new member states or regional neighbors, envoys from member state data privacy authorities engaged in twinning missions. Bureaucrats from member state authorities went to those countries in order to assist in legislative development and implementation. In other cases, the Article 29 Working Party, which is comprised primarily of national regulators, examined the policies of other countries to determine whether they met adequacy requirements. The Working Party has determined that a number of countries such as Argentina, Canada, and Switzerland meet the standard while at the same time refusing to give Australia or the USA a similar evaluation. From direct twinning to adequacy ruling, the EU uses its regulatory expertise to teach and model for other jurisdictions while at the same time holding the stick of market access in the background of negotiations (Newman 2008b).

It is clear that the EU efforts have been far from universal. The USA remains committed to the limited system and has resisted EU pressures (Farrell 2003). Nevertheless, the international regulatory landscape concerning privacy has changed dramatically in the last twenty years with a threefold increase in the number of countries with comprehensive regimes. While formal rules are not the only governance tool to manage privacy issues, it is clear that the baseline in terms of regulation has shifted significantly. This shift is in a significant part the result of a sequence of events taking place first nationally, then regionally, and finally spilling over transnationally.

New competing alternatives

Since the turn of the millennium, a number of governments and multinational companies have started to explore alternatives to the European privacy directive. The most advanced effort is the APEC Privacy Framework (APEC 2004). Developed within the Asian Pacific Economic Cooperation (APEC), the framework builds on the FIPP principles. But in contrast to the EU privacy directive, it relies on self-implementation and self-certification. Countries would, hypothetically, be in a position to determine whether their rules met the adequacy standards of other countries. This effort is supported by the USA and Australia. While it offers a potentially flexible set of principles to build domestic privacy rules, it is unclear if it will drive policy debates at either the domestic or the international level. The Article 29 Working Party has not yet recognized the standard, and, given the considerable amount of self-certification and self-implementation, it seems doubtful that they will.

Another alternative that has gained considerable attention in the private sector is binding corporate codes of conduct. These binding corporate codes spell out a set of practices maintained by a company and its affiliates. If breaches occur, the company has committed itself through legal contracts to resolving the matter. Seen as a potentially flexible solution for MNCs, few have actually adopted the measure. The most difficult part of such binding corporate codes are the set of legal obligations that might arise across multiple jurisdictions. They thus pose a significant regulatory burden on companies operating transnationally. At the same time, they offer an important example of how private sector authority might be brought to bear to resolve a transnational governance dilemma.

A final model for dealing with such issues is the Safe Harbor Agreement between the USA and the EU. The Agreement was concluded in July 2000, and went into force in November 2000. It is based on a set of Safe Harbor Principles that companies apply to data transferred from the EU to the USA (Farrell 2003). Firms that pledge to follow these principles receive Safe Harbor from the application of the European Directive. The US Department of Commerce maintains a list of firms that have agreed to follow the Agreement.[1] The principles of the Agreement are binding on companies and businesses must choose whether they will be monitored and enforced by self-regulation or a self-certification. Under self-regulation, the company agrees to comply with the principles and joins an independent dispute settlement body that processes and mediates complaints. The Federal Trade Commission agrees to act as a regulatory backstop, monitoring firm compliance with their self-regulatory agreements. Under self-certification, firms register with a national European data privacy authority and agree to regulation by that agency. If companies transfer human resources data, they are required to self-certify. A 2004 review of the Agreement's implementation found that 75 percent of firms self-certified, de facto placing themselves under the supervision of data privacy authorities in Europe (Commission of the European Communities 2004). In short, the Agreement creates a framework for multinational companies to share data across the Atlantic without requiring these firms to adjust data processing practices of domestic customers. Data coming from Europe, however, is guaranteed a similar level of protection to that it would enjoy at home. While it is still unclear how successful the Agreement has been, it offers a potentially innovative governance tool in which a network of regulators from multiple jurisdictions share the monitoring and enforcement of their rules vis-à-vis transnational companies.

CONCLUSION

Since the middle of the last century, the governance of privacy has changed dramatically. In parallel with many other sectors, governments have come to rely on a set of similar regulatory tools to manage a broad range of potential conflicts that arise as personal information collection and exchange have become more widespread. This has included the creation of formal rules on the use of such data and in some countries the establishment of independent regulatory agencies that monitor and enforce these rules. At the same time, private sector actors have explored a number of self-regulatory tools and technologies to deal with emerging privacy challenges (See Rhodes, Chapter 3, this volume; Peters, Chapter 2, this volume).

While many of these discussions started largely as national decisions, in the last twenty years they have spilled over in regional and transnational debates. Importantly, data privacy authorities worked collaboratively in transgovernmental networks within Europe to promote the passage of regional rules. Once in place, the EU was able to use its well-developed regulatory capacity in the issue area to promote comprehensive rules in other jurisdictions. Although regulations continue to vary in terms of their oversight structure, there has been a general movement toward the comprehensive model globally.

Despite these efforts, conflict within or across systems is far from over. New government-sponsored surveillance efforts have raised questions as to the limits of privacy protection within comprehensive systems. Alternative regulatory models such as the APEC privacy framework draw into question the long-term staying power of the current harmonization trend. New technologies such as cloud computing and radio frequency identification raise new monitoring capabilities and pose new challenges to individuals attempting to manage their personal information.

In terms of the literature on governance, the area of data privacy offers several important points of comparison. Most generally, it signals the general trend towards arm's length oversight structures (Jordana and Levi-Faur 2004; Rhodes, Chapter 3, this volume). At the same time, international and regional solutions have tended to rely on networks of regulators in contrast to traditional command and control centralized authority. The Article 29 Working Party offers an example of a novel form of network governance that is also being experimented with in other sectors such as international financial regulation (Eberlein and Newman 2008; Sabel and Zeitlin 2010). Such transnational governance based in collaborative networks of non-elected regulators, however, posses clear questions concerning democratic accountability. Finally, data privacy offers a puzzling case of the EU successfully promoting strict standards in the face of globalization and against the wishes of the USA. The area then signals the important role that regulatory capacity both in terms of control over market access and issue expertise plays in international regulatory negotiations.

NOTE

1. The list is available at http://www.export.gov/safeharbor/doc_safeharbor_index.asp.

REFERENCES

APEC (Asian Pacific Economic Cooperation). 2004. APEC Privacy Framework. Santiago. Singapore: APEC Secretariat.
Bach, D. and Newman, A. 2007. The European regulatory state and global public policy: Micro-institutions and macro-influence. *Journal of European Public Policy* 16: 827–846.

Bennett, C. 1992. *Regulating Privacy: Data Protection and Public Policy in Europe and the United States*. Ithaca, NY: Cornell University Press.

Bennett, C. and Raab, C. 2006. *The Governance of Privacy: Policy Instruments in Global Perspective*. Boston, MA: MIT Press.

Commission of the European Communities. 2004. The implementation of Commission Decision 520/2000/EC on the adequate protection of personal data provided by the Safe Harbour privacy principles and related frequently asked questions issued by the US Department of Commerce. October 20. Brussels: European Commission.

Eberlein, B. and Newman, A. 2008. Escaping the international governance dilemma? Incorporated transgovernmental networks in the European Union. *Governance* 21: 25–52.

Farrell, H. 2003. Constructing the international foundations of E-commerce: The EU–US safe harbor arrangement. *International Organization* 2: 277–306.

Flaherty, D. 1989. *Protecting Privacy in Surveillance Societies*. Chapel Hill: University of North Carolina Press.

Hondius, F. 1975. *Emerging Data Protection in Europe*. New York: Elsevier.

Jordana, J. and Levi-Faur, D. 2004. *The Politics of Regulation: Institutions and Regulatory Reforms for the Age of Governance*. Cheltenham: Edward Elgar.

Long, J. W. and Quek, M. P. 2002. Personal data privacy protection in an age of globalization: The US–EU safe harbor compromise. *Journal of European Public Policy* 9: 325–344.

Newman, A. 2008a. Building transnational civil Lliberties: Transgovernmental entrepreneurs and the European data privacy directive. *International Organization* 62: 103–130.

Newman, A. 2008b. *Protectors of Privacy: Regulating Personal Data in the Global Economy*. Ithaca, NY: Cornell University Press.

Newman, A. 2010. What you want depends on what you know: Firm preferences in an information age. *Comparative Political Studies* 43: 1286–1312.

Newman, A. and Bach, D. 2004. Self-regulatory trajectories in the shadow of public power: Resolving digital dilemmas in Europe and the United States. *Governance* 17: 387–413.

OECD (Organisation for Economic Co-operation and Development). 1980. *Guidelines on the Protection of Privacy and Transborder Flows of Personal Data*. Paris: OECD.

Regan, P. 1995. *Legislating Privacy: Technology, Social Values, and Public Policy*. Raleigh: University of North Carolina Press.

Sabel, C. and Zeitlin, J. 2010. *Experimentalist Governance*. Oxford: Oxford University Press.

Scharpf, F. 1999. *Governing in Europe: Effective and Democratic*. Oxford: Oxford University Press.

Schwartz, P. and Reidenberg, J. 1996. *Data Privacy Law: A Study of United States Data Protection*. Charlottesville, VA: Michie.

Swire, P. and Litan R. 1998. *None of Your Business: World Data Flows, Electronic Communication, and the European Privacy Directive*. Washington, DC: Brookings.

Turner, M. and Buc, L. 2002. The Imiact of data restrictions on fundraising for charitable and nonprofit institutions: Privacy leadership initiative. New York: Privacy Leadership Initiative.

PART VIII

EUROPEAN GOVERNANCE

CHAPTER 43

....

THE EUROPEAN
UNION—A UNIQUE
GOVERNANCE MIX?

....

TANJA A. BÖRZEL*

1. INTRODUCTION

....

THE European Union (EU) used to be considered as a unique supranational organization that could not be compared to any other form of political order we are familiar with at the national or international level. There is broad agreement that the EU is and has always been more than an international organization of states; but it is not and probably never will be a state (Wallace 1983). Political scientists have shown a remarkable creativity in developing new concepts to describe the alleged sui generis nature of the EU. This changed in the 1990s, when students of European Politics discovered the governance literature. The governance perspective seemed to finally capture the nature of the EU as "a unique set of multi-level, non-hierarchical and regulatory institutions, and a hybrid mix of state and non-state actors" (Hix 1998: 39) "network governance" (Kohler-Koch 1996)—without having to invent new labels.

Governance concepts are indeed more appropriate to study the political institutions and policy-making processes of the EU than traditional approaches of both International Relations and Comparative Politics. Yet the EU does not present a unique type of governance. Like its member states, the EU features different combinations of market, networks, and hierarchy. The analysis of this governance mix reveals several characteristics of the EU that have been largely overlooked in the literature. This chapter argues that, first, the EU heavily relies on hierarchy in the making of its policies. Its supranational institutions allow for the adoption and enforcement of legally binding decisions without the consent of (individual) member states. Second, network governance, which systematically involves private actors in the policy process, is hard to find. EU policies are largely formulated and implemented by governmental actors. Third, political competition among member states and their subnational authorities has gained importance in European governance. Member states increasingly resort to mutual recognition and the open method of coordination where their heterogeneity renders harmonization difficult. Overall, the EU is less characterized by network governance and private interest government than by inter- and transgovernmental negotiations, on the one hand, and political competition between member states and subnational authorities, on the other. Both operate in a shadow of hierarchy cast by supranational institutions. This governance mix does not render the EU unique but does distinguish it from both international organizations and national states.

2. FROM PROTOTYPE TO GOVERNANCE MIX

Governance research took off from studies on EU policy-making in the field of structural policy, where supranational, national and subnational actors have to pool their competencies to formulate and implement EU policies. Such forms of *multi-level governance* seemed to be characteristic for other policy areas, too (see Bache, Chapter 44, this volume). While early works described the EU as a whole as a prototype of network governance (Kohler-Koch and Eising 1999), the more recent literature on what is often referred to as "new modes of governance" (cf. Héritier and Rhodes 2010) explores to what extent the EU has made use of networks to govern its affairs. A systematic analysis of EU policy-making reveals that the EU does not represent a particular type of governance but features different combinations of market, networks, and hierarchy.

Studying the governance mix in the EU requires a typology that combines different forms of governance rather than treating them as ideal types. The literature usually distinguishes between hierarchy, market (competition system), and network (negotiation system). These differ with regard to the type of actors involved and the degree of coupling between them. While *political hierarchies* are confined to public actors, negotiation and competition systems may vary in their actor constellations. *Inter- or transgovernnmental negotiation* systems consist of public actors only, who may come from different policy sectors and/or levels of government. *Intermediate negotiation systems* bring together public actors with representatives of business and/or societal interests (Mayntz 1993). They are often referred to as "network governance" (Rhodes 1997). *Private negotiation systems* do not include public actors. They take the form of "private interest-government" in associations (Streeck and Schmitter 1985).

Not only private actors compete for the provision of public goods and services in competition systems, for example, when they are contracted out; public actors, such as state universities, also often participate in the political competition. *Regulatory or tax competition systems*, by contrast, are exclusively confined to public actors (states, regions, municipalities), since only they hold the competencies for setting collectively binding regulations and taxation.

The different governance structures feature distinct modes of social coordination by which actors seek to achieve changes in (mutual) behavior. *Hierarchical coordination* usually takes the form of authoritative decisions (e.g. administrative ordinances and court decisions that actors must obey), which is only possible for *political hierarchies*. *Non-hierarchical coordination* in *negotiation systems*, by contrast, is based on voluntary compliance. Conflicts of interests are solved by negotiation. *Voluntary agreement* is either achieved by negotiating a compromise and granting mutual concessions (side-payments and issue-linkage) on the basis of fixed preferences (bargaining), or actors engage in processes of non-manipulative persuasion (arguing), through which they develop common interests and change their preferences accordingly. Coordination in *competition systems* is also non-hierarchical. Actors compete over meeting certain performance criteria, to which they adjust their behavior accordingly. They are largely motivated by egoistic self-interests. However, they pursue a common goal or some scarce resources of which they wish to obtain as much as possible by performing better than their competitors. *Political competition* induces actors to contribute to the provision of collective goods and services by pursuing their self-interests. Unlike under private competition, their performance is evaluated and rewarded by institutionally defined criteria legitimized by public authorities.

The institutionalized rule structures and their modes of coordination are ideal types that hardly exist in reality. Rather, we find combinations, both within and beyond the state. Such governance mixes feature different combinations of ideal types, embedding one in the other by making one subordinate to the other ("shadow").

Combining governance structures, governance processes and types of actors, we arrive at a typology that allows to systematically map the governance mix in the EU. In order to label the different possible mixes, I draw on the EU governance typology of Fritz Scharpf (Scharpf 2001), which, however, focuses on public actors and neglects the combination of different governance forms. Not all combinations are theoretically feasible or exist empirically in the EU. Figure 43.1 provides an overview of the governance forms that are referred to throughout the chapter, with numbers in parentheses.

3. THE EU GOVERNANCE MIX

Hierarchy and its shadow

Unlike modern states, the EU lacks a legitimate monopoly of force to bring its member states into compliance with European law. Yet the supranational institutions of the Treaty establishing the European Communities (EC Treaty) provide ample possibility for hierarchical coordination by public actors. *Supranational centralization* (1) or centralized regulation (Eckert 2011) reigns where supranational actors can set and enforce legally binding decisions without requiring the consent of the member states. Thus, the European Central Bank (ECB) authoritatively defines EU monetary policy. In competi-

institutionalized rule structures	HIERARCHY		NEGOTIATION SYSTEM		COMPETITION SYSTEM
	hierarchical (asymmetrical influence)		non-hierarchical (mutual influence)		Non-hierarchical (mutual adjustment)
modes of coordination	AUTHORITATIVE DECISION		AGREEMENT VIA BARGAINING,		POLITICAL COMPETITION
	negotiation in the shadow of hierarchy	political competition in the shadow of hierarchy		political competition in the shadow of negotiation	
actors involved					
public	(1) supranational centralization	(4) mutual recognition	(6) intergovernmental cooperation	(7) open method of coordination–governmental	(5) regulatory-/tax competition
public–private	(2) supranational joint decision-making –majority–unanimity		(9) network governance (public–private co-regulation)	(8) open method of coordination–intermediate	
private	(3) private self-coordination in the shadow of hierarchy (regulated/delegated self-regulation)		(10) private interest government (private self-regulation)		

FORMS OF GOVERNANCE (INSTITUTIONALIZED FORMS OF POLITICAL COORDINATION) IN THE EU

FIGURE 43.1 The governance mix in the EU.

tion law, the Commission can conduct investigations against cases of suspected distortions of competition caused by member states (e.g. by state aid) and anti-competitive practices of private actors (e.g. cartel formation), impose sanctions and take legal recourse to the European Court of Justice (ECJ). The Commission not only enforces competition rules of the EU treaties and a series of directives and regulations, which have been adopted by qualified majority in the Council (since the Amsterdam Treaty). In case of public undertakings, it can also adopt legally binding regulations without the consent of the member states if privileges of public undertakings constitute a major obstacle to the completion of the single market. The Commission has only invoked these powers as a regulatory lever to shape markets once, when it sought to break open national monopolies in the telecommunication sector (Schneider 2001). However, it alluded to the possibility of using the coercive force of EU law several times when member states and public undertakings were unwilling to negotiate a subsequent liberalization of the energy sector (Eberlein 2008). This shadow of supranational hierarchy is reinforced by the right of the Commission to bring infringement proceedings against member states that violate the principles of free and fair competition. Finally, the ECJ can bind the member states against their will by interpreting European law. While ECJ case law is a direct form of *supranational centralization*, it also has a significant indirect effect by casting a *shadow of supranational hierarchy on inter- and transgovernmental negotiation systems*.

Public negotiation in the shadow of hierarchy

The shadow of hierarchy cast by supranational centralization is significantly enlarged in the areas subject to *supranational joint decision-making* (2), in which the Council decides by qualified majority and supranational institutions set the rules for implementation. This applies to almost all policies of the single market but also to the framework in justice and home affairs. In other words, the core areas of EU policy-making are embedded in hierarchical structures constituted by majority rule and the enforcement powers of the Commission and the ECJ. Supranational hierarchy provides the institutional framework for inter- and transgovernmental negotiation systems, which dominate the supranational policy process. While the Community Method grants the Commission and the European Parliament a significant say, EU decision-making is still dominated by the Council. The Committee of Permanent Representatives, numerous Council working groups as well as the expert committees of the Commission prepare legal proposals and execute Council decisions (comitology; see Héritier and Moury, Chapter 45, this volume). These formalized negotiation systems are embedded in transgovernmental networks, which span across several levels of government and stages of the policy process. The networks help supranational, national and subnational public actors to informally coordinate their interests and reach agreements through the exchange of resources and arguments.

The shadow of supranational hierarchy generated by majority rule in the Council significantly influences the dynamics and outcomes of inter- and transgovernmental negotiation systems. On the one hand, the perceived "threat" of a majority decision in the Council increases the willingness of governmental actors to come to an agreement. On the other hand, inter- and transgovernmental actors have to make sure that their agreements are likely to stand scrutiny by the Commission and the ECJ. The parameters set by their interpretation of European law are not always oriented towards mere market liberalization and free competition but may also support market correcting policies. The "dual mechanism of anticipated reactions and the fleet in being" (Scharpf 1997: 200) is particularly prevalent in the single market but also has an impact on other policy sectors, such as the environment, social policy and tax policy (Héritier and Lehmkuhl 2008).

Private negotiation in the shadow of hierarchy

The social dialogue is the most prominent form of *private self-coordination in the shadow of supranational hierarchy* (3). In selected areas of social policy, social partners have the right to conclude agreements which can be turned into European law. Moreover, the EU cannot take legal action without consulting the social partners. If the latter abstain from collective bargaining, however, the EU is free to legislate. While this form of Euro-corporatism is unique, the negotiation procedure under the social dialogue has hardly been invoked. Despite qualified majority voting in the Council, member states still appear too diverse to agree on EU legal standards. In the absence of a credible shadow of hierarchy, employers have had little incentive to negotiate with the trade unions. Moreover, the social partners themselves have faced problems in reaching agreement among their members since industrial relations are still organized along national lines (Falkner 2000). The European Employment Strategy and the Lisbon Process, both based on the Open Method of Coordination (OMC), were an attempt to deal with the ideological divisions and sovereignty disputes among the member states, which have blocked both the negotiations in the Council and among the social partners (see below).

Other forms of *delegated or regulated private self-regulation* are equally rare. While voluntary agreements at the national level abound, they have been hardly used by European business organizations to prevent EU regulation. If at all, they are found in the area of environmental and consumer protection (Héritier and Eckert 2008). Voluntary agreements are negotiated without the participation of Commission, Council, and Parliament. They have, however, to conform to certain parameters formulated by European legislation.

Technical standardization is another example of private regulatory activities under the hierarchical supervision of supranational actors. EU technical standardization is mostly voluntary since supranational harmonization of health and security standards is confined to national regulations concerning the public interest (Gehring and Kerler 2008). For the other areas, the Council has delegated the task to develop technical standards to three European private organizations (European Committee for Standardization [CEN], European Committee for Electrotechnical Standardization [Cenelec], and European Telecommunications Standard Institute [ETSI]). The technical standards are not legally binding but are subject to a "conformity assumption," which only applies, however, if the member states do not voice objections during the comitology procedure. The standardizing organizations have—with the exception of ETSI— only one representative per member state. Since national standardizing organizations are not always private, self-regulation is not only regulated by the EU and subject to the control of the member states through comitology, but it also involves mostly public actors.

This also holds for other areas of risk regulation, where regulatory networks have emerged in response to liberalization and privatization in the single market. Since the member states have been reluctant to transfer regulatory powers to supranational institutions, particularly in the area of economic regulation, market-creating and market-correcting, competencies are usually delegated to independent regulatory agencies or ministries at the national level (Coen and Héritier 2006). To fill the "regulatory gap" at the EU level, national regulatory authorities have formed informal networks to exchange information and develop "best practice" rules and procedures to address common problems (Coen and Thatcher 2008). While these regulatory and operational networks may be open to the participation of private actors (e.g. providers and consumers), they are transgovernmental rather than transnational in character (Eberlein and Grande 2005). Moreover, even if the member states have not delegated regulatory competencies to the EU, transgovernmental networks operate under the shadow of supranational framework regulation, which "regulates the regulators" (Eberlein and Grande 2005: 98) by setting minimum requirements for the regulatory regimes in the member states (Levi-Faur 1999).

Political competition in the shadow of hierarchy

The shadow of supranational hierarchy becomes weaker if the Council decides by unanimity and the codecision or cooperation procedure does not apply. In these cases, the institutionalized rule structures resemble inter- and transgovernmental negotiation systems as we find them in the area of foreign, security, and defense policy (see below). Where the member states wish to coordinate under the shadow of supranational hierarchy but have been unable to agree on a harmonization of their national policies and on granting the EU the necessary competencies, respectively, the *principle of mutual recognition* has provided an alternative mode of governance (4).

Markets can be conceptualized as a hierarchically regulated competition system. What is special about the European market is the *principle of mutual recognition* as a supranational competition rule that does not have to rely on the harmonization of national regulations. It was established by the ECJ in 1979 with its seminal *Cassis de Dijon* decision and constitutes the framework for a moderate regulatory competition between the member states in the shadow of supranational hierarchy (Sun and Pelkmans 1995: 68f.). European law mandates the opening of national markets and generates competitive pressure not only on domestic companies but also on public regulation within the member states. In a nutshell, the principle of mutual recognition allows high-regulating countries to maintain their regulatory standards but prevents them from using those standards as non-tariff trade barriers. A good produced in one member state has to be granted access to the markets of any other member state, even if the product standards are higher in the importing than in the exporting member state. The access can only be denied if compliance with the higher standards is in the imminent public interest of the receiving country. Such a decision is subject to judicial review by the ECJ. Thus, while fostering competition, the principle of mutual recognition constrains the dynamics of a race to the bottom by requiring that states (implicitly) agree on minimum standards. It thereby significantly expands the shadow of supranational hierarchy in the single market since the dismantling of non-tariff barriers does not require the consent of the member states—unlike the harmonization of national standards at the EU level.

This form of "horizontal transfer of sovereignty" (Nicolaidis and Shaffer 2005) has been increasingly invoked in justice and home affairs, for example, in the area of asylum and immigration policy or criminal law, where the national regulations of member states are too divergent to allow for agreement in the inter- and transgovernmental negotiation systems (Schmidt 2007). Unlike in the single market, however, the principle of mutual recognition is not to facilitate the removal of non-tariff barriers but, on the contrary, to help establish market correcting policies (Lavenex 2007). It may sound cynical to conceive of asylum seekers, migrants and criminals as undesired market outcomes, but the completion of the single market does indeed create a need for coordination in the area of internal security and immigration. The removal of border controls, envisioned already by the Schengen Treaty of 1985 and made European primary law with the Amsterdam, renders the control of illegal immigration and trans-border crime extremely difficult. The functional interdependence between market integration and internal security has led to a spillover effect as a result of which significant parts of justice and home affairs have been subsequently supranationalized, that is, made subject to supranational joint decision-making. For sensitive areas, such as police and judicial cooperation in criminal matters, the principle of mutual recognition serves as a functional equivalent for supranational joint decision-making. The principle of mutual recognition facilitates cross-border law enforcement since different national standards with regard to criminal codes can no longer obstruct judicial cooperation between member states (Lavenex 2007). The absence of the supranational shadow of hierarchy, however, has significant (normative) implications, which resemble the asymmetry between positive and negative integration in the single market (Lavenex and Wagner 2007). Mutual recognition facilitates the coordination of national security policies on the "lowest common denominator." While member states can maintain higher standards to protect the civil liberties of their citizens, these may be undermined by the police and judicial cooperation in criminal matters. The European arrest warrant is a case in point. As long as they cannot agree on a harmonization at the EU level, the principle of mutual recognition allows the member states to circumvent their national standards (Lavenex and Wagner 2007). Under the exchange of personal data regime in European Police Office (EUROPOL), for instance, a member state could request data that it may not be allowed collect under its own laws. This is particularly problematic if the data were collected by a member state that has not ratified the Convention on Data Protection of the European Council. Moreover, the ECJ has no power to monitor compliance in the member states. Unlike in the single market, the treaties so far do not contain any provisions that would allow supranational institutions to interfere with policing competencies operating under inter- and transgovernmental cooperation and mutual recognition. Finally, the principle of mutual recognition requires that member states trust each other in maintaining and controlling equivalent regulations (Schmidt 2007). Such trust is less likely to emerge in policy areas that are highly politicized by redistributive or normative conflicts among (increasingly heterogeneous) member states. It remains to be seen to what extent the principle of mutual recognition in the policy areas covered by the area of freedom, security and justice to ensure security, rights and free movement within the EU will result in a regulatory competition undermining the individual rights of EU citizens.

Political competition

There are areas of competition between the member states that are neither regulated by supranational institutions nor placed under the shadow of inter- and transgovernmental negotiation systems (on the latter see below), nor operate outside any political coordination by the EU. Instead, member states adjust their social and tax policies in order to avoid competitive disadvantages and gain competitive advantages, respectively (Scharpf 2001: 7–8). While *regulatory competition* (5) in the Single Market has been mitigated by supranational institutions (Sun and Pelkmans 1995; Radaelli 2004), market integration has given rise to a rather unmitigated *tax competition* (5), particularly in the area of corporate taxation (Radaelli 1995). The ECJ has not seen any legal reason to allow national corporate taxation interfere with the freedom of movement and capital, and the member states have been unable to agree on a tax harmonization to stop the competitive race to the bottom (Ganghof and Genschel 2008). They did, however, adopt a code of conduct against harmful tax competition which should ensure fair competition among the member states (Radaelli 2003). It remains to be seen whether the member states will manage to achieve some regulation of tax competition through political coordination at the informal level (Radaelli and Kraemer 2008). The developments in justice and home affairs shed serious doubts that political competition without a supranational shadow of hierarchy can contain the progressive dismantling of national standards.

Public negotiations

The member state governments have no or only limited formal decision-making powers under supranational centralization and supranational joint decision-making. The opposite is true for *inter- and transgovernmental cooperation* (6) in the fields of external and internal security. The (European) Council usually decides by unanimity and shares the right of initiative with the Commission. The Parliament is at best consulted and the ECJ has only limited power of judicial review. The areas of inter- and transgovernmental cooperation, which the member states explicitly sealed against the shadow of supranational hierarchy, largely correspond to the ideal type of (public) negotiation systems. European decisions rest on the voluntary coordination of the member states (unanimity or consent) and often do not have legally binding character (*soft law*). They are prepared and accompanied by inter- and transgovernmental networks, which act free from the shadow of hierarchy. This is not only true for the foreign, security and defense policy and parts of justice and home affairs, but also for selected areas of the single market (parts of social policy, macroeconomic and employment policy, research and development, culture, education, taxation), in which the EU has no or only very limited competencies and the influence of the supranational troika (Commission, Parliament, and Court) is severely restricted. Moreover, a new form of transgovernmental negotiation system or "state-centred multi-level governance" (Levi-Faur 1999: 201) has emerged, again in the single market, in which national authorities coordinate their regulatory activities, although they still operate under some shadow of supranational hierarchy (see above) and are not necessarily controlled by their governments. Where the shadow of supranational hierarchy is absent, member states have increasingly resorted to the *Open Method of Coordination* (OMC) in order to generate the necessary coordination at the EU level.

Political competition in the shadow of inter- and transgovernmental negotiation

OMC (7) was first applied in EU employment policy. It emerged as a "new mode of governance" to implement the so called Lisbon Strategy, which the European Council adopted in 2000 in order to promote economic growth and competitiveness in the EU (cf. Armstrong, Begg and Zeitlin 2008). OMC has allowed to coordinate national policies in areas where member states have been unwilling to grant the EU political powers and additional spending capacity, particularly in the field of economic and social policy. In the meantime, OMC has traveled beyond Lisbon and is applied in justice and home affairs, health policy, environmental policy, and tax policy. OMC works through inter- and transgovernmental negotiations, in which the member states strike voluntary agreements on joint goals that are not legally binding. In order to realize these goals, the member states develop national action plans whose implementation is monitored and evaluated on the basis of common indicators. The member states compete for best practices that are to trigger processes of mutual learning. By outperforming other member states, they gain a competitive advantage in attracting or keeping economic activities. OMC is in principle open to the participation of non-state actors (8). Yet, in practice, it has largely taken the form of inter- and transgovernmental negotiations with hardly any involvement of private actors, either in the formulation of joint goals at the EU level or in their implementation at the national level (Hodson and Maher 2001; Rhodes 2005: 295–300). This is not very surprising since it is precisely the intergovernmental and voluntaristic nature that makes OMC an acceptable mode of policy coordination for the member states in sensitive areas.

Public–private (intermediate) negotiations

Formal and informal EU-institutions often provide for the consultation of economic and societal interests by the Commission, the Parliament, and the representatives of the member states. In some cases, the EU treaties even allow for the participation of non-state actors in EU negotiation systems on equal basis. Most prominently, the partnership principle in structural policy explicitly requires the involvement of private actors in inter- and transgovernmental negotiation systems (see Bache, Chapter 4, this volume). The EU treaties prescribe the involvement of the social partners—beyond the consultation of the Economic and Social Committee—for the management of the European Social Fund. The social partners' representatives are members of the management committee, in which the member state governments are represented as well, and which is chaired by the European Commission. There are also several EU regulations specifying the partnership principle and providing for the participation of the social and economic partners at the various stages of programming under the Social and the Regional Development Funds. Moreover, a recent regulation extends the partnership principle to include civil society. The extent to which private actors are actually involved is contested in the literature and varies significantly across the member states. Governmental actors have largely defended their position as the central policy-makers. In any case, there is certainly not enough empirical evidence to speak of *network governance* (9) in structural policy.

Private negotiations

Private interest government (10) as the ideal type of private negotiation system is as rare as its public–private counterpart of network governance. Private actors may coordinate themselves without having a mandate from or being under supervision of supranational institutions. The EU is crowded with a multitude of private actors, representing both civil society and business. They have organized themselves at the EU level in umbrella organizations (Greenwood 2007). The so called Euro-groups are able to take binding decisions for their members, for example, by adopting codes of conduct, negotiating voluntary agreements, and monitoring compliance, but they seldom have embarked on collective action—and if they do, the shadow of hierarchy looms. The few EU-level voluntary agreements have been negotiated to avoid stricter EU regulation (Héritier and Eckert 2008). Rather than engaging in private interest government, business and civil society organizations focus on individual and collective lobbying of decision-makers, both at the EU and the national level (Eising 2007; Coen 2008). The emergence of private interest government is further impaired by European peak associations and umbrella groups being organized around and often divided along national lines, which in turn renders consensus among its members difficult.

4. CONCLUSION

The EU features a governance mix that is not unique but different both from any international organization and modern states. While it lacks the monopoly of force, supranational institutions can resort to hierarchical coordination to make individual member states act against their interests. Member state governments do not monopolize EU policy-making but share powers with the European Commission, the European Parliament, or (trans-) national regulatory authorities. Private actors do play a role but political decisions are largely taken and implemented by inter- and transgovernmental actors. Thus, the EU is governed in, rather than by networks, and these networks are not only managed but clearly dominated by public actors. Finally, political competition as a mode by which the member states seek to coordinate their policies is complementing inter- and transgovernmental negotiations operating under and outside the supranational shadow of hierarchy. The principle of mutual recognition and the Open Method of Coordination have gained importance in an ever more heterogeneous EU, where harmonizing national policies by supranational centralization and supranational joint decision-making is increasingly difficult.

Conceptualizing the EU as a specific mix of different forms of governance not only allows for a more nuanced analysis of its nature, it also makes the EU look less unique and facilitates comparison with other governance systems entailing different combinations of hierarchy, negotiation, and competition across different levels of government. Finally, the governance mix sheds some light on the governance functions the EU can perform. The EU governs the largest market in the world. The combination of negotiation and competition in the shadow of hierarchy provides a comprehensive regulatory framework that has successfully prevented and corrected market failures (on the EU model of regulatory governance see Eckert 2011; Finger 2011). Yet, particularly in (re-) distributive policy areas, the member states have not been willing to resort to supranational joint decision-making and supranational centralization in order to counteract politically undesired outcomes of the single market. At the same time, EU market integration impedes the member states in maintaining such functions. The single currency largely deprives the member states of their major instruments for national macroeconomic stabilization, while the Maastricht convergence criteria put serious constraints on state expenditures. Softer modes of governance (intergovernmental negotiations and competition) are unlikely to respond to this "European problem-solving gap" (Scharpf 2006: 855), elucidated once again by the financial crisis. Attempts to use the OMC for institutionalizing member state coordination in areas such as taxation of mobile capital, employment, social policy, or economic governance where the heterogeneity and political salience of member state preferences prohibits supranational forms of governance, pale in light of the redistributive effects of supranational centralization in monetary policy, on the one hand, and political competition with regard to taxes and labor costs, on the other. The principle of mutual recognition only contains the progressive dismantling of national standards if it operates under the shadow of supranational hierarchy. This is particularly the case for highly politicized issues. Redistributive or normative conflicts are hard to solve without the possibility of resorting to authoritative decision-making. The dilemma of European governance may be that "soft" forms appear to require a shadow of supranational hierarchy to address policy problems, which the member states refuse to make subject to "hard" supranational forms of governance in the first place.

Note

* I thank David Levi-Faur and Catherine Moury for their useful comments on earlier versions of this chapter. The chapter builds on Börzel 2010.

References

Armstrong, K. A., Begg, I., and Zeitlin, J. 2008. JCMS Symposium: EU governance after Lisbon. *Journal of Common Market Studies* 46: 413–450.

Börzel, T. A. 2010. European governance: Negotiation and competition in the shadow of hierarchy. *Journal of Common Market Studies* 48: 191–219.

Coen, D. 2008. *Lobbying in the European Union: Institutions, Actors and Policy*. Oxford. Oxford University Press.

Coen, D. and Héritier, A. (eds.) 2006. *Refining Regulatory Regimes in Europe: The Creation and Correction of Markets*. Cheltenham: Edward Elgar.

Coen, D. and Thatcher, M. 2008. Network governance and multi-level delegation: European networks of regulatory agencies. *Journal of Public Policy* 28: 49–71.

Eberlein, B. 2008. The making of the European energy market: The interplay of governance and government. *Journal of Public Policy* 28: 73–92.

Eberlein, B. and Grande, E. 2005. Beyond delegation: Transnational regulatory regimes and the EU regulatory state. *Journal of European Public Policy* 12: 89–112.

Eckert, S. 2011. European regulatory governance. In *Regulatory Governance in the European Union*, ed. D. Levi-Faur, Cheltenham: Edward Elgar, 00–00.

Eising, R. 2007. The access of business interests to the EU institutions: Towards elite pluralism? *Journal of European Public Policy* 14: 384–403.

Falkner, G. 2000. The council or the social partners? EC social policy between diplomacy and collective bargaining. *Journal of European Public Policy* 7: 705–724.

Finger, M. 2011. Towards a European model of regulatory governance? In *Regulatory Governance in the European Union*, ed. D. Levi-faur. Cheltenham: Edward Elgar, 00–00.

Ganghof, S. and Genschel, P. 2008. Taxation and democracy in the EU. *Journal of European Public Policy* 15: 58–77.

Gehring, T. and Kerler, M. 2008. Institutional stimulation of deliberative decision-making: Division of labour, deliberative legitimacy and technical regulation in the European single market. *Journal of Common Market Studies* 46: 1001–1023.

Greenwood, J. 2007. *Interest Representation in the European Union*. Houndmills. Palgrave Macmillian.

Héritier, A. and Eckert, S. 2008. New modes of governance in the shadow of hierarchy: Self-regulation by industry in Europe. *Journal of Public Policy* 28: 113–138.

Héritier, A. and Lehmkuhl, D. (eds.) 2008. *The Shadow of Hierarchy and New Modes of Governance. Special Issue Journal of Public Policy* 28: 1–17.

Héritier, A. and Rhodes, M. (eds.) 2010. *New Modes of Governance in Europe. Governing in the Shadow of Hierarchy*. Houndmills: Palgrave Macmillan.

Hix, S. 1998. The study of the European Union II: The "new governance" agenda and its revival. *Journal of European Public Policy* 5: 38–65.

Hodson, D. and Maher, I. 2001. The open method as a new mode of governance: The case of soft economic policy co-ordination. *Journal of Common Market Studies* 39: 719–746.

Kohler-Koch, B. 1996. Catching up with change: The transformation of governance in the European Union. *Journal of European Public Policy* 3: 359–380.

Kohler-Koch, B. and Eising, R. (eds.) 1999. *The Transformation of Governance in Europe*. London: Routledge.

Lavenex, S. 2007. Mutual recognition and the monopoly of force: Limits of the single market analogy. *Journal of European Public Policy* 15: 762–779.

Lavenex, S. and Wagner, W. 2007. Which European public order? Sources of imbalance in the European area of freedom, security, and justice. *European Security* 16: 225–243.

Levi-Faur, D. 1999. The governance of competition: The interplay of technology, economics, and politics in European Union electricity and telecom regimes. *Journal of Public Policy* 19: 175–207.

Mayntz, R. 1993. Modernization and the logic of interorganizational networks. In J. Child, M. Crozier, and R. Mayntz (eds.), *Societal Change between Market and Organization*. Aldershot: Avebury: 3–18.

Nicolaidis, K. and Shaffer, G. 2005. Transnational mutual recognition regimes: Governance without global government. *Law and Contemporary Problems* 68: 263–318.

Radaelli, C. 1995. Corporate direct taxation in the European Union. Explaining the policy process. *Journal of Public Policy* 15: 153–181.

Radaelli, C. M. 2003. The code of conduct against harmful tax competition: Open method of coordination in disguise? *Public Administration* 81: 513–531.

Radaelli, C. M. 2004. The puzzle of regulatory competition. *Journal of Public Policy* 24: 1–23.

Radaelli, C. M. and Kraemer, U. S. 2008. Governance areas in EU direct tax policy. *Journal of Common Market Studies* 46: 315–336.

Rhodes, M. 2005. Employment policy. In H. Wallace, W. Wallace, and M. A. Pollack (eds.), *Policy-Making in the European Union*. Oxford: Oxford University Press: 279–304.

Rhodes, R. A. W. 1997. *Understanding Governance. Policy Networks, Governance, Reflexivity and Accountability*. Buckingham, Philadelphia: Open University Press.

Scharpf, F. W. 1997. *Games real Actors Play: Actor-Centered Institutionalism in Policy Research*. Boulder, CO: Westview Press.

Scharpf, F. W. 2001. Notes toward a theory of multilevel governing in Europe. *Scandinavian Political Studies* 24: 1–26.

Scharpf, F. W 2006. The joint-decision trap revisited. *Journal of Common Market Studies* 44: 845–864.

Schmidt, S. K. 2007. Mutual recognition as a new mode of governance. *Journal of European Public Policy, Special Issue* 14: 667–681.

Schneider, V. 2001. Institutional reform in telecommunications: The European Union in transnational policy diffusion. In M. G. Cowles, J. A. Caporaso and T. Risse (eds.), *Transforming Europe. Europeanization and Domestic Change.* Ithaca, NY: Cornell University Press: 60–78.

Streeck, W. and Schmitter, P. C. (eds.) 1985. *Private Interest Government: Beyond Market and State.* London et al.: Sage.

Sun, J.-M. and Pelkmans, J. 1995. Regulatory competition in the single market. *Journal of Common Market Studies* 33: 67–89.

Wallace, W. 1983. Less than a federation, more than a regime: The community as a political system. In H. Wallace, W. Wallace and C. Webb (eds.), *Policy-Making in the European Community.* Chichester: John Willey, 43–80.

CHAPTER 44

....

MULTI-LEVEL GOVERNANCE
IN THE EUROPEAN UNION

....

IAN BACHE[*]

UNTIL the mid-1980s, the study of the European Union (EU) was dominated by approaches developed from the study of international relations (IR) that were concerned with understanding the process of European integration. From the IR tradition of pluralism, neofunctionalists (Haas 1958; Lindberg 1963) argued that the national governments who had initiated the integration process were losing control in an increasingly complex web of interdependence, a web that involved supranational, subnational, and non-state actors. The counterview came from intergovernmentalism (Hoffman 1964, 1966), informed by realist approaches in IR.

The neofunctionalist argument fitted neatly with events until the mid-1960s, when the reassertion of national authority strengthened the counterclaims of intergovernmentalists that governments retained control over the important issues—not least through the persistence of the national veto in most areas. The period from the mid-1960s to the mid-1980s is generally seen as one in which the pace of integration slowed and intergovernmentalist explanations prevailed.

The turning point in relation to theorizing the EU came with a renewed push for integration in the form of the single market program, expressed in the Single European Act of 1986. This initiative led to an expansion in EU competences and revised decision-making procedures, most notably to eliminate the national veto in a number of areas to facilitate faster integration. The effects of the single market program on the process of integration and, in turn, on the nature of the EU as a political system prompted a new wave of theory challenging the dominant intergovernmental-supranational debate. As the EU's competences expanded, parallels were increasingly drawn between the EU and domestic political systems, and tools and approaches from the study of domestic and comparative politics were utilized (Hix 1994).

Multi-level governance emerged in this period and drew upon both the old and new contributions to EU debates. Gary Marks (1992) first used the phrase multi-level governance to capture developments in EU cohesion policy. Later, Marks and others developed the multi-level governance approach to apply to EU decision-making more broadly (e.g. Marks, Hooghe, and Blank 1996; Hooghe and Marks 2001). The approach drew insights from both the study of domestic/comparative politics and the study of international politics. In particular, it had connections to the work by Fritz Scharpf (1988) and others on German federalism, resembled aspects of neofunctionalism, and was replete with network metaphors.

ORIGINS

Cohesion policy can be understood as the governing principles of various funding instruments aimed at addressing social and economic inequalities in the EU. It focuses in particular on developing disadvantaged regions in the context of market integration, and the structural funds are the main financial instruments for this purpose. The reform of the structural funds in 1988 introduced new governing principles that were central to the emergence of multi-level governance (MLG), in particular, the principles of partnership and additionality.

The partnership principle required that the bulk of structural funding be administered through partnerships established in each assisted region. These partnerships were to consist of national, subnational (regional and/or local), and supranational (EU Commission) actors. This decision gave subnational actors a formal role in the EU policy-making process for the first time and was central to the *multi-level* notion of MLG. In subsequent years the Commission pushed for and secured agreement to a greater role in the partnerships for non-state actors (trade unions, environmental organizations, voluntary and community groups, and so on). This indicated a greater cross-sectoral dimension to EU governing arrangements, which strengthened the *governance* dimension of MLG (below).

The additionality principle required that EU funds be spent in addition to any planned expenditure in the member states. The requirement had been in place since the introduction of EU regional policy in 1975 but was strengthened in 1988, having been regularly ignored to that point—in particular by the British government, which treated EU funds as a reimbursement to the Treasury for its payments to the EU budget. Following the 1988 reform, the Commission took the British government to task over its implementation of the additionality principle and—with the support of British local authorities—brought about a change in the government's approach. This case of joint supranational-subnational action was taken as further evidence of an emerging multi-level polity. Marks (1993: 403) suggested that "Several aspects of the conflict—the way in which local actors were mobilized, their alliance with the Commission, and the effectiveness of their efforts in shifting the government's position—confirm the claim that structural policy has provided subnational governments and the Commission with new political resources and opportunities in an emerging Multi-level policy arena."

From seeking to capture the dynamics of cohesion policy, MLG has since become extensively used to characterize the EU polity as a whole. It has been described by Schmitter (2004: 49) as "the most omnipresent and acceptable label one can stick on the contemporary EU." Indeed, it is a label that has been widely adopted by EU actors, illustrated by its use in the European Commission's White Paper on EU Governance in 2001 (COM 91) and by the publication of Committee of the Region's White Paper on Multi-level Governance of 2009 (CoR 2009).

DEFINITIONS AND TYPOLOGIES

In its early manifestation, multi-level governance referred to "continuous negotiation among nested governments at several territorial tiers" and described how "supranational, national, regional and local governments are enmeshed in territorially overarching policy networks" (Marks 1993: 392 and 402–403). Yet despite its reference to networks, multi-level governance at this stage focused on intergovernmental relations, highlighting the role of subnational governments as an important the "third level" in EU politics. MLG theorists claimed that competencies had "slipped away from central states both up to the supranational level and down to the subnational level" (Marks, Hooghe and Blank 1996: 167).

Yet this conceptualization ignored the increasing role of non-state actors in EU policy-making, which were central to the concept of governance for scholars in the public policy tradition. Without this dimension, what it described was multi-level *government*, not multi-level *governance*. This highlighted a tension in the debate on governance that remains central between those who use the term governance to describe the activity of governing, irrespective of the actors (e.g. Zürn, Chatper 51, this volume) and those who use the term to connote also changes in the actor constellations involved in governance (e.g. Rhodes, Chapter 3, this volume). However, in the field of cohesion policy and more generally in EU studies, it became increasingly commonplace for the "multi-level" part of the concept to be taken to refer to the increased vertical interactions between governments operating at different territorial levels, while "governance" signaled intensified interactions between governments and non-governmental actors.

In developing the approach—partly in response to criticisms over the lack of specificity in its *governance* dimension—Hooghe and Marks (2003; also Marks and Hooghe 2004) outlined a twofold typology of MLG. Type I has echoes of federalism. It describes system-wide governing arrangements in which the dispersion of authority is restricted to a limited number of clearly defined, non-overlapping jurisdictions at a limited number of territorial levels, each of which has responsibility for a "bundle" of functions. By contrast, Type II describes governing arrangements in which the jurisdiction of authority is task-specific, where jurisdictions operate at numerous territorial levels and may be overlapping. In Type I, authority is relatively stable, but in Type II it is more flexible, to deal with the changing demands of governance (see Table 44.1).

Table 44.1 Types of multi-level governance

Type I	Type II
General-purpose jurisdictions	Task-specific jurisdictions
Nonintersecting memberships	Intersecting memberships
Jurisdictions at a limited number of levels	No limit to the number of jurisdictional levels
System-wide architecture	Flexible design

Source: Marks and Hooghe (2004, 17).

These types of multi-level governance are not mutually exclusive, but coexist in modern polities: formal general purpose institutions of government operate alongside, and indeed create, special-purpose bodies designed to carry out particular tasks. The main Type I entities in the EU are the Commission, the Council of Ministers, and the European Parliament, while there is a vast array of Type II bodies that include agencies, partnerships and quangos (see also below).

Skelcher (2005: 101) identified four different relationships between Type I and Type II entities: parallel; complementary; incorporated; and oppositional (see Table 44.2).

Type I entitles are seen to operate more to a logic of appropriateness and Type 2 entities to a problem-solving logic. Type I and Type II relations can be either or both formal and informal depending on the nature of the Type II entity and specific issue. However, Type I entities take a greater responsibility for steering contemporary governance, while Type II entities do most of the rowing.

Table 44.2 The relationship between Type 1 and Type 2 entities in the EU[1]

Type of relationship	Characteristics of T2 body	Nature of relations
Parallel	An alternative to existing governmental organizations (eg regional partnership bodies for EU cohesion policy)	Mainly informal, but periodic reporting to T1 bodies (national and EU)
Complementary	Independent but undertakes activities that add to those carried out by government (eg European Central Bank)	Mainly formal, reporting directly to EU institutions
Incorporated	A formal extension of government (European Aviation Safety Agency)	Mainly formal, accountable to EU institutions
Oppositional	Challenges government and advocates for particular interests (eg, European Trade Union Confederation)	Mainly informal, sometimes formal (eg corporatist arrangements)

(Developed from Skelcher 2005: 101).

Table 44.3 The transformation of governance and the nature of regulatory capitalism

	Laissez-faire capitalism (1800s-1930s)	Welfare capitalism (1940s-1970s)	Regulatory capitalism (1980s-)
Steering	Business	State	State
Rowing	Business	State	Business

STEERING AND ROWING

Elaborating on Braithwaite (2000), David Levi-Faur (2005: 15) outlines how the locations of two major functions of governance, steering and rowing, have shifted across distinct phases of capitalism and how the current phase of *regulatory capitalism* is characterized by "a new division of labor between state and society and in particular between state and business" (Table 44.3).

In relation to this phase, a multi-level governance perspective on developments in Europe would identify not only a different mix of sectors involved in rowing (public, private and voluntary) but also steering taking place at different territorial levels (especially supranational and national). Moreover, while steering may now be supranational, much of the rowing remains national (and subnational) where responsibility for implementation remains (Table 44.4).

Empirical applications

Empirical studies of MLG have been at the level of policy sectors and most often on EU cohesion policy: the "home turf" of the concept (examples of applications to other

Table 44.4 The transformation of governance and the nature of regulatory capitalism in Europe: a multi-level governance perspective

	Laissez-faire capitalism (1800s-1930s)	Welfare capitalism (1940s-1970s)	Regulatory capitalism (1980s-)
Steering	Business (mainly national)	National state (sometimes in corporatist collaboration)	National state, international and subnational levels (i.e. mainly Type I governance)
Rowing	Business (mainly national)	National state	Public, private and voluntary sectors (mainly Type II governance)

policy sectors include Fairbrass and Jordan (2004) and Walti (2010) on the environment; Perraton and Wells [2004] and Enderlein [2010] on economic policy; and Piattoni [(2010] on higher education policy). Most studies show a marked increase in both multi-level and multi-actor interactions over time, but there is more contention over the effects on the distribution of power in this changing context as a brief survey of the cohesion policy research illustrates.

Hooghe's (1996) edited volume on cohesion policy implementation found considerable variation in the evidence for multi-level governance across states, and indeed *within* some states, with the pre-existing balance of territorial relations a key part of the explanation. In centralized member states, where central government actively sought to play a gatekeeper role over the political impact of the new arrangements, as in Britain, it met with considerable success. Here, subnational actors were mobilized, but not necessarily empowered. In more decentralized member states, subnational authorities—normally regional governments—were better placed to take advantage of the opportunities provided by the partnership requirement. Later research (Tavistock Institute 1999) confirmed this pattern of differentiated multi-level governance emerging through EU cohesion policy.

A study of the additionality issue in Britain (see above) found that the change in the government's approach to implementation failed to lead to the anticipated extra spending in Britain's regions. Policy control that the government "gatekeeper" lost through pressure from joint supranational-subnational action identified by Marks (1993) was clawed back at the (domestic) implementation stage of the policy process (Bache 1999). Here again, the implication was that increased supranational and subnational activity did not have a substantive effect on the distribution of power in relation to policy outcomes.

As EU funding shifted towards Central and East European states in the approach to the 2004 enlargement, so did the focus academic research on MLG. A study of the Czech Republic, Estonia, Hungary, Poland, and Slovenia identified national government "gatekeepers" as generally "firmly in control" of subnational actors, who were able to participate in but not significantly influence the policy process (Bailey and De Propris 2002). Research on Estonia, Hungary, Poland, and Slovenia emphasized the importance of institutional traditions in each state in shaping the degree of regionalization emerging (Hughes, Sasse, and Gordon 2004, 2005), echoing the findings of earlier research on the EU15 (Hooghe 1996).

Bachtler and McMaster (2008: 420–421) identified several points to support the argument that the role of regions in cohesion policy had increased "in terms of their legitimacy, institutional capacity and stability," but also suggested that "the limitations and barriers to regional participation in the funds currently outweighs the opportunities." Their bottom line was to challenge the idea that cohesion policy necessarily strengthens regions. Brustz (2008) explained how the Commission's turn to (re)centralization for administering funds in the pre-accession period was resisted in some states, and thus features of multi-level governance emerged. Here, the governance changes were described as "layering": "the emergence of change on the margins, implying local rule transformation within a basically unchanged institution that does not challenge the dominant characteristics of the mode of governance" (Brustz 2008: 620).

The study by Bache (2008) of the EU25 considered the impact of cohesion policy on Type I and Type II multi-level governance. It identified a trend towards multi-level governance across Europe, although this remained uneven. Moreover, the study indicated that while this trend was generally not due to states' engagement with the EU, it was not possible to understand the nature and pace of the changes evident without reference to the EU and its cohesion policy. However, the effects of EU cohesion policy seemed more pronounced on Type II multi-level governance than on Type I, with ad hoc functionally specific governance arrangements emerging at various territorial levels as a direct response. For the most part, this effect was driven by rational responses to EU financial incentives, although there was also evidence that deeper learning could take place in the longer term, characterized by the voluntary adoption of EU practices in the domestic sphere.

Key issues

In the ongoing academic debates on MLG a number of key issues can be identified. These relate to: definitions and understandings of MLG; its conceptual clarity; what MLG means for the role and power of the state; whether the concept is being overstretched; and its normative dimension. We deal with each of these issues in turn.

DEFINITIONAL ISSUES

As MLG has become more widely adopted it has been understood and applied in quite different ways with the consequence that, as Stein and Turkewitsch (2010: 197) observe, "there is no single definition of MLG that is currently broadly accepted by the academic community." However, a broad distinction can be made between those who emphasize the focus on "levels" and Type I relations (i.e. generally, more state-focused) and those more interested in the "governance as networks" and Type II dimensions.

The first category includes scholars who use the term MLG when they are talking primarily about intergovernmental relations. This includes scholars of the EU, often in the federalist tradition, who are "trying to understand the simultaneous shift of competences to supranational and subnational bodies" (Hooghe and Marks 2010: 2). Similarly, some domestic politics scholars employ MLG to highlight the "relevance of additional authority levels," either international or (in Europe) supranational (Braun 2010, 168), as do scholars of global governance seeking to bring a focus on "the interplay of different levels" in the context of "the rise of political authority beyond the nation state" (Zurn 2012).

The second category of scholars see the distinctive contribution of MLG to be in either the two types that highlight the relationship between territorial and functional governance (Schmitter 2000; Slaughter and Hale 2010) and/or the changing dynamics of the state-society relationships embedded in "territorially overarching" or "transgovernmental" networks (Stein and Turkewitsch 2010; Walti 2010). Indeed, Sbragia (2010: 267) speaks of the appeal of MLG to EU scholars being "that it seemed to capture the lack of 'stateness' that characterizes the EU".

A neat observation that brings the two strands together in the EU context comes from Borzel (2012) who suggests that "the EU is governed in, rather than by networks, and these networks are not only managed but clearly dominated by public actors."

CONCEPTUAL CLARITY

Beyond definitional issues, MLG has been criticized for its lack of conceptual clarity. Jessop (2005: 61) pointed to the "marked ambiguity in the referents of multi-level governance." More specifically, Benz (2010: 215) stated:

> Hooghe and Marks provided a framework for analysis but did not elaborate a theory that explains how multi-level governance works. Although they rightly emphasized the dynamics and flexibility of the European political structure, they did not clearly carve out mechanisms which may explain these dynamics and the outcomes of policy-making.

Critics have argued that MLG has not clearly distinguished its claims from those of the concepts of participation (Bache 1999), mobilization (Jeffery 2000), or dialogue (Wilson 2003). These three concepts also highlight increased interactions in the policy process but also evidence that suggests the effect of increased interactions on substantive outcomes is often marginal. In particular, evidence of control slipping away from states was not as clear as MLG initially inferred as the role of the state began to change in response to developments.

THE ROLE OF THE STATE

While MLG suggests that empirical developments present a challenge to state control—inferring the seepage of competences upwards, downwards and sideways—this is a challenge that states have often met with some success. In this new context, states seek to exercise control through a variety of steering mechanisms and through setting the ground rules for governance (metagovernance). Indeed, in some cases, the promotion of (multi-level) governance can be a strategy for enhancing state power; for example, where this allows central government to bypass powerful subnational institutions (on the case of the UK's reform of local education governance, see Bache 2003).

States' role in metagovernance has been seen as increasingly important (Jessop 2004; see also Rhodes, Chapter 3, this volume). At both national and international levels, state actors are engaged in "redesigning markets, in constitutional change and the juridical re-regulation of organizational forms and objectives, in organizing the conditions for self-organization, and, most importantly, in the overall process of collibration" (Jessop 2004: 65). An important illustration of metagovernance in the EU context is the Open Method of Coordination (OMC), which is an intergovernmental procedure for coordinating national actions in areas such as employment policy. While Jessop does at times seem to conflate EU institutions with "states," thus neglecting a potentially important supranational (if not subnational and non-state) influence over metagovernance, there is little dispute that states retain pivotal positions in processes such as the OMC.

Through the exercise of state power via steering and metagovernance, multi-level governance is said to take place in "the shadow of hierarchy" (Scharpf 1994: 40; Jessop 2004: 65). However, while a critique of the MLG perspective, this argument has echoes in the MLG literature where Marks and Hooghe (2004: 24) suggest that "Type II multi-level governance tends to be embedded in legal frameworks determined by Type I jurisdictions." Moreover, while MLG emphasizes the increased role of subnational authorities, theorists have also been clear to state their view of the EU as a Europe *with* the regions, rather than the more ambitious a Europe *of* the regions (Piattoni 2010: 125). In other words, while suggesting that some competences have slipped away from states, MLG theorists have also acknowledged that states remain an important part of contemporary governance.

TRAVELING OR STRETCHING?

MLG has been seen to have analytical purchase in an increasing number of contexts (see Bache and Flinders 2004; and Enderlein, Walti, and Zurn 2010). At perhaps its most successful in terms of "traveling" has been its emergence as a "new mantra" in the study of British politics (Marsh, Richards, and Smith 2003: 314). The ability of MLG to travel well is arguably connected to its conceptual imprecision: as Sartori (1970: 1035) put it "we can cover more—in travelling terms—only by saying less, and by saying less in a far less precise manner."

Stubbs (2005: 68) has been skeptical of applying the concept in southeast Europe, arguing that "The complex, shifting configuration of actors, agencies, themes, and initiatives found in the region stretches the 'mainstream' multi-level governance literature to breaking point." Here, MLG is understood as a "broadly consensual notion" that "does not fit the complexities and paradoxes of 'failed', 'weak', 'authoritarian', and 'captured/clientelist' states in South East Europe" (Stubbs 2005: 73). This perceived weakness is attributed to "Western European/European Union bias" in the literature. This is an interesting argument and perhaps demands clarification from MLG theorists on the extent to which consensus is a key feature of the concept: empirical studies certainly reveal conflict as well as cooperation in MLG arrangements.

However, when MLG has been examined empirically in south east Europe—in relation to cohesion policy and pre-accession aid—many of the issues identified as problematic for the concept were common to states such as the UK in their early engagement with EU funding: excessive central control; state (and party political) dominance of governance arrangements; bias in the selection of societal actors to engage in partnership processes; and central government denying resources to subnational authorities, nongovernmental organizations and other potential partners to deliberately undermine their ability to participate effectively. In this early phase of structural funding in the UK, MLG offered little analytical purchase on developments as central state actors blocked, stifled and controlled new governance arrangements. Over time, however, such arrangements became more accepted and MLG provided a better fit with events (Bache and Andreou 2011).

THE NORMATIVE DIMENSION

In addition to seeking to capture empirical developments, MLG theorists see it as a "normatively superior" way of organizing public decision-making, compared to central state dominance. (Marks and Hooghe 2004: 16). The core argument here is that governance should operate at multiple territorial levels to capture variations in the reach of policy externalities, which vary from global to local levels: thus, only through scale flexibility in governance can such externalities be effectively internalized. Other advantages identified are that more decentralized jurisdictions can better reflect heterogeneity of preferences among citizens and that multiple jurisdictions can facilitate credible policy commitments, allow for jurisdictional competition and facilitate innovation and experimentation (Marks and Hooghe 2004: 16). Of course, no one suggests that MLG is a panacea for the challenges of modern governance. As Jessop (2004, 2009) reminds us, all modes of governance fails in some respect and there is no reason to assume that MLG is or should be any different: old problems may be solved, but new problems inevitably emerge.

In relation to MLG, high on the list of emerging problems are the implications it has for democratic accountability. Peters and Pierre (2004) argued that MLG could be a type of "Faustian bargain" in which the purported advantages of MLG in terms of functional efficiency are traded for core democratic values as authority seeps away from the formal institutions where democratic accountability is exercised; or where political actors use these informal and opaque processes to escape accountability for their decisions.

In a similar vein, Jan Olsson (2003) considered the "democracy paradoxes" in MLG in relation to cohesion policy. He suggested that one way to address the democratic challenges inherent in the partnership arrangements established to administer structural funds would be to allocate a greater role to the formal institutions in the region, which were directly elected. This could be done by abolishing the institutions of MLG (multilevel and cross-sectoral partnerships) and allocating their functions to elected institutions; or, more realistically, by allowing elected institutions to play a greater role in regulating partnerships. This idea of "loose coupling" between Type I and Type II institutions has regularly been advanced as a way of securing the best of both worlds: flexibility with accountability. Depending on how well this is done though, there is the danger that the advantages of both could be lost.

Building on Olsson's work, Bache and Chapman (2008) examined three models of democracy—electoral, pluralist and elite-democratic—through which to evaluate the democratic credentials of multi-level governance. Their case study of the structural funds in South Yorkshire (UK) illustrated that among the expected complexity and technocracy at this stage of policy-making there were also experiments in local democracy—community-level elections for partnership representatives—that had not previously been identified in the academic literature. As such, there was evidence that while some traditional mechanisms of accountability may be undermined by MLG, other mechanisms may provide a valuable alternative.

Most recently, Piattoni (2010: 246) suggested that MLG could contribute to democracy in the EU in three ways: through entrenching the right of the "peripheries" to be involved in decisions affecting them; to do so in a way (loose coupling) that might avoid the deadlock often associated with federalist systems; and by fostering the development of more organic ties between subnational authorities and their local societies.

Conclusions

MLG has made a significant contribution to understanding the nature of governance in the EU. It directs attention to increasingly complex relations between actors from different sectors organized at different territorial levels and raises important questions about the mechanisms, strategies, and tactics through which decisions are made in contemporary politics and their implications for democratic accountability. It foregrounds concerns with changes to the role, power, and nature of the state within and beyond national boundaries. And, while MLG highlights competences slipping away from central states, this does not always mean that state power is undermined: this remains an empirical question that finds different answers in different cases. Indeed, state adaptation and innovation is a characteristic feature of complex multi-level governance. That this last point is often misunderstood may point to a lack of conceptual specification within the MLG framework.

As it stands, MLG remains at least a "compelling description" of the EU polity (Jordan 2001) and increasingly of others. It draws attention to important changes along a number of dimensions: domestic and international, state and society and centre and periphery (Piattoni 2010, 26) and highlights the importance of understanding the critical relationship between territorial and functional jurisdictions in this changing landscape. To go beyond this, the next stage of conceptual development must be to respond to the challenge of theorizing the dynamics of multi-level governance. This would include a clearer delineation of Type I and Type II entities and the incorporation of analytical tools that offer insights on the relationships between them and how they shape outcomes.

Notes

* I am very grateful to the editor David Levi-Faur and to Ian Bartle for their helpful comments on this chapter.
1. There is surprisingly little work that attempts to put flesh on the bones of the Type I and Type II categories or on the relations between them. Skelcher's work is a rare and helpful contribution in this respect. However, in trying to use this table for illustrative purposes it raised a number of issues about the nature of Type II entities (e.g. should interest groups acting as lobby groups be defined as Type II entities or only when the are incorporated formally into governance arrangements?) and about Type I-Type II relations (e.g. how distinctive are the categories of "complementary" and "incorporated"). These issues cannot be resolved here but are addressed by Bache, Bartle, and Flinders (forthcoming).

References

Bache, I. 1999. The extended gatekeeper: Central government and the implementation of EC regional policy in the UK. *Journal of European Public Policy* 6: 28–45.

Bache, I. 2003. Governing through governance: Education policy control under new labour. *Political Studies* 51: 300–314.

Bache, I. 2008. *Europeanization and Multi-level Governance: Cohesion Policy in the European Union and Britain*. Lanham: Rowman and Littlefield.

Bache, and Andreou, G. (eds.) 2011. *Cohesion Policy and Multi-level Governance in South East Europe*. Oxford: Routledge.

Bache, I., Bartle. I., and Flinders, M. (forthcoming). Unravelling multi-level governance: beyond the binary divide.

Bache, I. and Chapman, R. 2008. Democracy through multi-level governance? The implementation of the structural funds in South Yorkshire. *Governance* 21: 397–318.

Bache, I. and Flinders, M. (2004). *Multi-level Governance*. Oxford: Oxford University Press.

Bachtler, J. and McMaster, I. 2008. EU Cohesion policy and the role of the regions: investigating the influence of Structural Funds in the new member states. *Environment and Planning C* 26: 398–427.

Bailey, D. and De Propris, L. 2002. EU structural funds, regional capabilities and enlargement: Towards multi-level governance? *Journal of European Integration* 24: 303–324.

Benz, A. 2010. The European Union as a loosely coupled multi-level system. In H. Enderlein, S. Walti and M. Zürn (eds.), *Handbook on Multi-level Governance*. Cheltenham: Edward Elgar, 214–226.

Börzel, T. 2012. The European Union:A unique governance mix. In *Handbook on Governance*, ed. D. Levi-Faur. Oxford: Oxford University Press.

Braithwaite, J. 2000. The new regulatory state and the transformation of criminology. *British Journal of Criminology* 40: 222–238.

Braun, D. 2010. Multi-level governance in Germany and Switzerland. In H. Enderlein, S. Walti, and M. Zürn (eds.), *Handbook on Multi-level Governance*. Cheltenham: Edward Elgar, 166–181.

Brustz, L. 2008. Multi-level governance: The eastern versions: Emerging patterns of developmental governance in the new member states. *Regional and Federal Studies* 18: 607–627.

CoR 2009. *The Committee of the Regions White Paper on Multi-Level Governance.* CdR 89/2009 fin FR/EXT/RS/GW/ym/ms, Brussels: Committee of the Regions.

Enderlein, H. 2010. Economic policy-making and multi-level governance. In H. Enderlein, S. Walti, and M. Zürn (eds.), *Handbook on Multi-level Governance.* Cheltenham: Edward Elgar, 423–40.

Enderlein, H., Walti, S., and Zürn, M. 2010. *Handbook on Multi-level Governance.* Cheltenham: Edward Elgar.

Fairbrass, J. and Jordan, A. 2004. European Union environmental policy: A case of multi-level governance? In I. Bache and M. Flinders (eds.), *Multi-Level Governance.* Oxford: Oxford University Press, 147–164.

Haas, E. 1958. *The Uniting of Europe: Political, Social and Economic Forces 1950–57.* London: Library of World Affairs.

Hix, S. 1994. The study of the European Community: The challenge to comparative politics. *West European Politics* 17: 1–30.

Hoffmann, S. 1964. The European process at Atlantic cross-purposes. *Journal of Common Market Studies* 3: 85–101.

Hoffmann, S. 1966. Obstinate or obsolete? The fate of the nation state and the case of western Europe. *Daedalus* 95: 862–915.

Hooghe, L. (ed.) 1996. *Cohesion Policy and European Integration: Building Multi-level Governance.* Oxford: Oxford University Press.

Hooghe, L. and Marks, G. 2001. *Multi-Level Governance and European Integration.* London: Rowman and Littlefield.

Hooghe, L. and Marks, G. 2003. Unravelling the central state, but how? Types of multi-level governance. *American Political Science Review* 97: 233–243.

Hooghe, L. and Marks, G. 2010. Types of multi-level governance. In H. Enderlein, S. Walti and M. Zürn (eds.), *Handbook on Multi-level Governance.* Cheltenham: Edward Elgar, 17–31.

Hughes, J. Sasse, G. and Gordon, C. 2004. Conditionality and compliance in the EU's eastward enlargement. *Journal of Common Market Studies* 42: 523–551.

Jeffery, C. 2000. Sub-national mobilization and European integration: Does it make any difference? *Journal of Common Market Studies* 38: 1–23.

Jessop, B. 2005. Multi-level governance and multi-level metagovernance. In I. Bache and M. Flinders (eds.), *Multi-Level Governance.* Oxford: Oxford University Press, 49–74.

Jessop, B. 2009. From governance to governance failure and from multi-level governance to multi-scalar meta-governance. *Environment and Policy* 49: 79–98.

Jordan, A. 2001. The European Union: An evolving system of multi-level governance... or government? *Policy and Politics* 29: 193–208.

Levi-Faur, D. 2005. The global diffusion of regulatory capitalism. *Annals, AAPS,* 598: 12–32.

Lindberg, L. 1963. *The Political Dynamics of European Economic Integration.* Stanford, CA: Stanford University Press; London: Oxford University Press.

Marks, G. 1992. Structural policy in the European Community in *Euro-Politics: Institutions and Policymaking in the "New" European Community,* ed. A. Sbragia. Washington, D.C.: Brookings Institution: 191–224.

Marks, G. 1993. Structural policy and multilevel governance in the EC. In A. Cafruny and G. Rosenthal (eds.), *The State of the European Community,* Vol. 2: *The Maastricht Debates and Beyond.* Boulder, CO: Lynne Rienner; Harlow: Longman, 391–410.

Marks, G. and Hooghe, L. 2004. Contrasting visions of multi-level governance. In I. Bache and M. Flinders (eds.), *Multi-level Governance.* Oxford: Oxford University Press, 15–30.

Marks, G., Hooghe, L., and Blank, K. 1996. European integration from the 1980s: State-centric v. multi-level governance. *Journal of Common Market Studies* 34: 341–378.

Marsh, D., Richards, D., and Smith, M. 2003. Unequal plurality: Towards an asymmetric power model of the British polity. *Government and Opposition* 38: 306–332.

Olsson, J. 2003. Democracy paradoxes in multi-level governance. *Journal of European Public Policy* 10: 283–300.

Perraton, J. and Wells, P. 2004. Multi-level governance and economic policy. In I. Bache and M. Flinders (eds.), *Multi-Level Governance*. Oxford: Oxford University Press: 179–194.

Peters, G. and Pierre, J. 2004. Multi-level governance and democracy: A Faustian bargain? In I. Bache and M. Flinders (eds.), *Multi-Level Governance*. Oxford: Oxford University Press, 75–89.

Piattoni, S. 2010. *The Theory of Multi-level Governance: Conceptual, Empirical, and Normative Challenges*. Oxford: Oxford University Press.

Sartori, G. 1970. Concept misinformation in comparative politics. *American Political Science Review* LXIV: 1033–1053.

Sbragia, A. 2010. Multi-level governance and comparative regionalism. In H Enderlein, S. Walti and M. Zürn (eds.), *Handbook on Multi-level Governance*. Cheltenham: Edward Elgar, 267–278.

Scharpf, F. 1988. The joint decision trap: Lessons from German federalism and European integration. *Public Administration* 66: 239–278.

Scharpf, F. 1994. Games real actors could play: Positive and negative coordination in embedded negotiations. *Journal of Theoretical Politics* 6: 27–53.

Schmitter, P. 2000. How to democratize the European Union ... and why bother? Boulder, CO: Rowman and Littlefield.

Schmitter, P. 2004. Neo-neofunctionalism. In A. Wiener and T. Diez (eds.), *European Integration Theory*. Oxford: Oxford University Press, 45–74.

Skelcher, C. 2005. Jurisdictional integrity, polycentrism, and the design of democratic governance. *Governance* 18: 89–110.

Stein, M. and Turkewitsch, L. 2010. Multi-level governance in Canadian and American intergovernmental relations. In H. Enderlein, S. Walti, and M. Zürn (eds.), *Handbook on Multi-level Governance*. Cheltenham: Edward Elgar, 184–200.

Slaughter, A-M. and Hale, T. N. 2010. Transgovernmental networks and multi-level governance. In H. Enderlein, S. Walti, and M. Zürn (eds.), *Handbook on Multi-level Governance*. Cheltenham: Edward Elgar, 358–382.

Stubbs, P. 2005. Stretching concepts too far? Multi-level governance, policy transfer and the politics of scale in Southeast Europe. *Southeast European Politics* 6: 66–87.

Tavistock Institute. 1999. *The Thematic Evaluation of the Partnership Principle: Final Synthesis Report*. London: The Tavistock Institute Evaluation, Development and Review Unit.

Walti, S. 2010. Multi-level environmental governance. In H. Enderlein, S. Walti, and M. Zürn (eds.), *Handbook on Multi-level Governance*. Cheltenham: Edward Elgar, 411–422.

Wilson, D. 2003. Unravelling control freakery: Redefining central–local government relations. *British Journal of Politics and International Relations* 5: 317–346.

Zürn, M., Walti, S., and Enderlein, H. 2010. Introduction. In H. Enderlein, S. Walti, and M. Zürn (eds.), *Handbook on Multi-level Governance*. Cheltenham: Edward Elgar, 1–16.

....

CHAPTER 45

INSTITUTIONAL CHANGE IN EUROPEAN GOVERNANCE: THE COMMISSION'S IMPLEMENTING POWERS AND THE EUROPEAN PARLIAMENT

....

ADRIENNE HÉRITIER &
CATHERINE MOURY

1. INTRODUCTION

....

AT an abstract level, governance may be defined as a "co-production mode of decision-making among different types of actors" (Bartolini 2011:11) in distinct contexts and under different institutional arrangements. Institutional rules define the terms of interaction between the different actors engaged in joint decision-making. In European governance, these decision-making rules have been constantly subject to change and power shifts. The European Union (EU) is a political system of governance in which member states share power with the Commission and the Parliament in producing and implementing decisions. The distribution of competences between the Council of Ministers, the European Parliament, and the Commission have significantly changed over time. The Parliament, in particular, has made enormous gains in decision-making power. In this chapter we focus on the increasing role of the Parliament and explain the process and factors that have made it possible.

The comitology system dates back to the 1960s when the Council, overburdened with the implementation of the common agricultural policy, decided to delegate implementing powers to the Commission. However, member states still wanted to retain some control over the Commission by setting up "comitology committees" to supervise its implementing activities. After a lengthy contest of power, the European Parliament, whose role in comitology had long been very limited, obtained coequal rights with the Council to object to delegated acts (Art. 290) under the Lisbon Treaty. How did this change come about?

The changes can be explained by rational choice institutionalism and distributive bargaining theory. We start by summarize the literature explaining why delegation to comitology took place and why it developed specific governance rules. We *then* explain how and why Parliament's power increased under these rules. We empirically illustrate how these changes unfolded over time and assess to what extent our theoretical argument is able to grasp the change of rules.

2. THEORETICAL FRAMEWORK

First, why did member governments delegate implementing powers to the Commission to begin with? Principal–agent theory analyzes the motives of delegation and shows how the principal(s) seek(s) to control the agent by developing governance. Second, why did these governance rules change over time? A power-based bargaining theory of institutional change allows us to account for this change. Since institutional rules are incomplete contracts—they will be subject to a process of renegotiation as they are applied and thereby transformed. Both explanations of the why of delegation and the why of change of delegation rules are based on the assumptions of utility maximizing, boundedly rational actors that interact in the context of institutional rules that represent incomplete contracts. But while the principal–agent approach emphasizes efficiency aspects of delegation, the distributive bargaining goes beyond this and focuses on the shifting of power after the formal adoption of a rule. Since the first question of the why of delegation to comitology has been extensively studied by Pollack (2003), Franchino (2002, 2004, 2007) and Epstein and O'Halloran (1999), our empirical investigation focuses on the change of rules governing comitology.

Why delegate and how to control the agent

Why delegate?

The principal–agent approach conceptualizes the relationship between the Council and the Commission as a relationship of *delegation*. The Council charges the Commission with the task of adopting secondary legislation while at the same time establishing comitology procedures with the participation of member government representatives as control mechanisms. Principal–agent theory assumes that the agent acts on behalf of the principal in a particular domain of decision-making (Ross 1973: 134), that the agent has more information than the principal and takes actions that impact both players' payoffs.

The most important motives of delegation distinguished in the literature are (McCubbins 1985: 721) policy uncertainty or the need of expertise, political uncertainty, policy credibility, and blame shifting. Substantive *policy uncertainty, the need for expertise*, and the linked costs of information gathering constitute important reasons for delegation (Miller 2005, 2004; Fiorina 1982, 1986; McCubbins 1985; McCubbins, Noll and Weingast 1987; and Horn and Shepsle 1989). *Political uncertainty* as a cause of delegation exists in two different forms: (i) governments may wish to protect their policy choices from being dismantled by their successors (Moe 1990; Majone 1996; Gilardi 2005); (ii) political uncertainty may also derive from the uncertainty that a political decision comes about in the first place, as interest groups and their political representatives might block the legislative process (Fiorina 1982). In order to avoid gridlock, political actors may decide on framework legislation only and delegate detailed decisions to agents. The shifting of responsibility or *blame shifting* (Fiorina 1982) is considered another political motive for delegation. If the constituency costs of regulation are higher than its benefits, a rational legislator would delegate rather than legislate (Pollack 2003).

How to control the agent

After delegation, the principal wishes to ensure that the agent does not deviate from the original mandate of delegation. He may offer incentives to align the agent's preferences to those of the principals (Miller 2005: 204), or issue rules controlling the agent's behavior during contract application. (McCubbins, Noll, and Weingast 1989; Epstein and O'Halloran 1999: 25). Such "deckstacking" rules may ask the agent to privilege particular constituents' interests, assign the burden of proof to one specific party, prescribe consultation, transparency and disclosure rules, all preventing the agent to act against the principals' political objectives (McCubbins, Noll, and Weingast 1987; Epstein and O'Halloran 1999). *The comitology rules are the institutional rules that control the Commission when applying its implementing powers.* Through the comitology system, member states participate in secondary legislation and control the Commission in its implementing function. It is the change of these governance rules which are at the center of our empirical analysis.

Delegation rules transformed

While principal–agent theory asks why and how delegation occurs, distributive bargaining theory focuses on the contest of power implied in the choice of a rule on delegation. Which actors are gaining or losing from the adoption of a specific rule governing the application of comitology? If they stand to lose, by which means do they try to claw back power? This approach distinguishes between the intentional, designed changes of formal rules *and* of a subsequent alteration of these formal rules in the course of their application leading to informal institutional rules which subsequently may be formalized. Hence two processes are conceivable: (i) after the original design of a formal rule, it may be subject to subsequent formal change, or be redesigned, resulting in an amended formal rule. Or (ii) the formal rule may be specified and altered in the course of application leading to an informal rule which may subsequently be formalized.[1]

The institutional design of formal delegation rules

The institutional design of rules governing delegation is the result of an intentional and formal act of two or more actors. The contract, in our case the treaty or the Council Comitology decision, is based on a voluntary agreement, an exchange between actors that facilitates overall mutually beneficial outcomes. However, delegation rules can often have unequal distributional consequences for the actors involved (Knight 1992; Héritier 2007; Farrell and Héritier 2007). Why some actors win out and others lose in the designing of an institutional rule is accounted for by the relative power of actors in the bargaining over institutional rules (Krasner 1991; Sebenius 1992; Knight 1995). Actors are more powerful in the negotiations when they dispose of a comfortable fall-back position rendering them less risk averse and pressed for time (Knight 1995: 109; Knight 1992; Elster 1989: 111–112). Hence, the delegation rules will reflect the relative bargaining power of the actors.

The emergence of informal institutions: incomplete contracts and informal institutional rules

Since actors are assumed to be boundedly rational, institutional rules are almost always incomplete contracts(Farrell and Héritier 2003, 2004, 2006; Stacey and Rittberger 2003).[2] Rules are ambiguous and so will be transformed in the course of application. These changes may be of a mere efficiency enhancing nature equally beneficial to all, or involve a shift of decision-making power among actors. (Ullman-Margalit 1978; Sugden 1986). Alternatively, they may implicate a shift of decision-making power among actors; distributive negotiation theory expects that the losers under the existing rule will seek to renegotiate the rule in the course of its application hoping to transform it to their advantage. The outcome will be determined by the relative power of the actors: the actors' formal institutional positions in the decision-making process at t1 and the available fall-back position. Once a new rule has been created it will be sustained if (1) the rule is efficiency enhancing and beneficial to all actors, if (2) in the case of a power shift it enjoys the continuing support of the coalition of actors benefiting from the rule (Farrell and Héritier 2004); or if (3) it is "cheap" and easily conceded to those actors demanding formalization (Moury 2007).

3. The Parliament's long struggle for power in comitology: an empirical illustration

The Council has passed much of its responsibility for implementing legislation to the Commission. In doing so, it formulated requirements which provide for the use of committees obliging the Commission to cooperate with national representatives (comitology). While initially the Parliament had no formal voice in the implementation of legislation, today it has a co-equal right with the Council in supervising and, possibly, objecting to Commission decisions (Art. 290). How did this change in the governance of comitology governance come about? We will present the most important empirical changes to illustrate the plausibility of our theoretical argument.

In the *shaping of the original comitology system between 1957 and 1961*, after a period of institutional conflict between the Commission and the Council was followed by the latter's decision (Council Regulations 19–24/62/EEC) to establish common organizations (management committees) to issue decisions for the markets in cereals, pork, eggs, poultry, fruit and vegetables, and wine. In management committees, member governments could disagree (by qualified majority) with the implementation of the measure proposed by the Commission whereupon the Commission had to forward it to the Council. When the Parliament became aware of this plan to create "new organs," it issued a resolution demanding that no decision be taken before it had given its opinion on the grounds that it has political supervisory power over the Commission (Deringer Report pp.33, 36). However, the Commission insisted that the Regulation should not be subject to parliamentarian consultation. Hence, the Parliment did not play a role in the Commission's and Council's implicit bargaining of the Council Regulation of 1962, and the Parliament did not play a role in establishing the comitology system.

The comitology procedure was quickly extended from CAP to trade policy (GATT), common commercial policy and foodstuff regulation where management committees became the normal procedure of decision-making. But, increasingly, some member states insisted on more restrictive procedures and the Council introduced the regulatory committees in which the Commission's draft decision had to be *approved* by a qualified majority of member governments. Again, the Parliament did not have a voice in the shaping of the regulatory committee procedure and therefore expressed its concerns about being bypassed in various reports pointing out that it could be argued that many legislative matters were dealt with as implementing measures. The Jozeau–Marigné Report, in 1968,[3] defined different implementing measures and criteria to allocate different types of committee. It also requested a *droit de regard* (right of information) of decisions of management and regulatory committees. Yet these requests were ignored when the Commission and the Council agreed upon the rules of the regulatory committees. The legal action that Parliament brought to the ECJ against a number of Commission decisions it considered to be of a legislative nature was also unsuccessful.[4] The Court confirmed a wide interpretation of what constitutes an implementing measure. Thus an additional important actor entered the scene, throwing its weight into the bargaining process and influencing the outcome in favor of the Commission and the Council.

Having been unsuccessful in shaping the rules of comitology until that time, the Parliament sought to achieve its ends at the higher level by proposing a draft on a Treaty of the European Union. New "laws" should be introduced to be adopted jointly by Council and Parliament; regulatory committees would be abolished; a *droit de regard* would allow the Parliament to issue its opinion on draft decisions. In order to underline its requests, it resorted to its powers of budgetary control (which had been increased in

1975), and froze the funding for committees. However, member states preferred to focus on economic and monetary union and only subsequently tackled an institutional reform under the Single European Act (SEA). Nevertheless, member states accepted that the advisory committee should be given priority to speed up the establishing of the internal market.

The SEA asked the Council to revise the existing comitology regulation. The Parliament quickly proposed to link advisory, management, and regulatory committees to particular matters, then went further and called for the abolition of the regulatory committee. The Commission anticipated the resistance of the Council so refrained from proposing fixed criteria. In response, the Parliament delayed its (consultative) opinion on the Commission draft of a comitology decision. The Commission obliged the EP's requests and "stated its willingness to bring its (statement) more into line with the position of Parliament" (EP Resolution 23.10. 1986): advisory committees should have a predominant place in internal market measures and *a droit de regard* should be introduced. As a result, the Parliament delivered its opinion. Here the Parliament made direct use of its delaying power to wield influence on the substance of the institutional rule. However, the Comitology Decision of 1987, with the Council as the sole decision-maker, reflected almost nothing of the Commission's and Parliament's proposals: it did not define principles of categorizing cases, but preserved the flexible nature of implementing powers and even introduced more restrictive management and regulatory committee procedures, the *contre-filet* procedures.

Since the 1987 Comitology Decision had ignored its demands, when consulted, the Parliament systematically asked to eliminate committee procedures or to use less restrictive ones. Its internal guidelines stated: "In first reading, Parliament should systematically delete any provisions for procedure III (a) or (b) (filet et contre-filet) and for proposals concerning the internal market put forward under Art. 100a of the EEC Treaty..." (Guidelines EP cited in Corbett 1998: 258). However, under the consultation and cooperation procedures, the Parliament had no leverage to put pressure on the Council.

The introduction of *co-decision* under the Maastricht Treaty 1991 brought a sea change. It gave the Parliament the necessary instrument to wield influence over changing the governance rules of comitology. Moreover, as an equal partner in legislation, it no longer accepted that the Council had exclusive competences in the control over implementing powers. It requested that the exclusive use of only consultative committees, a hierarchy of legal acts and the formalization of the *droit de regard*. To lend pressure to its claims, it launched an offensive against regulatory committee procedures. During the first year of co-decision, the "issue was fought out on each individual item of legislation" (Corbett 1998: 258, 347, and 348). The precedent was set in the very first case dealt with under co-decision, the Open network provision to voice telephony. The Council Presidency attempted to attenuate the conflict by proposing a modus vivendi accepting the Parliament's right for information, while preserving the existing arrangements for implementing powers. Parliament underlined its role in the negotiation of the modus vivendi by placing part of the budget for committees in the reserve and only released them when the right for information was formally accepted.

Under the modus vivendi, the Parliament sought to extend the *droit de regard* to consultation and cooperation procedures by postponing votes. To improve the application of *the droit de regard* it again placed committee funding in the reserve and requested a list of the committee decision items from the previous year. Parliament released the funds when it was obliged to do so by the Commission. Once more the Parliament had resorted to arena linking, withholding its support in the budgetary arena until its request had been met in the arena shaping comitology rules.

The Amsterdam Treaty did not produce any changes in the governance of comitology, but requested a revision of the first Comitology Decision. The corresponding draft submitted by the Commission included a new set of rules: general criteria for choosing different procedures for legislation and executive implementation and a formalization of the Parliament's *droit de regard* and a reform of the regulatory procedure. In case of rejection, the Commission would present a legislative proposal. The Parliament asked for a formal voice in comitology decisions under co-decision and a repeal or safeguard mechanism. It forced the Commission to take the requests into account by delaying its Opinion and putting part of the committee budgets in the reserve, threatening "we will continue in legislative procedure after legislative procedure to block the comitology measures and resist the adoption of such restrictive measures and we will be very restrictive on voting the budgets and the credits to allow comitology-type committees to continue to meet..... unless agreement is reached in this matter. I can tell the Council that codecision procedure after codecision procedure we will have to go all the way to conciliation and time after time there will be difficulty on this problem".[5]

The conflict ended in the Council accepting the elimination of the restrictive variant of the management committee and a simplification of the regulatory committee procedure (with the Council still having to approve a draft before adoption). Parliament was not yet entirely satisfied so threatened renewed conflicts in co-decision whereupon member states finally conceded the Parliament the right to "blow the whistle" if a draft implementing measure should exceed the powers conferred on the Commission. Moreover, Parliament's right of information was replaced by a legally binding commitment.

After the adoption of the Second Comitology Decision (1999) a significant institutional change occurred which provided the Parliament with additional leverage to wield influence through arena linkage. The Lamfalussy reform (2001), providing for a speedy adoption of legislation on financial securities markets, was to be adopted as framework legislation giving delegating powers to the Commission subject to comitology under the regulatory procedure and based on a consultation of market actors. In the negotiation of the legislation, the Parliament successfully introduced a "sunset clause" providing for its reconsideration after five years.

With the extensive round of eastern enlargement, the Commission's White Paper on Governance indicated the need for new reform of the delegation system; it requested that legislation be reduced to framework legislation jointly adopted by Council and Parliament. The regulations or decisions necessary to implement legislation would be adopted by the Commission, subject to the supervision of the Council and the Parliament by means of a "call-back system." A reform of the Second Comitology Decision brought clear criteria for the choice of committee procedure. The regulatory committee was to be used for executive measures to implement essential aspects of laws, the advisory committee for executive measures of individual scope. In case of the rejection of a measure under the regulatory procedure by the Council or the Parliament, the Commission could enact the measure, amend it, or present a legislative proposal under co-decision. Not surprisingly, during consultation Parliament rejected the provision that the Commission *could*, but *did not have to* take into account the amendments of the Parliament and the Council. It then unexpectedly accepted the Commission's proposal, probably because it placed all its hopes in the Convention working on a reform of the Nice Treaty.

Under the Convention, the legislative acts were to take the form of law, while nonlegislative acts were to be regulations or decisions. The Commission was to be controlled by (1) a case-by-case control mechanism through a right of "call-back," by the Council or Parliament; (2) a period of tacit approval; (3) and a sunset clause: delegated acts were to have a limited duration that could be extended by the Parliament *and* the Council. During the IGC on the Constitutional Treaty, the hierarchy of legal acts was not taken up and renegotiated.

After the rejection of the Constitutional Treaty in 2005, the revision of the Second Comitology Decision returned to center stage. In negotiating the revision, the Parliament used the opportunity to withhold its support for the necessary renewal of the Lamfalussy legislation (sunset clause) and, additionally, blocked individual legislative items in financial market regulation. It also withheld part of the budget for comitology committees (Interview, EP February 2006). It thereby boosted its indirect influence on the revision of the Comitology Decision in which it had no formal voice but was only consulted. As a result, the Commission revised its proposal for a revision of the comitology decision and defined criteria for the choice of committees and introduced a reform of the regulatory committee procedure providing for the two legislators' equal control over Commission drafts. While the Council was aware that some reforms had to be undertaken to "buy" the Parliament's support for the Lamfalussy legislation, it was only willing to change the regulatory committees, the definition of the scope for implementing measures of "legislative" or "quasi-legislative" and to give the Parliament the right to block quasi-legislative decisions on procedural grounds (Interview, Council February. 2006).

The graph in Figure 45.1 illustrates the Parliament's implicit reasoning in the bargaining strategy to widen its competences under comitology: in order to gain concessions in the negotiations over the revision of the Second Comitology Decision, it launched an offensive by systematically introducing amendments to restrict the scope of delegation (Bergström, Farrell, and Héritier 2007; Corbett 1998: 258). The success of this strategy culminated in the regulatory procedure with scrutiny under which the Parliament obtained important competences in 2006 (Bergström and Héritier 2007; Bergström, Farrell, and Héritier 2007) (see Figure 45.1).

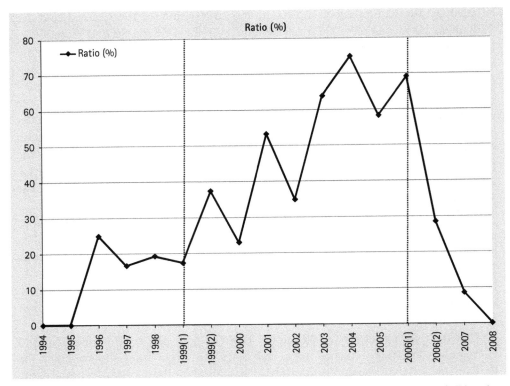

FIGURE 45.1 Percentage of legislative reports restricting delegation as a percentage of all legislative reports on delegation proposals (N=315 reports).

The recent entry into force of the Lisbon Treaty breaks new ground by distinguishing between legislative delegation and executive delegation for the first time. It established two separate procedures for delegated acts and implementing acts. Under delegated acts, the Commission—by legislation—may be delegated the power to adopt acts supplementing or amending certain non-essential elements of the legislation in question. Both the Council and the Parliament may prevent the entering into force of the delegated acts within a certain period of time ("objection"); or withdraw the delegation of powers ("revocation"). Under implementing acts, the Commission—by legislation—can be delegated the power to detail legislation which needs to be uniformly implemented across member states, under control of the member states (comitology). The Lisbon Treaty also provides that the new comitology decision on how to execute implementing or executive acts (Art.291) shall be decided upon by *both* the Council and the Parliament. The Council is clearly losing competences in relative terms: as we have shown, cross-arena linkage between co-decision and the comitology process and the sunset clause of the Lamfalussy system and the comitology has been crucial for the Parliament to achieve this gain in competences.

Table 45.1 summarizes the EP's main successes.

Table 45.1 EP's use of leverage in linked arenas and its outcomes

Linked arenas	EP strategy	Outcome
Consultation	1. Under consultation: amendments to delete or restrict delegation.	No outcome
Second Budgetary treaty (1975): partial budgetary power granted over non-compulsory spending	1. Froze budget for committees 2. Delayed its opinion for Council 1987 decision 3. stated internal guidelines to systematically use the "safeguard procedures"	1) Commission forced to justify increase of funds for comitology committees (1975); 2) Plumb–Delors agreement: EP's *droit de regard*
Co-decision (1992)	1. systematically asked for advisory or management procedures 2. Froze budget for committees	1) Klepsch–Millan agreement 1993: Commission shall forward to the EP *all* drafts decisions to be adopted in comitology. 2) Modus Vivendi (1994): under co-decision: Parliament has the right to be informed, and the Council and the Commission should "take into account" the opinion of the former. 3) Samland Williamson Agreement (1995): more rights of information for the EP
Abolition of third reading in the co-decision procedure (1997)	1. Froze budget for committee 2. Threatens not to vote the financial market regulation/Lamfalussy system (2005) 1. systematically introduced amendments to restrict the scope of delegation	Council decision (1999): EP's right of information; EP's right to vote a resolution opposing the measure which would oblige the Commission to reconsider it, and in regulatory committee, the Council may act on the proposal. Extension of time to examine Commission draft; introduction of a sunset clause.in "Lamfalussy system" Council decision 2006: new regulatory procedure with scrutiny (for quasi-legislative measures), in co-decision: EP's right to block the Commission's decisions if it deems that the

Continued

Table 45.1 Continued

Linked arenas	EP strategy	Outcome
	2. often go to conciliation to restrict the scope of delegation	executive body has exceeded its mandate. The Commission can respond either by presenting new draft measures or a new legislative proposal
	3. refused renewl of Lamfalussy legislation under the sunset clause and blocking of individual items under Lamfalussy system	Lisbon Treaty, 2007: introduction of delegated acts and executive acts. Right of revocation of member states and EP; under executive/implementing acts abolishing of regulatory committees; new comitology decision to be decided by Council and EP
	4. Froze the budget for committees	

Conclusion

We have presented a theoretical account of why institutional rules or governance rules change over time and applied this account to the development of the role of the European Parliament under the comitology system delegating powers of implementation to the Commission. While principal–agent theory plausibly explains the why and how of delegation, power based bargaining theory helps explain why the rules governing comitology have changed over time. Actors are assumed to be boundedly rational competence-maximizers and, therefore, will press for procedures that increase their own competences. Whether actors are successful in obtaining a rule change beneficial to them depends on the given formal institutional rule, the actor's fallback position in case of a failure of negotiations. Set in a context of linked decision-making arenas, the threat of veto by an actor may allow to exert influence in another linked arena in which the actor does not have a formal voice. We empirically show that the Parliament's long struggle for power under the comitology system was ultimately successful precisely because it successfully applied arena linkages. In other words, it held one arena hostage to obtain influence in another arena. We show that while the Parliament had no such leverage, i.e. no formal power in legislation and the budgetary process, it wielded little influence over the shaping of the comitology rules. Once it was granted budgetary powers and legislative power under codecision, it used these competences to indirectly influence the shaping of comitology rules, an arena in which it had no formal voice. It repeatedly threatened to freeze the budget for comitology and to withhold its support for a substantive legislative matter in the co-decision in order to influence the rules governing comitology—rules which are formally decided by the Council only. This strategy, as we have seen, was ultimately very successful.

Notes

1. The difference between a formal and an informal institutional rule is that the former is subject to formal sanctioning and third-party dispute resolution while the latter is not.
2. Bounded rationality implies that actors—when designing institutional rules (contracts)— are unable to take every relevant contingency into account, therefore contracts will remain ambiguous and will need to be adjusted to changing external conditions. Given actors' diversity of preferences, ambiguity may also be intentional.
3. PE DOC 115/68, cited in Bergström 2005.
4. Case 41/69 *Chemiefarma v. Commission* and case 25/70 *Einfuhr-und Vorratsstelle fur Getreide-und Futtermittel v. Koester, Berodt and Co.*
5. Cited in Bergström 2005.

References

Bartolini, S. 2011. New modes of European governance: An introduction. In A. Héritier and M. Rhodes (eds.), *New Modes of Governance in Europe: Governing in the Shadow of Hierarchy*. Basingstoke: Palgrave Macmillan, 1–18.

Bergström, C. F. 2005.Comitology: *Delegation of Powers in the European Union and the Committee System.* New York: Oxford University Press.

Bergström, C. F. and Héritier, A. 2007. Institutional Rule Five: Controlling the implementation powers of the Commission (Comitology). In *Explaining Institutional Change in Europe*, ed. A. Héritier. Oxford: Oxford University Press, 171–227.

Bergström, C. F., Farrell, H., and Héritier, A. 2007. Legislate or delegate? Bargaining over implementation and legislative authority in the EU. *West European Politics* 30: 338–366.

Corbett, R. 1998. *The European Parliament's Role in Closer EU Integration.* Basingstoke: Macmillan.

Elster, J. 1989. *Nuts and Bolts for the Social Sciences.* Cambridge: Cambridge University Press.

Epstein, D. and O'Halloran, S. 1999. *Delegating Powers: A Transaction Cost Politics Approach to Policy Making under Separate Powers.* New York: Cambridge University Press.

European Parliament, *European Parliament reports*, 1962–63, p. 36.

European Parliament, *Resolution of the 23 / 10 / 1986,* OJ 1986 C 297 / 94 final.

Farrell, H. and Héritier, A. 2003. Formal and informal institutions under codecision: Continuous constitution building in Europe. *Governance* 16: 577–600.

Farrell, H. and Héritier, A. 2004. Interorganizational cooperation and intraorganizational power: Early agreements under codecision and their impact on the parliament and the council. *Comparative Political Studies* 37: 1184–1212.

Farrell, H. and Héritier, A. 2006. Codecision and institutional change. *RSCAS Working Papers*, 2006/41.

Farrell, H. and Héritier, A. 2007. Introduction: contested competences in the European Union. *West European Politics* 38: 227–243.

Fiorina, M. 1982. Legislative choice of regulatory forms: legal process or administrative process. *Public Choice* 39: 33–66.

Fiorina, M. 1986. Legislator uncertainty, legislative control, and the delegation of legislative power. *Journal of Law, Economics and Organization* 2: 33–51.

Franchino, F. 2002. Efficiency or credibility? Testing the two logics of delegation to the European Commission. *Journal of European Public Policy* 9: 677–694.

Franchino, F. 2004. Delegating powers in the European Community. *British Journal of Political Science* 34: 276–293.

Franchino, F. 2007. *The Powers of the Union: Delegation in the EU.* Cambridge: Cambridge University Press.

Gilardi, F. 2005. The institutional foundations of regulatory capitalism. The diffusion of independent regulatory agencies in Western Europe. *Annals of the American Academy of Social and Political Sciences* 598: 84–101.

Héritier, A. 2007. *Explaining Institutional Change in Europe.* Oxford and New York: Oxford University Press.

Horn, M. J. and Shepsle, K. A. 1989. Commentary on "administrative arrangements and the political control of agencies": Administrative process and organizational form as legislative responses to agency costs. *Virginia Law Review* 75: 499–508.

Knight, J. 1992. *Institutions and Social Conflict.* Cambridge: Cambridge University Press.

Knight, J. 1995. Models, interpretations, and theories: Contructing explanations of institutional emergence and change. In J. Knight and I. Sened (eds.), *Explaining Social Institutions.* Ann Arbor, MI: University of Michigan Press, 95–120.

Krasner, S. D. 1991. Global communication and national power: Life on the Pareto frontier. *World Politics* 43: 336–366.

McCubbins, M. D. 1985. The legislative design of regulatory structure. *American Journal of Political Science* 29: 721–748.

McCubbins, M. D., Noll, R., and Weingast, B. 1987. Administrative procedures as instruments of political control. *Journal of Law, Economics, and Organization* 3: 243–277.

McCubbins, M. D., Noll, R., and Weingast, B. 1989. Structure and process, politics and policy: Administrative arrangements and the political control of agencies. *Virgina Law Review* 75: 431–482.

Majone, G. 1996. *Regulating Europe*. New York: Routledge.

Miller, G. J. 2005. The political evolution of principal–agent models. *Annual Review of Political Science* 8: 203–225.

Moe, T. M. 1990. Political institutions: The neglected side of the story. *Journal of Law, Economics, and Organization* 6: 213–261.

Moury, C. 2007. Explaining the European Parliament's right to appoint and invest the Commission. *West European Politics* 30: 367–391.

Pollack, M. A. 2003. *The Engines of European Integration: Delegation, Agency and Agenda-Setting in the EU*. New York: Oxford University Press.

Ross, S. 1973. The economic theory of agency: The principal's problem. *American Economic Review* 63: 134–139.

Sebenius, J. K. 1992. Challenging conventional explanations of international cooperation: Negotiation analysis and the case of epistemic communities. *International Organization* 46: 323–365.

Stacey, J. and Rittberger, B. 2003. Dynamics of formal and informal institutional change in the EU. *Journal of European Public Policy* 10: 858–883.

Sugden, R. 1986. *The Economics of Rights, Co-Operation and Welfare*. Oxford: Basil Blackwell.

Ullman-Margalit, E. 1978. Invisible hand explanations. *Synthese* 39: 263–291.

CHAPTER 46

....

EU EXTERNAL GOVERNANCE AND EUROPEANIZATION BEYOND THE EU

....

FRANK SCHIMMELFENNIG[*]

WHEN speaking of "European governance," we usually have in mind that the European Union (EU) provides rules and mechanisms to regulate the behavior of public and private actors across a great variety of integrated policy areas. "Europeanization" is then generally understood as the domestic impact of, and adaptation to, European governance. First and foremost, European governance applies to the EU's member states, and Europeanization research analyzes its impact on their domestic systems. Since the 1990s, however, EU scholars have begun to look beyond the formal borders of the EU to study the impact of European governance on external actors. This widening of the horizon was a result of three major developments in European integration.

1. The single market program deepened the EU's internal market. The size and attractiveness of this market accorded the EU considerable power to shape the economic and public policy rules of global governance and of its trading partners.
2. The eastern enlargement, which was bigger and considerably more intrusive and transformative than previous enlargement rounds. The EU pursued the ambitious goal of ensuring that the accession countries would transpose the entire *acquis communautaire*—the body of EU law—*ahead* of joining the EU, and accession negotiations were mostly about planning and monitoring this Europeanization process.
3. The novel institutional arrangements for countries that are either not willing to become members—the European Economic Area and the bilateral treaties with Switzerland—or not eligible for membership. The latter group comprises, for

example, the European Neighborhood Policy (ENP) for the Eastern European, Middle Eastern and Northern African neighbors. At their core, these institutional arrangements are directed at managing interdependence by aligning neighboring countries with EU policies and rules in the absence of formal membership.

In sum, we can speak of the EU's "external governance" in the sense that the EU projects its own regulatory model(s), institutions, and rules of governance beyond the borders of formal membership and does so in institutionalized forms of coordinated action that aim at the production of collectively binding agreements (Lavenex and Schimmelfennig 2009: 795). If successful, external governance results in Europeanization. However, Europeanization may also be the outcome of non-institutionalized and possibly even unintended diffusion processes.

This chapter first discusses the contents of Europeanization beyond the EU. Which are the "European" modes and rules of governance that the EU projects beyond its borders? The second part presents mechanisms of Europeanization and the conditions under which these have an impact on outside actors. The third section describes diverse international settings in which different mechanisms of Europeanization are operative.

The comparison of EU relations with "quasi-member states," candidate countries, the European neighborhood, other Organisation for Economic Co-operation and Development (OECD) countries, and far-away regions shows that EU market power and supranational regulation are the most important factors in making non-member states adopt the modes and rules of EU governance—either as a result of direct conditionality or through indirect externalization. Where these factors are absent or weak, the EU needs to rely on socialization and imitation—albeit with limited and superficial effects.

CONTENTS OF EUROPEANIZATION

What are the European models and rules of governance that the EU pursues or produces beyond its borders?

For the EU as a regionally integrated system of liberal democracies, "European governance" is in essence defined by regionalism, supranational integration, multilateralism, transnational markets, the regulatory state, and democratic constitutionalism.

1. The EU typifies regional integration. It proposes regional economic integration and the establishment of supranational organizations as the pathway to peace and welfare in other parts of the world (Farrell 2007). At the global level, the EU seeks to reproduce its own model of "intensive multilateralism" (Wallace 1999) by working within and strengthening multilateral international organizations (Laatikainen and Smith 2006).

2. The EU stands for the creation and regulation of transnational markets. In a critical perspective, the EU has been described to propagate a "neoliberal" economic

model, which reflects the EU's internal commitment to market-building and economic liberalization (e.g. Hurt 2003). Others point out, however, that the EU rather advocates a multilaterally managed "regulatory framework for liberal markets" according to its own model (Grugel 2004: 616). The EU is further seen to embody the "regulatory model" of policy-making (Majone 1996; Orbie 2008), which it projects abroad and uses to spread its rules beyond its borders.

3. Finally, the EU promotes constitutional norms such as human rights, the rule of law and democracy in its external relations (e.g. Manners 2002: 240–241). They mirror the constitutional principles of its member states and its accession criteria. Since the late 1980s and early 1990s, the EU has made the promotion of democracy and human rights a standard feature of its external relations across the globe.

Although these general principles have attracted high attention in the literature on the EU's external action, everyday EU external governance and its impact on third countries are arguably much more shaped by the issue-specific regimes of the EU in a broad variety of areas of public policy constituting the EU's *acquis communautaire*. They are too numerous to be listed here as they not only embody issue-specific sets of policy rules but also varying modes of regulation and governance (Börzel, Chapter 43, this volume; Eckert 2011). Yet the basic assumption of the external projection of internal models holds for issue-specific governance as well. Not only does the EU transfer its internal rules beyond its borders, but there is evidence that the modes of external governance also correspond to the modes of internal governance (hierarchy, market competition, or network governance) for the same issues (Lavenex, Lehmkuhl, and Wichmann 2009).

Mechanisms of Europeanization

What are the mechanisms and processes through which the EU disseminates its institutions and rules of governance in the wider international system? And what are the conditions of success? Several largely overlapping classifications of Europeanization mechanisms have been proposed in the literature (Bauer, Knill, and Pitschel 2007; Diez, Stetter, and Albert 2006; Lavenex and Uçarer 2004; see also Schimmelfennig 2009). I propose a simple 2x2 table of Europeanization mechanisms that distinguishes direct from indirect mechanisms (Schimmelfennig and Sedelmeier 2005a), and those that follow a logic of consequences from those that build on a logic of appropriateness (March and Olsen 1989: 160–62; see Table 46.1).

Direct mechanisms are those in which the EU takes a proactive stance and purposefully seeks to disseminate its model and rules of governance beyond its borders. By contrast, indirect ones are those in which either non-EU actors have the active part or the presence of the EU generates unintended external effects. According to the

Table 46.1 Mechanisms of Europeanization

	Direct	Indirect
Logic of consequences	Conditionality	Externalization
Logic of appropriateness	Socialization	Imitation

instrumentally rational logic of consequences, Europeanization proceeds through the manipulation of incentives and the change of cost–benefit calculations. By contrast, according to the logic of appropriateness, which assumes actors to be role-players and rule-followers, Europeanization is an effect of the legitimacy of the EU, its model of governance, or its norms and rules.

Conditionality is a direct mechanism of Europeanization based on the EU's manipulation of other actors' cost–benefit calculations. The EU proactively disseminates its system and rules of governance by setting them as conditions that external actors have to meet in order to obtain rewards and avoid sanctions. The most relevant EU rewards are different types of agreements ranging from trade agreements to accession treaties and the provisions of market access and financial aid that come with them. Correspondingly, the EU's sanctions comprise the suspension or termination of such agreements. Typically, however, the EU sanctions non-compliance by keeping countries in the waiting room for higher forms of agreement until they meet the conditions. The impact of this mode of Europeanization increases with the size of the EU's rewards and the credibility of the EU's conditionality. Credibility results from superior bargaining power and a consistent use of conditionality. The EU needs to be less dependent on or interested in the agreement than its partner, and the partner needs to be certain that it will receive the rewards when the conditions are met and not obtain them otherwise (Schimmelfennig and Sedelmeier 2005a). In addition, domestic adaptation costs must not be higher than the rewards because otherwise a rational target state of conditionality will not comply.

Externalization is an indirect mechanism of Europeanization based on the EU's impact on the cost–benefit calculations of external actors. In contrast with conditionality, the EU does not proactively promote its model or rules of governance beyond its own borders. Yet its sheer "presence" (Allen and Smith 1990) as a market and a regional system of governance produces (sometimes unintended or unanticipated) externalities. External actors adopt and comply with EU rules because ignoring or violating them would generate net costs. Firms interested in participating in the EU market must follow the EU's rules. Countries whose economies are strongly interconnected with the EU make their internal rules compatible with those of the EU. In general, the effects of Europeanization through externalization increase with the market share of the EU and the strength of its regulatory institutions (Bach and Newman 2007).

Socialization comprises all EU efforts to disseminate the modes and rules of European governance by persuading outside actors of the ideas and norms behind them. This is a direct mechanism of Europeanization based on the logic of appropriateness. External actors adopt and comply with EU rules if they are convinced by their legitimacy and appropriateness. This is more likely to be the case if the external actors are in a novel and uncertain environment, identify with and aspire to belong to "Europe." A process characterized by deliberation and frequent as well as dense contacts between the EU and external actors is also thought to help. Finally, high resonance of EU governance with domestic traditions, norms, and practices provides favorable conditions for effective socialization (Checkel 2001: 562–563).

Imitation works similarly but without a proactive role of the EU. Rather, the EU serves as a role model of governance, which outside actors emulate. Non-member actors imitate the EU because they recognize EU rules and policies as appropriate solutions to their own problems. Again, novices in the international system and states in an uncertain environment are more likely to look for and emulate role models. They are more likely to select the EU as their model if they identify with the EU, are in close contact with the EU, and find EU governance to resonate with their prior beliefs and practices.

THE SCOPE OF EUROPEANIZATION

The external governance of the EU and its Europeanization effects are patchy. The contents and mechanisms of EU external governance as well as its Europeanization impact vary across regions, countries, organizations, and policies. Most fundamentally, we can think of EU external governance as developing in five circles (see also Lavenex 2011): the quasi-member states of Western Europe, the candidate countries for membership, the neighborhood countries, the other OECD countries, and the rest of the world (see Table 46.2).

Table 46.2 Circles of external governance and Europeanization

	Principles	Mechanisms	Conditions	Strength and scope of impact
Quasi-members	Market regulation	Conditionality and Externalization	Strong dependence	Strong but partial
Candidate countries	All	Conditionality	Strong dependence, strong incentives	Strong and general
Neighborhood countries	All	Conditionality and Socialization	Medium dependence, weak incentives	Medium and partial
OECD countries	Market regulation	Externalization	Medium interdependence	Medium and partial
Other regions	Regionalism	Imitiation	Weak interdependence	Weak and partial

The quasi-member states

In 1992, the EU concluded the European Economic Area (EEA) agreement with the countries of the European Free Trade Association. According to the agreement, the EEA countries (Iceland, Norway, and Liechtenstein) are formally obliged to adopt all EU legislation regarding the Single Market and several related policy fields as well as the case law of the European Court of Justice. A Surveillance Authority and the EFTA Court enforce EU rules in the EEA countries. The EEA countries also participate in the informal preparation of EU legislation that concerns them ("decision-shaping"), but in contrast to full members, they do not take part in the formal decision-making process. Nevertheless, the EEA countries comply extremely well with their legal obligations and, for all practical purposes, they can be regarded as "quasi-members" that are subject to the core of EU rules and governance in almost the same way as the member states.

By contrast, Switzerland has opted for the "bilateral way," which comprises a series of sixteen interlinked policy-specific agreements with the EU. It envisages neither general decision-shaping nor automatic adoption of subsequent EU laws nor supranational monitoring and enforcement. Switzerland's far-reaching regulatory alignment with the EU rather results from coordination in bilateral committees and the unilateral adoption of EU law and EU-compatible adaptation of Swiss law. Although the bilateral arrangements allow Switzerland to formally preserve its sovereignty *de jure* and be more selective regarding "Europeanization," its *de facto* alignment with EU rules is similar to that of the EEA countries (Lavenex and Lehmkuhl 2009).

Quasi-membership results from a combination of high economic interdependence with the EU and strong popular opposition to full membership. In Norway and Switzerland, formal EU accession as desired by the political and economic elites was blocked by negative popular referendums and required these countries to manage their intense market and policy relationships with the EU below the level of full supranational integration. At the same time, the strong asymmetry in market size and trade shares results in the strong (but partial) formal or informal adoption of EU rules by the quasi-members. The basic mechanism behind the Europeanization of the quasi-members is a highly institutionalized form of conditionality (granting equal market access in return for rule adoption) tending toward externalization in the case of Switzerland.

The candidate countries

The EU's relations with the candidate countries for membership are another case of deep external governance and Europeanization beyond the formal borders of the EU. The objective is complete Europeanization. Ahead of starting membership negotiations with prospective new members, the EU focuses on the general principles of

European governance, in particular the liberal–democratic political criteria stipulated by the Treaty on European Union as the main principles of eligibility for membership (Art. 49).

By contrast, during the accession negotiations the focus is on the issue-specific rules of European governance. The concept of "negotiations," however, suggests an openness that does not exist in the accession process. The substantive outcome of the negotiations is largely predetermined: the applicants' adoption of the entire body of EU legislation and policies codified in the *acquis communautaire*. Accession negotiations then mainly consist in a process of rule transfer, "screening" and "reporting," in which the EU explains the *acquis* to the applicants, assesses their deficits, and monitors their progress in transposing EU law. The only true negotiations concern the possibility and length of "transition periods" during which the application of EU rules is suspended after accession.

The Europeanization of candidate countries relies predominantly on conditionality. The EU's main activities of external governance consist in setting conditions for membership, monitoring candidates' progress in compliance, and granting or withholding the reward accordingly. The conditions for effective conditionality are generally favorable in EU-candidate country relations. Membership is the highest reward the EU can offer to outsider countries. It gives them full and equal access to the internal market, the funds, the decision-making institutions, and the legal remedies of the most important economic and political organization of the continent. In addition, the credibility of conditionality is generally high as well. Usually, interdependence is highly asymmetrical in favor of the EU because the candidates are of lesser importance to the EU economy than the EU market is to the candidates. The EU can thus afford setting strict conditions and saying no. With a few exceptions (regarding, for instance, Cyprus and Turkey), the EU has also been rather consistent in applying its conditions, and candidates could expect to be admitted after fulfilling them. In the case of the Central and Eastern European countries, we can observe that their adoption of EU policy rules was selective and patchy during the early transition period and often followed domestic traditions or the rules of other international organizations. Once they had been offered a credible membership perspective, their public policies converged toward the EU—except for those issues in which the EU has only weak competencies or indeterminate rules (Schimmelfennig and Sedelmeier 2005b: 215–220).

The main obstacle to effective conditionality in the candidate countries is the domestic political costs of compliance for the target governments. Regarding political conditionality, these costs have been prohibitive for regimes whose power depends on undemocratic institutions and practices. Even a credible and attractive offer of EU membership cannot turn the benefit calculations of such regimes positive. Moreover, national identity issues (such as minority rights and ethnic conflict in the Baltic countries and the Balkans) have also proven difficult to overcome (Schimmelfennig, Engert, and Knobel 2006). As concerns *acquis* conditionality, domestic interest groups adversely affected by European integration are the major problem. In the case of eastern enlargement, however, they have been absent or weak.

The neighborhood countries

The European Neighborhood Policy (ENP) was introduced by the EU during the time of its "big bang" enlargement of 2004 in order to expand and strengthen its relationship with neighboring countries that would not be considered as candidates for membership—at least for the foreseeable future. Originally conceived to encompass the enlarged EU's Eastern European neighbors, it was later extended to the Middle Eastern and North African partner countries of the Euro-Mediterranean Partnership and further to the Southern Caucasus.

In principle, the ENP is based on the same encompassing notion of Europeanization as accession policy. "Everything but institutions" was the promise of Commission President Romano Prodi, when the ENP idea was launched, that is, full participation of the neighboring countries in material European governance if not in formal decision-making. In practice, however, the alignment has been unequal and partial. Whereas accession obliges prospective members to adopt the entire *acquis*, and the old members to grant the new ones equal rights and entitlements, the ENP allows for flexibility that both sides can use to avoid costly obligations. Rather than being uniformly based on the EU *acquis*, the Action Plans at the core of ENP programming are negotiated and monitored between the EU and its partners bilaterally and according to the principle of "joint ownership."

In addition, the ENP appears to copy the EU's accession conditionality. "Differentiation" is a fundamental principle. The ENP strategy documents tie both participation in the ENP as such and the intensity and level of cooperation to the ENP partners' adherence to liberal values and norms. Moreover, the EU uses planning, reporting and assistance procedures similar to those used for candidate countries. The conditions of effective impact, however, are clearly weaker. First, the most attractive "carrot"—EU membership—is not on offer. The major incentives designed to induce Europeanization in ENP countries are a liberalized access of goods and persons to the EU. Second, conditionality is inconsistent. Comparisons of ENP Action Plans show the absence of a coherent democracy promotion policy and the overriding importance of the EU's geostrategic and partner countries' political interests. Finally, the domestic costs of liberalization and democratization are prohibitive in the predominantly authoritarian regimes of the neighborhood. As a result, democratic conditionality proves ineffective in the ENP context (Maier and Schimmelfennig 2007: 45–48).

The EU's *acquis* conditionality in the Neighborhood has also suffered from weaknesses because the credibility of the market access incentive has been undermined by protectionist interest groups in the EU, the exclusion of sectors such as agriculture in which the ENP partners have a competitive edge, and fears of crime and uncontrolled immigration to the EU (Weber, Smith, and Baun 2007). In addition, the EU does not enjoy the same uncontested bargaining power as in its relationship with candidates for membership. This is particularly true for the energy-exporting countries of the region. Moreover, the EU competes with other powerful providers of external governance, namely Russia. As a result, the EU only has a chance to export its own rules to the

Neighborhood if the target countries are dependent on the EU and more dependent on the EU than on other actors (Dimitrova and Dragneva 2009). Alternatively, "self-conditionality" appears to work. Countries that would like to become members behave as if they were subject to accession conditionality, adopt EU rules in order to signal their readiness to join, and seek to persuade the EU to consider them as candidates (e.g. Verdun and Chira 2008).

Given the weak conditions for effective conditionality, many authors suggest that despite the appearances of conditionality the ENP is based de facto on a socialization mechanism of Europeanization. In this view, EU rules promoted in the context of ENP negotiations and policy networks may serve as a reference point for longer-term domestic political processes (Freyburg et al. 2009; Sasse 2008). It is questionable, however, whether the domestic conditions in the ENP countries are on the whole conducive to socialization-driven change. Recent studies find abundant evidence of transgovernmental networks engaged in extending EU governance to the Neighborhood. However, they also come to the conclusion that the operation and effectiveness of these networks is hampered by incompatible administrative structures, cultures, expertise and lack of trust (Lavenex and Wichmann 2009), and that EU norms, which have entered the legislation of some neighboring countries, face severe obstacles to effective application (Freyburg et al. 2009).

Other OECD countries

The quasi-member, candidate and neighborhood countries are the domains of direct Europeanization. Here, the EU proactively promotes its modes and rules of governance as part of an overarching strategy of regulatory alignment and common policies. Direct mechanisms of Europeanization are much less in evidence beyond the neighborhood. Here, we find two typical contexts of indirect mechanisms of Europeanization: the externalization of EU governance through economic interdependence and competition, and the imitation of EU governance in other regions of the world.

Governance by externalization is typical for the export of EU rules in its relations with the democratic, market-oriented, and highly industrialized OECD countries. Here, the EU has neither the goal nor the means to embark on a wholesale export of the EU *acquis*. The larger OECD region is much less dependent on the single market than the neighboring countries and lies beyond the zone of stability that the EU attempts to create in its surroundings. Enlargement is not even potentially on the agenda. The EU deals with the other OECD countries, above all the USA, either bilaterally or in the context of global organizations such as the UN or the World Trade Organization (WTO).

EU export rules mostly concern issue-specific matters relating to its internal market. Case studies converge on the finding that EU impact is a function of both the size of the EU market (and its relevance for outsiders) and the strength of EU regulation (e.g. Bach and Newman 2007; Princen 2003). Whereas market size can be understood as a necessary condition because it creates an interest of market actors to get access to the EU market, it is not sufficient alone if the EU's rules and their administration are weak, fragmented, and incoherent. Rather, the EU's impact depends on the EU regulatory state and increases with the supranationalization of EU governance. The more legally binding and centrally administered EU rules are, the more the EU can transform latent market power into manifest political clout. The highly centralized competition policy with its extraterritorial impact on mergers and acquisitions and its multi-million euro fines imposed on non-EU firms provides the most visible evidence for this relationship. Although initially set up to liberalize and strengthen the internal market, the regulatory powers of the EU provide it with the means to shape international standards, too.

Studies of multilateral negotiations also come to the conclusion that both size and institutions matter. The EU's sheer size as a market, a provider of development aid, and so on, as well as the number of participants and votes it can muster in global negotiations give it considerable power resources (Bretherton and Vogler 2006; Orbie 2008). Whether and how the EU can convert these resources into power over outcomes, however, depends on institutions. One issue is whether the EU has exclusive competence in a policy area. As a rule, exclusive competence increases EU impact. Where it does not exist, it can be partially compensated by homogeneous preferences or informal coordination leading to a united stand of its member states. This has, for instance, been the case in global environmental policy (Bretherton and Vogler 2006: 89–99).

Other regions: Latin America, Asia, Africa

The indirect mechanism of imitation is best seen in the impact that the EU model has had on regional institution-building and economic integration in other parts of the world. The EU has not directly encouraged or induced the establishment of major regional organizations such as the Andean Community and Mercosur in Latin America, ASEAN in Southeast Asia, or the African Union. Nor have these organizations and their reforms been a response to critical interdependence with the EU. But all of them have emulated EU institutions and policies. In the meantime, the EU has established institutionalized relationships, funds cooperation programs, and maintains a political dialogue with these regional organizations so that an element of socialization is involved alongside imitation (Börzel and Risse 2009).

The uncertainty of the emulators and the legitimacy of the EU appear to be the main conditions for the imitation of EU institutions. Embracing the apparently successful EU model is perceived as a way to overcome crises of multilateral cooperation and integration in the regions. For instance, the Andean Pact was founded in 1969 as a response to the deficiencies of the Latin American Free Trade Association. To correct for its failures, the founders of the Pact leapfrogged towards the Community model of supranational integration including, among other features, majority voting, legal integration with a court and the direct applicability and supremacy of supranational law, and—later on—a directly elected Andean Parliament (Malamud and De Sousa 2007: 93–94). Similarly, ASEAN reacted to its shortcomings in dealing with the financial crisis of 1997 and related problems by questioning its decidedly non-European "ASEAN way" of informal, consensual intergovernmental consultation and cooperation and of eschewing supranational economic integration. In the aftermath of this crisis, ASEAN policy-makers perceived the need for stronger formalization and institutionalization as well as more economic integration and started a process that eventually led to the adoption of a charter in 2005. In this process, the EU served as a source of inspiration for the constitutional structure as well as the project of a single market (Hwee 2008: 91–92; cf. Börzel and Risse 2009: 13–15).

As described by the notion of "decoupling" in the neo-institutionalist sociology of organizations (Meyer and Rowan 1977), the emulated formal structures as responses to crisis and uncertainty were, however, either never truly implemented or coexisted with practices reflecting "old habits." The first option is most clearly seen in the Andean Community, whereas the second seems typical for the tendency of the member states of ASEAN to retain the practices of sovereignty, informality, and intergovernmentalism (Hwee 2008: 97–98). At any rate, mimicry in formal appearance and emulation of actual practice need to be distinguished. In particular, the EU remains unique with regard to supranational integration, that is, the pooling and delegation of sovereignty. For this reason, many institutions that bear the same name in other regional organizations—Commission, Council, Court, Committee of Permanent Representatives, or Parliament—perform different functions. The most striking example of decoupling is the African Union. Whereas the former Organization of African Unity (OAU) not only adapted the EU's name but also its supranational institutions and policy programs (such as monetary union), its practices could not be more different from the EU's.

Conclusions

The EU has become a major player in global governance. Its "external governance" consists in exporting its internal rules and modes of regulatory governance to non-member countries and other international organizations, thereby contributing to the "Europeanization" of governance beyond the EU's borders. The overview has also shown, however, that the mechanisms and conditions of Europeanization vary across the circles of EU external governance. If we extended the analysis to issue-specific modes and rules of governance, the picture would even be more multi-faceted.

At the same time, the comparison reveals that supranational regulation and relevant market size are generally the most important conditions of Europeanization beyond the EU. Relevant market interactions and the material, economic incentives that come with them generate the need for external actors to adapt to the rules of European governance. But only to the extent that there is a clearly defined European rule—and one that is centrally decided and hierarchically enforced—can the EU speak with the necessary unity and authority to the outside world. The strong impact that the EU has in the quasi-member and candidate countries is predicated upon the high and asymmetric interdependence with these countries, the substantial incentives of membership or full market access, and the hierarchical organization of the accession process as well as the EEA. The difference between quasi-members and candidates can also generally be explained by the degree of dependence on the EU or the sustainability of economic autonomy. Relationships with the neighborhood and the rest of the OECD world (e.g. the USA) are characterized by weaker and more symmetrical interdependence, weaker incentives, and a non-hierarchical institutional setting. Whereas the EU cannot impose its entire model in these relationships, it can still have a Europeanizing impact with regard to specific governance rules where the conditions of critical market size and supranational regulation are present. Where these are absent, however, the EU's institutions can merely serve as a model for imitation or as a socialization agency. The biggest challenge for research on Europeanization beyond the EU is the establishment of causality. The models and rules of governance disseminated by the EU are not exclusively EU models and rules. Regionalism, regulatory governance, and liberal democracy have also diffused across the globe as local responses to similar domestic or international challenges such as modernization and globalization or as a result of dissemination policies by other international organizations and states (Levi-Faur 2005). To show that Europeanization rather than globalization or Americanization was the cause of diffusion requires a focus on the uniquely European features of regionalism and regulation (its supranational institutionalization) as well as liberal democracy (e.g. the prohibition of the death penalty) and careful process-tracing analysis establishing an unambiguous link between the EU and the outside world.

Note

* The author wishes to thank David Levi-Faur as well as Tina Freyburg and Michael Zürn for comments on an earlier version of this chapter. The chapter builds on Schimmelfennig (2010).

References

Allen, D. and Smith, M. 1990. Western Europe's presence in the contemporary international arena. *Review of International Studies* 16: 19–39.

Bach, D. and Newman, A. L. 2007. The European regulatory state and global public policy: Micro-institutions, macro-influence. *Journal of European Public Policy* 14: 827–846.

Bauer, M., Knill, C., and Pitschel, D. 2007. Differential Europeanisation in Eastern Europe: The impact of diverse EU regulatory governance patterns. *Journal of European Integration* 29: 405–423.

Börzel, T. and Risse, T. 2009. Diffusing (inter-)regionalism. The EU as a model of regional integration. KFG Working Paper Series, No.7. Berlin.

Bretherton, C., and Vogler, J. 2006. *The European Union as a Global Actor*. London: Routledge.

Checkel, J. T. 2001. Why comply? Social learning and European identity change. *International Organization* 55: 553–588.

Diez, T., Stetter, S., and Albert, M. 2006. The European Union and border conflicts: The transformative power of integration. *International Organization* 60: 563–593.

Dimitrova, A. and Dragneva, R. 2009. Constraining external governance: Interdependence with Russia and the CIS as limits to the EU's rule transfer in the Ukraine. *Journal of European Public Policy* 16: 853–872.

Eckert, S. 2011. European regulatory governance. In D. Levi-Faur (ed.), *Handbook on the Politics of Regulation*. Cheltenham: Edward Elgar, 513–524.

Farrell, M. 2007. From EU model to external policy? Promoting regional integration in the rest of the world. In S. Meunier and K. R. McNamara (eds.), *Making History: European Integration and Institutional Change at Fifty.*, Oxford: Oxford University Press, 299–315.

Freyburg, T., Lavenex, S., Schimmelfennig, F., Skripka, T., and Wetzel A. 2009. EU promotion of democratic governance in the neighbourhood. *Journal of European Public Policy* 16: 916–934.

Grugel, J. 2004. New regionalism and modes of governance - Comparing US and EU strategies in Latin America. *European Journal of International Relations* 10: 603–626.

Hurt, S. R. 2003. Co-operation and coercion? The Cotonou Agreement between the European Union and ACP states and the end of the Lomé Convention. *Third World Quarterly* 24: 161–176.

Hwee, Y. 2008. EU-ASEAN relations and policy-learning. In R. Balme and B. Bridges (eds.), *Europe-Asia Relations. Building Multilateralisms*. Basingstoke: Palgrave, 83–102.

Laatikainen, K. V., and Smith, K. E. 2006. Introduction. The European Union at the United Nations: Leader, partner or failure? In K. V. Laatikainen and K. E. Smith (eds.), *The European Union at the United Nations: Intersecting Multilateralisms*. Basingstoke: Palgrave, 1–23.

Lavenex, S. 2011. Concentric circles of flexible 'European' integration: A typology of EU external governance relations. *Comparative European Politics* 9: 372–393.

Lavenex, S. and Lehmkuhl, D. (eds.) 2009. Switzerland's flexible integration in the EU. *Swiss Political Science Review* 15: 547–712.

Lavenex, S., Lehmkuhl, D., and Wichmann, N. 2009 Modes of external governance: A cross-national and cross-sectoral comparison. *Journal of European Public Policy* 16: 813–833.

Lavenex, S. and Schimmelfennig, F. 2009. EU rules beyond EU borders: Theorizing external governance in European politics. *Journal of European Public Policy* 16: 791–812.

Lavenex, S. and Ucarer, E. 2004. The external dimension of Europeanization. *Cooperation and Conflict* 39: 417–443.

Lavenex, S. and Wichmann, N. 2009. The external governance of EU internal security. *Journal of European Integration* 33: 83–102.

Levi-Faur, D. 2005. The global diffusion of regulatory capitalism. *Annals of the American Academy of Political and Social Sciences* 598: 12–32.

Maier, S. and Schimmelfennig, F. 2007. Shared values: Democracy and human rights. In K. Weber, M. E. Smith, and M. Baun (eds.), *Governing Europe's Neighbourhood: Partners or Periphery?* Manchester: Manchester University Press, 39–57.

Majone, G. 1996. *Regulating Europe*. London: Routledge.

Malamud, A., and De Sousa, L. 2007. Regional parliaments in Europe and Latin America: Between empowerment and irrelevance. In A. Ribeiro Hoffmann and A. van der Vleuten, A. (eds.), *Closing or Widening the Gap? Legitimacy and Democracy in Regional Integration Organizations,* eds. Aldershot: Ashgate, 85–102.

Manners, I. 2002. Normative power Europe: A contradiction in terms? *Journal of Common Market Studies* 40: 235–258.

March, J., and Olsen, J. 1989. *Rediscovering Institutions: The Organizational Basis of Politics.* New York: Free Press.

Meyer, J. and Rowan, B. 1977. Institutionalized organizations: Formal structures as myth and ceremony. *American Journal of Sociology* 83: 340–363.

Orbie, J. 2008. A civilian power in the world? Instruments and objectives in European Union external policies. In J. Orbie (ed.), *Europe's Global Role*, Aldershot: Ashgate, 1–33.

Princen, S. 2003. Exporting regulatory standards: The cases of trapping and data protection. In M. Knodt and S. Princen (eds.), *Understanding the European Union's External Relations*. London: Routledge, 142–57.

Sasse, G. 2008. The European neighbourhood policy: Conditionality revisited for the EU's eastern neighbours. *Europe-Asia Studies* 60: 295–316.

Schimmelfennig, F. 2009. Europeanization beyond Europe. *Living Reviews in European Governance* 4. Available at http://www.livingreviews.org/lreg-2009-3 (accessed 19 September 2011).

Schimmelfennig, F. 2010. Europeanization beyond the member states. *Zeitschrift für Staats- und Europawissenschaften* 8: 319–339.

Schimmelfennig, F. Engert, S., and Knobel H. 2006. *International Socialization in Europe. Regional Organizations, Political Conditionality, and Democratic Change.* Basingstoke: Palgrave.

Schimmelfennig, F. and Sedelmeier, U. 2005a. Introduction: Conceptualizing the Europeanization of Central and Eastern Europe. In F. Schimmelfennig and U. Sedelmeier (eds.), *The Europeanization of Central and Eastern Europe*. Ithaca, NY: Cornell University Press, 1–28.

Schimmelfennig, F. and Sedelmeier, U. 2005b. Conclusions: The impact of the EU on the accession countries. In F. Schimmelfennig and U. Sedelmeier (eds.), *The Europeanization of Central and Eastern Europe*. Ithaca, NY: Cornell University Press, 210–228.

Verdun, A., and Chira, G. E. 2008. From neighbourhood to membership: Moldova's persuasion strategy towards the EU. *Southeast European and Black Sea Studies* 8: 431–444.

Wallace, W. 1999. Europe after the Cold War: Interstate order or post-sovereign regional system? *Review of International Studies* 25: 201–223.

Weber, K., Smith, M. E., and Baun, M. (eds.) 2007. *Governing Europe's Neighbourhood: Partners or Periphery?* Manchester: Manchester University Press.

PART IX

GLOBAL GOVERNANCE

CHAPTER 47

··

GOVERNANCE AND
GLOBAL PUBLIC POLICY

··

WILLIAM D. COLEMAN

In the current phase of globalization, ever-changing complex interconnections across the world have led to the strengthening of global sites of authority on the one side, and greater coordination between states on the other. Arising from these processes, we can now identify more and more instances of *global policy-making*. By this term, I refer to policy-making that takes place on the global rather than the regional or the national scale and that is expected to affect, if not be part of, governance of all parts of the world. The global character of the policy-making involved raises particular challenges for how we conceptualize and how we research public policy. In particular, the growing importance of global policy poses challenges for theories of governance and of policy-making, respectively. These theories were often designed based on assumptions that states would be the primary and dominant sites of authority and that policies would be designed specifically for territorially delineated national communities governed by those states. In this contribution, I review attempts to reconceptualize public policy for a global scale and make some suggestions about how we might proceed analytically in order to move beyond a state-centric model of governance.

The chapter begins with a brief discussion of globalization and how the concept is defined and used in the analysis that follows. Next, I review key contributions to the conceptualization of global public policy by Wolfgang Reinicke, Diane Stone, and Phil Cerny. I draw inspiration from such ideas as vertical and horizontal subsidiarity (Reinicke), policy agoras, and global policy-making personnel (Stone), and transnational pluralism and policy pentangles (Cerny) in looking for conceptual tools that might orient the development of the field. This review is followed by a summary statement of the defining features of global policy-making. These features, in turn, are illustrated with an example of global public policy, the 2007 United Nations Declaration on the Rights of Indigenous Peoples.

GLOBALIZATION

How researchers understand and study globalization varies considerably, given their disciplinary backgrounds and the varying theoretical paradigms within which they work. In addition, scholars need to take into account that, like many other concepts in the humanities and social sciences, globalization has become part of daily life in the mass media, and a common term used by politicians, corporate executives, and a wide range of non-governmental organizations (NGOs) (Brydon and Coleman 2008: 6).

As the academic literature on globalization has evolved, certain commonalities in thinking have emerged. The word *global* is used as a reference to scale and to phenomena that are somehow *transplanetary*, to use Scholte's (2005) term. Researchers generally agree that the growth of transplanetary connections has accelerated since World War II, particularly since the late 1970s. There are various explanations for this acceleration. At the heart of most of them is the dynamism of capitalism that resulted from the rapid growth of fully global financial markets. The predominant position of finance capital has led to a type of global capitalism not seen before (Castells 1999). This change in capitalism is linked in complex ways with innovations in information and communication technologies that have permitted transplanetary connections to become more supraterritorial: these technologies are less bound by the physical location or the nation-state boundaries within which people live. As a result, these technologies have permitted more planet-wide connections to develop, and their growth has led to ever greater intrusions into the daily lives of more persons than ever before.

Drawing then from this discussion, I define globalization as follows, for the purposes of this chapter. *Globalization is the transformative growth of connections among people across the planet. In the contemporary era, many of these connections take a supraterritorial form. In ever more profound ways, globalization ties together what people do, what they experience, how they perceive that experience, and how they reshape their lives.*

DEFINING GLOBAL PUBLIC POLICY

Two aspects of this definition of globalization are helpful in thinking about what we might mean by "global" public policy: transplanetary connections (scale) and supraterritoriality. To explore this meaning, however, we need to bring into the discussion two other sets of terms that are often invoked: international/internationalization and transnational/transnationalization (see Table 47.1). As a concept, "international" has the longest history of the three. The use of the term became increasingly common in the nineteenth century and was used to speak about the growing number of relationships between (mainly European) nation-states. When states felt a need to coordinate activities or to cooperate in developing new institutions, they were said to be engaging in

Table 47.1 Forms of public policy beyond the nation–state

	International public policy	Transnational public policy	Global public policy
Key actors	States	States, non-governmental organizations, corporations, social movements, individuals	States, non-governmental organizations, corporations, social movements, individuals
Scale of activity	Intra-regional Interregional Global	Intra-regional Interregional	Global

"international relations." Setting up organizations in the nineteenth and early twentieth centuries such as the World Meteorological Association or the International Telegraph Union, or signing trade agreements or even agreeing upon policies such as the "International Sanitary Regulations" were examples of this international political and policy activity.

The term "transnational" has sometimes been used as a synonym of "international" but increasingly the word has taken on a different meaning that involves the notion of supraterritoriality: relations are formed and transactions are made without being limited by the territorial boundaries of states. Transnational also refers to transactions that include not only states, but also various non-state actors such as corporations, interest groups, and social movements, as well as governance institutions whose mandate is broader than that of states. For example, the term is often used to characterize decision-making in the European Union (EU), which includes member states, but also the European Commission, the European Parliament, and varying non-state actors. Other examples might include the exercise of private authority where various non-state actors fill governance voids not covered by states. Examples here would be the regulation of over-the-counter derivatives or the employment of accounting rules or the rules for merchant shipping (Coleman 2003; Cutler 2003; Eaton and Porter 2008).

Use of the adjective "global" often overlaps with that of "transnational" in the literature in the sense that scholars employ the term to speak of processes that may involve states but also include other non-state actors. Where the term differs from "transnational" is in being more specific about the scale of the activity. "Transnational" can be used to refer to various scales including the regional scale such as the EU; arrangements involving several regions like the EU and the South American trade group, Mercosur, agreeing on trade matters, or the global scale. When I use the term "global" in relation to public policy, I am referring to policy made on a global scale that is transnational. I reserve the term "international" for those instances where policy is being made by states alone. And, of course, "international" policy-making may also take place at various scales: regional, transregional, or global. The negotiations that led to the Marrakesh agreements and the founding of the World Trade Organization (WTO) were "international," conducted on a global scale. Subsequent negotiations in the Doha Round, however, are "global" in that they involve not only states, but also the WTO itself through the office of the director general and some limited participation by non-state actors. Finally, these terms are not mutually exclusive. At any given time, we can expect to observe global, transnational, and international processes in play. These processes may reinforce, contradict, or be independent of one another.

When speaking of policy on a global scale, the term "public" differs from its normal usage in nation-state policy-making. In this usage, the term referred generally to policies made by state actors, whether at the countrywide, subregion or province, and municipal or city/town scales. In this respect, "public" policies were different from those made by private organizations such as unions, business associations, corporations, voluntary organizations, and so on. This understanding of "public" versus "private" becomes complicated when we move to transnational global policy-making. In these realms of policy-making, as we have noted, not only are states involved, but a potentially large and rather heterogeneous number of non-state actors are also. Accordingly, for global public policy, we understand "public" to refer to policies that are directed to the whole of the global polity, however disorganized and difficult the definition of its borders might be. As Cerny (2010: 98) observes, "the constitution of the public itself is being transformed in the context of political (as well as economic and social) globalizing trends."

For example, the Framework Convention on Tobacco Control negotiated under the auspices of the World Health Organization (WHO) between 1999 and 2003 is a "public" policy in this sense. Its provisions are designed to tightly regulate the behavior of transnational tobacco corporations as well as domestic practices by individuals and governments. Its target group includes anyone in the world who uses, sells, and trades in tobacco products. Like all global public policies, pursuit of these goals requires strong participation by states but also by other non-state actors. And coming to an agreement on the Convention involved not only states, but also NGOs, professional groups such as those representing medical professions, and tobacco corporations.

CONCEPTUAL FRAMEWORKS FOR STUDYING GLOBAL PUBLIC POLICY

Explicit conceptual reflections on what global public policy entails and how scholars might approach its study are not numerous. In this section, I review three of the more extensive attempts to wrestle with these issues and then I add another conceptual tool from my own work. I begin with the presentation of perhaps the earliest analysis in this field, Wolfgang Reinicke's (1998) book entitled *Global Public Policy*. I then consider a contribution by Diane Stone, who introduces the concept of an "agora" as a way to think about the phenomenon. I consider next Philip Cerny's (2010) concept of "transnational pluralism" and its implications for policy analysis.

Reinicke builds his approach by reflecting on the implications of intensifying economic globalization for policy-making. He begins by arguing against a common position among economists who see globalization and growing interdependence (i.e. internationalization) between states as the same thing. He counters by noting changes in the form of trade that have become more dominant in cross-border flows of goods and services: intra-firm trade and trade related to the international sourcing of intermediate inputs. Both these changes "reflect the progressive structuring of international trade around the operations of global corporations and international interfirm arrangements for production and supply" (1998: 24). Accompanying these changes is financial globalization: the "creation of a global pool of highly liquid capital that can move quickly and freely between countries and assets. The major actors in this landscape are a relatively small number of highly capitalized financial conglomerates operating in a range of markets across a number of locations" (1998: 29). In effect, globalization has led to the emergence of a parallel, even competing, set of linkages at the level of production that are transnational and global rather than international in form.

Reinicke analyzes the policy challenges posed by economic globalization by distinguishing between two forms of sovereignty (1998: 56–58). "External" sovereignty is the central constitutive rule of the international system: states are mutually exclusive and disjointed, follow the principle of self-help, and maintain their own security. "Internal" sovereignty refers to the ability of a government of a state to formulate, implement, and manage public policy. Globalization, he argues, poses a fundamental challenge to internal sovereignty. The reach of operational internal sovereignty extends only to the territorial borders of a given state, but the economic wellbeing of the citizens of this state is increasingly affected, if not determined, by global markets, transnational trade relations, and global corporations. The isomorphic fit between economic and political geography that had developed over the nineteenth and twentieth centuries no longer exists in many policy areas.

After considering various solutions to this conundrum, Reinicke suggests that "global public policy" is the only one that is sustainable in the long term: "the delinking of some elements of the operational aspects of internal sovereignty (governance) from its territorial foundation (the nation-state) and its institutional and legal environment (the government) and their reapplication on a sectoral—that is, functional—basis" (1998: 87). In doing so, policies could "cut across" state boundaries in order to match up political geography with economic geography.

Accordingly, Reinicke is suggesting that sovereignty is divisible both in its territorial and its legal forms. This divisibility is put into practice through subsidiarity, the idea that policy decisions should be made by lower-level jurisdictions unless there is a clear rationale and need for the decisions to be made at higher-level ones. He innovates further by suggesting that subsidiarity can also be horizontal. In the vertical form, public policy decision-making is delegated to higher or lower levels of governance; in the horizontal situation, it is delegated to non-state actors such as business associations, NGOs, and labor groups. Reinicke adds that when confronted with globalization, vertical subsidiarity is likely to involve delegations of internal sovereignty to international governance institutions.

Reinicke's contribution has been very important but also has two limitations. First, it focuses on economic globalization only, and thus may underestimate the extent of the need for global public policy in noneconomic areas such as culture and the environment. Second, its conceptualization remains close to internationalization in seeing states as the dominant drivers of the policy process. As studies of the politics of globalization have developed since the late 1990s, when he wrote his book, scholars have looked for ways to move further away from state-centrism in conceptualizing global public policy.

In a journal article published in 2008, Diane Stone addresses both these limitations. She opens her argument by noting that nation-state institutions no longer serve as the sole organizing center for policy. Quoting Philip Cerny (to whom I return below), she postulates that it is now necessary to look at the "restructuring of the playing field itself" (2008: 20). In this respect, her advice is similar to that of Jan Aart Scholte, who argues for a move from "state-centric" to "polycentric" models of global governance (2005: ch. 6). As a starting point, Stone adapts the Ancient Athenian concept of the "agora" as an organizing tool for analysis. This concept is used

> to identify a growing global public space of fluid, dynamic, and intermeshed relations of politics, markets, culture, and society. This public space is shaped by the interactions of its actors—that is, multiple publics and plural institutions. Some actors are more visible, persuasive, or powerful than others. However, the global agora is a social and political space—generated by globalization—rather than a physical place. (Stone 2008: 21)

Stone suggests that the agora is a site of relative disorder and uncertainty because institutions are underdeveloped and the sources of political authority are unclear, being dispersed through increasing numbers of institutions and networks.

This conceptual starting point, therefore, departs from Reinicke by allowing for a far greater role, in some instances, by non-state actors, depending on circumstances. In addition, the agora concept leaves room for an increasingly common aspect of global policy-making: the active presence in a policy field of several international organizations, with divergent interests, leading to difficulties in coordinating policy discussions and policy development and in implementing policy outcomes. The presence of several authority structures within the global agora means "far greater time and effort is also spent convening, debating, and negotiating in arenas created by interlocutors in order to promote compliance rather than exert enforcement" (2008: 28).

Stone goes on to identify three types of political actors that are central to global public policy in the agora (2008: 30). First, there are "internationalized public officials": public officials working for nation-state bureaucracies who are delegated responsibility for engaging in policy discussions at the global level on behalf of their country. Anne-Marie Slaughter carried out an extensive study of the varying roles (regulatory, harmonization, information sharing) of these networks of public officials in her book *A New World Order* (2004). Stone terms the second group "international civil servants": persons employed by international organizations who staff their secretariats and institutional operations. These persons are not delegates of states like those in the first category, nor do they have their first loyalty to states. They meet less regularly with one another, being quite geographically dispersed, highly reliant on information technologies, and traveling frequently. They are more likely than other actors in the agora to adopt a globalized identity and outlook (Stone 2008: 33). The third category includes "transnational policy professionals," a diverse group that might include consultants, NGO leaders, corporate executives, and leading scientific experts, among others. Stone postulates that the policy interchanges in the global agora are dominated by interactions among actors drawn from these three categories.

Stone's discussion of global public policy is useful not only in moving conceptually away from a state-centric perspective, but also in identifying the new types of political actors involved in policy-making. But the agora concept is a general one, looking at policy-making in a holistic way, on a global plane. It leaves open the question about whether there is one agora or different agoras for varying policy problems. Philip Cerny's recent work moves in the latter direction and he offers some further conceptual tools for studying the variance in processes of global policy-making across different policy spaces.

Cerny observes that world politics is being "transformed into a polycentric or multi-nucleated global political system, operating within an increasingly continuous geographical space and/or set of overlapping spaces" (2010: 98). He thus opens the door to using the concept of a "policy space" as an analytical tool and notes the possibility of multiple spaces, with no single center of power. As part of this transformation, domestic political forces are no longer the dominant players. Rather, power accrues to those actors that can coordinate their activities across borders, at multiple levels, and multiple nodes of power (2010: 5). This observation is also useful because it points to the likelihood that new "spaces" will contain several centers of power. In these circumstances, circuits of power are organized more and more around issue areas, rather than states. And in these issue areas, power accrues to those actors whose interests and values allow them to build transnational coalitions (2010: 103). Such actors will also be skilled at defining their goals, interests, and values in ways that permit the building of cross-border networks, and at coordinating and organizing their actions at a variety of scales from the local to the global (2010: 106).

Cerny theorizes these developments by drawing upon a long-standing political science concept for the study of group politics: pluralism. He adapts this concept for the new world politics and terms it "transnational pluralism." In these new, more global, spaces, "groups" need to be highly flexible in responding to political challenges. They must be able to build and rebuild coalitions and to be skilled in selecting short and long-term allies with whom they might work. And they have to develop the capacity for coordinating policy development and policy-making across borders. Traditional left–right politics and blocs of states give way to more mixed, complex, and looser coalitions (2010: 109).

Cerny also suggests building on a conceptual tool developed in US politics for studying policy-making: the iron triangle. In US policy studies, the iron triangle included the executive branch, Congress, and interest groups who entered into longer-standing, informal relationships with politicians and bureaucratic officials to conceive, adopt, and implement public policies in particular sectors. Cerny stresses that political executives and legislatures at the nation-state level remain key participants in global public policy, as do interest groups. But, as noted above, each of these actor categories will need to build networks to be effective in global policy-making. He pushes further and suggests that the triangle concept be replaced by a "flexible pentangle" (2010: 116–117). Added to the iron triangle mix are two categories also mentioned by Stone: the transnational public sector (international public servants) and the transnational private sector (somewhat analogous to Stone's transnational policy professionals).

Characteristics of global public policy

In reflecting upon these scholarly contributions, it becomes clearer that the use of the concept of "global policy spaces" becomes helpful (Coleman 2005: 94–98). The choice of the word "space" coincides with the epistemological position that borders around global policy are variable and are being created and recreated in response to globalizing processes and global problems. These spaces take form as different institutions or political groupings seek to engage in policy-making, and as various institutions and networks of actors gather at nodes in the policy space. Ultimately, a given set of global public policies may emerge as a result of interactions between these nodes. Such spaces may exist for short or longer periods of time depending on the policy problems at issue. Participants in such policy spaces will include not only states, but, as Reinicke, Stone, and Cerny all suggest, a host of other transnational actors, often working in networks, which also endure for shorter or longer times depending on the policy issue. In choosing the concept of space, I am not suggesting that "places" are unimportant. As Sassen (2006, 2007) has argued repeatedly, the material infrastructure for creating global spaces is located in places. What is changing is the multiplication of sites of power (nodes) that are contributing to the creation of spaces. And the degree of cooperation or the intensity of relationships between different place-based nodes in the policy space will be variable.

These global policy spaces will include varying international institutions, intergovernmental organizations, and non-governmental actors, which have membership bases that are more or less inclusive of the world, which uphold and manage global actions that are more or less anchored in law, and which have material and intellectual resources that give them more or less capacity for autonomous action in given policy spaces. There is no hierarchy in the usual sense structuring the activities of these varying institutions, no "executive branch" controlling them, and no meta-legal structures establishing hierarchies among given bodies of international and global law.

With this understanding of global policy spaces at hand, we are in a position to highlight several distinguishing characteristics of global public policy. In presenting these characteristics, I draw on an example of global public policy-making: the development and approval in 2007 by the United Nations General Assembly of the Declaration on the Rights of Indigenous Peoples. The seed for the policy was sown in 1948 when the idea of *human* rights was institutionalized, at least symbolically, at the United Nations (UN), in the Universal Declaration of Human Rights and built upon further in the International

Covenant on Economic, Social and Cultural Rights (ICESCR) and the International Covenant on Civil and Political Rights (ICCPR) in 1966. Indigenous peoples saw these ideas of rights as potential tools for decolonizing their oppressed lives (Battiste and Henderson 2000: 1).

To get to the point of even being able to think about, let alone pursue, a policy like the Declaration, these peoples had to think beyond their existing community identities by defining what they had in common. The identities of peoples in most places in the world are very specific and place-based. Only very gradually over the twentieth century did peoples come to recognize that there were "others" like them across the planet. The use of the word "indigenous," which means "from this place" or "native," points to the core characteristics that these peoples have in common: they have inhabited a particular place or territory for a long time or since "time immemorial." For example, it took a long time before those persons who see themselves as Waskapi, who speak a language called "Cree" in English, and who are located in the northwest part of the province of Québec in Canada, knew about and recognized what they have in common with the Aymara in present-day Bolivia or the "Scheduled Tribes" in India. Eventually they came to an understanding of a meaning of "indigenous" that captured what they shared with similar peoples, wherever they lived on the planet. The identity is based on an attachment that all participants share to some form of subsistence economy, to a territory or homeland that predates the arrival of settlers and surveyors, to a spiritual system that predates the arrival of missionaries, and to a language that expresses everything that is important and distinct about their place in the universe. Most importantly, they share the destruction and loss of these things (Niezen 2003: 86–93).

Some of this destruction has come at the hands of nation-state policies (2003: 87):

- assimilative state education which has led to a loss of language, culture, and traditional knowledge;
- loss of a subsistence economy due to resource development, which has undermined severely a culture and set of political institutions very closely tied to the land;
- state abrogation of treaties, which has led to further losses of land and to rapacious resource development on those lands.

With this example in front of us, we return to discuss and illustrate the distinguishing characteristics of global public policy.

First, *the policy problem to be solved is global in scope, not national, nor regional, nor even interregional in scale.* Stone and Cerny try to address this aspect through the use of concepts of "agora" or "policy spaces," respectively. Such global policy problems arise in several different ways.

- The *policy problems* are *transboundary or supraterritorial* on a *global scale*. For indigenous peoples, the global institutionalization of the nation-state form of governance, complete with the pursuit of "national" identities and the establishment of individual property rights led everywhere to the dispossession of their lands and the denigration of their cultures. The very definitions of "territory" and "borders" applied to their traditional lands by nation-states everywhere created a problem of dispossession on a global scale. They needed a policy instrument that would permit some overriding of these notions of national territory and boundaries. Other examples of policy problems of this type include agreeing on environmental policies to curb the emission of greenhouse gases to the point that changes in climate are arrested; finding ways to set international standards for food products such that the global trade in those products is not hindered by states using different sanitary or phytosanitary measures to block trade; and setting up rules for banks active across the world when it comes to how much core capital they must have before engaging in lending and related transactions in global markets.

- The problems relate to *common global property*. For example, outer space is common to all states and persons living on Earth. No one country or organization can privately own outer space. If it is agreed that there needs to be a policy limiting the weaponization of space, then by definition this policy is global in scope. A second example might be reducing levels of pollution in oceans. Because the oceans are fluid and interlinked on a global scale, solving the problem of excessive pollution in the oceans becomes a global policy problem.

- The policy problem arises *independently in a number of different places in the world* but cannot be systematically addressed without acting on a global scale. As indicated above, this situation relates to the experience of indigenous peoples. When the Anishinabe lost control of their lands in Canada, it was not directly linked to the dispossession of the Saami in Scandinavia or the Berber population of present-day Morocco. Gradually, various communities like these ones came to the conclusion that acting together despite their differences in culture, language, and physical location was the only avenue that could stop their disappearance from the Earth.

Another example addressed recently by the WHO is tobacco addiction. The medical evidence on the serious health problems created by tobacco addiction is incontrovertible. As a result, the cost in human lives and illness arising from tobacco is very high, putting immense strains on health care systems in every country. Although individual states can take action to reduce tobacco consumption, they still face a highly globalized and concentrated global corporate sector committed to selling the product. The problems posed by the mismatch between nation-state powers and the global tobacco industry were such that eventually the WHO was able to negotiate a Framework Convention on Tobacco Control between 1998 and 2003 (Holden and Lee 2009).

Second, *decision-making* is *polycentric*, not *state-centric*. As we have seen in the discussion of concepts like the "agora," "policy spaces," or a "multinucleated political system," there is no single focus for the formulation and implementation of global public policies. There are likely to be various nodes of power in play. And gathering at these nodes will be nation-state politicians, nation-state bureaucratic officials, NGOs operating at national, regional, and global scales, transnational public officials, and transnational private actors, whether corporations, consultants, scientific experts, or professional managers. The solution of the given policy problem will almost invariably involve states and they may have an important role in implementing any policy agreed upon. But they will not be able to act on their own. In situations of polycentric decision-making, lines between public and private become blurred. In many instances, private authority and public authority become enmeshed and work together in any policy outcome.

The movement toward the Declaration on the Rights of Indigenous Peoples also illustrates well these characteristics of global public policy. In 1982, the UN responded to increasing pressure from the growing cognitive and social justice networks of indigenous persons by setting up a "Working Group on Indigenous Populations" as a subgroup of the UN Commission on Human Rights Sub-Commission on Prevention of Discrimination and Protection of Minorities (Battiste and Henderson 2000: 3). This Working Group and its activities marked the beginning of the building of a "global policy space" where the notion of indigenous rights could be discussed on a global scale. Using this platform, indigenous peoples were able to push for new standards in UN law, the most comprehensive being the 1989 International Labour Organization (ILO) Convention on Indigenous and Tribal Peoples. They lobbied successfully for a special chapter for indigenous peoples' programs in Agenda 21, which was adopted by the UN Conference on the Environment in 1992, and for the inclusion of traditional ecological knowledge of indigenous peoples in the UN Convention on Biological Diversity in 1993. The same year was proclaimed the International Year of the World's Indigenous Peoples in 1993. Two years later, an International Decade for Indigenous Peoples was declared by the UN.

These events culminated in the formalization of a global policy space, with the setting up of a Permanent Forum for Indigenous Peoples in 2000. The *policy problem* at issue had taken on a global scope because it involved the mobilization of indigenous communities across the world who had experienced the kind of losses noted above, which ultimately provided the basis for an indigenous identity. The actions of indigenous peoples and their allies had led to the pushing out of a policy space in which conceptions of indigenous peoples' rights could be debated and ultimately translated into legal terms. Clearly, states were present and very active in the policy space but they were not alone. Consistent with the definition of global policy-making, *decision-making* was *polycentric* not state-centric. NGOs of indigenous peoples from all parts of the world participated, as did transnational organizations devoted to promoting human rights such as Amnesty International. UN officials who worked in the human rights area, whom Stone termed "international civil servants," also participated. Similarly, the *boundaries of the policy area* were blurred because of the mixing of issues of rights, economic development, cultural preservation, and language revitalization, among other issues. The complexity of such a space is anticipated in Stone's agora concept and in Cerny's notion of multinucleated processes involving policy "pentangles": nation-state bureaucrats; nation-state politicians; indigenous peoples' organizations operating on local, national, regional, and global scales; transnational officials from the UN, the ILO, and the World Bank (WB); transnational private actors including representatives of transnational corporations "developing" natural resource sites; and experts in international law.

Third, like nation-state level policy-making, the *boundaries between policy areas are often blurred* in global policy-making to the point that it is difficult to determine which agency, organization, or department is responsible for addressing a given problem. At the nation-state level, this situation involves bureaucratic competition but that competition can be mitigated by the intervention of executive authorities. In global policy-making, however, no such overall executive authority exists with these kinds of powers.

The complexity of the Indigenous Peoples declaration illustrates this dimension of global public policy-making. The issues addressed included: human rights, culture, religion, education, communication technologies, social welfare provisions, health care, and language use. The scope of the issues involved required participation by nation-state officials from a range of departments and agencies with different relations with indigenous peoples and often competing policy objectives. Another example is illustrated by the regulation of genetically modified organisms (Coleman 2005). Nation-state ministries of agriculture, health, environment, and industry ministries all could plausibly claim to be responsible for defining regulations. In these circumstances, the central executive can intervene by naming one of these agencies to be responsible or, more commonly, by creating a special agency to deal with the problem. In the absence of this kind of executive power, global policy-making becomes more protracted in being defined as competing sites of authority come into play. Reaching agreement on the Declaration on the Rights of Indigenous Peoples took over five years, and even then a number of key countries refused to sign.

Conclusion

From the standpoint of nation-states or smaller units like provinces and cities, global public policy-making is messy, often incomprehensible, and seldom satisfactory. But from the same standpoint, such policy-making is ever more essential. The intensification of globalizing processes and their impacts on more and more aspects of the lives of humans and nonhumans alike characterize our present world. Academic study is just beginning to wrestle with the normative questions arising from the need to decide on more important matters at a planetary scale. Similarly, scholars studying global public policy face the challenge of thinking outside the analytical box of concepts honed and refined during the nation-state era. This analytical frame assumes that nation-states are solely responsible for conceiving, formulating, bringing into law, implementing, and evaluating public policies. This assumption also dominates other social science disciplines—when sociologists speak about "society," they are referring to nation-state societies; when economists speak about "the economy," they are thinking about a given national economy. Globalization scholars like Scholte (2005) and Beck (2005) refer to this epistemological position as "methodological nationalism." They argue that a full understanding of global phenomena requires scholars to reframe their epistemologies and their approaches to theory.

The analysis of global public policy is at its very early stages. Breaking out of methodological nationalism thinking is immensely difficult because nation-states have been the center of our analytical universe since the inception of policy studies. Copernicus challenged the world by asking that we think of a solar system where the Earth was not at its center. Global public policy challenges the social sciences to think of a political world where the nation-state is no longer the standpoint from which we begin our studies. Can we meet this challenge?

REFERENCES

Battiste, M. A. and Henderson, J. Y. 2000. *Protecting Indigenous Knowledge and Heritage: A Global Challenge*. Saskatoon, Canada: Purich.

Beck, U. 2005. *Power in the Global Age: A New Global Political Economy*, trans. Kathleen Cross. London: Polity.

Brydon, D. and Coleman, W. D. 2008. Globalization, autonomy, and community. In D. Brydon and W. D. Coleman (eds.), *Renegotiating Community: Interdisciplinary Perspectives, Global Contexts*. Vancouver, BC: University of British Columbia Press, 1–28.

Castells, M. 1999. *The Rise of the Network Society*, 2nd ed. Cambridge, MA: Blackwell.

Cerny, P. G. 2010. *Rethinking World Politics: A Theory of Transnational Neopluralism*. Oxford: Oxford University Press.

Coleman, W. D. 2003. Governing global finance: Financial derivatives, liberal states and transformative capacity. In L. Weiss (ed.), *States in the Global Economy: Bringing Domestic Institutions Back*. Cambridge: Cambridge University Press, 271–292.

Coleman, W. D. 2005. Globality and transnational policy-making in agriculture: Complexity, contradiction, and conflict. In E. Grande and L. W. Pauly (eds.), *Complex Sovereignty: Reconstituting Political Authority in the Twenty-First Century*. Toronto, ON: University of Toronto Press, 93–119.

Cutler, A. C. 2003. *Private Power and Global Authority: Transnational Merchant Law in the Global Political Economy*. Cambridge: Cambridge University Press.

Eaton, S. and Porter, T. 2008. Globalization, autonomy and global institutions: Accounting for accounting. In Louis W. Pauly and William D. Coleman (eds.), *Global Ordering: Institutions and Autonomy in a Changing World*. Vancouver: University of British Columbia Press, 125–43.

Holden, C. and Lee, K. 2009. Corporate power and social policy: The political economy of the transnational tobacco companies. *Global Social Policy* 9: 328–354.

Niezen, R. 2003. *The Origins of Indigenism: Human Rights and the Politics of Identity*. Berkeley, CA: University of California Press.

Reinicke, W. 1998. *Global Public Policy: Governing Without Government?* Washington, DC: Brookings.

Sassen, S. 2006. *Territory, Authority, Rights: From Medieval to Global Assemblages*. Princeton, NJ: Princeton University Press.

Sassen, S. 2007. *A Sociology of Globalization*. New York: W.W. Norton.

Scholte, J. A. 2005. *Globalization: A Critical Introduction*, 2nd ed. Basingstoke: Palgrave Macmillan.

Slaughter, A-M. 2004. *A New World Order*. Princeton, NJ: Princeton University Press.

Stone, D. 2008. Global public policy, transnational policy communities, and their networks. *Policy Studies Journal* 36: 19–38.

CHAPTER 48

GLOBAL GOVERNANCE, INTERNATIONAL ORDER, AND WORLD ORDER

ARIE M. KACOWICZ*

INTRODUCTION: ASSESSING GLOBAL GOVERNANCE

THIS chapter explores the concept of global governance by looking at its analytical, theoretical, and normative implications. I present two major arguments. First, in an age of globalization there is an increasing need for global governance, as, in the previous period of "complex independence," as depicted by Keohane and Nye (1977), there was a functional need for international regimes and other international institutions to manage complex independence. Second, global governance should be understood alongside a possible continuum of governance ranging from international order (Bull's "anarchical society") to world government. Along that continuum, there are different ways of assessing and examining global governance, so it might take several institutional forms and denominations, including world order, "new medievalism," and cosmopolitanism. Moreover, these theoretical and social constructs can coexist simultaneously since they do not necessarily contradict, but rather complement, each other.

The first argument refers to the fact that economic globalization and global problems demand the establishment or creation of new political mechanisms that transcend the state system in order to cope with the complexities of our world. Thus, global governance mechanisms are necessary in order to manage the new world order of economic and environmental globalization and global challenges. As James Rosenau pointed out cogently, "Reinforced by the collapse of time and distance, the weaknesses of states, the vast movements of people and the ever greater complexities of modern life, the question of how to infuse a modicum of order, a measure of effective authority and a potential for improving the human condition into the course of events looms as increasingly urgent" (Rosenau 2002: 70–71). Hence, we should address questions such as: What do we mean by governance on a global scale ("global governance")? How is the world governed, in the absence of a world government, to produce norms, codes of conduct, and regulatory, surveillance, and compliance mechanisms? How is that different, if at all, from "international regimes" (see Rosenau 1992: 1; Duggett 2005: xi; Weiss and Thakur 2010: 1; and Hurrell 2007: 1)? The section on "Defining global governance" spells out the first argument and attempts to answer those questions.

The second argument implies that in order to make sense of global governance we should pay attention to the larger context of both the discipline of international relations (IR) and especially of its real-world context. In the absence of world government, the concept of global governance provides us with a proper theoretical terminology to describe and analyze the *complex* of systems of rule-making, political coordination, and problem-solving that transcends states and societies, constructing new political realities and reconstructing old ones. Global governance does that by describing the structures and processes of governing beyond the state where there is no single supreme supranational political authority (Held and McGrew 2002: 8). Yet, as the phenomena and processes of globalization still remain ambiguous and ill-defined, there is a great confusion in the IR literature regarding the possible meanings, dynamics, and scope of global governance. In this context, the possible relationships among global governance and different types of international and world order might clarify the relevance, and limitations, of the concept of "global governance." Thus, we should address questions such as: What is the relationship among global governance, international order, and world order? How is the world organized politically? How should it be organized? What forms of political organizations are required to meet the challenges faced by humankind in the twenty-first century? The section on "The continuum of global governance" illustrates this second argument. Finally, in the section on "The limitations of global government" I wrap up the two main arguments of this chapter.

Any discussion of global governance in the context of IR should start with an understanding of the significant changes that have taken place in the international society and system. Three major developments are relevant: first, the end of the Cold War; second, the complex processes of economic, political, and cultural globalization; and third, the possible relocation of political authority away from the nation-state and international organizations (IGOs) in the direction of private, non-state actors, including multinational corporations (MNCs) and non-governmental organizations (NGOs) as participants and components of an emerging transnational civil society (see Yunker 2005: 202; Hewson and Sinclair 1999: 3–4; and Ruggie 2010: xvii).

Economic and environmental globalization has not occurred in a political vacuum. There has also been a concomitant shift in the nature and form of political organizations, with a re-articulation of political authority occurring in many and multiple possible directions through a dense web of networks and linkages: supranational, international (through the enhancement of international organizations and institutions), transnational, and subnational; as well as public, private, and public–private partnerships. Thus, the idea of global governance is of growing concern among scholars and practitioners alike, with regard to the political dimensions of globalization and of global change (although one can question cause and effect relations in this context). This *global governance complex* embraces states, international institutions, transnational networks, and agencies (both public and private) that function, with variable effect and effectiveness, to promote, regulate, and manage the common affairs of humanity (see Held and McGrew 2002: 1, 5; Selby 2003: 4; Wilkinson 2005: 6; and Duffield 2001: 44).

DEFINING GLOBAL GOVERNANCE

Global governance in the international relations literature: old wine in new bottles?

The term "global governance" was apparently introduced in the late 1980s, in the context of the *international regimes* literature, which had a significant impact on scholarly thinking. At the time of the emergence of the neoliberal institutional paradigm, the emphasis was upon the possibility of nation-states cooperating under anarchy, by establishing international institutions. A related theme in the literature dealt with enhancing the capacity of international governance to address problems of global concern ("global problems"), first and foremost through the action of international institutions such as the United Nations (UN). The concept of global governance came into wide public usage in the early 1990s with the establishment of the United Nations Commission on Global Governance (UNCGG) in 1992 and the publication of such seminal works as *Governance without Government: Order and Change in World Politics* (1992) edited by James N. Rosenau and Ernst-Otto Czempiel (see Wilkinson 2005: 4–5; Hewson and Sinclair 1999: 11–12; Weiss and Thakur 2010: 30; and Yunker 2005: 202).

The concept of "global governance" initially overlapped with that of "international regimes," "international institutions," "multilateralism," and "international governance." Yet contemporary usage in the early twenty-first century refers, in the literature of IR, to a qualitative change embedded in the demand of political globalization to cope with the challenges of economic globalization and global problems (such as environmental degradation or nuclear proliferation). The result has been a movement from government to "governance," and a concomitant transformation from IR to "global politics."

As for the concept of "governance," as suggested by Rhodes and by Zürn in their respective chapters in this book (Chapters 3 and 51, respectively), the reference is to the rise of political authority in the framework of institutions different from the nation-state, which help in the process of governing. Adding "governance" to the "global" we can then spell out alternative definitions, as follows.

Alternative definitions of global governance in international relations literature

James Rosenau, a pioneer intellectual in the field of global governance, refers to the concept as the need for a *new ontology* to make sense of world politics (Rosenau 1999: 288–289). This "new ontology" is built on the premise that the world is nowadays comprised of spheres of authority that are not necessarily consistent with the division of territorial space that is the traditional international order of sovereign states. Rosenau, who coined the original term of *fragmengration* to point out the simultaneous forces of integration and disintegration that shape our world, defines global governance as "a summary term for a highly complex and widely disparate activities that may culminate in a modicum of worldwide coherence or that may collapse into pervasive disarray. In the event of either outcome, it would still be global governance in the sense that the sum of efforts by widely disaggregated goal-seeking entities will have supplemented, perhaps even supplanted, states as the primary sources of governance on a global scale" (Rosenau 1999: 294; see also Rosenau 2005: 45–46). The mechanisms and rules of global governance are then created by the actions and agreements of key actors and institutions involved in the global system, including state and non-state entities (see O'Brien et al. 2000: 125).

According to the UNCGG (1995), governance "is the sum of the many ways individuals and institutions, public and private, manage their common affairs. It is a continuing process through which conflicting or diverse interests may be accommodated and cooperative action may be taken. It includes formal institutions and regimes empowered to enforce compliance, as well as informal arrangements that people and institutions either have agreed to or perceive to be in their interest" (CGG 1995: 2). At the *global level*, "governance has been viewed primarily as intergovernmental relationships, but it must now be understood as also involving non-governmental organizations (NGOs), citizens' movements, MNCs, and the global capital market" (CGG 1995: 3). In this encompassing definition, the process of global governance includes a broad range of actors, both public and private. Private firms, associations of firms, non-governmental organizations and associations of NGOs all engage in it, often in association and unison with governmental bodies, to create (global) governance without government (Keohane and Nye 2000: 12).

Similarly, according to Weiss and Thakur, global governance is "the sum of laws, norms, policies, and institutions that define, constitute, and mediate trans-border relations among citizens, society, markets, and the state in the international arena—the wielders and objects of international public power. Even in the absence of an overarching central authority, existing collective arrangements bring more predictability, stability, and order to trans-boundary problems than we might expect" (Weiss and Thakur 2010: 6). In this sense, global governance is conceived as a system of rules and norms that ensures order on a voluntary, purposive way. Unlike the first definition by Rosenau, this definition, like the UNCGG's one, still emphasizes the paramount role of the states and international institutions composed of states, such as the UN.

For John Ruggie, governance "refers to the workings of the system of authoritative rules, norms, institutions, and practices by means of which any collectivity manages its common affairs" (Ruggie 2010: xv). In the specific case of global governance, Ruggie follows Rosenau by referring to "global governance as an instance of governance in the absence of government." Furthermore, Ruggie draws the important distinction between "politics" and "governance" (despite their close relationship); whereas politics always refers to the competition in the pursuit of particular interests, governance is always about producing public goods (Ruggie 2010: xv; see also Zürn, Chapter 51, this volume).

To sum up, all those definitions share the concern of global governance with the possible (or potential) regulation of the global sphere, the multiplicity of spheres of authority, and the nature of actors and institutions, both public and private, involved in the regulative process and the production of public global goods. We view the concept as under the slogan of "governance without government" or as a kind of intermediary stage between the management of global problems through traditional interstate politics and the operation of a world government (see Hakovirta 2004a: 14). In other words, as I specify below, global governance can be located in a continuum ranging from international order to world government.

Dynamics and types of global governance

To describe and analyze the dynamics of global governance is a daunting task, since there is no single model or form of global governance, nor is there a single structure or set of structures. In fact, global governance is a broad, dynamic, and complex process of interactive decision-making that is constantly in flux. The emerging complex of global governance encompasses a rich mixture of actors, institutions, and processes that take place on at least at three different levels: supranational (MNCs, IGOs, and NGOs); national (firms, central governments of nation-states, and civil society); and subnational (local firms, local governments, and local civil society) (see Keohane and Nye 2000: 12–13; see also CGG 1995: 4; Woods 2002: 26; and Rosenau 2002: 76–77).

A number of dynamics of global governance have contributed to the erosion and diminution of state capabilities. At the same time, one can argue the other way around; namely, that the erosion of state capacities contributed to the enhancement of global governance. In any case, one of the most relevant dynamics of global governance has been the shifting balance between hierarchical and network forms of organization, and between vertical and horizontal flows of authority. Associated with this relocation of authority from the public to the private we can discern an important shift in the principal modalities of global rule-making and implementation. Thus, although much of the formal modalities of global governance are still dominated by the interaction among states (traditional IR) and by international institutions such as the UN, we can trace the formulation and implementation of global public policy within an expanding web of political networks that involve non-state actors as well, as in the Global Compact agreement that involves MNCs, or the Kimberley Process that involves both states and non-state actors (see Held and McGrew 2002: 11; and Risse 2009).

Following Rosenau (2002) and Risse (2009), for analytical purpose we can establish a typology of six forms of global governance, according to three categories: formal structures (hierarchical); informal structures (nonhierarchical); and mixed formal and informal structures (such as public–private networks and partnerships). The directional flows of authority may be unidirectional (either vertical, top-down or bottom-up; or horizontal, nonhierarchical). Alternatively, the direction can follow multiple flows of authority transmission, both vertical and horizontal. The actors involved might include governments, transnational corporations (TNCs), IGOs, NGOs, business alliances, and public–private, and private–private partnerships. While traditional IR are best typified in Table 48.1 by cell # 1, global governance is best typified in the hybrid of mixed formal and informal structures and multidirectional flows of authority in cell # 6. We should add that all the six cells in Table 48.1 represent different forms and ways of global governance. This typology is summarized in the table (adapted from Rosenau 2002and Risse 2009).

From the reading of the table we can get a better understanding of the multi-level character of global governance as well as the multiplicity of the relevant political actors and institutions. Furthermore, we should locate the complex processes of global governance within an imaginary continuum running from the traditional form of inter-

Table 48.1 A typology of global governance

	Unidirectional: vertical or horizontal flows of authority	Multidirectional: vertical and horizontal flows of authority
Formal structures	*Top-down (hierarchical):* [Cell # 1] Governments of nation-states and supranational institutions (IGOs); TNCs (corporate hierarchies); contracting out and outsourcing	*Network governance* [Cell # 2] Governments of nation-states; international institutions (IGOs); NGOs; business alliances; contracting out and outsourcing
Informal structures	*Bottom-up governance* [Cell # 3] Impact of civil society and networks of advocacy; NGOs and INGOs; positive incentives and bargaining	*Side-by-side governance* [Cell # 4] NGOs and INGOs; governments; positive incentives and bargaining; international regimes; private interest government/private regimes; private–private partnerships.
Mixed formal and informal structures	*Market-type governance* [Cell # 5] Governments of nation-states; IGOs; elites; markets; mass publics; TNCs; public–private networks and partnerships	*Web/network governance* [Cell # 6] Governments of nation-states; IGOs; elites; mass publics; TNCs; NGOs; INGOs; networks of advocacy; civil society

national order (the Westphalian system of sovereign states) all the way to the utopian ideal of a world government. This leads to the discussion of the second main argument in this chapter.

THE DIFFERENT PHASES (AND FACES) OF GLOBAL GOVERNANCE: FROM INTERNATIONAL ORDER TO WORLD GOVERNMENT

There is a long tradition in the discipline of IR of studying the future of international politics by imagining alternative "institutional designs" of alternative world orders as objects of interest in themselves (see Hakovirta 2004b: 47). In this sense, global governance should be located along a continuum of the changing architecture of world politics in terms of governance, as the newest, most sophisticated, but also ambiguous, classification of "world order." Since global governance aims at providing public goods in the global realm, "governance is order plus intentionality" (Rosenau 1992: 5).

The continuum offered in this chapter is an analytical prism. Within the two extremes of "international order" and "world government" we might find the different phases (and faces) of global governance. Thus, in reality, we might find hybrid modes of global orders, as is reflected in Table 48.1, above, which describe the typology of global governance. In other words, as the concept and reality of global governance are ambiguous and encompassing, they might include different typologies, configurations, and forms. Consequently, all six cells depicted in Table 48.1 can be accommodated in these different phases.

In this continuum, we start discussing the idea of a pluralist and limited society of sovereign states, as formulated by Bull in his seminal work on the international society as an *anarchical society* as a form of *international order*. This international society might evolve into a *world* or *global society*, due to the impact of *globalization*. Moreover, we no longer refer to an international order, but rather to *world order*, encompassing a larger number and character of actors, not just nation-states, but first and foremost human beings themselves embedded in a *global society*. Furthermore, the world order under globalization leads us to the metaphor (again coined by Bull back in 1977) of *new medievalism*. Finally, at the right end of the continuum, and propelled by a cosmopolitan ideology, we might approximate the liberal ideal of a *world government*. As we learned previously in the chapter, the concept of *global governance* might correspond to any of those phases. This argument is summarized in Figure 48.1.

There is an interesting parallel between the stages of Figure 48.1 and the typologies of global governance of Table 48.1 above. Thus, cells # 1 and # 2 roughly correspond to the definition of "international order." Similarly, cells # 3 and # 4 parallel the concepts of "world society" and "world order," while "new medievalism" is best reflected in cells # 5 and # 6. We do not have a good example of "world government," which ideally might reflect a diagonal direction from cell # 1 to cell # 6.

```
Intl. Order  -> World Society  -> World Order  -> New Medievalism  -> World Government
       G  L  O  B  A  L                   G  O  V  E  R  N  A  N  C  E
```

FIGURE 48.1 The continuum of global governance.

At the first phase of the continuum, the initial form of global governance takes the form of a pluralist and limited society of sovereign states, which embodies the idea of *international order* within an *anarchical international society* (see Bull 1977). There is an interesting parallel or analogy between the idea of an "anarchical international society" and the concept of "global governance." Both concepts suggest the feasibility of a peaceful, progressive, benign, and well-ordered international regime in the absence of a unifying governmental, supranational entity (despite the connotation of the society being "anarchic"). Similarly, both ideas are imperfect, voluntaristic, lacking a real government, and aiming at the regulation of norms and the creation of common expectations (see Hurrell 2007: 3; and Yunker 2005: 213).

At a second phase in the continuum, with the impact of globalization, international society might evolve into a *world or global society*. As a result of the dynamics of globalization, which imply more than just increased interstate interdependence but rather the de-territorialization of IR, world entities other than states are, nowadays, crucial components of contemporary society, which is global rather than international, though it is far from being universal (see Keohane 2005: 123).

Moreover, moving into the direction of world government, it is obvious that globalization implies that we cannot still refer to an international order, but rather to a *world order*. By "world order" Bull meant "those patterns or dispositions of human activity that sustain the elementary or primary goals of social life among mankind [humankind] as a whole." Thus, world order is a wider category of order than the international order. It takes as its units of order not just nation-states, but rather individual human beings, and assesses the degree of order on the basis of the delivery of certain kinds of public goods (such as security, human rights, basic needs, or justice) for humanity as a whole (Bull 1977: 20; Clark 2005: 730; see also Whitman 2005: 27; Hakovirta 2004a: 15; and Rosenau 1992: 5).

World order can mean alternative "architectural" designs that include the international order itself (such as the ephemeral unipolar structure of the international system), but since they include humanity as a whole they might as well refer to processes of globalization, transcending the traditional structure of the state system. For instance, there are several scenarios of world order that have been discussed in the IR literature and for policy purposes, such as (1) neo-medievalism and the overlapping of authority and identity; (2) the North–South divide; (3) Huntington's "clash of civilizations"; and (4) Kaplan's "coming anarchy" (see Huntington 1996; Kaplan 2006; and Clark 2005).

It is important to notice that the concern with "global governance" since the 1990s, following the end of the Cold War and the advent of the contemporary age of globalization, has replaced an earlier exploration of what was called "world order studies," which several scholars criticized as too static and top-down (Weiss and Thakur 2010: 29). In the early 1960s, the utopian World Order Models Project (WOMP) initiated by Richard Falk and others, adapted the world federalist idea to suit a postcolonial setting, and toward the direction of a potential world government (see Falk 1999: 7). While not directly critical of world order studies, many contemporary scholars (including Falk himself) prefer to use the term "global governance" and "global democracy" in a conscious effort to expand the epistemic community of academics and practitioners who embrace the key assumptions and principles of world order (see Tehranian and Reed 1999: 62). As a matter of fact, global governance incorporates the same *problématique* of world order, heading in the direction of distancing or deviance from world anarchy and chaos (see Hakovirta 2004a: 14). Thus, the concept here becomes more normative than analytic, or at least it carries a strong normative bias.

One possible manifestation of world order, as epitomized by global governance in still another phase (and face) is the idea of *new medievalism*. In 1977, Bull coined the term to refer to a "modern and secular equivalent of the kind of universal political organization that existed in Western Christendom in the Middle Ages. In that system no ruler or state was sovereign in the sense of being supreme over a given territory and a given segment of the Christian population; each had to share authority with vassals beneath, and with the Pope and (in Germany and Italy) the Holy Roman Emperor above" (Bull 1977: 254).

Thus, neo-medievalism encompasses an ideal political order in which individuals are governed by a number of overlapping authorities and identities. Bull spoke of a "new medievalism" to connote the fragmentation of authority reminiscent of the pre-Westphalian era, although he did not believe that other political actors were yet strong enough to offer a serious challenge to the nation-state in global politics. More than thirty years later, the image of "neo-medievalism" and the overlapping of political authority and identities have become more and more relevant to make sense of our current world order and as a depiction of global governance. Thus, the relocation and delegation of political authority among the several layers of global governance, as depicted in Table 48.1 above, resembles the complexity of competing and overlapping jurisdictions and spheres of political action and responsibility that characterized medieval Europe (see Held and McGrew 2002: 10; and Linklater 2005).

If new medievalism is a form of global governance, the logical end of the continuum should lead us into the cosmopolitan ideal of world government. In (political) theory, we could imagine a world government that would arise "as the consequence of a social contract among states, and thus it would be a universal republic or cosmopolis founded upon some form of consent or consensus" (Bull 1977: 253). And yet, since we do not really have a universal global society, cosmopolitan democracy is very unlikely, if not impossible to fulfill on a global scale. Thus, the concept of global governance implicitly assumes that a world government, while idyllic in theory, might be disastrous in practice, as well as morally wrong, by infringing the self-determination and freedom of both the nation-states, and the liberties of individuals (see Keohane 2005: 124; Yunker 2005: 203; and Bull 1977: 253).

CONCLUSIONS: THE LIMITATIONS
OF GLOBAL GOVERNANCE

Global governance is a fascinating and useful concept to make sense of our complex world, the challenges we face, and the various institutions that can deal with globalization, given the impracticality and/or undesirability of a world government. Yet, it is far from being perfect, and there are several problems and limitations that should be pointed out in the concluding section of this chapter, at the theoretical, practical, and ethical levels.

On *theoretical grounds*, there are at least two embedded biases in the mainstream literature and analysis of global governance. First, in general terms, the concept of global governance starts with several neoliberal institutionalist premises, similarly to the previous literature on international regimes, although it somehow transcends them. Those premises refer to the possibility of cooperation under anarchy, and the feasibility of international institutions (mainly IGOs). Second, many of the approaches toward global governance tend to be mainstream, and state-centric, and downplay the possibilities of conflict and resistance to globalization and to political governance (see Selby 2003: 4–7; Gilpin 2002: 238; Duffield 2001; and Tehranian and Reed 1999: 76). At the same time, some critical writers reject the basic premises of the state as the main political unit, downgrading its relevance in the discourse of global governance, in opposition to IR theory (see Mitrani 2010; Held and McGrew 2002).

On *practical grounds*, realist critics like Robert Gilpin, following in Bull's footsteps, point out the *political limitations* inherent in the translation of global governance from theory to praxis: How can change and peaceful change be achieved? What are the goals of global governance? How can the provision of public (global) goods in the world arena be reconciled with the lingering realities of power politics? Who are "we the people" among the myriad of actors involved in the dynamic process? (see Gilpin 2002: 247; Keohane and Nye 2000: 32–33; and Ruggie 2010: xix).

Conversely, advocates of world government criticize the realities of global governance as being inefficient, insufficient, and anemic. They object the "benign" recommendations of the UNGG (1995) and ask themselves, "Within the present world structure, how can 'citizens' movements' or NGOs possibly participate with superpower nation-states or multinational corporations in something called 'consensual democratic global governance?'" (Martin 1999: 14). From this standpoint, the idea and reality of global governance is a strained compromise that is subservient to the realities of traditional power politics (see also Held and McGrew 2002: 13). Hence, attempts to impose policy features on it are anchored in an explicit normative bias.

Finally, on *ethical grounds*, the concept of global governance does not pay enough attention to the ethical and moral connotations of world order and of globalization (see Murphy 2005: 90; and Franceschet 2009). There are several paradigmatic moral visions of the politics of global governance, including an *ethics of reform*, which attempt to "civilize globalization" and suggest a social-democratic compromise (see Sandbrook 2003); an *ethics of responsible governance*, geared toward the provision of adequate governance on a global basis; an *ethics of cosmopolitan community*, which crowns a logic of world order for humanity as a whole as trumping any particular interests of given actors or groups; and an *ethics of critique*, that follows a Foucauldian premise of referring to global governance as another site of politics, power, and domination (see Franceschet 2009).

There are two major normative themes concerned with the dynamics and realities of global governance. First, there is the issue of democratizing global governance and overcoming the inherent problem of "democratic deficit," making global governance accountable (to whom?) Second, there is the issue of promoting global distributive justice and overcoming poverty and inequality, while keeping a modicum of order in world politics (see Held and McGrew 2002: 14; Falk 2005: 106, 118; and Dower 2004: 116).

With all the imperfections and limitations of both the theoretical concept and the realities it should reflect, global governance remains an essential and indispensable ingredient to make sense of our world. If world government is an unfeasible ideal, while the anarchy (or laissez-faire) of the markets is a recipe for financial global crises, then we have to compromise on an intermediate solution, ranging between international order and world government. Thirty years ago the realities (not the theory!) of complex interdependence demanded the creation of functional international institutions (including international regimes) to cope with it. Nowadays and similarly, in our post-Cold War age of economic globalization and global issues we have to explain and understand that set of political practices, actors, and institutions, both public and private, which improve coordination, provide global public goods, and compete and coexist with the still vibrant and vivid nation-states (themselves major agents of global governance) in providing a political equivalent and response to the functional demands of globalization. It is not just a "new world order" as proclaimed by George Bush twenty years ago; it is actually a new world of actors, networks, alliances, and overlapping authorities and identities, messy but vital, under the umbrella concept of "global governance." And our job remains to make sense of it, both in analytical and in normative terms.

NOTE

* I would like to thank David Levi-Faur, Claudia Kedar, Mor Mitrani, and Nilgun Onder for their comments on and insights into previous versions of this chapter.

REFERENCES

Bull, H. 1977. *The Anarchical Society: A Study of Order in World Politics*. New York: Columbia University Press.

Clark, I. 2005. Globalization and the post-Cold War order. In J. Baylis and S. Smith (eds.), *The Globalization of World Politics: An Introduction to International Relations*. Oxford: Oxford University Press, 727–742.

Commission on Global Governance (CGG) 1995. *Our Global Neighborhood: The Report of the Commission on Global Governance*. Oxford: Oxford University Press.

Dower, N. 2004. The ethics of globalization or the globalization of ethics? In H. Hakovirta (ed.), *Six Essays on Global Order and Governance*. Turku, Finland: Figare/Safir, 99–125.

Duffield, M. 2001. *Global Governance and the New Wars: The Merging of Development and Security*. London: Zed Books.

Duggett, M. 2005. Defining terms and delineating the debate in global governance. In G. Fraser-Moleketi (ed.), *The World We Could Win: Administering Global Governance*. Amsterdam: IOS Press, xi–xvii.

Falk, R. 1999. Pursuing the quest for human security. In M. Tehranian (ed.), *Worlds Apart: Human Security and Global Governance*. London: I. B. Taurus, 1–22.

Falk, R. 2005. Humane governance for the world: Reviving the quest. In R. Wilkinson (ed.), *The Global Governance Reader*. London: Routledge, 105–119.

Franceschet, A. 2009. Ethics, politics, and global governance. In A. Franceschet (ed.), *The Ethics of Global Governance*. Boulder, CO: Lynne Rienner Publishers, 1–20.

Gilpin, R. 2002. A realist perspective on international governance. In D. Held and A. McGrew (eds.), *Governing Globalization: Power, Authority, and Global Governance*. Cambridge: Polity, 237–248.

Hakovirta, H. 2004a. Introduction. In H. Hakovirta (ed.), *Six Essays on Global Order and Governance*. Turku, Finland: Figare/Safir, 11–21.

Hakovirta, H. 2004b. Alternative world orders and the governance of global problems. In H. Hakovirta (ed.), *Six Essays on Global Order and Governance*. Turku, Finland: Fgare/Safir, 47–67.

Held, D. and McGrew, A. 2002. Introduction. In D. Held and A. McGrew (eds.), *Governing Globalization: Power, Authority, and Global Governance*. Cambridge: Polity, 1–21.

Hewson, M. and Sinclair, T. J. 1999. The emergence of global governance theory. In M. Hewson and T. J. Sinclair (eds.), *Approaches to Global Governance Theory*. New York: SUNY Press, 3–22.

Huntington, S. P. 1996. *The Clash of Civilizations and the Remaking of World Order*. New York: Simon and Schuster.

Hurrell, A. 2007. *On Global Order: Power, Values, and the Constitution of International Society*. Oxford: Oxford University Press.

Kaplan, R. D. 2006. The coming anarchy. In P. Williams, D. M. Goldstein, and J. M. Shafritz (eds.), *Classic Readings and Contemporary Debates in International Relations*. Belmont, CA: Thomson, 601–617.

Keohane, R. O. 2005. Global governance and democratic accountability. In R. Wilkinson (ed.), *The Global Governance Reader*. London: Routledge, 120–137.

Keohane, R. O. and Nye, J. S. 1977. *Power and Interdependence: World Politics in Transition*. Boston: Little Brown.

Keohane, R. O. and Nye, J. S. 2000. Introduction. In J. S. Nye and J. D. Donnahue (eds.), *Governance in a Globalizing World*. Washington, DC: Brookings, 1–41.

Linklater, A. 2005. Globalization and the transformation of political community. In J. Baylis and S. Smith (eds.), *The Globalization of World Politics: An Introduction to International Relations*. Oxford: Oxford University Press, 709–725.

Martin, G. T. 1999. A planetary paradigm for global governance. In E. E. Harris and J. A. Yunker (eds.), *Toward Genuine Global Governance: Critical Reactions to "Our Global Neighborhood"*. Westport, CT: Praeger, 1–18.

Mitrani, M. 2010. Bringing international relations back in: Globalization and the political adaptation of international relations. Paper presented at the International PhD Workshop on International Order: Transnational Processes and their Effects. Berlin Graduate School for Transnational Studies, Berlin, 11–12 November.

Murphy, C. N. 2005. Global governance: Poorly done and poorly understood. In R. Wilkinson (ed.), *The Global Governance Reader*. London: Routledge, 90–104.

O'Brien, R. O., Goetz, A. M., Scholte, J. A. and Williams, M. 2000. *Contesting Global Governance: Multilateral Economic Institutions and Global Social Movements*. Cambridge: Cambridge University Press.

Risse, T. 2009. Notes on "global governance" and prospects for Israeli–German academic exchange. In A. M. Kacowicz (ed.), *In the Spirit of Einstein: Germans and Israelis on Ethics and International Order*. Jerusalem: The Leonard Davis Institute for International and the Einstein Center, Hebrew University of Jerusalem, 57–70.

Rosenau, J. N. 1992. Governance, order, and change in world politics. In J. N. Rosenau and E. Czempiel (eds.), *Governance without Government: Order and Change in World Politics*. Cambridge: Cambridge University Press, 1–29.

Rosenau, J. N. 1999. Toward an ontology for global governance. In M. Hewson and T. J. Sinclair (eds.), *Approaches to Global Governance Theory*. New York: State University of New York Press, 287–301.

Rosenau, J. N. 2002. Governance in a new global order. In D. Held and A. McGrew (eds.), *Governing Globalization: Power, Authority, and Global Governance*. Cambridge: Polity, 70–86.

Rosenau, J. N. 2005. Governance in the 21st century. In R. Wilkinson (ed.), *The Global Governance Reader*. London: Routledge, 45–67.

Ruggie, J. 2010. Foreword. In T. G. Weiss and R. Thakur, *Global Governance and the United Nations: An Unfinished Journey*. Bloomington: Indiana University Press, xv–xx.

Sandbrook, R. (ed.) 2003. *Civilizing Globalization*. Toronto, ON: Toronto University Press.

Selby, J. 2003. Introduction. In F. Cochrane, R. Duffy, and J. Selby (eds.), *Global Governance, Conflict and Resistance*. New York: Palgrave Macmillan, 1–18.

Tehranian, M. and Reed, L. 1999. Evolving governance regimes. In M. Tehranian (ed.), *Worlds Apart: Human Security and Global Governance*. London: I. B. Taurus, 54–78.

Weiss, T. G. and Thakur, R. 2010. *Global Governance and the United Nations: An Unfinished Journey*. Bloomington, IN: Indiana University Press.

Whitman, J. 2005. *The Limits of Global Governance*. London: Routledge.

Wilkinson, R. 2005. Introduction: Concepts and issues in global governance. In R. Wilkinson (ed.), *The Global Governance Reader*. London: Routledge, 1–22.

Woods, N. 2002. Global governance and the role of institutions. In D. Held and A. McGrew (eds.), *Governing Globalization: Power, Authority, and Global Governance*. Cambridge: Polity, 25–45.

Yunker, J. A. 2005. *Rethinking World Government: A New Approach*. Lanham, MD: University Press of America.

CHAPTER 49

···

GOVERNANCE IN AREAS OF LIMITED STATEHOOD

···

THOMAS RISSE

IN the twenty-first century, it is increasingly clear that conventional modes of political steering by the nation-states and international intergovernmental organizations (IOs) are not living up to global challenges such as environmental issues, humanitarian catastrophes, and new security threats.[1] This is one of the reasons why governance has become such a central topic of research within the social sciences, focusing in particular on non-state actors who participate in rule-making and implementation. Yet the governance discourse remains centered on an "ideal type" of modern statehood—with full internal and external sovereignty, a legitimate monopoly on the use of force, and checks and balances that constrain political rule and authority. Similarly, most of the "global governance" debate in international relations, while focusing on "governance without government" and the rise of private authority in world politics (e.g. Cutler, Haufler, and Porter 1999; O'Brien et al. 2000; Hall and Biersteker 2002; Grande and Pauly 2005), is based on the assumption that functioning states are capable of implementing and enforcing global norms and rules. Even the discourse on failed, failing, and fragile states centers on state-building as the main remedy for establishing or restoring political and social order (see, e.g. Rotberg 2003, 2004; Schneckener 2004).

From a global as well as a historical perspective, however, the modern and consolidated nation-state with a full monopoly over the means of violence and the capacity to effectively enforce central decisions is rather exceptional. Outside the developed Organisation for Economic Co-operation and Development (OECD) world, we find areas of "limited statehood," from developing and transition countries to failing and failed states, in today's conflict zones and—historically—in colonial societies. Areas of limited statehood lack the capacity to implement and enforce central decisions and/or a monopoly on the use of force.

If "limited statehood" is not a historical accident or some deplorable deficit of most Third World and transition countries that has to be overcome by the relentless forces of economic and political modernization in an era of globalization, the concept and the empirical reality of governance have to be reconceptualized. We have to ask ourselves how effective and legitimate governance is possible under conditions of limited statehood and how security and other collective goods can be provided under these circumstances.

This chapter begins by introducing the concept of limited statehood. Second, I show that we can observe governance and the provision of collective goods even under conditions of limited statehood. Third, I discuss conceptual issues that arise when governance is applied to areas of limited statehood. I reveal the Western and Eurocentric bias of contemporary social science notions of statehood and governance. I conclude by discussing some of the political consequences that would arise if we took the concept of limited statehood more seriously.

Before I proceed, however, the concept of governance must be clarified (see also David Levi-Faur's introduction to this volume). In its most general version, governance refers to all modes of coordinating social action in human society. Williamson, for example, distinguished between governance by markets and governance by hierarchy (i.e. the state); later scholars added governance by networks to this list (see e.g. Williamson 1975; Rhodes 1997). However, these distinctions identify governance with all kinds of social ordering and therefore are too broad. I use a somewhat narrower concept that is linked to politics. I define governance as the various *institutionalized modes of social coordination to produce and implement collectively binding rules, or to provide collective goods*. This conceptualization follows closely the understanding of governance that is widespread within the social sciences (e.g. Mayntz 2004, 2008; Kohler-Koch 1998; Benz 2004; Schuppert and Zürn 2008). My understanding of governance includes hierarchies and networks, but excludes markets whereby social order follows from individual choices as non-intentional externalites. In contrast, my understanding of governance is confined to intentional action. Here, governance refers to the intentional provision of rules and collective goods for a particular community. Spontaneous social order does not constitute governance. Note, however, that effective and legitimate problem-solving is not part of the definition. Intentional action (not motivation!) toward rule-making and service provision is all that is needed to qualify as governance. Whether or not governance is effective and/or legitimate is an empirical question that should be studied separately.

Governance encompasses process ("modes of social coordination") as well as structural ("institutionalized") dimensions. As to the actors involved, governance covers steering by state actors or by non-state actors, or self-regulation by civil society as well as governance via cooperative networks of public and private actors (cf. Benz 2004; Grande and Pauly 2005; Zürn 1998). As to the modes of social coordination, governance includes hierarchical steering through authoritative rule-making (*Herrschaft*), but also nonhierarchical modes of social coordination, such as bargaining, persuasion, deliberation (Risse 2000), and social learning (see Göhler, Höppner, and de la Rosa 2009).

WHAT IS LIMITED STATEHOOD?

Before I can discuss the governance *problématique* in the context of weak state institutions, the concept of "limited statehood" requires clarification. Most typologies in the literature and data sets on fragile states and "states at risk" reveal a normative orientation toward highly developed and democratic statehood and, thus, toward the Western model (e.g. Rotberg 2003, 2004). The benchmark is usually the liberal capitalist state governed by the rule of law (Leibfried and Zürn 2005). This is problematic on both normative and analytical grounds. It is normatively questionable, because it reveals Eurocentrism and a bias toward Western concepts, as if statehood equals Western liberal statehood and market economy. We might find the political and economic systems of the People's Republic of China and of Russia morally questionable, but they certainly constitute states. Confounding statehood with a particular Western understanding is analytically problematic, too, because it tends to confuse definitional issues and research questions. Such conceptualizations of statehood obscure what I consider the relevant research questions: Who governs for whom, and how are governance services provided?

In the following, "limited statehood" is based on a rather narrow concept of statehood. It follows closely Max Weber's conceptualization of statehood as an institutionalized rule structure with the ability to rule authoritatively (*Herrschaftsverband*) and to legitimately control the means of violence (*Gewaltmonopol*, cf. Weber 1980 [1921]; on statehood in general see Benz 2001; Schuppert 2009). Consolidated states at least possess the ability to authoritatively make, implement, and enforce central decisions for a collectivity. In other words, consolidated states command what Stephen Krasner calls "domestic sovereignty," that is, "the formal organization of political authority within the state and the ability of public authorities to exercise effective control within the borders of their own polity" (Krasner 1999: 4). This does not imply that consolidated states rule authoritatively or hierarchically all the time. On the contrary, the huge literature on the transformation of the modern (Western) state demonstrates quite a degree of decentralization and privatization (e.g. Leibfried and Zürn 2005; Hurrelmann et al. 2007; Schuppert 2009). Yet, consolidated states still retain the option of hierarchical steering—if only to cast a "shadow of hierarchy" (see below).

This narrow understanding of statehood as an institutionalized monopoly over the means of violence and/or the ability to make and enforce central decisions allows us to distinguish between statehood as a structure of authority, on the one hand, and the kind of governance and public services it provides, on the other. The latter is an empirical, not a definitional question. The literature on failing and failed states, for example, suffers from a conflation of statehood with governance. Failed states are then defined as lacking governance (see e.g. Rotberg 2003, 2004), as a result of which we can no longer investigate how much statehood is necessary to insure the provision of governance and public services.

We can now define more precisely what "limited statehood" means. In short, while areas of limited statehood still belong to internationally recognized states (even the failed state Somalia still commands international sovereignty), it is their domestic sovereignty that is severely circumscribed. Areas of limited statehood, then, concern those parts of a country in which central authorities (governments) lack the ability to implement and enforce rules and decisions and/or in which the legitimate monopoly over the means of violence is lacking, at least temporarily. It follows that the opposite of "limited statehood" is not "unlimited" but "consolidated" statehood, that is, those areas of a country in which the state enjoys the monopoly over the means of violence and/or the ability to make and enforce central decisions. Thinking in terms of configurations of limited statehood also implies thinking in degrees of limited statehood rather than using the term in a dichotomous sense.

This conceptualization allows for distinguishing quite different types of limited statehood. As argued above, "limited statehood" is not confined to failing and failed states that have all but lost the ability to govern and to control their territory. Failed states such as Somalia comprise only a small percentage of the world's areas of limited statehood. Most developing and transition states, for example, encompass areas of limited statehood as they only partially control the instruments of force and are only partially able to enforce decisions, mainly for reasons of insufficient political and administrative capacities. Brazil and Mexico, on the one hand, and Somalia and Sudan, on the other, constitute opposite ends of a continuum of states containing areas of limited statehood. Moreover, and except for failed states, "limited statehood" usually does not encompass a state as a whole, but "areas," that is, territorial or functional spaces within otherwise functioning states in which the latter have lost their ability to govern. While the Pakistani government, for example, enjoys a monopoly over the use of force in many parts of its territory, the so-called tribal areas in the country's northeast regions are beyond the control of the central government and, thus, are areas of limited statehood. It also follows that limited statehood is by no means confined to the developing world. The Italian state, for example, lacks the institutional capacity to deal effectively with the Mafia in Southern Italy.

If we conceptualize limited statehood in such a way, it becomes clear that areas of limited statehood are an almost ubiquitous phenomenon in the contemporary international system, and also in historical comparison (Conrad and Stange 2011; Lehmkuhl 2007). After all, the state monopoly over the means of violence has only been around for a little more than 150 years. Most contemporary states contain "areas of limited statehood" in the sense that central authorities do not control the entire territory, do not completely enjoy the monopoly over the means of violence, and/or have limited capacities to enforce and implement decisions, at least in some policy areas or with regard to parts of the population. According to the Bertelsmann Transformation Index 2010, for example, which focuses on 129 transition and developing countries, about 100 states in the contemporary international system contain at least some areas of limited statehood.[2]

These considerations have serious consequences for the way in which we think about statehood and governance. The world today, as an international community of states, is largely based on the fiction that it is populated by fully consolidated states. International law embodies the idea of sovereign nation-states, which the international community assumes are functioning states that command "effective authority" over their territories. International law and the legalization of world politics have increasingly embedded states in a net of legal and other binding obligations in almost every policy area (Goldstein et al. 2000; Zangl and Zürn 2004). Yet, legalization assumes that states are fully capable of implementing and enforcing the law.

Most international donor agencies and most international state-building and democratization programs—from the World Bank (WB) to the European Union (EU) and the United States—also presuppose that the modern Western nation-state is the model for "good governance" (Magen, Risse, and McFaul 2009). Underneath these programs and strategies are the assumptions of modernization theory that the modern state comes as a package consisting of an effective government, the rule of law, human rights, democracy, market economy, and some degree of social welfare. This "governance package" constitutes a world cultural script (Meyer 1987) and is applied to developing and transition countries as well as to failing and failed states. But the goal of these measures is always the same: the institutionalization of fully consolidated, democratic, Western-style nation-states.

GOVERNANCE IN THE CONTEXT OF LIMITED STATEHOOD

Limited statehood does not imply the absence of political, social, or economic order. Limited statehood does not mean anarchy in a Hobbesian sense. We even find failed states such as Somalia where limited statehood is all-pervasive, but where governance takes place regularly and collective goods are provided (Menkhaus 2006/2007; Debiel et al. 2010). Effective governance and service provision occur even under the seemingly adverse conditions of limited statehood. To give a very rough indicator: if we use the Human Development Index 2009 (HDI)[3] as an indicator for governance and the provision of collective goods, and map the transition and developing countries contained in the Bertelsmann Transformation Index 2010 according to their degree of statehood unto it, this is what the world looks like (see Figure 49.1; each dot represents a country). Only the darkly shaded dots at either end of the statehood continuum—failed and failing states on the left-hand side, consolidated states on the right-hand side of the graph—perform in a way expected by modernization theory: while governance and public services are very poor in failed and failing states, consolidated states are among the top performers. Yet the variation is enormous in the middle of the graph, which represents countries with various degrees of limited statehood. Among those, the HDI ranges from 0.3 to 0.9—that is, almost across the entire spectrum.

In the context of limited statehood, forms of governance emerge which the contemporary social science literature discusses as "new" modes of governance or the

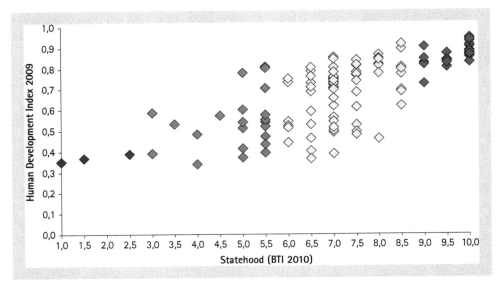

FIGURE 49.1 Human Development Index and degrees of statehood.

privatization of authority (for details see Risse 2011). However, these "new" modes of governance are not specific to the contemporary international system (Conrad and Stange 2011). The colonial state, for example, constituted an area of limited statehood as a result of which governance took place through colonial rulers ("states"), transnational "public–private" companies (cf. the Hudson Bay Company in North America or the East India Company in Asia), and local "private" actors such as settlers (Lehmkuhl 2007).

As to the actor dimension of governance, we find various combinations of state and non-state actors "governing" areas of limited statehood. These can be public–private partnerships (PPP, see Schäferhoff, Campe, and Kaan 2009; Liese and Beisheim 2011; Börzel and Risse 2005) in which national governments, international (interstate) organizations, as well as (multinational) firms and (international) non-governmental organizations ((I)NGOs) co-govern. But governance can also be provided by the self-regulation of firms (Börzel et al. 2011) and even by warlords and other violent actors (Chojnacki and Branovic 2011).

Concerning modes of steering, we even find hierarchical steering in areas of limited statehood. Warlords and local "big men" sometimes exert hierarchical control in war-torn areas of limited statehood. In addition, international organizations as well as— mostly Western—states often interfere authoritatively, particularly in modern protectorates such as Kosovo or Afghanistan. Much more common, however, are nonhierarchical modes of social coordination in areas of limited statehood (Göhler, Höppner, and de la Rosa 2009). This includes creating and manipulating incentives and "benchmarking," as well as initiating communicative learning processes.

Last but not least, governance in areas of limited statehood constitutes "multi-level governance" par excellence in the sense that external actors such as international organizations, foreign states, INGOs, and transnational corporations are systematically involved in rule-making processes and the provision of public goods.

When governance travels: the implicit (Western) bias of social science concepts

The understanding of governance outlined in the introduction largely follows the conceptualizations in American and European social sciences. However, applying this concept to areas of limited statehood reveals some implicit biases. The way in which the governance concept has been developed in the social sciences (and has become part of political practice) is strongly influenced by the experiences of Western modernity and of modern statehood. In the following, I discuss this with regard to three problems of governance theory, namely the distinction between the "public" and the "private" spheres, the implicit intentionality and normative biases of the governance concept, and the question of the "shadow of hierarchy."

The distinction between the "public" and the "private" spheres

Defining governance and the modes of governance in terms of including state and non-state actors in the provision of collective goods more often than not relies on the distinction between the "public" and "private" realms. This distinction, however, stems from modern statehood in its Western and Eurocentric understandings. This is problematic when we apply the governance concept to other historical contexts and/or to other cultural experiences in the contemporary international system. Historically speaking, the modern Western notion of the "private sphere" is connected to processes of individualization and personalization that only emerged in the second half of the eighteenth century in Europe, leading to the separation of the public and the private (e.g. Böckenförde 1976; Keane 1988). As Conrad and Stange argue, thinking of the "public" and the "private" spheres as binary categories is inherently problematic outside Western or European modernity (Conrad and Stange 2011). They demonstrate, for example, that the differences between state-funded administrative personnel and "private" actors among the colonizers were marginal at best. For example, the "private" East India Company exercised "public" authority on behalf of the British Empire.

Applying the public–private distinction to contemporary areas of limited statehood is as difficult. Of course, we can still distinguish formally between the state and the non-state sector including for-profit companies, on the one hand, and the not-for-profit NGO and civil society sector, on the other. But what does this mean in countries in which state institutions are so weak that government actors can easily exploit state resources for private purposes, while so-called "private" actors such as companies, and NGOs, but also clans and tribes, provide much-needed collective goods with regard to education, public health, or infrastructure (e.g. Börzel, Héritier, and Müller-Debus 2007; Fuhr, Lederer, and Schröder 2007). In other words, the implicit assumption of the public–private distinction according to which governments govern and private actors mind their own business, is often turned on its head in areas of limited statehood.

The distinction that comes with Western modernity, according to which "state = public" and "non-state = private" is often problematic in areas of limited statehood. Rent-seeking governments, for example, distribute state revenues, including development aid, to maintain their rule via clientelistic networks (the so-called "neo-patrimonial state" in sub-Saharan Africa, the Southern Caucasus, and elsewhere, see Erdmann 2002; Erdmann and Engel 2007). In other words, they transform public goods into club or even private goods. The emergence of "shadow" or "quasi states" has to be considered here, too (Koehler and Zürcher 2004; Zürcher 2007). On the one hand, formal state institutions have ceased to exist or to provide governance services in failing and failed states. On the other hand, informal governance institutions often emerge, providing social and political order as well as collective goods, thereby preventing the country or the region from completely collapsing into anarchy. In some cases, such as the Southern Caucasus, shadow states survive over extended periods of time.

These examples challenge the way in which the concepts of "state" and "public" as well as "non-state" and "private" are often used interchangeably in the social sciences, which originated from and are based on the historical experiences of Western and European modernity. The examples also show the implicit normative connotations of these concepts. We usually expect that state actors contribute to governance, that is, that they act in the public rather than the private interest. At least, they are supposed to justify their actions with regard to the common good (Zürn 2008). While policy-makers might be power-seeking, state institutions in a consolidated state—no matter how "transformed"—are supposed to direct their practices toward governance in the common interest. And if they abuse their power, we can throw them out through democratic procedures or, in the worst case, through the judicial system. Limited statehood, however, consists of weak political institutions lacking the capacity to constrain power-maximizing actors. As a result, it becomes problematic to speak of "public" actors in such cases or to assume that state actors promote the public interest. As to private actors, we usually assume that private companies pursue their narrow self-interest, even if their business practices produce positive externalities for the community (jobs, welfare, etc.). But we also assume that private actors act within the confines of the law—and if not, that the courts will take care of them.

These assumptions can no longer be taken for granted in areas of limited statehood. The conceptual problem cannot be solved easily. A possible way out is to investigate empirically who serves as a governance actor—irrespective of a formal position in the political system or in society. In other words, one would search for functional equivalents of "public" actors (Draude 2007, 2008). Companies, NGOs, tribal clans, and other so-called "private" actors might provide governance and public services, while state actors might abuse public resources for their own private purposes. Neo-patrimonial rule in many African as well as Central Asian countries is a case in point (Erdmann and Engel 2007).

Intentionality and normativity of governance

There is a second problem with regard to the applicability of the governance concept to areas of limited statehood. The governance concept as defined above is geared toward producing and implementing collectively binding rules and/or providing collective goods. In other words, governance implies intentional action toward providing public services for a given community (Mayntz 2004: 67). This does not mean that governance actors have to be necessarily motivated toward the public interest, only that their behavior includes the intention to govern. Governance implies intentional action, not some positive externality of behavior that is intended to produce, say, private goods. Policy-makers, for example, can still be motivated as rational power-maximizers. Yet, in a con-solidated state, they are usually embedded in governance structures that "civilize" them and institutionalize the intentionality of governance toward providing services for the community. The inherent intentionality of governance becomes tricky when applied to areas of limited statehood. First, as noted above, we can no longer assume that govern-ance institutions such as the state embody intentions toward providing collective goods. Second, we need to distinguish between the provision of some collective goods or serv-ices as the unintended consequence of "private" activities, on the one hand, and the explicit regulation of social issues and intentional provision of collective goods, on the other hand. Only the second understanding would qualify as governance, if we stick to the conceptualization above.

To illustrate the point with an example: oil companies routinely use private security firms to protect their production facilities in areas of limited statehood. This transforms security into a private good. Protecting such facilities might have positive externalities for the surrounding neighborhoods insofar as the security firms might unintentionally deter armed gangs or militias from attacking nearby villages, too. In this sense, the firms, while primarily providing a private good for an oil company, would also contribute to public security, albeit indirectly. But we would not call this security governance because of the lack of intentionality. Only if the oil company explicitly instructs the security firm to protecting not only the oil facilities, but also the surrounding villages, could this activity be called governance.

In other cases, we are faced with a continuum ranging from governance in the above-defined sense to "racketeering". An Afghan warlord who uses his militias to provide public security for the area of his rule, can be regarded a governance actor. However, the more he uses the same militias to threaten the safety of the community and then resells security to clientelistic networks for a protection fee, the more he would transform public security into a club or private good. The latter would be "racketeering" (Chojnacki and Branovic 2011).

Thus, applying the governance concept to areas of limited statehood highlights its unavoidable intentionality and normativity. If we mean by governance—as is common in the social sciences—that collectively binding rules are made and implemented and that collective goods are provided, we cannot refrain from acknowledging that governance is linked normatively toward what is supposed to be in the common interest. But who are those, in areas of limited statehood, in whose name the "common interest" is being articulated? What is the relevant community or collectivity for whom governance is provided? Once again, these issues are clearly decided in the ideal typical modern Western state: in most cases, governance is provided for the people or the citizens living in a given territory. While some services are only accessible to the citizens rather than the residents, even noncitizen residents enjoy some basic rights as well as access to at least some public services.

All this becomes problematic in areas of limited statehood. In many cases, it remains unclear who are the addressees of governance, who is entitled to which governance services, and who actually receives them in practice. Take border regions in sub-Saharan Africa, for example, that are beyond the control of central governments. Are the people living on a given territory those entitled to receiving governance? Or are members of particular tribal and/or ethnic communities so entitled? And who decides who is entitled to what, particularly in cases of extremely scarce resources? Is it governance if collective goods become club goods in the sense that only particular ethnic, religious, or gendered communities are entitled to receive them? The latter constitutes a common practice in many areas of limited statehood, both historically and in the contemporary international system.

Applying governance to areas of limited statehood, thus requires taking a step back and refraining from "either everything or nothing" conceptual solutions. Rather, we should consider governance as both a process and a continuum. The more inclusive the social group for which goods are provided or regulations are formulated, the more we should consider this as governance. After all, this approximates the definition of public goods in terms of non-rivalry in consumption and non-exclusivity in access. In contrast, the more certain services are only provided for exclusive groups and the more collective goods are transformed into club or private goods accessible only to those who pay for them or who belong to specific ethnic or religious groups, the less we should conceptualize this as governance. Applying the notion of collective goods to areas of limited statehood requires a more differentiated conceptualization of the collectivity for which governance is provided. In many cases, those entitled to receiving collective goods such as security are distinct from the addressees of governance services, who also differ from those who actually receive governance (de la Rosa, Höppner, and Kötter 2008).

It follows that the borders between governance and "racketeering" are rather fluid in areas of limited statehood. The weaker and the more fragile the state, the less it makes sense to judge governance services according to benchmarks derived from modern developed states.

Governance in areas of limited statehood and the "shadow of hierarchy"

A third *problématique* with regard to the application of the governance concept to areas of limited statehood concerns what has been called the "shadow of hierarchy" (Scharpf 1993). Research on modes of governance in the OECD world and on the transformation of (modern) statehood has demonstrated that public–private cooperation (such as PPP) and private self-regulation are usually most effective under the "shadow of hierarchy" (see Börzel, Chapter 43, this volume; also Börzel and Risse 2010). This means that state agencies supervise private regulatory efforts and/or that governments threaten to legislate if private actors do not get their act together or do not provide the collective goods. Hierarchical steering or the threat to do so appears to be a precondition for the successful implementation and effectiveness of "new" modes of governance in the modern nation-state and beyond.

If these findings are universally applicable, then governance in areas of limited statehood is doomed. Areas of limited statehood are by definition characterized by weak state capacities to implement and enforce decisions, that is, by weak "shadows of hierarchy." Moreover, the contribution of non-state actors to the provision of collective goods has to substitute for governance by governments rather than to complement it. If the Bill & Melinda Gates Foundation (BMGF) decides to withdraw from providing services in the area of public health—for example, the immunization of children—in sub-Saharan Africa, these services will not be provided at all (for details see Schäferhoff 2011; Liese and Beisheim 2011). Private actors as well as the international community substitute for, rather than complement, governance by the state.

As demonstrated above, however, we do find governance and the provision of collective goods even under the adverse conditions of limited statehood. How can this be explained? I argue that there are functional equivalents to the "shadow of hierarchy" provided by consolidated statehood (see Börzel 2010; Börzel and Risse 2010 for the following). First, in the case of modern protectorates such as Afghanistan or Kosovo, the international community not only rules authoritatively in areas of limited statehood, but also supplies a "shadow of hierarchy," inducing other actors to provide governance. More generally, governance in areas of limited statehood often constitutes a form of multi-level governance insofar as external actors—international organizations, donor agencies, and others—directly contribute to public services and the like (on multi-level governance in general, see e.g. Hooghe and Marks 2001).

Second, international legal standards on good governance, human rights, and the rule of law hold actors accountable in areas of limited statehood, be it through governments, NGOs, firms, or even rebel groups (Ladwig and Rudolf 2011). While enforcement of these standards is inherently problematic, the increased legalization of these standards, including the international "responsibility to protect" (R2P), casts a shadow of hierarchy in areas of limited statehood. Firms investing in areas of limited statehood, for example, may be subjected to transnational NGO campaigns if they are caught violating international legal standards such as human and social rights (see e.g. Flohr et al. 2010).

Empirical evidence also suggests that when rebel groups and warlords start complying with international law, the closer they are to victory and to taking over the state (Jo and Bryant 2012), since compliance increases their legitimacy.

Last but not least, there are various incentive structures available to commit non-state actors to the provision of collective goods even under most dire circumstances of limited statehood. Even warlords, local "big men," or rebel groups sometimes provide security as a collective good in security markets, if faced with an opportunity structure by which they benefit from protecting the local population rather than exploiting it (Jo and Bryant 2012; Chojnacki and Branovic 2011). As to firms, there are several market-based mechanisms inducing companies to engage in self-regulation. If, for example, brand name firms target high-end markets or are subjected to NGO campaigns, they are likely to provide collective goods in the framework of corporate social responsibility (CSR; see e.g. Prakash and Potoski 2006; Börzel et al. 2011). In other cases, it is in the instrumental self-interest of firms to contribute to governance. Multinational companies in South Africa, for example, have substantially contributed to public health and to the fight against HIV/AIDS in the absence of state action, because they had made huge investments in human resources that they could not afford to lose (Börzel, Héritier, and Müller-Debus 2007; Thauer 2009).

CONCLUSIONS

I have argued in this chapter that the social science debate on governance implicitly or explicitly remains wedded to an ideal type of modern statehood—with full domestic sovereignty and the capacity to make, implement, and enforce decisions. From a global as well as a historical perspective, however, the Western modern nation-state constitutes the exception rather than the rule. Outside the developed OECD world, we find areas of limited statehood that lack domestic sovereignty. Under such conditions, governance requires the inclusion of non-state as well as external actors in the provision of collective goods and the regulation of social issues.

Yet, our conceptual apparatus is ill-equipped to deal with the governance *problématique* in areas of limited statehood. The Western governance discourse is not only heavily influenced by modernization theory. It also assumes modern statehood and a fully functioning state as a background condition. I have tried to illustrate this point with regard to the applicability of the governance concept to areas of limited statehood. In particular, I have discussed problems with regard to the distinction between the "public" and the "private" spheres, the implicit intentionality and normativity of the governance concept, and concerning the "shadow of hierarchy." Discussing governance under conditions of limited statehood reveals several blind spots with regard to implicit and explicit theoretical and normative assumptions. These assumptions concern the modernization bias of the governance concept as currently used in the social sciences, which requires some conceptual innovation.

However, one should not throw out the baby with the bathwater. The governance concept provides a useful tool to analyze policies and politics in areas of limited statehood, precisely because it directs our attention to the role of non-state actors, on the one hand, and nonhierarchical modes of steering, on the other. As a result, governance overcomes the state-centric bias implicit in the literature on failed and failing states as well as the modernization bias of most development studies.

In conclusion, I would like to highlight the political consequences of thinking systematically about governance in areas of limited statehood. The international community is oriented almost completely toward the ideal of developed and democratic Western statehood in its state-building efforts and its democratization and development strategies (see e.g. Magen, Risse, and McFaul 2009). If, however, areas of limited statehood are here to stay for the time being, this strategic orientation of the international community becomes problematic for practical as well as normative reasons. We need to think anew about the international democratization, development, and state-building strategies, if only to counter the widespread suspicion that "good governance" is nothing more than Western neocolonialism in disguise. State-building efforts that simply try to reproduce the modernization package of the Western developed and liberal nation-state in areas of limited statehood are bound to fail. Rather, the international community should help to improve the capacity of states to enforce and implement decisions, and see to it that the preconditions of governance are enabled in areas of limited statehood. This implies a "light footprint," but also the need to be more innovative with regard to strengthening functional equivalents to consolidated statehood within the framework of governance.

NOTES

1. This chapter represents a summary version of Risse 2011. It is based on research conducted within the framework of the Collaborative Research Center 700 "Governance in Areas of Limited Statehood" at the Freie Universität Berlin, funded by the German Research Foundation (*Deutsche Forschungsgemeinschaft*). For critical comments and suggestions I thank David Levi-Faur and Arie Kacowicz.
2. This is calculated from two indicators of the Bertelsmann Transformation Index 2010, namely "state monopoly over the means of violence" and "basic administration." Data according to "Detaillierte_Werte_BTI2010.xls," downloaded from http://www.bertelsmann-transformation-index.de/bti/ranking/.
3. See http://hdr.undp.org. The Human Development Index is a composite indicator measuring education, public health, poverty reduction, and other development goals.

REFERENCES

Benz, A. 2001. *Der moderne Staat: Grundlagen der politologischen Analyse*. Munich and Vienna. Oldenbourg.

Benz, A. 2004. *Governance: Regieren in komplexen Regelsystemen*. Wiesbaden, Germany: VS Verlag für Sozialwissenschaften.

Böckenförde, E. W. 1976. Die Bedeutung der Unterscheidung von Staat und Gesellschaft im demokratischen Sozialstaat der Gegenwart. In E. W. Böckenförde (ed.), *Staat, Gesellschaft, Freiheit.* Frankfurt-am-Main: Suhrkamp, 395–431.

Börzel, T. A. 2010. Governance without government: False promises or flawed premises? SFB-700 Working Paper Series, Berlin: Freie Universität Berlin.

Börzel, T. A. and Risse, T. 2005. Public private partnerships: Effective and legitimate tools of international governance? In E. Grande and L. W. Pauly, *Complex Sovereignty: Reconstituting Political Authority in the Twenty-First Century.* Toronto, ON: University of Toronto Press, 195–216.

Börzel, T. A. and Risse, T. 2010. Governance without a state: Can it work? *Regulation and Governance* 4(2): 1–22.

Börzel, T. A., Héritier, A. and Müller-Debus, A. K. 2007. Der Regulierungsbeitrag von Großunternehmen im Kampf gegen HIV/AIDS in Südafrika. In T. Risse and U. Lehmkuhl (eds.), *Regieren ohne Staat? Governance in Räumen begrenzter Staatlichkeit.* Baden-Baden: Nomos, 272–291.

Börzel, T. A., Héritier, A., Kranz, N. and Thauer, C. 2011. Racing to the top? Regulatory competition among firms in areas of limited statehood. In T. Risse (ed.), *Governance Without a State? Policies and Politics in Areas of Limited Statehood.* New York: Columbia University Press.

Chojnacki, S. and Branovic, Z. 2011. New modes of security: The violent making and unmaking of governance in war-torn areas of limited statehood. In T. Risse (ed.), *Governance Without a State? Policies and Politics in Areas of Limited Statehood.* New York: Columbia University Press.

Conrad, S. and Stange, M. 2011. Governance and colonial rule. In T. Risse (ed.), *Governance Without a State? Policies and Politics in Areas of Limited Statehood.* New York: Columbia University Press.

Cutler, C. A., Haulfer, V. and Porter, T. (eds.) 1999. *Private Authority and International Affairs.* Albany, NY: SUNY Press.

Debiel, T., Glassner, R., Schetter, C. and Terlinden, U. 2010. Local state-building in Afghanistan and Somaliland. *Peace Review: A Journal of Social Justice* 21: 38–44.

De la Rosa, S., Höppner, U. and Kötter, M. (eds.) 2008. *Transdisziplinäre Governanceforschung: Gemeinsam hinter den Staat blicken.* Baden-Baden: Nomos.

Draude, A. 2007. Wer regiert wie? Für eine äquivalenzfunktionalistische Beobachtung von Governance in Räumen begrenzter Staatlichkeit. SFB 700 Working Paper Series. Berlin: Freie Universität Berlin.

Draude, A. 2008. Wer regiert wie? Eurozentrismus in der Governanceforschung und der Versuch einer methodischen Grenzüberschreitung. In S. De La Rosa and M. Kötter (eds.), *Transdisziplinäre Governanceforschung. Gemeinsam hinter den Staat blicken.* Baden-Baden: Nomos, 100–118.

Erdmann, G. 2002. Neopatrimoniale herrschaft—oder: Warum es in Afrika so viele Hybridregime gibt. In P. Bendel, A. Croissant, and F. W. Rüb (eds.), *Hybride Regime: Zur Konzeption und Empirie demokratischer Grauzonen.* Opladen, Germany: Leske and Budrich, 323–342.

Erdmann, G. and Engel, U. 2007. Neopatrimonialism reconsidered: Critical review and elaboration of an elusive concept. *Commonwealth and Comparative Politics* 45(1): 95–119.

Flohr, A., Rieth, L., Schwindenhammer, S. and Wolf, K. D. 2010. *The Role of Business in Global Governance: Corporations as Norm-Entrepreneurs.* Basingstoke. Palgrave Macmillan.

Fuhr, H., Lederer, M. and Schröder, M. 2007. Klimaschutz und Entwicklungspolitik: Der Beitrag privater Unternehmen. In T. Risse and U. Lehmkuhl (eds.), *Regieren ohne Staat? Governance in Räumen begrenzter Staatlichkeit.* Baden-Baden: Nomos, 292–308.

Göhler, G., Höppner, U. and de la Rosa, S. (eds.) 2009. *Weiche Steuerung: Studien zur Steuerung durch diskursive Praktiken, Argumente und Symbole.* Baden-Baden: Nomos.

Goldstein, J. L., Kahler, M, Keohane, R. O. and Slaughter, A-M. (eds.) 2000. *Legalization and World Politics: Special Issue of International Organization.* Cambridge, MA: MIT Press.

Grande, E. and Pauly, L. W. (eds.) 2005. *Complex Sovereignty: Reconstituting Political Authority in the Twenty-First Century.* Toronto, ON: Toronto University Press.

Hall, R. B. and Biersteker, T. J. (eds.) 2002. *The Emergence of Private Authority in Global Governance.* Cambridge: Cambridge University Press.

Hooghe, L. and Marks, G. 2001. *Multi-Level Governance and European Integration.* Lanham, MD: Rowman and Littlefield.

Hurrelmann, A., Leibfried, S, Martens, K. and Peter, M. (eds.) 2007. *Transforming the Golden-Age Nation State.* Basingstoke: Palgrave Macmillan.

Jo, H. and Bryant, K. 2012. Taming the rebels. Commitment and compliance by armed opposition groups. In T. Risse, S. S. Ropp, and K. Sikkink (eds.), *From Commitment to Compliance: The Persistent Power of Human Rights* (Cambridge UK: Cambridge University Press).

Keane, J. 1988. Despotism and democracy: The origins of the distinction between civil society and the state 1750–1850. In J. Keane (ed.), *Civil Society and the State.* London: Verso, 35–72.

Koehler, J. and Zürcher, C. 2004. Der Staat und sein Schatten: Zur Institutionalisierung hybrider Staatlichkeit im Südkaukasus. *WeltTrends* 12(45): 84–96.

Kohler-Koch, B. 1998. Einleitung: Effizienz und Demokratie: Probleme des Regierens in entgrenzten Räumen. In B. Kohler-Koch (ed.), *Regieren in entgrenzten Räumen: PVS—Sonderheft 29.* Opladen, Germany: Westdeutscher Verlag, 11–25.

Krasner, S. D. 1999. *Sovereignty: Organized Hypocrisy.* Princeton, NJ. Princeton University Press.

Ladwig, B. and Rudolf, B. 2011. International legal and moral standards of good governance in fragile states. In T. Risse (ed.), *Governance Without a State? Policies and Politics in Areas of Limited Statehood.* New York: Columbia University Press.

Lehmkuhl, U. 2007. Regieren im kolonialen Amerika: *Colonial Governance* und koloniale *Gouvernementalité* in französischen und englischen Siedlungskolonien. In T. Risse and U. Lehmkuhl (eds.), *Regieren ohne Staat? Governance in Räumen begrenzter Staatlichkeit.* Baden-Baden: Nomos, 111–133.

Leibfried, S. and Zürn, M. (eds.) 2005. *Transformations of the State?* Cambridge: Cambridge University Press.

Liese, A. and Beishem, M. 2011. Transnational public–private partnerships and the provision of collective goods in developing countries. In T. Risse (ed.), *Governance Without a State? Policies and Politics in Areas of Limited Statehood.* New York: Columbia University Press.

Magen, A., Risse, T. and McFaul, M. (eds.) 2009. *Promoting Democracy and the Rule of Law: American and European Strategies.* Basingstoke: Palgrave Macmillan.

Mayntz, R. 2004. Governance im modernen Staat. In A. Benz (ed.), *Governance: Regieren in komplexen Regelsystemen.* Wiesbaden, Germany: VS Verlag für Sozialwissenschaften, 65–76.

Mayntz, R. 2008. Von der Steuerungstheorie zu Global Governance. In G. Folke Schuppert and M. Zürn (eds.), *Governance in einer sich wandelnden Welt. PVS-Politische Vierteljahresschrift, Sonderheft 41.* Wiesbaden: VS Verlag für Sozialwissenschaften, 43–60.

Menkhaus, K. 2006/2007. Governance without government in Somalia: Spoilers, state building, and the politics of coping. *International Security* 31(3): 74–106.

Meyer, J. M. 1987. The world polity and the authority of the nation state. In G. M. Thomas, J. W. Meyer, F. O. Ramirez, and J. Boli (eds.), *International Structure: Constituting State, Society and the Individual*. London: Sage, 41–70.

O'Brien, R., Goetz, A-M., Scholte, J. A. and Williams, M. 2000. *Contesting Global Governance: Multilateral Economic Institutions and Global Social Movements*. Cambridge: Cambridge University Press.

Prakash, A. and Potoski, M. 2006. Racing to the bottom? Trade, environmental governance, and ISO 14001. *American Journal of Political Science* 50(2): 350–364.

Rhodes, R. A. W.1997. *Understanding Governance: Policy Networks, Governance, Reflexivity and Accountability*. Buckingham and Philadelphia: Open University Press.

Risse, T. 2000. "Let's argue!" Communicative action in international relations. *International Organization* 54(1): 1–39.

Risse, T. 2011. Governance in areas of limited statehood: Introduction and overview. In T. Risse (ed.), *Governance Without a State? Policies and Politics in Areas of Limited Statehood*. New York: Columbia University Press.

Rotberg, R. I.(ed.) 2003. *State Failure and State Weakness in a Time of Terror*. Washington, DC: Brookings.

Rotberg, R. I. (ed.) 2004. *When States Fail: Causes and Consequences*. Princeton, NJ: Princeton University Press.

Schäferhoff, M. 2011. Die Bereitstellung von Gesundheitsleistungen in Räumen begrenzter Staatlichkeit: Wie viel Staat ist zur effektiven Erbringung von Governance-Leistungen notwendig? In M. Beisheim, T. A. Börzel, P. Genschel, and B. Zangl (eds.), *Was vom Staate übrig bleibt? Der staatliche Beitrag zu Governance*. Baden-Baden: Nomos.

Schäferhoff, M., Campe, S. and Kaan, C. 2009. Transnational public–private partnerships in international relations: Making sense of concepts, research frameworks, and results. *International Studies Review* 11(3): 451–474.

Scharpf, F. 1993. Positive und negative Koordination in Verhandlungssystemen. In A Héritier (ed.), *Policy-Analyse, Politische Vierteljahresschrift, Sonderheft 24*. Opladen, Germany: Westdeutscher Verlag, 57–83.

Schneckener, U.(ed.) 2004. *States at Risk: Fragile Staaten als Sicherheits- und Entwicklungsproblem*. Berlin: Stiftung Wissenschaft und Politik.

Schuppert, G. F. 2009. *Staat als Prozess: Eine staatstheoretische Skizze in sieben Aufzügen*. Frankfurt-am-Main: Campus Verlag.

Schuppert, G. F. and Zürn, M. (eds.) 2008. *Governance in einer sich wandelnden Welt: PVS—Politische Vierteljahresschrift, Sonderheft 41*. Wiesbaden, Germany: VS Verlag für Sozialwissenschaften.

Thauer, C. 2009. Corporate social responsibility in the regulatory void: Does the promise hold? self-regulation by business in South Africa and China. PhD Dissertation, Florence, European University Institute.

Weber, M. 1980. *Wirtschaft und Gesellschaft*. Tübingen, Germany: J. C. B. Mohr.

Williamson, O. E. 1975. *Markets and Hierachies: Analysis and Anti-Trust*. New York. Free Press.

Zangl, B. and Zürn, M. (eds.) 2004. *Verrechtlichung: Baustein für Global Governance?* Bonn: Dietz.

Zürcher, C. 2007. When governance meets troubled states. In M. Beisheim and G. F. Schuppert (eds.), *Staatszerfall und Governance*. Baden-Baden: Nomos, 11–28.

Zürn, M. 1998. *Regieren Jenseits des Nationalstaates: Globalisierung und Denationalisierung als Chance*. Frankfurt-am-Main: Suhrkamp.

Zürn, M. 2008. Governance in einer sich wandelnden welt: Eine zwischenbilanz. In G. F. Schuppert and M. Zürn (eds.), *Governance in einer Sich Wandelnden Welt: PVS— Politische Vierteljahresschrift, Sonderheft 41*. Wiesbaden, Germany: VS Verlag für Sozialwissenschaften, 553–580.

CHAPTER 50

GOVERNMENTALITY IN GLOBAL GOVERNANCE

ALEXANDRIA JAYNE INNES &
BRENT J. STEELE

THIS chapter considers the utility of the concept of governmentality, introduced by Michel Foucault but developed by a multitude of authors, scholars, and theorists, in shedding light on mechanisms of global governance as practices of regulation. We conceptualize regulation not as the "command and control" of populations, but rather as notions of responsibilizing individuals through new instruments of management that emerge from the market-driven logic of neoliberal governance. We begin by examining some of the work on governmentality, and then move to a broader review of the use of governmentality as offering insight into the workings of global governance at three levels: (1) global governance that creates space for the political effects of substate actors, transnational networks, and global governmental and non-governmental institutions; (2) the challenge to the role of the state and the conventional understanding of sovereignty; and (3) the idea of global governance and global subjects or citizens.

The role of government and governance in international relations (IR) has been consistently debated and widely studied (Hardt and Negri 2001; Held and McGrew 2002; Risse 2002; Levi-Faur 2005; Sassen 2006; Neumann and Sending 2010; Bevir and Hall 2011), with attention to global governance growing recently, toward the conceptualization of regulatory mechanisms of global governance as practiced *upon* and *amongst* a variety of actors: states, individuals, regional institutions, intergovernmental organizations (IGOs), supranational and international institutions, non-governmental organizations (NGOs), for-profit agencies, and private militaries, to name a few. Existing scholarship has provided conceptualizations such as "new governance," which focuses on institutional design for efficient regulation and is discussed further in this volume (Lobel, Chapter 5); and "meta-governance," which focuses on the mechanisms and institutions that manage self-governance, in other words "the governance of governance" (Jessop 2011). The concept of governmentality sees governance as a field of power relations that are strategic in their "mobility, transformability, and reversibility," and which "refer to an ethics of the subject defined by the relationship of self to self" (Foucault 2001 [1982]: 252). The mechanisms of these strategic power relations function as a form of governance that relies on *tactics*. This governance is not necessarily state-centered, given that the power relations are strategic and are not statically defined as emanating from the top down. Instead, power can emanate from the actions and practices of various actors that are not traditionally considered as "the state" (Rose and Miller 1992). In this manner, Foucault conceptualized governmentality not as a "question not of imposing laws on men, but of disposing things: that is to say, of employing tactics rather than laws, and even of using laws themselves as tactics—to arrange things in such a way that, through a certain number of means, such and such ends may be achieved" (Foucault 1991). These tactics can be thought of as "a form of political power that consists of various technologies, mentalities, and rationalities of governing others *and* oneself" (Foucault 1991; Löwenheim 2007).

The "governance of the self" is key to governmentality—as a notion of "regulation" operating in governmentality is key to self-regulation—it is an embedded logic of "responsibility" to perform actions representing the self within fields of governmental power relations. Governmentality can, of course, be applied at the state level—and indeed much work in IR has appropriated governmentality to understand the state–citizen relationship. Yet understandings of global governance incorporate a multitude of supra-state and substate actors, which represent the agents that self-govern as well as the agencies that disseminate the rules and tactics. Governmentality then offers insight into a concept of global governance that does not prioritize the state. Rather, it situates the state within a network of governance, representing an actor that governs itself and others.

Theories of global governance have been advanced in IR through the study of states, international institutions, and transnational organizations, networks, and agencies, and through the analysis of their capacity to govern global affairs. The use of the term *governance* rather than *government* carries connotations of decentralization, reflecting the incorporation of several different actors, moving away from a hierarchical understanding of government, and allowing an identification of *governance* as a multi-level and multijurisdictional process. It follows that the mechanisms of global governance can be understood at different levels of interaction and through analysis of diverse relationships between actors, institutions, and public spheres (Neumann and Sending 2010; Jessop 2011; Kacowitz, Chapter 48; Lobel, Chapter 5; Rhodes, Chapter 3; Zürn, Chapter 51, all this volume). The theory of governmentality, with the focus on the subject, or the self-to-self relationship, offers unique insight into how these interactions operate at the level of the agent, be it individuals, groups, states, or other corporate actors. Rather than looking at the institutions of governance, governmentality focuses on the tactics that the array of global actors employ to achieve self-governance at the level of the governed.

Governmentality is attached to the mechanisms of a form of global governance that is predicated upon the assumptions of the neoliberal economic system. Indeed, Foucault's lectures on governmentality analyzed the rise of neoliberalism, and following work adopted neoliberalism as the framework to understand rationalities of government

(Dean 2010). The mechanisms and tactics that characterize governmentality can be broadly understood as regulations and rules of conduct that encourage self-governance. They are managed through statistical and actuarial technologies. The agents of regulation are not understood in a top-down hierarchical way, but comply with a horizontal or networked understanding of power relations that are mobile, transformable, and reversible. Self-governance is encouraged through *tactics that shift responsibility for behavior to the subject*. These tactics reward certain types of behavior and punish others, provoking individuals, states, or other agents to *assume responsibility* for their compliance with a particular type of behavior or set of norms that are informed by a liberal rationality of governance (Larner 2000; Neumann and Sending 2010).

In a very recent and vibrant study, Iver Neumann and Ole Jacob Sending draw our attention to these operations in a variety of ways. For one, they look at the utility of governmentality applied to global governance as a burgeoning phenomenon. They recognize the liberal rationale as extant within liberal states and build on this to recognize the mechanisms, agents, and subjects of governmentality at the global level, which they describe as global governance, thus complying with Rhodes's differentiation between government and governance (Rhodes, Chapter 3, this volume). A further contribution of Neumann and Sending looks at the relationship between sovereignty and governmentality as it is understood at the global level, given the disruption to the assumption that sovereign states are like units and principal actors (Neumann and Sending 2010).

This relationship is explored in more detail by theorists such as Giorgio Agamben (1998, 2000) and Judith Butler (2004). Foucault posited the difference between sovereignty and governmentality: sovereignty represents power and obedience, while governmentality represents a code of conduct or set of regulations under which one self-governs (Butler 2004; Neumann and Sending 2010). The distinction between those with the capacity to self-govern and those without is where these authors posit sovereignty, that is, with the police or, globally, with those actors who police others through force (Pratt 1999; Stenson 1999; Bonelli 2005; Neumann and Sending 2010). However, Neumann and Sending's position further complicates such a distinction at the global level in asserting that the state requires a form of sovereignty in order for it to be considered a global actor able to "self-govern" and incorporated into the power relations of governmentality. In other words, the state has to be understood as sovereign in its territory in order to self-govern. Yet, a global sovereignty can be asserted over those states without the capacity to self-govern. Consequently, the concept of sovereignty and its interaction with governmentality is complex at the global level.

The following sections provide examples of how governmentality has been used to give new insight into global governance. The first examines the actors, agents, and subjects who are evident in global governmentality, presenting examples of the mechanisms in action. The ensuing section problematizes the role of the state, the understanding of sovereignty that can be seen domestically acting on citizens, and how this transfers to the global system. The connection between the bounded state and the global is then developed further in the third section, which explores how one can understand the citizen, that is, global governance operating on the individual.

GLOBAL GOVERNMENTALITY: ACTORS, AGENTS, AND SUBJECTS

Governmentality rethinks the role of power in conventionally understood IR, or within the realm of global governance. Power is evident in global governance—but rather than emanating from the state to all other actors that are below the state, it is understood as *relational*. Rather than disciplinary power that aims for final control, power operating under governmentality is laissez-faire; it disposes people in their relation to desired ends and hence creates an environment of self-governance (de Boever 2009). Power exists in tandem with resistance: subjects have the scope to act differently. Governmentality manages the conduct of the governed, and at the global level the governed can be understood as individuals, states, agencies, international and transnational organizations, private authorities, and so on. According to Foucault, disciplined conduct is the outcome of three processes: "1) training individuals in various routines; 2) putting them under panoptic surveillance; and 3) punishing them for proscribed or deviant behaviour" (Löwenheim 2008: 258). This understanding of disciplined conduct differs from disciplinary power in that the conduct is managed rather than enforced and is related to a rethinking of global political behavior as fueled by potential risk rather than threat (Aradau, Lobo-Guerrero, and van Muster 2008).

The management of risk is seen in third parties such as private authorities, networks, and agencies who participate in the construction of truths through statistics and actuarial technologies. Such agents can play an authoritative role in truth construction in IR if that role is legitimized and given power by hegemonic states, or by the underlying "higher power" of the liberal rationality of governance. The question of democracy and the democratic capacity of states is representative of this technology measuring and managing risk; for example, international organizations such as the World Bank "actively seek to set up and build a global grid of performance indicators and benchmarks," which can be seen as tactics of governmentality coercing the state to govern in a way that complies with these indicators and benchmarks (Neumann and Sending 2010).

For instance, in the context of scales of democracy, the agents frequently act independently of a given state: "the main impetus for the spread of rating and ranking is the growth of international neoliberalism" (Löwenheim 2008: 265). Growing international investment in developing countries, perceived negative externalities of bad governance in the Third World such as the debt crisis, the failure of aid programs and policy reforms, and the institutional analyses that demonstrate the social and economic importance of a country's governing institutions reveal the motivation for more pervasive rating and ranking. The democratic indicators reduce risk for potential investors; a high ranking will encourage investment and therefore economic growth via the international economy. The agencies that compose these scales create the state as an ethical subject that is responsible for the choices it makes and consequently for the score it receives (Löwenheim 2008: 259). The ratings (and therefore the agencies that create the ratings) become important forces in international politics because of the power they carry. For example, the ratings can become a determinant of "aid selectivity" in which developing states have to achieve at least a rate of improvement in corruption and democracy scores in order to continue to qualify for aid (Löwenheim 2008: 261). Hegemonic states thus equally rely on these rankings to determine where aid should be sent, and where investments should be made. If developing states reject evaluation then they are categorized as undemocratic or corrupt. Consequently, more states are acquiescing to examination, sometimes actively soliciting evaluation, and committing themselves to improving their ranking, indicative of the governance of the "self."

Rather than being disciplinary mechanisms, rankings can be seen as a tactic of governmentality because the disciplining in question is not applied by "formal and restrictive hierarchies" (Löwenheim 2008: 258). States are not obliged to take part in the governance indicator data and they are not formally punished for negative results or deviant behavior. The "training" and "panoptic surveillance" are carried out by a combination of actors that operate at the level of global governance: institutions such as the World Bank (WB), the International Monetary Fund (IMF), and the Organisation for Economic Co-operation and Development (OECD); as well as NGOs such as Freedom House and Transparency International (Löwenheim 2008: 266). This reflects the mechanisms of global governance operating though a variety of actors and levels, and reproduced at multiple levels of authority (Kacowitz, Chapter 48, this volume).

Governmentality offers additional insight into the shift in the role and behavior of the governed, as Löwenheim emphasizes: "The 'state' addressed in these examinations [of democracy] is a subject in the sense that it is both an object of research and an actor deemed capable of action and responsible for choices and policies—and, consequently, for the scores it receives" (Löwenheim 2008: 259). As the state is responsibilized on these levels, other actors are absolved from responsibility for social, economic, and political problems that might be present. This observation is reinforced in studies by Bonelli (2005), and Hardt and Negri (2001).

Risk management as a technology of governmentality is seen in the context of mobile populations, who are often characterized as high risk (Bigo 2002; Salter 2008). Salter discusses this in terms of the use of new security technologies that are seen to minimize risk in aviation security practices. This is visible in the interaction between government policy and private risk managers, such as consulting firms, in the realm of things like border screening and airport security (Amoore 2006; Salter 2008). Salter posits that aviation has become an imagined space of risk for populations and the use of statistics renders that imagined risk "real." The effect is that individuals who self-govern will submit to the security technologies as their responsibility to minimize risk to themselves and others (Salter 2008).

The extension over individual mobility can also be seen in the practice of issuing travel warnings. States may have political motivations in the travel warnings they issue. Political implications may also come out of these warnings if the states against which they are issued perceive them to be making a particular statement, regardless of intentions. For example, despite issuing travel warnings after terrorist attacks in other locations, the US did not issue warnings against travel to the UK or Spain after terrorist attacks in those countries. Additionally, the UK government did not issue a travel warning against the US as a possible country of "revenge attacks on British citizens" after the 2002 invasion of Afghanistan, despite the US recognizing possible revenge attacks on its own territory (Löwenheim 2007: 207). The effect of this suggests political and economic motivation in issuing travel warnings. This possible bias also shows "how travel warnings are part of the construction of geographies of danger in world politics: they *authoritatively* emphasize or deemphasize risk and threat in various locations (an act that might indeed have observable material consequences)" (Löwenheim 2007: 207). Thus the lack of warnings in Western states that perceive each other as safe authoritatively perpetuates the assumption that they are secure, while the notion of insecurity in other locations is equally perpetuated.

In the case of travel warnings, the mode of diffusion of power is particularly apparent. The travel warnings disseminate from the state to travel companies and insurance agencies that, in turn, are responsibilized, and these companies and agencies tend to take the warnings very seriously. Examples include travel operators cancelling tours to warned-against locations and refunding money (Löwenheim 2007: 216). On the other hand, insurance companies are seen to further transfer responsibility to the individual travelers. This action is not relegated simply to travel insurance providers, life insurance policies often use travel warnings as a criterion to measure "willful exposure to risk," and raise premiums based on foreign travel to warned-against states (Löwenheim 2007, citing Avari 2004; Tunnah 2005; Foreign Affairs and International Trade Canada 2006). The mechanism of responsibilization on the part of insurance agencies is made all the more complex by the withdrawal of state responsibility. The state recommends that travelers take out insurance policies, citing examples of travelers who were harmed and faced extensive costs. However, the insurance agencies will not cover states that have government-issued travel warnings against them. State authorities are generally aware of this. For example, the British Foreign and Commonwealth Office recognizes that if it does not publish warnings, the insurance companies are likely to find some alternative reference point (Löwenheim 2007: 217). Thus responsibility is transferred to the individual on two simultaneous, interconnected levels, making the individual a subject at the global level, which will be discussed further below.

GOVERNMENTALITY AND SOVEREIGNTY

Understanding governmentality in global governance includes additional actors that hold power other than the state—governmentality can be understood, again, as a "regulatory" set of mechanisms—but in this case such regulatory power is not simply held *within states or over non-state actors*, but is exercised *in a relational way* between states, individuals, and other agents. Sovereignty in a system of global governance, then, looks different from that in conventional IR theory, which posits states as like sovereign units.

The presence of sovereignty in a system of governmentality is directed at subjects deemed incapable of self-governance according to the liberal rationale (Stenson 1999; Pratt 1999; Neumann and Sending 2010). Giorgio Agamben incorporates the locales of sovereignty under a system of governmentality in conjunction with the Schmittean "state of exception," identifying individuals and groups that remain outside the underlying liberal mode of governance and thus remain on the margins of political and social participation (Agamben 1998). Agamben considers the *homo sacer* as the converse of the sovereign: the *homo sacer* is a body who has been exiled from society and is considered human only in his capacity to be killed. The sovereign is separate from society in his ability to suspend the law (Agamben 1998). Sovereignty then is manifested in the state of exception that exists in conjunction with the rule of law in governmentality: the existence of a state of exception makes the rule of law apparent, and the presence of a state of exception becomes normal practice and can be seen as a locale of sovereignty. However, there are contentions due to the mechanisms of international norms understood under theories of global governance, which offer some constraints to the suggested sovereignty, and contentions regarding the lack of agency attributed to refugees (Hindess 2000; Budz 2009; Owens 2009; Squire 2009).

Judith Butler utilizes the notion of disseminated or relational power to understand the role of what she terms "petty sovereigns" in domestic politics with regard to the use of indefinite detention, although the concept is certainly more broadly applicable (Butler 2004: 56). Butler revises the distinction between governmentality and sovereignty. She understands governmentality as operating "through state and non-state institutions and discourses that are legitimated neither through direct elections nor through established authority" (Butler 2004: 52). As is demonstrated in the above examples, governmentality instead operates diffusely; furthermore, rather than replacing sovereignty, it relocates it, allowing for the suspension of the rule of law "in order to heighten the discretionary power of those who are asked to rely on their own judgment to decide fundamental matters of justice, life, and death" (Butler 2004: 54). The agents in question become petty sovereigns who can exercise authority on certain occasions and in certain matters without holding legitimate or absolute authority but through the suspension of the rule of law in particular cases. While Butler uses the specific example of this momentary and particularized authority in the case of decisions of indefinite detention, thus demonstrating the suspension of law, the mechanism can be understood more broadly. The diffusion of power into substate agents or specialized agents is visible within international and domestic politics. For instance, Roxanne Lynn Doty (2007) demonstrates that vigilantes on the Mexico–US border can be understood as "petty sovereigns" who suspend the rule of law. The role of substate or non-state agents is not confined only to adopting disseminated state power in domestic politics. Agents are not confined within a particular state and can diffuse power outside sovereign borders, thus making themselves relevant in international politics and demonstrating governmentality on an international scale.

Examination of governmentality as exercised over immigrants and non-citizen incomers can benefit from Butler's description of petty sovereigns, as the suspension of state law when it applies to non-citizens is an established practice. With regard to governmentality in state–citizen relations, Didier Bigo looks into threat construction mechanisms as a means of politicizing immigration debates. He looks at the dispersal of threat construction through three levels in order to explain the development of petty sovereigns in the area of border controls. As Bigo points out, "the professionals of politics … cannot channel the millions of individual decisions of border crossing" (Bigo 2005: 50). While the politicians have the will but not the capacity to act, that capacity is transferred to border agents and immigration officials who exercise localized sovereignty. Bigo looks in particular at the context of Schengen Europe, in which traditionally delineated frontiers have been undermined. Instead, there are "new technologies and new loci of controls in addition or in replacement of internal border controls" (Bigo 2005: 70). Examples of these include visa requirements (before appearance at the border), the right of refusal without explanation, carrier sanctions, and biometrics. Bigo describes the construction of fear and insecurity in the population as a mechanism of governmentality that speaks both to Butler's view of petty sovereigns and Aradau and colleagues' emphasis on the management of risk. Politicians themselves are incapacitated but act within this "discourse of truth" that migrants present an active threat, while the technologies of power incorporate additional actors who generate and perpetuate the discourse. Bigo characterizes these actors as security professionals, such as the military and the police—for whom immigrants present a national security threat—and "fear-mongers" who portray this threat to the population, such as the media (Bigo 2002). Thus the power is dispersed and resides within a variety of actors who each take a responsibilized role in the maintenance of national security, against incomers. The location of sovereignty then is upon the incomers who represent risk to the society and remain on the margins of or outside the social and political space, representing Agamben's spaces of exception at the border.

The concept of governmentality is used in studies of criminology, given that the penal system is often understood as a location of sovereignty within a system of governmentality, following Agamben's theorizing. For example, Pratt outlines the underlying liberal rationale that sees the penal system as a location of exception. The incarcerated criminal is understood to be responsible for his or her behavior, and the rationale governing the penal system shifts from one of rehabilitation and welfare toward one of punishment. This use of discipline represents sovereignty present within liberal governance: the disagreeable nature of imprisonment will encourage the prisoner to self-govern in the future. Programs such as the "three strikes" law enacted by several US states suggest that those individuals who demonstrate themselves as unable to self-govern ought to be subject to incarceration in order to protect the public (Pratt 1999). Thus sovereignty and governmentality coexist in different spaces and on different subjects yet within the liberal rationality of government.

Further to this, the coexistence of sovereignty and governmentality, or of disciplinary and relational power, can be seen in the global system, and offer insight in two ways. First, similar to the understanding within the bounds of a liberal state, states that are deemed incapable of self-governance are labeled "failed" and are subject to disciplinary power. This type of power can be seen as a manifestation of sovereignty, although it does not emanate from a hierarchical greater power but the greater power of the liberal rationale of governance (Neumann and Sending 2010). Understanding this as disciplinary power and sovereignty can offer insight into the mechanisms of global governance as they differ between the states where the assumption of modernity and the functioning of modern statehood holds, and those where this assumption does not: conditions Risse terms "limited statehood" (Risse, Chapter 49, this volume). However, Neumann and Sending offer a second insight into the role of sovereignty in global governmentality. Rather than understanding governmentality and sovereignty as co-existing in different spaces, they see them as mutually constitutive at the global level, in particular with regard to fragile states (Neumann and Sending 2010). For example, governmentality emerges after the state has proved capable of managing "in-house" wisely, to one where it interacts globally with the market as the reference point for governing (Hardt and Negri 2001; Neumann and Sending 2010). Consequently the capacity to manage in-house must be encouraged and globally oriented agencies such as the IMF and WB thus shift their attention from the economy to the state, with the aim of creating a sovereign unit capable of self-management (Neumann and Sending 2010). Thus two different understandings of sovereignty emerge. The first follows the understanding of sovereignty in the literature at the (liberal) state level and is associated with disciplinary power that functions in spaces outside the system of governmentality on those actors deemed incapable of self-governance. The second is the more benign understanding of sovereign states as self-governing units. For the state to be understood as a cohesive agent or subject in a system of governmentality, the second understanding of sovereignty is required. Thus the interaction and coexistence of sovereignty and governmentality is evident on two levels: through disciplinary power and policing, and through the capacity of the state to act as a unitary cohesive agent in the global system.

GOVERNMENTALITY AND CITIZENS

Governmentality can be used to demonstrate the interactions and relationship between the state and its citizens. Traditional assumptions regarding state sovereignty see citizens constrained by the rule of law because the state has a monopoly on the legitimate use of force. The notion of governmentality differs because, as detailed above, it represents a relationship with state authority that is internalized by the citizen through tactics of government. Governmental authorities provoke the citizen to act in a particular way within the bounds of acceptable, normalized, *regulated* behavior. This can be understood as *responsibilization*, in which the government consciously acts to construct the individual as calculating, prudent, and rational (Löwenheim 2007). This regulation is thus a self-regulation, a self-governance by the individual to scale their behavior "up" to the "standards" assumed within a field of governmentality. Put another way, responsibilized individuals are capable of assuming risk and acting within the boundaries of behavior established and maintained by the state through policy, and through the reproduction of societal norms. In other words, they are capable of self-governance. The responsibilized citizen retains this rationality when he or she is not within the territory and so arguably not subject to the law enforcement of the state in question. For example, state mechanisms affect the way in which individuals perceive their own security and this perception normalizes individuals into taking responsibility for their actions. The process can be seen to reflect a given political agenda of a state, or of particular political elites (Bigo 2002). The mechanism sees responsibility for particular action shifted from the state to the individual.

While governmentality offers insight into the changing state–citizen relations or role of sovereignty at the domestic level, it is useful at the level of global governance because the responsibilized individual remains outside state borders. This can be observed in Löwenheim's discussion of government-issued travel warnings. Travel warnings shift the responsibility for the decision to travel to certain locations that the state deems dangerous from the state to the individual. Responsibilization can be seen in the issuing of travel warnings and the subsequent actions of states with regards to those travelers who did not heed the warnings. The state shifts the responsibility for travel decisions to citizens. This is seen in the compensation given to victims of crime abroad. Governments such as the USA and the UK may give different amounts of compensation if a citizen has failed to heed a travel warning. Additionally, states may charge for evacuation procedures that might be required from a state against which a travel warning has been issued.

The tactics of the state are applied to the individual, channeling him or her to adapt the perception of the particular destination accordingly (whether the traveler assumes that the state view is accurate, or assumes that the state view is exaggerated). Travel warnings became common in the late 1990s and early 2000s and since then the use of travel warning information has expanded (Löwenheim 2007). This demonstrates a normalizing process whereby individual travelers accept the authoritative assertion of the state in travel decisions. Even if travelers are not deterred, an increasing number of travelers access travel warning websites and helplines, demonstrating that consideration of the information is becoming more common (Löwenheim 2007). Thus the normalization of the travel warning procedure is seen as it becomes a part of the normal travel process. This also reflects the tactics of the state as it places freedom of movement at the level of decision-making, rather than at legal border restrictions.

Bonelli (2005) observes a similar phenomenon of responsibilization in government tactics toward citizens with regards to crime. He looks at governmentality in the "management of fears." Bonelli points to the fear of crime being used to create space for technologies of power that can replace the postwar welfare state as the governmental institution to relieve insecurity among the population. He asserts that agency-based rational choice approaches to the study of crime posit that the delinquent is *"homo oeconomicus ... a rational being who chooses criminality according to a cost–benefit calculation"* (Bonelli 2005: 204). Therefore, the supposition is that "adolescents in the poor neighborhoods make an easy choice that is rational and consistent in a system of delinquent values" (Bonelli 2005: 204). The technology of power transfers the responsibility of the decision to partake in criminal behavior to the rational individual who has made a choice, rejecting the value of hard work in favor of delinquent values. The criminal is at least attributed with responsibility and the social causes of crime are disguised or perceived as irrelevant.

The concept of governmentality present in state–citizen relations also can be seen in the growing use of citizenship tests for those who are residing in a state and have the intention of becoming a citizen. This perception looks in particular at the process of the examination and the role of observation in creating disciplined conduct. The citizenship tests function to subjectivize citizens to state authority relatively quickly, reflecting Foucault's conception of the mechanism of examination, which functions as "(i) a sign of authority, (ii) a technology used to naturalize authority, and (iii) as a disciplinary tool" (Löwenheim and Gazit 2009: 149). With regard to governmentality, this serves as a normalizing instrument, through exposure to the content of the examination that schools the examinee in how to behave within the given society he or she wants to enter. The citizenship tests are, in some cases, voluntary, in that individuals who want to become citizens seek to take them, and in all cases the potential citizens acquiesce to the tests as opposed to being compelled to take them in a controlled environment. Residence in a state does not depend on passing the test but certain benefits of full citizenship do. Thus, in choosing to seek citizenship and take the test, the examinees can be seen to engage with the process of self-optimization that is inherent in governmentality (Foucault 1991), a process whereby individuals come to be "moral beings" (Foucault 1991: 91). Additionally, the individual seeking citizenship becomes an examinee who is under the gaze of the governmental authorities. As Löwenheim and Gazit point out, the process of the examination allows the examiner to intervene into the life of the examinee, giving recommendations and instructions and treating certain aspects of behavior as abnormalities or malfunctions (Löwenheim and Gazit 2009: 159). It is claimed that these interventions are done to the people "for their own good," which demonstrates power exercised over them to change behavior (Löwenheim and Gazit 2009: 152, citing Hanson 1994). This can be seen to work on the potential citizen in the same way that travel warnings responsibilize citizens and extend power over them even when they are not within the national territory.

The responsibilization of potential citizens is also seen in the interaction between the state and asylum seekers. Christie and Sidhu (2006) observe asylum processes in Australia, with particular attention toward the education of children. They find that asylum seekers who are minors are detained and are not given access to education as a result of the technologies of management applied to asylum seekers, which in Australia includes mandatory detention for all people who arrive "illegally" (Christie and Sidhu 2006). The authors observe regulations and rationalities governing asylum seekers and the resultant normalization of illiberal and repressive practices, particularly as applied to those asylum seekers who arrive by boat and are subject to stigmatization and social exclusion (Christie and Sidhu 2006). This can be understood to spread the expectation of self-governance outside state borders, as detention is applied on entry to the state, which suggests that deviance and the inability to self-govern is assumed. Furthermore, Squire refers to the program of dispersal in Britain, where asylum seekers are placed in particular locations throughout a state by the government. In this process, asylum seekers are warned that they are responsible for complying with state directives in pursuing their asylum claim. In Britain asylum seekers are warned that if they fail to travel to the location to which the National Asylum Support Services (NASS) directs them, all support will be withdrawn and they will be expelled from their current accommodation. Additionally, the NASS expends considerable funds in observing asylum seekers in their accommodations, verifying that they are living there and not housing additional people (Squire 2009: 126). Thus, asylum seekers are not fully responsibilized, but are subjectivized under relations of power and authority established by the state. The asylum seeker must submit to this authority in order to continue to receive benefits. If an asylum seeker does not comply, the authorities withdraw their responsibility of care.

Conclusion

In conclusion, governmentality offers a conceptual understanding of global governance that is comprised of tactics that normalize behavior and responsibilize actors. This force operates on the domestic level in liberal states and can be observed at the global level, representing liberalism as a higher power than the sovereign state. Thus, it confounds traditional assumptions of the international state system as anarchic; states, substate actors, and individuals are compelled to act in a particular way despite there being no single hierarchical agent of force. Power inherent in discourses of truth represents the force that can compel particular action, and punish deviant behavior.

Governmentality, as the tactics of governance, is operative on different actors at different levels and in different jurisdictions. Citizens are responsibilized to act in accordance with the state's needs, but the power of governmentality is distinct from sovereign force. Individuals remain subject to the power of their state of citizenship even when they are outside its territory. Individuals who seek to become citizens submit to beliefs of what is normal and what is deviant behavior and are compelled to adjust their behavior accordingly. Substate actors can induce particular behavior in states, as seen in the discourses of truth generated with regard to immigration and, more significantly, the use of scales of democracy. In this case the state, conventionally understood as the highest sovereign authority in the neoliberal system, changes its behavior subject to both non-state actors and hegemonic powers. This may be the clearest example of governmentality at the international level, showing it to be a salient force that should be taken into account in discussions regarding the development and potential growth of global governance.

References

Agamben, G. 1998. *Homo Sacer: Sovereign Power and Bare Life*, trans. D. Heller-Roazen. Stanford, CA: Stanford University Press.

Agamben, G. 2000. *Means Without End: Notes on Politics*, trans. V. Binetti and C. Casarino. Minneapolis, MN: University of Minnesota Press.

Amoore, L. 2006 Biometric borders: Governing mobility in the war on terror. *Political Geography* 25: 336–351.

Aradau, C., Lobo-Guerrero, L. and van Muster, R. 2008. Security, technologies of risk, and the political: Guest editors' introduction. *Security Dialogue* 39: 147–154.

Avari, S. 2004. Travel advisory. *Advisor's Edge* 7: 29–32.

Bevir, M. and Hall, I. 2011. Global governance. In M. Bevir (ed.), *The Sage Handbook of Governance*. Berkeley, CA: Sage, 352–366.

Bigo, D. 2002. Security and immigration: Toward a critique of the governmentality of unease. *Alternatives* 27: 63–92.

Bigo, D. 2005. Frontier controls in the European Union: Who is in control? In D. Bigo and E. Guild (eds.), *Controlling Frontiers: Free Movement into and within Europe*. Burlington, VT: Ashgate, 49–99.

Bigo, D. and Guild, E. 2005. (eds.) *Controlling Frontiers: Free Movement into and within Europe*. Burlington, VT: Ashgate.

Bonelli, L. 2005. The control of the enemy within? Police intelligence in the French suburbs (banlieues) and its relevance for globalization. In D. Bigo and E. Guild (eds.), *Controlling Frontiers: Free Movement into and within Europe*. Burlington, VT: Ashgate 193–208.

Budz, M. 2009. A heterotopian analysis of maritime refugee incidents. *International Political Sociology* 3:18–35.

Butler, J. 2004. *Precarious Life: The Powers of Mourning and Violence*. London and New York: Verso.

Christie, P. and Sidhu, R. 2006. Governmentality and "fearless speech": Framing the education of asylum seeker and refugee children in Australia. *Oxford Review of Education* 32: 449–465.

Dean, M. 2010 *Governmentality: Power and Rule in Modern Society*. London: Sage.

De Boever, A. 2009. Agamben and Marx: Sovereignty, governmentality, economy. *Law and Critique* 20: 259–270.

Doty, R. L. 2007. States of exception on the Mexico–U.S. Border: Security, "decisions" and civilian border patrols. *International Political Sociology* 1: 113–127.

Foreign Affairs and International Trade Canada. 2006. Available at http://www.tbs-sct.gc.ca/dpr-rmr/2006-2007/inst/ext/ext03-eng.asp (accessed 19 September 2011).

Foucault, M. 1991 Governmentality. In G. Burchell, C. Gordon, and P. Miller (eds.), *The Foucault Effect*. Chicago: University of Chicago Press, 87–104.

Foucault, M. 2001 *The Hermaneutics of the Subject: Lectures at the Collège de France 1981–1982*, trans. G. Burchell. New York: Picador.

Hanson, F. A. 1994. *Testing Testing: Social Consequences of the Examined Life*. Berkeley, CA: University of California Press.

Hardt, M. and Negri, A. 2001. *Empire*. Cambridge, MA: Harvard University Press.

Held, D. and McGrew, A. (eds.) 2002. *The Global Transformation Reader*. London: Polity.

Hindess, B. 2000. Citizenship in the international management of populations. *American Behavioural Scientist* 43: 1486–1497.

Jessop, B. 2011. Metagovernance. In M. Bevir and I. Hall (eds.), *The Sage Handbook of Governance*. Berkeley, CA: Sage, 106–123.

Larner, W. 2000. Neoliberalism: Policy, ideology, governmentality. *Studies in Political Economy* 63: 5–25.

Levi-Faur, D. 2005. The global diffusion of regulatory capitalism. *Annals of the American Academy of Political and Social Science* 598: 12–32.

Löwenheim, O. 2007. The responsibility to responsibilize: Foreign offices and the issuing of travel warnings. *International Political Sociology* 1: 203–221.

Löwenheim, O. 2008. Examining the state: A Foucauldian perspective on international "governance indicators." *Third World Quarterly* 29: 255–274.

Löwenheim, O. and Gazit, O. 2009. Power and examination: A critique of citizenship tests. *Security Dialogue* 40: 145–167.

Neumann, I. B. and Sending, O. J. 2010. *Governing the Global Polity: Practice, Mentality, Rationality.* Ann Arbor, MI: University of Michigan Press.

Owens, P. 2009. Reclaiming "bare life"? Against Agamben on refugees. *International Relations* 23: 567–582.

Pratt, J. 1999. Governmentality, neoliberalism, and dangerousness. In R. Smandych, *Governable Places: Readings on Governmentality and Crime Control.* London and Brookfield, VT: Ashgate, 133–162.

Risse, T. 2002 Transnational actors and world politics. In W. Carlsnaes, T. Risse, and B. Simmons (eds.), *Handbook of International Relations.* London: Sage, 225–274.

Rose, N. and Miller, P. 1992. Political power beyond the state: Problematic of government. *The British Journal of Sociology* 43: 173–205.

Salter, M. B. 2008. Risk, quantification, and aviation security. *Security Dialogue, Special Issue on Security, Technologies of Risk and the Political* 39: 243–265.

Sassen, S. 2006 *Territory, Authority, Rights: From Medieval to Global Assemblages.* Princeton, NJ: Princeton University Press.

Smandych, R. 1999. *Governable Places: Readings on Governmentality and Crime Control.* London and Brookfield, VT: Ashgate.

Squire, V. 2009. *The Exclusionary Politics of Asylum.* New York: Palgrave Macmillan.

Stenson, K. 1999. Crime control, governmentality, and sovereignty. In R. Smandych, *Governable Places: Readings on Governmentality and Crime Control.* London and Brookfield, VT: Ashgate, 45–74.

Tunnah, H. 2005 Insurer says no to Bali terror cover. *The New Zealand Herald*, 8 October.

CHAPTER 51

GLOBAL GOVERNANCE AS MULTI-LEVEL GOVERNANCE

MICHAEL ZÜRN*

1. INTRODUCTION

GLOBAL *governance refers to the entirety of regulations put forward with reference to solving specific denationalized and deregionalized problems or providing transnational common goods.* The entirety of regulations includes the substantial norms, rules, and programs, the processes by which norms, rules, and programs are adapted, monitored, and enforced, as well as the structures in which they operate. The term governance thus encompasses structures, processes, and policy content, which the common distinction between policy, polity, and politics may help to disentangle. Governance activities are justified with reference to the common good, but they do not necessarily serve it. Global governance points to those sets of regulations that address denationalized problems, that is, problems which reach beyond national borders. While government refers to one public actor, governance describes an activity independent of the numbers and kinds of actors carrying it out.

This concept of global governance has two important implications. To begin with, by distinguishing governance structure from contents and actors, it becomes obvious that governance beyond the nation-state is possible, despite the absence of a central authority or a "world state" equipped with a legitimate monopoly of the use of force (Rosenau 1992). In the absence of a world state or at least an empire with a global reach, global governance cannot take on the form of governance by government. Governance with (many) governments such as we see it in intergovernmental institutions, or governance without government as in the case of transnational institutions are, however, conceivable alternatives that are extensively used on the level beyond the nation-state. Second, by requiring a common goods-oriented justification of norms and rules, the concept of global governance also refers to a certain quality of international regulation.

Accordingly, international cooperation includes more than just simple coordination between states to achieve a *modus vivendi* of interaction. Rather, international regulatory governance often aims actively at achieving normatively laden political goals when handling common problems of the international community. In this sense, governance presupposes some common interests and goal orientations beyond the nation-state, at least in a rudimentary form, without—of course—denying the persistence of fundamental conflicts.

Conceptualized this way, global governance is not necessarily identical with multi-level governance. In order to speak of global governance as "multi-level" two additional conditions have to be met. First, the global level must possess some authority of its own. It must be more than just intergovernmental coordination with no delegation of powers to spheres outside the member states. As long as international relations are structured by the consensus principle, according to which states only comply with what they have agreed to, it does not make sense to speak of multi-level governance. Second, the global level must be part of a system that is characterized by the interplay of different levels rather than works independently from other governance levels. Before we can speak of a multi-level governance system, it thus needs to be shown that the system includes some form of division of labor. The whole notion of a multi-level governance system is based on the idea that segmentary differentiation of similar states, each of which controls a certain territorially defined part of the world, gets replaced by a concept that is at least to some extent characterized by functional and stratificatory differentiation.

Against this conceptual backdrop, I want to argue that global governance can indeed be described as a specific form of multi-level governance. In doing so, three issues will be tackled in the ensuing sections. It is argued first that political institutions on the global level today possess a significant level of authority and that those international institutions only achieve their effect by interacting with other political levels. Next, the specific features of global multi-level governance compared to other national or regional multi-level governance systems are discussed. Finally, the built-in deficiencies of such a system are examined.

2. POLITICAL AUTHORITY BEYOND THE NATION-STATE

The traditional, Westphalian notion of sovereignty emphasized the principle of nonintervention into domestic affairs and—closely related—the consensus principle. This notion involved three norms: first, that the ruler of a state exercises sole authority over the territory of that state; second, that all states are judicially equal; and third, that state parties are not subject to any law other than their own. In this view, international institutions are considered as instruments of the territorial state, without possessing political authority in their own right (Kahler 2004).

The last two to three decades, however, brought changes that undermined Westphalian sovereignty. Most importantly, *supranationalization* describes a process in which international institutions developed procedures that contradict the consensus principle and the principle of nonintervention. In this way, some international norms and rules create obligations for national governments to take measures even when they have not agreed to do so. Supranationalization thus leads to political authority beyond the nation-state (cf. also Kahler and Lake 2009: 246; Rittberger and Nettesheim 2008: 3). "International institutions have authority *when states recognize in principle or in practice, their ability to make...binding decisions on matters relating to a state's domestic jurisdiction, even if those decisions are contrary to a state's own policies and preferences*" (Cooper et al. 2008: 505). Such a political authority requires legitimation.[1]

Political authority beyond the nation-state does not necessarily require autonomous international organizations. Both international institutions with an international organization that has been delegated autonomous power to make decisions (e.g. the International Criminal Court) and international institutions without such a formal delegation of power (e.g. majority decisions in the United Nations Security Council) can possess authority in the defined sense. In the former case, one can speak of delegated authority; the latter is a case of pooled authority (Moravcsik 1998: 67; Hawkins et al. 2006). The authority of international institutions thus points to another feature other than the autonomy of international organizations.

What evidence is there that the described changes in international relations governance have indeed come about? A preliminary indicator for this dynamic is the simple increase in the number of international agreements concluded. For example, the number of United Nations (UN) registered international agreements grew from a total of 8,776 treaties in 1960 to 63,419 as of 25 March 2010. If we consider only the most important multilateral agreements officially drawn up and countersigned in the UN, then we obtain a comparable level of growth, namely, from 942 such agreements in 1969 to 6,154 by 2010.[2] Underlying this increase is a corresponding growth in the issue areas to be dealt with by international institutions. For a long time, security issues and economic relations have dominated as the focal points of international cooperation; today, however, international institutions deal with a much broader range of issue areas.

In addition to the growing quantity and extended range of international agreements, a second indicator can be seen in the new, authority-generating quality of international institutions at different phases of the policy cycle. A policy cycle is a sequence of distinct phases in the life-course of a regulation. At the international level, we can differentiate between the following phases: agenda-setting—decision-making—implementation/rule interpretation—monitoring—enforcement—evaluation/new agenda-setting (see e.g. Abbott and Snidal 2009: 63).

Focusing, first, on the *negotiation* or *decision phase*, we can observe an increase of majoritarian decision-making in international institutions. There is a growing need for regulation at international level and growing demands on international institutions to accommodate this need. Majoritarian decision-making increases the ability of international institutions to act, by canceling the vetoes of individual states and overcoming blockades. Today, roughly two-thirds of all international organizations with the participation of at least one great power have the possibility to decide by majority (see Blake and Payton 2008). Even if decision by majority is employed far less often than could be, it exerts pressure on veto players and increases their readiness to seek compromise. The formal possibility of international institutions implementing decisions by majority, in connection with a *de facto* preference of states for consensus decision-making, represents an attempt to balance the contradictory aims of maintaining international institutions' ability to act and fostering states' readiness to implement measures decided upon. The result of seeking such a balance is that the probability of individual states implementing environmental measures, even when doing so runs counter to those states' original will or intent, increases.

Monitoring and verification of international rules are, likewise, increasingly carried out by actors who are not directly under the control of states. In general, the need for monitoring is greater if international norms no longer just apply to the borders between countries but, instead, begin to regulate activities within the boundaries of sovereign territories. The monitoring of customs regulations, for instance, which occurs at state borders, is a comparatively simple task. Monitoring to prevent a state from subsidizing its own national enterprises, on the other hand, is more difficult because this involves *behind-the-border* issues. Mutual observation by the states party to an agreement is, in such cases, often not sufficient to guarantee compliance. Thus, the need for independent actors who process information on treaty compliance and make it available is steadily growing. Such information could be provided by autonomous organizations established as part of a treaty regime's safeguards. Two prominent examples of such organizations are the International Monetary Fund (IMF) (for the global financial system) and the International Atomic Energy Agency (IAEA) (for the Nuclear Nonproliferation Treaty) (Dai 2007: 50–53). In addition to such bodies, the role of international secretariats in regulatory monitoring has increased notably in recent years (see Siebenhüner and Biermann 2009).

Equally important in this regard is the growing significance of transnational non-governmental organizations (NGOs). Transnational NGOs collaborate with societal actors who have been negatively impacted by rule violations. Together they undertake informal, independent regulatory monitoring. For example, the monitoring of internationally standardized human rights has long since been transferred informally to human rights organizations like Human Rights Watch. The proliferation of transnational NGOs accredited by the United Nations' Economic and Social Council (ECOSOC) can thus be taken as an indicator for this development. In 1948, only fifty NGOs were approved by ECOSOC; by 1996, this number had climbed to 1041; and in 2009 it had reached no less than 3,287.[3]

Regarding disputed cases of *rule interpretation*, we find that there has been a significant increase in international judicial bodies. To the extent that the quantity of international obligations has grown, so, too, have the number of collisions between international and national regulations, and the number of conflicts between different international regulations. The establishment of court-like proceedings is one possibility for dealing with such problems. At the same time, however, this would lead to a situation where states would be, by and large, stripped of their authority to interpret rules. For example, the World Trade Organization's Dispute Settlement Body (WTO–DSB) decides matters of controversy over the application of the rules in international trade. A judgment by the Dispute Settlement Body can only be overturned by a unanimous vote of all WTO member states. In 1960, there were, worldwide, only twenty-seven quasi-judicial bodies; by 2004, this number had grown to ninety-seven. If we narrow the definition and include only those bodies that meet all of the prerequisites for formal judicial proceedings, then only five such bodies existed worldwide in 1960, climbing to twenty-eight by 2004.[4]

Concerning *rule enforcement*, we can observe an increased readiness to levy material sanctions against violators. *Jus cogens* (independent and binding international law, not requiring the consent of states) in the meantime reaches beyond the prohibition of wars of aggression, including *inter alia* the prohibition of crimes against humanity, genocide, and apartheid. Furthermore, especially since 1989, the international community has increasingly begun to respond to cases of gross violation of human rights with military force and economic sanctions (Binder 2009: 340). After 1989, in some cases (like Kosovo or East Timor) the UN even set up transitional administrations with far-reaching executive, legislative, and judicial powers (Caplan 2004). But developments of this sort are not limited just to the area of security policy. For instance, for a good two decades, the World Bank (WB) has increasingly employed conditional loans—that is, loans which are tied to the recipient state fulfilling certain conditions, like carrying out specific economic or political reforms (Mosley, Harrigan, and Toye 1995).

Finally, other actors have begun to compete with states in the field of *policy evaluation and related agenda-setting*. The set of organizations that evaluate the effectiveness of existing regulations and place new problem areas on the international agenda has widened in accordance with the extent to which the addressees of international regulation have become societal actors. Again, international secretariats and transnational NGOs are the actors who have increasingly taken up these governance functions. In conjunction with this tendency, so-called *knowledge bodies* affiliated with the secretariats of international organizations, like the Intergovernmental Panel for Climate Change (IPCC), have gained in importance. To a comparable extent, those NGOs that identify international problems and call for international regulation have also clearly taken on greater significance. The role of Transparency International in the development of the Anti-Bribery Convention (see Metzges 2006) is just one example. In any case, the normative pressure resulting from the authority of such knowledge bodies and agenda-setting actors weakens the ability of individual governments to oppose international norm development processes (see Meyer 2005).

Overall, a dense network of international and transnational institutions of unprecedented quality and quantity has developed in recent decades. Many of these new institutions are far more intrusive than conventional international institutions. They can circumvent the resistance of most governments *via* majoritarian decision-making, or by dispute settlement procedures through the interaction of monitoring agencies with transnational society, and by dominating the process of knowledge interpretation in some fields. With the—most often consensual—decision to install international institutions with such features, state parties become subject to a law other than their own, to which they have either not agreed upon (mission creep) or do not agree any more (costly exit option). Given the extent of the intrusion of these new international institutions into the affairs of national societies, the notion of "delegated, and therefore controlled authority" no longer holds.[5] At least in some issue areas, the global level has achieved a certain degree of authority and has thus partially replaced the consensus principle of the traditional international system.

3. FUNCTIONAL DIFFERENTIATION IN GLOBAL GOVERNANCE

The rise of political authority beyond the nation-state should, however, by no means be read as an indication of the demise of the nation-state. First, the developments described here apply only to denationalized issue areas. Second, it is hard to see how governance goals can be achieved without the nation-state, even in strongly denationalized issue areas. For instance, the elimination of the problems relating to global financial markets, organized crime, or global environmental risks is hardly conceivable without nation-states. For the implementation of policies, especially, the nation-state seems to be indispensable. This is due to its control of resources based on its legal monopoly on the use of force and its capacity to raise taxes. Third, the nation-state remains, with respect to many issues, the first point of address for political demands, even in highly denationalized issue areas. Whereas transnational NGOs and even traditional interest groups increasingly address international institutions directly with their political demands, the nation-state remains, in this respect, the default option. Nation-states still aggregate territorial interests and put them forward in international negotiations.

The concept of multi-level governance promises to better grasp the complex arrangements of governing institutions than the concept of sovereign states does (see Bache, Chapter 44, this volume for an exploration of the term multi-level governance with respect to the European Union (EU)).[6] In such a multi-level constellation, nation-states will not relinquish their resources such as monopoly on the use of force or the right to exact taxes in a given territory. Nevertheless, while the nation-state will play a significant role in multi-level governance, it will no longer be the paramount political institution able to perform all functions, but only one among others carrying out some of these tasks (Zürn and Leibfried 2005). The nation-state has lost its monopoly on political authority. The state remains pivotal, however, increasingly playing the role of an authority manager (Genschel and Zangl 2008).

In denationalized issue areas, effective and legitimate governance depends on the interplay of different political levels. It often requires transnational recognition of problems, decision-making in global forums, and the implementation of these decisions at the national level. Global governance thus does not run parallel to other levels of governance; rather, it is constituted by the interplay of different levels and organizations, whereby each level and organization cannot work unilaterally. In this sense, the Westphalian system of segmentary differentiation has transformed into a multi-level entity characterized by functional differentiation.[7]

Each of these levels exercises authority, that is, they can make decisions and take measures in a given issue area, which cannot be unilaterally reversed by other levels without violating accepted governance procedures. Authority beyond the nation-state means that some governance tasks are taken over on the supranational or transnational level and cannot be hindered in this by single states affected by these decisions and measures. Authority on the lower level means that some governance tasks can be carried out by decentralized units without a legitimate possibility for the higher levels to intervene. If more than one level exhibits authority, then there is a "need to coordinate decisions between different levels" and one can thus speak of multi-level governance (Benz 2004).

4. FEATURES OF GLOBAL MULTI-LEVEL GOVERNANCE

There are, however, different types of multi-level governance (Hooghe and Marks 2010; Scharpf 2009). Global multi-level governance is different from both unitary federal political systems (Scharpf, Reissert, and Schnabel 1976) and the European multi-level system (Marks et al. 1996; Jachtenfuchs and Kohler-Koch 1996; see also Bache, Chapter 44, this volume). The specific features of global multi-level governance point simultaneously to the structural deficiencies of global governance.

All these three types of multi-level governance are characterized by a *two-stage implementation* process.[8] In all these cases, norms and rules developed by the higher level will be mostly implemented by decentralized units. An international or European regulation asking, for instance, for a reduction of emissions, needs to be implemented by national governments and administrations. And all laws legislated, for instance by the government of the Federal Republic of Germany, will be implemented by the decentralized state administrations.

With respect to *legitimation processes*, significant differences among these three multi-level systems can be observed. In a unitary federal system, there is a direct relationship between the societal addressees of a regulation and the central decision-making units. The government and the parliament are directly accountable to the citizens. They are elected by the citizens and address them directly when justifying laws and measures. Here we can speak of a direct, or one-stage, legitimation process. In the European multi-level system, any direct contact between the central decision units and the citizens is limited. Whereas elections to the European Parliament constitute a direct relationship, other—more important—decision units such as the Commission and the Council are, as a collective, not directly accountable. This is even less so, when it comes to international institutions. The executive board of the World Bank, for example, does not turn directly to the affected people when justifying their decisions; and, in turn, the people do not have many possibilities to sanction the board directly. They normally need to take a detour through their national governments.

Multi-level governance with such a two-stage legitimation process has mainly developed beyond the nation-state. In these cases, societal actors confer legitimacy to constituent members of the system, which interact with each other to constitute the higher level beyond the nation-state. In return, almost any decision taken at the higher level needs to be organized and implemented through the lower levels. Citizens of nation-states therefore rarely have direct contact with the higher levels of multi-level governance systems, which reach beyond the nation-state.[9]

In addition, global multi-level governance differs with respect to the *coordination of different policies and societal subsystems*. Since regulations always produce effects in other issue areas beyond the ones to which they are directed, governance also involves the coordination of different policies which have been formulated on the same level or at different levels. In unitary federalism, coordination takes place via formal procedures on the side of central decision-makers, for instance, via Cabinet rules or supreme courts, and through public debate on the side of the addressees of a regulation. Public debates are characterized by an exchange of opinions in which views and positions are not just issued, but a discourse among competing claims occurs. *Broad* public debate refers to an ideal-typical democratic discourse among citizens of a given political community about vital political issues of general interest in mass media such as newspapers, radio, and television. Broad publics often debate conflicting goals and thus the coordination of different sectors. Sectoral publics, in turn, comprise formal and informal groups generated through functional differentiation, which devote themselves to specific issues. Here, the medium of interaction is often the Internet, specialized press, or personal exchanges or communications at conferences and meetings (Zürn and Neyer 2005: 201). Sectoral publics by definition are not able to mediate intersectoral conflicts.

Regarding coordination, the EU can be described as a multi-issue arrangement with a limited number of nonoverlapping jurisdictional boundaries and some built-in coordination mechanisms such as the Commission and the Council. Such a governance structure follows a system-wide architecture that is relatively stable and clearly public in character. Whereas broad public debate is possible, such debates occur most frequently at the constituent member level and are therefore often fragmented. They nevertheless provide for some policy coordination through the expression of a minimal sense of a polity.[10]

By contrast, global multi-level governance describes a complex and fluid patchwork of overlapping jurisdictions. In these cases, each issue area has developed its own norms and rules, and the membership varies from issue area to issue area. The membership of the Organisation for Economic Co-operation and Development (OECD), for instance, is significantly different from the WTO. Debates and discourses take place almost exclusively within sectoral publics that do not address the side effects of certain measures for other issue areas. In addition, there are no constitutionalized mechanisms for the coordination of different issue-area-specific regimes; at best, informal mechanisms exist. Thus, global multi-level governance stands out due to a very loose coupling of different issue areas.

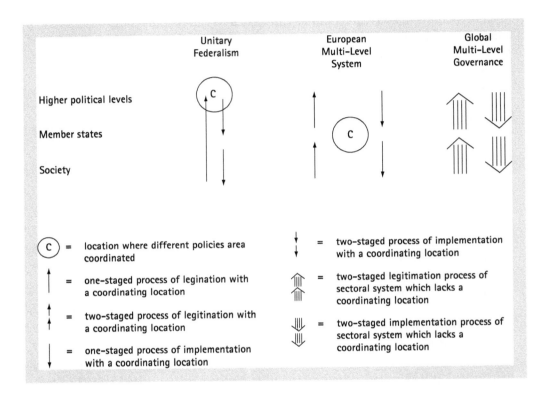

Types / MLG Features	Unitary Federalism	EU MLG System	Global Governance
Implementation	2-staged	2-staged	2-staged
Legitimation	1-staged	1-staged/2-staged	2-staged
Coordination	Centralized	Decentralized	Missing/rudimentary

FIGURE 51.1 Three types of multi-level arrangements.

5. DEFICIENCIES OF GLOBAL MULTI-LEVEL GOVERNANCE

From the specific features of global multi-level governance, we now can derive some conjectures about structural deficiencies. First, global multi-level governance is permanently confronted with a *significant likelihood of non-compliance*. While many consider the legitimate monopoly on the use of force as a necessary prerequisite for compliance, the case of the EU demonstrates that alternative mechanisms such as legitimacy, legalization, and nonhierarchical enforcement can be used to successfully induce sufficient levels of compliance (Tallberg 2002; Zürn and Joerges 2005). All of the alternatives mentioned for ensuring compliance depend, however, on specific conditions of scope, which are not regularly given on the global level. The appeal to legitimacy grounded in law-like procedures depends on the willingness of a non-compliant actor to be responsive to good reason and concerns of legitimacy. In cases of nonhierarchical enforcement mechanisms, the enforcing actors need to be willing to bear the costs of enforcement, and the addressees of sanctions and blame need to be vulnerable to such strategies. Obviously, these conditions do not always hold on the global level. As a result global multi-level governance is inherently selective vis-à-vis the implementation of norms and rules. The selectivity of interventions authorized by the United Nations Security Council illustrates the point (Binder 2009).

In addition, global multi-level governance produces specific *legitimation problems*. As long as the intergovernmental level was restricted to merely developing a *modus vivendi* of interaction, requiring the consent of each member state, the two-stage process of legitimation was sufficient. The decisions taken on the level beyond the constituent members were legitimated through the legitimacy of their representatives. With the rise of a multi-level system and the authority of international institutions undermining the consensus principle, this has changed. There is an increasing need to legitimate decisions more directly.

Free elections, discursive will formation, party systems favoring those parties that represent a broad range of interests, and majority decision-making are mechanisms that made the political participation of broad segments of the public possible in the territorial state, and through which legitimacy was transferred to the central decision bodies. Only through these mechanisms has it been possible to strengthen and broaden the public interest orientation of democratic nation-states during the nineteenth and twentieth centuries. Beyond the nation-state such mechanisms are, to a large extent, lacking.

There are two developments which can be seen as institutional responses to the deficits of the two-stage legitimation process. First, there is the rising number and importance of transnational NGOs—that is, societal groups directly influencing international decisions by arguing mainly in terms of the global common good (as opposed to member interests). NGOs are an important element of sectoral publics, which help to directly connect the global level of regulation with the societal addressees of the regulations. In this way, the two-stage legitimation process gets informally complemented with a direct link.

Second, decision-making in global networks often emphasizes consensus beyond the point that formal procedures require. Even when majority decisions are possible, real-world negotiations seek consensus. Adjudication mechanisms also take great care to hear all addressees and to strike a compromise if possible. There are very few direct interventions at the global level without prior consultation at the constituent member level. In this sense, the system is more autonomy-preserving than some formal rules seem to suggest.[11]

However, this comes at a cost. Given this inclusive and consensual orientation of multi-level arrangements, it can be expected that global multi-level governance will rarely lead to redistributive or strongly interventionist measures. To the extent that market-making and compatible regulations are more easily achieved consensually than are market-correcting policies (Streeck 1995), a liberalizing bias is introduced into global governance. In any case, it means that global multi-level governance tends to be slow and hardly able to take decisive steps.

The *lack of a central place for the coordination of different policies* points to a third deficiency in global multi-level governance. Global governance does not have a central government that is responsible for the coordination of different policies. Moreover, one of the major functions of a broad public—namely, to decide in cases of goal conflicts between different sectors such as growth and clean environment, or security and freedom—cannot be fulfilled by sectoral publics which, by definition, are tied exclusively to either growth, environmental protection, security, or freedom. Given the functional and to some extent technocratic limits of such sectoral publics, there is a tendency to neglect the effects of regulations on other societal subsystems that are not part of the decision networks.

Against this background, the global multi-level governance system has—again informally—produced some substitute institutions that sometimes seem to assume such a coordinating role. The UN Security Council in particular has aspired to such a role by deciding on all those issues in which the goal of peace and the protection of human rights seem to contradict each other. Also, the G8/20 seem to define themselves as central coordinators by giving other international institutions a sense of direction, and by identifying issues and assigning the governance of those issues to specific international institutions.[12] These attempts, however, have remained limited. Moreover, they generate resistance on the side of many other actors, because membership in these institutions is not only restricted, but highly exclusive. The members of these institutions are self-nominated in the role as coordinators, and lack authorization to act in this way.

All three mechanisms available for coordination between different sectors and levels—the UN Security Council, the G8/20, and the dispute settlement bodies—share two features. First, they are completely detached from societies. There are no formal and hardly any informal channels available through which societal actors can make these institutions responsive to their demands. Moreover, these institutions were not created for the purpose of coordination. They are probably the most emergent elements of an emergent order. Global governance therefore is troubled by a strange lack of subjects: something happens, but no one has done it (Offe 2008). If no one governs, however, no one can be made responsible. This lack of accountability in the global multi-level governance system is another deficiency, which affects its ability to gain social acceptance.

6. CONCLUSIONS

Global governance can be described and fruitfully analyzed as a multi-level governance system. The global level contains a sufficient degree of authority, and the interaction between levels is functionally differentiated. In this way, the rise of global multi-level governance seems to be the logical response to the process of societal denationalization.

The construction principles of global multi-level governance differ, however, from other multi-level systems. It is those specific features—the lack of direct relationships between the higher level and the societies of the constituent members, and the lack of a location for the coordination of the policies—which cause the major deficits in global governance, namely, compliance problems, legitimacy problems, and unrestricted sectoral externalities. Two questions directly follow from this: Do these observations reflect structural deficits in multi-level systems of governance, or do they represent problems of transformation? And what can be done about this? Being skeptical about structural explanations and believing in the importance of social reflectivity, I tend to believe that civil society and public interests will in the long run find ways to bind multi-level governance more closely to the attainment of the common good. There are increasing signs that the institutions of global multi-level governance are becoming politicized (see Zürn and Ecker-Ehrhardt 2011). People and societal actors are beginning to bring transnational and international issues which were previously handled by mainly administrative or technocratic bodies into the public realm. International institutions are confronted with more societal resistance than ever, but they are also used more often by interest groups and non-governmental institutions. They are increasingly judged by political criteria such as legitimacy and fairness, in addition to efficiency and functionality—the yardstick of international affairs so far. In this sense, the future is open, as it has always been. If so, one of the most important tasks will certainly be to investigate the ways in which and the extent to which new ideas and intelligent institutional designs that help to avoid the inadequate attainment of governance goals in global multi-level governance can be developed.

NOTES

* This contribution builds on Zürn (2010). I would like to thank Jack Donelly and Sonja Wälti for most helpful comments on an earlier version.
1. *Transnationalization of governance* refers to a process in which transnational non-state actors develop political regulations and activities without being formally authorized by

states. Such regulations are based on the principle of self-governance and create *private authority* (cf. Cutler, Haufler, and Porter 1999; Biersteker and Hall 2002). Examples are *codes of conduct*, which are agreed upon between multinational corporations (MNCs) and possibly contain obligations not liked by all the governments affected by them (cf. Scherer and Palazzo 2008). The informal adoption of functions through NGOs within international institutions—for example, Amnesty International's role as primary monitoring agency in the human rights regime—is another case of transnationalization. Transnationalization can lead as well to *de facto* circumvention of the consensus and nonintervention principle. For the purposes of this chapter, I will focus on supranationalization, however.

2. See http://treaties.un.org/Pages/Home.aspx?lang=en.

3. See http://esango.un.org/paperless/content/E2009INF4.pdf.

4. See http://www.pict-pcti.org/matrix/matrixintro.html; see also Alter (2009).

5. See also Haftel and Thompson (2006) who define the independence of international organizations as the absence of complete control by other actors, and consider autonomy, together with neutrality and the delegation of authority, as constitutive elements.

6. Arguably, the arrangement is—given the parallel process of supranationalization and transnationalization—better described as multi-level and multi-actor governance, since on each of the levels, different actors—public ones and private ones—independent of each other are relevant. In this contribution, the conceptual focus is on the interplay of different levels (each of them consisting of more than one actor), which makes it possible to use the simpler, yet still not very elegant term, multi-level governance.

7. Functional differentiation as used here refers merely to the assignment of specific roles within—to use the language of Luhmann—the societal subsystem "politics." Functional differentiation writ large means, according to Luhmann, that different societal subsystems work more or less independently of each other. Arguably, there is, however, a close connection between these two forms of functional differentiation.

8. Dualist federal systems—such as the one in the United States before the New Deal—are different in this respect. In dualist—as opposed to unitary—federal systems, two completely developed governance systems operate—at least in the ideal world—in parallel. They take full responsibility for different policy fields. Here, the division of labor is exclusively along different issue areas, with the central level responsible for, for example, foreign policy, and the state level for, for example, educational policy.

9. There are, however, notable exceptions to this rule such as the international administration of war-torn societies (see Heupel 2009) and the International Criminal Court of Justice (Deitelhoff 2006).

10. Hooghe and Marks (2010) describe this as MLG type 1. Similar concepts are used by Mayntz (2001) to argue that the EU differs fundamentally from global governance.

11. The famous comitology in the EU highlights this point. In conjunction with more formal EU decision-making, a parallel apparatus has developed, which assures the participation of the member states in the implementation process (Joerges and Neyer 1997; Huster 2008).

12. The rise of transnational and national dispute settlement bodies points as well to the lack of coordination in global multi-level governance. While such adjudicatory bodies still rarely mediate between different issue areas—with the exception of the WTO–DSB—they play an important role in the coordination between the global and the national level. The quantitative rise of such dispute settlement bodies indicates the growing autonomy of the global level, but also the lack of coordination between different sectors of it.

References

Abbott, K. W. and Snidal, D. 2009. The governance triangle: Regulatory standards institutions and the shadow of the state. In W. Mattli and N. Woods (eds.), *The Politics of Global Regulation*. Princeton, NJ: Princeton University Press, 44–88.

Alter, K. J. 2009. *The European Court's Political Power: Selected Essays*. Oxford: Oxford University Press.

Benz, A. (ed.) 2004. *Governance—Regieren in komplexen Regelsystemen: Eine Einführung*. Wiesbaden, Germany: VS Verlag.

Biersteker, T. J. and Hall, J. A. (eds.) 2002. *The Emergence of Private Authority in Global Governance*. Cambridge: Cambridge University Press.

Binder, M. 2009. Humanitarian crises and the international politics of selectivity. *Human Rights Review* 10: 327–348.

Blake, D. and Payton, A. 2008. Voting Rules in International Organizations: Reflections of Power or Facilitators of Cooperation? Paper presented at ISA's 49th Annual Convention. San Francisco, CA.

Caplan, R. 2004. International authority and state building: The case of Bosnia and Herzegovina. *Global Governance* 10: 53–65.

Cooper, S., Hawkins, D. G., Jacoby, W. and Nielson, D. 2008. Yielding sovereignty to international institutions: Bringing system structure back in. *International Studies Review* 10: 501–524.

Cutler, A. C., Haufler, V. and Porter, T. (eds.) 1999. *Private Authority and International Affairs*. Albany, NY: State University of New York Press.

Dai, X. 2007. *International Institutions and National Policies*. Cambridge: Cambridge University Press.

Deitelhoff, N. 2006. *Überzeugung in der Politik: Grundzüge einer Diskurstheorie internationalen Regierens*, Frankfurt-am-Main: Suhrkamp.

Genschel, P. and Zangl, B. 2008. Metamorphosen des Staates: Vom Herrschaftsmonopolisten zum Herrschaftsmanager. *Leviathan* 36: 430–454.

Haftel, Y. and Thompson, A. 2006. The independence of international organizations: Concepts and applications. *Journal of Conflict Resolution* 50: 253–275.

Hawkins, D. G., Lake, D. A., Nielson, D., and Tierney, M. (eds.) 2006. *Delegation and Agency in International Organizations*. Cambridge: Cambridge University Press.

Heupel, M. 2009. Multilateral sanctions against terror suspects and the violation of due process standards. *International Affairs* 85: 307–321.

Hooghe, L. and Marks, G. 2009. A postfunctionalist theory of European integration: From permissive consensus to constraining dissensus. *British Journal of Political Science* 39: 1–23.

Huster, S. 2008. *Europapolitik aus dem Ausschuss: Innenansichten des Ausschusswesens der EU*. Wiesbaden: Deutscher Universitätsverlag.

Jachtenfuchs, M. and Kohler-Koch, B. 1996. *Europäische Integration*. Opladen: Leske & Budrich.

Joerges, C. and Neyer, J. 1997. Transforming strategic interaction into deliberative problem-solving: European comitology in the foodstuffs sector. *Journal of European Public Policy* 4: 609–625.

Kahler, M. 2004. Defining accountability up: The global economic multilaterals. *Government and Opposition* 39: 132–158.

Kahler, M. and Lake, D. A. 2009. Economic integration and global governance: Why so little supranationalism? In W. Mattli and N. Woods (eds.), *The Politics of Global Regulation*. Princeton, NJ: Princeton University Press, 242–275.

Marks, G., Schmitter, P. C., Scharpf, F. W. and Streeck, W. 1996. *Governance in the European Union*. London: Sage.

Mayntz, R. 2001. Politikwissenschaft in einer entgrenzten Welt. In C. Landfried (ed.), *Politik in einer entgrenzten Welt, 21. Wissenschaftlicher Kongress der DVPW*. Cologne: Verlag Wissenschaft und Politik, 29–48.

Metzges, G. 2006. *NGO-Kampagnen und ihr Einfluss auf Internationale Verhandlungen*. Baden-Baden: Nomos.

Meyer, J. W. 2005. *Weltkultur: Wie die westlichen Prinzipien die Welt durchdringen*. Frankfurt-am-Main: Suhrkamp.

Moravcsik, A. 1998. *The Choice for Europe: Social Purpose and State Power from Messina to Maastricht*. Ithaca, NY: Cornell University Press.

Mosley, P., Harrigan, J. and Toye, J. F. J. 1995. *Aid and Power: The World Bank and Policy-Based Lending*. London: Routledge.

Offe, C. 2008. Governance: "Empty signifier" oder sozialwissenschaftliches Forschungsprogramm? In G. F. Schuppert and M. Zürn (eds.), *Governance in einer sich wandelnden Welt*. Wiesbaden: VS Verlag, 61–76.

Rittberger, V. and Nettesheim, M. 2008. *Authority in the Global Political Economy*. Basingstoke: Palgrave Macmillan.

Rosenau, J. N. 1992. Governance, order, and change in world politics. In E.-O. Czempiel and J. N. Rosenau (eds.), *Governance Without Government: Order and Change in World Politics*. Cambridge: Cambridge University Press, 1–29.

Scharpf, F. W. 2009. Legitimität im europäischen Mehrebenensystem. *Leviathan* 37: 244–280.

Scharpf, F. W., Reissert, B. and Schnabel, F. 1976. *Politikverflechtung: Theorie und Empirie des kooperativen Föderalismus in der Bundesrepublik*. Regensburg, Germany: Scriptor.

Scherer, A. G. and Palazzo, G. (eds.) 2008. *Handbook of Research on Global Governance Citizenship*. Cheltenham: Edward Elgar.

Siebenhüner, B. and Biermann, F. 2009. International organizations in global environmental governance: epilogue. In F. Biermann, B. Siebenhüner, and A. Schreyögg (eds.), *International Organizations in Global Environmental Governance*. Abingdon: Routledge, 264–269.

Streeck, W. 1995. From market making to state building? Reflections on the political economy of European social policy. In S. Leibfried and P. Pierson (eds.), *European Social Policy: Between Fragmentation and Integration*. Washington, DC: Brookings, 389–431.

Tallberg, J. 2002. Paths to compliance: Enforcement, management, and the European Union paths. *International Organization*. 56: 609–644.

Zürn, M. 2010. Global governance as multi-level governance. In H. Enderlein, S. Wälti, and M- Zürn (eds.), *Handbook on Multi-Level Governance*. Cheltenham: Edward Elgar, 80–102.

Zürn M. and Joerges C. (eds.) 2005. *Law and Governance in Postnational Europe: Compliance Beyond the Nation-State*. Cambridge: Cambridge University Press.

Zürn, M. and Leibfried, S. 2005. A new perspective on the state: Reconfiguring the national constellation. In S. Leibfried and M. Zürn (eds.), *Transformations of the State*. Cambridge: Cambridge University Press, 1–36.

Zürn, M. and Neyer, J. 2005. Conclusions: The conditions of compliance. In M. Zürn and C. Joerges (eds.), *Law and Governance in Postnational Europe*. Cambridge: Cambridge University Press, 183–217.

Zürn, M. and Ecker-Ehrhardt, M. (eds.) 2011. *Gesellschaftliche Politisierung und internationale Institutionen*. Berlin: Suhrkamp.

....

CHAPTER 52

REORDERING THE WORLD: TRANSNATIONAL REGULATORY GOVERNANCE AND ITS CHALLENGES

....

MARIE-LAURE DJELIC &
KERSTIN SAHLIN

THE financial and economic crisis that has shaken the world since 2008 has generated calls for more regulation and order at the transnational level (G20 2009; House of Commons Treasury Committee 2009; Bartley and Schneiberg 2010). The media, politicians, and various analysts have often described this crisis as, in part, the consequence of the deregulation that marked the last decades of the twentieth century (Obama 2008). This argument is not convincing, we argue, as this period was in reality "a golden era of regulation," characterized by intense transnational "regulatory activism" (Levi-Faur and Jordana 2005; Djelic and Sahlin-Andersson 2006; Graz and Nölke 2008; Mattli and Woods 2009). Instead, we choose, with others, to talk about a period of consequential reregulation or reordering (Brunsson and Jacobsson 2000; Slaughter 2004).

This consequential reordering mostly came about through the proliferation of soft law, which increasingly had a transnational reach (Mörth 2004; Brütsch and Lehmkhul 2007; Tamm-Hallström and Boström 2010). Extensive elements of self-regulation (Ayres and Braithwaite 1992) were involved in the process but associated mechanisms of audit and control also deserve scrutiny (Power 1997; Boström and Garsten 2008). In turn, evaluation, accreditation, certification, and ranking schemes helped stabilize and reinforce the impact of those mechanisms (Boli 2006; Wedlin 2006). Another striking characteristic of this intense reregulation process has been that regulatory boundaries do not necessarily coincide, any more, with national boundaries. Some of the new regulations stem from the initiative of states or intergovernmental bodies. But governance constellations that bridge the state/non-state divide proliferate at rapid pace (Djelic and Sahlin-Andersson 2006; Graz and Nölke 2008; Djelic and Quack 2010). National states remain involved in this redefined governance game but they increasingly have to compose and interact and come to terms with many other actors.

In the meantime, the conceptual frameworks at our disposal for understanding processes of regulatory governance are mostly inadequate. They are often mere extensions of the conceptual frameworks originally developed to understand rule-making and monitoring in a Westphalian world—where sovereign nation-states with supreme jurisdiction over demarcated territorial areas functioned in an essentially anomic international arena (Martin 2005). As such, those frameworks have a tendency to marginalize processes of transnational regulatory governance (Cutler 2002; Kobrin 2002). We propose that a contemporary goal for social scientific research is to extend and reinvent our analytical tools in order to approach regulatory governance as a complex compound of activities bridging the global and the local and taking place at the same time within, between, and across national boundaries.

Taking transnational regulatory governance seriously, we propose in this chapter to treat it as a dependent variable. Processes of emergence and stabilization are of particular interest. We emphasize the complex, step-by-step, sometimes bumpy and highly historical dimension of these processes. Regulatory change, as it characterizes our contemporary transnational world is generally associated with struggles, conflicts, resistance, negotiations, and painful integration. It is often incremental yet, nevertheless, potentially highly consequential, with a strong transformative impact (Djelic and Quack 2003; Thelen and Streeck 2005).

In order to characterize the dynamics of transnational regulatory governance, we revisit some key conceptual debates. We begin this chapter with an exploration of the nature of the actors involved and of the nature and dynamics of the rules produced. Taken separately, these theoretical repertoires give, we claim, important but only partial insights into the dynamics at work. A combination of perspectives then allows us, in the following section, to better capture the multiple levels and dimensions of transnational regulatory governance in the making. We conclude the chapter with a brief discussion of the more recent challenges to transnational governance, particularly in a post-crisis world.

KEY ELEMENTS OF CONTEMPORARY REORDERING: THE NATURE OF ACTORS AND RULES

In order to capture the multi-level complexity of transnational regulatory governance in the making, we need first to take into consideration some key constitutive elements. We build upon different debates and discussions across social science disciplines to characterize the situation with respect to the actors involved and the nature of rules produced.

The consequential reordering of our world has meant the multiplication of actors, but also their transformation. It has also come with a profound transformation of the nature of rules and compliance mechanisms.

The actors of transnational governance

Traditionally, regulatory issues have been approached, in political science and in the international relations literature, from a state-centered perspective. The idea that states are the central pillars of regulation within but also across national boundaries is still shaping quite a share of that literature (Martin 2005). Theories of governance emerged in reaction to the perspective that social control was mobilized by and confined in states (Keohane 1982; Baldwin 1993). The catchphrase "governance without government" (Rosenau and Czempiel 1992) was coined precisely to express this reaction, and as such should not be taken literally.

Transnational regulatory governance suggests that territorial grounds and national autonomy or sovereignty cannot be taken for granted; it is increasingly difficult to sepa-rate what takes place within national boundaries from what takes place across and beyond nations (Sassen 2003). Although the term "transnational" does not imply the disappear-ance of nation-states, it suggests that states are only one type of actors amongst others (Katzenstein, Keohane, and Krasner 1999; Pierre 2000). As Hannerz (1996: 6) put it "(i)n the transnational arena, the actors may now be individuals, groups, movements, business enterprises, and in no small part it is this diversity of organizations that we need to con-sider." This fits with our conviction, buttressed by the increasing availability of rich empir-ical evidence, that the exploration of a reordering world should neither neglect states nor treat them as the only or central mainsprings of the reordering process (Djelic and Sahlin-Andersson 2006; Graz and Nölke 2008; Mattli and Woods 2009; Djelic and Quack 2010). Kobrin (2002: 64) saw parallels between present transnational regulatory governance structures and the medieval situation, where "borders were diffuse, representing a pro-jection of power rather than a limit of sovereignty. In that context, power and authority could not be based on mutual exclusive geography." Building on Ruggie (1983), Kobrin characterized such political structures as patchworks. "Patchwork" political structures mean interdependence and entanglement across fluid boundaries. As they pursue their interests, actors connect with others and hence have to interact and come to terms with diverse goals and interests in the process. Interdependence and entanglement drive changing patterns of regulatory governance. In turn, changing regulatory governance only deepens interdependence and entanglement.

The role of states and governments in contemporary processes of regulatory govern-ance should, hence, not be taken for granted (Rose and Miller 1992; Kohler-Koch 1996; Moran 2002); rather, they should become the object of serious scholarly scrutiny (e.g. Zürn 2005). States have not withered away; still, they may be changing, potentially quite significantly. As used by Majone (1996) and others (for a review see Moran 2002), the concept of "regulatory states" points indeed to a significant evolution of states and of the way they control or influence activities and actors. Regulatory states are not less influential or powerful but they are increasingly embedded in complex constellations of actors and structures (i.e. Higgott, Underhill, and Bieler 2000; O'Brien et al. 2000). Going one step further, Moran (2002) argues that the concept of "regulatory state" itself may be somewhat misleading as it sends the signal, still, of a central role for states in regulatory governance. Along the same lines, Scott (2004) criticized a state-centered bias and introduced the idea of "post-regulatory states." The defining characteristic here is the blurring of the distinction between public and private actors, and the introduction of a much more decentered view of regulation that relies on mechanisms not directly associated with state authority or sanctioning power (see also Risse, Chapter 49, this volume).

While research on regulatory governance needs to further document the changing nature and role of states, it also needs to capture the rising importance of new actors. Contributions on the widespread expansion of various forms of private authority are, in that respect, highly relevant (Cutler, Haufler, and Porter 1999; Hall and Biersteker 2002). Since the 1980s, mention of the importance of transnational social networks has been made in the international relations literature. Using the concept of "social network" in its simple descriptive sense, Kees van der Pijl and the Amsterdam school explored the sociology and political economy of transnational class formation (van der Pijl 1984, 1998). Haas (1989, 1992), on his part, focused on the role of social networks as key mechanisms of governance crossing state boundaries. He used the label of "epistemic communities" to describe increasingly transnational communities of expertise and practice, where individuals still retained some form of local or national embeddedness and authority (Haas 1992). More recent contributions identify "regulatory networks," underscoring the broad variety of public and private actors involved in transnational regulatory governance (e.g. Schmidt 2004). Regulatory networks imply connected actors—individuals and organizations—but also common discursive patterns (Marcussen 2000). Knowledge claims and various forms of expertise shape the authority of governance actors and the legitimacy of their activities. In other words, networks and governance processes are all institutionally embedded. Hence, research on regulatory governance needs to be sensitive to this institutional contextualization (cf. Lynn, Heinrich, and Hill 2001; Johnston 2001).

The concept of "soft actors" captures this idea of multiple identities in flux quite well. With this concept, Meyer (1996) emphasized a view of actors—be they organizations, states, or individuals—as culturally and institutionally constrained and dependent (see also March 1981). Hence, transnational regulatory governance should not be looked at only through the prism of network connections and nodes. Activities, and relationships, but also actors or the development of actorhood itself, are constituted and shaped by more diffuse cultural and institutional processes. John Meyer and colleagues have repeatedly documented the importance of integrating those processes, if we are to understand how organizations, states, or individuals change. Studies within this tradition show that states remain important regulators but that they are embedded in, shaped, and fashioned by a powerful world society and its associated templates (Meyer et al. 1997; Jacobsson 2006). These templates diffuse as global models, along which states and other actors are benchmarked and possibly transformed (Finnemore 1993, 1996). The stateless but rational, organized, and universalist character of world society may in fact add to rather than detract from the speed of diffusion and the global pervasiveness of standardized models (Finnemore and Sikkink 1998).

A focus on the multiplicity of non-state actors in transnational processes of regulatory governance—working with, along or even without state actors—cannot but beg the question of the legitimacy of private authority (see also Zürn, Chapter 51, this volume). With a broadening set of rule-makers, the way of authorizing rules is likely to broaden as well. Coercive rules that rest on the monopoly of states over legal authority and physical violence, or on citizens' habitual obedience, come to represent only one among several forms of authorization.

From the rule of law to the law of rules

In parallel with the expansion of transnational regulatory governance, empirical studies and theories have multiplied (see Baldwin et al. 1998; Levi-Faur 2005). Different definitions and conceptions of regulation run through these studies. Rule-making has traditionally been associated, in a Westphalian world, with the coercive power of the nation-state. As such, it has generally been expressed in "hard laws" and directives. In contemporary transnational regulatory governance, new legally non-binding "soft" rules (e.g. Mörth 2004) or norms—such as contractual arrangements, standards, rankings, and monitoring frames—appear to be taking over and are, in fact, increasingly being used by states themselves (Hood et al. 1999).

Many new rules are voluntary. This means that those who are to comply should voluntarily follow the rules rather than be forced to do so. In the background to the multiplication of soft rules, we find the potential threat of states issuing harder rules—both more restrictive and less open to interpretation and adjustment by those following the rules. In fact, soft rules can be either a way to buffer the field from harder forms of regulation or a first step toward harder forms of regulation. This suggests important dynamics where regulations develop and expand in response and reaction to each other. These dynamics clearly involve power relations and structures of authority, including when the latter are hidden under the apparent neutrality of references to science and expertise (Drori, Meyer, and Hwang 2006).

While many rule-makers in transnational constellations do not have the type of regulatory authority traditionally associated with states, they can still develop mechanisms of social control that can be more or less coercive. Compliance can be ensured through the connection between certain rules or standards and access to membership, resources, or certifications. It can also rest on socialization, acculturation, or peer pressure, often through organizing, reference to expertise, or the linking of rules to each other (Jacobsson and Sahlin-Andersson 2006). Compliance needs to be verified and monitored, which means increasing demands for transparency and the deployment of various kinds of audit and control mechanisms. Regulation and rule-making, in their contemporary forms, come together with intense organizing and monitoring activities that sustain and reproduce emerging rules as well as targeting their adoption and implementation.

Even when they lean on the shoulders of potentially harder modes of control, soft rules are typically formed in general terms. They are open, as a consequence, to negotiations and translations by those they regulate, whether at the moment of elaboration or during monitoring (Kirton and Trebilcock 2004; Sahlin-Andersson 2004). Soft rules are generally associated with complex and costly procedures of self-presentation, self-reporting, and self-monitoring. So, what could appear to be at first sight a "softening" of the rule system, in fact fosters most of the time extended reregulation and increased organizing and formalization (Brunsson and Jacobsson 2000). This certainly resonates with Power's (1997) characterization of the audit society, where audits explode everywhere and operations and organizations are increasingly structured in ways that make them "auditable" (see also Strathern 2000; Shore and Wright 2000).

Explaining supply and demand: the dynamics of regulatory governance

The rise of governance is not simply the consequence of weaker states or transformed economic orders. In fact, those latter trends could themselves be driven in part by the rise of governance on a transnational scale (Djelic and Quack 2003; Djelic and Sahlin-Andersson 2006). Combining the conceptual repertoires presented above, we outline some of the core dynamics of transnational regulatory activism.

A spiral of distrust

Power (1997, 2004), Hood and colleagues (1999), and Moran (2002) suggest that expanded monitoring and auditing activities generate spirals of distrust. Widespread distrust prompts activities that reveal, make transparent, and set rules with a view to rebuilding trust. These activities, however, may in turn reveal and suggest new problems. Hence, rather than building trust, they could be undermining it further, leading to still more requests for auditing, monitoring, and regulation. This seems particularly true in the case of transnational regulatory governance, due to two specific features.

First, the absence of a formal and sovereign holder of legitimacy in the transnational arena entails the relative fragility of rules and monitoring activities. There is competition out there for claims to authority, and the regulatory arena can be described as a regulatory market—where demand and supply stimulate and reinforce each other. Some of it may even have the feel of a regulatory bubble! In some of the new regulatory "markets," the incentives for following rules are essentially financial. The new market for CO_2

emissions rights is a good illustration (Engels 2006). In other regulatory "markets," reputation, trust, or legitimacy will play the role of incentives. This is the case with accreditation and rankings of higher education (Hedmo, Sahlin-Andersson, and Wedlin 2006), forestry certification schemes (McNichol 2006), or the United Nations (UN) global compact for corporate responsibility (Jacobsson and Sahlin-Andersson 2006; Wedlin, Buhr, and Sahlin 2010).

Second, this "market-like" competition is reinforced by the trend toward deliberative and participative democracy so characteristic of transnational regulatory governance (Mörth 2006). Deliberative democracy means expanded claims to be involved and contribute in rule-making and rule-monitoring. Ultimately, this is bound to generate regulatory or governance "inflation"—where "your" regulation fosters "my" monitoring or counter-regulation, and so forth. Thus self-regulation, if not controlled, tends to be replaced by or developed into regulated and framed counter-regulation (Ayres and Braithwaite 1992).

Hence, behind exploding governance activities and activism we find evidence of a distrust spiral. This distrust spiral reveals the problem of legitimate authority and is certainly a major challenge for transnational governance. It is vividly illustrated by the striking ambivalence, in the transnational governance context, to science and expertise. New modes of governance tend to be expert-based; they are often legitimized by references to science and translated into measurement scales (Power 2004; Wälti, Kübler, and Papadopoulos 2004). A general societal trust in science and expertise is certainly a driving force behind transnational governance (Drori and Meyer 2006). In parallel, though, Hood and colleagues (1999) and Moran (2002) point to distrust in experts, expertise, and measurement as one driver for extended governance. While science in general is legitimate and legitimating, individual experts and individual pieces of expertise are often contested. For example, scandals around health, safety, environmental, or other issues generate profound distrust and a demand for even more transparency and regulation as well as closer monitoring. This contemporary ambivalence toward expertise and science not only stimulates denser governance activities, but favors more universal types of rules, as abstract expertise tends to be highly legitimate while practicing and individual experts often suggest distrust instead.

Responsibility and control spirals

This distrust spiral, which arguably is a powerful motor of contemporary governance, combines and articulates with two other "spirals"—a responsibility and a control spiral.

Governance and regulation are, in part, about the allocation of responsibility. When rules are precise and focused, responsibilities tend to be clear. With the multiplication of regulatory and governance activities, and with the increasing complexity of regulatory constellations, responsibilities get diffused and dispersed. The movement toward soft regulation has a tendency, furthermore, to reroute responsibility away from rule-setters and toward rule-followers. Voluntary rules that are open to translation mean that those who choose to follow the rules and to follow them in certain ways are held responsible. This double blurring of responsibilities may drive the need for regulation and governance still further, and at the local level expanded soft regulation may foster a culture of defensiveness (see Power 2004). Organizational representatives then have to allocate resources not only to follow rules but also to explain why they choose to follow certain rules in particular ways or why they should not be held responsible.

A third mechanism feeding the governance activism is a spiral for control. We have pictured the transnational world as a world in motion, with unclear and shifting boundaries and organizations in flux. On the regulatory market, the way to reach control or to react to regulations that are not favorable to one's own position and strategy is essentially to organize and drive a competing regulatory setup. We can find examples of this in the field of management education (Hedmo, Sahlin-Andersson, and Wedlin 2006). When European business schools realized that US accreditation and ranking systems increasingly shaped the norms for what counted as good management education, they reacted. Feeling marginalized within the existing governance frame, they structured and defined competing and complementary ranking and accreditation systems. Similar control spirals have emerged in many other areas, particularly with the development of the European Union (EU). In a world where transnational regulation expands, the way to seek control is not to avoid regulation but to be actively involved in the development of a satisfactory alternative scheme.

Processes of institutional stabilization

We are interested, in this chapter, in the genesis of transnational governance—why and how new modes of governance, with a transnational scope and reach, come to impose themselves. But it is also important to explore the ways in which these modes of governance are stabilized and appropriated.

Czarniawska and Sevón (1996) propose that ideas and institutions do not flow or homogenize spontaneously, but that the "travel of ideas" is an active social process of translation. Ideas are picked up by actors, packaged into objects, sent to other places than those where they emerged, and translated, as they are embedded into new settings. Similar notions of activity are alluded to with terms such as hybridization, performative processes, editing, or creolization (Sahlin-Andersson and Engwall 2002). The theoretical repertoire around the "travel of ideas" was originally developed to describe what happened to management ideas as they spread. We propose that this repertoire can easily be extended to other types of ideas and practices, in particular those shaping processes of regulatory governance. This makes all the more sense as there is an important direct connection between management ideas and transnational governance. We noted above that transnational governance largely builds upon soft law—standards, norms, and guidelines. Many of those standards, norms, or guidelines relate to organizational, administrative, or management issues, and quite a number, in fact, derive from popular management ideas (Brunsson and Jacobsson 2000; Beck and Walgenbach 2002). Ultimately, it is often not easy to distinguish between management ideas and soft regulation. As an illustration, the package of reforms known as New Public Management (NPM) started out as a "management idea" along which countries reformed their state administration (Hood 1995). After being appropriated by many countries and key international organizations, such as the Organisation for Economic Co-operation and Development (OECD), the World Bank (WB), or the International Monetary Fund (IMF), NPM turned into a standard (Sahlin-Andersson 2000). When ideas and practices associated with NPM became strict requirements that countries had to meet to receive IMF loans, a management idea had turned into a harder form of regulatory governance.

The above accounts of how management ideas translate into soft regulations show that contemporary governance does not start from scratch. Much transnational governance is in reaction and relation to earlier, national systems of rules and modes of governance (Whitley 1999; Hall and Soskice 2001). However, in a world where transactions and interactions increasingly take on a transnational dimension, a conceptual framework that interprets action merely as the expression of national logics becomes too restrictive. Transnational pressures—the multiplication of multinational companies, the progress of Europeanization, the intensification of transnational competition, the increasing number of international organizations and institutions, and the explosion of transnational regulation—challenge national business systems and their systemic complementarities (Djelic and Quack 2003; Morgan, Whitley, and Moen 2005). The multiple ("soft") actors involved in transnational regulatory governance—corporations, state agencies, non-governmental organizations (NGOs), civil society groups, professions and epistemic communities, standardizing bodies, international organizations—are themselves to various degrees associated with, embedded in, or in close interaction with national regulatory traditions and institutional frames (Djelic and Quack 2003; Marcusen 2006). Those actors can mobilize bits and pieces of their national legacies in the negotiation around transnational governance. Some of them may even be purely and simply fighting for the transformation of a national regulatory framework into a transnational one (Djelic and Kleiner 2006). In the process, though, of interaction, those actors that come in contact with each other—both those regulating and those regulated—are likely to develop shared identities and to become increasingly similar, at least to some extent (Djelic and Quack 2010). States have reformed to become more business-like as they incorporate management tools and modes of organizing (e.g. Hood 1991). Non-profit and non-governmental organizations are also restructuring to become more business-like (e.g. Powell et al. 2006). Corporations, on the other hand, are expected to act as "citizens" of the global society (e.g. Zadek 2001) and to claim and assume a degree of political power and responsibility. Distinctions between public and private sectors are getting blurred and a clear tendency is for these various kinds of actors to be all defined, controlled, and governed as organizations (Brunsson and Sahlin-Andersson 2000).

CONCLUDING REMARKS: THE FATE OF TRANSNATIONAL GOVERNANCE IN TIMES OF CRISIS

We argued, at the beginning of this chapter, that the reordering of our world is not new. It largely predates the recent financial and economic crisis. Still, it is fair to ask, in closing, how the recent crisis might come to reflect upon transnational regulatory governance and its dynamics as described here. We identify three main scenarios.

First, increasing calls for reregulation today could bring us back to tighter forms of governance and oversight at the national level. A consequence would then be a return of national states to the front stage when it comes to regulatory activity and governance. This, in turn, would probably mean the deployment of more coercive systems and processes. Such a scenario would impact quite significantly on the types of dynamics described in this chapter. National hard regulatory oversight could represent a major challenge to transnational governance.

In a second scenario, calls for tighter governance and oversight would combine to preserve the advantages of transnationalization. This would suggest the need for strong and centralized authority in matters of governance and would therefore imply the partial transfer of Westphalian state power to a number of international institutions—such as the UN, the World Trade Organization (WTO), or even the IMF. Those institutions would become, in the process, building blocks of a kind of "global state." This scenario would require a serious collective political project to be formed involving a number of nation-states. It would also call for an expressed and real will to delegate, at that level, resources, legitimacy, and some tools for coercive control. The analysis we proposed above leads us to conclude that this scenario is, in fact, not very plausible!

A third possible response to the crisis and to calls for extended regulatory oversight would be to build upon the existing architecture of transnational governance—as described above—but to overcome, as much as possible, its limitations and shortcomings. Those limitations are quite significant and the task, as a consequence, is not an easy one! First, there is a clear need to build up and solidify the legitimacy of transnational governance and transnational governance processes. Second, it appears necessary to create mechanisms that can make those governance processes more democratic and hence more socially acceptable. A third issue has to do with the need to find a balance between the elaboration of transnational rules and principles and the degree of local/national contextualization that might be necessary and would be acceptable. Last but not least, naturally, there is the question of implementation and control. There is a need to ensure that governance rules defined at a transnational level become more than a discourse, and that they get translated and embedded into the everyday behavior of concerned actors.

REFERENCES

Ayres, I. and Braithwaite, J. 1992. *Responsive Regulation*. Oxford: Oxford University Press.

Baldwin, D. (ed.) 1993. *Neorealism and Neoliberalism*. New York: Columbia University Press.

Baldwin, R., Scott, C., and Hood, C. (eds) 1998. *A Reader on Regulation*. Oxford: Oxford University Press.

Bartley, T. and Schneiberg, M. 2010. Regulating or redesigning finance? Market architectures, normal accidents, and dilemmas of regulatory reform. In M. Lounsbury and P. Hirsch (eds.), *Markets on Trial, Research in the Sociology of Organizations*, vol. 30a . Bingley: Emerald Group Publishing, 281–307.

Beck, N. and Walgenbach, P. 2002. The institutionalization of the quality management approach in Germany. In K. Sahlin-Andersson and L. Engwall (eds.), *The Expansion of Management Knowledge*. Stanford: Stanford University Press, 145–174.

Boli, J. 2006. The rationalization of virtue and virtuosity in world society. In M. L. Djelic and K. Sahlin-Andersson (eds.), *Transnational Governance*. Cambridge: Cambridge University Press, 95–118.

Boström, M. and Garsten, K. (eds.) 2008. *Organizing Transnational Accountability*. Cheltenham: Edward Elgar.

Brunsson, N. and Jacobsson, B. (eds.) 2000. *A World of Standards*. Oxford: Oxford University Press.

Brunsson, N. and Sahlin-Andersson, K. 2000. Constructing organizations: The example of public sector reform. *Organization Studies* 21: 721–746.

Brütsch, C. and Lehmkuhl (eds.) 2007. *Law and Legalization in Transnational Relations*. London: Routledge.

Cutler, A. C. 2002. Private international regimes and interfirm cooperation. In R. D. Hall and T. J. Biersteker (eds.), *The Emergence of Private Authority in Global Governance*. Cambridge: Cambridge University Press, 23–42.

Cutler, A. C., Haufler, V., and Porter, T. (eds.) 1999. *Private Authority and International Affairs*. Albany: State University of New York Press.

Czarniawska, B., and Sevón, G. (eds.) 1996. *Translating Organizational Change*. Berlin: De Gruyter.

Djelic, M. L. and Quack, S. (eds.) 2003. *Globalization and Institutions*. Cheltenham: Edward Elgar.

Djelic, M. L. and Sahlin-Andersson, K. (eds.) 2006. *Transnational Governance*. Cambridge: Cambridge University Press.

Djelic, M. L. and Kleiner, T. 2006. The international competition network: Moving towards transnational governance. In M. L. Djelic and K. Sahlin-Andersson (eds.), *Transnational Governance*. Cambridge: Cambridge University Press, 287–307.

Djelic, M. L. and Quack, S. (eds.) 2010. *Transnational Communities*. Cambridge: Cambridge University Press.

Drori, G. S. and Meyer, J. W. 2006. Scientization: Making a world safe for organizing. In M. L. Djelic and K. Sahlin-Andersson (eds.), *Transnational Governance*. Cambridge: Cambridge University Press, 31–52.

Drori, G., Meyer, J. and Hwang, H. (2006). *Globalization and Organization*. Oxford: Oxford University Press.

Engels, A. 2006. Market creation and transnational rule-making: The case of CO_2 emissions trading. In M. L. Djelic and K. Sahlin-Andersson (eds.), *Transnational Governance*. Cambridge: Cambridge University Press, 329–348.

Finnemore, M. 1993. International organization as teachers of norms: The United Nations educational, scientific, and cultural organization and science policy. *International Organization* 47: 567–597.

Finnemore, M. 1996. *National Interests in International Society*. Ithaca, NY: Cornell University Press.

Finnemore, M. and Sikkink, K. 1998. International norm dynamics and political change. *International Organization* 52: 887–917.

G20. 2009. "Leaders' statement: The global plan for recovery and reform." Communiqué of the G20 meeting in London, 2 April; available at http://www.g20.org/Documents/final-communique.pdf.

Graz, J. C. and Nölke, A. (eds.) 2008. *Transnational Private Governance and Its Limits*. London: Routledge.

Haas, P. 1989. Do regimes matter? Epistemic communities and Mediterranean pollution control. *International Organization* 43: 377–403.

Haas, P. 1992. Introduction: Epistemic communities and international policy coordination. *International Organization* 46: 1–35.

Hall, P. and Soskice, D. 2001. *Varieties of Capitalism*. Oxford: Oxford University Press.

Hall, R. D. and Biersteker, T. J. (eds.) 2002. *The Emergence of Private Authority in Global Governance*. Cambridge: Cambridge University Press.

Hannerz, U. 1996. *Transnational Connections*. London: Routledge

Hedmo, T., Sahlin-Andersson, K. and Wedlin, L. 2006. The emergence of a European regulatory field of management education. In M. L. Djelic and K. Sahlin-Andersson (eds.), *Transnational Governance*. Cambridge: Cambridge University Press, 308–328.

Higgott, R., Underhill, G. R. and Bieler, A. 2000. *Non-State Actors and Authority in the Global System*. London: Routledge.

Hood, C. 1991. A public management for all seasons? *Public Administration* 69: 3–19.

Hood, C. 1995. The new public management in the 1980s: Variations on a theme. *Accounting, Organization and Society* 20: 93–109.

Hood, C., Scott, C., James, O., Jones, G. and Travers, T. 1999. *Regulation Inside Government*. Oxford: Oxford University Press.

House of Commons Treasury Committee. 2009. *Banking Crisis: Regulation and Supervision*. London: Stationery Office Books.

Jacobsson, B. 2000. Standardization and expert knowledge. In N. Brunsson, B. Jacobsson, and associates (eds.), *A World of Standards*. Oxford: Oxford University Press, 40–49.

Jacobsson, B. 2006. Regulated regulators: Global trends of state transformation. In M. L. Djelic and K. Sahlin-Andersson (eds.), *Transnational Governance*. Cambridge: Cambridge University Press, 205–224.

Jacobsson, B. and Sahlin-Andersson, K. 2006. Dynamics of soft regulation. In M. L. Djelic and K. Sahlin-Andersson (eds), *Transnational Governance*. Cambridge: Cambridge University Press. 247–265.

Johnston, A. I. 2001. Treating international institutions as social environments. *International Studies Quarterly* 45: 487–515.

Katzenstein, P., Keohane, R. and Krasner, S. 1999. International organizations and the study of world politics. In P. Katzenstein, R. Keohane and S. Krasner (eds.), *Explorations and Contestations in the Study of World Politics*. Cambridge, MA: MIT Press, 5–46.

Keohane, R. 1982. The demand for international regimes. *International Organization* 36: 325–355.

Kirton, J. J. and Trebilcock, M. J. 2004. *Hard Choices, Soft Law*. Aldershot: Ashgate.

Kobrin, S. J. 2002. Economic governance in an electronically networked global economy. In R. D. Hall and T. J. Biersteker (eds.), *The Emergence of Private Authority in Global Governance*. Cambridge: Cambridge University Press, 43–75.

Kohler-Koch, B. 1996. The strength of weakness: The transformation of governance in the EU. In S. Gustavsson and L. Lewin (eds.), *The Future of the Nation-State*. Stockholm: Nerenius and Santérus, 169–210.

Levi-Faur, D. 2005. The global diffusion of regulatory capitalism. *The Annals of the American Academy of Political and Social Science* 598(1): 12–32.

Levi-Faur, D. and Jordana, J. 2005. The rise of regulatory capitalism: The global diffusion of a new order. *The Annals of the American Academy of Political and Social Science* 598(1): 200–217.

Lynn, E. L., Heinrich, C. J. and Hill, C. J. 2001. *Improving Governance*. Washington, DC: Georgetown University Press.

Majone, G. (ed.) 1996. *Regulating Europe*. London: Routledge.

March, J. G. 1981. Footnotes to organizational change. *Administrative Science Quarterly* 26: 563–577.

Marcussen, M. 2000. *Ideas and Elites: The Social Construction of Economic and Monetary Union*. Aalborg, Denmark: Aalborg University Press.

Marcussen, M. 2006. The Transnational network of central bankers. In M. L. Djelic and K. Sahlin-Andersson (eds), *Transnational Governance*. Cambridge: Cambridge University Press, 180–204.

Martin, L. (ed.) 2005. *International Institutions in the New Global Economy*. Cheltenham: Edward Elgar.

Mattli, W. and Woods, N. (eds.) 2009. *The Politics of Global Regulation*. Princeton, NJ: Princeton University Press.

McNichol, J. 2006. Transnational NGO certification programs as new regulatory forms: Lessons from the forestry sector. In M. L. Djelic and K. Sahlin-Andersson (eds.), *Transnational Governance*. Cambridge: Cambridge University Press, 330–374.

Meyer, J. 1996. Otherhood: The promulgation and transmission of ideas in the modern organizational environment. In B. Czarniawska and G. Sevón (eds.), *Translating Organizational Change*. Berlin: De Gruyter, 241–252.

Meyer, J., Boli, J., Thomas, G. and Ramirez, R. 1997. World society and the nation-state. *American Journal of Sociology* 103: 144–181.

Moran, M. 2002. Understanding the regulatory state. *British Journal of Political Science* 32: 391–413.

Morgan, G., Whitley, R. and Moen, E. (eds.) 2005. *Changing Capitalism?* Oxford: Oxford University Press.

Mörth, U. (ed.) 2004. *Soft Law in Governance and Regulation*. Cheltenham: Edward Elgar.

Mörth, U. 2006. Soft regulation and global democracy. In M. L. Djelic and K. Sahlin-Andersson (eds.), *Transnational Governance*. Cambridge: Cambridge University Press, 119–136.

Obama, B. 2008. Remarks of Senator Barack Obama: Renewing the American economy. Speech, 27 March. New York: Cooper Union.

O'Brien, R., Goetz, A. M., Scholte, J. A. and Williams, M. 2000. *Contesting Global Governance*. Cambridge: Cambridge University Press

Pierre, J. 2000. *Debating Governance*. Oxford: Oxford University Press.

Powell, W. W., Gammal, D. L. and Simard, C. 2006. Close encounters: The circulation and reception of managerial practices in the San Francisco Bay area nonprofit community. In B. Czarniawska and G. Sevón (eds.), *Global Ideas*. Lund, Sweden: Liber, 233–258.

Power, M. 1997. *The Audit Society*. Oxford: Oxford University Press.

Power, M. 2004. *The Risk Management of Everything*. London: DEMOS.

Rose, N. and Miller, P. 1992. Political power beyond the state: Problematics of government. *The British Journal of Sociology* 43: 173–205.

Rosenau, J. and Czempiel, E-O. (eds.) 1992. *Governance without Government*. Cambridge: Cambridge University Press.

Ruggie, J. G. 1983. Continuity and transformation in world politics: Towards a neorealist synthesis. *World Politics* 35: 261–285.

Sahlin-Andersson, K. 2000. Arenas as standardizers. In N. Brunsson and B. Jacobsson (eds.), *A World of Standards*. Oxford: Oxford University Press, 101–114.

Sahlin-Andersson, K. 2004. Emergent cross-sectional soft regulations: Dynamics at play in the global compact initiative. In U. Mörth (ed.), *Soft Law in Governance and Regulation*. Cheltenham: Edward Elgar, 129–154.

Sahlin-Andersson, K. and Engwall, L. (eds.) 2002. *The Expansion of Management Knowledge*. Stanford, CA: Stanford University Press.

Sassen, S. 2003. Globalization or denationalization? Review of International Political Economy 10: 1–22.

Schmidt, P. 2004. Law in the age of governance: Regulation, networks and lawyers. In J. Jordana and D. Levi-Faur (eds.), *The Politics of Regulation: Institutions and Regulatory Reforms for the Age of Governance*. The CRC Series on Competition, Regulation and Development. Cheltenham: Edward Elgar, 273–295.

Scott, C. 2004. Regulation in the age of governance: The rise of the post-regulatory state. In J. Jordana and D. Levi-Faur (ed.), *The Politics of Regulation: Institutions and Regulatory Reforms for the Age of Governance*. The CRC Series on Competition, Regulation and Development. Cheltenham: Edward Elgar, 145–174.

Shore, C. and Wright, S. 2000. Coercive accountability. The rise of audit culture in higher education. In M. Strathern (ed.), *Audit Cultures*. London: Routledge, 57–89.

Slaughter, A-M. 2004. *A New World Order*. Princeton, NJ: Princeton University Press.

Strathern, M. 2000. The tyranny of transparency. *British Educational Research Journal* 26: 309–321.

Tamm-Hallström, K. and Boström, M. 2010. *Transnational Multi-stakeholder Standardization*. Cheltenham: Edward Elgar.

Thelen, K. and Streeck, W. 2005. *Beyond Continuity*. Oxford: Oxford University Press.

Van der Pijl, K. 1984. *The Making of an Atlantic Ruling Class*. London: Verso.

Van der Pijl, K. 1998. *Transnational Classes and International Relations*. London: Routledge.

Wälti, S., Kübler, S. and Papadopoulos, Y. 2004. How democratic is governance. *Governance* 17: 83–113.

Wedlin, L. 2006. *Ranking Business Schools*. Cheltenham: Edward Elgar.

Wedlin, L., Buhr, K. and Sahlin, K. 2010. Regulators. In L. Engwall et al., *Corporate Governance in Action: A Field Approach*. Manuscript Dep. of Business Studies, Uppsala University.

Whitley, R. 1999. *Divergent Capitalism*. Oxford: Oxford University Press.

Zadek, S. 2001. *The Civil Corporation*. London: Earthscan.

Zürn, M. 2005. Law and compliance at different levels. In M. Zürn and C. Joerges (eds.), *Law and Governance in Postnational Europe: Compliance beyond the Nation-State*. Cambridge: Cambridge University Press.

INDEX

collaborative governance (*cont.*)
  and factors affecting success of 505–7
    commitment to process 505–6
    incentives for collaboration 505–6
    institutional design 506–7
    leadership 506
    representativeness 507
    trust 506
  and high-conflict situations 498
  and institutional flexibility 187
  and instrumental goal of 514
  and legitimacy 518, 519
  and network governance 500
  and organization of 499
  and participants in 499, 512–13
  and quality of policy-making 518, 519
    legitimacy of majority decisions 520–1
    nature of deliberation 519–20
    other-regardingness of 520–1
  as response to social complexity 513
  and sponsorship of 499
  as strategy of last resort 505
  and types of 500–2
    collaborative planning 501, 502
    exercise of voice 501–2
    regulatory negotiation 501, 502, 507–8
    watershed partnerships 501, 502
  and wicked problems 504, 505
collaborative management 499–500
collaborative network organizations (CNOs) 593
collaborative planning 501, 502
collective action:
  and governance 20
  and regulatory governance 556–7
collective bargaining 541, 542, 545, 547, 549
Collins, H 420
colonialism, and limited statehood 704
command-and-control regulation 554, 557
  and criticism of 376–7
  and environmental regulation 557–8
  and limitations of 68–9, 70, 71, 172, 243
  and politicians' motivations 557
  and trend away from 540
command, and decision-making 9
Common Implementation Strategy (CIS, European Union) 171–2

common pool resources, and good governance 143–4
Commons, John R 387
Commonwealth Scientific and Industrial Research Organisation (CSIRO, Australia) 342, 345
communication, and e-governance 572–4
community service organizations 56
comparative advantage, and modes of economic governance 390
comparative politics, and governance 131–2
competition:
  and innovation in public sector 219, 220, 222, 223
  and regulation for 376
complexity theory 118, 129–30
  and adaptation 137–8
    coevolution 138
    fitness landscapes 137–8
  and agents 135–6
  and application to social sciences 138
  and conceptual diversity 129
  and conceptual fuzziness 134
  and critical mass and threshold effects 135, 138
  and definition of **134**–5
  and dynamic and adaptive nature of systems 135
  and emergence of order 133, 134, 135, 138
    order from below 135
  and evolution 133–4
  and facets of **134**
  and governance, implications for 139–40
  and influences on 134
  and multiplexity 136
  and networks 136
  and nonlinearity 138
    butterfly effect 138
    unpredictability 138
  and reflexive learning 156
  and rules 136–7
  and unified theory 134
compliance:
  and compliance programs 75
  and corporate compliance systems 543
  and global multi-level governance 739
  and transnational governance 749

Helmke, G 24
Héritier, A:
  and definition of governance 355
  and failure of centralized steering 311–12
  and self-regulation 560, 563
  and shadow of hierarchy 317
  and state-centered governance 12
heterarchy 283
hierarchy:
  and continued importance of 244, 490
  and European Union 613, 615–17
    mutual recognition 619–21
    political competition in shadow of
      619–21
    private self-coordination in shadow
      of 618–19
    supranational centralization 615–17
    supranational joint decision-
      making 617–18
  and limitations of 99
  and persistence of 313
  and 'shadow' of 244, 317
    limited statehood 709–10
Hill, C J:
  and governance in United States 488–9
  and hierarchical governance 196
  and multi-level governance 57
  and structures 8
Hill, Gregory 55
Hindmoor, A 277
  and criticism of first wave theory 287
  and hard vs soft policy instruments 244
  and policy instrument mixes 249
  and state capacity 285, 287
  and state-centered governance 12
historical institutionalism, and
    interdependence theory 105
history, and governance 88
Hix, S 8, 613
Hobbes, Thomas 358
Hogg, C 535
Holland, J H 136–7
Holliday, I 285
Holmes, Oliver Wendell 368
Hong Kong, and corruption 150
Hood, Christopher 117
Hoogenboom, Ari 271

Hooghe, L 278
  and multi-level governance 630, 634,
    636, 637
  EU cohesion policy 633
Howlett, M 248
Huang, H 145
Huang, K 306
Hulme, D 325
human development, and participation 459
Human Development Index, and degrees of
  statehood 703, **704**
human rights, and institutionalization
  of 680–1
Humrich, C 9
Hungary 633
Huntington, S P 693
Hysing, Erik 56–7, 57–8

Ice land 376
  and European Union 661
ideas, and travel of 752
Idema, T 321
ideology:
  and administrative reform 61, 192
  as barrier to responsiveness 123
Imboden, D 450
imitation, and Europeanization 660,
  665–6
impartiality, and good governance 151–2
implementation:
  and European Union 320–1
  and governance 22
  and information 117–18
India, and participatory governance 459, 465,
  466, 467
indigenous peoples, and global public
  policy 681–2, 683, 684
individual behavior, and governance 28
industrial policy 379
inflation:
  and central bank independence 402,
    404–6
  and inflation targeting 408
  and unemployment 402–3
informal communities, and market
  governance 360–2

and relationship between firms and
    regulators 556
  dynamic nature of 554
  and reporting pyramid 76, 77
  and reregulation 746
  and social enforcement 73–7
    avoidable harm doctrine 74
    compliance programs 75
    internal reporting procedures 73–5, 546
    reasonable inaction 74
    whistleblowing 73, 75–7, 546
  and soft law 67, 72
  as third-way approach to regulation 69–71
  see also command-and-control regulation;
    experimental governance; self-
    regulation; transnational regulatory
    governance
Regulatory Impact Assessment (RIA) 375
regulatory markets 750–1
regulatory negotiation:
  and collaborative governance 501, 502
  and criteria for success:
    achieving agreement 507
    efficiency 507–8
    social capital and knowledge benefits 508
    stakeholder satisfaction 508
regulatory networks, and transnational
    governance 748
regulatory state 13, 69, 490, 747–8
  and rise of 54, 375
  and state capacity 285
reinforcement politics, and the Internet 588
Reinicke, Wolfgang 673
  and global public policy 676, 677–8
relational contracting, and regulatory
    governance 71
representative democracy:
  and challenge to 518–19
  and collaborative governance 517–18
  and governance 208, 210
    tensions between 303
  and New Public Management 210
  and techno-scientific knowledge 435
representative institutions, and challenge
    to 473–4
reregulation 745
  and transnational governance 750

resource distribution, and steering 37
responsibility, and regulation 751–2
responsive regulation 544
  and market governance 366–8
Rhodes, Martin 311–12, 355
Rhodes, Rod 6
  and definition of governance 206, 311, 319,
    339
  and finance in governance 246
  and governance and change 7
  and governance without government 51, 257
  and hollowing out of the state 10, 11, 230
  and interpretive governance 40
  and meta-governance 69
  and network governance 355, 485
  and path dependence of evolution of
    governance 58
  and (re)construction of governance 55
  and self-governance 283
  and waves of governance 282
Richardson, J 244, 248
  and policy styles 311
  and post-parliamentary thesis 314–15
Riksbank (Sweden) 401
risk:
  and definition of 418
  and disciplinary understandings of 420
  and environmental policy-making 421
  and European Union 422, 619
  and governance 420–4
    accountability 425
    co-production 422–3, 425–6
    efficacy as technique of 424
    framing 423–4
    meta-governance 421–2
    public administration 421
    relationship between 417, 420–1, 424, 426
    as technique of 417
  and governing 418–20
    analysis of information 420
    decision-making 420
    enforcement and criminal justice 419
    explaining and justifying role of the
      state 419
    institutional context 420
    public sector management
      reform 418–19